The Globalization of World Politics

THE GLOBALIZATION OF WORLD POLITICS

An introduction to international relations

THIRD EDITION

Edited by

John Baylis and Steve Smith

with the assistance of Patricia Owens

OXFORD
UNIVERSITY PRESS

OXFORD

UNIVERSITY PRESS

Great Clarendon Street, Oxford OX2 6DP

Oxford University Press is a department of the University of Oxford.
It furthers the University's objective of excellence in research, scholarship,
and education by publishing worldwide in

Oxford New York

Auckland Cape Town Dar es Salaam Hong Kong Karachi Kuala Lumpur
Madrid Melbourne Mexico City Nairobi New Delhi Shanghai Taipei Toronto

With offices in

Argentina Austria Brazil Chile Czech Republic France Greece
Guatemala Hungary Italy Japan South Korea Poland Portugal
Singapore Switzerland Thailand Turkey Ukraine Vietnam

Oxford is a registered trade mark of Oxford University Press
in the UK and in certain other countries

Published in the United States
by Oxford University Press Inc., New York

British Library Cataloguing in Publication Data

Data available

Library of Congress Cataloging in Publication Data

Data available

ISBN-13: 978-0-19-927118-4
ISBN-10: 0-19-927118-6

10 9 8 7 6 5 4 3 2

Typeset by RefineCatch Limited, Bungay, Suffolk
Printed and bound in Great Britain by
Ashford Colour Press Ltd., Gosport, Hants.

Dedicated with love to Marion and Jeannie

EDITORS' PREFACE

The first two editions of this book proved to be much more successful than either of the editors expected. We hoped that a text that combined history, theory, structure, and process, together with contemporary international issues, would prove popular with students and their teachers. What we did not expect was that the book would be adopted as a major text in such a short time in a wide range of international/world politics courses in thirty-three countries, including the United States, United Kingdom, Australia, Canada, Denmark, Sweden, Finland, Germany, France, Spain, Belgium, South Africa, Japan, Brazil, and India. Nor did we expect the book to sell nearly 100,000 copies since its first publication in 1997. This has put it into the category of one of the two best selling IR books available and we are delighted that it is one of the most successful texts published by Oxford University Press.

We have also been greatly heartened by all the very helpful comments we have received from teachers of International Relations in many countries. Some of these were solicited by our publishers and some have been sent to us quite independently. For the third edition OUP undertook a major review of attitudes towards the book by scholars in the field in a range of countries. This review was more comprehensive than anything either of the editors had experienced in the past with their other publications. The overwhelming judgement was that the book continues to 'work' in the contemporary teaching environment. Teachers liked the combination of history and theory, in particular, and students found the chapters interesting, easy to understand and, to use a hackneyed phrase, 'user friendly'. We also received some very useful suggestions on how the book could be made even better.

In the light of these comments we decided to use much the same structure and format for the third edition, while at the same time bringing the text up to date (especially in the light of 9/11 and the events which have taken place since 2001) and adding some new material which we, and a number of our reviewers, felt had been neglected in the first two editions. We have also added a number of other new chapters, including a new opening chapter on the globalization theme. In Part Two a new chapter on 'Social Constructivism' has been added and significant changes have been made to the chapter on 'Reflectivist and Constructivist approaches to international theory'. In response to comments made by reviewers we have also added a chapter on 'International law' in Part Three and a chapter on 'International terrorism' in Part Four.

Finally, we have added more links to the World Wide Web at the ends of chapters (to further emphasize the globalization theme), which we hope will encourage students to use the new, exciting technology available to them, to further their studies and acquire new transferable skills so essential in the new (globalized) world we live in!

ACKNOWLEDGEMENTS

We would like to thank all those who sent us or OUP comments on the strengths and weaknesses of the second edition: we hope that they can see that we have tried to deal with all the suggestions we received. We would also like to thank all anonymous referees who commented in detail for OUP on the second edition. Special thanks are also due to Patricia Owens who did the editorial work on this third edition and prepared the parallel web pages: as with the second edition she has been superbly efficient in all that she has done, and she has contributed in her own right to a number of the chapters. We both owe her a great debt and we hope that by putting her name on the title-page we can reflect our gratitude. Thanks also go to Sue Dempsey, Ruth Anderson, and Helen Adams at OUP for their professionalism and assistance during the preparation of this new edition.

Steve Smith and John Baylis
Exeter and Swansea
June 2004

Grateful acknowledgement is made to the following sources for permission to reproduce material in this book.

Figure 18.1 reproduced with the permission of the United Nations Department of Public Information.

Box 25.4 reproduced with the permission of Her Majesty the Queen in Right of Canada, represented by the Minister of Foreign Affairs, 2004.

Table 30.1 reproduced with the permission of the Centre for Reproductive Rights.

Box 30.1 reproduced with the permission of the International Labour Organization.

Figure 30.1 reproduced with the permission of The Inter-Parliamentary Union.

The third edition of *The Globalization of World Politics* is a pedagogically rich learning resource. **About the book** will show you how to fully utilize your text by illustrating each of the features.

Chapter opener

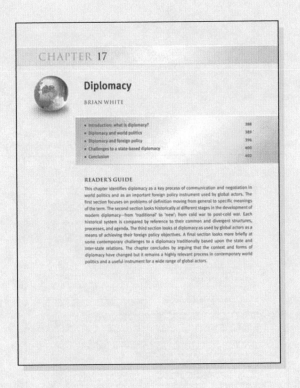

Reader's guide

Each chapter opens with a guide that outlines its focus and sets up key questions and issues.

In the chapter

Figures

Figures in each chapter help to illustrate key principles. Here, the figure illustrates the configuration of International Relations theory today.

Key points

Each section of the chapter ends with a summary of the main points.

Key concepts

The field of International Relations has its own language. Key concepts are presented in boxes to help you learn this language.

Boxes

Boxes feature throughout the text. These include chronologies of key events, facts and figures, big debates or theories, quotes and case studies. Here the box illustrates how international trade can be used to evade taxation.

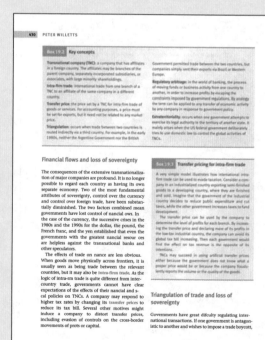

End of chapter

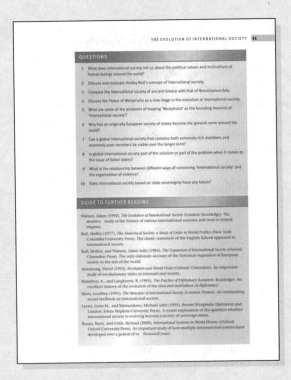

Questions

These questions allow you to revisit key themes and ideas raised throughout the chapter.

Guide to further reading

An annotated list of key books allows you to research topics of particular interest.

Web links

An annotated list of key web links allows you to explore different subjects further.

End of book

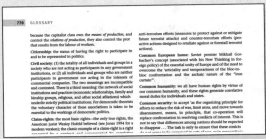

Glossary

Key terms are highlighted in green throughout the text and then presented and defined in the Glossary at the end of the book.

Companion web sites are developed to provide students and lecturers with ready-to-use teaching and learning resources. They are free of charge, designed to complement the textbook and offer additional materials which are suited to electronic delivery.

All these resources can be downloaded and are fully customisable allowing them to be incorporated into your institution's existing virtual learning environment.

Lecturer resources

PowerPoint slides

These complement each chapter of the book and are a useful resource for preparing lectures and handouts. They allow you to guide the student through the key concepts, ideas, and theories and can be fully customized to meet the needs of your course, enabling you to focus on the areas most relevant to your students.

Student resources

Case studies

Additional case studies show the theory of International Relations in real-life situations. These are ideal for tutorial discussions and prompting debate on important issues within the subject.

Multiple choice questions

Self-test multiple choice questions are available for each chapter allowing you to monitor your grasp of key concepts, theories, and ideas as you progress through the course. Each is submitted online giving you an immediate mark and instant feedback.

Review questions

Additional questions allow you to test yourself and your knowledge or provide valuable exam practise.

Web links

A selection of annotated web links, organized by chapter to allow you to easily research those topics that are of particular interest. Checked regularly to ensure links remain up to date.

CONTENTS

Part Three Structures and processes

Part Four International issues

Part Five Globalization in the future

DETAILED CONTENTS

Part Two Theories of world politics

Part Three Structures and processes

Part Four International issues

Part Five Globalization in the future

LIST OF FIGURES

LIST OF BOXES

LIST OF TABLES

ABOUT THE CONTRIBUTORS

Jonathan D. Aronson is a professor in the Annenberg School for Communication and in the School of International Relations at the University of Southern California. His books include *Managing the World-Economy: The Consequences of International Corporate Alliances* (Council on Foreign Relations, 1993), *When Countries Talk: International Trade in Telecommunications Services* (Ballinger, 1988) and *Trade Talks: America Better Listen!* (Council on Foreign Relations, 1985). His most recent writings consider the implications of new communications technologies for globalization and international communications competition.

Michael Barnett is the Harold Stassen Chair of International Affairs at the Hubert Humphrey School of Public Affairs at the University of Minnesota. He teaches and publishes in the areas of international relations, international organizations, and Middle Eastern politics. Among his books are *Dialogues in Arab Politics: Negotiations in Regional Order* (Columbia University Press, 1998), *Security Communities* (Cambridge University Press, 1998, and co-edited with Emanuel Adler), *Confronting the Costs of War: Military Power, State, and Society in Egypt and Israel* (Princeton University Press, 1992), *Eyewitness to a Genocide: The United Nations and Rwanda* (Cornell University Press, 2002), with Martha Finnemore, *Rules for the World: International Organizations and World Politics* (Cornell University Press, 2004), and, with his co-editor Raymond Duvall, *Power in Global Governance* (Cambridge University Press, forthcoming).

John Baylis is Pro-Vice-Chancellor and Head of the Department of Politics and International Relations at Swansea University. He was formerly Dean of Social Sciences and a Professor in the Department of International Politics at the University of Wales, Aberystwyth. He is the author and editor of more than twenty books, including *Anglo-American Defence Relations, 1939–1984* (Macmillan, 1984), *Ambiguity and Deterrence* (Oxford University Press, 1995) and *Strategy in the Contemporary World* (Oxford University Press, 2002).

Alex J. Bellamy is Lecturer in Peace and Conflict Studies at the University of Queensland, Australia. He is the author of *Kosovo and International Society* (Palgrave Macmillan, 2002), *The Formation of Croatian National Identity* (Manchester University Press, 2003), *Understanding Peacekeeping* (with Paul Williams and Stuart Griffin) (Polity, 2004), and *Security Communities and their Neighbours* (Palgrave Macmillan, 2004). He is editor of *International Society and its Critics* (Oxford University Press, 2004) and *Peace Operations and Global Order* (with Paul Williams and Frank Cass, 2004). He has also published articles in *Review of International Studies*, *Millennium*, *Journal of Peace Research*, and *International Affairs*. He is currently working on the ethics of war and writing a book on *Just Wars* (Polity, forthcoming).

Chris Brown is Professor of International Relations at the London School of Economics. Prior to taking up this post in 1999 he taught at the Universities of Kent and Southampton. He was Chair of the British International Studies Association in 1997 and 1998, and has served on the Governing Council and Executive Committee of the (US) International Studies Association. He is the author of *International Relations Theory: New Normative Approaches* (Harvester Wheatsheaf/Columbia University Press, 1992), *Understanding International Relations* (Macmillan, 1997; 2nd edn Palgrave, 2001), *Sovereignty, Rights and Justice* (Polity, 2002) and editor of *Political Restructuring In Europe: Ethical Perspectives* (Routledge, 1994) and (with Terry Nardin and N. J. Rengger) *International Relations in Political Thought: Texts from the Greeks to the First World War* (Cambridge University Press, 2002).

Susan L. Carruthers is an Associate Professor of History at Rutgers, the State University of New Jersey in the USA. Her area of teaching specialization is 'the United States and the World', but she writes more widely on cultural and communicative dimensions of international history. Her publications include *Winning Hearts and Minds: British Governments, the Media and Colonial Counterinsurgency* (Leicester University Press, 1995) and *The Media at War: Communication and Conflict in the Twentieth Century* (Palgrave Macmillan, 2000). She is at present completing a book on captivity and the early cold war.

Thomas Christiansen is Senior Lecturer in the EU Decision-making Unit at the European Institute for Public Administration in Maastricht. His research interests cover institutional issues in European governance and the constitutional dimension of EU reform as well as theoretical questions of European integration. He is a member of the editorial board of the *Journal of European Public Policy* and co-editor of the Europe in Change series at Manchester University Press. He has published widely on the institutional politics of the European Union and is currently co-authoring a book on *Constitutionalising the European Union* for Palgrave Macmillan.

Ian Clark is Professor of International Politics at the University of Wales, Aberystwyth. His teaching and research interests combine international history with the theory of international relations. His works on globalization include *Globalization and Fragmentation: International Relations in the Twentieth Century* (Oxford University Press, 1997) and *Globalization and International Relations Theory* (Oxford University Press, 1999). His last book was *The Post-Cold War Order: The Spoils of Peace* (Oxford University Press, 2001) and he is now completing *Legitimacy in International Society*, to be published by Oxford University Press in 2005.

Michael Cox was formerly of the Department of International Politics, University of Wales, Aberystwyth before taking up a Chair in International Relations at the London School of Economics in 2002. He has been an Associate Research Fellow at Chatham House since 1994, served on the Executive Committee of the British International Studies Association between 1996 and 2000, was Senior Fellow at the Nobel Institute in Oslo in 2002, and is currently an Executive Committee member of the European Consortium for Political Research. He is the author, editor, and co-editor of over ten books, including *US Foreign Policy after the Cold War: Superpower Without a Mission?* (Chatham House Papers) (Thomson Learning, 1995), *Rethinking the Soviet Collapse: Sovietology, the Death of Communism and the New Russia* (Pinter, 1998), *E. H. Carr: A Critical Appraisal* (Palgrave Macmillan, 2000), and *Empires, Systems and States: Great Transformations in International Politics* (Cambridge University Press, 2002). He is also editor of the journal *International Politics*, serves on the Editorial Board of the Cambridge Studies in International Relations series, and is General Editor of the Palgrave book series *Rethinking World Politics*.

Richard Crockatt is Professor of American History at the University of East Anglia where he also teaches international relations. His publications include *The Fifty Years War: The United States and the Soviet Union in World Politics, 1941–1991* (Routledge, 1995) and *America Embattled: September 11, Anti-Americanism and the Global Order* (Routledge, 2003).

Devon Curtis is a Research Fellow at the Center for International Security and Cooperation at Stanford University and a doctoral candidate in the Department of International Relations at the London School of Economics. In 2004–2005, she will be a Post-doctoral Fellow at the School of International and Public Affairs at Columbia University. Her research focuses on the external promotion of power-sharing agreements in civil conflict, democratization, and the peace processes in the Great Lakes region of Africa. Previously she has worked for the Canadian Government and for the United Nations Staff College.

Tim Dunne is Reader in International Relations and Head of the Department of Politics, University of Exeter. He is author of *Inventing International Society* (Palgrave Macmillan, 1998) and was associate editor of the *Review of International Studies* from 1998 to 2002. He has edited six books including *Human Rights in Global Politics* (with Nicholas J. Wheeler, Cambridge University Press, 1998), and *Worlds in Collision: Terror and the Future of Global Order* (with Ken Booth, Palgrave Macmillan, 2002).

Owen Greene is Senior Lecturer in International Relations and Security Studies at the Department of Peace Studies, Bradford University. He trained in mathematics and physics, and conducted research in theoretical physics for several years before turning to international relations. He is author or co-author of ten books and over 150 other research works on international environmental issues and international security problems. His recent work has focused on the development, implementation, and effectiveness of international regimes, particularly in the areas of climate change, ozone depletion, regional sea pollution, and the significance of monitoring, transparency, and review processes.

Fred Halliday is Professor of International Relations at the London School of Economics. His books include *Revolution and World Politics, The Rise and Fall of the Sixth Great Power* (1999), *Nation and Religion in the Middle East* (2000), and *The World at 2000. Perils and Promises* (2000).

Stephen Hobden was formerly lecturer in the Department of International Politics, University of Wales, Aberystwyth and his research and teaching interests are theories of large-scale social change, the international politics of Latin America, and the international drug trade.

Darryl Howlett is Senior Lecturer in the Division of Politics and International Relations at the University of Southampton. His current publications include: co-edited with John Glenn and Stuart Poore, *Neo-realism Verus Strategic Culture* (Ashgate, 2004).

Robert H. Jackson is a Professor at the University of British Columbia. His publications include: *The Global Covenant: Human Conduct in a World of States* (Oxford University Press, 2000), (ed.), *Sovereignty at the Millennium* (Political Studies, Special Issue, July 1999); co-author with Georg Sorensen, *Introduction to International Relations* (Oxford University Press, 1999); *Quasi-States* (Cambridge University Press, 1990); and co-edited with A. James, *States in a Changing World* (Clarendon Press, 1993). He is completing a book entitled *Sovereignty: Evolution of an Idea*.

Richard Wyn Jones is Senior Lecturer in International Politics at the University of Wales, Aberystwyth where he has special responsibility for teaching through the medium of the Welsh language. He is author of *Security, Strategy and Critical Theory* (Lynne Rienner, 1999) and editor of *Critical Theory and World Politics* (Lynne Rienner, 2000).

James D. Kiras is an Assistant Professor at the School of Advanced Air and Space Studies at Maxwell Air Force Base, Alabama. His experience includes several years as a defence consultant providing studies and analysis support to a variety of offices within the US Department of Defense. His areas of expertise include strategic theory and aspects of irregular warfare such as counter-terrorism, counter-insurgency, and special operations. His most recent works on the subject include 'Terrorism and Irregular Warfare', in *Strategy in the Contemporary World: An Introduction to Strategic Studies* (Oxford University Press, 2002) and 'US Special Operations Forces, Transformation, and its Implications for Canadian Special Operations Doctrine', in David Last and Bernd Horn (eds), *Choosing Force? Special Operations for Canada* (McGill-Queen's, 2004). The opinions expressed are those of the author, and are not necessarily representative of those of the US Department of Defense or the United States Air Force.

Steven L. Lamy is Professor and Director in the University of Southern California's School of International Relations. His areas of expertise include international relations theory, foreign policy analysis, the foreign policies of Western advanced industrial states, and teaching and curriculum development in international relations. Dr Lamy has published over thirty articles and book chapters in these areas and has edited a book on contemporary international issues. His current work is on the domestic sources of foreign policy in European states.

Andrew Linklater is Woodrow Wilson Professor of International Politics at the University of Wales, Aberystwyth. His main publications include *Men and Citizens in the Theory of International Relations* (Macmillan, 1982/1990), *Beyond Realism and Marxism: Critical Theory and International Relations* (Macmillan, 1990), and *The Transformation of World Politics: Ethical Foundations of the Post-Westphalian Era* (Polity Press, 1998). His next book, *The English School: A Contemporary Assessment*, co-written with Hidemi Suganami, will be published in 2005.

Richard Little is Professor in the Department of International Politics at the University of Bristol. He is a former editor of the *Review of International Studies*. His latest book, co-authored with Barry Buzan, is *International Systems in World History: Remaking the Study of International Relations* (Oxford University Press, 2000).

Anthony McGrew is Professor of International Relations at the University of Southampton and Fellow of the Centre for Global Governance at the London School of Economics. His research interests embrace globalization, global governance (with particular reference to issues of accountability and democracy), and international relations theory. His recent publications include (ed.) *The Transformation of Democracy? Democracy Beyond Borders* (Polity Press, 1997), *Global Transformations* (with D. Held) (Polity Press, 1999), *The Global Transformations Reader* (co-edited with D. Held) (Polity Press, 2003), (ed.) *Empire—The United States in the Twentieth Century* (Hodder & Stoughton, 2000), and *Governing the Global Polity: From Government to Global Governance* (2002, co-edited with D. Held).

Simon Murden received his doctorate from the University of Exeter in 1993 for work on international relations and political economy in the Gulf. He specializes in the study of contemporary globalization in the Middle East, as well as on security issues in the region. He has been a lecturer in International Relations at the University of Plymouth and University of Wales, Aberystwyth, and is now Senior Lecturer in the Department of Strategic Studies and International Affairs at Britannia Royal Naval College, Dartmouth, as well as an honorary fellow at the University of Exeter. He is the author of *Emergent Regional Powers and International Relations in the Gulf, 1988–1991* (Cornell University Press, 1995) and of *Islam, the Middle East and the New Global Hegemony* (Lynne Reinner, 2002). He is currently writing a book on US intervention in the Middle East since 11 September 2001.

Patricia Owens is Lecturer in the Department of Politics and International Relations, Oxford University and Research Fellow of Oriel College. She teaches and researches the history and theory of strategy, especially war and society, and international and political theory. She has published in *Millennium* and *International Affairs* and is currently working on a book on public spheres and the politics of 'humanitarian' military force.

Jan Jindy Pettman is Professor in Women's Studies at the Australian National University, and foundation editor of the *International Feminist Journal of Politics*. She is the author of *Worlding Women: A Feminist International Politics* (Routledge, 1996). Her current research focuses on gender and globalization in Asia, and gender, identity, and conflict in post-9/11 international politics.

Christian Reus-Smit is Professor and Head in the Department of International Relations, Research School of Pacific and Asian Studies, Australian National University. He is author of *American Power and World Order* (Polity, 2004) and *The Moral Purpose of the State* (Princeton University Press, 1999), co-author of *Theories of International Relations* (Palgrave Macmillan, 2001), editor of *The Politics of International Law* (Cambridge University Press, 2004), and co-editor of *Between Sovereignty and Global Governance* (Macmillan, 1998). His articles have appeared in a range of journals, including *International Organization, Review of International Studies, Millennium,* and the *European Journal of International Relations.*

Brian C. Schmidt is Assistant Professor in the Department of Political Science at Carleton University, Canada. His research interests are in international relations theory and disciplinary history. He is author of *The Political Discourse of Anarchy: A Disciplinary History of International Relations* (State University of New York Press, 1998) and *Imperialism and Internationalism in the Discipline of International Relations,* co-edited with David Long (State University of New York Press 2005).

Jan Aart Scholte is Professor in the Department of Politics and International Studies at the University of Warwick, where he currently also directs the Centre for the Study of Globalisation and Regionalisation. He is author of *International Relations of Social Change* (Open University Press, 1993), *Globalization: A Critical Introduction* (Palgrave Macmillan, 2nd edn 2005), co-author of *Contesting Global Governance* (Cambridge University Press, 2000), and co-editor of *Civil Society and Global Finance* (Routledge, 2002) and *The Encyclopedia of Globalization* (Routledge, forthcoming 2006).

Len Scott is Professor of International Politics in the Department of International Politics at the University of Wales, Aberystwyth, where he is also Director of the Centre for Intelligence and International Security Studies. His recent publications include *Understanding Intelligence in the Twenty-first Century: Journeys in Shadows,* co-edited with Peter Jackson (Routledge, 2004) and *Planning Armageddon: Britain, the United States and the Command of Nuclear Forces, 1945–1964,* with Stephen Twigge (Routledge, 2000).

Steve Smith is Vice-Chancellor of the University of Exeter. He has held Professorships of International Relations at the University of Wales, Aberystwyth and the University of East Anglia, and has also taught at the State University of New York (Albany), and Huddersfield Polytechnic. He was President of the International Studies Association for 2003–4, and was elected to be an Academician of the Social Sciences (AcSS) in 2000. He is the author or editor of 13 books, including (with Martin Hollis) *Explaining and Understanding International Relations* (Oxford University Press, 1989) and (co-edited with Ken Booth and Marysia Zelewski) *International Theory: Positivism and Beyond* (Cambridge University Press, 1995), and of some 90 academic papers and chapters in major international journals and edited collections.

Paul Taylor is Professor of International Relations at the London School of Economics and Political Science, where he specializes in international organization, particularly the economic and social arrangements of the United Nations and the politics of the institutions of the European Union. He published *International Organization in the Modern World* (Pinter, 1993) and *The European Union in the 1990s* (Oxford University Press, 1996). He has edited and contributed to a number of books on international organization, especially with A. J. R. Groom, most recently on the *United Nations at the Millennium* (Continuum, 2000).

Caroline Thomas is Professor of Global Politics at, and Deputy Vice-Chancellor of, Southampton University. She specializes in North–South relations. Her publications include work on global governance and development *Global Governance, Development and Human Security* (Pluto Press, 2000), the politics of global health governance (*Third World Quarterly* and *Global Governance*), and the marginalisation of the South in the study of International Relations (with Peter Wilkin, *British Journal of Politics and International Relations*). Her current focus is US–Africa relations.

Nicholas J. Wheeler is Reader in the Department of International Politics at the University of Wales, Aberystwyth. His most recent book is *Saving Strangers: Humanitarian Intervention in International Society* (Oxford University Press, 2000). He is currently researching the impact of the 'war on terror' on the future of humanitarian intervention.

Brian White is a Professor of International Relations at Warwick and Staffordshire Universities. He is also an Associate Professor in the Institut d'Etudes Politiques, University of Toulouse, France. He is the author of *Understanding European Foreign Policy* (Palgrave Macmillan, 2001) and *Britain, Detente and Changing East-West Relations* (Routledge, 1992). He has also co-edited and contributed to *British Foreign Policy: Tradition, Change and Transformation* (Unwin Hyman, 1988), *Understanding Foreign Policy* (Edward Elgar, 1989), *Issues in World Politics* (Palgrave Macmillan, 2nd edn 2001) and *Contemporary European Foreign Policy* (Sage, 2004).

Peter Willetts is Professor of Global Politics at City University (London). He has written extensively on international organizations, including editing two books on non-governmental organizations, *Pressure Groups in the Global System* (Pinter, 1982) and *'The Conscience of the World': The Influence of Non-Governmental Organizations in the UN System* (Hurst, 1996).

Ngaire Woods is Fellow in Politics and International Relations and Director of the Global Economic Governance Programme at University College, Oxford. She has written extensively on international relations and globalization, including *The Political Economy of Globalization* (Macmillan, 2000), (with Andrew Hurrell) *Inequality, Globalization, and World Politics* (Oxford University Press, 1999), *Explaining International Relations since 1945* (Oxford University Press, 1986), and numerous journal articles on the reform of global economic institutions. She is at present completing a book on the politics of the IMF and World Bank.

Introduction

STEVE SMITH • JOHN BAYLIS

The events of 11 September 2001 (hereafter, 9/11), probably more than any other single event, brought home just how globalized is the contemporary world; the subsequent war in Afghanistan (2001–2) and the particularly controversial attack on Iraq in 2003 have been further clear examples of what it means to call the current era a globalized one, as both involved international coalitions in conflicts that seemed to link events in seemingly unrelated parts of the world. Let us open up some aspects of how these events illustrate globalization, using 9/11 as an example.

First, 9/11 was an event taking place in one country, the United States, but immediately observed throughout the world: the television pictures of the second plane crashing into the World Trade Center are probably the most widely seen images in television history. Thus 9/11 was a world event, which had far more of an effect than represented by the simple fact of the number of deaths involved (about 3,000 died in the four attacks that day; on an average day 30,000 children throughout the world die of malnutrition, though not of course in front of the gaze of the television cameras). Second, the attacks were carried out by 19 individuals in the name of an until-then shadowy organization known as Al Qaeda. This organization was not a state, was not a formal international body, but instead was a loose

coalition of committed Muslims based, it is claimed, in over fifty countries. This was a truly globalized organization. Third, the attacks were coordinated by using some of the most powerful technologies of the globalized world, namely mobile phones, international bank accounts, and the Internet. Moreover, the key personnel travelled regularly between continents, using yet another symbol of globalization, mass air travel. Fourth, the reactions to the events throughout the world were intense, instantaneous, and very mixed: in some Arab and Muslim countries there was jubilation that the West generally, and the United States specifically, had been hit; in many other countries there was profound shock and an immediate empathy with the United States. Fifth, although the attacks were on buildings in the United States, these were not ordinary buildings; while the Pentagon is the symbol of the United States' military power, the World Trade Center was (as the name implies) an iconic symbol of the world financial network. Sixth, it is worth noting that although these were attacks on the United States, many individuals of other nationalities were killed; it is estimated that citizens from about ninety countries were killed in the attacks on the World Trade Center. Finally, though there is a lot of disagreement over why Osama bin Laden ordered the attacks, the main reasons seem to have concerned events in yet other parts of the world: bin Laden himself cited the plight of the Palestinians as a reason, though most specialists point to the continued support of the United States for the current Saudi regime, and the presence of their advisers on that country's (holy) soil. Therefore, though there are many indicators that the world has been becoming increasingly globalized over the last thirty years, 9/11 in many ways best symbolizes globalization.

The aim of this book is to provide the reader with an overview of world politics in this globalized world, and in the chapters that follow you might like to think through how these shed light on some aspects of events such as 9/11. Let us start though with a few words about the title of this book. The title is not accidental; first, we want to introduce you to world politics, as distinct from international politics or international relations; second, many think that the contemporary, post-cold war world is distinctly different from previous periods because of globalization. We think that it is especially difficult to explain world politics in such an era because globalization is a particularly controversial term. It is controversial because there is considerable dispute over just what it means to talk of this being an era of globalization, and whether that means that the main features of world politics are any different from those of previous eras. In this Introduction we want to explain how we propose to deal with the concept of globalization and offer you some arguments in favour of seeing it as an important new development in world politics and also some arguments against such a view.

Before turning to look at globalization in order to set the scene for the chapters that follow, we want to do two things. We will first say something about the various terms used to describe global politics, and then we will spend some time looking at the main ways in which global politics has been explained. We need to do both of these things because our aim in this Introduction is not to put forward one view of how to think about globalization, agreed by all the contributors to this volume; rather we want to give the reader a context within which to read the chapters that follow and that means giving a variety of views on globalization and how to think about it. Our central concern is to point out that the main theoretical accounts of world politics all see globalization differently; some treat it as nothing more than a temporary phase in human history, and one which does not mean that we need to rethink how we understand world politics; others see it as but the latest manifestation of the growth of Western capitalism and modernization; and others see it as representing a fundamental transformation of world politics, one that requires new ways of understanding. The contributors to this book hold no one agreed view, and in fact there are representatives of all the responses just mentioned, and thus, for example, they would each have a slightly different take on the events of 9/11. From what we have said so far you should note that there are three main aims of this book:

- To offer an overview of world politics in an era of globalization.

- To summarize the main theoretical approaches available to explain contemporary world politics.

- To provide the material necessary to answer the question of whether globalization marks a fundamental transformation in world politics.

From international politics to world politics

Why does the main title of this book refer to world politics rather than international politics or international relations? These are the traditional names used to describe the kinds of interactions and processes that are the concern of this book. Indeed, you could look at the table of contents of many other introductory books and find a similar listing of main topics dealt with, yet often these books would have either international relations or international politics as their main title. Furthermore, the discipline that studies these issues is nearly always called International Politics or International Relations. Our reason for choosing the phrase 'world politics' is that we think it is more inclusive than either of the alternative terms. It is meant to denote the fact that our interest is in the politics and political patterns in the world, and not only those between **nation-states** (as the term international politics implies). Thus, we are interested in relations between organizations that may or may not be states (such as, for example, multinational companies, terrorist groups, or human rights **non-governmental organizations** (NGOs); these are all known as transnational actors). Similarly, the term 'international relations' seems too exclusive; of course, it does represent a widening of our concern from simply the political relations between nation-states, but it still restricts our focus to *inter-national* relations, whereas we think that relations between, say, cities and other governments or **international organizations** can be equally important to what states do. So we prefer to characterize the

relations we are interested in as those of world politics, with the important proviso that we do not want the reader to define politics too narrowly. You will see this issue arising time and time again in the chapters that follow, since many contributors want to define politics very widely. One obvious example concerns the relationship between politics and economics; there is clearly an overlap, and a lot of bargaining power goes to the person who can persuade others that the existing distribution of resources is 'simply' economic rather than a political issue. So, we want you to think about politics very loosely for the time being, and several of the chapters will describe as political, features of the contemporary world that you may not have previously thought of as such. Our focus, then, is with the patterns of political relations, defined broadly, that characterize the contemporary world. Many will be between states, but many, perhaps most, will not.

Theories of world politics

The basic problem facing anyone trying to understand contemporary world politics is that there is so much material to look at that it is difficult to know which things matter and which do not. Where on earth would you start if you wanted to explain the most important political processes? How, for example, would you explain 9/11, or the 2003 war in Iraq? Why did Al Qaeda attack the United States? Why did President Bush and Prime Minister Tony Blair authorize the attack on Saddam Hussein's Iraq? As you will know there are very different answers to questions such as these and there seems no easy way of arriving at a definitive answer to them. Was the attack on Iraq motivated by a concern with human rights, with oil, with unfinished business, with **imperialism**, with the 'war against terrorism'? Whenever individuals are faced with such a problem they have to resort to **theories**, whether they are aware of them or not. A theory is not simply some grand formal model with hypotheses and assumptions; rather **a theory is some kind of simplifying device that allows you to decide which facts matter and which do not**. A good analogy

is with sunglasses with different coloured lenses; put on the red pair and the world looks red, put on the yellow pair and it looks yellow. The world is not any different, it just looks different. Well, so it is with theories. Shortly we are going to summarize the four main theoretical views that have dominated the study of world politics, so you will get an idea of which 'colours' they paint world politics. But before we do so, please note that we do not think that theory is an option. It is not as if you can say that you do not want to bother with a theory, all you want to do is to look at the 'facts'. We believe that this is simply impossible, since the only way in which you can decide which of the millions of possible facts to look at is by adhering to some simplifying device which tells you which ones matter the most. We think of theory as such a simplifying device. Note also that you may well not be aware of your theory, it may just be the view of the world that you have inherited from family, peer group, or the media. It may just seem common sense to you and not at all anything complicated like a theory. But we fervently believe that all that is happening in such a case is that your theoretical assumptions are **implicit** rather than **explicit**, and we prefer to try and be as explicit as possible when it comes to thinking about world politics; otherwise we may be looking at the world through the equivalent of red sunglasses without even being aware that we are wearing them.

People have tried to make sense of world politics for centuries, and especially so since the separate academic discipline of International Politics was formed in 1919 when the Department of International Politics was set up at Aberystwyth. Interestingly, the man who set up that department, a Welsh industrialist called David Davies, saw its purpose as being to help prevent war. By studying international politics scientifically, academics could find the causes of the world's main political problems and put forward solutions to help politicians solve them. For the next twenty years, the discipline was marked by such a commitment to change the world. This is known as a **normative** position, with the task of academic study being one of making the world a better place. Its opponents characterized it as **Idealism**, in that it had a view of how the world ought to be and tried to assist events to turn out that way. In its place its opponents preferred an approach they called **Realism**, which, rather unsurprisingly, stressed seeing the world as it really is rather than how we would like it to be. And, the world as it really is is not seen by Realists as a very pleasant place; human beings are at best selfish and probably much worse. Notions such as the perfectibility of human beings and the possibility of an improvement of world politics seem far fetched. This debate between Idealism and Realism has continued to the present day, but it is fair to say that Realism has tended to have the upper hand. This is mainly because it appears to accord more with common sense than does Idealism, especially when the media bombard us daily with images of how awful humans can be to one another. Having said which we would like you to think about whether such a Realist view is as neutral as it is commonsensical. After all, if we teach world politics to generations of students and tell them that people are selfish, then doesn't that become common sense and don't they, when they go off into the media or to work for government departments or the military or even when they talk to their children over the dinner table, simply repeat what they have been taught and, if in positions of power, act accordingly? We will leave you to think about this as you read the rest of this book; for now we would like to keep the issue open and simply point out that we are not convinced that Realism is as objective or non-normative as it is portrayed as being.

What is certainly true is that Realism has been the dominant way of explaining world politics in the last one hundred years. What we are now going to do is to summarize the main assumptions underlying Realism and then do the same for its three main rivals as theories of world politics, **Liberalism**, **Marxism**, and **Constructivism**. These theories will be discussed in much more detail in Part Two of this book, along with a chapter dealing with some of the more recent alternative approaches that seek to explain contemporary world politics. They will also be reflected in three of the other four parts that comprise the book. In Part One we look at the **historical** background to the contemporary world. In Part Three we will look at the main **structures** and processes of contemporary world politics. In Part Four we will deal with some of the main issues in the globalized world. So although we will not go into much depth now about these theories, we do need to give you a flavour of their main themes since we want, after summarizing them, to say something about how each might think about globalization.

Realism and world politics

For Realists the main actors on the world stage are **states**, which are legally sovereign actors. **Sovereignty** means that there is no actor above the state that can compel it to act in specific ways. Other actors such as multinational corporations or international organizations all have to work within the framework of inter-state relations. As for what propels states to act as they do, Realists see human nature as centrally important. For Realists, human nature is fixed and crucially it is selfish. To think otherwise is to make a mistake, and it was such a mistake that the Realists accused the Idealists of making. As a result, world politics (or more accurately for Realists international politics) represents a struggle for **power** between states each trying to maximize their **national interests**. Such order as exists in world politics is the result of the workings of a mechanism known as the **balance of power**, whereby states act so as to prevent any one state dominating. Thus world politics is all about bargaining and alliances, with **diplomacy** a key mechanism for balancing various national interests, but finally the most important tool available for implementing states' foreign policies is military force. Ultimately, since there is no sovereign body above the states that make up the international political system, world politics is a **self-help** system in which states must rely on their own military resources to achieve their ends. Often these ends can be achieved through **cooperation**, but the potential for conflict is ever present. In recent years, an important variant of Realism, known as **Neo-realism**, has developed. This view stresses the importance of the **structure** of the international political system in affecting the behaviour of all states; thus during the cold war there were two main powers dominating the **international system** and this led to certain **rules** of behaviour; now that the cold war has ended the structure of world politics is said to be moving towards **multipolarity** which for neo-realists will involve very different rules of the game.

Liberalism and world politics

Liberals have a different view of world politics, and like Realists, have a long tradition. Earlier we mentioned Idealism, and this was really one rather extreme version of Liberalism. There are many variants of Liberalism (or, as it is often known, Pluralism) as you will see when you read the chapter on it in Part Two, but the main themes that run through Liberal thought are that human beings are perfectible, that democracy is necessary for that perfectibility to develop, and that ideas matter. Behind all this lies a belief in **progress**. Accordingly, Liberals reject the Realist notion that war is the natural condition of world politics. They also question the idea that the state is the main actor on the world political stage, although they do not deny that it is important. But they do see multinational corporations, **transnational actors** such as terrorist groups, and inter-

national organizations as central actors in some issue-areas of world politics. In those issue-areas in which the state acts, they tend to think of the state not as a unitary or united actor but as a set of bureaucracies each with its own interests. Therefore there can be no such thing as a national interest, since it merely represents the result of whatever bureaucratic organizations dominate the domestic decision-making process. In relations between states, Liberals stress the possibilities for cooperation, and the key issue becomes devising international settings in which cooperation can be best achieved. The picture of world politics that results from the liberal view is of a complex system of bargaining between many different types of actors. Military force is still important but the liberal agenda is not as restricted as is the Realist one. Liberals see national interests in much more than military terms, and stress the importance of economic, environmental, and technological issues. Order in world politics emerges not from a balance of power but from the interactions between many layers of governing arrangements, comprising laws, agreed **norms**, **international regimes**, and institutional rules. Fundamentally, Liberals do not think that sovereignty is as important in practice as Realists think it is in theory. States may be legally sovereign, but in practice they have to negotiate with all sorts of other actors, with the result that their freedom to act as they might wish is seriously curtailed. **Interdependence** between states is a critically important feature of world politics.

Marxist theories and world politics

The third main theoretical position we want to mention, **Marxist theory**, is also known as **structuralism** or **world-system theory**, which immediately gives you clues as to its main assumptions. We want to point out that Marxist theory has been historically less influential than either Realism or liberalism, and has less in common with either Realism or Liberalism than they do with each other. For Marxist theory, the most important feature of world politics is that it takes place within a world capitalist economy. In this world-economy the most important actors are not states but classes, and the behaviour of all other actors is ultimately explicable by class forces. Thus states, multinational corporations, and even international organizations represent the dominant class interest in the world economic system. Marxist theorists differ over how much leeway actors such as states have, but all agree that the world-economy severely constrains the freedom of manoeuvre of states. Rather than world politics being an arena of conflict between national interests or an arena with many different issue-areas, Marxist theorists conceive of world politics as the setting in which **class conflicts** are played out. As for order in world politics, Marxist theorists think of it primarily in economic rather than in military terms. The key feature of the international economy is the division of the world into core, semi-periphery, and periphery areas. Within the semi-periphery and the periphery there exist cores which are tied into the capitalist world-economy, while within even the core area there are peripheral economic areas. In all of this what matters is the dominance of the power not of states but of **international capitalism**, and it is these forces that ultimately determine the main political patterns in world politics. Sovereignty is not nearly as important for Marxist theorists as for Realists since it refers to political and legal matters, whereas the most important feature of world politics is the degree of economic autonomy, and here Marxist theorists see all states as having to play by the rules of the international capitalist economy.

Constructivism

Social Constructivism; is a relatively new theory about world politics. It is an optimistic account, one developed in the late 1980s and becoming increasingly influential since the mid-1990s. The approach arose out of a set of events in world politics, notably the disintegration of the Soviet empire, as symbolized most notably by the fall of the Berlin Wall in 1989. This indicated that human agency had a much greater potential role in world politics than implied by Realism, Liberalism, and Marxism. But the theoretical underpinnings of the approach are much older, and relate to a series of social scientific and philosophical works that dispute the notion that the social world both is external to the people that live in it, and is not easily changed. Realism, Liberalism, and Marxism, to different degrees, stress the regularities and 'certainties' of political life (though Liberalism is somewhat less adamant than the other two theories). By contrast, Constructivism argues that we make and re-make the social world and that therefore there is much more role for human agency than other theories suggest. Moreover, Constructivists note that those who see the world as fixed underestimate the possibilities for human progress and for the betterment of the lives of people. In the words of one of the most influential Constructivists theorists (Alexander Wendt) even the self-help international system portrayed by Realists is in fact something that we make and re-make: as he puts it, '**anarchy** is what states make of it'. Therefore, the world that Realists portray as 'natural' or 'given' is in fact far more open to change, and Constructivists think that self-help is only one possible response to the anarchical structure of world politics. Even more subversively, they think that not only is the structure of world politics amenable to change, but so are the identities and interests that the other theories take as given. In other words, Constructivists think that it is a fundamental mistake to think of world politics as something that we cannot change. The seemingly 'natural' structures, processes, identities, and interests of world politics could in fact be different from what they currently are, and implying otherwise is a political act.

The four theories and globalization

The first three of these theoretical perspectives have tended to be the main theories that have been used to understand world politics, with Constructivism becoming increasingly influential since the mid-1990s. In the 1980s it became common to talk of there being an **inter-paradigm** debate between Realism, Liberalism, and Marxism; that is to say that the three theories (known as paradigms after the influential philosopher of natural science, Thomas Kuhn) were in competition, and that the 'truth' about world politics lay in the debate between them. At first sight each seems to be particularly good at explaining some aspects of world politics better than the others, and an obvious temptation would be to try and combine them into some overall account. But we need to warn you that this is not the easy option it may seem. This is because the four theories are not so much different views of the same world, but are instead **four views of different worlds**. Let us explain this briefly: while it is clear that each of the four focuses on different aspects of world politics (Realism on the power relations between states, Liberalism on a much wider set of interactions between states and **non-state actors**, Marxist theory on the patterns of the world-economy, and Constructivism on the ways in which we can develop different social structures and processes) each is saying more than this. Each view is claiming that it is picking out **the most important features** of world politics and that it offers a **better account** than do the rival theories. Thus, the four approaches are really in competition with one another; and, while you can certainly choose between them it is not so easy to add bits from one to the others. For example, if you are a Marxist theorist, you think that state behaviour is ultimately determined by class forces: forces that the Realist; does not think affect state behaviour. Similarly, Constructivism suggests that actors do not face a world that is fixed, and thus it is one that they can in principle change, in direct contrast to the core beliefs of Realists and Marxists alike. In other words these four theories are really versions of what world politics is like rather than partial pictures of it. They do not agree on what the 'it' is!

We now need to make it clear that we do not think that any one of these theories has all the answers when it comes to explaining world politics in an era of globalization. In fact each sees globalization differently. We do not want to tell you which theory seems best, since the purpose of this book is to give you a variety of conceptual lenses through which you might want to look at globalization. All we will do is to say a few words about how each theory might respond to globalization. We will then go on to say something about the rise of globalization and offer some ideas on its strengths and weaknesses as a description of contemporary world politics.

1. For **Realists**, globalization does not alter the most significant feature of world politics, namely the territorial division of the world into nation-states. While the increased interconnectedness between economies and societies might make them more dependent on one another, the same cannot be said about the states-system. Here, states retain sovereignty, and globalization does not render obsolete the struggle for political power between states. Nor does it undermine the importance of the threat of the use of force, or the importance of the balance of power. Globalization, then, may affect our social, economic, and cultural lives, but it does not transcend the international political system of states.

2. For **Liberals**, the picture looks very different. They tend to see globalization as the end product of a long-running transformation of world politics. For them, globalization fundamentally undermines Realist accounts of world politics since it shows that states are no longer such central actors as they once were. In their place are numerous actors, of differing importance according to the issue-area concerned. Liberals are particularly interested in the revolution in technology and communications represented by globalization. This increased interconnectedness between societies which is economically and technologically led results in a very different pattern of world political relations from that which

has gone before. States are no longer sealed units, if ever they were, and as a result the world looks more like a cobweb of relations than like the state model of Realism or the class model of Marxist theory.

3. For **Marxist** theorists, globalization is a bit of a sham. It is nothing particularly new, and is really only the latest stage in the development of international capitalism. It does not mark a qualitative shift in world politics, nor does it render all our existing theories and concepts redundant. Above all it is a Western-led phenomenon which basically simply furthers the development of international capitalism. Rather than make the world more alike, it further deepens the existing divide between the core, the semi-periphery, and the periphery.

4. For **Constructivist** theorists, globalization tends to be presented as an external force acting on states, which leaders often argue is a reality that they cannot challenge. This, Constructivists argue, is a very political act, since it underestimates the ability of leaders to challenge and shape globalization, and instead allows them to duck responsibility by blaming 'the way the world is'. Instead, Constructivists think that we can mould globalization in a variety of ways, notably because it offers us very real chances to create cross-national social movements aided by modern technological forms of communication such as the Internet.

By the end of the book we hope you will work out which of these theories (if any) best explains globalization. We spend a lot of time in Part Two outlining these theories in more detail so as to give you much more of an idea of the main ideas involved. We will also introduce you to a set of other theories that many believe are crucial in explaining globalization, but which have not been the dominant theories in the discipline of International Relations. However, the central point we want to make here is to reinforce our comment earlier that theories do not portray 'the' truth. In other words, the theories we have mentioned will see globalization differently because they have a **prior** view of what is most important in world politics. Therefore the option is not available of simply answering the tempting question of which theory has the 'truest' or 'correct' view of globalization.

Globalization and its precursors

The focus of this book is globalization, and as we have already said our concern is with offering you an overview of world politics in a globalized era. **By globalization we simply mean the process of increasing interconnectedness between societies such that events in one part of the world more and more have effects on peoples and societies far away.** A globalized world is one in which political, economic, cultural, and social events become more and more interconnected, and also one in which they have more impact. In other words, societies are affected more and more extensively and more and more deeply by events of other societies. These events can conveniently be divided into three types, **social, economic,** and **political.** In each case, the world seems to be 'shrinking', and people are increasingly aware of this. The World Wide Web is but the most graphic example of this, since it allows you to sit at home and have instant communication with web sites around the world. Electronic mail has also transformed communications in a way that the editors of this book would not have envisaged fifteen years ago. But these are only the most obvious examples. Others would include: worldwide television communications, global newspapers, international social movements such as Amnesty International or Greenpeace, global franchises such as McDonald's, Coca-Cola, and Pizza Hut, the global economy (go and look in your nearest supermarket and work out the number of countries' products represented there), and global risks such as pollution, AIDS, etc. There are, of course, many other examples, but we are sure that you get the picture. It is this pattern of events that seems to have changed the nature of world politics from what it was just a few years ago. The important point to stress is that it is not just that the world has changed but that the changes are qualitative and not merely quantitative; a strong case can be made that a 'new' world political system has emerged as a result of globalization.

Having said which, we want to point out that globalization is not some entirely new phenomenon in world history; indeed, as we will note later on, many argue that it is merely a new name for a long-term feature. While we want to leave it to you to judge whether in its current manifestation it represents a new phase in world history or merely a continuation of processes that have been around for a long time, we do want to note that there have been several precursors to globalization. In other words, globalization bears a marked similarity to at least nine features of world politics discussed by writers before the contemporary period. We will now note these briefly.

First, globalization has many features in common with the **theory of modernization** (see Modelski 1972 and Morse 1976). According to these writers, industrialization brings into existence a whole new set of contacts between societies, and changes the political, economic, and social processes that characterized the pre-modernized world. Crucially, industrialization alters the nature of the state, both widening its responsibilities and weakening its control over outcomes. The result is that the old power-politics model of international relations becomes outmoded. Force becomes less usable, states have to negotiate with other actors to achieve their goals, and the very identity of the state as an actor is called into question. In many respects it seems that modernization is part of the globalization process, differing only in that it applied more to the developed world and involved nothing like as extensive a set of transactions.

Second, there are clear similarities with the arguments of influential writers such as Walt Rostow (1960) who argued that **economic growth** followed a pattern in all economies as they went through industrialization. Their economies developed in the shadow of more 'developed' econ-

omies until they reached the stage where they were capable of self-sustained economic growth. What this has in common with globalization is that Rostow saw a clear pattern to economic development, one marked by stages which all economies would follow as they adopted capitalist policies. There was an automaticity to history that globalization theory tends also to rely on.

Third, there was the important literature emerging out of the Liberal paradigm discussed above. Specifically there were very influential works on the nature of **economic interdependence** (Cooper 1968), the role of transnational actors (Keohane and Nye 1971), and the resulting cobweb model of world politics (Mansbach, Ferguson, and Lampert 1976). Much of this literature anticipates the main theoretical themes of globalization, although again it tends to be applied much more to the developed world than is the case with globalization.

Fourth, there are notable similarities between the picture of the world painted by globalization and that portrayed in Marshall McLuhan's influential work on the **'global village'** (1964). According to McLuhan, advances in electronic communications resulted in a world where we could see in real time events that were occurring in distant parts of the world. For McLuhan, the main effects of this development were that time and space become compressed to such an extent that everything loses its traditional identity. As a result, the old groupings of political, economic, and social organization simply do not work any more. Without doubt, McLuhan's work significantly anticipates some of the main themes of globalization, although it should be noted that he was talking primarily about the communications revolution, whereas the globalization literature tends to be much more extensive.

Fifth, there are significant overlaps between some of the main themes of globalization and the work of writers such as John Burton (1972), who spoke of the emergence of a **'world society'**. According to Burton, the old **states-system** was becoming outmoded, as increasingly significant interactions took place between non-state actors. It was Burton who coined the phrase the 'cobweb' model of world politics. The central message here was that the most important patterns in world politics were those created by trade, communications, language, ideology, etc., along with the more traditional focus on the political relations between states.

Sixth, in the 1960s, 1970s, and 1980s, there was the visionary work of those associated with the **World Order Models Project** (WOMP), which was an organization set up in 1968 to promote the development of alternatives to the inter-**state system** which would result in the elimination of war. What is most interesting about their many studies (see, for example, Mendlovitz (1975) and Falk (1975; 1995b)), is that they focused on the questions of global government that today are central to much work going on under the name of globalization. For WOMPers (as they were known), the unit of analysis is the individual, and the level of analysis is the global. Interestingly by the mid-1990s WOMP had become much wider in its focus, concentrating on the world's most vulnerable people and the environment.

Seventh, there are important parallels between some of the ideas of globalization and the thoughts of those who argued for the existence of an **international society**. Prominent amongst these was Hedley Bull (1977), who pointed to the development over the centuries of a set of agreed norms and common understandings between state leaders, such that they effectively formed a society rather than merely an international system. However, although Bull was perturbed by the emergence of what he called the 'new medievalism', in which a series of sub-national and inter-national organizations vied with the state for authority, he did not feel that the nation-state was about to be replaced by the development of a world society.

Eighth, globalization theory has several points in common with the infamous argument of Francis Fukuyama (1992) about the 'end of history'. Fukuyama's main claim is that the power of the economic market is resulting in liberal democracy replacing all other types of government. Though he recognizes that there are other types of political regimes to challenge liberal democracy, he does not think that any of the alternatives such as communism, fascism, or Islam will be able to deliver the economic goods in the way that liberal democracy can. In this sense there is a direction to history and that direction is towards the expansion of the economic market throughout the world.

Finally, there are very marked similarities between some of the political aspects of globalization and long-standing ideas of liberal progress. These have most recently been expressed in the '**liberal peace' theory** of writers such as Bruce Russett (1993) and Michael Doyle (1983a and 1983b), although they go back centuries to writers such as Immanuel Kant. The main idea is that liberal democracies do not fight one another, and although of course there can be dispute as to what is a liberal democracy, adherents to this view claim quite plausibly that there is no case where two democracies have ever gone to war. The reason they claim this is that public accountability is so central in democratic systems that publics will not allow leaders easily to engage in wars with other democratic nations. Again the main link with globalization is the assumption that there is progress to history, and that this is making it far more difficult to start wars.

Globalization: myth or reality?

Our final task in this Introduction is to offer you a summary of the main arguments for and against globalization as a distinct new phase in world politics. We do not expect you to decide where you stand on the issue at this stage, but we think that we have to give you some of the main arguments so that you can keep them in mind as you read the rest of this book. Because the arguments for globalization being an important new phase of world politics have been rehearsed above, and also because they are most effectively summarized in the chapter that follows, we will spend a little more time on the criticisms. The main arguments in favour of globalization comprising a new era of world politics are:

1. The pace of **economic transformation** is so

great that it has created a new world politics. States are no longer closed units and they cannot control their economies. The world-economy is more interdependent than ever, with trade and finances ever expanding.

2. **Communications** have fundamentally revolutionized the way we deal with the rest of the world. We now live in a world where events in one location can be immediately observed on the other side of the world. Electronic communications alter our notions of the social groups we work and live in.

3. There is now, more than ever before, a **global culture**, so that most urban areas resemble one another. The world shares a common culture, much of it emanating from Hollywood.

4. The world is becoming more **homogeneous**. Differences between peoples are diminishing.

5. **Time and space seem to be collapsing.** Our old ideas of geographical space and of chronological time are undermined by the speed of modern communications and media.

6. There is emerging a **global polity**, with transnational social and political movements and the beginnings of a transfer of allegiance from the state to sub-state, transnational, and international bodies.

7. A **cosmopolitan culture** is developing. People are beginning to 'think globally and act locally'.

8. A **risk culture** is emerging with people realizing both that the main risks that face them are global (pollution and AIDS) and that states are unable to deal with the problems.

However, just as there are powerful reasons for seeing globalization as a new stage in world politics, often allied to the view that globalization is progressive, that is to say that it improves the lives of people, there are also arguments that suggest the opposite. Some of the main ones are given below.

1. One obvious objection to the globalization thesis is that it is merely a buzzword to denote the latest phase of capitalism. In a very powerful critique of the globalization theory, Hirst and Thompson (1996) argue that one effect of the globalization thesis is that it makes it appear as if national gov-

ernments are powerless in the face of global trends. This ends up paralysing governmental attempts to subject global economic forces to control and regulation. Believing that most globalization theory lacks historical depth they point out that it paints the current situation as **more unique than it is** and also as more firmly entrenched than it might in fact be. Current trends may well be reversible. They conclude that the more extreme versions of globalization are 'a myth', and they support this claim with five main conclusions from their study of the contemporary world-economy (1996: 2–3): **First**, the present internationalized economy is not unique in history. In some respects they say it is less open than the international economy was between 1870 and 1914. **Second**, they find that 'genuinely' transnational companies are relatively rare, most are national companies trading internationally. There is no trend towards the development of international companies. **Third**, there is no shift of finance and capital from the developed to the underdeveloped worlds. Direct investment is highly concentrated amongst the countries of the developed world. **Fourth**, the world-economy is not global, rather trade, investment, and financial flows are concentrated in and between three blocs—Europe, North America, and Japan. **Finally**, they argue that this group of three blocs could, if they coordinated policies, regulate global economic markets and forces. Note that Hirst and Thompson are only looking at economic theories of globalization, and many of the main accounts deal with factors such as communications and culture more than economics; nonetheless, theirs is a very powerful critique of one of the main planks of the more extreme globalization thesis, with their central criticism being that seeing the global economy as something beyond our control both misleads us and prevents us from developing policies to control the national economy. All too often we are told that our economy must obey 'the global market', but Hirst and Thompson believe that this is a myth.

2. Another obvious objection is that globalization is very **uneven in its effects**. At times it sounds very much like a Western theory applicable only to a small part of humankind. To pretend that

even a small minority of the world's population can connect to the World Wide Web is clearly an exaggeration when in reality most people on the planet have probably never made a telephone call in their lives. In other words, globalization only applies to the developed world. In the rest of the world, there is nothing like the degree of globalization. We are in danger of overestimating the extent and the depth of globalization.

3. A related objection is that globalization may well be simply **the latest stage of Western imperialism**. It is the old modernization theory discussed above in new guise. The forces that are being globalized are conveniently those found in the Western world. What about non-Western values? Where do they fit into this emerging global world? The worry is that they do not fit in at all, and what is being celebrated in globalization is the triumph of a Western worldview, at the expense of the worldviews of other cultures.

4. Critics have also noted that there are very considerable **losers** as the world becomes more globalized. This is because it represents the success of liberal capitalism in an economically divided world. Perhaps one outcome is that globalization allows the more efficient exploitation of less well-off nations, and all in the name of openness. The technologies accompanying globalization are technologies that automatically benefit the richest economies in the world, and allow their interests to override local ones. So, not only is globalization imperialist, it is also exploitative.

5. We also need to make the straightforward point that not all globalized forces are necessarily **'good' ones**. Globalization makes it easier for drug cartels and terrorists to operate, and the World Wide Web's anarchy raises crucial questions of censorship and preventing access to certain kinds of material.

6. Turning to the so-called **global governance** aspects of globalization, the main worry here is, to whom are the transnational social movements responsible and democratically accountable? If IBM or Shell becomes more and more powerful in the world, does this not raise the issue of how accountable it is to democratic control? David Held has made a strong case for the development

of what he calls 'cosmopolitan democracy' (1995), but this has clearly defined legal and democratic features. The worry is that most of the emerging powerful actors in a globalized world precisely are NOT accountable. This argument also applies to seemingly 'good' global actors such as Amnesty International and Greenpeace.

7. Finally, there seems to us to be a **paradox** at the heart of the globalization thesis. On the one hand it is usually portrayed as the triumph of Western, market-led values, but how do we then explain the tremendous economic success that some national economies have had in the globalized world? We are thinking here in the main of the so-called 'Tigers' of Asia, countries such as Singapore, Taiwan, Malaysia, and Korea, which have enjoyed some of the highest growth rates in the international economy, but subscribe to very different 'Asian' values. These nations emphatically reject Western values, and yet they have had enormous economic success. The paradox then is whether these countries can continue to modernize so successfully without adopting Western values. If they can, then what does this do to one of the main themes of globalization, namely the argument that globalization represents the spreading across the globe of a set of values? If these countries do continue to follow their own roads towards economic and social modernization, then we must anticipate future disputes between 'Western' and 'Asian' values over issues like human rights, **gender**, and religion.

We hope that these arguments for and against globalization will cause you to think deeply about the utility of the concept of globalization in explaining contemporary world politics. The chapters that follow do not take a common stance **for** or **against globalization**. We will end by posing some questions that we would like you to keep in mind as you read the remaining chapters:

- Is globalization a new phenomenon in world politics?

- Which theory discussed above best explains globalization?

- Is globalization a positive or a negative development?

- Is globalization merely the latest stage of capitalist development?

- Does globalization make the state obsolete?

- Does globalization make the world more or less democratic?

- Is globalization merely Western imperialism in a new guise?

- Does globalization make war less likely?

We hope that this Introduction and the chapters that follow help you to answer these questions, and that this book as a whole provides you with a good overview of the politics of the contemporary world. Whether or not you conclude that globalization is a new phase in world politics, and whether you think it is a positive or a negative development, we will now leave you to decide. But, returning to 9/11, we think it important to conclude this chapter by stressing that globalization, be it a new form of world politics or merely a new name for an age-old set of features, clearly has a very complex set of features that together make it contradictory and difficult to comprehend. Just as the Internet is for most of us a liberating force, so was it the way in which those who planned the attacks communicated. Similarly, television can bring live stories right into our living rooms so that we understand more about the world, but on 9/11 it was also a means of communicating a very specific message about the vulnerability of the United States, and ultimately a way of constructing the categories within which we reacted. Finally, maybe the most fundamental lesson of 9/11 is that not all people in the world share a view of globalization as a progressive force in world politics, since what those who undertook the attacks were rejecting was in part the globalization-as-westernization project. Globalization is therefore not one thing; how we think about it will reflect not merely the theories we accept, but, rather, our own positions in this globalized world. In this sense, the ultimate paradox of 9/11 is that the answers to questions such as what it was, what it meant, how to respond to it, etc., may themselves be ultimately dependent on the social, cultural, economic, and political spaces we occupy in a globalized world. In other words, world politics suddenly becomes very personal: how does your economic position, your ethnicity, your gender, your culture, or your religion determine what globalization means to you?

GUIDE TO FURTHER READING

There are several good introductory guides to globalization. The most comprehensive discussion is found in D. Held *et al.* (1999), *Global Transformations* (Cambridge: Polity Press). See also D. Held and A. McGrew (eds) (2003), *The Global Transformations Reader*, 2nd edn (Cambridge: Polity Press). M. Waters (1995), *Globalization* (London: Routledge) is a clear overview, written by a sociologist. J. A. Scholte (1993), *International Relations of Social Change* (Buckingham: Open University Press) is an extremely clear and comprehensive introduction to the social relations aspects of globalization. His latest book (2000), *Globalization: A Critical Introduction* (London: Macmillan) offers an excellent overview.

A. McGrew and P. Lewis (1992), *Global Politics* (Cambridge: Polity Press) is a good collection of essays about global politics and contains some very relevant chapters on the relationship between the three theories discussed above and globalization. R. Robertson (1992), *Globalization: Social Theory and Global Culture* (London: Sage) is a very widely cited survey of the relations between globalization and global culture. J. N. Rosenau and E.-D. Czempiel (1992), *Governance without Government* (Cambridge: Cambridge University Press) is a good collection of essays dealing with the political aspects of globalization. J. N. Rosenau (1990), *Turbulence in World Politics* (Princeton: Princeton University Press) and J. A. Camilleri and J. Falk (1992), *The End of Sovereignty* (Aldershot: Edward Elgar) are both very good at looking at the main trends in world politics at the beginning of the 1990s.

Excellent critiques of the globalization thesis are David Held and Anthony McGrew (2002), *Globalization and Anti-globalization* (Cambridge: Polity Press), Barry Gills (ed.) (2002), *Globalization and the Politics of Resistance* (London: Palgrave Macmillan), Joseph Stiglitz (2003), *Globalization and its Discontents* (London: Penguin), R. Falk (1999), *Predatory Globalization: A Critique* (Cambridge: Polity Press), L. Weiss (1998), *The Myth of the Powerless State* (Cambridge: Polity Press), and P. Hirst and G. Thompson (2000), *Globalization in Question*, 2nd edn (Cambridge: Polity Press).

Mary Kaldor (2003) has written a powerful account of the relationship between globalization and international civil society in her *Global Civil Society: An Answer to War* (Cambridge: Polity Press). See also the series of yearbooks she and others have edited on global civil society: Helmut Anheier, Marlies Glasius, and Mary Kaldor (eds) (2001), *Global Civil Society* (Oxford: Oxford University Press), Marlies Glasius, Mary Kaldor, and Helmut Anheier (eds) (2002), *Global Civil Society Yearbook 2002* (Oxford: Oxford University Press), and Mary Kaldor, Helmut Anheier, and Marlies Glasius (eds) (2003), *Global Civil Society Yearbook 2003* (Oxford: Oxford University Press). For another very influential analysis of the relationship between globalization and governance see David Held and Anthony McGrew (2002), *Governing Globalization: Power, Authority and Global Governance* (Cambridge: Polity Press).

Fig. 1 World Map

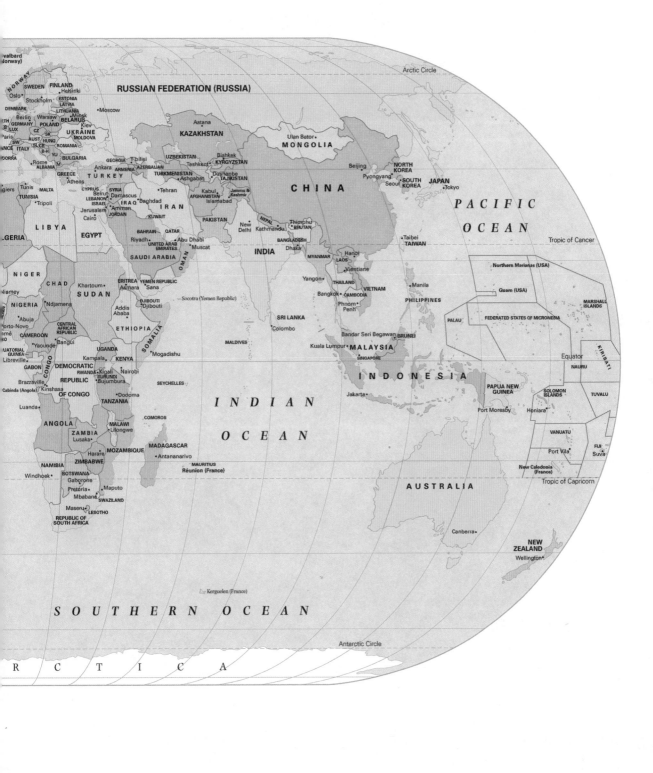

CHAPTER 1

Globalization and global politics

ANTHONY MCGREW

READER'S GUIDE

This chapter offers an account of globalization and its consequences for world politics. It considers globalization as a historical process which involves the widening, deepening, speeding up and growing impact of worldwide interconnectedness. This process, however, is highly uneven such that far from implying the evolution of a more cooperative world it generates powerful sources of tension, conflict, and fragmentation. Nor does it prefigure the demise of the state. Yet it has not left world politics unaltered. This chapter explores some of the significant transformations brought about by the current phase of globalization. In particular it concludes that a conceptual shift in our thinking is required fully to grasp the nature of the changes that are under way. This conceptual shift involves embracing the idea of global politics: the politics of an embryonic global society in which domestic and world politics are no longer discrete spheres of activity. In the process many of the traditional organizing assumptions and institutions of modern political life—from sovereignty to democracy—require rethinking since power is no longer simply organized along national or territorial lines. Furthermore the existence of enormous global inequalities of economic, military, and social power have created a distorted global politics in which the interests of the few more often than not take precedence over the interests of the majority of humankind. Whether a more just and democratic global politics can be fashioned out of the contemporary global condition is a matter of intense debate among theorists, practioners, and activists alike. The chapter has three interrelated objectives: to elucidate and elaborate the concept of globalization; to examine and explore its implications for world politics; and to discuss and reflect upon the key normative issues posed by globalization for the study of world politics.

Introduction

Globalization—simply the widening, deepening, and speeding up of worldwide interconnectedness—is a contentious issue in the study of world politics. Some—the **hyperglobalists**—argue that it is bringing about the demise of the sovereign nation-state as global forces undermine the ability of governments to control their own economies and societies (Ohmae 1995; Scholte 2000). Others—the **sceptics**—reject the idea of globalization as so much 'globaloney', and argue that states and geopolitics remain the principal forces shaping world order (Krasner 1999; Gilpin 2001). This chapter takes a rather different approach—a **transformationalist** perspective—arguing that both the hyperglobalists and sceptics alike exaggerate their arguments and thereby misconstrue the contemporary world order. By contrast while the transformationalist perspective takes globalization seriously it acknowledges that it is leading not so much to the demise of the sovereign state but to a globalization of politics: to the emergence of a conspicuously global politics in which the traditional distinction between domestic and international affairs is no longer valid. Under these conditions 'politics everywhere, it would seem, are related to politics everywhere else' such that orthodox approaches to the study of international relations—which are constructed upon this very distinction—provide at best only a partial insight into the real nature and functioning of the current world order (Rosenau in Mansbach, Ferguson, and Lamperst 1976: 22).

Since it is such a 'slippery' and misused concept it is hardly surprising that globalization should engender such intense debate. Accordingly, this chapter commences by elucidating the concept of globalization before exploring its implications for the study of world politics. The chapter is organized into three main sections: section one will address several interrelated questions, namely: What is globalization? How is it best conceptualized and defined? How is it manifest today, most especially given the events of 9/11? Is it really all that new? Section two will discuss the ways in which globalization is contributing to the emergence of a distorted global politics which is highly skewed in favour of a global elite and to the exclusion of the majority of humankind. Finally, section three will reflect upon the ethical challenges posed by the realities of this distorted global politics and current normative thinking about the conditions, and prospects for, a more humane global politics which is both more inclusive of, and responsive to, those in greatest need in the global community.

Making sense of globalization

Over the last three decades the sheer scale and scope of global interconnectedness has become increasingly evident in every sphere from the economic to the cultural.

Worldwide economic integration has intensified as the expansion of global commerce, finance, and production links together the fate of nations, communities, and households across the world's major economic regions and beyond within an emerging global market economy. Crises in one region, whether the collapse of the Argentinean economy in 2002 or the East Asian recession of 1997, take their toll on jobs, production, savings, and investment many thousands of miles away, while a slowdown in the US economy is felt everywhere from Birmingham to Bangkok.

Everyday over $1.2 trillion flows across the world's foreign exchange markets so that no government, even the most powerful, has the resources to resist sustained speculation against its currency and thereby the credibility of its economic policy (see Ch.27). In 1992 the British Government was forced to abandon its economic strategy and devalue the pound as it came under sustained attack from currency speculators.

Transnational corporations now account for between 25 and 33 per cent of world output, 70 per cent of world trade, and 80 per cent of international investment, while overseas production by these firms exceeds considerably the level of world exports, making them key players in the global economy controlling the location and distribution of economic and technological resources.

New modes and infrastructures of global communication have made it possible to organize and mobilize like-minded people across the globe in virtual real time as expressed in coordinated worldwide protests in early 2003 against military intervention in Iraq and the 45,000 international NGOs, from Greenpeace to the Climate Action Network, not to mention the activities of transnational criminal and terrorist networks, from drugs cartels to Al Qaeda (see Ch.28).

With a global communications infrastructure has also come the transnational spread of ideas, cultures, and information, from Madonna to Muhammad, both amongst like-minded peoples and between different cultural groups—reinforcing simultaneous tendencies towards both an expanded sense of global solidarity amongst the like minded and difference, if not outright, hostility between different cultures, nations, and ethnic groupings.

People—with their cultures—are also on the move in their millions—whether legally or illegally—with global migration almost on a scale of the great nineteenth-century movements but transcending all continents, from south to north and east to west, while over 550 million tourists are on the move every year.

As globalization has proceeded so has the recognition of transnational problems requiring global regulation, from climate change to the proliferation of weapons of mass destruction. Dealing with these transnational issues has led to an explosive growth of transnational and global forms of rule-making and regulation through both the expanding jurisdiction of established international organizations, such as the International Monetary Fund or the Inter-

national Civil Aviation Organization, and the literally thousands of informal networks of cooperation between parallel government agencies in different countries, from the Financial Action Task Force (which brings together government experts on money-laundering from different countries) and the Dublin Group (which brings together drug enforcement agencies from the EU, USA, and other countries).

With the recognition of global problems and global interconnectedness has come a growing awareness of the multiple ways in which the security and prosperity of communities in different regions of the world is bound together. A single terrorist bombing in Bali has repercussions for public perceptions of security in Europe and the USA, while agricultural subsidies in the USA and the EU have significant consequences for the livelihoods of farmers in Africa, Latin America, and the Caribbean.

We inhabit a world in which the most distant events can rapidly, if not almost instantaneously, come to have very profound consequences for our individual and collective prosperity and perceptions of security. For those of a sceptical persuasion, however, this is far from a novel condition nor is it necessarily evidence of globalization if that term means something more than simply international interdependence, i.e. linkages between countries.

What then distinguishes the concept of globalization from notions of internationalization or interdependence? What, in other words, is globalization?

Key points

- Over the last three decades the sheer scale and scope of global interconnectedness has become increasingly evident in every sphere from the economic to the cultural. Sceptics do not regard this as evidence of globalization if that term means something more than simply international interdependence, i.e. linkages between countries. The key issue becomes what we understand by the term 'globalization'.

Conceptualizing globalization

Initially it might be helpful to think of **globalization** as a process characterized by:

- a *stretching* of social, political, and economic activities across political frontiers so that events, decisions, and activities in one region of the world come to have significance for individuals and communities in distant regions of the globe. Civil wars and conflict in the world's poorest regions increase the flow of asylum seekers and illegal migrants into the world's affluent countries;

- the intensification, or the growing *magnitude*, of interconnectedness, in almost every sphere of social existence from the economic to the ecological, from the activities of Microsoft to the spread of harmful microbes, such as the SARS virus, from the intensification of world trade to the spread of weapons of mass destruction;

- the *accelerating pace* of global interactions and processes as the evolution of worldwide systems of transport and communication increases the rapidity or velocity with which ideas, news, goods, information, capital, and technology move around the world. Routine telephone banking transactions in the UK are dealt with by call centres in India in real time;

- the growing *extensity*, *intensity*, and *velocity* of global interactions is associated with a *deepening* enmeshment of the local and global in so far as local events may come to have global consequences and global events can have serious local consequences creating a growing collective awareness or consciousness of the world as a shared social space, i.e. globality or **globalism** This is expressed, amongst other ways, in the worldwide diffusion of the very idea of globalization itself as it becomes incorporated into the world's many languages from Mandarin to Gaelic.

As this brief description suggests there is more to the concept of globalization than simply interconnectedness. It implies that the cumulative scale, scope, velocity, and depth of contemporary interconnectedness is dissolving the significance of the borders and boundaries which separate the world into its some 193 constituent states or national economic and political spaces (Rosenau 1997). Rather than growing interdependence between discrete bounded national states, or **internationalization** as the sceptics refer to it, the concept of globalization seeks to capture the dramatic shift that is underway in the organization of human affairs: from a world of discrete but interdependent national states to the world as a shared social space. The concept of globalization therefore carries with it the implication of an unfolding process of structural change in the scale of human social and economic organization. Rather than social, economic, and political activities being organized primarily on a local or national scale today they are also increasingly organized on a transnational or global scale (see Box 1.1). Globalization therefore denotes a significant shift in the scale of social organization, in every sphere from the economic to the security, transcending the world's major regions and continents.

Central to this structural change are contemporary informatics technologies and infrastructures of communication and transportation. These have greatly facilitated new forms and possibilities of virtual real-time worldwide organization and **coordination** from the operations of multinational corporations to the worldwide mobilization and demonstrations of the anti-globalization movement. Although geography and distance still matter it is nevertheless the case that globalization is synonymous with a process of **time-space compression**— literally a shrinking world—in which the sources of even very local **developments**, from unemployment to ethnic conflict, may be traced to distant conditions or decisions. In this respect globalization embodies a process of **deterritorialization**: as social, political, and economic activities are increasingly 'stretched' across the globe they become in a significant sense no longer organized solely according to a strictly territorial logic. Terrorist and criminal networks, for instance, operate both locally and globally. National economic space, under conditions of globalization, is no longer coterminous with

| Box 1.1 | Political globalization |

Stretching: in the political sphere globalization is evident in the way turmoil on the West Bank ripples out across the globe or in how the decisions of the World Trade Organization may dramatically affect the livelihoods of steel workers in Europe, rice farmers in Japan, or access to medicines for the world's poorest communities. Politics is effectively 'stretched' across frontiers as developments or decisions in one locality come to have significant (intended and unintended) consequences for distant communities.

Thickening: associated with this stretching is a thickening of the infrastructures of worldwide political interaction. Since the mid-twentieth century, there has been a phenomenal expansion of global, regional, and transnational institutions or networks of rule-making and surveillance, from the World Trade Organization to the World Toilet Organization. More than 6,400 multilateral organizations or networks of officials seek to monitor and regulate every sector of global activity, from the Missile Technology Control regime—which seeks to prevent the diffusion of missile technologies to unstable regimes—to the International Telecommunications Union which sets global communications standards. Beyond governments and their officials, citizens and private organizations too have also acquired a global presence (with official sources recording the existence of some 47,098 international NGOs in 2001) as they organize across national borders to promote and pursue their common interests.

Speeding up: furthermore, instantaneous communications and almost real-time media reporting alter, sometimes quite

fundamentally, the context and dynamics of politics and policymaking. An incautious remark at a daily press briefing in Washington may require instant rebuttal from No. 10 Downing Street lest it undermine the British Government's official position. For governments, no less for many transnational corporations, reaction and decision times have shrunk under the pressures of 24-hour-a-day global media reporting and global markets. Moreover, decisions in one organization rapidly cascade through global systems, with cumulative worldwide effects often magnifying their unintended and adverse consequences. When the Thai monetary authorities decided to de-link the Thai Baht from the US dollar in July 1997, they could not have predicated that this would trigger the worst financial crisis throughout East Asia since the Great Depression and threaten global financial stability. Global communications are transforming the context of politics, speeding up political processes and the diffusion of political ideas, and amplifying the worldwide impacts of political action and decisionmaking.

Deepening: with this stretching, thickening, and speeding up of political processes comes a significant blurring of the local–global or domestic–foreign divide. Managing the domestic economy increasingly requires concerted multilateral cooperation while dealing with global warming demands coordinated local actions. Domestic issues are becoming internationalized and world affairs are becoming domesticated, creating a new breed of 'intermestic' (i.e. **inter**(national)(do)**mestic**) policy problems arising from the globalization of economic, social, and cultural life.

national territorial space since, for example, many of the UK's largest companies have their headquarters abroad while many domestic companies now outsource their production to China and East Asia amongst other locations. Territorial borders no longer demarcate the boundaries of national economic or political space. This is not to argue that territory and borders are now irrelevant but rather to acknowledge that under conditions of globalization their *relative significance*, as constraints upon social action and the exercise of power, is declining. In an era of instantaneous real-time global communication and organization the distinction between the domestic and the international, inside and outside the state breaks down.

A 'shrinking world' implies that sites of power and the subjects of power quite literally may be continents apart. Under these conditions the location of power cannot be disclosed simply by reference to local circumstances. As the East Asian economic collapse of 1997/8 demonstrated, key sites of global power, such as the International Monetary Fund and the World Bank, are quite literally oceans apart from the communities whose destiny they shape (see Ch.14). In this regard globalization involves the idea that power, whether economic, political, and cultural or military is increasingly organized and exercised at a distance. As such the concept of globalization denotes the **relative denationalization** of power in so far as, in an increasingly interconnected

Globalization is variously defined in the literature as:

1. 'The intensification of worldwide social relations which link distant localities in such a way that local happenings are shaped by events occurring many miles away and vice versa' (Giddens 1990: 21).

2. 'The integration of the world-economy' (Gilpin 2001: 364).

3. 'De-territorialization—or . . . the growth of supraterritorial relations between people' (Scholte 2000: 46).

4. 'time-space compression' (Harvey 1999).

global system, power is organized and exercised on a trans-regional, transnational, or transcontinental basis while—as noted in the discussion of political globalization–many other actors, from international organizations to criminal networks, exercise power within, across, and against states. States no longer have a monopoly of power resources whether economic, coercive, or political.

To summarize: globalization is a process which involves much more than simply growing connections or interdependence between states. It can be defined as:

> A historical process involving a fundamental shift or transformation in the spatial scale of human social organization that links distant communities and expands the reach of power relations across regions and continents.

Such a definition enables us to distinguish globalization from more spatially delimited processes such as **internationalization** and **regionalization**. Whereas internationalization refers to growing interdependence between states, the very idea of *internationalization* presumes that they remain discrete national units with clearly demarcated borders. By contrast globalization refers to a process in which the very distinction between the domestic and the external breaks down. Distance and time are collapsed, so that events many thousands of miles away can come to have almost immediate local consequences while the impacts of even more localized developments may be diffused rapidly around the globe. This is not to argue that distance and borders are now irrelevant but rather to acknowledge that under conditions of globalization their *relative significance*, as constraints upon social activity and the exercise of power, is declining.

If globalization refers to transcontinental or transregional networks, flows, or interconnectedness then **regionalization** can be conceived as the intensification of patterns of interconnectedness and integration amongst states which share common borders or are geographically proximate as in the European Union (see Ch.26). Accordingly, whereas flows of trade and finance between the world's three major economic blocs—North America, Asia Pacific, and Europe—constitute globalization by contrast such flows within these blocs are best described as regionalization.

Key points

- Globalization is evident in the growing extensity, intensity, velocity, and deepening impact of worldwide interconnectedness.

- Globalization denotes a shift in the scale of social organization, the emergence of the world as a shared social space, the relative deterritorialization of social, economic, and political activity, and the relative denationalization of power.

- Globalization can be conceptualized as a fundamental shift or transformation in the spatial scale of human social organization that links distant communities and expands the reach of power relations across regions and continents.

- Globalization is to be distinguished from internationalization and regionalization.

Box 1.3   Key concepts

Transnational civil society: a political arena in which citizens and private interests collaborate across borders to advance their mutual goals or to bring governments and the formal institutions of global governance to account for their activities.

Globalization: a historical process involving a fundamental shift or transformation in the spatial scale of human social organization that links distant communities and expands the reach of power relations across regions and continents.

Asymmetrical globalization: describes the way in which contemporary globalization is experienced unequally across the world and among different social groups, so that it produces a distinctive geography of inclusion in, and exclusion from, the global system.

Globalism: the condition of globalization at any particular time, usually gauged by its thickness or thinness.

Internationalization: growing interactions between national states.

Regionalization: growing interdependence between geographically contiguous states, as in the European Union (EU).

Institutionalization: the degree to which networks or patterns of social interaction are formally constituted as organizations with specific purposes.

Deterritorialization: a process in which the organization of social activities is increasingly less constrained by geographical proximity and national territorial boundaries.

Time-space compression: the technologically induced erosion of distance and time giving the appearance of a world that is in communication terms shrinking.

Global governance: the evolving system of (formal and informal) political coordination—across multiple levels from the local to the global—amongst public authorities (states and IGOs) and private agencies (NGOs and corporate actors) seeking to realize common purposes or resolve collective problems through the making and implementing of global or transnational norms, rules, programmes, and policies.

Global politics: the politics of global social relations in which the pursuit of power, interests, order, and justice transcends regions and continents.

Global polity: the collective structures and processes by which 'interests are articulated and aggregated, decisions are made, values allocated and policies conducted through international or transnational political processes' (Ougaard 2004: 5).

Transgovernmental networks: formal and informal mechanisms which link government officials in one agency with their foreign counterparts for purposes of policy coordination, harmonization, dialogue, and enforcement.

Global policy networks: complexes which bring together the representatives of governments, international organizations NGOs, and the corporate sector for the formulation and implementation of global public policy.

Normative theory: systematic analyses of the ethical, moral, and political principles which either govern or ought to govern the organization or conduct of global politics.

The disaggregated state: the tendency for states to become increasingly fragmented actors in global politics as every part of the government machine becomes entangled with its foreign counterparts and others in dealing with global issues through proliferating transgovernmental and global policy networks.

Sovereignty: the rightful entitlement to exclusive, unqualified, and supreme rule within a delimited territory.

Contemporary globalization

According to John Gray the cataclysmic attacks on the United States, on 11 September 2001, herald a new epoch in world affairs, 'The era of globalization is over' (Naim 2002). States have reasserted their power and borders have been sealed, however imperfectly, in response to the perceived worldwide terrorist threat. Measured in terms of flows within the circuits of the world-economy, economic globalization has undoubtedly stalled by comparison with the position at the turn of the century. This has been seized upon by those of a sceptical persuasion as confirmation of their argument (Hirst and

Thompson 2003). Sceptics conclude that not only has globalization been highly exaggerated but it is a myth which has concealed the reality of a world which is less interdependent than it was in the nineteenth century and one which is increasingly regionalized rather than globalized (Hirst and Thompson 1999; Gilpin 2002). By contrast, for many of a more globalist persuasion, 9/11 and the climate of insecurity it has engendered are evidence of a pervasive 'clash of globalizations'. This is expressed in the form of a heightening confrontation between the globalization of Western modernity (i.e. ways of life) and the globalization of reactions against it. What is at issue here, at least in part, are differing theoretical and historical interpretations of globalization.

One of the problems of the sceptical argument is that it tends to conflate globalization solely with economic trends. It thus tends to overlook other evidence. Indeed contemporary globalization is not a singular process: it operates within all aspects of social life from politics to production, culture to crime, and economics to education. It is implicated directly and indirectly in many aspects of our daily lives, from the clothes we wear, the food we eat, the knowledge we accumulate, through to our individual and collective sense of security in an uncertain world. Evidence of globalization is all around us: universities are literally global institutions from the recruitment of students to the dissemination of academic research. To understand contemporary globalization therefore requires a mapping of the distinctive patterns of worldwide interconnectedness in all of the key sectors of social activity from the economic and the political through to the military, the cultural, and the ecological.

As Box 1.5 illustrates globalization is occurring, albeit with varying intensity and at a varying pace, in every domain of social activity. Of course it is more advanced in some domains than others. For instance economic globalization is much more extensive and intensive than is cultural or military globalization. To this extent contemporary globalization is highly *uneven*, with the result that in seeking to understand it we have to ask the prior question: the globalization of what? Contrary to the sceptics it is crucial to recognize that globalization is a complex *multidimensional process*: patterns of economic globalization and cultural globalization are not identical. In this respect to draw general conclusions about globalizing trends simply from one domain produces a false picture. As noted, in the aftermath of 9/11 the slowdown in economic globalization was heralded by sceptics as marking the end of globalization yet this ignored the accelerating pace of globalization in the military, technological, and cultural domains. Moreover what is highly distinctive about contemporary globalization is the confluence of globalizing tendencies across all the key domains of social activity. Significantly, these tendencies have proved remarkably robust in the face of global instability and military conflicts.

If patterns of contemporary globalization are uneven they are also highly *asymmetrical*. It is a

---

Box 1.4   The sceptical view of globalization

Sceptical accounts of globalization tend to dismiss its significance for the study of world politics. They do so on the grounds that:

1. By comparison with the period 1870 to 1914 the world is much less globalized economically, politically, and culturally.

2. Rather than globalization the contemporary world is marked by intensifying regionalization and internationalization.

3. The vast bulk of international economic and political activity is concentrated within the group of OECD states.

4. By comparison with the heyday of European global empires the majority of the world's population and countries in the South are now much less integrated into the global system.

5. State power, nationalism, and territorial boundaries are of growing, not less, importance in world politics.

6. Internationalization and regionalization are creatures of states not corporations or capitalism

7. Globalization is at best a self-serving myth or ideology which reinforces Western and particularly US hegemony in world politics.

(Hirst and Thompson 1999; Hay 2000; Hoogvelt 2001; Gilpin 2002; Hirst and Thompson 2003)

Box 1.5   Patterns of contemporary globalization

Globalization, to varying degrees, is evident in all the principal sectors of social activity:

Economic: in the economic sphere, patterns of worldwide trade, finance, and production are creating global markets and, in the process, a single global capitalist economy—what Castells (2000) calls 'global informational capitalism'. Multinational corporations organize production and marketing on a global basis while the operation of global financial markets determines which countries get credit and upon what terms.

Military: in the military domain the global arms trade, the proliferation of weapons of mass destruction, the growth of transnational terrorism, the growing significance of transnational military corporations, and the discourse of global insecurity point to the existence of a global military order.

Legal: the expansion of transnational and international law from trade to human rights alongside the creation of new world legal institutions such as the International Criminal Court is indicative of an emerging global legal order.

Ecological: a shared ecology involves shared environmental problems, from global warming to species protection, alongside the creation of multilateral responses and regimes of global environmental governance.

Cultural: involves a complex mix of homogenization and increased heterogeneity given the global diffusion of popular culture, global media corporations, communications networks, etc., simultaneously with the reassertion of nationalism, ethnicity, and difference. But few cultures are hermetically sealed off from cultural interaction.

Social: shifting patterns of migration from South to North and East to West have turned migration into a major global issue as movements come close to the record levels of the great nineteenth-century movements of people.

Box 1.6   The engines of globalization

Explanations of globalization tend to focus on three inter-related factors, namely: technics (technological change and social organization); economics (markets and capitalism); and politics (power, interests, and institutions).

Technics is central to any account of globalization since it is a truism that without modern communications infrastructures, in particular, a global system or worldwide economy would not be possible.

Economics—crucial as technology is, so too is its specifically **economic** logic. Capitalism's insatiable requirement for new markets and profits lead inevitably to the globalization of economic activity.

Politics—shorthand here for ideas, interests, and power—constitutes the third logic of globalization. If technology provides the physical infrastructure of globalization politics provides its normative infrastructure. Governments, such as those of the USA and the UK, have been critical actors in nurturing the process of globalization.

Box 1.7   Globalization since 9/11

'Before anyone rushes to give the last rites to globalization, keep in mind that we've heard it all before. In the months following the September 11, 2001 terrorist attacks, pundits were predicting the end of globalization as we knew it. The porous borders that made possible the unprecedented global movement of money, goods, people, and ideas were to be encircled by barbed wire and checkpoints, bringing trade and travel to a halt. . . . Despite all its travails, the world was more—not less—integrated at the end of 2002 than it had ever been before.'

(*Foreign Policy*, Feb. 2004)

common misconception of many sceptics that globalization implies universalism: that the 'global' in globalization implies that all regions or countries must be similarly enmeshed in worldwide processes. This is plainly not the case for it very markedly involves differential patterns of enmeshment, giving it what Castells calls its 'variable geometry' (Castells 2000). The rich OECD countries are much more globalized than many of the poorest sub-Saharan African states. Globalization is not uniformly experienced across all regions, countries, or even communities since it is inevitably a highly asymmetrical process. Even within OECD states and sub-Saharan African states many elites are in the vanguard of globalization while others find themselves excluded. As a highly asymmetrical process globalization exhibits a distinctive geography of inclusion and exclusion resulting in clear winners and losers not just between countries but within and across them. For the most affluent it may very well entail a shrinking world—jet travel, global television and the World Wide Web—but for the largest slice of humanity it tends to be associated with a profound sense of disempowerment. Inequality is inscribed deeply in the very processes of contemporary globalization such that it is more accurately described as **asymmetrical globalization**.

Given such asymmetries it should not be surprising to learn that globalization does not prefigure the emergence of a global community or an ethic of global cooperation. On the contrary, as 9/11 tragically demonstrated, the more the world becomes a shared social space the greater the sense of division, difference, and contest it creates. Asymmetrical globalization is principally perceived beyond the OECD core as Western globalization, provoking fears of a new **imperialism** and significant counter-reactions, from the protests of the anti-globalization movement to the actions of different cultural or national communities seeking to protect their indigenous culture and way of life. Rather than a more cooperative world order contemporary globalization, in many respects, has exacerbated existing tensions and conflicts, generated new divisions and insecurities, creating a more unruly world. Globalization is a complex process embodying contradictory tendencies towards global integration and fragmentation, cooperation and conflict, order and disorder. This has been its history.

By comparison with previous periods, contemporary globalization combines a remarkable confluence of dense patterns of global interconnectedness, alongside their unprecedented **institutionalization** through new global and regional infrastructures of control and communication, from the WTO to the transnational corporations. In nearly all domains contemporary patterns of globalization have not

Box 1.8   The three waves of globalization

Globalization is not a novel phenomenon. Viewed as a secular historical process by which human civilizations have come to form a single world system it has occurred in three distinct waves.

In the first wave, the age of discovery (1450–1850), globalization was decisively shaped by European expansion and conquest.

The second wave (1850–1945) evidenced a major expansion in the spread and entrenchment of European empires.

By comparison contemporary globalization (1960 on) marks a new epoch in human affairs. Just as the industrial revolution and the expansion of the West in the nineteenth century defined a new age in world history so today the microchip and the satellite are icons of a globalized world order.

only surpassed those of earlier epochs, but also displayed unparalleled qualitative differences—that is in terms of how globalization is organized and managed. The existence of new real-time global communications infrastructures, in which the world literally is transformed into a single social space, distinguishes very clearly contemporary globalization from that of the past. In these respects it is best described as a thick form of globalization or globalism (Held, McGrew *et al.* 1999; Keohane and Nye 2003).

As such it delineates the set of constraints and opportunities which confront governments and thereby conditions their freedom of action or autonomy, most especially in the economic realm. For instance the unprecedented scale of global financial flows at over $1.2 trillion a day imposes a significant discipline on any government, even the most economically powerful, in its conduct of national economic policy. Thick globalization embodies a powerful systemic logic in so far as it structures the context in which states operate and thereby defines the parameters of state power. It therefore has significant consequences for how we think about world politics.

Key points

- The contemporary phase of globalization has proved more robust in the aftermath of 9/11 than the sceptics recognize.

- Contemporary globalization is a multidimensional, uneven, and asymmetrical process.

- Contemporary globalization is best described as a thick form of globalization or globalism.

A world transformed: globalization and distorted global politics

Consider a political map of the world: its most striking feature is the division of the entire earth's surface into over 190 neatly defined territorial units, namely states. To a student of politics in the Middle Ages such a representation of the world, which gave primacy to borders and boundaries, would make little sense. Historically borders are a relatively recent invention as is the idea that states are sovereign, self-governing, territorially delimited political communities or polities. Although today a convenient fiction, this presumption remains central to orthodox state-centric conceptions of world politics as the pursuit of power and interests between sovereign states. Globalization, however, calls this state-centric conception of world politics into question. Taking globalization seriously therefore requires a conceptual shift in the way we think about world politics.

The Westphalian Constitution of world order

The Peace Treaties of Westphalia and Osnabruck (1648) established the legal basis of modern statehood and by implication the fundamental rules or constitution of modern world politics. Although Pope Innocent referred to the Westphalian settlement at the time as a 'null, reprobate and devoid of meaning for all time', in the course of the subsequent four centuries it has formed the normative structure or constitution of the modern world order At the heart of the Westphalian settlement was

agreement amongst Europe's rulers to recognize each other's right to rule their own territories free from outside interference. This was codified over time in the doctrine of sovereign statehood. But it was only in the twentieth century, as global empires collapsed, that sovereign statehood and with it national self-determination finally acquired the status of universal organizing principles of world politics. Contrary to Pope Innocent's desires the Westphalian constitution by then had come to colonize the entire planet.

Constitutions are important because they establish the location of legitimate political authority within a polity and the rules which inform the exercise and limits of political power. In codifying and legitimating the principle of sovereign statehood the Westphalian constitution gave birth to the modern

| Box 1.9 | The Westphalian Constitution of world politics |

1. **Territoriality**: humankind is organized principally into exclusive territorial (political) communities with fixed borders.

2. **Sovereignty**: within its borders the state or government has an entitlement to supreme, unqualified, and exclusive political and legal authority.

3. **Autonomy**: countries appear as autonomous containers of political, social, and economic activity in that fixed borders separate the domestic sphere from the world outside.

states-system. It welded together the idea of **territoriality** with the notion of legitimate sovereign rule. Westphalian sovereignty located supreme legal and political authority with territorially delimited states. Sovereignty involved the rightful entitlement to exclusive, unqualified, and supreme rule within a delimited territory. It was exclusive in so far as no ruler had the right to intervene in the sovereign affairs of other nations; unqualified in that within their territories rulers had complete authority over their subjects; and supreme in that there was no legal or political authority beyond the state. Of course for many, especially weak states, sovereignty—as the legitimate claim to rule—has not always translated into effective control within their territories. As Krasner recognizes, the Westphalian system has for many states been little more than a form of 'organized hypocrisy' (Krasner 1999). Nevertheless this never fundamentally compromised its **influence** upon the developmental trajectory of world politics. Although the UN Charter and the Universal Declaration on Human Rights modified aspects of the Westphalian Constitution, in qualifying aspects of **state sovereignty**, it remains the founding covenant of world politics. However many argue that contemporary globalization presents a fundamental challenge to the Westphalian ideal of sovereign statehood and in so doing is transforming world order.

From (state-centric) geopolitics to (geocentric) global politics

As globalization has intensified over the last five decades, it has become increasingly difficult to maintain the popular fiction of the 'great divide': that is, treating political life as having two quite separate spheres of action, the domestic and the international, which operate according to different logics with different rules, actors, and agendas. There is a growing recognition that, as former President Clinton described it, 'the once bright line between domestic and foreign policy is blurring. If I could do anything to change the speech patterns of those of us in public life, I would like almost to stop hearing people talk about foreign policy and domestic policy, and instead start discussing economic policy, security policy,

environmental policy' (quoted Cusimano 2000: 6). As the substantive issues of political life consistently ignore the artificial foreign/domestic divide, from the worldwide coordination of anti-globalization protests to national courts enforcing the rulings of the World Trade Organization, the Westphalian Constitution appears increasingly anachronistic. A post-Westphalian world order is emerging and with it a distinctive form of **global politics**.

To talk of global politics is to recognize that politics itself has been globalized and that as a consequence there is much more to the study of world politics than conflict and cooperation between states. In other words globalization challenges the one-dimensionality of orthodox accounts of world politics which conceive it purely in terms of geopolitics and the struggle for power between states. By contrast the concept of global politics focuses our attention upon the global structures and processes of rule-making, problem-solving, and the maintenance of security and order in the world system (Brown 1992). It requires us to acknowledge the importance of states and geopolitics but not a priori to grant them a privileged status in understanding and explaining contemporary world affairs. For, as noted (Box 1.1), under conditions of political globalization states are increasingly embedded in thickening and overlapping worldwide webs of: multilateral institutions and multilateral politics such as NATO and to the World Bank; transnational associations and networks, from the International Chamber of Commerce to the World Muslim Congress; **global policy networks** of officials, corporate and non-governmental actors, dealing with global issues, such as the Global AIDS Fund and the Roll Back Malaria Initiative; and those formal and informal (transgovernmental) networks of government officials dealing with shared global problems, including the Basle Committee of central bankers and the Financial Action Task Force on money-laundering (Fig. 1.1).

Global politics directs our attention to the emergence of a fragile **global polity** within which 'interests are articulated and aggregated, decisions are made, values allocated and policies conducted through international or transnational political processes' (Ougaard 2004: 5). In other words to how the global order is, or is not, governed.

Since the UN's creation in 1945 a vast nexus of

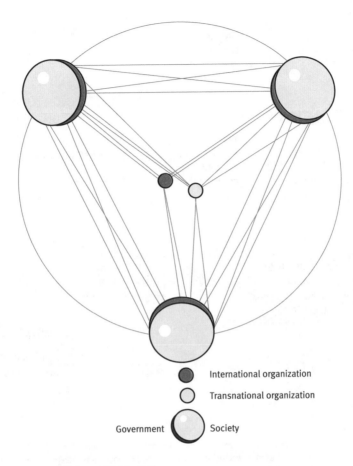

Fig. 1.1 The World Wide Web

global and regional institutions has evolved surrounded by a proliferation of non-governmental
agencies and networks seeking to influence the governance of global affairs. Whilst world government
remains a fanciful idea, there does exist an evolving
global governance complex—embracing states,
international institutions, transnational networks
and agencies (both public and private)—which functions, with variable effect, to promote, regulate, or
intervene in, the common affairs of humanity. Over
the last five decades, its scope and impact have
expanded dramatically with the result that its activities have become significantly politicized, as global
protests against the WTO attest.

This evolving global governance complex
encompasses the multitude of formal and informal
structures of political coordination amongst gov-

ernments; intergovernmental and transnational
agencies—public and private—designed to realize
common purposes or collectively agreed goals
through the making or implementing of global or
transnational rules, and the regulation of transborder problems. A good illustration of this is the
creation of international labour codes to protect
vulnerable workers. The international Convention
on the Elimination of Child Labour, for instance, was
the product of a complex politics involving public
and private actors from trade unions, industrial
associations, humanitarian groups, governments,
legal experts, not forgetting officials and experts
within the International Labour Organization.

Within this global governance complex private
or non-governmental agencies have become
increasingly influential in the formulation and

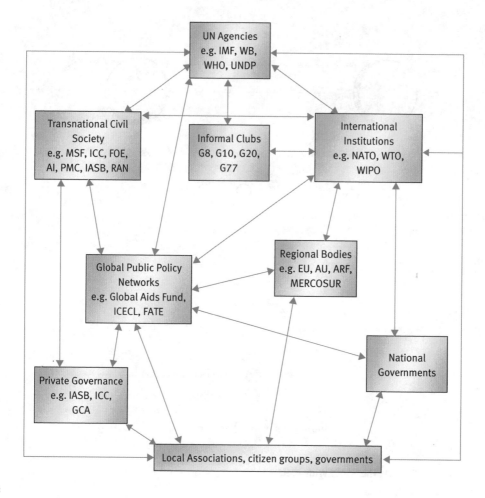

KEY:

IMF	International Monetary Fund
WB	World Bank
WHO	World Health Organization
UNDP	UN Development Programme
G8	Group of 8 (US, Italy, UK, France, Germany, Russia, Canada, Japan & EU)
G77	Group of 77 developing countries
MSF	Medecin sans Frontieres
ICC	International Chamber of Commerce
FOE	Friends of the Earth
AI	Amnesty International
PMC	Private Military Companies, e.g. Sandline
MWNC	Multinational Corporations, e.g. Shell
RAN	Rainforest Action Network

IASB	International Accounting Standards Board
ICECL	International Convention on the Elimination of Child Labour
FATF	Financial Action Task Force (on money laundering)
GCA	Global Credit Agencies, e.g. Moodies, Standard and Poor
ARF	Asean Regional Forum
EU	European Union
MERCOSUR	Southern American Common Market
AU	African Union
NATO	North Atlantic Treaty Organization
WTO	World Trade Organization
WIPO	World Intellectual Property Rights Organization

Fig. 1.2 **The global governance complex**

implementation of global public policy. The International Accounting Standards Board establishes global accounting rules, while the major **bond-rating** agencies, such as Moodys and Standard and Poor, determine the credit status of governments and corporations around the globe. This is a form of private global governance in which private organizations regulate, often in the shadow of global public authorities, aspects of global economic and social affairs. In those realms in which it has become highly significant, mainly the economic and the technological, this private global governance involves a relocation of authority from states and multilateral bodies to non-governmental organizations and private agencies.

Coextensive with the global governance complex is an embryonic **transnational civil society**. In recent decades a plethora of NGOs, transnational organizations (from the International Chamber of Commerce, international trade unions, the Rainforest Network, to the Catholic Church), advocacy networks—from the women's movement to Nazis on the net—and citizens' groups have come to play a significant role in mobilizing, organizing, and exercising political power across national boundaries. This has been facilitated by the speed and ease of modern global communications and a growing awareness of common interests between groups in different countries and regions of the world. At the UN Earth Summit in Rio de Janeiro in 1992, the key representatives of environmental, corporate, and other interested parties outnumbered the formal representatives of government. Of course, not all the members of transnational civil society are either civil or representative; some seek to further dubious, reactionary, or criminal causes while many lack effective accountability. Furthermore, there are considerable inequalities between the agencies of transnational civil society in terms of resources, influence and access to key centres of global decisionmaking. Multinational corporations, like Rupert Murdoch's News International, have much greater access to centres of power, and capacity to shape the global agenda, than does the Rainforest Action Network.

If global politics involves a diversity of actors and institutions it is also marked by a diversity of political concerns. The agenda of global politics is anchored not just to traditional geopolitical concerns but also to a proliferation of economic, social, cultural, and ecological questions. Pollution, drugs, human rights, and terrorism are among an increasing number of transnational policy issues which, because of globalization, transcend territorial borders and existing political jurisdictions, and thereby require international cooperation for their effective resolution. Politics today is marked by a proliferation of new types of 'boundary problem'. In the past, of course, nation-states principally resolved their differences over boundary matters by pursuing reasons of state backed by diplomatic initiatives and, ultimately, by coercive means. But this geopolitical logic appears singularly inadequate and inappropriate to resolve the many complex issues, from economic regulation to resource depletion and environmental degradation to chemical weapons proliferation, which engender—at seemingly ever-greater speeds—an intermeshing of 'national fortunes'.

This is not to argue that the sovereign state is in decline. The sovereign power and authority of national government—the entitlement of states to rule within their own territorial space—is being transformed but by no means eroded. Locked into systems of global and regional governance, states now assert their sovereignty less in the form of a legal claim to supreme power than as a bargaining tool, in the context of transnational systems of rule making, with other agencies and social forces. Sovereignty is bartered, shared, and divided amongst the agencies of public power at different levels from the local to the global. The Westphalian conception of sovereignty as an indivisible, territorially exclusive form of public power is being displaced by a new sovereignty regime—in which sovereignty is understood as the shared exercise of public power and authority. In this respect we are witnessing the emergence of a post-Westphalian world order.

Furthermore, far from globalization leading to 'the end of the state', it elicits a more activist state. This is because, in a world of global enmeshment, simply to achieve domestic objectives national governments are forced to engage in extensive multilateral **collaboration** and cooperation. But in becoming more embedded in frameworks of global and regional governance, states confront a real dilemma: in return for more effective public policy and meeting their citizens' demands, their capacity for self-governance—

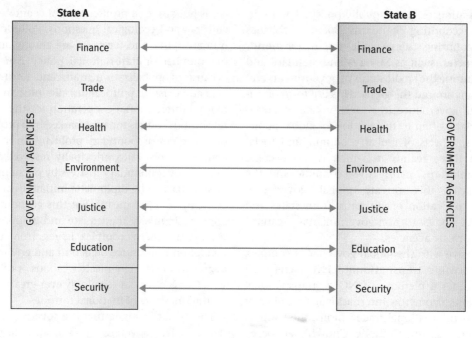

Patterns of Direct Communication Interaction and Transgovernmental Networks

Fig. 1.3 The disaggregated state

that is, **state autonomy**—is compromised. Today difficult trade-off is posed between effective governance and self-governance. In this respect, the Westphalian image of the monolithic, unitary state is being displaced by the image of the **disaggregated state** in which its constituent agencies increasingly interact with their counterparts abroad, international agencies, and NGOs in the management of common and global affairs (Slaughter 2004).

Global politics is a term which acknowledges that the scale of political life has fundamentally altered: politics understood as that set of activities concerned primarily with the achievement of order and justice does not recognize territorial boundaries. It asserts the growing irrelevance of the distinction between the domestic and the foreign, inside and outside the **territorial state**, the national and the international as decisions and actions taken in one region impact upon the welfare of communities in distant parts of the globe, with the result that domestic politics is internationalized and world politics becomes domesticated. It acknowledges that power in the global system is not the sole preserve of states but is distributed (unevenly) among a diverse array of public and private actors and networks (from international agencies, through corporations to NGOs) with important consequences for who gets what, how, when, and where. It recognizes that political authority has been diffused not only upwards to supra-state bodies, such as the EU, but also downwards to sub-state bodies, such as regional assemblies, and beyond the state to private agencies, such as the International Accounting Standards Board. It accepts that sovereignty remains a principal juridical attribute of states but concludes that it is increasingly divided and shared between local, national, regional, and global authorities. Finally, it affirms that, in an age of globalization, national polities no longer function as closed systems. On the contrary, it asserts that all politics—understood as the pursuit of order and justice—are played out in a global context.

However, as with globalization, inequality and exclusion are endemic features of contemporary

The post-Westphalian order

State sovereignty

The sovereign power and authority of national government—the entitlement of states to rule within their own territorial space—is being transformed but not necessarily eroded. Sovereignty today is increasingly understood as the shared exercise of public power and authority between national, regional, and global authorities.

State autonomy

In a more interdependent world, simply to achieve domestic objectives national governments are forced to engage in extensive multilateral collaboration and co-operation. But in becoming more embedded in frameworks of global and regional governance states confront a real dilemma: in return for more effective public policy and meeting their citizens' demands, whether in relation to the drugs trade or employment, their capacity for self-governance—that is state autonomy—is compromised.

Territoriality

Borders and territory still remain important, not least for administrative purposes. Under conditions of globalization, however, a new geography of political organization and political power is emerging which transcends territories and borders.

global politics. There are many reasons for this but three factors in particular are crucial: first, enormous inequalities of power between states; second, global governance is shaped by an unwritten constitution that tends to privilege the interests and agenda of global capitalism; third, the technocratic nature of much global decisionmaking, from health to security, tends to exclude many with a legitimate stake in the outcomes.

These three factors produce cumulative inequalities of power and exclusion—reflecting the inequalities of power between North and South—with the result that contemporary global politics is more accurately described as '**distorted global politics**': 'distorted' in the sense that inevitably those states and groups with greater power resources and access to key sites of global decisionmaking tend to have the greatest control or influence over the agenda and outcomes of global politics. In short, global politics has few democratic qualities. Whether a more democratic global politics is imaginable and what it might look like is the concern of normative theorists and is the subject of the concluding section of this chapter.

Key points

- Globalization is transforming but not burying the Westphalian ideal of sovereign statehood.

- Globalization requires a conceptual shift in our thinking about world politics from a primarily geopolitical perspective to the perspective of geocentric or global politics—the politics of worldwide social relations.

- Global politics is more accurately described as distorted global politics because it is afflicted by significant power asymmetries.

From distorted global politics to cosmopolitan global politics?

Globalization, it can be argued, is associated with a double democratic deficit. On the one hand it has compounded the tension between democracy, as a territoriality rooted system of rule, and the operation of global markets and transnational networks of corporate power. For if democratic governments are losing the capacity to manage transnational forces in accordance with the expressed preferences of their citizens then the very essence of democracy, namely self-governance, is decidedly compromised. On the other hand, it is associated with the emergence of a distorted global politics in which power asymmetries and global institutions more often than not enhance the interests of global elites at the expense of the wider world community. Many of the agencies of global civil society too are highly unrepresentative of the world's peoples. Distorted global politics in other words has weak democratic credentials. Arguably

Guiding ethical principles/core values	Global social justice, democracy, universal human rights, human security, rule of law, transnational solidarity
Short-term measures	*Governance* • Reform of global governance: representative Security Council; establishment of Human Security Council (to coordinate global development policies); Global Civil Society Forum; strengthened systems of global accountability; enhancement of national and regional governance infrastructures and capacities; enhanced parliamentary scrutiny *Economy* • Regulating global markets: selective capital controls; regulation of offshore financial centres; voluntary codes of conduct for MNCs • Promoting development: abolition of debt for highly indebted poor countries (HIPCs); meeting UN aid targets of 0.7% GNP; fair trade rules; removal of EU and US subsidies of agriculture and textiles *Security* • Strengthening global humanitarian protection capacities; implementation of existing global poverty reduction and human development commitments and policies; strengthening of arms control and arms trade regulation
Long-term transformations	*Governance* • Double democratization (national to supra-state governance); enhanced global public goods provision; global citizenship *Economy* • Taming global markets: World Financial Authority; mandatory codes of conduct for MNCs; global tax mechanism; global competition authority • Market correcting: mandatory global labour and environmental standards; foreign investment codes and standards; redistributive and compensatory measures; commodity price and supply agreements • Market promoting: privileged market access for developing countries; convention on global labour mobility *Security* • Global social charter; permanent peacekeeping and humanitarian emergency forces; social exclusion and equity impact reviews of all global development measures
Institutional/political conditions	Activist states, global progressive coalition (involving key Western and developing states and civil society forces), strong multilateral institutions, open regionalism, global civil society, redistributive regimes, regulation of global markets, transnational public sphere

Fig. 1.4 Cosmopolitan democracy

redressing this double democratic deficit, alongside global poverty reduction, are the greatest ethical and political challenges of the twenty-first century.

Within the **normative theory** of world politics (see Ch.12) one particular approach speaks directly to the failings of distorted global politics, namely, **cosmopolitanism** (Held 2002; Moellendorf 2002). Cosmopolitanism presents a radical critique of distorted global politics for the manner in which it perpetuates global inequalities and therefore global injustices. Realizing a more humane and just world order requires a reformed and more democratic system of global governance, which can at a minimum regulate global markets and prevent transnational harm to the most vulnerable. This might be termed the project of **cosmopolitan democracy**.

Cosmopolitan democracy can be conceived as a basis for combining the democratization of global governance with the pursuit of global social justice (see Ch.32). It seeks to nurture and institutionalize some of the core values of social democracy—the rule of law, political equality, democratic governance, social justice, social solidarity, and economic efficiency—within global power systems. Cosmopolitan democracy seeks to reinvigorate democracy within states by extending democracy to relations between and across states. Only through such a double democratization will the double democratic deficit created by globalization be addressed. In effect, those global sites and transnational networks of power which at present escape effective national democratic control will be brought to account, so establishing the conditions befitting the realization of a more humane and democratic global politics. In the context of a deeply divided world, in which violence is endemic and might seeks to impose right, the prospects for its realization might currently appear somewhat remote. Yet its advocates argue that it is rooted in the actually existing conditions of global politics.

Cosmopolitanism builds upon the argument that globalization is bringing about a post-Westphalian order. As a result the present world order combines, in an unstable mix, elements of both paradise and power: that is, of democratic principles and realpolitik (see Ch.7 and Ch.8). Thus the principles of self-determination, the rule of law, popular sovereignty, democratic legitimacy, the legal equality of states, and even redistribution (through aid) are embedded in distorted global politics juxtaposed with the idea that might is right and the primacy of the **national interest**. Moreover globalization has provoked major political reactions which in their more progressive manifestations have engendered a wider political debate about the democratic credentials of the existing global governance complex. Regulating globalization in the public and global interest has become a paramount political issue across the world. There is now increased political pressure on **G8** governments especially to bring good governance to global governance by making it more transparent, accountable, and legitimate. A broader global consensus appears to be emerging on the need for such reform, drawing political support from across the North–South divide and among diverse constituencies of transnational civil society. In short, distorted global politics gives expression to diverse democratic impulses and constituencies. However, it would be foolish to assume that such impulses and constituencies will triumph in the near future since arrayed against them are powerful global forces which resist the creation of a more cosmopolitan or humane global politics.

Arguably, distorted global politics embodies a historic struggle between the logic of power politics (statism) and the logic of cosmopolitanism, between power and paradise. Its future trajectory, however, remains wholly speculative. That it is so is a source of both intellectual despair and huge relief: despair since it reaffirms the limits of our current theories of world politics in so far as they offer scant guide to the future, relief because it confirms that the future remains to be made, even if, to paraphrase Marx, it is not within the conditions of our own choosing. Therefore globalization undoubtedly will remain a powerful force for global change, hopefully for the better but quite possibly for the worse.

Key points

- Globalization creates a double democratic deficit in that it places limits on democracy within states and new mechanisms of global governance which lack democratic credentials.

- Global politics has engendered its own global political theory which draws upon cosmopolitan thinking.

- Cosmopolitanism offers an account of the desirability and feasibility of the democratization of global politics.

- Distorted global politics can be interpreted as expressing a contest between the forces of statism and cosmopolitanism in the conduct and management of world affairs.

Conclusion

This chapter has sought to elucidate the concept of globalization and identify its implications for the study of world politics. It has argued that globalization reconstructs the world as a shared social space. But it does so in a far from uniform manner: contemporary globalization is highly uneven—it varies in its intensity and extensity between different spheres of activity; and highly asymmetrical—it engenders a highly unequal geography of global inclusion and exclusion. In doing so it is as much a source of conflict as of cooperation in world affairs.

In focusing upon the consequences of globalization for the study of international relations, this chapter has argued that it engenders a fundamental shift in the constitution of world politics. A post-Westphalian world order is in the making as sovereign statehood is transformed by the dynamics of globalization. A conceptual shift in our thinking is therefore required: from geopolitics (or inter-state politics) to global politics—the politics of state and non-state actors within a shared global social space. But global politics reflects deep inequalities of power with the result that in its current configuration it is more accurately described as distorted global politics. Cosmopolitan theory, it was noted, suggests that a more democratic form of global politics is both desirable and feasible. To this extent the trajectory of global politics will be shaped significantly by the struggle between the forces of statism and cosmopolitanism, or might is right versus right is might. The outcome of this contest will determine whether twenty-first-century global politics will be a politics of hope or of fear; in other words, whether a more humane and democratic global politics can be fashioned out of today's distorted global politics.

For further information and case studies on this subject, please visit the companion web site at www.oup.com/uk/booksites/politics.

CWS

QUESTIONS

1 Distinguish the concept of globalization from that of regionalization and internationalization

2 What do you understand by the Westphalian Constitution of World Order

3 Why is global politics today more accurately described as distorted global politics?

4 Outline the principal causes of globalization.

5 Review the sceptical argument and critically evaluate it.

6 What are the principal characteristics of the post-Westphalian order

7 Identify some of the key elements of political globalization.

8 What are the principal characteristics of contemporary globalization?

9 Distinguish the concept of global politics from that of geopolitics and international politics.

10 Outline the main elements of cosmopolitan global politics.

11 Is the state being eclipsed by the forces of globalization and global governance

12 Is state sovereignty being eroded or transformed? Explain your answer.

GUIDE TO FURTHER READING

Castells, M. (2000), *The Rise of the Network Society* (Oxford: Blackwells). This is now contemporary classic account of the political economy of globalization which is comprehensive in its analysis of the new global informational capitalism

Duffield, M. (2001), *Global Governance and the New Wars* (London: Zed Press). A very readable account of how globalization is leading to the fusion of the development and security agendas within the global governance complex.

Gilpin, R. (2001), *Global Political Economy* (Princeton: Princeton University Press). A more sceptical view of economic globalization which although taking it seriously conceives it as an expression of Americanization or American hegemony

Held, D., McGrew, A., *et al.* (1999), *Global Transformations: Politics, Economics and Culture* (Cambridge: Polity Press). A comprehensive exploration of the nature and dynamics of globalization as a historical process which is transforming the nature of world order and the landscape of the global political economy.

Held, D., and McGrew, A. (2002), *Globalization/Anti-Globalization* (Cambridge: Polity Press). A short introduction to all aspects of the current globalization debate and its implications for the study for world politics.

Hirst, P., and Thompson, G. (1999), *Globalization in Question*, 2nd edn (Cambridge: Polity Press). An excellent and sober critique of the hyperglobalist arguments which is thoroughly sceptical about the globalization thesis, viewing it as a return to the *belle époque* and heavily shaped by states.

Holton, R. (1998), *Globalization and the Nation-State* (London: Palgrave). A comprehensive overview of the implications of globalization for the state and state power written from a sociological perspective.

Kennedy, P., *et al.* (2002), *Global Trends and Global Governance* (London: Pluto Press). A good introduction to how globalization is reshaping world politics and the nature of global governance.

Robertson, R. (2003), *The Three Waves of Globalization—A History of Developing Global Consciousness* (London: Zed Press). A very good account of globalization as a long-term historical process driven by a combination of economic and political factors.

Scholte, J. A. (2000), *Globalization—a critical introduction* (London: Macmillan). An excellent introduction to the globalization debate from its causes to its consequences for the global political economy from within a critical political economy perspective.

Slaughter, A. M. (2004), *A New World Order* (Princeton: Princeton University Press). A very accessible discussion of the disaggregated state and global governance networks and their implications for the study of world politics.

Waters, M. (2000), *Globalization* (London: Routledge). An introduction to the globalization debate which is comprehensive in its coverage.

WEB LINKS

www.isn.ethz.ch/linkslib/ Good links to security and global politics nexus.

www.theglobalsite.ac.uk Good site for the globalization debate and related links.

www.polity.co.uk/global Good site for the globalization debate and many good links.

www.csf.colorado.edu Good site for general material on all aspects of global politics.

www.foreignaffairs.org Link to key journal on world politics and a host of other sources and links.

www.cfr.org US Council of Foreign Relations web site with resources on globalization, global governance, and global politics.

www.globalpolicy.org Global Policy Forum site which hosts many useful resources on globalization, global policy issues, and governance.

Part One

THE HISTORICAL CONTEXT

In this part of the book, we want to provide you with a historical context within which to make sense of globalization. We have two main aims: **first**, we want to introduce you to the main aspects of international history and we will do this by giving you an increasingly more chronologically concentrated set of chapters. We start with an overview of international society from its origins in Ancient Greece through to the twentieth century. We think that you need to have some basic understanding of the main developments in the history of world politics, as well as some kind of context for thinking about the contemporary period of world history. This is followed by two chapters that look at the main themes of twentieth-century history, one dealing with the period before the Second World War, the other dealing with the period after it. We then have a chapter that is specifically concerned with the period since the late 1980s, and that concentrates on the most significant historical development of that period, namely the end of the cold war. Our final chapter looks at developments within international history since 1990. We want these chapters to give you a lot of historical information which will be of interest in its own right, but our **second** aim is to draw to your attention the main themes of international history so that you can develop a deeper understanding of the issues both theoretical and empirical, that are dealt with in the remaining four parts of this book. We think that an overview of international history gives you a context within which to begin thinking about globalization: is it a new phenomenon that fundamentally changes the main patterns of international history or are there precedents for it that make it seem less revolutionary?

CHAPTER 2

The evolution of international society

ROBERT H. JACKSON • PATRICIA OWENS

READER'S GUIDE

This chapter discusses the idea of 'international society' and some of its historical manifestations. The starting point is human beings organized into geographically separate political communities and the horizontal relations of conflict and cooperation that ensue from their joint political existences. International society can be understood as a distinctive institutional response to accommodate this dimension of political coexistence. It has assumed different forms from ancient times to the present era but it also discloses common features the most important being a relationship of both independence and interconnectedness between political communities, usually conceived as states.

Introduction: origins and definitions

In order to understand the contemporary world and the significance of globalization we need to consider the evolution of what has been called 'international society'. The social reality of group relations on a horizontal plane could be considered, figuratively speaking, as the core problem of international relations. If there were no horizontal lines of territorial division between 'we' and 'they' there could still be human societies: perhaps isolated political communities, perhaps a vertical society such as an empire, possibly even a cosmopolitan world society of all humankind, or some other social formation. But there could not be international relations in the usual meaning of the term. In short, international relations as historically and conventionally understood are relations of territorially based and delimited political groups.

We now begin to arrive at a definition of 'international society'. It stands for relations between politically organized human groupings, which occupy distinctive territories and enjoy and exercise a measure of independence from each other. International society can thus be conceived as a society of political communities that are not under any higher juridical political authority. In the language of international relations these communities are referred to as states which are usually conceptualized in 'ideal-type' terms as consisting of (1) a permanent population (2) occupying a defined territory (3) under a central government (4) which is independent of all other governments of a similar kind (Brownlie 1979). That condition of constitutional or political independence is ordinarily spoken of as state sovereignty (James 1986: 25). Of course, not all approaches to international relations accept this model of state sovereignty, but it is central to the 'international society' approach (see Ch.12).

Hedley Bull (1977: 8), one of the founders of the 'international society' approach, sums up the foundation of the subject: 'The starting point of international relations is the existence of states, or independent political communities, each of which possesses a government and asserts sovereignty in relation to a particular portion of the earth's surface

---

Box 2.1	Key concepts

Coexistence: the doctrine of live and let live between political communities, or states.

Territory: a portion of the earth's surface appropriated by a political community, or state.

State sovereignty: a state's characteristic being politically independent of all other states.

Suzerain state: a state which dominates and subordinates neighbouring states, without taking them over.

Empire: a distinct type of political entity, which may or may not be a state, possessing both a home territory and foreign territories.

Theocracy: a state based on religion.

Hegemony: power and control exercised by a leading state over other states.

Reason of state: the practical application of the doctrine of Realism and virtually synonymous with it.

Balance of power: a doctrine and an arrangement whereby the power of one state (or group of states) is checked by the countervailing power of other states.

National security: a fundamental value in the foreign policy of states.

Society of states: an association of sovereign state based on their common interests, values, and norms.

Imperialism: the practice of foreign conquest and rule in the context of global relations of hierarchy and subordination. It can lead to the establishment of an empire.

International law: the formal rules of conduct that state acknowledge or contract between themselves.

International order: a shared value and condition of stability and predictability in the relations of states.

Non-discrimination: a doctrine of equal treatment between states.

Self-determination: the right of a political community or state to become a sovereign state.

Right of self-defence: a state's right to wage war in its own defence.

World society: the society produced by globalization.

Global covenant: the rules, values, and norms which govern the global society of states.

and a particular segment of the human population.' Bull (1977: 13) offers the following definition of international society: 'A society of states (or international society) exists when a group of states, conscious of certain common interests and common values, form a society in the sense that they conceive themselves to be bound by a common set of rules in their relations with one another, and share in the working of common institutions.' When understood this way, 'international society' is basically a Pluralist-ig;ic or 'liberal' political arrangement. In other words, the core value is the political opportunity of people to enjoy a geographically separate group existence free from unsolicited interference from neighbouring groups. Independence is the core value in a cluster of important international values, including self-determination, non-intervention, and right of self-defence (see Ch.8). The basic institutional arrangement that embodies and expresses those values is state sovereignty. This is not to suggest that all groups of people have enjoyed unsolicited interference from neighbouring groups. But it is a basic theoretical assumption of the international society approach.

One of the most noteworthy and characteristic arrangements between sovereign states is diplomacy, which obviously is intended primarily to facilitate and smooth their relations. Of course diplomatic arrangements have been expressed differently from one time or place to the next: diplomacy in ancient Greece was not the same as diplomacy in Renaissance Italy which was different again from the classical diplomacy of the eighteenth century or the global diplomacy of the twentieth and twenty-first centuries (Nicolson 1954). Another arrangement is international law, which is a more recent innovation dating back only as far as the sixteenth and seventeenth centuries when the first recognizable international legal texts were written that sought to document the rather novel legal practices of what at that time were recently discerned entities known as sovereign states (see Ch.15). Other such arrangements include recognition, reciprocity, and the laws of war, international conferences, and much else. In the past century an increasingly important arrangement is the large and extensive complex of international organizations—universal, regional, and functional—by means of which much of the

---

> **Box 2.2   Edward Keene on the origins of the 'anarchical society'**
>
> Bull developed his position primarily to challenge the popular belief that international relations should be understood in 'Machiavellian' or 'Hobbesian' terms. In other words, he was taking issue with the argument that, because the international system is anarchic, all state have to obey the brutal logic of realpolitik and must devote themselves to the pursuit of their own interests (see Ch.7). Bull acknowledged that this perspective captures some aspects of international relations, as does the alternative 'Kantian' perspective that highlights the importance of transnational or ideological solidarity and conflict, but he insisted that neither tells the whole story (see Ch.8). In particular, they underestimate the importance and frequency of cooperation and regulated intercourse among states, based on the norms, rules, and institutions of the modern 'anarchical society' of equal and independent sovereign states. While it is important to explain how the logic of anarchy influences the behaviour of states, it is just as important to understand the normative structure of the order that has been created in this international society (see Ch.11) (Keene 2002: xi).

---

business of international relations is nowadays conducted (see Ch.18).

One point deserves particular emphasis so that the idea and expression of international society is understood in its proper historical context. As Edward Keene has suggested of Hedley Bull, but it can be applied to much of the 'international society' literature, 'Bull's work provides a description of . . . the pattern of order that developed in the European states-system . . . He almost completely ignored the other pattern of order, which developed roughly simultaneously in the colonial and imperial systems that were established beyond Europe. [T]he extra-European order was based on the principle that sovereignty should be divided across national and territorial boundaries, creating hierarchical institutions through which colonial and imperial powers transmitted the supposed benefits of their civilization to the rest of the world' (2002: xi). Indeed, vertical or hierarchical relations between political groups are a historical commonplace throughout most of the world throughout recorded history. Political empire is the prevalent form of group

Box 2.3	The earliest records of 'international society'

There are recorded formal agreements among ancient city-states which date as far back as 2400 BC, alliances dating to 1390 BC, and envoys as early as 653 BC

(Barber 1979: 8–9).

relations and recently many have argued that imperialism, understood here as international relations of hierarchy and subordination, continues to be prevalent (Barkawi and Laffey 2002). Horizontal relations between political groups, in addition to hierarchical ones, are comparatively rare. The ancient Greeks constructed an international society that survived for several centuries in a surrounding political environment of various hegemonic empires, including Persia, Macedonia, and the Roman Empire. At that time there were also great empires and suzerain-state systems beyond Europe and the Middle East, including the Chinese empire, which was the greatest of them all and which lasted for millennia, albeit in different dynastic incarnations.

Empire, then, was the prevalent mode of large-scale political group relations in Western Europe throughout the era of the Roman Empire and that of its successor, medieval Christendom, which lasted until about the sixteenth century. In the late Middle Ages (1300–1500) the Renaissance Italians constructed and operated a small regional international society based on the city-states of northern and central Italy. The first modern international society based on large-scale territorial states came into existence a little later in north-western Europe out of which the contemporary global international society has evolved (see chronology in Box 2.4). But empires continued to exist in Europe and many other parts of

the world down to the twentieth century. Some even argue that today new forms of empire are emerging (Hardt and Negri 2000; Mann 2003). Empires clearly dominated Eastern Europe until the end of the First World War. Although Europeans created a society of states among themselves which was the very definition of political modernity, at the very same time they constructed vast empires to rule non-European political communities in the rest of the world. Indeed, this was a process of **mutual penetration**. For example, the military dimensions of colonization directly affected the social and political organization of the colonial powers back at 'home' (Bond 1998). What has traditionally been described in terms of 'international society' is thus uncommon in history even though it became globalized in the twentieth century.

Key points

- International society is an association of member states who not only interact across international borders but also share common purposes, organizations, and standards of conduct.

- There are different historical versions of international society, the most important of which is the contemporary global international society.

- Political independence is the core value of international society.

- In understanding international society it is important to keep in mind contrasting group relations, such as empires, which are far more common historically. Some argue that the concept of international society is not incompatible with forms of imperial power, understood as hierarchal relations between states in the global North and South.

Ancient Greece and Renaissance Italy

In an important survey of international society Adam Watson (1992) identified, among others, the independent city-states of Classical Greece, the states-system of Renaissance Italy, the anti-hegemonial Peace of Westphalia, the Concert of Europe, the globalization of the European states-system, the era of the two superpowers, and the contemporary international society. So we are dealing with a large historical subject of which only a few highlights can be examined here.

This section briefly discusses two incipient and important forerunners of the idea and institution of international society: ancient Greece and Renaissance Italy. The first historical manifestation of an international society is ancient Greece, then known as Hellas, which was a geographical area and a cultural unity but not a single political entity or state. Hellenic international society comprised a large number of city-states based geographically on the lower Balkan peninsula and the many islands in the surrounding Aegean, Adriatic, and Mediterranean seas. The Hellenes thought of themselves as sharing a common ancestry, language, religion, and way of life, all of which distinguished them from neighbours whom they regarded as 'barbarians'—those who did not speak Greek—of whom the Persians were the defining case (Wight 1977: 46–7, 85). Athens was the most famous of the **Greek city-states** but there were also many others, such as Sparta and Corinth, which taken together formed the first international society in Western history. It is important to emphasize, then, that ancient Greece was not a state: the Greeks referred to themselves as Hellenes. Hellenic international society consisted of city-states that were more or less independent of each other but shared a common culture that was essential to their cohesion as an international society. Furthermore, as indicated, the ancient Greeks sharply distinguished Hellas from neighbouring non-Greek 'barbarians', such as the Persians, with whom they had political relations but no cultural affinities or political association.

There were extensive and elaborate relations between the city-states of Hellas. Even though each city-state had its own identity, ceremonies, cults, oracles, and political arrangements, their religion, customs, traditions, and politics were similar. The Oracle at Delphi was consulted as a source of authority in disputes between city-states. A special political vocabulary also evolved among the ancient Greeks that included 'reconciliation', 'truce', 'convention', 'alliance', 'coalition', 'arbitration', 'treaty', and 'peace', among other translated words. They had a concept of neutrality, which was expressed by a word that translates to 'stay quiet' (Nicolson 1954: 3–14). However, they did not possess an institution of diplomacy based on resident ambassadors, which was an invention of the Italian Renaissance. But nevertheless they developed a comparable institution, known as proxeny, which served the same basic function and involved local residents from other Greek cities (Wight 1977: 53–6).

Whether there existed an international society as defined above by Hedley Bull, of which the Greek cities were self-consciously members, is less clear and more controversial. The ancient Greeks did not articulate a body of international law because they could not conceive of the polis—the city-state political communities in which they lived—as having rights and obligations in relation to other city-states on some basis of rough equality (Wight 1977: 51). The ancient Greek city-states were politically self-contained even though they were based on a common culture and religion; they were not part of a larger political association consisting, for example, of a common body of international law. Their international society, to the extent that it existed, was cultural-religious rather than legal-political.

Even though the ancient Greeks had no explicit conception of international law as such, they did nevertheless recognize that certain principles ordained by the gods or dictated by practical reality should govern the conduct of international affairs between the city-states of Hellas. Treaties were under the special custody of Zeus, the all-powerful ruler of gods and men, and it was considered an offence to break a treaty without a recognized justification, or to abandon an ally in the middle of a military campaign. According to Harold Nicolson (1954: 5), among the ancient Greeks 'there seems ... to have existed a religious sanction, mitigating the unrestrained barbarities of war and analogous to our

Box 2.4	Approximate chronology of international society
500–100 BC	Ancient Greek or Hellenic
1300–1500	Renaissance Italian
1500–1650	Early modern European
1650–1950	European-cum-Western
1950–	Global

Geneva Convention'. That analogy might be misplaced because the Geneva Conventions are an elaborate and explicit body of international law. But narrow expediency and strict opportunism in both war and foreign policy were considered wrong: it was immoral to engage in a surprise military attack; atrocities were associated with the conduct expected of barbarians but not Greeks. Some states, such as Sparta, were censured for their diplomatic unreliability. And apart from the laws and customs which obtained among the cities of Hellas, according to Nicolson (1954: 10) the Greeks did dimly recognize the existence of certain standards of conduct which applied to all mankind, civilized and barbarian alike.

These practices obviously come close to Hedley Bull's concept and so it is not surprising that ancient Greece is often seen as the first significant international society in the Western tradition. But it should again be emphasized that the Greeks did not operate with a concept of equal sovereignty. Some states clearly were more equal than others: there were a few major powers, such as Athens and Sparta, and many lesser powers that often became entangled in their rivalries, coalitions, and wars. Minor states were not the equals of major powers. Thucydides makes that clear in his account of the **Peloponnesian war** (431–404 BC) between Athens and Sparta that polarized Greek international society. In a famous dialogue, the people of Melos, a small city-state, appeal for justice from the powerful Athenians, who have presented them with an ultimatum. But the Athenians spurn this appeal with the response that justice between states depends on equality of power: 'the strong do what they have the power to do and the weak accept what they have to accept . . . This is the safe rule—to stand up to one's equals, to behave with deference towards one's superiors, and to treat one's inferiors with moderation' (**Thucydides**, trans. Warner 1972: 402, 407). Here is the classic statement of the political ethics of Realism in the Western tradition (see Ch.7).

Hellas was finally overwhelmed by imperial Macedonia, which was a continental state based on the Balkan peninsula. Even the greatest power in the ancient Greek world, Athens, lacked the power to withstand the Macedonian bid for supremacy over the Hellenes. That ushered in an age of hierarchy and empire in the relations of political communities in that part of the world. The Romans, who eventually displaced the Macedonians, developed an even greater empire in the course of conquering, occupying, and ruling most of Europe and a large part of the Middle East and North Africa. Although the Romans recognized a primitive law of **nations** (*jus gentium*) it was not an express law for independent or sovereign states. Rome was the only sovereign and its relations with all other political communities in its domain were imperial rather than international. Instead of dialogue and conciliation between independent states, under the Roman imperium there was only the alternative of obedience or revolt.

After a long period of decline the (Western) empire at **Rome** disintegrated in the fourth century AD under the impact of 'barbarian' assaults from the imperial peripheries. It was eventually succeeded by a **theocracy**—that is, a government based on organized religion, in this case Latin Christendom, which was one of two successor empires to that of Rome. The (Eastern) empire at Constantinople—which also was a theocracy—was not overthrown but lived on for another thousand years in the incarnation of Greek—i.e. Orthodox—Christianity (Byzantium). The Ottoman Turks, a rising Muslim imperial state, finally destroyed it in the mid-fifteenth century. In North Africa, the Roman Empire was eventually succeeded, after the passing of several centuries, by rising Islamic states. That same area came to be dominated much later by the **Ottoman Empire**. The Middle Ages were thus an age of empire, and the relations and conflicts of different empires, and not an age of international society based on sovereign states.

Medieval Europe in the West, which lasted for about a thousand years from the year 500 until about 1500, has been called a **Respublica Christiana**: a universal society based on a joint **structure** of religious authority (*sacerdotium*) and political authority (*regnum*) which gave at least minimal unity and cohesion to Europeans whatever their language and wherever their homeland happened to be (Wight 1977: 47). That at least was the formal arrangement acknowledged in medieval political theory (Gierke 1987: 13). In practice, of course, medieval Europe was fragmented along feudal lines at both the regional and local level of society. Medieval Europeans had a customary political loyalty to their immediate feudal superiors in those numerous local communities in which the vast majority lived out their lives. Their loyalty to the king (or in other words the secular state) was weak. Medieval Europeans as a whole nevertheless did have a customary religious obedience to the (Western) Church which was an overarching hierarchy of bishops and priests headed by the Bishop of Rome, the Pope. The Pope could also assert, and occasionally he did assert, his vocation as judge in disputes between secular rulers. Even as late as the start of the early modern period (1500–1650) the Pope was still revered in many parts of Europe and periodically he performed the role of a mediator between sovereign rulers, as when Pope Alexander VI settled the division of the newly discovered American continent and surrounding oceans between Spain and Portugal.

In the course of time, however, the European kings beat down the feudal barons and challenged the Pope and in that way they became state defenders against internal disorder and external intervention or threat. This political transformation is summarized by Martin Wight (1986: 25): 'The common man's inner circle of loyalty expanded, his outer circle of loyalty shrank, and the two met and coincided in a doubly definite circle between, where loyalty before had been vague. Thus the modern state came into existence; a narrower and at the same time a stronger unit of loyalty than medieval Christendom'. The medieval ecclesiastical-political order began to unravel during the sixteenth century under the impact of the **Protestant Reformation** and the new political theology of Martin Luther, which enhanced the authority of kings and the legitimacy of their kingdoms. By that time the papacy itself had long since become a state and indeed a significant power: one among several rival Italian powers (Burckhardt 1958: 120–42). The Renaissance papacy, infamous for nepotism and corruption, nevertheless went on to contribute innovations in diplomacy, such as resident ambassadors and rules for the diplomatic corps at Rome. It is one of the curious paradoxes of European history that the papacy acted not only to resist and undermine but also to foster the institution and expansion of early modern international society.

The second noteworthy historical experiment in the evolution of international society involved the small states of the **Italian Renaissance**, which were the first to break free from the medieval empire and flourished in northern Italy between the fourteenth and sixteenth centuries. The Renaissance saw enlightenment in the arts and sciences launched by the recovery of ancient learning, particularly that of Greece and Rome, which Arabic scholars in the Muslim world had kept alive during the Middle Ages. In inventing the Renaissance the Italians also invented the modern independent state, or *stato*, of which the most prominent examples were Venice, Florence, Milan, and the Papal states. They were usually based on a city and its environs—although they sometimes extended farther, as in the case of the Venetian republic that occupied extensive territories along the northern and eastern Adriatic Sea. By instituting their own free-standing political systems the new Italians of the *stato* were of course defying and breaking free from medieval religious-political authority (Burckhardt 1958: 26–44). The republic of Venice, the predominant trading state of that era, brought many diplomatic practices and institutions of international society to Europe, having acquired them from its political and trading relations with Byzantium. The Venetian republic set the standard for other Italian states, later for France and Spain, and eventually for Europe as a whole (Nicolson 1954: 24).

The conviction that the interests of the state and the conduct of statecraft must be guided by a separate political ethics was given a free rein by the

---

Box 2.5   Renaissance theories of statecraft

Statecraft was theorized by Machiavelli (1469–1527), particularly in his classic study of 'The Prince', as an instrumental foreign policy outlook in which political virtue was equated with astuteness in the development and employment of state power, and political vice was a naive (i.e. Christian) faith in justice. Honour, glory, fortune, necessity, and above all virtue—in the strictly secular sense of adroit statecraft—are central ideas for Machiavelli and other Renaissance political commentators (such as Francesco Guicciardini, the political historian of Florence). These ideas form an important part of what has come to be known as the classical theory of realism (Angelo 1969: ch.7).

Italians. That Realist kind of political thinking based on what we would term 'power politics' and the 'national interest' came to be known as reason of state and later as realpolitik in which the morality of the state and the ethics of statecraft are distinguished from universal religious ethics or common morality and are elevated above them (Vincent 1982: 74). The Italian city-states did nevertheless institute among themselves for about a century (1420–1527) a social order based on diplomatic dialogue. The Renaissance Italians also had an acute insight into the importance of the balance of power for maintaining order But the agreements they made were all too often based on expediency, which was an inadequate foundation for the development of a permanent international society. It also encouraged intervention by external powers in the support of one Italian state (or combination of states) against another, which eventually destroyed the society of Italian states and put in its place a system of foreign domination from across the Alps.

In the end the Italian city-states were too small, too weak, and too divided to defend themselves against the far larger territorial states that were being politically engineered by ambitious rulers in Western Europe. Both France and Spain alone were as large as all the Italian states put together. The Italian states were thus confronted by a new and altogether more dangerous external challenge to their independence than had ever come from among themselves. They might have resisted the new territorial states more effectively had they been able to unite politically and militarily into one large territorial state of their own. **Machiavelli**, in a book on the art of war (1965), called for a united Italy in the early years of

the sixteenth century, and devoted much thought to how it might be brought about not only politically but also militarily. He saw the organization of violence as *the* 'political technology for the reconstitution of the republic and the citizen' (Drake 2002: 241). But Italian rulers were unable or unwilling to do that, probably owing to the exceptionally well-entrenched rivalries between their various city-states and the extent of their personal or dynastic ambitions. They were overwhelmed in the sixteenth century by the Austro-Spanish Habsburgs and the French whose long hegemony over the Italian peninsula did not finally end until the mid-nineteenth century.

Key points

- Two forerunner international societies were ancient Greece and Renaissance Italy.

- Two empires that contrasted with these international societies and also served as a historical bridge between them were the Roman Empire and its direct Christian successor in the West, the medieval Respublica Christiana.

- Greek international society was based on the polis and Hellenic culture.

- Italian international society was based on the stato and the strong urban identities and rivalries of Renaissance Italians.

- These small international societies were eventually overwhelmed by neighbouring hegemonic powers.

European international society

Medieval cathedrals took many years, sometimes centuries, to reach their final form; similarly, the classical European international society which began to be constructed as early as the sixteenth and seventeenth centuries was only completed in the eighteenth and nineteenth. The modern territorial state upon which it was based was a derivative of the

Italian Renaissance and the Protestant Reformation. The rulers of the new European states took their cue from the Italians and, as a result, the arts and sciences of the Renaissance, including the art of statecraft, spread to all of Western Europe. The political theology of **Martin Luther**—with its 'impulse towards disengaging political elements from religious modes of thought' (Wolin 1960: 143)—also disengaged the political legitimacy of the state from the religious sanction of the medieval Respublica Christiana. Machiavelli and Luther are important architects of the modern society of states.

In the modern era, secular politics, and particularly the politics of the state and the art of statecraft, was liberated from the moral inhibitions and religious constraints of the medieval Christian world. The sovereign state now shaped the relations of the main political groupings of Europe, and given the competition for colonial possessions outside Europe, those relations were now recognizable as international relations. Many European rulers were ambitious to expand their territories, while many others were anxious to defend their realms against external encroachments. As a result international rivalries developed which often resulted in wars and the enlargement of some countries at the expense of others. At various times France, Spain, Austria, England, the Netherlands, Denmark, Sweden, Poland, Prussia, Russia, and other states of the new European international society were at war. Some wars were spawned by the Protestant Reformation, which profoundly divided the European Christian population in the sixteenth and seventeenth centuries. But other wars (increasingly a majority) were provoked by the mere existence of independent states whose rulers resorted to war as a principal means of defending their interests, pursuing their ambitions, and, if possible, expanding their territorial holdings. Indeed, changing modes of organizing violence itself became an impetus to the organization of the state as a polity entity. As Charles Tilly famously asserted, war made the state and the state made war (1990). And **war**, the clash of armed forced in a given territory, became an international institution for resolving conflicts between sovereign states.

The Catholic Habsburgs, who controlled a sprawling dynastic state which comprised extensive disjointed territories in Austria, Spain, the Netherlands, Italy, Bohemia, Hungary, and other parts of Western and Eastern Europe, tried—in the name of the Respublica Christiana—to impose their imperium on a Europe that was fracturing into religious-cum-political communities, some Catholic and some Protestant, under the impact of the Protestant

Reformation and the Catholic **Counter-Reformation**. That bid for European supremacy led to the devastating Thirty Years War (1618–48) in which the Habsburgs were defeated and peace treaties were negotiated at Westphalia in 1648 (Wedgwood 1992). That was not the first gamble for political mastery in Europe and it would not be the last. But after 1648 the language of international justification would gradually change, away from Christian unity and religious orthodoxy and towards international diversity based on a secular society of sovereign states in Europe. The Treaties of Westphalia and those of Utrecht (1713) still referred to the Respublica Christiana, but they were the last to do so. For what had come into historical existence in the meantime was a secular European society of states in which overarching political and religious authority was no longer in existence in any substantive sense.

The Reformation and Counter-Reformation conflicts made it clear by the mid-seventeenth century that Protestant states and Catholic states must co-exist. The fundamental problem of their relations was thus recognized to be political and not religious. The war itself was not fought along religious lines: it was fought along political–territorial lines with some Catholic states, most notably France, aligned with Protestant states such as Sweden in an alliance against the Catholic Habsburgs. Indeed, the centrality of the changing organization of military power to the viability of this model of a society of European states must be noted. As Paul Hirst (2001) has argued, the introduction of gunpowder and the primacy of defensive technologies over offensive technologies made war in early modern Europe less than decisive and such developments helped make possible a Europe of many states.

The anti-Habsburg alliance also demonstrated the doctrine of the balance of power: the organization of a coalition of states whose joint military power is intended to operate as a counterweight against bids for political hegemony and empire. The doctrine of reason of state took precedence over any residual obligation to support the Respublica Christiana, which was now seen in many quarters as merely the ideology of one side in the conflict. That secular move away from religious legitimacy has been a cornerstone of international society ever since. The treaties of Westphalia formally recognized the existence of **separate sovereignties** in one international society. Religion was no longer a legal ground for intervention or war among European states. The settlement thus created a new international covenant based on state sovereignty, which displaced the medieval idea of the Respublica Christiana. The seeds of state sovereignty and non-intervention that those seventeenth-century statespeople planted would eventually evolve into the Charter of the United Nations, the Geneva Conventions, and other contemporary bodies of international law.

The procedural starting point of modern European international society, speaking very generally, is thus usually identified with the Peace of Westphalia. That at least is the conventional view. Martin Wight (1977: 150–2) argues, somewhat to the contrary, that

Westphalia is the coming of age but not the coming into existence of European international society, the beginnings of which he traces to the Council of Constance (1415) which, in effect, transformed the papacy into a quasi-secular political power with its own territory. F. H. Hinsley (1967: 153) argues, on the other side, that modern international society only fully emerged in the eighteenth century, because prior to that time the Respublica Christiana was still in existence. But however we choose to look at it, the multinational treaties of Westphalia, and those which came after, were conceived as the foundation of secular international law or what came to be known as the 'public law of Europe' (Hinsley 1967: 168).

Adam Watson (1992: ch.17) captures the Westphalian moment very aptly: 'the charter of a Europe permanently organized on an anti-hegemonial principle'. The European society of states had several prominent characteristics that can be summarized as follows:

- First, it consisted of member states whose political independence and juridical equality was acknowledged by international law.

- Second, every member state was legitimate in the eyes of all other members.

- Third, the relations between sovereign states were managed, increasingly, by a professional corps of diplomats and conducted by means of an organized multilateral system of diplomatic communication.

- Fourth, the religion of international society was still Christian but that was increasingly indistinguishable from the culture, which was European.

- Fifth, a balance of power between member states was conceived, which was intended to prevent any one state from making a bid for hegemony.

- Finally, and as a result, wars between European states would from now on tend to be fought in the global South in the competition for colonial influence.

The **anti-hegemonial** notion of a countervailing alliance of major powers aimed at preserving the freedom of all member states and maintaining the Pluralist European society of states as a whole was

---

Box 2.6	**Westphalian international society**

Westphalian international society was based on three principles. The first principle was *rex est imperator in regno suo* (the king is emperor in his own realm). This norm specifies that sovereigns are not subject to any higher political authority. Every king is independent and equal to every other king. The second principle was *cuius regio, eius religio* (the ruler determines the religion of his realm). This norm specifies that outsiders have no right to intervene in a sovereign jurisdiction on religious grounds. The third principle was the balance of power: that was intended to prevent any hegemon from arising and dominating everybody else.

Box 2.7	**Grotius and international law**

The emerging idea of international law was spelled out by Hugo Grotius, a Dutch Protestant diplomat and philosopher, whose *Laws of War and Peace* (1625; (1925)) provided an intellectual foundation for the subject that was enormously influential and is still regarded as a founding text. Grotius hoped to restrict war and expand peace by clarifying standards of conduct which were insulated against all religious doctrines and could therefore govern the relations of all independent states, Protestant and Catholic alike.

only worked out by trial and error and fully theorized much later. The greatest historical threat to the European balance of power before the twentieth century was posed by Napoleon's bid for continental hegemony (1795–1815). British and later American foreign policy can be read as historical lessons in attempting to preserve or restore the balance of power. In the eighteenth and nineteenth centuries Britain often played the role of the defender of the balance of power by adding military (especially naval) weight to the coalition, which formed against the **hegemon**, most notably in the case of post-revolutionary Napoleonic France. The United States played a similar role in the Second World War against Nazi Germany and Imperial Japan, and in the cold war against communist Russia. In so far as both Britain and the United States accepted and indeed defended the principles of international society against contrary revolutionary ideologies, they could not themselves be regarded as hegemons in the classical political meaning of the term.

It should be noted, of course, that some scholars have suggested that this understanding of the origins of the European society of states is not historically accurate. For example, Stephen Krasner (1999) has argued that that the features most often associated with the sovereign state—territory, autonomy, recognition, and control—are inaccurate descriptions of the reality of statehood throughout European and world history. Krasner suggests that the absence of authoritative international institutions and power asymmetries between states mean that Westphalian and international legal sovereignty are best conceived as 'organized hypocrisy' on a grand scale—powerful leaders abide by them only when it is in their interests to do so. States have never been quite as sovereign as many have assumed. One task for students of international politics is to assess the historical accuracy of the theoretical models, in this instance the concept of 'international society', which we use to describe the world.

In sum, however, the first fully articulated conception of the theory and practice of international society as an explicit covenant with a legal and political foundation was worked out in Europe among its sovereign states. Edmund Burke, with his eye on the alleged threat posed to monarchical and dynastic Europe by republican and revolutionary France, went so far as to refer to eighteenth-century Europe as 'virtually one great state having the same basis of general law, with some diversity of provincial customs and local establishments'. Burke saw European international society as based on two fundamental principles: a 'law of neighbourhood'—recognition of neighbouring states and respect for their independence, and 'rules of prudence'—the responsibility of statespeople not only to safeguard the national interest but also to preserve international society (Raffety 1928: 156–61). Similar ideas were expressed by many European publicists of the day and there is little doubt that modern international society is rooted in the political culture and political thought of the European peoples.

Key points

- The Peace of Westphalia was the first explicit expression of a European society of states, which served as a precedent for all subsequent developments of international society.

- That international society displaced and succeeded the medieval Respublica Christiana.

- It was the external aspect of the development of modern secular states that had to find an orderly and legitimate way to conduct mutual relations without submitting to either superior authority or hegemonic domination from abroad.

- It was the first completely explicit international society, even though it was centred in Europe, with its own diplomatic institutions, formal body of law, and enunciated practices of prudential statecraft, including the balance of power.

The globalization of international society

The spread of European political control beyond Europe which began in the late fifteenth century and only came to an end in the early twentieth century proved to be an expansion not only of European imperialism but also, later, of international society (Bull and Watson 1984). Indeed, the history of European imperialism and the 'globalization of international society' are fundamentally intertwined. The history of modern Europe is—in very significant part—a history of political and economic rivalry, particularly war between sovereign states, and subsequent expansion into and engagement with the non-European world. European rivalries were conducted wherever European ambitions and power could be projected—i.e. eventually on a global scale. During this period, the logic of capitalism meant that European states entered into competition with each other to penetrate and control economically desirable and militarily useful areas in other parts of the world. To an important extent, then, the histories of the European and non-European worlds are fundamentally intertwined in ways not always captured by traditional understandings of the European 'society of states' (Keene 2002).

| Box 2.8 | Buzan and Little on Eurocentrism |

Eurocentrism has bedevilled every aspect of the social sciences . . . At first glance, it might appear that there is nothing untoward about the familiar Eurocentric account of how the contemporary international system emerged . . . Europeans . . . occupied whole continents and stamped upon them a system of territorial boundaries, trading economies, and colonial administrations. The few places that they did not reduce to colonial status (Japan, Siam, Persia, Turkey, China) were forced to adapt to European models to preserve themselves. But . . . this story can only be told in this way by ignoring or distorting great swaths of the past . . . Indeed, one can only explore the origins and significance of the idea of international system, and fully understand what is happening to it now, by comprehending its non-European dimension (Buzan and Little 2000: 20).

Until the nineteenth century large-scale wars were fought by the militarily and economically powerful European states **outside Europe**. Non-European territories and populations came under the control of European governments by conquest or occupation, and were sometimes transferred from one European state to another as happened in the case of French Canada which the British annexed at the end of their successful Seven Years War with France (1756–63). From the perspective of the Europeans a 'remarkable achievement' of the nineteenth-century Concert of Europe—a balance-of-power coalition originally formed by the Great Powers that defeated Napoleon (Britain, Austria, Prussia, and Russia)—was their avoidance of war in the course of their competitive expansion outside Europe. This was in marked contrast to 'the incessant acts of war against each other overseas in previous centuries' (Watson 1992: 272). It was also in contrast to the social and economic devastation suffered by non-Europeans as a result. European definitions of international law, diplomacy, and the balance of power thus came to be applied around the world and not only in Europe or the West. By the late nineteenth century continents previously inaccessible to European penetration, like the interior of Africa, were under the jurisdiction and manipulation of European powers.

Not every non-Western country fell under the political control of a Western imperial state. But those countries that escaped were still obliged to accept international law and follow the other diplomatic practices of European-defined international society. For a discussion of the resistance of the **Ottoman Empire** see Box 2.9. Japan elected to do the same a little later although without the same compulsion and humiliation. Japan successfully acquired the persona and substance of a modern power and by the early twentieth century had defeated the Russian Empire in a major war and had become a colonial power itself. China was subjected to extensive territorial encroachments by European states, the United States, and Japan, and did not acquire full membership in international society until 1945 at which time China became a permanent member of the UN

Resistance to the expansion of European international society

The Ottoman Empire (Turkey), which geographically and ethnically was a partly European state, had for centuries been in close contact with European states but had never accepted the conduct requirements of their definition of international society. Instead, the Ottomans insisted on treating European states on their own Islamic terms. Although for several centuries the Ottoman Empire regularly intervened in Europe with the aim, usually, of undercutting their Habsburg enemies, they held aloof from the conventions of Christian and later European international society with regard to which, as Muslims, they considered themselves superior. At the height of their power between the mid-fifteenth century and the turn of the seventeenth century the Ottomans were able to dictate terms to European states. By the mid-nineteenth century, however, they had long been in decline and were obliged by what were now clearly militarily superior European powers to accept international law and other dictates of Western states.

The right of self-determination

The principle of legitimacy that sanctioned decolonization was spelled out in the celebrated 1960 UN General Assembly Declaration on the Granting of Independence to Colonial Countries and Peoples (Resolution 1514) which declared not only that 'all peoples have the right to self-determination' and thus membership of international society but also that 'the further continuation of colonialism . . . is a crime which constitutes a violation of the Charter of the United Nations'.

Security Council. Most other non-Western political systems were not able to resist Western imperialism and lost their independence as a result. That proved to be the case throughout South Asia, South-East Asia, most of the Middle East, and virtually all of Africa, the Caribbean, and the Pacific.

The second stage of the globalization of international society was via reactive nationalism and often violent anti-colonial struggles. In that reaction, indigenous political leaders often made the political calculation to base their claims for **decolonization** and independence, in part, on European and American ideas of **self-determination**. That involved a further claim for subsequent equal membership of a universal international society open to all cultures and civilizations without discrimination (Jackson 1990). This anti-colonial 'revolt against the West', as Hedley Bull put it, was the main vehicle by which international society expanded after the Second World War. In a short period of some twenty years, beginning with the independence of India and Pakistan in 1947, most colonies in Asia and Africa became sovereign states and full members of the United Nations. European decolonization in the

Third World more than tripled the membership of the society of states from about fifty to over one hundred and sixty. To some extent, however, the penetration of the global South by European and Western interests, economic and military, *after* decolonization has matched that experienced under direct colonialism (Duffield 2001).

The final act of European decolonization that completed the globalization of international society was the dissolution of the Soviet Union at the end of the cold war. Here self-determination was based not on overseas colonies but, rather, on the internal borders of the former Russian (Tsarist) Empire which the communists took over and preserved after their revolution in 1917. Those old Russian imperial frontiers thus became new international boundaries. The dissolution of the Soviet Union together with the simultaneous break-up of Yugoslavia, Ethiopia, and Czechoslovakia increased the number of international states to well over one hundred and eighty. Until the US occupation of Iraq in 2003, there emerged one continuous international society of global extent—without any intervening gaps of isolated aboriginal government or imposed colonial jurisdiction and also without any external hegemons. This juridical international society was based on local territorial sovereignty and a common set of rules the most important of which are embodied by the United Nations Charter. Since the invasion and occupation of Iraq, however, questions have been raised about the viability of the notion of 'international society' in the context of US hegemony and absolute military preponderance (Dunne 2003; Barkawi 2004).

Key points

- Through their rivalries and wars European states developed the military organization and technology to project their power on a global scale and few non-European political systems could block their expansion.

- European international law, diplomacy, and the balance of power came to be applied around the world.

- Indigenous non-Western nationalists eventually went into revolt and claimed a right of self-determination which led to decolonization and the expansion of international society.

- That was followed by a further expansion after the cold war, brought about by the disintegration of the Soviet Union and several other communist states.

- During the 1990s, for the first time in history, there was one inclusive international society of global extent.

- Whether this model of international society can endure under US hegemony is the subject of some dispute.

Conclusion: problems of global international society

As written in the UN Charter, the core values and norms of the contemporary global society of states are international peace and security, state sovereignty, self-determination, non-intervention, **non-discrimination** and generally the sanctity, integrity, and inviolability of all existing states regardless of their level of development, form of government, political ideology, pattern of culture, or any other domestic characteristic or condition. When understood this way, these values and norms can be seen as embodying and expressing the **global covenant** of contemporary international society. However, serious questions about this construct of universal state sovereignty can be raised, some of which are unprecedented in history. Only the most important can be discussed briefly as a conclusion to this chapter.

First, given the European origins of 'international society' there is a noteworthy absence of a common underlying culture to support any global international society that might cut across all the major cultures and civilizations. There is no worldwide cultural support comparable to Christianity or European civilization, which helped sustain European-cum-Western international society. Perhaps the **Western norms** and values of capitalism,

human rights discourses, and liberal democracy can provide that support if they become universalized or imposed. They are certainly avowed by the most powerful states of the present era, such as the members of the OECD. And as witnessed with the US-led invasions of Afghanistan (2001–2) and Iraq (2003), where Western-style democracy has been forcibly imposed, the willingness of powerful **regimes** to extend political influence in the non-Western world endures. But the fact remains that other important states including some in East Asia and many in the Middle East dispute some of these norms and values and the suggestion that they are always observed by Western states themselves. Moreover, as **9/11** made clear, the once seemingly inexorable process of cultural assimilation under globalization has not prevented the emergence of an Islamic resistance movement to Western influence in the Middle East.

Second, if the global covenant is going to be supported in the future, that support is likely to be widely forthcoming only if its core norms and values respond to the interests and concerns of the vast majority if not all the members of contemporary international society and the people whom these states ostensibly represent. This probably requires that the currently dominant norms of capitalism and Western-style liberal democracy be divorced or at least distanced from the norms and values of any particular culture, including that of the West. All members still clearly and publicly avow the wider range of core norms such as the rule of law most of which are incorporated into regional international organizations, such as the Charter of the Organization for African Unity (Brownlie 1971: 2–8). However, the Western origins of these 'international society' norms seem all too evident given the extent to which they also uphold the continuing economic and political subornation of the global North over the **global South**.

Third, although in juridical terms the world is divided into formally equal sovereign states, it in fact contains huge **substantive inequalities** between member states, particularly between the rich OECD states and the poorest Asian and African states. Moreover, there is great inequality within the oil-rich states of the Middle East. An unprecedented theory and practice of international aid has emerged alongside this socio-economic disparity in which rich states are called upon to help ameliorate poverty in poor states. On one level, this has changed the ethos of international society. The traditional ethos in relation to poor states, immediately after the period of colonial exploitation, was national self-reliance and reciprocity. The new ethos and self-perception of wealthy states is international benevolence and non-reciprocity. This is ironic, as Ch.29 of this volume suggests, for despite unprecedented official development policies, 'global polarization is increasing, with the economic gap between rich and poor states and people growing'.

Fourth, the regional diversity of contemporary global social relations is far more pronounced than that of European international society or any other previous society of states. The result is a form of international Pluralism based on the social construction of **regions** or groupings of states, such as South-East Asia, Western Europe, Latin America, or Africa, which share a geographical region and may also have cultural affinities and an interconnected economic life. If the **regional-cultural Pluralism** of the world is to be accommodated then global social relations cannot be encumbered with intrusive norms and values of a particular culture, including those of the Western democracies. This is currently not the case.

Fifth, since 1945 there has been a definite freezing and sanctifying of international **boundaries** as the globe has been enclosed by local sovereign jurisdiction. For this and other reasons, states have been discouraged from engaging in acts of overt aggression or armed intervention in other states with a view to territorial expansion. These were not uncommon practices of historical European international society, with recurrent wars fought between them in the global South over territory and other issues. Moreover, the penetration of Western power and interests into the global South has not ceased with the end of territorial expansion; it has simply taken on different forms. However, what the establishment of juridical sovereignty has created is a barrier to the formation of new jurisdictions and this has directly contributed to some of the violent conflict we see today. For example, the effective prohibition on reshuffling certain territorial jurisdictions in response to changing socio-political identities and demands for national self-determination have led to **wars** in places such as Bosnia-Herzegovina and Kosovo.

Sixth, the doctrine of non-intervention has created an inversion of the traditional **security dilemma** in many states (see Ch.13), particularly post-colonial and post-communist states. In those states the security threat is more likely to come from within: the prevailing pattern of warfare is internal rather than international (Holsti 1996). In more than a few sub-Saharan African countries, for example, the main security threat comes from armed rebels or from the government, or both, which often hold citizens hostage in what are referred to as failed or **collapsed states** (Zartman 1995). Although powerful states have frequently superceded the 'right' to state sovereignty of weaker states, the doctrine of non-intervention has in other instances appeared to make it difficult for international society to address the problem. It is also difficult to institute some kind of international trusteeship for obviously failed states, such as Somalia, owing to the fact that the institution and law of trusteeship which currently exists is designed for colonies and not for independent countries. This partly explains the legal quandary surrounding the US occupation of Iraq after the 2003 invasion. International society currently has no generally accepted procedures for dealing with the problem of failed states. Only when it seems to be in the geostrategic interest of powerful states such as the United States is there an effort to force 'regime change', such as the intervention to facilitate the exile of elected President Aristide from Haiti in 2004.

Seventh, global international society may be evolving into some form of world society, both organizationally and normatively, which differs significantly in several important respects from previous international societies. For some this involves **cosmopolitan norms**, such as human rights, which sanctify and indemnify human beings regardless of their citizenship. It involves global norms such as environmental protection, which place new responsibilities, legal as well as moral, on sovereign states, particularly those states with the greatest capacity to cause pollution. And it involves a rapidly expanding role for non-governmental organizations (NGOs), such as Greenpeace or Amnesty International, which are assuming growing importance in world politics. For many, however, the notion of world society also involves **new threats and inequalities**, which seem to coexist easily with the more positive norms just mentioned. We have already referred to great disparities in wealth. In addition, the apparent unwillingness of some powerful states to abide by international environmental agreements was made evident by the US decision to withdraw from the Kyoto Protocol (see Ch.20). The United States has also refused to participate in the International Criminal Court.

Finally, this tendency for international society to evolve into a world society raises important questions about the continuing primacy of state sovereignty. Many of these issues are raised in other chapters in this book and cannot be dealt with at length here. Suffice it to say, state sovereignty has been a defining characteristic of international politics for three hundred and fifty years. However, it is not a static institution. On the contrary, it is a dynamic institution and it continues to evolve. For example, at one time dynastic families held state sovereignty, but today it is the collective entitlement of entire national populations. At one time sovereign

states had a right to initiate aggressive war in pursuit of their self-defined interests, but that right has usually been denied and extinguished by the twenty-first century. At one time sovereign states could control foreign populated territory as colonial dependencies. That right has been extinguished for all states apart from the United States or a coalition of US-led states under the authority of the UN. Many other examples of state sovereignty as a dynamic, evolving institution could also be given. But perhaps these examples are sufficient to make us sceptical about claims that world politics is moving beyond state sovereignty. It is far more likely that state sovereignty is evolving yet again. Martin Shaw (2000), for example, argues that supranational institutions represent the beginning of a new form of 'international' state power or a 'global-Western state conglomerate'. Still others point to the emergence of new form of 'empire', with the United States at its core, that is made up of a new form of 'post-modern' sovereignty (Hardt and Negri 2000; see Ch.1).

Historical change is ongoing, the dust is swirling all about, and it will be some time before anyone can get a clear view of this fundamentally important issue of state sovereignty and changing forms of global power.

> **Key points**
>
> - Today international society is usually conceived as a global social framework of shared norms and values based on state sovereignty.
>
> - An important manifestation of that social framework is the UN Charter.
>
> - But those shared norms and values have provoked unprecedented problems and predicaments of contemporary world politics.
>
> - There is a current debate about the future of state sovereignty and thus also about the future of the contemporary global international society.

For further information and case studies on this subject, please visit the companion web site at www.oup.com/uk/booksites/politics.

QUESTIONS

1   What does international society tell us about the political values and inclinations of human beings around the world?

2   Discuss and evaluate Hedley Bull's concept of international society.

3   Compare the international society of ancient Greece with that of Renaissance Italy.

4   Discuss the Peace of Westphalia as a new stage in the evolution of international society.

5   What are some of the problems of treating 'Westphalia' as the founding moment of 'international society'?

6   Why has an originally European society of states become the general norm around the world?

7   Can a global international society that contains both extremely rich members and extremely poor members be viable over the longer term?

8   Is global international society part of the solution or part of the problem when it comes to the issue of failed states

9   What is the relationship between different ways of conceiving 'international society' and the organization of violence?

10   Does international society based on state sovereignty have any future?

GUIDE TO FURTHER READING

Watson, Adam (1992), *The Evolution of International Society* (London: Routledge). The definitive study of the history of various international societies and rival or related empires

Bull, Hedley (1977), *The Anarchical Society: a Study of Order in World Politics* (New York: Columbia University Press). The classic statement of the English School approach to international society.

Bull, Hedley, and Watson, Adam (eds) (1984), *The Expansion of International Society* (Oxford: Clarendon Press). The only elaborate account of the historical expansion of European society to the rest of the world.

Armstrong, David (1993), *Revolution and World Order* (Oxford: Clarendon). An important study of revolutionary states in international society.

Hamilton, K., and Langhorne, R. (1995), *The Practice of Diplomacy* (London: Routledge). An excellent history of the evolution of the idea and institution of diplomacy.

Stern, Geoffrey (1995), *The Structure of International Society* (London: Pinter). An outstanding recent textbook on international society.

Lyons, Gene M., and Mastanduno, Michael (eds) (1995), *Beyond Westphalia* (Baltimore and London: Johns Hopkins University Press). A recent exploration of the question whether international society is evolving beyond a society of sovereign states.

Buzan, Barry, and Little, Richard (2000), *International Systems in World History* (Oxford: Oxford University Press). An important study of how multiple international systems have developed over a period of five thousand years.

Keene, Edward (2002), *Beyond the Anarchical Society: Grotius, Colonialism and Order in World Politics* (Cambridge: Cambridge University Press). A recent look at the interpenetration between the European society of states and imperial and colonial order.

Drake, Michael (2002), *Problematics of Military Power: Government, Discipline and the Subject of Violence* (London: Frank Cass). For more advanced students interested in how the organization of violence is central to the constitution of social relations from the Roman Republic to the Early Modern period.

WEB LINKS

www.hyperhistory.com/online_n2/History_n2/a.html This site has over 2000 files covering over 3000 years of world history.

www.leeds.ac.uk/polis/englishschool/wg-his.htm This is the site of a UK-based working group on the English School approach to 'international society'. It contains a variety of useful documents and papers for more advanced readers.

www.yale.edu/lawweb/avalon/westphal.htm Here is the transcript of the Treaty of Westphalia, 24 October 1648, the 'Peace Treaty between the Holy Roman Emperor and the King of France and their respective Allies'.

CHAPTER 3

International history, 1900–1945

SUSAN L. CARRUTHERS

READER'S GUIDE

This chapter seeks to elucidate key transformations in international relations between 1900 and 1945. Within 45 years, the world experienced two 'Total Wars', a global economic crisis, and the disintegration of four major empires, with Tsarist Russia being overthrown by a Bolshevik Revolution. This chapter identifies the passing of global hegemony from the European 'Great Powers' (particularly Britain, as the hub of world trade and finance) to the United States as the most significant systemic change that occurred during the first half of the twentieth century. By 1945, Europe was shattered by its long crisis. The continent was divided between two emergent superpowers—the United States and the USSR. How do we account for the decline of Europe? The chapter looks at developments both within the continent and further afield, paying particular attention to the historiographical controversy surrounding the two world wars. It concludes by considering how far 'globalization' intensified or was impeded during this turbulent period of world history.

Introduction

The year 1900 forms a convenient, but not necessarily the most helpful, starting point for an analysis of **modern** international history. Eric Hobsbawm has suggested that the twentieth century really only began in 1914, with a cataclysmic war which swept away the nineteenth-century status quo, whereby a handful of European states dominated the affairs of the world (Hobsbawm 1994: 3). Before the First World War, Europe had not experienced a major war involving most of its dominant states for a century. The world had **never** experienced a conflict that enmeshed so many different countries and peoples. Not only was this war truly a 'world war', but also it was the century's first 'Total War', during which the major protagonists mobilized virtually their whole populations, male and female alike—whether as soldiers at the front line or as workers on the 'Home Front'.

The consequences of the First World War were enormous. After over four years of war, the diplomats and political leaders who gathered at Versailles in 1919 to forge a peace settlement were adamant that their endeavours must not just resolve the immediate post-war issues (what to do with the vanquished countries, especially Germany, and with the Austro-Hungarian and Ottoman empires which had collapsed during the war) but also make war impossible in the future. 'Never again' was the overwhelming popular sentiment. And yet only twenty years after the **Treaty of Versailles**, another world war was under way—this one even more global in its reach than the first. The years 1900–45 thus mark the most destructive period in human history. Not only did human beings kill one another in greater numbers than in any other span of four decades, but also they found more barbaric methods of doing so: from the Nazi genocide of six million Jews carried out in the concentration camps, to America's dropping of atomic bombs on the Japanese cities of Hiroshima and Nagasaki in August 1945.

The world of 1945 was almost unrecognizable from that of 1900 (as Boxes 3.1 and 3.2 suggest). The story of these years appears to be one of disintegration. A series of empires collapsed in Austro-Hungary, Turkey, and Russia in the course of the First

---

Box 3.1	Key features of the world in 1900

European states dominate the global pattern of international relations

- One in four of the world's population lives in Europe (approximately 400m. of a 1,600m. total).
- The European 'Great Powers' (Britain, France, Italy, Germany, Austria-Hungary, and Russia) have a concentration of military power, as well as dominating world trade.
- Colonial empires of European states (especially Britain and France, but also Belgium, the Netherlands, and Portugal) cover much of the world.
- Approximately 500m. people live under European colonial rule.
- Search for colonies continues; especially Germany in Africa, and Tsarist Russia in Asia.

Several territorial empires in a protracted state of collapse

- The Habsburg Empire (covering Austria-Hungary and much of central Europe and the Balkans).
- The Ottoman Empire (centred on Turkey, and encompassing much of the Middle East and the Balkans).
- Tsarist Russia.
- Imperial China.

Global capitalist economy

- In 1900 centred primarily on the UK, as the world's largest imperial and trading power, but increasingly under threat.
- Rapid industrial expansion in North America.
- Japan modernizing and industrializing.

Box 3.2	Key features of the world in 1945

Prominence of the USA and USSR

- The USA the first nuclear superpower, after the explosion of atomic bombs on Hiroshima and Nagasaki, August 1945.

- The USA emerges from the Second World War as a major creditor nation, and the centre of the international economy.

- The USSR in economic ruin after the war, but the Red Army occupies all Eastern and much of Central Europe, to Berlin and beyond.

Collapse of Europe

- Rapidly divided between East and West; Germany split until 1989.

- National economies in ruin; large debts owing to the USA.

- European colonial empires undermined by war; by Japanese overrunning of colonies in South-East Asia.

Growing nationalism in the colonial empires

- Wartime 'Atlantic Charter' makes commitment to national self-determination.

- India seeking independence (achieved in 1947).

- Ho Chi Minh declares Vietnam an independent republic in 1945.

Civil war in China

- Ended with the victory of Mao and the establishment of the People's Republic of China in 1949.

- Together with the population of the USSR, one-third of the world now lives under communist rule.

World War. Imperial China, long subject to foreign incursions, also slid into prolonged civil war. The international economy collapsed after the **Wall Street Crash** of 1929. And, partly as a result of the ensuing Depression, democracies crumbled in the 1930s, while extreme right-wing dictatorships flourished in Germany, Italy, Spain, Japan, and many countries of South America. The culmination of these turbulent years, which with hindsight we call the 'inter-war period', was another Total War which left few of the world's citizens entirely untouched.

The most globally significant transformation during the first half of the twentieth century was Europe's demotion as pre-eminent continent. A world dominated in 1900 by a small group of economically prosperous, industrialized European states, whose empires encompassed much of the globe, by 1945 had been replaced by one in which the major arbiters of international affairs were the two new 'superpowers'—the United States of America and the Soviet Union. Europe, at least temporarily, was in a state of ruin and indebtedness, with Eastern and Central Europe lying under Soviet occupation. The Second World War further intensified Europe's disintegration. But in fact that war only accentuated a process several decades old. Many historians would argue that the Second World War was essentially a continuation of the First. Europe was not so much suffering a '**Twenty Year Crisis**' (E. H. Carr's description of the period 1919–39 (Carr 1939)) as undergoing a '**Thirty-Year War**', whose roots stretched back to the 1870s.

The origins of the First World War

Why did Europe lose its predominant place in the world in the years between 1900 and 1945? The answer lies partly in Europe itself and partly beyond. European states fought viciously with one another on their own soil. However, the continent which had given birth to the industrial revolution, and had

formed the hub of global financial activity, also faced economic challenges from rapidly industrializing states—most obviously the United States. Similarly, in the East Asia, Japan underwent rapid expansion in the early twentieth century, posing a significant economic and military challenge to both

America's and the European powers' trading and colonial interests in East Asia.

We will consider global economic developments in due course, but first we will examine the **internal roots** of Europe's instability. These are frequently dated to the 1870s, when the continent's relative tranquillity following the Napoleonic Wars was disturbed by the creation of a single, unified German nation-state.

Germany's bid for world power status

The unified Germany's territorial ambitions rapidly became apparent. Although Bismarck himself had cautioned against further German expansionism, his successors were less circumspect, and sought to secure German's 'place in the sun' through acquisition of overseas empire. **Imperial disputes** were thus an important contributory factor to the outbreak of war in 1914, and in Marxist accounts of the war's origins are allotted causal primacy. Certainly, Britain was not keen to see its own position as the world's most powerful trading nation overshadowed by Germany, with which it was now engaged in fierce naval rivalry. France had equally compelling reasons to fear German expansion. The opening years of the twentieth century thus saw a hitherto unlikely alliance of Britain, France, and Tsarist Russia merging in an attempt to halt Germany's determined search for **territory** and markets. Germans, however, saw themselves not as the aggressors but rather as the victims of an imperial system which operated entirely to their disadvantage: Britain and France dominated Africa, Asia, and the Middle East; Russia, Japan, and Britain competed in China, while the USA held sway in Latin America. Between them, these powers appeared to have carved up the international market to their exclusive satisfaction. Gaining colonies was thus not solely a matter of prestige or status but regarded as an economic imperative for Germany. The main areas of contention were **North Africa**, where clashes occurred with France and Britain over Morocco in 1906 and in 1911, and the **Middle East**, as Germany sought to build a railway from Berlin to Baghdad.

Does inter-imperial rivalry alone explain the war? The evaluation of various explanatory factors—imperialism, nationalism, disruption of the European balance of power—continues to generate much historiographical debate, as does the question of how far war was planned or resulted (at least in part) from the working out of various unforeseen chain reactions. Some historians concur with, others dispute, the verdict of the war's victors—that 'war guilt' belonged to Germany alone. The most famous explication of this view was Fritz Fischer's *Griff nach der Weltmacht* (*Bid for World Power*), published in 1961, which emphasized the extent of Germany's annexationist aims in the war, arguing that the German Government deliberately went to war in their pursuit. Others insist that a general war came about more by accident than design, partly due to the way in which military plans had been drawn up. German strategy, devised by Count Alfred von Schlieffen, was designed to counter the prospect of Germany fighting a war on two fronts against France and Russia. His plan therefore envisaged a decisive blow against France before German troops turned to the tardily mobilized Russians. Thus the '**Schlieffen plan**' served to widen the war rapidly once the opening shots had been fired. Those opening shots were fired, not by Germany, but in Sarajevo at Archduke Franz Ferdinand (the heir to the throne of the Austro-Hungarian Empire) by a Serb nationalist. This assassination should alert us to other deep-seated origins of Europe's crisis, and ultimately of the war itself.

The 'Eastern Question'

Besides the 'German problem' the other main source of instability in late nineteenth- and early twentieth-century Europe was the so-called 'Eastern Question', which arose from the slow collapse of the Muslim Ottoman Empire centred in present-day Turkey. The European Great Powers each took considerable interest in how the power vacuum that was spreading from the Balkans to the Middle East would be filled. But the peoples over whom the Ottoman dynasty had presided were also keen to assert, in the **age of nationalism**, their right to self-rule. In the Balkans, rival national groups clashed in a series of wars, with the backing of various European Great Powers. Consequently, the Tsarist Russian Empire (although

Box 3.3	The 'German problem'

Germany before unification

- Until 1871, 'Germany' did not exist in anything like the shape we know it today.

- 'Germany' was a collection of 25 states, ranging in size from small principalities to the economically and militarily assertive Prussia with a population of some 30m. (Bavaria, the second largest, contained 5.5m.).

- Some ethnic Germans lived under the sovereignty of other states; as in Alsace-Lorraine, which was part of France, and Schleswig-Holstein, ruled by Denmark.

Unification

- The bringing together of these states, and the annexation of 'foreign' lands containing ethnic Germans, was the work of the Prussian Chancellor Otto von Bismarck.

- Three wars were fought to secure German unification, and to ensure that Prussia predominated to Austria's exclusion: against Denmark (1864) over Schleswig-Holstein; Austria-Hungary (1866); and France (1870) over Alsace-Lorraine.

Germany after unification

- For the first time in modern history, the centre of Europe was dominated by a single, vast state.

- Germany's population of nearly 67m. (by 1913) was second in size only to the Russian Empire.

- Germany underwent rapid industrialization. Its coal, iron, and steel production (in the 1870s well below the UK's) outstripped Britain's by 1914.

- From 1871 to 1914, the value of Germany's agricultural output doubled; industrial production quadrupled; and overseas trade more than tripled.

- With such great reserves of territory, population, military, and industrial strength, Germany had the capacity—and the inclination, many believed—for outward expansion. The birth of a unified Germany thus constituted the birth of 'the German problem', as far as other European states were concerned, by fundamentally disrupting the balance of power in Europe. Other states were accordingly disposed to enter into alliances in order to prevent Germany from using its central geostrategic location and economic resources to achieve further territorial enlargement.

itself in a state of terminal collapse) refused to watch impassively while Austro-Hungary threatened Russia's fellow Slavs in Serbia after the assassination of Franz Ferdinand in June 1914. What might have been a localized incident quickly sparked a general war. The complicated alliance system built up over the previous two decades rapidly ensured that Austria-Hungary and Germany, on the one side, confronted Britain, France, and Russia on the other. The ensuing war was to last for over four years. Much of it was marked by a military stalemate—most vividly, and horrifically, epitomized by the trench warfare which decimated a generation of young European men, and which also claimed casualties from continents further afield, with the United States entering the war in 1917, and the European empires making use of colonial forces.

Key points

- Europe's instability can be traced back to the creation of a unified Germany in the 1870s, which disrupted the balance of power.

- The European powers clashed over imperial issues in the late nineteenth and early twentieth centuries, as Germany sought colonies and markets.

- A number of European dynasties were in a state of collapse, leaving open the question of what territorial and constitutional arrangements would replace these empires when they finally disintegrated.

- At the same time, nationalism was growing, particularly in the Balkans and Central Europe, with nationalist movements asserting their claims to statehood in the decaying Ottoman and Austro-Hungarian empires.

- A combination of imperial, nationalist, and economic tensions ultimately resulted in the First World War.

Peacemaking, 1919: the Versailles settlement

Post-war problems

When the war finally ended, the peacemakers who gathered at Versailles in 1919 confronted a daunting set of problems. The war generated millions of individual casualties, through either death, or injury or the loss of homes and livelihoods. The teetering Austro-Hungarian and Ottoman empires also expired, while a Bolshevik revolution overthrew the Tsarist regime in Russia. Had anyone really **won** the war? Certainly the victors' economies, no less than those of the vanquished, were decimated. On all sides, the combatants had sought to pursue this war until their enemies were utterly defeated. Total War demanded Total Victory, but the cost of totally defeating an enemy was near ruination of one's own state. The domestic devastation facing France in particular, on whose soil much of the fighting had occurred, added a retributive dimension to the peacemakers' agenda: how could **reparations** (money, goods, or raw materials) be extracted from Germany to finance domestic reconstruction? How, most critically, could the peacemakers ensure that Germany did not seek to dominate Europe ever again?

It should come as no surprise, given both the intractability of Europe's problems and the diversity of the victorious coalition, that the peacemakers failed to agree among themselves on the shape of the post-war order. The principal European victors, Britain and France, concurred over German responsibility for the war, which justified a harsh settlement, but they differed over its terms. However, the guiding force at Versailles was not one (or more) of the European powers, but the President of the United States.

President Wilson's 'Fourteen Points'

America joined the war in its latter stages, having offered escalating support to the Western powers prior to formal entry into the war in 1917. Eager to play a pivotal role in post-war re-ordering, President Wilson provided a set of **principles** around which he hoped peace would be constructed. The overall vision promoted free trade and liberalized markets while resting on a political basis of expanded sovereign statehood. Woodrow Wilson's 'Fourteen Points' called for a new approach to international **diplomacy**: 'open covenants, openly arrived at' would replace the old-style secret diplomacy which produced various private inter-state deals over who would gain what territory after the First World War. Wilson also hoped that future wars could be averted by creation of an **international organization** based on the principle of '**collective security**' (see Ch.13). His scheme for a **League of Nations** was premised on 'peaceloving' member states taking any threat to international peace—any violation of the sovereignty of one member by another state—as an act of aggression which ultimately threatened them all, and therefore had to be responded to collectively. Ideally, however, the very existence of the League would serve to ensure that aggressive states desisted from expansionist actions. The League was thus one of the distinctive features of the post-1919 world: the first formalized attempt to create an international body designed to mediate disputes with permanent **structures** and a codified Charter. Despite its failure to take assertive action against Japanese, Italian, and German aggression in the 1930s, the League provided a model for the United Nations Organization in 1945.

CWS

Self-determination: the creation of new states

Just as significant as Wilson's insistence on an international collective security body was his commitment to the principle of 'national self-determination'. To each nation a state: this was ostensibly Wilson's ideal. But his views were a good deal more contradictory both in theory and in practice. Who were the 'peoples' for whom this principle might be sanctioned by a new international body? Unless one adopts an organic, essentialist view of nations as rooted in 'blood and soil', it is not

---

Box 3.4   Wilson's 'Fourteen Points': a summary

1. Open covenants of peace, openly arrived at; international diplomacy to be carried on publicly.

2. Absolute freedom of navigation on the seas.

3. The removal, as far as possible, of all economic barriers.

4. Disarmament undertaken, and guaranteed, by states to the lowest point consistent with domestic safety.

5. A free, open-minded, and impartial adjustment of all colonial claims, based on the principle that the interests of the population concerned must have equal weight with the equitable claims of the government whose title is to be determined.

6. The evacuation of all Russian territory and the settlement of questions affecting Russia.

7. Belgium must be evacuated and restored.

8. French territory to be evacuated and restored, and Alsace-Lorraine to be returned to French rule.

9. Italian frontiers to be adjusted along clearly recognizable lines of nationality.

10. The peoples of Austria-Hungary to be given the opportunity for autonomous development.

11. Romania, Serbia, and Montenegro to be evacuated; Serbia to be given access to the sea; and international guarantees of the independence and territorial integrity of the Balkan states to be made.

12. The Turkish portions of the Ottoman Empire to be assured a secure sovereignty; other nationalities to be allowed to develop autonomously; the Dardanelles to be permanently open to shipping.

13. An independent Polish state to be established, with free and secure access to the sea.

14. A general association of nations to be formed to afford mutual guarantees of political independence and territorial integrity to all states.

---

self-evident where the boundaries of nationhood lie, in terms of either population or territory. Who is entitled to citizenship? (One might question whether ethnically exclusive states of the kind Wilson apparently envisaged are, in any case, a desirable ideal. Why not multi-ethnic or multi-national states with a more cosmopolitan character?) How are national boundaries to be arbitrated (and by whom?), when two or more nations simultaneously insist on their historic entitlement to sovereignty over the same piece of territory? In Europe peoples claiming shared nationhood, especially where empires had recently crumbled—in the Balkans, and Central and Eastern Europe—were not neatly parcelled into distinct territorial areas. The peacemakers therefore faced a difficult task of drawing the boundaries of the new states of Europe, some of which had never existed before. Often the boundaries reflected uneasy compromises: for example, Czechoslovakia, a state for the first time in 1919, was composed of so many national groups that Mussolini scornfully referred to it as 'Czecho-Germano-Polono-Magyaro-Rutheno-Romano-Slovakia'.

Wilson's insistence on self-determination in Europe, given messy human realities, generated as many contradictions as it solved: sixty million people being awarded a state of their own while another twenty-five million were transformed into minorities within these imperfect nation-states. Not surprisingly, the new states in Southern, Eastern, and Central Europe—Hungary, Yugoslavia, Romania, Bulgaria, Czechoslovakia, Poland—suffered serious problems. They had to contend not only with ethnic cleavages but also with weak economies and fledgling political institutions. Why, given the problems of boundary drawing, and the weakness of the resulting states (leaving Germany surrounded by relatively defenceless neighbours), did the peacemakers demur to Wilson's insistence on self-determination? The answer lies in the West European powers' preoccupation with a new threat. At Versailles, the peacemakers certainly feared a possible future resurgence of Germany. Perhaps equally vividly, however, they were haunted by the spectre of Bolshevism spreading from Lenin's newly created Union of Soviet Socialist Republics (USSR) into Western Europe. Lenin, after all, explicitly stated that the Soviet revolution was but the start of a world revolution—a historical inevitability which the Moscow-led Communist International (**Comintern**) was dedicated to hastening. Moreover, the war seemed to have provided the ideal breeding ground for communist parties in Western Europe, which the Soviets could infiltrate and use as vehicles of world revolution.

Fear of Bolshevism thus explains British and French politicians' enthusiasm for self-determination. After all, these new states were virtually bound to be anti-Soviet since they were largely created from land formerly belonging to Russia: Finland, the Baltic Republics, Poland, and Romania. They were the ideal 'quarantine belt' for the USSR. But they did not address the threat which Germany posed to European security: thus the inter-war era saw another period of alliance building and treaty signing, as France and Britain (and Italy, after 1925) extended guarantees to various Eastern and Central European states, promising action if their boundaries were violated by an aggressor.

If Wilson's enthusiasm for self-determination struck a responsive chord in Europe (however vexed its implementation), the American President himself was considerably less committed to its application to non-white peoples. Extolled as a universal ideal, self-rule in practice was limited by Wilson to Europeans, as the only peoples sufficiently mature for self-rule. Those in the colonized territories of the European Great Powers, who hoped that Wilson's commitment to self-determination applied throughout the globe, were sorely disappointed. Some peoples, in Wilson's eyes, were clearly more equal than others, and it is worth bearing in mind that the USA—during Wilson's presidency and after—intensified its use of military force in the Caribbean and Central America, maintaining a military occupation of Haiti (1915–40) and continuing to rule the Philippines as a colony until after the Second World War. Those peoples whom Wilson did not deem equal to the challenge of self-governance, in particular Germany's former colonies in Africa (such as present-day Namibia) and areas of the Middle East, were turned into League **Mandates**. Although these territories were ostensibly only temporary protectorates of the League, pending their maturation into independent states, the mandated territories remained colonies in all but name—their governance switched from defeated powers to the European victors (primarily Britain and France). Key portions of the Middle East—including Palestine, Iran, Iraq,

Syria and Jordan—thus fell under more invasive European dominance as the last vestige of transnational Muslim governance, in the shape of the Ottoman Empire, crumbled away.

The future of Germany

In many ways the territorial settlement which Versailles established stored up problems for the future, not least in its reshaping of Germany. When the peacemakers came to determine Germany's fate, they did not apply the principle of self-determination rigidly. Largely at French insistence, France regained the lost province of Alsace-Lorraine and occupied the Saar—the key industrial area on Germany's Western flank—in order to extract coal, steel, and iron. French troops also occupied the Rhineland, to ensure that Germany remained demilitarized, as the treaty insisted. Additionally, German politicians (and much of the population) resented the inclusion of Germans in the reconstituted Poland. Poland had not existed as an independent state since the eighteenth century, but now it divided the vast bulk of Germany from East Prussia. This anomalous situation resulted from the peacemakers' determination that Poland should have an outlet to the sea at the port of Danzig (or Gdansk). Where was Danzig's right to self-determination, Germans demanded.

The territorial arrangements of 1919, under which Germany lost 13 per cent of her land and nearly seven million people, angered many Germans, providing a potent grievance for Hitler's National Socialists to manipulate in the 1930s. But what perhaps hurt even more was the inscription of German 'war guilt' into the treaty.

'War guilt' and reparations

The victors included the 'war guilt' clause largely in order to justify the extraction of swingeing reparations from Germany. Popular pressure in Britain and France encouraged the peacemakers to 'squeeze the German lemon until the pips squeak', a line most vigorously pursued by the French premier, Georges Clemenceau. The British Prime Minister, Lloyd

Fig. 3.1 Europe after the First World War

Map reproduced from Keylor (1992: 93).

George, also agreed that reparations should be exacted from Germany, though not at such a punitive level as France sought. The issue of exactly **how much** Germany should pay in reparations was in fact never settled at Versailles. Unable to agree, the Allies left the matter to a Reparations Commission (and ultimately, the sum was scaled ever downwards).

While it is easy to understand why the economic dismemberment of Germany appealed to these leaders—punishing Germany was electorally popular, and also seemed to guarantee future German inability to launch all-out wars—the wisdom of such a move was questionable. It was indeed called into question almost before the ink had dried on the treaty. In 1919, a women's international congress in Zurich predicted that the settlement would 'create all over Europe discords and animositites which can only lead to future wars' (Pettman 1996: 109). In the same year, if from a rather different perspective, the eminent British economist, John Maynard Keynes (an adviser to the British delegation at Versailles) produced an influential indictment of the treaty entitled *The Economic Consequences of the Peace*. Keynes propounded a compelling thesis: economic ruination of Germany—the result of punitive reparations—would prevent the recovery of Europe as a whole. Germany was the motor of the European economic engine. In punishing Germany, the Allies were effectively prolonging their own wartime privations.

To sum up, then, as the French general Foch acutely predicted after the signing of the treaty, Versailles would not bring peace, only an armistice for twenty years. It had solved none of Europe's fundamental problems. In economic terms, it was (if one followed Keynes's reasoning) too hard on Germany, and consequently on Europe as a whole. The interwar years thus saw Europe's economic position decline further relative to that of the United States, which emerged from the war as the net beneficiary, being owed huge sums by Britain and France, which Wilson insisted they repay. In its territorial arrangements, and the selective application of Wilsonian principles, the peace was also arguably too severe on Germany. (This was certainly the argument many Germans advanced, most vehemently under Hitler's regime.) Moreover, a growing number of non-Germans had some sympathy with the view that Versailles bequeathed Germany legitimate grievances: this in part explains the policy of **appeasement** pursued by British governments in the 1930s. But, according to another line of reasoning (expounded by, among others, the historian A. J. P. Taylor), the real problem with Versailles was that it was **not hard enough**. The 'German problem' was unresolved, in so far as Germany still remained the largest unitary state in the heart of Europe. Moreover, Germany's potential to wage war again had not been absolutely destroyed. However viewed—whether as too punitive or insufficiently so—the Treaty of Versailles was almost bound to fail, not least in the absence of any major power absolutely committed to upholding it.

> ### Key points
>
> - Many of the terms of the peace treaties concluded following the First World War (referred to as the Versailles settlement) were shaped by the 'Fourteen Points' supplied by the American President, Woodrow Wilson, but the points themselves were both problematic and inconsistently applied.
>
> - Future wars were to be deterred by the League of Nations, which would take collective action against aggressor states.
>
> - A series of new states was created in the Balkans and Eastern and Central Europe, where the Ottoman and Austro-Hungarian empires had collapsed. Colonial territories of Germany and portions of the collapsed Ottoman Empire were turned into League Mandates, administered by Britain and France.
>
> - Germany was found 'guilty' of having begun the war: Germany lost land to Poland; Alsace-Lorraine was returned to France; Germany was to be disarmed, with France occupying the Rhineland as a security zone; and reparations were to be repaid to the victorious powers.
>
> - Many critics found fault with the settlement, either because it was too hard, or not hard enough, on Germany.

The global economic crisis, 1929–1933

From the very turn of the new century, America occupied the pivotal position in the global economy that Britain had held for over a century. As early as 1902, Europeans were speaking of an 'American invasion', as US corporations—having achieved monopolies at home—cast their eyes hungrily overseas for new markets, and as US financiers looked for sites in which to invest surplus capital. By 1914, US direct investment abroad amounted to 7 per cent of US GNP: the same percentage as in 1966 (Arrighi 1994: 241). By 1929, the USA generated 42 per cent of the world's industrial output, with Germany, Britain, and France together accounting for only 28 per cent (Hobsbawm 1994: 97). The passing of global capitalist hegemony from the UK to the USA was also accompanied by an intensification of economic interconnectedness, with Norman Angell announcing in 1910 that the **international order** was integrated to an unprecedented degree: the 'economically civilized world' tied together by 'credit and commercial contract'. The Wall Street stock-market crash of 29 October 1929 revealed not only the fragility of post-war economic regeneration but also, in the devastating impact of the US Depression on much of the world, the truth of Angell's assertion (Hopkins 2002: 35).

The underlying causes of 'the largest global earthquake ever to be measured on the economic historians' Richter Scale—the Great Inter-War **Depression**' (Hobsbawm 1994: 86) continue to be disputed, and cannot be rehearsed at any length here. Beyond argument, however, is the truly global impact of the Depression. The results of the Depression in America and Europe are familiar enough to Western readers. The drying up of US loans and the sudden shrinkage of transatlantic trade generated spiralling inflation and a decline in manufacturing industry as consumers had ever less disposable income to spend, and as foreign markets disappeared. This in turn occasioned massive unemployment. In the era before social welfare provision was widely established as a social compact between state and citizens, unemployment meant utter destitution and grinding **poverty** for millions. Even for those who remained employed, hyperinflation—and in some countries the complete collapse of currencies—led to the overnight elimination of savings, and to paper money becoming virtually worthless, as in Weimar Germany.

Perhaps less well known in Europe or America are the results of the Depression elsewhere in the world. Every country that participated in international trade was affected—whether they were independent states (as in South America) or colonial territories under the rule of Western European powers. The precipitous drop in the Western world's demand for luxury goods, foodstuffs, and raw materials did not just mean unemployment for workers in factories in the industrialized states of Europe and North America. It also spelled ruin for the producers of primary materials from which consumer goods were manufactured. To take but one example, Japanese silk

Table 3.1 Major wartime and post-war foreign loans of the US Government (in millions of dollars)

Recipient nation	Pre-Armistice (cash)	Post-Armistice (cash & supplies)	Total indebtedness
Great Britain	3,696.0	581.0	4,277.0
France	1,970.0	1,434.8	3,404.8
Italy	1,031.0	617.0	1,648.0
Russia	187.7	4.9	192.6
Belgium	171.8	207.3	379.1

Source: Harold Moulton and Leo Pasvolsky, *War Debts and World Prosperity* (1932: 426), and Thomas A. Bailey, *A Diplomatic History of the American People* (1974: 657).

Box 3.5   The USA and the USSR between the wars

One reason why the 1919 peace settlement did not last, it is often argued, was the failure of any major power, particularly the USA, to sponsor it. After the Second World War, the USA and the USSR emerged as 'superpowers', and their mutual hostility—the cold war—dominated the world for forty years. Why were both relatively inactive on the international scene in the twenty years after the First World War?

The USSR

Nov. 1917   The **Bolshevik Revolution** brought a Marxist-Leninist regime to power in the former Tsarist empire.

Mar. 1918   Lenin concluded a **separate peace treaty** with Germany (in which a quarter of Russian territory and a third of its population were surrendered), in order to concentrate on consolidating the revolution.

1918–20   Before consolidation could occur, **civil war** broke out. Trotsky's Red Army quelled the counter-revolutionary forces of the White Russians, who were aided by interventions from France, Britain, Japan, and the USA.

1924   Josef Stalin came to power, following Lenin's death, and concentrated on building 'socialism in one country'.

1929   The first **Five-Year Plan** for the Soviet economy was introduced, and Stalin stepped up the pace of state planning of industry, together with the collectivization of agriculture.

1936–8   Stalin undertook the **Great Purge** of the enemies of his dictatorship.

Aug. 1939   Stalin signed a **non-aggression pact with Nazi Germany**. This suggests how small a role ideology now played in Soviet foreign policy (although Stalin did not altogether abandon the USSR's support for communist parties around the world). Instead Soviet security concerns were uppermost, and the Pact promised the USSR land in the Baltic, in return for Soviet acquiescence towards Hitler's march into Poland.

The USA

Mar. 1920   The US **Senate refused to ratify the Treaty of Versailles**, concluding a separate peace with Germany in 1921 which did not include the 'war guilt' clause, or the terms of the League of Nations. The USA had thus embarked upon an essentially isolationist foreign policy, which it pursued until the Japanese attack on Pearl Harbor. However, the US government did remain concerned with, and involved in, a number of international issues, particularly those relating to disarmament and security—not least in the Pacific, a traditional area of US concern, where Japan was in the ascendant.

1921–2   The Washington Disarmament Conference was notable for the manner in which it dealt with Japan's growing power in the Pacific. The relative strength of the navies of the USA, the UK, Japan, France, and Italy was fixed in a ratio of 5 : 5 : 3 : 1.75 : 1.75. The sovereignty of China was also affirmed, and an 'Open Door' policy of trade with China maintained.

1931   The US Government's concern with Japanese aggression against China was evident in its response to the **Manchurian crisis**, beginning in 1931, when Japanese forces occupied an ever greater part of the North Chinese province of Manchuria. Although not a member of the League of Nations, the USA did offer to assist its efforts to establish the origins of the crisis. However, the USA stopped far short of actually using—or encouraging the League to use—force to reverse Japan's aggression.

Throughout the inter-war years, America's primary influence on the world lay not so much in the diplomatic sphere, as in the realm of economics, where the US economy was emerging as the world's strongest. US capital helped rebuild Germany, with loans enabling Germany to make reparations to Britain and France, who could then repay their own debts to the USA.

farmers suddenly found their livelihoods ruined as Americans ceased to buy silk stockings in the Depression of the early 1930s. Similarly growers of crops farmed in what we now know as the Global South for the world market found that the prices they received for their commodities plummeted. Brazil's coffee growers attempted to prevent the coffee price from collapsing by selling it to Brazilian railway companies as an alternative fuel to coal.

In economic terms, the result of the Depression was that the globalization of the world-economy stuttered as states attempted to reverse the process. Rather than a global free trade system continuing to develop (as it had from the industrial revolution up to 1914), the major capitalist states now sought to isolate their national economies as far as possible from the vagaries of the international market and cross-border capital flows. Free trade was abandoned in favour of protectionist policies and high tariff barriers, as states attempted to make their economies as self-sufficient as possible. As a result the volume of international trade fell sharply. America led the way in protectionism, being in the fortunate position of needing other countries' products less than did Britain, for example, and many other industrialized states.

The economic crisis of the 1930s was accompanied by profound political upheavals. We might question whether, without the Depression, Hitler would have found such fertile soil for Nazism in Germany. Although it is overly reductive to argue that the Depression alone accounts for Hitler's accession to power in 1933, nevertheless the human costs of economic collapse certainly made extremist political solutions appear attractive during the 1930s. Having secured power in Germany, Hitler proceeded to encourage Nazi movements on Germany's borders, especially in Austria and Czechoslovakia. Meanwhile, Mussolini completed the construction of the 'Fascist State' in Italy in the 1930s, while in Spain Franco ultimately defeated the Popular Front ranged against him. But the emergence of more radicalized (and often also racialized) forms of politics was not simply a European phenomenon. Several South American **regimes** toppled during the 1930s, to be replaced with new ones of either a pronounced left- or right-wing complexion. In the colonized world, nationalist movements were also given a powerful impetus by the Depression. In India, for example, Gandhi mobilized a mass campaign of civil disobedience against British rule, while in French Indo-China, Ho Chi Minh's communist nationalists embarked on the long road to independence which would ultimately entail protracted wars with both France and America after 1945.

Key points

- Since the industrial revolution, a global capitalist economy had been developing, drawing all parts of the world into transnational flows of finance and trade.

- The First World War disrupted this development, with a profound negative impact on the international economic system, which was initially masked by the vibrancy of the US economy in the 1920s.

- In 1929, the Wall Street stock-market crash induced a world Depression, illustrating the degree to which national economics were enmeshed in a global system.

- Depressions in many countries around the world resulted in extremist political movements gaining strength, and, more generally, in an upsurge of introverted nationalism and the pursuit of economic autarky.

The origins of the Second World War in Asia and the Pacific

Europeans sometimes display a tendency to regard the Second World War as primarily a European phenomenon, while Americans may insist that the war began in December 1941. In Asia, however, war began well before 1939. To understand how conflicts in Asia and Europe merged into a 'world war' (albeit with distinct 'theatres'), we must clearly examine inter-war developments in Asia, particularly in Japan and China.

In some respects Japan's position in Asia during the first decades of the twentieth century was akin to Germany's in Europe. After unification, Germany underwent rapid modernization and industrialization. It had sought an enlarged empire, challenging those of France and Britain in the years prior to 1914. Germany emerged from the First World War aggrieved at the treatment meted out by the victors and determined to reverse key aspects of the Versailles Settlement—a 'revisionism' heightened by the catastrophic consequences of the Depression. Under an extreme right-wing regime, Germany sought a solution to its problems through outward expansion, and found its path eased by the weakness of the states geographically closest to it. Much of this could also be said of Japan.

Japan and the 'Meiji Restoration'

During the reign of Emperor Meiji (from around 1868 to 1912), Japan's rulers fostered rapid industrialization, borrowing a model from Western Europe and North America. This was accompanied by a modernization of Japanese society and political life: the feudal agricultural system was abolished; the army was reorganized and conscription introduced, heralding the disintegration of the Samurai caste; education and foreign travel were encouraged; and a new parliamentary system was implemented. Like those of Germany, Japan's rulers in the late nineteenth century turned to imperial expansion to resolve domestic tensions; to control access to foreign resources; to secure cheap labour; and to open new markets. Both shared a belief that their popula-tion was growing so rapidly that the populace would soon outstrip the state's geographical and financial capacity to support it. Thus Hitler sought *Lebensraum* (living space) for the German people in Central and Eastern Europe, while Japan looked towards China, Korea, and South-East Asia as areas for expansion.

Japanese expansion in China

Just as Germany profited from the decline of its imperial neighbours (in Austria-Hungary, Turkey, and Russia), Japan's expansionism was likewise eased by the state of near-extinction in which China languished. China, once a great dynastic empire, by the late nineteenth century barely remained a sovereign state, having been forced to concede jurisdiction over coastal cities to foreign states and commercial interests, who between them determined to wrest control over the lucrative 'China trade' from China itself. The last emperor was toppled in 1911, and China slid into a protracted state of civil war. As provincial warlords fought one another, the Nationalist Guomindang movement under Sun Yat Sen (and latterly Chiang Kai Shek) clashed with Mao Zedong's Chinese Communist Party, which ultimately triumphed in 1949. Such internal chaos, and the absence of strong central government, provided fresh opportunities for foreign 'profiteers'. China had long been infiltrated by outside powers, anxious for a share of its 'exotic' goods—tea, spices, opium, silk—and to trade with the world's most populous state. Britain in the nineteenth century had the most extensive China trade, having used its heavily armed gunboats to forcibly open the market. But by the turn of the century, Tsarist Russia was heavily involved in railway building in northern China, while the United States was an increasingly prominent actor, insisting that imperial China adhere to America's preferred policy: that of the 'Open Door' (by which was meant the extension of equal trading rights to all foreign powers who wanted access to China's market, rather than granting monopoly privileges to single states in particular port cities and

Box 3.6	The origins of the war in the Pacific: a chronology

18 Sept. 1930	Mukden incident in Manchuria between Japanese troops and Chinese 'bandits'. Marks the start of Japan's conquest of Manchuria.	25 Nov. 1936	Germany and Japan sign the Anti-Comintern Pact.
		7 July 1937	Outbreak of war between Japan and China.
24 Feb. 1933	League of Nations adopts the Lytton Report, which recommends international mediation in the dispute between Japan and China, and urges League members not to recognize the Japanese puppet state in Manchuria (Manchuguo), but does not seek to impose sanctions on Japan.	6 Nov. 1937	Italy joins the Anti-Comintern Pact.
		14 June 1939	Japan begins a blockade of the Chinese city of Tientsin.
		26 July 1939	America retracts 1911 trade treaty with Japan.
		30 Aug. 1940	Japan occupies northern Indo-China.
		13 April 1941	Japan signs neutrality pact with USSR.
27 March 1933	Japan announces her withdrawal from the League.	21 July 1941	Vichy France permits Japan to occupy the whole of Indo-China.
29 Dec. 1934	Japan denounces the 1922 Washington naval treaty.	26 July 1941	America freezes Japanese assets.
		7 Dec. 1941	Japan attacks the US Navy at Pearl Harbor.
15 Jan. 1936	Japan withdraws from London naval conference.	8 Dec. 1941	Britain and America declare war on Japan.
		11 Dec. 1941	Germany and Italy declare war on the USA.

provinces). As US interests in China grew, Japan was also taking particular interest in the region of Manchuria, and clashed with Russia during 1904–5 in a war which marked the first major defeat in modern times of a European power by an Asian state. Japan's position in China was strengthened still further as a result of the First World War, during which Japan fought against Germany, using the opportunity to secure Germany's Chinese possessions.

Although Japan opposed Germany in the First World War, both felt dissatisfied by the terms of the Versailles settlement. Japan had tried, and failed, to have the principle of racial equality written into the terms of the treaties. That the Western powers were indeed racially prejudiced against the Japanese seemed to be confirmed by America's 1924 immigration legislation, which virtually prevented further Japanese immigration into the USA. The Japanese Government also felt that the country had not received adequate territory in recognition of its part in the war. As the 1920s progressed, Tokyo additionally protested against the way in which America and Britain sought, through the **Washington treaties**, both to limit Japan's naval construction and to pre-

vent China falling more effectively under Japanese domination.

Some Japanese policymakers remained committed to an internationalist policy during the 1920s. In particular they believed that Japan should take an active role in the League of Nations. But increasingly the army gained prominence in Japanese political life. The officer class (especially that part of it stationed in northern China following Japan's victory in the 1904–5 war with Russia) pressed ever more forcibly for Japanese expansion in China. Japan's experience of social upheaval strengthened the appeal of militarism. In the late 1920s, Japan suffered from two destabilizing tremors, one literal, the other figurative. The Great Kanto Earthquake of 1923 resulted in nearly a hundred thousand deaths and the destruction of about two million homes. The volcanic eruption seemed to symbolize the volatility of Japanese society during a period of rapid modernization. The second, metaphorical, great tremor to hit Japanese society was the Depression. As in Europe, the socio-economic conditions of Japan's depression provided fertile soil for radicalism. Outward expansionism looked even more attractive, and

Japanese political and military leaders increasingly talked of establishing a 'co-prosperity sphere' in Asia. This phrase was a euphemism for Japanese economic hegemony (if not outright rule) over various neighbouring states. Such imperialistic aspirations were fuelled by rising Japanese nationalism, the ideological foundation of which was Shintoism: a belief in the divinity and infallibility of the emperor, to whom each citizen owed personal allegiance.

The Manchurian crisis and after

Japan's foreign policy thus became increasingly assertive. The 'Manchurian crisis' of 1931 demonstrated this, and is sometimes regarded as the opening shot of the Second World War. Japan used a minor skirmish between Japanese soldiers and Chinese 'bandits' as a pretext to occupy a greater portion of Manchuria. Despite Chinese protests to the League of Nations, Japan was unrepentant, and by 1932 had established a puppet state in the whole of Manchuria, called **Manchuguo**. The League's response to the first blatant act of aggression by one of its member states against another was insipid: a Commission under the British Earl Lytton was dispatched to investigate the initial Sino-Japanese incident which had sparked the crisis. Its Report was a year in the making, and even then recommended moderation—urging both non-recognition of Manchuguo and international mediation of Japan and China's differences, but not any forcible action against Japan for its violation of international law.

Would Hitler's aggression in Europe and Mussolini's in East Africa (where he tried to capture Abyssinia, the last independent African state) have been deterred had the League acted decisively over Manchuria? The answer seems almost certainly not. Neither one had much regard for the niceties of international law, and most historians agree that both had long-term territorial ambitions which would scarcely have been deflected by a firmer League response to the Manchurian crisis. However, the League's abject failure to check Japanese aggression did perhaps help create a permissive atmosphere, which emboldened the European dictators to

disrespect international law in the expectation that they would not incur international sanctions. Certainly, in East Asia, Japan's rulers were not deterred from further aggression by the upshot of the Manchurian crisis.

By 1937, Japan was involved in full-scale war with China, and this too lasted until 1945. But Japan's mounting incursions into neighbours' territory— the so-called **'New Order'** in East Asia—were certainly not ignored by the Western powers. The United States, deeply invested (both commercially and psychologically) in the 'China trade' and in intensive Christian proselytizing activity there, grew increasingly agitated in the face of Japan's attempt to make China into its exclusive sphere of interest. Over the course of the 1930s, Washington wavered between a variety of measures intended to curb Japanese expansionism, provide some limited military assistance to the Chinese, and to protect America's own interests in the region, without taking on Japan's military directly. As these attempts failed, so Washington moved towards a more confrontational posture, and the application of ever more stringent economic sanctions and trade embargoes. In 1939, the US Government cancelled its 1911 trade agreement with Japan, thus restricting the latter's ability to import raw materials necessary to its war machine. Particularly damaging to Japan was the restriction this imposed on its access to oil. In the eyes of some historians, US actions pushed (more or less deliberately) Tokyo into more and more aggressive actions. Cut off from the vital lubricants of an industrialized economy, Japan had few choices but to extract them from South-East Asia.

Did the USA miscalculate, or did Washington deliberately try to push Japan south in order to avert a looming clash between Japan and Russia? Historians also debate how far Franklin Delano Roosevelt may have known of—hence tacitly encouraged—a Japanese retaliatory strike on US territory as the kind of galvanizing action that would rally American support for entry into a war in which the President was keen to play a leading part, but for which his citizens exhibited considerably less enthusiasm (Merrill and Paterson 1995: 127–84). The debate over whether Japanese intentions were known, or could have been anticipated, by US intelligence before the bombing of Pearl Harbor in December 1941 continues, now in parallel with the contemporary dispute over what the Bush White House and the CIA may, or may not, have known about Al Qaeda's plans prior to 9/11. But however one apportions responsibility for the deterioration of US-Japanese relations, the breakdown was both swift and decisive after the application of US sanctions. When Japan responded with its 'sneak attack' on the US Navy in Hawaii, Britain and the USA swiftly declared war on Japan on 8 December. Germany and Italy reciprocated with a declaration of war on the USA three days later. The Second World War was thereafter unquestionably global in scope. However, for many months there had been no doubt as to where the main lines of division lay in Asia, nor that an axis was emerging between Japan, Germany, and Italy. A Three-Power Pact was concluded in 1940, which was transformed into a military alliance in 1942. Thus while the German army overran huge swathes of continental Europe, Japan occupied large parts of Asia hitherto colonized by European states. The Dutch East Indies and French Indo-China fell to Japan, just as the Netherlands and France lay under Nazi rule. And although Britain itself repelled German invasion, the same was not true of its South-East Asian colonies, Burma, Ceylon, and Malaya.

Key points

- From 1868 onwards, Japan underwent a rapid period of industrialization and modernization, with profound social, economic, and political consequences.

- To find new markets, raw materials, and land for Japan's growing population, Japan began to expand into northern China, while China was in a protracted state of civil war.

- Japan, although it fought against Germany during the First World War, emerged from that war similarly dissatisfied with the post-war settlement.

- Between 1931 and 1933, Japan consolidated its hold over Manchuria, establishing a puppet state, Manchuguo: the League of Nations' response to the most blatant act of aggression it had thus far faced was minimal.

- By 1937, Japan was at war with China, which caused worsening relations with the USA, also with a strong imperial interest in China. When the USA limited Japan's ability to import oil and other vital strategic commodities in 1939, relations between those two powers drastically deteriorated—culminating in the bombing of Pearl Harbor in December 1941.

The path to war in Europe

As the crisis in the Far East deepened during the 1930s, Europe lurched from one crisis to the next: Italy's invasion of Abyssinia (Ethiopia); Germany's remilitarization of the Rhineland; civil war in Spain; Germany's expansion into Austria, then Czechoslovakia, followed by Poland, at which point Britain and France declared war on Germany in September 1939.

The controversy over the origins of the Second World War

It was suggested earlier in this chapter that in many ways the Second World War was a continuation of the First: another manifestation of Europe's deep-rooted instability, and a reflection of the imbalance of power which had existed on the continent ever since the unification of Germany. However, many historians would argue that besides the profound structural forces which were at work undermining the stability of Europe, human agency also played a role in bringing about the Second World War. Indeed, some maintain that to narrate the origins of that war without reference to Hitler would be akin to telling the story of Adam and Eve without the serpent. To many the Second World War was, quite simply, 'Hitler's war', which he planned, and which was the conscious result of his determination to achieve world mastery.

However, the origins of the Second World War have been—perhaps surprisingly—a matter of considerable historiographical dispute. While most historians agree that immediate responsibility for the war rests with Hitler and Nazi Germany, they have differed over whether Hitler actually **planned** the war, and what the extent of his territorial ambitions was—mastery of Europe, or German hegemony of the world? Did Hitler have a timetable for the expansionist ambitions he had set out in his autobiography-cum-manifesto *Mein Kampf*? Had he decided, by 1937, to take Czechoslovakia and then Poland, before turning to Western Europe, as a document (entitled the Hossbach Memorandum) used in the Nuremberg tribunal seemed to suggest? Did he think he could expand German power in Europe **without** causing a major war? Or did he believe that a Total War was inevitable, but did not foresee this coming about until the 1940s, when the German economy would be fully mobilized for such a war? All these questions have been posed by historians, and divergent answers given (Robertson 1971; Finney 1997).

The most controversial treatment of the war's origins by a serious historian remains A. J. P. Taylor's *The Origins of the Second World War*, first published in 1961 to a barrage of criticism. The cause of the furore was Taylor's suggestion that Hitler essentially resembled any other European statesman. Nazi ideology—though responsible for the 'evil of the gas chambers'—did not suffice to explain the war. Hitler, like his Weimar predecessors, had merely sought to enhance Germany's position after the Versailles settlement, and to reverse its unfavourable, and unfair, aspects. Far from having a timetable for expansion and general war, Hitler was an opportunist, who capitalized on the blunders of others, and the opportunities afforded him by the appeasers in Britain and France. War in September 1939 caught Hitler essentially by surprise. Although Taylor later claimed in his autobiography that his view of Hitler as blunderer and opportunist had become the new orthodoxy, this is something of an exaggeration (Taylor 1983: 299). It is probably truer to say that most historians believe that Hitler had a long-term fixity of purpose—expansion in Europe, if not further afield—coupled with a short-term flexibility in his tactics and timing.

The rise of Fascism and Nazism in Europe

A. J. P. Taylor aside, most liberal historians regard Nazi and fascist ideology as essential to understanding both the origins and practices of the war. Fuelled by popular dissatisfaction with the 1919 settlement, extreme right-wing movements arose in the 1920s and 1930s. These fed on the social, economic, and political instabilities engendered by the First World War. Italy had never really achieved stable central government despite unification in the nineteenth century. Although Fascist mythology claimed that Mussolini seized power with his '**March on Rome**', in reality he was invited to form a parliament by the king and conservative politicians in 1922, because the traditional right-wing parties had failed to form a stable government. Far from marching on Rome, he was brought to the capital by special train. Once Prime Minister, Mussolini set about conducting a 'Fascist revolution' in Italian life, which no doubt horrified at least some of those responsible for bringing him to power.

As many historians and political theorists have pointed out, 'fascism' evades easy definition—arguably so incoherent as not to constitute a political philosophy at all. As practised in Italy, it entailed the establishment of a type of state popularly termed '**totalitarian**' (especially after 1945), in which almost all aspects of its citizens' lives were subject to invasive regulation. In the sphere of employment, trade unions were abolished and 'corporations' of employers and employees established, overseen by fascist bureaucrats. Whatever the legitimation in terms of harmonious labour relations, 'corporatism' in practice ensured that the interests of big business prevailed over those of organized labour. In politics, opposition parties were eliminated, and a personality cult was built around the figure of Mussolini, 'Il Duce'. Social life was heavily imbued with fascist ideology—from women's institutes, to football clubs and youth leagues.

Fascist precepts also influenced foreign policy, although there was some continuity of purpose between Mussolini and his predecessors. Fascism glorified violence and struggle, within society and between states, as natural and heroic. War was the ultimate test not only of individual 'manhood' but of a state's maturity and position in the international hierarchy. Mussolini was thus committed to overturning that part of the Versailles settlement which had subtracted territory from Italy in the Adriatic. In addition, he strove to expand his 'New Roman Empire' into North Africa, by war if necessary. The obvious target was Abyssinia—the last remaining independent state in Africa—and in 1935, Italian troops moved to seize control of the country from Haile Selassie. This became a more protracted campaign than Mussolini had probably envisaged. Its most obvious beneficiary was not Il Duce himself, but Adolf Hitler, who used the cover of Mussolini's North African adventure to proceed with his own plans for dismantling the 1919 settlement in Europe.

Hitler came to power in Germany over a decade after Mussolini's accession in Italy. After years of street fighting and rabble rousing in beer cellars, Hitler's National Socialist party achieved success at the German polls in 1933. Once in power as Reich Chancellor, Hitler—like Mussolini—moved to consolidate the grip of his party over both the organs of the state, and the German people as a whole. Nazis assumed power in central and local government; the state directed industry, and controlled the German mass media. Opposition parties were abolished, and dissent stifled, either by physical punishment or the fear of it. Hitler's particular targets of detestation—the Jews, gypsies, and homosexuals—were sent in ever increasing numbers to concentration camps. No aspect of German life was left untouched by the Nazi party and ideology. Even the most intimate aspects of private life—relating to reproduction and child rearing—were subordinated to the imperatives of the Third Reich. German women were accordingly exhorted to produce genetically pure children for the greater good of the Reich.

In this regard, as in others, Nazism closely resembled Italian fascism, Mussolini also insisting that 'Maternity is the patriotism of women' (Mazower 1999: 82). But Nazism exhibited distinct, and more virulent, strains, especially in its genocidal anti-Semitism. At the heart of Hitler's worldview was his racist belief in the superiority of the pure German people—the Aryan race. Not only did he believe that Germany had been unfairly robbed of land and people in 1919, but his territorial aims went far beyond mere rectification of the wrongs of Versailles. In pursuit of more **Lebensraum** (living space), Aryan Germans must fufil racial and historical destiny, by expanding eastwards (the **Drang nach Osten**), at the expense of the slavonic **Untermenschen** ('subhumans') who inhabited Eastern Europe, and the Soviet Union in particular. Hitler's worldview thus rested on a debased Social Darwinism, in which the 'fittest' race was compelled to expand at the expense of its genetically inferior neighbours.

From appeasement to war

The Nazis made no secret of their territorial ambitions; *Mein Kampf* spelled out Hitler's racial views and expansionist plans quite explicitly. Why, therefore, did the governments of Britain and France not do more to prevent Hitler from realizing these plans? Why was Hitler allowed to remilitarize the Rhineland, annex Austria, and invade Czechoslovakia before the Allies confronted him over his incursion into Poland in September 1939? Why, in short, was Hitler appeased for so long?

The policy of **appeasement** pursued by the Western powers throughout much of the 1930s has received considerable scholarly attention, and remains a potent source of historical analogies for politicians. The first generation of post-war historians was extremely (if understandably) harsh in its verdict on the appeasers: Chamberlain and his French counterparts were the '**Guilty Men of Munich**'. By cravenly appeasing Hitler, the leaders of France and Britain simply fed his appetite, and emboldened the Führer to believe that he could successfully carry off ever more audacious violations of the Treaty of Versailles.

A number of subsequent historians have been somewhat kinder to the 'appeasers'. Certainly we should not underestimate the magnitude of the domestic and international crises confronting West European policymakers and diplomats in the 1930s. Japan's violations of Chinese sovereignty were a source of concern in the Far East. Events in Asia thus provided a convenient cover for Hitler to leave the Geneva disarmament conference and the League in 1933, and to begin the process of German rearmament. Germany also profited from Italy's invasion of Abyssinia, and was a far from reliable ally to Mussolini during the ensuing war there. Although Mussolini announced the formation of a '**Rome-Berlin Axis**' between Germany and Italy in November 1936, in fact, Hitler had sent some arms to Haile Selassie's beleaguered forces in Abyssinia—precisely to protract the war, enabling Germany to tear more gaping holes in the fabric of the Versailles settlement, while British and French attention was still focused on north-east Africa. As the League grappled with the issue of whether or not to apply sanctions to Italy over Abyssinia, civil war broke out in Spain. The ideological fissures in Europe were now unmistakable.

British and French politicians accordingly faced the daunting scenario of war on three fronts: in the Pacific (against Japan); the Mediterranean (against Italy); and Central Europe (against Germany). Neither Britain nor France was prepared militarily for such an eventuality. Nor, for much of the 1930s, did a majority of British and French citizens appear to favour going to war to prevent or reverse acts of aggression. There were after all pressing domestic issues to be attended to: the Depression had created chronic unemployment and poverty. Moreover, the memory of the First World War was still vivid, and this made politicians, mindful of the publics they served, cautious about embarking on military solutions to international problems. Appeasement, some historians would thus argue, was in certain respects a justifiable attempt to 'buy time'. It enabled British and French rearmament to proceed, and public opinion to be mobilized, so that if Germany did have to be challenged militarily, and Hitler's pose as a 'man of peace' was proved a sham, then at least a serious military effort could be mounted against him.

However, this more charitable interpretation of appeasement might be criticized on the grounds that it credits the appeasers with considerable foresight—with seeking a breathing space which would enable them, ultimately, to wage more effective war against Hitler, whereas in fact they tended to believe that if they gave in to his demands, the Führer would cease to make them. Chamberlain not only accepted that Germany did have some legitimate grievances but additionally regarded Hitler in the same light as other statesmen. The British premier therefore assumed that differences between European statesmen could be ironed out through negotiation and compromise, as all essentially wanted peace. This underestimation of Nazi intentions consequently enabled Hitler to launch a spectacular series of assaults on the Versailles settlement with impunity. He reoccupied the Rhineland in 1936, with surprisingly little response from France. He encouraged Nazi movements in Austria, and pressurized the Austrian chancellor Schuschnigg to include Nazis in his government. Then in March 1938 he dispatched German troops over the border to secure the 'unification' of Austria with Germany (*Anschluss*). Czechoslovakia was next. Here, Hitler again deployed as legitimation the fact that Germany had been wronged in 1919, when three and a half million Germans of the Sudetenland had been incorporated within the new Czech state. German troop movements against Czechoslovakia began in May 1938. While British and French leaders were clearly alarmed by this development, they nevertheless continued to appease Hitler, and indeed the high point of the policy was the now notorious **Munich conference** of September 1938. At Munich, the British and French premiers agreed to German occupation of the Sudetenland, but offered a guarantee (with Italy and Germany) of the borders of the remaining Czech state. Hitler also promised Chamberlain that their two countries would 'never go to war with one another again'—the famous piece of paper which Chamberlain claimed would secure '**peace for our time**'.

As we know, it did not. In March 1939, Germany invaded the remainder of Czechoslovakia, and Britain and France ignored their pledges made at Munich, with Chamberlain having decided some months earlier that Czechoslovakia was indefensible. However, in the wake of Germany's effective occupation of all Central Europe, the Western powers showered guarantees on the remaining free states of Eastern Europe and the Balkans. Why this sudden diplomatic revolution? The answer seems to be that appeasement no longer appeared credible once Hitler's ambitions had clearly outstripped revision of German grievances outstanding from 1919. By sending German troops into Prague, Hitler revealed that his territorial ambition was not just for 'Germanic' lands. Why assume that he would be satisfied with Czechoslovakia? Poland, the Low Countries, and France all now appeared in imminent danger of German expansionism. Fearing for their own territorial integrity and confronting a complete reordering of the global system, the leaders of Britain and France determined to go to war with Hitler over Poland in September 1939.

Box 3.7	The origins of the Second World War in Europe: a chronology

30 Oct. 1922	Mussolini becomes Prime Minister of Italy.	22 Sept. 1938	Chamberlain and Hitler meet at Godesburg.
30 Jan. 1933	Hitler becomes Chancellor of Germany.	29/30 Sept. 1938	Munich Conference.
14 Oct. 1933	Germany leaves the Geneva disarmament conference and walks out of the League of Nations.	28 March 1939	End of Spanish Civil War.
		31 March 1939	Britain and France extend a guarantee to Poland that they will defend Poland's territorial integrity from German attack, after Germany occupies the remainder of Czechoslovakia.
14/15 June 1934	Hitler and Mussolini meet in Venice.		
25 July 1934	Murder of Austrian Chancellor, Dollfuss, by Austrian Nazis.	17 April 1939	USSR proposes alliance to Britain and France.
16 March 1935	Germany reintroduces conscription.	22 May 1939	Pact of Steel signed between Italy and Germany.
3 Oct. 1935	Italy invades Abyssinia (Ethiopia).		
11 Oct. 1935	League decides to impose sanctions against Italy.	12 Aug. 1939	Britain and France begin military talks with USSR.
7 March 1936	Germany reoccupies the Rhineland (which the Treaty of Versailles had established as a demilitarized zone).	23 Aug. 1939	Stalin signs Nazi-Soviet Pact.
		25 Aug. 1939	Britain signs treaty with Poland.
9 May 1936	Italy annexes Abyssinia.	1 Sept. 1939	Germany invades Poland; Italy remains neutral.
17 July 1936	Civil war breaks out in Spain between Franco's fascist forces and the communist/socialist/syndicalist Popular Front.	3 Sept. 1939	Britain and France declare war on Germany.
1 Nov. 1936	Mussolini announces the existence of the Rome-Berlin Axis.	17 Sept. 1939	USSR invades Poland.
11 Dec. 1937	Italy leaves the League of Nations.	30 Nov. 1939	USSR invades Finland.
13 March 1938	Austria united with Germany (*Anschluss*).	9 April 1940	Germany invades Denmark and Norway.
20 May 1938	Rumours of German troop movements against Czechoslovakia.	10 June 1940	Italy enters the war.
		22 June 1940	France signs armistice with Germany.
15 Sept. 1938	British PM Chamberlain meets Hitler at Berchtesgaden.	22 June 1941	Germany invades USSR.
		8 Dec. 1941	USA enters the war.

Key points

- The origins of the Second World War have been the subject of particular historiographical controversy. Historians still dispute how far Hitler actually planned the war; whether he foresaw the extent of the war that began in 1939; and how ambitious Nazi territorial expansionism actually was (European hegemony or world domination?).

- Fascism and Nazism, as practised in Italy and Germany, led to a complete reordering of those societies, eliminating any notion of a private sphere.

  In foreign policy terms, ambitious territorial plans were mapped which went far beyond the revision of aspects of the Treaty of Versailles.
- Confronted with numerous international crises—in China, Abyssinia, and Europe—policymakers in Britain and France adopted a policy of appeasing Hitler.
- Once Germany occupied Prague in March 1939, appeasement was abandoned, and Britain and France declared war on Germany once it invaded Poland in September 1939.

Theorizing global history, 1900–1945

This chapter has offered an account of Europe's eclipse and the reorientation of the global system around increasing US leadership. In so doing, it has largely followed diplomatic history's conventional, state-centred approach, accentuating shifts in political and economic power, and noting the interconnectedness of national economies within a global economy that experienced a sclerotic (but temporary) contraction in the wake of 1929's crash. But of course the narrative offered here, although alert to controversies among historians over particular issues (most prominently the origins of the two world wars), constitutes only one way of recounting the history of these chaotic years. Like any historical era, this one can be both narrated and explicated in a multiplicity of different ways, depending on the epistemological commitments and theoretic preferences of the author (see Ch.12). By way of conclusion, then, let us consider—in necessarily condensed form—the ways in which the three central theoretical traditions in International Relations emplot and interpret the events of these years.

Realism

Interpretation of the years 1900–45 plays an important role in texts often most closely associated with

Selfish

the **Realist tradition**, such as E. H. Carr's *The Twenty Years' Crisis* (1939) and Hans Morgenthau's *Politics Among Nations* (1948) (see Ch.7). Stressing the need to understand the eternal clash of national interests—given the state's dynamic compulsion to maximize power by outward expansion—Realists conceive this period as one in which the virtues of their approach are self-evident. 'Idealist' aspirations to foster world peace, after the 'war to end all wars', ended in thoroughly predictable collapse, with Wilson's League of Nations foundering on states' persistent privileging of calculations of **national self-interest** above any sense of a global collective good. Accordingly, Liberal internationalists' attempts to give 'power politics' a bad name had proven naively misguided, Carr insisted in 1939 (1939: 103).

If politics are 'in one sense always power politics', then explaining the two world wars is perhaps not so difficult a task. Indeed, in the Realist view, the anarchical nature of world politics makes war appear the typical—not aberrant—condition of human life. Ideology and public opinion plays some role in explaining the particular complexion of foreign policies as pursued by particular states at particular times, but the more important issues for analysis lie in the structure and distribution of power within the international system. Hence, for Realists, the key to understanding Europe's long crisis lies in the profound disruption to its **balance of power** occasioned first by German unification at the end of the nineteenth century, and then by Germany's ongoing search to outstrip its competitors as they all sought to maximize national wealth, and secure the military, territorial, imperial and trading conditions under which this might best occur.

Liberalism/Idealism

cooperative

The **Liberal tradition**, rooted in a very different ontology, in which humans are regarded as essentially cooperative creatures despite their confinement within states that often behave as though they were not, finds quite distinct significance in the years 1900–45 (see Ch.8). While clearly the most significant inter-state attempt at international organization failed to prevent war in either Asia or Europe, Liberal theorists have nevertheless found more positive signs of internationalism.

These years are often assumed to be ones of ever greater isolationism (on the part of the USA) and xenophobic nationalism in much of the rest of the world. But for all that these and other '-isms' should be taken with due seriousness—as Liberals attach greater significance to the realm of ideas than their Realist counterparts—other ideational forces were also visibly at work, connecting people across national boundaries at a **sub-state level**. Given the growing density of communication and transport links crossing continents, it is scarcely surprising that ideas travelled along with people and products, and that **transnational social and political movements** intensified (Iriye 1997). Radical African-American activists, struggling against the intersection of race and class oppression at home, found common cause with anti-imperialists battling colonialism in Africa, the Caribbean, and Asia. Nationalists in India looked for both moral inspiration and practical guidance in anti-imperial tactics to the Irish republican tradition, especially after Britain conceded an Irish Republic in 1919. Likewise, suffragist ideas, and the women who espoused them, circumnavigated the Atlantic, and beyond. And in the 1930s, socialist and communist ideas found considerable support not only among incipient nationalist movements but among many in industrialized

states looking for a radical transformation of a capitalist system chronically incapable of delivering social justice and economic **equity**.

World systems theory

World systems theory stresses the global capitalist economy—developing over 500 years—as the central structure binding geographically disparate parts of the world into a single whole (see Ch.10). The system is marked by a functional and hierarchical **division of labour** between its industrialized, wealthy **core** and an exploited, under-developed **periphery**, from whom assets (whether cheap labour, raw materials, or other forms of surplus) are constantly stripped. Given to looking at historical processes over extremely long cycles, world systems theorists would tend not to conceive the years 1900–45 as a discrete period in their own right.

Rather, according to the interpretation offered by Giovanni Arrighi in *The Long Twentieth Century*, the first half of the twentieth century can be viewed as the most turbulent phase of a protracted crisis during which **hegemony** over the global capitalist system passed from the United Kingdom to the United States. This process was already under way by the 1890s, when US corporations began to assume a more prominent role in global trade, and as more American capital was directly invested overseas. However, no hegemonic succession (and he traces four since the Genovese flowering of finance capital in the Middle Ages) occurs rapidly. Nor does leadership pass from one city or state to another without considerable turbulence, as **capitalism** is inherently generative of instability and punctuated by crises of over-accumulation. Systemic crises thus periodically recur as the flowering of one phase of finance capital implodes in transnationalized chaos, engendered by the system's multiple contradictions but also necessary to its ongoing regeneration under reconstructed hegemony. In the inter-war period, US finance capital underwrote the militarization of European politics, seeing the opportunity for profit in European inter-capitalist competition, irrespective of the possibility that generalized war would lead to the system's total meltdown. While a global conflagration did indeed ensue, it turned out not, in fact, to be the ruination of US capital—but rather the moment at which American hegemony over the global economy crystallized. America emerged from the war as the only leading protagonist to have strengthened its economic position in both relative and absolute terms. The Soviets might have shouldered most of the burden of defeating the *Wehrmacht* in Europe, but American loans had made the Russian war-effort possible. After the Second World War, as billions of dollars were pumped into the regeneration of Western Europe and Japan, American primacy within the global economy was assured, and visibly on display.

Key points

- The three predominant traditions in International Relations offer quite distinct interpretations of large-scale historical events over the period 1900–45.

- Realists emphasize states' ruthlessly self-interested search for territorial, military, and economic resources whereas Liberal/Idealists point to efforts—however fruitless they may ultimately appear—to foster internationalism during the inter-war period. World-systems theorists, for their part, accentuate the role of the global capitalist economy is bringing states and people into often dislocating proximity.

Conclusion: 1900–1945, an era of deglobalization?

Viewed from a distance, the first half of the last century seems overwhelmingly fragmented and fissiparous: marked by imperial dissolutions, the emergence of violently exclusive nationalisms, and global economic collapse. In some accounts, these are regarded as years of 'deglobalization'. Many analyses fail even to consider, let alone historicize, the processes productive of global 'shrinkage', asserting that globalization properly denotes only the heightened phase of economic, cultural, and political interconnectivity since the 1970s, or even since the post-cold war 1990s.

Despite the disintegrative trends so visible during this era, one could nevertheless find considerable evidence of many phenomena that we now commonly associate with globalization. Indeed, as Ian Clark has argued, globalization and fragmentation are not one another's antitheses but rather exist in dialectical relationship with one another: connectedness and asymmetric co-dependencies generate tensions, counter-reactions, and the possibility for ostensibly localized crises to ripple across space rapidly, as the Depression did (Clark 1997).

Certainly, time- and space-compressing modes of communication and transport expanded rapidly in the first half of the twentieth century. These were the years in which both the radio and cinema enjoyed their heyday. Although many European states and their North American counterparts developed national media (whether privately or publicly funded), neither radio broadcasts nor films were consumed by solely domestic audiences. By the end of the 1920s, the USSR had already pioneered international radio broadcasting, soon to be joined by the BBC's External Services (later its World Service). While French companies developed the newsreel as a visual catalogue of current affairs and curios, Hollywood films enjoyed growing popularity with European audiences—so much so that Hitler ultimately banned them from German cinemas, while privately relishing screenings of Disney cartoons and *Gone With the Wind*, just as the Soviet Union greeted transgressive imports such as American jazz and swing music with alarm, while nevertheless instituting American-style Fordist production techniques in its state-run factories.

Attempts at cultural protectionism may only have confirmed the impression among certain US commentators that the export of consumer culture was a more effective route to spreading admiration for the

'American way of life' than conventional forms of diplomacy (Rosenberg 1999). If unfriendly states exhibited alarm, this surely attested films' ability to stimulate popular emulation of American lifestyles and appetite for the products so essential to 'freedom' conceived along consumerist lines. We might, then, trace what would later be called 'cultural imperialism' back to the inter-war years of dollar diplomacy, though it remains debatable how far non-Americans' enthusiastic consumption of US products translates into ready approval of US policy.

Box 3.8   Key Concepts

Appeasement: a policy of making concessions to revanchist (or otherwise territorially acquisitive state) in the hope that settlement of more modest claims will assuage that state's expansionist appetites. Appeasement remains most (in)famously associated with British Prime Minister Neville Chamberlain's acquiescence to Hitler's incursions into Austria and then Czechoslovakia, culminating in the Munich Agreement of September 1938. Since then, appeasement has generally been seen as synonymous with a craven collapse before the demands of dictators—encouraging, not disarming, their aggressive designs.

Autarky: the pursuit of national economic self-sufficiency—a policy pursued by several states in the wake of the Depression, as they sought to disentangle their economies from reliance on unstable global commodity markets and foreign loans.

Collective security: the foundational principle of the League of Nations: namely, that member states would take a threat or attack on one member as an assault on them all (and on international norms more generally). The League would accordingly respond in unison to such violations of international law. Appreciating that such concerted action would ensue, putative violators—the League's framers hoped—would be duly deterred from launching aggressive strikes in the first place. As the 1920s and 1930s showed, however, theory and practice diverged wildly, with League members failing to take concerted action against Japanese imperialism in Asia, and German and Italian expansionism in Europe and Africa.

Great Depression: a byword for the global economic collapse that ensued following the US Wall Street stock-market crash in October 1929. Economic shockwaves soon rippled around a world already densely interconnected by webs of trade and foreign direct investment such that the events of October 1929 were felt in countries as distant as Brazil and Japan.

'Open Door' policy: pursuit of an 'Open Door' was the aspiration of US foreign policy in China since 1900. What this meant was that China would agree to cede equal access and commercial opportunities to all foreign powers that sought to participate in the lucrative 'China trade', rather than surrendering exclusive access to single foreign states in its many treaty ports. The 'Open Door' has also, however, been taken as a signifier more broadly for the US approach to the pursuit of asymmetric advantage in trading relations, often involving a bulldozing down of barriers to 'free trade' erected by those less economically powerful than itself.

Reparations: dues owed (as money or *matériel*) by vanquished nations to their victorious former enemies at a war's end. In 1919, the issue of reparations owed by Germany caused the peacemakers considerable difficulty, with much debate over the precise amount that Germany be expected to repay, and with what consequences for that country's economic reconstruction. Whether or not Germany should be squeezed dry—and the economic sense that made (or did not make) for Europe's wider recovery—was coupled with the contentious issue of 'war guilt'. Germans thus smarted not only at the punitively high scale of the reparations bill with which they were confronted but also at its coupling to a clause insisting on Germany's singular responsibility for the war.

Self-determination: a principle ardently, but selectively, espoused by US President Woodrow Wilson in the peacemaking that followed the First World War: namely that each 'people' should enjoy self-government over its own sovereign nation-state. Wilson pressed for application of this principle to East/Central Europe, but did not believe that other nationalities (in colonized Asia, Africa, the Pacific, and the Caribbean) were fit for self-rule.

Total War: a term given to the twentieth century's two world wars to denote not only their global scale but also the combatants' pursuit of their opponents' 'unconditional surrender' (a phrase particularly associated with the Western allies in the Second World War). Total War also signifies the mobilization of whole populations—including women into factory work and in auxiliary civil defence units, and as paramilitaries and paramedics—as part of total call-up of all able-bodied citizens in pursuit of victory.

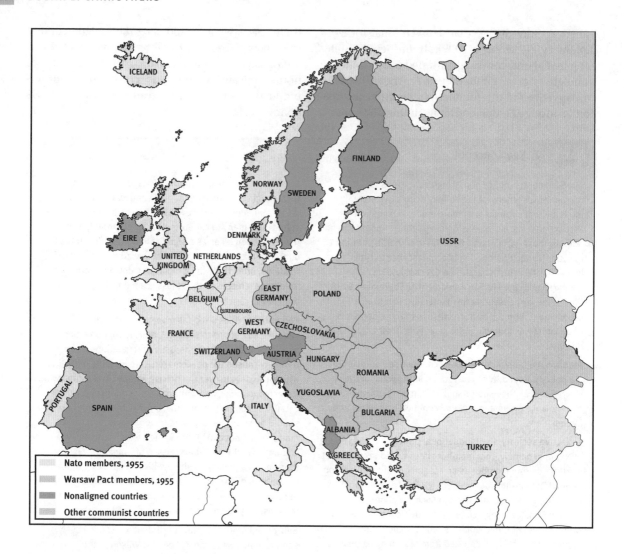

Fig. 3.2 Europe after the Second World War

The ability to traverse the globe with greater ease was not confined to cultural and consumer products alone. Individuals with disposable income and surplus leisure time could themselves travel to foreign destinations ever more readily. In both Western Europe and North America, tourism—hitherto a preserve of leisured elites for whom acquaintance with the treasures of Renaissance Europe was mandatory—expanded to the bourgeoisie. But of course the vast majority of those who travelled across continents in the nineteenth and early twentieth centuries did so not as tourists but as migrants in search of better life opportunities elsewhere, whether fleeing political persecution or poverty, or (as was often the case) both in tandem. Between 1891 and 1920, over 27 million people left turbulent, emiserated Europe, heading (particularly from Ireland, Italy, Spain and Eastern Europe) to destinations in the New World (notably the USA, Argentina, Brazil, and Australasia). By 1920, after which point immigration was substantially curtailed until after the Second World War, nearly one in seven residents of the USA was foreign born. Of these, it is impossible to determine how many relocated eagerly and how many reluctantly left their destitute homelands.

Clearly, however, not all this reshuffling of population was willingly undertaken by those who moved. Europe's imperial powers continued to operate schemes of indentured labour in a **global network** that encompassed over forty countries. Britain alone transplanted over thirty million Indians in Trinidad, Guyana, and Fiji as agricultural labourers, and imperial Japan also drew heavily on forced labour (including so-called 'comfort women') from Korea (Ponting 1998: 46–7). To the extent that imperialism and war have been key engines of globalization, and continue to be (albeit in altered forms), the years 1900–45 offer some salutary correctives to globalization's more myopic and optimistic boosters. The world's becoming a 'single space' has been in process for a very long time: five hundred years or five thousand, according to varieties of world systems theory. As the retreat to economic **autarky** in the 1930s suggests, interconnectedness proceeds in fits and starts, not along an ever-thickening linear line. Finally, as the case of indentured labour should remind us, if (as Roland Robertson (1992) and others insist) globalization requires individuals' **awareness** of the world's smallness, then this realization was often impressed upon people with particular violence— not so much as global shrinkage as the stripping of local and personal autonomy.

For further information and case studies on this subject, please visit the companion web site at www.oup.com/uk/booksites/politics.

QUESTIONS

1   In what ways did Europe dominate international politics at the start of the twentieth century?

2   Why was Germany regarded as a 'problem' after its unification in 1871?

3   What factors resulted in the outbreak of the First World War in 1914?

4   What were the main weaknesses with the post-war peace settlement?

5   Was Germany treated unfairly by the Treaty of Versailles?

6   Why were the USA and the USSR not more active in international politics between the First and Second World Wars?

7   Why did the Wall Street stock-market crash of October 1929 have such profound international consequences?

8   How far and in what ways did the European Great Powers and the USA regard Japan as a threat in the first three decades of the twentieth century?

9   Is it fair to regard the Second World War as 'Hitler's War'?

10   In what ways do different theoretical positions yield different interpretations of these years?

11   To what extent is it appropriate to regard the period 1900–45 as an era of 'deglobalization'?

GUIDE TO FURTHER READING

General

Hobsbawm, E. (1999), *Age of Extremes: The Short Twentieth Century 1914–91* (London: Michael Joseph). This is an engagingly readable look at the century which Hobsbawm regards as beginning in 1914.

Keylor, W. (1992), *The Twentieth Century World: An International History* (New York: Oxford University Press). This book provides an excellent overview of the entire century, with lengthy sections of the period up to 1945. Economic factors are dealt with particularly well.

Mazower, M. (1999), *Dark Continent: Europe's Twentieth Century* (London: Penguin). An incisive and provocative history of Europe in the twentieth century, synthesizing a great deal of material with engaging verve.

Merrill, D. and Paterson, T. (eds) (2000), *Major Problems in American Foreign Relations: Vol. II*, 6th edn (Boston, Mass.: Houghton Mifflin). A useful collection of primary source documents and interpretive essays, covering key issues in US global relations from the First World War.

The First World War and after

Henig, R. (1984), *Versailles and After, 1919–33* (London: Methuen). A pamphlet setting out the main terms of the post-war peace settlement.

Joll, J. (1984), *The Origins of the First World War* (London: Longmans). A useful synthesis of the debate on the origins of the war.

The Second World War

Iriye, A. (1987), *The Origins of the Second World War in Asia and the Pacific* (London: Longmans). In the same series as Joll's book, this volume examines the growth of Japanese imperialism and the onset of the war.

Finney, P. (1997), *The Origins of the Second World War* (London: Arnold). A recent assemblage of key articles, covering the range of historiographical debates over the origins of the Second World War, interpretations of the nature of the 'dictatorships', and appraisals of appeasement

Robertson, E. M. (ed.) (1971), *The Origins of the Second World War: Historical Interpretations* (London: Macmillan). A useful collection of articles illustrating the extent of the row over Taylor's thesis; including a vicious exchange between Taylor and his chief opponent, Hugh Trevor-Roper.

Taylor, A. J. P. (1961), *The Origins of the Second World War* (Harmondsworth: Penguin). This book sparked a huge controversy on account of Taylor's claim that Hitler—an ordinary European statesman—blundered into the war. Taylor also has much to say about Versailles and appeasement.

WEB LINKS

www.etown.edu/vl www Virtual library, international affairs resources.

www.hartford-hwp.com/archives/ World history archives.

www.history.ac.uk/ihr/Resources History online.

www.besthistorysites.net/index.shtml The best of history websites.

CHAPTER 4

International history, 1945–1990

LEN SCOTT

READER'S GUIDE

This chapter examines some of the principal developments in international politics from 1945 to 1990. Fundamental changes in politics, technology, and ideology took place in this period, with enormous consequences for world affairs. The onset of the cold war, the creation of nuclear weapons, and the end of European imperialism are the principal developments explored in the chapter. Since 1945 world politics has been greatly influenced by the conflict between the United States and the Soviet Union, each of which emerged as 'superpowers'. The ideological, political, and military interests of these two states, and their allies, extended around the globe. How far, and in what ways, conflict in Europe, Asia, and elsewhere was promoted or prevented by the cold war are central questions. Similarly, how the process of decolonization became intermingled with cold war conflicts is a central issue in understanding many wars and conflicts in the 'Third World'. Finally, how dangerous was the nuclear confrontation between East and West? Did nuclear weapons keep the peace between the superpowers or did they provoke conflict and risk global catastrophe? The chapter raises these questions, and explores the relationship between nuclear weapons development and phases in East–West relations, first with détente, and then with the deterioration of Soviet–American relations in the 1980s.

Introduction

The Second World War was global in scope and total in nature. It helped bring about fundamental changes in world politics after 1945. Before 1939 Europe had been the arbiter of world affairs, and both the Soviet Union and the United States remained, for different reasons, preoccupied with internal development at the expense of any significant global role. The war brought the Soviets and the Americans militarily and politically deep into Europe, and helped transform their relations with each other. This transformation was soon reflected in their relations outside Europe where various confrontations developed. Like the Second World War, the cold war had its origins in Europe, but quickly spread, with enormous consequences for countries and peoples around the world.

After 1945, European power was increasingly in eclipse, although this was not always apparent to those in government or their supporters. The economic plight of the wartime belligerents, including those Western European countries that had emerged as victors, was nevertheless increasingly and transparently obvious, as was the growing realization of the military and economic potential of the United States and the Soviet Union. Both countries emerged as 'superpowers', combining global political objectives with military capabilities that included weapons of mass destruction and the means to deliver them over intercontinental distances. In Europe, the military involvement of the superpowers soon took the form of enduring political commitments, notwithstanding early American intentions to withdraw and demobilize their troops after 1945. European political, economic, and military weakness contrasted with the appearance of Soviet strength and the growing Western perception of malign Soviet intent. The onset of the cold war in Europe marked the collapse of the wartime alliance between the UK, the USSR, and the USA. How far this alliance had been a marriage of convenience, and how far its breakdown was inevitable after 1945 remain crucial and contentious issues. What is beyond doubt is that the legacies of the Second World War provided a heavy burden for succeeding generations. Arguably the most notable, and certainly the most dramatic, legacy was the atomic bomb, built at enormous cost and driven by fear that Nazi Germany might win this first nuclear arms race, with terrifying consequences. After 1945, nuclear weapons presented unprecedented challenges to world politics and to the leaders responsible for conducting post-war diplomacy. The cold war provided context and pretext for the growth of nuclear arsenals which threatened the very existence of humankind, and which have continued (and continued to spread) beyond the end of the cold war and the East–West confrontation.

Since 1945 world politics has been transformed in a variety of ways. These changes reflected political, technological, and ideological developments, of which three are examined in this chapter: (1) the end of empire: the withdrawal of European countries from their empires in Africa and Asia; (2) the cold war: the political and military confrontation between the United States and the Soviet Union; (3) the bomb: the development of the atomic bomb and the hydrogen bomb, and the means of their delivery. There have, of course, been other important changes, and indeed equally important continuities, some of which are explored in other chapters. The transformation of the international political economy and the creation of the United Nations are among several key developments. Nevertheless, the three principal changes outlined above provide a framework for exploring events and trends which have shaped post-war international politics and the world we now inhabit.

Box 4.1	Key concepts

Superpower: term used to describe the United States and the Soviet Union after 1945, denoting their global political involvements and military capabilities, including in particular their nuclear arsenals.

'Wind of change': reference by British Prime Minister Harold Macmillan in a speech in South Africa in 1960 to the political changes taking place across Africa heralding the end of European imperialism.

Apartheid: system of racial segregation introduced in South Africa in 1948, designed to ensure white minority domination.

Hegemony: political (and/or economic) domination of region, usually by a superpower.

Truman doctrine: statement made by President Harry Truman in March 1947 that it 'must be the policy of the United States to support free people who are resisting attempted subjugation by armed minorities or by outside pressures'. Intended to persuade Congress to support limited aid to Turkey and Greece, the doctrine came to underpin the policy of containment and American economic and political support for its allies.

Containment: American political strategy for resisting perceived Soviet expansion, first publicly espoused by an American diplomat, George Kennan, in 1947. Containment became a powerful factor in American policy towards the Soviet Union for the next forty years, and a self-image of Western policymakers.

North Atlantic Treaty Organization (NATO): organization established by treaty in April 1949 comprising 12 (later 16) countries from Western Europe and North America. The most important aspect of the NATO alliance was the American commitment to the defence of Western Europe.

Détente: relaxation of tension between East and West; Soviet–American détente lasted from the late 1960s to the late 1970s, and was characterized by negotiations and nuclear arms control agreements.

Rapprochement: re-establishment of more friendly relations between the People's Republic of China and the United States in the early 1970s.

Ostpolitik: the West German Government's 'Eastern Policy' of the mid- to late 1960s, designed to develop relations between West Germany and members of the Warsaw Pact.

Glasnost: policy of greater openness pursued by Soviet President Mikhail Gorbachev from 1985, involving greater toleration of internal dissent and criticism.

Perestroika: policy of restructuring, pursued by Gorbachev in tandem with Glasnost, and intended to modernize the Soviet political and economic system.

Brezhnev doctrine: declaration by Soviet premier Leonid Brezhnev in November 1968 that members of the Warsaw Pact would enjoy only 'limited sovereignty' in their political development.

Sinatra doctrine: statement by the Soviet foreign ministry in October 1989 that countries of Eastern Europe were 'doing it their way' (a reference to Frank Sinatra's song, 'I did it my way') and which marked the end of the Brezhnev doctrine and Soviet hegemony in Eastern Europe.

Mutually Assured Destruction (MAD): condition in which both superpowers possessed the capacity to destroy their adversary even after being attacked first with nuclear weapons.

End of empire

The demise of imperialism in the twentieth century was a fundamental change in world politics. It reflected and contributed to the decreasing importance of Europe as the arbiter of world affairs. The belief that national **self-determination** should be a guiding principle in international politics marked a transformation of attitudes and values. During the age of imperialism political status had accrued to imperial powers. After 1945, imperialism was viewed with growing international hostility. Colonialism and the United Nations Charter were increasingly recognized as incompatible, though independence

Table 4.1 Principal acts of European decolonization, 1945–1980

Country	Colonial state	Year of independence
India	Britain	1947
Pakistan	Britain	1947
Burma	Britain	1948
Sri Lanka	Britain	1948
Indonesia	Holland	1949
Ghana	Britain	1957
Malaya	Britain	1957
French African colonies*	France	1960
Zaire	Belgium	1960
Nigeria	Britain	1960
Sierra Leone	Britain	1961
Tanganyika	Britain	1961
Uganda	Britain	1962
Algeria	France	1962
Rwanda	Belgium	1962
Kenya	Britain	1963
Guinea-Bissau	Portugal	1974
Mozambique	Portugal	1975
Cape Verde	Portugal	1975
São Tomé	Portugal	1975
Angola	Portugal	1975
Zimbabwe	Britain	1980

* Including Cameroon, Central African Republic, Chad, Gabon, Ivory Coast, Madagascar, Mali, Mauritania, Niger, Senegal and Upper Volta.

was often slow and sometimes marked by prolonged conflict and war. The cold war often complicated and hindered the transition to independence. Various factors influenced the process of decolonization: the attitude of the colonial power; the ideology and strategy of the anti-imperialist forces; and the role of external powers. Political, economic, and military factors played various roles in shaping the transfer of power. Different imperial powers and newly emerging independent states had different experiences of withdrawal from empire. Three of the principal European experiences of withdrawal from empire are discussed below.

Britain

In 1945, the British empire extended across the globe. Between 1947 and 1980, 49 territories were granted their independence. There was debate within Britain over Britain's imperial role, which can be traced back to the nineteenth century, but after 1945 growing recognition of the justice of self-determination combined with recognition of the strength of nationalism brought about a reappraisal of policy. Withdrawal from India, the 'Jewel in the Crown' of the empire, in 1947 was the most dramatic, and in (most) British eyes, successful, act of decolonization, and one which paved the way for the creation of the world's largest democracy. How far the ensuing hostility between India and Pakistan was avoidable, and how far it reflected previous British efforts to divide and rule, remain matters for debate. What is clear is that India was something of an exception in the early post-war years, and that successive British governments were reluctant to rush toward decolonization. The key period for the British empire in Africa came toward the end of the 1950s and early 1960s, symbolized by Prime Minister Harold Macmillan's speech in South Africa in 1960 when he warned his hosts of the 'wind of change' blowing through their continent.

The transition from empire was relatively peaceful, and led to the creation of democratic and stable states. There were some conflicts with indigenous revolutionary elements, notably in Kenya (1952–6) and Malaya (1948–60). Yet, from a European perspective, the British experience was more successful than the French. In Rhodesia (Zimbabwe), however, the transition to 'one person one vote', and black majority rule, was prevented by a white minority prepared to disregard both the British Government and world opinion. This minority was aided and abetted by the South African Government. Under apartheid, after 1948, the South Africans engaged in what many saw as the racial equivalent of imperialism. South Africa also conducted more traditional imperialist practices in its occupation of Namibia, and exercised an important influence in post-colonial/cold war struggles in Angola and Mozambique.

Britain, like France, sought to ensure that independence was granted on terms advantageous to the colonial power, even where the decision to leave often reflected the judgement that the cost of fighting the nationalists was too great. Britain and France sought to maximize their interests by economic and political frameworks designed to serve their advantage. The British Commonwealth and the French Union in Africa were the main instruments of this, though the British Commonwealth developed its own identity, and frequently voiced views and concerns at variance with those of the British Government. In the 1980s for example the Commonwealth played a major part in the campaigns against apartheid South Africa, bringing it into conflict with the Thatcher Government in Britain.

France

The British experience of decolonization stood in contrast to that of the French. France had been occupied during the Second World War, and successive governments sought to preserve French prestige in international affairs by maintaining her imperial status. In Indo-China after 1945, the French attempted to preserve their colonial role, only withdrawing after prolonged guerrilla war and military defeat at the hands of the Vietnamese revolutionary forces, the Viet Minh, led by Ho Chi Minh. In Africa, the picture was different. The wind of change also blew through French Africa, and under President Charles de Gaulle, France withdrew from empire, while attempting to preserve its influence by means of the French Union and later the French Community. In Algeria, however, the French refused to leave. Algeria was regarded by many French people to be part of France itself. The resulting war, from 1954 to 1962, led to up to 45,000 deaths, and France itself was brought to the edge of civil war.

Portugal

The last European empire in Africa was that of Portugal, and when the military dictatorship was overthrown in Lisbon, withdrawal from empire followed swiftly. The transition to independence occurred with relative ease in Guinea-Bissau, Cape Verde, and São Tomé, but in Mozambique and Angola the anti-colonial struggle was already giving way to conflict among the different anti-colonial groups. These organizations received support from various external powers (America, the Soviet Union, Cuba, and South Africa) which helped arm and finance them. The pattern of resulting conflict reflected a complex of anti-colonial, tribal, and ideological allegiances. In Angola, Cuban troops supported the MPLA (the Popular Movement for the Liberation of Angola) who were opposed by invading South African forces, while the United States provided various types of assistance, including sophisticated weapons, to the anti-communist UNITA (National Union for the Total Independence of Angola). Cold war perspectives and antagonisms thus fuelled regional instability, while prolongation and escalation of the conflict exacerbated global Soviet–American tensions (see below).

The consequences for the populations concerned were continuing civil war and, eventually, in the case of Mozambique, famine and mass starvation. How far political and ideological divisions, and how far tribal factors were responsible for conflict is one question, and one that was to be asked of many newly emergent African states. Indeed, in general, how far tribal divisions were created or exacerbated by the imperial powers is an important question in examining the political stability of the newly independent states. Equally important is how capable the new political leaderships in these societies were in tackling their political and economic problems.

Legacies and consequences: nationalism or communism

The pattern of decolonization in Africa was thus diverse, reflecting the attitudes of the colonial powers, the nature of the local nationalist or revolutionary movements, and in some cases the involvement of external states, including the main cold war protagonists. In Asia, the relationship between nationalism and revolutionary Marxism was a potent force. In Malaya the British defeated an insurgent communist movement (1948–60). In Indo-China (1946–54) the French failed to do likewise. For the Vietnamese, centuries of foreign oppression—Chinese, Japanese, French—soon focused on a new 'imperialist' adversary, the United States. For the Americans, early reluctance to support European imperialism gave way to incremental and covert involvement, and from 1965, growing open commitment to the newly created state of South Vietnam. The American aim of containing communism was soon applied to the conflicts of Indo-China. Chinese and Soviet support for North Vietnam and the 'Viet Cong' (the communist guerrillas) were part of the cold war context of the war. The United States, however, failed to coordinate limited war objectives with a political strategy for defeating these forces. North Vietnamese success in revolutionary warfare eventually led Washington to search for 'peace with honour' once political objectives could not be achieved, and 'victory' was no longer possible. The 'Viet Cong's' *Tet* (Vietnamese New Year) offensive in 1968 marked a decisive event in the war, though it was not until 1973 that American forces were finally withdrawn, two years before South Vietnam was defeated.

The global trend towards decolonization has been a key development since 1945, but one frequently offset by local circumstances. Some countries have lost their independence since 1945, such as Tibet, invaded by China in 1950, and East Timor, invaded by Indonesia in 1975. Yet, while imperialism has generally withered, other forms of domination or hegemony have appeared. The notion of hegemony has been used as criticism of the behaviour of the superpowers, most notably with Soviet hegemony in Eastern Europe, and American hegemony in Central America. European retreat from empire did not result in isolationism: Britain, and particularly France, sought to intervene, both overtly and covertly, in post-colonial affairs using a variety of methods including economic development assistance.

Key points

- Different European powers had different attitudes to decolonization after 1945: some, such as the British, decided to leave while others wished to preserve their empires, in part (the French) or in whole (the Portuguese).

- European powers adopted different attitudes to different regions and countries; e.g. British withdrawal from Asia came much more quickly after 1945 than from Africa.

- The process of decolonization was relatively peaceful in many cases; it led to revolutionary wars in others (Algeria, Malaya, and Angola), whose scale and ferocity depended on the attitudes of the colonial power and the nationalist movements.

- The struggle for independence or national liberation became embroiled in cold war conflicts when the superpowers and/or their allies became involved, e.g. Vietnam.

- Whether decolonization was judged successful depends, in part, on whose perspective you adopt—that of the European power, or the independence movement, or the people themselves.

The cold war

The rise of the United States as a world power after 1945 was of paramount importance in international politics. Its conflict with the Soviet Union provided one of the crucial dynamics in world affairs, and one which affected—directly or indirectly—every part of the globe. In the West, historians have debated, with vigour and acrimony, who was responsible for the collapse of the wartime relationship between the United States and the Soviet Union. The rise of the Soviet Union as a global power after 1945 is equally crucial in understanding international affairs in this period. Relations between the Union of Soviet Socialist Republics (USSR) and its Eastern European 'allies', with the People's Republic of China (PRC), and with various revolutionary movements and governments in the Third World, have been vital issues in world politics, as well as key factors in Soviet–American affairs.

Discerning phases in East–West relations casts light on key characteristics of the cold war. How such phases are defined is a matter of debate. The issue of when the cold war began, for example, is closely bound up with the question of who (if anyone) was responsible. Some historians date the origins of the cold war back to the 'Russian revolution' of 1917, while most focus on various events between 1945 and 1950. Whether the cold war was inevitable, whether it was the consequence of mistakes and misperceptions by political leaders, or whether it was the response of courageous Western leaders to malign and aggressive Soviet intent, are central issues in debates about the origins of the cold war, and its subsequent development. Hitherto, these debates have drawn from Western archives and sources, and are often focused on Western actions and reactions. With the end of the cold war, greater evidence is appearing about Soviet actions, and how Moscow perceived the issues. The following section sets out various key phases of the cold war (with which not all historians would agree), but which help identify key features and changes in East–West relations after 1945.

1945–1953: onset of the cold war

The onset of the cold war in Europe reflected failure to implement the **principles** agreed at the wartime conferences of Yalta and Potsdam. The future of Germany, and of various Central and Eastern European countries, notably Poland, were issues of growing tension between the former wartime allies. Reconciling the principles of national self-determination with the concerns of **national security** was a formidable task. In the West there was a growing feeling that Soviet policy towards Eastern Europe was guided not by historic concern with security but by ideological expansion. In March 1947 the Truman administration sought to justify limited aid to Turkey and Greece with a rhetoric designed to arouse awareness of Soviet ambitions, and a declaration that America would support those threatened by Soviet subversion or expansion. The **Truman doctrine** and the associated policy of **containment** expressed the self-image of the United States as inherently defensive, and were underpinned by the

Marshall Plan for European economic recovery, proclaimed in June 1947, which was essential to the economic rebuilding of Western Europe. In Eastern Europe, democratic socialist and other anti-communist forces were systematically undermined and eliminated as Marxist-Leninist **regimes** loyal to Moscow were installed. The only exception was in Yugoslavia, where the Marxist leader, Marshal Tito, consolidated his position while maintaining independence from Moscow. Subsequently Tito's Yugoslavia was to play an important role in the Third World's Non-Aligned Movement.

The first major confrontation of the cold war took place over Berlin in 1948. The former German capital had been left deep in the heart of the Soviet zone of occupation, and in June 1948 Stalin sought to resolve its status by severing road and rail communications. West Berlin's population and political autonomy were kept alive by a massive airlift. Stalin ended the blockade in May 1949. The crisis also saw the deployment of American long-range bombers in Britain, officially described as 'atomic capable', though none were actually armed with nuclear weapons. The American military deployment was followed by the political commitment enshrined in the **North Atlantic Treaty Organisation (NATO)** treaty signed in April 1949. The key principle of the treaty—that an attack on one member would be treated as an attack on all—accorded with the principle of collective self-defence enshrined in Article 51 of the United Nations Charter. In practice, the cornerstone of the alliance was the commitment of the United States to defend Western Europe. In reality, this came to mean the willingness of the United States to use nuclear weapons to deter Soviet 'aggression'. For the Soviet Union 'political encirclement' soon entailed a growing military, and specifically nuclear, threat.

While the origins of the cold war were in Europe, events and conflicts in Asia and elsewhere were also crucial. In 1949, the thirty-year-long Chinese civil war ended in victory for the communists under Mao Zedong. This had a major impact on Asian affairs and on perceptions in both Moscow and Washington. In 1950, the North Korean attack on South Korea was interpreted as part of a general communist offensive, and a test case for American resolve, and the will of the United Nations to withstand aggression. The resulting American and UN commitment, followed in October 1950 by Chinese involvement, led to a war lasting three years, in which over three million people died before pre-war borders were restored. North and South Korea themselves remained locked in seemingly perpetual hostility, even after the end of the cold war.

1953–1969: conflict, confrontation, and compromise

One consequence of the Korean War was the build-up of American conventional forces in Western Europe, in case communist aggression in Asia was a feint to detract from the real intent in Europe. The idea that communism was a monolithic political entity controlled from Moscow became an enduring American fixation, not shared in London and elsewhere. Western Europeans nevertheless depended on the United States for military security and this dependence deepened as the cold war confrontation in Europe was consolidated. The rearmament of the Federal Republic of Germany in 1954 precipitated the creation of the Warsaw Pact in 1955. The military build-up continued apace, with unprecedented concentrations of conventional and moreover nuclear forces. By the 1960s there were some 7,000 nuclear weapons in Western Europe alone. NATO deployed these nuclear weapons to offset Soviet conventional superiority, while Soviet 'theatre nuclear' forces in Europe compensated for overall American nuclear superiority. Towards the end of the 1950s the United States also deployed nuclear missiles in Europe.

The death of Stalin in 1953 was an important event, and had significant consequences for the USSR, at home and abroad. Stalin's eventual successor, Nikita Khrushchev, strove to modernize Soviet society, but helped unleash reformist tendencies in Eastern Europe. While Polish reformism was controlled, the position in Hungary threatened Soviet hegemony, and in 1956 Soviet intervention brought bloodshed to the streets of Budapest, and international condemnation on Moscow. The Soviet intervention coincided with an attack on Egypt by Britain, France, and Israel, precipitated by Colonel Nasser's seizure of the Suez Canal. The

British Government's actions provoked fierce domestic and international criticism, and the most serious rift in the 'special relationship' between Britain and the United States. The Eisenhower administration was strongly opposed to the actions of its allies, and in the face of what were effectively US economic sanctions, the British abandoned the operation (and their support for the French and Israelis). International opprobrium at the Soviet action in Budapest was lessened and deflected by what many saw as the final spasms of European imperialism.

Khrushchev's policy towards the West was a mixture of seeking coexistence while pursuing confrontation. Soviet support for movements of national liberation aroused fears in the West of a global communist challenge and further strengthened American determination to support friends and subvert enemies in the Third World. American commitments to liberal democracy and national self-determination were mediated by cold war perspectives, as well as by perceptions of American economic and political interest. The cold war saw the growth of large permanent intelligence organizations, whose roles ranged from discerning the intentions and capabilities of adversaries to covert intervention in the affairs of other states. Crises over Berlin in 1961 and Cuba in 1962 (see Box 4.2) marked the most dangerous moments of the cold war. In both, there was risk of direct military confrontation, and certainly in October 1962 the possibility of nuclear war. How close the world came to Armageddon during the Cuban missile crisis, and exactly why peace was preserved remain matters of great debate among historians and surviving officials.

The events of 1962 were followed by a more stable period of coexistence and competition. Nuclear arsenals continued to grow and both superpowers continued to support friends and subvert enemies. At the same time as America's commitment in Vietnam was deepening, Soviet–Chinese relations were deteriorating. Indeed, by 1969 China and the USSR fought a minor border war over a territorial dispute. Despite (or because of) these tensions, the foundations for what became known as détente were laid between the USSR and USA, and for what became known as rapprochement between China and the

Box 4.2	The Cuban missile crisis

In October 1962 the United States discovered that, contrary to public and private assurances, the Soviet leadership had secretly deployed nuclear missiles in Cuba. President Kennedy responded by imposing a partial blockade or 'quarantine' of the island, and US nuclear forces moved to unprecedented states of alert. The superpowers stood 'eyeball to eyeball', and most historians believe that this was the moment during the cold war when the risk of nuclear war was at its greatest. Indeed, recent evidence suggests that the risk of inadvertent nuclear war, arising from a concatenation of misperceptions, insubordinate actions, and organizational failures, may well have been greater than was realized. The diplomatic impasse was resolved six days after Kennedy announced the 'quarantine' of Cuba, when Nikita Khrushchev undertook to withdraw the missiles in return for assurances that the United States would not invade Cuba. It has also now emerged that President Kennedy provided a secret undertaking to remove equivalent NATO nuclear missiles from Europe.

United States. Détente in Europe had its origins in the *Ostpolitik* of the German Socialist Chancellor, Willy Brandt, and resulted in agreements that recognized the peculiar status of Berlin, and the sovereignty of East Germany. Soviet–American détente had its roots in mutual recognition of the need to avoid nuclear crises, and in the economic and military incentives in avoiding an unconstrained arms race. Both Washington and Moscow also looked towards Beijing when making their 'bilateral' calculations.

Table 4.2 Cold war crises

1948–9	Berlin	USSR/USA/UK
1954–5	Taiwan straits crisis	USA/PRC
1961	Berlin	USSR/USA/NATO
1962	Cuba	USSR/USA/Cuba
1973	Arab–Israeli war	Egypt/Israel/Syria/ USA/USSR
1983	Exercise *Able Archer*	USSR/USA/NATO

1969–1979: the rise and fall of détente

The period known as détente represented an attempt by both superpowers to manage their relations with each other within a framework of negotiation and agreement. In the West détente was associated with the political leadership of President Richard Nixon and his adviser Henry Kissinger, who were also instrumental in Sino-American rapprochement. This new phase in Soviet–American relations did not mark an end to political conflict, as each side sought to pursue political goals, some of which were to prove increasingly incompatible with the aspirations of the other superpower. Both sides maintained support for friendly regimes and movements, and this came when various political upheavals were taking place in the Third World (see Table 4.3). How far the superpowers were able to control their friends, and how far they were entangled by their commitments was underlined in 1973 when the Arab–Israeli war embroiled both the USA and the USSR in what became a potentially dangerous confrontation.

In Washington, Soviet support for revolutionary movements in the Third World was seen as evidence of duplicity. Some Americans claim that Moscow's support for revolutionary forces in Ethiopia in 1975 killed détente. Others cite the Soviet role in Angola in 1978. Furthermore, the perception that the USSR was using arms control agreements to gain military advantage was linked to Soviet behaviour in the Third World. Growing Soviet military superiority was reflected in growing Soviet influence, it was argued. The view from Moscow was different, reflecting different assumptions about the scope and purpose of détente. Other events were also seen to weaken American influence. The overthrow of the Shah of Iran in 1979 resulted in the loss of an important Western ally in the region, though the ensuing militant Islamic Government was as hostile to the USSR as to the USA.

December 1979 marked a point of transition in East–West affairs. NATO agreed to deploy land-based Cruise and Pershing II missiles in Europe if negotiations with the Soviets did not reduce what NATO saw as a serious imbalance. Later in the month, Soviet armed forces intervened in Afghanistan to support their revolutionary allies. The USSR was bitterly condemned in the West and in the Third World

Table 4.3 Revolutionary upheavals in the Third World, 1974–1980

Ethiopia	Overthrow of Haile Selassie	Sept. 1974
Cambodia	Khmer Rouge takes Phnom Penh	April 1975
Vietnam	North Vietnam/'Viet Cong' take Saigon	April 1975
Laos	Pathet Lao takes over state	May 1975
Guinea-Bissau	Independence from Portugal	Sept. 1974
Mozambique	Independence from Portugal	June 1975
Cape Verde	Independence from Portugal	July 1975
São Tomé	Independence from Portugal	July 1975
Angola	Independence from Portugal	Nov. 1975
Afghanistan	Military coup in Afghanistan	April 1978
Iran	Ayatollah Khomeini installed in power	Feb. 1979
Grenada	New Jewel Movement takes power	March 1979
Nicaragua	Sandinistas take Managua	July 1979
Zimbabwe	Independence from Britain	April 1980

Source: F. Halliday, *The Making of the Second Cold War* (London: Verso, 1986), 92.

for its actions, and soon became committed to a protracted and bloody struggle which many compared to the American war in Vietnam. In the United States, the impact on the Carter administration was to change the President's view of the Soviet Union. Republican and other critics had increasingly used foreign and defence policy issues to attack the Carter presidency. Perceptions of American weakness in foreign policy permeated domestic politics. And in 1980, Ronald Reagan was elected President, committed to a more confrontational approach with the Soviets on arms control, Third World conflicts, and East–West relations in general.

1979–1986: 'the second cold war'

The resulting period of tension and confrontation between the superpowers has been described as the **'second cold war'** and compared to the early period of confrontation and tension between 1946 and 1953. In Western Europe and the Soviet Union there was real fear of nuclear war. Much of this was a reaction to the rhetoric and policies of the Reagan administration. American statements on nuclear weapons (see below) and military intervention in Grenada in 1983, and against Libya in 1986, were seen as evidence of a new belligerence. Reagan's policy towards Central America, and support for the rebel Contras in Nicaragua, were sources of controversy within the United States and internationally. In 1986, the International Court of Justice found the United States guilty of violating **international law** for the CIA's covert attacks on Nicaraguan harbours.

The Reagan administration's use of military power was nonetheless limited: the rhetoric and the perception were at variance with the reality. Some operations ended in humiliating failure, notably in the Lebanon in 1983. Nevertheless, there is evidence that the Soviet leadership took very seriously the words (and deeds) of the Reagan administration and believed that the US leadership was planning a nuclear first strike. In 1983 Soviet air defences shot down a South Korean civilian airliner in Soviet airspace. The American reaction, and the imminent deployment of US nuclear missiles in Europe, created a climate of great tension in East–West relations. And in November 1983 Soviet intelligence misinterpreted a NATO training exercise (codenamed *Able Archer*) and led the Soviet leadership to believe that NATO was preparing to attack them. How close the world came to a serious nuclear confrontation in 1983 is not yet clear.

Throughout the early 1980s, the Soviets were handicapped by a succession of ageing political leaders (Brezhnev, Andropov, and Chernenko) whose ill health further inhibited Soviet responses to the American challenge and the American threat. This changed dramatically after Mikhail Gorbachev became President in 1985. Gorbachev's **'new thinking'** in foreign policy, and his domestic reforms, created a revolution, both in the USSR's foreign relations and within Soviet society. At home the policies of *glasnost* (or openness) and *perestroika* (or restructuring) unleashed nationalist and other forces which, to Gorbachev's dismay, were to destroy the Union of Soviet Socialist Republics.

Gorbachev's aim in foreign policy was to transform relations with the United States and Western Europe (on the latter, for example, see Box 4.3). His domestic reforms were also a catalyst for change in Eastern Europe, though unlike Khrushchev, Gorbachev was not prepared to react with force or coercion. When confronted with revolt in Eastern Europe, Gorbachev's foreign ministry invoked Frank Sinatra's song, 'I did it my way', to mark the end of the Brezhnev doctrine which had limited Eastern European sovereignty and political development. The Sinatra doctrine meant that Eastern Europeans were now allowed to 'do it their way'. Throughout Eastern Europe Moscow-aligned regimes gave way to democracies, in what for the most part was a peaceful as well as speedy transition (see Ch.5).

Most dramatically, Germany became united and East Germany (the German Democratic Republic) disappeared.

Gorbachev's policy toward the West used agreements on nuclear weapons as a means of building trust, and demonstrating the serious and radical nature of his purpose. However, despite similar radical agreements on conventional forces in Europe (culminating in the Paris agreement of 1990), the end of the cold war marked success in nuclear *arms control* rather than the beginning of nuclear *disarmament*. The histories of the cold war and of the bomb are very closely connected, but while the cold war is now over, nuclear weapons are still very much in existence.

Box 4.3 Mikhail Gorbachev's 1987 vision of European security

'We are firmly opposed to the division of the continent into military blocs facing each other, against the accumulation of military arsenals in Europe, against everything that is the source of the threat of war. In the spirit of the new thinking we advanced the idea of the "common European home" . . . [with] the recognition of a certain integral whole, although the states in question belong to different social systems and are members of opposing military-political blocs ranged against each other.'

(Sakwa 1998: 337–8)

Key points

- There are disagreements about when the cold war started, why, and who was responsible.

- The cold war began (or accelerated) in Europe with the failure to implement the agreements reached at Potsdam and Yalta.

- Distinct phases can be seen in East–West relations during which tension and the risk of direct confrontation grew and receded.

- Some civil and regional wars were intensified and prolonged by superpower involvement; others may have been prevented or shortened.

- The end of the cold war has not resulted in the abolition of nuclear weapons.

The bomb

Dropping the bomb in 1945

Nuclear weapons preceded and post-dated the cold war. The Western allies developed the atomic bomb in the war against Nazi Germany and imperial Japan, and intended to use the weapon in much the same way as they had used strategic bombing against German and Japanese cities. The destruction of the

Japanese cities of Hiroshima and Nagasaki was of great significance in post-war affairs, but, as Table 4.4 shows, the scale of the casualties and the extent of the devastation were not exceptional. The precise importance of Hiroshima and Nagasaki in post-war affairs remains a matter of continuing controversy. Aside from the moral issues involved in attacking civilian populations, the destruction of the two cities

Table 4.4 Second World War estimated casualties

> **Hiroshima** (6 August 1945): 70–80,000 'prompt'; 140,000 by end 1945; 200,000 by 1950
>
> **Nagasaki** (9 August 1945): 30–40,000 'prompt'; 70,000 by end 1945; 140,000 by 1950
>
> **Tokyo** (9 March 1945): 100,000+
>
> **Dresden** (13–15 February 1945): 25–135,000
>
> **Coventry** (14 November 1940): 568
>
> **Leningrad** (siege 1941–4): 1,000,000+

Sources: R. Rhodes, *The Making of the Atomic Bomb* (Harmondsworth: Penguin, 1986); Committee for the Compilation of Materials, *Damage Caused by the Atomic Bombs in Hiroshima and Nagasaki* and *Hiroshima and Nagasaki: The Physical, Medical, and Social Effects of the Atomic Bombings* (London: Hutchinson, 1981); M. Gilbert, *Churchill: A Life* (London: Heinemann, 1991).

has generated fierce debate, particularly among American historians, about why the bomb was dropped. Gar Alperovitz in his celebrated book *Atomic Diplomacy*, first published in 1965, claimed that, as President Truman knew Japan was defeated, his real motive was to coerce the Soviet Union to serve post-war American interests in Europe and Asia. Such claims generated angry and dismissive responses from other historians. Ensuing debates have benefited from more historical evidence, though this has only partially resolved the controversies. Inasmuch as a consensus now exists among historians, it is that Truman's decision reflected various considerations. Controversy remains over how far Truman dropped the bomb simply to end the war, and how far other factors, including the coercion of the Soviet Union in post-war affairs, entered his calculations.

CWS

Whether Hiroshima and Nagasaki should have been destroyed nevertheless remains a matter for debate. So too does the question of what were the effects of their destruction. Whether the use of nuclear weapons demonstrated the awesome power of such weapons to post-war decisionmakers and thereby inhibited their use, or whether by accelerating the development of the Soviet atomic bomb Hiroshima speeded up or even started the nuclear arms race are questions to consider.

Towards the global battlefield

The bomb dropped on Hiroshima was equivalent in destructive power to 12,500 tons of TNT. In 1952, the United States exploded a thermonuclear or hydrogen bomb, equivalent to 10,400,000 tons of TNT. Subsequent nuclear weapons were measured in this new megaton range, each capable of destroying the largest of cities in a single explosion. Equally significant was the development of the means to deliver them. In 1945, the American bomber that destroyed Hiroshima took some six hours to cross the Pacific and reach its target. Initially the United States did not possess bombers that had the range to reach the USSR from the USA, and used British and other bases to hold at risk Soviet targets. Both superpowers developed long-range bombers, and then ballistic missiles that could target the other superpower from their own **territory**. In 1957, the USSR tested an Intercontinental Ballistic Missile (ICBM) and later that year launched a satellite, *Sputnik*, into space using such a missile. In 1960, the United States began deploying ballistic missiles on submarines. (For details of the technological arms race see Table 4.5.)

By then the world was potentially a global battlefield in which both superpowers could strike each other's territory from their own, and in no more

Table 4.5 The nuclear technology race

Weapon	Date of testing or deployment	
	USA	USSR
Atomic bomb	1945	1949
Intercontinental bomber	1948	1955
Jet bomber	1951	1954
Hydrogen bomb	1952	1953
Intercontinental Ballistic Missile	1958	1957
Submarine Launched Ballistic Missile	1960	1964
Anti-Ballistic Missile	1974	1966
Multiple Independently Targetable Re-entry Vehicle	1970	1975

Source: R. McNamara, *Blundering into Disaster* (London: Bloomsbury, 1987), 60.

than the 20–40 minutes it took a ballistic missile to strike its target. The global dimension was increased by the emergence of other nuclear weapon states—Britain in 1952, France in 1960, and China in 1964. In the 1950s, there was growing concern at the spread or **proliferation** of nuclear weapons and in the 1960s, a nuclear Non-Proliferation Treaty (NPT) was negotiated in which those states which had nuclear weapons committed themselves to halt the arms race, while those states which did not have nuclear weapons promised not to develop them (see Ch.22). Despite the apparent success of the NPT agreement, several states are known to have developed nuclear weapons (Israel, India, Pakistan, and apartheid South Africa) and others have invested considerable effort in doing so (Iraq and North Korea). There is also disquieting evidence that India and Pakistan came close to a nuclear confrontation in 1990.

Both the Soviet Union and the United States also made some attempt to develop weapons that could shoot down incoming ballistic missiles and thereby provide defence against nuclear attack. These anti-ballistic missiles (ABMs) were technologically ineffective and both sides continued to rely on offensive nuclear weapons for their security. In 1972, an agreement was concluded which limited ABM defences to a token level. However in 1983, President Reagan cast doubt on the principles of this agreement by launching the Strategic Defense Initiative (SDI) (see below).

The growth in Soviet and American arsenals is often characterized as an arms race, though how far perception of the adversary, and how far internal political and bureaucratic pressures caused the growth of nuclear arsenals, is a matter for debate. For the United States, commitments to its NATO allies also provided pressures and opportunities to develop and deploy shorter-range ('tactical' and 'theatre') nuclear weapons. At the strategic (or long-range) level, qualitative change was as significant as quantitative change. In particular, the fear that one side would have sufficient weapons of sufficient accuracy to destroy the other side's nuclear arsenal became a mutual fear. Robert Oppenheimer, one of the scientists who created the American atomic bomb, characterized the atomic age as like two scorpions trapped in a glass jar. The scorpions have no means

of escape and no alternative but to threaten that which it would be suicidal to carry out. Yet the logic of what became known in the West as **Mutually Assured Destruction (MAD)** depended upon each side being able to destroy their adversary *after* being attacked. For much of the cold war both sides feared that the other was moving, or believed it was moving, to a position of meaningful superiority. What is clear is that ideas of MAD were of only limited relevance to the military force structures and strategies adopted by the superpowers.

The situation was further complicated by the differences in the attitude of the two superpowers. The Soviet Union was confronted, first by a situation of American monopoly, and then by enduring US superiority. This was coupled with political encirclement and growing antagonism with a nuclear-armed China. From the American side, misperception of Soviet nuclear strength in the 1950s was allied with concern about Soviet political ambitions. This was further complicated by US military and political commitments, especially to NATO, and its determination to use nuclear weapons against, and thereby to deter, Soviet aggression towards Western Europe. Even if a nuclear war could never be won, the policies and strategies of both superpowers, and of NATO, can be seen to be ambiguous on these critical issues.

Rise and fall of détente; fall and rise of arms control

How far the arms race was the result of mutual misperceptions, how far the unavoidable outcome of irreconcilable political differences, are central questions. Some influential Americans believed that the Soviets were bent on world domination, which the communist rhetoric of world revolution certainly encouraged. What is clear is that nuclear weapons provided context and pretext for their more dangerous confrontations, most notably when the Soviets deployed nuclear missiles in Cuba in 1962. It is also clear that when political confrontation gave way to Soviet–American détente, agreements on nuclear weapons became the most tangible achievement of détente. Yet, just as détente was a way of managing East–West conflict, and did not resolve the basis of disagreement, so too, arms control was a means of regulating the growth of nuclear arsenals, not eliminating them (see Table 4.6). On the other hand, critics argued, arms control served to legitimize the existence and growth of nuclear arsenals. Disarmament meant getting rid of weapons. While arms control was sometimes presented as a first step to disarmament it was more generally recognized as a means of managing nuclear weapons.

Yet, just as détente collapsed in the 1970s, the achievements of the SALT (Strategic Arms Limitation Talks) gave way to renewed conflict and debate over nuclear weapons. In the West, critics of détente and arms control argued that the Soviets were acquiring nuclear superiority. Some of these critics also urged that the United States should pursue policies and strategies based on the idea that victory in nuclear war was possible. The election of Ronald Reagan to the American presidency in 1980 was a watershed in Soviet–American relations. The period of the 'second cold war' marked a new phase in the political and nuclear relationship between East and West. One issue which Reagan inherited, and which loomed large in the breakdown of relations between East and West, was nuclear missiles in Europe. NATO's decision to deploy land-based missiles, capable of striking Soviet territory, precipitated a period of great tension in relations between NATO and the USSR, and political friction within NATO. Reagan's own incautious public remarks reinforced perceptions that he was as ill informed as he was dangerous in matters nuclear, though some of his arms policies were consistent with those of his predecessor, Jimmy Carter. On arms control, Reagan was not interested in agreements that would freeze the status quo for the sake of getting an agreement, and

Soviet and American negotiators proved unable to make progress in talks on long-range and intermediate-range weapons. One particular initiative had significant consequences for arms control and for the USA's relations with both the Soviets and its allies. The **Strategic Defense Initiative** (SDI), quickly dubbed 'Star Wars', was a research programme designed to explore the feasibility of space-based defences against ballistic missiles. The Soviets appear to have taken SDI very seriously, and claimed that President Reagan's real purpose was to regain the nuclear monopoly of the 1950s. The technological advances claimed by SDI proponents did not materialize, however, and the programme was reduced and marginalized. A second debate has now emerged concerning possible limited US national as well as theatre defence against ballistic missiles, and has focused on concerns about the proliferation of weapons of mass destruction and the ballistic missiles capable of delivering them.

The advent of Mikhail Gorbachev paved the way for agreements on nuclear and conventional forces, which helped ease the tensions that had characterized the early 1980s. In 1987, Gorbachev travelled to Washington to sign the Intermediate Nuclear Forces (INF) Treaty banning intermediate-range nuclear missiles, including Cruise and Pershing II. This agreement was heralded as a triumph for the Soviet President, but NATO leaders, including Thatcher and Reagan, argued that it was vindication of the policies pursued by NATO since 1979. The INF treaty was concluded more quickly than a new agreement on cutting strategic nuclear weapons, in part because of Soviet opposition to SDI. And it was Reagan's successor, George Bush, who concluded a Strategic Arms Reductions Treaty (START) agreement that reduced long-range nuclear weapons (though only back to

Table 4.6 The arms race: American and Soviet nuclear bombs and warheads, 1945–1990

	1945	1950	1955	1960	1965	1970	1975	1980	1985	1990
USA	2	450	4,750	6,068	5,550	4,000	8,500	10,100	11,200	9,680
USSR	0	0	20	300	600	1,800	2,800	6,000	9,900	10,999

Sources: R. McNamara, *Blundering into Disaster* (London: Bloomsbury, 1987) 154–5; International Institute for Strategic Studies, *The Military Balance 1990–1991* (Oxford: IISS, 1991). Soviet figures given here are based on Western estimates.

Table 4.7 Principal arms control and disarmament agreements

Treaty	Purpose of agreement	Signed	Parties
Geneva protocol	Chemical weapons: bans use	1925	100+
Limited Test Ban Treaty	Bans atmospheric, underwater, outer-space nuclear tests	1963	100+
Nuclear Non-Proliferation Treaty	Limits spread of nuclear weapons	1968	100+
Biological Weapons Convention	Bans production/use	1972	80+
SALT I	Limits strategic arms*	1972	USA/USSR
ABM Treaty	Limits anti-ballistic missiles	1972	USA/USSR
SALT II	Limits strategic arms*	1979	USA/USSR
Intermediate Nuclear Forces Treaty	Bans two categories of land-based missiles	1987	USA/USSR
START 1	Reduces strategic arms*	1990	USA/USSR

* Strategic arms are long-range weapons.
Source: adapted from Harvard Nuclear Study Group, 'Arms Control and Disarmament: What Can and Can't be Done', in F. Holroyd (ed.), *Thinking About Nuclear Weapons* (Milton Keynes: Open University, 1985), 96.

the level they had been in the early 1980s). By the time that a follow-on START 2 agreement was reached in 1992, the USSR had disintegrated. The collapse of the Soviet Union risked the creation of four nuclear weapons states (Russia, Kazakhstan, Belarus, and Ukraine). Nevertheless, all the new states made clear their commitment to the treaty and to the new cordial relations with the West. On the other hand, the disintegration of the Soviet Union raised fears about the spread of nuclear technologies (and nuclear technologists). Moreover, the continuing proliferation of nuclear weapons raised the prospect of regional arms races and crises, such as when India and Pakistan are believed to have come close to nuclear confrontation in 1990. The end of the cold war may have reduced some nuclear problems. It may well have increased others. It certainly did not solve the problem of nuclear weapons.

Key points

- There remains debate about the use of the bomb in 1945, and the effect that this had on the cold war.

- Nuclear weapons were an important factor in the cold war. How far the arms race has had a momentum of its own is a matter of debate.

- Agreements on limiting and controlling the growth of nuclear arsenals played an important role in Soviet–American (and East–West) relations.

- States with nuclear weapons agreed on the desirability of preventing the spread of nuclear weapons to other states.

- Various international crises occurred in which there was the risk of nuclear war. Judging how close we came to nuclear war at these times remains a matter for debate.

Conclusion

The changes that took place in world politics after 1945 were enormous. Assessing their significance raises many complex issues about the nature of international history and international relations.

The question of who won the cold war, how, and with what implications, is a matter on which fierce controversy has been generated. Several points are emphasized in this conclusion concerning the relationship between the three trends explored in the chapter (the end of empire, the cold war, and the bomb). The period of history since 1945 has witnessed the end of European empires constructed before, and in the early part of, the twentieth century, and has also witnessed the rise and fall of the cold war. The end of the cold war has also been followed by the collapse of one of the two principal protagonists in that conflict, the USSR. The relationship between the end of empire and cold war conflicts in the Third World is a close, though problematic, one. In some cases involvement of the superpowers helped bring about change. In others, direct superpower involvement resulted in escalation and prolongation of the conflict. Marxist ideology in various forms provided inspiration to many Third World liberation movements, but provocation to the United States (and others). The example of Vietnam is most obvious in these respects, but in a range of anti-colonial struggles the cold war played a major part. Precisely how the cold war influenced decolonization is best assessed on a case-by-case basis. One key issue is how far the values and objectives of revolutionary leaders and their movements were nationalist rather than Marxist. It is claimed that both Ho Chi Minh in Vietnam and Fidel Castro in Cuba were primarily nationalists who could have been won over to the West, but turned to Moscow and to communism in the face of American and Western hostility. The divisions between the Soviet Union and the People's Republic of China also demonstrate the diverging trends within the practice of Marxism. In several instances, conflict between communists became as bitter as conflict between communists and capitalists.

Similarly, the relationship between the cold war and the history of nuclear weapons is a close, though problematic one. Some historians contend that the use of atomic weapons by the United States played a decisive part in the origins of the cold war. Others would see the paranoia generated by the threat of total annihilation as central to understanding Soviet defence and foreign policy: the unprecedented threat of devastation is crucial to understanding the mutual hostility and fear of leaders in the nuclear age. It is also argued that without nuclear weapons direct Soviet–American conflict would have been much more likely, and that had nuclear weapons not acted as a deterrent then war in Europe would have been much more likely. On the other hand there are those who contend that nuclear weapons have played a relatively limited role in East–West relations, and that in political terms their importance is exaggerated.

Nuclear weapons have been a focus for political agreement, and during détente, nuclear arms agreements acted as the currency of international politics. How far, and why, nuclear weapons have helped keep the peace (if indeed they have) raises very important questions not only for assessing the cold war but for contemplating the proliferation of nuclear and other weapons of mass destruction into the twenty-first century. How close we came to nuclear war in 1961 (Berlin) or 1962 (Cuba) or 1973 (Arab–Israeli war) or 1983 (Exercise *Able Archer*) and what lessons might be learned from these events are crucial questions for historians and policymakers alike. One central issue is how far cold war perspectives and the involvement of nuclear-armed superpowers imposed stability in regions where previous instability led to war and conflict. The cold war may have led to unprecedented concentrations of military and nuclear forces in Europe, but this was a period characterized by stability and great economic prosperity, certainly in the West. How far this stability was bought at the risk of an ever-present danger of nuclear confrontation is a question historians are still exploring and debating.

Both the cold war and the age of empire are over, though across the globe their legacies, good and bad, seen and unseen, persist. The age of 'the bomb', and of other weapons of mass destruction (chemical and biological) continues. How far the clash of communist and liberal/capitalist ideologies helped facilitate and/or retard the process of **globalization** is a matter for debate. Despite the limitations of the human imagination the global consequences of nuclear war remain all too real. The accident at the Soviet nuclear reactor at Chernobyl in 1986 showed that radioactivity knows no boundaries. In the 1980s some scientists suggested that only a fraction of the world's nuclear weapons exploded over a fraction of the world's cities could bring an end to life itself in the northern hemisphere. While the threat of strategic nuclear war has receded the global problem of nuclear weapons remains a common and urgent concern as humanity enters the twenty-first century.

For further information and case studies on this subject, please visit the companion web site at www.oup.com/uk/booksites/politics.

QUESTIONS

1   Was Harry Truman to blame for the collapse of the wartime alliance after 1945 and the onset of the cold war?

2   Why did the United States become involved in wars in Asia after 1945? Illustrate your answer by reference to either the Korean or Vietnam wars.

3   Did détente succeed?

4   Should Ronald Reagan or Mikhail Gorbachev claim the greater credit for the ending of the cold war?

5   Why did France try to remain an imperial power in Indo-China and Algeria?

6   What were the consequences of the collapse of the Portuguese Empire in Africa?

7   Were the British successful at decolonization after 1945?

8   Compare and contrast the end of empire in Africa with that in Asia after 1945.

9   Why were atomic bombs dropped on Hiroshima and Nagasaki?

10   Did nuclear weapons help prevent war in Europe after 1945?

11   How close did we come to nuclear war during either the Berlin crisis (1961) or the Cuban missile crisis (1962)?

12   What role did nuclear weapons play in Soviet–American relations during the 1980s?

GUIDE TO FURTHER READING

General

Young, J., and Kent, J. (2003), *International Relations since 1945* (Oxford: Oxford University Press). Provides a comprehensive survey of the impact of the cold war on world politics since 1945, and includes analysis of such regional issues as the Middle East wars, the development of European integration, and the demise of the European empires in Africa and Asia.

Bell, P. M. H. (2001), *The World since 1945: An International History* (London: Arnold). Provides a comprehensive account of principal developments in international politics since 1945, covering superpower conflict in the cold war, regional issues, and the post-cold war order.

The cold war

Gaddis, J. (1997), *We Now Know: Rethinking Cold War History* (Oxford: Clarendon Press). Provides an overview, and reassessment, of relations between the Soviet Union and the United States, and explores how understanding of the cold war has changed (or not changed) with disclosures from Soviet and Chinese archival sources.

Halliday, F. (1986), *The Making of the Second Cold War* (London: Verso, 2nd edn). Explores the phase in the cold war of Soviet–American antagonism, 1979–85, and places this within a broader thematic and critical analysis of the cold war.

The bomb

Lebow, R. N., and Stein, J. G. (1994), *We All Lost the Cold War* (Princeton: Princeton University Press). Provides a revisionist interpretation of the cold war, which reassesses the role and risks of nuclear deterrence by detailed examination of two case studies: the Cuban missile crisis and the Arab–Israeli war of 1973.

Newhouse, J. (1989), *The Nuclear Age* (London: Michael Joseph). Provides a history of nuclear weapons which examines the technological and political dimensions of the arms race, from the use of the bomb at Hiroshima to the debates and issues of the 1980s.

Bird, K., and Lifschultz, L. (eds) (1998), *Hiroshima's Shadow* (Stony Creek, Conn.: The Pamphleteer's Press). A wide-ranging collection of articles on the destruction of Hiroshima and Nagasaki, which provide comprehensive coverage of the military, political, ethical, and historiographical issues and debates about the use of atomic weapons in 1945.

Decolonization

Chamberlain, M. E. (1999), *Decolonization: the Fall of the European Empires* (Oxford: Blackwell). Provides an analysis of the end of British, French, and smaller European empires on a region-by-region basis.

Betts, R. (1998), *Decolonization* (London: Routledge). Provides an introductory theoretical overview that examines the forces that drove decolonization, and explores interpretations of post-colonial legacies.

WEB LINKS

www.pro.gov.uk/ The UK National Archives.

www.archives.gov/ United States National Archives and Record Administration.

www.gwu.edu/~nsarchiv/ The National Security Archive, The George Washington University, USA.

http://cwihp.si.edu Woodrow Wilson International Center for Scholars: Cold War International History Project. Washington, USA.

CHAPTER 5

The end of the cold war

RICHARD CROCKATT

READER'S GUIDE

The end of the cold war represented a turning point in the structures of international politics, in the roles and functions of nation-states, and in international organizations The chief cause of the end of the cold war was the collapse of communism in the Soviet Union and Eastern Europe. This had deep internal roots in the history of Soviet bloc societies but a full explanation of the end of the cold war must include examination of external pressures, particularly the policies of the United States, and growing relative economic disadvantage experienced by the Soviet bloc over the post-war period. Close attention is given in this chapter to the policies and personality of Mikhail Gorbachev but due emphasis is also given to historical and systemic factors in the international environment. Opinions on the implications of the end of the cold war have been varied and often conflicting, but in the new millennium it was evident that globalization and above all terrorism had replaced the characteristic cold war concerns with superpower bipolarity, the nuclear arms race, and ideology.

Introduction

Historical events do not come with labels upon them, telling us precisely how important they are. Only the passage of time can do that, and it may take years. Communist Chinese Prime Minister Zho Enlai is reported to have said, in reply to a question about the significance of the French Revolution, that 'it's too soon to tell'. Nevertheless, some events are sufficiently momentous in their immediate effects for us to be able to say with confidence that something important has happened, even if full explanations are as yet unattainable.

The events of 1989–91, from the collapse of the Iron Curtain to the dismantling of the Soviet Union in December 1991, represent a turning point in three respects. **First**, they marked the end of the broadly bipolar structure, based on US–Soviet rivalry, which the international system had assumed since the late 1940s.

A **second** set of important changes took place at the level of the nation-state. Former communist states experienced serious problems of transition ranging from economic collapse, which affected them all, to (in the case of the Soviet Union, Czechoslovakia, and most explosively Yugoslavia) the disintegration of the state itself. Even those states which maintained communist systems, such as China, North Korea, and Cuba, faced enormous challenges, since they had to accommodate themselves to positions of increased marginality. Yet those states not in the throes of post-communist transition were also forced to redefine their national interests and roles in the light of the radical change in the international balance of power. This applied as much to large states such as the United States, whose policies had been premised on the Soviet threat, as to small states in the Third World which had been to greater or lesser degree 'client' states of the superpowers. In short, the end of the cold war enforced redefinition of national interests on all states and in some cases a reshaping of the states themselves.

The **third** important indicator of change in the end of the cold war lay in new or modified roles for international organizations. Most obviously the ending of the virtually automatic split in the United Nations (UN) Security Council along cold war lines released the potential for the UN to work as a genuinely collective body. The novel possibility of consensus on major issues in the Security Council did not ensure that the UN would act decisively or with authority—it was still a creature of the states which composed it and they continued to guard their national sovereignties—but it did remove one obstacle to collective decisionmaking and one which had crippled the UN during the cold war (see Ch.18).

The end of the cold war also had an impact on various multilateral treaty organizations. The Warsaw Pact (or Warsaw Treaty Organization) was disbanded, while the North Atlantic Treaty Organization (NATO) struggled to reconceive itself in a context in which European security as a whole was being redefined. Questions too were raised about possible roles for other existing European security organizations such as the Western European Union (WEU) and the Conference on Security and Co-operation in Europe (CSCE). The European Union (EU) debated expansion of its membership to include nations from Eastern Europe. However tentative these gestures, however unrealized the ambition to create a new European and a new international order, the end of the cold war forced such questions on to the agenda (see Ch.26).

In sum, the end of the cold war saw radical change at the system level, at the level of the nation-state, and in international organizations.

Before examining the causes and consequences of these transformations, it is important to establish what is meant by the term 'cold war'. It has been used in two distinct senses: first, in a narrow sense to refer to the years between the Truman doctrine (1947) and the Khrushchev thaw of the mid-1950s, during which virtually unrelieved antagonism existed between the superpowers. To the extent that the open antagonisms of these years were reproduced later in, for example, the Kennedy years and the first Reagan administration, then the term cold war is also applied to these instances. The term refers to a certain kind of **behaviour**, characterized by open ideological confrontation. Such periods of cold war alternated with periods of *détente* (1953–60, 1969–75, 1985–9), during which negotiations and tension reduction were firmly on the agenda.

The second meaning of 'cold war', and the one which is adopted here, has to do with the **structure** rather than the behaviour of East–West relations. To the extent that key elements of that structure remained continuous throughout the post-war period, then cold war refers to the whole period from the late 1940s to the late 1980s. Viewed from this perspective, détente was part of the cold war rather than a departure from it, in that while there was behavioural change in periods of détente, the fundamental structure of US–Soviet relations remained constant. When we talk of the end of the cold war we therefore mean the end of that structural condition which was defined by political and military rivalry between the United States and the Soviet Union, ideological antagonism between **capitalism** and communism, the division of Europe, and the extension of conflict at the centre to the periphery of the international system.

The most obvious cause of the end of the cold war was the collapse of communism but we need to look beyond the communist system to find the sources of its failure. In what follows we shall analyse the end of the cold war with reference to three sets of factors: (1) internal **developments** in the Soviet bloc; (2) external forces in the form of Western policies

towards the Soviet bloc; and (3) the changing relative position of the Soviet bloc with respect to the West. This will be followed by a discussion of the immediate global consequences of the end of the cold war. The chapter will end with some inevitably tentative ideas about possible futures.

> ### Key points
>
> - The end of the cold war was a major historical turning point as measured by changes in the international system, the nation-state, and international organizations.
>
> - The term 'cold war' can refer both to the behavioural characteristics of US–Soviet relations, which fluctuated over the period 1945–89, or to the basic structure of their relations, which remained constant.
>
> - The key structural elements of the cold war are political and military (above all, nuclear) rivalry between the United States and the Soviet Union, ideological conflict between capitalism and communism, the division of Europe, and the extension of superpower conflict to the Third World.
>
> - The explanation for the end of the cold war is to be found in the interaction between the Soviet bloc failure and the external environment.

Internal factors: the collapse of communism in the Soviet Union

Structural problems in the Soviet system

Among the most striking features of communism's collapse was its suddenness, a surprise as much to most Western experts on the Soviet Union and Eastern Europe as to political leaders and the public. One Western Soviet expert, whose views are fairly representative, wrote in a study published in 1986, that 'it is unlikely that the [Soviet] state is now, or will be in the late 1980s, in danger of social or political disintegration. Thus we must study the factors which made the regime stable in the post-Stalin era and are still at

work at the present' (Bialer 1986: 19). It is true that revolutionary change by its nature contains a large element of the incalculable. Institutional inertia, social customs, and psychological habit ensure that systems can maintain their outer shapes long after they have begun to decay internally. Perhaps the most useful general observation on the causes of revolution remains that of the French political philosopher Alexis de Tocqueville: that 'the most dangerous moment for a bad government is generally that in which it sets about reform' (Tocqueville 1933: 186). This model, generalized as it is, is a useful starting point for an understanding of Mikhail Gorbachev's revolutionary period in power.

Gorbachev's accession to power in March 1985 was itself an event of considerable significance. He was the first General Secretary of the Soviet Communist Party to have reached maturity after the Second World War. He had little adult experience of the Stalinist period and was less beholden to the Stalinist legacy than his predecessors. He had been appointed to the ruling Politburo as recently as 1978 towards the end of the **era of stagnation** under Brezhnev. In projecting a new dynamism as a representative of the rising class of educated professionals, he presented a striking contrast to the ageing and intellectually stultified leaders of the Brezhnev period. His path to leadership was not immediate on Brezhnev's death. Following the latter's death in 1982 an interregnum ensued during which first Yuri Andropov and then Konstantin Chernenko were appointed and died in each case within little more than a year of taking office. The passing of the old guard, combined with Gorbachev's power base among advocates of change, which enabled him to make key changes in personnel, conveyed the sense that Gorbachev was inaugurating a new era in Soviet history.

Crucially, however, it was evidently not his intention to dismantle the Soviet Union. His widely read political credo, **Perestroika** (1988), was firmly anti-Stalinist but not anti-socialist. 'Through *perestroika* and *glasnost*,' he wrote, 'the ideals of socialism will gain fresh impetus'; and they would do so through a return to the ideals of Lenin, who 'lives on in the minds and hearts of millions of people' (Gorbachev 1988: 131, 25). Indeed the sense of renewal which Gorbachev projected did not seem to presage the end of the cold war. On the contrary, it was felt by many on the Right in the United States that a reinvigorated Soviet Union would present a more severe challenge to the West than the old sclerotic leadership.

How, then, are we to explain the transformation of the next few years? We can usefully distinguish between long-term and short-term causes. The chief long-term problem was economic, though arguably it had political roots, in that economic policies and practices were dictated by political ideology. Structural weaknesses were built into the system of the command economy which relied on inflexible

Box 5.1	Change in the Soviet Union
March 1985	On the death of Konstantin Chernenko, Mikhail Gorbachev becomes General Secretary of the Soviet Communist Party.
1987	Publication of Gorbachev's book *Perestroika*.
April 1988	The Soviet Union undertakes to withdraw troops from Afghanistan by February 1989; in October Gorbachev becomes President of the USSR, replacing Andrei Gromyko.
March 1989	Elections held for the Congress of People's Deputies.
March 1990	Congress of People's Deputies abolishes the leading role of the Communist Party; Lithuania declares independence from the USSR.
Aug. 1991	Coup against Gorbachev.
Dec. 1991	USSR ceases to exist and CIS (Commonwealth of Independent States) comes into being.

central planning, rewarded gross output of goods rather than productivity, and offered disincentives to innovation in management and production techniques. In place of a market relation between consumer demand and supply, from the late 1920s the centre dictated what kinds of goods should be produced and at what prices, according pre-eminence to heavy industrial production with a view to forced-marching the Soviet economy into the twentieth century. Arguably, this approach succeeded up to a point; the Soviet Union's ability to withstand Germany's onslaught in 1941 and ultimately to defeat the Third Reich owed a good deal to the brutal pace at which Stalin pushed the Soviet economy and the Soviet people in the 1930s. Such success came at enormous human cost and at the cost of entrenching the primacy of heavy industry in Soviet economic thinking far beyond the point of utility. That point was reached somewhere in the 1970s when the computer and automation revolution overtook the West but virtually bypassed the Soviet Union except in the military sector. Even there the Soviet Union found it hard to keep pace with the West (Dibb 1988: 266). Furthermore, agriculture was a notoriously weak sector of the Soviet economy. In agriculture, as in industry, central planning stifled productivity and promoted inflexible practices.

These problems were **systemic** and of long-standing. If so, why was the Soviet Union able to survive so long and why did these problems become critical in the 1980s? The answers to both questions have political as well as economic components. **Survival** was possible economically because, as mentioned above, the Soviet economy performed well in certain fields such as the production of heavy industrial goods and military equipment. It also had large reserves of oil which could be sold for hard currency. Politically, the legacy of discipline and repression supplied by the Communist Party served to stifle dissent and more positively to promote an ethos of collective sacrifice such as is undertaken by governments in wartime. Indeed, the Soviet system could be described as essentially a war economy. As for the question of why conditions became critical in the 1980s, economically, as we have seen, the failure to modernize in line with the West was of paramount importance. Furthermore, a serious decline in harvests in the late 1970s and a slowdown in production in some key industries suggested a general climate of economic stagnation. Commentary also began to appear in the West during the early 1980s on a decline in general health in the Soviet Union, with rising death rates and infant mortality rates (Hobsbawm 1994: 472).

The effects of Gorbachev's reforms: *glasnost* and political restructuring

However, even these problems might not have been critical, given the capacity of the Soviet system to sustain itself despite handicaps. It took specific initiatives by Gorbachev to turn these systemic problems into a systemic crisis. The first of these initiatives was the decision to permit dissemination of knowledge about the realities of Soviet life (*glasnost* or 'openness'), the second and third were political and economic restructuring (*perestroika*). Elements of these programmes had been present in previous reform efforts in the Soviet Union, for example during the Khrushchev period. If there was one element which differentiated Gorbachev's approach from that of his predecessors it was his conviction that consent rather than coercion should, as far as possible, guide implementation of these changes.

Glasnost was in one sense the old communist tradition of self-criticism writ large. The difference was that *glasnost* was less purely ritualistic, less hedged around with restrictions, and more open-ended than the usual forms of self-criticism which took place in the pages of *Pravda* and similar publications. Designed to purify and cleanse rather than destroy, to serve as a means of gaining public support for Gorbachev's reforms rather than as a vehicle for attacks on the system itself, *glasnost* quickly exceeded the bounds set for it. Once controls on the press, radio, television, and the film industry were loosened, control of public opinion began to slip from Gorbachev's grasp. (Indeed only now could one begin to speak of public opinion in the Soviet Union.) Freedom of expression gave a voice to those who opposed Gorbachev as well as to those who wanted to go farther and faster than he did. While *glasnost* did not of itself create opposition parties, the logic of *glasnost* was ultimately to undermine the fundamental principle of the Party's leading role. Although the Party's privileged position, guaranteed by Article 6 of the Soviet Constitution, was not abolished until 1990, a sequence of reforms, culminating in major changes proposed at the 19th Party Congress in June 1988, effected a fundamental shift in the balance of political forces with the Soviet state. Perhaps it would be truer to say that in these reforms Gorbachev was acknowledging the existence of a newly emerging civil society distinct from the interest of the Communist Party and the government.

Gorbachev's major proposal was for a new legislature, only one-third of whose delegates would be reserved for the Communist Party and its affiliated organizations. The other delegates to the Congress of People's Deputies, as the new body was known, would be directly elected on the basis of popular choice. At a stroke, following the elections of 1989, the political system was transformed by the entry into public life of a mass of new participants, a large proportion of whom were not beholden to the Communist Party. Indeed huge numbers of Communist candidates were defeated. The first meeting of the Congress in May 1989 has been described as 'the most momentous event in the Soviet Union

---

Box 5.2   Internal causes of the collapse of Soviet communism

Long-term causes

- structural weaknesses in the economy, including:
- inflexible central planning system
- inability to modernize
- inefficiency and absence of incentives in agricultural production

Short-term causes

- economic stagnation in the 1970s and 1980s
- poor harvests in the late 1970s and early 1980s
- Gorbachev's political and economic reforms

Box 5.3   Essentials of *glasnost* and *perestroika*

Essentials of *glasnost* (openness)

- promotion of principle of freedom to criticize
- loosening of controls on media and publishing
- freedom of worship

Essentials of *perestroika* (restructuring)

- new legislature, two-thirds of which was to be elected on the basis of popular choice (i.e. allowing non-communists to be elected)
- creation of an executive presidency
- ending of the 'leading role' of the Communist Party
- Enterprise Law, allowing state enterprises to sell part of their product on the open market
- Joint Ventures Law, allowing foreign companies to own Soviet enterprises

---

since the 1917 Revolution'. There took place 'a whirlwind of free debate that scattered every known communist taboo' (Roxburgh 1991: 135).

The other major element of political restructuring was the creation of an executive presidency, a post for which Gorbachev insisted he be allowed to stand unopposed. His aim was to maintain a grip on the direction of change, but it was inevitable that his critics, and even some of his supporters, should note the irony of a leader who preached democracy but claimed the right to stand above it himself. Arguably, however, Gorbachev's pursuit of reform from the top down, self-serving though it was, was both very much in the Russian/Soviet tradition and understandable in a country which was subject to growing splits. The erosion of the integrative force of the Communist Party transformed the dynamics of the political **institutions** at the centre but also threatened the structure of the Soviet Union itself.

The collapse of the Soviet Empire

A multi-ethnic, multilingual entity, composed of 15 'autonomous' republics and numerous sub-units within them, the Soviet Union was in all but name an **empire**, held together by powerful central institutions, pressure for ideological conformity, and the threat of force. The Communist Party played a key role in each of these areas and the erosion of the

Party's power released aspirations for freedom which had been suppressed but not destroyed by seventy years of Soviet rule. Demands for independence came in particular from the Baltic republics, Estonia, Latvia, and Lithuania, and from Georgia, but the power of example supplied by these movements affected virtually all the Soviet republics. A more tangled and bloody conflict arose in Azerbaijan, resulting from the desire of Armenians in Ngorny Karabakh (an Armenian region administered by Azerbaijan) for incorporation into the Soviet Republic of Armenia.

For the purposes of understanding the collapse of Soviet rule **two** points are important about these events:

1. The 'nationalities question' was evidently a blind spot of Mikhail Gorbachev's. He was noticeably unsympathetic to their demands and, though keen to maintain his credibility as a liberal by claiming that the more violent attempts to suppress nationalism in the republics had been undertaken without his orders, he insisted that Moscow could not countenance secession.

2. However, when faced with the reality of secessionist actions (above all in the Baltic republics),

he was unwilling in practice to use the full force of Soviet military power to suppress them. The result was that Gorbachev succeeded in alienating both Liberals, who argued that Russia should not stand in the way of independence movements, and conservatives, who saw in Gorbachev's concessions to nationalism a betrayal of the integrity of the Soviet Union.

During 1990 and 1991 Gorbachev oscillated between trying to satisfy conservatives and Liberals. To the former he promised suppression of nationalism by force. Swinging to the latter in the early months of 1991, he announced a proposal for a new 'Union treaty' which would devolve power substantially to the Soviet republics. It was this move which provoked conservatives to mount the coup of August 1991, during which Gorbachev was held for several days in the Crimea, while Boris Yeltsin defied the coup plotters in Moscow and thus laid the basis for his subsequent career as President of Russia. The coup's failure did not, contrary to Gorbachev's hopes and expectations, restore his position and status in the eyes of the Soviet people, not least because it was felt that Gorbachev's indulgence of the Right had helped to make the coup attempt possible. Furthermore, Gorbachev seemed unaware of how far public opinion had moved under the stimulus of the movement he had set in motion. In a press conference on his return to Moscow after the coup, he continued to defend the Communist Party. He seemed clearly yesterday's man. Within a few months the logic of *perestroika* and nationalism was followed through with the dismantling of the Soviet Union and its replacement by a loose Confederation of Independent States (CIS).

Economic restructuring

Economic restructuring in a sense cannot be separated from politics since, as was suggested above, under the Soviet system economics, like all areas of social life, was subject to a political and ideologically derived rationale. Nevertheless, economic initiatives were important in their own right under Gorbachev, in that their goal was precisely to effect a separation of the economic from the political, or at least to go some way in that direction. Real changes began in 1987 with the legalization (within clearly specified limits) of private farming and business cooperatives. A year later the Enterprise Law granted limited freedom to managers of state enterprises to sell a proportion of their products on the open market rather than, as had been the practice, having to sell all of it to the government (Goldman 1992: 111–17).

In all these measures there was a partial move towards a free market or, more precisely, an attempt to straddle the gap between the stifling command economy and an incentive-led market system. In the sphere of foreign economic policy, a new law on Joint Ventures allowed foreign companies ownership of enterprises in the Soviet Union (initially 49 per cent and then, following amendment in 1990, 100 per cent). This was a huge innovation for an economy which had generally sought to insulate itself from capitalism. Such trade as had taken place with the West had been tightly controlled by the Ministry of Foreign Trade. Now individual companies could make their own arrangements (Hough 1988: 66–72).

The effect of these economic changes was catastrophic. The reforms managed to cut the ground from under the old system without putting in its place viable new economic mechanisms. State planning was in abeyance but there was no fully operating market mechanism in its place; price levels were inconsistent, some reflecting the input of government subsidies and some reflecting what consumers would pay. Inflation, shortages, and declining production were the harvest of five years of *perestroika* and *glasnost*. To these could be added rising crime rates, a sense of social disarray, and a general feeling of uncertainty about the future. By the time Gorbachev left office in 1991 much of the exhilaration which had attended the liberation from communist oppression had been expended. Destructuring perhaps inevitably proved easier than restructuring. That this was to remain a continuing problem is evident in the efforts of Gorbachev's successor, Boris Yeltsin, to make the transition to a market economy during 1992–3 by means of 'shock therapy', the result of which was rampant inflation (Phillips 2000: 123–8).

Key points

- The suddenness of the collapse of communism defied the predictions of experts.

- Gorbachev's accession to power represented the advent of a new generation in the Soviet leadership, though Gorbachev gave little indication early on that he would break the mould of Soviet politics.

- The Soviet Union suffered from systemic economic problems which were compounded in the 1980s by poor harvests and a failure to meet the challenge of the computer revolution.

- *Glasnost* began with relaxation of censorship which Gorbachev hoped to be able to control, but the process soon eluded his grasp as something approaching a genuine public opinion emerged.

- A combination of *glasnost* and political restructuring undermined the role of the Communist Party and ultimately the Soviet Union itself which by the end of 1991 had dissolved into separate republics.

- Economic restructuring had the effect of destroying the rationale of the old system without putting viable new mechanisms in its place.

The collapse of communism in Eastern Europe

The collapse of communism in Eastern Europe, marked most graphically by the destruction of the Berlin Wall in November 1989, was intimately related to events in the Soviet Union but also had roots of its own. The nations of Eastern Europe had experienced only forty years of communist rule as opposed to the seventy of the Soviet Union and in all cases except Yugoslavia had had communism imposed on them rather than choosing it themselves. The suddenness of communist collapse in Eastern Europe, and the relative ease with which citizens shed the habits of forty years, suggests that those habits were to a considerable extent a matter of form. One important force which had held them in place since the late 1940s was the threat of Soviet intervention to reimpose orthodoxy should Eastern Europeans stray from the path set down for them. **Two** things therefore need explaining:

1. The sources of opposition in Eastern Europe to communist rule.

2. The Soviet Union's decision not to intervene to check the uprisings which took place in the summer and autumn of 1989.

The legacy of protest in Eastern Europe

After Stalin's draconian imposition of Soviet rule between 1947 and 1953 Khrushchev had acknowledged the principle of separate paths to socialism though within strict limits. In practice this meant that where socialism and the integrity of the bloc itself seemed at risk, as in the popular uprisings in Hungary in 1956 and Czechoslovakia in 1968, Moscow would act uncompromisingly. The crushing of the Czechoslovak revolt in August 1968 was justified on the principle of **'limited sovereignty'** for Eastern bloc nations (also known as the Brezhnev doctrine). Where, as in Poland in 1956 and 1980–1, indigenous leaders could be found to enforce Moscow's will, direct intervention could be avoided. Where, however, as in Romania and Albania, communism developed distinctively national forms but within the framework of rigid dictatorships, Moscow was prepared to tolerate, or at least grudgingly accept, a greater or lesser degree of detachment from Moscow. In the case of Albania, a small nation with no border with the Soviet Union, this went as far as alignment with China in the growing split between the Soviet Union and China. Romania under Ceauşescu maintained a somewhat ambiguous relationship with Moscow and the Warsaw Pact, not unlike

France's with NATO: political and military independence within the framework of broad bloc alignment. In short, the Eastern bloc was more diverse and potentially more fragile than the word 'bloc' would suggest.

In accounting for the events of 1989 it would be hard to overestimate the importance of the rise of Solidarity in Poland in 1980. Poland had always been critical to Moscow both because of its strategic position on the Soviet border and because of the legacy of hatred between the Poles and the Russians. Formed in the shipyards of Gdansk as a union of workers, Solidarity quickly assumed the status of a quasi-political body independent of the Communist Party, its membership comprising one-third of the Polish people. It called for a referendum on

Box 5.4	Revolutions in Eastern Europe
1988	
May	Janos Kadar replaced as General Secretary of the Czechoslovak Communist Party.
1989	
Jan.	Hungarian Parliament permits independent parties.
April	Ban on Solidarity in Poland repealed.
June	Elections in Poland won overwhelmingly by Solidarity candidates.
July	Solidarity invited by General Jaruselski to form coalition government.
Sept.	Hungary allows East German refugees to cross into Austria.
Oct.	Hungary adopts new constitution which guarantees multiparty democracy. East German leader Erich Honecker resigns and is replaced by Egon Krenz.
Nov.	3rd: Czechoslovakia opens border for Easterners seeking to go to the West. 10th: Berlin Wall dismantled; General Secretary of the Bulgarian Community Party, Zhivkov, resigns. 24th: Czechoslovak leadership resigns.
Dec.	6th: East German Government resigns. 22nd: Ceauşescu overthrown in Romania and executed (on the 25th).

Polish membership of the WTO and on the principle of one-party rule. With alarm bells ringing furiously in Moscow, Soviet military intervention was forestalled only by the insertion of a new Polish leader, General Jaruselski, who was willing to do Moscow's bidding by declaring martial law and banning Solidarity. However, the difference from earlier instances of suppression of opposition was that Solidarity continued a thriving underground existence during the 1980s, while the Catholic Church carried on public opposition along lines laid down by Solidarity. Dissidence thus achieved momentum and extended beyond small groups of intellectuals.

Beyond Poland, though events were less dramatic, dissidence also had a history and gained some new stimulus from the development of organizations designed to monitor compliance of Eastern bloc governments with the human rights provisions of the Helsinki Accords, agreed at the Conference on Security and Co-operation in Europe (1975). Particularly important was **Charter 77** in Czechoslovakia. A similar group existed in Moscow itself. Though these organizations were hounded by the authorities, their members imprisoned and in some cases deported, they attracted enormous attention in the West and exerted some leverage over Soviet bloc governments. They were after all simply demanding that their governments make good the promises they had made on human rights in signing the Helsinki Accords. In this way the détente agreements proved to have important subterranean effects in the Soviet bloc.

Flowing directly from this point, and of crucial significance in accounting for the timing of the collapse of communism in Eastern Europe, was the demonstration effect of *glasnost* and *perestroika* in the Soviet Union. After 1985, above all in Poland and Hungary, while dissidents demanded the same— indeed more—from their governments as Gorbachev was giving to the Soviet people, the Eastern European leaderships were bereft of the instrument on which they had always been able to rely in the past—the threat of Soviet intervention. By the middle of 1988 the opposition in Hungary had forced the removal of the Communist Party leader, Janos Kadar. In January 1989 General Jaruselski was forced to repeal the ban on Solidarity and hold elections. In the elections, which were won decisively by Solidarity, Jaruselski found himself being urged by Gorbachev to accede to a Solidarity-led government (Gati 1990: 167; Dawisha 1990: 155).

Gorbachev and the end of the Brezhnev doctrine

Why did Gorbachev abandon the **Brezhnev doctrine**? Doubtless there were many reasons, but the chief one was probably the recognition that suppression of change in Eastern Europe would have been totally inconsistent with his domestic reforms in the Soviet Union. His credibility at home, which was fragile enough once the economy began to fail, required that he endorse similar policies in the Soviet Union's 'internal empire', though it is doubtful that he foresaw the radically destabilizing effect which such changes would have on the governments of Eastern Europe. If reform in the Soviet Union was led from the top, at least initially, in Eastern Europe it had a popular base which immediately threatened the communist leaderships and created a revolutionary situation.

A further reason for Gorbachev's reluctance to enforce the Brezhnev doctrine was that he had made much in his speeches and writings of his vision of a common European home which would bring to an end the division of Europe. Again one wonders whether he foresaw that this would entail the end of communism; it is more likely that he envisaged a reformed and reinvigorated communist system pursuing moderate policies of genuinely peaceful coexistence with the West, expanded trade, and greatly increased contacts across the board. In any event, the logic of his non-interventionist position was to preclude direct Soviet control over the processes of change in Eastern Europe.

There were foreign policy considerations too in the policy of **laissez-faire** towards Eastern Europe. Retrenchment, in the form of withdrawal from the costly, increasingly unpopular, and futile intervention in Afghanistan (1979), was the order of the day rather than new ventures. Revision of military policy

in line with **new thinking** in foreign policy generally (treated below in greater detail) ruled out the kind of aggressive and interventionist policies which had characterized the later Brezhnev years. Finally, Gorbachev could hardly expect to maintain good relations with the West, and achieve arms agreements and improved trade terms if he was seen to be engaging in the suppression of freedom in Eastern Europe.

It was in these circumstances that governmental authority decayed in Poland and Hungary during the early months of 1989 and finally collapsed in all of Eastern Europe by the end of the year. Collapse was initiated by the removal of the security fence between Austria and Hungary, allowing thousands of East Germans to pass over the border and through to West Germany during September. Suddenly, with Hungary's connivance in this flight from East to West, the illusion of communism, which had been sustained by the Iron Curtain, evaporated. Efforts to check the process of collapse in East Germany, then Czechoslovakia and Bulgaria, by bringing in new leaders proved futile. Changes of personnel only delayed the inevitable briefly. The Berlin Wall was breached by demonstrators in November, opening up the possibility, which had been unthinkable for close to a generation, of German unification. In Czechoslovakia, in the face of massive popular protest, the government fell in November and Václav Havel, playwright and dissident, was elected President. Only in Romania did violence take place, as President Ceauşescu's security police undertook a savage and short-lived attempt to defend his rule and destroy the popular opposition. By the end of December Ceauşescu and his wife had been captured and executed. Only in Albania did communism linger on, but there too during 1990 the old leadership fell to the inexorable logic of events.

The manner of communist collapse in Eastern Europe suggested that their systems were both rigid and brittle and that they had relied on the ultimate threat of Soviet force to maintain their shapes. With that threat removed, the stimulus to change which had always been present was able to express itself.

Key points

- The end of communism in Eastern Europe was sudden but protest against communist rule was nothing new.

- The Soviet Union had always been forced to acknowledge the existence of national differences and desires for autonomy among Eastern European nations and had tried to maintain a balance between maintaining the integrity of the Soviet bloc and allowing some diversity.

- The Polish union Solidarity illustrated the deep currents of dissent, whose momentum was maintained even after the banning of the organization in 1981.

- A catalyst for the revolutionary process was Gorbachev's abandonment of the Brezhnev doctrine of limited sovereignty for Eastern Europe.

- Failure of the attempts by Eastern European leaders to stem the tide of revolution in 1989 by installing new personnel illustrated the degree to which the crisis of communism was systemic.

External factors: relations with the United States

Debate about US policy and the end of the cold war

Debate about who or what was responsible for ending the cold war began as soon as it had happened and quickly generated a large literature (see Hogan 1992). It became an issue in the US presidential election of 1992 (Kennan 1992; Pipes 1992). The Republican Party's claim, stripped to essentials, was that President Reagan's tough stance towards the Soviet Union, especially his refusal to compromise on the development of the Strategic Defense Initiative (SDI), had been decisive in forcing the Soviet Union to the negotiating table and subsequently bringing about the fall of communism itself. The United States had proved that it was prepared to outspend the Soviet Union, particularly in nuclear arms, thereby forcing the Soviet Union either to match the West and bankrupt itself or come to terms and negotiate real reductions in nuclear arms. Gorbachev chose the latter course, signalled by his signing of the Intermediate Nuclear Forces (INF) Treaty in December 1987, by his unilateral reduction in conventional forces announced at the UN in 1988, and by progress towards the Strategic Arms Reduction Treaty (START) 1, signed in 1991. Without these agreements, Gorbachev could not hope to fund his domestic renewal plans. Ultimately, it was argued, Reagan's policies, which built on the legacy of Truman's **containment**, brought Gorbachev and the Soviet Union to their knees.

There were **two** responses to this argument:

The **first** was to say, as did Raymond Garthoff, author of the most substantial analysis of the end of the cold war, *The Great Transition*, that the West did not win the cold war through geopolitical

Box 5.5	US–Soviet summitry, 1985–1991
Nov. 1985	Geneva Summit (Gorbachev and Reagan)
Oct. 1986	Reykjavik Summit (Gorbachev and Reagan)
Dec. 1987	Washington Summit (Gorbachev and Reagan) at which INF (Intermediate Nuclear Forces) Treaty is signed
May–June 1988	Moscow Summit (Gorbachev and Reagan)
Dec. 1989	Malta Summit (Gorbachev and Bush)
May 1990	Washington Summit (Gorbachev and Bush)
July 1991	START (Strategic Arms Reduction Treaty) signed in Moscow (Gorbachev and Bush)

containment and military deterrence. Still less was the cold war won by the Reagan military build-up. Instead '"victory" came when a new generation of Soviet leaders realized how badly their system at home and their policies abroad had failed. What containment did do was to successfully preclude any temptation by Moscow to advance Soviet hegemony by military means' (Garthoff 1994: 753).

The **second** response to the Western triumphalist argument is the claim that Reagan's policies not only did not end the cold war but actually delayed its end. 'The Carter–Reagan build-up did not defeat the Soviet Union,' wrote Richard Ned Lebow and Janet Gross Stein, 'on the contrary it prolonged the Cold War. Gorbachev's determination to reform an economy crippled in part by defense spending urged by special interests, but far more by structural rigidities, fuelled his persistent search for an accommodation with the West. That persistence, not SDI, ended the Cold War' (Lebow and Stein 1994: 37).

These two responses have in common a conviction that internal factors were primarily responsible for the end of the cold war. Neither discounts external pressures but they interpret them quite differently.

Was Reaganism of no account in the collapse of communism, as Garthoff claims, or was it an active hindrance, as Lebow and Stein argue? We can evaluate the significance of external pressures by looking at the record of diplomacy between 1985 and 1991.

Soviet–American diplomacy, 1985–1991

It must be emphasized at the outset that relations between the USA and the Soviet Union did not change overnight on the accession of Gorbachev. On the American side deep scepticism prevailed towards Gorbachev until as late as autumn 1989. Despite the signature of the INF Treaty in December 1987, which was the first arms reduction as opposed to arms control treaty of the cold war period, progress was slow in other areas. Reagan was evidently inclined to reach arms agreements but not at the cost of what he considered to be essential elements of security. Bush took no initiatives towards the Soviet Union during the first nine months of his presidency (January–September 1989). Bush's Secretary of Defense,

Richard Cheney, remarked in May 1989 that he felt Gorbachev could easily fail with *perestroika* and be overthrown by hardliners. It was therefore dangerous to put much trust in Gorbachev (*Guardian*, 3 May 1989: 26). Bush indicated that he did not share these views but they were evidently common in some government circles. It was only with the collapse of communism in Eastern Europe that the entire structure of East–West relations can be said to have changed.

Nevertheless, the advent of Gorbachev to power brought a qualitative difference to US–Soviet relations. As recently as 1983 Reagan had labelled the Soviet Union an evil empire. (Nor, incidentally, did he abandon his hatred of communism, however much he moderated his policies towards the Soviet Union.) Furthermore, among his chief foreign policy priorities during his first term as president were a massive nuclear and conventional arms build-up and support for groups in the Third World—most notably the Contras in Nicaragua and the Mujaheddin in Afghanistan—which were opposing Soviet power or governments of what were taken to be Soviet client states. The Soviet Union for its part was heavily embroiled in Afghanistan and was assuming an intransigent stand on the issue of intermediate and theatre nuclear forces in Europe. The latter years of the Carter administration and much of Reagan's first term indeed represented what has been called the **second cold war** (Halliday 1983).

One important stimulus for change was the new philosophy of foreign affairs which Gorbachev brought to bear on US–Soviet relations. New thinking in foreign policy meant in the first place acknowledging that in an age of weapons of mass destruction, against which there was no reliable defence, security could not be achieved by amassing more and more weapons. Achieving security was a political rather than a military task and could be undertaken only in cooperation between the contending parties. Recognition of **common security** interest, of interdependence, and of common global challenges replaced the traditional Soviet assumption of the inevitability of conflict between capitalism and communism. Associated with this revision of Soviet orthodoxy was the military doctrine of **reasonable sufficiency** which involved an explicit renunciation of aggressive motives and enabled the

Soviet leadership for the first time to contemplate asymmetrical cuts in troops and weaponry. Without this change in philosophy the INF Treaty could not have been signed, since it involved the abandonment of **principles**—such as the insistence that the British and French nuclear deterrents be considered in conjunction with American weapons—which had been integral to the Soviet negotiating position since the 1960s.

In other areas of foreign policy too concession seemed the order of the day. In August 1989 it was announced that Soviet troops would be withdrawn from Afghanistan. During the following year in a speech to the United Nations Gorbachev restated his new foreign policy doctrines and added a commitment to nuclear disarmament by the year 2000 and a unilateral reduction of Soviet armed forces by 500,000 (White 1990: 159–61; Oberdorfer 1992: 316–19). There can be little doubt, first, that Gorbachev had indeed abandoned principles and practices which had been integral to Soviet policy until the 1980s and, second, that these concessions were responsible in large part for the sea change in US–Soviet relations during these years.

It seems clear also that Reagan's refusal to move on SDI and other issues faced Gorbachev with the choice of either failing to reach any agreement or making concessions in order to reach agreements. Even if, as some claim, Reagan's intransigence initially delayed agreements, Gorbachev seems to have calculated that the further forward he went with domestic *perestroika* the less flexibility he had in foreign policy. To that extent, Reagan's maintenance of a hard line on key issues did have the effect of forcing concessions from the Soviet Union.

That is not the whole story, however. Movement was not all one-way, nor did all the advantage in these agreements lie with the United States. On the critical question, for example, of Gorbachev's decision not to make Soviet agreement to the INF Treaty conditional on abandonment of SDI, Gorbachev evidently recognized that SDI was a politically contentious issue in the United States and that he had more to gain by moderating his position. This proved to be the case, since following signature of the INF Treaty the American Congress moved to limit funds for SDI. Furthermore, the issue of verification of the Treaty was as problematic for the

American military as for the Soviet military, both of whom harboured deep suspicions of intrusive verification **regimes**. Most significant, however, was the character of Ronald Reagan, whose stance on nuclear weapons was more complex and contradictory than his most aggressive public statements would suggest.

We have to reckon with a Reagan who came close at the Reykjavik summit of 1986 to agreeing with Gorbachev to the establishment of a nuclear-free world, who regarded SDI, with evident sincerity, as a wholly peaceful (because **defensive**) initiative which would render offensive weapons redundant once both sides were supplied with it, and who above all, again with evident sincerity, had a visceral hatred of nuclear weapons and an equally strong desire to be rid of them. Indeed according to one carefully argued interpretation, Reagan signalled a historic turn towards a more conciliatory posture towards the Soviet Union in a speech of January 1984, well before Gorbachev came to power. Prompted by a growing horror at the possibility of nuclear war, Reagan evidently became deeply troubled about the theory of nuclear deterrence and its associated concept of **Mutually Assured Destruction (MAD)**. On a visit to the US nuclear command centre in the run-up to the 1980 election he had been shocked to discover that the centre could be destroyed by a direct hit from a Soviet missile. Hence his determination to promote the development of SDI which he regarded as pacific in intent. Later revelations about the likelihood of nuclear accidents deepened his conviction that MAD was truly dangerous (Fischer 1997). In short, like many on the Left, but for quite different reasons, Reagan had emancipated himself to a degree from inherited nuclear doctrines. True, he was not prepared to give ground unilaterally or put American security at risk. Nor was he prepared to compromise on SDI which was regarded by the Soviets (and indeed Reagan's critics in the West) as deeply provocative rather than pacific. Indeed he had shown during his first term that he was willing to commit vast new sums of money to American defence. However, he was in many respects bolder in seeking arms agreements (or more foolhardy, as some of his critics suggested) than many of his advisers who had been schooled in the orthodoxy of nuclear deterrence. Besides, it was easier for a known conservative to reach agreements with the Soviet Union than for a liberal. Richard Nixon's promotion of détente was another example. Since there could be no doubt about their American-ism and commitment to anti-communism, they had a freedom to reach accommodations with the Soviet Union which would have been the object of deep suspicion if they had been made by Liberals.

The conclusion must be that, while the main story is of Soviet concessions to the United States, there was some movement on the American side too. Rea-gan's signature of the INF Treaty was not without political risks. The Treaty encountered considerable opposition from conservatives in the United States and from some European leaders too who felt that it represented a reduced American commitment to the nuclear defence of Europe. The departure from the Reagan administration during his second term of well-known foreign policy 'hawks'—among them Defense Secretary Weinberger and Assistant Sec-retary of Defense Richard Perle—demonstrates a mel-lowing of policy towards the Soviet Union as com-pared with the years 1981–5. There was thus an element of interaction between the Reagan adminis-tration and the new leadership in the Soviet Union, which casts doubt on those explanations of the end of the cold war which see it as a simple either/or: either Reagan's policies were the catalyst or Gorbachev's policies were wholly responsible.

Key points

- Opinion about the American role in ending the cold war has tended to polarize: either the Reagan hard line forced the Soviet Union to its knees or Reagan's policies were immaterial or actually served to pro-long the cold war.

- Soviet–American relations did not change overnight with the advent of Gorbachev. The United States responded cautiously to his initiatives.

- Gorbachev's new thinking in foreign policy over-threw the conventional wisdom of Soviet foreign policy.

- Gorbachev's concessions, which helped to produce the INF Treaty and generally improve the climate of Soviet–American relations, were promoted initially in a controlled fashion but tended to become more unilateral and sweeping as the pace of domestic reform quickened.

- The story is not simply one of Soviet concessions. The United States made some significant move-ment too, indicating that a polarized interpretation of the end of the cold war is too simple and schematic.

The interaction between internal and external environments

Isolation of the communist system from the global capitalist system

The end of the cold war is not to be explained only in terms of specific decisions or policies of the super-powers. There are some factors which are given in the underlying conditions of the relationship between East and West. The most important of these was the isolation of the Soviet Union and the com-munist bloc from the modernizing current of capital-ism. Initially, communist doctrine had held that the success of the Bolshevik Revolution could only be guaranteed by the spread of revolution, preferably throughout the world but in any event to the

developed nations of Europe. When this did not hap-pen in the years immediately following 1917 Stalin invented the doctrine of socialism in one country to justify the restriction of the Revolution to Russia. The subsequent extension of communism to Eastern Europe, China, North Korea, and Cuba after the Sec-ond World War was in theory a stepping stone to world revolution but in practice the advance of communism coincided with the expansion of world capitalism in what Eric Hobsbawm has called 'the golden years' (Hobsbawm 1994). The clash of these two processes, of course, gave the cold war its global character during and after the 1950s (see Ch.4).

For our purposes the most important feature of

these developments was the continued separation of the communist and capitalist blocs, a symbol of which was the Soviet Union's refusal to participate in the US Marshall Plan for post-war reconstruction (1948–52). The Soviet Union believed, with justification, that the conditions for participation demanded by the United States, which involved opening the Soviet bloc to Western investment and hence to Western economic and political leverage, would undermine the autonomy of the Soviet system and leave it at a disadvantage with respect to the West. Nor did the decision to undertake separate development initially seem to harm the Soviet bloc. During the 1950s Soviet growth rates actually exceeded those of all the capitalist nations except West Germany and Japan (Munting 1982: 132, 137; Van der Wee 1987: 50). Clearly this was from a low starting point and barely hid structural weaknesses in industrial production and agriculture. Nevertheless, the gross figures were impressive, and the launch of Sputnik in 1957 ahead of the US space satellite programme appeared to suggest considerable dynamism in the Soviet economy, sufficient at least to offer a real military threat to the West. Khrushchev announced in 1960 that he expected the Soviet economy to out-produce the United States within ten years and there were many in the West across the political spectrum who believed him.

From the perspective of the end of the cold war, the West's anxiety in the 1950s and early 1960s looks misplaced. We know that Soviet growth rates slowed in the 1960s and fell sharply in the 1970s and 1980s, and that the Soviet leadership's motive for détente with the West in the 1970s was in part to gain imports of 'high-tech' goods in recognition of the Soviet Union's increasing backwardness. The key conclusion to be drawn is that the Soviet bloc suffered not merely from low levels of growth and productivity in absolute terms but from increasing **relative** disadvantage with respect to the West. The world was changing around the Soviet bloc, bearing out Trotsky's prediction (considered heretical by Stalin in the late 1920s) that a Soviet island of communism could not survive in a capitalist sea.

Crucially too, Soviet bloc efforts to develop fuller trade links, greater travel opportunities, and cultural exchanges with the West exposed the vulnerability of communism to Western economic and cultural **influence** rather than strengthening it. Economically this was manifested in the debts owed by such

---

Box 5.6	**Key concepts**

Brezhnev doctrine: the idea of 'limited sovereignty' for Soviet bloc nations, which was used to justify the crushing of the reform movement in Czechoslovakia in 1968.

Civil society: the network of social institutions and practices (economic relationships, family and kinship groups, religious and other social affiliations) which underlie strictly political institutions. For democratic theorists the voluntary character of the above associations is taken to be essential to the workings of democratic politics.

Common European home: Gorbachev's concept (associated with his new thinking in foreign policy) of the essential unity of Europe and of the need to overcome the 'artificiality and temporariness of the bloc-to-bloc confrontation and the archaic nature of the "iron curtain" '.

Evil empire: Reagan's term, used in a speech of 1983, to describe the Soviet Union.

New thinking: the general label given by Gorbachev to his reforms in domestic and foreign policy.

Pax Americana: Latin phrase (literally American peace, adapted from Pax Romana) implying a global peace dictated by American power.

Reasonable sufficiency: Gorbachev's term (associated with his new thinking in foreign policy) for a defence policy which relied on the minimum necessary level of weaponry consistent with national security, and designed to overcome the spiralling dynamics of the nuclear arms race.

Separate paths to socialism: Khrushchev' acknowledgement of the existence of diversity in the Soviet bloc and of the validity (within strict limits) of separate routes to the common socialist goal.

Socialism in one country: Stalin's term used to justify the Soviet Union's departure from the orthodox Marxist view that socialism in the Soviet Union could succeed only in conjunction with socialist revolutions in advanced industrial nations.

nations as Poland and Hungary to Western banks. Culturally, citizens of Eastern Europe were increasingly able to make comparisons between their own lives and those lived in the West. West German television, for example, was widely viewed in East Germany and Czechoslovakia; Radio Free Europe and similar stations beamed their programmes to the Eastern bloc. One must also take account of the growth of the trans-European peace movement in the 1970s, which linked anti-nuclear and pro-democracy forces on both sides of the Iron Curtain. While there is dispute about how far such pressures influenced government policies in the West, it is plausible to assume that they helped to generate the ferment in Eastern Europe (Thompson 1990; Kaldor 1995). In short, isolationism and economic autarky (separate development in isolation from world trade), which had arguably fostered growth and ideological cohesion in the Eastern bloc in the early post-war period, later became a liability and was ultimately impossible to sustain.

It is helpful to view the cold war as having been composed of two distinct but overlapping systems:

1. A **cold war system** which was defined by US–Soviet antagonism, the nuclear stand-off, and the extension of these central conflicts to the periphery of the international system.

2. The **global capitalist system** which was defined by the expansion of production and trade and growing economic interdependence.

The Soviet Union's existence was defined and limited by the cold war, while the United States was a full, indeed the chief, participant in the growth of world capitalism. However great the United States' economic problems from the 1970s onwards—and they were considerable—they were not such as to produce the disabling crisis of political legitimacy experienced by the Soviet Union. One way of putting this is to say that the United States was never wholly consumed by the cold war, politically or economically. By contrast, the Soviet Union, limited as it was by ideology and history to a debilitating isolationism, was unable to meet the challenge posed by the globalization of the capitalist political economy and Western consumer culture (Crockatt 1995: 370–1).

Key points

- The causes of the end of the cold war are to be found not only in internal and external conditions considered separately but in the interaction between the two.

- The separation of the communist bloc from capitalism, though not apparently disadvantageous to communism until the 1970s, left it at an increasing relative disadvantage to the capitalist West.

- Growing consciousness of relative disadvantage was a factor in the collapse of communism.

Conclusion

The end of the cold war removed more or less at a stroke the **structural** and **ideological** conditions which underlay superpower conflict over the previous forty years. This in itself seemed to promise a general relaxation of tension and a reduction in the threat of major, especially nuclear, war. To the extent that superpower conflict lay behind regional conflicts in various parts of the world, then the end of the cold war held out the possibility of resolution of these conflicts. On the most optimistic reading, conditions were now present for a new world order in which American power, in concert with other members of the UN Security Council, would serve as a global stabilizer. One writer, expressing the triumphalism which characterized some early American reactions to the end of the cold war, talked of a 'unipolar moment' (Krauthammer 1990–1). The Gulf War of 1991 was taken by some to be the model for a new type of collective international action in which the UN, with strong US backing, would act as its founders had intended as a genuine **collective security** organization. Beyond this, the end of the cold war would bring a 'peace dividend' both financial and political. Nations could now afford to expend fewer resources on military and foreign policy, and devote them to domestic growth.

At the opposite extreme was the view that the cold war had served to stabilize international politics, that indeed it had fostered the **long peace** of the post-war years, defined as the absence of war between the major powers (Gaddis 1986). From this perspective the end of the cold war was therefore a destabilizing event, however much one might welcome the collapse of communism. The most pessimistic predictions were of chaos and violence in the successor states of the Soviet Union and Eastern Europe, as long-suppressed national and ethnic forces achieved expression, and a general rise in global instability (Mearsheimer 1990).

There is little point in attempting to draw up a simple balance sheet between these two positions, since both optimists and pessimists could find evidence to support their contentions. Each new development in international politics contained potentially positive and negative tendencies and events moved swiftly in the decade following the end of the cold war. It is more appropriate to ask how the end of the cold war affected the broad environment in which international conflict took place. More specifically, what principles of order, if any, now underpinned the international system?

In the immediate aftermath of the end of the cold war, analysts tended to focus on the disappearance of cold war structures and agendas. Ideas about possible futures of the international system, as outlined above, were initially either vague or reflective of assumptions born in the cold war. As the dust settled from the cold war, however, a number of possible ways of describing the new realities, not all of them mutually exclusive, emerged. Some envisaged **multipolarity** based either on three major economic blocs—North America, especially after the signing of the North American Free Trade Association (NAFTA) in 1993, the European Union, and East Asia—or on a larger number of dominant powers (Rusi 1997; Kegley and Wittkopf 1999) while others favoured 'unipolarity', based on the dominance of the United States in the international system. George Bush's

'new world order' promised a Wilsonian scheme of internationalism, based (like Woodrow Wilson's) on the assumption of strong American backing for mechanisms for settling international disputes, preventing aggression, and securing international justice. If this concept lasted for only a short time, it was because it was so closely associated with prosecution of the Gulf War. The ambiguous outcome of the war, which raised a host of questions about the motives and effects of the UN-backed coalition's intervention in Iraq and left Saddam Hussein in power, failed to substantiate the claims made for the 'new world order'. Nevertheless, discussion of developments in global 'governance', at the core of which lay the UN and its associated institutions, suggested an increasing role for internationalist ideas and institutions (Halliday 1999: 121–4).

Undoubtedly, as the new millennium approached, the most discussed paradigm for the post-cold war international order was 'globalization'. Its attractiveness lay in its ability to encompass at once **processes**, especially transnational exchanges of information, goods, and finance, and **structures**, including those based on relations between non-governmental organizations as well as nation-states. Furthermore, globalization could be shown to have had a history and to that extent it could be employed to link the period of cold war with what preceded it and followed it (Clark 1997). Finally, globalization could be linked to the central question of the role of the United States in the post-cold war world since the United States was the most globalizing of all world powers in the extent of its economic, cultural, political, and military reach.

In the early 1990s, estimates of the United States varied greatly. Despite the prevalence of 'triumphalists' such as Charles Krauthammer (1990–1) and Francis Fukuyama (1992), the influence of 'declinists' such as Paul Kennedy (1998) remained strong and he was joined by other interpreters from across the political spectrum, including Samuel Huntington (1993 and 1996). To many observers, 'winning the cold war' did not remove the challenges to American power from rival economies such as Japan's or (in Huntington's interpretation) from cultural antagonists in the form of the Muslim world. In the second half of the 1990s, however, the combination of crisis in the Asian economies and a sustained boom in the United States economy led to a revised assessment of the United States and of its role in international politics. While some observers asked 'whatever happened to the Pacific century?' (Foot and Walter 1999) others noted that the 'American century' (announced in 1941 by Henry Luce) was far from over. Whether the American century was to be praised or deplored was scarcely the issue, wrote one American scholar of the Left. The fact was that 'American standards of all kinds are the standard of globalization' (Cumings 1999: 294).

The terrorist attacks of 9/11, while shattering many of the assumptions about the possibility of order in the international system, reinforced the centrality of American power in global politics, even if there was fierce debate about how long it could last or even whether it was a good thing (Kupchan 2002; Garton Ash 2002). The terrorist attacks also seemingly resolved the issue of America's 'grand strategy' in the post-cold war world. For the Bush administration, it was often said, the war against terror performed a role analogous to that of containment in the cold war. Questions remained, however, about whether terrorism, dangerous and destabilizing as it was, could really be considered comparable to the Soviet threat during the cold war. 'Terrorism,' wrote one analyst, 'is to geopolitics what a strong wind is to geography—a potent, spectacular and destructive element, but one that affects surface features, not underlying tectonic forces and the location of fault-lines' (Kupchan 2002: 109). Meanwhile the challenge to practitioners and analysts alike remained, in the absence of the apparent simplicities of the cold war, of finding terms to describe the fault-lines of post-cold war international politics and of devising strategies to meet them. As for the cold war, it was now firmly a part of history.

> **Key points**
>
> - The end of the cold war offered grounds for both pessimistic and optimistic speculation.
>
> - Both the above approaches could find evidence for their contentions in the varied and conflicting tendencies in post-cold war international developments.
>
> - The novelty of the post-cold war international system lay not in the existence of instability and conflict but in the environment in which conflict took place.
>
> - In the aftermath of the cold war, globalization and the future of the United States were considered by many scholars to be closely linked, though countervailing processes to both could be expected to develop.

For further information and case studies on this subject, please visit the companion web site at www.oup.com/uk/booksites/politics.

QUESTIONS

1 Does an examination of the end of the cold war help in understanding how systemic change occurs in world politics?

2 What do you think Gorbachev hoped to achieve through *glasnost* and *perestroika*?

3 What are the connections between change in the Soviet Union and the revolutions in Eastern Europe?

4 Why did changes of leadership in Eastern Europe in the summer and autumn of 1989 fail to stem the collapse of communism?

5 Can you find ways, other than those presented in this chapter, of conceptualizing the relationship between external and internal causes of the collapse of communism in the Soviet Union?

6 Did the West 'win' the cold war?

7 What role, if any, did the Reagan administration play in bringing about the end of the cold war?

8 Why did experts by and large fail to anticipate the collapse of communism?

9 Is the post-cold war international system more unstable than the cold war international system?

10 What ordering principles, if any, operate in post-cold war international politics?

11 Can communism be regarded as a victim of the 'globalization of world politics'?

GUIDE TO FURTHER READING

General

Beschloss, M. and Talbott, S. (1993), *At the Highest Levels: The Inside Story of the End of the Cold War* (Boston: Little Brown). A well-written blow-by-blow account of the high politics of the years 1989–91.

Garthoff, R. (1994), *The Great Transition: American-Soviet Relations and the End of the Cold War* (Washington, DC: Brookings Institution). This is still the fullest international history of the subject.

Hogan, M. (ed.) (1992), *The End of the Cold War: Its Meaning and Implications* (Cambridge: Cambridge University Press). A lively collection of essays containing a variety of perspectives.

Oberdorfer, D. (1992), *The Turn: From the Cold War to a New Era* (New York: Touchstone Books). A finely observed narrative which captures the flavour of events and also conveys a sense of the big picture of structural change.

On the Soviet Union

Bowker, M. (1997), *Russian Foreign Policy and the End of the Cold War* (Aldershot: Dartmouth). A comprehensive and scholarly account.

Remnick, D. (1993), *Lenin's Tomb: The Last Days of the Soviet Empire* (London: Viking). Eyewitness commentary by a first-rate journalist who also grasps the bigger picture.

Goldman, M. (1992), *What Went Wrong with Perestroika* (New York: Norton). Especially valuable for its coverage of economic issues

Eastern Europe

Gati, C. (1990), *The Bloc that Failed: Soviet–East European Relations in Transition* (Bloomington: Indiana University Press). A clearly written analytical account.

Stokes, G. (1993), *The Walls Come Tumbling Down: The Collapse of Communism in Eastern Europe* (New York: Oxford University Press). The work of a historian which combines narrative of the collapse of communism with longer term perspectives.

The United States

Fischer, B. (1997), *The Reagan Reversal: Foreign Policy and the End of the Cold War* (Columbia, Mo.: University of Missouri Press). Presents a challenging interpretation of Reagan's foreign policy and its impact on bringing about the end of the cold war.

Gaddis, J. (1992), *The United States and the End of the Cold War: Implications, Reconsiderations, Provocations* (New York: Oxford University Press). Characteristically incisive and thoughtful essays by a leading historian of the cold war.

Hutchings, R. (1997), *American Diplomacy and the End of the Cold War* (Baltimore: Johns Hopkins University Press). A valuable perspective by an American diplomat.

WEB LINKS

http://cwihp.si.edu The Cold War International History Project disseminates new information and perspectives on the history of the cold war.

CHAPTER 6

From the cold war to the war on terror

MICHAEL COX

READER'S GUIDE

This chapter argues that the way we now look at the period after 1989 is increasingly being conditioned by the most important event of the last few years: the attack on the United States on 11 September 2001. This has not only made historians rethink the years that defined the post-cold war era but also compelled them to look for clues to why the attack may have happened in the first place. This is an understandable response. However, we should be careful not to look at the period entirely through one prism. There were many developments in the period following the end of the cold war, and we need to study these in their own right and not reduce the complexities of a whole era to one where we are merely searching for clues to what happened to the USA on that fatal day in autumn 2001. The chapter begins therefore with the unexpected end of the cold war and how writers thought about the new world order after communism; it then goes on to discuss the main trends of the 1990s; and it concludes with a brief look at 9/11 and its aftermath. The thesis advanced at the end is that in spite of America's overwhelming power, because of 9/11 we have entered into more dangerous times: we have thus left behind the relatively calm waters of the post-cold war era. A new world disorder beckons.

Introduction

Before 11 September 2001 historians generally thought of the world after the fall of communism in terms of what it was not and what it came after—and what it was not, and what it came after, most obviously, was the cold war. This is why we referred to the period as the post-cold war era. Indeed, so powerful was this rather negative characterization, that the image or images which stuck in our minds most for many years were those inspired by the events of 1989 in Eastern Europe, to be followed two years later by the collapse of the USSR. This has now changed completely, and with one or two minor exceptions, most writers now tend to view the period less in its own terms and increasingly through the prism of the Twin Towers falling and the events which then unfolded, beginning with America's muscular military response against the Taleban regime in Afghanistan, followed just over a year later by its controversial invasion of Iraq.

Historians today thus view the 1990s in rather different ways than they did before. Indeed, according to some, the decade should now be regarded as little more than an interregnum—almost an interwar period—marked at one end by the conclusion of one kind of war and at the other by the beginning of another, new kind of global conflict. In fact, some would argue that the years before 9/11 should be also seen as some prolonged moment of rest during which the West quite literally slept while others plotted its downfall. In the United States this kind of thinking has now become especially popular on the conservative Right. The 1990s, they argue, were years when history quite literally took a holiday; a period when many assumed (or at least hoped) that the impact of global economic integration on the one hand and the spread of democracy on the other, would make the world a far less dangerous place. If nothing else, 9/11 put paid to such fantasies, and reminded people that swords could not be turned into ploughshares without a price being paid. Many who argue thus have also taken aim at one of their great bogeymen of the period: President Bill Clinton who occupied the White House between 1992 and 2000. This American champion of globalization and democracy, they argue, took the United States on what they have called an extended 'beach party', which like all good parties ended badly with an especially painful hangover on 9/11.

The present crisis therefore casts a huge shadow over how many now look back at the years after 1989. But we should take care. After all, during the 1990s itself the world appeared to be a relatively benign place—unless of course you happened to be Rwandan, Bosnian, or poor. There also seemed to be many possible outcomes once the cold war had come to an end, only one of which needed to conclude with the attack on the United States. Nor should we be so mesmerized by 9/11 as to think of everything that went on before it in terms of some logical preparation for what happened on that terrible day. This is not only bad history. It also makes us blind to the complexities of the period. As historians always like to remind people, history can only be explained once it has come to an end. However, how it 'ends'—in this case with 9/11—should not lead us to assume that this was the only possible outcome. We should, in other words, beware the twin sins of determinism and hindsight.

In this chapter we shall thus treat the years after the end of the cold war in at least two ways: as ones

---

Box 6.1   Getting it right: getting it wrong

'Who called the East Asian crisis? Or the collapse of the Soviet Union? Yugoslavia's demise or Mexico's crash? Japan's swift transformation from global economic powerhouse to financial wreck? No one. A theory's value is proportional to its predictive power. As these examples illustrate, the theories we bank to interpret world affairs, or that heads of governments and corporations use to guide their decisions, sometimes fall flat. Indeed, the flood of events that have caught the experts by surprise in recent years has heightened awareness about the poverty of the theoretical apparatus at our disposal.'

(Moises Nam, Editor, *Foreign Policy* (Spring 1998), 9)

that need to be analysed in their own right, and as a critical phase in international history that contained within it a series of unresolved tensions that finally produced the attack of 9/11. Let us be clear: 9/11 was a shock. However, it should have come as no surprise to those who had been studying the post-cold war era properly. Even less surprising should have been the American reaction. Indeed, if we were to identify one central dynamic of global politics since 9/11 it would have to be the profound shift in the nature of American foreign policy. But as our discussion will show, this shift to a more assertive stance—one that has been termed neo-

imperial by a few observers—has only been made possible because the United States was already in a position of enormous strength. This points to something else as well: that we should not think of history in terms of separate bits of discrete time. Thus what the United States was able to do after 9/11 was conditioned by what had happened to it during the post-cold war era: but the power it accumulated during this period was only made possible by the victory it achieved in the cold war. We might like to present history in nice neat packages; history itself though knows no such boundaries.

The cold war ends

The cold war was composed of five different levels of reality: a strategic confrontation between the USSR and the United States; an ideological stand-off between communism and capitalism; a geographical and military confrontation that kept Europe and Germany divided for the best part of forty years; an ongoing struggle for the future control of the Third World; and finally, a wider opposition between two material civilizations both of which insisted that they, and they alone, represented the wave of the future. Yet in spite of its confrontational character the cold war also had its own unwritten rules of engagement. These not only helped regulate the relationship—especially important in an age of nuclear weapons—but introduced a degree of order to international relations that had been absent before the cold war began in the immediate post-war years. This is why many practitioners of foreign policy, not to mention most theorists of world politics, came to the not illogical conclusion that something so stable, or as some claimed so peaceful, was bound to continue into the indefinite future.

This of course did not happen, and left historians asking one of two questions: most divisively, why did all the so-called experts fail to predict what happened in the form of the end of the cold war; and, more generally, how do we actually explain what actually took place in 1989? Neither question has been adequately answered, especially that concern-

ing causation. Indeed, there are by now several different ways in which historians have tried to explain the end of the cold war, with some insisting that it was the result of American pressure, others that it was the consequence of Soviet economic decline, a few more that it was the result of imperial over-stretch, some that communism simply could not compete with capitalism, and quite a number that it was the product of agency and choice—in particular the kind of choices made by Soviet reformer Mikhail Gorbachev to improve the position of the Soviet system by establishing a less confrontational and less costly relationship with the capitalist world. Ironically, though, instead of renovating the Soviet system, his efforts weakened it severely and set in train a series of developments that finally (and quite unplanned) brought the whole edifice of the cold war tumbling down (see Ch.5).

Confronted with such an upheaval historians have again responded in one of two ways: either by suggesting that very little changed because of 1989 or that the whole world was turned upside down. Thus the United States, it has been argued by the former, continued to remain extraordinarily powerful in spite of the end of communist power in Europe; Europe itself continued along the same path of integration; the North–South divide remained intact; wars continued to blight the new international landscape; and institutions built in one era continued to remain central to management of the international system in another. Thus why all the fuss? And why repeat the standard cliché that the end of the cold war signified a truly critical turning point in history? This is not a view which commands majority support, however. In fact, most analysts now concede that the events of 1989 constituted a true historical turning point. After all, an international system that had once been balanced because it was **bipolar**, now gave way to a new **unipolar** world in which there was hardly any balance at all. The possibility of revolution in the Third World was now replaced with the realities of structural adjustment. Anti-capitalism became ideologically unfashionable. Europe quite literally was redefined both geographically and politically. And the way we began to think about economic choices and strategic possibilities was transformed. The historical future in the form of planning and Soviet power had been tried. It had failed. And all we could look forward to now—it seemed—was a world dominated by the market and shaped by American choices.

Key points

- The cold war was a complex relationship combining elements of both conflict and stability.

- Most experts assumed that the cold war would go on.

- The end of the cold war has been interpreted in at least five different ways.

- While some historians argue that 1989 did not turn the world upside down, most accept that it was a crucial turning point.

Three theories in search of the post-cold war world

A Liberal peace?

After all great wars there is inevitably (and understandably) a period when optimism reigns supreme; and in the context of the post-cold war era, much of this was expressed through the writings of theorists of a liberal persuasion: and one of the most politically influential of these was Francis Fukuyama, a former US State Department official. An expert on the Third World with a penchant for philosophical speculation, Fukuyama shot to fame in the late 1980s with an article bearing the challenging title, 'The End of History'. The basic thesis he put forward in 1989 consisted of a set of simple, but highly important assertions. These can be summarized thus: that 'history' since the French Revolution had been driven by a core dynamic conflict between the forces supporting collectivism and those endorsing the ideals of 'bourgeois' individualism; that with the Russian Revolution of 1917 the balance clearly tilted towards the former; that by the late 1970s, however, the balance began to tilt the other way as the various efforts at economic planning in the Third World started to show signs of fatigue; that this shift became even more pronounced, though, when Gorbachev assumed office in the USSR in 1985 and began to challenge traditional Soviet assumptions; and it became clearer still when Gorbachev finally decided to abandon Eastern Europe and the peoples of these countries opted for 'bourgeois' democracy and market economics—thus ending the cold war on terms entirely favourable to the West. This, according to Fukuyama, represented a historic victory for the forces of individualism, marking what he termed the 'end' of one phase in 'history', and the beginning of another where Liberal economic values would prevail globally. There was now no alternative to bourgeois democracy.

This view of a new and more pacific world in formation was supported by at least three key Liberal arguments. The first had to do with democracy and the idea—going back to Kant—that while authoritarianism bred war, democracies bred peace; hence, the more democracies there were (as there were after the fall of communism), the more peaceful the world was bound to become. This assumption was linked to another hypothesis concerning the role of institutions: these it was asserted not only helped organize the modern world more efficiently but did much to overcome the logic of **anarchy** by mediating conflict between states. This in turn went hand in hand with a third argument that linked the cause of peace with the existence of capitalism. Naturally enough, liberals agreed that capitalism had its dark underside. But, they argued, as world trade grew, as financial ties between different geographical zones deepened, and countries invested more heavily in each other's economies, this would create a powerful set of material incentives that would compel **nations** to get on with each other. The possibility of conflict remained, but in an increasingly integrated economic system, the likelihood of its actually occurring was bound to diminish rapidly.

Box 6.2	**The triumph of Liberalism?**

'The twentieth century saw the developed world descend into a paroxysm of ideological violence, as Liberalism contended first with the remnants of absolutism, then bolshevism and fascism, and finally an updated Marxism that threatened to lead to the ultimate apocalypse of nuclear war. But the century that began full of self-confidence in the ultimate triumph of Western liberal democracy seems at its close to be returning full circle to where it started: not to an "end of ideology" or a convergence between capitalism and socialism, but to an unabashed victory of economic and political Liberalism.'

(Francis Fukuyama, 'The End of History?', *National Interest*, Summer 1989)

Key points

- The 1990s are now viewed as the high moment of Liberalism and Francis Fukuyama's concept of the 'end of history' as the most influential Liberal theory of the post-cold war era.

- Liberal optimism about the post-cold war era rested on three assumptions: that democracies do not go to war with one another; that institutions can overcome the logic of anarchy; and that modern globalized capitalism binds states more closely together.

Realist warnings

If Liberals looked forward to more peaceful times, others of a more Realist persuasion painted a much bleaker picture of the world in formation. Not for them visions of **security**, stability, and economic order, but rather chaos and conflict. This assessment drew its inspiration from three main sources: a more general theory of world politics which argued that the international system had always been, and would continue to remain competitive and anarchic; a reading of history that pointed to past failures of building new world orders—most obviously after the First World War; and an assessment of the world as it was after 1989 with its new barbaric wars, **failed states** and collapsing regions. From this a few drew the not unreasonable conclusion that there was really little to be too optimistic about.

One of the leading thinkers who helped define Realism in the post-cold war period was John Mearsheimer, a professor of political science in the University of Chicago. A military historian by background, and an international relations scholar by training, Mearsheimer took issue with what he felt was the simple-minded optimism that was sweeping the United States after 1989. In his view this new-found happiness was premised upon a major misreading of history in general and the cold war in particular. He spelled out the reasons why in one of the most cited articles of the post-cold war period.

Box 6.3	**Why Realism is right**

'There is much well worth criticizing in the classically Realist theory of the international relations and what was once eponymously called statecraft; many of us have bored first-year tutorials with our skilful skewering of the balance-of-power theory, the concept of power, and—of course—the national interest. The problem is that with our intellectual rigour, all too often we correct the grammar but forget the plot. Flawed though the principal texts of classical Realism may be, when compared with our contemporary would-be master-mistress-works, they have an overriding virtue. To risk the vernacular; they got the big things right enough.'

(Colin Gray, 'Clausewitz rules OK?', *Review of International Studies*, December 1999, 162)

Published in the major American journal *International Security* in the summer of 1990, his 'Back to the Future: Instability in Europe after the Cold War' spawned a furious debate.

Mearsheimer's pessimism was based in very large part on an analysis of the structure of the international system during the cold war. His thesis was neither original nor new; yet it was one with which other Realists (including Kenneth Waltz) readily concurred. Bipolarity, he argued, had produced stability and order after the Second World War: its collapse therefore could only generate new problems—further nuclear proliferation being perhaps the most dangerous. Mearsheimer also felt that the division of Europe and Germany after 1946 had contributed to a new continental order; hence the unification of both was likely to introduce uncertainty. Finally, he believed (along with many others) that with the collapse of communism in the East, old ethnic hatreds would once again resurface and thrust the continent back into the chaos and the bloodshed that had marked its none-too-happy history between the two world wars. As the Balkans descended into barbarity after 1990, Meirsheimer's gloomy prognosis about Europe (or at least one part of it) going 'back to the future' looked prescient indeed.

If Mearsheimer's argument drew inspiration from his study of the cold war in Europe, Robert D. Kaplan's derived succour from his observations about those parts of the world experiencing collapse and disintegration. His argument formed the second central challenge to liberal optimism in the 1990s. 'The Coming Anarchy' was first published in the influential magazine, *Atlantic Monthly*, in 1994. Building upon the work of other writers, Kaplan's vision of the future was perhaps the least sustained empirically but without question one of the most sobering readings of the post-cold war era—unsurprisingly so given his core working assumption that economic and human collapse in parts of Africa were as relevant to our understanding of the future character of world politics.

The picture drawn of the new world by Kaplan was a desperate one indeed. In his world, the real world he felt, old structures and traditional certainties were rapidly dissolving, producing chaos and misery, notably (but not only) in countries like Sierra Leone and Zaire in West Africa where life for ordinary people had become virtually intolerable. Meanwhile, in other parts of the world, old-fashioned conflicts between ideologies such as communism and capitalism were giving way to less easily regulated—and possibly more fundamental—clashes over resources such as water, cropland forests, and even fish. Scarcer resources in turn were placing an even greater strain on several of the poorer countries in the world, countries whose populations were increasing at an alarming rate, and where few mechanisms existed for settling disputes peacefully. Of course, not all of the countries of the world were experiencing such horrors, as Kaplan readily admitted. In fact, according to Kaplan, the world was rapidly dividing after the cold war into those areas and regions whose inhabitants in the main were 'healthy, well fed and pampered by technology' and those whose people were condemned to a Hobbesian life where conditions were 'nasty, brutish and short'. However, the have-nots would not stay put and would soon come hammering on the doors of the more prosperous zones fuelling even more tensions in a world without meaning or welfare for the vast majority.

The third writer who helped place Realism in the forefront of the post-cold war debate was the American political scientist based at Harvard, Samuel Huntington. An important figure in many debates over a number of years (who has become more influential still since 9/11) Huntington always had a good eye for the big trends. Never far from power, and always keen to use his influence to shape the policy debate in the United States, Huntington gave warnings about the world after 1989 that were read at the time as indicative of at least one strand of tough-minded opinion in the US policy-making elite. Some in fact suspected, or feared, that the Huntington thesis was not merely a reflection of the world 'out there', but instead an attempt by the United States to find a new and useful enemy that would give it a role and provide justification for its continued hegemony in a post-Soviet world.

At the heart of Huntington's argument was a powerful refutation of the Liberal argument that the world now faced more tranquil times. Not so, opined Huntington: the cold war clash of secular economic ideologies might have come to a conclusion. But this did not mean the end of conflict as such. This, he insisted, would simply assume a new form; and this he argued could be most accurately defined as a 'clash of civilizations'. This would be the latest phase in what he termed the evolution in conflict in the modern world. However, instead of this occurring within a pre-existing set of Western norms—even communism he accepted was a secular political ideology that had arisen under Western conditions—it would be between the 'West' and those other countries and regions in the world that did not adhere to such values as respect for the individual, human rights, democracy, and secularism. Identity and culture thus lay at the heart of the new antagonisms according to Huntington; and it was this that would be the new fault-line in the post-cold war world, pitting those nations in Western Europe and the USA that embodied one form of 'civilization' against those in the Middle East, China, and Asia (even post-communist Russia) where the value systems were profoundly different.

Nor, he continued, was there much the West could do to avoid this clash. The differences between civilizations were real and they were important. They were not an invention of the West, or even of Samuel Huntington for that matter. Huntington indeed made it clear that he did not actually advocate such a conflict. He simply felt that these profound oppositions existed—witness, he said, the ongoing struggle between militant Islam and the liberal democracies, and the very real tensions that existed between the more traditional value system in the countries of the Middle East and those in the more developed West. These were proof enough of difference, and until the West recognized this reality, it would be unable to deal with it wisely.

Key points

- Realists are not Realists because they are 'realistic', but rather because they have what they believe is a more historically rooted analysis about the way the international system has always operated and operates now.

- Mearsheimer's argument about going 'back to the future' is built upon the basic Realist argument that the cold war system of bipolarity led to a 'long peace' that might now be undermined by its dissolution.

- Kaplan's 'coming anarchy' builds on the experience of what he terms the 'dying regions' of the world—like parts of Africa—and asserts that the West ignores what is happening in these areas at its risk.

- Huntington's thesis about the 'clash of civilizations' takes as its starting point the inevitability of conflict as a historically proven fact, and goes on to argue that the next key conflicts in the world will be not economic or ideological but cultural.

Radical alternatives

One of the more interesting intellectual features of the post-cold war world was that while classical Marxism suffered a major setback because of its perceived association with the old communist regimes radical theory in its various guises actually managed to flourish. Of course, what constitutes and does not constitute radical theory remains unclear. Radical after all can come in all shapes and sizes. But one such figure whose radical credentials cannot be doubted is the brilliant American linguistic theorist Noam Chomsky of the Massachusetts Institute of Technology. Marginalized in his own country—he once referred to himself as a dissident in the land of the deaf and the blind—Chomsky was and remains perhaps the most significant critical voice in what he has always regarded as an American academic wilderness peopled by those either too spineless or too dependent to attack the status quo. But from his position on the edges of the mainstream, Chomsky has always managed to influence and inspire many young students. A best-selling author who has refused to keep quiet (and has become more vociferous still since the war on terror began) Chomsky has painted an impressionistic, but powerfully realistic picture of an international order where the powerful exploit the powerless, the rich manipulate the masses, and the Great Powers dominate the weak.

CWS

Chomsky has written on most things it seems: but what he has concentrated on most is the United States. His views of the last remaining superpower can hardly be described as flattering. On the contrary. The international system he believes is an American creation. This system is not a benign one. That far from representing a force for good in the world, the USA is an aggressive and ruthless hegemon whose principal aim has always been to make the world safe for the multinationals. Moreover, even when it does promote moral policies such as democracy and human rights it only does so for self-interested reasons. Furthermore, whatever its own citizens might think, the United States is an empire one of whose great successes has been to convince the world—not to mention itself—that it is not an empire! Naturally, like any good radical, Chomsky sees no divide between foreign policy and domestic politics: thus the former he argues can be used to frame and discipline what is discussed at home; and what is discussed at home will always be conditioned by the interests of an elite keen to export American values to the rest of the world.

A very different kind of radical theorist is Robert Cox, a Canadian who originally worked at the International Labour Office before finally moving to York University in Canada. Like Chomsky he developed his iconoclastic views not within but apart from what he later termed 'the dominant currents of thought in international relations'. Unlike Chomsky though he was over time able to build up quite a large following within the international relations

community proper. Influenced by several different writers—Vico, Sorel, Weber, Polanyi, Braudel, Antonio Gramsci, and E. H. Carr—Cox also went on to shape the outlook of a number other critical political economists, including most prominently Stephen Gill, Kees van der Pijl, and Craig Murphy.

Though much of Cox's most important work appeared before the end of the cold war, he still has much to say about the nature of the new world order in general. In schematic terms his main arguments can be summarized thus: first, the essential transformation in world politics did not take place in 1989 or even 1991 but rather in the mid-1970s following the world economic crisis. At this point there was a decisive shift from Keynesian industrial growth policies organized in and around a welfare state to those which laid much greater stress on the free market; second, that while this transformation produced much wealth for the wealthy and those states with the economic power, it generated an enormous degree of poverty and misery for the majority; third, that even though much might have changed since 1989, much more has not: the obfuscating ideologies, the many controls and state apparatuses—all built up during the cold war—have remained more or less the same; and finally, that while working-class revolution in the traditional Marxist sense is most unlikely, the possibility of new emancipatory challenges to globalization remains on the political agenda.

This last theme was to be taken up by our third radical: the publicist and lecturer, Naomi Klein. Though possessing neither the intellectual power of a Chomsky nor the systematic line of analysis developed by Cox, Klein, who originally trained as a journalist in Canada, nonetheless had a huge—though perhaps temporary—impact on the way in which a new generation of activists thought about modern material culture. Klein might be best characterized as a public intellectual from outside of the academic mainstream, who by dint of a wonderfully accessible writing style and sheer energy (wedded to a brilliant use of websites and public lectures) possibly did more to make the case against globalization than most academic critics put together. She also had the very great wisdom of writing short books with catchy titles—especially *No Logo* (2000)—rather than long ones with uninteresting titles, and so made her

---

| Box 6.4 | **Noam Chomsky takes a sceptical look at 'humanitarian intervention' after the cold war** |

'From a contrasting perspective, the "new interventionism" is replaying an old record. It is an updated variant of traditional practices that were impeded in a bipolar world system that allowed some space for nonalignment—a concept that effectively vanishes when one of the two poles disappears. The Soviet Union and to some extent China, set limits on the actions of the Western powers in their traditional domains, not only by virtue of the military deterrent, but also because of their occasional willingness, however opportunistic, to lend support to targets of Western subversion and aggression. With the Soviet deterrent in decline, the Cold War victors are more free to exercise their will under the cloak of good intentions but in pursuit of interests that have a very familiar ring outside the realm of enlightenment.'

(Noam Chomsky, *The New Military Humanism* (Monroe, Me.: Common Courage Press, 1999), 11)

ideas available to very wide audience. *No Logo* in fact became an overnight publishing sensation, referred to by one admirer as 'the Das Kapital of the growing anti-corporate movement' and another as a 'stylishly argued indictment of post-modern capitalism'. Translated into 21 languages and published in over 25 countries, it became in effect a manifesto of its time.

Her message in *No Logo* was as simple as some academics said it was simple-minded: the new world order, she argued, brought global pillage not global emancipation. The information age's global economy of 'groovy Gaps, Starbucks and Microsofts isn't as cool as it is pledged to be', she opined. But hope was at hand in the shape of rising anti-corporate sentiment driven forward by a new ethical consciousness increasingly hostile to a world dominated by labels and logos. This in turn was bound to produce a 'vast wave of opposition squarely targeting transnational corporations particularly those with very high name-brand recognition'. And out of this would emerge a new political order—neither obviously socialist nor particularly capitalist—that would help check the excesses of globalization and by so doing lay the foundations for a more meaningful, more authentic politics.

> ### Key points
>
> - Some of the more significant radical writers on world politics developed their ideas outside of—and in opposition to—mainstream international relations.
>
> - Noam Chomsky is a famous best-selling author in the United States whose critique of what he terms the 'American empire' takes as its point of intellectual departure the notion that in the new world order very little has fundamentally changed—other than America's increased capacity to get its own way.
>
> - Robert Cox has a more established reputation in the field of international political economy, but like Chomsky believes that the structures of hegemony established in one era still remain intact.
>
> - Naomi Klein is less a systematic thinker than the self-defined activist voice of an anti-globalization movement opposed to consumerism and faceless corporations.

Key trends in the post-cold war era

The globalization of capitalism

Globalization did not merely become the most discussed phenomenon of the 1990s—though few could agree precisely on what it meant, when it began, or what its consequences were likely to be; for many writers it came to define the international system itself. Globalization in its modern form could not have come about of course without the end of the cold war and the collapse of previously planned economies. Globalization, however, did not just define a more open world-economy: it described a more internationalized one where the **nation-state** more generally was fast being undermined by transnational movements of capital, and where every government—including those from former com-

munist and nationalist Third World countries—were compelled to play by a single set of economic rules set by an **International Monetary Fund**. These rules moreover were tough, advocating as they did productivity over social protection, the logic of profit over the needs of workers and peasants, and strict financial targets that often worked to the disadvantage of industry. There was little room for social concern in this brave new world of privatization, **deregulation**, and cut-throat competition.

Of course, the neo-liberal economic agenda was not specifically American. However, by the early 1990s it had become known, quite simply, as the 'Washington consensus', the obvious conclusion to be drawn that behind the drive towards globalization stood the power of the United States using its great leverage to make the world permanently safe for capitalism by ensuring that no country could either escape the system or buck it by challenging its logic. And there was little doubt about it: globalization did define the way in which states now operated. It would be too simple to say that international relations during the cold war was basically about military security, and that in the new era it was primarily concerned with economic survival. Nevertheless, there was definitely a much greater stress now laid on ensuring that your own national 'team' competed effectively in an increasingly harsh world where, to paraphrase the title of one book, major powers were compelled to go head to head in order to decide who would prevail in international markets. In a world where only the fit survived and the weak went under, there was no room for compassion. Nor was there much space for inefficiency. Indeed, one of the more interesting features of the new world was the increase in the bureaucratic weight of those government departments whose primary purpose was to help companies win markets abroad. Even national intelligence agencies found themselves under increasing pressure to define a new role for themselves, and while they continued to carry out their 'normal' assignments of specifying traditional threats to national security, some of them did start to take on new missions, one of which was to help their countries compete more effectively.

As the world-economy went global, politics in the main tended to shift to the centre and right. Indeed, the whole character of political discourse changed. The anti-capitalist Left in particular now had to rethink its position in a post-communist era, and those who managed to survive only did so largely because they abandoned previous beliefs and came to terms with new economic realities. Politics, as Fukuyama had anticipated, was fast becoming a debate about how to manage the market rather than thinking of ways of going beyond it. This in turn had a huge impact on the way people lived, thought, and entertained themselves. Even the heroes of popular literature became very different kinds of people. Thus whereas in the days of the superpower standoff the most respected individual was the brave warrior or the wily spy—witness here the cult of the soldier and the popularity of the Bond movies—now

the new men (and women) of distinction were the entrepreneurs and the new get-rich whizzkids of the computer world. The way people worked altered too as they adjusted to the new environment. Certainly, they had to work a good deal harder in these new Darwinian times, and realized they had to. After all, if their company failed to compete globally, then what followed was as inevitable as it was bound to be painful. Nothing it seemed was sacrosanct in the new international economy where globalization did not just seem to describe the way the world operated, but in a very important sense was deployed by governments to spur on people and firms to ever greater efforts.

Capitalism in its new post-communist manifestation thus assumed an increasingly intensive form. Naturally, the system did not meet all expectations. Nor was it without its own problems as the financial crisis of 1997 and 1998 showed only too vividly. Moreover, even those who were its beneficiaries—like the financier George Soros—were well aware that the new 'unfettered capitalism' was at heart a very unstable entity. That said, the critics (and there were many more radical than Soros) faced two fairly obvious problems. The first was that whatever its limits, it still managed to generate vast quantities of wealth; and the second was that hardly anybody could conceive of anything different, other than a more humane and possibly more

---

Box 6.5	**William Greider describes the 'manic logic of one world capitalism'**

'The logic of commerce and capital has overpowered the inertia of politics and launched an epoch of great social transformations. Settled facts of material life are being revised for rich and poor nations alike. Social understandings that were formed by the hard political struggles of the twentieth century are put in doubt. Old verities about the rank ordering of nations are revised and a new map of the world is gradually being drawn. These great changes sweep over the affairs of mere governments and destabilize the established political orders in both advanced and primitive societies. Everything seems new, and strange. Nothing seems certain.'

(William Greider, *One World Ready or Not* (Harmondsworth: Penguin, 1998), 11)

regulated form of the same. Herein was one of the more obvious consequences of what had happened back in 1989 in Eastern Europe when planning collapsed under the weight of its own contradictions. It was true: the new 'turbo-charged capitalism' was decidedly ruthless and manifestly unfair. But what was the alternative? As Susan Strange once observed in her normally pithy way, in the end the system was bound to go on—not because it worked perfectly or delivered justice—but because of the difficulty of finding, and building, something different.

Key points

- The existence of communism limited the geographic range of capitalism; the end of the cold war therefore led to globalization and the more rapid spread of market principles around the whole world.

- The short-hand term used to define global economic policy in the post-communist era was the 'Washington consensus', describing a strict set of economic criteria that all countries had to adhere to, whatever the welfare consequences.

- After the cold war, there was a detectable trend in the advanced capitalist countries towards a more economically driven foreign policy.

- Critics of globalization made a powerful case, but were unable to provide a serious economic alternative to the market.

The United States—from decline to hegemony

If a triumphant capitalism was one result of the end of the cold war, another was a resurgence of American self-confidence. This was a development that few had foretold in the late 1980s, when all the talk then had been about US decline and the inability of the United States to compete effectively in the world-economy. Significantly, one of the best-selling books of the late Reagan years, *The Rise and Fall of the Great Powers* (1988) by Paul Kennedy, warned US

leaders that the nation faced what all other empires had confronted before: an erosion in its global position that would over time turn the United States from a superpower into what Richard Rosecrance of the University of California had earlier called an 'ordinary country'. And though the USA still had many assets (probably more than any of its nearest rivals), ultimately it could not avoid its fate.

Things however turned out rather differently. Indeed, as events unfolded, it very much looked that that far from being an ordinary kind of country, the United States was in fact a place apart with some fairly extraordinary attributes. At least three events after 1989 made this idea seem credible. The first occurred in 1989 when the USA invaded Panama and arrested its dictator (a former ally), Manuel Noriega. The conclusion to be drawn was obvious: America would not hesitate to use force if required to do so. This lesson in statecraft was driven home more forcefully still a couple of years later following Iraq's decision to invade and occupy the oil-rich state of Kuwait. The United States responded with an even more massive display of force that quickly destroyed what many had hitherto regarded as one of the more significant armies in the world. The message was once again clear: the United States had the capacity and the will to destroy those who challenged world order. How much that order was likely to be US dominated became only too obvious when the USSR most unexpectedly disintegrated in late 1991. The implications of this event were more seismic still as the old world order of two superpowers collapsed, leaving the United States in a position of almost unrivalled dominance in an international system where its reach seemed unlimited and its freedom of manoeuvre unprecedented.

But America's recovery did not end there. After a shaky economic start to the decade (one that helped lose Bush senior the 1992 election) the situation began to turn round. In fact, not only did the USA recover from a brief bout of the blues, but then went on to boom—in part because George Bush's successor, Bill Clinton, set as one of his goals the regeneration of the American economic system. And regenerate it did. Indeed, between 1992 and 2000, the USA experienced one of the longest booms in its long economic history. During this period the value

Box 6.6	Whatever happened to American decline?

'At the inception of the twenty-first century, books on "the American century" proliferate monthly if not daily. We now have *The American Century Dictionary*, *The American Century Thesaurus*, and even *The American Century Cookbook*; perhaps the American baseball cap or cologne is not far behind . . . If this intoxicating optimism is commonplace today, it would have seemed demented just a few short years ago: back then scholars and popular pundits who are supposed to know the occult science of international affairs were full of dread about American decline and Japanese and German advance. The American century looked like an accountably short one.'

(Bruce Cumings, 'Still the American Century', *Review of International Studies*, 25 (December 1999), 271)

of American stocks doubled and then doubled again, unemployment dropped dramatically as tens of millions of new jobs were created, and the US deficit finally disappeared. Under Clinton, the United States also did well in international terms; and by the turn of the century was still the most significant economic actor in the world, accounting for just over 30 per cent of global economic output while being home to nearly half of the world's biggest 500 corporations. Certainly, by the time Clinton left the White House in 2000, few were speaking any longer of the United States being in economic decline.

All roads in the end however lead to hard power, and American policymakers remained as determined as ever—even in a world where the United States confronted no serious military threat—to retain a decisive margin of military superiority over friend and enemy alike. Even a self-defined Liberal like Clinton accepted the logic of supremacy: indeed, for someone as apparently inclined to multilateralism as he, he continued to believe in the virtues of a strong military. He even allowed military expenditure to rise again after 1997 in spite of the fact that the USA already possessed overwhelming preponderance, and by the beginning of the new century (and this long before 9/11) the United States—unsurprisingly—found itself in the quite unprecedented, but hardly unplanned, situation of spending as much on national security as

most of the rest of the world put together—if not more.

Nor did its dominance end there. As the decade wore on, it became obvious—even to those who did not want to admit as much—that without the United States the likelihood of achieving any degree of international security was limited. In fact, in many instances, it was clear that without the USA a number of dangerous conflicts might well have continued or even got worse. Thus it was American mediation between Pakistan and India in 1990 that defused tension between these two nuclear powers. American intervention was equally important in Northern Ireland. And it was more significant still in the case of Bosnia where decisive intervention in 1994—after European and UN dithering—finally brought that particular phase of the conflict in former Yugoslavia to an end. Of course, it could not pull rabbits out of the hat all of the time: and there were some conflicts (Israel–Palestine) to which there were perhaps no solution at all. But in a world where serious power, rather than diplomatic niceties, still counted, the United States remained what US Secretary of State Madelaine Albright once termed the 'indispensable nation'.

Naturally, with all these assets at its disposal, there was some concern that the United States would not use its formidable power wisely or well. Some even feared a new assertive and aggressive phase in American foreign policy. This, however, was only one worry: others were concerned not that the USA would be tempted to act in an imperial fashion, but rather that it would not act at all. Its initial decision not to get drawn into Yugoslavia, its blank refusal to do anything in Rwanda, and its more general fear of losing US lives in combat, were all good examples of America the reluctant being unwilling, or unable, to deploy its forces in countries where American public opinion would not support such action. This hardly made the United States isolationist. But it did point to a certain lack of grand strategy. The world may indeed have been a safer place because of American actions in the post-cold war era; and America itself might have looked increasingly like the new Rome. But in the absence of a specific and well-defined enemy, it had all the appearances of a superpower without a mission.

Key points

- In the late 1980s there were many writers like Paul Kennedy who argued that the United States was in decline.

- This once fashionable view virtually disappeared during the 1990s. A combination of factors including the early defeat of Iraq in 1991, the collapse of the USSR, the long economic boom in America, and high levels of military expenditure, continued to guarantee US hegemony.

- The major problem facing US foreign policy after the cold war was not isolationism but an inability in the absence of a defining enemy to formulate a clear grand strategy.

Russia—reform or decline?

While the United States prospered in a world increasingly organized along economic lines consonant with American interests and values, post-communist Russia appeared to lurch from one near-fatal crisis to another. This, however, was not how things were meant to be immediately after the break-up of the USSR and the election of the then popular (but now almost unknown) Boris Yeltsin. Indeed, according to the prevalent line of the time, Russia, with a good deal of political support from its new-found allies in the West—and even more direct financial assistance from the IMF—would emerge at some time in the future as a stable democratic entity with a functioning capitalist economy. The **transition** from authoritarian communism and planning would not be painless. Nor would it be without its ups and downs. But in time, day, Russia would become what the reformers liked to refer to as a 'normal country'.

That at least was the theory. The actual outcome was rather different, and in the years following the collapse of the USSR, Russian industrial production dropped by nearly 40 per cent, over 80 per cent of Russians experienced a reduction in their living standards, health care disintegrated, life expectancy fell along with the birth rate, and morale overall plummeted. Clearly, this had not been part of the original plan. To make matters worse, the only

people who seemed to benefit from what some critics increasingly came to refer to as Russian 'criminal capitalism' were the new super-rich, the overwhelming majority of whom were simply members of the old Soviet *nomenklatura* who had used their position of privilege under the previous order to enrich themselves under the new one. Nor, in the end, did Russia become a proper democracy either. Indeed, after having quite literally bought one election in 1996, Yeltsin was then replaced three years later not by a true democrat but by a former KGB officer—Vladimir Putin—a man with little interest in human rights, even less in democratic norms, and who came to power after having waged a brutal war of ethnic destruction in the republic of Chechnya.

At least two reasons have been suggested by analysts to explain the failure of Russia to make the transition. One, interestingly enough, concerns the kind of advice provided by the West itself. Russia, according to this thesis, had the misfortune to enter the world order in 1991 at a time when market triumphalism was in the ascendant. Irresponsible policies, which had little to do with Russian conditions and everything to do with what some felt was neo-liberal hubris, were foisted on the country. Predictably, the results of this irresponsible intervention were ruinous. Not so, argue the IMF and Russian reformers themselves. The real failure, they insist, was not the medicine but the failure to apply it properly. Thus what had worked in countries like Poland and the Czech Republic—so-called shock therapy—was not fully implemented in Russia. Russia thus drifted and suffered the consequences of having abandoned planning without then going for a proper market. As an IMF official is reported to have remarked, 'Russia had its chance and it blew it'.

Whichever of the different explanations we favour, the fact remains that the situation in Russia post-USSR was always going to be extremely challenging. With over seventy years' experience of communism, an imperial past, a vast military-industrial complex now with little purpose, and no democratic tradition worth speaking of, Russia was, in many ways, an improbable candidate for liberal democratic capitalism. Indeed, at a very early stage, it was evident to observers abroad that events within the country were not unfolding as planned. In December 1993, for instance, the USA woke up to

Box 6.7   Russia's ruin

'Only a few years ago, American policy-makers were confidently predicting that a regimen of privatization and market reform would in due course transform Russia into a stable and prosperous democracy . . . Today all that has passed away. Far from fulfilling their promise of a better life, the US-sponsored reforms of the 1990s have left many, if not most Russians worse off. For this state of affairs many Russians today blame the Western aid and advice they had received. Some indeed believe that the United States set out deliberately to destroy their economy.'

(Janine R. Wedel, 'Tainted Transactions', *The National Interest*, 59 (Spring 2000), 23)

discover that nearly one-quarter of all Russians had voted for an extreme nationalist called Vladimir Zhironovsky. Five years later, it then had to come to terms with a more material crisis when the Russian financial system collapsed, in the process wiping out the savings of many aspiring middle-class Russians. And less than two years on, it had to accept the decision of the Russian people when they actually showed their support for a leader in the form of Putin who had only a few years earlier been warning that America had a sinister plan of reducing Russia to the level of a Third World dependency.

Given these many problems the West had to be prepared to take the long view. The United States especially stressed that one simply had to keep faith, even if Russia at times did things of which it disapproved. Better a constructive relationship with an errant ally, it was reasoned, than a return to the days of the cold war. Even Putin's subsequent consolidation of power did not provoke much of a response. US Secretary of State, Madelaine Albright, was unambiguously clear: Putin, she insisted, would be judged by his actions in the here and now, not by his associations and words of the past. British Prime Minister Blair adopted exactly the same outlook. Putin, he agreed, was not perfect but he promised to bring order to Russia and to pursue a pro-Western foreign policy—reasons enough to give him a chance. Realism rather than Idealism thus shaped the Western response to Russia. The new Russia may not have been ideal; but because of its nuclear arsenal and its permanent membership of the UN Security Council (not to mention its later support for the USA in the war against terror), it remained a force to be reckoned with. Indeed, long before the war on terror, it was evident that Russia retained enough political and economic assets—especially oil—to continue to make it a significant factor in world politics. Meanwhile, the cynical could at least console themselves with the thought that even if reform had not managed to improve life for ordinary Russians (let alone a viable capitalist democracy), Russia at least was no longer a threat. As one observer later remarked, better perhaps a frail Russia than a capable Soviet Union.

Key points

- The attempt to build a popular functioning market economy in Russia thus far has been unsuccessful.

- However, there is too much at stake for the West to abandon Russia now—in spite of human rights abuses in Chechnya and the election of Vladimir Putin, a former KGB officer, to the office of President.

- Even if economic reform has been unable to restore Russia, because Russia is now so weak it does not represent a serious problem internationally.

China—Asian tiger: regional threat

When analysts talk of an end to the cold war taking place in 1989, they are normally referring to the course of events in Eastern and Central Europe. But in the same year in which communist authority collapsed on the European continent, it was being reaffirmed in China. The two processes were intimately connected. In fact, there is every likelihood that if Gorbachev had decided to crack down in Poland or East Germany, the Chinese Communist Party might have been persuaded to act with less severity itself. But seeing the destruction of state authority in the other socialist countries convinced leaders in Beijing that unless it took swift action, they too might go the same way. Out of such brutal calculations was born the massacre of Tiananmen Square in June 1989—a decisive, effective, and bloody action that sent a clear and simple message to those who cared to listen: that in spite (and perhaps even because) of economic reform, there would be no tinkering with the fundamentals of the Chinese political system.

The modern history of China begins therefore when a number of Western pundits like Fukuyama were talking rather too easily about history coming to an end. China thereafter remained what the American foreign policy guru, Zbigniew Brzezinski, rather aptly termed 'unfinished business', with strong residues of communist ideology articulated by a powerful party bureaucracy with an inefficient but still important state sector coexisting uneasily alongside a highly dynamic, open capitalist system driven forward by foreign investment. Many experts took the view that this combination of opposites—communism and commercialism—was simply not viable over the longer term. Others felt that the two could not only exist side by side, but that the success of one actually presupposed the other, and that China's great strides forward economically, which made it one of the most dynamic regions of the world capitalist system by the beginning of the twenty-first century, would have been inconceivable without a powerful state holding the ring. Either way, this peculiar form of 'market Stalinism' or what some have termed 'Leninism with capitalist characteristics', did not easily fit into simple pre-existing socio-economic categories.

Historically, the origins of this hybrid can be traced back to the 1970s and the twin decisions taken then to open up relations with the United States and integrate at least parts of China into the global economy—partly as a way of offsetting the power of the former USSR and partly as a means of renovating China's moribund economic system. At around the same time, China took the equally momentous decision to privatize agriculture, thus laying the foundation for a great upsurge of economic activity in the Chinese countryside, to be followed later by serious and equally important reform of the economic system as a whole. In purely material terms the results were striking, and within two decades—hardly anything in the life of China—the nation was being referred to by outsiders even as one of the great success stories of modern capitalism. Indeed, so successful did it become, that it was increasingly talked about as one of the miracles of the new world-economy. Its almost insatiable demand for raw materials, its vast monetary reserves, its demand for foreign investment, and its ability to produce cheap, well-produced consumer goods for the American and Japanese markets, were clearly making it a key player whose own prosperity and that of the international economy as a whole were becoming increasingly intertwined.

But economic change was not neutral, and as China boomed and its middle class grew, Chinese leaders started to redefine their relationship with the West in a far more positive way. Indeed, as its economy grew, so too did its weight within the international system. This not only caused quite a stir in the Asia-Pacific region but generated one of the great foreign policy debates in the United States. To many versed in the truths of Realism of course, a rising China was bound to be a problem. Indeed, during the first months of the Bush administration in 2001, many started to view China as the major rival of the USA. One commentator, Nicholas Kristoff of the *New York Times* even compared China to the Germany of old—resentful, ruthless and expansionary with a growing military capability to match its ambitions. This was not a view, though, that recommended itself to all, or even the majority, of senior Americans. China was hardly an ally. On the other

Box 6.8	China rising

'For those with an interest in thinking strategically about modern international affairs, there is no more important challenge than to understand the nature and implications of a rising China. As this reality dawns on the public policy community, the debate has often been simplistic. The exchange seems to be between those who assert that China will soon rise to be the world's largest economy and those who argue that it cannot sustain current levels of growth. Some suggest that China will muddle through difficulties, while others suggest it faces a major crisis of governance. It is argued by some that China can only be wrapped in the warm embrace of "engagement", whereas others stress the need to "contain" Chinese power. While the issues raised by these clusters of questions are undoubtedly important, the debates about their accuracy have rarely been sufficiently sophisticated.'

(Gerald Segal and David S. G. Goodman quoted in their (edited) volume, *China Rising* (London: Routledge, 1997), 1)

hand, it could hardly be viewed as an enemy. Its failure to veto UN actions against Iraq in 1991. Its lack of real opposition to NATO actions in Kosovo. Its peaceful reacquisition of Hong Kong. Its approval of the deployment of UN peacekeepers to East Timor. Its cautious diplomacy during the Asia financial crisis of 1998. And its implicit support for America's war on terror. All pointed to a nation seeking to put the cold war well and truly behind it.

But the great debate about China, was, in effect, part of a much deeper discussion; and this revolved around a simple but fundamental question: namely, what impact would rapid market change and global economic integration have upon the functioning of political systems in general and repressive polities in particular? Inevitably, the supporters of capitalism saw only positive political outcomes, arguing with some justification that once the market genie had been let out of the bottle there could be no putting it back in again. Others were always more sceptical, feeling that this was little more than a fancy rationalization used by Western governments and their multinational allies to justify doing business with dictators and dictatorships like China. Only time would tell who was right. Meanwhile, out there in the 'real world', Western policymakers could see only economic opportunities; and if they did not take them, their competitors would. A vast China market comprising a billion consumers beckoned; new orders were there to be won and vast investments made as China continued in its headlong rush towards market modernity. And there was no time to lose. It was these very material considerations, rather than liberal concerns about free speech and human rights, that increasingly determined the West's attitude towards China in an era of geo-economics.

Key points

- China's rise in the 1990s has been on the basis of an economic system that is an almost unique blend of capitalism and communism.

- Policymakers in the United States in particular are more concerned about the great business opportunities in China than about political freedom.

- However, over time, many predict that market reform and China's integration in the global economy will lead to irreversible political change.

- Meanwhile, many in the Asia-Pacific region regard China as the number one threat.

Whatever happened to the Pacific century?

The modern image of an economically dynamic China driving the world capitalist system forward is indeed a most enthralling one. Yet only a few years ago, the Asian nation that was talked about most was not China but Japan. This image in turn was often wedded to a much larger idea about the Asia-Pacific region with Japan (more than China) at its heart redefining the character of international politics for many years to come. Indeed, it was most fashionable in the late 1980s to talk of a new Pacific century in the making, one that would not only bring unheard-of prosperity to this once troubled region, but over time challenge European and American pre-eminence. Japan in particular became the subject of much wild analysis as its economy boomed and its trade surpluses with the rest of the world grew. Hardly a day went by in fact when one 'expert' or another did not engage in some fairly fanciful observations about either the peculiar work habits of the Japanese, or the even more bizarre character of its protected economic system that threatened to out-produce its competitors and lay the foundation for a new Japanese hegemony in the twenty-first century. In this way Japan, the model Asian democracy of the cold war years, which had relinquished all claims to great power status, that had willingly subordinated itself to the United States, that had even had a clause inserted into its constitution preventing it from deploying Japanese troops abroad, which had quite consciously turned itself into a semi-sovereign state more interested in producing cars and tape decks than battleships and guns, was now portrayed as a potential threat. It must all have seemed quite galling.

The speed with which these various truths and half-truths, myths, and semi-educated speculations about Japan specifically, and the region generally,

Box 6.9   **The trouble with Asian tigers**

'Like revolution, financial mayhem is a major historical event. In the post-Cold War era, and particularly in East Asia, where geoeconomy has largely displaced geopolitics as the major agent of change.'

(François Godemont, *The Downsizing of Asia*
(London: Routledge, 1999), 1)

collapsed, is one of the great stories of the 1990s. But like many great events, when the bubble burst— initially in Japan itself and then later along the Pacific Rim as a whole—so preoccupied were most analysts with the idea of a new Pacific century, that when the fall came, all eyes were looking the other way. What followed must have seemed utterly bewildering. Certainly, hardly anybody of note (with a few exceptions) foresaw the financial crisis in Japan: fewer still the chain of events that unravelled after 2 July 1997, the day when Thailand's government gave up the struggle to defend the parity of its own currency, the baht, against the dollar. Within a few months the contagion had spread, and by the end of the year it was calculated that the wave of financial and monetary destruction had destroyed somewhere close to $700bn. of capital. To all intents and purposes, by the middle of 1997, the region's economy had more or less ground to a halt. This was not the first bust experienced by the booming Asia Pacific. Nor did it prove fatal. However, it was without doubt the biggest economic collapse in the area's turbulent history, one that undermined local business confidence and set off a chain reaction globally that for a time appeared to threaten the very survival of the international financial system as a whole. For a very brief moment the edifice of post-cold war global capitalism looked as if it was gazing over a very steep precipice.

The several post mortems held on the crash have not arrived at a settled consensus, and opinion has veered wildly between what Richard Higgot has called 'domesticist explanations' that stress cronyism, inadequate banking supervision, and lack of transparency, to 'internationalist' ones that point to excessive deregulation in global financial markets, the extent of economic integration in the modern world-economy where shocks in one country can

have an enormous and speedy impact in others, and the end of the cold war and the failure of the United States to take remedial action early enough to prop up an area no longer threatened by communism. No doubt that particular discussion will run and run. More important (and more measurable) though have been the consequences. One has been to shake old political norms to the core. In some countries this simply led to a change in government; in others to a questioning of the normal rules of the political game. It assumed its most acute form however in Indonesia—significantly the region's worst-hit economy—where the thirty-five-year-old military dictatorship finally went under in 1998. But this was not all. The crisis also undermined the glamour and attractiveness of the once highly esteemed Asian way to prosperity, and after 1997 one tended to hear far fewer lengthy perorations from local elites about the superiority of the Asian system and its accompanying set of authoritarian values. The crisis thus had the unintended outcome of strengthening the champions of the Anglo-Saxon liberal model with its greater stress on individualism, choice, and anarchic competition, while delivering what many saw as a fatal blow to the Asian model with its emphasis on community, tradition, hierarchy, and consensus.

Of course, a recovery of a kind did take place. South Korea came back after 2000. Malaysia too. Even Japan began to see its economic fortunes improve as one century gave way to another. Clearly, there was still a good deal of economic life left in the Asia Pacific. However, by the time the twenty-first century began to gather pace, it was evident that one very important thing had changed: the new driver in the region was not just (or even) Japan but China too.

Key points

- Until the second half of the 1990s the accepted wisdom was that the Asia Pacific had achieved economic take-off: many even predicted a new 'Pacific century'.

- The Asian economic crisis that began in 1997 has led to a massive shake-out and profound social and political consequences.

- The crisis also had a major impact on the stability of the world financial system.

- Since 2000 there has been economic recovery in the region; however, this is now being driven by China as much as by Japan.

Europe: integration, expansion, and paralysis

During the twentieth century **Europe** has been one of the great testing grounds for theories of international relations. Thus out of the carnage of the First World War was born that greatest of all expressions of Liberal faith in international institutions, the League of Nations. Created in a flush of post-war optimism, the League represented a laboratory on a large scale for what many—including E. H. Carr— later regarded as a deeply flawed utopian experiment in organized **collective security**. The collapse of the inter-war system followed in quick order by world war and cold war not only put paid to such schemes but also appeared to confirm one of the basic truths of Realism: that in the real world of opposing nation-states, the only thing standing between the European **state system** and the breakdown of order, was not fine words or legal documents condemning aggression—these after all had not stopped Italy, Germany, or Japan—but raw military power and the willingness to deploy this to deter expansion.

The rebirth of Western Europe after 1947 provided what many saw as a refutation of this hard-nosed view. The speedy **rapprochement** between France and Germany, and the creation of a zone of **democratic peace** were, it was now argued, powerful confirmation of the Liberal thesis that states were not fixed things bound to collide, but rather active entities able to negotiate a new set of cooperative relationships. **Liberalism** also worked economically and one of its most significant triumphs—it was suggested—was the creation of a zone of prosperity in the West that by 1989 had totally exposed the economic pretensions of Soviet-style communism in the East. In this way, the theory of Liberalism, when translated into practice, did more than military pressure, and possibly even more than the Atlantic alliance, in winning the cold war and so overcoming the division of Europe.

Far from settling the great debate between Realists and Liberals, the birth of a new Europe only seemed to provide new empirical evidence which the two sides could deploy in order to confirm their own particular claims of truth. There was very little give— and even less take—in the debate which ensued. Thus whereas Liberals emphasized the central importance of a non-military organization like the European Union in helping stabilize the continent after 1989, Realists pointed to NATO. Realists insisted that the disaster in former Yugoslavia—as Mearsheimer might have predicted—only confirmed their thesis that the end of the cold war would bring chaos in its wake. Liberals however emphasized the important ways in which institutions like the Council of Europe and the Organization for Security and Co-operation in Europe had helped establish new democratic norms, thus laying the foundation stone for better times ahead. And while Realists stressed that we had to prepare for the worst because the worst was always likely to happens, Liberals took an altogether more sanguine view, arguing that the history of the post-cold war decade (the former Yugoslavia aside) proved that Europe as a whole was bound for peace rather than war, further integration rather than economic conflict, and increased **cooperation** rather than hostility.

At least four important events shaped the course of European history during the first decade of the post-cold war period: German unification; European expansion and integration; the war in the former Yugoslavia; and the decision to expand NATO. Let us deal briefly with each.

German unification

German unification was neither welcomed by the other European powers, who worried about its impact on the peace, nor much looked forward to by many in West Germany who feared that the economic costs of unity were bound to outweigh the alleged political benefits. The first set of concerns proved groundless: the second did not. Indeed, if anything, people seriously underestimated the price that Germany as a whole would have to pay. The shock was especially sharp in the early 1990s as factory after factory closed down in the East, causing large-scale unemployment there and thrusting Western Germany into its deepest recession of the entire post-war period. True, by 1996, some of the gloom had lifted. However, it had not been dispelled, and as Germany entered the twenty-first century, the human costs and output losses associated with the economic collapse of the old command economy had left a profound mark that would take many years to overcome.

The short-term pain endured by Germany should not however obscure our understanding of the historical significance of unification: Germany, in the end, was one of the more obvious international 'winners' of the 1990s. It had not just become the largest country in Europe with new interests in the East. It was also transformed from having been a divided nation, effectively controlled by the two superpowers, into a more independent actor. Indeed, as the events in 2003 revealed only too graphically, the new Germany was even now prepared to stand up to the United States and oppose its desire to go to war with Iraq. This was of crucial significance with consequences that over time would be likely to have impact not just on Europe and Germany, but and the world as a whole.

Integration and expansion

If the birth of a new Germany was one of the most immediate consequences of 1989, another was an accelerated process of European integration combined with the equally significant expansion of the EU to the East. The various processes were closely connected. Thus if Germany was to remain stable inside Europe, a new security architecture was required, one part of which would be provided by a more powerful European Union. But Europe in turn had to comprise more than just the West: it had to open its doors to the East as well. The two missions went hand in hand. A more integrated Europe would, it was reasoned, be a more effective Europe: an enlarged Europe however would mean that the legacy of the cold war could finally be laid to rest. Indeed, it was significant that when enlargement finally took place in early 2004—thus taking the EU from 15 to 25 members—many in the former communist countries celebrated by declaring that Europe was now truly whole and free.

The end of the cold war therefore generated new and bolder demands for both a deeper and a wider conception of Europe, one that would possess not only its own currency (later launched as the Euro) but its own common foreign and security policy as well. This was perhaps a bridge too far: in fact, it soon became plain that while Europe was fast becoming a serious economic player in global terms (one with the largest GNP in the world) it remained a political pygmy unable to act in international politics. Europe thus presented a dual image. In trade and economics, and in dealing with the emerging economies of Central Europe, it gave every appearance of being a strong and dynamic force. But in the realms of security and diplomacy—what is sometimes talked of as 'high politics'—it was basically paralysed. The extent of this paralysis soon became obvious when the former Yugoslavia began to implode—our third area of concern.

The war in former Yugoslavia

The disintegration of Yugoslavia—the most ethnically diverse but politically most plural of the former communist countries of East-Central Europe—is a tragic story that many have interpreted as morally emblematic of our time with its parade of 'good guys' on one side (normally the Bosnian Muslims and sometimes the Croats) and its line-up of political ogres and monsters on the other, invariably the Serbs, the Yugoslav army, and key Serb leaders like Slobodan Milošović and Radovan Karadzić. The bare facts are by now well known. In September 1990 Slovenia declared its independence; this was followed a few months later by a Croatian decision to do the same. In February 1992, a referendum was then held to decide the fate of Bosnia-Hercegovina, and even though the Bosnian Serbs (comprising nearly 36 per cent of the electorate) boycotted the election, the Bosnian Muslims and Croats voted in favour of leaving Yugoslavia and forming a new state. Thereafter this most tragic of post-cold war European conflicts unfolded with great speed and intensity, exacting an appalling price in terms of lives lost, peoples displaced, and property destroyed. Finally, on 22 December 1995, a US-brokered peace deal was signed by the warring parties at Dayton. Unfortunately, this left unresolved a number of key issues, one being Kosovo which remained under Serbian rule. The status of Kosovo, however, was finally resolved in 1999 after an extensive air war conducted by NATO against Serbia, following which Kosovo was made into a formal protectorate under the protection of the West.

What happened in the former Yugoslavia has been variously interpreted as a war of civilizations between Muslim and Christians (a view favoured by those influenced by the work of Samuel Huntington), the inevitable consequence of Balkan history, the by-product of the collapse of communism and the end of the cold war in one particularly diverse part of Europe, and a monument to Western indifference and the West's refusal to intervene early enough or decisively enough to prevent ethnic cleansing in a part of the world where it did not have—or said it did not have—a vital interest. Certainly, the role of the West has come under intense scrutiny and neither the EU (which was early handed the responsibility of dealing with the situation) nor the UN came out of the whole thing with very much credit. The war also exposed deep divisions on the European side, with some countries being much more in favour of self-determination and the break-up of Yugoslavia than others. Germany in particular appeared to act with what some saw as almost total indifference towards the concerns of its allies when it insisted on recognizing Bosnian independence—a move which some felt at the time (and have argued since) only exacerbated the situation rather than calming it down.

The expansion of NATO

If the third Balkan War exposed the foreign policy pretensions of the Europeans, it also served to highlight the still central role played by the United States in the new European order. And if we are looking for continuities in history, then one of the most obvious is the extent to which Europe after the cold war remained every bit as dependent on the USA for its security as it had been before. By the same token, if one action speaks louder than a thousand words, then among the most critical actions in Europe after 1989 were the American decisions to expand NATO and to offer full membership to several former members of the Warsaw Pact including Poland, the Czech Republic, and Hungary—who joined in 1994—and the three Baltic republics, Bulgaria, and Romania, who joined ten year later. The supreme irony was that this had never been Washington's intention in the immediate aftermath of 1989. However, a combination of events—uncertainty in Russia, domestic pressure upon Clinton from his Republican opponents at home, and what the Americans saw as the abject failure of the Europeans to provide a European answer to a European problem in the former Yugoslavia—convinced the USA that it really had no alternative. Thus in 1994, the decision was taken in principle; and on 12 March 1999, Madelaine Albright formally welcomed NATO's new Central European members into the alliance. A critically important corner had been turned confirming what many had always wanted, some had not anticipated, and a few vehemently resented: a strong American presence in Europe. With or without a Soviet threat, the USA remained the number one power on the continent—by invitation.

Box 6.10   A new European security architecture?

'Twice this century, America sent its young men to Europe to fight and often die, for Europe's freedom. It is worth remembering that on neither occasion was communism or the Soviet Union the enemy. The demise of both will not result in a loss of common commitment since that predated the Cold War and will live on after it. The United States continues to need Europe as much as Europe needs the United States.'

(Malcolm Rifkind in *NATO Review*, 2 (March 1995), 8)

Key points

- Europe has been a major testing ground for Liberal and Realist international relations theories.

- The key political question facing Europe after 1989 was how to manage the process of German unification.

- The expansion and integration of the European economic space has not been accompanied by a parallel development of a Common Foreign and Security Policy.

- The collapse of Yugoslavia was a major test which the European Union failed to pass.

- The United States remains the key provider of security in Europe.

Still the North: still the South

Often the most significant facts about the international system are those sometimes least talked about by the discipline of international relations—at least that used to be the case during the cold war when most academics were almost completely fixated (and in some ways legitimately so) on the strategic dimensions of the superpower relationship and the impact which the conflict more generally was having upon the different regions of the world. The world, from this point of view, mattered not for its own sake, but in terms of the part it played in the larger drama involving the two principal actors, the United States and the USSR. Nowhere was this more true than in the 'Third World', a vague and loose term conceived in the 1950s which, if nothing else, did at least have the advantage from the point of view of the other two worlds (the democratic and capitalist, and the communist and planned) of putting the less developed countries in their rightful place at the end of the political and economic line.

Several factors have led some analysts at least to doubt the very utility of the term 'Third World'. The most obvious perhaps has been the collapse of what might generically be termed the Third World project of achieving independent economic development outside of the world market system. This retreat began in the early 1980s and continued thereafter as one country after another, from Mexico to India, decided to abandon the policies of economic **autarky** and adopt the type of market-led strategies most favoured in the West. Another reason for dispensing with the term was the end of the cold war itself. This not only undermined the cause of non-alignment, but rendered illogical the whole idea of a Third World—a concept that only made sense in an international system where there were two other poles and not just one. There was a third objection: that the term was far too broad, including countries as different as Botswana and Argentina, continents as diverse as Africa and Latin America, and regions as far apart economically and culturally as the oil-rich Middle East and the oil-dependent Asian sub-continent. Many analysts therefore (though not all) drew the not unreasonable conclusion that the concept ought to be abandoned altogether.

Getting rid of the concept however did not change the basic conditions under which the vast majority of the world's people continued to live in the 1990s; and while different commentators would identify very different reasons, it would involve denial on an unprecedented scale not to recognize the simple fact that the world still remains divided between a relatively rich 'North' within which the overwhelming bulk of the world's economic activity takes place, and a very poor 'South' where it does not. To this extent, the end of the cold war and the collapse of communism changed very little. Indeed, according to many critics it might have made it a good deal worse: first, by bringing the less-developed countries more completely under the control of the West and its various economic institutions; second, by leading to a reduction in foreign aid; and, finally, by making it increasingly difficult for some Third World states to exploit the superpower rivalry to their own advantage. The cold war may have produced much misery in a number of the more backward countries (think here of its impact in places like Angola, Mozambique, and Afghanistan). On the other hand, some were especially adept at manipulating the old East–West rivalry to their own advantage.

The triumph of capitalism therefore did not necessarily lead to an improvement in the lives of billions of people, a point made not just by radicals critical of the status quo, but also by those who insist that after the failure of planning, capitalism stands alone as the only feasible way rationally of organizing a modern economy. One such observer is the well-known Peruvian economist Hernando de Soto. Admired by many on the Right, and listened to by several governments (many of whom he advises) de

---

> **Box 6.11   Still the North–South divide**
>
> 'Today across the world, 1.3 billion people live on less than one dollar a day; 3 billion live on under two dollars a day; 3 billion have no access to clean water; 3 billion have no access to sanitation; 2 billion have no access to electricity. We talk of financial crises while in Jakarta, in Moscow, in sub-Saharan Africa, in the slums of India and in the barrios of Latin America, the human pain of poverty is all around us.'
>
> (James D. Wolfensohn of the World Bank, quoted in *The Reality of Aid 2000* (London: Earthscan, 2000), 10)

Soto has a blunt message—which is delivered in great style in his best-selling study, *The Mystery of Capital* published in 2001. 'The hour of capitalism's triumph', he has argued, is also 'its hour of crisis'. After ten years of reform, restructuring, and dancing to the 'economic tune' of the experts at the IMF, the masses are still waiting. Communism has been seen off, he accepts, and possibly for good. But its demise has not for the most part seen a viable capitalism kick-started in those parts of the world where it was not already well established. The 'new world order' thus looks very much like the old one with North America, Europe, and parts of Asia still in economic command. Everything has changed, or so it seems, but the fundamentals remain the same.

De Soto's bleak message that capitalism has triumphed in the 'West' but failed nearly everywhere else, is not one likely to be greeted with universal approval by those more optimistic than he. Their argument is not without some foundation. The West, they point out, has tried to improve things and in some instances succeeded. For example, it has linked economic reform and structural adjustment to what it has termed 'good governance'. In many places—the Middle East and southern Africa being good examples—the end of the cold war has also created a new context that has made possible the settlement of long-standing disputes. In other regions too, like Central America, it made some form of negotiated peace feasible. Vietnam and Cambodia have also come in from the cold. Moreover, there are winners in the 'South', as well as losers. India, for example, is now experiencing a boom of sorts, while

Mexico is rapidly altering as a result of foreign investment. It is not all doom and gloom.

But it is difficult to be too sanguine. In sub-Saharan Africa a number of states have simply imploded from within, while in others—such as Ethiopia and Eritrea—long-standing disputes inherited from the old world continue. Nor should we assume that these problems—amongst the many others facing the Third World—can be kept outside the citadels of power and wealth. Poor people frequently move, and invariably their point of destination is Western Europe or the United States. They also grow drugs which then find their way inside the walls of the West, often wreaking havoc on their inner cities. And if things become too desperate, they may even commit acts of 'terrorism'. Uneven development in the world-economy will always come back to haunt us, as some would say it finally did on 9/11.

Key points

- Many experts now question the use of the term 'Third World'.

- In the 1990s, poverty remains a reality for the majority of people.

- The end of the cold war has produced contradictory results in the less-developed countries.

- The political tensions caused by underdevelopment cannot be isolated from the advanced countries.

Conclusion: 9/11 and after

9/11 has been variously interpreted: as a symbolic yet savage protest by the dispossessed of the Third World; as a shrewd move undertaken by those who knew where to hit the hegemon most; and as the opening of a new Third World War between a radicalized Islam and the modern West. There can be little doubt though about its historical significance. Indeed, on that fateful and fatal day, many would argue that the post-cold war era effectively came to

an end. Naturally, this did not mean that everything changed at once, or in some cases at all. Thus China did not stop developing, Russia did not immediately decide to become a normal bourgeois democracy, and the distribution of wealth in the world did not alter because of what happened. But there was no getting away from its significance—or the fact that this was a disaster waiting to happen. In fact, any reasonable understanding of the post-cold

---

Box 6.12 **New wars**

'Today the international security environment is far more complex than it was in the Cold War era of bipolarity. The radically diminished threat of a world war has been replaced by the reality of intra-state conflicts which undermine stability security at the domestic and regional levels. A serious challenge for the international system is the increasing number of weak or even failed states and their inability to control developments on their own territory.'

(Adam Daniel Rotfeld in *SIPRI Yearbook 1998*
(Oxford: Oxford University Press, 1998), 1)

Box 6.13 **Jihad**

'First, for over seven years the United States has been occupying the lands of Islam in the holiest of places, the Arabian peninsula . . . Second, despite the great devastations inflicted on the Iraqi people by the crusader-Zionist alliance, the Americans are once again trying to repeat the horrific massacres; Third, if the Americans' aims behind these wars are religious and economic, the aim is also to serve the Jews' petty state and divert attention from its occupation of Jerusalem and murder of Moslems there.'

(Declaration of the World Islamic Front for Jihad against the
Jews and the Crusaders, 23 February 1998)

---

war period would suggest that 9/11, or at least something very much like it, was always a very strong possibility. After all, those who planned it had for a long time been vowing to attack the United States. Indeed, they had already bombed the World Trade Center once in 1993, and had made it clear that they would return. This they most certainly did on 11 September 2001 when two of the four planes carrying twenty Islamists (the overwhelming majority of them Saudis) slammed into the Twin Towers in lower Manhattan, killing over 3,000, people and probably changing the course of American history for ever.

9/11 therefore should not have come as a great surprise. The rise of radical Islam since the late 1970s, continued instability in the Middle East as a whole, America's close association with Israel, several other attacks associated with the name of bin Laden, and the blind eye the United States had turned for some time to dangerous developments in countries such as Pakistan, Saudi Arabia, and Afghanistan, all pointed to the kind of atrocity that brought terror home to the city streets of New York and Washington. What was more surprising perhaps was the way in which the United States now decided to interpret and respond to the attack itself; and within days a new 'war' was declared against international terrorism, one which according to President Bush at least would be just as dangerous, and just as long, as the cold war itself. The **war on terror** moreover would be fought at several different levels and in several different stage. The first phase would necessitate occupation of Afghanistan and the elimination of

the regime which had supported and given shelter to bin Laden in the first place. But that would be only one part of a wider, more assertive American strategy that would attack Islamic terrorism in not only one country but all those—including various states—which had in the past endorsed, terrorism in any shape or form, and continued to endorse it. A new era was in the making.

How new became only too evident in January 2002 when President Bush spoke pointedly about a so-called **axis of evil** states—Iran, Iraq, and North Korea—which stood outside of the community of nations supporting those who threatened the civilized world. Bush did not mince his words. These illegitimate entities with the potential to go nuclear (if they had not already done so) would no longer be tolerated. There could be no compromise. Countries had one of two choices: either to be with the United States or to be against it. There could be no middle way when it came to fighting terror and its presumed state backers—like Iraq. Indeed, no sooner had the USA dealt with Afghanistan (however incompletely) than it began to prepare for war against Iraq. Using the kind of high moral rhetoric that had not been heard since the early days of the cold war, Bush stressed—some would argue seriously exaggerated—the menace that was represented by Iraq, a monster of a regime he claimed that had not just repressed its own people (true) and backed the attack of 11 September (untrue) but accumulated a vast store of weapons of mass destruction that its leader could easily pass over to its terrorist surrogates. Evidently, in the central front against terror, of which Iraq was

Box 6.14   War on terror

'In defending the peace, we face a threat with no prece-dent. Enemies in the past needed great armies and great industrial capabilities to endanger the American people and our nation. The attacks of September 11th required a few hundred thousand dollars in the hands of a few dozen evil and deluded men. All of the chaos and suffering they caused came at much less than the cost of a single tank. The dangers have not passed. The government and the American people are on the watch, we are ready, because we know the terrorists have more money and more men and more plans.'

(George W. Bush, Speech at West Point, 1 June 2002)

now assumed to be a major part, everything it seemed—including a great deal of hyperbole—was permissible.

But it was not just American language that changed. As the United States started to flex its not inconsiderable military muscle it was evident that in this new and more dangerous era, its notion of enemies, its concept of its own interests, and its def-inition of strategy began to expand most dramatic-ally. In fact, within a year of the original attack, the USA not only found itself planning for yet another war, but also had carried through something of a strategic revolution that assumed that the best form of military defence was offence and that even when one was not immediately threatened by another state it was still legitimate to attack it. Indeed, when faced with ruthless people it was even justified to employ less than ethical or moral means in order to prevent them doing you damage. Radicals not surprisingly were appalled, Liberals outraged, while even hard-nosed Realists felt this was going too far. In fact, as the United States prepared for war against Iraq, some of the more articulate American critics, including Realists like John Mearsheimer, argued that far from making the world a safer place, the new tough line (which verged close to a new form of imperialism) could only make things a good deal worse. It was not even clear that it would do much to deal with the original problem of terrorism.

The international reaction to these trains of dra-matic events assumed many different forms. Many of course decided to throw in their lot with the United States, either because like Tony Blair they agreed with America's analysis or simply because they calculated that it was better to go along with the hegemon—especially an angry one—than to oppose it. Others, though, took a decidedly different kind of position. It was entirely legitimate, they argued, for the USA to wage war against those who had attacked it on 11 September. It was not, however, wise to see this a green light for the settlement of scores against all those who had upset or annoyed it in the past. There was a very real danger indeed of one of three very unfortunate things happening as a result: one would be to fall into bin Laden's trap and alien-ate Muslims around the world; another was that international opinion might turn against you; or, finally you ran the risk of doing what other Great Powers had done in the past when enraged and vengeful—get sucked into positions from which there was no easy retreat. Within a year the USA had successfully managed to do all three, especi-ally once its wholly successful war against Iraq turned into a bloody and increasingly unpopular occupation.

Thus as the war on terror unfolded the world as a whole began to look a far less stable place—to such a degree that some began to look back on the post-cold war years as a genuine moment of respite. Much of this change of course was caused by those who had attacked the United States on 11 September, and having committed one atrocity going on to commit a string of others, many of them against self-defined Muslim states such as Morocco, Indonesia, Saudi Arabia, Pakistan, and Turkey. Yet part of the problem it seemed was not just the nature of the menace but the character of the American response that to some at least—including those not unsympathetic to the USA—smacked of a new form of imperialism

Box 6.15   War with Iraq

'Iraq's behaviour shows that Saddam Hussein and his regime are concealing their efforts to produce weapons of mass destruction . . . [but] our concern is not just about these illicit weapons. It's the way these weapons can be connected to terrorism and terrorist organizations.'

(Secretary of State Colin Powell at the UN, 6 February 2003)

Indeed, one of the many consequences of the new war on terror was to generate an intense debate within and without the United States as to whether (or not) it was in the process of becoming (if it had not become already) a new kind of **empire**. Whether this was (or was not) an accurate way of thinking about American power remains an open question What is less in dispute is the degree to which this debate reflected an increasing concern about the direction in which US foreign policy was moving.

No one doubted the United States faced some tough opponents; nor that it had vast capabilities. But it remained to be seen whether this power would bring the USA the security it desired in an age of terror. As George W. Bush prepared for his second and more difficult campaign to win the White House in 2004, it certainly did not look like it. The post-cold war era had ended: tragically it very much seemed as if a new world disorder was going to replace it.

Box 6.16	**Key concepts**

Axis of evil: phrase deliberately used by George W. Bush in January 2001 to characterize Iran, North Korea, and Iraq.

Bipolarity: term employed by scholars of International Relations to describe the post-war order before the USSR fell apart in 1991, leaving the United States as the only sole superpower.

Clash of civilizations: controversial idea first used by Samuel Huntington in 1993 to describe the main cultural fault-line of international conflict in a world without communism; the notion has become more popular still since 9/11.

Cold war: extended worldwide conflict between communism and capitalism that is normally taken to have begun in 1947 and concluded in 1989 with the collapse of Soviet power in Europe.

Empire: a disputed concept that some have tried to apply to the United States to describe its international reach, huge capabilities, and vital global role of underwriting world order

End of History: famous phrase employed by Francis Fukuyama in summer 1989; this argued that one phase of history shaped by the antagonism between collectivism and individualism had (two hundred years after the French Revolution) come to an end leaving Liberalism triumphant.

Europe: a geographical expression that during the course of the cold war came to be identified with Western Europe, but since 1989 has once again come to be associated with the whole of the European continent.

Globalization: a catch-all phrase often used to describe single world-economy after the collapse of communism, though sometimes employed to define the growing integration of the international capitalist system in the post-war period.

Islam: a religious faith developed by the Prophet Muhammad which in the present period functions as a form of political identity for millions and the inspiration of what some at least now regard as the most important ideological opposition to Western modern values.

Market Stalinism: ironic coupling of two words sometimes used by critics to describe the system in China which combines an authoritarian political order with a highly dynamic capitalism.

11 September: referred to as '9/11', the day when four aircraft were hijacked by Islamic terrorists in the United States—two of which destroyed the World Trade Center in New York, one which partially destroyed the Pentagon, and a fourth which crash-landed in a field in Pennsylvania.

Third World: a notion that was first used in the late 1950s to define both the underdeveloped world and the political and economic project that would help overcome underdevelopment; employed less in the post-cold war era.

Transition: usually taken to mean the lengthy period between the end of communist planning in the Soviet bloc and the final emergence of a fully functioning democratic capitalist system.

Unipolarity: theoretical notion that takes as its working assumption the fact that the United States has now become and is likely to remain the only major power in the world.

US decline: an argument that gained currency in the United States in the 1970s, subsequently made popular by historian Paul Kennedy who in 1987 suggested that because of domestic economic problems and imperial overextension, America was entering a period of global retreat.

War on terror: announced after 9/11 to suggest an extensive and global struggle to combat and finally defeat international terrorism.

Key points

- 11 September 2001 marked the end of the post-cold war era.

- The two key factors shaping world politics since 9/11 have been Islamic terrorism and the United States-led war on terror.

- US foreign policy has come under sustained attack after it decided to go to war against Iraq.

- The world is now a less stable place than it was before 9/11.

 For further information and case studies on this subject, please visit the companion web site at www.oup.com/uk/booksites/politics.

QUESTIONS

1   Identify the most likely causes of the end of the cold war.

2   Which of the two theories—Liberal or Realist—do you find the most convincing when looking at the world after the cold war?

3   Has radical theory anything to tell us about the course of international history since 1989?

4   'Globalization means exploitative capitalism with American characteristics.' Would you agree?

5   Why did the United States experience such a renaissance after 1989?

6   Has reform failed in post-communist Russia: should the West be worried about it?

7   Should US policymakers aim to engage with China or contain it?

8   Whatever happened to the Pacific century?

9   Outline the main issues facing Europe after the cold war

10   Was 9/11 a disaster waiting to happen?

11   Has US foreign policy become imperialist since 9/11?

GUIDE TO FURTHER READING

Sifry, Micah L. and Cerf, Christopher (eds) (2003), *The Iraq Reader* (New York: Touchstone Books) is the best collection on the debate to go to war.

Woodward, Bob (2004), *Plan of Attack* (New York: Simon & Schuster) is the most detailed insider account of the Bush team's decision to go to war with Iraq.

Mann, James (2004), *Rise of the Vulcans: the History of Bush's War Cabinet* (New York: Viking Press) is indispensable background on how the Bush administration viewed the world at large after 2001.

Pillar, Paul R. (2001), *Terrorism and U.S. Foreign Policy* (Washington, DC: Brookings Institution Press) is a useful guide.

Ruthven, Malise (2002), *A Fury for God: The Islamist Attack On America* (London: Granta Books) is a fine analysis of the ideology of radical Islamism.

Cox, Michael, Booth, Ken and Dunne, Tim (eds) (1999), *The Interregnum: Controversies in World Politics, 1989–1999* (Cambridge: Cambridge University Press) is a wide-ranging survey of most of the key issues facing the world after 1989.

Cox, Michael, Ikenberry, G. John and Inoguchi, Takashi (eds) (2000), *American Democracy Promotion: Impulses, Strategies, and Impacts* (Oxford: Oxford University Press) looks at critically important and neglected facet of US foreign policy.

Booth, Ken (ed.) (1998), *Statecraft and Security: The Cold War and Beyond* (Cambridge: Cambridge University Press) brings together a number of well-known experts who reflect widely on the 'real world' before 9/11.

Booth, Ken and Dunne, Tim (eds) (2002), *Worlds in Collision* (Basingstoke: Palgrave) is a collection of short, well-written essays on the world after 9/11.

Chomsky, Noam (1994), *World Orders, Old and New* (London: Pluto Press) is a refreshing and iconoclastic look at the international system by the 'old man' of American radicalism.

Greider, William (1997), *One World Ready or Not: the Manic Logic of Global Capitalism* (Harmondsworth: Penguin Books) is a racy but highly readable account which argues there is a fundamental instability at the heart of the new global economy.

Kapstein, Ethan and Mastanduno, Michael (eds) (1999), *Unipolar Politics: Realism and State Strategies After the Cold War* (New York: Columbia University Press) is an empirically rooted attempt to show that the struggle for power between states did not stop when the cold war ended.

O'Meara, Patrick, Mehlinger, Howard D. and Krain, Matthew (eds) (2000), *Globalization and the Challenges of a New Century* (Bloomington: Indiana University Press) is a very useful collection of many well-known essays about global order and disorder.

Godement, François (1999), *The Downsizing of Asia* (London: Routledge) provides a lively and critical view of the Asian crash and its consequences.

Burstein, Daniel and de Keijzer, Arne (1998), *Big Dragon—The Future of China* (New York: Simon & Schuster), in spite of the title, is a relatively balanced account of China.

Kaldor, Mary (1999), *New and Old Wars: Organized Violence in a Global Era* (Cambridge: Polity Press) explains why millions have died in 'small' wars since the end of the cold war.

WEB LINKS

http://usinfo.state.gov US Department of State international information.

http://csis.org/ Centre for Strategic and International Studies.

http://fas.org/man/crs US Congressional Research Report and Military Analysis Network

Part Two

THEORIES OF
WORLD POLITICS

In this part of the book we introduce you to the main theories that try to explain world politics. We have two main aims: **first**, we want you to be able to grasp the main themes of the theories that have been most influential in explaining world politics. To this end, we have included in this section chapters on the three main theoretical perspectives on world politics: Realism, Liberalism, and Marxism. Of these, Realism has been by far the most influential theory but, as we mentioned in the Introduction, it has also attracted fierce criticism for being an ideology masquerading as an objective theory. Most of the history of International Relations theory has seen a dispute between Realism and its two main rivals, with the debate between Realism and Liberalism being the most long-standing and well-developed. For this reason we have a chapter on contemporary mainstream debates between neo-realists and neo-liberals. We then want to introduce you to other recent theoretical work in world politics, thereby giving you an up-to-date survey of the Reflectivist and Constructivist theoretical literature. Given the growing importance of Social Constructivism we have decided to add a new chapter on this subject in this edition. So, by the end of this part we hope that you will be able to understand the main themes of the various theories and be able to assess their comparative strengths and weaknesses. Our **second** aim is to give you the overview of theory that you need to be able to assess the significance of globalization for our understanding of world politics. After reading these chapters on theory we hope that you will be in a better position to see how these theories of world politics might interpret globalization in different ways. We feel that you should then be able to decide for yourself both which interpretation you find most convincing and what kind of evidence you might find in the remaining sections of the book to enable you to be able to work out just how much globalization marks a new distinct stage in world politics, requiring new theories, or whether it is simply a fad or fashion which might alter the surface of world politics but not its main underlying features.

Realism

TIM DUNNE • BRIAN C. SCHMIDT

READER'S GUIDE

Realism is the dominant theory of International Relations. Why? Because it provides the most powerful explanation for the state of war which is the regular condition of life in the international system. This is the bold claim made by Realists in defence of their tradition, claim which will be critically examined in this chapter. The second section will ask whether there is one Realism or a variety of Realisms. The argument presented below suggests that despite important differences, particularly between classical and structural Realism, it is possible to identify a shared core set of assumptions and ideas. Section three outlines these common elements which we identify as self-help, statism, and survival. In the final section, we return to the question of how far Realism is relevant for explaining or understanding the globalization of world politics. Although there are many voices claiming that a new set of actors and forces are collectively challenging the Westphalian sovereign state system, Realists are generally sceptical of these claims, arguing that the same basic patterns that have shaped international politics in the past remain just as relevant today.

Introduction: the timeless wisdom of Realism

The story of Realism most often begins with a mythical tale of the idealist or utopian writers of the inter-war period (1919–39). Writing in the aftermath of the First World War, the 'idealists', a term that realist writers have retrospectively imposed on the inter-war scholars, focused much of their attention on understanding the cause of war so as to find a remedy for its existence. Yet according to the realists, the inter-war scholars' approach was flawed in a number of respects. They, for example, ignored the role of power, overestimated the degree to which human beings were rational, mistakenly believed that nation-states shared a set of common interests, and were overly passionate in their belief in the capacity of humankind to overcome the scourge of war. The outbreak of the Second World War in 1939 confirmed, for the realists at least, the inadequacies of the inter-war idealists' approach to studying international politics.

A new approach, one based on the timeless insights of Realism, rose from the ashes of the discredited idealist approach.[1] Histories of the academic field of International Relations describe a Great Debate that took place in the late 1930s and early 1940s between the inter-war idealists and a new generation of realist writers, which included E. H. Carr, Hans J. Morgenthau, Reinhold Niebuhr, Frederick Schuman, George Kennan, and others, who all emphasized the ubiquity of power and the competitive nature of politics among nations. The standard account of the Great Debate is that the realists emerged victorious, and the rest of the International Relations story is, in many respects, a footnote to Realism.[2] It is important to note, however, that at its inception, there was a need for Realism to define itself against an alleged 'idealist' position. From 1939 to the present, leading theorists and policymakers have continued to view the world through realist lenses. The prescriptions it offered were particularly well suited to the United States' rise to become the global hegemon (or leader). Realism taught American leaders to focus on interests rather than ideology, to seek peace through strength, and to recognize that Great Powers can coexist even if they have

antithetical values and beliefs. The fact that Realism offers something of a 'manual' for maximizing the interests of the **state** in a hostile environment explains in part why it remains 'the central tradition in the study of world politics' (Keohane 1989a: 36). This also helps to explain why alternative perspectives (see Ch.12) must of necessity engage with, and attempt to go beyond, Realism.

The theory of Realism that became dominant after the Second World War is often claimed to rest on an older, classical tradition of thought. The very idea of the timeless wisdom of Realism suggests that modern versions of realism have a long history. Indeed, many contemporary realist writers often claim to be part of an ancient tradition of thought that includes such illustrious figures as Thucydides (c.460–406 BC), Niccolo Machiavelli (1469–1527), Thomas Hobbes (1588–1679), and Jean-Jacques Rousseau (1712–78). The insights that these realists offered on the way in which state leaders should conduct themselves in the realm of international politics are often grouped under the doctrine of *raison d'état*, or **reason of state** Together, writers associated with *raison d'état* are seen as providing a set of maxims to leaders on how to conduct their foreign affairs so as to ensure the **security** of the state. Many successful leaders of the nineteenth and twentieth centuries have claimed to follow the timeless **principles** of classical realism.

According to the historian Friedrich Meinecke, '*Raison d'état* is the fundamental principle of international conduct, the State's First Law of Motion. It tells the statesman what he must do to preserve the health and strength of the State' (Meinecke 1957: 1). Most importantly, the state, which is identified as the key actor in international politics, must pursue power, and it is the duty of the statesperson to calculate rationally the most appropriate steps that should be taken so as to perpetuate the life of the state in a hostile and threatening environment. For realists of all stripes, the survival of the state can never be guaranteed, because the use of force culminating in war is a legitimate instrument of statecraft. As we will see, the assumption that the state is the principal actor coupled with the view that the environment which states inhabit is a perilous place help to define the essential core of Realism. There is, however, one issue in particular that theorists associated with *raison d'état*, and classical realism more generally, were concerned with; that is, the role, if any, that morals and ethics occupy in international politics.

Realists are sceptical of the idea that universal moral principles exist and, therefore, warn state leaders against sacrificing their own self-interests in order to adhere to some indeterminate notion of 'ethical' conduct. Moreover, realists argue that the need for survival requires state leaders to distance themselves from traditional morality which attaches a positive value to caution, piety, and the greater good of humankind as a whole. Machiavelli argued that these principles were positively harmful if adhered to by state leaders. It was imperative that state leaders learned a different kind of morality which accorded not to traditional Christian virtues but to political necessity and prudence. Proponents of *raison d'état* often speak of a dual moral standard: one moral standard for individual citizens living inside the state and a different standard for the state in its external relations with other states. Justification for the two moral standards stems from the fact that the condition of international politics often make it necessary for state leaders to act in a manner (for example, cheating, lying, killing) that would be entirely unacceptable for the individual. But before we reach the conclusion that Realism is completely immoral, it is important to add that proponents of *raison d'état* argue that the state itself represents a moral force, for it is the existence of the state that creates the possibility for an ethical political community to exist domestically. Preserving the life of the state and the ethical community it envelops becomes a moral duty of the statesperson. Thus it is not the case that realists are unethical, rather they find that sometimes 'it is kind to be cruel'.[3]

Although the advanced student might be able to detect some subtle differences, it is fair to say that there is a significant degree of continuity between older realists and modern variants. Indeed, the three core elements that we identify with Realism—statism, survival, and self-help—are present in the work of a classical realist such as Thucydides and structural Realists such as Kenneth Waltz. We argue that these 'three Ss' constitute the corners of the realist triangle. While we will expand on the meaning of these 'three Ss' later in the chapter, it is important to be clear at the outset what these terms signify.

Realism identifies the group as the fundamental unit of political analysis. During earlier times, such as when Thucydides and Machiavelli were writing, the basic unit was the *polis* or city-state, but since the Treaty of Westphalia (1648) realists consider the sovereign state as the principal actor in international politics. This is often referred to as the state-centric assumption of Realism. Statism is the term given to the idea of the state as the legitimate representative of the collective will of the people. The legitimacy of the state is what enables it to exercise authority internally as manifest, for example, in the making and enforcement of law. Yet outside the boundaries of the state, realists argue that a condition of anarchy exists. By anarchy what is most often meant is that international politics takes place in an arena that has no overarching central authority above the individual collection of sovereign states. Thus rather than necessarily denoting complete chaos and lawlessness, the concept of anarchy is used by realists to emphasize the point that the international realm is distinguished by the lack of a central authority. As we will see, realists draw a variety of conclusions about the effect that anarchy has on shaping the basic character of international politics.

Following from this, realists draw a sharp distinction between domestic and international politics. Thus while Hans J. Morgenthau argues that 'international politics, like all politics, is a struggle for power', he goes to great lengths to demonstrate the qualitatively different result this struggle has on international politics as compared to domestic politics (Morgenthau [1948] 1955: 25). One major factor that realists argue sets international politics apart from domestic politics is that while the latter is able to constrain and channel the power-seeking ambitions of individuals in a less violent direction (for example, the pursuit of wealth), the former is much less able to do so. For realists, it is self-evident that the incidence of violence is greater at the international than the domestic level. A prominent explanation that realists provide for this difference in behaviour relates to the different organizational structure of domestic and international politics. Realists argue that the basic structure of international politics is one of anarchy in that each of the independent sovereign states consider themselves to be their own highest authority and do not recognize a higher power above them. Conversely, domestic politics is often described as a hierarchical structure in which different political actors stand in various relations of super- and subordination.

It is largely on the basis of how realists depict the international environment that they conclude that the first priority for state leaders is to ensure the survival of their state. Under anarchy, the survival of the state cannot be guaranteed. Realists correctly assume that all states wish to perpetuate their existence. Looking back at history, however, realists note that the actions of some states resulted in other states losing their existence (for example, Poland has experienced this fate four times in the past three centuries). This is partly explained in light of the power differentials of states. Intuitively, states with more power stand a better chance of surviving than states with less power. Power is crucial to the realist lexicon and traditionally has been defined narrowly in military strategic terms. It is the ability to get what you want either through the threat or use of force. Yet irrespective of how much power a state may possess, the core national interest of all states must be survival. While states obviously have various interests, such as economic, environmental, and humanitarian, if their existence was to be jeopardized, then these other interests would not stand a chance of ever being realized. Like the pursuit of power, the promotion of the national interest is an iron law of necessity.

Self-help is the principle of action in an anarchical system where there is no global government. According to Realism, each state actor is responsible for ensuring their own well-being and survival. Realists do not believe it is prudent for a state to entrust its safety and survival to another actor or international institution such as the League of Nations or the United Nations. States, in short, should not depend on other states or institutions to ensure their own security. Unlike in domestic politics, there is no emergency number that states can dial when they are in mortal danger.

You may at this point be asking what options are available to states to ensure their own security. Consistent with the principle of self-help, if a state feels threatened it should seek to augment its own power capabilities by engaging, for example, in a military arms build-up. Yet this may prove to be insufficient for a number of smaller states that feel threatened by a much larger state. This brings us to one of the crucial mechanisms that realists throughout the ages have considered to be essential to preserving the liberty of states—the balance of power. Although various meanings have been attributed to the concept of the balance of power, the most common definition holds that if the survival of a state or a number of weaker states is threatened by a hegemonic state or coalition of stronger states, they should join forces, establish a formal alliance, and seek to preserve their own independence by checking the power of the opposing side. The mechanism of the balance of power seeks to ensure an equilibrium of power in which case no one state or coalition of states is in a position to dominate all the others. The cold war competition between the East and West, as institutionalized through the formal alliance system of the Warsaw Pact and the North Atlantic Treaty Organization (NATO), provides a prominent example of the balance of power mechanism in action.

The peaceful conclusion of the cold war caught many realists off guard. Given that realists claim a scientific basis to their causal account of the world, it is not surprising that their inability to foresee the dynamics that led to the end of the bipolar cold war system sparked the publication of several powerful critiques of realist theory. Various scholars emphasized the importance of individuals and the role of ideational factors in changing the behaviour of the Soviet Union. If realism was in trouble explaining the dynamics of the inter-state system, it was in even deeper water in providing a persuasive account of new developments such as regional integration, humanitarian intervention, and the emergence of a security community in Western Europe. In addition, proponents of globalization argued that realism's privileged actor, the state, was in decline relative to non-state actors such as transnational corporations and powerful regional institutions. The cumulative weight of these criticisms led many to question the analytical and moral adequacy of realist thought.

By way of a response to the critics, it is worth reminding them that the death-knell of Realism has been sounded a number of times already, by the scientific approach in the 1960s and transnationalism in the 1970s, only to see the resurgence of a robust form of structural realism in the 1980s (commonly termed 'neo-realism'). In this respect Realism shares with Conservatism (its ideological godfather) the recognition that a theory without the means to change is without the means of its own preservation. The question of Realism's resilience touches upon one of its central claims, namely, that it is the embodiment of laws of international politics which remain true across time (history) and space (geo-politics). This argument is made by a leading contemporary realist, Robert Gilpin, who cast doubt on 'whether or not twentieth-century students of international relations know anything that Thucydides and his fifth-century BC compatriots did not know about the behaviour of states' (1981: 227–8).

The question whether Realism does embody 'timeless truths' about politics will be returned to in the conclusion of the chapter. Could a scholar who understood the history of international conflict in the fifth century BC really apply the same conceptual tools to global politics at the beginning of the third millennium? In the following section we will begin to unravel Realism in order to reveal the way in which the tradition has evolved over the last twenty-five centuries. After considering the main tributaries which flow into the realist stream of thinking, the third section will establish a core set of realist principles to which all realists could subscribe.

Key points

- Realism has been the dominant theory of world politics since the beginning of academic International Relations.

- Outside of the academy, Realism has a much longer history. Scepticism about the capacity of human reason to deliver moral progress resonates through the work of classical political theorists such as Thucydides, Machiavelli, Hobbes, and Rousseau.

- The unifying theme around which all realist thinking converges is that states find themselves in the shadow of anarchy with the result that their security cannot be taken for granted. In such circumstances, it is rational for states to compete for power and security.

- At the end of the second millennium, Realism continues to attract academicians and inform policy-makers, although in the period since the end of the cold war we have seen heightened criticism of realist assumptions on the grounds that they are of declining relevance in a globalized world.

One Realism, or many?

The intellectual exercise of articulating a unified theory of Realism has been criticized by writers who are both sympathetic to and critical of the tradition (Doyle 1997; M. J. Smith 1986). The belief that there is not one realism, but many, leads logically to a delineation of different types of realism. In the last few years a number of alternative thematic classifications have been offered to differentiate realism into a variety of distinct categories. The most simple distinction is a form of periodization that commonly differentiates realism into three historical periods: classical realism (up to the twentieth century), which is frequently depicted as beginning with Thucydides' text on the Peloponnesian War between Athens and Sparta and incorporating the ideas of many of those included in the classic canon of Western political thought, modern realism (1939–79), which typically takes the so-called First Great Debate between the scholars of the inter-war period and a new wave of scholars who began to enter the field immediately before and after the Second World War as its point of departure; and structural or neo-realism (1979 onwards) that officially entered the picture following the publication of Kenneth Waltz's landmark text, *Theory of International Politics*. While these different periods

Table 7.1 A taxonomy of Realisms

Type of Realism	Key thinkers	Key texts	'Big idea'
Classical realism (Human nature)	Thucydides (c.460–406 BC)	The Peloponnesian War	International politics is driven by an endless struggle for power which has its roots in human nature. Justice, law, and society either have no place or are circumscribed.
	Machiavelli (1532)	The Prince	Political realism recognizes that principles are subordinated to policies; the ultimate skill of the state leader is to accept, and adapt to, the changing power-political configurations in world politics.
	Morgenthau (1948)	Politics Among Nations	Politics is governed by laws that are created by human nature. The mechanism we use to understand international politics is through the concept of interests, defined in terms of power.
Structural realism (International system)	Rousseau (c.1750)	The State of War	It is not human nature, but the anarchical system which fosters fear, jealousy, suspicion, and insecurity
	Waltz (1979)	Theory of International Politics	Anarchy leads to a logic of self-help in which states seek to maximize their security. The most stable distribution of power in the system is bipolarity.
	Mearsheimer (2001)	Tragedy of Great Power Politics	The anarchical, self-help system compels states to maximize their relative power position.
Contemporary responses to structural realism	Key thinkers		'Big idea'
Neoclassical realism	Schweller (1997), Zakaria (1998)		The systemic account of world politics provided by structural realism is incomplete. It needs to be supplemented with better accounts of unit-level variables such as how power is perceived, and how leadership is exercised.
Rational choice realism	Grieco (1993a), Krasner (1999)		Advocates of this position claim that institutions matter although the problem of relative gains means that they exert less of causal force than neo-liberals contend. Rational choice realists use advanced social science methodologies such as game theory in order to test realist hypotheses.

suggest a neat historical sequence, they are problematic in so far as they close down the important question about divergence within each historical phase. For example, not all classical, modern, or structural realists agree on the causes of war, on what the proper relationship between power and morality should be, or on whether states are primarily motivated by defensive or aggressive impulses. Rather than opt for the neat but intellectually unsatisfactory system of historical periodization, we outline below our own representation of realisms that makes important connections with existing categories deployed by other thinkers in the field. A summary of the varieties of Realism outlined below is contained in Table 7.1.

Classical Realism

The classical realist lineage begins with Thucydides' representation of power politics as a law of human behaviour. The drive for power and the will to dominate are held to be fundamental aspects of human nature. The behaviour of the state as a self-seeking egoist is understood to be merely a reflection of the characteristics of the people that comprise the state. It is human nature that explains why international politics is necessarily power politics. This reduction of Realism to a condition of human nature is one which frequently reappears in the leading works of the realist canon, most famously in the work of the high priest of post-war Realism, Hans J. Morgenthau. Classical realists argue that it is from the nature of man that the essential features of international politics, such as competition, fear, and war can be explained. Morgenthau notes, 'politics, like society in general, is governed by objective laws that have their roots in human nature' (Morgenthau [1948] 1955: 4). The important point for Morgenthau is, first, to recognize that these laws exist and second, to devise the most appropriate policies that are consistent with the basic fact that human beings are flawed creatures. For both Thucydides and Morgenthau, the essential continuity of the power-seeking behaviour of states is rooted in the biological drives of human beings.

Another distinguishing characteristic of classical realism is its adherents' belief in the primordial character of power and ethics. Classical realism is fundamentally about the struggle for belonging, a struggle that is often violent. Patriotic virtue is required in order for communities to survive in this historic battle between good and evil, a virtue that long predates the emergence of sovereignty-based notions of community in the mid-seventeenth century. Classical realists therefore differ from contemporary realists in the sense that they engaged with moral philosophy and sought to reconstruct an understanding of virtue in light of practice and historical circumstance. Two paradigmatic classical realists who wrestled with the degree to which state leaders could be guided by ethical considerations were Thucydides and Machiavelli.

Thucydides was the historian of the Peloponnesian War, a conflict between two Great Powers in the ancient Greek world, Athens and Sparta. Thucydides' work has been admired by subsequent generations of realists for the insights he raised about many of the perennial issues of international politics. Thucydides' explanation of the underlying cause of the war was 'the growth of Athenian power and the fear which this caused in Sparta' (1.23) is considered to be a classic example of the impact that the anarchical structure of international politics has on the behaviour of state actors. On this reading, Thucydides makes it clear that Sparta's national interest, like that of all states, was survival, and the changing distribution of power represented a direct threat to its existence. Sparta was, therefore, compelled by necessity to go to war in order to forestall being vanquished by Athens. Thucydides also makes it clear that Athens felt equally compelled to pursue power in order to preserve the empire it had acquired. The famous Athenian leader, Pericles, claimed to be acting on the basis of the most fundamental of human motivations: ambition, fear, and self-interest.

One of the significant episodes of the war between Athens and Sparta is known as the 'Melian dialogue' and represents a fascinating illustration of a number of key realist principles. Case study 1 (Box 7.1) reconstructs the dialogue between the Athenian leaders who arrived on the island of Melos to assert their right of conquest over the islanders, and the response this provoked. In short, what the Athenians are asserting over the Melians is the logic of power

| Box 7.1 | Case study 1: The Melian dialogue—Realism and the preparation for war |

ATHENIANS. Then we on our side will use no fine phrases saying, for example, that we have a right to our empire because we defeated the Persians. . . . And we ask you on your side not to imagine that you will influence us by saying that you, though a colony of Sparta, have not joined Sparta in the war, or that you have never done us any harm . . . you know as well as we do that, when these matters are discussed by practical people, **the standard of justice depends on the equality of power to compel and that in fact the strong do what they have the power to do and the weak accept what they have to accept.**

MELIANS. Then in our view (since you force us to leave justice out of account and to confine ourselves to self-interest) . . . you should not destroy a principle that is to the general good of all men—namely, that in the case of all who fall into danger there should be such a thing as fair play and just dealing.

ATHENIANS. We do not want any trouble in bringing you into our empire, and we want you to be spared for the good both of yourselves and of ourselves.

MELIANS. And how could it be just as good for us to be the slaves as for you to be the masters?

ATHENIANS. You, by giving in, would save yourselves from disaster; we by not destroying you, would be able to profit from you.

MELIANS. So you do not agree to our being neutral, friends instead of enemies, but allies of neither side?

ATHENIANS. No . . . if we were on friendly terms with you, our subjects would regard that as a sign of weakness in us, whereas your hatred is evidence of our power. . . . So that **by conquering you we shall increase not only the size but the security of our empire.**

MELIANS. But do you think there is no security for you in what we suggest? For here again, since you will not let us mention justice, but tell us to give in to your interests, we, too, must tell you what our interests are and, if yours and ours happen to coincide, we must try to persuade you of the fact. Is it not certain that you will make enemies of all states who are at present neutral, when they see what is happening here and naturally conclude that in course of time you will attack them too? . . . Yet we know that in war, fortune sometimes makes the odds more level.

ATHENIANS. Hope, that comforter in danger!

MELIANS. We trust that the gods will give us fortune as good as yours, because we are standing for what is right against what is wrong; and as for what we lack in power, we trust that it will be made up for by our alliance with the Spartans, who are bound, if for no other reason, then for honour's sake, and because we are their kinsman, to come to our help.

ATHENIANS. So far as the favour of the gods is concerned, we think we have as much right to that as you have. . . . Our opinion of the gods and our knowledge of men lead us to conclude that **it is a general and necessary law of nature to rule whatever one can.** This is not a law that we made ourselves, nor were we the first to act upon it when it was made. We found it already in existence, and we shall leave it to exist forever among those who come after us. We are merely acting in accordance with it, and we know that you or anybody else with the same power as ours would be acting in precisely the same way. And therefore, so far as the gods are concerned, we see no good reason why we should fear to be at a disadvantage. But with regard to your views about Sparta and your confidence that she, out of a sense of honour, will come to your aid, we must say that we congratulate you on your simplicity but do not envy you your folly . . . of all people we know the Spartans are most conspicuous for believing that what they like doing is honourable and what suits their interests is just.

MELIANS. But this is the very point where we can feel most sure. Their own self-interest will make them refuse to betray their own colonists, the Melians.

ATHENIANS. You seem to forget that if one follows one's self-interest one wants to be safe, whereas **the path of justice and honour involves one in danger.** . . . Do not be led astray by a false sense of honour. . . . You, if you take the right view, will be careful to avoid this. And, when you are allowed to choose between war and safety, you will not be so insensitively arrogant as to make the wrong choice. You will see that there is nothing disgraceful in giving way to the greatest city in Hellas when she is offering you such reasonable terms—alliance on a tribute-paying basis and liberty to enjoy your own property. **This is the safe rule—to stand up to one's equals, to behave with deference to one's superiors, and to treat one's inferiors with moderation.**

MELIANS. Our decision, Athenians, is just the same as it was at first. We are not prepared to give up in a short moment the liberty which our city has enjoyed from its foundation for 700 years.

ATHENIANS. You seem to us . . . to see uncertainties as realities, simply because you would like them to be so.

(This is an edited extract from Thucydides, *The Peloponnesian War*, trans. Rex Warner (London: Penguin Classics, 1954), 360–5)

politics. Because of their vastly superior military force, they are able to present a *fait accompli* to the Melians: either submit peacefully or be exterminated. The Melians for their part try and buck the logic of power politics, appealing in turn with arguments grounded in justice, God, and their allies the Spartans. As the dialogue makes clear, the Melians were forced to submit to the realist iron law that 'the strong do what they have the power to do and the weak accept what they have to accept'.

Later classical realists—notably Machiavelli and Morgenthau—would concur with Thucydides' suggestion that the logic of power politics has universal applicability. Instead of Athens and Melos, we could just as easily substitute the vulnerability of Machiavelli's beloved Florence to the expansionist policies of external Great Powers. In Morgenthau's era, there were many examples where the innate drive for more power and territory seemed to confirm the realist iron law: for example, Nazi Germany and Czechoslovakia in 1939, and the Soviet Union and Hungary in 1956. The seemingly endless cycle of war and conflict confirmed in the minds of twentieth-century classical realists the essentially aggressive impulses in human nature. For Morgenthau, 'the 'drives to live, to propagate, and to dominate are common to all men' (Morgenthau [1948] 1955: 30). How is a leader supposed to act in a world animated by such dark forces? The answer given by Machiavelli is that all obligations and treaties with other states must be disregarded if the security of the community is under threat. Moreover, imperial expansion is legitimate as it is a means of gaining greater security. Other classical realists, however, advocate a more temperate understanding of moral conduct. Mid-twentieth-century realists such as Butterfield, Carr, Morgenthau, and Wolfers believed that anarchy could be mitigated by wise leadership and the pursuit of the national interest in ways that are compatible with international order. Taking their lead from Thucydides, they recognized that acting purely on the basis of power and self-interest without any consideration of moral and ethical principles frequently results in self-defeating policies. After all, as Thucydides showed, Athens suffered an epic defeat while following the realist tenet of self-interest.

Structural realism

Structural realists concur that international politics is essentially a struggle for power but they do not endorse the classical realist assumption that this is a result of human nature. Instead, structural realists attribute security competition and inter-state conflict to the lack of an overarching authority above states and the distribution of power in the international system. This form of realism is most commonly associated with Waltz's *Theory of International Politics*. Waltz defined the structure of the international system in terms of three elements – organizing principle, differentiation of units, and distribution of capabilities. Waltz identifies two different organising principles: anarchy, which corresponds to the decentralized reality of international politics, and hierarchy, which is the basis of domestic order. He argues that the units of the international system are functionally similar sovereign states, hence unit-level variation is irrelevant in explaining international outcomes. It is the third tier, the distribution of capabilities across units, that is, according to Waltz, of fundamental importance to understanding crucial international outcomes. According to structural realists, the distribution of power in the international system is the key independent variable to understanding important international outcomes such as war and peace, alliance politics, and the balance of power. Structural realists are interested in providing a rank-ordering of states so as to be able to differentiate and count the number of Great Powers that exist at any particular point in time. The number of Great Powers, in turn, determines the structure of the international system. For example, during the cold war from 1945 to 1989 there were two Great Powers—the United States and the Soviet Union—that constituted the bipolar international system.

How does the international distribution of power impact on the behaviour of states, particularly their power-seeking behaviour? In the most general sense, Waltz argues that states, especially the Great Powers, have to be sensitive to the capabilities of other states. The possibility that any state may use force to advance its interests results in all states being worried about their survival. According to Waltz, power is a means to the end of security. In a significant passage, Waltz writes, 'because power is a possibly useful means, sensible statesmen try to have an appropriate amount of it'. He adds, 'in crucial situations, however, the ultimate concern of states is not for power but for security' (Waltz 1989: 40). In other words, rather than being power maximizers, states, according to Waltz, are security maximizers. Waltz argues that power maximization often proves to be dysfunctional because it triggers a counterbalancing coalition of states.

A different account of the power dynamics that operate in the anarchical system is provided by John Mearsheimer's theory of offensive realism, which is another variant of structural realism. While sharing many of the same basic assumptions with Waltz's structural realist theory, which is frequently termed defensive realism, Mearsheimer differs from Waltz when it comes to describing the behaviour of states. Most fundamentally, 'offensive realism parts company with defensive realism over the question of how much power states want' (Mearsheimer 2001: 21). According to Mearsheimer, the structure of the international system compels states to maximize their relative power position. Under anarchy, he agrees that self-help is the basic principle of action. Yet he also argues that not only do all states possess some offensive military capability, but there is a great deal of uncertainty about the intentions of other states. Consequently, Mearsheimer concludes that there are no satisfied or status quo states; rather all states are continuously searching for opportunities to gain power at the expense of other states. Contrary to Waltz, Mearsheimer argues that states recognize that the best path to peace is to accumulate more power than anyone else. Indeed the ideal position, although one that Mearsheimer argues is virtually impossible to achieve, is to be the global hegemon of the international system. Since he does not consider global hegemony to be feasible, primarily because of the difficulty of projecting power across large bodies of water, 'the world is condemned to perpetual great-power competition' (2001: 2).

Contemporary realist challenges to structural realism

While offensive realism does represent an important contribution to realism, some contemporary realists are sceptical of the notion that the international distribution of power alone can explain the behaviour of states. Since the end of the cold war a group of scholars have attempted to move beyond the parsimonious assumptions of structural realism and incorporated a number of additional factors located at the individual and domestic level into their explanation of international politics. While systemic factors are recognized to be an important influence on the behaviour of states, so are factors such as the perceptions of state leaders, state-society relationships, and the motivation of states. In attempting to build a bridge between structural and unit-level factors (which many classical realists emphasized), this group of scholars has been characterized by Gideon Rose (1998) as 'neoclassical realists'. According to Stephen Walt the causal logic of neoclassical realism 'places domestic politics as an intervening variable between the distribution of power and foreign policy behavior' (Walt 2002: 211).

One such important intervening variable is leaders themselves, namely how they perceive the international distribution of power. There is no objective, independent reading of the distribution of power: rather, what matters is how state leaders derive an understanding of the distribution of power. While structural realists assume that all states have a similar set of interests, neoclassical realists such as Randall Schweller argue that historically this is not the case. He argues that with respect to Waltz, the assumption that all states have an interest in security results in neo-realism exhibiting a profoundly status quo basis (Schweller 1996). Schweller returns to the writings of realists such as Carr, Morgenthau, and Kissinger to remind us of the key distinction that they made between status quo and revisionist states. Neoclassical realists would argue that the fact that Germany was a revisionist state in the 1930s and a status quo state since the end of the Second World War is of fundamental importance to understanding its role in the international system. Not only do states differ in terms of their interests, but they also differ in terms of their ability to extract and direct resources from the societies that they rule. Fareed Zakaria (1998) introduces the intervening variable of state strength into his theory of state-centered realism. State strength is defined as the ability of a state to mobilize and direct the resources at its disposal in the pursuit of particular interests. Neoclassical realists argue that different types of states possess different capacities to translate the various elements of national power into state power. Thus, contrary to Waltz, all states cannot be treated as 'like units'.

There is still another group of realist thinkers who accept the basic assumptions of Realism and yet are aware of the fact that the theory is incomplete. These figures—whom we call **rational choice** realists—recognize that anarchy does not prevent durable patterns of **cooperation** from occurring under certain specified conditions. The key difference between structural realists and rational choice realists turns on the role of international institutions. While Mearsheimer believes that institutions 'have mattered rather little' in international politics (Mearsheimer 1994/5: 49), rational choice realists see institutions playing an important role. Even for realists, institutions can fulfil several important functions such as binding weak states into the international order and providing a bargaining chip to encourage unstable states to give up dangerous military technologies for membership in a regime or institution. What is immediately apparent here is that rational choice realists are seeking to apply realism to all states rather than just the Great Powers.

Rational choice realists have much in common with **neo-liberals**. Both assume that units (whether individuals or states) are rational and that they seek to maximize their utility (see Ch.9). Both point to widespread evidence of cooperation across a range of economic and security issue-areas. Set against this overlap, key differences remain. Rational choice realists recognize that anarchy casts a permanent shadow over cooperative arrangements. Under anarchy, there is a continual fear of cheating, and a concern with uneven distributional gains. Even here,

rational choice realists argue that relative gains problems can potentially be overcome. Joe Grieco argues, for example, that side payments can be made to disadvantaged states in order to alter their incentives to cooperate (Grieco 1993*a*). While rational choice realists are not a cohesive group of scholars with a clearly identified position, it is apparent that their method-driven approach to Realism is opening up a significant research programme that engages with neo-liberalism without losing sight of enduring features of the realist tradition such as the primacy of state power and the problem of anarchy.

Given the varieties of Realism that exist, it is hardly surprising that the overall coherence of Realism as a tradition of inquiry into international relations has been questioned (Forde 1992: 62). The answer to the question of 'coherence' is, of course, contingent upon how strict the criteria are for judging the continuities which underpin a particular theory. Here it is perhaps a mistake to understand traditions as a single stream of thought, handed down in a neatly wrapped package from one generation of realists to another. Instead it is preferable to think of living traditions like Realism as the embodiment of both continuities and conflicts. For this reason it is important for students to read realists in their historical and political contexts, to try and understand the world they were speaking to and the forces they were reacting against.

While there is intellectual merit in dividing Realism into distinct categories, there are good pedagogical reasons for attempting to identify a shared core of propositions to which all realists subscribe (see section below, 'The essential Realism'). In the first instance, there is virtue in simplicity; complex ideas can be filtered, leaving a residual substance which may not conform to any one of the ingredients but is nevertheless a virtual representation of all of them. A second reason for attempting to arrive at a composite Realism is that, despite the different strands running through the tradition, there is a sense in which all realists share a common set of propositions. These will be considered in the third section of this chapter.

Key points

- There is a lack of consensus in the literature as to whether we can meaningfully speak about Realism as a single coherent theory.

- There are good reasons for delineating different types of Realism. The most important cleavage is between those who grant theoretical primacy to human nature and those who accentuate the importance of international anarchy and the distribution of power in the international system.

- Structural realism divides into two camps: those who argue that states are security maximizers (defensive realism) and those who argue that states are power maximizers (offensive realism).

- There are contemporary realists who dissent from both defensive and offensive variants of structural realism. Neoclassical realists bring individual and unit variation back into the theory while rational choice realists recognize the importance of international institutions.

The essential Realism

The previous paragraphs have argued that Realism is a theoretical broad church, embracing a variety of authors and texts. Despite the numerous denominations, we argue that all realists subscribe to the following 'three Ss': statism, survival, self-help.[4] Each of these elements is considered in more detail in the subsections below.

Statism

For realists, the state is the main actor and sovereignty is its distinguishing trait. The meaning of the sovereign state is inextricably bound up with the use of force. In terms of its internal dimension, to illustrate this relationship between violence and the state we need look no further than Max Weber's famous definition of the state as 'the monopoly of the legitimate use of physical force within a given territory'.[5] Within this territorial space, sovereignty means that the state has supreme authority to make and enforce laws. This is the basis of the unwritten contract between individuals and the state. According to Hobbes, for example, we trade our liberty in return for a guarantee of security. Once security has been established, civil society can begin. But in the absence of security, there can be no art, no culture, no society. The first move, then, for the realist is to organize power domestically. In this respect, 'every state is fundamentally a Machstaat' or power state

(Donelan 1990: 25). Only after power has been organized, can community begin.

Realist international theory appears to operate according to the assumption that, domestically, the problem of order and security is solved. The presence of a sovereign authority domestically implies that individuals need not worry about their own security, since this is provided for them in the form of a system of law, police protection, prisons, and other coercive measures. This allows members of the political community living 'inside' the state to pursue the good life. However, on the 'outside', in the relations among independent sovereign states, insecurities, dangers, and threats to the very existence of the state loom large. Realists largely explain this on the basis that the very condition for order and security—namely, the existence of a sovereign—is missing from the international realm. Yet it is worthwhile to evaluate critically the assumptions that are being made here. In the aftermath of 11 September 2001, is it really the case that you always feel secure inside your own state? Is the inside/outside distinction that realists draw between peace and security on the one hand, and violence and insecurity on the other hand defensible?

Realists claim that in anarchy, states compete with other states for security, markets, influence, and so on. And the nature of the competition is viewed in zero-sum terms; in other words, more for one actor means less for another. This competitive logic of power politics makes agreement on universal principles difficult, apart from the principle of non-intervention in the internal affairs of other sovereign states. This international legal aspect of sovereignty functions as a 'no trespass sign' placed on the border between states. But even this principle, designed to facilitate coexistence, is suspended by realists who argue that in practice non-intervention does not apply in relations between Great Powers and their 'near abroad'. As evidenced by the most recent behaviour of the United States in Afghanistan and Iraq, powerful states are able to overturn the non-intervention principle on the grounds of national security and international order.

Given that the first move of the state is to organize power domestically, and the second is to accumulate **power** internationally, it is self-evidently important to consider in more depth what realists mean by their ubiquitous fusion of politics with power. It is one thing to say that international politics is a struggle for power, but this merely begs the question of what realists mean by power. Morgenthau offers the following definition of power: 'man's control over the minds and actions of other men' ([1948] 1955: 26). There are two important points that realists make about the elusive concept of power. First, power is a relational concept; one does not exercise power in a vacuum, but in relation to another entity. Second, power is a relative concept; calculations need to be made not only about one's own power capabilities, but about the power that other state actors possess. Yet the task of accurately assessing the power of states is infinitely complex, and often is reduced to counting the number of troops, tanks, aircraft, and naval ships a country possesses in the belief that this translates to the ability to get other actors to do something they would not otherwise do.

There have been a number of criticisms of how realists define and measure power. Critics argue that Realism has been purchased at a discount precisely because its currency, power, has remained under-theorized and inconsistently used. Simply by asserting that states seek power provides no answer to crucial questions. Why do states struggle for power? Why is the accumulation of power, as Morgenthau argued, 'always the immediate aim'? Surely power is a means to an end rather than an end in itself? How much power do states want? Is there not a difference between the mere possession of power and the ability to change the behaviour of others?

Contemporary structural realists have in recent years sought to bring more conceptual clarity to bear on the meaning of power in the realist discourse. Waltz tries to overcome the problem by shifting the focus from power to capabilities. He suggests that capabilities can be ranked according to their strength in the following areas: 'size of population and territory, resource endowment, economic capability, military strength, political stability and competence' (1979: 131). The difficulty here is that resource strength does not always lead to military victory. For example, in the 1967 Six Day War between Israel and Egypt, Jordan, and Syria, the distribution of resources clearly favoured the Arab coalition and yet the supposedly weaker side annihilated its enemies' forces and seized their territory. The definition of power as capabilities is even less successful at explaining the relative economic success of Japan over China. A more sophisticated understanding of power would focus on the ability of a state to control or influence its environment in situations that are not necessarily conflictual.

An additional weakness with the realist treatment of power concerns its exclusive focus upon state power. For realists, states are the only actors that really 'count'. Transnational corporations, international organizations, and ideology-driven terrorist networks, such as Al Qaeda, rise and fall but the state is the one permanent feature in the landscape of modern global politics. The extent to which non-state actors bear the imprint of a statist identity is further endorsed by the fact that these actors have to make their way in an international system whose rules are made by states. There is no better example of this than the importance of American hegemonic power 'underwriting' the Bretton Woods trading system which has set the framework for international economic relations since 1945. The motivation for this was not altruism on the part of the USA but the rational calculation that it had more to gain from managing the international system than to lose by refusing to exercise leadership. Moreover, realists argue that an open, free-trade economic system, such as that which was established at Bretton Woods, depends on the existence of a hegemon who is willing to shoulder the financial burdens of managing the system. This realist argument, popularly known as hegemonic stability theory, maintains that international economic order is dependent on the existence of a dominant state.

Survival

The second principle which unites realists of all persuasions is the assertion that, in international politics, the pre-eminent goal is **survival**. Although there is an ambiguity in the works of the realists as to whether the accumulation of power is an end in itself, one would think that there is no dissenting from the argument that the ultimate concern of states is for security. Survival is held to be a precondition for attaining all other goals, whether these involve conquest or merely independence. According to Waltz, 'beyond the survival motive, the aims of states may be endlessly varied' (1979: 91). Yet as we mentioned in the previous section, a recent controversy among structural realists has arisen over the question of whether states are in fact principally security or power maximizers. Defensive realists such as Waltz and Joseph Grieco (1997) argue that states have security as their principal interest and therefore only seek the requisite amount of power to ensure their own survival. According to this view, states are profoundly defensive actors and will not seek to gain greater amounts of power if that means jeopardizing their own security. Offensive realists such as Mearsheimer argue that the ultimate goal of all states is to achieve a hegemonic position in the international system. States, according to this view, always desire more power and are willing, if the opportunity arises, to alter the existing distribution of power even if such an action may jeopardize their own security. In terms of survival, defensive realists hold that the existence of status quo powers lessens the competition for power while offensive realists argue that the competition is always keen because revisionist states and aspiring hegemons are always willing to take risks with the aim of improving their position in the international system.

Niccolo Machiavelli tried to make a 'science' out of his reflections on the art of survival. His short and engaging book, *The Prince*, was written with the explicit intention of codifying a set of maxims that will enable leaders to maintain their hold on power. Machiavelli derived these maxims from his experience as a diplomat and his studies of ancient history. One of the most important maxims was that princes or sovereigns must be prepared to break their promises if it is in their interests, and to conquer neighbouring states before the latter (inevitably) attack them.

In important respects, we find two related Machiavellian themes recurring in the writings of modern realists, both of which derive from the idea that the realm of international politics requires different moral and political rules from those which apply in domestic politics. The task of understanding the real nature of international politics, and the need to protect the state at all costs (even if this may mean the sacrifice of one's own citizens) places a heavy burden on the shoulders of state leaders. In the words of Henry Kissinger, the academic realist who became Secretary of State during the Nixon presidency, 'a nation's survival is its first and ultimate responsibility; it cannot be compromised or put to risk' (1977: 204). Their guide must be an **ethic of responsibility**: the careful weighing up of consequences; the realization that individual acts of an immoral kind might have to be taken for the greater good. By way of an example, think of the ways in which governments frequently suspend the legal and political rights of 'suspected terrorists' in view of the threat they pose to '**national security**'. An ethic of responsibility is frequently used as a justification for breaking the laws of war, as in the case of the United States' decision to drop nuclear bombs on Hiroshima and Nagasaki in 1945. The principal difficulty with the realist formulation of an 'ethics of responsibility' is that, while instructing leaders to consider the consequences of their actions, it does not provide a guide to how state leaders should weigh the consequences (M. J. Smith 1986: 51).

Not only does Realism provide an alternative moral code for state leaders, it suggests a wider objection to the whole enterprise of bringing ethics into international politics. Starting from the assumption that each state has its own particular values and beliefs, realists argue that the state is the supreme good and there can be no community beyond borders. Without a common culture, and common institutions, the idea of an 'international community', so frequently articulated by journalists, is seriously premature. E. H. Carr turned scepticism about moral universals into a 'critical weapon' which he wielded in order to reveal how the supposedly universal principles adumbrated by the Great Powers (such as the virtue of free trade or self-determination) were really 'unconscious reflexions of national policy' (Carr 1946: 87). This moral relativism has generated a substantial body of criticism, particularly from liberal theorists who endorse the notion of universal human rights.

Self-help

Kenneth Waltz's *Theory of International Politics* (1979) brought to the realist tradition a deeper understanding of the international system within which states coexist. Unlike many other realists, Waltz argued that international politics was not unique because of the regularity of war and conflict, since this was also familiar in domestic politics. The key difference between domestic and international orders lies in their **structure**. In the domestic polity, citizens do not have to defend themselves. In the international system, there is no higher authority to prevent and counter the use of force. Security can therefore only be realized through **self-help**. In an anarchic structure, 'self-help is necessarily the principle of action' (Waltz 1979: 111). But in the course of providing for one's own security, the state in question will automatically be fuelling the insecurity of other states.

The term given to this spiral of insecurity is the **security dilemma**.[6] According to Wheeler and Booth, security dilemmas exist 'when the military preparations of one state create an unresolvable uncertainty in the mind of another as to whether those preparations are for "defensive" purposes only (to enhance its security in an uncertain world) or whether they are for offensive purposes (to change the status quo to its advantage)' (1992: 30). This scenario suggests that one state's quest for security is often another state's source of insecurity. States find it very difficult to trust one another and often view the intentions of others in a negative light. Thus the military preparations of one state are likely to be matched by neighbouring states. The irony is that in the end, states often feel no more secure than before they undertook measures to enhance their own security.

In a self-help system, structural realists argue that the balance of power will emerge even in the absence of a conscious policy to maintain the balance (i.e. prudent statecraft). Waltz argues that balances of power result irrespective of the intentions of any particular state. In an anarchical system populated by states that seek to perpetuate themselves, alliances will be formed that seek to check and balance the power against threatening states. A fortuitous balance will be established through the interactions of states in the same way that an equilibrium is established between firms and consumers in a free economic market (according to classical liberal economic theory). Classical realists are more likely to emphasize the crucial role state leaders and diplomats play in maintaining the balance of power. In other words, the balance of power is not natural or inevitable, it must be constructed.

There is a lively debate among realists concerning the stability of the balance of power system. This is especially the case today in that many argue that the balance of power has been replaced by an unbalanced unipolar order. It is questionable whether other countries will actively attempt to balance against the United States as structural realism would predict. Whether it is the contrived balance of the Concert of Europe in the early nineteenth century, or the more fortuitous balance of the cold war, balances of power are broken—either through war or through peaceful change—and new balances emerge. What the perennial collapsing of the balance of power demonstrates is that states are at best able to mitigate the worst consequences of the security dilemma but are not able to escape it. The reason for this terminal condition is the absence of trust in international relations.

Historically realists have illustrated the lack of trust among states by reference to the parable of the 'stag hunt'. In *Man, the State and War*, Kenneth Waltz revisits Rousseau's parable:

Assume that five men who have acquired a rudimentary ability to speak and to understand each other happen to come together at a time when all of them suffer from hunger. The hunger of each will be satisfied by the fifth part of a stag, so they 'agree' to cooperate in a project to trap one. But also the hunger of any one of them will be satisfied by a hare, so, as a hare comes within reach, one of them grabs it. The defector obtains the means of satisfying his hunger but in doing so permits the stag to escape. His immediate interest prevails over consideration for his fellows. (1959: 167–8)

Waltz argues that the metaphor of the stag hunt provides not only a justification for the establishment of government, but a basis for understanding the problem of coordinating the interests of the individual versus the interests of the common good, and the pay-off between short-term interests and long-term interests. In the self-help system of international politics, the logic of self-interest mitigates against the provision of collective goods such as 'security' or 'free trade'. In the case of the latter, according to the theory of comparative advantage, all states would be wealthier in a world that allowed freedom of goods and services across borders. But individual states, or groups of states like the European Union, can increase their wealth by pursuing protectionist policies provided other states do not respond in kind. Of course the logical outcome is for the remaining states to become protectionist, international trade collapses, and a world recession reduces the wealth of each state.

The contemporary liberal solution to this problem of collective action in self-help systems is through the construction of **regimes** (see Ch.16). In other words, by establishing patterns of rules, **norms** and procedures, such as those embodied in the World Trade Organization (WTO), states are likely to be more confident that other states will comply with the rules and that defectors will be punished. Contemporary structural realists agree with liberals that regimes can facilitate cooperation under certain circumstances, although realists believe that in a self-help system cooperation is 'harder to achieve, more difficult to maintain, and more dependent on state power' (Grieco 1993b: 302). One reason for this is that structural realists argue that states are more concerned about relative than absolute gains. Thus the question is not whether all will be better off through cooperation, but rather who is likely to gain more than another. It is because of this concern with relative gains issues that realists argue that cooperation is difficult to achieve in a self-help system (see Ch.9).

Key points

- **Statism** is the centrepiece of Realism. This involves two claims. First, for the theorist, the state is the pre-eminent actor and all other actors in world politics are of lesser significance. Second, state 'sovereignty' signifies the existence of an independent political community, one which has juridical authority over its territory.

- **Key criticism**: statism is flawed both on empirical (challenges to state power from 'above' and 'below') and normative grounds (the inability of sovereign states to respond to collective global problems such as famine, environmental degradation, and human rights abuses).

- **Survival**: the primary objective of all states is survival; this is the supreme national interest to which all political leaders must adhere. All other goals such as economic prosperity are secondary (or 'low politics'). In order to preserve the security of their state, leaders must adopt an ethical code which judges actions according to the outcome rather than in terms of a judgement about whether the individual act is right or wrong. If there are any moral universals for political realists, these can only be concretized in particular communities.

- **Key criticism**: are there no limits to what actions a state can take in the name of necessity?

- **Self-help**: no other state or institution can be relied upon to guarantee your survival. In international politics, the structure of the system does not permit friendship, trust, and honour; only a perennial condition of uncertainty generated by the absence of a global government. Coexistence is achieved through the maintenance of the balance of power, and limited cooperation is possible in interactions where the realist state stands to gain more than other states.

- **Key criticism**: self-help is not an inevitable consequence of the absence of a world government; self-help is a logic that states have selected. Moreover, there are historical and contemporary examples where states have preferred collective security systems, or forms of regional security communities, in preference to self-help.

Conclusion: Realism and the globalization of world politics

The chapter opened by considering the often repeated realist claim that the pattern of international politics—wars interrupted for periods characterized by the preparation for future wars—have remained constant over the preceding twenty-five centuries. Realists have consistently held that the continuities in international relations are more important than the changes, but many find this to be increasingly problematic in the present age of globalization. In the concluding paragraphs below, we will briefly argue that the importance of Realism has not been diminished by the dynamics of globalization. We will do so by initially challenging the argument that economic **interdependence** has made war less likely. We then argue that the state continues to be the dominant unit in world politics. Finally, we claim that globalization should not be seen as a process that is disconnected from the distribution of power in the international system; in this sense, this current phase of globalization is fundamentally tied to Westernization and, to be even more specific, Americanization.

One variant of the globalization thesis, propounded by Francis Fukuyama, was that the end of the cold war represented the logical triumph of Liberalism. According to this thesis, Realism was increasingly seen to be an anachronism—a cold war way of thinking whose time had passed. The fact that structural realists in particular believed the bipolar system would continue well into the twenty-first century (Waltz 1979: 210), further contributed to the sense that realism was in decay. Critics of structural realism were right in pointing to its inability to anticipate the great upheavals of 1989–91. Yet many realists have provided explanations to account for the end of the cold war and do not regard it to be a major anomaly for realism. For a more detailed discussion of this controversy, see Case study 2 (Box 7.2).

Realism's strongest riposte lies not so much in challenging a liberal interpretation of the end of the cold war as in questioning the extent to which liberals' optimism in the spread of democracy, in the growth of free trade, and the general pacification of

---

Box 7.2   Case study 2: After the cold war—Realism's eternal return?

- Leading non-realist theorists have argued that the end of the cold war represents a failure for Realism in general, and neo- or structural realism in particular. Why? First, Waltz's 1979 book *Theory of International Politics* aligns structural realism with positivism, and the objective of all positivist theories is to predict. Despite this clear scientific objective, most realists were unwilling to specify when and how the international system was going to change, although Waltz believed it was likely to last well into the twenty-first century. This in itself suggests that Realism is a conservative theory, privileging an explanation of continuity over theorizing alternative future orders.

- While realists could claim that all branches of IR theory were caught out by the collapse of bipolarity at the end of the 1980s, there is a second and more weighty criticism of Realism, and that concerns its failure to *explain* the end of the cold war. The most common realist reply is to argue that a state in decline will try to reverse this process by curtailing its external commitments. In other words, the Soviet Union retreated, and in this sense, was defeated. The problem here is that, when they did make general predictions, contemporary realists expected the opposite.

- Again, we find that Realism lends itself to any number of possible consequences. Realism can lend itself to an expansionist foreign policy or to **appeasement**; to a retreat from empire or to expanding the frontier for security reasons. The ambiguity of this point is put very succinctly by John Vazquez (in his excellent critique of neo-realism and the end of the cold war): 'The great virtue of realism is that it can explain almost any foreign policy event. Its great defect is that it tends to do this after the fact, rather than before' (Vazquez 1998: 324).

---

world politics will have traction in the future. The crucial moment that brought the post-cold war era to an end was of course that fateful Tuesday morning in September 2001 when Al Qaeda terrorists flew hijacked planes into the World Trade Center and the

Pentagon. In the days immediately after the attack, President George W. Bush and a coalition of leaders from other states declared themselves to be fighting a war against **terrorism**. The two US-led wars against Afghanistan and Iraq, and the general climate of fear and insecurity caused by acts of terror, suggests a serious flaw in the liberal argument that war had become obsolescent.

Not surprisingly, leading realist thinkers have been quick to seize on the apparent convergence between our experience since 9/11 and the cycle of violence predicted by the theory. There were, however, some apparent contradictions in the realist account of the conflict. To begin with, the attacks on the US homeland were committed by a non-state actor. Had one of the significant norms of the Westphalian order become unhinged, namely, that war happens between sovereign states? Not only was the enemy a **global network** of Al Qaeda operatives, their goal was unconventional in that they did not seek to conquer territory but to challenge by force the ideological supremacy of the West. Set against these anomalies, the leading states in the system were quick to identify the network with certain **territorial states**—the Taliban Government of Afghanistan being the most immediate example, but also other pariah states which allegedly harboured terrorists. The United States was quick to link the overthrow of Saddam Hussein's Iraq with its global **war on terror** Moreover, rather than identifying the terrorists as transnational criminals and using police enforcement methods to counter their threat, the USA and its allies defined them as enemies of the state who had to be targeted and defeated using conventional military means.

For realists such as John Gray and Kenneth Waltz, 9/11 was not the beginning of a new era in world politics so much as a case of 'business as usual' (see their essays in Booth and Dunne 2002). What matters most, argues Waltz, are the continuities in the structural imbalance of power in the system and the distribution of nuclear weapons. Crises are to be expected because the logic of self-help generates periodic crises. Their analysis is a stark rejoinder to the more idealist defenders of globalization who see a new pacific **world order** emerging out of the ashes of the previous order. According to realists, 9/11 was never going to trigger a new era in governance: the

coalition of the willing that was forged in the immediate aftermath was, in Waltz's terms, 'a mile wide', but only 'an inch deep'. How prophetic those words have proven to be. The war against Iraq was executed by the USA with the UK being the only significant diplomatic and military ally. Not only did most states in the world oppose the war, leading American realists were public in their condemnation (see Box 7.3). Iraq, they argued, could have been

---

Box 7.3 | **Realism against wars: an unlikely alliance?**

Realists are often portrayed as being advocates of an aggressive foreign policy. Such a representation has always lacked credibility. E. H. Carr defended a negotiated settlement with Germany in the late 1930s on the grounds that the absorption of part of Czechoslovakia constituted an example of peaceful change. The Munich Agreement embodied, in his words, both elements of power (the military costs of defending Czechoslovakia) and morality (self-determination of the German-speaking peoples of that country). Hans Morgenthau opposed the US war against the North Vietnamese on the grounds that it defied a rational understanding of the national interest. He believed that US goals were not attainable 'without unreasonable moral liabilities and military risks' (M. J. Smith 1986: 158). The US-led war against Iraq in 2003 is the most recent example of Realism's counsel against the use of force. As the intense round of negotiations were under way in the Security Council, in the autumn of 2002, 34 leading realist thinkers co-signed an advertisement in the *New York Times* entitled 'War with Iraq is *Not* [emphasis in original] in America's National Interest'. John J. Mearsheimer and Stephen M. Walt developed this position further in early 2003. Why, they asked, had the USA given up on the policy of deterrence which proved to be successful during the cold war? They end the article with a bold, and some might say prescient, conclusion:

This war would be one the Bush administration chose to fight but did not have to fight. Even if such a war goes well and has positive long-range consequences, it will still have been unnecessary. And if it goes badly— whether in the form of high U.S. casualties, significant civilian deaths, a heightened risk of terrorism, or increased hatred of the United States in the Arab and Islamic world—then its architects will have even more to answer for. (Mearsheimer and Walt 2003: 59)

deterred from threatening both the security of the United States and its neighbours in the Middle East. Furthermore, a costly military intervention followed by a lengthy occupation in the Middle East has weakened the USA's ability to contain the rising threat from China. In short, the Bush presidency has not exercised power in a responsible and sensible manner.

The above is not to suggest that Realism is only useful as a guide to understanding seemingly enduring patterns of war and conflict. It will continue to serve as a critical weapon for revealing the interplay of national interests beneath the rhetoric of universalist sentiments. There is no better example of this in contemporary world politics than the foreign policy of the USA. The war on terror is frequently defended in universalist terms—in his State of the Union address in the run-up to the Iraq war, President George W. Bush described the gathering storm as a fight between the forces of good versus evil. Behind the rhetoric of universal values, the USA has used the war to justify a wide range of policy positions that strengthen its economic and military power while undermining various multilateral agreements on arms control, the environment, human rights, and trade.

Realists do not have to situate their theory of world politics in opposition to globalization *per se*, rather, what they offer is a very different conceptualization of the process. What is important about a realist view of globalization is the claim that rudimentary transnational governance is possible but at the same time it is entirely dependent on the distribution of power. Given the preponderance of power that the USA holds, it should not be a surprise that it has been one of the foremost proponents of globalization. The core values of globalization—liberalism, capitalism, and consumerism—are exactly those espoused by the United States. At a deeper cultural level, realists argue that modernity is not, as liberals hope, dissolving the boundaries of difference among the peoples of the world. From classical realists such as Rousseau to structural realists such as Waltz, protagonists have argued that **interdependence** is as likely to breed 'mutual vulnerability' as peace and prosperity. And while questioning the extent to which the world has become any more interdependent in relative terms, realists insist that the state is not going to be eclipsed by global forces operating either below or above the nation-state. Nationalism, realists have continuously reminded us, remains a potent force in world politics.

There are good reasons for thinking that the twenty-first century will be a realist century. Despite efforts of federalists to rekindle the idealist flame, Europe continues to be as divided by different national interests as it is united by a common good. As Jacques Chirac put it in 2000, a 'united Europe of states' was much more likely than a 'United States of Europe'. Outside of Europe and North America, many of the assumptions which underpinned the post-war international order, particularly those associated with human rights, are increasingly being seen as nothing more than a Western idea backed by economic dollars and military 'divisions'. If China continues its rate of economic growth, it will be more economically powerful than the USA by 2020 (Mearsheimer 1991: 398). By then, realism leads us to predict, Western norms of individual rights and responsibilities will be under threat. Rather than transforming global politics in its own image, as Liberalism has sought to do in the twentieth century, the West may need to become more realist in order for its traditions and values to survive the twenty-first.

For further information and case studies on this subject, please visit the companion web site at www.oup.com/uk/booksites/politics.

Box 7.4   Key concepts in realist thought

Anarchy: does not imply chaos, but the absence of political authority.

Anarchical system: the 'ordering principle' of international politics, and that which defines its structure.

Balance of power: refers to an equilibrium between states; historical realists regard it as the product of diplomacy (contrived balance) whereas structural realists regard the system as having a tendency towards a natural equilibrium (fortuitous balance).

Capabilities: population and size of territory, resources, economic strength, military capability, and competence (Waltz 1979: 131).

Defensive realism: a structural theory of realism that views states as security maximizers.

Dual moral standards: the idea that there are two principles or standards of right and wrong: one for the individual citizen and a different one for the state.

Ethic of responsibility: for historical realists, an ethic of responsibility is the limits of ethics in international politics; it involves the weighing up of consequences and the realization that positive outcomes may result from amoral actions.

Idealism: holds that ideas have important causal effect on events in international politics, and that ideas can change. Referred to by realists as utopianism since it underestimates the logic of power politics and the constraints this imposes upon political action.

Inter-dependence: a condition where the actions of one state impact upon other states (can be strategic interdependence or economic). Realists equate interdependence with vulnerability.

Hegemony: the influence a great power is able to establish on other states in the system; extent of influence ranges from leadership to dominance.

Hegemonic stability theory: a realist based explanation for cooperation that argues that a dominant state is required to ensure a liberal, free-trade international political economy.

International system: a set of interrelated parts connected to form a whole. Systems have defining principles such as hierarchy (in domestic politics) and anarchy (in international politics).

National interest: invoked by realists and state leaders to

signify that which is most important to the state—survival being at the top of the list.

Neoclassical realism: a version of realism that combines both structural factors such as the distribution of power and unit-level factors such as the interests of states (status quo or revisionist).

Offensive realism: a structural theory of realism that views states as power maximizers.

Power: Defined by most realists in terms of the important resources such as size of armed forces, gross national product, and population that a state possesses. There is the implicit belief that material resources translate into influence.

Relative gains: one of the factors that realists argue constrains the willingness of states to cooperate. States are less concerned about whether everyone benefits (absolute gains) and more concerned about whether someone may benefit more than someone else.

Self-help: in an anarchical environment, states cannot assume other states will come to their defence even if they are allies. *Each state must take care of itself*.

Sovereignty: the state has supreme authority domestically and independence internationally.

State: a legal territorial entity composed of a stable population and a government; it possesses a monopoly over the legitimate use of force; its sovereignty is recognized by other states in the international system.

Statism: the ideology which supports the organization of humankind into particular communities; the values and beliefs of that community are protected and sustained by the state.

State of war: the conditions (often described by classical realists) where there is no actual conflict, but a permanent cold war that could become a 'hot' war at any time.

Structure: in the philosophy of the social sciences a structure is something which exists independently of the actor (e.g. social class) but is an important determinant in the nature of the action (e.g. revolution). For contemporary structural realists, the number of Great Powers in the international system constitutes the structure.

Survival: the first priority for state leaders, emphasized by historical realists such as Machiavelli, Meinecke, and Weber.

QUESTIONS

1 How does the Melian dialogue represent key concepts such as self-interest, the balance of power alliances, capabilities, empires, and justice?

2 Do you think there is one Real*ism*, or many?

3 Do you know more about international relations than an Athenian student during the time of *The Peloponnesian War*?

4 Do realists confuse a *description* of war and conflict with an *explanation* of why it occurs?

5 Is Realism anything more than the ideology of powerful, satisfied states

6 How would a realist explain the war on terrorism

7 Will the West have to learn to be more realist, and not less, if its civilization is to survive in the twenty-first century?

8 What is at stake in the debate between defensive and offensive realism

9 Is structural realism sufficient to account for the variation in the behaviour of states?

10 Can realism help us to understand the globalization of world politics?

11 Were realists right to oppose the 2003 war against Iraq?

12 Do the foreign policies of states conform to realist prescriptions?

GUIDE TO FURTHER READING

For a general survey of the realist tradition

Smith, Michael Joseph (1986), *Realist Thought from Weber to Kissinger* (Baton Rouge: Louisiana State University Press). An excellent discussion of many of the seminal realist thinkers.

Grieco, Joseph M. (1997), 'Realist International Theory and the Study of World Politics', in Michael W. Doyle and G. John Ikenberry (eds), *New Thinking in International Relations Theory* (Boulder, Col.: Westview Press). A comprehensive critical appreciation of realist international theory.

Walt, Stephen M. (2002), 'The Enduring Relevance of the Realist Tradition', in I. Katznelson and H. V. Milner (eds), *Political Science: The State of the Discipline* (New York: W. W. Norton). A state-of-the-art exposition of the realist tradition.

Guzzini, Stefano (1998), *Realism in International Relations and International Political Economy* (London: Routledge). Provides an understanding of the evolution of the realist tradition.

Classical Realism

Doyle, Michael (1997), *Ways of War and Peace* (New York: W. W. Norton). A clever interpretation of the classical realist theory of Thucydides, Machiavelli, Hobbes, and Rousseau is provided.

Original sources

Thucydides (1954), *The Peloponnesian War*, trans. Rex Warner (London: Penguin Classics).

Machiavelli, Niccolo (1988), *The Prince*, ed. Q. Skinner (Cambridge: Cambridge University Press).

Hobbes, Thomas (1985), *Leviathan*, ed. C. B. Macpherson (London: Penguin Classics).

Rousseau, Jean-Jacques (1987) *The Basic Political Writings*, trans. Donald A. Cress (Cambridge: Hackett).

Twentieth-century classical realism

Carr, E. H. (2001), *The Twenty Years' Crisis 1919–1939: An Introduction to the Study of International Relations* (London: Palgrave).

Morgenthau, Hans J. (1946), *Scientific Man Versus Power Politics* (Chicago: University of Chicago Press).

Morgenthau, Hans J. ([1948] 1955), *Politics Among Nations: The Struggle for Power and Peace* (New York: Alfred A. Knopf).

Structural realism

Waltz, Kenneth (1979), *Theory of International Politics* (Reading, Mass.: Addison-Wesley). This is the exemplar for structural Realism.

Keohane, Robert (ed.) (1986), *Neo-realism and its Critics* (New York: Columbia University Press). This collection of essays includes key chapters by Waltz, an interesting defence of Realism by Robert Gilpin, and powerful critiques by Richard Ashley, Robert Cox, and J. G. Ruggie.

Baldwin, David A. (1993), *Neo-realism and Neo-liberalism: The Contemporary Debate* (New York: Columbia University Press). This fine collection takes the debate further.

Wendt, Alexander (1992), 'Anarchy is What States Make of it', *International Organization*, 46: 2: 395–421. Provides a penetrating constructivist challenge to Realism.

Mearsheimer, John (2001), *The Tragedy of Great Power Politics* (New York: W. W. Norton). This is the definitive account of offensive realism.

Neoclassical Realism

Rose, G. (1998), 'Neoclassical Realism and Theories of Foreign Policy', *World Politics*, 51: 144–72. An important review article that is credited with coining the term 'neoclassical realism'.

Schweller, R. L. (1996), 'Neo-realism's Status-Quo Bias: What Security Dilemma?', *Security Studies*, 5: 90–121. One of the leading neoclassical realists attempts to demonstrate the status quo bias of Waltz's version of structural realism.

Zakaria, Fareed (1998), *From Wealth to Power: The Unusual Origins of America's World Role* (Princeton: Princeton University Press). Puts forth his theory of state-centric realism.

WEB LINKS

www.geocities.com/virtualwarcollege/ir_realism.htm An introduction to the realist tradition in IR.

http://globetrotter.berkeley.edu/people2/Mearsheimer/mearsheimer-con0.html An interesting interview with leading realist, John Mearsheimer.

NOTES

1. Realism, *realpolitik*, and *raison d'état* are broadly interchangeable. In this chapter, Realism with an upper case 'R' will be used to signify the general tradition. When discussing particular realists, or types of realism (such as classical realism), lower case 'r' will be used.

2. A number of critical histories of the field of International Relations have recently challenged the notion that the inter-war period was essentially 'idealist' in character. Both Peter Wilson (1998) and Brian C. Schmidt (1998) argue that it is simply a myth that an idealist paradigm dominated the study of international relations during the inter-war period of the field's history.

3. See Desch 2003.

4. There are a number of similar versions of this idea of a 'shared core' to Realism in the literature. Keohane distils the core into: state as actor, state as rational, state as power maximizer. Keohane (1989*b*: 39) and Gilpin (1986: 304–5) are two examples among many.

5. M. J. Smith (1986: 23). Weber is rightly regarded by Smith as the theorist who has shaped twentieth-century realist thought, principally because of his fusion of politics with power.

6. It is important to note that not all conflict results from the security dilemma (since both parties have benign intent); historically, more conflicts have been caused through predator states.

CHAPTER 8

Liberalism

TIM DUNNE

READER'S GUIDE

The practice of international relations has not been accommodating to Liberalism. Whereas the domestic political realm in many states has witnessed an impressive degree of progress, with institutions providing for order *and* justice, the international realm in the era of the modern states-system has been characterized by a precarious order and the *absence* of justice. The introductory section of the chapter will address this dilemma before providing a definition of Liberalism as it is understood by international relations scholars. Section two considers the core concepts of Liberalism, beginning with the visionary internationalism of the Enlightenment, through to the Idealism of the inter-war period, and the institutionalism which became dominant in the second half of the twentieth century. This discussion is a prelude to the analysis in the third and final section on Liberalism in an era of globalization. The argument returns to the definition set out at the beginning in order to show how tensions underpinning Liberalism as a political theory are exacerbated by social and economic forces of globalization.

I would like to warmly thank Amrita Narlikar and Brian Schmidt for their comments on an earlier draft. In addition, Steve Smith gave me typically pertinent advice on how to rework the chapter for this edition.

Introduction

Although Realism is regarded as the dominant theory of international relations, **Liberalism** has a strong claim to being the historic alternative. Rather like political parties, Realism is the 'natural' party of government and Liberalism is the leader of the opposition, whose main function is to censure those in power for their complicity in maintaining the status quo. And like historic parties of 'opposition', Liberalism has occasionally found itself in the ascendancy, when its ideas and values set the agenda for international relations. In the twentieth century, liberal thinking influenced policymaking elites and public opinion in a number of Western states after the First World War, an era often referred to in academic international relations as idealism. There was a brief resurgence of liberal sentiment at the end of the Second World War with the birth of the United Nations, although this beacon of hope was soon extinguished by the return of **cold war** power politics. In the 1990s, Liberalism appeared resurgent as Western state leaders proclaimed a 'New World Order' and intellectuals provided theoretical justifications for the inherent supremacy of their liberal ideas over all other competing ideologies. After 9/11, the pendulum has once again swung towards the Realist pole as the USA and its allies have sought to consolidate their power and punish those whom they define as terrorists and the states that provide them with shelter.

How do we explain the divergent fortunes of Liberalism in the domestic and international domains? While liberal values and institutions have become deeply embedded in **Europe** and North America, the same values and institutions lack legitimacy worldwide. To invoke the famous phrase of Stanley Hoffmann's, 'international affairs have been the nemesis of Liberalism'. 'The essence of Liberalism', Hoffmann continues, 'is self-restraint, moderation, compromise and peace' whereas 'the essence of international politics is exactly the opposite: troubled peace, at best, or the **state of war**' (Hoffmann 1987: 396). This explanation comes as no surprise to Realists, who argue that there can be no progress, no law, and no justice, where there is no common power. Despite the weight of this Realist argument, those who believe in the liberal project have not conceded defeat. Liberals argue that power politics itself is the product of ideas, and crucially, ideas can change. Therefore, even if the world has been inhospitable to Liberalism, this does not mean that it cannot be remade in its image.

While the belief in the possibility of progress is one identifier of a liberal approach to politics, (Clark 1989: 49–66) there are other general propositions that define the broad tradition of Liberalism. Perhaps the appropriate way to begin this discussion is with a four-dimensional definition (Doyle 1997: 207). First, all citizens are juridically equal and possess certain basic rights to education, access to a free press, and religious toleration. Second, the legislative assembly of the state possesses only the authority invested in it by the people, whose basic rights it is not permitted to abuse. Third, a key dimension of the liberty of the individual is the right to own property including productive forces. Fourth, Liberalism contends that the most effective system of economic exchange is one that is largely market driven and not one that is subordinate to bureaucratic regulation and control either domestically or internationally. Liberal values such as individualism, tolerance, freedom, and constitutionalism, can be contrasted with conservatism, which places a higher value on order and authority and is willing to sacrifice the liberty of the individual for the stability of the **community**.

There are two striking aspects about this four-dimensional definition; each will be taken up in detail in the main sections of the chapter. First, although many writers have tended to view Liberalism as a theory of government, what is becoming increasingly apparent is the explicit connection between Liberalism as a political and economic theory and Liberalism as an international theory. Many Enlightenment thinkers foresaw this connection. Jean Jacques Rousseau realized the force of this argument. Progress in the realm of **civil society** would not be possible without an end to the state of war on the 'outside'. Immanuel Kant sought a way out of this dilemma with his pamphlet 'Perpetual Peace' (1970), one of the great liberal treatises of the modern era. The time to reflect on Kant's argument in more detail is not yet upon us; instead, what matters is the claim that domestic and international variants of Liberalism have all too often been written in isolation, a tendency that became more pronounced in late-twentieth-century writings. The treatment in this chapter explicitly rejects such a separation. Properly conceived, Liberal thought on a global scale embodies a **domestic analogy** operating at multiple levels.[1] Like individuals, states have different characteristics—some are bellicose and war-prone, others are tolerant and peaceful: in short, the identity of the state determines its outward orientation. Liberals see a further parallel between individuals and sovereign states. Although the character of states may differ, all states are accorded certain 'natural' rights, such as the generalized right to non-intervention in their domestic affairs. On another level, the domestic analogy refers to the extension of ideas that originated inside liberal states to the international realm, such as the coordinating role played by institutions and the centrality of the rule of law to the idea of a just order. In a sense, the historical project of Liberalism is the domestication of the international.

Liberals concede that we have far to go before this goal has been reached. International order in the modern period has indeed been defined by a state of anarchy, as the Realists proclaim. But the absence of a legitimate global authority with the power to enforce the law does not mean we are in a state of war. If anarchy is not the permissive cause of war, as it is for structural Realists, how then do Liberals explain the causes of war (and its corollary, the vexed question of the conditions of peace)? As Box 8.1 demonstrates, certain strands of Liberalism see the causes of war located in imperialism, others in the failure of the balance of power, and still others in the problem of undemocratic regimes. And ought this to be remedied through collective security

---

Box 8.1	Liberalism and the causes of war, determinants of peace

One of the most useful analytical tools for thinking about differences between individual thinkers or particular variations on a broad theme such as Liberalism is to differentiate between levels of analysis. For example, Kenneth Waltz's *Man, The State and War* (1959) examined the causes of conflict operating at the level of the individual, the state, and the international system itself. The table below turns Waltz on his head, as it were, in order to show how different liberal thinkers have provided competing explanations (across the three levels of analysis) for the causes of war and the determinants of peace.

'Images' of Liberalism	Public figure/period	Causes of conflict	Determinants of peace
First image (Human nature)	Richard Cobden (mid-19th century)	Interventions by governments domestically and internationally disturbing the natural order	Individual liberty, free trade, prosperity, interdependence
Second image (The state)	Woodrow Wilson (early 20th century)	Undemocratic nature of international politics, especially foreign policy and the balance of power	National self-determination; open governments responsive to public opinion; collective security
Third image (The structure of the system)	J. A. Hobson (early 20th century)	The balance of power system	A world government, with powers to mediate and enforce decisions

commerce, or world government? While it can be productive to think about the various strands of liberal thought and their differing prescriptions (Doyle 1997: 205–300), given the limited space permitted to deal with a broad and complex tradition, the emphasis below will be on the core concepts of international Liberalism and the way in which these relate to the goals of order and justice on a global scale.[2]

In the third and final section of the chapter, the discussion will return to a tension that lies in the heart of the liberal theory of politics. As can be seen from a critical appraisal of the four-fold definition presented above, Liberalism pulls in two directions: its commitment to freedom in the economic and social spheres leans in the direction of a minimalist role for governing institutions, while the democratic political culture required for basic freedoms to be safeguarded requires robust and interventionist institutions. This has variously been interpreted as a tension between different liberal goals, or more broadly as a sign of rival and incompatible conceptions of Liberalism. Should a liberal polity—no matter what the size or scale—preserve the right of individuals to retain property and privilege, or should Liberalism elevate equality over liberty so that resources are redistributed from the strong to the weak? When we are looking at politics on a global scale it is clear that inequalities are far greater while at the same time our institutional capacity to do something about them is that much less. As writers on globalization remind us, the intensification of global flows in trade, resources and people has weakened the state's capacity to govern. Closing this gap requires nothing short of a radical reconfiguration of the relationship between territoriality and governance.

Key points

- The liberal tradition in political thought goes back at least as far as the thinking of John Locke in the late seventeenth century. From then on, liberal ideas have profoundly shaped how we think about the relationship between government and citizens.

- Liberalism is a theory of both government within states and good governance between states and peoples worldwide. Unlike Realism, which regards the 'international' as an anarchic realm, Liberals seek to project values of order, liberty, justice, and toleration into international relations.

- The high water mark of liberal thinking in international relations was reached in the inter-war period in the work of Idealists who believed that warfare was an unnecessary and outmoded way of settling disputes between states.

- Domestic and international institutions are required to protect and nurture these values. But note that these values and institutions allow for significant variations which accounts for the fact that there are heated debates within Liberalism.

- Liberals disagree on fundamental issues such as the causes of war and what kind of institutions are required to deliver liberal values in a decentralized multicultural international system.

- An important cleavage within Liberalism, which has become more pronounced in our globalized world, is between those operating with a positive conception of Liberalism who advocate interventionist foreign policies and stronger international institutions, as against those who incline towards a negative conception which places a priority on toleration and non-intervention.

Core ideas in Liberal thinking on international relations

Immanuel Kant and Jeremy Bentham were two of the leading Liberals of the Enlightenment. Both were reacting to the barbarity of international relations, or what Kant graphically described as 'the lawless state of savagery', at a time when domestic politics was at the cusp of a new age of rights, citizenship and constitutionalism. Their abhorrence of the lawless savagery led them individually to elaborate plans for 'perpetual peace'. Although written over two centuries ago, these manifestos contain the seeds of core liberal ideas, in particular the belief that reason could deliver freedom and justice in international relations. For Kant the imperative to achieve perpetual peace required the transformation of individual consciousness, republican constitutionalism, and a federal contract between states to abolish war (rather than to regulate it as earlier international lawyers had argued). This federation can be likened to a permanent peace treaty, rather than a 'superstate' actor or world government. The three components of Kant's hypothetical treaty for a permanent peace are outlined in Box 8.2.

Kant's claim that liberal states are pacific in their international relations with other liberal states was revived in the 1980s. In a much cited article, Michael Doyle argued that liberal states have created a 'separate peace' (1986: 1151). According to Doyle, there are two elements to the Kantian legacy: restraint among liberal states and 'international imprudence' in relations with non-liberal states. Although the empirical evidence seems to support the democratic peace thesis, it is important to bear in mind the limitations of the argument. In the first instance, for the theory to be compelling, supporters of the 'democratic peace thesis' must provide an explanation as to why war has become unthinkable between liberal states. Kant had argued that if the decision to use force was taken by the people, rather than by the prince, then the frequency of conflicts would be drastically reduced. But logically this argument implies a lower frequency of conflicts between liberal and non-liberal states, and this has proven to be contrary to the historical evidence. An alternative explanation for the 'democratic peace' thesis might be that liberal states tend to be wealthy, and therefore have less to gain (and more to lose) by engaging in conflicts than poorer authoritarian states. Perhaps the most convincing explanation of all is the simple fact that liberal states tend to be in relations of amity with other liberal states. War between Canada and the USA is unthinkable, perhaps not because of their liberal democratic constitutions, but because they are friends (Wendt 1999: 298–9) with a high degree of convergence in economic and political matters. Indeed, war between states with contrasting political and economic systems may also be unthinkable because they have a history of friendly relations. An example here is

---

Box 8.2 Immanuel Kant's 'Perpetual Peace: A Philosophical Sketch'

First Definitive Article: *The Civil Constitution of Every State shall be Republican*

If, as is inevitably the case under this constitution, the consent of the citizens is required to decide whether or not war is to be declared, it is very natural that they will have great hesitation in embarking on so dangerous an enterprise . . . But under a constitution where the subject is not a citizen, and which is therefore not republican, it is the simplest thing in the world to go to war. For the head of state is not a fellow citizen, but the owner of the state, and a war will not force him to make the slightest sacrifice so far as his banquets, hunts, pleasure palaces and court festivals are concerned. (Kant 1991: 99–102)

Second Definitive Article: *The Right of Nations shall be based on a Federation of Free States*

Each nation, for the sake of its own security, can and ought to demand of the others that they should enter along with it into a constitution, similar to a civil one, within which the rights of each could be secured . . . But peace can neither be inaugurated nor secured without a general agreement between the nations; thus a particular kind of league, which we will call a *pacific federation* is required. It would be different from *a peace treaty* in that the latter terminates *one* war, whereas the former would seek to end *all wars* for good . . . It can be shown that this idea of *federalism*, extending gradually to encompass all states and thus leading to perpetual peace, is practicable and has objective reality. (Kant 1991: 102–5)

Third Definitive Article: *Cosmopolitan Right shall be limited to Conditions of Universal Hospitality*

The peoples of the earth have thus entered in varying degrees into a universal community, and it has developed to the point where a violation of rights in one part of the world is felt *everywhere*. The idea of a cosmopolitan right is therefore not fantastic and overstrained; it is a necessary complement to the unwritten code of political and international right, transforming it into a universal right of humanity. (Kant 1991: 105–8)

Mexico and Cuba, who maintain close bilateral relations despite their history of divergent economic ideologies.

Irrespective of the scholarly search for an answer to the reasons why liberal democratic states are more peaceful, it is important to note the political consequences of this hypothesis. In 1989 Francis Fukuyama wrote an article entitled 'The **End of History**' which celebrated the triumph of Liberalism over all other ideologies, contending that liberal states were more stable internally and more peaceful in their international relations (Fukuyama 1989: 3–18). Other defenders of the democratic peace thesis were more circumspect. As Doyle recognized, liberal democracies are as aggressive as any other type of state in their relations with authoritarian regimes and stateless peoples (Doyle 1995*b*: 100). How, then, should states inside the liberal zone of peace conduct their relations with non-liberal regimes? How can the positive Kantian legacy of restraint triumph over the historical legacy of international imprudence on the part of liberal states? These are fascinating and timely questions which will be taken up in the final section of the chapter.

Two centuries after Kant first called for a 'pacific federation', the validity of the idea that democracies are more pacific continues to attract a great deal of scholarly interest. The claim has also found its way into the public discourse of Western states' foreign policy, appearing in speeches made by US presidents as diverse as Ronald Reagan and William Jefferson Clinton. Less crusading voices within the liberal tradition believe that a legal and institutional framework must be established that includes states with different cultures and traditions. Such a belief in the power of law to solve the problem of war was advocated by Jeremy Bentham at the end of the eighteenth century. 'Establish a common tribunal' and 'the necessity for war no longer follows from a difference of opinion' (Luard 1992: 416). Like many liberal thinkers after him, Bentham showed that federal states such as the German Diet, the American Confederation, and the Swiss League were able to transform their identity from one based on conflicting interests to a more peaceful federation. As Bentham famously argued, 'between the interests of nations there is nowhere any real conflict'.

The idea of a natural order underpinning human society underpins the contribution of another Enlightenment figure to liberal thought. Adam Smith, the Scottish political economist and moral philosopher, argued that by pursuing their own self-interest, individuals are inadvertently promoting the public good. The mechanism which intervenes between the motives of the individual and the 'ends' of society as a whole, is what Smith referred to as 'an invisible hand'. Although Smith believed that the natural harmony between individual and state did not extend to a harmony between states (Wyatt-Walter 1996: 28) this is precisely what was emphasized by mid-nineteenth-century thinkers such as Richard Cobden. In common with many key figures in the liberal tradition, Cobden was a political activist as well as a writer and commentator on public affairs. He was an eloquent opponent of the exercise of arbitrary power by governments the world over. 'The progress of freedom', he compellingly argued, 'depends more upon the maintenance of peace, the spread of commerce, and the diffusion of education, than upon the labours of cabinets and foreign offices' (Hill 1996: 114).

Cobden's belief that **free trade** would create a more peaceful world order is a core idea of nineteenth-century Liberalism. Trade brings mutual gains to all the players irrespective of their size or the nature of their economies. It is perhaps not surprising that it was in Britain that this argument found its most vocal supporters. The supposed universal value of free trade brought disproportionate gains to the hegemonic power. There was never an admission that free trade among countries at different stages of **development** would lead to relations of dominance and subservience.

The idea of a natural '**harmony of interests**' in international political and economic relations came under challenge in the early part of the twentieth century. The fact that Britain and Germany had highly interdependent economies before the Great War (1914–18) seemed to confirm the fatal flaw in the association of economic interdependence with peace. From the turn of the century, the contradictions within European civilization, of progress and exemplarism on the one hand and the harnessing of industrial power for military purposes on the other, could no longer be contained. Europe stumbled into a horrific war killing fifteen million people. The war not only brought an end to three **empires** but also was a contributing factor to the Russian Revolution of 1917.

The First World War shifted liberal thinking towards a recognition that peace is not a natural condition but is one which must be constructed. In a powerful critique of the idea that peace and prosperity were part of a latent natural order, the publicist and author Leonard Woolf argued that peace and prosperity required 'consciously devised machinery' (Luard 1992: 465). But perhaps the most famous advocate of an international authority for the management of international relations was Woodrow Wilson. According to this US President, peace could only be secured with the creation of an **international organization** to regulate the international anarchy Security could not be left to secret bilateral diplomatic deals and a blind faith in the balance of power. Just as peace had to be enforced in domestic society,

the international domain had to have a system of regulation for coping with disputes and an international force which could be mobilized if non-violent conflict resolution failed. In this sense, more than any other strand of Liberalism, Idealism rests on the **domestic analogy** (Suganami 1989: 94–113).

In his famous 'Fourteen Points' speech, addressed to Congress in January 1918, Wilson argued that 'a general association of nations must be formed' to preserve the coming peace (see Box 8.3)—the League of Nations was to be that general association. For the League to be effective, it had to have the military power to deter aggression and, when necessary, to use a preponderance of power to enforce its will. This was the idea behind the **collective security** system which was central to the League of Nations (see Ch.13). Collective security refers to an arrangement where 'each state in the system accepts that the

---

| Box 8.3 | Woodrow Wilson's 'Fourteen Points' and the realism of Idealism |

1. Open covenants openly arrived at.

2. Freedom of the seas alike in peace and war.

3. The removal of all economic barriers to trade.

4. Reduction of national armaments.

5. A readjustment of all colonial claims.

6. The evacuation of Russian **territory** and the independent determination by Russia of her own political development and national policy.

7. The evacuation and restoration of Belgium.

8. The evacuation and restoration of France and the return of Alsace-Lorraine.

9. A readjustment of the frontiers of Italy along national lines.

10. Self-determination for the peoples of Austria-Hungary.

11. A redrawing of the boundaries of the Balkan states along historically established lines of nationality.

12. Self-determination for the peoples under Turkish rule.

13. The independence of Poland with free access to the sea guaranteed by international covenant.

14. The formation of a general association of nations under specific covenants for the purpose of affording mutual guarantees of political independence and territorial integrity to great and small states alike.

These 'Fourteen Points' contain many Idealist **principles**, in particular the importance of self-determination from colonial rule as well as the need for an international organization to maintain peace and security. But a close reading not just of the 14 points, but of the political context of the time, suggests that there was more than a twist of realism to the Idealist principles articulated by Woodrow Wilson. This comes through strongly in the following excerpt:

> As a number of historians have shown, Wilson advanced his Fourteen Points for many reasons, but one, obviously, was a shrewd appreciation that liberal democracy was the best antidote to Bolshevism and reaction in a world turned upside down by global war. Even his support for self-determination was as much a strategic ploy as a moral demand. As the record reveals, the ultimate purpose of the slogan was not to free all nations, but rather to undermine the remaining empires on the European continent and win America friends in east and central Europe. Wilson understood, even if his later realist critics did not, the power of values and **norms** in international relations. (Cox *et al.* 2000: 6–7)

security of one is the concern of all, and agrees to join in a collective response to aggression' (Roberts and Kingsbury 1993: 30). It can be contrasted with an alliance system of security, where a number of states join together usually as a response to a specific external threat (sometimes known as collective defence). In the case of the League of Nations, Article 16 of the League's Charter noted the obligation that, in the event of war, all member states must cease normal relations with the offending state, impose sanctions, and if necessary, commit their armed forces to the disposal of the League Council should the use of force be required to restore the status quo.

The League's constitution also called for the **self-determination** of all nations, another founding characteristic of liberal thinking on international relations. Going back to the mid-nineteenth century, self-determination movements in Greece, Hungary, and Italy received support among liberal powers and public opinion. Yet the default support for self-determination masked a host of practical and moral problems that were laid bare after Woodrow Wilson issued his proclamation. What would happen to newly created minorities who felt no allegiance to the self-determining state? Could a democratic process adequately deal with questions of identity—who was to decide what constituency was to participate in a ballot? And what if a newly self-determined state rejected liberal democratic norms.

The experience of the League of Nations was a disaster. While the moral rhetoric at the creation of the League was decidedly Idealist, in practice states remained imprisoned by self-interest. There is no better example of this than the United States' decision not to join the institution it had created. With the Soviet Union outside the system for ideological reasons, the League of Nations quickly became a talking shop for the 'satisfied' powers. Hitler's decision in March 1936 to reoccupy the Rhineland, a designated demilitarized zone according to the terms of the Treaty of Versailles, effectively pulled the plug on the League's life-support system (it had been put on the 'critical' list following the Manchurian crisis in 1931 and the Ethiopian crisis in 1935). Indeed, throughout the 1930s, the term crisis had become the most familiar one in international affairs. The word was used by E. H. Carr in the title of his polemical introduction to international relations, *The*

Twenty Years' Crisis 1919–1939 (1939). Carr brilliantly attacked the moral double standards of the League's supporters. In common with previous peace settlements, the overriding aim had been to create an order convenient to the victor powers—what was new in 1919 was the spin that sought to persuade the rest of the world that the new institutional arrangement was to everyone's advantage. James L. Richardson neatly sums up Carr's argument against liberal Idealists: 'the defence of the status quo in the name of peace was not necessarily more legitimate than challenging it in the name of justice' (1997: 17).

Although the League of Nations was the principal organ of the Idealist inter-war order, it is important to note other ideas which dominated liberal thinking in the early part of the twentieth century. Education became a vital addition to the liberal agenda, hence the origins of the study of International Relations as a discipline in Aberystwyth in 1919 with the founding of the Woodrow Wilson professorship. One of the tasks of the Wilson Professor was to promote the League of Nations as well as contributing to 'the truer understanding of civilizations other than our own' (John *et al.* 1972: 86). It is this self-consciously **normative** approach to the discipline of International Relations, the belief that scholarship is about what ought to be and not just what is, that sets the Idealists apart from the dominant strand of post-1945 liberal thinking with its emphasis upon the creation of regimes and institutions for the management of international order.

According to the history of the discipline of International Relations, the collapse of the League of Nations dealt a fatal blow to **Idealism**. There is no doubt that the language of Liberalism after 1945 was more pragmatic; how could anyone living in the shadow of the Holocaust be optimistic? Yet familiar core ideas of Liberalism remained. Even in the early 1940s, there was a recognition of the need to replace the League with another international institution with responsibility for international peace and security. Only this time, in the case of the United Nations there was an awareness among the framers of the Charter of the need for a consensus between the great powers in order for enforcement action to be taken, hence the veto system (Article 27 of the UN Charter) which allowed any of the five permanent members of the Security Council the power of veto. This revision constituted an important modification to the classical model of **collective security** (Roberts 1996: 315). With the ideological polarity of the cold war, the UN procedures for collective security were still-born (as either of the **superpowers** and their allies would veto any action proposed by the other).[3] It was not until the end of the cold war that a collective security system was put into operation, following the invasion of Kuwait by Iraq on 2 August 1990 (see Box 8.4).

An important argument advanced by Liberals in the early post-war period concerned the state's inability to cope with modernization. David Mitrany, a pioneer **integration** theorist, argued that transnational **cooperation** was required in order to resolve common problems (Mitrany 1943). His core concept was ramification, meaning the likelihood that cooperation in one sector would lead governments to extend the range of **collaboration** across other sectors. As states become more embedded in an **integration** process, the 'cost' of withdrawing from cooperative ventures increases.

This argument about the positive benefits from transnational cooperation is one which informed a new generation of scholars (particularly in the USA) in the 1960s and 1970s. Their argument was not simply about the mutual gains from trade, but that other **transnational actors** were beginning to challenge the dominance of sovereign states. World pol-

itics, according to **Pluralists** (as they are often referred to) was no longer an exclusive arena for states, as it had been for the first three hundred years of the Westphalian states-system. In one of the central texts of this genre, Robert Keohane and Joseph Nye argued that the centrality of other actors, such as interest groups, transnational corporations, and international non-governmental organizations (INGOs), had to be taken into consideration (1972). Here the overriding image of international relations is one of a cobweb of diverse actors linked through multiple channels of interaction.

Although the phenomenon of **transnationalism** was an important addition to the international relations theorists' vocabulary, it remained underdeveloped as a theoretical concept. Perhaps the most important contribution of **Pluralism** was its elaboration of **interdependence**. Due to the expansion of **capitalism** and the emergence of a global culture, Pluralists recognized a growing interconnectedness in which 'changes in one part of the system have direct and indirect consequences for the rest of the system' (Little 1996: 77). Absolute **state autonomy** so keenly entrenched in the minds of state leaders, was being circumscribed by interdependence. Such a development brought with it enhanced potential for cooperation as well as increased levels of vulnerability.

Interdependence not only challenged Realist

Box 8.4   **Case study 1: The Gulf War, 1990–1991 and collective security**

Iraq had always argued that the sovereign state of Kuwait was an artificial creation of the imperial powers. When this political motive was allied to an economic imperative, caused primarily by the accumulated war debts following the eight-year war with Iran, the annexation of Kuwait seemed to be a solution to Iraq's problems. The Iraqi President, Saddam Hussein, also assumed that the West would not use force to defend Kuwait, a miscalculation which was fuelled by the memory of the support the West had given Iraq during the Iran–Iraq war (the so-called 'fundamentalism' of Iran was considered to be a graver threat to international order than the extreme nationalism of the Iraqi regime).

The invasion of Kuwait on 2 August 1990 led to a series of UN resolutions calling for Iraq to withdraw unconditionally. Economic sanctions were applied while the US-led coalition

of international forces gathered in Saudi Arabia. Operation 'Desert Storm' crushed the Iraqi resistance in a matter of six weeks (16 January to 28 February 1991). The 1990–1 Gulf War had certainly revived the UN doctrine of collective security, although a number of doubts remained about the underlying motivations for the war and the way in which it was fought (for instance, the coalition of national armies was controlled by the USA rather than by a UN military command as envisaged in the Charter). President George Bush declared that the war was about more than one small country, it was about a 'big idea; **a new world order**'. The content of this new world order was 'peaceful settlement of disputes, solidarity against aggression, reduced and controlled arsenals, and just treatment of all peoples'.

theory, but also undermined liberal theories of justice which assumed that the boundaries of community coincided with the borders around sovereign territory. In a book that many believe to be the most important work of political theory in the twentieth century, John Rawls perpetuates the myth of self-sufficiency: according to his *Theory of Justice*, it was for each state to resolve the problem of inequality. Cosmopolitan critics of Rawls believe that such a premise of self-sufficiency is deficient on practical and moral grounds. A resolution to the problem of inequality, on this reading, must be international in scope. Why should we tolerate massive inequalities between communities that we would not tolerate within them? In so far as Rawls takes for granted the fact that the basis for global social justice does not exist (Brown 2000: 131), he is inadvertently aligning himself with the Realist conception of states coexisting in an anarchic environment.

One such Realist took great delight in attacking the Pluralist argument about the decline of the state. In his 1979 work *Theory of International Politics*, Kenneth Waltz argued that the degree of interdependence internationally was far lower than the constituent parts in a national political system. Moreover, the level of economic interdependence—especially between the greater powers—was less than that which existed in the early part of the twentieth century. Waltz concludes: 'if one is thinking of the international-political world, it is odd in the extreme that "interdependence" has become the word commonly used to describe it' (1979: 144). In the course of their engagement with Waltz and other neo-realists, early Pluralists modified their position. **Neo-Liberals**,[4] as they came to be known, conceded that the core assumptions of **neo-realism** were indeed correct: the anarchic international structure, the centrality of states, and a rationalist approach to social scientific inquiry. Where they differed was

apparent primarily in the argument that anarchy does not mean durable patterns of cooperation are impossible: the creation of **international regimes** matters here as they facilitate cooperation by sharing information, reinforcing **reciprocity**, and making defection from norms easier to punish (see Ch.16). Moreover, in what was to become the most important difference between neo-realists and neo-liberals (developed further in Ch.9), the latter argued that actors would enter into cooperative agreements if the gains were evenly shared. Neo-Realists dispute this hypothesis: what matters is a question not so much of mutual gains as of **relative gains**: in other words, a neo-realist state has to be sure that it has more to gain than its rivals from a particular bargain or regime.

There are two important arguments that set neo-liberalism apart from democratic peace Liberals and liberal Idealists of the inter-war period. First, academic inquiry should be guided by a commitment to a scientific approach to theory building. Whatever deeply held personal values scholars maintain, their task must be to observe regularities, formulate hypotheses as to why that relationship holds, and subject these to critical scrutiny. This separation of fact and value puts neo-liberals on the positivist side of the methodological divide. Second, writers such as Keohane and Axelrod are justly critical of the naive assumption of nineteenth-century Liberals that commerce breeds peace. A free-trade system, according to Keohane, provides incentives for cooperation but does not guarantee it. Here he is making an important distinction between cooperation and harmony. 'Co-operation is not automatic', Keohane argues, 'but requires planning and negotiation' (1989: 11). In the following section we see how contemporary liberal thinking maintains that the institutions of world politics after 1945 successfully embedded all states into a cooperative order.

Key points

- Early liberal thought on international relations took the view that the natural order had been corrupted by undemocratic state leaders and outdated policies such as the balance of power. Prescriptively, Enlightenment liberals believed that a latent cosmopolitan morality could be achieved through the exercise of reason and through the creation of constitutional states. In addition, the unfettered movement of people and goods could further facilitate more peaceful international relations.

- Although there are important continuities between Enlightenment liberal thought and twentieth-century ideas, such as the belief in the power of world public opinion to tame the interests of states, liberal Idealism was more programmatic. For Idealists, the freedom of states is part of the problem of international relations and not part of the solution. Two requirements follow from their diagnosis. The first is the need for explicitly normative thinking: how to promote peace and build a better world. Second, states must be part of an international organization, and be bound by its rules and norms

- Central to Idealism was the formation of an international organization to facilitate peaceful change, disarmament, arbitration, and (where necessary) enforcement. The League of Nations was founded in 1920 but its collective security system failed to prevent the descent into world war in the 1930s.

The victor states in the wartime alliance against Nazi Germany pushed for a new international institution to be created: the United Nations Charter was signed in June 1945 by fifty states in San Francisco. It represented a departure from the League in two important respects. Membership was near universal, and the great powers were able to prevent any enforcement action from taking place which might be contrary to their interests.

- In the post-1945 period, liberals; turned to international institutions to carry out a number of functions the state could not perform. This was the catalyst for integration theory in Europe and Pluralism in the United States. By the early 1970s Pluralism had mounted a significant challenge to Realism. It focused on new actors (transnational corporations, nongovernmental organizations) and new patterns of interaction (interdependence, integration).

- Neo-liberalism represents a more sophisticated theoretical challenge to contemporary Realism. Neo-liberals explain the durability of institutions despite significant changes in context. According to neo-liberals, institutions exert a causal force on international relations, shaping state preferences and locking them into cooperative arrangements

- Democratic peace Liberalism and neo-liberalism are the dominant strands in liberal thinking today.

Liberalism and globalization

When applying liberal ideas to international relations today, we find two clusters of responses to the problems and possibilities posed by globalization. Before outlining these, let us briefly return to the definition of Liberalism set out at greater length earlier, the four components being: juridical equality, democracy, liberty, and the free market. As we will see below, these same values can be pursued by very different political strategies.

The first alternative is that of 'the **Liberalism of privilege**' (Richardson 1997: 18). According to this perspective, the problems of globalization need to be addressed by a combination of strong democratic states in the core of the international system, robust regimes, and open markets and institutions. For an example of the working out of such a strategy in practice, we need to look no further than the success of the liberal **hegemony** of the post-1945 era. The US writer, G. John Ikenberry, is an articulate defender of this liberal order. In the aftermath of the Second World War, the USA took the opportunity to 'embed' certain fundamental liberal principles into the regulatory rules and institutions of international society. Most importantly, and contrary to Realist thinking, the USA chose to forsake short-run gains in return for a durable settlement that benefited all states. According to Ikenberry, the USA signalled the cooperative basis of its power in a number of ways. First, in common with liberal democratic principles, the USA was an example to other members of international society in so far as its political system is open and allows different voices to be heard. Foreign policy, like domestic policy, is closely scrutinized by the media, public opinion, and political committees and opposition parties. Second, the USA advocated a global free-trade regime in accordance with the idea that free trade brings benefits to all participants (it also has the added advantage, from the hegemon's point of view, of being cheap to manage). Third, the USA appeared to its allies at least as a reluctant hegemon that would not seek to exploit its significant power-political advantage. Fourth, and most importantly, the USA created and participated in a range of important international institutions that constrained its actions. The Bretton Woods system of economic and financial accords, and the **NATO** security alliance, are the best examples of the highly institutionalized character of American power in the post-1945 period. Advocates of this liberal hegemonic order note wryly that it was so successful that allies were more worried about abandonment than domination.

The post-1945 system of regulatory regimes and institutions has been successful in part due to the fact that they exist. In other words, once one set of institutional arrangements becomes embedded it is very difficult for alternatives to make inroads. There are two implications that need to be teased out here. One is the narrow historical 'window' that exists for new institutional design; the other is the durability of existing institutions. 'In terms of American hegemony, this means that, short of a major war or a global economic collapse, it is very difficult to envisage the type of historical breakpoint needed to replace the existing order' (Ikenberry 1999: 137).

Let us accept for a moment that the **neo-liberal** argument is basically correct: the post-1945 international order has been successful and durable because US hegemony has been of a liberal character. The logic of this position is one of institutional con-

servatism. In order to respond effectively to global economic and security problems, there is no alternative to working within the existing institutional structure. This is a manifesto for managing an international order in which the Western states who paid the start-up costs of the institutions are now experiencing significant returns on their institutional investment. At the other end of the spectrum, the current order is highly unresponsive to the needs of weaker states and peoples. According to the United Nations Development Programme, the resulting global inequality is 'grotesque'. One statistic is particularly graphic: the richest 1 per cent of the world's population receives as much income as the poorest 57 per cent.[5]

Given that Liberalism has produced such unequal gains for the West and the rest, it is not surprising that the hegemonic power has become obsessed with the question of preserving and extending its control of institutions, markets, and resources. When this hegemonic liberal order comes under challenge, as it did on 9/11, the response is uncompromising. It is noticeable in this respect that President George W. Bush mobilized the language of Liberalism against Al Qaeda, the Taliban, and also Iraq. He referred to the 2003 war against Iraq as 'freedom's war' and the term 'liberation' is frequently used by defenders of 'Operation Iraqi Freedom'.

Given the primacy of a neo-conservative ideology in the Bush cabinet, one needs to proceed with caution when stumbling upon liberal principles in contemporary American foreign policy. Nevertheless, the official discourse of US foreign policy overlaps in interesting ways with a number of liberal values and ideas (Rhodes 2003) as can be seen in Bush's speech at the West Point graduation ceremony in June 2002. A key opening theme in the speech is how force can be used for freedom: 'we fight, as we always fight, for a just peace'. Bush then goes on to locate this argument in historical context. Prior to the twenty-first century, great power competition manifested itself in war. Today, 'the Great Powers share common values' such as 'a deep commitment to human freedom'. In his State of the Union address of 2004, he even declared that 'our aim is a democratic peace'. Box 8.5 further illustrates the connections between Liberalism, **democracy promotion**, and the Bush foreign policy.

Box 8.5 **George W. Bush and Liberalism in American foreign policy**

'The twentieth century ended with a single surviving model of human progress, based on non-negotiable demands of human dignity, the rule of law, limits on the power of the state, respect for women and private property and free speech and equal justice and religious tolerance. America cannot impose this vision—yet we can support and reward governments that make the right choices for their own people. In our development aid, in our diplomatic efforts, in our international broadcasting, and in our educational assistance, the United States will promote moderation and tolerance and human rights. And we defend the peace that makes all progress possible.

'When it comes to the common rights and needs of men and women, there is no clash of civilizations. The requirements of freedom apply fully to Africa and Latin America and the entire Islamic world. The peoples of the Islamic nations want and deserve the same freedoms and opportunities as people in every nation. And their governments should listen to their hopes.'

(Excerpt from President George W. Bush, Graduation Speech at West Point, US Military Academy, New York, 1 June 2002. Available at: **www.whitehouse.gov/news/releases**)

The potential for Liberalism to embrace **imperialism** is a tendency that has a long history (Doyle 1986: 1151–69). We find in Machiavelli a number of arguments for the necessity for republics to expand. Liberty increases wealth and the concomitant drive for new markets; soldiers who are at the same time citizens are better fighters than slaves or mercenaries; and expansion is often the best means to promote a state's security. In this sense, contemporary US foreign policy is no different from the great expansionist republican states of the pre-modern period such as Athens and Rome. Few Liberals today would openly advocate **imperialism** although the line between interventionist strategies to defend liberal values and privileges and **imperialism** is very finely drawn. Michael Doyle advocates a policy mix of forcible and non-forcible instruments that ought to be deployed in seeking regime change in illiberal parts of the world (see Box 8.6).

CWS

This strategy of preserving and extending liberal institutions is open to a number of criticisms. For the sake of simplicity, these will be gathered up into an alternative to the **Liberalism of privilege** that we will call **radical Liberalism**. An opening objection concerns the understanding of Liberalism embodied in the neo-liberal defence of international institu-

Box 8.6 **Defending and extending the liberal zone of peace**

As we have seen, advocates of the democratic peace thesis believe that liberal states act peacefully towards one another. Yet this empirical law does not tell liberal states how to behave towards non-liberal states. Should they try to convert them, thereby bringing them into the zone of peace, or should they pursue a more defensive strategy? The former has not been successful in the past, and in a world of many nuclear weapons states, crusading could be suicidal. For this reason, Michael Doyle suggests a dual-track approach.

- The first track is preserving the liberal community which means forging strong alliances with other like-minded states and defending itself against illiberal regimes This may require liberal states to include in their foreign policy strategies like the balance of power in order to contain authoritarian states.

- The second track is more expansionist and aims to extend the liberal zone by a variety of economic and

diplomatic instruments. Doyle categorizes these in terms of 'inspiration' (hoping peoples living in non-democratic regimes will struggle for their liberty), 'instigation' (peace building and economic restructuring), and 'intervention' (legitimate if the majority of a polity is demonstrating widespread disaffection with their government and/or their basic rights are being systematically violated).

Doyle concludes with the warning that the march of Liberalism will not necessarily continue unabated. It is in our hands, he argues, whether the international system becomes more pacific and stable, or whether antagonisms deepen. We must be willing to pay the price—in institutional costs and development aid—to increase the prospects for a peaceful future. This might be cheap when compared with the alternative of dealing with hostile and unstable authoritarian states (Doyle 1999).

tions. The liberal character of those institutions is assumed rather than subjected to critical scrutiny. As a result, the incoherence of the purposes underpinning these institutions is often overlooked. The kind of economic **liberalization** advocated by Western financial institutions, particularly in economically impoverished countries, frequently comes into conflict with the norms of democracy and human rights. Three examples illustrate this dilemma. First, the more the West becomes involved in the organization of developing states' political and economic infrastructure, the less those states are able to be accountable to their domestic constituencies, thereby cutting through the link between the government and the people which is so central to modern liberal forms of representative democracy (Hurrell and Woods 1995: 463). Second, in order to qualify for Western aid and loans, states are often required to meet harsh economic criteria requiring cuts in many welfare programmes; the example of the poorest children in parts of Africa having to pay for primary school education (Booth and Dunne 1999: 310)—which is their right according to the Universal Declaration of Human Rights—is a stark reminder of the fact that economic liberty and political equality are frequently opposed. Third, the inflexible response of international financial institutions to various crises in the world-economy, such as the East Asian financial crisis, has contributed to a backlash against Liberalism *per se*. Richard Falk puts this dilemma starkly: there is, he argues, a tension between 'the ethical imperatives of the global neighbourhood and the dynamics of economic globalisation' (1995a: 573). **Radical liberals** argue that the hegemonic institutional order has fallen prey to the neo-liberal consensus which minimizes the role of the public sector in providing for welfare, and elevates the market as the appropriate mechanism for allocating resources, investment, and employment opportunities.

A second line of critique pursued by **radical liberals** concerns not so much the contradictory outcomes but the illiberal nature of the regimes and institutions. To put the point bluntly, there is a massive **democratic deficit** at the global level. Issues of international peace and security are determined by only 15 members of international society, of whom only five can exercise a power of veto. In other words, it is hypothetically possible for up to 200

states in the world to believe that military action ought to be taken but such an action would contravene the UN Charter if one of the permanent members was to cast a veto. If we take the area of political economy, the power exerted by the West and its international financial institutions perpetuates structural inequality. A good example here is the issue of free trade, which the West has pushed in areas where it gains from an open policy (such as in manufactured goods and financial services) but resisted in areas that it stands to lose (agriculture and textiles). At a deeper level, radical liberals worry that *all* statist models of governance are undemocratic as elites are notoriously self-serving.

These sentiments underpin the approach to globalization taken by writers such as Danielle Archibugi, David Held, Mary Kaldor, and Jan Aart Scholte, among others, who believe that **global politics** must be democratized (Held and McGrew 2002). Held's argument is illustrative of the analytical and prescriptive character of radical Liberalism in an era of globalization. His diagnosis begins by revealing the inadequacies of the 'Westphalian order' (or the modern states-system which is conventionally dated from the middle of the seventeenth century). During the latter stages of this period, we have witnessed rapid democratization in a number of states, but this has not been accompanied by democratization of the **society of states** (Held 1993). This task is increasingly urgent given the current levels of interconnectedness, since 'national' governments are no longer in control of the forces which shape their citizens' lives (for example, the decision by one state to permit deforestation has environmental consequences for all states). After 1945, the UN Charter set limits to the **sovereignty** of states by recognizing the rights of individuals in a whole series of human rights conventions. But even if the UN had lived up to its Charter in the post-1945 period, it would still have left the building blocks of the Westphalian order largely intact, namely: the hierarchy between great powers and the rest (symbolized by the permanent membership of the Security Council); massive inequalities of wealth between states; and a minimal role for **non-state actors** to **influence** decisionmaking in international relations.

In place of the Westphalian and UN models, Held outlines a '**cosmopolitan model of democracy**'.

This requires, in the first instance, the creation of regional parliaments and the extension of the authority of such regional bodies (like the European Union) which are already in existence. Second, human rights conventions must be entrenched in national parliaments and monitored by a new International Court of Human Rights. Third, reform of the UN, or the replacement of it, with a genuinely democratic and accountable global parliament. Without appearing to be too sanguine about the prospects for the realization of the cosmopolitan model of democracy, Held is nevertheless adamant that if democracy is to thrive, it must penetrate the institutions and regimes which manage global politics.

Radical liberals place great importance on the civilizing capacity of global society. While the rule of law and the democratization of international institutions is a core component of the liberal project, it is also vital that citizens' **networks** are broadened and deepened to monitor and cajole these institutions. These groups form a linkage between individuals, states, and global institutions). It is easy to portray radical liberal thinking as 'utopian' but we should not forget the many achievements of global civil society so far. The evolution of international humanitarian law, and the extent to which these laws are complied with, is largely down to the millions of individuals who are active supporters of human rights groups like Amnesty International and Human Rights Watch (Falk 1995*b*: 164). Similarly,

global protest movements have been responsible for the heightened sensitivity to environmental degradation everywhere.

This emphasis on what Richard Falk calls 'globalization from below' is an important antidote to neo-liberalism's somewhat status quo oriented worldview. But just as Imperialism can emerge from a complacent Liberalism of privilege, the danger for radical liberals is naivety. How is it that global institutions can be reformed in such a way that the voices of ordinary people will be heard? And what if the views of 'peoples' rather than 'states' turn out to be similarly indifferent to global injustice? There is a sense in which radical liberal thought wants to turn back the clock of globalization to an era in which local producers cooperated to produce socially responsible food in the day and wove baskets or watched street theatre in the evening. It is not clear that such an organic lifestyle is preferable to purchasing relatively inexpensive goods from a multinational supermarket outlet or finding entertainment on multichannel television (Brown 2002: 238–9). Perhaps the least plausible aspect of the radical liberal project is the injunction to reform global capitalism. Just how much of a civilizing effect is global civil society able to exert upon the juggernaut of capitalism? And can this movement bridge the globalization divide in which democratic institutions are territorially located while forces of production and destruction are global?

Conclusion

The euphoria with which Liberals greeted the end of the cold war in 1989 has to a large extent been dissipated by 9/11 and the **war on terror** triggered by it. The pattern of conflict and insecurity that we have seen at the beginning of the twenty-first century suggests that liberal democratic values continue to lack traction in practice. Images and narratives from Afghanistan, Liberia, Chechnya, Burundi, the Democratic Republic of Congo, Iraq, and Zimbabwe remind us that in many parts of the world, anti-liberal values of warlordism, torture,

intolerance, and injustice are daily occurrences. Stanley Hoffmann is surely right to argue that the case of degenerating states reveals how sovereignty, democracy, national self-determination, and human rights 'are four norms in conflict and a source of complete liberal disarray' (1995: 169).

A deeper reason for the crisis in Liberalism is that it is bound up with an increasingly discredited Enlightenment view of the world. Contrary to the hopes of Bentham, Hume, Kant, Mill, and Paine, the application of reason and science to politics has not

Box 8.7   Key concepts of Liberalism

Collective security: refers to an arrangement where 'each state in the system accepts that the security of one is the concern of all, and agrees to join in a collective response to aggression' (Roberts and Kingsbury 1993: 30).

Cosmopolitan model of democracy: associated with David Held, Daniele Archibugi, Mary Kaldor, and others, a cosmopolitan model of democracy requires the following: the creation of regional parliaments and the extension of the authority of such regional bodies (like the European Union) which are already in existence; human rights conventions must be entrenched in national parliaments and monitored by a new International Court of Human Rights; the UN must be replaced with a genuinely democratic and accountable global parliament.

Democratic peace: a central plank of liberal internationalist thought, the democratic peace thesis makes two claims: first, liberal polities exhibit restraint in their relations with other liberal polities (the so-called separate peace) but are imprudent in relations with authoritarian states. The validity of the democratic peace thesis has been fiercely debated in the international relations literature.

Democracy promotion: the strategy adopted by leading Western states and institutions—particularly the USA—to use instruments of foreign and economic policy to spread liberal values. Advocates make an explicit linkage between the mutually reinforcing effects of democratization and open markets.

Enlightenment: associated with rationalist thinkers of the eighteenth century. Key ideas include: secularism, progress, reason, science, knowledge, and freedom. The motto of the Enlightenment is: 'Sapere aude! Have courage to use your own understanding' (Reiss 1991: 54).

Harmony of interests: common among nineteenth-century Liberals was the idea of a natural order between peoples which had been corrupted by undemocratic state leaders and outdated policies such as the balance of power. If these distortions could be swept away we would find that there were no real conflicts between peoples.

Idealism: Idealists seek to apply liberal thinking in domestic politics to international relations, in other words, institutionalize the rule of law. This reasoning is known as the **domestic analogy**. According to Idealists in the early twentieth century, there were two principal requirements for a new world order. First: state leaders, intellectuals, and public opinion had to believe that progress was possible.

Second: an international organization had to be created to facilitate peaceful change, disarmament, arbitration, and (where necessary) enforcement. The League of Nations was founded in 1920 but its collective security system failed to prevent the descent into world war in the 1930s.

Integration: a process of ever-closer union between states, in a regional or international context. The process often begins by cooperation to solve technical problems, referred to by Mitrany as ramification.

Interdependence: a condition where states (or peoples) are affected by decisions taken by others; for example, a decision to raise interest rates in the USA automatically exerts upward pressure on interest rates in other states. Interdependence can be symmetric, i.e. both sets of actors are affected equally, or it can be asymmetric, where the impact varies between actors.

Liberalism: according to Doyle (1997: 207), Liberalism includes the following four claims. First, all citizens are juridically equal and have equal rights to education, access to a free press, and religious toleration. Second, the legislative assembly of the state possesses only the authority invested in it by the people, whose basic rights it is not permitted to abuse. Third, a key dimension of the liberty of the individual is the right to own property including productive forces. Fourth, Liberalism contends that the most effective system of economic exchange is one that is largely market driven and not one that is subordinate to bureaucratic regulation and control either domestically or internationally.

Normative: the belief that theories should be concerned with what ought to be, rather than merely diagnosing what is. Norm creation refers to the setting of standards in international relations which governments (and other actors) ought to meet.

Pluralism: an umbrella term, borrowed from American political science, used to signify international relations theorists who rejected the Realist view of the primacy of the state, the priority of national security, and the assumption that states are unitary actors.

World government: associated in particular with those Idealists who believe that peace can never be achieved in a world divided into separate sovereign states. Just as the state of nature in civil society was abolished by governments, the state of war in international society must be ended by the establishment of a world government.

brought communities together. Indeed, it has arguably shown the fragmented nature of the **political community**, which is regularly expressed in terms of ethnic, linguistic, or religious differences. Critics of Liberalism argue that the universalizing mission of liberal values, such as democracy, capitalism, and secularism, undermines the traditions and practices of non-Western cultures (Gray 1995: 146). When it comes to doing inter-cultural politics, somehow Liberals just don't seem to take 'no' for an answer. The Marxist writer Immanuel Wallerstein has a nice way of expressing the dilemma over universalism. Liberals view it as 'a "gift" of the powerful to the weak' which places them in a double bind: 'to refuse the gift is to lose; to accept the gift is to lose' (in Brown 1999).

At the outset, the chapter pointed to a tension within Liberalism. The emphasis on personal liberty, unfettered trade, and the accumulation of property can lend itself to a society riven with inequality, suspicion, and rivalry. Pulling in the opposite direction, Liberalism contains within it a set of values that seek to provide for the conditions of a just society through democratic institutions and welfare-

oriented economies. Projecting this tension on to a global stage leads to two possibilities for Liberalism in an era of globalization. The neo-liberal variant is one where international rules would be minimal and institutions relatively weak and status quo oriented. In this world economic growth would be strong but unevenly distributed. As a consequence, preventive military action remains an ever-present possibility in order to deal with chaos and violence produced by dispossessed communities and networks. The more progressive model, advocated by radical Liberals, seeks to heighten regulation through the strengthening of international institutions. This is to be done by making institutions more democratic and accountable for the negative consequences of globalization. The charge of utopianism is one that is easy to make against this position and hard to refute. In so doing, Liberals of a radical persuasion should invoke Kant's axiom that 'ought' must imply 'can'.

For further information and case studies on this subject, please visit the companion web site at www.oup.com/uk/booksites/politics.

QUESTIONS

1 Do you agree with Stanley Hoffmann that international affairs are 'inhospitable' to Liberalism? What arguments might one draw upon to support or refute this proposition?

2 Was the language of international morality, used by liberal Idealists in the inter-war period, a way of masking the interests of Britain and France in maintaining their dominance of the international system after the First World War?

3 Should liberal states promote their values abroad? Is force a legitimate instrument in securing this goal?

4 How much progress (if any) has there been in liberal thinking on international relations since Kant?

5 Are democratic peace theorists right, but for the wrong reasons?

6 Which strategy of dealing with globalization do you find more convincing: those who believe that states and institutions should maintain the current order or those who believe in reform driven by global civil society

7 Is there a fundamental tension at the heart of Liberalism between liberty and democracy? If so, how is this tension played out in the international domain?

8 Are liberal values and institutions in the contemporary international system as deeply embedded as neo-liberals claim?

9 What liberal ideas, if any, inform the George W. Bush government's foreign policy?

GUIDE TO FURTHER READING

Liberalism in International Relations

Brown, C., Nartin, T., and Rengger, N. (eds) (2002), *International Relations in Political Thought: Texts from the Ancient Greeks to the First World War* (Cambridge: Cambridge University Press). See especially the readings from classical liberal thought in Sections 7, 8, and 9.

Doyle, M. (1997), *Ways of War and Peace* (New York: W. W. Norton). The best textbook on the principal theories of international relations. There are over 100 pages of analysis on Liberalism in the book. See also, in a shorter and modified form, his article: Doyle, M. (1986), 'Liberalism and World Politics', *American Political Science Review*, 80:4: 1151–69.

Hoffmann, S. (1987), *Janus and Minerva* (Boulder, Col.: Westview), 394–436. An excellent account of Liberalism and its troubled relationship to international relations.

Smith, M. J. (1992), 'Liberalism and International Reform', in T. Nardin and D. Mapel (eds), *Traditions of International Ethics* (Cambridge: Cambridge University Press), 201–24. A comprehensive piece that draws out the premises of Liberalism and in particular the belief in international organization

Richardson, J. L. (1997), 'Contending Liberalisms: Past and Present', *European Journal of International Relations*, 3:1: 5–33. A thorough overview of Liberalism in political thought and in international relations. Parts of the argument in this chapter mirror Richardson's article.

Walt, S. (1998), 'International Relations: One World, Many Theories', *Foreign Policy*, 110: 29–46. Not only does this contain a useful short overview of Liberalism, it highlights the imperfect application of liberal theory in practice.

Liberalism in American and British foreign policy

Cox, M., Ikenberry, G. J., and Inoguchi, T. (eds) (2000), *American Democracy Promotion Impulses, Strategies and Impacts* (Oxford: Oxford University Press), 1–17. See especially the introduction which puts US democracy promotion in context.

Cox, M., Booth, K., and Dunne, T. (eds) (1999), *The Interregnum: Controversies in World Politics 1989–1999* (Cambridge: Cambridge University Press). Contains a range of perspectives on the pattern of world power in the 1990s.

Paul, T. V., and Hall, J. A. (eds) (1999), *International Order and the Future of World Politics* (Cambridge: Cambridge University Press). See especially the essay on the role of liberal institutions by G. John Ikenberry, 'Liberal Hegemony and the Future of American Post-war Order', 123–45.

Rhodes, E. (2003), 'The Imperial Logic of Bush's Liberal Agenda', *Survival*, 45: 131–54. The article advances an important argument about the liberal values incorporated in the Republican presidency of George W. Bush.

Held, D., and McGrew, A. (eds) (2002), *The Global Transformation Reader* (Cambridge: Polity Press, 2nd edn). A useful collection of essays with many contributors who represent radical Liberalism.

NOTES

1. The term domestic analogy was used by Hedley Bull and later developed by Hidemi Suganami.

2. Doyle classifies Liberalism into the following strands: liberal pacifism, liberal imperialism, and liberal internationalism (1986: 1151–69).

3. Between 1945 and 1990, there were 232 resolutions vetoed, between 1990 and April 2004 there were only seventeen vetoed.

4. Many of the leading Pluralists of the 1970s embraced neo-liberalism in the 1980s. Neo-liberalism is often referred to in the literature as neo-liberal institutionalism.

5. This is one statistic among many that throws the naive optimism of some liberal internationalists into sharp relief. For a detailed empirical analysis of globalization and development, see the UN *Human Development Report 2003*, freely available on the Web at: www.undp.org/hdr2003/pdf/hdr03_chapter_2.pdf.

CHAPTER 9

Contemporary mainstream approaches: neo-realism and neo-liberalism

STEVEN L. LAMY

READER'S GUIDE

This chapter reviews the core assumptions of neo-realism and neo-liberalism and explores the debate between these intellectual siblings that has dominated mainstream academic scholarship in international relations in the United States. Realism and neo-realism, and to some extent neo-liberalism, have also had a profound impact on US foreign policy. Neo-realists dominate the world of security studies and neo-liberals focus on political economy and more recently on issues like human rights and the environment. These theories do not offer starkly contrasting images of the world. Neo-realists state that they are concerned with issues of survival. They claim that neo-liberals are too optimistic about the possibilities for cooperation among states. Neo-liberals counter with claims that all states have mutual interests and can gain from cooperation. Both are normative theories of a sort, biased towards the state, the capitalist market, and the status quo. The processes of globalization have forced neo-realists and neo-liberals to consider similar issues and address new challenges to international order. In the introduction, I discuss the various versions of neo-liberalism and neo-realism and ask the reader to consider how theory shapes our image of the world. Each theory represents an attempt by scholars to offer a better explanation for the behaviour of states and describe the nature of international politics. Similarly, the more policy-relevant versions of these theories prescribe competing policy agendas. The next section of the chapter reviews three versions of neo-realism: Waltz's structural Realism; Grieco's neo-realism or modern Realism with its focus on absolute and relative gains; and, third, what security scholars call offensive and defensive Realism or neo-realism. The third section of the chapter reviews the assumptions of neo-liberal and neo-liberal Institutionalist perspectives. The fourth section focuses on the 'neo-neo-debate'. This is a debate that many US scholars think is the most important intellectual issue in international relations today. Many other scholars see it as not much of a debate at all. It is a debate about refining common assumptions and about the future role and effectiveness of international institutions and the possibilities of cooperation. However, it is not a debate between mainstream and critical perspectives. It is a debate between 'rulemakers' and it leaves out the voices on the margins or the 'ruletakers'. In the fifth section of the chapter, I review how neo-realists and neo-liberal thinkers react to the processes of globalization. The chapter concludes with a suggestion that we are only seeing part of the world if we limit our studies to the neo perspectives and the neo-neo debate. A neo-neo agenda is not a global agenda and it offers a myopic view of human relations, the state, and the international system. Yet, these theories remain dominant in US academic and policy communities and, therefore, it is important that they are understood.

Introduction

The debate between neo-realists and neo-liberals has dominated mainstream international relations scholarship in the United States since the mid-1980s. Two of the major US journals in the field, Inter-national Organization and *International Security*, are dominated by articles that address the relative merits of each theory and its value in explaining the world of international politics. Neo-realism and neo-liberalism are the progeny of Realism and Liberalism respectively. They are more than theories; they are paradigms or conceptual frameworks that define a field of study, limit our conception of reality, and define an agenda for research and policymaking. As previous chapters on Liberalism and Realism have suggested, there are many versions and interpret-ations of each paradigm or theory. Some Realists are more 'hard-line' on issues such as defence or partici-pation in international agreements, while other Real-ists take more accommodating positions on these same issues. The previous chapter on Liberalism pro-vides a useful description of the varieties of this the-ory, and this chapter will explore those that have the greatest impact on academic discourse in the United States and on the people who develop US foreign policy. This chapter will also show the considerable differences in how the scholarly and policy world define and use the labels neo-realism and neo-liberalism.

For most academics, neo-realism refers to Kenneth Waltz's *Theory of International Politics* (1979). Waltz's theory emphasizes the importance of the structure of the international system and its role as the primary determinant of state behaviour. Yet, most scholars and policymakers use neo-realism to describe a recent or updated version of Realism. Recently, in the area of security studies, some scholars use the terms offensive and defensive Realism when discussing the current version of Realism; or neo-realism.

In the academic world, neo-liberal generally refers to neo-liberal Institutionalism or what is now called Institutional theory by those writing in this theoretical domain. However, in the policy world, neo-liberalism means something different. A neo-liberal foreign policy promotes free trade or open markets and Western democratic values and institu-tions. Most of the leading Western states have joined the US-led chorus, calling for the 'enlargement' of the community of democratic and capitalist nation-states. There is no other game in town, the financial and political institutions created after the Second World War have survived and these provide the foundation for current political and economic power arrangements. These are institutions created by policymakers who embrace neo-liberal or Realist/neo-realist assumptions about the world.

In reality, neo-liberal foreign policies tend not to be as wedded to the ideals of democratic peace, free trade, and open borders. National interests take pre-cedence over morality and universal ideals and, much to the dismay of traditional Realists, economic interests are given priority over geopolitical ones.

For students beginning their study of Inter-national Relations, these labels and contending def-initions can be confusing and frustrating. Yet, as you have learned in your reading of previous chapters in this volume, understanding these perspectives and theories is the only way you can hope to understand and explain how leaders and citizens alike see the world and respond to issues and events. This under-standing may be more important when discussing neo-realism and neo-liberalism because they repre-sent dominant perspectives in the policy world and in the US academic community.

There are clear differences between neo-realism and neo-liberalism; however, these differences should not be exaggerated. Robert Keohane (in Baldwin 1993), a neo-liberal Iinstitutionalist, has stated that neo-liberal Institutionalism borrows equally from Realism and Liberalism. Both theories represent status-quo perspectives and are what Robert Cox calls problem-solving theories (see Chs 10 and 12). This means that both neo-realism and neo-liberalism address issues and problems that could disrupt the status quo, namely, the issues of security, conflict, and cooperation.

Neither theory advances prescriptions for major reform or radical transformation of the international system. Rather, they are system maintainer theories, meaning that adherents are generally satisfied with the current international system and its actors, values, and power arrangements. These theories address different sets of issues. In general, neo-realist theory focuses on issues of military security and war. Neo-liberal theorists focus on issues of cooperation, international political economy, and, most recently, the environment. For neo-liberal Institutionalists, the core question for research is how to promote and support cooperation in an anarchic and competitive international system. For neo-realists, the core research question is how to survive in this system.

A review of the assumptions of each theory and an analysis of the contending positions in the so-called neos debate and a discussion of how neo-liberals and neo-realists react to the processes of globalization follows.

Key points

- The neo-neo debate has been the dominant focus in international relations theory scholarship in the USA for the last 10–15 years.

- More than just theories, neo-realism and neo-liberalism represent paradigms or conceptual frameworks that shape individuals' images of the world and influence research priorities and policy debates and choices.

- There are several versions of neo-realism or neo-liberalism.

- Neo-liberalism in the academic world refers most often to neo-liberal Institutionalism. In the policy world, neo-liberalism is identified with the promotion of capitalism and Western democratic values and institutions.

- Rational choice approaches and game theory have been integrated into neo-realist and neo-liberal theory to explain policy choices and the behaviour of states in conflict and cooperative situations. These present more rigorous and scientific versions of the theories.

- Neo-realist and neo-liberal theories are status-quo oriented problem-solving theories. They share many assumptions about actors, values, issues, and power arrangements in the international system. Neo-realists and neo-liberals study different worlds. Neo-realists study security issues and are concerned with issues of power and survival. Neo-liberals study political economy and focus on cooperation and institutions.

Neo-realism

Kenneth Waltz's theory of **structural Realism** is only one version of neo-realism. A second group of neo-realists, represented by the scholarly contributions of Joseph Grieco (1988*a* and 1988*b*), have integrated Waltz's ideas with the ideas of more traditional Realists such as Hans Morgenthau, Raymond Aron, Stanley Hoffmann, and Robert Gilpin to construct a contemporary or **modern Realist** profile. A third version of neo-realism is found in security studies. Here scholars talk about offensive and defensive Realists. These versions of neo-realism are briefly reviewed in the next few pages.

Structural realism

Waltz's neo-realism is distinctive from traditional or classical Realism in a number of ways. **First**, Realism is primarily an inductive theory. For example, Hans Morgenthau would explain international politics by looking at the actions and interactions of the states in the system. Thus, the decision by Pakistan and India to test nuclear weapons would be explained by looking at the influence of military leaders in both states and the long-standing differences compounded by their geographic proximity. All of these explanations are unit or bottom-up explanations.

Neo-Realists, such as Waltz, do not deny the importance of unit-level explanations; however, they believe that the effects of structure must be considered. According to Waltz, structure is defined by the ordering principle of the international system, which is anarchy, and the distribution of capabilities across units, which are states. Waltz also assumes that there is no differentiation of function between different units.

The structure of the international system shapes all foreign policy choices. For a neo-realist, a better explanation for India and Pakistan's nuclear testing would be anarchy or the lack of a common power or central authority to enforce rules and maintain order in the system. In a competitive system, this condition creates a need for weapons to survive. Additionally, in an anarchic system, states with greater power tend to have greater influence.

A second difference between traditional Realists and Waltz's neo-realism is found in their view of power. To Realists, power is an end in itself. Hans Morgenthau describes the Realist view:

The main signpost that helps political realism to find its way through the landscape of international politics is the concept of interest defined in terms of power. . . . We assume that statesmen think and act in terms of interest defined as power, and the evidence of history bears that assumption out. (1962: 5)

Although traditional Realists recognize different elements of power (for example, economic resources, and technology), military power is considered the most obvious element of a state's power. Waltz would not agree with those who say that military force is not as essential as it once was as a tool of statecraft. As recent conflicts in the Balkans, Russia, the Middle East, Africa, and Asia suggest, many leaders still believe that they can resolve their differences with force.

For neo-realists, power is more than the accumulation of military resources and the ability to use this power to coerce and control other states in the system. Waltz and other neo-realists see power as the combined capabilities of a state. States are differentiated in the system by their power and not by their function. Power gives a state a place or position in the international system and that shapes the state's behaviour. During the cold war, the USA and the USSR were positioned as the only two superpowers. Neo-Realists would say that such positioning explains the similarities in their behaviour. The distribution of power and any dramatic changes in that distribution of power help to explain the structure of the international system. Specifically, states will seek to maintain their position or placement in the system. The end of the cold war and the disintegration of the Soviet empire upset the balance of power and, in the eyes of many neo-realists, increased uncertainty and instability in the international system. Waltz concurs with traditional Realists when he states that the central mechanism for order in the system is balance of power. The renewed emphasis on the importance of the UN and NATO and their interventions in crisis areas around the world may be indicative of the major powers' current search for order in the international system. Waltz would challenge neo-liberal Institutionalists who believe that we can manage the processes of globalization merely by building effective international institutions. He would argue that their effectiveness depends on the support of major powers.

A third difference between Realism and Waltz's neo-realism is each one's view on how states react to the condition of anarchy. To Realists, anarchy is a condition of the system, and states react to it according to their size, location, domestic politics, and leadership qualities. In contrast, neo-realists suggest that anarchy defines the system. Further, all states are functionally similar units, meaning that they all experience the same constraints presented by anarchy and strive to maintain their position in the system. Neo-Realists explain any differences in policy by differences in power or capabilities. Both Belgium and China recognize that one of the constraints of anarchy is the need for security to protect their national interests. Leaders in these countries may select different policy paths to achieve that security. A small country such as Belgium, with limited resources, responds to anarchy and the resulting security dilemma by joining alliances and taking an activist role in regional and international organizations, seeking to control the arms race. China, a major power and a large country, would most likely pursue a unilateral strategy of increasing military strength to protect and secure its interests.

Relative and absolute gains

CWS

Joseph Grieco (1988*a*) is one of several Realist/neo-realist scholars who focuses on the concepts of relative and absolute gains. Grieco claims that states are interested in increasing their power and influence (absolute gains) and, thus, will cooperate with other states or actors in the system to increase their capabilities. However, Grieco claims that states are also concerned with how much power and influence other states might achieve (relative gains) in any cooperative endeavour. This situation can be used to show a key difference between neo-liberals and neo-realists. Neo-Liberals claim that cooperation does not work when states fail to follow the rules and 'cheat' to secure their national interests. Neo-Realists claim that there are two barriers to international cooperation: cheating and the relative gains of other actors. Further, when states fail to comply with rules that encourage cooperation, other states may abandon multilateral activity and act unilaterally.

The likelihood of states abandoning international cooperative efforts is increased if participants see other states gaining more from the arrangement. If states agree to a ban on the production and use of landmines, all of the signatories to the treaty will be concerned about compliance. Institutions will be established to enforce the treaty. Neo-Realists argue that leaders must be vigilant for cheaters and must focus on those states that could gain a military advantage when this weapon system is removed. In some security situations, landmines may be the only effective deterrent against a neighbouring state with superior land forces. In this situation, the relative gains issue is one of survival. In a world of uncertainty and competition, the fundamental question, according to Grieco and others who share his view of neo-realism, is not whether all parties gain from the cooperation; but, who will gain more if we cooperate?

Security studies and neo-realism

Recently, security studies scholars, primarily in the USA, have suggested a more nuanced version of a Realism that reflects their interests in understanding the nature of the security threats presented by the

---

Box 9.1   Core assumptions of neo-realists

- States and other actors interact in an anarchic environment. This means that there is no central authority to enforce rules and norms or protect the interests of the larger global community.

- The structure of the system is a major determinant of actor behaviour.

- States are self-interest oriented, and an anarchic and competitive system pushes them to favour self-help over cooperative behaviour.

- States are rational actors, selecting strategies to maximize benefits and minimize losses.

- The most critical problem presented by anarchy is survival.

- States see all other states as potential enemies and threats to their national security. This distrust and fear creates a security dilemma, and this motivates the policies of most states.

---

international system and the strategy options states must pursue to survive and prosper in the system. These two versions of neo-realism, offensive and defensive Realism (many scholars in this area prefer to be called modern Realists and not neo-realists), are more policy relevant than Waltz and Grieco's version of neo-realism and, thus, may be seen as more prescriptive than the other versions (Jervis 1999).

Offensive neo-realists appear to accept most of Waltz's ideas and a good portion of the assumptions of traditional Realism. Defensive neo-realists suggest that our assumptions of relations with other states depend on whether they are friends or enemies. When dealing with friends such as the European Union, the assumptions governing US leaders are more akin to those promoted by neo-liberals. However, there is little difference between defensive and offensive neo-realists when they are dealing with expansionary or pariah states or traditional enemies.

John Mearsheimer (1990, 1994/5), an offensive Realist in security studies, suggests that relative power and not absolute power is most important to states. He would suggest that leaders of countries should pursue security policies that weaken their potential enemies and increase their power relative to all others. To offensive neo-realists, international relations is a prisoner's dilemma game. In this era of globalization, the incompatibility of states' goals and interests enhances the competitive nature of an anarchic system and makes conflict as inevitable as cooperation. Thus, talk of reducing military budgets at the end of the cold war was considered by offensive neo-realists to be pure folly. Leaders must always be prepared for an expansionary state that will challenge the global order. Moreover, if the major powers begin a campaign of disarmament and reduce their power relative to other states, they are simply inviting these expansionary states to attack.

John Mearsheimer and Stephen Walt (2003) were very critical of the recent decision by George W. Bush to go to war in Iraq. They argue that the Bush Administration 'inflated the threat' by misleading the world about Iraq's weapons of mass destruction and its links to terrorists who might attack the USA in the future.

More importantly for security neo-realists, this war was unnecessary because the containment of Iraq was working effectively and there was no 'compelling strategic rationale' for this war. The war with Iraq is likely to cost the USA billions of dollars and it has already required a tremendous commitment of US military forces. With Iraq, Afghanistan, and the global war on terrorism, the US military is overextended. The unilateralism of the Bush Administration concerns both offensive and defensive neo-realists because it hurts the absolute and relative power of the USA.

Defensive neo-realists Robert Jervis (1999) and Jack Snyder (1991) claim that most leaders understand that the costs of war clearly outweigh the benefits. The use of military force for conquest and expansion is a security strategy that most leaders reject in this age of complex interdependence and globalization. War remains a tool of statecraft for some; however, most wars are seen by citizens and leaders alike to be caused by irrational or dysfunctional forces within a society, such as excessive militarism or ethnonationalism.

Defensive neo-realists are often confused with neo-liberals. Although they have some sympathy for the neo-liberal argument that war can be avoided by creating security institutions (for example, alliances or arms control treaties) that diminish the security dilemma and provide mutual security for participating states, they do not see institutions as the most effective way to prevent all wars. Defensive neo-realists share some of the pessimism of offensive neo-realists. Most believe that conflict is simply unavoidable in some situations. First, aggressive and expansionary states do exist and they challenge world order and, second, simply in pursuit of their national interests, some states may make conflict with others unavoidable.

Defensive neo-realists are more optimistic than are offensive neo-realists; however, they are considerably less optimistic than neo-liberals for several reasons (Jervis 1999). First, defensive neo-realists see conflict as unnecessary only in a subset of situations (for example, economic relations). Second, leaders can never be certain that an aggressive move by a state (for example, support for a revolutionary movement in a neighbouring state) is an expansionary action intended to challenge the existing order or simply a preventive policy aimed at protecting their security. Third, defensive Realists challenge the neo-liberal view that it is relatively easy to find areas where national interests might converge and become the basis for cooperation and institution building. Although they recognize that areas of common or mutual interests exist, defensive neo-realists are concerned about non-compliance or cheating by states, especially in security policy areas.

Key points

- Kenneth Waltz's structural Realism has had a major impact on scholars in International Relations. Waltz claims that the structure of the international system is the key factor in shaping the behaviour of states. Waltz's neo-realism also expands our view of power and capabilities; however, he agrees with traditional Realists when he states that major powers still determine the nature of the international system.

- Structural Realists minimize the importance of national attributes as determinants of a state's foreign policy behaviour. To these neo-realists, all states are functionally similar units, experiencing the same constraints presented by anarchy.

- Structural Realists accept many assumptions of traditional Realism. They believe that force remains an important and effective tool of statecraft and balance of power is still the central mechanism for order in the system.

- Joseph Grieco represents a group of neo-realists or modern Realists who are critical of neo-liberal Institutionalists who claim states are mainly interested in absolute gains. Grieco claims that all states are interested in both absolute and relative gains. How gains are distributed is an important issue. Thus, there are two barriers to international cooperation, fear of those who might not follow the rules and the relative gains of others.

- Scholars in security studies present two versions of neo-realism or modern Realism. Offensive neo-realists emphasize the importance of relative power. Like traditional Realists, they believe that conflict is inevitable in the international system and leaders must always be wary of expansionary powers. Defensive Realists are often confused with neo-liberal Institutionalists. They recognize the costs of war and assume that it usually results from irrational forces in a society. However, they admit that expansionary states willing to use military force make it impossible to live in a world without weapons. Cooperation is possible, but, it is more likely to succeed in relations with friendly states.

Neo-Liberalism

As the previous chapter on Liberalism indicates, there are a number of versions of the theory and all have their progeny in contemporary neo-liberal debates. David Baldwin (1993) identified four varieties of Liberalism that influence contemporary international relations: commercial, republican, sociological, and Liberal Institutionalism.

The first, **commercial Liberalism**, advocates free trade and a market or capitalist economy as the way towards peace and prosperity. Today, this view is promoted by global financial institutions, most of the major trading states, and multinational corporations. **Republican Liberalism** states that democratic states are more inclined to respect the rights of their citizens and are less likely to go to war with their democratic neighbours. In current scholarship, this view is presented as democratic peace theory.

These two forms of Liberalism, commercial and republican, have been combined to form the core foreign policy goals of many of the world's major powers. This neo-liberal Internationalism is promoted by the USA and its G8 partners, the UK, France, Germany, and Japan, in trade, aid, and security policies.

In **sociological Liberalism**, the notion of community and the process of interdependence are important elements. As transnational activities increase, people in distant lands are linked and their governments become more interdependent. As a result, it becomes more difficult and more costly for states to act unilaterally and to avoid cooperation with neighbours. The cost of war or other deviant behaviour increases for all states and, eventually, a peaceful international community is built. Many of the assumptions of sociological Liberalism are represented in the current globalization literature dealing with popular culture and civil society. Much of the globalization literature suggests that it is a transnational process and that it builds communities of scholars, producers, consumers, musicians, artists, activists, and others, who transcend the boundaries of states.

Liberal Institutionalism or **neo-liberal Institutionalism** is considered by many scholars to present the most convincing challenge to Realist and neo-realist thinking. The roots of this version of neo-liberalism are found in the functional integration scholarship of the 1940s and the 1950s and regional integration studies of the 1960s. These studies suggest that the way towards peace and prosperity is to have independent states pool their resources and even surrender some of their sovereignty to create integrated communities to promote economic growth or respond to regional problems (see Ch.26). The European Union is one such institution that began as regional community for encouraging multilateral cooperation in the production of coal and steel. Proponents of integration and community building were motivated to challenge dominant Realist thinking because of the experiences of the two world wars. Rooted in liberal thinking, integration theories promoted after the Second World War were less Idealistic and more pragmatic than the Liberal Internationalism that dominated policy debates after the First World War.

The third generation of liberal institutional scholarship was the transnationalism and complex interdependence of the 1970s (Keohane and Nye 1972, 1977). Theorists in these camps presented arguments that suggested that the world had become more Pluralistic in terms of actors involved in international interactions and that these actors had become more dependent on each other. Complex interdependence presented a world with four characteristics: (1) increasing linkages among states and non-state actors; (2) a new agenda of international issues with no distinction between low and high politics; (3) a recognition of multiple channels for interaction among actors across national boundaries; and (4) the decline of the efficacy of military force as a tool of statecraft. Complex interdependence scholars would suggest that globalization represents an increase in linkages and channels for interaction, as well as in the number of interconnections.

Neo-liberal Institutionalism or Institutional theory shares many of the assumptions of neo-realism; however, its adherents claim that neo-realists focus excessively on conflict and competition and minimize the chances for cooperation even in an anarchic international system. Neo-liberal Institutionalists see 'institutions' as the mediator and the means to achieve cooperation among actors in the system. Currently, neo-liberal Institutionalists are focusing their research on issues of global governance and the creation and maintenance of institutions associated with managing the processes of globalization.

For neo-liberal Institutionalists the focus on mutual interests extends beyond trade and development issues. With the end of the cold war, states were forced to address new security concerns like the threat of terrorism, the proliferation of weapons of mass destruction, and an increasing number of internal conflicts that threatened regional and global security. Graham Allison (2000) states that one of the consequences of the globalization of security concerns like terrorism, drug trafficking, and pandemics like HIV/AIDS is the realization that threats to any country's security cannot be addressed unilaterally. Successful responses to security threats require the creation of regional and global regimes that promote cooperation among states and the coordination of policy responses to these new security threats.

Robert Keohane (2002) suggests that one result of the 9/11 terrorist attacks on the USA was the creation of a very broad coalition against terrorism involving a large number of states and key global and regional institutions. Neo-Liberals support cooperative multilateralism and are generally critical of the preemptive and unilateral use of force as is condoned in the 2002 Bush Doctrine. Most neo-liberals would believe that the US-led war with Iraq did more to undermine the legitimacy and influence of global and regional security institutions that operated so successfully in the first Gulf War (1990–1) and continue to work effectively in Afghanistan.

The core assumptions of neo-liberal Institutionalists include:

- States are key actors in international relations, but not the only significant actors. States are rational or instrumental actors, always seeking to maximize their interests in all issue-areas.

| Box 9.2 | Neo-liberal views on institutions and regimes |

- **Institutions** are seen as persistent and as connected sets of rules and practices that prescribe roles, constrain activity, and shape the expectations of actors. Institutions may include organizations, bureaucratic agencies, treaties and agreements, and informal practices that states accept as binding. The balance of power in the international system is an example of an institution.

    (Adapted from Haas, Keohane, and Levy (1993: 4–5))

- **Regimes** are social institutions that are based on agreed rules, norms, principles, and decisionmaking procedures. These govern the interactions of various state and non-state actors in issue-areas such as the environment or human rights. The global market in coffee, for example, is governed by a variety of treaties, trade agreements, scientific and research protocols, market protocols, and the interests of producers, consumers, and distributors. States organize these interests and consider the practices, rules, and procedures to create a governing arrangement or regime that controls the production of coffee, monitors its distribution, and ultimately determines the price for consumers.

    (Adapted from Young 1997: 6)

- In this competitive environment, states seek to maximize absolute gains through cooperation. Rational behaviour leads states to see value in cooperative behaviour. States are less concerned with gains or advantages achieved by other states in cooperative arrangements.

- The greatest obstacle to successful cooperation is non-compliance or cheating by states.

- Cooperation is never without problems, but states will shift loyalty and resources to institutions if these are seen as mutually beneficial and if they provide states with increasing opportunities to secure their international interests.

The neo-liberal institutional perspective is more relevant in issue-areas where states have mutual interests. For example, most world leaders believe that we will all benefit from an open trade system, and many support trade rules that protect the environment. Institutions have been created to manage international behaviour in both areas. The neo-liberal view may have less relevance in areas in which states have no mutual interests. Thus, cooperation in military or national security areas, where someone's gain is perceived as someone else's loss (a zero-sum perspective), may be more difficult to achieve.

Key points

- Contemporary neo-liberalism has been shaped by the assumptions of commercial, republican, sociological, and institutional Liberalism.

- Commercial and republican Liberalism provide the foundation for current neo-liberal thinking in Western governments. These countries promote free trade and democracy in their foreign policy programmes.

- Neo-liberal Institutionalism, the other side of the neo-neo debate, is rooted in the functional integration theoretical work of the 1950s and 1960s and the complex interdependence and transnational studies literature of the 1970s and 1980s.

- Neo-liberal Institutionalists see institutions as the mediator and the means to achieve cooperation in the international system. Regimes and institutions help govern a competitive and anarchic international system and they encourage, and at times require, multilateralism and cooperation as a means of securing national interests.

- Neo-liberal Institutionalists recognize that cooperation may be harder to achieve in areas where leaders perceive they have no mutual interests.

- Neo-liberals believe that states cooperate to achieve absolute gains and the greatest obstacle to cooperation is 'cheating' or non-compliance by other states.

The neo-neo debate

By now it should be clear that the neos debate is not particularly contentious, nor is the intellectual difference between the two theories significant. As was suggested earlier in the chapter, neo-realists and neo-liberals share an epistemology; they focus on similar questions and agree on a number of assumptions about man, the state, and the international system. A summary of the major points of contention is presented in Box 9.3.

If anything, the current neo-liberal Institutionalist literature appears to try hard to prove that they are a part of the neo-realist/Realist family. As Robert Jervis (1999: 43) states, there is not much of a gap between the two theories. As evidence of this, he quotes Robert Keohane and Lisa Martin (1995): 'for better or worse institutional theory is a half-sibling of neo-realism'.

The following reviews key aspects of this debate. With regard to anarchy, both theories share several assumptions. First, they agree that anarchy means that there is no common authority to enforce any rules or laws constraining the behaviour of states or other actors. Neo-liberal institutionalists and neo-realists agree that anarchy encourages states to act unilaterally and to promote self-help behaviour. The condition of anarchy also makes cooperation more difficult to achieve. However, neo-realists tend to be more pessimistic and to see the world as much more competitive and conflictive. To most neo-realists, international relations is a struggle for survival, and in every interaction, there is a chance of a loss of power to a future competitor or enemy. For neo-liberal Institutionalists, international relations is competitive; however, the opportunities for cooperation in areas of mutual interest may mitigate the effects of anarchy.

Some scholars suggest that the real difference between the neos is that they study different worlds.

| Box 9.3 | **The main features of the neo-realist/neo-liberal debate** |

1. Both agree that the international system is anarchic. Neo-realists say that anarchy puts more constraints on foreign policy and that neo-liberals minimize the importance of survival as the goal of each state. Neo-liberals claim that neo-realists minimize the importance of international interdependence, globalization, and the regimes created to manage these interactions.

2. Neo-realists believe that international cooperation will not happen unless states make it happen. They feel that it is hard to achieve, difficult to maintain, and dependent on state power. Neo-liberals believe that cooperation is easy to achieve in areas where states have mutual interests.

3. Neo-liberals think that actors with common interests try to maximize absolute gains. Neo-realists claim that neo-liberals overlook the importance of relative gains. Neo-liberals want to maximize the total amount of gains for all parties involved, whereas the neo-realists believe that the fundamental goal of states in cooperative relationships is to prevent others from gaining more.

4. Neo-realists state that anarchy requires states to be pre-occupied with relative power, security, and survival in a competitive international system. Neo-liberals are more concerned with economic welfare or international political economy issues and other non-military issue-areas such as international environmental concerns.

5. Neo-realists emphasize the capabilities (power) of state over the intentions and interests of states. Capabilities are essential for security and independence. Neo-realists claim that uncertainty about the intentions of other states forces states to focus on their capabilities. Neo-liberals emphasize intentions and preferences.

6. Neo-liberals see institutions and regimes as significant forces in international relations. Neo-realists state that neo-liberals exaggerate the impact of regimes and institutions on state behaviour. Neo-liberals claim that they facilitate cooperation, and neo-realists say that they do not mitigate the constraining effects of anarchy on cooperation.

(Adapted from Baldwin 1993: 4–8)

The neo-liberal Institutionalists focus their scholarship on political economy, the environment, and human rights issues. Neo-Liberals work in what we once called the low politics arena, issues related to human security and the good life. Their assumptions work better in these issue-areas.

Neo-Realists tend to dominate the security studies area. They study issues of international security or what was once called the high politics issues. Many neo-realists assume that what distinguishes the study of international relations from political science is the emphasis on issues of survival. Moreover, high politics issues are the real issues, and the low politics of economic welfare and other good life issues are seen as lesser issues than international relations mainstream issues.

For neo-liberal Institutionalists, foreign policy is now about managing complex interdependence and the various processes of globalization. It is also about responding to problems that threaten the economic well-being, if not the survival, of people around the world. Foreign policy leaders must find ways to manage financial markets so that the gap between rich and poor does not become insurmountable. These same leaders must find ways to deal with toxic waste dumping that threaten clean water supplies in developing states. The anodyne for neo-liberal Institutionalists is to create institutions to manage issue-areas where states have mutual interests. Creating, maintaining, and further empowering these institutions is the future of foreign policy for neo-liberal Institutionalists.

Neo-Realists take a more state-centric view of foreign policy. They recognize international relations as a world of cooperation and conflict. However, close to their traditional Realist roots, neo-realists see foreign policy as dominated by issues of national security and survival. The most effective tool of statecraft is still force or the threat of force and, even in these times of globalization, states must continue to look after their own interests. All states, in the language of the neo-realists, are egoistic value maximizers.

Neo-Realists accept the existence of institutions and regimes (see Box 9.2) and recognize their role as tools or instruments of statecraft. From a neo-realist view, states work to establish these regimes and institutions if they serve their interests (absolute gain), and they continue to support these same regimes and institutions if the cooperative activities promoted by the institution do not unfairly advantage other states (relative gains). Neo-Realists also would agree that institutions can shape the content and direction of foreign policy in certain issue-areas and when the issue at hand is not central to the security interests of a given state.

Neo-Liberals agree that, once established, institutions can do more than shape or influence the foreign policy of states. Institutions can promote a foreign policy agenda by providing critical information and expertise. Institutions also may facilitate policymaking and encourage more cooperation at local, national, and international levels. They often serve as a catalyst for coalition building among state and non-state actors. Recent work on environmental institutions suggests that they can promote changes in national policies and actually encourage both national and international policies that address environmental problems (Haas, Keohane, and Levy 1993).

A major issue of contention in the debate is the notion that institutions have become significant in international relations. Further, they can make a difference by helping to resolve global and regional problems and encourage cooperation rather than conflict. Neo-liberal Institutionalists expect an increase in the number of institutions and an increase in cooperative behaviour. They predict that these institutions will have a greater role in managing the processes of globalization and that states will come to the point where they realize that acting unilaterally or limiting cooperative behaviour will not lead to the resolution or management of critical global problems. Ultimately, neo-liberal Institutionalists claim that the significance of these institutions as players in the game of international politics will increase substantially.

Neo-Realists recognize that that these institutions are likely to become more significant in areas of mutual interest, where national security interests are not at stake. However, the emphasis that states place on relative gains will limit the growth of institutions and will always make cooperation difficult. For neo-realists, the important question is not will we all gain from this cooperation, but, who will gain more?

What is left out of the debate?

One could argue that the neo-neo debate leaves out a great number of issues. Perhaps with a purpose, it narrows the agenda of international relations. It is not a debate about some of the most critical questions like 'Why war?' or 'Why inequality in the international system?' Remember this is a debate that occurs within the mainstream of international relations scholarship. Neo-Realists and neo-liberal Institutionalists agree on the questions; they simply offer different responses. Some important issues are left out and assumptions about international politics may be overlooked. As a student of international relations, you should be able to identify the strengths and weaknesses of a theory. Let us consider three possible areas for discussion: the role of domestic politics, learning, and political globalization.

Both theories assume that states are value maximizers and that anarchy constrains the behaviour of states. But, what about domestic forces that might promote a more cooperative strategy to address moral or ethical issues? Neo-Realist assumptions suggest a sameness in foreign policy that may not be true. How do we account for the moral dimensions of foreign policy such as development assistance given to poor states who have no strategic or economic value to the donor? Or how do we explain domestic interests that promote isolationist policies in the USA at a time when system changes would suggest international activism might result in both absolute and relative gains? We may need to challenge Waltz and ask if the internal make-up of a state

matters. All politics is now glocal (global and local) and neo-realists especially, but also neo-liberals, must pay attention to what goes on inside a state. Issues of political culture, identity, and domestic political games must be considered.

We must assume that leaders and citizens alike learn something from their experiences. The lessons of two world wars prompted Europeans to set aside issues of sovereignty and nationalism and build an economic community. Although some neo-liberal Institutionalists recognize the importance of learning, in general neither theory explores the possibility that states will learn and may shift from a traditional self-interest perspective to an emphasis on common interests. There may be a momentum to cooperation and institution building that both theories underestimate. Can we assume that institutions and cooperation have had some impact on conditions of anarchy?

Both neo-realists and neo-liberals neglect the fact the political activities may be shifting away from the state. A number of scholars have suggested that one of the most significant outcomes of globalization is the emergence of global or transnational political advocacy networks (Keck and Sikkink 1998). Institutions promoted primarily by these advocacy networks have had a major impact on human rights issues such as child labour and security. The recent campaign against the further use of landmines was initiated outside the state and challenged power centres, namely the military and military industries, within states. How will these successful transnational political campaigns affect neo-liberal and neo-realist thinking?

Key points

- The neo-neo debate is not a debate between two polar opposite worldviews. They share an epistemology, focus on similar questions, and agree on a number of assumptions about international politics. This is an intra-paradigm debate.

- Neo-liberal Institutionalists and neo-realists study different worlds of international politics. Neo-realists focus on security and military issues—the high politics issue-area. Neo-liberal Institutionalists focus

on political economy, environmental issues, and, lately, human rights issues. These issues have been called the low politics issue agenda.

- Neo-realists explain that all states must be concerned with the absolute and relative gains that result from international agreements and cooperative efforts. Neo-liberal Institutionalists are less concerned about relative gains and consider that all will benefit from absolute gains.

- Neo-realists are more cautious about cooperation and remind us that the world is still a competitive place where self-interest rules.

- Neo-liberal Institutionalists believe that states and other actors can be persuaded to cooperate if they are convinced that all states will comply with rules and cooperation will result in absolute gains.

- This debate does not discuss many important issues that challenge some of the core assumptions of each theory. For example, neo-realism cannot explain foreign policy behaviour that challenges the norm of national interest over human interests. Neither theory addresses the impact of learning on the foreign policy behaviour of states.

- Globalization has contributed to a shift in political activity away from the state. Transnational social movements have forced states to address critical international issues and in several situations that have supported the establishment of institutions that promote further cooperation, and fundamentally challenge the power of states.

Neo-Liberals and neo-realists on globalization

As I suggested earlier in this chapter, most neo-realists do not think that globalization changes the game of international politics much at all. States might require more resources and expertise to maintain their sovereignty, but neo-realists think most evidence suggests that states are increasing their expenditures and their jurisdictions over a wide variety of areas. Ultimately, we still all look to the state to solve the problems we face, and the state still has a monopoly over the legal use of coercive power. Most neo-realists assume that conditions of anarchy and competition accentuate the concerns for absolute and relative gains. As Waltz (see Box 9.4) suggested in a recent article on the topic, 'The terms of political, economic and military competition are set by the larger units of the international political system' (Waltz 2000: 53).

States remain the primary actors and the only actors with enough power to control or manage the processes of globalization. What neo-realists are most concerned with is the new security challenges presented by globalization. Two examples follow.

Neo-Realists are concerned with the uneven nature of economic globalization. Inequality in the international system may be the greatest security threat in the future. People without food are inclined to seek change, and often that change will be violent. Global economic forces often look for the lowest

| Box 9.4 | **Waltz on globalization** |

Kenneth Waltz, a prominent structural Realist/neo-realist, accepts that globalization presents new challenges for national leaders; however, he denies that the state is being pushed aside by new global actors. According to Waltz, globalization is the fad of the 1990s. It is exaggerated and much of the world has been left out of the process. Globalization is made in America, that is, current institutions and rules that sustain and promote the global economy are under American control. The state has not lost power; in fact, the state has expanded its functions and its control over societies and economies at home and abroad. Waltz claims that states adapt to new environments and transform their power and authority to respond to new policy issues. Ultimately, he states, international politics is still *inter-national*. Waltz makes a strong case against those who argue that states are less important than corporations, markets, or other non-state actors. Waltz argues that no other actor can match the state in terms of its capabilities and successes: 'States perform essential political, social and economic functions, and no other organization rivals them in these respects. They foster the institutions that make internal peace and prosperity possible' (Waltz 2000: 51).

What matters most in shaping international politics is the capabilities of states and not globalization.

(Adapted from Waltz 2000: 46–56)

common denominator in terms of labour costs, safety, and environmental rules. This could create two security problems for states. First, the push and pull of globalization and the search for the lowest common denominator could lead to the loss of key industries and resources that are important for national security. Second, economic globalization can accentuate existing differences in societies, creating instability in strategic regions, thereby challenging world order.

Most neo-realists would claim that forces of globalization challenge sovereignty; however, states have not lost their authority and control. Yet, globalization has had a significant impact on domestic politics and the existing power structures. Transnational social movements (TSMOS) and global advocacy networks have successfully shifted many political issues away from the state. For example, some neo-realists are concerned that the power and security of the state are being undermined by political movements seeking to force states to make new rules that control the use of nuclear and conventional weapons. These movements deftly use the press, the Internet, and activist networks to challenge many of the core assumptions of the dominant Realist/neo-realist policy perspective. Realists and neo-realists tend to favour elitist models of decisionmaking, especially in security areas. Some neo-realists have expressed concern that globalization might contribute to an unwanted democratization of politics in critical security areas (see Ch.13). Their concern is that expertise will be overwhelmed by public emotions.

Most of the discussion of globalization among neo-liberals falls into two categories: (1) a free market commercial neo-liberalism that dominates policy circles throughout the world and (2) academic neo-liberal Institutionalism that promotes regimes and institutions as the most effective means of managing the globalization process.

The end of the cold war was the end of the Soviet experiment in command economics and it left capitalism and free market ideas with few challengers in international economic institutions and national governments. Free market neo-liberals believe that governments should not fight globalization or attempt to slow it down. These neo-liberals want

---

Box 9.5   Neo-liberalism and its current critics

Critical voices

'Free trade theorists claimed that the *rising tide will lift all boats*, providing broad economic benefits to all levels of society. The evidence so far clearly shows that it lifts only yachts' (Barker and Mander 1999: 4).

Critics of the World Trade Organization (WTO) and economic globalization are primarily concerned with the centralization of the world's political and economic institutions. The critics see the WTO as an undemocratic organization that represents the interests of global corporations. In December 1999, representatives from over 1,000 organizations, from over eighty countries, took to the streets in Seattle, Washington, to protest at WTO rulings against national trade laws or regulations that consider issues related to health, the environment, and human rights. The WTO has consistently ruled against governments that pass legislation that impedes the free flow of goods, services, and capital. Critics have called for an open decisionmaking process and they want their political leaders to pressure the officials who govern the global economic institutions (for example, WTO, IMF, and the World Bank), to consider more than market factors in their decisionmaking.

Neo-liberal defenders

The benefits of globalization are clear to neo-liberal free market advocates, and they believe that those who fight against these processes suffer from globalphobia. First, the more global the economy, the more manufacturers or producers in a given country can take advantage of commodities, production processes, and markets in other countries. Second, globalization encourages the diffusion of knowledge and technology, which increases the opportunities for economic growth worldwide. Most neo-liberals have incredible faith in the market and believe that globalization will encourage further economic integration among public and private actors in the economy. Economic integration is seen in giant corporations in Europe merging with their US counterparts. Neo-liberals predict that the globalization momentum will increase due to the declining costs of transportation and communications. Distance is disappearing.

(Adapted from Burtless *et al.* 1998)

minimal government interference in the national or global market. From this perspective, institutions should promote rules and norms that keep the market open and discourage states which attempt to interfere with market forces. Other more social democratic neo-liberals support institutions and regimes that manage the economic processes of globalization as a means to prevent the uneven flow of capital and other resources that might widen the gap between rich and poor states.

Recent demonstrations against global economic institutions in the USA and Europe suggest that there are many who feel that the market is anything but fair. People marching in the streets of London and Seattle called for global institutions that provide economic well-being for all and for reformed institutions that promote social justice, ecological balance, and human rights (see Box 9.5). The critics of economic globalization state that governments will have to extend their jurisdictions and intervene more extensively in the market to address these concerns, as well as open the market and all of its opportunities to those people now left out. Given the current neo-liberal thinking, this kind of radical change is unlikely.

Key points

- Neo-realists think that states are still the principal actors in international politics. Globalization challenges some areas of state authority and control; but politics is still inter-national.

- Neo-realists are concerned about new security challenges resulting from uneven globalization, namely, inequality and conflict.

- Globalization provides opportunities and resources for transnational social movements that challenge the authority of states in various policy areas. Neo-realists are not supportive of any movement that seeks to open critical security issues to public debate.

- Free market neo-liberals believe globalization is a positive force. Eventually, all states will benefit from the economic growth promoted by the forces of globalization. They believe that states should not fight globalization or attempt to control it with unwanted political interventions.

- Some neo-liberals believe that states should intervene to promote capitalism with a human face or a market that is more sensitive to the needs and interests of all the people. New institutions can be created and older ones reformed to prevent the uneven flow of capital, promote environmental sustainability, and protect the rights of citizens.

Conclusion: narrowing the agenda of international relations

Neo-Realism and neo-liberal Institutionalism are status quo rationalist theories. They are theories firmly embraced by mainstream scholars and by key decisionmakers in many countries. There are some differences between these theories; however, these differences are minor compared to the issues that divide reflectivist and rationalist theories and critical and problem-solving theories (see Ch.12).

In scholarly communities, neo-realism generally represents an attempt to make Realism more theoretically rigorous. Waltz's emphasis on system structure and its impact on the behaviour of states leads one to conclude that international relations is not explained by looking inside the state. Neo-Realists who reduce international politics to microeconomic rational choice or instrumental thinking also minimize the idiosyncratic attributes of individual decisionmakers and the different cultural and historical factors that shape politics within a state. These more scientific and parsimonious versions of neo-realism offer researchers some powerful explanations of state behaviour. However, do these explanations offer a complete picture of a given event or a policy choice? Does neo-realist scholarship narrow the research agenda? Recently, neo-realist scholars were criticized for their inability to explain the end of the cold war and other major transformations in the international system. Neo-Realists minimize the importance of culture, traditions, and identity—all factors that shaped the emergence of new communities that helped to transform the Soviet empire.

Contributions by neo-realists in security studies have had a significant impact on the policy community. Both defensive and offensive neo-realists claim that the world remains competitive and uncertain and the structure of the international system makes power politics the dominant policy paradigm. This fits with the interests and belief systems of most military strategists and foreign policy decisionmakers in positions of power in the world today. This continues the Realist tradition that has dominated international politics for centuries and it suggests that the criticisms of the Realist/neo-realist tradition may be limited to the academic world. However critical perspectives, inside and outside the academic world, are causing some Realists/neo-realists to re-examine their assumptions about how this world works. Certainly, defensive neo-realists represent a group of scholars and potential policy advisers who understand the importance of multilateralism and the need to build effective institutions to prevent arms races that might lead to war. There is some change, but the agenda remains state-centric and focused on military security issues.

Neo-Liberalism, whether the policy variety or the academic neo-liberal Institutionalism, is a rejection of the more utopian or cosmopolitan versions of Liberalism. US foreign policy since the end of the cold war has involved a careful use of power to spread an American version of liberal democracy: peace through trade, investment, and commerce. In the last few years, US foreign policy has promoted business and markets over human rights, the environment, and social justice. Washington's brand of neo-liberalism has been endorsed by many of the world's major powers and smaller trading states. The dominant philosophy of statecraft has become a form of 'pragmatic meliorism' with markets and Western democratic institutions as the chosen means for improving our lives. Again, we see a narrowing of choices and a narrowing of the issues

and ideas that define our study of international politics.

Neo-liberal Institutionalism, with its focus on cooperation, institutions, and regimes, may offer the broadest agenda of issues and ideas for scholars and policymakers. Neo-liberal Institutionalists are now asking if institutions matter in a variety of issue-areas. Scholars are asking important questions about the impact of **international regimes** and institutions on domestic politics and the ability of institutions to promote rules and norms that encourage environmental sustainability, human rights, and economic development. It is interesting that many neo-liberal Institutionalists in the USA find it necessary to emphasize their intellectual relationship with neo-realists and ignore their connections with the English School (see Ch.8) and more cosmopolitan versions of Liberalism (see Ch.32). The emphasis on the shared assumptions with neo-realism presents a further narrowing of the agenda of international politics. A neo-liberal institutional perspective that focuses on the nature of international society or community and the importance of institutions as promoters of norms and values may be more appropriate for understanding and explaining contemporary international politics.

Every theory leaves something out. No theories can claim to offer a picture of the world that is complete. No theory has exclusive claims to the truth. Theories in international politics offer insights into the behaviour of states. Realists and neo-realists give great insights into power, conflict, and the politics of survival. However, neo-realism does not help us understand the impact of economic interdependence on state behaviour or the potential effects of institutions and regimes on domestic politics. Here is where neo-liberal Institutionalism helps us construct a picture of international politics. Theories empower some actors and policy strategies and dismiss others. Neo-Realism and neo-liberal Institutionalism are theories that address status quo issues and consider questions about how to keep the system operating. These theories do not raise questions about the dominant belief system or the distribution of power and how these may be connected to conditions of **poverty** and violence. As you continue your studies in international politics, be critical of the theories being presented. Which theories explain the most?

Which theory helps you make sense of this world? What does your theory leave out? Who or what perspective does the theory empower? Who or what view of the world is left out?

For further information and case studies on this subject, please visit the companion web site at www.oup.com/uk/booksites/politics.

 CWS

QUESTIONS

1   What are the similarities between traditional Realism and neo-realism?

2   What are the intellectual foundations of neo-liberal Institutionalism?

3   What assumptions about international politics are shared by neo-liberals and neo-realists? What are the significant differences between these two theories?

4   How do you react to those who say that the neo-neo debate is not much of a debate at all? Is this merely an academic debate or has this discussion had any influence on foreign policy?

5   Do you think globalization will have any impact on neo-realist and neo-liberal thinking? Is either theory useful in trying to explain and understand the globalization process?

6   What do defensive and offensive neo-realists believe? How important are their theories to military strategists?

7   What is the difference between relative and absolute gains? What role do these concepts play in neo-realist thinking? In neo-liberal thinking?

8   How might the proliferation of institutions in various policy areas influence the foreign policy process in major, middle-ranking, and small states? Do you think these institutions will mitigate the effects of anarchy as neo-liberals claim?

9   Why do you think neo-realism and neo-liberalism maintain such dominance in US International Relations scholarship?

10   If we study international politics as defined by neo-realists and neo-liberal Institutionalists, what are the issues and controversies we would focus on? What is left out of our study of international politics?

GUIDE TO FURTHER READING

General surveys with excellent coverage of the neo-realist and neo-liberal perspectives

Burchill, S., Linklater, A., *et al.* (1996), *Theories of International Relations* (Basingstoke: Macmillan). This collection of essays is particularly good on Liberal Internationalism and neo-realism.

Doyle, Michael (1997), *Ways of War and Peace* (New York: W. W. Norton). Discusses the antecedents to neo-realism and neo-liberalism. Excellent sections on Hobbes and structural Realism and varieties of Liberalism;.

Halliday, F. (1994), *Rethinking International Relations* (Vancouver: University of British Columbia Press). Lively and honest analysis of the current theoretical debates.

Luard, E. (ed.) (1997), *Basic Texts in International Relations* (New York: St Martins). An excellent collection of classical, modern, and contemporary essays in international relations presented in three sections: the nature of man; the state; and the international system.

Mandelbaum, M. (2002), *The Ideas That Conquered the World* (New York: Public Affairs). An excellent review of the core ideas of peace, democracy, and free market capitalism Liberalism is discussed as the sole surviving ideology as the cold war ended.

For the more advanced student of International Relations

Smith, S., Booth, K., and Zalewski, M. (eds) (1996), *International Relations Theory and Beyond* (Cambridge: Cambridge University Press). Excellent on critical theory and challenges to rationalist approaches.

For more information on the neo-liberal/neo-realist debate

Baldwin, D. (ed.) (1993), *Neo-realism and Neo-liberalism: The Contemporary Debate* (New York: Columbia University Press). Includes reflections on the debate section with articles by Grieco and Keohane.

Doyle, M., and Ikenberry, G. J. (eds) (1997), *New Thinking in International Relations Theory* (Boulder, Col.: Westview Press). The chapters by Grieco on Realism and world politics and Weber on institutions and change are very useful.

Kegley, C. (ed.) (1995), *Controversies in International Relations Theory: Realism and the Neoliberal Challenge* (New York: St Martins). The first part of the text includes excellent chapters by Waltz, Holsti, Doyle, and Grieco.

Security and neo-realism

Brown, M. E., Lynn-Jones, S. M., and Miller, S. E. (eds) (1995), *The Perils of Anarchy: Contemporary Realism and International Security* (Cambridge, Mass.: MIT Press). A collection of essays from *International Security*.

Mearsheimer, J., and Walt, S. (2003), 'An Unnecessary War', *Foreign Policy* (Jan.–Feb.), 51–9. The article raises several serious concerns about how the Bush Administration distorted the facts to justify the war with Iraq.

Mearsheimer, J. (2003), *The Tragedy of Great Power Politics* (New York: W. W. Norton). The author presents the basics of his offensive Realist theory of world politics and uses historical evidence to support his position that all states seek to survive by maximizing their power.

Pastor, R. (ed.) (1999), *A Century's Journey* (New York: Basic Books). A study of the role the principal actors or Great Powers played in designing and maintaining the current world order.

Snyder, J. (1991), *Myths of Empire: Domestic Politics and International Ambition* (Ithaca, NY: Cornell University Press). A defensive Realist view of war and expansion or overextension. An excellent use of case studies to test competing explanations of overextension.

Neo-Liberalism and neo-liberal institutionalism

Allison, G. (2000), 'The Impact of Globalization on National and International Security', in J. S. Nye and J. D. Donahue (eds), *Governance in a Globalizing World* (Washington, DC: Brookings Institution Press), 72–85.

Haas, P., Keohane, R., and Levy, M. (eds) (1993), *Institutions for the Earth* (Cambridge, Mass.: MIT Press). An excellent collection of case studies asking if institutions have any impact on international, regional, and domestic environmental policies.

Kahler, M. (ed.) (1997), *Liberalization and Foreign Policy* (New York: Columbia University Press). Excellent essays on political and economic liberalization and their impact on foreign policy.

Keohane, R. (2002), 'The Public Delegitimation of Terrorism and Coalitional Politics', in K. Booth and T. Dunne, *Worlds in Collision* (Basingstoke: Palgrave), 141–51.

Milner, H. (1997), *Interests, Institutions, and Information* (Princeton: Princeton University Press). Explores how two-level games influence international cooperation. The reader is introduced to how neo-liberals use rational choice approaches to explain state behaviour.

Nye, J., and Donahue, J. (eds) (2000), *Governance in a Globalizing World* (Washington, DC: Brookings Institution Press). Explores the meaning of globalization, its impact on nation-states, and how globalization might be managed to solve global problems and interests of mankind.

Yergin, D., and Stanislaw, J. (2002), *The Commanding Heights: The Battle for the World Economy* (New York: Touchstone). A basic review of the global economy that covers every region in the world. It has been developed as a very accessible television series.

WEB LINKS

www.isn.ethz.ch The International Relations and Security Network. The Swiss contribution to NATO's Partnership for Peace, it offers extensive information on global security issues.

http://bcsia.ksg.harvard.edu The Belfer Center for Science and International Affairs at Harvard sponsors an international security programme and is the home for the journal *International Security*. Most neo-realist security specialists publish in this journal.

www.iie.com The Institute for International Economics includes useful analysis of major global economic issues from China's exchange rate problems to labour standards and development. Excellent discussions on the role and effectiveness of global economic institutions.

www.pbs.org/wgbh/commandingheights The site offers additional information on 'the battle for the world-economy' and the institutions that manage and promote global trade and economic development.

CHAPTER 10

Marxist theories of international relations

STEPHEN HOBDEN • RICHARD WYN JONES

READER'S GUIDE

This chapter will introduce, outline, and assess the Marxist contribution to the study of International Relations. Having identified a number of core features common to Marxist approaches, the chapter discusses four strands within contemporary Marxism which make particularly significant contributions to our understanding of world politics: world-system theory; Gramscianism; critical theory; and New Marxism. The chapter argues that no analysis of globalization is complete without an input from Marxist theory. Indeed, Marx can be depicted as the *first* theorist of globalization, and from the perspective of Marxism, the features often pointed to as evidence of globalization are hardly novel, but are rather the modern manifestations of long-term tendencies within the development of capitalism.

The authors would like to acknowledge the advice and assistance of Michael Cox and Adam Morton.

Introduction: the continuing relevance of Marxism

With the end of the cold war, the collapse of Communist Party rule in Russia and throughout Eastern Europe, and the global triumph of 'free market' capitalism, it became commonplace to assume that the ideas of Marx, and his numerous disciples, could be safely consigned to the dustbin of history. The 'great experiment' had clearly failed. While Communist parties retained power in China, Vietnam, and Cuba, they did not now constitute a threat to the hegemony of the global capitalist system. Rather, in order to try and retain power, these parties were themselves being forced to submit to the apparently unassailable logic of 'the market' by aping many of the central features of contemporary capitalist societies. In North Korea, where a Communist government has tried to maintain a particularly brutal and idiosyncratic form of central control over its economy and society, credible reports of mass famine served only to confirm the perception that communism no longer offered a viable or attractive alternative. One of the key lessons of the twentieth century, therefore, would appear to be that Marxist thought leads only to a historical dead end. The future is liberal and capitalist.

Yet despite this, Marx, and Marxist thought more generally, refuses to go away. The end of the Soviet experiment, and the apparent lack of a credible alternative to capitalism may have led to a crisis in Marxism, but ten years later there appears to be something of a renaissance. There are probably two reasons why this renaissance is occurring, and why Marxists walk with a renewed spring in their step.

First, for many Marxists the communist experiment in the Soviet Union and in its East European client states, had become a major embarrassment. In the decades immediately after the October Revolution, most had felt an allegiance to the Soviet Union as the first 'Workers' State'; subsequently, however, this loyalty had been stretched beyond breaking point by the depravities of Stalinism, and by Soviet behaviour in its post-Second World War satellites in Eastern Europe. 'Actually existing socialism' was plainly not the communist utopia that many dreamed of and that Marx had apparently promised. Some Marxists were openly critical of the Soviet Union. Others just kept quiet and hoped that the situation, and the human rights record, would improve.

The break-up of the Eastern bloc and the demise of the Soviet Union have in a sense wiped the slate clean. They have reopened the possibility of being able to argue in favour of Marx's ideas without having to defend the actions of governments that justify their behaviour with reference to them. Moreover, the disappearance of the Soviet Union has encouraged an appreciation of Marx's work less encumbered by the baggage of Marxism-Leninism as a state ideology. The significance of this is underlined when it is realized that many of the concepts and practices that are often taken as being axiomatic of Marxism do not in fact figure in Marx's writings: these include the 'vanguard party', 'democratic centralism', and the centrally directed 'command economy'.

Second, and perhaps more importantly, Marx's social theory still retains formidable analytical purchase on the world we inhabit. The vast bulk of his theoretical efforts consisted of a painstaking analysis of capitalism as a mode of production (key Marxist terminology is defined in Box 10.1), and the basic elements of his account have not been bettered. Indeed, with the ever-increasing penetration of the market mechanism into all aspects of life, it is arguable that Marx's forensic examination of both the extraordinary dynamism and the inherent contradictions of capitalism is even more relevant now than in his own time. There is certainly much in his writings that is extraordinarily prescient. A particular strength of Marx's work is his analysis of crisis. Orthodox accounts of capitalism suggest that free markets will move towards equilibrium and will be inherently stable. Our day-to-day lived experience suggests otherwise. The 1987 stock-market crash and the Asian financial crisis of the late 1990s demonstrate that global capitalism continues to be rocked by massive convulsions which have

Box 10.1   A glossary of Marxist terms

Capitalism: the capitalist mode of production, in Marx' analysis, involved a specific set of social relations that were particular to a specific historical period. For Marx there were three main characteristics of capitalism: (1) Everything involved in production (e.g. raw materials, machines, labour involved in the creation of commodities, and the commodities themselves) is given an exchange value, and all can be exchanged, one for the other. In essence, under capitalism everything has its price, including people's working time. (2) Everything that is needed to undertake production (i.e. the factories, and the raw materials) is owned by one class—the capitalists. (3) Workers are 'free', but in order to survive must sell their labour to the capitalist class in order to survive, and because the capitalist class own the *means of production*, and control the *relations of*

production, they also control the profit that results from the labour of workers.

Means (or forces) of production: these are the elements that combine in the production process. They include labour as well as the tools and technology available during any given historical period.

Relations of production: these link and organize the means of production in the production process. They involve both the technical and institutional relationships necessary to allow the production process to proceed, as well as the broader structures that govern the control of the means of production, and control of the end product(s) of that process. Private property and wage labour are two of the key features of the relations of production in capitalist society.

enormous implications for the lives of individuals around the globe. On Marx's account, such convulsions, and their baleful human consequences, are an inherent and inescapable part of the very system itself.

But while much of Marx's analysis of capitalism has stood the test of time, history has treated other elements of his ideas less kindly. His belief that capitalism would be superseded, just as previous modes of production such as feudalism had been, and moreover, would be superseded by socialism, has proven to be at the very least premature. And as has already been mentioned, attempts to date to construct alternative societies based on Marxist ideas have been less than successful. Nevertheless, much of the conceptual armoury developed by Marx in his analysis of capitalism still retains an enormous utility in a world increasingly dominated by free markets.

Compared to Realism and Liberalism, Marxist thought presents a rather unfamiliar view of international relations. While the former portray world politics in ways which resonate with those presented in the foreign news pages of our newspapers and magazines, Marxist theories aim to expose a deeper, underlying—indeed hidden—truth. This is that the familiar events of world politics—wars, treaties, international aid operations, etc.—all occur within structures which have an enormous influence on

those events. These are the structures of a global capitalist system. Thus, Marxists would argue, any attempt to understand world politics must be based on a broader understanding of the processes which operate within global capitalism.

In addition to presenting a rather unfamiliar view of world politics, Marxist theories are also discomfiting, for they argue that the effects of global capitalism are to ensure that the powerful and wealthy continue to prosper at the expense of the powerless and the poor. We are all aware that there is gross inequality in the world. Statistics concerning the human costs of poverty are truly numbing in their awfulness (see Box 10.2). Approximately a third of the world's population use up the vast bulk of the world's resources with the rest having to make do as best they can. Indeed, according to the UNDP *Human Development Report 1996*, the total wealth of the world's 358 billionaires is equal to the combined incomes of the poorest 45 per cent of the world's population. Marxist theorists argue that the relative prosperity of the few is dependent on the destitution of the many. In Marx's own words, 'Accumulation of wealth at one pole is, therefore, at the same time accumulation of misery, agony of toil, slavery, ignorance, brutality at the opposite pole'.

In the next section we will outline some of the central features of the Marxist approach—or

---

Box 10.2   Indicators of world inequality

- One-fifth of the world's population are living in extreme poverty.

- Average incomes in the richest 20 countries are 37 times higher than in the poorest 20—this ratio has doubled in the last 20 years.

- In the developed world subsidies to agricultural producers are six times higher than overseas development aid.

- Tariffs on manufactured goods from the developing world are four times higher than those on manufactured goods from other OECD countries.

- 70 per cent of the world's poor and two-thirds of the world's illiterates are women.

- In 34 countries in the world life expectancy is now lower than it was in 1990.

- More than 30,000 children die every day from easily preventable diseases.

- In Africa only one child in three completes primary education.

- In Sub-Saharan Africa a woman is 100 times more likely to die in childbirth than women in high-income OECD countries.

- One billion people lack access to clean water.

- African countries pay out $US40 million every day on debt repayment.

(Sources: World Bank, United Nations Development Programme, Jubilee Research)

---

historical **materialism** as it is often known. Following on from this, subsequent sections will explore some of the most important strands in contemporary Marx-inspired thinking about world politics. We should note, however, that given the richness and variety of Marxist thinking about world politics, the account that follows is inevitably destined to be partial and to some extent arbitrary. Our aim in the following is to provide a route map that we hope will encourage readers themselves to explore further the work of Marx and of those who have built on the foundations he laid.

Key points

- Marx's work retains its relevance despite the collapse of Communist Party rule in the former Soviet Union.

- Of particular importance is Marx's analysis of capitalism, which has yet to be bettered.

- Marxist analyses of international relations aim to reveal the hidden workings of global capitalism. These hidden workings provide the context in which international events occur.

The essential elements of Marxist theories of world politics

In his inaugural address to the Working Men's International Association in London in 1864, Karl Marx told his audience that history had 'taught the working classes the duty to master [for] themselves the mysteries of international politics'. However, despite the fact that Marx himself wrote copiously about international affairs, most of this writing was jour-nalistic in character. He did not incorporate the international dimension into his theoretical mapping of the contours of capitalism. Given the vast scope of Marx's work, this 'omission' should perhaps not surprise us. The sheer scale of the theoretical enterprise in which he was engaged, as well as the nature of his own methodology, inevitably meant that Marx's work would be contingent and unfinished. That said, since his death many of those who have taken inspiration from Marx's approach have attempted to apply his theoretical insights to international relations.

Given that Marx was an enormously prolific writer, and given also that his ideas developed and changed over time in significant ways, it is not surprising that his legacy has been open to numerous—and often contradictory—interpretations. In addition, real-world developments have also led some of those influenced by Marx to revise his ideas in the light of experience. Hence a variety of different schools of thought have emerged, which claim Marx as a direct inspiration, or whose work can be linked to Marx's legacy. This chapter will focus on four strands of contemporary Marxist thought that have all made major contributions to thinking about world politics. These are world-system theory, Gramscianism, critical theory, and New Marxism. But before we move to discuss what is distinctive about these approaches, it is important that we first examine the essential elements of commonality that lie between them.

First, all the theorists discussed in this chapter share with Marx the view that the social world should be analysed as a **totality**. For them the academic division of the social world into different areas of enquiry—history, philosophy, economics, political science, sociology, international relations, etc.—is both arbitrary and unhelpful. Rather, none can be understood without knowledge of the others: the social world had to be studied as a whole. Given the scale and complexity of the social world, this entreaty clearly makes great demands of the analyst. In his *magnum opus*, volume one of *Capital*, Marx's methodological solution was to start with the simplest of social relations and then proceed to build them up into a more and more complex picture. But however the need to address the totality of relationships in a social world is operationalized, there can be no doubt that for Marxist theorists, the disciplinary boundaries that characterize the contemporary social sciences need to be transcended if we are to generate a proper understanding of the dynamics of world politics.

Another key element of Marxist thought, which serves further to underline this concern with inter-

connection and context, is the **materialist conception of history**. The central contention here is that processes of historical change are ultimately a reflection of the economic development of society. That is, economic development is effectively the motor of history. The central dynamic that Marx identifies is tension between the **means of production** and **relations of production** that together form the **economic base** of a given society. As the means of production develop, for example through technological advancement, previous relations of production become outmoded, and indeed become fetters restricting the most effective utilization of the new productive capacity. This in turn leads to a process of social change whereby relations of production are transformed in order to better accommodate the new configuration of means.

Developments in the economic base act as a catalyst for the broader transformation of society as a whole. This is because, as Marx argues in the Preface to his *Contribution to the Critique of Political Economy*, 'the mode of production of material life conditions the social, political and intellectual life process in general'. Thus the legal, political, and cultural **institutions** and practices of a given society reflect and reinforce—in a more or less mediated form—the pattern of power and control in the economy. It follows logically, therefore, that change in the economic base ultimately leads to change in the 'legal and political **superstructure**'. (For a diagrammatical representation of the **base–superstructure model** see Fig. 10.1).

Class plays a key role in Marxist analysis. In contrast to Liberals who believe that there is an essential harmony of interest between various social groups, Marxists hold that society is systematically prone to class conflict. Indeed in the *Communist Manifesto*, which Marx co-authored with Engels, it is argued that 'the history of all hitherto existing societies is the history of class struggle'. In capitalist society, the main axis of conflict is between the bourgeoisie (the capitalist) and the proletariat (the workers).

Despite his commitment to rigorous scholarship, Marx did not think it either possible or desirable for the analyst to remain a detached or neutral observer of this great clash between capital and labour. Rather, in one of his most frequently cited

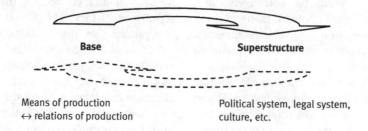

Base   Superstructure

Means of production   Political system, legal system,
↔ relations of production   culture, etc.

Fig. 10.1 The base–superstructure model

comments, he argued that 'philosophers have only interpreted the world in various ways; the point, however, is to change it'. Marx was committed to the cause of **emancipation**. It is clear from Marx's own work, however, that this commitment is emphatically NOT a justification for the uncritical acceptance of some party line, or an excuse dogmatically to ignore facts which cast doubt on some long-cherished belief. Marx insisted on the deployment of solid evidence in order to support (and refute) arguments, and indeed pioneered the use of official statistics in social science writing. Nonetheless, Marx was not interested in developing an understanding of the dynamics of capitalist society simply for the sake of it. Rather he expected such an understanding to make it easier to overthrow the prevailing order and replace it with a communist society—a society in which wage labour and private property are abolished and social relations transformed.

It is important to emphasize that the essential elements of Marxist thought, all too briefly discussed in this section, are also essentially contested. That is, they are subject to much discussion and disagreement even among those contemporary writers who have been influenced by Marxist writings. There is disagreement as to how these ideas and concepts should be interpreted and how they should be put into operation. Analysts also differ over which elements of Marxist thought are most relevant, which have been proven to be mistaken, and which should now be considered as outmoded or in need of radical overhaul. So, for example, while proponents of the four strands of contemporary Marxism discussed in

the following sections would all share Marx's classical commitment to emancipation, few would share Marx's apparent belief that the replacement of capitalism by socialism is inevitable. Moreover, there are substantial differences between them in terms of their attitudes to the legacy of Marx's ideas. The work of the New Marxists draws far more directly on Marx's original ideas than does the work of the Critical Theorists. Indeed the latter would probably be more comfortable being viewed as post-Marxists than as straightforward Marxists. But even for them, as the very term post-Marxism suggests, the ideas of Marx remain a basic point of departure.

Having considered what unites different Marxist approaches to the study of international relations, we will now turn to the task of examining their distinguishing features, as well as their major claims and contributions.

Key points

- Marx himself provided little in terms of a theoretical analysis of International Relations.

- His ideas have been interpreted and appropriated in a number of different and contradictory ways, resulting in a number of competing schools of Marxism.

- Underlying these different schools are several common elements that can be traced back to Marx's writings.

World-system theory

The origins of world-system theory

The origins of world-system theory can be traced back to the first systematic attempt to apply the ideas of Marx to the international sphere, that is to the critique of imperialism advanced by such thinkers as Hobson, Luxemburg, Bukharin, and Hilferding, and Lenin at the start of the twentieth century (see Brewer 1990). Without doubt, the most well-known and influential work to emerge from this debate is the pamphlet written by Lenin, and published in 1917, called *Imperialism, the Highest Stage of Capitalism*. Lenin accepted Marx's basic thesis that the economic mode of production ultimately determines broader social and political relations: a relationship usually summarized via the famous base–superstructure model. Lenin also accepted Marx's contention that history can only be correctly understood in terms of class conflict.

However, Lenin argued that the character of capitalism had changed since Marx published the first volume of *Capital* in 1867. Capitalism had entered a new stage—its highest and final stage—with the development of **monopoly capitalism**. Under monopoly capitalism, a two-tier structure had developed within the world-economy with a dominant **core** exploiting a less-developed **periphery**. Such a structure dramatically complicates Marx's view of a simple divergence of interests between the proletariat and the bourgeoisie. With the development of a core and periphery, there was no longer an automatic harmony of interests between all workers. The bourgeoisie in the core countries could use profits derived from exploiting the periphery to improve the lot of their own proletariat. In other words, the capitalists of the core could pacify—or bluntly, buy off—their own working class through the further exploitation of the periphery. Thus, the structural division between the core and periphery determines the character of the relationship between the bourgeoisie and proletariat of each country.

This summary of Lenin's theory of imperialism should alert us to two important features of the world-system approach to the understanding of world politics. The first is that all politics, international and domestic, takes place within the framework of a capitalist world-economy. The second is the contention that states are not the only important actors in world politics, rather social classes are also very significant. Moreover, it is the location of these states and classes within the structure of the capitalist world-economy that constrains their behaviour and determines patterns of interaction and domination between them.

Lenin's views were developed by the Latin American Dependency School, the writers of which developed the notion of core and periphery in greater depth. In particular the work of Raul Prebisch was especially significant. He argued that countries in the periphery were suffering as a result of what he called 'the declining terms of trade'. Put simply he suggested that the price of manufactured goods increased more rapidly than that of raw materials. So, for example, year by year it requires more tons of coffee to pay for a refrigerator. As a result of their reliance on primary goods, each year countries of the periphery are becoming poorer relative to the core. These arguments were developed further by writers such as André Gunder Frank, and Henrique Fernando Cardoso. It is from the framework developed by such writers that contemporary world-system theory can be seen to have emerged.

The key features of Wallerstein's world-system theory

In order to outline the key features of world-system theory, we shall concentrate on the work of perhaps its most prominent protagonist, Immanuel Wallerstein.

For Wallerstein the dominant form of social organization has been what he calls 'world-systems'. History has witnessed two types of world-system: **world-empires**, and **world-economies**. The main distinction between a world-empire and a world-economy relates to how decisions about resource distribution—crudely, who gets what—are made. In a world-empire a centralized political system uses its power to redistribute resources from peripheral areas to the central core area. In the Roman Empire this took the form of the payment of 'tributes' by the outlying provinces back to the Roman heartland. By contrast, in a world-economy there is no single centre of political authority, but rather we find multiple competing centres of power. Resources are not distributed by central decree but rather through the medium of a **market**. However, although the mechanism for resource distribution is different, the net effect of both types of system is the same, and that is the transfer of resources from the periphery to the core.

The modern world-system is an example of a world-economy. According to Wallerstein this system emerged in Europe at around the turn of the sixteenth century. It subsequently expanded to encompass the entire globe. The driving force behind this seemingly relentless process of expansion and incorporation has been capitalism, defined by Wallerstein as 'a system of production for sale in a market for profit and appropriation of this profit on the basis of individual or collective ownership' (1979: 66). He argues that within the context of this system, specific institutions are continually being created and re-created. This state of flux not only extends to what are normally considered to be narrowly economic institutions such as particular companies or even industries. It is equally true for what are often thought to be permanent, even primordial institutions, such as the family unit, ethnic groups, and states. According to Wallerstein, none of these is timeless—none remains the same. To claim otherwise is to adopt an **ahistoric** attitude, that is, to fail to understand that the characteristics of social institutions are historically specific. For Wallerstein all social institutions, large and small, are continually adapting and changing within the context of a dynamic world-system. Furthermore, and crucially, it is not only the elements within the system which change. Wallerstein argues that the system itself is historically bounded. It had a beginning, has a middle, and will have an end.

The modern world-system has features which can be described in terms of space and time. The **spatial** dimension focuses on the differing economic roles played by different regions within the world-economy. To the core–periphery distinction Wallerstein has (somewhat controversially) added another economic zone in his description of the world-economy, an intermediate **semi-periphery**. According to Wallerstein, the semi-peripheral zone has an intermediate role within the world-system displaying certain features characteristic of the core and others characteristic of the periphery. For example, although penetrated by core economic interests, the semi-periphery has its own relatively vibrant indigenously owned industrial base (see Fig. 10.2). Because of this hybrid nature, the semi-periphery plays important economic and political roles within the modern world-system. In particular, it provides a source of labour that counteracts any upward pressure on wages in the core and also provides a new home for those industries that can no longer function profitably in the core (for example, car assembly and textiles). The semi-periphery also plays a vital role in stabilizing the political structure of the world-system.

According to world-system theorists, the three zones of the world-economy are linked together in an exploitative relationship in which wealth is drained away from the periphery to the centre. As a consequence, the relative positions of the zones become ever more deeply entrenched: the rich get richer while the poor become poorer.

Together, the core, semi-periphery, and periphery make up the spatial dimension of the world-economy. However, described in isolation they provide a rather static portrayal of the world-system. In order to understand the dynamics of their interaction over time we must turn our attention to the **temporal** dimensions of Wallerstein's description of the world-economy. These are cyclical rhythms, secular trends, contradictions, and crisis. It is these, when combined with the spatial dimensions, which determine the historical trajectory of the system.

The first temporal dimension, **cyclical rhythms**, is concerned with the tendency of the capitalist world-economy to go through recurrent periods of expansion and subsequent contraction, or more colloquially, boom and bust. Whatever the underlying processes responsible for these waves of growth and depression, it is important to note that each cycle

CWS

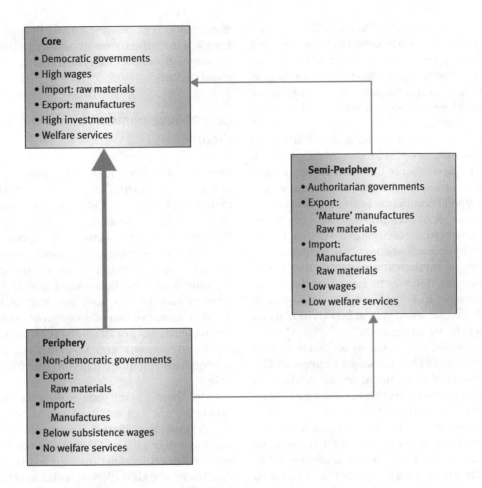

Fig. 10.2 Interrelationships in the world-economy

does not simply return the system to the point from which it started. Rather, if we plot the end point of each wave we discover the **secular trends** within the system. Secular trends refer to the long-term growth or contraction of the world-economy.

The third temporal feature of the world-system is **contradictions**. These arise because of 'constraints imposed by systemic structures which make one set of behavior optimal for actors in the short run and a different, even opposite, set of behavior optimal for the same actors in the middle run' (1991a: 261). These constraints can best be illustrated by examining a problem that Wallerstein regards as one of the main contradictions confronting the capitalist world-system: under-consumption.

In the short term it is in the interests of capitalists

to maximize profits through driving down the wages of the producers, i.e. their workers. However, to realize their profits, capitalists need to sell the products that their workers produce to consumers who are willing and able to buy them. The contradiction arises from the fact that the workers (the producers) are also the potential consumers, and the more wage levels are driven down in the quest to maximize profits, the less purchasing power the workers enjoy. Thus, capitalists end up with shelves full of things that they are unable to sell and no way of getting their hands on the profits. So, although in the short term it might be beneficial for capitalists to depress wage levels, in the longer term this might well lead to a fall in profits because wage earners would be able to purchase fewer goods: in other words, it would create a crisis of under-consumption. Thus, contradictions in the world-economy arise from the fact that the structure of the system can mean that apparently sensible actions by individuals can, in combination or over time, result in very different—and possibly unwelcome—outcomes from the ones originally intended.

In everyday language we tend to use the word **crisis** to dramatize even relatively minor problems. However, in the context of the world-system, Wallerstein wishes to reserve the term to refer to a very specific temporal occurrence. For him, a crisis constitutes a unique set of circumstances that can only be manifested once in the lifetime of a world-system. It occurs when the contradictions, the secular trends, and the cyclical rhythms at work within that system combine in such a way as to mean that the system cannot continue to reproduce itself. Thus, a crisis within a particular world-system heralds its end and replacement by another system.

Controversially, Wallerstein argues that the end of the cold war, rather than marking a triumph for Liberalism, indicates its imminent demise (Wallerstein 1995). This has sparked a crisis in the current world-system that will involve its demise and replacement by another system. Such a period of crisis is also a time of opportunity. When a system is operating smoothly behaviour is very much determined by its structure. In a time of crisis, however, actors have far greater agency to determine the character of the replacement structure. Much of Wallerstein's recent work has been an attempt to develop a political programme to promote a new world-system that is more equitable and just than the current one (Wallerstein 1998, 1999). Even more contentious, particularly in the light of recent discussion of an 'imperial United States', is his claim that the American power is in rapid decline, and that its recent military adventures are a confirmation of such a decline (Wallerstein 2003). From this perspective, to focus on globalization is to miss out on what is truly novel about the contemporary era. Indeed, for Wallerstein, current globalization discourse represents a 'gigantic misreading of current reality' (Wallerstein 2003: 45). Those phenomena evoked by 'globalization' are manifestations of a world-system that emerged in Europe during the sixteenth century to incorporate the entire globe; a world-system that is now in terminal decline.

Recent developments in world-system theory

Various writers have built on the framework established by Wallerstein (Denemark et al. 2000). Christopher Chase-Dunn, for example, lays much more emphasis on the role of the inter-state system than Wallerstein. He argues that the capitalist mode of production has a single logic in which both politico-military and exploitative economic relations play key roles. In a sense he attempts to bridge the gap between Wallerstein's work and that of the New Marxists (discussed in a subsequent section), by placing much more of an emphasis on production in the world-economy and how this influences its development and future trajectory (see Chase-Dunn 1998).

André Gunder Frank (one of the most significant Dependency School writers) has launched a significant critique of Wallerstein's work, and of Western social theory in general. He argues not only that the world-system is far older than suggested by Wallerstein (Frank and Gills 1996), it is also an offshoot of a system that originated in Asia (Frank 1998). His work builds on that of Janet Abu-Lughod. She has challenged Wallerstein's account of the emergence of the modern world-system in the sixteenth century arguing that, during the medieval period, Europe was a peripheral area to a world-economy centred on the Middle East (Abu-Lughold 1989). Frank argues that the source of the capitalist world-economy was not in Europe, rather, the rise of Europe occurred within the context of an existing world-system. Hence social theory, including Marxism, which tries to examine 'Western exceptionalism', is making the mistake of looking for the causes of that rise to dominance in the wrong place, Europe, rather than within the wider, global context in which it occurred.

Key points

- World-system theory can be seen as a direct development of Lenin's work on imperialism and the Latin American Dependency School.

- Immanuel Wallerstein and his work on the modern world-system makes a key contribution to this school.

- Wallerstein's work has been developed by a number of other writers who have built on his initial foundational work.

Gramscianism

In this section we discuss the strand of Marxist theory that has emerged from the work of the Italian Marxist Antonio Gramsci. Gramsci's work has become particularly influential in the study of International Political Economy, where a neo-Gramscian or 'Italian' school is flourishing. Here we will discuss Gramsci's legacy, and the work of Robert W. Cox, a contemporary theorist who has been instrumental in introducing his work to an International Relations audience.

Antonio Gramsci

Antonio Gramsci (1891–1937) was a Sardinian and one of the founding members of the Italian Communist Party. He was jailed in 1926 for his political activities, and spent the remainder of his life in prison, suffering the most appalling privations under a regime personally supervised by Mussolini. Although he is regarded by many as the most creative Marxist thinker of the twentieth century, he produced no single, integrated theoretical treatise. Rather his intellectual legacy has been transmitted primarily through his remarkable *Prison Notebooks* (Gramsci 1971). As their title suggests, these are a collection of notes and some longer essays which Gramsci produced during his long period in captivity. They contain reflections not only on political theory, but also on a wide range of other subjects including economics, philosophy, history, and literary criticism. Given the circumstances under which

they were written, where, with failing health, Gramsci had to work without access to books, and had to write in code in order to confuse the prison censor, it is not surprising that the ideas contained in the *Notebooks* are somewhat fragmentary and are sometimes opaque. They are suggestive rather than definitive statements, and as such open to a range of different interpretations.

The key question which animated Gramsci's theoretical work was why had it proven to be so difficult to promote revolution in Western Europe. Marx, after all, had predicted that revolution, and the transition to socialism, would occur first in the most advanced capitalist societies. But, in the event, it was the Bolsheviks of comparatively backward Russia that had made the first 'breakthrough' while all the subsequent efforts by putative revolutionaries in Western and Central Europe to emulate their success had ended in failure. The history of the early twentieth century seemed to suggest, therefore, that there was a flaw in classic Marxist analysis. But where had they gone wrong?

Gramsci's answer to this question revolves around his use of the concept of **hegemony**. Hegemony is a term widely used in International Relations theory, most frequently in order to describe the most powerful state in the international system, or the dominant state in a particular region. So, for example, the United Kingdom is regarded as having been the hegemonic power in the international system of the nineteenth century, while India is widely viewed as the current regional hegemon in South Asia.

CWS

Gramsci's use of hegemony is also related to his understanding of power, but it reflects a conceptualization of power that is broader and richer than that usually encountered in the work of contemporary Realists.

Gramsci adopts Machiavelli's view of power as a centaur, half beast, half man: a mixture of coercion and consent. In understanding how the prevailing order was maintained, Marxists had concentrated almost exclusively on the coercive practices and **capabilities** of the state, an institution that Engels once described as 'nothing but a machine for the oppression of one class by another'. On this understanding, it was simply coercion, or the fear of coercion, that kept the exploited and alienated majority in society from rising up and overthrowing the system that was the cause of their suffering. Gramsci recognized that while this characterization may have held true in less developed societies, such as pre-revolutionary Russia, it was not the case in the more developed countries of the West. Here the system was maintained not merely by coercion, but also through consent.

Consent, on Gramsci's reading, is created and recreated by the hegemony of the ruling stratum in society. It is this hegemony that allows the moral, political, and cultural values of the dominant group to become widely dispersed throughout society and to be accepted by subordinate groups and classes as their own. Indeed, according to Gramsci's analysis, dominant ideologies become sedimented in society to the extent that they take on the status of unquestioned 'common sense'. All this takes place through the institutions of **civil society**. Civil society is the **network** of institutions and practices in society that enjoy some autonomy from the state, and through which groups and individuals organize, represent, and express themselves to each other and to the state. These include, for example, the media, the education system, churches, voluntary organizations, etc.

Several important implications flow from this analysis. The first is that Marxist theory needs to take superstructural phenomena seriously, because while the structure of society may ultimately be a reflection of social relations of production in the economic base, the nature of relations in the super-structure are of great relevance in determining how susceptible that society is to change and transformation. Gramsci used the term **historic bloc** to describe the mutually reinforcing and reciprocal relationships between the socio-economic relations (base) and political and cultural practices (superstructure) that *together* underpin a given order. Its use serves as a reminder that for Gramsci and Gramscians, to reduce analysis to the narrow consideration of economic relationships, on the one hand, or solely to politics and ideas on the other, is deeply mistaken. It is the interaction that matters.

Another crucial implication is for political practice. If the hegemony of the ruling class or stratum is a key element in the perpetuation of its dominance, then society can only be transformed if that hegemonic position is successfully challenged. This entails a **counter-hegemonic** struggle in civil society, in which the prevailing hegemony is undermined, allowing an alternative historic bloc to be constructed.

Gramsci's writing reflects a particular time and a particular, and in many ways unique, set of circumstances. This has led several writers to question the broader applicability of his ideas. Their central argument is that Gramsci was primarily concerned with a specific national society, that is Italy, rather than the analysis of international circumstances more generally, and that his thinking was relevant to a particular historical epoch, and cannot therefore be regarded as a source of 'transhistorical' concepts (see Burnham 1991; Germain and Kenny 1998). We would suggest, however, that a careful analysis of the *Prison Notebooks* reveals that Gramsci was indeed attempting to develop a conceptual framework that, while certainly not claiming universal, timeless validity, would certainly be applicable to other societies. Furthermore, and as his analysis of Italian society demonstrates, he was very well aware of the significance of developments in the international sphere. But the most important test, of course, is how useful ideas and concepts derived from Gramsci's work prove to be when they are removed from their original context and applied to other **issues** and problems? It is to this that we now turn our attention.

Robert Cox—the analysis of 'world order'

The person who has done most to introduce Gramsci to the study of world politics is the Canadian scholar Robert W. Cox. He has developed a Gramscian approach that involves both a critique of prevailing theories of International Relations and International Political Economy and the development of an alternative framework for the analysis of world politics.

To explain Cox's ideas we would like to begin by discussing one particular sentence in his seminal 1981 article 'Social Forces, States, and World Orders: Beyond International Relations Theory'. The sentence, which has become one of the most often-quoted lines in all of contemporary International Relations theory, reads as follows: 'Theory is always *for* some one, and *for* some purpose' (1981: 128). It expresses a worldview that follows logically from the Gramscian, and broader Marxist position, that has been explored in this chapter. If ideas and values are (ultimately) a reflection of a particular set of social relations, and are transformed as those relations are themselves transformed, then this suggests that all knowledge (of the social world at least) must reflect a certain context, a certain time, a certain space. Knowledge, in other words, cannot be objective and timeless in the sense that some contemporary Realists, for example, would like to claim.

One key implication of this is that there can be no simple separation between facts and values. Whether consciously or not, all theorists inevitably bring their values to bear on their analysis. This leads Cox to suggest that we need to look closely at those theories, those ideas, those analyses that claim to be objective or value free, and ask who or what is it for, and what purpose does it serve? He subjects Realism, and in particular its contemporary variant **neo-realism** to thoroughgoing critique in these grounds. According to Cox, these theories are for—or serve the interests of—those who prosper under the prevailing order, that is the inhabitants of the developed states, and in particular the ruling elites. Their purpose, whether consciously or not, is to reinforce and legitimate the status quo. They do this by making the current configuration of International Relations appear natural and immutable. When Realists (falsely) claim to be describing the world as it is, as it has been, and as it always will be, what they are in fact doing is reinforcing the ruling hegemony in the current world order.

Cox contrasts **problem-solving theory**, that is theory which accepts the parameters of the present order, and thus helps legitimate an unjust and deeply iniquitous system, with **critical theory**. Critical theory attempts to challenge the prevailing order by seeking out, analysing, and, where possible, assisting social processes that can potentially lead to emancipatory change.

One way in which theory can contribute to these emancipatory goals is by developing a theoretical understanding of world orders that grasps both the sources of stability in a given system, and also the dynamics of processes of transformation. In this context, Cox draws upon Gramsci's notion of hegemony and transposes it to the international realm, arguing that hegemony is as important for maintaining stability and continuity here as it is at the domestic level. According to Cox, successive dominant powers in the international system have shaped a world order that suits their interests, and have done so not only as a result of their coercive capabilities, but also because they have managed to generate broad consent for that order even among those who are disadvantaged by it.

For the two hegemons that Cox analyses (the United Kingdom and the United States) the ruling, hegemonic idea has been 'free trade'. The claim that this system benefits everybody has been so widely accepted that it has attained 'commonsense' status. Yet the reality is that while 'free trade' is very much in the interests of the hegemon (which, as the most efficient producer in the global economy, can produce goods which are competitive in all markets, so long as they have access to them), its benefits for peripheral states and regions are far less apparent. Indeed many would argue that 'free trade' is a hindrance to their economic and social development. The degree to which a state can successfully produce and reproduce its hegemony is an indication of the extent of its power. The success of the United States in gaining worldwide acceptance for neo-liberalism suggests just how dominant the current hegemon has become (see Box 10.3).

Box 10.3   The politics of neo-liberalism

A very good example of the hegemonic power of the United States, many Marxists would argue, is the success that it has had in getting neo-liberal policies accepted as the norm throughout the world. The set of policies most closely associated with the neo-liberal project (in particular reduction of state spending, currency devaluation, privatization, and the promotion of free markets) are, revealingly, known as the 'Washington consensus'. Many would argue that these are 'commonsense' policies and that those Third World countries that have adopted them have merely realized that such economic policies best reflect their interests. However, Marxists would argue that an analysis of the self-interest of the hegemon, and the use of coercive power, provide a more convincing explanation of why such policies have been adopted.

The adoption of neo-liberal policies by Third World countries has had a number of implications. Spending on health and education has been reduced, they have been forced to rely more on the export of raw materials, and their markets have been saturated with manufactured goods from the industrialized world. It does not take a conspiracy theorist to suggest that these neo-liberal policies are in the interests of capitalists in the developed world. There are three main areas where the adoption of neo-liberal policies in the Third World is in the direct interest of the developed world. First there is the area of free trade. We need not enter into arguments about the benefits of free trade, but it is clear that it will always be in the interest of the hegemon to promote free trade—this is because, assuming it is the most efficient producer, its goods will be the cheapest anywhere in the world. It is only if countries put up barriers to trade, to protect their own production, that the hegemon's products will be more expensive than theirs. Second, there is the area of raw materials. If Third World countries are going to compete in a free trade situation the usual result is that they become more reliant on the export of raw materials (because their industrial products cannot compete in a free trade situation with those of the developed world). Again this is in

the interest of the hegemon, as increases in the supply of raw material exports mean that the price falls. Additionally where Third World countries have devalued their currency as part of a neo-liberal package the price of their exported raw materials goes down. Finally, when Third World governments have privatized industries, investors from North America and Europe have frequently been able to snap up airlines, telecommunications companies, and oil industries at bargain prices. Duncan Green (1995) gives an eloquent description of the impacts of neo-liberalism on Latin American counties.

If neo-liberal policies appear to have such negative results for Third World countries why have they been so widely adopted? This is where the coercive element comes in. Through the 1970s and 1980s and continuing to today there has been a major debt crisis between the Third World and the West. This debt crisis came about primarily as a result of excessive and unwise lending by Western banks. Third World countries were unable to pay-off the interest on these debts, let alone the debt itself. They turned to the major global financial institutions such as the International Monetary Fund for assistance. Although the IMF is a part of the United Nations it is heavily controlled by Western countries, in particular the United States. For example, the United States has 18 per cent of the votes, while Mozambique has only 0.07 per cent. In total the 10 most industrialized countries have over 50 per cent of the votes. For Third World countries, the price of getting assistance was that they would implement neo-liberal policies. Only once these were implemented, and only on condition that the policies were maintained, would the IMF agree to provide aid to continue with debt repayment.

Hence Marxists would argue that a deeper analysis of the adoption of neo-liberal policies is required. Such an analysis would suggest that the global acceptance of neo-liberalism is very much in the interests of the developed world and has involved a large degree of coercion. That such policies seem 'natural' and 'commonsense' is an indication of the hegemonic power of the United States.

But despite the dominance of the present world order, Cox does not expect it to remain unchallenged. Rather, he maintains Marx's view that capitalism is an inherently unstable system, riven by inescapable contradictions. Inevitable economic crises will act as a catalyst for the emergence of counter-

hegemonic movements. The success of such movements is however far from assured. In this sense, thinkers like Cox face the future on the basis of a dictum popularized by Gramsci, that is, combining 'pessimism of the intellect' with 'optimism of the will'.

Critical theory

Critical theory has been an enormously influential school of thought in fields of academic endeavour that range from aesthetics and psychoanalysis, to sociology and ethics. Nevertheless, it is only relatively recently that its influence has begun to be felt on the discipline of International Relations. There are, without doubt, many overlaps between critical theory and Gramscian approaches to the study of world politics. Most obviously, of course, there is the overlap in terminology. As we have seen in the previous section, Robert W. Cox refers to his own Gramsci-influenced approach as critical theory. Moreover, both Gramscianism and critical theory have their roots in Western Europe of the 1920s and 1930s—a place and a time in which Marxism was forced to come to terms not only with the failure of a series of attempted revolutionary uprisings, but also with the rise of fascism. Indeed, both critical theory and Gramscianism grew out of attempts from within the Marxist tradition to understand why the optimism of an earlier generation, who had believed in the inevitability of emancipatory transformation, had proven to be so disastrously misplaced. We would certainly argue, therefore, that it is a mistake to draw too strong a dividing line between the two schools of thought. Indeed, it is understandable that many commentators regard them as, to all intents and purposes, identical.

Nevertheless, there are differences between them. Contemporary critical theory and Gramscian thoughts about International Relations draw upon the ideas of different thinkers, with differing intellectual concerns. In addition, there is a clear difference in focus between the two strands, with those influenced by Gramsci tending to be much more concerned with issues relating to the subfield of international political economy than are the critical theorists. Critical theorists, on the other hand, have involved themselves with questions concerning international society and **security**. In this section, therefore, we will briefly introduce critical theory and the thought of one of its main proponents in the field of International Relations, Andrew Linklater. In addition, we will briefly introduce Critical Security Studies, an approach to the study of security that draws on both critical theory and Gramscian influences.

Critical theory has developed out of the work of the **Frankfurt School**. This was an extraordinarily talented group of thinkers who began to work with each other in the 1920s and 1930s. As left-wing German Jews, the members of the school were forced into exile by the Nazis' rise to power in the early 1930s, and much of their most creative work was produced after they had successfully sought refuge in the United States. At the end of the Second World War some returned to Germany while others remained in the United States. The leading lights of the first generation of the Frankfurt School included **Max Horkheimer, Theodor Adorno,** and

Herbert Marcuse. A subsequent generation has taken up the legacy of these thinkers and developed it in important and innovative ways. The best known is **Jürgen Habermas**, who is regarded by many as the most influential of all contemporary social theorists. Given the vast scope of critical theory writing, we can do no more here than introduce some of the key features.

The first point to note is that their intellectual concerns are rather different from those of most other Marxists in that they have not been much interested in the further development of analysis of the economic base of society. They have instead concentrated on questions relating to culture, bureaucracy, the social basis and nature of authoritarianism, and the structure of the family, and on exploring such concepts as reason and **rationality** theories of knowledge, etc. Frankfurt School theorists have been particularly innovative in terms of their analysis of the role of the media, and what they have famously termed the 'culture industry'. In other words, in classical Marxist terms, the focus of critical theory is almost entirely superstructural.

Another key feature is that critical theorists have been highly dubious as to whether the proletariat in contemporary society does in fact embody the potential for emancipatory transformation in the way that Marx had believed. Rather, with the rise of mass culture and the increasing commodification of every element of social life, Frankfurt School thinkers have argued that the working class has simply been absorbed by the system and no longer represents a threat to it. This, to use Marcuse's famous phrase, is a **'one dimensional'** society to which the vast majority simply cannot begin to conceive an alternative.

Critical theorists have made some of their most important contributions through their explorations of the meaning of **emancipation**. Emancipation, as we have seen, is a key concern of Marxist thinkers, but the meaning that they give to the term is often very unclear and deeply ambiguous. Emancipation clearly means different things to different people. In addition, the historical record is unfortunately replete with examples of unspeakably barbaric behaviour being justified in the name of emancipation, of which imperialism and Stalinism are but

two. Critical theorists have given sustained consideration to what human capacities and capabilities are being invoked in calls for emancipation, and, on this basis, sketching the contours of a more emancipated world. Two interesting themes have emerged from these deliberations.

For the first generation of critical theorists, emancipation had to be conceived of in terms of a **reconciliation with nature**. This formulation is in stark contrast with more traditional Marxist approaches which have equated emancipation with the process of humanity gaining ever greater mastery over nature. Marx spoke of the desirability of moving 'from the age of necessity to an age of freedom', which meant in part moving from a period where men and women were dominated by, and in thrall to, natural processes, to a period in which they enjoyed dominion. Horkheimer, Adorno, and Marcuse argued, however, that humanity's increased domination over nature had been bought at a very heavy price. This is because the kind of mind-set that is required for conquering nature slips all too easily into the domination of other human beings. It also leads to the hollowing out of some of the finest sensibilities of which humankind is capable. Nothing is valued in and for itself, but is viewed solely in terms of instrumental calculation.

It must be admitted that these critical theorists were extremely vague about what reconciliation might mean in practice, although one might reasonably argue that simply formulating the problem in this way is actually a major contribution in its own right as it forces us to think about familiar things in a very different light. The contemporary German sociologist **Ulrich Beck** has pursued a similar theme with his discussion of **'ecological enlightenment'**. The ideas of the Frankfurt School on this issue also chime with sections of the contemporary Green movement.

The second strand of thought arises from the work of a more recent generation of critical theorists, and in particular the work of Habermas, with his stress on the centrality of communication and dialogue to processes of emancipation. In contrast to classical Marxists who locate the potential for emancipation in the economic base of society—that is, the realm of production—Habermas argues that the promise of a better society lies in the realm of communication. Setting aside the various twists and turns of his argument, Habermas's central point as far as political practice is concerned is that the route to emancipation lies through **radical democracy**. That is, it is through a system in which the widest possible participation is encouraged not only in word (as is the case in many Western democracies) but also in deed, by actively identifying barriers to participation—be they social, economic, or cultural—and overcoming them. For Habermas and his many followers, participation is not to be confined within the borders of a particular sovereign state. Rights and obligations extend beyond state frontiers. This, of course, leads him directly to the concerns of International Relations, and it is striking that Habermas's recent writings have begun to focus on the international realm. However, thus far, the most systematic attempt to think through some of the key issues in world politics from a recognizably Habermasian perspective has been made by **Andrew Linklater**.

 CWS

Andrew Linklater is one of the most distinguished contemporary International Relations theorists, and certainly the most significant critical theorist writing in the field. He has used some of the key **principles** and precepts developed in Habermas's work in order to argue that emancipation in the realm of international relations should be understood in terms of the expansion of the moral boundaries of a **political community** (see Ch.32). In other words, he equates emancipation with a process in which the borders of the sovereign state lose their ethical and moral significance.

Since the establishment of the present international system—an event which is usually traced back to 1648 and the signing of the Treaty of Westphalia—state borders have acted as an ethical boundary. They denote the furthest extent of our sense of duty and obligation, or at best, the point where our sense of duty and obligation is radically transformed, only proceeding further in a very attenuated form. For critical theorists, this situation is simply indefensible. The goal is therefore to move towards a situation in which citizens share the same duties and obligations towards non-citizens as they do towards their fellow citizens.

To arrive at such a situation would, of course, entail a wholesale transformation of the present insitutions of governance—a transformation which most of us would find very unlikely at present. But an important element of the critical theory method is to identify—and, if possible, nurture—tendencies that exist within the present conjuncture that point in the direction of emancipation. The technical term for this is **immanent critique**. On this basis, Linklater identifies the development of the European Union as representing a progressive, or emancipatory tendency in contemporary world politics. It suggests that an important part of the international system is entering a **post-Westphalian era** in which the sovereign state, which has for so long claimed an exclusive hold on its citizens, is beginning to lose some of its pre-eminence. Given the notorious pessimism of the thinkers of the Frankfurt School, the guarded optimism of Linklater in this context is indeed striking.

Critical security studies

Critical Security Studies (CSS) is the name given to a trend in the study of security issues that has gained prominence in recent years (in particular through the work of Keith Krause and Mike Williams (1997), Ken Booth (1991, 2004) and Richard Wyn Jones (1995, 1999)). CSS combines influences from Gramscianism and critical theory with aspects of peace research and the so-called 'alternative defence thinking' of the early 1980s. In contrast to much mainstream security thinking (in the West at least), CSS refuses to accept the state as the 'natural' object of analysis, arguing that, for much of the world's population, states are part of the security problem rather than a provider of security. Instead, proponents of CSS tend to argue that it is beholden on security analysts to place individual human beings at the centre of their analysis. Like Linklater, they regard their work as supporting and nurturing emancipatory tendencies, for it is only through emancipation that security can ultimately be assured.

Key points

- Critical theory has its roots in the work of the Frankfurt School, a group of thinkers including Max Horkheimer, Theodor Adorno, Herbert Marcuse, and Jürgen Habermas.

- Among the key concerns of critical theorists is emancipation, and, in particular, the human capacities and capabilities appealed to in calls for emancipatory action.

- Several different understandings of emancipation have emerged from the critical theory tradition. The first generation of the Frankfurt School equated

emancipation with a reconciliation with nature. Habermas has argued that emancipatory potential lies in the realm of communication and that radical democracy is the way in which that potential can be unlocked.

- Andrew Linklater has developed on critical theory themes to argue in favour of the expansion of the moral boundaries of the political community and has pointed to the European Union as an example of a post-Westphalian institution of governance.

New Marxism

In our exploration of world-system theory, Gramscianism, and critical theory, we have been discussing thinkers whose engagement with Marx's ideas has been mediated through the work of early or mid-twentieth-century interpreters. In this section, by contrast, we examine the work of writers who derive their ideas more directly from Marx's own writings. These New Marxists have returned to the fundamental tenets of Marxist thought and sought to reappropriate ideas that they regard as having been neglected or somehow misinterpreted by subsequent generations. On this basis they have sought both to criticize other developments within Marxism, and to make their own original theoretical contributions to the understanding of contemporary trends. In this section we will introduce the work of two writers associated with this strand of Marxist thought: Bill Warren, a trenchant critic of dependency and world-system approaches; and Justin Rosenberg, who has used key elements of Marx's writings to critique both Realist approaches to International Relations and globalization theory.

Bill Warren—imperialism and the rise of third world capitalism

It is often forgotten that Marx's analysis of capitalism was far more than some simplistic, one-sided condemnation. In addition to pointing forcefully to the inhumanity of capitalist society, Marx was also keenly aware of its great dynamism. As is clear from the *Communist Manifesto*, for example, Marx regarded capitalism as a **necessary** stage in human development. Through its development of the productive capacities of society, capitalism both lays the economic foundation upon which an emancipated society can subsequently be built, and generates the intense class struggle which is the necessary catalyst for such a transformation. As a result of this view, Marx argued that the introduction of capitalism by the colonial powers into the colonies should be regarded as a positive development. Just as capitalism had ended the 'folly of feudalism' in Britain and other European countries, so its progressive characteristics would overthrow backward modes of production throughout the world. This would not be a cost-free or painless process. Marx noted that it was 'sickening . . . to human feeling to witness these myriad of industrious patriarchal and inoffensive social organisations disorganized and dissolved into their units, thrown into a sea of woes, and their individual members losing at the same time their ancient form of civilisation'. However, while the resulting human misery was to be bitterly regretted, it was unavoidable and historically necessary. Capitalism was a phase of world history that had to be endured if a socialist order was to emerge in the longer term.

As we saw earlier, Lenin did not so much reject Marx's view as argue that the character of capitalism had changed by the start of the twentieth century. As a result capitalism could no longer be regarded as playing a progressive role—indeed for the colonies it was deeply regressive. It was regressive, not only in the sense that it was not developing the productive base of what has come to be known as the Third World in the way that Marx had expected, but also because the profits that it was possible to extract through the exploitation of the colonies allowed capitalists to deflect the revolutionary potential of the working classes in the developed core states. For Lenin, therefore, imperialism represented the phase where capitalism definitively ceased to play any progressive function—imperialism was both 'the highest stage of capitalism' and its final stage. This view became the standard Marxist and neo-Marxist position through much of the twentieth century.

The British Marxist, Bill Warren, rejected this view. In his book *Imperialism: Pioneer of Capitalism* (1980) he argued that Lenin had been both empirically and theoretically mistaken. In contrast, he argued that the line argued by Marx remained essentially valid. Capitalism, according to Warren, was fulfilling its historic role in the periphery by rapidly developing the means of production and, crucially for a future transition to socialism, facilitating the emergence of an urban working class. Imperialism should therefore be seen as 'the pioneer of capitalism' rather than its 'highest stage'.

To back up his view Warren examined in depth the development of capitalism in a range of Third World countries. Colonialism, he argued, had brought about a marked improvement in material welfare throughout the world. This improvement took three main forms—better health care, better education, and greater access to consumer goods. Each of these was crucial in laying the foundations for the long-term development of productive forces. In terms of health care, Warren notes that throughout the

colonial world, life expectancy increased and child mortality decreased, resulting in large increases in population. Likewise with education, Warren argued that in Third World countries the percentage of the population attending primary, secondary, and, in particular, tertiary levels of education was higher than it had been in Europe at an equivalent level of development. So, for example, the Third World secondary school enrolment rate of 20 per cent, achieved in 1970, had only been reached in the developed world between 1930 and 1950. Finally, provision of consumer goods increased enormously during the colonial period, stimulating a large increase in domestic production.

Furthermore, Warren argues that in the post-colonial era there has been an enormous increase in the wealth and productive capacity of Third World countries. This process has, of course, been uneven, and there have been winners and losers, but such irregularities are inherent in capitalist development. In particular, growth rates in the Third World have increased significantly since the Second World War. Warren argues that they compare favourably with growth rates in Europe during the eighteenth and nineteenth centuries—an equivalent period in terms of the level of industrial development.

Overall, Warren suggests that the picture of North–South relations depicted by dependency theorists and world-systems theorists is an incomplete one. Certainly the introduction of capitalism throughout the world has had its costs, but it is not leading to the 'development of underdevelopment' as many have argued. Making direct reference to Marx, Warren argues that we should not be anti-capitalist in those situations where capitalist development is increasing levels of productivity and making material improvements to living standards—these are part of capitalism's historic mission as a precursor to a transition to socialism.

Warren's argument is clearly a contentious one. Evidence provided by, for example, World Bank reports, indicates a growing immiseration of much of the Third World. Nonetheless, in one important sense he could be viewed as being essentially correct. Imperialism was not the 'highest stage' of capitalism as Lenin had claimed, it was rather 'the pioneer' by which the capitalist mode of production expanded from its European heartland throughout the globe—

leading directly to the globalized capitalist world of today.

Justin Rosenberg—capitalism and global social relations

Warren focuses primarily on the economic possibilities that the expansion of capitalism provides for Third World countries. By contrast, the focus of Rosenberg's analysis is the character of the international system and its relationship to the changing character of social relations.

Rosenberg's starting point is a critique of Realist International Relations theory. His particular objection is to Realism's claim to provide an ahistorical, essentially timeless account of international relations. Rosenberg argues that we need a theory that allows the development of a historical account of how international relations have developed. He analyses the differences in the character of international relations between the Greek and Italian city-states. A touchstone of Realist theory is the similarity between these two historical cases. Rosenberg, however, describes the alleged resemblances between these two eras as a 'gigantic optical illusion'. Instead his analysis suggests that the character of the international system in each of these periods was completely different. In addition, he charges that attempts to provide an explanation of historical outcomes during these periods working purely from the inter-state level is not feasible (as, for example, in Realist accounts of the Peloponnesian War). Finally, Rosenberg argues that Realist attempts to portray international systems as autonomous, entirely political realms founder because in the Greek and Italian examples this external autonomy was based on the character of internal—and in each case different—sets of social relations.

As an alternative, Rosenberg argues for the development of a theory of international relations that is sensitive to the changing character of world politics. This theory must also recognize that international relations are part of a broader pattern of social relations. His starting point is Marx's observation (Rosenberg 1994: 51) that

it is always the direct relationship of the owners of the conditions of production to the direct producers . . . which reveals

the innermost secret, the hidden basis of the entire social structure, and with it the political form of the relation of sovereignty and dependence, in short, the corresponding specific form of the state.

In other words, the character of the relations of production permeate the whole of society—right up to, *and including*, relations between states. The form of the state will be different under different modes of production, and as a result the characteristics of inter-state relations will also vary. Hence if we want to understand the way that international relations operate in any particular era, our starting point has to be an examination of the mode of production, and in particular the relations of production.

Turning to the contemporary era, Rosenberg argues that two of the core concepts in Realist theorizing, sovereignty and anarchy, can fruitfully be re-evaluated in the light of Marx's method. Indeed, for Rosenberg, both sovereignty and anarchy reflect particular features of the capitalist era. Sovereignty reflects the way in which the state has become separated from the production process under capitalism, with its role becoming purely 'political'. Although states are involved in the regulation of production, they tend not to be directly embroiled in the process of surplus extraction. In all previous eras, by contrast, states were involved directly in production. But with the separation of sovereign territorial governance and production, capitalist enterprises are now able to operate internationally with much greater autonomy from state control. The current situation is therefore a novel and very significant development in social arrangements.

Likewise, Rosenberg suggests that a Marxist approach facilitates a rethinking of that other keystone of Realist thought, anarchy. Rosenberg argues that a theory of anarchy is contained within Marx's analysis of capitalism. This posits that anarchy is a key feature of capitalist production. All wage-earners and capitalists, after all, exist in a condition of competition with each other. In Marx's own words, 'in the society where the capitalist mode of production prevails, anarchy in the social division of labour and despotism in the manufacturing division of labour mutually condition each other' (Rosenberg 1994: 143). The conclusion drawn by Rosenberg is that anarchy is a condition of capitalist relations and not a set of circumstances confined to international relations: it is inherent in social relations within the capitalist mode of production rather than a trans-historical feature of relations between states.

In his more recent work Rosenberg has turned his attention to globalization, or more specifically 'globalization theory' (Rosenberg 2000). He argues that globalization is a descriptive category denoting 'the geographical extension of social processes'. That such social processes have become a global phenomenon is beyond dispute, and a 'theory of globalization' is needed to explain what and why this is happening. Such a theory, for Rosenberg, should be rooted in classical social theory. Instead, he argues, a body of 'globalization theory' has emerged. Globalization theory has put claims about the categories of time and space at its core. The supposed compression of time and space that typifies globalization requires a whole new social theory in order to explain contemporary developments. Rosenberg argues that it is an error to focus a social theory on claims about the character of time and space. Time and space are ultimately social phenomena, and particular spatio-temporal divisions can only be understood in relation to certain sets of social relations. As a result

globalization theory will be a limited and self-defeating exercise able to explain very little about the social world. By contrast a theory of globalization, rooted in classical social theory, would examine the underlying social relations which have led to the capitalist system becoming dominant throughout the globe.

Key points

- New Marxism is characterized by a direct (re)appropriation of the concepts and categories developed by Marx.

- Warren deploys Marx's analysis of capitalism and colonialism to criticize some of the central ideas of dependency and world-system theorists.

- Rosenberg uses Marx's ideas to criticize Realist theories of international relations, and globalization theory. He seeks to develop an alternative approach which understands historical change in world politics as a reflection of transformations in the prevailing relations of production.

Conclusion: Marxist theories of international relations and globalization

In this chapter, we have attempted to outline some of the fundamental tenets of Marxist thinking, and to introduce four contemporary strands of thought that have in different ways attempted to build on these principles and precepts in order to develop an understanding of world politics. In this concluding section we will discuss how Marxist theorists, in general, view the phenomenon of globalization.

As was outlined in the first chapter of this book, globalization is the name given to the process whereby social transactions of all kinds increasingly take place without account for national or state boundaries, with the result that the world has become 'one relatively borderless social sphere'. The particular trends pointed to as typifying globaliza-

tion include: the growing integration of national economies; a growing awareness of ecological interdependence; the proliferation of companies, social movements, and intergovernmental agencies operating on a global scale; and a communications revolution which has aided the development of a global consciousness.

Marxist theorists would certainly not seek to deny that these developments are taking place, nor would they deny their importance, but they would reject any notion that they are somehow novel. Rather, in the words of Chase-Dunn, they are 'continuations of trends that have long accompanied the expansion of capitalism' (1994: 97). Marx and Engels were clearly aware not only of the global scope of capitalism, but also of its potential for social transformation. In a particularly prescient section of the *Communist Manifesto* (Marx and Engels 1967: 83–4), for example, they argue that:

The bourgeoisie has through its exploitation of the world market given a cosmopolitan character to production and consumption in every country ... All old-established national industries have been destroyed or are daily being destroyed. They are dislodged by new industries, whose introduction becomes a life and death question for all civilized nations, by industries that no longer work up indigenous raw material, but raw material drawn from the remotest zones; industries whose products are consumed, not only at home, but in every quarter of the globe. ... National one-sidedness and narrow-mindedness become more and more impossible, and from the numerous local literatures, there arises a world literature.

According to Marxist theorists, the globe has long been dominated by a single integrated economic and political entity—a global capitalist system—which has gradually incorporated all of humanity within its grasp. Within this system, all elements have always been interrelated and interdependent. 'National economies' have long been integrated to such an extent that their very nature has been dependent on their position within a capitalist world-economy. The only thing 'new' is an increased awareness of these linkages. Similarly, ecological processes have always ignored state boundaries, even if it is only recently that growing environmental degradation has finally allowed this fact to permeate into public consciousness.

The growth of multinational corporations certainly does not signify any major change in the structure of the modern capitalist system. Rather, they form part of a long-term trend towards the further integration of the global economy. Neither is international contact between those movements who oppose the prevailing political and economic order a new development. In fact, as even the most cursory examination of the historical record will amply attest, such movements, be they socialist, nationalist, or ecological in character, have always drawn inspiration from, and forged links with, similar groups in other countries. Finally, the much-vaunted communications revolution is the latest manifestation of a long-term trend under capitalism

whereby space and time are becoming increasingly compressed.

While the intensity of cross-border flows may be increasing, this does not necessarily signify the fundamental change in the nature of world politics proclaimed by so many of those who argue that we have entered an era of globalization. Marxist theorists insist that the only way to discover how significant contemporary developments really are is to view them in the context of the deeper structural processes at work. When this is done, we may well discover indications that important changes are afoot. Many Marxists, for example, regard the delegitimation of the sovereign state as a very important contemporary development. However, the essential first step in generating any understanding of those trends regarded as evidence of globalization must be to map out the contours of global capitalism itself. If we fail to do so, we will inevitably fail to gauge the real significance of the changes that are occurring.

Another danger of adopting an ahistoric and uncritical attitude to globalization is that it can blind us to the way in which reference to globalization is increasingly becoming part of the ideological armoury of elites within the contemporary world. Globalization is now regularly cited as a reason to promote measures to reduce workers' rights and lessen other constraints on business. Many politicians and business leaders argue that unless businesses are allowed to function without constraints, they will not be able to compete in a globalizing economy.

Such ideological justifications for policies which favour the interests of business can only be countered through a broader understanding of the relationship between the political and economic structures of capitalism. As we have seen, the understanding proffered by the Marxist theorists suggests that there is nothing natural or inevitable about a world order based on a global market. The current organization of global capitalism is in a constant state of change and crisis. Therefore, rather than accept the inevitability of the present order, the task facing us is to lay the foundations for a new way of organizing society—a global society which is more just and more humane than our own.

Key points

- Marxists are rather sceptical about the emphasis currently being placed on the notion of globalization.

- They see the recent manifestations of globalization as not a recent phenomenon but part of long-term trends in the development of capitalism.

- Furthermore the notion of globalization is increasingly being used as an ideological tool to justify reductions in workers' rights and welfare provision.

 For further information and case studies on this subject, please visit the companion web site at www.oup.com/uk/booksites/politics

For further information and case studies on this subject, please visit the companion web site at www.oup.com/uk/booksites/politics

QUESTIONS

1   How would you account for the continuing vitality of Marxist thought?

2   How did Lenin's approach to international relations differ from that of Marx?

3   How useful is Wallerstein's notion of a semi-periphery?

4   Assess Warren's criticisms of world-system theory.

5   Evaluate Rosenberg's critique of globalization theory.

6   In what ways does Gramsci's notion of hegemony differ from that employed by Realist International Relations writers?

7   How has Linklater developed critical theory for an International Relations audience?

8   How do Marxist theorists view the notion of 'globalization'?

9   What do you regard as the main contribution of Marxist theory to our understanding of world politics?

10   How useful is the notion of emancipation used by critical theorists?

11   Do you agree with Cox's distinction between 'problem-solving theory' and 'critical theory'?

12   Assess Wallerstein's claim that the power of the United States is in decline.

GUIDE TO FURTHER READING

In order to develop an understanding of the basic elements of Marx's ideas, and the origins of Marxism in general, we strongly suggest that you start by reading Marx and Engels' *Communist Manifesto*. Numerous editions are available, some of which are very reasonably priced. Despite having been first published in 1848, the Manifesto remains a very powerful statement, whose impact has scarcely been dulled by the passage of time. The more ambitious may then wish to tackle *Capital*, volume one of which is the most readable by some distance, and the only one that was completed in Marx's lifetime. Again many different editions are available. C. J. Arthur (1992) has produced a helpful 'Student's Edition' that sensitively abridges the text and supplies a useful introduction (*Capital: Student Edition*, London: Lawrence & Wishart). For those of a more historical bent, Perry Anderson's (1974) *Passages from Antiquity to Feudalism* and (1974), *Lineages of the Absolutist State* (both London: New Left Books) are a stunning demonstration of the analytical power of the Marxist approach. While undoubtedly challenging, both are well worth the investment of time and energy.

On Marx himself, Francis Wheen's recent biography (1999), simply titled *Karl Marx* (London: Fourth Estate), has been rightly praised for its liveliness and lightness of touch. It is both enjoyable and highly informative and can be wholeheartedly recommended. There are also a number of short introductions to Marx's ideas available. P. Singer's (1985), *Marx* (Oxford: Oxford University Press) is especially worthwhile. The most important recent discussion of Marx's ideas it to be found in Allan Megill's (2002), *Karl Marx: The Burden of Reason (Why Marx Rejected Politics and the Market)* (Oxford: Rowman and Littlefield): a model of respectful scholarship that is also devastatingly critical.

On Marxism and International Relations, see the excellent discussion by John Hobson (2000), in *The State and International Relations* (Cambridge: Cambridge University Press), ch.4. Michael Cox's article (1998) 'Rebels without a Cause? Radical Theorists and the World System after the Cold War', *New Political Economy* 3:3: 445–60, provides a wide-ranging and notably accessible overview of contemporary Marxist writing about international relations. Andrew Gamble (1999), *Timewalkers: The Prehistory of Global Colonisation* (Cambridge, Mass.: Harvard University Press) also discusses the fate of Marxist approaches to International Relations after the cold war.

The most complete account of the world-system approach to the study of International Relations is to be found in the work of Immanuel Wallerstein. If you have the time and energy the three volumes (1974, 1980, 1989), of *The Modern World-System*, are well worth studying (San Diego: Academic Press). Shorter summaries of Wallerstein's approach to world-system theorizing can be found in: S. Hobden (1998), *International Relations and Historical Sociology: Breaking down Boundaries* (London: Routledge), ch.7; and T. R. Shannon (1996), *An Introduction to the World System Perspective* (Boulder, Col.: Westview). For an excellent introduction to the various contemporary writers within world-system theory see Denemark, R.A., Friedman, J., Gills, B. K., and Modelski, G. (eds) (2000), *World System History* (London: Routledge).

Stephen Gill's edited volume (1993) *Gramsci, Historical Materialism and International Relations* (Cambridge: Cambridge University Press) draws together an important series of essays on Gramscian approaches to the study of world politics. The best introduction to Robert Cox's work is Robert Cox with Timothy J. Sinclair (1996), *Approaches to World Order* (Cambridge: Cambridge University Press), which reproduces most of his key essays including the seminal 1981 article 'Social Forces, States, and World Orders: Beyond International Relations Theory'. For a brief and very useful survey of Gramscian approaches see also A. Morton (1999), 'On Gramsci', *Politics*, 19:1: 1–8. Those interested in discovering more about Gramsci's life and ideas should read Giuseppe Friori's (1990) deeply moving biography, *Antonio Gramsci: Life of a Revolutionary*, trans. Tom Nairn (London: Verso).

The first three chapters of Richard Wyn Jones (1999), *Security, Strategy and Critical Theory* (Boulder, Col.: Lynne Rienner), provide an introduction to, and overview of, some of the key intellectual concerns of the Frankfurt School. All three of Andrew Linklater's books can be highly recommended: (1990), *Men and Citizens in the Theory of International Relations* and (1990), *Beyond Realism and Marxism: Critical Theory and International Relations* (both London: Macmillan); and (1998), *The Transformation of Political Community* (Cambridge: Polity Press). Also very useful is his essay 'The Achievements of Critical Theory', in Smith, S., Booth, K., and Zalewski, M. (eds) (1996), *International Theory: Positivism and Beyond* (Cambridge: Cambridge University Press). The collection (2000) *Critical Theory and World Politics* (Boulder, Col.: Lynne Rienner), edited by Richard Wyn Jones, brings together the key critical theorists in International Relations as well as Gramscians such as Robert Cox. This book also contains two important critiques of critical theory by Chris Brown and Alexander Wendt. On New Marxism, see B. Warren (1980), *Imperialism: Pioneer of Capitalism* (London: New Left Books), and J. Rosenberg (1994), *The Empire of Civil Society: A Critique of the Realist Theory of International Relations* (London: Verso). In addition, the journal *Historical Materialism* provides a forum for New Marxist writing.

WEB LINKS

www.marxists.org.uk The Marx and Engels Internet Archive: a large collection of works (including the *Communist Manifesto*), letters, and images relating to Marx and Engels.

www.yorku.ca/socreg *The Socialist Register*: an annual academic socialist journal. Edited by Leo Panitch and Colin Leys. The site includes links to selected articles from current and past volumes.

www.monthlyreview.org *The Monthly Review*: a long-established Marxist journal from the USA, edited by Harry Magdoff and John Bellamy Foster.

www.newleftreview.com *The New Left Review*: a leading Marxist theoretical journal. Founded in 1960, NLR has been called 'the flagship of the Western intellectual left'.

www.victoryiscertain.con/gramsci Gramsci Links Archive: includes links to a variety of Gramsci-related sites.

www.uta.edu/huma/illuminations Illuminations: The Critical Theory Web Site: firmly based in Frankfurt School thought, this site maintains a collection of articles, excerpts, and chapters from many contemporary writers of and about critical theory.

CHAPTER 11

Social Constructivism

MICHAEL BARNETT

READER'S GUIDE

This chapter provides an overview of Constructivist approaches to international relations theory. Constructivism's antecedents are located in the 1980s and in a series of critical reactions to mainstream international relations theory in the United States, namely neo-realism and neo-liberal Institutionalism. These theories emphasized the distribution of power and the unwavering pursuit by states of power and wealth, and minimized the power of ideas. Constructivism countered by highlighting how ideas define and can transform the organization of world politics, shape the identity and interests of states, and determine what counts as legitimate action. Although initially given a cold reception, Constructivism quickly gained credibility and popularity in the 1990s due to the end of the cold war, the enduring insights of sociological and critical theory, and the ability to generate novel accounts of world politics. Although there are important differences among Constructivists, they share several commitments that generate a distinctive approach for understanding how the world is made and re-made through human action and intervention.

Introduction

Constructivism is a success story. It rose very quickly from rather humble beginnings to become one of the leading schools in International Relations. Twenty years ago Constructivism did not exist. Ten years ago Constructivism was recognized as an exciting, but still unproven, paradigm. Seven years ago the leading American journal of International Relations, International Organization, exclaimed that the next great debate in the discipline would be between Rationalism and Constructivism. Although still received rather coolly in many quarters in the United States Constructivism is widely accepted in Canada and Europe, and its survival is assured for the foreseeable future. The very fact that a chapter on Constructivism is included in this volume is testimony to its prominence and ability to capture important features of global politics.

My goal in this chapter is not to provide the definitive account of the life and times of Constructivism. Instead, it is to consider its origins, its fight for disciplinary acceptability, its core commitments, and features of its research agenda as it relates to global change. I will highlight two factors surrounding its birth, one theoretical and the other sociological. The midwives of Constructivism are an unlikely pairing: neo-realism and neo-liberalism, on the one hand, and sociological and critical theory, on the other. The 1980s were dominated by the 'neos', as recalled in Ch.9. Notwithstanding their substantive differences, they shared two fundamental assumptions. Both assumed that states have innate and fixed interests and are constrained in their ability to further those interests because of material forces such as geography, technology, and the distribution of power. Critics drew from sociological and critical theory to argue for greater attention to ideational forces such as ideas, knowledge, norms, and rules in order to deepen our interpretation of the origins of states' interests, and the organization of world politics. These claims later became part of Constructivism's intellectual oeuvre.

Constructivism's birth and development also was shaped by an American context. To call attention to this dimension is not to claim that Americans cre-

ated Constructivism. Indeed, as with the development of Realism in the United States, most of its leading figures either were born in Europe and now teach in the United States or currently teach at non-American universities. Nor is it to say that the ideas that animate Constructivism are quintessentially American. Indeed, many of Constructivism's core beliefs, including the claim that societies shape the identities, interests, and capacities of individuals, run counter to the American culture that emphasizes individualism and autonomy, and hail from European social and political thought. Nor is it to suggest that only this version of Constructivism was interested in the role of international norms and conceptualizing international politics not as a system but as a society. After all, there were important traditions that predated Constructivism that made similar kinds of claims, including feminist approaches to international relations, and the English School and its recognition of the society of states, as discussed in Ch.8.

My decision to emphasize the American context is intended to highlight how the struggle for acceptance in the American disciplinary context shaped Constructivism's conceptual contours and its research agenda. In order to prove itself, it had to transform its considerable theoretical erudition into workmanlike empirical research that mattered to neo-liberal institutionalism and neo-realism. A consequence of this fight for recognition was not only an engagement with the mainstream but also a disengagement from other social theories, including post-structuralism and some variants of critical theory, that inspired many of its claims, a point made in Ch.12. Although there are rival camps, they are unified by a common concern with how ideas define the international structure that constructs the identities, interests, and foreign policy practices of states, how state and non-state actors reproduce that structure—and at times transform it. The concern with the making and re-making of world politics underscores Constructivism's strong interest in issues of global change. A defining feature of the contemporary world is the diffusion of institutional models and the internationalization of norms, which points to the role of international processes in shaping the identities and interests of actors around the world, the possibility of convergence around similar models and norms, and the homogenization of world politics.

In the beginning . . .

Constructivism's origins can be traced to the 1980s when neo-realism and neo-liberal Institutionalism dominated American international relations theory. Waltz aspired to make Realism more rigorous, scientific, and amenable to hypothesis testing. He did so by specifying the nature of the units and their preferences, and how the structure of the international system constrains those preferences. The most important actors are states. Although Waltz was unclear whether they pursued survival, security, or power, and whether they maximized or satisfied, he is very clear that these interests suffocated any possibility that ideas, norms, or values might shape state behaviour. He argued that the structure of the international system had three elements: anarchy (the absence of a supranational authority); functional non-differentiation of the units (because anarchy created a self-help system, all states had to be self-reliant and safeguard their security), and the distribution of power. But because the world has always been an anarchy and states have always been obsessed about their survival, to understand enduring tendencies in world politics required scholars to focus only on the position of the state in international hierarchy and the distribution of power. Waltz depicted a dreary world in which states were suspicious, misanthropic, and aggressive not necessarily because they were born that way but because the environment punished anything else (see Ch.7).

Neo-Liberal Institutionalism responded to neo-realism's pessimistic view of international politics by demonstrating that states had the capacity to cooperate on a range of issues. States did not always have conflicting interests; they often had convergent interests and realized that they might be able to cooperate in ways that improved their lives. If states could not necessarily trust each other to abide by their agreements, then they could construct international institutions to discourage cheating and encourage compliance and cooperation. International institutions can perform various functions that help states cooperate. They can clarify the nature of agreements, make states' behaviour transparent, monitor compliance, and publicize cheaters. Neo-liberals also highlighted how international norms can enhance the prospect of cooperation by establishing expectations of behaviour and regulating state action.

Neo-realism and neo-liberal Institutionalism dominated international relations theory in the United States during the 1990s. As recounted in Ch.9, these camps disagreed over the effects of anarchy, whether state interests varied, whether states sought absolute or relative gains, whether institutions can shape state behaviour, and whether and how cooperation was possible. Yet for all their heated disagreements, they shared a commitment to individualism and materialism. Individualism is the view that actors have a set of innate interests that are fixed and that the structure that constrains their behaviour derives from the aggregation of the properties of the actors. Although neo-realists and neo-liberals differ because the former believe that the pursuit of security is primary while the latter can envision other goals such as the pursuit of wealth, for empirical and theoretical reasons they proceed on the assumption that state interests are hard-wired and fixed forever. Materialism is the view that the structure that constrains behaviour is defined by factors such as the distribution of power, technology, and geography. Neo-realism denies that ideas and norms can trump interests. Neo-liberal Institutionalism, though, does recognize that states might willingly construct norms and institutions to regulate their behaviour because to do so will enhance their long-term interests. But neither approach can imagine that ideas and norms might not only constrain but actually construct how states define their interests.

The 1980s was characterized not only by the dominance of neo-realism and neo-liberal Institutionalism but also by a growing interest in social theory, that is, how to conceptualize the structure and its organizing principles, the actors and the rules that regulate their relations, and the relationship between the structure and the actors. Neo-realism and neo-liberalism adopted an individualist approach to states as they examined how the international structure, largely defined in material terms, constrained the ability of states to pursue their interests. Various scholars, however, began to utilize alternative social theories to challenge these claims. At this point the critiques did not come from a single school. Some drew from sociological theory, emphasizing how structures not only constrain but also constitute (or construct) the identities and interests of actors. Others drew from critical theory and the general interest in uncovering the power behind seemingly value-neutral concepts and recovering the interpretations and meanings that actors give to their activities. Nor were the protagonists conspiring to promote any single research programme. Instead, they were daring international relations to imagine how the structure of international politics constructs the identities and interests of states, to recover the meanings that states give to their activities, and to consider how relations between self-reflective states can transform the very structure of world politics.

There were many important contributions in the 1980s, but arguably four were most influential for establishing Constructivism's theoretical orientation and conceptual vocabulary. Although for over a decade John Ruggie had been writing on the centrality of ideas and norms in international politics, his review essay (1983) of Kenneth Waltz's *Theory of International Politics* helped to establish a countermovement. He directed his critique at the very foundation of Waltz's conceptual architecture: structure. As already discussed, Waltz's conception of international structure has three elements: anarchy; functional non-differentiation between states; and the distribution of power. Any genuine transformation in the structure, in his view, required a movement from anarchy to hierarchy. Because the world has always been anarchic and because states have always operated according to a self-help logic, scholars need

focus only on the distribution of power. Ruggie, though, directed attention at the second element, differentiation. The states-system, he observed, has been organized according to alternative principles. What marked the movement from the feudal to the modern states-system was the shift from heteronomy and overlapping authorities to state sovereignty and the centralization of authority in the modern state. Waltz's approach to international politics, then, led him to overlook the defining organizing principle of modern states-system—sovereignty. Moreover, Waltz's approach provided no way for understanding this great transformation because his framework argued that all change came from the top, that is, the states-system. Ruggie challenged Waltz on this point and argued that to understand international change and transformation required a consideration of the growing density of interactions among actors located at the inter-state, transnational, and domestic levels.

The following year Richard Ashley (1984) published a wide-ranging and immensely influential critique of neo-realism. He levelled a variety of charges. It is so fixated on the state that it cannot see a world populated by non-state actors. It treats states as having fixed interests and thus cannot see how their interests are created, constructed, and transformed by global-historical forces. It is so committed to individualism and the presumption of the individual coming prior to society rather than society creating the social person that it cannot see how global-historical forces are responsible for creating the very identities, interests, and capacities of states. It is so committed to materialism that it constructs an artificial view of society that is completely devoid of ideas, beliefs, and rules. It is so willing to treat the basic concepts of international relations, such as sovereignty, as if they are natural objects that it fails to recognize how they are socially and culturally produced. Drawing from post-structural and critical theory, Ashley's devastating critique of the underpinnings of neo-realism revealed not only its limitations but also the power of post-structural and critical theory (see Ch.12).

In 1987 Alexander Wendt introduced international relations scholars to the agent-structure problem and its relationship to international politics. The question is: how should international relations scholars conceptualize the relationship between agents (states) and structures (the international structure)? Waltz's approach, he argued, began with states, examined the aggregate properties of states' capabilities to determine a structure defined by the international distribution of military power, and then posited that this structure constrains what states can do and generates patterns of inter-state behaviour. The problem, according to Wendt, is that Waltz fails to see how structures do more than constrain agents; they also construct or constitute the identities and interests of agents. An alternative formulation, one closely associated with Immanuel Wallerstein's world-system theory and the claim that there is a structure to the world system that is defined by capitalism, argues that the structure determines what states are and what they do. The virtue of this approach is also its vice. It recognizes that structures can constitute the agents but treats the agents as little more than structural dupes because they can do little more than mechanically reproduce that structure. Although these theories offer alternative understandings of the relationship between agents and structures, both treated structures in strictly material terms. For Waltz it was the distribution of military power and for Wallerstein it was capitalism. Yet structures are also defined by ideas, norms, and rules; in other words, structures contain normative and material elements. The challenge, therefore, is to recognize that the normative structures can create agents and that agents can create and possibly transform those structures.

Employing Anthony Giddens' concept of **structuration**, Wendt argued that an international normative structure shapes the identities and interests of states, and through their practices and interactions states re-create that very structure. This points to the importance of the actions of states for understanding what sustains and transforms normative structures. Norms do not operate behind the backs of actors; rather, actors determine what they are. Frequently actors reproduce these norms without much thought, acting reflexively as a consequence of taken-for-granted knowledge, habits, and routines. Yet at other times they self-consciously attempt to construct new norms that might affect not only the incentives for certain behaviour but also the very structure itself. They are certainly con-

strained by the underlying structure and must overcome resistance by other actors who either have a vested interest in the underlying rules, a preferred alternative, or just cannot imagine anything else. Yet no structure is so determining that it eliminates the capacity for critical reflection and the possibility that agents might knowingly attempt to transform the structure. Wendt expertly used sociological theory to expose conceptual problems in contemporary theorizing and to identify tractable solutions.

Drawing from legal, sociological, and linguistic theories, Friedrich Kratochwil offered one of the first systematic treatments of rules and norms in international relations. He introduced international relations scholars to the distinction between regulative and constitutive rules. **Regulative rules** are those rules that regulate already existing activities. Rules for the road determine how to drive. The World Trade Organization's rules regulate trade. **Constitutive rules**, however, do not merely regulate but in fact create the very possibility for these activities. The rules of rugby not only prohibit blocking but also help to define the very game (and distinguish it from American football); after all, if forwards began to block for backs not only would this be a penalty but it would change the game itself. The rules of sovereignty not only regulate state practices but also make possible the very idea of a sovereign state. He also advised scholars to adopt interpretive methods to recover how actors bring meaning to and understand these norms. Furthermore, he cautioned that rules should not be treated as naturally existing because they are created and revised through practice, reasoned reflection, and arguments over how best to apply these rules to new situations. Scholars, therefore, should use interpretive approaches to understand how actors debate what counts as a valid and appropriate act as applied to a specific setting.

By drawing from critical and sociological theory to demonstrate the limitations of neo-realism and neo-liberal Institutionalism, these and other scholars were opening space for an alternative research programme. These ideas did not receive a warm reception. To some extent this is how the intellectual elite always treat challengers. The critics did not always help their cause, though. They frequently belittled the theories and research agendas of the mainstream. They could write in highly alienating ways,

---

Box 11.1   Robert Keohane's early views on the reflectivist challenge

Students of international institutions should direct their attention to the relative merits of two approaches, the rationalistic and the reflective. Until we understand the strengths and weaknesses of each, we will be unable to design research strategies that are sufficiently multifaceted to encompass our subject-matter, and our empirical work will suffer accordingly . . . [T]he greatest weakness of the reflective school lies not in deficiencies in their critical arguments but in the lack of a clear reflective program that could be employed by students of world politics. Waltzian neo-realism has such a research program; so does neo-liberal institutionalism. [U]ntil the reflective scholars or others sympathetic to their arguments have delineated such a research program and shown in particular studies that

it can illuminate important issues of world politics they will remain on the margins of the field . . . [R]eflective approaches are less well specified as theories: their advocates have been more adept at pointing out what is omitted in rationalist theory than in developing theories of their own with a priori content. Supporters of this research program need to develop testable theories and to be explicit about their scope . . . above all, students of world politics who are sympathetic to this position need to carry out systematic empirical investigations, guided by their ideas. Without such detailed studies, it will be impossible to evaluate their research program. Eventually, we may hope for a synthesis between the rationalistic and reflective approaches.

(Keohane 1988: 161, 173–4)

---

hardly encouraging a wide readership or a sympathetic reading. Moreover, the critiques were long on erudition but short on empirical analysis. Those being asked to learn a second language rather late in life understandably wanted evidence that doing so would enrich empirical analysis. Robert Keohane's response in his presidential address to the International Studies Association captured the mood. He simultaneously recognized the insights of what he called the 'reflectivist' research programme and issued a challenge. As recalled in Box 11.1, he acknowledged that reflectivists offered important critiques that could not ignored. Yet until these critics transformed their criticisms into a positive research agenda that used careful research designs and standard social science methodologies to generate empirical pay-offs, then the jury was out.

Key points

- International relations theory in the 1980s was dominated by neo-realism and neo-liberal Institutionalism; both theories ascribed to materialism and individualism.

- Various scholars critical of neo-realism and neo-liberalism drew from critical and sociological theory to demonstrate the effect of normative structures on world politics.

- The mainstream responded coolly to these challenges, demanding that critics demonstrate the superiority of these alternative claims through empirical research.

The rise of Constructivism

Constructivism, a term coined by Nicholas Onuf in his important book, *The World of Our Making* (1989), met that challenge. Four background factors sponsored its meteoric rise in the 1990s. The first was the end of the cold war. Although only a handful of scholars had even contemplated the possibility that the cold war would end with a whimper and not a

bang, neo-realists and neo-liberal Institutionalists were especially hard-pressed to explain this outcome. Their commitment to individualism and materialism meant that they could not begin to grasp what appeared to reside at the heart of this stunning development: the revolutionary impact of ideas to transform the organization of world politics and state identities. Nor did these approaches provide insight into what might come next. The USA was enjoying a unipolar moment, but the distribution of power could not determine whether the USA would aspire to become a global hegemon or would opt to work through multilateral institutions. States clearly expected the new international order to further their interests. But the end of the cold war triggered national debates over what were those interests, which were frequently tied to a consideration of their national identity, which presupposed, as well, a discussion of critical similarities and differences. In other words, states were actively debating their national identity—who are 'we' and where do 'we' belong?—in order to determine their interests and the desired regional and international order. To understand the dissolution and creation of new international orders required, so it seemed, a Constructivist sensibility. Finally, the end of the cold war clipped the prominence of traditional security themes, neo-realism's comparative advantage, and raised the importance of non-traditional security issues, transnationalism, human rights, and other subjects that seemingly played to Constructivism's strengths.

Constructivists also convinced the mainstream in the United States that they were committed to 'science'. At first, many mainstream scholars dismissively labelled Constructivism as 'anti-science' and post-modern—a remarkable claim that only highlighted how quaint was their conception of social science, which cleaved to positivism and the search for timeless laws. In response, Constructivists worked to widen and modernize the concept of social science, to show careful attention to the logic of inquiry, and to insist that their differences were around what the world was made of and not necessarily whether they tested their claims in relationship to the evidence and alternative explanations. Over time the relations between Constructivists and the mainstream improved. The same could not be said for relations between Constructivists and those subscribing to post-structural and critical theory.

After all, Constructivists had gained considerable intellectual insights from these approaches, but they were insisting that they held the 'middle ground' because they could address these crucial issues within social science (Adler 2000).

Constructivism's reliance on sociological theory also furthered its rise to respectability. The debates in international relations regarding how to conceptualize the relationship between states and the international system had been played (and replayed) in sociology for over a century as it debated how to conceptualize the relationship between the individual and society. Max Weber wrote against individualism and claimed that sociology was concerned with how culture shaped the meanings and significance that actors gave to their actions. George Herbert Mead encouraged sociologists to examine how interactions between individuals are mediated by symbols. Talcott Parsons slammed individualism. Constructivists resurrected these arguments and applied them to their own debates with neo-realists and neo-liberals; the latter could not easily dismiss the ideas of such eminent sociologists that had influenced various areas of political science.

Ultimately, Constructivism's success derived from its ability to further empirical analysis in matters of central concern to neo-realism and neo-liberal Institutionalism. The epistemic community literature carefully explored how expert groupings help states discover their interests and ways for producing durable cooperation. Peter Katzenstein's *The Culture of National Security* (1996) challenged standard neo-realist claims in a series of critical areas—including alliance patterns, military intervention, arms racing, Great Power transformation—and demonstrated how identity and norms shape state interests and must be incorporated to generate superior explanations. By the end of the 1990s Constructivism was no longer a fad or something attributed to the wild innocence of youth but instead was an increasingly accepted form of analysis.

Key points

- The end of the cold war meant that there was a new intellectual space for scholars to challenge existing theories of international politics.

- Constructivists drew from established sociological theory to demonstrate how social science could help international relations scholars understand the importance of identity and norms in world politics.

- Constructivists demonstrated how attention to norms and states identities could help uncover important issues neglected by neo-realism and neo-liberalism.

Constructivism

Before proceeding to identify Constructivism's tenets, two caveats are in order. Constructivism is a social theory and not a substantive theory of international politics. Social theory is broadly concerned with how to conceptualize the relationship between agents and structures and substantive theory offers specific claims and hypotheses about patterns in world politics. In this way Constructivism is best compared to rational choice. Rational choice is social theory that offers a framework for understanding the relationship between actors and their environment. Briefly, actors operate with fixed preferences, and they attempt to maximize those preferences under a set of constraints. It makes no claims about the content of those preferences; they could be wealth or religious salvation. Nor does it assume anything about the content of these constraints; they could be guns or ideas. Rational choice offers no claims about the actual patterns of world politics. For instance, neo-realism and neo-liberalism subscribe to rational choice, but they arrive at rival claims about patterns of conflict and cooperation in world politics because they make different assumptions about the effects of anarchy. Like rational choice, Constructivism is a social theory that is broadly concerned with the relationship between agents and structures, but it is not a substantive theory. In order to generate substantive claims, scholars must delineate who are the principal actors, what are their interests and social capacities, and what is the content of the normative structures.

Also, while Constructivism might appear to be one, big, happy, family, in fact the family members have lots of divisions. Differences derive from the fact that some use the insights of James March, John Meyer, and organizational theory and others Michel Foucault and discourse analysis. Some prioritize agents and others structures. Some focus on inter-state politics and others transnationalism. There are differences over the possibility of social science. Different empirical puzzles drive different approaches. These fault-lines have spawned a proliferating number of labels. Neoclassical. Modernist. Post-modern. Naturalistic. Thick. Thin. Linguistic. Narrative. Weak. Strong. Systemic. Holistic. This development should not be surprising. As the other chapters on international relations theory in this volume suggest, all schools have internal rivalries.

Still, there is unity within such diversity. 'Constructivism is about human consciousness and its role in international life' (Ruggie 1998: 856). This suggests a commitment to a form of Idealism. The world is defined by material and ideational forces. But these ideas are not akin to mental beliefs or psychological states that reside inside our heads. Instead, these ideas are social. Our mental maps are shaped by collectively held ideas such as knowledge, symbols, language, and rules. In this way, Constructivism also accepts some form of holism or Structuralism. The world is irreducibly social and cannot be decomposed to the properties of already existing actors. Shared ideas, then, shape the organization of world politics. Idealism and holism, according to Wendt (1999), are Constructivism's core commitments. The emphasis on Idealism does not mean a rejection of material reality. Instead, it recognizes that the meaning and construction of that material reality is dependent on ideas and interpretation. The **balance of power** does not objectively exist out there waiting to be discovered; instead states themselves debate what is the balance of power, what is its meaning, and how they should respond. Nor does the emphasis on holism deny agency. Instead, it recognizes that agents have some autonomy and their practices and interactions help to construct, reproduce, and transform those structures. Although the structure of the cold war seemingly locked the United States and the Soviet Union into a fight to the death, leaders on both sides creatively transformed their relations and, with it, the very structure of global politics.

Below I explore some of Constructivism's conceptual vocabulary and contrast its claims with those of rational choice. The core observation is the **social construction of reality**. This has a number of related elements. One is to emphasize the socially constructed nature of actors and their identities and interests. Instead of assuming that actors are born outside of and prior to society, as individualism does, the claim is that individuals are produced and created by their cultural environment. Nurture, not nature. For instance, what makes an Arab state an *Arab* state is not the fact that the populations speak Arabic but rather that there are rules associated with Arabism that shape the Arab states' identity, interests, and foreign policies that are deemed legitimate and illegitimate. Another element is how knowledge, that is, symbols, rules, concepts, categories, and meanings, shapes how individuals construct and interpret their world. Reality does not exist out there waiting to be discovered; instead, historically produced and culturally bound knowledge enables individuals to construct and give meaning to reality.

The possibility that this constructed reality presents itself as an objective reality relates to the concept of **social facts**. There are those things whose existence is dependent on human agreement and those things whose existence is not. Brute facts such as rocks, flowers, gravity, and oceans exist independent of human agreement and will continue to exist even if humans disappear or deny their existence. Social facts are dependent on human agreement and are taken for granted. Money, refugees, terrorism human rights, and sovereignty are social facts. Even though they are wholly dependent on human agreement and will only exist so long as that agreement exists, we treat them as objective facts and thus as constraints on action.

The social construction of reality concerns not only how we see the world but also how we see ourselves, define our interests, and determine what constitutes acceptable action. As already discussed, the concept of structuration captures how the underlying normative structure shapes the identities and interests of actors, and how through their practices and interactions actors recreate that structure. The rules that help to define that structure, in other words, do more than regulate the practices of actors with already existing interests; they construct their interests and define what counts as appropriate behaviour. This distinction between constitutive and regulative rules parallels the conceptual distinction between the **logic of consequences** and the **logic of appropriateness**. The logic of consequences attributes human behaviour to the anticipated costs and benefits of particular action, mindful that other actors are doing just the same. This logic, then, highlights how action is driven by an actor's calculation of how a particular strategy is likely to further her preferences. The logic of appropriateness, however, suggests that actors are rule following. They determine their course of action depending on a sense of self and what is appropriate for the situation.

To emphasize the social construction of reality is to denaturalize what is frequently taken for granted. This points to several issues. One is with the origins of those social constructs that are now taken for granted. Sovereignty did not always exist; it was a product of historical forces and human interactions that generated new distinctions regarding where political authority resided. The category of weapons of mass destruction is a modern invention. Although individuals have been forced to flee their homes ever since Adam and Eve were exiled from Eden, the political and legal category of 'refugees' is only a century old. To understand the origins of these concepts requires attention to the interplay between existing ideas and institutions, the political calculations by leaders who had ulterior motives, and morally minded actors who were attempting to improve

Nuclear Weapons

humanity. Also of concern are alternative pathways. Although history is path dependent, there are contingencies, historical accidents, the conjunction of material and ideational forces, and human intervention that can force history to jump the proverbial train tracks. The events of 11 September 2001 and the response by the Bush Administration arguably transformed the direction of world politics. This interest in possible and counterfactual worlds works against historical determinism. When Alexander Wendt (1992) famously argued that 'anarchy is what states make of it' he was not, as some ridiculed, suggesting that wishing the world was different would make it so, but rather calling attention to how existing beliefs and practices make the world and if they change then so, too, would the organization of world politics. A world of Mahtma Gandhis will be very different from a world populated by Osama bin Ladens.

Constructivists also examine how actors make their activities meaningful. Following Max Weber's (1949: 81) insight that 'we are cultural beings with the capacity and the will to take a deliberate attitude toward the world and to lend it *significance*', Constructivists attempt to recover the meanings that actors give to their practices and the objects that they construct. The meanings that actors lend to their activities derive not from private beliefs but rather from society or culture. In contrast to the Rationalist presumption that culture, at most, is a constraint on action, Constructivists argue that culture informs the meanings that people give to their action. Sometimes Constructivists have presumed that such meanings derive from a hardened culture. But because culture is fractured and because society is comprised of different interpretations of what is meaningful activity, scholars need to consider these cultural fault-lines and treat the fixing of meanings as an accomplishment that is at the essence of politics. Some of the most important debates in world politics revolve around the meanings of particular activities. Development, human rights, humanitarian intervention, sovereignty are all important orienting concepts that can have any number of meanings. Individuals fight to fix the meanings of these concepts, and their rival interpretations frequently derive from their different cultural settings.

The very fact that these meanings are fixed through politics and that once these meanings are fixed they have consequences for the ability to determine the fates of people suggests an alternative way of thinking about **power**. Most international relations theorists treat power as the ability of one state to compel another state to do what it otherwise would not. The assumption is that the means of power, such as military technology and economic statecraft, are material, and that evidence of power exists when states are forced to alter their behaviour. Yet the forces of power go beyond material, they also can be ideational. When human rights activists 'name and shame' they are attempting to embarrass law-breaking governments into changing their conduct by demonstrating how their conduct is not consistent with existing legal norms. Moreover, the effects of power go beyond the ability to change behaviour. Power also includes how knowledge, the fixing of meanings, and the construction of identities allocate differential rewards and capacities. If development is defined as per capita income then some actors, namely states, and some activities, namely industrialization, are privileged; however, if development is defined as basic needs, then other actors, namely peasants and women, gain voice, and other activities, namely small-scale agricultural initiatives and cottage industries, are visible.

Power also exists when identities and interests are constructed in ways that benefit some to the disadvantage of others. Most scholars who work on **gender** have evidenced careful attention to the relationship between gender and power; indeed, V. Spike Peterson (2003) has recently argued that a hallmark of gender analysis is attention to power. Most gender scholars accept the presumed differences between men and women are socially constructed, and the social construction of these differences generates differential social capacities and opportunities. The importance of thinking about gender as a social construct is highlighted in Box 11.2. (Also see Ch.12 for a fuller discussion.) As scholars of gender have deployed their approaches to the study of international relations, they have made two central contributions of relevance here. One is to push Constructivist analysis to consider more fully how power operates in international politics. Until recently, Constructivists have been relatively inattentive to questions of power, and scholars of

---

Box 11.2 | **Charli Carpenter on the effects of gender on the lives of individuals in war-torn societies**

International agencies mandated with the protection of war-affected civilians generally aim to provide protection in a neutral manner, but when necessary they prioritize the protection of the 'especially vulnerable.' According to professional standards recently articulated by the International Committee for the Red Cross 'special attention by organizations for specific groups should be determined on the basis of an assessment of their needs and vulnerability as well as the risks to which they are exposed.' If adult men are most likely to lose their lives directly as a result of the fall of a beseiged town, one would expect that, given these standards, such agencies would emphasize protection of civilian men in areas under siege by armed forces. Nonetheless, in places where civilians have been evacuated from besieged areas in an effort to save lives, it is typically women, children, and the elderly who have composed the evacuee population . . . While in principle all civilians are to be protected on the basis of their actions and social roles, in practice only certain categories of population (women, elderly, sick, and disabled) are presumed to be civilians regardless of context . . . Thus . . . gender is encoded within the parameters of the immunity norm: while in principle the 'innocent civilian' may include other groups, such as adult men, the presumption that women and children are innocents, whereas adult men may not be means that 'women and children' signifies 'civilian' in a way that 'unarmed adult male' does not . . . Similarly, gender beliefs are embedded in . . . the concept of 'especially vulnerable populations' . . . In this context it never would have occurred to protection agencies to evacuate men and boys first, even if they had had the chance.

(Carpenter 2003: 662, 671, 673–4)

---

gender, who have been highly attentive to power, have pushed Constructivists to remedy this omission. The other is to see how many of the international institutions and norms that Constructivists identify are also gendered and leave men and women with differential capacities and opportunities. Sandra Whitworth (1994), for instance, has demonstrated how the very international organizations transmit norms, such as particular meanings of development, that leave women differentially advantaged.

There is tremendous debate among Constructivists over whether and how they are committed to social science. Still, there is some common ground. To begin, they reject the unity of science thesis, that is, that the methods of the natural sciences are appropriate for understanding the social world. Instead, they argue that the objects of the natural world and the social world are different in one crucial respect: in the social world the subject knows herself through reflection upon her actions as a subject not simply of experience but of intentional action as well. Humans reflect on their experiences and use these experiences to inform their reasons for their behaviour. Atoms do not. What necessitates a human science, therefore, is the need to understand how individuals give significance and meaning to their actions. Only then will we be able to explain

human action. Consequently, the human sciences require methods that can capture the interpretations that actors bring to their activities. Max Weber, a leading advocate of this position, advocated that scholars employ vershten to recreate how people understand and interpret the world. To do so, scholars need to exhibit empathy, to locate the practice within the collectivity so that one knows how this practice or activity counts, and to unify these individual experiences into objectively, though time-bound, explanations (Ruggie 1998: 860).

There is considerable debate among Constructivists (and beyond) about whether the human sciences abandon causality and explanation for description, and the position of scholars in this debate depends on the definition of causality and explanation. Constructivists generally argue that they *are* offering causal explanations. But they reject the claim that the only legitimate form of causality is when scholars have uncovered an enduring sequenced connection between an independent and a dependent variable. It is virtually impossible to find such laws in international politics. The reason for their absence is not because of some odd characteristic of international politics. Instead, this elusiveness exists for all the human sciences. As Karl Popper observed, the search for timeless laws in the human sciences will be forever elusive because of the ability of humans to accumulate knowledge of their activities, to reflect on their practices and acquire new knowledge, and to change their practices as a consequence. Accordingly, <u>Constructivists reject the search for laws in favour of contingent generalizations</u> (Price and Reus-Smit 1998).

Constitutive theory is explanatory theory, but of a particular sort. There are 'why' and 'how' questions, as Wendt explores in Box 11.3. Standard causal analysis asks 'why' questions as it treats independent and dependent variables as unrelated entities. Constitutive theories ask 'how' questions. They want to know how structures constitute social kinds and make possible certain tendencies. Sovereignty does not cause states with certain capacities; instead, it produces them and invests them with certain capacities that make possible certain kinds of behaviours. Being a sovereign state, after all, means that states have certain rights and privileges that other actors in world politics do not. Knowing something about the structure does important explanatory work.

Constructivists use a variety of methods. They adopt ethnographic and interpretive techniques in order to re-create the meanings that actors bring to their practices and how these practices relate to social worlds. They employ large-n quantitative studies in order to demonstrate the emergence of a world culture that spreads specific practices, values, and models. They use genealogical methods to identify the contingent factors that produced the categories of world politics that are subsequently taken for granted. They utilize structured, focused comparisons in order better to understand the conditions under which norms diffuse from one context to another. They even use computer simulations in order to model the emergent properties and enduring actors of world politics.

Throughout, though, Constructivists have attempted to interpret evidence as it relates to alternative explanations. Although they have largely positioned their substantive arguments against neo-realism and neo-liberal Institutionalism, they have clarified the differences by contrasting Constructivism with rational choice analysis. The presumption, then, is that these are rival social theories. In many ways, they are. Whereas rational choice treats actors as pre-social, Constructivism treats them as social. Whereas rational choice treats interests as fixed, Constructivism treats interests as constructed by the environment and interactions. Whereas rational choice sees the environment as limited to constraining and regulating the actions of already constituted actors, Constructivism sees it as constituting the actors' identities and interests. Whereas rational choice uses the logic of consequences to understand behaviour, Constructivism adopts the logic of appropriateness.

The juxtaposition of these Rationalist and Constructivist claims raises the issue of their relationship to one another. One line of argument is that different social theories are incommensurable. Another is that any claim that one social theory might subsume the other is misguided since different social theories can rarely be integrated in this way because they capture different features of reality. Consequently, the best that can be obtained is some form of **Pluralism** and any attempt at a grand synthesis, the mother of all social theories, is likely to produce either a theoretic mutant or theoretical **Imperialism**. For much the same reason, a gladiatorial, winner-take-all, competition makes little sense.

A more promising avenue is to identify points of connection and to identify the relative strengths of

---

| **Box 11.3** | **Alexander Wendt on explanation** |

In the philosophy of science a common way to characterize the difference between kinds of explanations is in terms of the kinds of questions which they answer . . . Causal theories answer questions of the form 'why?' and, in some cases, 'how?'. In providing answers to causal questions, in saying that 'X causes Y', we assume . . . that X and Y exist independent of each other . . . that X precedes Y in time, and . . . that but for X, Y would not have occurred . . . Constitutive theories have a different objective, which is to account for the properties of things by reference to the structures in virtue of which they exist . . . As such, constitutive questions usually take the form of 'how-possible?' . . . The answers to constitutive questions must support a counterfactual claim of necessity, namely that in the absence of the structures to which we are appealing the properties in question would not exist . . . Constitutive theories provide *explanations*. These explanations are not causal, but they are explanations just the same.

(Wendt 1998: 4–5, 8)

each approach in order to see whether they might be combined to enrich our understanding of the world. Exemplary are recent attempts to consider the relationship between the normative structure and strategic behaviour. Some begin by identifying how identity shapes the state's interests and then turn to rational choice for understanding strategic behaviour. In this view, the American identity shapes **national interests**, and then the structure of the international system informs its strategies for pursuing those interests. Others consider strategic social construction (Finnemore and Sikkink 1998). Actors can attempt to change the norms that subsequently guide and constitute state identities and interests. Human rights activists try to encourage compliance with human rights norms not only by naming and shaming those who violate these norms but also by encouraging states to identify with these norms because it is the right thing to do.

Finally, strategic interaction occurs in a cultural context. Strategic interaction exists when the ability of actors to achieve their goals is dependent on the behaviour of others. In such a situation of **interdependence**, they must incorporate the strategies of others before determining their strategy, and are likely to try and **influence** their rival's strategies in order to further their goals. Social scientists typically liken such strategic settings to a 'game'. For scholars of international relations, such game metaphors are closely associated with **game theory**, which examines the strategic choices of rational actors in a particular situation. Constructivists, however, define the game as a normative structure that is simultaneously external and internal to the players. The game is external because it is a constraint on their ability to achieve their goals. It also is internal because the normative structure establishes the culturally and historically specific ways in which actors think and the norms that guide what is acceptable play. Not all is fair in love, war, or any other social endeavour. For decades Arab nationalism shaped the identities and interests of Arab states, contained norms that guided how Arab leaders could play the game of Arab politics, and encouraged Arab leaders to draw from the symbols of Arab politics to try and manoeuvre around their Arab rivals and further their own interests. How Arab leaders played out their regional games was structured by the norms of Arab politics. They had very intense rivalries and as they vied for prestige and status they frequently accused each other of being a traitor to the Arab **nation** or harming the cause of Arabism. But rarely did they use military force. In general, these examples of how the connections between Constructivism and rational choice might further our analysis remind us that we should be open to and utilize as many approaches as possible as we try to enrich our understanding of how the world works.

Key points

- Constructivists are concerned with human consciousness, treat ideas as structural factors, consider the dynamic relationship between ideas and material forces as a consequence of how actors interpret their material reality, and are interested in how agents produce structures and how structures produce agents.

- Knowledge shapes how actors interpret and construct their social reality.

- The normative structure shapes the identity and interests of actors such as states.

- Social facts such as sovereignty and human rights

- exist because of human agreement while brute facts such as mountains are independent of such agreements.

- Social rules are regulative, regulating already existing activities, and constitutive, making possible and defining those very activities.

- Social construction denaturalizes what is taken for granted, asks questions about the origins of what is now accepted as a fact of life and considers the alternative pathways that might have produced and can produce alternative worlds.

- Power can be understood not only as the ability of

one actor to get another actor to do what they would not do otherwise but also as the production of identities and interests that limit the ability to control their fate.

- Although the meanings that actors bring to their activities are shaped by the underlying culture,

meanings are not always fixed but are a central feature of politics.

- Although Constructivism and rational choice are generally viewed as competing approaches, at times they can be combined to deepen our understanding of global politics.

Constructivism and global change

Constructivism's focus on how the world hangs together, how normative structures construct the identities and interests of actors, and how actors are rule following, might seem ideal for explaining reproduction but useless at transformation. This is hardly true. Because Constructivism claims that what exists need not have and need not—that is, it invites us to think of alternative worlds and the conditions that make them more or less possible, it is attentive to issues of transformation. Indeed, Constructivism scolded neo-realism and neo-liberal Institutionalism for their failure to explain contemporary global transformations. The Peace of Westphalia helped to establish sovereignty and the norm of non-interference, but in recent decades various processes have worked against the principle of non-interference and suggested how state sovereignty is conditional on how states treat their populations. **World orders** are created and sustained not only by Great Power preferences but also by changing understandings of what constitutes a legitimate international order. Until the Second World War the idea of a world organized around **empires** was hardly illegitimate; now it is.

A central theme in any discussion of global change is diffusion. Stories about diffusion are explanations of how particular organizational models, practices, norms, strategies, or beliefs spread within a population. As Constructivists have considered matters of diffusion, they have highlighted two important issues. One is institutional isomorphism, which observes how actors and institutions that are subjected to the same environment will frequently acquire identical forms. In other words, if once there was a diversity of models within the population,

over time that diversity yields to conformity and convergence around a single model. There used to be various ways to organize state structures, economic activity, education systems, free trade agreements, and on and on. But now the world is organized around the **nation-state**, modern states increasingly adopt democratic forms of governance, economies are increasingly organized around markets, most international organizations now have a multilateral form, and a growing number of regional trade agreements now have labour and environmental side-agreements. This convergence might be driven by the fact that the world now knows that some institutions are just far superior to others. Yet there is the additional possibility that this convergence is driven not by the search for efficiency but rather by the desire for acceptance, symbolic legitimacy, and status. The other issue is the origins, rise, and widespread acceptance of various international norms. Norms of humanitarianism, **citizenship**, military intervention, human rights, trade, arms control, and the environment have helped to organize world politics, define the purpose of state activities, and have shaped what counts as acceptable behaviour. The Constructivist concern with diffusion, then, touches centrally on global change because of the interest in the world in motion and transformation.

There are various causes of the diffusion of social institutions. It can occur from coercion. Colonialism and Great Power imposition figured centrally in the spread of capitalism. It can occur from strategic competition. Heated rivals are likely to adopt similar weapons systems and military organizations in order to try and stay even on the military battlefield. But diffusion and convergence occur not only because of

CWS

imposition and competition. States will adopt similar institutional forms for at least four other reasons. Formal and informal pressures can cause states to adopt those models that are deemed superior because doing so will bring them needed resources. States, like all organizations, require resources to survive and sustain their various activities. In order to attract these resources, states will adopt and reform their institutions in order to signal to various communities that they are part of the club and are utilizing modern techniques. In other words, they value these new institutions not because they believe that they are superior but rather because they are symbols that will attract resources. **Third World** states accept the IMF's recommendations not only to secure IMF loans but also to receive its seal of approval to facilitate access to global capital markets. Eastern European countries seeking entry into the European Union adopt various reforms not only because they believe that they are superior but also because they are the price of admission.

Also, during periods of uncertainty when states are unsure of how to address existing challenges they are likely to adopt those models that are perceived as successful or legitimate. In other words, they frequently adopt these models even in the absence of evidence that they are superior to existing practices. Political candidates in newly democratizing countries reorganize their party and campaign organizations in order to increase their chances on election day. Toward that end, they draw from those models of success, largely from the American context, not necessarily because they have empirical evidence that the American campaign model will increase their prospect of victory but often because it appears modern, sophisticated, and superior. Furthermore, frequently states adopt these models because of their symbolic standing. For instance, many Third World governments have adopted weapons systems that have very little military value because they convey to others that they are sophisticates and are a part of the 'club'.

Finally, professional associations and expert communities also diffuse organizational models. Most associations and **networks** have established techniques, codes of conduct, and methodologies for determining how to confront challenges in their area of expertise. They learn these techniques

through informal interactions and in formal settings such as in universities and postgraduate programmes. Once these standards are established, they become the 'industry standard' and the accepted way of addressing problems in an area. Part of the job of professional associations and expert networks is to communicate these standards to others; doing so makes them agents of diffusion. Economists, lawyers, military officials, arms control experts diffuse practices, standards, and models through networks and associations. If the American way of campaigning is becoming increasingly accepted around the world it is in part due to a new class of professional campaign consultants that have converged around a set of accepted techniques and are ready to peddle their wares to willing customers. The diffusion of the 'Washington Model' around the world is due not only to demands imposed by the United States and the IMF but also to the fact that the economists in the other countries' finance ministries are trained in broadly similar ways in postgraduate programmes in the West.

Discussions of diffusion also draw attention to the internationalization of norms. Norms are generally understood as a standard of appropriate behaviour for actors with a given identity. Norms not only constrain behaviour because actors are worried about the costs of doing so; they also constrain behaviour because they are connected to a sense of self. 'Civilized' states are expected to avoid settling their difference through violence not because war might not pay but rather because it violates how 'civilized' states are expected to act. These expectations of proper behaviour can diffuse across the population and become institutionalized to the point that they are taken for granted. Human rights activists aspire to reduce human rights violations not only by 'naming and shaming' those who violate these rights but also by persuading potential violators that the observation of human rights is tied to their identity as a modern, responsible state.

Norms do not simply erupt but rather evolve through a political process. A central issue, therefore, is the internationalization and **institutionalization** of norms, or what is now called the **life cycle of norms** (see Box 11.4). Although many international norms have a taken-for-granted quality, they have to come from somewhere and their path to acceptance

| Box 11.4 | Finnemore and Sikkink on the three stages of the life cycle of norms |

Norm emergence

This stage is typified by persuasion by norm entrepreneurs. 'Norm entrepreneurs attempt to convince a critical mass of states (norm leaders) to embrace new norms. Norm entrepreneurs call attention to issues or even "create" issues by using language that names, interprets, and dramatizes them.' Norm entrepreneurs attempt to establish 'frames ... that resonate with broader public understandings and are adopted as new ways of talking about and understanding issues'. Norm entrepreneurs need a launching pad to promote their norms, and will frequently work from non-governmental organizations and with international organizations and states. 'In most cases for an emergent norm to reach a threshold and move toward the second stage, it must become institutionalized in specific sets of international rules and organizations ... After norm entrepreneurs have persuaded a critical mass of states to become norm leaders and adopt new norms, we can say the norm reaches a critical threshold or tipping point.'

Norm cascade

'The second stage is characterized more by a dynamic of imitation as the norm leaders attempt to socialize other states to become norm followers. The exact motivation for

this second stage where the norm "cascades" through the rest of the population (in this case, states) may vary, but we argue that a combination of pressure for conformity, desire to enhance international legitimation, and the desire of state leaders to enhance their self-esteem facilitate norm cascades.' These processes can be likened to socialization. 'To the degree that states and state elites fashion a political self or identity in relationship to the international community the concept of socialization suggests that the cumulative effect of many countries in a region adopting new norms' is akin to peer pressure.

Norm internalization

The third stage is 'norm internalization ... norms acquire a taken-for-granted quality and are no longer a matter of broad public debate' and thus are automatically honoured. 'Precisely because they are not controversial, however, these norms are often not the centerpiece of political debate and for that reason tend to be ignored by political scientists' ... 'For example, few people today discuss whether women should be allowed to vote, whether slavery is useful, or whether medical personnel should be granted immunity during war.'

(Adapted from Finnemore and Sikkink 1998: 894–905)

is nearly always rough and rocky. Although most states now recognize that prisoners of war have certain rights and cannot be subjected to summary executions on the battlefield, this was not always the case. These rights originated with the emergence of international humanitarian law in the late nineteenth century, and then slowly spread and became increasingly taken for granted over the next several decades in response to considerable debate regarding how to minimize the horrors of war. Now the existence of rights for prisoners of war is largely accepted, even if they are not fully observed.

Among the various consequences of institutional isomorphism and the internationalization of norms, three are worth highlighting. There used to be a myriad of ways to organize human activities, but that diversity has slowly but impressively yielded to conformity. Yet just because states are converging on the same institutional forms does not mean that they act in identical ways. After all, many states adopt these institutions not because they will be more efficient

for achieving their stated goals but rather because they like the symbolic legitimacy that is conferred by these institutional forms. These states, then, can be expected to act in ways that are inconsistent with the demands of the institution. For instance, if governments are adopting democratic forms of governance and elections solely for symbolic reasons, then we should expect the presence of democratic institutions to exist alongside authoritarian and illiberal practices. A second consequence is the deepening of a sense of international community. The internationalization of norms suggests that actors are increasingly accepting standards of behaviour because they are connected to a sense of self that is tied to the international community. These norms, in other words, are bound up with the values of the international community. To the extent that these values are shared then it becomes possible to speak of an international community.

Institutional isomorphism and norm internationalization also point to processes of

Box 11.5	Key concepts of Constructivism

Agent-structure problem: the problem is how to think about the relationship between agents and structures. One view is that agents are born with already formed identities and interests and then treat other actors and the broad structure that their interactions produce as a constraint on their interests. But this suggests that actors are pre-social to the extent that there is little interest in their identities or possibility that they might change their interests through their interactions with others. Another view is to treat the structure not as a constraint but rather as constituting the actors themselves. Yet this might treat agents as cultural dupes because they are nothing more than artifacts of that structure. The proposed solution to the agent-structure problem is to try and find a way to understand how agents and structures constitute each other.

Constructivism: an approach to international politics that concerns itself with the centrality of ideas and human consciousness and stresses a holistic and Idealist view of structures. As Constructivists have examined world politics they have been broadly interested in how the structure constructs the actors' identities and interests, how their interaction are organized and constrained by that structure, and how their very interaction serves to either reproduce or transform that structure.

Holism: the view that structures cannot be decomposed to the individual units and their interactions because structures are more than the sum of their parts and are irreducibly social. The effects of structures, moreover, go beyond merely constraining the actors but also construct them. Constructivism holds that the international structure shapes the identities and interests of the actors.

Idealism: idealism as a substantive theory of international relations is generally associated with the claim that it is possible to create a world of peace. But Idealism as a social theory refers to the claim that the most fundamental feature of society is social consciousness. Ideas shape how we see ourselves and our interests, the knowledge that we use to categorize and understand the world, the beliefs we have of others, and the possible and impossible solutions to challenges and threats. The emphasis on ideas does not mean a neglect of material forces such as technology and geography. Instead it is to suggest that the meanings and consequences of these material forces are not given by nature but rather driven by human interpretations and understandings.

Identity: the understanding of the self in relationship to an 'other.' Identities are social and thus are always formed in relationship to others. Constructivists generally hold that identities shape interests; we cannot know what we want unless we know who we are. But because identities are social and are produced through interactions, identities can change.

Individualism: the view that structures can be reduced to the aggregation of individuals and their interactions. International relations theories that ascribe to individualism begin with some assumption of the nature of the units and their interests, usually states and the pursuit of power or wealth, and then examine how the broad structure, usually the distribution of power, constrains how states can act and generates certain patterns in international politics. Individualism stands in contrast to holism.

Materialism: the view that the most fundamental feature of society is the organization of material forces. Material forces include natural resources, geography, military power, and technology. To understand how the world works, therefore, requires taking these fundamentals into account. For international relations scholars, this leads to forms of technological determinism or the distribution of military power for understanding the state's foreign policy and patterns of international politics.

Normative structure: international relations theory traditionally defines structure in material terms, such as the distribution of power, and then treats structure as a constraint on actors. By identifying a normative structure, Constructivists are noting how structures also are defined by collectively held ideas such as knowledge, rules, beliefs, and norms that not only constrain actors—they also construct categories of meaning, constitute their identities and interests, and define standards of appropriate conduct. Critical here is the concept of a norm, a standard of appropriate behaviour for actors with a given identity. Actors adhere to norms not only because of benefits and costs for doing so but also because they are related to a sense of self.

Rational choice: an approach that emphasizes how actors attempt to maximize their interests, how they attempt to select the most efficient means to achieve those interests, and endeavours to explain collective outcomes by virtue of the attempt by actors to maximize their preferences under a set of actors to maximize their preferences under a set of constraints. Deriving largely from economic theorizing, the rational choice approach to politics and international politics has been immensely influential and applied to a range of issues.

socialization. To speak of socialization in world politics is to consider the process by which states and their societies are taking on the identities and interests of the dominant peer group in international society. When examining relations between Western Third World states, therefore, a central issue is whether and how Third World states have slowly accepted, for a variety of reasons, the habits and expectations of Western states. The international society of states began as a European society and then expanded outward; the internationalization of this society and its norms shaped the identities and foreign policy practices of new members. In other words, the convergence on similar models, the internationalization of norms, and the possible emergence of an international community should not be mistaken for a world without power and hierarchy.

Key points

- The recognition that the world is socially constructed means that Constructivists can investigate global change and transformation

- A key issue in any study of global change is diffusion, captured by the concern with institutional isomorphism and the life cycle of norms.

- Although diffusion sometimes occurs because of the view that the model is superior, frequently actors adopt a model either because of external pressures or its symbolic legitimacy.

- Institutional isomorphism and the internationalization of norms raise issues of growing homogeneity in world politics, a deepening international community, and socialization processes.

Conclusion

In this chapter I have tried to capture the global-historical, intellectual, and disciplinary forces that made Constructivism a particularly attractive way for thinking about international politics. It invites students to imagine the continuities and transformations of international politics. It looks into why the world is organized in the way it is, considers the different factors that shape the durable forms of world politics, and seeks alternative worlds. In doing so, it challenges the received wisdoms and opens up new lines of enquiry. Although many in the discipline treated as strange the claim that ideas can shape how the world works, in fact what is strange is a view of a world devoid of ideas. After all, is it even possible to imagine such a world? What would it look like? Is it even possible to imagine a world driven only by materialist forces? What would it look like?

Constructivism challenged the discipline's mainstream on its own terms and on issues that were at the heart of its research agenda. Scholars of neo-realism and neo-liberal Institutionalism demanded

that Constructivists demonstrate how unpacking state interests and imagining the constitution of actors' identities, interests, and capacities would matter for illuminating fundamental issues surrounding war and peace, and cooperation and conflict. Constructivists answered the challenge.

The ability to challenge substantive theories on their home ground has sometimes led to the false impression that Constructivism is a substantive theory and not the social theory that it is. As such, it is much more and much less than meets they eye. It is much less because it is not properly a theory that can be viewed as a rival to already existing theories. It offers no predictions about enduring regularities or tendencies in world politics. Instead, it suggests how to investigate them. Consequently, it is much more than meets the eye because it offers alternative ways of thinking about a range of issues. Constructivists have offered alternative formulations of the basic concepts and theories that matter to Realists, including the nature of power, alliance formation, war termination, and military intervention. They have offered important insights into the liberal peace. They have offered critical amendments to neo-liberal Institutionalism as they have investigated alternative causes and consequences of international institutions and organizations. Although Constructivism does not have the same analytical rigour that is one of rational choice's strengths, its thematic reach is comparable.

What of the future of Constructivism? It depends on which version of Constructivism we are discussing. Constructivists generally accept certain commitments, including Idealism, holism, and an interest in the relationship between agents and structures. They also accept certain basic claims, such as the social construction of reality, the existence and importance of social facts, the constitu-

tion of actors' identities, interests, and subjectivities, and importance of recovering the meaning actors give to their activities. But they also exhibit tremendous differences. Although sometimes these disagreements can appear to derive from academic posturing, the search for status, and the narcissism of minor differences, in fact there also can be much at stake, as suggested in Ch.12. These differences will exist as long as Constructivism exists. This is healthy because it will guard against complacency and enrich our understanding of the world.

For further information and case studies on this subject, please visit the companion web site at www.oup.com/uk/booksites/politics.

QUESTIONS

1 What were the silences of neo-realism and neo-liberal Institutionalism?

2 How did international relations scholars use critical and sociological theory to address important issues overlooked by neo-realism and neo-liberal Institutionalism?

3 What is the core of Constructivism?

4 Do you find Constructivism a useful approach for thinking about world politics?

5 Do you agree that we should try to understand how actors make meaningful their behaviour in world politics? Or is it enough to examine behaviour?

6 How are meanings fixed in world politics?

7 Do you think that Constructivism adds richness and complexity at the expense of our desire to understand patterns in world politics?

8 What sort of relationship can exist between rational choice and Constructivism

9 What do you think are the core issues for the study of global change and how does Constructivism help you address those issues? Alternatively, how does a Constructivist framework help you identify new issues that you had not previously considered?

10 What sorts of questions are opened up by thinking about socialization in world politics?

11 How does the concept of diffusion help you understand why and how the world has changed?

GUIDE TO FURTHER READING

Adler, E. (2003), 'Constructivism', in Walter Carlneas, Beth Simmons, and Thomas Risse (eds), *Handbook of International Relations* (Thousand Oaks, Cal.: Sage). A terrific overview of the origins and fundamentals of Constructivism and its relationship to existing theories of international politics.

Barnett, M. (1998), *Dialogues in Arab Politics: Negotiations in Regional Order* (New York: Columbia University Press). Examines how Arab leaders played the game of Arab politics and, in doing so, transformed the very nature of Arab politics. An example of how Constructivists might think about how strategic action is shaped by a normative structure.

Carpenter, C. (2003), ' "Women and Children First": Gender, Norms, and Humanitarian Evacuation in the Balkans 1991–1995', *International Organization*, 57:4 (Fall): 661–94.

Fearon, J., and Wendt, A. (2003), 'Rationalism vs. Constructivism', in Walter Carlneas, Beth Simmons, and Thomas Risse (eds), *Handbook of International Relations* (Thousand Oaks, Cal.: Sage). A very useful exposition of how rational choice and Constructivism overlap, written by two of the leading proponents of each approach in international relations.

Finnemore, M., and Sikkink, K. (2001), 'Taking Stock: The Constructivist Research Program in International Relations and Comparative Politics', *Annual Review of Political Science*, 4: 391–416. A highly insightful account of Constructivism's insights and future directions of research.

—— and —— (1999), 'International Norms and Political Change', in P. Katzenstein *et al.* (eds), *Explorations and Controversies in World Politics* (Cambridge, Mass.: MIT Press).

Hollis, M., and Smith, S. (1990), *Explaining and Understanding International Relations* (New York: Oxford University Press). Explains in an exceptionally clear fashion the contrast between a conception of world politics driven by self-interested action and a conception informed by rules and interpretive methods.

Katzenstein, P. (ed.) (1996), *The Culture of National Security* (New York: Columbia University Press). An edited collection that clearly identified why we need to examine how identities and norms shape state interests, and explored those claims in a range of critical security areas.

Wendt, A. (1999), *A Social Theory of International Politics* (Cambridge: Cambridge University Press). The seminal text that explains the central elements and dissects the important controversies of Constructivism.

CHAPTER 12

Alternative approaches to international theory

STEVE SMITH • PATRICIA OWENS

READER'S GUIDE

Following from the preceding five chapters, which very broadly might be described as the new 'mainstream' theories of international relations, this chapter outlines other important contributions to thinking about world politics. The main theories dealt with are: historical sociology, normative theory, feminist theory, post-modernism, and post-colonialism. The chapter begins by establishing some important preliminary distinctions between theories that are explanatory and foundationalist (like Realism, Liberalism, and most of all Marxism) and those that are constitutive and non-foundationalist. Explanatory/ foundationalist theories are termed rationalist. Constitutive/non-foundationalist theories have developed in two broad versions, one is known as Social Constructivism (dealt with in Ch.11) and the other group is termed for convenience here 'alternative' approaches. The latter theories are the main concern of this chapter. Although both Social Construc- tivism and these alternative approaches reject the main assumptions of rationalist theories and see theories as constituting the social world, the alternative approaches are more critical of the mainstream and move beyond it in more far-reaching ways.

Introduction

The previous five chapters have given you over-views of the four most dominant theories of inter-national relations (Realism, Liberalism, Marxism, and Constructivism) and the contemporary debate between the two leading mainstream theories, **neo-realism** and **neo-liberalism**. With the exception of Social Constructivism, which is relatively new, these approaches have governed the discipline for the last fifty years, and the debate between their adherents has defined the areas of disagreement in international theory. The **'inter-paradigm debate'** between Realism, Liberalism, and Marxism has been extremely influential, with generations of students told that the debate between the various elements effectively exhausts the kinds of questions that can be asked about international relations. However, the inter-paradigm debate by no means covers the range of issues that any contemporary theory of world politics needs to deal with. Instead this 'debate' ends up being a rather conservative political move because it gives the impression of open-mindedness and intellectual **Pluralism** whereas, in fact, Realism has tended to dominate. Indeed, one factor supporting the dominance of Realism has been that it seems to portray the world as common-sensically understood. Thus alternative views can be dismissed as **normative** or **value-laden**, to be negatively compared with the so-called **objectivity** of Realism.

In the last decade or so this picture has changed dramatically in two ways. First, there has been a major debate between **neo-realism** and **neo-liberalism** (see Ch.9), known as the **neo-neo** debate or the **neo-neo synthesis**. The second change has been the appearance of a range of new approaches developed to understand world politics. In part this reflects a changing world. The end of the cold war system significantly reduced the credit-ability of Realism, especially in its neo-realist guise where the stability of the bipolar system was seen as a continuing feature of world politics. As that **bipolarity** dramatically disappeared, so too did the explanatory power of the theory that most relied on it. But this was not by any means the only reason for the rise of new approaches. There are three other obvious reasons. First, Realism's dominance was called into question by a resurgence of its historical main competitor, Liberalism, in the form of **neo-liberal Institutionalism**, as discussed in Ch.8, with this debate now comprising the mainstream of the discipline. Second, there were other changes under way in world politics that made the **develop-ment** of new approaches important, such as the kinds of features discussed under the heading 'globalization'. Whatever the explanatory power of Realism, it did not seem very good at dealing with issues such as the rise of **non-state actors** transnational **social movements**, and information technology. In short, new approaches were needed to explain these features of world politics, even if Realism still claimed to be good at dealing with power politics. Third, there were major develop-ments under way in other academic disciplines in the social sciences, but also in the philosophy of science and social science, that attacked the under-lying methodological (i.e. how to undertake study) assumption of Realism, a position known as **posi-tivism** (discussed below). In its place a whole host of alternative ways of thinking about the social sciences were being proposed, and International Relations simply caught up. Since then a series of alternative approaches have been proposed as more relevant to world politics in the twenty-first century.

Key points

- Realism, Liberalism, and Marxism together comprised the **inter-paradigm debate** of the 1980s, with Realism dominant amongst the three theories.

- Despite promising intellectual openness, however, the inter-paradigm debate ended up naturalizing the dominance of Realism by pretending that there was real contestation.

- In recent years, the dominance of Realism has been undermined by three developments: first, **neo-liberal Institutionalism** has become increasingly important; second, **globalization** has brought a host of other features of world politics to centre-stage; third, **positivism**, the underlying methodological assumption of Realism, has been significantly undermined by developments in the social sciences and in philosophy.

Explanatory/constitutive theories and foundational/anti-foundational theories

In order to understand the current situation with regard to international theory it is important to introduce two distinctions. The terms can be a little unsettling, but they are merely convenient words for discussing what in fact are fairly straightforward ideas. The first distinction is between **explanatory** and **constitutive** theory. An explanatory theory is one that sees the world as something external to our theories of it. In contrast, a constitutive theory is one that thinks our theories actually help construct the world. This is actually a distinction adopted in both scientific and non-scientific disciplines. But a moments thought should make you realize why it is more appealing in the non-scientific world. In a very obvious way our theories about the world make us act in certain ways, and thereby make those theories become self-confirming. For example, if we think that individuals are naturally aggressive then we are likely to adopt a different posture towards them than if we think they are naturally peaceful. However, you should not regard this claim as self-evidently true, since it assumes that our ability to think and reason makes us able to determine our choices (i.e. that we have free will rather than having our 'choices' determined behind our backs). What if our human nature is such that we desire certain things 'naturally', and that our language and seemingly 'free choices' are simply our rationalizations for our needs? This is only the opening stage of a very com-

plex but fascinating debate about what it is to be human (Hollis and Smith 1990). However, the upshot, whichever position you eventually adopt, is that there is a genuine debate between those theories that think of the social world as like the natural world, and those theories that see our language and concepts as helping create that reality. Theories claiming the natural and the social worlds are the same are known as **naturalist**.

In International Relations, the more structural Realist and Structuralist theories dealt with in Chs 7 and 10 tend to be explanatory theories, which see the task of theory as being to report on a world that is external to our theories. Their concern is to uncover **regularities** in human behaviour and thereby explain the social world in much the same way as a natural scientist might explain the physical world. By contrast, nearly all the approaches developed in the last 15 years or so tend to be constitutive theories, and interestingly the same is true of some Liberal thought. Here theory is not external to the things it is trying to explain, and instead may construct how we think about the world. Or, to put it another way, our theories define what we see as the external world. Thus the very concepts we use to think about the world help to make that world what it is (think about the concepts that matter in your own life, such as love, happiness, wealth, status, etc.).

The **foundational/anti-foundational** distinction refers to the simple-sounding issue of whether our beliefs about the world can be tested or evaluated against any neutral or objective procedures. This is a distinction central to the branch of the philosophy of social science known as **epistemology** (the study of how we can claim to know something). A foundationalist position is one that thinks that all truth claims (about some feature of the world) can be judged true or false. An anti-foundationalist thinks that truth claims cannot be so judged since there are never neutral grounds for so doing. Instead each theory will define what counts as the facts and so there will be no neutral position available to determine between rival claims. Think for example of a Marxist and a Liberal arguing about the 'true' state of the economy, or a feminist and an Islamic Fundamentalist discussing the 'true' status of women. Foundationalists look for what are termed **meta-theoretical** (or above any particular theory) grounds for choosing between truth claims. In contrast, anti-foundationalists think that there are no such positions available, and that believing there to be some is itself simply a reflection of an adherence to a particular view of epistemology.

In many senses most of the new approaches to international theory discussed later are much less wedded to foundationalism than were the traditional theories that comprised the inter-paradigm debate. Thus, **post-modernism**, **post-colonialism**, some **feminist theory**, and some normative theory would tend towards anti-foundationalism. However, the **neo-neo debate**, some **historical sociology**, some normative theory, and some **critical theory** would tend towards foundationalism (see Ch.10). Interestingly, **Social Constructivism** wishes to portray itself as occupying the middle ground (see Ch.11). On the whole, and as a rough guide, explanatory theories tend to be foundational while constitutive theories tend to be anti-foundational. The point at this stage is not to construct some checklist, nor to get you thinking yet about the differences. Rather we want to draw your attention to the role that these assumptions about the nature of knowledge have on the theories that we are going to discuss. The central point at this stage is that the two distinctions mentioned in this section were never really discussed in the literature of International

Relations until very recently. The last 15 years has seen these underlying assumptions brought more into the open and the most important effect of this has been to undermine Realism's claim to be delivering **the** truth.

The distinctions between explanatory and constitutive theories and between foundational and anti-foundational theories have been brought into the open because of a massively important reversal in the way in which social scientists have thought about their ways of constructing knowledge. Until the late 1980s, most social scientists in International Relations tended to be **positivists**. But since then positivism has been under attack. Positivism is best defined as a view of how to create knowledge that relies on four main assumptions. The first is a belief in the unity of science, i.e. that roughly the same methodologies apply in both the scientific and non-scientific worlds. Second, there is a distinction between facts and values, with facts being neutral between theories. Third, that the social world, like the natural one, has regularities, and that these can be 'discovered' by our theories in much the same way as a scientist does in looking for the regularities in nature. Finally, that the way to determine the truth of statements is by appeal to these neutral facts; this is known as an **empiricist** epistemology.

It is the rejection of these assumptions that has characterized the debate in international theory in the last 20 years or so. Yosef Lapid (1989) has termed this 'a post-positivist era'. In simple terms, traditional international theory was dominated by the four kinds of positivistic assumptions noted above. Since the late 1980s, the new approaches that have emerged have tended to question these same assumptions. The resulting map of international theory at the beginning of the twenty-first century has three main features: first, the continuing dominance of the three theories that together made up the inter-paradigm debate, this can be termed the **rationalist** position, and is epitomized by the **neo-neo debate**; second, the emergence of non-positivistic theories, which together can be termed **alternative** approaches, and epitomized by much **critical theory** (discussed in Ch.10), **historical sociology**, **normative theory**, much **feminist work**, **post-modernism**, and **post-colonialism**,

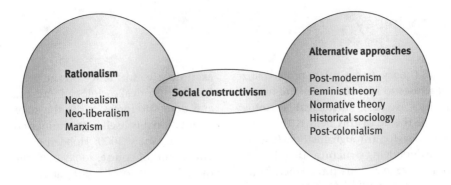

Fig. 12.1 International theory at the beginning of the twenty-first century

to be discussed below; and third, the development of an approach that tries to speak to both rationalist and alternative approaches known as **Social Constructivism**. Figure 12.1 illustrates the resulting configuration of the theories today.

Note that this is a very rough representation of how the various theories can be categorized. It is misleading in some respects since, as the previous five chapters have shown, there are quite different versions of the main theories and some of these are less rationalistic than others. Moreover, **critical theory**, which is discussed in Ch.10, can seem like quite a radical departure from the mainstream. Similarly, some of the approaches classified as 'alternative' in

this chapter are markedly less so than others. For example, work in historical sociology often adopts similar theoretical methods to rationalist approaches, though this is not always the case. Because historical sociology tends to reject the central unit of rationalism, the state, and is compatible with much post-positivism we discuss it in this chapter. In other words, the classifications are broadly illustrative of the theoretical landscape, and are best considered a useful starting point for thinking about the differences between theories. As you learn more about them you will see how rough and ready a picture this is, but it is as good a categorization as any other.

Key points

- Theories can be distinguished according to whether they are **explanatory** or **constitutive** and whether they are **foundational** or **anti-foundational**. As a rough guide, explanatory theories tend to be foundational and constitutive theories tend to be anti-foundational.

- The three main theories comprising the **inter-paradigm debate** were based on a set of positivist assumptions, namely a denial of the idea that social science theories can use the same methodologies as theories of the natural sciences, that facts and values can be distinguished, that neutral facts can act as arbiters between rival truth claims, and that the social world has regularities which theories can 'discover'.

- Since the late 1980s there has been a rejection of

positivism, with the main new approaches tending more towards **constitutive and anti-foundational** assumptions.

- The current theoretical situation is one in which there are three main positions: first, **Rationalist** theories that are essentially the latest versions of the **Realist** and **Liberal** theories; second, **alternative** theories that are **post-positivist**; and third, **Social Constructivist** theories that try to bridge the gap.

- Alternative approaches at once differ considerably from one another, and at the same time overlap in some important ways. One thing that they do share is a rejection of the core assumptions of **Rationalist** theories.

Historical sociology

Just as **critical theory** (see Ch.10) problematizes the state and refuses to see it as some kind of given in world politics, so does **historical sociology**. Indeed the main theme of this field is the way in which societies develop through history. It is concerned with the underlying structures that shape the institutions and organizations into which human society is arranged, including violence, economy, and gender (Hall 1992; Skocpol 1992). Historical sociology has a long history. The first wave, which was a response to the great events of the eighteenth century—the American and French revolutions, the processes of industrialization, and nation building— ran until the 1920s (Smith 1991). The second wave has been of particular interest to international theory, because the key writers, Michael Mann (1986; 1993), Theda Skocpol (1979; 1984), Immanuel Wallerstein (1974; 1984), Charles Tilly (1981; 1990), John Hall (1985; 1994), and Martin Shaw (1984; 2003) have all to various degrees focused their sociological analyses on the relationship between the domestic and the international (Hobden 1998). Tilly has neatly summarized this interest with the statement that 'states made war but war made the state'. In short, the central feature of historical sociology has been an interest in how the structures that we take for granted (as 'natural') are the products of a set of complex social processes.

Thus, whereas **neo-realism** takes the state as a given, historical sociology asks how specific kinds of states have been produced by the various forces at work in domestic and international societies. Historical sociologists show just how complex the state is as an organization, thereby undermining the rather simple view of the state found in neo-realism. They also fundamentally undermine the notion that a state is a state is a state through time and across the world. States differ—they are not functionally similar as neo-realism portrays them. Furthermore, historical sociologists show that there can be no simple distinction between international and domestic societies. They are inevitably interlinked. There is no such thing as 'an international system', as suggested by Waltz, which is self-contained and thereby able to

exert decisive influence on the behaviour of states. Finally, historical sociology shows that international and domestic forces create the state, and that the international is itself a determinant of the nature of the state (Shaw 2000; Hobden and Hobson 2002). This claim, of course, looks particularly relevant to the debate on globalization, since, as discussed in the Introduction to the book, one of its dominant themes is that the international economic system places demands on states such that only certain kinds of states can prosper.

Charles Tilly's work is particularly interesting because it is a clear example of the complexity of the state as an entity. In his 1990 book, *Coercion, Capital and European States, AD 900–1990*, Tilly poses the following question: 'What accounts for the great variation over time and space in the kinds of states that have prevailed in Europe since AD 990, and why did European states eventually converge on different variants of the national state?' (1990: 5). The answer he gives is that the national state eventually dominated because of its role in fighting wars. Distinguishing between capital-intensive and coercion-intensive regimes (or economic power-based and military power-based systems), Tilly notes that three types of states resulted from the combinations of these forms of power, tribute-making empires, systems of fragmented sovereignty (city-states), and national states. These states were the result of the different class structures that resulted from the concentrations of capital and coercion. Broadly speaking, coercion-intensive regimes had fewer cities and more agricultural class systems than did capital-intensive systems, which led to the development of classes representing commercial and trading interests. Where capital accumulation was high relative to the ability of the state to coerce its citizens, then city-states developed. On the other hand, where there was coercion but not capital accumulation then tribute-making empires developed. As Dennis Smith notes (1991: 83), each of these is a form of indirect rule, requiring the ruler to rely on the cooperation of relatively autonomous local powers. But with the rise in the scale of war, the result was that national states started to acquire a decisive advantage over the other kinds of state organizations. This was because national states could afford large armies and could respond to the demands of the classes representing both agricultural and commercial interests.

Through about a 350-year period starting around 1500, national states became the norm, as they were the only states that could afford the military means to fight the kind of large-scale wars that were occurring. States, in other words, became transformed by war. Tilly notes that the three types of states noted above all converged on one version of the state, so now that is seen as the norm. Yet, in contrast to neo-realism, Tilly notes that the state has not been of one form throughout its history. His work shows how different types of states have existed, all with different combinations of class structures and modes

of operating. And, crucially, it is **war** that explains the convergence of these types of states into the national state form. War plays this central role because it is through preparing for war that states gain their powers as they have to build up an infrastructure of taxation, supply, and administration (McNeill 1982). The national state thus acquires more and more power over its population by its involvement in war, and therefore could dominate other state forms because they were more efficient than either tribute-gathering empires or city-states in this process.

The second example of historical sociology is the work of Michael Mann. Mann is involved in a four-volume study of the sources of social power dealing with the whole of human history. (The first two volumes have appeared dealing with the period up to 1914, see his (1986) and (1993).) This is an

---

Box 12.1   Mann's IEMP model of power organization

Mann differentiates between three aspects of power:

1. Between distributive power and collective power, where distributive power is the power of *a* over *b* (for *a* to acquire more distributive power, *b* must lose some), and collective power is the joint power of actors (where *a* and *b* can cooperate to exploit nature or another actor, *c*).

2. Power may be extensive or intensive. Extensive power can organize large numbers of people over far-flung territories. Intensive power mobilizes a high level of commitment from participants.

3. Power may be authoritative or diffused. Authoritative power comprises willed commands by an actor and conscious obedience by subordinates. It is found most typically in military and political power organizations. Diffused power is not directly commanded; it spreads in a relatively spontaneous, unconscious, and decentred way. People are constrained to act in different ways but not by command of any particular person or organization. Diffused power is found most typically in ideological and economic power organizations.

Mann argues that the most effective exercise of power combines all three elements. He argues that there are four sources of social power, which together may determine the overall structure of societies. The four are:

1. Ideological power derives from the human need to find ultimate meaning in life, to share norms and values, and to participate in aesthetic and ritual practices. Control over ideology brings general social power.

2. Economic power derives from the need to extract, transform, distribute, and consume the resources of nature. It is peculiarly powerful because it combines intensive cooperation with extensive circuits of distribution, exchange, and consumption. This provides a stable blend of intensive and extensive power and normally of authoritative and diffused power.

3. Military power is the social organization of physical force. It derives from the necessity of organized defence and the utility of aggression. Military power has both intensive and extensive aspects, and it can also organize people over large areas. Those who monopolize it can wield a degree of general social power.

4. Political power derives from the usefulness of territorial and centralized regulation. Political power means state power. It is essentially authoritative, commanded, and willed from a centre.

The struggle to control ideological, economic, military, and political power organizations provides the central drama of social development. Societies are structured primarily by entwined ideological, economic, military, and political power.

(Mann 1993: 6–10)

enormously ambitious project, aimed at showing just how states have taken the forms that they have. In other words, Mann studies the ways in which the various forms of power have combined in specific historical circumstances. He makes a major contribution to our thinking of how states have come into existence and about how they have related to the international political system. In this sense his work is similar to that of Tilly, but the major innovation of Mann's work is that he has developed a sophisticated account of the forms of power that combine to form certain types of states. This is his IEMP model (Ideological, Economic, Military, and Political forms of power). This argument is summarized in Box 12.1 to give you an idea of its potential to shed light on how the state has taken the form that it has throughout history. It should make you think that the version of the state presented by **neo-realism** is very simple, but note also that there is some overlap between the focus of neo-realism on war and the focus of historical sociology on how states, classes, and war interact.

Historical sociology is a method and focus of research. It is possible, therefore, to be both a historical-sociologist and a Realist, and a critical theorist, and a feminist concerned with how gender and patriarchy have shaped states and societies (Miller 1998). It is also possible to be a post-modern historical sociologist; for example, Foucault's method of **genealogy** (see Box 12.4) has much in common with the concerns of the field (Dean 1994; Kendall and Wickham 1999). Though Foucault is most famously a 'post-modern' theorist, there is no contradiction between drawing on his understanding of

power and knowledge (discussed later) and approaching questions such as the organization of violence historically (Drake 2001).

> ### Key points
>
> - **Historical sociology** has a long history, having been a subject of study for several centuries. Its central focus is with **how societies develop the forms that they do**.
>
> - Contemporary historical sociology is concerned above all with how the state has developed since the Middle Ages. It is basically a study of the **interactions between states, classes, capitalism, and war**.
>
> - **Charles Tilly** looks at how the three main kinds of state forms that existed at the end of the Middle Ages eventually converged on one form, namely the **national state**. He argues that the decisive reason was the ability of the national state to **fight wars**.
>
> - **Michael Mann** has developed a powerful model of the sources of state power, known as the **IEMP model**.
>
> - Like Realism, historical sociology is interested in **war**. But it undercuts **neo-realism** because it shows that the state is not one functionally similar organization, but instead has altered over time.
>
> - The concerns of historical sociology are compatible with a number of the other approaches surveyed in this chapter including **feminism** and **post-modernism**.

Normative theory

The last 15 years or so have witnessed the re-emergence of normative approaches to international theory. For a long time this work was out of fashion as the mainstream fell under the spell of positivism. One of the main claims of positivism is that there exists a clear division between 'facts' and 'values'. It is, therefore, simply not scholarly to spend too much time on debates about what the world should look like. Instead what is preferred is looking at the way things '**really**' are. From the perspective of normative theory, there are two basic problems with this position. First, it is a very narrow definition of what politics is about. For thousands of years political actors and students have been fascinated with the search for '**the good life**', with the strengths and weaknesses of specific ways of life and forms of political arrangement. Thus, defining politics as limited to what 'really' already exists in the social world, as if it had nothing to do with ethics, is a very restricting move. Moreover, it is a very political move designed to support existing political arrangements. After all, if the only thing we can do is to discuss how things operate and not why, then existing power divisions are naturalized. As a result, questions about the origins of power can be immediately delegitimized and dismissed as 'value-laden' or 'normative'.

A second problem with the marginalizing of normative work is the rather serious objection that all theories reflect values, the only question being whether or not we are explicit about what they are. If we tell you things just 'are the way they are', then this clearly represents our view of what the social world is like and which features of it are fixed and which are not. In our view, all theories have values running throughout their analysis, from what they choose to focus on as the 'facts' to be explained, through the methods they use to study these 'facts', down to the policy prescriptions they suggest. Thus, it is not that normative theory is odd, or optional. All theories have normative assumptions and implications, but in most cases these are hidden. Indeed, ethical assumptions about the world not only shape our theories. Scholars in IR have also begun systematically to address how the process and content of ethical argument actually help construct and constitute the world in which we live (Crawford 2002).

A good survey of normative theory about world politics is by Chris Brown (1992) (see Box 12.2), who

---

<table>
<tr><td>Box 12.2</td><td>Chris Brown's view of normative theory</td></tr>
</table>

By normative international relations theory is meant that body of work which addresses the moral dimension of international relations and the wider questions of meaning and interpretation generated by the discipline. At its most basic it addresses the ethical nature of the relations between communities/states, whether in the context of the old agenda, which focused on violence and war, or the new(er) agenda, which mixes these traditional concerns with the modern demand for international distributive justice.

(Brown 1992)

---

outlines two main normative positions, **cosmopolitanism** and **communitarianism**. Cosmopolitanism is the view that the central focus of any normative theory of world politics should concentrate either on humanity as a whole or on individuals. On the other hand, communitarianism maintains that the appropriate focus is the political community (usually the state). The terms of this cosmopolitanism/communitarianism debate are whether there is a basis for rights and obligations between states in world politics or whether the bearers of these rights and obligations are individuals, that is, either as individuals, or as a whole in the sense of humanity (also see Ch.32). For example, do states have the right to hold large nuclear stockpiles if these weapons could potentially wipe out humanity? Or, is it acceptable for some cultures to perform 'female circumcision' because 'that is their way of doing things'? Or do the women concerned have rights that are more important than the rights of the community to make its own decision? This leads us into complex questions about intervention, gender, and human rights, but you can quickly see how massive normative debates might ensue when we open up these kinds of discussions.

Brown uses the distinction between cosmopolitanism and communitarianism to examine three main focal points of normative international theory: the moral value to be assigned to state autonomy (Beitz 1979; Frost 1996; and Nardin 1983); the ethics of inter-state violence, otherwise known as **Just War Theory** (Walzer 1977, Elshtain 2003), and the issue of international justice with specific regard to the obligations that the richer states of the world have to poorer countries (Rawls 1971; Barry 1989). As you can imagine, cosmopolitans and communitarians have rather different views on these issues. To take the first question, cosmopolitanism clearly rejects the notion that states have a right to autonomy if it allows them to undertake actions that conflict with the moral rights of either individuals within the state or humanity as a whole. Communitarianism on the other hand opposes any restrictions on autonomy that do not arise out of the community itself. Similarly, cosmopolitans and communitarians will differ over when it is right for states to intervene in the affairs of others and over how we should evaluate calls for a more just distribution of economic resources. Two particularly good overviews of the main debates can be found in Cochran (1999) and Hutchings (1999).

Normative questions have become more 'policy relevant' in the last few years as governments have felt the need to justify their positions in moral terms. This has led to a renewed interest in normative theory and an increasing dissatisfaction with theories that (proudly) claim to be non-normative or 'Realistic'. Particularly powerful examples of this new normative agenda are the debates over **humanitarian intervention** (see Ch.25), and the moralistic rhetoric of George W. Bush's Administration in the United States. The former example led to explicit discussions about the 'right' moral stance to take, for example over the wars in former Yugoslavia, or over Western intervention in Somalia or East Timor (Lang 2002). A related question is whether international institutions have **moral responsibilities** (Erksine 2003). This became a central question around debates about the failure of the West, including the UN, to prevent the 1994 genocide in Rwanda. Also consider the normative assumptions behind US President Bush's justifications of the conduct of his war on terror. He has not hesitated to frame his foreign policy in religious terms as a battle between 'good' and 'evil'. In this sense, normative theory is more obviously relevant to foreign policy than it has been for several generations. And note the consequence, which is that those theorists who claim

that theory should NOT be normative may be unable to debate central issues of foreign policy.

CWS

Key points

- Normative theory was out of fashion for decades because of the dominance of positivism, which portrayed it as 'value-laden' and 'unscientific'.

- In the last 15 years or so there has been a resurgence of interest in normative theory. It is now more widely accepted that all theories have normative assumptions either explicitly or implicitly.

- The key distinction in normative theory is between cosmopolitanism and communitarianism. The former sees the bearers of rights and obligations as individuals; the latter sees them as being the community (usually the state).

- Main areas of debate in contemporary normative theory include the autonomy of the state, the ethics of the use of force, and international justice.

- In the last two decades, normative issues have become more relevant to debates about foreign policy, for example in discussions of how to respond to calls for humanitarian intervention and whether war should be framed in terms of a battle between good and evil.

Feminist theory

Chapter 30 details some of the main varieties of feminisms and gender issues in world politics. Here we offer an overview of five main types of feminist theory, which have become common since the mid-1980s. These are liberal, socialist/Marxist, standpoint, post-modern, and post-colonial. We also refer you to the very brief discussion of gender and Constructivism in Ch.11. Although this section is titled 'feminist theory' it is both a deliberate and misleading heading. It is deliberate in that it focuses on the socially constructed roles that 'women' occupy in world politics. It is misleading because this ques-

tion has to be understood in the context of the construction of differences between women and men and contingent understandings of masculinity and femininity. In other words, the focus could more accurately be on **gender** rather than on 'women' because the very categories of 'women' and 'men', and the concepts of masculinity and femininity, are highly contested in much feminist research. Similarly, the distinctions of liberal/socialist, etc., are slightly misleading for as you will discover below these categories do not exactly correspond to the diverse work of feminist scholars, especially in contemporary work in which elements from each 'type' are often integrated.

The term gender usually refers to the social construction of difference between 'men' and 'women'. Some of the theories covered in this section assume natural and biological (e.g. sex) differences between men and women. Some of the approaches do not. What all of the most interesting work in this subfield does, however, is analyse how gender both affects world politics and is an effect of world politics; in other words, how different concepts (such as the state or sovereignty) are gendered and, in turn, how this gendering of concepts can have differential consequences for 'men' and 'women' (Steans 1998). It is important to note that feminists have always been interested in how understandings of gender affect men's lives as well as women. Indeed, there is also a field of research known as **men's studies** that models itself after, and was made possible by the emergence of, 'women's studies' (see Seidler 1989; Brittan 1989; Connell 1995; Carver 1996; for a feminist discussion see Zalewski and Parpart (eds) 1998).

Feminist theory in international relations originally developed in work on the politics of development and in peace research. But by the late 1980s a first wave of feminism, **liberal feminism**, was more forcefully posing the question of 'where are the women in world politics?' The meaning of 'liberal' in this context is decidedly NOT the same as the meaning of the term in Ch.8. In the context of feminism, the term starts from the notion that the key units of society are individuals, that these individuals are biologically determined either men or women, and that these individuals possess specific rights and are equal. Thus, one strong argument of liberal feminism is that all rights should be granted to women equally with men. Here we can see how **the state** is gendered in that rights, such as voting rights, right to possess property, etc., were predicated solely on the experiences and expectations of men— and, typically, a certain ethnic/racial class of men. Thus, taking women seriously made a difference to the standard view of world politics. Liberal feminists look at the ways in which women are excluded from power and prevented from playing a full part in political activity. They examine how women have been restricted to roles critically important for the functioning of things (such as reproductive economies)

but that are not usually deemed to be important for theories of world politics.

To ask 'where are the women?' was at the time quite a radical political act, precisely because women were absent from the canonical texts of international relations, and thus appeared invisible. Writers such as **Cynthia Enloe** (1989; 1993; 2000) began from the premise that if we simply started to ask 'where are the women?' we would be able to see their presence and importance to world politics, as well as the ways in which their exclusion from world politics was presumed a 'natural' consequence of their biological or natural roles. After all, it was not that women were actually absent from world politics. Indeed, they played absolutely central roles, either as cheap factory labour, as prostitutes around military bases, or as the wives of diplomats. The point is that the conventional picture painted by traditional international theory both ignored these contributions and, if recognized, designated them as less important than the actions of states-'men'. Enloe demonstrated just how critically important were the activities of women to the functioning of the international economic and political systems. She illustrated exactly how crucial women, and the conventional arrangements of 'women's and men's work' were to the continued functioning of international politics. Most specifically, Enloe documented how the concepts and practice of militarization influenced the lives and choices of men and women around the world. 'Militarization', she writes, 'is a step-by-step process by which a person or a thing gradually comes to be controlled by the military or comes to depend for its well-being on militaristic ideas' (2000: 3; also see Elshtain 1987; Elshtain and Tobias 1990). Enloe is an example of a scholar who begins from a liberal premise, that is that women and men should have equal rights and responsibilities in world politics, but draws upon socialist feminism to analyse the role of economic structures and standpoint feminism to highlight the unique and particular contributions of women.

A second strand of feminist theory is **socialist/ Marxist feminism**, with its insistence on the role of material, primarily economic, forces in determining the lives of women (see Ch.10). This approach is also sometimes known as materialist feminism (Lise 1995; Hennessy and Ingraham 1997). For Marxist feminism, the cause of women's inequality is to be found in the capitalist system; overthrowing **capitalism** is the necessary route for the achievement of the equal treatment of women (Sargent 1981). Socialist feminism, noting that the oppression of women occurred in pre-capitalist societies, and continues in socialist societies, differs from Marxist feminism in that it introduces a second central material cause in determining women's unequal treatment, namely the patriarchal system of male dominance (Braun 1987; Gottlieb 1989). For Marxist feminists, then, capitalism is the primary oppressor, for socialist feminists it is capitalism plus patriarchy. For socialist/Marxist feminists the focus of a theory of world politics would be on the patterns by which the world capitalist system and the patriarchal system of power lead to women being systematically disadvantaged compared to men. The approach, therefore, has much in common with **post-colonial feminism** (discussed below); both are especially insightful when it comes to looking at the nature of the world-economy and its differential advantages and disadvantages that apply to women. But post-colonial feminism critiques socialist/Marxist feminism for presuming the 'sameness' of patriarchy throughout the world and across time; rather than seeing the ways in which patriarchy both falsely presumes a universal experience of male domination and obscures the intersections of oppression of both men and women of colour.

The third version of feminist theory is **standpoint feminism** (Zalewski 1993a; Hartsock 1998). This variant emerged out of socialist feminism and the idea of a particular class system. The goal was to try to think about how women as a class might be able to 'envision' or see politics from a perspective denied to those who benefited from the subordination of women. Radical feminism was premised upon the unique qualities and individuality of women. Drawing upon socialist feminist interpretations of structure, standpoint feminism began to identify how the subordination of women, as a particular class by virtue of their sex rather than economic standing (although the two were related) possessed a unqiue perspective—or standpoint—on world politics as a result of their subordination. This first insight was later developed to consider also how the knowledge, concepts, and categories of world

politics were predicated upon a norm of masculine behaviour and masculine experiences and, therefore, represented not a universal standard—but a highly specific, particular standard. Standpoint feminists argue that seeing the world from the standpoint of women radically alters our understanding of that world. Standpoint feminism has undergone dramatic changes since its first articulation to incorporate the critiques of women of colour who argued that, like socialism, it presumed that class **identity** (or in this case, sex identity) was the primary affiliation of all women and, accordingly, the single source of their oppression. The standpoint position also runs the risk of essentializing and fixing the views and nature of women, by saying that **this** is how women see the world (Gioseffi 2003). Nonetheless despite these dangers, standpoint feminism has been very influential in showing just how male-dominated the main theories of world politics are—in part because it is grounded in a simple premise. In an important early essay, for example, **J. Ann Tickner** (1988) reformulated the famous 'Six **principles** of political realism' developed by the 'godfather' of Realism, Hans Morgenthau. Tickner showed how the seemingly 'objective' **rules** of Morgenthau in fact reflect male values and definitions of reality, rather than female ones. As a riposte Tickner reformulated these same rules taking women's (as opposed to men's) experiences as the starting point.

The fourth version is post-modern feminism, which develops the work of post-structuralism (especially that of Foucault and Derrida) to analyse specifically the concept of gender. Therefore, it might help to read the following in conjunction with the section on post-modernism below. Essentially, post-modern feminism critiques the basic distinction between 'sex' and 'gender' that earlier feminist theories found so useful in thinking about the roles/lives of men and women in world politics and in analysing the gendered concepts of world politics itself. This distinction between sex and gender was useful because it allowed feminists to argue that the position of women and men in the world was not natural, but highly contingent and dependent upon the meaning given to biological differences. Yet, while extremely useful, the acceptance of the sex–gender distinction retained the binary opposition of male–female, and presumed that while gender was

| Box 12.3 | V. Spike Peterson on the global political economy and the sex/gender distinction |

In her book on the global political economy, feminist V. Spike Peterson focuses upon two roughly simultaneous occurrences—the 'explosive growth in financial markets that shape business decision-making and flexible work arrangements' and the 'dramatic growth in informal and flexible work arrangements that shapes income generation and family well being'. She notes that 'informalization reaps higher profits for capital, depresses formal wages, disciplines all workers and through the isolation of informalized workers impedes collective resistance' while 'flexibilization **feminizes the workforce**: an increasing number of jobs require few skills and the most desirable workers are those deemed to be unorganized, docile, but reliable [and] available for part time and temporary work and willing to accept low wages'. Taken together, Spike Peterson argues, these developments render 'women, the poor, migrants, and recent immigrants the prototypical workers of the informal economy and arguably the future of all but elite workers worldwide'.

'It is here that the distinction between (positivist) sex and (constructivist) gender is crucial. In contrast to positivist notions of sex (as a biologically natural binary of male–female) gender is a systematic social construction that dichotomizes . . . As a social construct, gender is not "given" but learned (and therefore mutable). Most significantly, gender is not simply a trait of individuals, but an institutionalized structural feature of social life . . . In short, gender is not simply an empirical category (referring to embodied men and women) but an analytical one, such that all social life is *gendered* . . . [Gender] structures divisions of power and authority, which determine whose voices and experiences dominate culturally and coercively . . . and it structures divisions of labor which determine what *counts as work, who does what kind of work and how different kinds of work are valued.*'

(V. Spike Peterson 2003: 1, 111, 31)

---

constructed, sex was wholly natural. However, as a number of scholars demonstrated, what we understood sex to be, what biological differences were, was heavily influenced by our understanding of gender—that is, that sex was as constructed as gender (Fausto-Sterling 1992; 2000; Haraway 1989; 1991; Fox-Keller 1985; Longino 1990). Thus as Helen M. Kinsella argues, 'it is an increasingly difficult position to defend that sex is prior to gender. The more one searches for the brute reality of sex, the more one finds that is gendered—that is, that the understanding of sex as a fact is itself a "cultural conceit" (Haraway 1991: 197). In other words, this understanding of sex and sex difference is paradigmatic for a way of thinking about difference—as binary, as complementary, as given in nature. What are obscured, then, is the relations of power and politics which produce, distinguish, and regulate these concepts of "gender" and of "sex" ' (2003: 295). This does not mean that our biological bodies or 'the determination of sex' is not important. Rather it suggests that 'understanding this process leads to questions concerning how sex and gender operate to create the reality through which bodies materialize as sexed, as sexualised . . . as objects of knowledge and subjects of power' (Kinsella 2003: 296).

In questioning the sex–gender distinction, in argu-

ing that sex is not the origin of gender but an effect of gender, post-modern feminists introduced the concept 'gender performativity' (Butler 1990). Performativity is itself a tricky concept, and one that is easily misunderstood. However, a good place to begin is thinking about an act that is repeatable, yet alterable, and an act or a production that can only make sense within a larger social construct of agreed-upon norms. To think about gender performativity is to think about gender as not given or rooted in sex, but as something that is enacted and produced in social relations. In Judith Butler's famous phrase 'gender is a doing'. This is still a difficult concept in feminist theory, and it is highly contested as well. Nonetheless, the concept of gender performativity opens the sex–gender distinction to analysis while, simultaneously, displacing the subject of 'woman' from the centre of feminist theorizing and introducing the question of identity. For, rather than presuming women are the subjects of feminism, Butler asks how subjects are produced. To try to understand this process in world politics is to ask, to put it simply, how world politics produces certain kinds of 'soldiers,' certain kinds of 'workers,' certain kinds of 'states' that are not simply men or women, male or female, but complexly positioned states that seem, to us, completely natural.

The final form of feminism to mention is **post-colonial** feminism. There is some overlap between this approach and what is discussed under the heading 'Gender in the global political economy' in Ch.30. In addition, it might help to read the following in conjunction with the discussion of post-colonialism in this chapter. Post-colonial feminists work at the intersection of class, race, and gender on a global scale and especially analyse the gendered effects of transnational culture and the unequal division of labour in the global political economy. From this perspective, it is not good enough to simply demand (as liberal feminists do) that men and women should have equal rights in a Western-style democracy. Such a move ignores the way in which poor women of colour in the global South remain subordinated by the global economic system; a system that liberal feminists were slow to challenge in a systematic way. In other words, the concerns and interests of feminists in the West and those in the rest of the world may not, therefore, so easily fit. Post-colonial feminists are also critical of Western, privileged academic intellectuals (men and women) who claim to be able to 'speak for' the oppressed, a form of cultural **imperialism** with important material effects. Perhaps the most influential post-colonial feminist scholar in this vein is Gayatri Spivak who combines **Marxism**, **feminism**, and **deconstruction** (discussed below) to interpret imperialism, past and present, and ongoing struggles for decolonization. In an influential 1988 essay 'Can the **Subaltern** Speak?' Spivak acknowledged the ambiguity of her own position in a privileged Western university and argued that elite scholars should be wary of homogenizing the 'subaltern' and try to speak *for* them in their 'true' voice (what she calls a form of 'epistemic violence'). The concept of the subaltern is discussed below, but it essentially refers to subordinated groups and in this instance to underprivileged women in the global South. In not recognizing the **heterogeneity** of experience and opinion of these diverse women, seemingly benevolent and well-meaning academics are at once patron-izing in their desire to redeem them and unwittingly complicit in new forms of colonialism. Some post-modernists have also been criticized along similar lines for being too Western-centric and gender-blind. The combination of colonialism and **patriarchy** has made it doubly difficult for the resistance and agency of the subaltern to be heard and recognized.

Key points

- **Liberal** feminism looks at the roles women play in world politics and asks why they are marginalized. It wants the same opportunities afforded to women as are afforded to men.

- **Marxist/socialist** feminists focus on the **international capitalist system**. Marxist feminists see the oppression of women as a by-product of capitalism, whereas socialist feminists see both capitalism and **patriarchy** as the structures to be overcome if women are to have any hope of equality.

- **Standpoint** feminists, such as **J. Ann Tickner,** want to correct the male dominance of our knowledge of the world. Tickner does this by re-describing the six 'objective' principles of international politics developed by **Hans Morgenthau** according to a female version of the world.

- **Post-modernist** feminists are concerned with gender as opposed to the position of women as such. They look into the ways in which **masculinity** and **femininity** get constructed, and are especially interested in how world politics constructs certain types of 'men' and 'women'.

- **Post-colonial** feminists, such as Gayatri Spivak, work at the intersection of gender, race, and class on a global scale. They suggest that liberal feminists and others have ignored the interests and opinions of women in the global South, often preferring to speak on their behalf. This is a form of cultural imperialism with important material effects.

Post-modernism

Post-modernism has been a particularly influential theoretical development throughout the social sciences in the last 25 years. It reached international theory in the mid-1980s, but can only be said to have really arrived in the past 15 years. Nonetheless, it is probably as popular a theoretical approach as any discussed in this chapter and overlaps with a number of them. Part of the difficulty, however, is precisely defining post-modernism. This is in addition to the fact, of course, that there are substantial theoretical differences within its various strands. One useful definition is by Jean-François Lyotard: 'Simplifying to the extreme, I define *post-modern* as incredulity towards metanarratives' (1984: xxiv). Incredulity simply means scepticism; 'metanarrative' means any theory that asserts it has clear foundations for making knowledge claims and involves a **foundational** epistemology. Post-modernism, then, is essentially concerned with **deconstructing** and distrusting any account of human life that claims to have direct access to 'the truth'. Thus, Marxism (including critical theory), Freudian psychoanalysis, and standpoint feminisms are all suspect from a post-modern perspective because they claim to have uncovered some fundamental truth about the world.

Three central themes in post-modern work will be briefly discussed: the power-knowledge relationship, the performative nature of identity, and various textual strategies used by post-modern thinkers. Work on the **power-knowledge** relationship has been most influenced by **Michel Foucault** (1977; 1978; 1984; 1994). (Note, however, that this relationship is also a key concern of **critical theory** (see Ch.10).) Foucault was opposed to the notion dominant in **rationalist** theories and **positivism** that knowledge is immune from the workings of power. Instead, Foucault argued that power in fact **produces knowledge**. All power requires knowledge and all knowledge relies on and reinforces existing power relations. Thus, there is no such thing as 'truth' existing outside of power. To paraphrase Foucault, how can history have a truth if truth has a history? Truth is not something external to social settings but is instead part of them.

Accordingly, post-modernists look at what power relations are supported by 'truths' and knowledge practices. Post-modern international theorists have used this insight to examine the 'truths' of international relations theory to see how the concepts and knowledge claims that dominate the discipline in fact are highly contingent on specific power relations. Three recent examples on the concept of **sovereignty** in the history and theory of international politics are by Cynthia Weber (1995), Jens Bartelson (1995), and Jenny Edkins *et al.* (1999). In each book the concept of sovereignty is revealed to be both historically variable despite the attempts of mainstream scholars to imbue it artificially with a fixed meaning, and itself caught up in the practice of sovereignty by producing the discourse about it.

How do post-modernists study history in the light of this relationship between power and knowledge? Foucault's approach is known as **genealogy**, which is to undertake a 'history of the present' and turn what we accept as natural into a question. Box 12.4 reproduces Richard Ashley's (1987) summary of this. The central message of genealogy is that various **regimes of truth** merely reflect the ways in which through history both power and truth develop together in a mutually sustaining relationship. The way to uncover the workings of power is to undertake a **detailed historical analysis** of how the practices and statements about the social world are only 'true' within specific **discourses**. Accordingly, post-modernism is concerned with how some discourses and therefore some truths dominate others in very concrete ways (see, for example, Edwards 1996). It is for this reason that post-modernists are opposed to any metanarratives, since they imply that there are conditions for establishing the truth or falsity of knowledge claims that are not the product of any discourse, and thereby not the product of power.

A second theme is how post-modernists view identity not as a fixed 'thing' but as a **performative** site (you may with to refer back to the discussion of post-modern feminism in the previous section). One way to approach this is to make a comparison with how

| Box 12.4 | Foucault's notion of genealogy |

First, adopting a genealogical attitude involves a radical shift in one's analytical focus. It involves a shift away from an interest in uncovering the structures of history and towards an interest in understanding the movement and clashes of historical practices that would impose or resist structure. . . . with this shift . . . social enquiry is increasingly disposed to find its focus in the posing of 'how' questions, not 'what' questions. How . . . are structures of history produced, differentiated, reified, and transformed? How . . . are fields of practice prised open, bounded and secured? How . . . are regions of silence established?

Second, having refused any notion of universal truth or deep identities transcending differences, a genealogical attitude is disposed to comprehend all history, including the production of order, in terms of the endless power political clash of multiple wills. Only a single drama is ever staged in this non-place, the endlessly repeated play of dominations. Practices . . . are to be understood to contain their own strategies, their own political technologies . . . for the disciplining of plural historical practices in the production of historical modes of domination.

Third, a genealogical attitude disposes one to be especially attentive to the historical emergence, bounding, conquest, and administration of social spaces . . . one might think, for example, of divisions of territory and populations among nation states . . . one might also think of the separation of spheres of politics and economics, the distinction between high and low politics, the differentiation of public and private spaces, the line of demarcation between domestic and international, the disciplinary division between science and philosophy, the boundary between the social and the natural, or the separation of the normal and legitimate from the abnormal and criminal . . . a genealogical

posture entails a readiness to approach a field of practice historically, as an historically emergent and always contested product of multiple practices . . . as such, a field of practice . . . is seen as a field of clashes, a battlefield . . . one is supposed to look for the strategies, techniques, and rituals of power by which multiple themes, concepts, narratives, and practices are excluded, silenced, dispersed, recombined, or given new or reverse emphases, thereby to privilege some elements over others, impose boundaries, and discipline practice in a manner producing just this normalised division of practical space.

Fourth, what goes for the production and disciplining of social space goes also for the production and disciplining of subjects. From a genealogical standpoint there are no subjects, no fully formed identical egos, having an existence prior to practice and then implicated in power political struggles. Like fields of practice, subjects emerge in history . . . as such, the subject is itself a site of political power contest and ceaselessly so.

Fifth, a genealogical posture does not sustain an interest in those noble enterprises—such as philosophy, religion, positive social science, or the utopian political crusade—that would embark on searches for the hidden essences, the universal truths, the profound insights into the secret identity that transcends difference . . . from a genealogical standpoint . . . they are instead resituated right on the surface of political life. They are seen as political practice intimately engaged in the interpretation, production, and normalisation of modes of imposed order, modes of domination. They are seen as means by which practices are disciplined and domination advances in history.

(Ashley 1987: 409–11)

---

identity is understood in mainstream Constructivism in International Relations (see Ch.11). David Campbell has summarized the approach to identity by a leading Constructivist Alexander Wendt: 'identity is said to come in two basic forms, one of which is "those [deemed] *intrinsic* to an actor . . .". As an instance of this, [Wendt] claims that "being democratic . . . is an intrinsic feature of the U.S. state relative to the structure of the international system." It is not difficult to appreciate that a position that regards certain identities as "intrinsic," and includes among the[m] highly contestable concepts such as "democracy," is reductionist in its representation of polit-

ics' (1998: 279). Campbell is suggesting that in mainstream Constructivism identity is regarded as a kind of object or substance that can be observed and measured. But for post-modernists, identity ought to be conceived as having 'no ontological status apart from the various acts which constitute its reality' (Campbell 1992: 9). In contrast, stressing the performative make-up of identity and the constitutive nature of **political agency** reveals culture as 'a relational site for the politics of identity, rather than a substantive phenomen[on] in its own right' (Campbell 1998: 221; also see Campbell 1992; 1993). Constructivism, then, while appropriating some of the labels and terms of post-modernism, only vaguely destabilizes the dominant discourse about identity.

A third post-modern theme concerns **textual strategies**. The main claim is that, following **Jacques Derrida** (1976), the very way in which we construct the social world is textual. For Derrida the world is constituted like a text in the sense that interpreting the world reflects the concepts and structures of language, what he terms textual interplay. Derrida has two main ways of exposing these textual interplays, **deconstruction** and **double reading**. Deconstruction is based on the idea that seemingly stable and natural concepts and relations within language are in fact artificial constructs. They are arranged hierarchically in the case of opposites in language where one term is always privileged over the other. Therefore, deconstruction is a way of showing how all theories and discourses rely on artificial stabilities produced by the use of seemingly objective and natural oppositions (such as public/private, good/bad, male/female, civilized/barbaric, right/wrong). Double reading is Derrida's way of showing how these stabilizations operate by subjecting the text to two readings. The first is a repetition of the dominant reading to show how it achieves its coherence. The second points to the internal tensions within a text that result from the use of seemingly natural stabilizations. The aim is not to come to a 'correct' or even 'one' reading of a text, but instead to show how there is always more than one reading.

In international theory, Richard Ashley (1988) has performed exactly such a **double reading** of the concept of anarchy by providing first a reading of the anarchy problematique according to the traditional IR literature. He then undertook a second reading showing how the seemingly natural opposition between anarchy and sovereignty in the first reading is in fact a false opposition. By disrupting the first reading Ashley shows just how arbitrary is the 'truth' of the traditional assumptions made about anarchy and the kind of logic of state action that it requires. In a similar move, Rob Walker (1993) looks at the construction of the tradition of **Realism** and shows how this is only possible by ignoring the major nuances and complexities within the thought of the key thinkers of this tradition, such as Machiavelli and Hobbes. James Der Derian (1987; 1992;

2001) suggests that the revolution in surveillance **technology** and information gathering has rendered the media presentation of world politics virtually as important as 'real' events on the ground to the extent that we have lost the capacity to distinguish 'reality' from simulation, existence from make-believe. And, as a final example, Jenny Edkins (1999; 2000; 2003) has used post-modern insights to look at famine and practices of aid, and also the way in which the experience of trauma, from the world wars to 9/11, shapes and re-shapes politics. As you can see from this brief survey, post-modernism is taking apart the very concepts and methods of our thinking. It helps us think about the conditions under which we are able to theorize about world politics and for many is the most appropriate theory for a globalized world.

Key points

- **Lyotard** defines **post-modernism** as **incredulity towards metanarratives,** meaning that it denies the possibility of foundations for establishing the truth of statements existing outside of **discourse**.

- **Foucault** focuses on the **power-knowledge relationship** and sees the two as mutually constituted. It implies that there can be no truth outside of **regimes of truth**. How can history have a truth if truth has a history?

- **Foucault** proposes a **genealogical** approach to look at history, and this approach uncovers how certain regimes of truth have dominated others.

- **Derrida** argues that the world is like a text in that it cannot simply be grasped, but has to be interpreted. He looks at how texts are constructed, and proposes two main tools to enable us to see how arbitrary are the seemingly 'natural' oppositions of language. These are **deconstruction** and **double reading**.

- **Post-modern** approaches have been accused of being 'too theoretical' and not concerned with the 'real world'. They reply, however, that in the social world there is no such thing as the 'real' world in the sense of a reality that is not interpreted by us; they have done a great deal of work on important empirical questions such as war and famine.

Post-colonialism

Post-colonialism has been an important approach in cultural studies, literary theory, and anthropology for some time now, and has a long and distinguished pedigree. Founding texts arguably date back as far as the first oral histories and journals of freed African slaves in the United States (Gates 1987) and the political writing of W. E. B. DuBois, the leading African-American intellectual of his generation (1993 [1903]). Despite such ancestry, post-colonial scholarship has only recently begun to make an impact in the discipline of IR. This might seem especially odd given that the diverse subject matter of post-colonialism is intimately connected to the structure and processes of world politics—the transnational flows of peoples and identity constructions, issues of nation and nationalism, the effects of **cultural chauvinism**, how culture makes **imperialism** possible, and the cultures of **diasporas** to name just a few. A diaspora is the voluntary or forcible movement of peoples from their homelands into new regions.

Despite this overlap of subject mater, post-colonial approaches have been largely ignored in IR given its **state-centrism** and **positivism**. But this is now changing, not least because old disciplinary boundaries are breaking down and since the attacks of 11 September scholars in IR are beginning to understand how the histories of the West and the global South have always been intertwined (Barkawi 2004). Post-colonialism, given its interdisciplinary origins, has made a significant contribution to the destruction of these disciplinary boundaries. And as a result, IR scholars have begun to see the world in new 'post-colonial' ways, also making use of both traditional and non-traditional sources for understanding the world such as literature, poetry, and film (Holden and Ruppel 2003).

As with the other approaches surveyed in this chapter there is no one satisfactory definition of post-colonialism. For a start, the prefix 'post' might seem to imply the end of colonial practices. This would be a mistake. **Colonialism** is 'the political control, physical occupation, and domination of people over another people and their land for pur-

poses of extraction and settlement to benefit the occupiers' (Crawford 2002: 131). In many ways, of course, this **juridical** practice of controlling territory and peoples has ended. And a number of post-colonial scholars have looked at how this major transformation altered the politics and society of both the metropole (e.g. Britain) and the former colony (e.g. India) (Hall 2002). But much post-colonial scholarship also highlights the important degree of **continuity** and **persistence** of colonial forms of power in contemporary world politics. For example, the level of economic and military control of Western interests in the global South is in many ways actually greater now than it was under direct control—a form of **'neo'-colonialism** (Grovogui 1996; Duffield 2001). So although the era of formal colonial imposition by force of arms is apparently over (with the exception of the US occupation of Iraq in 2003–4), an important starting point for post-colonial scholarship is the issue of vast inequality on a global scale, the forms of power that make this systematic inequality possible, and the continued domination of **subaltern** peoples. The term subaltern was originally used by **Gramsci** to describe the classes dominated under hegemony (see Ch.10). More recently, feminist post-colonial scholars such as **Gayatri Spivak** (1987; 1988; 1998) have used it to describe poor rural women in the global South. Spivak's work was briefly discussed in the feminist theory section (above), but note again how she writes at the intersection of three literatures, **Marxism**, feminism, and post-modernism.

In fact, for many, the 'post' is actually more indicative of the **'post-positivist'** assumptions of the field. Most post-colonial scholars reject the assumptions of the explanatory and foundational theories described earlier in this chapter because they obscure how identities are not fixed and essential but are produced through essentially social processes and practices. Homi K. Bhabha writes, for example, that 'Terms of cultural engagement, whether antagonistic or affiliative, are produced **performatively**. The representation of difference must not be hastily read as the reflection of pre-given ethnic or cultural traits set in the fixed tablet of tradition. The social articulation of difference, from the minority perspective, is a complex, ongoing negotiation that seeks to authorize **cultural hybridities** that emerge in moments of historical transformation' (1994: 2). Hybridity is the idea that the identities of the colonized and colonizers are constantly in flux and mutually constituted. This is missed in positivist IR scholarship. Indeed, positivist assumptions, post-colonial writers claim, are not neutral in terms of race, gender, and class but have helped secure the domination of the Western world over the global South (Doty 1996). For example, in his influential book *Orientalism*, Edward Said argued that knowledge and material power could not be separated; Western culture (literally in the form of novels, etc.) was fundamentally entwined with imperialism and specifically the domination of the Islamic world of the Middle East (1979; 1993). Orientalism, for Said, refers to the hegemonic ways of representing 'the East' and its people from the beginning of 'Western' civilization. These **representations** have been absolutely crucial to the success of the economic and military domination of the West over the East and the construction of identities (be it race, class, or gender) in both.

Box 12.5   Edward Said on Orientalism

Unlike the Americans, the French and British . . . have had a long tradition of what I shall be calling Orientalism, a way of coming to terms with the Orient that is based on the Orient's special place in European Western Experience. The Orient is not only adjacent to Europe; it is also the place of Europe's greatest and richest and oldest colonies, the source of its civilizations and languages, its cultural contestant, and one of its deepest and most recurring images of the Other. In addition, the Orient has helped to define Europe (or the West) as its contrasting image, idea, personality, experience. Yet none of this Orient is merely imaginative. The Orient is an integral part of European material civilization and culture. Orientalism expresses and represents that part culturally and even ideologically as a mode of discourse with supporting institutions, vocabulary, scholarship, imagery, doctrines, even colonial bureaucracies and colonial styles.

(Said 1979: 1).

Thus, an important claim of post-colonialism is that global hierarchies of subordination and control, past and present, are made possible through the social construction of racial, gendered, and class differences (Spivak 1987; 1998; Bhabha 1990). As other chapters in this volume suggest, International Relations has been slightly more comfortable with issues of class (Chs 10, 14, 29) and gender (Ch.30). But the issue of race has been almost entirely ignored. This is even though race and **racism** continue to shape the contemporary theory and practice of world politics in far-reaching ways (Doty 1993; Castles 2000; Vitalis 2000; Persaud 2002). As an international institution, racism has historically been part of the emergence of humanitarian norms sanctioning obligations as a kind of colonial mission. But racism may also help explain the lack of 'humanitarian' action by the West in the 1994 Rwanda genocide. It has been an important factor in garnering support for the increased militarization of Western **immigration policies** (Simon 1998). And the unprecedented increase in US prison growth in recent years, which has overwhelmingly relied on racist assumptions about crime and conviction rates, is intimately connected to structural adjustments in the domestic economy associated with globalization (Gilmore 1998). In 1903, W. E. B. DuBois famously argued that the problem of the twentieth century would be the problem of the 'colour-line'. How will transnational racism continue to shape the twenty-first?

It is absolutely crucial to bear in mind that for post-colonial scholars imperial and other forms of power really operate at the **intersection** of **gender**, **race**, and **class**. Consider, for example, how it is possible for nations in the West to perceive of themselves as '**civilized**' and their enemies as '**barbaric**'. As a way to justify imperial rule in India the British employed both racist and sexist assumptions in pointing to the 'uncivilized' way woman were being treated by Indian men. The enlightened (white) British males would bring civilization to (dark) India at the same time as they exploited the country economically. The issue at stake, however, was not so much the freedom of women in either Victorian Britain or India, as effective strategies of imperial rule (Metcalf 1997).

Post-colonial scholars do not only focus on issues of domination, though this surely is important. For example, Franz Fanon used **psychoanalytical** theory to suggest how colonialism and Western stereotypes warped the psyche of colonized subjects (1967*a*). But post-colonial scholars also look at how forms of power have been resisted in both violent and non-violent ways. Antonio Gramsci argued that even though powerful ideologies (hegemony) subordinated some classes of people there would always be counterhegemonies of **resistance** (see Ch.10). In *The Wretched of the Earth* (1967*b*), Fanon, who was a revolutionary during the Algerian independence struggles against France, identified what he saw as the inherent **violence** in struggles for decolonization. But resistance has also taken more peaceful forms, with some arguing that post-colonial scholarship itself is an example of effective dissidence (Chowdhry and Nair 2002). Post-colonial scholars, therefore, also investigate the multiple and diverse forms of resistance to colonizing ideologies and offer strategies of empowerment and not only critique.

> **Key points**
>
> - Given the state-centrism and positivism of IR, post-colonial approaches have been largely ignored until recently as old disciplinary boundaries are breaking down.
>
> - Post-colonialism essentially focuses on the persistence of colonial forms of power in contemporary world politics, especially how the social construction of racial, gendered, and class differences uphold relations of power and subordination.
>
> - Most post-colonial research rejects positivism, given its claims to produce knowledge devoid of race, gender, and class-power hierarchies.
>
> - Racism, in particular, continues to operate in both obvious and sometimes subtle ways in contemporary world politics but this is not captured in traditional approaches to international theory.
>
> - Post-colonial research seeks to offer positive resources for resistance to imperial and other forms of power and not just critique.

Conclusion

This chapter has summarized the main alternatives accounts of world politics to the dominant **rationalist** mainstream of international theory. Each has clear strengths, and probably the best place for you to start thinking about which is most useful is to cast your mind back to the Introduction of the book and to Chapter 1 on Globalization. Crucially, you now need to think about which of the theoretical perspectives discussed in this chapter gives you the best overview of the globalized world we have been discussing.

The **rationalist** perspective, and particularly the **neo-neo synthesis**, as discussed in Ch.9, dominates the literature in the discipline of International Relations. That is the theoretical debate you will find in most of the journals, particularly in the USA. It focuses on the kinds of international political relations that concern many Western governments, particularly the debate about the future **security**

structure of the international system and economic foreign policy. But do you think that it is wide enough a perspective to capture what are to you the most important features of world politics? You might think that we need theories that define the political realm rather more widely, to take in identity, ethnicity, and culture. You might also think that the alternative theoretical perspectives outlined here are actually even better than rationalist accounts for thinking about security and economics.

Alternative theories obviously differ enormously with regard to what they are 'alternative' about. As noted above they are really very different, but they were put together in one category because they all reject the central concerns of rationalism. Do you think that any one of them gives you a better understanding of the main features of world politics than that provided by the rationalist mainstream? Or do you think that they are not really dealing with what are 'obviously' the most important features of world politics? Of course, these alternative theories do not cohere to one theoretical position in the way that the rationalist theories do. In some important ways, if you are a liberal feminist then you do not necessarily agree with post-modernism or some forms of normative theory. More fundamentally still, you cannot be **both** a post-modernist and a normative-communitarian. In short, some theories gathered under 'alternative' here have a set of mutually exclusive assumptions and there is no easy way to see the theories being combined. Some combinations are possible (a feminist post-modernism, or a normative historical sociology) but the one thing that is clearly correct is that the whole lot cannot be added together to form one theoretical agenda in the way that the neo-neo debate serves on the rationalist side. Moreover, some of these alternative theories do not have the same idea of how to construct knowledge as the rationalists, and therefore often reject the notion of coming up with testable hypotheses to compare with those provided by the rationalist position (see Keohane 1989*a*). This means that the prospect of a rationalist—post-modern debate, for example, is very low. The two sides simply see world politics in very different ways. You have to decide which side (or which subdivision) you think explains world politics most effectively.

There is no one theory of world politics that is right simply because it deals with the **truth**. What you should take from the theoretical positions outlined here is scepticism any time a theorist tells you that they are dealing with 'reality' or with 'how the world really is'. This is where the values of the theorist (or lecturer, etc.) can be smuggled in through the back door. World politics in an era of globalization is very complex and there are a variety of theories that try to account for different parts of that complexity. You should work out which theories both explain best the things you are concerned with and also offer you the chance to reflect on their own assumptions. One thing is for sure: there are enough theories to choose between and they paint very different pictures of world politics.

For further information and case studies on this subject, please visit the companion web site at **www.oup.com/uk/booksites/politics**.

QUESTIONS

1 Why do the post-positivist theories reject positivism?

2 What does it mean to say that the main difference between theories is whether they are explanatory or constitutive?

3 Why have alternative theoretical approaches to Realism become more popular in recent years?

4 What are the main implications of historical sociology for the study of world politics?

5 Is normative theory anything more than an optional extra for the study of world politics?

6 Which variant of feminist theory, or any combination of them, seems to capture most accurately the way 'gender makes the world go around' (Enloe)?

7 What might adopting a genealogical approach to the history of the present do for our understanding of world politics?

8 Why has IR ignored issues concerning race for so long? What does post-colonialism have to say on the subject?

9   What is it about some of the theories outlined in the chapter that makes them incompatible with others and why are some theories often used together?

10 Which of the main alternatives discussed in this chapter do you think offers the best account of world politics? Why?

GUIDE TO FURTHER READING

General

Burchill, S., and Linklater, A. (1996), *Theories of International Relations* (Basingstoke: Macmillan). This is a very good survey book dealing with contemporary international theory.

Smith, S., Booth, K., and Zalewski, M. (eds) (1996), *International Theory: Positivism and Beyond* (Cambridge: Cambridge University Press). A key text in the movement in IR away from positivism towards the theoretical approaches covered in this chapter.

Historical sociology

Hobden, Stephen, and Hobson, John M. (2002), *Historical Sociology of International Relations* (Cambridge: Cambridge University Press). An excellent survey of opinion on the connections between the two fields.

Mann, Michael (1986, 1993), *The Sources of Social Power*, vols 1 and 2 (Cambridge: Cambridge University Press). Two monumental texts of historical sociology.

Normative theory

Brown, C. (1992), *International Relations Theory: New Normative Approaches* (Hemel Hempstead: Harvester Wheatsheaf). A good introductory guide to the main strands of normative thinking in IR.

Frost, M. (1996), *Ethics in International Relations: A Constitutive Theory* (Cambridge: Cambridge University Press). A slightly more advanced analysis of normative theory, which offers its own Hegel-derived ethical theory, constitutive theory for world politics.

Feminist theory

Enloe, C. (1989), *Bananas, Beaches and Bases: Making Feminist Sense of International Politics* (London: Pandora). This was the classic text charting the way forward for feminist IR.

Post-modernism

Walker, R. J. B. (1993), *Inside/Outside: International Relations as Political Theory* (Cambridge: Cambridge University Press). An important early contribution to post-modern IR theory, which challenged some of the central categories of the discipline.

Campbell, D. (1998), *Writing Security: United States Foreign Policy and the Politics of Identity* (Manchester: Manchester University Press, rev. edn). This important book shows how the identity of the United States is constructed through perceptions of danger in foreign policy discourse.

Post-colonialism

Chowdhry, Geeta, and Nair, Sheila (eds) (2002), *Power, Post-colonialism and International Relations: Reading Race, Gender and Class* (London: Routledge). An edited volume looking at how the intersection of race, class, and gender structure much of world politics.

Said, Edward (1979), *Orientalism* (New York: Vintage). A seminal post-colonial text showing how colonial literary and artistic texts create the 'other' with devastating material consequences.

Gilroy, Paul (1993), *The Black Atlantic: Modernity and Double Consciousness* (Cambridge, Mass.: Harvard University Press). A look at the unique racial and cultural identity of those black people forced to move from their native countries to the West and how Europeans were also affected by this cultural exchange.

WEB LINKS

www.watsoninstitute.org/infopeace/index2.cfm The InfoTechWarPeace Project site, which examines the impact of information technology on world politics, often from a post-modern perspective.

www.postcolonialweb.org/index.html A collection of definitions, essays, and commentaries on and about post-colonialism.

www.bartleby.com/114/ W. E. B DuBois' influential 1903 book, *The Souls of Black Folk*, can be accessed online here.

Part Three

STRUCTURES AND PROCESSES

In this part of the book we want to introduce you to the main underlying structures and processes in contemporary world politics. There is obviously going to be some overlap between this part and the next, since the division between structures and processes, and international issues is largely one of perspective. For us, the difference is that by structures and processes we mean relatively stable features of world politics that are more enduring and constant than are the issues dealt with in the next part. Again we have two aims in this part: **first**, we want you to get a good overview of some of the most important structures and processes in world politics at the end of the twentieth century. We therefore have chosen a series of ways of thinking about world politics that draw attention to these underlying features. Again, note that we realize that what is a structure and what is a process is largely a matter of debate, but it may help to say that together these provide the setting in which the issues dealt with in the next part of the book have to be played out. All of the features examined in this part of the book will be important for the resolution of the issues we deal with in the next part, since they comprise both the main structures of world politics that these issues have to face and the main processes that will determine their fate. Our **second** aim is that these structures and processes will help you to think about globalization by forcing you to ask again whether or not it is a qualitatively different form of world politics than hitherto. Does globalization require or represent an overthrow of the structures and processes that have been central in world politics to date?

CHAPTER 13

International and global security
in the post-cold war era

JOHN BAYLIS

READER'S GUIDE

This chapter focuses on two central arguments about the effects of the end of the cold war on international security. The first argument suggests that very little of substance has changed: international relations, especially in an era of increasing globalization, are likely to be as violent in the future as they have been in the past. The second argument suggests that cooperation as well as competition has been a feature of international politics in the past and that, despite the violence of the contemporary era, opportunities nevertheless exist for a much safer and more secure world order to develop. In the context of this debate the chapter begins by looking at disagreements that exist about the causes of war and whether violence is always likely to be with us. We then turn to traditional/ classical Realist and more contemporary neo-realist perspectives on international security. Refinements of the neo-realist perspective (which reflect a more optimistic view of future international security) are then considered under the headings of 'contingent Realism', 'mature anarchy', 'Liberal Institutionalism', and 'democratic peace'. Other perspectives are developed under the headings of 'collective security', 'Constructivist' theory, critical security theory, feminist approaches, 'post-modernist' approaches, and 'globalist views'. The chapter ends by considering the continuing tension between national and international security and suggests that, despite the important changes associated with the processes of globalization, it remains too early to make a definitive judgement about whether a fundamentally different paradigm of international politics is emerging, or whether it is possible for such a transformation to occur. Globalization is undoubtedly affecting security in a number of important ways, but there are also many traditional issues and concerns.

Introduction

Students of international politics deal with some of the most profound questions it is possible to consider. Amongst the most important of these is whether international security is possible to achieve in the kind of world in which we live. For much of the intellectual history of the subject a debate has raged about the causes of war.

For some writers, especially historians, the causes of war are unique to each case: 'Hannibal's need for revenge pushed him to attack Rome in 218 BC; religious differences between Protestant and Catholic states drove the Thirty Years War (1618–48); Napoleon's charges across Europe reflected his egomania and his lust for power; states stumbled into war in 1914 for fear that others would strike first; nazi ideology and Hitler's personality caused the Second World War' (Copeland 2000: 1). In contrast, other writers believe that it is possible to provide a wider, more generalized explanation. Some analysts, for example, see the causes lying in human nature, others in the outcome of the internal organization of states, and yet others in international anarchy. In major work on the causes of war, Kenneth Waltz considers what he calls the three 'images' of war (man, the state, and the international system) in terms of what thinkers have said about the origins of conflict throughout the history of Western civilization (Waltz 1954). Waltz himself puts particular emphasis on the nature of international anarchy ('wars occur because there is nothing to stop them from occurring') but he also recognizes that a comprehensive explanation requires an understanding of all three. In his words: 'The third image describes the framework of world politics, but without the first and second images there can be no knowledge of the forces that determine policy, the first and second images describe the forces in world politics, but without the third image it is impossible to assess their importance or predict their results' (Waltz 1954: 238).

In this ongoing debate, as Waltz points out, there is a fundamental difference between political philosophers over whether conflict can be transcended or mitigated. In particular, there has been a difference between **Realists** and **Idealist** thinkers, who have been respectively pessimistic and optimistic in their response to this central question in the international politics field (see Ch.7). In the period after the First World War **Idealism** claimed widespread support as the League of **Nations** seemed to offer some hope for greater **international order**. In contrast, during the cold war which developed after 1945, Realism became the dominant school of thought. War and violent conflict were seen as perennial features of inter-state relations stretching back through human history. With the end of the cold war, however, the debate began again. For some, the end of the intense ideological confrontation between East and West was a major turning point in international history, ushering in a new paradigm in which inter-state violence would gradually become a thing of the past and new communitarian values would bring greater **cooperation** between individuals and human collectivities of various kinds (including states). This reflected more optimistic views about the development of a peaceful global society. For others, however, Realism remained the best approach to thinking about international security. In their view, very little of substance had changed as a result of the events of 1989. The end of the cold war initially brought a new, more cooperative era between the **superpowers** into existence, but it was only temporary as states and other **non-state actors** (including international terrorist groups) continued to use force to achieve their objectives.

This chapter focuses on this debate, highlighting the different strands of thinking within these two optimistic and pessimistic schools of thought. Before this can be done, however, it is necessary to consider what is meant by 'security' and to probe the relationship between national security and international security. Attention will then shift to traditional ways of thinking about national security and the influence which these ideas have had on contemporary thinking. This will be followed by a survey of alternative ideas and approaches which have emerged in the literature in recent years. The conclusion will then provide an assessment of these ideas before we return to the central question of whether or not greater international security is more, or less, likely in the new century.

What is meant by the concept of security?

Most writers agree that security is a 'contested concept'. There is a consensus that it implies freedom from threats to core values (for both individuals and groups) but there is a major disagreement about whether the main focus of enquiry should be on 'individual', 'national', or 'international' security. For much of the cold war period most writing on the subject was dominated by the idea of **national** security, which was largely defined in militarized terms. The main area of interest for both academics and statesmen tended to be on the military **capabilities** that their own states should develop to deal with the threats that faced them. More recently, however, this idea of security has been criticized for being **ethnocentric** (culturally biased) and too narrowly defined. Instead a number of contemporary writers have argued for an expanded conception of security outward from the limits of parochial national security to include a range of other considerations. Barry Buzan, in his study, *People, States and Fear*, argues for a view of security which includes political, economic, societal, environmental, as well as military aspects, and which is also defined in broader international terms (see Box 13.2). This involves states overcoming 'excessively self-referenced security policies' and thinking instead about the security interests of their neighbours (Buzan 1983: 214–42). Buzan's work raises interesting and important questions about whether national and international security considerations can be compatible and whether states, given the nature of the **international system**, are capable of thinking in more cooperative international and global terms.

This focus on the tension between national and international security is not accepted by all writers on security. There are those who argue that the emphasis on the state and inter-state relations ignores the fundamental changes which have been

> **Box 13.1   Notions of 'security'**
>
> 'A nation is secure to the extent to which it is not in danger of having to sacrifice core values if it wishes to avoid war, and is able, if challenged, to maintain them by victory in such a war.'
>
> (Walter Lippmann)
>
> 'Security, in any objective sense, measures the absence of threats to acquired values and in a subjective sense, the absence of fear that such values will be attacked.'
>
> (Arnold Wolfers)
>
> 'In the case of security, the discussion is about the pursuit of freedom from threat. When this discussion is in the context of the international system, security is about the ability of states and societies to maintain their independent **identity** and their functional integrity.'
>
> (Barry Buzan)
>
> 'Stable security can only be achieved by people and groups if they do not deprive others of it; this can be achieved if security is conceived as a process of emancipation.'
>
> (Wheeler and Booth)

taking place in world politics especially in the aftermath of the cold war. For some, the dual processes of **integration** and fragmentation which characterize the contemporary world mean that much more attention should be given to 'societal security'. According to this view, growing integration in regions like Europe is undermining the classical political **order** based on **nation-states**, leaving nations exposed within larger political frameworks (like the EU). At the same time, the fragmentation of various states, like the Soviet Union and Yugoslavia, has created new problems of boundaries, minorities, and organizing ideologies which are causing

Box 13.2	Different dimensions of international security

At the political level there has been a growing recognition that systems of government and ideologies have a powerful influence not only on domestic stability but also on international security. Authoritarian governments often seek to divert attention away from problems at home by pursuing foreign adventures. This appears to have been one of the major reasons for the Malvinas/Falklands war in 1982 between Argentina and Britain. The contemporary trend towards the fragmentation of states also poses wider security problems. This has been evident with the disintegration of the Soviet Union and Yugoslavia in the 1990s and could become a major problem if the Chinese Communist Party began to lose effective control in the years ahead.

Population growth and problems over access to resources and markets [have] also led to greater attention being given to economic security issues. Deprivation and poverty are not only a source of internal conflict but can also spill over into tension between states. An example of this can be seen in the late 1980s in relations between Senegal and Mauritania. Disputes over agricultural land, together with population pressures gave rise to the expulsion of minority groups and ethnic violence in the Senegal River Valley bordering on Mauritania. The dispute did not lead to war between the two states but considerable diplomatic tensions were generated, demonstrating the growing importance of economic interdependence and the potential for conflict which can be created as a result.

Economic pressures can also encourage social tensions within states which can have implications for international security. In recent years large migration movements between states [have] produced group-identity conflicts. One of the most serious has been the migration from Bangladesh to north-east India. In the last twenty years the population of Assam has risen from 7 million to 22 million people causing major social changes which have altered the balance of political power between religious and ethnic groups in the state. This resulted in intergroup conflict which has caused difficulties between India and Bangladesh.

Many of the economic and social sources of insecurity in the contemporary world are linked to environmental scarcity. As Thomas Homer-Dixon has shown, scarcities of cropland, water, forests and fish, together with atmospheric changes such as global warming have an important impact on international security. Control over oil was a major cause of the Gulf War in 1991 and tension over the control of water resources in the occupied West Bank has helped heighten tension between Arabs and Jews in Israel complicating the efforts to achieve a durable peace settlement in the region.

(Homer-Dixon 1994: 18)

increasing regional instability (Waever *et al.* 1993: 196). This has led to the argument that ethno-national groups, rather than states, should become the centre of attention for security analysts.

At the same time, there are other commentators who argue that the stress on national and international security is less appropriate because of the emergence of an embryonic global society in the post-cold war era. Like the 'societal security' theorists they point to the fragmentation of the nation-state but they argue that more attention should be given, not to society at the ethno-national level, but to global society. These writers argue that one of the most important contemporary trends is the broad process of globalization which is taking place. They accept that this process brings new risks and dangers. These include the risks associated with such things as international terrorism, a breakdown of the global monetary system, global warming, and the dangers of nuclear accidents. These threats to security, on a planetary level, are viewed as being largely outside the control of nation-states. Only the development of a global community, they believe, can deal with this adequately.

At the same time, there are other writers on globalization who stress the transformation of the state (rather than its demise) and the new security agenda in the early years of the new century. In the aftermath of what has become known as '9/11' in September 2001 and the new era of violence which followed it, Jonathan Friedman argued that we are living in a world 'where polarization, both vertical and horizontal, both class and ethnic, has become rampant, and where violence has become more globalized and fragmented at the same time, and is no longer a question of wars between states but of sub-state conflicts, globally networked and financed, in which states have become one actor, increasingly privatized, amongst others.' (Friedman 2003: ix). For many of those who feel like this, the post-9/11 era is a new and extremely dangerous period in world history. Whether the world is so different today from what it was in the past is a matter of much contemporary discussion. In order to consider this issue we need to begin by looking at the way 'security' has been traditionally conceived.

Key points

- Security is a 'contested concept'.
- The meaning of security has been broadened to include political, economic, societal, and environmental, as well as military, aspects.
- Differing arguments exist about the tension between national and international security.
- Different views have emerged about the significance of 9/11 for the future of international security.

The traditional approach to national security

As Chapter 2 has shown, from the Treaty of Westphalia in 1648 onwards states have been regarded as by far the most powerful actors in the international system. They have been 'the universal standard of political legitimacy' with no higher authority to regulate their relations with each other. This has meant that security has been seen as the priority obligation of state governments. They have taken the view that there is no alternative but to seek their own protection in what has been described as a self-help world.

In the historical debate about how best to achieve national security writers like Hobbes, Machiavelli, and Rousseau tended to paint a rather pessimistic picture of the implications of **state sovereignty**. The international system was viewed as a rather brutal arena in which states would seek to achieve their own security at the expense of their neighbours. Inter-state relations were seen as a struggle for power as states constantly attempted to take advantage of each other. According to this view **permanent peace** was unlikely to be achieved. All that states could do was to try and balance the power of other states to prevent any one from achieving overall **hegemony**. This was a view which was shared by writers, like E. H. Carr and Hans Morgenthau, who developed what became known as the Realist (or

'classical' Realist) school of thought in the aftermath of the Second World War.

This largely pessimistic view of international relations is shared by many contemporary writers like Kenneth Waltz and John Mearsheimer. The pessimism of these **neo-realists** rests on a number of key assumptions they make about the way the international system works (see Ch.7 and Ch.9).

Key neo-realist assumptions

- The international system is **anarchic**. They do not mean by this that it is necessarily chaotic. Rather, anarchy implies that there is no central authority capable of controlling state behaviour.

- States claiming **sovereignty** will inevitably develop **offensive military capabilities** to defend themselves and extend their power. As such they are potentially dangerous to each other.

- **Uncertainty**, leading to **a lack of trust**, is inherent in the international system. States can never be sure of the intentions of their neighbours and, therefore, they must always be on their guard.

- States will want to maintain their independence

and sovereignty, and, as a result, **survival** will be the most basic driving force influencing their behaviour.

- Although states are rational, there will always be **room for miscalculation**. In a world of imperfect information, potential antagonists will always have an incentive to misrepresent their own capabilities to keep their opponents guessing. This may lead to mistakes about 'real' state interests.

Taken together, neo-realists argue, these assumptions produce a tendency for states to act aggressively towards each other.

According to this view, national security, or insecurity, is largely the result of the **structure** of the international system (this is why these writers are sometimes called 'structural Realists'). The **structure** of anarchy is seen as being highly durable. The implication of this is that international politics in the future is likely to be as violent as international politics in the past. In an important article entitled 'Back to the Future' written in 1990 John Mearsheimer argued that the end of the cold war was likely to usher in a return to the traditional multilateral **balance of power** politics of the past in which extreme nationalism and ethnic rivalries would lead to widespread **instability** and **conflict**. Mearsheimer viewed the cold war as a period of peace and stability brought about by the bipolar structure of power which prevailed. With the collapse of this system, he argued, there would be a return to the kind of Great Power rivalries which had blighted international relations since the seventeenth century.

For neo-realist writers, like Mearsheimer, international politics may not be characterized by constant wars but there is nevertheless a relentless security competition which takes place, with war, like rain, always a possibility. It is accepted that cooperation among states can and does occur, but such cooperation has its limits. It is 'constrained by the dominating logic of security competition, which no amount of co-operation can eliminate' (Mearsheimer 1994/5: 9). Genuine long-lasting peace, or a world where states do not compete for power, therefore, is very unlikely to be achieved.

Key points

- Debates about security have traditionally focused on the role of the state in international relations.

- Realists and neo-realists emphasize the perennial problem of insecurity.

- The 'security dilemma' is seen by some writers as the essential source of conflict between states.

The 'security dilemma'

This view that war is a constant historical feature of international politics and is unlikely to disappear is based on the notion that states face what has been described as a **security dilemma** from which it is largely impossible to escape. The idea of a security dilemma was first clearly articulated in the 1950s by John Herz. It was, he said, 'a structural notion in which the **self-help** attempts of states to look after their security needs, tend regardless of intention to lead to rising insecurity for others as each interprets its own measures as defensive and the measures of others as potentially threatening' (Herz 1950: 157).

According to this view, in a self-help environment, like the international system, states are faced with an 'unresolvable uncertainty' about the military preparations made by other states. Are they designed simply for their own defence or are they part of a more aggressive design? Because the uncertainty is unresolvable, states are likely to remain mistrustful

---

Box 13.3 A statesman's view of the 'security dilemma'

'The distinction between preparations made with the intention of going to war and precautions against attack is a true distinction, clear and definite in the minds of those who build up armaments. But it is a distinction that is not obvious or certain to others. Each Government, therefore, while resenting any suggestion that its own measures are anything more than for defence, regards similar measures of another government as preparation to attack.'

(Lord Grey)

of each other. In turn, if mistrust is mutual, 'a dynamic **"action-reaction"** cycle may well result, which will take the fears of both to higher levels'. Insecurity will breed further insecurity, with the ever-present potential for war breaking out (Wheeler and Booth 1992: 29–31).

At the root of the security dilemma, therefore, are mistrust and fear. Even when states are believed to be benign in their intentions there is always the recognition that intentions can change. Being overly trusting opens up the prospects of being taken advantage of, with potentially disastrous consequences. This constant fear, according to Butterfield, creates an awful tragedy which afflicts international relations. 'Behind the great conflicts of mankind', he argues, there 'is a terrible predicament which lies at the heart of the story'. Writing in the 1950s Butterfield argued that there was no sign that mankind was capable of overcoming this 'irreducible dilemma' (Butterfield 1951: 20).

The difficulties of cooperation between states

For most contemporary neo-realist writers there is little prospect of a significant change in the nature of security in the post-cold war world. Pointing to the Gulf War in 1991, the violent disintegration of the former Yugoslavia and parts of the former Soviet Union, continuing violence in the Middle East, and the Iraq War in 2003, they argue that we continue to live in a world of mistrust and constant security competition. Cooperation between states occurs, but it is difficult to achieve and even more difficult to sustain. There are two main factors, it is suggested, which continue to make cooperation difficult, even after the changes of 1989. The first is the prospect of cheating; the second is the concern which states have about what are called relative gains.

The problem of cheating

Writers like Waltz and Mearsheimer do not deny that states often cooperate or that in the post-cold war era there are even greater opportunities than in the past for states to work together. They argue, however, that there are distinct limits to this cooperation because states have always been, and remain, fearful that others will cheat on any agreements reached and attempt to gain advantages over them. This risk is regarded as being particularly important, given the nature of modern military technology which can bring about very rapid shifts in the balance of power between states. 'Such a development', Mearsheimer has argued, 'could create a window of opportunity for the cheating side to inflict a decisive defeat on the victim state' (Mearsheimer 1994/5: 20). States realize that this is the case and although they join alliances and sign arms control agreements, they remain cautious and aware of the need to provide for their own national security in the last resort. This is one of the reasons why, despite the Strategic Arms Reduction Agreements of the early 1990s and the extension of the Non-Proliferation Treaty in 1995, the nuclear powers continue to maintain some of their nuclear weapons. The unilateralism of the Bush administration, and especially its growing disillusionment with arms control in general (illustrated by its abandonment of the 1972 ABM Treaty), has indicated a determination to put national security at the forefront of its strategic agenda.

The problem of relative gains

Cooperation is also inhibited, according to many neo-realist writers, because states tend to be concerned with 'relative gains', rather than 'absolute gains'. Instead of being interested in cooperation because it will benefit both partners, states, they suggest, always have to be aware of how much they are gaining compared with the state they are cooperating with. Because all states will be attempting to maximize their gains in a competitive, mistrustful, and uncertain international environment, cooperation will always be very difficult to achieve and hard to maintain.

Such a view of the problems of cooperation in the post-cold war world are not, however, shared by all writers, even within the neo-realist school. There is a wide body of opinion amongst scholars (and politicians) that the traditional or 'standard' neo-realist view of international relations should be modified or even replaced. Opposition to 'standard' neo-realism takes a wide variety of different forms. To illustrate alternative ways of thinking about contemporary international security, eight different approaches will be considered. Despite the differences which exist between writers in these fields they all share a common view that greater international security in the future is possible through cooperation. Many of

them have argued that international security has been undergoing significant changes which could bring greater opportunities for peace.

> **Key points**
>
> - Trust is often difficult between states, according to Realists, because of the problem of cheating
> - Realists also point out the problem of 'relative gains' whereby states compare their gains with those of other states when making their decisions about security.

The opportunities for cooperation between states

'Contingent Realism'

Contrary to the views of those neo-realists (like Waltz and Mearsheimer) who continue to remain pessimistic about cooperation between states in the post-cold war world, there are other neo-realist writers who present a rather more optimistic assessment. According to Charles Glaser, 'contrary to the conventional wisdom, the strong general propensity of adversaries to compete is not an inevitable logical consequence of structural realism's basic assumptions' (Glaser 1994/5: 51). Glaser accepts much of the analysis and assumptions of structural Realism, but he argues that there are a wide range of conditions in which adversaries can best achieve their security goals through cooperative policies, rather than competitive ones. In such circumstances states will choose to cooperate rather than to compete. Security is therefore seen to be 'contingent' on the circumstances prevailing at the time.

Contingent Realists argue that **standard** structural Realism is flawed for **three** main reasons.

1. They reject the competition bias inherent in the theory. Because international relations are characterized by self-help behaviour does not necessarily mean, they argue, that states are damned to perpetual competition which will result in war.

Faced with the uncertainties associated with being involved in an arms race, like that of the 1970s and 1980s, for example, states preferred to cooperate. There were distinct advantages in working together to reduce the risks and uncertainty in this period rather than engaging in relentless competition which characterized most of the cold war years.

2. A second, and related argument is that standard structural Realism is flawed because of its emphasis on 'relative gains'. States often pursue cooperation, it is argued, precisely because of the dangers of seeking relative advantages. As the security dilemma literature suggests, it is often best in security terms to accept rough parity rather than seek maximum gains which will spark off another round of the arms race leading to less security for all in the longer term.

3. The third flaw in the standard argument, according to contingent Realists, is that the emphasis on cheating is overdone. Cheating is a problem which poses risks, but so does arms racing. Schelling and Halperin (1961) have argued that 'it cannot be assumed that an agreement that leaves some possibility of cheating is unacceptable or that cheating would necessarily result in strategically important gains'. The risks involved in

---

Box 13.4   Key concepts

'A security community is a group of people which has become "integrated". By integration we mean the attainment, within a territory, of a "sense of community" and of institutions and practices strong enough and widespread enough to assure . . . dependable expectations of "peaceful change" among its population. By a "sense of community" we mean a belief . . . that common social problems must and can be resolved by processes of "peaceful change".'

(Karl Deutsch)

'Security regimes occur when a group of states cooperate to manage their disputes and avoid war by seeking to mute the security dilemma both by their own actions and by their assumptions about the behaviour of others.'

(Robert Jervis)

'A security complex involves a group of states whose primary security concerns link together sufficiently closely that their national securities cannot realistically be considered apart from one another.'

(Barry Buzan)

'Acceptance of common security as the organizing principle for efforts to reduce the risk of war, limit arms, and move towards disarmament, means, in principle, that co-operation will replace confrontation in resolving conflicts of interest. This is not to say that differences among nations should be expected to disappear . . . The task is only to ensure that these conflicts do not come to be expressed in acts of war, or in preparations for war. It means that nations must come to understand that the maintenance of world peace must be given a higher priority than the assertion of their own ideological or political positions.'

(*Palme Report* 1992)

---

arms control may be preferable to the risks involved in arms racing. Contingent Realists argue that this is often ignored by writers like Waltz and Mearsheimer. This was clearly the view of the superpowers in the late 1980s and early 1990s when a wide range of agreements were signed including the INF Treaty and the START 1 and 2 Treaties (see Ch.22).

The main thrust of the argument was that there is no need to be overly pessimistic about international security in the aftermath of the cold war.

Key points

- 'Contingent Realists' regard themselves as 'structural Realists' or 'neo-realists'.

- They believe standard 'neo-realism' is flawed for three main reasons: they reject the competition bias in the theory; they do not accept that states are only motivated by 'relative gains'; they believe the emphasis on cheating is exaggerated.

- 'Contingent Realists' tend to be more optimistic about cooperation between states than traditional 'neo-realists'.

Mature anarchy

The view that it is possible to ameliorate (if not necessarily to transcend) the security dilemma through greater cooperation between states is also shared by other writers who would describe themselves as 'neo-realists' or 'structural Realists'. Barry Buzan has argued that one of the interesting and important features of the 1980s and 1990s is the gradual emergence of a rather more 'mature anarchy' in which states recognize the intense dangers of continuing to compete aggressively in a nuclear world. While accepting the tendency of states to focus on their own narrow parochial security interests, Buzan argues that there is a growing recognition amongst the more 'mature' states in the international system that there are good (security) reasons for taking into account the interests of their neighbours when making their own policies. States, he suggests, are increasingly internalizing 'the understanding that national securities are interdependent and that excessively self-referenced security policies, whatever their jingoistic attractions, are ultimately self-defeating' (Buzan 1983: 208). He cites the Nordic countries as providing an example of a group of states that have moved, through 'a maturing process', from fierce military rivalry to a security community. Buzan accepts that such an evolutionary process for international society as a whole is likely to be slow and uneven in its achievements. A change away from the preoccupation with national security towards a greater emphasis on international security, however, is, in his view, at least possible, and certainly desirable.

It could be argued that this is exactly what has happened in Western Europe over the past fifty years. After centuries of hostile relations between France and Germany, as well as between other Western European states, a new sense of 'community' was established with the Treaty of Rome which turned former enemies into close allies. Unlike in the past these states no longer consider using violence or coercion to resolve their differences. Disagreements still occur but there is a consensus within the EU that these will always be resolved peacefully by political means. Supporters of the concept of 'mature anarchy' argue that this ongoing 'civilizing' process in Europe can be extended further to achieve a wider **security community** by embracing other regions with which economic and political cooperation is increasingly taking place.

Key points

- Supporters of the concept of 'mature anarchy' also accept that **structure** is a key element in determining state behaviour.

- There is, however, a trend towards 'mature anarchy', especially in Europe, which focuses on the growing importance of international security considerations.

- This is occurring because more states in the contemporary world are recognizing that their own security is interdependent with the security of other states.

- The more this happens the greater the chances of dampening down the security dilemma.

Liberal Institutionalism

One of the main characteristics of the standard neorealist approach to international security is the belief that international institutions do not have a very important part to play in the prevention of war. Institutions are seen as being the product of state interests and the constraints which are imposed by the international system itself. It is these interests and constraints, rather than the institutions to which they belong, which shape the decisions on whether to cooperate or compete.

Such views have been challenged by both statesmen and a number of international relations specialists, particularly following the end of the cold war. The British Foreign Secretary, Douglas Hurd, for example made the case in June 1992 that institutions themselves had played, and continued to play, a crucial role in **enhancing security**, particularly in Europe. He argued that the West had developed 'a set of international institutions which have proved their worth for one set of problems'. He went on to argue that the great challenge of the post-cold war era was to adapt these institutions to deal with the new circumstances which prevailed (Hurd, quoted in Mearsheimer 1994/5).

This view reflected a belief, widely shared among Western statesmen that a framework of complementary, mutually reinforcing institutions—the EU, NATO, WEU, and the Organization for Security and Co-operation in Europe (OSCE)—could be developed to promote a more durable and stable European security system for the post-cold war era. For many observers such an approach has considerable potential in achieving peace in other regions of the world as well. ASEAN is often cited as an institution which has an important role to play in helping to maintain stability in South-East Asia. Similarly the Organization of African States plays a part in helping to resolve differences between African states.

This is a view which is also shared by a distinctive group of academic writers which developed during the 1980s and early 1990s. These writers all share a conviction that the developing pattern of **institutionalized cooperation** between states opens up unprecedented opportunities to achieve greater international security in the years ahead. Although the past may have been characterized by constant wars and conflict, important changes are taking place in international relations at the beginning of the twenty-first century which create the opportunity to dampen down the traditional security competition between states.

This approach, known as **Liberal Institutionalism** (or neo-liberalism), operates largely within the Realist framework, but argues that international institutions are much more important in helping to achieve cooperation and stability than 'structural Realists' realize (see Ch.9). According to Keohane and Martin (1995: 42) 'institutions can provide information, reduce transaction costs, make commitments more credible, establish focal points for coordination and, in general, facilitate the operation of reciprocity'. Supporters of these ideas point to the importance of European economic and political institutions in overcoming the traditional hostility of European states. They also point to the developments within the EU and NATO in the post-cold war era to demonstrate that by investing major resources states themselves clearly believe in the importance of institutions. According to this line of argument, if states were influenced only by narrow calculations of power, the EU and NATO would have withered away at the end of the cold war. In fact, the reverse has happened. Both retain their vitality at the beginning of the new century and are engaged in a process of expansion. This is not to say that institutions can prevent wars from occurring, but they can help to mitigate the fears of cheating and alleviate fears which sometimes arise from unequal gains from cooperation.

It is suggested that in a world constrained by state power and divergent interests, international institutions operating on the basis of reciprocity at least will be a component of any lasting peace. In other words, international institutions themselves are unlikely to eradicate war from the international system but they can play a part in helping to achieve greater cooperation between states. This was reflected in Prime Minister Margaret Thatcher's call in 1990 to 'bring the new democracies of Eastern Europe into closer association with the institutions of Western Europe'. Despite some scepticism about the European Community, she argued that the EC had reconciled antagonisms within Western Europe in the post-Second World War period and it could be used to overcome divisions between East and West in Europe in the post-cold war period. This has been very much at the heart of the campaign to expand the EU in the early years of this century.

Key points

- Neo-realists reject the significance of international institutions in helping many to achieve peace and security.

- Contemporary politicians and academics, who write under the label of Liberal Institutionalism, however, see institutions as an important mechanism for achieving international security.

- Liberal Institutionalists accept many of the assumptions of Realism about the continuing importance of military power in international relations but argue that institutions can provide a framework for cooperation which can help to overcome the dangers of security competition between states.

Democratic peace theory

Another 'Liberal' approach to international security has gathered momentum in the post-cold war world. This centres on the argument that democratic states tend not to fight other democratic states. Democracy, therefore, is seen as a major source of peace (see Ch.8). As with 'Liberal Institutionalism', this is a notion which has received wide support in Western political and academic circles. In his State of the Union Address in 1994 President Bill Clinton went out of his way to point to the absence of war between democracies as a justification for American policies of promoting a process of democratization around the world. Support for this view can be seen in the Western policy of promoting democracy in Eastern and Central Europe following the end of the cold war and opening up the possibility of these states joining the EU.

'Democratic peace' theory has been largely associated with the writings of Michael Doyle and Bruce Russett. In the same way that contemporary Realists have been influenced by the work of Hobbes, Rousseau, and Machiavelli, Doyle points to the importance of the insights contained in Immanuel Kant's 1795 essay, *Perpetual Peace*. Doyle contends that democratic representation, an ideological commitment to human rights, and transnational interdependence provide an explanation for the 'peace-prone' tendencies of democratic states. (Doyle 1995a: 180–4) Equally, the absence of these attributes, he argues, provides a reason why non-democratic states tend to be 'war-prone'. Without these domestic values and restraints the logic of power replaces the liberal logic of accommodation.

Supporters of democratic peace ideas, as a way of promoting international security in the post-cold war era, do not only argue that wars between democracies are rare or non-existent. They also contend that democracies are more likely to settle mutual conflicts of interest short of the threat or use of any military force. It is accepted that conflicts of interest will, and do, arise between democratic states, but shared **norms** and institutional constraints mean that democracies rarely escalate those disputes to the point where they threaten to use military force against each other, or actually use force at all. Much more than other states, they settle their disagreement by mediation, negotiation, or other forms of peaceful **diplomacy**. One of the benefits of democracy, according to Doyle, is that differences will be managed long before they become violent disputes in the public arena. There is clearly a close link here with the arguments put forward by supporters of the concept of 'mature anarchy', discussed above.

These democratic peace arguments are not designed to reject Realism completely but to suggest that liberal democracies do make rather more of a difference in international politics than Realist writers accept. Bruce Russett has argued that there is no need to jettison the insights of Realism which tell us that power and strategic considerations affect states' decisions to fight each other. But neither should one deny the limitations of those insights, and their inability to explain many of the instances when liberal states have chosen not to fight or to threaten one another. For Russett the danger resides in 'vulgar realism's' vision of war of all against all, 'in which the threat that other states pose is unaffected by their internal norms and institutions' (Russett 1995: 175).

Russett argues that democratic values are not the only influence permitting states to avoid war; power and strategic influences undoubtedly affect the calculations of all states, including democracies. And sometimes these strategic considerations can be predominant. Shared democracy, however, he believes, is important in international affairs and should not be ignored in any attempt to dampen down the security dilemma and achieve greater security. He is not saying that shared democratic values by themselves will eliminate all wars but, like Liberal Institutionalists, he argues that such values will contribute to a more peaceful world.

> ### Key points
>
> - Democratic peace theory emerged in the 1980s. The main argument was that the spread of democracy would lead to greater international security.
>
> - Democratic peace theory is based on a Kantian logic—emphasizing three elements—republican democratic representation, an ideological commitment to human rights, and transnational interdependence.
>
> - Wars between democracies are seen as being rare and they are believed to settle mutual conflicts of interest without the threat or use of force more often than non-democratic states.
>
> - Supporters of democratic peace ideas do not reject the insights of Realism, but they reject 'vulgar realism's' preoccupation with the idea of war of all against all. They argue that internal norms and institutions matter.

Ideas of collective security

There are other approaches to contemporary international security which take realpolitik and power calculations seriously but which also argue that domestic politics, beliefs, and norms must also be included as important determinants of state behaviour. One such approach is that associated with collective securit ideas. Proponents of collective security argue that although military force remains an important characteristic of international life, there are nevertheless realistic opportunities to move beyond the self-help world of Realism, especially after the end of the cold war. They reject the idea that state behaviour is simply the product of the structure of the international system. Ideas, it is argued, are also important.

According to Charles and Clifford Kupchan, under collective security, states agree to abide by certain norms and **rules** to maintain stability, and when necessary, band together to stop aggression (Kupchan and Kupchan 1995). Defined in these terms collective security involves a recognition by states that to enhance their security they must agree to three main **principles** in their inter-state relations.

- **First**, they must renounce the use of military force to alter the status quo and agree instead to settle all of their disputes peacefully. Changes will be possible in international relations, but ought to be achieved by negotiation rather than force.

- **Second**, they must broaden their conception of **national interest** to take in the interests of the international community as a whole. This means that when a troublemaker appears in the system, all of the responsible states automatically and collectively confront the aggressor with overwhelming military power.

- **Third**, and most importantly, states must overcome the fear which dominates world politics

and learn to trust each other. Such a system of security, as Inis Claude has argued, depends on states entrusting 'their destinies to collective security'.

Supporters of collective security as a way forward to achieving greater global security accept that their ideas are not a panacea for preventing war. They argue, however, that by setting up collective security institutions some of the worst excesses of the perennial competition between states can be avoided. According to this view, 'regulated, institutionalized balancing is preferable to unregulated balancing under anarchy' (Kupchan and Kupchan 1995). Collective security is seen as a way of providing a more effective mechanism for balancing against an aggressor. By facing potential aggressors with preponderance, collective security arrangements are designed to provide **deterrence** and more effective action if deterrence breaks down.

It is also argued that collective security institutions contribute to the task of creating a more benign international system. They help create greater confidence so that states can concentrate their energies and resources on their own domestic welfare rather than on non-productive, excessive national security arrangements. Proponents argue that there are profound advantages to institutionalizing a security

---

Box 13.5   The problems with collective security

John Mearsheimer has argued that collective security is inescapably flawed. There are nine main reasons, he suggests, why it is likely to fail:

1. States often find it difficult, if not impossible, to distinguish between the 'aggressor' and the 'victim' in international conflicts.

2. Collective security assumes that all aggression is wrong, whereas there may be circumstances where conquest is warranted against a threatening neighbour.

3. Because some states are especially friendly for historical or ideological reasons they will be unlikely to join a coalition against their friends.

4. Historical enmity between states may complicate the effective working of a collective security system.

5. Because sovereign states have a tendency to 'pass the buck' in paying the price of dealing with aggression there is often difficulty in distributing the burden equitably.

6. Difficulties arise in securing a rapid response to aggression because of the unwillingness to engage in pre-crisis contingency planning.

7. States are often reluctant to join a coalition because collective action is likely to transform a local conflict into an international conflict.

8. Democracies are reluctant to make an automatic commitment to join collective action because of state sovereignty.

9. Collective security implies a contradiction in the way military force is viewed. It is seen as abhorrent and yet states must be willing to use it against an aggressor.

(Mearsheimer 1994/5)

system that promises to deepen the accord among states rather than letting a self-help system take its course and simply hoping that great power conflict will not re-emerge. The aim, as with Liberal Institutionalism and democratic peace ideas, is to ameliorate security competition between states by reducing the possibility that unintended spirals of hostility will escalate into war.

Supporters of these ideas argue that although collective security arrangements, like the League of Nations, have failed in the past there is no iron law which says they must fail in the future. The post-cold war era, they believe, has created a more conducive international environment in which greater opportunities exist than in the past for states to share similar values and interests. This is particularly so in Europe with the spread of democratic values and the collapse of confrontation politics between East and West. These conditions provide the essential foundations for the successful functioning of a collective security system. Supporters also point to the Gulf War in 1991 as an example of effective collective security action in the post-cold war period. Collective security has also been one part of the approach adopted by the Bush administration in the aftermath of 9/11 to try to build up a global coalition against the new phase of international terrorism linked to Al

Qaeda. (For a critique of collective security ideas see Box 13.5.)

Key points

- Collective security theorists take power seriously but argue that it is possible to move beyond the self-help world of Realism.

- Collective security is based on three main conditions—that states must renounce the use of military force to alter the status quo; that they must broaden their view of national interest to take in the interests of the international community; and that states must overcome their fear and learn to trust each other.

- Collective security aims to create a more effective system of 'regulated institutionalized balancing' rather than relying on the unregulated balancing which takes place under anarchy.

- Collective security is believed to contribute to the creation of a more benign international system.

- Despite past failures, supporters argue that there is an opportunity to try collective security again with more success in the post-cold war world.

Alternative views of international and global security

'Social Constructivist' theory

The notion that international relations are affected not only by power politics but also by ideas is also shared by writers who describe themselves as 'Social Constructivist theorists'. According to this view, the fundamental structures of international politics are **social** rather than strictly **material**. This leads Social Constructivists to argue that changing the way we **think** about international relations can bring a fundamental shift towards greater international security (see Ch.11).

At one level, Social Constructivists, like Alexander Wendt, share many of the major Realist assumptions about international politics. They accept that states

are the key referent in the study of international politics and international security; that international politics is anarchic; that states often have offensive capabilities; that states cannot be absolutely certain of the intentions of other states; that states have a fundamental wish to survive; and that states attempt to behave rationally. They also see themselves as structuralists; that is to say they believe that the interests of individual states are in an important sense constructed by the structure of the international system.

However, Social Constructivists think about international politics in a very different way to neorealists. The latter tend to view structure as being made up only of a distribution of material capabilities. On the other hand, they think that structure is the product of social relationships. Social structures, they argue, are made up of elements, such as **shared knowledge**, **material resources**, and **practices**. This means that social structures are defined, in part, by shared understandings, expectations, or knowledge. As an example of this, Alexander Wendt argues that the security dilemma is a social structure composed of **inter-subjective understandings** in which states are so distrustful that they make worst-case assumptions about each other's intentions, and, as a result, define their interests in 'self-help' terms (Wendt 1992). In contrast, a security community is a rather different social structure, composed of shared knowledge in which states trust one another to resolve disputes without war.

The emphasis on the structure of shared knowledge is important in Social Constructivist thinking. Social structures include material things, like tanks and economic resources, but these only acquire **meaning** through the structure of shared knowledge in which they are embedded. The idea of power politics, or **realpolitik**, has meaning to the extent that states accept the idea as a basic rule of international politics. According to Social Constructivist writers, power politics is an idea which does affect the way states behave, but it does not describe all inter-state behaviour. States are also influenced by other ideas, such as the rule of law and the importance of institutional cooperation and restraint. In his study, 'Anarchy is What States Make of it', Wendt (1992) argues that security dilemmas and wars are the result of self-fulfilling prophecies. The 'logic of reciprocity' means that states acquire a shared knowledge about the meaning of power and act accordingly. Equally, he argues, policies of reassurance can also help to bring about a structure of shared knowledge which can help to move states towards a more peaceful security community (see Wendt 1999).

Although Social Constructivists argue that security dilemmas are not acts of God, they differ over whether they can be escaped. For some, the fact that structures are socially constructed does not necessarily mean that they can be changed. This is reflected in Wendt's comment that 'sometimes social structures so constrain action that transformative strategies are impossible' (Wendt 1995: 80). Other Social Constructivist writers, however, are more optimistic.

They point to the changes in ideas introduced by Gorbachev during the second half of the 1980s which led to a shared knowledge about the end of the cold war. Once both sides accepted the cold war was over, it really was over. According to this view, understanding the crucial role of social structure is important in developing policies and processes of interaction which will lead towards cooperation rather than conflict. For the optimists, there is sufficient 'slack' in the international system which allows states to pursue policies of peaceful social change rather than engage in a perpetual competitive struggle for power. If there are opportunities for promoting social change most Social Constructivists believe it would be irresponsible not to pursue such policies.

Key points

- Social Constructivist thinkers base their ideas on two main assumptions: (1) that the fundamental structures of international politics are socially constructed; and (2) that changing the way we think about international relations can help to bring about greater international security.

- Social Constructivist thinkers accept many of the assumptions of neo-realism, but they reject the view that 'structure' consists only of material capabilities. They stress the importance of social structure defined in terms of shared knowledge and practices as well as material capabilities.

- Social Constructivists argue that material things acquire meaning only through the structure of shared knowledge in which they are embedded.

- Power politics and realpolitik, emphasized by Realists, are seen as being derived from shared knowledge which is self-fulfilling.

- Social Constructivists can be pessimistic or optimistic about changing international relations and achieving international security.

Critical security studies

Despite the differences between Social Constructivists and Realists about the relationship between ideas and material factors they agree on the central role of the state in debates about international security. There are other theorists, however, who believe that the state has been given too much prominence. Keith Krause and Michael Williams have defined critical security studies in the following terms: 'Contemporary debates over the nature of security often float on a sea of unvoiced assumptions and deeper theoretical issues concerning to what and to whom the term *security* refers . . . What most contributions to the debate thus share are two inter-related concerns: what security is and how we study it.' (Krause and Williams 1997: 34). What they also share is a wish to de-emphasize the role of the state and re-conceptualize security in a different way. What might be termed 'alternative' security studies includes a number of diferent approaches. These include 'critical theory and emancipation', 'feminist' approaches, and 'post-modernist' approaches.

Critical theory and emancipation

Robert Cox draws a distinction between **problem-solving theories** and **critical theories**. Problem-solving theorists work within the prevailing system. They take 'the existing social and political relations and institutions as starting points for analysis and then see how the problems rising from these can be solved and ameliorated' (Smith 2000). In contrast, critical theorists focus their attention on the way these existing relationships and institutions emerged and what might be done to change them (see Ch.10). For critical security theorists, states should not be the centre of analysis because they are not only extremely diverse in character but also often part of the problem of insecurity in the international system. They can be providers of security, but they can also be a source of threat to their own people. According to this view, therefore, attention should be focused on the individual rather than the state. With this as their main referent, writers like Booth and Wyn Jones argue that security can best be assured through **human emancipation**, defined in terms of 'freeing people, as individuals and groups, from the social, physical, economic, political, and other constraints that stop them from carrying out what they would freely choose to do'. This focus on emancipation is designed to provide 'a theory of progress', 'a politics of hope', and a guide to 'a

politics of resistance' (Booth 1999). Critics point to the vagueness of the concept of 'emancipation' and the difficulty of 'individual-based' theories to analyse international and global security (see Rengger 2000).

'Feminist' approaches

Feminist writers also challenge the traditional emphasis on the central role of the state in studies of international security. While there are significant differences between feminist theorists (including critical theory and post-modernist/post-structuralist perspectives), all share the view that works on international politics in general, and international security in particular, have been written from a 'masculine' point of view (see Chs 12 and 30). In her work, Tickner argues that women have 'seldom been recognized by the security literature' despite the fact that conflicts affect women, as much as, if not more than, men. The vast majority of casualties and refugees in war are women and children and, as the recent war in Bosnia confirms, the rape of women is often used as a tool of war (Tickner 1992).

In a major feminist study of security, entitled *Bananas, Beaches and Bombs* (1989), Enloe points to the patriarchal structure of privilege and control at all levels which, in her view, effectively legitimizes all forms of violence. Like Tickner, she highlights the traditional exclusion of women from international relations, suggesting 'that they are in fact crucial to it in practice and that nowhere is the state more gendered in the sense of how power is dispersed than in the security apparatus' (Terriff, Croft, James, and Morgan 1999: 91). She also challenges the concept of 'national security', arguing that the use of such terms is often designed to preserve the prevailing male-dominated order rather than to protect the state from external attack.

Feminist writers argue that if **gender** is brought more explicitly into the study of security, not only will new issues and alternative perspectives be added to the security agenda, but the result will be a fundamentally different view of the nature of international security. According to Jill Steans: 'Rethinking security . . . involves thinking about militarism and patriarchy, mal-development and environmental degradation. It involves thinking about the relationship between poverty, debt and population growth. It involves thinking about resources and

---

Box 13.6   **'Feminist' approaches to security**

'an obvious and simplistic retort to "what is to be secured against, under feminism?" would be "men". But for all but the most radical essentialist and separatist feminists this answer is deeply flawed. In terms of building a feminist idea of security, the threat is not men as a group, but the dynamics of power and hierarchy based on violence and inequality that feminists understand as intrinsically gendered. And it is this that makes a feminist understanding of security distinctive. While ideas such as structural violence and environmental security are used elsewhere, feminism understands these forms of security as following from a construction of power which is based on gendered divisions. The difference between male and female social roles, the public and private, and so on, predetermine the hierarchical and exploitative power relations which allow for an elevation, of say, scientific development over the renewal of natural resources, or "hard" economic policies over effective social welfare (a "soft" concern) By fully integrating the private what is deemed political/public, a gender-aware analysis highlights the divisive nature of traditional constructions of power and security.'

(Terriff, Croft, James, and Morgan 1999: 98)

---

how they are distributed' (Steans 1998. See also Smith 2000).

Post-modernist views

Recent years have seen the emergence of post-modernist approaches to international relations which has produced a somewhat distinctive perspective towards international security (see Ch.12). Post-modernist writers share the view that ideas, discourse, and 'the logic of interpretation' are crucial in understanding international politics and security. Like other writers who adopt a 'Critical security studies' approach, post-modernists see 'Realism' as one of the central problems of international insecurity. This is because Realism is a **discourse of power and rule** which has been dominant in international politics in the past and which has encouraged security competition between states. Power politics is seen as an image of the world that encourages behaviour that helps bring about war. The attempt to balance power is itself part of the very behaviour that leads to war. According to this view, alliances do not produce

peace, but lead to war. The aim, for many post-modernists, therefore, is to replace the discourse of Realism or power with a different discourse and alternative interpretations of concepts such as 'danger' and what counts as a threat to 'national security'. The idea is that once the 'software' program of Realism that people carry around in their heads has been replaced by a new 'software' program based on cooperative norms, individuals, states, and regions will learn to work with each other and **global politics** will become more peaceful.

For post-modern writers, security and subjectivity are closely connected. According to one leading scholar in the field, David Campbell:

Traditional discourses of international relations maintain that alliance is one where security is a goal to be achieved by a number of instrumentalities deployed by the state (defense and foreign policy, for example). But the linkage between the two can be understood in a different light, for just as Foreign Policy works to constitute the **identity** in whose name it operates, security functions to instantiate the subjectivity it purports to serve. Indeed, security (of which foreign policy/Foreign Policy is a part) is first and foremost a performance discourse constitutive of political order: after all 'Securing something requires its differentiation, classification and definition. It has, in short, to be identified' (Campbell 1992: 253).

One of the central differences between Realism and post-modernism is their very different **epistemologies** (ideas about knowledge). Post-modernists argue that there are no secure, timeless, and uncontested foundations for making choices about interpretations. This leads back to the view of theory as ideology, and as such there is no such thing as value-free enquiry (as they see it). Realism is also viewed not only as a statist ideology, largely out of touch with the globalizing tendencies which are occurring in world politics, but also as a dangerous discourse which is the main obstacle to efforts to establish a new and more peaceful hegemonic discourse. This is because it purports to provide a universal view of how the world is organized and what states have to do if they wish to survive. Post-modernists reject what they see as the 'preposterous certainty' of Realism. In their view the enormous complexity and indeterminacy of human behaviour, across all its cultural, religious, historical, and linguistic variations means that there can be no single interpretation of global reality. The problem with

| Box 16.4 | **The game of Prisoners' Dilemma** |

The Prisoners' Dilemma scenario

The governor of a prison once had two prisoners whom he could not hang without a voluntary confession of at least one. Accordingly, he summoned one prisoner and offered him his freedom and a sum of money if he would confess at least a day before the second prisoner did so, so that an indictment could be prepared and so that the second prisoner could be hanged. If the latter should confess at least a day before him, however, the first prisoner was told, then the prisoner would be freed and rewarded and he would be hanged. 'And what if we both should confess on the same day, your Excellency?', asked the first prisoner. 'Then you each will keep your life but will get ten years in prison.' 'And if neither of us should confess, your Excellency?' 'Then both of you will be set free—without any reward, of course. But will you bet your neck that your fellow prisoner—that crook—will not hurry to confess and pocket the reward? Now go back to your solitary cell and think about your answer until tomorrow.' The second prisoner in his interview was told the same, and each man spent the night alone considering his dilemma (Deutsch 1968: 120).

The two actors are confronted with two possible strategies, generating a situation with four possible outcomes. Being rational, the prisoners can place these outcomes on a preference ranking. The matrix below reveals the preference rankings for the two prisoners. Both prisoners will pursue the strategy which will optimize their position in the light of the strategies available to the other prisoner. To avoid being hanged, both prisoners will confess and end up in prison for ten years, thereby demonstrating how individual **rationality** leads to collective irrationality. The suboptimal outcome

could only be avoided if the two prisoners possessed a mechanism which allowed them to collaborate.

	A	
	Silent	Confess*
B Silent	3, 3‡	4, 1
B Confess*	1, 4	2, 2†

In this figure, cell numerals refer to ordinally ranked preferences: 4 = best, 1 = worst. The first number in each cell refers to A's preference and the second number refers to B's preference.

Key

* Dominant strategy: both players have dominant rather than contingent strategies. A strategy becomes dominant if it is preferable to the alternative strategy no matter which strategy the other player adopts.

† Denotes an equilibrium outcome.

‡ A Pareto optimal outcome: Vilfredo Pareto (1848–1923) was an Italian sociologist and economist who developed a criterion for identifying when an exchange between two parties has reached its most efficient or optimum point. He argued, in essence, that the point is reached when one party is better off and the other party is no worse off than before the exchange took place. An implication of this optimum is discussed later.

---

regimes. First, they have drawn on the work of microeconomists who have insisted that state intervention is not the only mechanism available to produce public goods. It is suggested that if there is a dominant or hegemonic actor operating within the market, then that actor may well be prepared to sustain the cost of producing a public good (Olson 1965). Liberal Institutionalists have had no difficulty extending this line of argument to the international arena. During the course of the nineteenth century, for example, a regime was established which outlawed the international traffic of slaves. States agreed to observe the humanitarian principle underpinning this regime because they expected other states to do

so. The expectation emerged because it was recognized that Great Britain intended to police the regime and possessed the naval capacity to do so. The regime was consolidated, therefore, because of Britain's hegemonic status within the international system.

As already indicated, it is widely accepted that the economic regimes established after the Second World War owe their existence to the presence of the United States as a hegemonic power. But when Liberal Institutionalists examined the consequences of hegemonic decline, they concluded that established regimes would persist. Although the Prisoners' Dilemma indicated that market failures occur because in an anarchic system there is an expectation that states will compete rather than collaborate, once states have moved away from the suboptimum outcome resulting from mutually competitive strategies, then there is no incentive to defect from the mutually collaborative strategies and return to the suboptimum outcome. Even in the absence of a hegemon, therefore, Liberal Institutionalists argue that established regimes will survive (Keohane 1984).

The second route explored by the Liberal Institutionalists has reinforced this conclusion. It is argued that the Prisoners' Dilemma exaggerates the difficulty of generating collaboration within the anarchic international system. The Prisoners' Dilemma presupposes that the game is only played once. But, in reality, because situations persist over time, it is more appropriate to think of the game being played over and over again. The 'shadow of the future' looms over the players, affecting their strategic calculations. Because the game will be played on future occasions, it becomes worthwhile taking a risk and pursuing a collaborative strategy in order to produce the optimum outcome. If all states can be persuaded to do the same, then there will be little incentive to defect in the future, because if one state defects, then, 'tit for tat', all the others will follow. Accepting this line of argument, then, the major mechanism for establishing and maintaining a regime is not the existence of a hegemon, but the principle of reciprocity. Liberal Institutionalists, therefore, have increasingly come to focus on factors that will strengthen reciprocity within the system. Inspection and surveillance facilities become very important for ensuing that states are operating within the parameters of a regime. The establishment of satellite surveillance, for example, was a significant factor in encouraging the United States and the Soviet Union to reach arms control agreements. Attention has also been drawn to the importance of scientific knowledge. States are unwilling to restrict their activities on the basis of speculation and respond much more effectively when scientists start to agree about the significance of their findings. With states becoming ever more open and the constant expansion in scientific understanding, so the international environment will become increasingly 'information rich'. It is this trend, Liberal Institution-

alists argue, that will do most to facilitate regime building in the future (Keohane 1984).

The Realist approach

From a Liberal Institutionalist perspective, Realism has little to contribute to the understanding of regimes. The traditional Realist emphasis on the inherently competitive nature of the international system is seen to inhibit rather than facilitate any explanation of how and why states collaborate to achieve the mutually advantageous benefits derived from the establishment of regimes. Indeed, the growth of regimes would seem to confirm that the Realist perspective is becoming increasingly anachronistic. Unsurprisingly, Realists contest such an evaluation. Two problems are identified with the Liberal Institutional approach. First, Realists attack the Liberal Institutional assumption that the activities of a hegemon in the international system can be compared to the role of the state when dealing with cases of market failure. Second, Realists deny that regimes emerge as the result of states endeavouring to overcome the pressure to compete under conditions of anarchy. Regimes form, Realists argue, in situations when uncoordinated strategies can interact to produce suboptimum outcomes. So, from the Realist perspective, the influence of microeconomics has encouraged the Liberal Institutionalists to advance an unsound assessment of regime formation. There is an irony here, because it was the neo-realists (Waltz 1979) who first drew the analogy between the market and the international system. The common starting point, however, can lead in very different directions.

Power and regimes

Realists, like Liberal Institutionalists, were very aware in the 1970s and 1980s that the hegemonic status of the United States was being questioned. But they did not conclude that this development might lead to an anomic world. Instead, they focused on Third World demands for a new set of principles and norms to underpin the regimes associated with the world-economy. Existing regimes were seen to work against the interests of Third World states, opening them up to unfair competition and malign economic forces. Realists took the case presented by the Third World seriously, but argued that the principles and norms demanded by the Third World would only come into operation if the balance of power moved against the West (Tucker 1977; Krasner 1985). This line of analysis runs directly counter to the image presented by the Liberal Institutionalists of the United States as a benign benefactor, underwriting a set of regimes which allowed the members of the anarchic international system to escape from a suboptimum outcome and into a position of Pareto optimality. In its place, it was necessary to view the United States as a hegemon using its power to sustain a regime which promoted its own long-term interests. Closer inspection of the Liberal Institutional position reveals tacit support for the way that public goods are defined by governments in the West. It may appear axiomatic to Liberal Institutionalists that states should wish to promote economic regimes built on liberal norms and principles. And the same argument applies to the promotion of human rights, the elimination of pollution, and all the other goals advanced by Liberals in the West. But this position disregards the fact that it is by no means universally agreed that liberal norms and principles should be underpinning the regimes that are emerging in the international system.

From the Realist perspective, therefore, the United States helped to ensure that regimes were underpinned by a particular set of principles and norms. But a full appreciation of the Realist's position also requires the recognition that a hegemon can effectively veto the formation of a regime. For example, in 1972, when the United States launched its first remote-sensing satellite, the event caused concern among a large range of countries. These satellites have the capacity to gather important and sensitive commercial and strategic data about countries all around the world. Not only can the satellites identify where military equipment is located, but they can also identify the size of a crop yield and the location of minerals. There were several attempts to establish a regime which would limit the right of states to acquire data without the permission of the state under surveillance (Brown *et al.* 1977). Many states have considered that they would benefit from such a regime. But because the balance of power was tilted in favour of states that possessed these satellites and

they were clear that such a regime would not work to their benefit they vetoed the proposed regime.

Regimes and coordination

As it stands, the Realist account of regimes is incomplete, because it fails to explain why states adhere to the principles and norms underlying a regime that they oppose. In accounting for this anomaly, Realists, like Liberal Institutionalists, resort to game theory. Realists insist, however, that states wishing to form a regime confront the problem of coordination, as illustrated by the Battle of the Sexes (see Box 16.5), not collaboration, as illustrated by the Prisoners' Dilemma. Here the problem is not associated with the danger of defection to a competitive strategy, but the possibility of failing to coordinate strategies, with the consequence that a mutually desired goal is unintentionally missed.

Coordination problems are very familiar to strategic thinkers. Schelling (1960) illustrates the problem with the example of a couple getting separated in a department store. Both wish to get back together again, but there is a danger that they will wait for each other in different places; situations of this kind generate a coordination problem. In the absence of communication, solving coordination problems can be difficult, even impossible. But with the aid of communication, a solution can be very straightforward and uncontroversial. For example, while communication between an aircraft and an air traffic control centre can occur in any mutually agreed language, it is obviously unacceptable for the pilot and the air traffic controller not to be able to speak a common language. Under the rules of the International Civil Aviation Organization, every international pilot and some personnel in every air traffic control centre must be able to speak English. This is a highly stable equilibrium and the rule undoubtedly contributes to air safety. But it is only one of a large body of rules which form the regime that regulates international civil aviation. It has major training implications and it is not an issue that can be constantly renegotiated. It needs to be embodied in a stable regime that all the involved parties can treat as a constant.

The decision to choose English under these circumstances may have been relatively uncontroversial, but it does not follow that a common

---

Box 16.5   **The Battle of the Sexes and Pareto's frontier**

The Battle of the Sexes

The scenario of this game envisages a couple who have just fallen in love and decide to go on holiday together. The problem is that one wants to go hiking in the mountains and the other wants to visit art galleries and museums in the city. But both much prefer to be with their partner than to go on holiday alone. When mapped on to a matrix, two stable equilibriums emerge from the scenario.

		A(male)	
		Holiday in city	Holiday in mountains
B(female)	Holiday in city	4, 3*	1, 2
	Holiday in mountains	2, 1	3, 4*

In this figure, cell numerals refer to ordinally ranked preferences: 4 = best, 1 = worst. The first number in each cell refers to A's preference and the second number refers to B's preference.

* Denotes an equilibrium outcome and a Pareto optimal strategy.

The Pareto frontier

Wishing to reach a compromise, the couple might decide to split their week's holiday, spending time in the city and in the mountains. Since the two extreme positions represent a Pareto optimum, so too must all the possible combinations and these can be mapped to form a Pareto frontier.

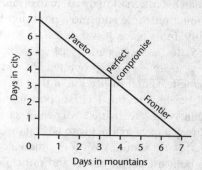

Realists argue that this line of analysis helps us to aversion to certain outcomes (a pilot speaking only German and the air traffic controller speaking only Japanese) will necessarily generate a common interest in a particular outcome (everyone speaking English). There is little doubt that the French would have preferred their language to English; and, of course, English has no intrinsic merit over French in this context. And this is the main lesson to be learned from the Battle of the Sexes game—there can be more than one outcome reflecting a Pareto optimum. Indeed, there can be many positions that represent a Pareto optimum and they can then be located on what is referred to as the Pareto frontier (see Box 16.5). So in the context of civil aviation, every spoken language can be located on the frontier because, in principle, any language could be chosen, provided that everyone spoke it. And the use of any common language is preferable to the alternative that would arise in the event of a failure to coordinate and identify a common language.

Realists argue that this line of analysis helps us to understand why states might conform to a regime while wishing to change the underlying principles. The explanation is that the states are already operating on the Pareto frontier. They observe the regime because they are operating in a coordination situation, and a failure to coordinate will move them into a less advantageous situation. The French can rail against the use of English in the civil aviation context, but they have no alternative but to persist with the policy. The same argument applies to Third World states; they wish to trade with the West, while preferring to do so on more advantageous terms. The application of new trade principles would represent another point on the Pareto frontier. But, as yet, because the balance of power continues to favour the West, there are few signs of new economic principles emerging that are more favourable to the Third World.

The situation is somewhat different in the area of communication regimes. All forms of electronic communication use electromagnetic waves that are emitted along an electromagnetic spectrum. Coordination here is essential, because interference occurs if more than one user adopts the same frequency of the spectrum at the same time over the same area. It is not possible, therefore, for states to operate on a unilateral basis, and the establishment of a regime was essential. Moreover, because the electromagnetic spectrum is a limited resource, principles and rules for partitioning the resource had to be determined. In the first instance, states agreed that the spectrum should be allocated on the basis of need. But by 1980 this principle had resulted in the Soviet Union and the United States claiming half of the available frequencies and 90 per cent of the spectrum was allocated to provide benefits for 10 per cent of the world's population (Krasner 1985). It is unsurprising to find this outcome being challenged by developing states, which argued that part of the spectrum should be reserved for future use. More surprisingly, this new principle has been accepted. But Realists argue that this is not the result of altruism on the part of the developed world. It is a consequence of the fact that developing states can interfere with the signals of neighbouring countries. This gave them access to a power lever, which they otherwise would not have possessed (Krasner 1991). Through the use of power, the developing states have managed to move in a more favourable direction along the Pareto frontier. By contrast, they have had little say over the allocation of geosynchronous orbits, which are the most efficient locations for broadcasting satellites. Here too coordination is required, but only among those states already in a position to launch the satellite. So a different balance of power is involved.

| Box 16.6 | Key concepts |

Anarchy: a system operating in the absence of any central government.

Anomie: a system operating in the absence of norms or rules.

'Battle of the Sexes': a scenario in game theory illustrating the need for a coordination strategy.

Collaboration: a form of cooperation requiring parties not to defect from a mutually desirable strategy for an individually preferable strategy.

Cooperation: is required in any situation where parties must act together in order to achieve a mutually acceptable outcome.

Coordination: a form of cooperation requiring parties to pursue a common strategy in order to avoid the mutually undesirable outcome arising from the pursuit of divergent strategies.

Exponential growth: a situation where the rate of growth is not constant or linear but increases over time.

Game theory: a branch of mathematics which explores strategic interaction.

Hegemony: a system regulated by a dominant leader.

Microeconomics: the branch of economics studying the behaviour of the firm in a market setting.

Market failure: results from the inability of the market to produce goods which require collaborative strategies.

'Prisoners' Dilemma': a scenario in game theory illustrating the need for a collaboration strategy.

Public goods: goods which can only be produced by collective decision, and cannot, therefore, be produced in the market place.

Public bads: the negative consequences which can arise when actors fail to collaborate.

Rationality: reflected in the ability of individuals to rank order their preferences and choose the best available preference.

Reciprocity: reflects a 'tit for tat' strategy, only cooperating if others do likewise.

Regimes: sets of implicit or explicit principles, norms, rules, and decisionmaking procedures around which actors' expectations converge in a given area of international relations.

'Shadow of the future': a metaphor indicating that decisionmakers are conscious of the future when making decisions.

Strategic interaction: occurs when an outcome is the product of decisions arrived at independently.

Key points

- The market is used by Liberal Institutionalists as an analogy for the anarchic international system.

- In a market/international setting, public goods get underproduced and public bads get overproduced.

- Liberal Institutionalists draw on the Prisoners' Dilemma game to account for the structural impediments to regime formation.

- A hegemon, 'the shadow of the future', and an information-rich environment promote collaboration and an escape route from Prisoners' Dilemmas.

- Realists argue that Liberal Institutionalists ignore the importance of power when examining regimes.

- Realists draw on the 'Battle of the Sexes' to illuminate the nature of coordination and its link to power in an anarchic setting.

Conclusion

Although Liberal Institutionalists and Realists acknowledge that regimes are an important feature of the international system, and draw on identical tools of analysis, they reach very different conclusions about the circumstances in which regimes emerge. For Liberal Institutionalists, the need for regimes arises because there is always a danger in the anarchic international system that competitive strategies will trump cooperative strategies. Their analysis, therefore, focuses on ways of deterring competitive strategies that are otherwise seen to be the rational response within an anarchically structured system. By contrast, and paradoxically, given conventional assessments, Realists link the emergence of regimes to situations where there is a mutual desire to cooperate, but where anarchy generates a problem of coordination. Again, in contrast to Liberal Institutionalists, Realists assume that there is no incentive to defect once coordination has taken place.

The two approaches also adhere to divergent conceptions of power. For Liberal Institutionalists, power may be used by a hegemon to pressure other states to collaborate and conform to a regime. But it is also acknowledged that states can establish and maintain regimes in the absence of hegemonic power. Collaborative strategies are pursued and maintained because of the 'shadow of the future'—a mutual recognition that if any state defects from a regime, it will result in mass defection on a 'tit for tat'

basis and states moving from an optimum to a sub-optimum outcome. There seems little doubt that 'lead' states do establish regimes in the expectation that other states will follow. For example, in 1987, 22 states signed the Montreal Protocol agreeing to reduce CFC gases—which erode the ozone layer—by 50 per cent by 1998. But in 1990, the timetable was accelerated and the signatories expanded to 81, all agreeing to eliminate all CFCs by 2000.

For Realists, on the other hand, power is seen to play a crucial role, not as a threat to discipline states caught defecting from a collaborative agreement, but in the bargaining process—to determine the shape of a regime around which all states will coordinate their actions. For Realists, the conflict over economic regimes reveals most clearly the importance of the role played by power in the establishment of regimes. It is the rich and powerful states in the North that have primarily determined the shape of these economic regimes. Third World states have had no alternative but to accept the regimes because of the need to engage in trade. By contrast, there have been massive violations of the human rights regimes that have emerged since the end of the Second World War. These dead-letter regimes have failed to become full-blown regimes, according to Realists, because there is no coordination involved. States can unilaterally violate human rights regimes without paying the automatic penalty incurred in coordination situations.

Stein (1983), who introduced the distinction between collaborative and coordination games into the regime literature, never assumed, however, that they represented mutually incompatible approaches to regime formation. It could be argued, therefore, that the debate between the Liberal Institutionalists and the Realists can be resolved by empirical investigation. Do decisionmakers who are responsible for establishing regimes see themselves in a 'Prisoners' Dilemma' or a 'Battle of the Sexes'? Liberal Institutionalists insist that the former represents the characteristic situation, whereas Realists focus on the latter. Although it is not possible to foreclose on this question, it is possible that the two types of games can be viewed in sequential terms. States may escape from the Prisoners' Dilemma by agreeing to collaborate, only to find that they then enter a Battle of the Sexes when the details come to be worked out.

For further information and case studies on this subject, please visit the companion web site at www.oup.com/uk/booksites/politics.

QUESTIONS

1 What are the defining elements of a regime?

2 Is a regime the same as an organization?

3 Why did the study of international regimes develop in the 1970s?

4 What characteristic features do the Realist and Liberal Institutionalist approaches to regime analysis share?

5 How has microeconomics influenced the Liberal Institutionalist approach to regimes?

6 What is meant by rationality in the context of game theory

7 What are the main implications of strategic interaction

8 What are the implications of the Prisoners' Dilemma game for regime analysis?

9 What major mechanisms do Liberal Institutionalists advance to promote regime formation?

10 How does the Realist approach to regime analysis differ from the Liberal Institutional approach?

11 What does the Battle of the Sexes game tell us about the role of power in regime formation?

12 What does operating at the Pareto frontier mean in the context of regime theory?

GUIDE TO FURTHER READING

Brown, S. *et al.* (1997), *Regimes for the Ocean, Outer Space and the Weather* (Washington, DC: Brookings Institution). An early attempt to examine areas which need to be regulated by regimes.

Cronin, B. (2003), *Institutions for the Common Good: International Protection Regimes in International Society* (Cambridge: Cambridge University Press). An important counter to rationalist-based accounts of regimes.

Hasenclever, A., Mayer, P., and Rittberger, V. (1997), *Theories of International Regimes* (Cambridge: Cambridge University Press). Argues that in addition to Realism that focuses on power, and neo-liberalism that focuses on interests, cognitivism, focusing on ideas, now forms a third school of thought in the regime literature.

Keohane, R. O. (1984), *After Hegemony: Cooperation and Discord in the World Political Economy* (Princeton: Princeton University Press). One of the most influential Liberal Institutional texts on the theory underlying regime formation.

Keohane, R. O., and Nye, J. S. (1977), *Power and Interdependence* (Boston: Little Brown). Examines the role of regimes in an interdependent world, advancing four models to account for regime change.

Krasner, S. D. (ed.) (1983), *International Regimes* (Ithaca, NY: Cornell University Press). A seminal text setting out the main theoretical issues

—— (1985), *Structural Conflict: The Third World Against Global Liberalism* (Berkeley: University of California Press). This is one of the major Realist texts. It explores North–South disputes over regimes.

Oye, K. A. (ed.) (1986), *Cooperation Under Anarchy* (Princeton: Princeton University Press). An influential set of theoretical essays on how cooperation takes place under anarchic conditions.

Rittberger, V. (ed.) (1993), *Regime Theory and International Relations* (Oxford: Clarendon Press). This important book examines regime theory from European and American perspectives.

Zacher, M. W., with Sutton, B. A. (1996), *Governing Global Networks: International Regimes for Transportation and Communications* (Cambridge: Cambridge University Press). A Liberal Institutional account of regimes, arguing that they are based on mutual interests, and not the dictates of the most powerful states.

WEB LINKS

www.state.gov/t/np/c10527.htm Information on the non-proliferation regime.

www.ciesin.org/TG/PI/TRADE/tradhmpg.html Information on trade regimes and the environment.

http://sedac.ciesin.columbia.edu/entri/index.jsp Environmental regimes.

www.cid.harvard.edu/cidtrade/site/tradeint.html Trade regimes.

CHAPTER 17

Diplomacy

BRIAN WHITE

READER'S GUIDE

This chapter identifies diplomacy as a key process of communication and negotiation in world politics and as an important foreign policy instrument used by global actors. The first section focuses on problems of definition moving from general to specific meanings of the term. The second section looks historically at different stages in the development of modern diplomacy—from 'traditional' to 'new'; from cold war to post-cold war. Each historical system is compared by reference to their common and divergent structures processes, and agenda. The third section looks at diplomacy as used by global actors as a means of achieving their foreign policy objectives. A final section looks more briefly at some contemporary challenges to a diplomacy traditionally based upon the state and inter-state relations. The chapter concludes by arguing that the context and forms of diplomacy have changed but it remains a highly relevant process in contemporary world politics and a useful instrument for a wide range of global actors.

Introduction: what is diplomacy?

Diplomacy is one of those infuriatingly vague terms that can have different meanings depending upon user and usage. We can begin to make sense of it in relation to two major perspectives on world politics that might be labelled 'macro' (the big picture) and 'micro' (the small picture). The macro perspective tries to make sense of world politics as a whole. What are its constituent parts? How do they all fit together? The micro perspective tries to explain world politics from the different but complementary perspective of the actors involved in world politics. Traditionally, the micro perspective focused on states and the governments that act on their behalf in world politics. But, as we shall see, this conventional state-centred focus is no longer adequate to cover the range of actors involved and the different processes that feature in a globalized system of world politics.

The conscientious reader will be able to find uses of this term elsewhere that are so general that 'diplomacy' appears to be synonymous with 'world politics' or 'foreign policy' as a whole. You will find references to, for example, **great power diplomacy**, summit diplomacy, or **development diplomacy** which—particularly in media reports—appear to describe a process that is much wider than a specific discussion of one facet of diplomacy. Links between international relations and international history—often referred to as diplomatic history—help to reinforce this notion of interchangeability of terms. Similarly, references to, for example, 'British diplomacy', 'Russian diplomacy', or 'South African diplomacy' often suggest that the writer is referring not just to diplomacy as such but to British, Russian, or South African foreign policy as a whole.

Uses of the term diplomacy in such general ways are a potentially misleading shorthand, but at least they alert us to the fact that diplomacy is central both to an understanding of a global system of world politics and to the foreign policies of states and other actors on the international stage. From the 'macro' perspective of world politics, diplomacy refers to a **process of communication** that is central

Box 17.1 Diplomacy in world politics

Diplomacy in world politics refers to a communications process between international actors that seeks through negotiation to resolve conflict short of war. This process has been refined, institutionalized, and professionalized over many centuries.

to the workings of the global system. Indeed, if world politics is characterized simply by the tension between conflict and cooperation, diplomacy together with war, can be said to represent its defining institutions (see Box 17.1). If conflict and cooperation are placed at two ends of a spectrum (see Fig. 17.1) diplomacy can be located at the cooperation end representing forms of interaction that focus on the **resolution of conflict by dialogue and negotiation**. Diplomacy therefore is fundamentally related to attempts to create stability and order within a global system, the object being to prevent conflict spilling over into war. This chapter characterizes the essential features of the diplomatic process.

From the 'micro' perspective of international actors like states, an understanding of diplomacy provides revealing insights into the behaviour of the actors themselves in the global system. From this perspective, however, diplomacy can be identified as a **policy instrument rather than a global process** (see Box 17.2). All actors have goals or ends towards which their foreign policy behaviour is directed. In

World politics	
Conflict	Cooperation
War	Diplomacy

Fig. 17.1 World politics

Diplomacy and foreign policy

Diplomacy in foreign policy refers to the use of diplomacy as a policy instrument possibly in association with other instruments such as economic or military force to enable an international actor to achieve its policy objectives.

order to achieve ends, actors clearly need means—often called policy instruments. Diplomacy provides one instrument that international actors use to implement their foreign policy. It may be used directly ('pure' diplomacy) with other parties or as a means of communicating the use or threatened use of other instruments ('mixed' diplomacy). A second major function of this chapter is to characterize the essential features of diplomacy as a policy instrument.

Diplomacy and world politics

Diplomacy as a communications process between political entities has existed for literally thousands of years. The earliest diplomatic document in our possession, discovered in the 1970s, is a letter inscribed on a tablet which has been dated some time around 2500 BC. It was sent from a kingdom called Ebla near the Mediterranean coast in what we would call the Middle East to the kingdom of Hamazi in what is now Northern Iran. It was carried by a messenger who made a round trip of almost 2,000 kilometres. In this one brief message, as Cohen (1995: 3) notes,

we have evidence of a fully-fledged diplomatic system: a working relationship between two distant kingdoms; the use of an emissary to convey a letter over a long distance; protocol, including the concept of equal status, an understood medium of communication, and a conventional form of address; a domestic organization for making and implementing foreign policy; an archive; a set of normative expectations about right and proper behaviour; a sense of . . . fellowship or brotherhood; trade or reciprocal gift-giving via envoys.

Traditional diplomacy

While the conventions and machinery of diplomacy have evolved over a long historical period—the city-states in Ancient Greece, for example, introduced a diplomatic system that had many remarkably modern features—our global diplomatic system has its origins in fifteenth-century Italy where permanent embassies were first established (Hamilton and Langhorne 1995: chs 1, 2). A **'traditional'** diplo-

matic **system** developed thereafter which had some distinctive features. These can be usefully characterized under the headings of **structure** **process**, and **agenda**—broadly relating to who was involved in diplomacy, how diplomatic activity was organized, and the substance of diplomacy. This framework will help us to compare traditional diplomacy with diplomatic systems that preceded it and those that followed.

Structure

Traditional diplomacy can be distinguished from its predecessors in the ancient and medieval worlds primarily because it constituted a communications process between recognizably modern states rather than between other forms of political organization like, for example, the Catholic Church. As relations between states expanded, political leaders (usually monarchs) found it increasingly necessary to negotiate with each other on a regular basis. But, given the distances involved, negotiations had to be indirect and diplomats were sent abroad for this purpose. If diplomacy as a state-based activity is central to the structure of traditional diplomacy, diplomatic agents acting on behalf of states later became institutionalized and eventually professionalized.

By **institutionalized**, we mean that particular institutions emerged which had diplomacy as their main function and diplomacy ceased to be an irregular activity undertaken by ad hoc representatives. As already noted, the Italian city-states were the first to establish permanent, resident missions or embassies abroad and other states in Europe soon followed their lead. The advantages of permanent representation abroad included practicality and continuity. Embassies became an important embodiment of state interests and a network of permanent embassies later became linked to specialized foreign departments established within home states. The institutionalization of diplomacy with a dedicated workforce of diplomats at home and abroad was followed by the professionalization of diplomacy as an occupation.

Processes

In the traditional system, diplomacy was organized largely on a bilateral (two-party) basis and usually undertaken in secrecy. When two states developed a relationship of mutual importance, it became normal to exchange permanent embassies and to conduct diplomacy through those embassies on a state-to-state basis. Unless one state forced the other to accept a position, mutual agreement was the only means of achieving a settlement of any disputes. Limiting the relationship to two parties, of course, made it easier to keep negotiations secret, although there were other good reasons in terms of the negotiating process itself for maintaining as much secrecy as possible. No good card or chess player reveals his or her 'hand' in advance, and diplomatic negotiations are similar to these games in important respects.

The traditional process of diplomacy also drew upon rules and procedures for behaviour from earlier diplomatic systems. From the fifteenth century onwards, **diplomacy became not just a regular process but also a regularized process**. Procedural rules known as diplomatic protocol were developed which included rather ostentatious ceremonies and also more practical procedures relating to such things as the order in which a treaty is signed by the parties involved in a negotiation. A series of rights, privileges, and immunities became attached both to diplomats and to diplomatic activities.

These derived from two principles. The first essentially practical consideration was that diplomats should be able to conduct their business without fear or hindrance. The popular phrase 'don't shoot the messenger!' not only suggests the need to safeguard the messenger who does not deserve to be blamed for

the content of the message carried, but also indicates the importance of safeguarding the whole system of communications between international actors. The second principle was derived from the idea that the ambassador in particular is the direct representative of a sovereign monarch and, therefore, should be treated with the same consideration that a monarch would receive. This idea of representation was expanded to include the controversial idea of extraterritoriality which in this context simply means that the resident embassy abroad is regarded as part of the territory of the home state and subject to the laws of that state and, likewise, that the resident diplomatic staff are subject only to the laws of the home state.

Agenda

Traditional diplomacy can be characterized finally by its agenda—what issues did diplomats negotiate about? The important point to note here is that the agenda of traditional diplomacy was narrow certainly by comparison with later periods. Not only was the agenda set by the relatively underdeveloped state of bilateral relations but, more importantly, the preoccupations of diplomacy reflected the preoccupations of political leaders themselves.

For hundreds of years, foreign policy was seen as the exclusive province of monarchs and their advisers and, not surprisingly, personal ambitions—the acquisition of territory perhaps, or another throne—together with more general issues of war and peace constituted the most important issues on the diplomatic agenda. In a highly personalized structure, diplomats in essence were sent abroad by one monarch to win over another. Less desirable aspects of diplomacy occasionally surfaced as diplomats came under pressure to 'get a result' whatever the means employed. This prompted at least one cynical definition of a diplomat as 'an honest man sent abroad to lie on behalf of his country' (a remark usually credited to Sir Henry Wotton, an Elizabethan diplomat). In general, however, it was quickly discovered that honesty rather than deceit is more likely to be effective in achieving objectives, whatever short-term gains might be made by more duplicitous behaviour. Traditional diplomacy reached its most developed form and was arguably most effective as a system for ordering international relations in nineteenth-century Europe. This is the period known, in a classic piece of historical overstatement, as the 'century of peace' in Europe.

New diplomacy

However successful traditional diplomacy may have been in promoting stability, order, and peace in nineteenth-century Europe, its failure to prevent the First World War and, for some indeed, its role in actually causing that war, led to a widespread belief that a new form of diplomacy was needed. Though this was commonly referred to after the First World War as the 'new' diplomacy, elements of this allegedly new form of diplomacy were already in evidence in the nineteenth century if not before, and there was a long transition period between traditional forms and the new system of diplomacy that evolved in the first half of the twentieth century. What was identifiably new about the 'new' diplomacy emerged from two important ideas (see Hamilton and Langhorne 1995: 137).

First, there was a demand that diplomacy should be more open to **public scrutiny and control**. This demand related less to a public involvement in the process than to the provision of information to the public about agreements reached. This focused attention on two interlinked elements of traditional diplomacy that were now seen to be problematic: excessive secrecy and the fact that diplomats were normally members of a closed social elite—the aristocracy. The **second** idea related to the importance of establishing **an** international organization— which initially took the form of the League of Nations after the First World War—that would act both as an international forum for the peaceful settlement of disputes and as a deterrent against another world war by the threat of collective action against potential aggressors. Historically then the new diplomacy represented the widespread hope for a new start after 1918.

Structure

The structure of the new diplomacy remained similar in form to traditional diplomacy to the extent that states and governments remained the major actors in this system and were represented internationally by what was now a well-established network of permanent embassies abroad attached to foreign departments at home. There are two important changes to note, however, that have implications not only for the structure but also for the processes and the issues that characterized the new diplomacy. First, **states were no longer the only actors** involved. Increasingly, they had to share the international stage with other actors such as international organizations which were also engaged in diplomacy. These organizations were of two types, intergovernmental (with governments only as members) and non-governmental (with private individuals and groups as members).

The second important change to note is that governments themselves were beginning to change in terms of the scope of their activities and the extent to which they sought to regulate the lives of their citizens. Where once they had simply provided for the physical security of their citizens they now had broader concern with their social and economic well-being. Thus, the twentieth century saw an important change from the so-called **'night-watchman state'** to the **'welfare state'**. This has implications for the range of issues that states needed to negotiate about in their international activity.

Processes

The changing interests of states as international actors and the growing number of non-state actors involved changed the nature of the new diplomacy as a process of negotiation. Most obviously, it made diplomacy a more complex activity involving more and different actors. States continued to negotiate bilaterally with each other on a state-to-state basis, but groups of states typically negotiated multilaterally through the auspices of intergovernmental organizations like the League of Nations and its successor the United Nations and, increasingly, with the growing range of non-governmental organizations which sought to influence inter-state behaviour to achieve their own objectives. Again, it must be stressed that multilateral diplomacy was not strictly new in the sense that what had been called conference diplomacy between the Great Powers had been an important feature of nineteenth-century European diplomacy. Nor did multilateral diplomacy replace bilateral diplomacy. But, to the extent that it was more difficult to keep secret a process involving so many different actors, it is fair to say that the new diplomacy was a more open process than its predecessor.

Agenda

The agenda of the new diplomacy contained a number of new issues as well as a reinforced emphasis on military security. The avoidance of war now became a priority as the 'new' diplomats sought to make the First World War 'the war to end all wars', but diplomatic activity also began to focus more on economic, social, and welfare issues relating to material well-being. These became known as **'low politics'** issues in contrast to the **'high politics'** issues associated with the traditional diplomatic agenda. These new issues reflected not only the wider interests and responsibilities of governments but also the often narrowly focused interests of non-state actors.

The other distinctive feature of the new agenda is that it increasingly featured **highly specialized issues** that raised questions about the adequacy of the training given to diplomats. If the specialization required of new diplomats challenged their competence, their distinctive role was also challenged by two other trends: the direct role political leaders themselves often played in diplomacy and the growing tendency of political leaders in the inter-war period to appoint personal envoys to represent them. Clearly, professional diplomats were no longer the only 'players' involved in the new diplomatic 'game' and they enjoyed far less autonomy than traditional diplomats had enjoyed in earlier periods.

Cold war diplomacy

Many of the characteristics of the new diplomacy continued to evolve in the period after the Second World War, indeed multilateralism and an increasingly specialized agenda now contained issues like the environment, technology, and arms control. In terms of changing structures and processes, a host of new states joined an already complex array of state and non-state actors as the former colonies of the

European powers gained their independence. The fact that these new states were unfamiliar with the established rules and principles of diplomacy led to the first important attempt to give them the status of international law, notably in the 1961 Vienna Convention on Diplomatic Relations (see Berridge 1995: 20–31).

The term 'cold war diplomacy' refers to some very specific aspects of diplomacy that emerged after the Second World War. From the late 1940s until the end of the 1980s, world politics was dominated by the ideological confrontation between the United States and the Soviet Union. Each superpower supported by a network of allies sought to undermine and 'defeat' the other by all means short of a real or a 'hot war'—hence the 'cold war' description of this confrontational system. The diplomatic activity associated with 'East–West' confrontation had a single dramatic focus—**the absolute necessity of avoiding a global, nuclear conflict** that could destroy the international system. The most important types of cold war diplomacy, nuclear, crisis, and summit diplomacy are defined in Box 17.3.

 CWS

There was nothing new about nuclear diplomacy to the extent that states have always hoped that the size of their military forces would help to persuade or dissuade potential adversaries. The distinctiveness of nuclear diplomacy, however, is the extent to which both sides of the East–West divide relied upon their

---

> **Box 17.3** Types of cold war diplomacy
>
> **Nuclear diplomacy:** refers to the interactions between nuclear-armed states where one or more of them threatens to use nuclear weapons either to dissuade an opponent from undertaking an action or to persuade them to call a halt to some action that has begun. The former is also known as deterrence and the latter as compellence.
>
> **Crisis diplomacy:** refers to the delicate communications and negotiations involved in a crisis. A **crisis** may be defined as a short, intensive period in which the possibility of (nuclear) war is perceived to increase dramatically.
>
> **Summit diplomacy:** refers to a direct meeting between heads of government (of the superpowers in particular) to resolve major problems. The 'summit' became a regular mode of contact during the cold war.

nuclear weapons in political and psychological terms to achieve their objectives, but also sought to avoid triggering a nuclear war. Given the destructive nature of nuclear weapons, however, there were unprecedented risks attached to this type of diplomacy and crises frequently emerged as a result, which in turn required a particular diplomatic response. The successful resolution of the most serious nuclear crisis in October 1962 over Soviet missiles in Cuba led political leaders and analysts to look for clues about behaviour in that crisis that might provide principles of crisis management (see Richardson 1994: ch.3).

But there are problems with the notion of 'crisis management'—as Richardson's extended comment explains (see Box 17.4)—and many analysts including Richardson prefer the more traditional term 'crisis diplomacy'. From this perspective, the most important outcome of the Cuban missile crisis was not a checklist of guidelines for future crisis management but the agreement to set up a 'hot line'—a direct communications link between Moscow and Washington—that would maximize the chances of negotiating a direct settlement between the principal parties. Another form of direct communication was the summit meeting between the superpowers pioneered by the Geneva summit in 1955. Initially, summit meetings had symbolic value only but, by the 1970s, they had become a useful forum for negotiating tangible agreements which contributed to a reduction of East–West tensions. By the mid-

1980s, a series of superpower summits played a significant role in bringing the cold war to an end.

Diplomacy after the cold war

The end of the cold war represented a dramatic change in the international context within which diplomacy is conducted. The end of the ideological East–West conflict and the demise of the Soviet Union raised popular expectations about what might now be achieved by diplomacy and negotiation. The successful ousting of the invading Iraqi forces from Kuwait in 1991 by a US-led military coalition sanctioned by a UN resolution appeared to provide a model for the future. But optimism was soon replaced by a realization that the end of the cold war may have resolved some problems but other problems had merely been hidden from view during the cold war period. The failure of diplomacy to resolve the breakdown of order in the former Yugoslavia (see Box 17.5) illustrates the intractable nature of many post-cold war problems on the international agenda.

CWS

At the beginning of the twenty-first century, diplomacy at the level of world politics could be characterized in two ways. First, diplomacy is now genuinely global in scope. Gone are the East–West ideological divisions that excluded a large number of states from 'normal' diplomatic intercourse during the cold war period. A good illustration of this is the extent to which 'North–South' dimensions of international diplomacy were obscured by the East–West focus. From a cold war perspective, developing states were the object of superpower attention only in so far as they might be tempted to side with one or the other. Problems of poverty and development were effectively sidelined. Since the end of the cold war, however, the specific concerns of development diplomacy (see Box 17.6) have occupied a much higher-profile position in global diplomacy. Second, contemporary diplomacy can also be characterized as complex and fragmented. In terms of the analytical categories used here, there are multiple actors involved, complex multilateral as well as bilateral processes at work, and the substance of global diplomacy covers a wider agenda of issues than ever before.

Box 17.4   Crisis management

'The term [crisis management] is often taken to mean the exercise of restraint in order to reduce the risk of war. However, this usage obscures the central problem confronting decision-makers in nuclear-age crises—that each party seeks to pursue simultaneously two potentially incompatible goals: to prevail over the adversary, while at the same time avoiding nuclear war. "Crisis management" must address the tension between the two goals, but this brings out the questionable character of the concept itself. The dilemmas of choice are glossed over by the use of the term "management", with its overtones of technical rationality and efficiency.'

(Richardson 1994: 25)

Box 17.5   Diplomacy in the Balkans

The breakdown of order in the Balkan region followed the disintegration of the federal state of Yugoslavia. The problems began in 1991 when Croatia and Slovenia declared their independence and Serbia used military force in an attempt to maintain the territorial integrity of Yugoslavia. Problems quickly spread to other members of the federation, to Bosnia-Hercegovina, and by 1998–9 to Kosovo. Instability in the region also sparked a crisis in Albania in 1997. Conflict took a conventional military form but was also complicated by inter-ethnic violence between different groups, Serbians, Croats, and Muslims in particular. Huge dislocations of population occurred with widespread evidence of attempts at 'ethnic cleansing'. The international community has struggled to use various forms of diplomacy to stabilize the region. The forms have included bilateral and multilateral (conference) diplomacy, peacekeeping with military observers, the use of economic and humanitarian aid to assist civilian reconstruction, and (particularly in Kosovo) peacemaking—the use of overt military force in an attempt to enforce a peace. A variety of different combinations of state and non-state actors have been involved, including the European Union, the United Nations, NATO, and the 'Contact Group' (the United States, Russia, Germany, Britain, and France). Diplomacy has had one qualified success—the 1995 Dayton Agreement on Bosnia-Hercegovina—and thereafter it has made a significant contribution to some semblance of stability and order in the region. However, complex problems remain unresolved.

Box 17.6   Developmental diplomacy

Developmental diplomacy: refers to 'the process whereby Third World countries attempt to negotiate improvements in their position in the international political economy. These negotiations largely take the form of bargaining with Western industrialized countries.'

(Williams 1994: 46)

Diplomacy and the 'war against terrorism'

If the end of the cold war spawned an optimistic mood about what might be achieved by diplomacy, the sudden and devastating attack on the World Trade Center in New York on 11 September 2001 produced the very opposite mood of deep pessimism. What became known as 9/11 symbolized a new phase of globalization in which the contribution that diplomacy might make to the resolution of terror-related conflict was unclear to say the least. This was partly because the perpetrating actor, Al Qaeda, is not a state or even a conventional non-state actor, but rather an amorphous transnational network with whom communication and negotiation would be inherently difficult even if the precise causes of 9/11 and subsequent attacks could be established. A second key reason for a sense of pessimism about diplomacy was the decision of the George W. Bush Adminstration to frame the response to 9/11 in terms of a 'war against terrorism' which suggested that military force and other coercive measures would be the instruments of choice.

Nevertheless, in the first few months after 11 September 2001 intense negotiations did produce a broad coalition which rallied to the side of the United States and supported a range of countermeasures which included the military invasion of Afghanistan, the main base of Al Qaeda and its leader Osama bin Laden. The subsequent invasion of Iraq in March 2003, however, split that coalition and, in particular, created an unprecedented rift in the transatlantic alliance. From a European perspective, there were three interrelated concerns that relate to diplomacy. First, unilateralism. It was apparent that the US Government was determined to invade Iraq, ostensibly in the cause of counterterrorism, whether or not its allies were in support and whether or not a legitimizing resolution could be obtained at the United Nations. The 'diplomacy window' was opened largely as a result of the concerns of the Blair Government but it quickly became clear that this was merely a cover to distract attention from the extensive military build-up in the Persian Gulf that preceded the invasion of Iraq (see Box 17.7). Second, there was concern

CWS

| Box 17.7 | Iraq: shutting the diplomacy window |

The long build-up to war in Iraq was punctuated on two occasions by attempts to use diplomacy to avert war or at least to provide international support for it, through the auspices of the United Nations. On both occasions the role of British Prime Minister Blair was significant. The first came in September 2002 at a meeting at Camp David when Blair backed Bush on Iraq but said that he needed to show that they had tried UN diplomacy. With the issue presented in terms of the threat posed by weapons of mass destruction in Iraq rather the need for 'regime change', the UN Security Council unanimously passed Resolution 1441 in November 2002. The second occasion resulted from Bush's apparent concern that the Blair Government might be in danger of falling because of its overt support for the hard US line on Iraq. He, therefore, acceded to Blair's request for a follow-up resolution that would spell out the 'serious consequences'

that Resolution 1441 had stated would follow Iraqi non-compliance with the UN arms inspectors. A second resolution declaring Iraq in material breach of its obligation to disarm was withdrawn on 17 March by its backers, the United States, Britain, and Spain, when it became clear that it would not attract sufficient support from other Security Council members. These attempts to reach a diplomatic solution need to be set against the US domestic process of deciding upon and implementing the decision to go to war in Iraq. This process began as early as December 2001, with intensive military and intelligence planning through 2002 creating its own momentum. The final decision by the president to go to war was taken in January 2003 with the planned attack delayed only to accommodate the forlorn attempt to get the second UN resolution passed.

(See Woodward 2004)

about the new US military doctrine of pre-emption which implied at least a rejection of both containment and deterrence, the twin pillars of US diplomacy in the cold war. The fear in Europe was that the invasion of Iraq would be followed by the use of military force against other 'rogue' states.

The third related concern refers more broadly to the relationship between what are called 'hard' and 'soft' instruments of power. As defined by Christopher Hill, 'hard' power refers to 'that which is targeted, coercive, often immediate and physical', whereas 'soft' power refers to 'that which is indirect, long term and works more through persuasion than force' (Hill 2003: 135; see also Nye 2004). This is not a new debate, of course, but the 'war against terror-

ism' has provided a dramatic new focus for it. Without denying that hard power has a place in an integrated counter-terrorist strategy, the Europeans have argued that excessive reliance on 'sticks' rather than 'carrots' is likely to be counterproductive. Twelve months after the military intervention in Iraq, the absence of a stable, secure post-Saddam Hussein state was posing major questions about the efficacy of military force and strong arguments were being made in favour of a soft power approach to the global problem of terror. These arguments were strengthened by some evidence of success for this approach in Iran and Libya. The role of diplomacy as a policy instrument and its relationship to other instruments is taken up in more detail in the next section.

Key points

- Diplomacy is a key concept in world politics. It refers to a process of communication and negotiation between states and other international actors.

- Diplomacy began in the ancient world but took on a recognizably modern form from the fifteenth century onwards with the establishment of the permanent embassy.

- By the end of the nineteenth century all states had a network of embassies abroad linked to foreign departments at home. Diplomacy had also become an established profession.

- The First World War was a 'watershed' in the history of diplomacy. The perceived failure of diplomacy to prevent this war led to a demand for a 'new' diplomacy that would be less secretive and more subject to democratic control. The outbreak of the Second World War revealed the limits of the 'new' diplomacy.

- Cold war diplomacy relates to the period after the Second World War when international relations were dominated by a global confrontation between the superpowers and their allies. The imperative need to avoid a nuclear war, but also to 'win' the cold war produced a very delicate, dangerous form of diplomacy.

- The end of the cold war produced a new mood of optimism that diplomacy could resolve all major international problems. Such optimism quickly dissipated when a host of new problems and old problems in a new guise emerged.

- The war against terrorism after 11 September 2001 has posed a major challenge to the role of diplomacy in global politics. This challenge has been framed within a debate about the appropriate relationship between hard and soft instruments of power.

Diplomacy and foreign policy

As noted in the introduction to this chapter, diplomacy not only helps us to understand the nature of world politics as a whole but, from a different perspective, **also reveals much about the behaviour of the actors in a global system of world politics**. The focus of this second major section of this chapter is the relationship between diplomacy and the foreign policies of states. While this section will generalize from the experience of developed states, it should be apparent from the discussion so far in this chapter that developed states are not the only state actors in the system. The role of diplomacy in the behaviour of developing states and other non-state actors will also be discussed.

The making and the implementation of foreign policy

We need first to locate diplomacy within the foreign policy process of states. There are two major stages in that process—the making and the implementation (or the carrying out) of policy. A simple view suggests that the making of foreign policy is the exclusive business of government. So important is foreign policy to the achievement of the 'national interests' of the state that the most senior members of government will oversee and control the policy process. Having made the key decisions, they then hand them over to their foreign departments for implementation. Diplomacy is one of a set of instruments through which decisions are implemented, policy activated, and policy objectives— also established by the political leadership— achieved.

This is a reassuring picture in that, while the difficulties of successful implementation are underplayed, it does suggest that it is the politicians who establish the policy objectives and make the important decisions. If they are elected, this suggests the possibility of democratic control of foreign policy— in principle at least. The foreign policy bureaucracy, not elected of course, plays a subordinate, non-political, essentially instrumental role. This picture, however, is an idealized one, unlikely to match the realities of the process, particularly in developed states with their highly bureaucratized systems of government. As we shall see in the next section, the making and the implementation of foreign policy cannot be so easily split. The two stages can be separated for analysis but in practice they are parts of a continuous and interactive process.

Diplomacy as policy instrument

There is a specialized section of every government devoted to foreign policy. This usually takes the institutionalized form of a foreign department with a dedicated staff. In Britain, for example, the relevant department is the Foreign and Commonwealth Office and, in the United States, the Department of State performs the same function. The specialized staff are known respectively as the Diplomatic Service and Foreign Service Officers. **Every foreign department is linked to a network of embassies abroad and this constitutes the diplomatic machinery of government.** If we identify the main functions performed by this 'machine', it will become apparent that they relate not only to the implementation but also to the actual making of foreign policy. **Diplomacy as a governmental activity then refers not only to a particular policy instrument but also to the whole process of policymaking and implementation.**

As listed in Box 17.8, there are five major functions performed by the diplomatic machine. The first two of these functions are essential to the making of foreign policy. Information and data are the raw materials of foreign policy and it is part of the job of diplomats abroad to gather information and report back to the political leadership via the foreign department at home. Information relevant to policymaking can be gathered from both formal and informal sources. The formal sources include the local media and government reports. Informal sources include personal contacts among the local political elite and the rest of the diplomatic corps—other states' diplomatic representatives based in that location. Given the expanded agenda of modern foreign policy, the scope and range of information required by government for policymaking purposes has increased dramatically. As much of this information is specialized, it is normal for trained representatives called attachés to be attached (as their name

suggests) to the larger embassies. These may include commercial, military, scientific, or cultural attachés, or some relevant mix of experts depending upon the precise nature of the relationship between the parties.

It is difficult in practice to separate the function of information gathering and political reporting from the expectation that diplomats will offer policy advice to government. Part of the purpose of having permanent representatives abroad is that they develop a familiarity with the country in which they are based and are able to use this together with other skills and experience to interpret data and to 'put a gloss' on their reports. They make assessments about likely developments and also make reports on the reception home government policies have received or are likely to receive. The distinction between giving advice and making policy is often blurred. The information and advice given by diplomats will certainly limit the perceived options available and may effectively structure the choices of the political leadership.

If diplomats contribute to policymaking by providing information and advice, the diplomatic machinery provides an important policy instrument relevant to policy implementation through the functions of representation, negotiation, and consular services. Embassies not only represent the government abroad but also represent the wider interests of the home state which go beyond the narrowly political realm. The ambassador and his/her staff will attempt to maintain good relations with the host state, to network with local elites, to be present at relevant ceremonial occasions and events where home interests need to be promoted—at trade fairs, for example. The status and size of the embassy provides a symbolic representation of the importance attached to relations with the host country. Increasing or decreasing the number of diplomats can be used politically to signal the current state of a relationship, or to indicate problems, as the cases in Box 17.9 illustrate.

Negotiation is perhaps the single most important function of the diplomatic machine. This covers a variety of activities from simple consultation—known as an 'exchange of views'—to detailed negotiations on a specific issue. Professional diplomats may take the lead on negotiations or they may play a

---

Box 17.8   Functions of the diplomatic machine

- Information gathering
- Policy advice
- Representation
- Negotiation
- Consular services

Box 17.9   Diplomacy by expulsion

In May 1996, the British Government both initiated and was on the receiving end of diplomatic actions designed to signal displeasure. In the first case, the Russian Government required the removal of four British diplomats in the Moscow embassy who had allegedly been involved in espionage. In a 'tit for tat' response, preserving honour on both sides, the British Government then required four Russian diplomats in London to be sent home. In a second, unrelated case, the British Government expelled three Sudanese diplomats in response to a United Nations Security Council resolution to impose diplomatic and travel sanctions on Sudan because of concerns over complicity by the Sudanese military regime in acts of terrorism. In addition to the expulsions, the remaining Sudanese diplomats were required to give prior notice of UK travel outside London and entry visas were denied to members of the Sudanese Government and military.

supportive role if political leaders themselves or other envoys are involved. Whenever states require the agreement of other states or third parties, diplomacy is the technique used to secure that agreement. The ability to persuade other parties is central to the art of diplomacy. On some issues, persuasion itself may suffice. But, not infrequently, some pressure may be required and the parties involved may then agree to compromise and to adjust their original positions. Pressure may take various forms including the imposition of time limits on the negotiation, seeking to isolate the other party diplomatically, or, in extreme circumstances, threatening to break off diplomatic relations.

The final function of the machine, the provision of consular services, has two elements of which the second is more directly related to diplomacy as a policy instrument. The first type of consular activity involves action to support and protect home citizens abroad. This work, together with the processing of immigration applications from host country citizens may be handled separately from embassy work. The second type of consular work is dedicated to commercial work, supporting trade relations with the host state. This type of work has increased dramatically in recent years and embassies are often evaluated in part at least in terms of their ability to boost home export promotion and trade activity generally.

The relationship between diplomacy and other policy instruments

It is clear that that diplomacy is an important policy instrument in its own right. Persuasion or 'pure diplomacy' may indeed be sufficient to achieve a state's policy objectives abroad. Typically, however, diplomacy is linked to other policy instruments to produce what is called 'mixed diplomacy'. Here, diplomacy becomes a communications channel through which the use or threatened use of other instruments is transmitted to other parties. States learned long ago that persuasion is often more successful if 'sticks' and/or 'carrots' are attached (a point made earlier in the context of the war against terrorism). There are three other types of policy instrument that may be used in various ways either as potential rewards or as punishments in the attempt to secure compliant behaviour in another party.

First, military force may be threatened or deployed to give 'muscle' to a negotiation. Diplomacy and military force, often in combination, have been used by states for so many centuries that they may be regarded as the traditional instruments of foreign policy. The growing costs of warfare, however, have led developed states at least to look for alternative instruments to strengthen their hand in negotiations. A second instrument, economic measures, is not new—trade diplomacy also has a long history. But trade and aid have been used increasingly since the Second World War to influence the outcome of negotiations. Both trade and aid can be threatened or used as a stick or as a carrot in the sense that either can be offered or withheld. The third instrument is the most recent in terms of regular usage and can be labelled subversion. Where the other instruments are used to target governments directly, subversion is rather different in that it is focused on particular groups within other states with the object of undermining or overthrowing the government of that state. Subversion may include a variety of techniques including propaganda, intelligence activities, and assisting rebel groups (see Box 17.10).

The effectiveness of mixed diplomacy in achieving policy objectives depends upon a variety of factors including the nature of the objective sought, the availability of relevant instruments, the nature of the

In September 1970, Salvador Allende was elected President of Chile, the first democratically elected Marxist leader. The United States Government decided thereafter to use all means short of military invasion to bring down the Allende Government. A combination of diplomatic, economic, and subversion instruments were used to support a policy of destabilization. Chile was isolated diplomatically from the international community. US influence with international banks was used to withhold economic loans and the Chilean economy was thrown into chaos. Trade in its principal export, copper, was effectively paralysed. Some $8 million was made available to the Central Intelligence Agency (CIA) for clandestine interference in Chile which was used to fund the activities of opposition political parties and paramilitary groups hostile to Allende. The Allende Government was finally ousted by a coup in September 1973 and Allende himself was killed.

(See Hersh 1983: chs 21, 22)

'mix' used, the costs attached to the use of particular instruments, and so on. In terms of selection, diplomacy continues to occupy a favoured position because it has certain comparative advantages—even though it may need to be supplemented by other instruments to be effective. First, diplomatic resources are readily available. All states and other actors have at least some capacity to communicate with other parties. Second, diplomacy has relatively few costs directly associated with it. While the use of other instruments may be regarded as politically unacceptable in certain circumstances—military force in particular—diplomacy, as Hocking and Smith suggest, is widely regarded as legitimate 'because of its association with negotiation and conciliation, which are valued as norms of international behaviour' (Hocking and Smith 1990: 205).

Diplomacy and developing states

The discussion in the previous sections has assumed that all states are similar with respect to diplomacy and foreign policy. There are however, important differences between developed and developing states which must qualify some of the generalizations we have made about 'states'. In particular, developing states are handicapped as effective international actors by having relatively underdeveloped diplomatic machines and by a restricted range of policy instruments. They tend to have a patchy system of representation abroad and limited resources available for policy analysis. They also have a limited range of policy instruments for bargaining with other actors and for implementing decisions made. For many developing states, the use of international organizations at both regional and global levels is crucial to compensate for weaknesses in national capabilities. We should note here the special role of the United Nations as a forum in which all developing states are represented and where they can attempt to coordinate their common interests and maximize their impact on world politics.

Key points

- Diplomacy plays a key role in the foreign policies of states and other international actors.

- A diplomatic 'machinery' (minimally a foreign department and overseas representation) performs important functions in the making and the implementation of foreign policy.

- Diplomacy involves persuading other actors to do (or not to do) what you want (do not want) them to do. To be effective, ('pure') diplomacy may need to be supplemented by other instruments, but negotiating skills are central to the traditional art of diplomacy.

- Diplomacy combined with other instruments (military, economic, subversion) is called mixed diplomacy. Here, diplomacy becomes a communications channel through which the use or threatened use of other instruments is transmitted to other parties.

- Diplomacy usually has comparative advantages over other instruments in terms of availability and cost.

- Developing states are handicapped as effective international actors by having a relatively underdeveloped diplomatic machinery and by a restricted range of policy instruments.

Challenges to a state-based diplomacy

The last section of this chapter focused on diplomacy as an instrument of state behaviour, whether we are talking about developed or developing states. Indeed, diplomacy used to be called 'statecraft' to emphasize the traditional dominance of states as international actors. However, even the most powerful states are no longer the only significant international actors in a global diplomatic system. Bilateral state-to-state diplomacy remains an important structural feature of that system but it has been increasingly supplemented by multilateral forms of diplomacy with a mixture of state and non-state actors involved. What forms does multilateral diplomacy take and how do actors seek to manage these complex relationships?

International organizations tend to act diplomatically in very much the same way as states. They may not have the extensive diplomatic apparatus performing a wide range of functions that is characteristic of developed states, but all have at least a rudimentary diplomatic machinery—whether they are intergovernmental organizations like the UN or non-governmental organizations like the major multinational corporations. They can communicate their interests and deploy their resources to influence the outcome of negotiations. Indeed, many of these actors have a greater ability to influence the diplomatic process at a global level than smaller states. At a regional level, complex multilateral types of diplomacy have evolved which have reached their most developed form in Europe and can be illustrated by looking at foreign or external policy making in the European Union (see Box 17.11).

These developments raise important questions about the extent to which the state and the state system remain, or indeed should remain, the main vehicles for a global diplomacy. At least one scholar has argued that diplomacy's linkage to the state is 'paradoxical and problematic' and that diplomacy should be tranformed into a 'concept that embodies social relationships which are ordered without the state' (Hoffman 2003: 526). This may be a radical position but other scholars have stressed the challenges that new developments pose to a

---

Box 17.11 External diplomacy of the European Union

The European Union (EU) is arguably a unique multilateral actor in world politics to the extent that state and non-state actors within the Union combine in different ways to act diplomatically on the international stage. The precise combination of actors and associated policy processes depend largely upon the nature of the issue. There are three major types of European foreign policy. Foreign policy 'proper', referred to in Euro-jargon as the 'Common Foreign and Security Policy', can be characterized as an intergovernmental process, largely though not exclusively controlled by the member states. Foreign economic policy or 'external relations', on the other hand, can be characterized as more of a transnational process, with EU institutions like the European Commission playing major role. In trade diplomacy, for example, the Commission acts on behalf of the member states though agreements with third parties need to be agreed by the Council of Ministers representing the member states. Finally, all 25 member states continue to pursue their own diplomatic activities though, over time, national foreign policies have been increasingly 'Europeanized'—adapted to a greater or lesser extent to conform to a common EU policy.

(See White 2001)

---

state-centred view of diplomacy. Hocking, for example, notes that the traditional 'identification of diplomacy as a means of securing the state from its international environment is being modified by diplomacy conceived of as a "boundary-spanning" activity. Here, diplomats are operating not so much within the well-defined "shell" of the state, but within shifting and reconstituting boundaries as state sovereignty is redefined in the face of globalising and regionalising pressures' (Hocking 2004: 92). It is worth noting that these pressures can in certain circumstances put diplomats and embassies in a dangerously exposed position, as illustrated in Box 17.12. Hocking goes on to conclude that 'there is an increasing recognition that the execution of international policy demands the construction of

Diplomats in danger

The importance of safeguarding diplomats and securing the whole system of communications between international actors was underlined in an earlier section of this chapter. One unfortunate consequence of terrorism has been the targeting of embassies by suicide bombers. Following the Al Qaeda attacks on United States embassies in Kenya and Tanzania in 1998, the British consulate (and a British bank) in Istanbul were attacked in November 2003. As a result, millions of dollars and pounds are being spent on moving embassies to safer sites and improving security. Britain has 230 overseas missions and those in the Middle East and North Africa are regarded as being most at risk. While the safety of embassy staff is an obvious priority, diplomats themselves are concerned about losing contact with the local population and remain opposed to the building of fortress-style embassies located outside capitals. This is bound to make the crucial information-gathering task of diplomats that much more difficult.

networks of interaction based on the exchange of resources which are no longer the sole preserve of government'. This recognizes the challenge posed to inter-state diplomacy by the growth of civil society and non-governmental organizations (NGOs) in particular (Hocking 2004: 94. See also Cooper and Hocking 2000).

But it is far too soon to conclude that state-based diplomacy does not remain highly significant. As Hill notes, 'most diplomatic agency is still the preserve of states' and intergovernmental relations as a whole remain important (Hill 2003: 138). Given the changing nature of foreign policy, many parts of the state machinery, apart from ministries of foreign affairs, now engage in international diplomacy. This may challenge the traditional 'gatekeeper' role of

foreign ministries and professional diplomats but it increases the volume of governmental agents involved in diplomacy broadly conceived. One interesting new area of diplomatic activity in which states have taken a lead is known as 'public diplomacy'. This has some similarities to the policy instrument described earlier as subversion, in that it seeks to influence foreign societies as much as other governments. But, often linked to older notions of commercial and cultural diplomacy, public diplomacy is less concerned to destabilize those societies by clandestine operations and more concerned openly to project a positive image of the state to the outside world in order to influence the policy of others towards it. As Hill comments, public diplomacy constitutes 'a curious revival of statism in this age of globalization. A state has become something to sell through an image which effectively promotes its strengths and downplays its weaknesses' (Hill 2003: 280. See also International Studies Perspectives 2004).

The demands of multilateral diplomacy today, however, impose constraints upon the ability of all actors to control outcomes. This is not only because it is a diverse and complex process with multiple actors negotiating about a wider range of issues than ever before. The international context within which those negotiations take place has also been radically transformed by levels of interconnectedness or interdependence between societies and the effect of the revolution in communications technology which has transformed diplomacy as process and as instrument. The result is that diplomacy has become less of a traditional art form with a premium on negotiating skills and 'winning' and more of a management process with actors seeking to reach agreements through a process of adjustment.

Key points

- Even the most powerful states are no longer the only significant international actors. Bilateral state-to-state diplomacy has been increasingly supplemented by multilateral forms of diplomacy.

- International organizations, both inter-governmental and non-governmental, have become significant diplomatic actors. With at least a rudimentary diplomatic machinery, they can communicate their interests and deploy their resources to influence the outcome of negotiations.

- Complex multilateral types of diplomacy have evolved at the regional level and have reached their most developed form in Europe.

- In complex, multilateral negotiations, diplomacy has become less an art form and more a management process reflecting high levels of interdependence between societies.

- There is now a lively debate about the extent to which states and the state system remain, or should remain, the major vehicles for global diplomacy. Globalization challenges a traditional state-based diplomacy but there are indications that states are adapting to these changes. It is certainly too soon to conclude that state-based diplomacy does not remain highly significant in global diplomacy.

Conclusion

This chapter has tried to demonstrate that diplomacy is neither a vague concept nor an international activity that is of interest only to diplomatic historians. As an international process and a policy instrument, diplomacy preceded the modern states-system. It then played a central role in the operation of that system for hundreds of years. Today, adapted to the demands of the contemporary global system, diplomacy continues to make an important contribution to cooperation and order in that system. But diplomacy is no panacea. It cannot guarantee international cooperation but, given goodwill on all sides, it can provide the means to make it happen through dialogue and negotiation. The problem now is that diplomatic systems have become so complex that a range of management skills beyond those deployed by the traditional diplomat is essential.

For further information and case studies on this subject, please visit the companion web site at www.oup.com/uk/booksites/politics.

QUESTIONS

1   What is the difference between diplomacy as a 'process' and diplomacy as an 'instrument'?

2   What are the essential elements of 'traditional' diplomacy?

3   What was 'new' about the 'new diplomacy'?

4   What is the difference between the 'nightwatchman state' and the 'welfare state' and why is this difference important to the diplomatic agenda?

5   What was distinctive about 'cold war diplomacy'?

6   What is 'development diplomacy'?

7   What is the difference between 'crisis management' and 'crisis diplomacy'?

8   What is the foreign policy 'machine'? What functions does it perform?

9   What is the difference between 'pure' and 'mixed' diplomacy?

10 What factors contribute to the successful use of diplomacy?

11 What are the characteristics of multilateral diplomacy in a global system of world politics in terms of actors, processes, and issues

12 To what extent do states and the state system remain the main vehicles for diplomatic activity in a globalized world?

GUIDE TO FURTHER READING

Barston, R. P. (1997), *Modern Diplomacy* (London: Longman, 2nd edn). A useful summary of diplomacy as a policy instrument of states. It is an updated textbook aimed specifically at undergraduates with little prior knowledge of diplomacy.

Berridge, G. R. (1995), *Diplomacy: Theory and Practice* (Hemel Hempstead: Harvester Wheatsheaf). This textbook is aimed at graduate students but it contains digestible material for undergraduates on forms of diplomacy and the negotiating process.

Berridge, G. R., and James, A. (2001), *A Dictionary of Diplomacy* (Basingstoke: Palgrave). A useful relatively recent reference source.

Hamilton, K., and Langhorne, R. (1995), *The Practice of Diplomacy* (London: Routledge). This scholarly book analyses the evolution and development of the modern diplomatic system. It is excellent on historical detail and the changing context of diplomacy.

Hocking, B. (ed.) (1999), *Foreign Ministries: Change and Adaptation* (Basingstoke: Macmillan). This is a useful, up-to-date, comparative study which analyses how effectively foreign ministries and the diplomatic machinery of states have adapted to the challenges of operating in a fragmented, multilateral policy environment.

Richardson, J. L. (1994), *Crisis Diplomacy: The Great Powers Since the Mid-nineteenth Century* (Cambridge: Cambridge University Press). The most comprehensive book on crisis diplomacy published to date. It considers a wide range of case studies from the pre-nuclear as well as the nuclear era and contains an important critique of 'crisis management'.

Watson, A. (1982), *Diplomacy: The Dialogue Between States* (London: Methuen). A 'classic' book on diplomacy written by a former practitioner. It makes a strong case for the continuing relevance of diplomacy to solving the problems of world politics. It still offers important insights into the world of the diplomat.

CHAPTER 18

The United Nations

PAUL TAYLOR • DEVON CURTIS

READER'S GUIDE

This chapter focuses on the development of the United Nations (UN) and the changes and challenges that it has faced since its establishment in 1945. The UN is a grouping of states, and is therefore premised on the notion that states are the primary units in the international system. The institutions of the United Nations reflect an uneasy hybrid between traditions of Great Power consensus, and traditions of universalism that stress the equality of states. Furthermore, while the UN was established as a grouping of sovereign states, the chapter argues that United Nations institutions have taken on an increasing range of functions, and have become much more involved within states. Justice for individuals is increasingly seen as a concomitant of international order. Serious deficiencies in human rights, or in economic welfare, can lead to international tensions. This development has led to challenges to traditional views about intervention within states. It has also led to the expansion of UN institutions to address an increased number of economic and social questions, and the search for better ways to coordinate these activities.

Introduction

The United Nations is made up of a group of international institutions, which include the central system located in New York, the Specialized Agencies such as the World Health Organization (WHO) and the International Labour Organization (ILO), and the Programmes and Funds, such as the United Nations Children's Emergency Fund (UNICEF) and the United Nations Development Programme (UNDP). When created more than half a century ago in the aftermath of the Second World War, the United Nations reflected the hope for a just and peaceful global community. It is the only global institution with the legitimacy that derives from universal membership, and a mandate that encompasses security, economic and social development, the protection of human rights, and the protection of the environment. Yet the UN was created by states for states and the relationship between state sovereignty and the protection of the needs and interests of people has not been fully resolved. Questions about the meaning of sovereignty and the limits of UN action have remained key issues. Nonetheless, since the founding of the UN, there has been an expansion of UN activities to address conditions within states, an improvement in UN capacity in its economic and social work, and an increased tendency to accord the UN a moral status. Threats to global security addressed by the UN now include inter-state conflict, threats by non-state actors, as well as political, economic, and social conditions within states. Despite the growth in UN activities however, there are some questions about the relevance and effectiveness of the UN. The failure to get clear UN Security Council authorization for the war in Iraq in 2003 led to well-publicized criticism of the UN and a crisis in international relations. Yet the aftermath of the invasion and persistent questions about the legitimacy of a war that was not sanctioned by the UN show that the UN has acquired important moral status in international society.

After describing the main organs of the UN, this chapter will look at the changing role of the UN in addressing matters of peace and security, and then matters of economic and social development. It will focus on how the UN's role has evolved in response to changes in the global political context, and on some of the problems that it still faces.

A brief history of the United Nations and its principal organs

The United Nations was established on 24 October 1945 by 51 countries, as a result of initiatives taken by the governments of the states that had led the war against Germany and Japan. By 2003, 191 countries were members of the United Nations, nearly every state in the world. When joining, member states agreed to accept the obligations of the UN Charter, an international treaty that set out basic principles of international relations. According to the Charter, the UN had four purposes: to maintain international peace and security; to develop friendly relations among nations; to cooperate in solving international problems and in promoting respect for human rights; and to be a centre for harmonizing the actions of nations. At the UN, all the member states—large and small, rich and poor, with differing political views and social systems—had a voice and a vote in this process. Interestingly, while the United Nations was clearly created as a grouping of states, the Charter referred to the needs and interests of peoples as well as those of states (see Box 18.1).

In many ways, the United Nations was set up to correct the problems of its predecessor, the League of Nations. The League of Nations had been estab-

| Box 18.1 | Selected Articles of the UN Charter |

The UN Charter contains references to both the rights of states and the rights of people.

The **Preamble** of the UN Charter asserts that 'We the peoples of the United Nations [are] determined to reaffirm faith in fundamental human rights, in the dignity and worth of the human person, in the equal rights of men and women and of nations large and small'.

Article 1(2) states that the purpose of the UN is to develop 'friendly relations among nations based on respect for the principle of equal rights and self-determination of peoples and to take other appropriate measures to strengthen universal peace'.

Article 2(7) states that 'Nothing contained in the present Charter shall authorize the United Nations to intervene in matters which are essentially within the domestic jurisdiction of any state'.

Chapter VI deals with the 'Pacific Settlement of Disputes'.

Article 33 states that 'The parties to any dispute, the continuance of which is likely to endanger the maintenance of international peace and security, shall, first of all, seek solution by negotiation, enquiry, mediation, conciliation, arbitration, judicial settlement, resort to regional agencies or arrangements, or other peaceful means of their own choice'.

Chapter VII deals with 'Action with Respect to Threats to the Peace, Breaches of the Peace, and Acts of Aggression'.

Article 42 states that the Security Council 'may take such action by air, sea, or land forces as may be necessary to maintain or restore international peace and security'. The Security Council has sometimes authorized member states to use 'all necessary means', and this has been accepted as a legitimate application of Chapter VII powers

Article 99 authorizes the Secretary-General to 'bring to the attention of the Security Council any matter which in his opinion may threaten the maintenance of international peace and security'.

lished after the First World War, and was intended to make future wars impossible, but a major problem was the League's lack of effective power. There was no clear division of responsibility between the main executive committee (the League Council) and the League Assembly that included all member states. Both the League Assembly and the League Council could only make recommendations, not binding resolutions, and these recommendations had to be unanimous. Any government was free to reject any recommendation. Furthermore, in the League there was no mechanism for coordinating military or economic actions against miscreant states, which further contributed to the League's weakness. Key states, such as the United States, were not members of the League. By the Second World War, the League had already failed to address a number of acts of aggression.

The **structure** of the United Nations was intended to avoid some of the problems faced by the League of Nations. The United Nations has six main organs: the Security Council, the General Assembly, the Secretariat, the Economic and Social Council, the Trusteeship Council, and the International Court of Justice (see Fig. 18.1).

The Security Council

In contrast to the League of Nations, the United Nations recognized Great Power prerogatives in the Security Council. The UN Security Council was given the main responsibility for maintaining international peace and security. It was made up initially of 11 states, and then, after 1965, of 15 states. It includes five permanent members, namely the USA, Britain, France, the Soviet Union (later Russia), and China, as well as 10 non-permanent members. Unlike the League, the decisions of the Security Council are binding, and must only be passed by a majority of nine out of the 15 members, as well as each of the five permanent members. These five permanent members therefore have **veto power** over all Security Council decisions.[1] There have been widespread calls for the reform of the Security Council, but this is very difficult (see Box 18.2). The five permanent members of the Security Council were seen as the major powers when the UN was founded, and they were granted a veto on the view that if big powers were not given a privileged position, the UN would not work. This view stems from Realist theory. Indeed, this tension between the recognition of

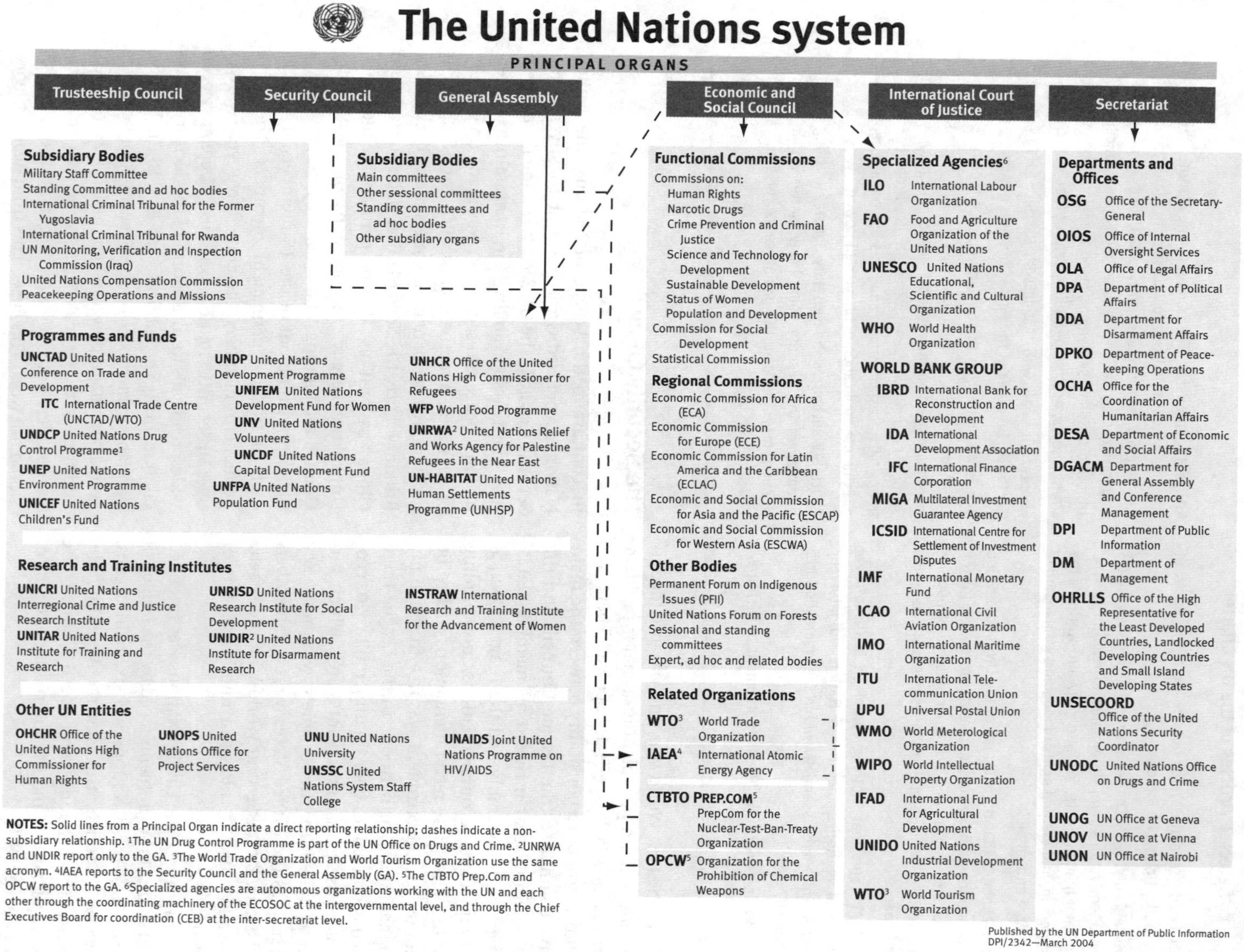

The United Nations system

PRINCIPAL ORGANS

| Trusteeship Council | Security Council | General Assembly | Economic and Social Council | International Court of Justice | Secretariat |

Subsidiary Bodies

Military Staff Committee
Standing Committee and ad hoc bodies
International Criminal Tribunal for the Former Yugoslavia
International Criminal Tribunal for Rwanda
UN Monitoring, Verification and Inspection Commission (Iraq)
United Nations Compensation Commission
Peacekeeping Operations and Missions

Subsidiary Bodies

Main committees
Other sessional committees
Standing committees and ad hoc bodies
Other subsidiary organs

Programmes and Funds

UNCTAD United Nations Conference on Trade and Development
ITC International Trade Centre (UNCTAD/WTO)
UNDCP United Nations Drug Control Programme[1]
UNEP United Nations Environment Programme
UNICEF United Nations Children's Fund
UNDP United Nations Development Programme
UNIFEM United Nations Development Fund for Women
UNV United Nations Volunteers
UNCDF United Nations Capital Development Fund
UNFPA United Nations Population Fund
UNHCR Office of the United Nations High Commissioner for Refugees
WFP World Food Programme
UNRWA[2] United Nations Relief and Works Agency for Palestine Refugees in the Near East
UN-HABITAT United Nations Human Settlements Programme (UNHSP)

Research and Training Institutes

UNICRI United Nations Interregional Crime and Justice Research Institute
UNITAR United Nations Institute for Training and Research
UNRISD United Nations Research Institute for Social Development
UNIDIR[2] United Nations Institute for Disarmament Research
INSTRAW International Research and Training Institute for the Advancement of Women

Other UN Entities

OHCHR Office of the United Nations High Commissioner for Human Rights
UNOPS United Nations Office for Project Services
UNU United Nations University
UNSSC United Nations System Staff College
UNAIDS Joint United Nations Programme on HIV/AIDS

Functional Commissions

Commissions on:
Human Rights
Narcotic Drugs
Crime Prevention and Criminal Justice
Science and Technology for Development
Sustainable Development
Status of Women
Population and Development
Commission for Social Development
Statistical Commission

Regional Commissions

Economic Commission for Africa (ECA)
Economic Commission for Europe (ECE)
Economic Commission for Latin America and the Caribbean (ECLAC)
Economic and Social Commission for Asia and the Pacific (ESCAP)
Economic and Social Commission for Western Asia (ESCWA)

Other Bodies

Permanent Forum on Indigenous Issues (PFII)
United Nations Forum on Forests
Sessional and standing committees
Expert, ad hoc and related bodies

Related Organizations

WTO[3] World Trade Organization
IAEA[4] International Atomic Energy Agency
CTBTO PREP.COM[5] PrepCom for the Nuclear-Test-Ban-Treaty Organization
OPCW[5] Organization for the Prohibition of Chemical Weapons

Specialized Agencies[6]

ILO International Labour Organization
FAO Food and Agriculture Organization of the United Nations
UNESCO United Nations Educational, Scientific and Cultural Organization
WHO World Health Organization

WORLD BANK GROUP
IBRD International Bank for Reconstruction and Development
IDA International Development Association
IFC International Finance Corporation
MIGA Multilateral Investment Guarantee Agency
ICSID International Centre for Settlement of Investment Disputes

IMF International Monetary Fund
ICAO International Civil Aviation Organization
IMO International Maritime Organization
ITU International Telecommunication Union
UPU Universal Postal Union
WMO World Meteorological Organization
WIPO World Intellectual Property Organization
IFAD International Fund for Agricultural Development
UNIDO United Nations Industrial Development Organization
WTO[3] World Tourism Organization

Departments and Offices

OSG Office of the Secretary-General
OIOS Office of Internal Oversight Services
OLA Office of Legal Affairs
DPA Department of Political Affairs
DDA Department for Disarmament Affairs
DPKO Department of Peacekeeping Operations
OCHA Office for the Coordination of Humanitarian Affairs
DESA Department of Economic and Social Affairs
DGACM Department for General Assembly and Conference Management
DPI Department of Public Information
DM Department of Management
OHRLLS Office of the High Representative for the Least Developed Countries, Landlocked Developing Countries and Small Island Developing States
UNSECOORD Office of the United Nations Security Coordinator
UNODC United Nations Office on Drugs and Crime
UNOG UN Office at Geneva
UNOV UN Office at Vienna
UNON UN Office at Nairobi

Published by the UN Department of Public Information
DPI/2342—March 2004

NOTES: Solid lines from a Principal Organ indicate a direct reporting relationship; dashes indicate a non-subsidiary relationship. [1]The UN Drug Control Programme is part of the UN Office on Drugs and Crime. [2]UNRWA and UNDIR report only to the GA. [3]The World Trade Organization and World Tourism Organization use the same acronym. [4]IAEA reports to the Security Council and the General Assembly (GA). [5]The CTBTO Prep.Com and OPCW report to the GA. [6]Specialized agencies are autonomous organizations working with the UN and each other through the coordinating machinery of the ECOSOC at the intergovernmental level, and through the Chief Executives Board for coordination (CEB) at the inter-secretariat level.

Fig. 18.1 The structure of the United Nations system

Published by the UN Department of Public Information. See www.un.org/aboutun/unchart.pdf.

Box 18.2 **The reform of the Security Council**

Since the Security Council is the main executive body within the United Nations with primary responsibility for maintaining international peace and security, it is not surprising that many discussions of UN reform have focused on the Security Council.

The founders of the UN deliberately established a universal General Assembly and a restricted Security Council that required unanimity among the Great Powers. Granting permanent seats and the right to a veto to the Great Powers of the time, the United States, the Soviet Union (now Russia), France, the United Kingdom, and China, was an essential feature of the deal.

The composition and decisionmaking procedures of the Security Council were increasingly challenged as membership of the United Nations grew, particularly after decolonization. Yet the only significant reform of the Security Council occurred in 1965, when the Council was enlarged from 11 to 15 members and the required majority from seven to nine votes. Nonetheless, the veto power of the permanent five (P-5) members was left intact.

The Security Council does not reflect today's distribution of military or economic power, and does not reflect a geographic balance. Germany and Japan have made strong cases for permanent membership. Developing countries have demanded a better reflection of their numbers in the Security Council, with countries such as India, Egypt, Brazil, and Nigeria making particular claims. However, it has proved to be impossible to reach agreement on new permanent members. Should the European Union be represented instead of Great Britain, France, and Germany individually? How would Pakistan feel about India's candidacy? How would South Africa feel about a Nigerian seat? What about representation by an Islamic country? These issues are not easy to resolve. Likewise, it is very unlikely that the P-5 countries will relinquish their veto.

Nonetheless, while large-scale reform has proved impossible, there have been changes in Security Council working procedures that have made it more transparent and accountable.

---

power politics through the Security Council veto, and the universal ideals underlying the United Nations, is a defining feature of the organization.

When the Security Council considers a threat to international peace, it first explores ways to settle the dispute peacefully under the terms of **Chapter VI** of the UN Charter (see Box 18.1). It may suggest principles for a settlement or may suggest mediation. In the event of fighting, the Security Council tries to secure a ceasefire. It may send a peacekeeping mission to help the parties maintain the truce and to keep opposing forces apart (see the discussion of peacekeeping below). The Council can also take measures to enforce its decisions under **Chapter VII** of the Charter. It can, for instance, impose economic sanctions or order an arms embargo.

On rare occasions, the Security Council has authorized member states to use '**all necessary means**', including collective military action, to see that its decisions are carried out. The Council also makes recommendations to the General Assembly on the appointment of a new Secretary-General and on the admission of new members to the UN.

The General Assembly

The recognition of power politics through veto power in the Security Council can be contrasted with the universalist principles underlying the other organs of the United Nations. All UN member states are represented in the General Assembly—a 'parliament of nations'—which meets to consider the world's most pressing problems. Each member state has one vote. A two-thirds majority in the General Assembly is required for decisions on key issues such as international peace and security, the admission of new members, and the UN budget. A simple majority is required for other matters, but in recent years, a special effort has been made to reach decisions through consensus, rather than by a formal vote. However, the decisions reached by the General Assembly only have the status of recommendations, rather than binding decisions. One of the few exceptions is the General Assembly's Fifth Committee, which makes decisions on the budget that are binding on members.

At its 2001/02 session, the General Assembly considered more than 180 different topics, including globalization, HIV/AIDS, conflict in Africa, the protection of the environment, and the consolidation of new democracies. Since the General Assembly resolutions are non-binding, they cannot force action by any state, but its recommendations are an important indication of world opinion and represent the moral authority of the community of nations.

The Secretariat

The Secretariat carries out the substantive and administrative work of the United Nations as directed by the General Assembly, the Security Council, and the other organs. At its head is the Secretary-General, who provides overall administrative guidance. The Secretariat consists of departments and offices with a total staff of 7,500 under the regular budget, and a nearly equal number under special funding. Duty stations include UN Headquarters in New York, as well as UN offices in Geneva, Vienna, Nairobi, and other locations.

On the recommendation of the other bodies, the Secretariat also carries out a number of research functions and some quasi-management functions. By the mid-1990s, support for peacekeeping activities had become especially important. Yet the role of the Secretariat remains primarily bureaucratic and it lacks the political power and the right of initiative of, for instance, the Commission of the European Union. The one exception to this is the power of the Secretary-General under Article 99 of the Charter, to bring situations that are likely to lead to a breakdown of international peace and security to the attention of the Security Council. This article, which may appear innocuous at first, was the legal basis for the remarkable expansion of the diplomatic role of the Secretary-General, compared with its League predecessor. Due to this, the Secretary-General is empowered to become involved in a large range of areas that can be loosely interpreted as threats to peace, including economic and social problems and humanitarian crises.

The Economic and Social Council

The Economic and Social Council (ECOSOC), under the overall authority of the General Assembly, is intended to coordinate the economic and social work of the United Nations and the UN family of organizations. It also consults with **non-governmental organizations** (NGOs), thereby maintaining a vital link between the United Nations and civil society.

Along with the Secretariat and the General Assembly, ECOSOC is responsible for overseeing the activities of a large number of other institutions that have come to be known as the **United Nations system**. This includes the Specialized Agencies and the Programmes and Funds (see Fig. 18.1). The **Specialized Agencies** such as the World Health Organization (WHO), the International Labour Organization (ILO), and the Food and Agriculture Organization (FAO), have their own constitutions, regularly assessed budgets, executive heads, and assemblies of state representatives. They are self-contained constitutionally, financially, and politically, and not subject to the management of the central system.

The **Programmes and Funds** are much closer to the central system in the sense that their management arrangements are subject to direct General Assembly supervision, can be modified by Assembly resolution, and most importantly, are largely funded on a voluntary basis. Overall, the Programmes and Funds respond to changes in global economic and social circumstances. Since the establishment of the United Nations in 1945, a number of new issues have come on to the international agenda, such as the rights and interests of women, climate change, resource depletion, population growth, terrorism the spread of HIV/AIDS, and so on. These issues often did not fall into the field of responsibility of the Specialized Agencies. Very frequently, a new organization in the Programmes and Funds was the fruit of a global conference, such as the United Nations Conference on the Human Environment in 1972, or the United Nations World Conference on Women held in Beijing in 1995. Examples of Programmes and Funds include the United Nations Development Programme (UNDP), and the United

Nations International Children's Emergency Fund (UNICEF).

Whereas the League of Nations attributed responsibility for economic and social questions to the League Assembly, the Charter of the United Nations established ECOSOC in order to carry out more specialized functions and to improve on the mechanisms to oversee economic and social institutions. These changes in the UN, compared with the League, were a consequence of thinking in more **functionalist** terms.[2] Organizations were set up to deal with specific economic and social problems. However, ECOSOC was not given the necessary management powers. It could only issue recommendations and receive reports from the Specialized Agencies. In consequence, the UN's economic and social organizations have continuously searched for better ways of achieving effective management (see the discussion of the reform process below).

The Trusteeship Council

When the United Nations was created, the Trusteeship Council was established to provide international supervision for 11 Trust Territories administered by seven member states and to ensure that adequate steps were taken to prepare the territories for self-government or independence. By 1994, all Trust Territories had attained self-government or independence, either as separate states or by joining neighbouring independent countries. The last to do so was the Trust Territory of the Pacific Islands, Palau, which had been previously administered by the United States. Its work completed, the Trusteeship

Council now consists of the five permanent members of the Security Council. It has amended its rules of procedure to allow it to meet when necessary.

The International Court of Justice

The International Court of Justice, also known as the World Court, is the main judicial organ of the UN. Consisting of 15 judges elected jointly by the General Assembly and the Security Council, the Court decides disputes between countries. Participation by states in a proceeding is voluntary, but if a state agrees to participate, it is obligated to comply with the Court's decision. The Court also provides advisory opinions to the General Assembly and the Security Council upon request.

Key points

- The United Nations was established to preserve peace between states after the Second World War.

- In a number of ways, the institutions of the United Nations reflected lessons learned from its predecessor, the League of Nations.

- The institutions and mechanisms of the United Nations reflect both the demands of Great Power politics (i.e. Security Council veto) and universalism. They also reflect demands to address the needs and interests of people, as well as the needs and interest of states. The tensions and balance between these various demands have been a key feature of UN development.

The United Nations and the maintenance of international peace and security

The performance of the United Nations in questions of peace and security has been shaped by the world political context. Clearly, there have been changes in international society since the UN was founded in 1945 that have had an impact on the UN system. The

cold war clash between the United States and the Soviet Union hampered the functioning of the UN Security Council, since the veto could be used whenever the major interests of the United States or Soviet Union were threatened. From 1945 to 1990,

193 substantive vetoes were invoked in the Security Council, compared to only 12 substantive vetoes from 1990 to 2003 (Malone 2004: 7). Furthermore, while the UN Charter provided for a standing army to be set up by agreement between the Security Council and consenting states, the East–West cold war rivalry made it impossible to implement such an army. The end result was that the UN Security Council could not function in the way in which the UN founders had expected.

Since member states could not agree upon the arrangements laid out in Chapter VII of the Charter, especially with regard to setting up a UN army for tackling an aggressor, there followed a series of improvizations to address matters of peace and security. First, an enforcement procedure was established under which the Security Council agreed to a **mandate for an agent to act on its behalf**. This occurred in the Korean conflict in 1950, and the Gulf War in 1990, when action was undertaken principally by the United States and its allies.

Second, there have been many instances of **classical peacekeeping**. No reference to peacekeeping exists in the UN Charter, but classical peacekeeping mandates and mechanisms are based on Chapter VI of the UN Charter. Classical peacekeeping involves the establishment of a UN force under UN command to be placed between the parties to a dispute after a ceasefire. Such a force only uses its weapons in self-defence, is established with the consent of the host state, and does not include forces from the major powers. This mechanism was first used in November 1956, when a UN force was sent to Egypt to facilitate the exodus of the British and French forces from the Suez canal area, and then to stand between Egyptian and Israeli forces. Since the Suez crisis, there have been a number of classical peacekeeping missions, for instance, monitoring the Green Line in Cyprus, and in the Golan Heights.

Third, there has been a new kind of peacekeeping, sometimes called **multidimensional peacekeeping** or peace enforcement, which emerged after the end of the cold war. These forces were more likely to use force to achieve humanitarian ends, more likely to have heavier military equipment, and more likely to include forces from major powers. Such forces were sometimes used when order had collapsed within states, and therefore addressed civil wars as well as international conflict. A key problem was that the forces found it increasingly difficult to maintain a neutral position and were targeted by all sides. Examples include the intervention in Somalia in the early 1990s and intervention in the former Yugoslavia in the mid-1990s. The new peacekeeping mandates were sometimes based on Chapter VII of the UN Charter. At their peak in 1994, UN peacekeeping operations involved nearly 80,000 military personnel around the world, seven times the figure for 1990 (Pugh 2001: 115).

Increased attention to conditions within states

The new peacekeeping was the product of a greater preparedness to intervene within states. The argument that what went on within states was of no concern to outsiders came to be strongly opposed. Many people believed that the international community, working through the UN, should address individual political and civil rights, as well as the right to basic provisions like food, water, health care, and accommodation. This challenged the traditional belief that diplomats should ignore the internal affairs of states in order to preserve international stability. On the contrary, many people came to believe that violations of individuals' rights were a major cause of disturbances in relations between states: a lack of internal justice risked international disorder. The UN reinforced this new perception that pursuing justice for individuals, or ensuring **human security**, was an aspect of national interest. If there was a clear-cut conflict between perceptions of national interest and the pursuit of justice, the former should have priority, but it was increasingly believed that the choice could not be put in such stark terms.

In some states, contributions to activities such as peacekeeping and humanitarian intervention were defended in terms of national interest. Indeed, states like Canada accepted an obligation to develop their capacity for peacekeeping. This was understood as a 'moral' course of action, but also one that could be justified by national interest since Canada gained status in the international community through such contributions. The Japanese also responded to moral pressure founded in hard national interest when they contributed substantially to defraying the cost of British involvement in the 1990–1 Gulf War. This extraordinary act could only be explained in terms of the synthesis of morality and interest. For some states, reputation in the United Nations has become an important national good.

These actions therefore reflected an increasing concern with questions of justice for individuals and conditions within states. Yet in the past, the United Nations had helped promote the traditional view of the primacy of international order between state over justice for individuals, so the new focus on individual rights was a significant change. What accounts for this change?

First, the international environment had changed. The cold war stand-off between the East and the West had meant that member states did not want to question the conditions of the sovereignty of states. Jean Kirkpatrick's notorious essay, which recommended tolerating abhorrent dictatorships in Latin America in order to fight communism, was a reasonable report of the situation at that time: unsavoury right-wing regimes in Latin America were tolerated because they were anti-Soviet, and interfering in the other's sphere by East or West risked escalation of conflict (Forsythe 1988: 259–60).

Second, the process of decolonization had privileged statehood over justice. The UN reflected the claims of colonies to become states, and had elevated the right to statehood above any tests of viability, such as the existence of a nation, adequate economic performance, defensibility, or a prospect for achieving justice for citizens. This unconditional right to independence was enunciated in the General Assembly Declaration on the Granting of Independence to Colonial Countries and Peoples in 1960. There emerged a convention that the claims of elites in the putative states could be a sufficient indication of popular enthusiasm, even when the elites were crooks and the claims misleading.

Charles Beitz was one of the first to question such insouciance on the part of the imperial states when he concluded, in defiance of political correctness in the 1970s, that statehood should not be unconditional: attention had to be given to the situation of individuals after independence (Beitz 1979). Michael Waltzer and Terry Nardin produced arguments leading to similar conclusions: states were

conditional entities in that their right to exist should be dependent on a criterion of performance with regard to the interests of their citizens (Walzer 1977; Nardin 1983). Such writings helped alter the moral content of diplomacy.

The new relationship between order and justice was, therefore, a product of particular circumstances. After the cold war, it was felt that threats to international peace and security did not only emanate from aggression between states. Rather, global peace was also threatened by civil conflict (including refugee flows and regional instability), humanitarian emergencies, violations of global standards of human rights, and other conditions such as poverty and inequality. In 1992, then Secretary-General Boutros Boutros-Ghali outlined a far more ambitious UN agenda for peace and security in a report called *An Agenda for Peace* (see Box 18.3). Other types of non-state based threats, such as terrorism and the proliferation of arms and weapons of mass destruction, also have an increasingly prominent place on

---

Box 18.3   An agenda for peace

In the early 1990s after the end of the cold war, the UN agenda for peace and security expanded quickly. Secretary-General Boutros Boutros-Ghali outlined the more ambitious role for the UN in his seminal report, *An Agenda for Peace*. The report described interconnected roles for the UN to maintain peace and security in the post-cold war context. These included:

- **Preventive diplomacy**: involving confidence-building measures, fact finding, and preventive deployment of UN authorized forces.

- **Peacemaking**: designed to bring hostile parties to agreement, essentially through peaceful means. However, when all peaceful means have failed, **peace enforcement** authorized under Chapter VII of the Charter may be necessary. Peace enforcement may occur without the consent of the parties.

- **Peacekeeping**: the deployment of a UN presence in the field with the consent of all parties (this refers to classical peacekeeping).

- **Post-conflict peacebuilding**: to develop the social, political, and economic infrastructure to prevent further violence and to consolidate peace.

(See: www.un.org/Docs/SG/agpeace.html)

the UN agenda.[3] Partly due to the terrorist attacks in the US in 2001 as well as the impasse reached in the UN Security Council over Iraq in 2003, Secretary-General Kofi Annan named a high-level panel to examine the major threats and challenges to global peace, and to make recommendations for elements of a collective response. The panel was formed in November 2003 and is due to make its recommendations by the end of 2004.

Key points

- The cold war and the decolonization process had discouraged more active involvement by the United Nations within states.

- After the cold war, it became more difficult for states and diplomats to accept that what happened within states was of no concern to outsiders.

- It became more common for governments to see active membership in the United Nations as serving their national interest as well as being morally right.

- By the mid-1990s the UN had become involved in maintaining international peace and security in three main ways: by resisting aggression between states, by attempting to resolve disputes within states (civil wars), and by focusing on conditions within states, including economic, social, and political conditions.

The United Nations and intervention within states

As issues of peace and security were increasingly understood to include human security and justice, the UN was expected to take on a stronger role in maintaining standards for individuals within states. A difficulty with carrying out the new tasks was that it seemed to run against the doctrine of non-intervention. **Intervention** was traditionally defined as a deliberate incursion into a state without its consent by some outside agency, in order to change the functioning, policies, and goals of its government and achieve effects that favour the intervening agency (Vincent 1974) (see Ch.25).[4]

At the founding of the UN, **sovereignty** was regarded as central to the system of states. States were equally members of international society, and were equal with regard to international law. Sovereignty also implied that states recognized no higher authority than themselves, and that there was no superior jurisdiction. The governments of states had exclusive jurisdiction within their own frontiers, a principle which was enshrined in Article 2(7) of the United Nations Charter. Intervention in the traditional sense was in opposition to the principles of international society, and it could only be tolerated as an exception to the rule.

In earlier periods however, states had intervened in each other's business and thought that they had a right to do so. The American Government refused to accept any curtailment of their right to intervene in the internal affairs of other states in their hemisphere until 1933, when they conceded the point at the seventh International Conference of American States. The US position was very similar to the Brezhnev doctrine of the 1970s, which held that the Soviet Union had the right to intervene in the member states of the socialist commonwealth to protect the principles of socialism.

Much earlier, the British had insisted on the abolition of slavery in their relations with other states. They stopped ships on the high seas, and imposed the abolition of slavery as a condition in treaties (Bethell 1970). There were also occasions when states tried to bind other states to respect certain principles in their internal affairs. A number of states in Eastern Europe, such as Hungary and Bulgaria, were bound to respect the rights of minorities within their frontiers based on agreements made at the Berlin Conference of 1878 by the Great Powers. In practice then, intervention was a common feature of international politics, sometimes for good cause.

By the 1990s, some people believed that there should be a return to this earlier period where intervention was justified, but it was felt that a wider range of instruments should be used to protect generally accepted standards. They insisted on a key role for the United Nations in granting a licence to intervene. The principle of non-intervention could only be challenged on the basis of a threat to universal values. It was pointed out that the UN Charter did not assert merely the rights of states, but also the rights of peoples: statehood could be interpreted as being conditional upon respect for such rights (see Box 18.4). There was ample evidence in the UN Charter to justify the view that extreme transgressions of human rights could be a justification for intervention by the international community.

The major pronouncements of the UN General Assembly on humanitarian assistance referred to the primary responsibility of the target states for dealing with complex crises within their frontiers; however a General Assembly resolution passed in 1991 implied some relaxation of this principle. The resolution

held that 'The sovereignty, territorial integrity and national unity of States must be fully respected in accordance with the Charter of the United Nations. In this context, humanitarian assistance should be provided with the consent of the affected country and in principle on the basis of an appeal by the affected country' (A/46/182). The use of the phrase 'in principle', and the term 'should', implied that there could be occasions where intervention was necessary even when government approval in the target state was not possible.

There was disagreement about whether the existing procedures of the United Nations, relying in particular on the approval of the Security Council, were adequate for the authorization of new forms of intervention, or whether further safeguards were necessary, such as a two-thirds majority in the General Assembly and the supervision of the International Court of Justice.[5] In most cases, the UN Security Council has not given explicit approval for such action. Rather, it uses indirect language such as authorizing member states to use 'all necessary means' under Chapter VII of the Charter to carry out its decisions.

Indeed, the number of occasions where a UN resolution justified intervention due to gross infringements of the rights of individuals in the target territories has remained limited.[6] The justification of intervention in Kosovo represented a break from the past in that it included a clear humanitarian element. Kosovo was arguably the first occasion in which international forces were used in defiance of a sovereign state in order to protect humanitarian standards.[7] The Iraq war in 2003 was questionably another case, although the legality of intervention under existing Security Council resolutions is contested, especially in view of the failure to obtain a second UN Security Council resolution to give an explicit mandate for the action (see Box 18.5). The US action against Afghanistan in 2001 is an exceptional case in which the UN Security Council acknowledged the right of a state which had been attacked—referring to the events of 11 September 2001 in the United States—to respond in its own defence.

It could be argued that earlier instances of intervention did not explicitly breach sovereignty. The 1991 Security Council resolution on Iraq did not

CWS

Box 18.4   Intervention and the responsibility to protect

In response to UN Secretary-General Kofi Annan's request to the international community to find a new consensus on issues of external military intervention for human protection purposes, the **International Commission on Intervention and State Sovereignty** was established by the Government of Canada in 2000. Its report, entitled *The Responsibility to Protect*, was presented to the Secretary-General in 2001. The central theme of the report is that sovereign states have a responsibility to protect their own citizens from avoidable catastrophe such as mass murder, rape, and starvation, but when they are unwilling or unable to do so, that responsibility must be borne by the broader community of states. Where a population is suffering serious harm and the state in question is unwilling or unable to halt it, the principle of non-intervention yields to the international responsibility to protect.

| Box 18.5 | Case study: the 2003 intervention in Iraq |

In March 2003, a US-led coalition launched a highly contro-versial war in Iraq, which removed Saddam Hussein from power. The justification for war stressed Iraq's possession of weapons of mass destruction, in defiance of earlier UN resolutions. Unlike in Kosovo, the gross violation of human rights was not given as a main justification for the invasion. One year after the war, the continued failure to find weapons of mass destruction in Iraq has fuelled the claims of critics that the war was unjustified.

There was no agreement over whether the UN Security Council authorized military action in Iraq. American and British diplomats pointed to UN Security Council Resolution 687 of 1991, which required the destruction of Iraqi weapons of mass destruction under UN supervision, and UN Security Council Resolution 1441 of 2002 which threatened 'serious consequences' if this were not done. Yet efforts to reach a Security Council resolution in the winter of 2003 that would clearly authorize the use of force against Iraq were

unsuccessful. France and Russia threatened to veto a second Security Council resolution authorizing force.

The credibility of the UN was damaged by the failure to agree on a second Security Council resolution, and by the decision of the US and British administrations, along with a small number of allies, to use force against Iraq without clear UN authorization. There are fears of an increased tendency for the USA to act without UN authorization. The Bush Administration's National Security Strategy of September 2002 states that '[W]e will be prepared to act apart when our interests and unique responsibilities require' (p. 31).

Nonetheless, the aftermath of the invasion and the dif-ficulties in establishing security in Iraq highlight the need for international cooperation. The UN enhances the legitimacy of military action, but it can also help share in global risks and burdens, such as stabilizing post-war Iraq and ensuring a reasonably smooth political transition.

breach Iraqi sovereignty in so far as its implementa-tion depended on Saddam Hussein's consent, which was given in a series of six-monthly agreements, known as a Memorandum of Understanding (Taylor and Groom 1992). Perhaps it can be better described as near-non-consensual intervention. The 1992 Security Council resolution that first sanctioned UN involvement in Somalia was based on a request by Somalia, even though the government of that coun-try had virtually collapsed. A later resolution for Somalia, which authorized the United States to dis-patch 30,000 troops to 'establish a secure environ-ment for Humanitarian Relief Operations in Somalia as soon as possible' did not mention the consent of Somali authorities, but by that time a central Somali Government did not exist.

The difficulty in relaxing the principle of non-intervention should not be underestimated. There is some fear of a slippery slope whereby a relaxation of the non-intervention principle by the UN will lead to military action by individual states without UN approval. It could be argued that the action against Iraq in 2003 illustrates the danger (see Box 18.5). Some newly independent states and some develop-ing countries have been suspicious of what appears to be the granting of a licence to Western developed states to intervene in their affairs.

In summary, an increasing readiness by the UN to intervene within states in order to pro-mote internal justice for individuals would indicate a movement towards global governance and away from unconditional sovereignty. There have been some signs of movement in this direction, but principles of state sovereignty and non-intervention remain important. There is no clear consensus on these points. There is still some sup-port for the view that Article 2(7) of the UN Charter should be interpreted strictly: that there can be no intervention within a state without the express con-sent of the government of that state. This position is probably most frequently seen in the arguments favoured by the government of the People's Republic of China. Others believe that intervention within a country to promote human rights is only justifiable on the basis of a threat to international peace and security. Evidence of a threat to international peace and security could be the appearance of sig-nificant numbers of refugees, or the judgement that other states might intervene militarily. Some Liberals argue that this condition is flexible enough to justify intervention to defend human rights whenever it seems prudent. There is also some support for a stronger position. In September 1999, UN Secretary-General Kofi Annan declared that

---

Development of the economic and social organizations

A/32/197, Dec. 1977. The first major General Assembly resolution on reform of the economic and social organizations.

A/48/162, Dec. 1993. A major step towards reform of the economic and social organization of the United Nations, especially the Economic and Social Council.

Development of the UN's role in maintaining international peace and security

SC Res. 678, Nov. 1990, sanctioned the use of force against Saddam Hussein.

SC Res. 743, Feb. 1992, established UNPROFOR in Croatia.

SC Res. 770, 13 Aug. 1992, created UNPROFOR2 in Bosnia-Hercegovina.

SC Res. 816, Apr. 1993, enforced the no-fly zone over Bosnia in that it permitted NATO war planes to intercept Bosnian Serb planes in the zones.

SC Res. 1160, 1199, and 1203, contained arguments relevant to the action on Kosovo. Resolution SC1244 contained the agreement at the end of the bombing.

Development of humanitarian action through the UN

SC Res. 688, Apr. 1991, sanctioned intervention in Iraq at the end of the Gulf War to protect the Kurds in north Iraq, and the Shia Muslims in the south, against the regime of Saddam Hussein.

SC Res. 733, Jan. 1992, first sanctioned UN involvement in Somalia. A/46/182, Apr. 1992, is the major document on the development of the machinery for humanitarian assistance.

SC Res. 794, Dec. 1992, sanctioned the American move into Somalia; by that stage the central government of Somalia had ceased to exist in the eyes of the member states of the Security Council which approved the resolution unanimously.

SC Res. 808, July 1993, set up an ad hoc war tribunal with regard to war crimes in the former Yugoslavia.

SC Res. 1441, Nov. 2002, the first resolution on Iraq which threatened serious consequences if Saddam Hussein failed to reveal his weapons of mass destruction to the team of UN inspectors.

Note: documents may be accessed via the Internet using the addresses indicated at the end of this chapter.

---

individual sovereignty may be as important as national sovereignty.

Overall then, the UN's record on the maintenance of international peace and security has been mixed. On the one hand, there have been positive changes since the end of the cold war. There has been a stronger assertion of the responsibility of international society, represented by the United Nations, for gross offences against populations. Nonetheless, the practice has been patchy. Intimations of a new world order in the aftermath of the Gulf War in 1991 quickly gave way to despondency with what were seen as failures in Somalia, Rwanda, other parts of Africa, and the former Yugoslavia, and increasing disagreement about the proper role of the UN in Kosovo and Iraq. Compared to the enthusiasm about the potential for the UN in the early 1990s, the debates and disagreements at the time of the war in Iraq in 2003 were striking.

Key points

- New justifications for intervention in states were being considered by the 1990s, but no consensus has been reached.

- Nonetheless, most operations of the United Nations were justified in the traditional way: as a response to a threat to international peace and security.

- Any relaxation of the traditional principle of non-intervention had to be treated very cautiously, and new methods of approval in the UN could be advisable.

The United Nations and economic and social questions

As described above, there has been an increased perception that issues of peace and security encompass traditional threats such as aggression between states, civil conflict within states, as well as economic and social conditions within states. There is the recognition that conditions within states, including human rights, justice, development, and equality have a bearing on global peace. The more integrated global context has meant that economic and social problems in one part of the world may have an impact on other areas.

The number of institutions within the UN system that address economic and social issues has significantly increased since the founding of the UN. Nonetheless, the main contributor states have been giving less and less to economic and social institutions, mostly well below the 0.7 per cent of Gross Domestic Product (GDP) that had been promised as part of the UN's Development Decade's agenda. By the mid-1990s, there was a crippling financial crisis in the regular Assessed Budget for the UN, and in the budget for peacekeeping operations. This was only mitigated when the USA agreed, under certain

conditions, to repay what it owed the UN and when it returned to full funding in December 2002.

Paradoxically, despite the shortage of funds, the changes in the economic and social machinery of the United Nations have been promising, and the UN's roles in economic and social areas have been largely positive. The UN has acquired skills and resources with regard to key economic and social problems, such as rebuilding failed states, supporting democratization, promoting human development, and addressing HIV/AIDS, poverty, and disease. These skills have made the UN an indispensable resource.

The United Nations family of economic and social organizations has always been a polycentric system. Historically there was no organization or agent within the system that was capable of defining a coherent overall agenda or coordinating and managing the wide range of economic and social activities under the UN umbrella. The Specialized Agencies, such as the Food and Agriculture Organization (FAO) or the International Labour Organization (ILO), were constitutionally independent of each

---

Box 18.7   **The UN Conference on Environment and Development: the Earth Summit**

The UN Conference on Environment and Development (Earth Summit) held in 1992 in **Rio de Janeiro** was unprecedented for a UN conference in both its size and its scope of concerns. Representatives of 172 countries, including 108 heads of state, as well as 2,400 NGO representatives, joined together to look for ways to help reach the goal of sustainable development.

The Rio Earth Summit was held 20 years after the first UN Conference on the Human Environment in Stockholm. That 1972 Conference had stimulated the creation of environmental ministries around the world, and established the United Nations Environment Programme (UNEP).

The central concern of the Rio Earth Summit was the need for broad-based, environmentally sustainable development. As a result of the Summit, 108 governments adopted three major agreements concerned with changing the traditional approach to development. These agreements included: the

Rio Declaration on Environment and Development (a series of principles defining the rights and responsibilities of states), the Statement of Forest Principles, and **Agenda 21** (a comprehensive programme of action to attain sustainable development on a global scale). In addition, the UN Framework Convention on Climate Change and the Convention on Biological Diversity were signed by many governments.

The **UN Commission on Sustainable Development** was formed after the 1992 Earth Summit to ensure follow-up and to report on the implementation of Earth Summit agreements at the local, national, regional, and international levels. A five-year review of Earth Summit progress took place in New York in 1997 and a ten-year review at the **World Summit on Sustainable Development** held in Johannesburg in 2002. The Johannesburg Summit did not aim to renegotiate Agenda 21, but it did address some of the gaps that have impeded its full implementation.

other and from the centre, and were only obliged to report to the Economic and Social Council (ECOSOC). There was no central institution with legal authority over them. The Administrative Committee on Coordination (ACC), which has now changed its name to the **United Nations System Chief Executives Board for Coordination** (CEB), was established in 1946 at the request of ECOSOC. It was intended to function as the main coordinating mechanism, but generally failed. Its members, the heads of the Specialized Agencies, used the ACC to defend their territories rather than to agree on management and coordination issues.

Over the past decade, a number of new issues were brought on to the international agenda and these were reflected in the economic and social organizations. Several **Global Conferences** were convened to discuss pressing problems, such as environmental issues at a conference in Rio de Janeiro (1992), human rights at a conference in Vienna (1993), population questions at a conference in Cairo (1994), and women's issues at a conference in Beijing (1995). Follow-up conferences on the same theme were planned ten years later to take stock of progress.

These conferences each spawned a Commission (discussed below) to carry forward the programme. Such conferences represented a growing sense of the **interdependence** of the globe, and the globalization of human concerns. They stimulated a renewed interest in translating broad concerns into more specific and more manageable programmes. (See Box 18.7.)

Key points

- The number of institutions within the UN system that address economic and social issues has significantly increased. Several Programmes and Funds were created in response to Global Conferences.

- Coordination between the various economic and social organizations has been problematic.

- Despite a shortage of funds and coordination problems, the UN has done important work in key economic and social areas.

The reform process in the economic and social arrangements of the United Nations

In the mid- to late 1990s, a reform of the UN's economic and social arrangements took place at two levels: first, reforms concerned with operations in the country (field) level; and second, reforms at the general or headquarters level, especially with respect to the role of the Economic and Social Council (ECOSOC).

Country level

A key feature of the reforms at the country (field) level was the adoption of Country Strategy Notes. These were statements about the overall development process tailored to the specific needs of individual countries. They were written on the basis of

discussions between the Specialized Agencies, Programmes and Funds, donors, and the host country, and were described as a 'tour de table' of all the plans of the various institutions and donors in a particular country.[8] The merit of the Country Strategy Notes is that they clearly set out targets, roles, and priorities.

Another reform at the country level was the strengthening of the Resident Coordinator. The Resident Coordinator, usually an employee of the United Nations Development Programme (UNDP), became the responsible officer at the country level, and was provided with more training to fulfil this role.

This reflected attempts to professionalize the way in which economic and social programmes were provided. It was recognized that in the past, UNDP officers had not always been good performers. The continuing complaints of NGOs about poor UN performance in the field served as a powerful stimulus for reform. The conclusion was that it was necessary to have a central coordinating figure at the field level, as well as agreement and monitoring of standards of performance. For instance, field-level officers were given enhanced authority, so that they could make decisions about the redeployment of funds within a programme without referring to headquarters. There was also an effort to introduce improved communication facilities and information sharing. Furthermore, the activities of the various UN organizations were brought together in single locations or 'UN houses', which brought officers together on a daily basis and facilitated inter-agency communication and collegiality. The new country-level approach was called an Integrated Programmes approach. It can be contrasted to earlier arrangements whereby the various agencies would work separately on distinct projects, often in ignorance of each other's presence in the same country.

Headquarters level

If the UN role in economic and social affairs at the country level was to be effective, reform was also required at the general or headquarters level. Reform efforts in the 1990s focused on the reorganization and rationalization of the work of the Economic and Social Council (ECOSOC).

One of ECOSOC's responsibilities was to review common themes in the work of the nine Functional Commissions (see Fig. 18.1). Examples of Functional Commissions include the Commission on Human

---

Box 18.8 | **Key concepts**

Human security: the security of people including their physical safety, their economic and social well-being, respect for their dignity, and the protection of their human rights.

Intergovernmental organization: an organization in which full legal membership is officially solely open to states and decisionmaking authority lies with government representatives.

International non-governmental organizations (INGOs): cross-national organizations in which membership is made up of non-state actors.

Intervention: when there is direct involvement within a state by an outside actor to achieve an outcome preferred by the intervening agency without the consent of the host state.

Involvement: when an outsider, such as an international organization, acts within a state with or without the consent of that state.

Justice: fair or morally defensible treatment for individuals, in the light of human rights standards or standards of economic or social well-being.

Order: when relationships between actors, such as states, are stable, predictable, controlled, and not characterized by violence, turbulence, or chaos. Justice may or may not be present.

Programmes and Funds: institutions which are subject to the supervision of the General Assembly and which depend upon voluntary funding by states and other donors.

Recognition: the act, at present carried out by governments individually and separately, of acknowledging the status of another entity as a legal person, thus granting it a licence to act in international society, and to enter into contracts with its members. At present recognition is symbolized by establishing diplomatic relations, exchanging ambassadors, and accepting the other's membership in the United Nations.

Sovereignty: a condition necessary for states in that they are not subject to any higher authority. The government of a sovereign state is ultimately responsible for its citizens. In practice sovereignty has often been conditional. Internally governments have been subject to conventional standards, and externally conditions may mean that governments are more or less free to act independently. A sovereign government is free to choose within the framework of these conventions and standards.

Specialized Agencies: international institutions which have a special relationship with the central system of the United Nations but which are constitutionally independent, having their own assessed budgets, executive heads and committees, and assemblies of the representatives of all state members.

Rights, the Commission on Narcotic Drugs, the Commission on Sustainable Development, and the Commission on the Status of Women.[9] Previously, there had been significant duplication and overlap in the work of the Functional Commissions, and the reform effort aimed to eliminate this duplication. ECOSOC would integrate the work of its Functional Commissions and provide input to the General Assembly, which was responsible for considering and establishing the broader economic and social policy framework.

In the UN Charter, the powers given to the General Assembly and ECOSOC were modest. According to the Charter, the General Assembly and ECOSOC could only issue recommendations and receive reports. By contrast, UN reform in the mid-1990s allowed ECOSOC to become more assertive and to take a leading role in the coordination of the UN system. ECOSOC was to ensure that General Assembly policies were appropriately implemented on a system-wide basis. ECOSOC was also given the power to fully implement its authority to take final decisions on the activities of its subsidiary bodies and on other matters relating to its system-wide coordination in economic, social, and related fields (A/50/227, para. 37).

The Boards of the Programmes and Funds were also reformed to enhance their day-to-day management. These developments followed from Secretary-General Kofi Annan's 1997 Report in which he promised to thin the UN administration, eliminate up to a thousand jobs, and put the savings towards development programmes.

Overall, economic and social reorganization meant that the two poles of the system were better coordinated: the pole where intentions are defined through global conferences and agendas, and the pole where programmes are implemented. Programmes at the field level were better integrated and field officers were given enhanced discretion. At the other end, Global Conferences encouraged greater agreement about what needed to be done. These agreements fed into Functional Commissions, and the reform of ECOSOC sharpened its capacity to shape these broad agreements into cross-sectoral programmes with well-defined objectives. At the same time, ECOSOC acquired greater capacity to act as a conduit through which the results of field-level monitoring could be conveyed upwards to the Functional Commissions. These new processes had the effect of strengthening the norms of a multilateral system.

Key points

- In the mid- to late 1990s under the leadership of Secretary-General Kofi Annan, the UN embarked on an overarching reform effort.

- Reform of the economic and social arrangements of the UN aimed at improving coordination, eliminating duplication, and clarifying spheres of responsibility.

- These efforts strengthened the norms of the multilateral system.

Conclusion

Changes in the role of the UN reflect the changes in perceptions of international society and the nature of sovereign states. Over the previous half century, the rules governing the international system have become increasingly numerous and specific, covering a large range of the activities of relations between states. Concerns have expanded to include not only the protection of the rights of states, but also the rights of individuals. Yet obtaining the agreement of governments to principles of individual rights is only a first step in building a more orderly and just world. It was also necessary to have instruments to trigger action when standards were breached. The instruments had to be consistent, impartial, and reliable.

The United Nations Security Council is the instrument that comes closest to meeting these aims. Despite the flaws of the Security Council, it is striking that even the largest states prefer to get authorization from the United Nations Security Council for any action they propose. In Kosovo, the states that participated in the NATO intervention wanted to demonstrate that they were acting according to the UN Charter and the relevant Security Council resolutions. In Iraq, the US and UK governments invested considerable diplomatic energy in getting a second Security Council resolution in support of military action. The effort failed, but nevertheless it was attempted. It remains to be seen whether the USA will persist with its declared policy of acting unilaterally, regardless of the view of the UN, when it believes that its interests are threatened.

Participation in the United Nations gives governments status in the international system. Membership and success in the UN has come to be regarded as legitimizing state autonomy. Hence office holding, initiative taking, providing personnel, and norm policing are seen to have value because they add to the self-esteem as well as to power of the state. The UN has become the essential club for states.

The capacity of the UN in its economic and social work, its development work, and its management of peacekeeping and post-conflict reconstruction has expanded and improved since the early 1990s. Nonetheless, the predominance of United States military power, the possibility that the USA will act again without clear UN authorization, the heightened concern over terrorism and weapons of mass destruction, and the pervasiveness of inequality and injustice across the world, signal that further changes and adaptations within the UN system will be necessary.

For further information and case studies on this subject, please visit the companion web site at www.oup.com/uk/booksites/politics.

QUESTIONS

1   How does the United Nations try to maintain international order?

2   Why have more states decided to support the work of the United Nations?

3   What are some of the barriers to UN Security Council reform?

4   How far have traditional restraints with regard to intervention within states been relaxed?

5   How have definitions of threats to peace and security changed in the post-cold war period?

6   How has UN peacekeeping evolved?

7   What problems prevent UN organizations from carrying out their roles more effectively?

8   Does increased UN activity undermine the sovereignty of states?

9   Why was there greater opposition to developing the international accountability of states during the cold war?

10   What lessons about the present role and future of the UN might be drawn from the experience of the war in Iraq?

GUIDE TO FURTHER READING

Archer, Clive (1992), *International Organisations*, 2nd edn (London: Routledge). A useful, succinct survey of the range of international institutions in terms of their main purpose and nature.

Claude, Inis L. Jr. (1971, 1984), *Swords into Plowshares: The Progress and Problems of International Organization*, 4th edn (New York: Random House). A classic text on the history of international institutions. Covers all the major themes, but particularly concerned with their role in war and peace. Useful for the history of the UN.

Dodds, Felix (ed.) (1997), *The Way Forward: Beyond Agenda 21* (London: Earthscan). An account of the involvement of the United Nations system in the issues raised in the Functional Commissions, such as social development, the status of women, and environmental protection.

Malone, David (ed.) (2004), *The UN Security Council: From the Cold War to the 21st Century* (Boulder, Col.: Lynne Rienner). Discusses the history of the UN Security Council and major UN operations.

Mayall, James (ed.) (1996), *The New Interventionism 1991–1994* (Cambridge: Cambridge University Press). A useful analysis of UN intervention in Cambodia, former Yugoslavia, and Somalia.

Roberts, Adam, and Kingsbury, Benedict (eds) (1993), *United Nations, Divided World: The UN's Roles in International Relations*, 2nd edn (Oxford: Clarendon Press). An important collection of readings by practitioners and academics.

Taylor, Paul, and Groom, A. J. R. (eds) (2000), *The United Nations at the Millennium* (London: Continuum). A detailed account of the institutions of the central United Nations system with chapters on the General Assembly, the Security Council, the Economic and Social Council, and others.

White, Nigel D. (1997), *Keeping the Peace: the UN and the Maintenance of International Peace and Security*, 2nd edn (Manchester: Manchester University Press). A useful account of the problems and achievements of the UN with regard to peacekeeping.

WEB LINKS

www.un.org The main UN web site.

www.unsystem.org For all parts of the UN system including all Agencies, Funds, and Programmes.

www.globalpolicy.org Global Policy Forum.

www.isn.ethz.ch International Relations and Security Network.

www.dfait-maeci.gc.ca/iciss-ciise/report-en.asp *The Responsibility to Protect*: Report of the International Commission on Intervention and State Sovereignty

www.whitehouse.gov/nsc/nss.pdf National Security Strategy of the United States of America.

NOTES

1. The convention emerged that abstention by a permanent member is not regarded as a veto.

2. For an interpretation of functionalism see Claude (1984).

3. After the terrorist attacks of 11 September 2001 on the United States, the Security Council established a UN counter-terrorism committee (CTC) in October 2001 (Resolution 1373).

4. See the excellent collection of essays on intervention in Lyons and Mastanduno (1995).

5. See Development Studies Association, evidence to the Foreign Affairs Select Committee of the House of Commons, entitled, 'The United Nations Humanitarian Response', Nov. 1992.

6. Well-known interventions, such as that of India in East Pakistan in 1971, Tanzania in the Uganda of Idi Amin, or of the United States in Panama, were justified by referring to the need to protect the citizens of the invading states, and their right of self-defence

7. NATO launched the air campaign in March 1999 in Kosovo against the Republic of Yugoslavia without a mandate from the Security Council, since Russia had declared that it would veto such action. Nonetheless, NATO states noted that by intervening to stop ethnic cleansing and crimes against humanity in Kosovo, they were acting in accordance with the principles of the UN Charter.

8. By an official, Danish mission to the UN, Sept. 1996.

9. Commissions were first created in the 1940s. Later, they were explicitly attached to the UN Global Conferences and their numbers increased.

CHAPTER 19

Transnational actors and international organizations in global politics

PETER WILLETTS

READER'S GUIDE

The subject of International Relations originally covered simply the relations between states. Economic bodies and social groups, such as banks, industrial companies, students, environmentalists, and women's organizations, were given secondary status as non-state actors. This two-tier approach has been challenged, particularly by the effects of globalization. First, ambiguities in the meaning given to 'a state', and its mismatch with the contemporary world, result in it not being a useful concept. Greater clarity is obtained by analysing intergovernmental and inter-society relations, with no presumption that one sector is more important than the other. Second, we can recognize governments are losing sovereignty when faced with the economic activities of transnational companies and the violent threat from criminals, terrorists, and guerrillas. Third, non-governmental organizations (NGOs) engage in such a web of global relations, including participation in diplomacy, that governments have lost their political independence. We conclude that events in any area of global policymaking have to be understood in terms of complex systems, containing governments, companies, and NGOs interacting in a variety of international organizations.

Introduction

In diplomacy, international law, journalism, and academic analysis, it is widely assumed that international relations consists of the relations between coherent units called states. This chapter will argue that better understanding of political change is obtained by analysing the relations between governments and many other actors from each country. Global politics also includes companies and non-governmental organizations. Thus the five main categories of political actors in the global system are:

1. nearly 200 governments, including 191 members of the UN;

2. 64,000 major transnational companies (TNCs), such as Shell, Microsoft, or Nestlé, with these

---

Box 19.1   Key concepts

Realism: the theoretical approach that analyses all international relations as the relations of states engaged in the pursuit of power. Realism cannot accommodate non-state actors within its analysis.

Neo-realism: modification of the Realist approach, which recognizes that economic resources—in addition to military capabilities—are a basis for exercising influence. Also, the concept of a single international system is abandoned in favour of analysing issue-specific systems, each characterized by their own power structure. Thus Saudi Arabia may be the most powerful state in the politics of oil, while Brazil is the most powerful in the politics of rainforests.

Pluralism: the theoretical approach that considers all organized groups as being potential political actors and analyses the processes by which actors mobilize support to achieve policy goals. Pluralists can accept that transnational actors and international organizations may influence governments. Elsewhere in this book, the approach is equated with Liberalism. This chapter adopts the term Pluralism and rejects any link to Liberalism, because the author denies that theory necessarily has a normative component and because writers who call themselves Liberals are still highly state-centric.

State: the one word is used to refer to three distinct concepts:

1. In international law, a **state** is an entity that is recognized to exist when a government is in control of a community of people within a defined territory. It is comparable to the idea in domestic law of a company being a legal person.
2. In the study of international politics, each state is a **country**. It is a community of people who interact in the same political system and who have some common values.

3. In philosophy and sociology, the state consists of the apparatus of **government**, in its broadest sense, covering the executive, the legislature, the administration, the judiciary, the armed forces, and the police.

Sovereignty: the condition of a state being free from any higher legal authority. It is related to, but distinct from, the condition of a government being free from any external political constraints.

Non-state actor: a term widely used to mean any actor that is not a government. Often it is not clear whether the term is being used to cover bodies such as the United Nations Ambiguity is best avoided by referring separately to two categories, transnational actors and international organizations.

Nation: a group of people who recognize each other as sharing a common identity, with a focus on homeland.

Nation-state: would exist if nearly all the members of single nation were organized in a single state, without any other national communities being present. Although the term is widely used, no such entities exist.

Civil society: (1) the totality of all individuals and groups in society who are not acting as participants in any government institutions, or (2) all individuals and groups who are neither participants in government nor acting in the interests of commercial companies. The two meanings are incompatible and contested. The first meaning is used in this chapter, because it is not possible to draw a clear line between the non-profit and the for-profit sectors.

Transnational actor: any civil society actor from one country that has relations with any actor from another country or with an international organization.

parent companies having just over 866,000 foreign affiliates;

3. 9,000 single-country non-governmental organizations (NGOs), such as Population Concern (UK) or the Sierra Club (USA), which have significant international activities;

4. 240 intergovernmental organizations (IGOs), such as the UN, NATO, the European Union, or the International Coffee Organization; and

5. 6,600 international non-governmental organizations (INGOs), such as Amnesty International, the Baptist World Alliance, or the International Chamber of Shipping, plus a similar number of less well-established international caucuses and networks of NGOs.

All these actors play a regular part in global politics and each government interacts with a diverse range of non-state actors. Sometimes guerrilla groups challenge the authority of particular governments. In addition, even though they are considered not to be legitimate participants in the system, terrorists and other criminal gangs have an impact, often minor, but sometimes in a major way. Very many more companies and NGOs only operate in a single country, but have the potential to expand into other countries.[1]

Nobody can deny the number of these organizations and the range of their activities. The controversial questions are whether the non-state world has significance in its own right and whether it makes any difference to the analysis of inter-state relations. It is possible to *define* international relations as covering the relations between states. This is known as the state-centric approach, or **Realism**. Then it is only a tautology (true by definition) to say that non-state actors are of secondary importance. A more open-ended approach, known as **Pluralism**, is based on the assumption that all types of actors can affect political outcomes. The very words, non-state actors, imply that states are dominant and other actors are secondary. An alternative word, **transnational**, has been coined by academics in order to assert forcefully that international relations are not limited to governments and other actors operate across country boundaries.

It is an unacceptable analytical bias to decide, before research starts, that only states have any influence. Until the evidence indicates otherwise, we must assume that governments and NGOs interact with each other, along with companies and international organizations. Who actually determines outcomes will vary from issue to issue. This chapter will first consider how assumptions made about 'states' inhibit analysis of transnational actors and international organizations. Then the nature of the different types of actors will be outlined. Finally, the case will be argued for always considering the activities of a diverse range of political actors.

Problems with the state-centric approach

The great advantage of the state-centric approach is that the bewildering complexity of world politics is reduced to the relative simplicity of the interactions of less than two hundred supposedly similar units. However, there are *four* major problems that suggest the benefits of simplification have been gained at the cost of the picture being distorted and blurred.

Ambiguity between different meanings of a 'state'

Writers who refer to the state often fail to use the term consistently and lack intellectual rigour by merging three concepts. The **state** as a legal person is a highly abstract fiction. This is easily confused with the concrete concept of a **country**, with a distinct political system of people sharing common values. Then there is a very dissimilar concept of a state as the apparatus of **government**. Unfortunately, no standard method exists to handle the ambiguity. From now on, this chapter will use the word, state, to indicate the abstract legal concept, while country and government will be used to analyse political behaviour. Conventional ambiguous usage will be indicated by inverted commas.

With the legal and political-community concepts, *civil society is part of the state*, whereas for philosophers and sociologists, focusing on the state as government, *civil society is separate from the state*. Thus, in international law or when the state means the whole country, there is very little room to acknowledge the existence of distinct transnational actors. Alternatively, when the state means the government and does not encompass civil society, we can investigate both intergovernmental relations and the inter-society relations of transnational actors.

The lack of similarity between countries

The second problem is that giving all 'states' the same legal status implies they are all essentially the same type of unit, when in fact they are not remotely similar. Orthodox analysis does acknowledge differences in size between 'the superpowers' and middle and small 'powers'. Nevertheless this does not suggest that at the end of the cold war the United State economy was twice the size of the Soviet Union's economy, nor that at the start of this century the US economy was eight times China's, 64 times Saudi Arabia's, more than 1,400 times Ethiopia's, and over 100,000 times greater than Kiribati's. In terms of population, the divergences are even greater. The small island countries of the Caribbean and the Pacific with populations measured in tens of thousands are not comparable entities to ordinary small countries, let alone China or India: they are truly 'micro-states'. Alternatively, comparing the governments of the world reveals a diverse range of democracies, feudal regimes, ethnic oligarchies, economic oligarchies, populist regimes, theocracies, military dictatorships, and idiosyncratic combinations. The only thing that the countries have in common is the general recognition of their right to have their own government. They are legally equal and politically very different.

The consequence of admitting the differences in size is to make it obvious that the largest transnational actors are considerably larger than many of the countries. The 50 largest transnational industrial companies each have an annual sales revenue greater than the GNP of 142 members of the United Nations. Using people as the measure, many NGOs, particularly trade unions, churches, and campaigning groups in the fields of human rights, women's rights, and the environment, have their membership measured in millions, whereas 40 of the 191 countries in the UN have populations of less than one million.[2] There is also great variation in the complexity and diversity of the economies and the societies of different countries and hence the extent to which they are each involved in transnational relations.

State systems and international systems

Third, there is an underlying analytical inconsistency in supposing 'states' are located in an anarchical international system. Whether it means legal entity, a country, or a government, the 'state' is seen as a coherent unit, acting with common purpose and existing as something more than the sum of its parts (the individual people). At the same time, most advocates of the state-centric approach deny the possibility of such collective entities existing at the global level. The phrase, 'the international system', is denied its full technical meaning of a collectivity in which the component elements (the individual 'states') lose some of their independence. No philosophical argument has been put forward to explain this inconsistency in the assumptions made about the different levels of analysis. By exaggerating the coherence of 'states' and downplaying the coherence of global politics, both transnational relations and intergovernmental relations are underestimated.

The difference between state and nation

Fourth, there is a behavioural assumption that politics within 'states' is significantly different from politics between 'states'. This is based on the idea that people's loyalty to their nation is more intense than other loyalties. Clearly, it cannot be denied that nationalism and national identity invoke powerful emotions for most people, but various caveats must be made about their political relevance. Communal identities form a hierarchy from the local through the nation to wider groupings. Thus, both local communities and intergovernmental bodies, such as the European Community, can also make claims on a person's loyalty.

There has been a long-standing linguistic conjuring trick whereby national loyalty is made to appear as if it is focused on the 'nation-state'. Both inter*national* relations and trans*national* relations cover relations across 'state' boundaries, although logically the words refer to relations between national groups, such as the Scots and the Welsh. In the real world, only a few countries, such as Iceland, Poland, and Japan, can make a reasonable claim that their people are from a single nation and in all such cases there are significant numbers of the national group resident in other countries, often in the USA. Most countries are multinational and many national groups are present in several countries. Thus national loyalty is actually quite different from loyalty to a country.

> ### Key points
>
> - The concept of the 'state' has three very different meanings: a legal person, a political community and a government.
>
> - The countries and governments around the world may be equal in law, but have few political similarities. Many governments control less resources than many transnational actors.
>
> - It cannot be assumed that all country-based political systems are more coherent than global systems, particularly as national loyalties do not match country boundaries.
>
> - By abandoning the language of 'states' and 'non-state' actors, we can admit the possibility of theorizing about many types of actors in global politics. By distinguishing government from society and nation from country, we can ask whether private groups, companies, and national minorities in each country engage in transnational relations.

Transnational companies as political actors

All companies that import or export are engaging in transnational economic activities and, if they lobby foreign governments about trade, they may become transnational political actors. However, they are not known as transnational companies (TNCs) until they have branches or subsidiaries outside their home country. The first companies to expand in this way were in agriculture, mining, or oil, operating in European colonies. From the 1960s there has been a massive expansion, with the other major industrial manufacturers establishing overseas subsidiaries. Banking also moved into the empires, and then from the 1970s onwards most of the service industries set up new operations around the world or formed global structures by mergers and acquisitions. Now transnational companies can be expected to operate in any major economic sector,

except for products that are specific to particular cultures.

The geographical spread has also widened, so industrialized countries that never had empires, such as Sweden and Canada, and many of the developing countries, have seen some of their companies expand transnationally. In 2001, among the 100 TNCs with the highest levels of assets outside their home country, 55 were from nine Western European countries, 28 from the USA, 8 from Japan, 3 from Canada, 2 from Australia, and one each from Mexico, Singapore, Hong Kong, and South Korea. While only developed countries, South-East Asia, a few Latin American countries, and South Africa host large TNCs, there are now transnational companies based in as many as 73 countries—51 of them being developing countries, including 21 African countries.[3]

Box 19.2 | **Key concepts**

Transnational company (TNC): a company that has affiliates in a foreign country. The affiliates may be branches of the parent company, separately incorporated subsidiaries, or associates, with large minority shareholdings.

Intra-firm trade: international trade from one branch of TNC to an affiliate of the same company in a different country.

Transfer price: the price set by a TNC for intra-firm trade of goods or services. For accounting purposes, a price must be set for exports, but it need not be related to any market price.

Triangulation: occurs when trade between two countries is routed indirectly via a third country. For example, in the early 1980s, neither the Argentine Government nor the British Government permitted trade between the two countries, but companies simply sent their exports via Brazil or Western Europe.

Regulatory arbitrage: in the world of banking, the process of moving funds or business activity from one country to another, in order to increase profits by escaping the constraints imposed by government regulations. By analogy the term can be applied to any transfer of economic activity by any company in response to government policy.

Extraterritoriality: occurs when one government attempts to exercise its legal authority in the territory of another state. It mainly arises when the US federal government deliberately tries to use domestic law to control the global activities of TNCs.

Financial flows and loss of sovereignty

The consequences of the extensive transnationalization of major companies are profound. It is no longer possible to regard each country as having its own separate economy. Two of the most fundamental attributes of sovereignty, control over the currency and control over foreign trade, have been substantially diminished. The two factors combined mean governments have lost control of financial flows. In the case of the currency, the successive crises in the 1980s and the 1990s for the dollar, the pound, the French franc, and the yen established that even the governments with the greatest financial resources are helpless against the transnational banks and other speculators.

The effects of trade on finance are less obvious. When goods move physically across frontiers, it is usually seen as being trade between the relevant countries, but it may also be intra-firm trade. As the logic of intra-firm trade is quite different from inter-country trade, governments cannot have clear expectations of the effects of their financial and fiscal policies on TNCs. A company may respond to higher tax rates by changing its transfer prices to reduce its tax bill. Several other motives might induce a company to distort transfer prices, including evasion of controls on the cross-border movements of profits or capital.

Box 19.3 | **Transfer pricing for intra-firm trade**

A very simple model illustrates how international intra-firm trade can be used to evade taxation. Consider a company in an industrialized country exporting semi-finished goods to a developing country, where they are finished and sold. Imagine that the government of the industrial country decides to reduce public expenditure and cut taxes, while the other government increases taxes to fund development.

The transfer price can be used by the company to determine the level of profits for each branch. By increasing the transfer price and declaring more of its profits in the low-tax industrial country, the company can avoid its global tax bill increasing. Then each government would find the effect on tax revenue is the opposite of its intentions.

TNCs may succeed in using artificial transfer prices either because the government does not know what a proper price would be or because the company fraudulently reports the volume or the quality of the goods.

Triangulation of trade and loss of sovereignty

Governments have great difficulty regulating international transactions. If one government is antagonistic to another and wishes to impose a trade boycott, it is totally impossible for the government on its own to prevent movement of information or people for business purposes. Even the US administration was unable to prevent its citizens visiting communist Cuba during the cold war. It may be possible to prevent the *direct* import or export of goods. However, there is no guaranteed method of preventing *indirect* trade from one country to another. This is known as **triangulation**. Only if a UN Security Council resolution obliges all the countries of the world to impose sanctions is there a reasonable prospect of a determined government preventing TNCs from evading sanctions. However, in such a situation sovereignty over the relevant trade then lies with the Security Council and not with the individual governments.

Regulatory arbitrage and loss of sovereignty

It is difficult for governments to regulate the commercial activities of companies within their country, because companies may choose to engage in **regulatory arbitrage**. If a company objects to one government's policy, it may threaten to limit or close down its local production and increase production in another country. The government that imposes the least demanding health, safety, welfare, or environmental standards will offer competitive advantages to less socially responsible companies. There is also a strong global trend towards the reduction of corporation taxes. It thus becomes difficult for any gov-

ernment to set high standards and maintain taxes. In the case of banking, the political dangers inherent in the risks of a bank collapsing through imprudent or criminal behaviour are so great that the major governments have set common capital standards. Under the Basle Committee **rules** all commercial banks must protect their viability by having capital to the value of 8 per cent of their outstanding loans. Whatever control is achieved does not represent the successful exercise of sovereignty over companies: it is the partial surrender of sovereignty to an intergovernmental body.

Extraterritoriality and sovereignty

In addition transnational companies generate clashes of sovereignty between different governments. Let us consider the example of a company that has its headquarters in the United States and a subsidiary company that it owns in the United Kingdom. Three lines of authority exist. The United States Government can control the main company and the United Kingdom Government can control the subsidiary. Each process would be the standard exercise of a government's sovereignty over its internal affairs. In addition, both governments would accept that the TNC can, within certain limits, control its own policies on purchasing, production, and sales. Under normal circumstances these three lines of authority can be exercised simultaneously and in harmony. However, when the US Government decisions cover the global operations of

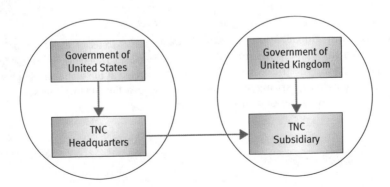

Fig. 19.1 Who controls the United Kingdom subsidiary of a United States TNC?

the TNC, there can be a clash of sovereignty. Does the subsidiary obey the UK Government or the orders of the US Government issued via its headquarters? This problem of **extraterritoriality** is inherent in the structure of all TNCs.

As a matter of routine policy implementation, clashes now have to be resolved between different decisions in different jurisdictions on competition policy, mergers and acquisitions, accounting procedures, and anti-corruption measures. Will the US Government or the European Community have the greater impact on what is included within Microsoft Windows software? Can the European Commission prevent one US company, Honeywell, taking control over another US company, General Electric, if this will result in their domination of the market for aircraft engines in Europe? Will US accounting standards apply to European companies, because some of their operations are in the USA? Can the directors of parent TNCs be prosecuted for the payment of bribes by their overseas branches? The long-term trend is for such questions to be resolved by global standardization of domestic policy.

From domestic deregulation to global re-regulation

For most companies most of the time, their interests in expanding their production, increasing their market share, and maximizing their profits will be in accord with the government's policy of increasing employment and promoting economic growth. Conflicts will arise over the regulation of markets to avoid the risks of **market failures** or externalization of social and environmental costs of production. Domestic **deregulation** and globalization of economic activity has moved these questions from the domestic agendas of each country to the global political agenda. As there were many strong political pressures that led to regulation in the past, it is not surprising that reactions against deregulation are growing. However, re-regulation (governments again seeking to control markets) is now occurring at the global level rather than within individual countries. The examples of the International Baby Foods Action Network (IBFAN), the World Rainforest Movement, and the Pesticides Action Network (PAN) indicate how the reaction against irresponsible behaviour by TNCs is often focused on the United Nations and its agencies. Three factors involving TNCs push towards the globalization of politics. First, governments can only reassert control by acting collectively. Second, consumer pressures are leading to global codes of conduct being accepted by companies and implemented in **collaboration** with NGOs. A third push is for global companies to submit to social and environmental auditing.

Key points

- The ability of TNCs to change transfer prices means that they can evade taxation or government controls on their international financial transactions.

- The ability of TNCs to use triangulation means individual governments cannot control their country's international trade.

- The ability of TNCs to move production from one country to another means individual governments are constrained in regulating and taxing companies.

- The structure of authority over TNCs generates the potential for intense conflict between governments, when the legal authority of one government has extraterritorial impact on the sovereignty of another government.

- In some areas of economic policy, governments have lost sovereignty and regulation now has to be exercised at the global level rather than by governments acting independently.

Non-legitimate groups and liberation movements as political actors

A variety of groups engage in violent and/or criminal behaviour on a transnational basis. A distinction can be made between activity that is considered criminal around the world, such as theft, fraud, personal violence, piracy, or drug-trafficking, and activity that is claimed by those undertaking it to have legitimate political motives. In reality, the distinction may sometimes be blurred, when criminals claim political motives or political groups are responsible for acts such as **terrorism**, torture, or involving children in violence. For all governments neither criminal activity nor political violence can be legitimate within their own jurisdiction and generally not in other countries.

Transnational criminals and their political impact

Politically, the most important criminal industries are illicit trading in arms and illicit trading in drugs. They have been estimated to be the two most valuable commodities in international trade. As travel has increased so much, trafficking in people has become easier and increased significantly in recent years. There is virtually a new slave trade, mainly for sexual exploitation of young women. Trade in stolen goods generally is limited to high-value, easily transported goods, such as diamonds. In addition, theft of intellectual property, particularly of music, video films, and computer software, and trade in counterfeit goods, are organized on a very large scale.

The same four sovereignty problems arise with tackling criminals as with regulating TNCs. **First**, criminal financial flows can be massive and money-laundering threatens the integrity of banking and other financial **institutions**. **Second**, criminal trade has been so extensively diversified through triangulation that no government could confidently claim that its country is not a transit route for drugs or arms. **Third**, as with regulatory arbitrage by TNCs, police action may displace well-organized gangs to another country, rather than stop their activities. **Fourth**, illicit drugs, money-laundering, and terror-

ism involve questions of extraterritorial jurisdiction. However, in contrast to the regulation of TNCs, transnational police activities achieve **cooperation** that would be unthinkable in other fields. As with TNCs, the global financial system, displacement, triangulation, and extraterritoriality, each limit the effective exercise of sovereignty over criminals. The difference is that in some fields, where the threat is felt to be most severe, there have been strenuous efforts to re-establish control by surrender of sovereignty through international agreement.

Terrorists, guerrillas, and national liberation movements

Political violence has been adopted by a variety of different groups. Violence is most common when broadly based nationalist movements or ethnic minorities reject the legitimacy of a government. These groups are often called **terrorists** to express disapproval, **guerrillas** by those who are more neutral, or **national liberation movements** by their supporters. In the past, nationalists were usually able to obtain some external support. Now, because of widespread revulsion against political violence, national groups and ethnic minorities are subject to pressure to negotiate instead of fighting. Governments have been very reluctant to accept the use of violence by transnational groups, even when the cause meets with their approval. Nevertheless, some groups do manage to move from the status of (bad) terrorists to (good) national liberation movements.

The concept of a terrorist is deeply controversial. It has generally been used as a term of abuse against groups who engage in violent behaviour, by people who oppose the goals of the group. US law has defined terrorism in a more precise abstract manner, as 'the unlawful use of force or violence against persons or property to intimidate or coerce a government, the civilian population, or any segment thereof, in furtherance of political or social objectives' (FBI 1999: i). The definition fails to resolve whether terrorism includes attacks by governments on civilians or excludes the use of force by dissidents against military targets.

Legitimacy in using violence is increased in *four* ways: (1) when a group appears to have widespread support within their constituency; (2) when political channels have been closed to them; (3) when the target government is exceptionally oppressive; and (4) when the violence is aimed at 'military targets' without civilian victims. Groups such as the Republican and Loyalist paramilitaries in Northern Ireland or the Basque separatists, *Euzkadi to Askatasuna* (ETA) that fail to match these four characteristics obtain very limited transnational support. Some other groups are able to gain legitimacy by winning respect on all four grounds. The African National Congress (ANC) and the South West African People's Organization (SWAPO) received widespread external support for their fight against the South African **apartheid** regime: they gained diplomatic status, money, and weapons supplies. The position of the Palestine Liberation Organization (PLO) has been more complex. When Palestinian groups used terrorist methods, such as hijacking of airliners, they gained attention, but not support. When terrorism stopped in the mid-1970s, they achieved membership of the Arab League, along with observer status in the UN General Assembly and at all UN conferences. However, adoption of suicide bombing by some Palestinians during the second *intifada* greatly reduced President Arafat's legitimacy, at least in the non-Arab world.

Since 11 September 2001, the political balance has changed substantially. The scale of the destruction wrought by Al Qaeda organizing 19 hijackers simultaneously taking control of four passenger aircraft and using these as weapons against New York and Washington did much to delegitimize all groups who use violence for political purposes. The US Government took the lead in announcing a 'war on terrorism' and many other governments sought to win support by branding their opponents as terrorists. Those who challenge the existing order similarly emphasized the need for change, to end the conditions of oppression and despair that cause people to resort to terrorism.

Historically, terrorism has mainly been an instrument of internal conflict within a single society.

While terrorism has often had transnational aspects, such as foreign funding, Al Qaeda suddenly presented the world with a new threat of a transnational **global network**. Within a few years they staged attacks in Kenya, Tanzania, Yemen, Saudi Arabia, the USA, Tunisia, Indonesia, Turkey, and Spain. Despite this, it is an analytical mistake to treat contemporary terrorism as a single phenomenon. The Irish, Basque, Palestinian, Kashmiri, Tamil, and Chechnya disputes clearly have roots that are totally independent of each other and have little or no connection to Al Qaeda. There are different transnational processes for different conflicts generating terrorism. Even Al Qaeda itself is a disparate coalition of anti-American fundamentalist groups rather than a coherent disciplined organization. (See Ch.21.)

The significance of criminals, terrorists, and guerrillas

Before September 2001, analysis of transnational criminals and guerrillas did not present a challenge to orthodox state-centric theory. On the one hand, criminals seemed to be marginal because they are not legitimate and are excluded from normal international transactions. On the other hand, the violent groups that gained military, political, and diplomatic status on a transnational basis were generally nationalist groups, aspiring to govern a particular territory. Therefore they could be presented as endorsing the basic **principles** of state-centric system.

Such an approach masks the way globalization has changed the nature of sovereignty and the processes of government. The operations of criminals and other non-legitimate groups have become more complex, spread over a wider geographical area and increased in scale, because the improvements in communications have made it so much easier to transfer people, money, weapons, and ideas on a transnational basis. Government attempts to control such activities have become correspondingly more difficult. The legal concept of statehood may not be affected, but the practice of sovereignty has become significantly different. Now virtually every government feels it has to mobilize external support, to exercise 'domestic jurisdiction' over criminals.

CWS

Finally, defeat of Al Qaeda will not be achieved by military counter-terrorism, but by global political change that delegitimizes fundamentalism and violence.

Key points

- Effective action against transnational criminals by individual governments is difficult for the same reasons as control of TNCs is difficult.

- Groups using violence to achieve political goals generally do not achieve legitimacy, but in exceptional circumstances they may be recognized as national liberation movements and take part in diplomacy.

- The transnational activities of criminals and guerrillas shift problems of the domestic policy of countries into the realm of global politics.

- Terrorism may be particular to individual countries, have transnational aspects, or be carried out by groups in a transnational network, but it is not a single political force.

Non-governmental organizations as political actors

The politics of an individual country cannot be understood without knowing what groups lobby the government and what debate there has been in the media. Similarly, international diplomacy does not operate on some separate planet, cut off from global civil society. Because diplomats like to claim that they are pursuing 'the national interest' of a united society, they will not admit to relations with interest groups or pressure groups and they prefer the bland title, non-governmental organizations or simply NGOs.

Consultative status at the UN for NGOs

As a result of pressure, primarily from American groups, the United Nations Charter contains an

---

Box 19.4 | Key concepts

Non-governmental organization (NGO): any group of people relating to each other regularly in some formal manner and engaging in collective action, provided that the activities are non-commercial and non-violent, and are not on behalf of a government. People are often baffled by the dry, bland term, 'non-governmental organization'. Nevertheless, some of the international NGOs, such as Amnesty International, Greenpeace, or the Red Cross, are better known than some of the smaller countries.

Community-based organization (CBO): any group of people organized in a local village, small town, or local district of a city. Logically, a CBO is a local NGO. However, in political debate, CBOs are sometimes contrasted with NGOs and seen as being more radical.

Network: any structure of communication for individuals and/or organizations to exchange information, share experiences, or discuss political goals and tactics. There is no clear boundary between a network and an NGO. A network is less likely than an NGO to become permanent, to have formal membership, to have identifiable leaders, or to engage in collective action.

Social movement: people with a diffuse sense of collective identity, solidarity, and common purpose that usually leads to collective political behaviour. The concept covers all the different NGOs and networks, plus all their members and all the other individuals who share the common value(s). Thus, the women's movement and the environmental movement are much more than the specific NGOs who provide leadership and focus the desire for social change.

article providing for the Economic and Social Council (ECOSOC) to consult with NGOs (Article 71). In 1950, the Council formally codified its practice, in a statute for NGOs. It recognized *three categories* of groups: (1) a small number of high-status NGOs, concerned with most of the Council's work; (2) specialist NGOs, concerned with a few fields of activity and having a high reputation in those fields; and (3) a Roster of other NGOs that are expected to make occasional contributions to the Council.[4] Since then the term NGO has, for diplomats, been synonymous with a group that is eligible for ECOSOC consultative status.

The UN definition of an acceptable NGO

The ECOSOC statute and the way it has been applied embodies six principles:

1. An NGO should support the aims and the work of the UN. This has been interpreted very broadly and it is very rare that objections are made to the political purposes of NGOs.

2. Officially, an NGO should be a representative body, with identifiable headquarters, and officers, responsible to a democratic policy-making confer-

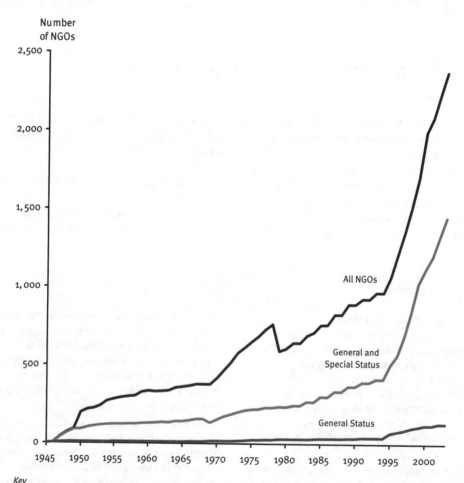

Key

General Status: having a large membership and working on most ECOSOC questions.
Special Status: large regional/national NGOs or specialist NGOs of high status.
All NGOs: including also the ECOSOC Roster of small or very specialist NGOs.

Fig. 19.2 The Growth of NGOs at the UN

ence. In practice many highly prestigious NGOs, particularly development and environment NGOs, are not membership organizations.

3. An NGO cannot be a profit-making body. Individual companies cannot gain consultative status, but trade federations of commercial interests are recognized as NGOs.

4. An NGO cannot use or advocate violence. A few guerrilla groups have been accepted as national liberation movements, but this is distinct from and of higher status than being an NGO.

5. An NGO must respect the norm of 'non-interference in the internal affairs of states'. This means an NGO cannot be a political party, but parties can, like companies, form international federations. Also, NGOs concerned with human rights should not restrict their activities to a particular group, nationality, or country. (Exception was made with respect to anti-apartheid groups.)

6. An international NGO is one that is not established by intergovernmental agreement. This is a technical legal expression of the property of being non-governmental.

Many NGO activists believe the UN should be more restrictive and only accept groups that are 'true' NGOs, contributing to 'progressive' social movements. Environmentalists are often upset that business federations are accepted and the whole NGO community at the UN agonized over the National Rifle Association being admitted to the Roster in November 1996.

Economic globalization and the expansion of NGOs

The creation of a complex global economy has had effects way beyond the international trade in goods and services. Most companies or employees, in each distinct area of activity, have formed organizations to facilitate communication, to harmonize standards, and to manage adaptation to complex change. For example, air, sea, road, and rail transport, banking, telecommunications, the media, and computing could not operate transnationally without the necessary infrastructure, which includes the organizational structures of international NGOs. Cooperation is not essential to other companies, but they find agreement on common standards and procedures is more efficient and hence cheaper. Equally the employees have found they face common problems in different countries and so trade unions and professional bodies have developed their own transnational links. Any form of international regime to formulate policy for an industry, whether it is non-governmental or intergovernmental, will encourage the strengthening of the global links among the NGOs concerned with its activities. An illustration is given in Box 19.5, with eight of the major NGOs involved in the commercial and safety regimes for aviation.

Box 19.5	International aviation organizations

The airlines have come together in the International Air Transport Association (IATA), forming a global NGO to manage their commercial relations.

Governments are members of the International Civil Aviation Organization (ICAO), providing an effective regime for navigation and setting safety standards. Because of the importance of weather forecasts for flight safety, close cooperation is maintained with another intergovernmental organization, the World Meteorological Organization (WMO). Both ICAO and WMO are UN specialized agencies.

The people most affected by questions of air safety are the pilots. They put forward their views at ICAO through their professional body, the International Federation of Air Line Pilots Associations (IFALPA). In September 1969 they move from safety 'into the political field', when they took the question of hijacking to the UN Secretary-General. Eventually IFALPA achieved a significant strengthening of the international law against hijacking.

ICAO has a less formal relationship with NGOs than does the UN. Both IATA and IFALPA have a permanent invitation to attend meetings. Other NGOs having strong working relationships include the trade unions through the International Transport Workers' Federation; a related commercial interest, the International Union of Aviation Insurers; a research forum, the Institute of Air Transport; scientists in the International Union of Geodesy and Geophysics; a sports body, the International Aeronautical Federation; and a standards body, the International Commission on Illumination.

The globalization of communications

For most of the twentieth century any individual with enough money and enough time could travel in person or communicate in writing to most parts of the world, unless communications were disrupted by war. The technical revolution in the last fifty years lies in the increased density, the increased speed, and the reduced cost of communication (see Ch.28). The political revolution lies in these changes bringing rapid global communication within the capabilities of most people. This includes even the poor, if they band together to fund a representative to articulate their case or gain access to the news media. Changes in communications constitute a fundamental change in the structure of world politics. Governments have lost sovereignty over the transnational relations of their citizens. They may attempt to monitor or control trans-boundary communications, but closing the border is no longer technologically possible.

The pattern of choices made by the news media helps explain changing priorities on political agendas in most countries. Some of the similarities between different countries are due to their separate responses to similar economic and social problems, but the decisions of the biggest transnational press agencies and satellite television networks also strengthen the similarities. The movement of ideas not only affects the agenda but also political outcomes. It is not a coincidence that individual human rights, women's rights, environmental concerns, monetarism, and privatization policies have gained increasing support in many countries around the same time. It cannot be argued that the boundaries separating the political cultures and political systems of each country have been totally eroded, but it is the case that each country is a subsystem within the global political system.

The shift of NGOs from the local to the global

One effect of the globalization of communication is to make it physically and financially feasible for small groups of people to establish and to maintain cooperation, even though they may be based thousands of miles apart from each other. Thus it is very easy for NGOs to operate transnationally, but not all NGOs make this choice. They vary from local organizations solely operating in one small town to large global bureaucracies with a presence in most countries. The crucial factor in determining whether an NGO goes transnational is the nature of its goals.

1. If the prime purpose is to offer a service to its own members, to pursue charitable activities locally, or to campaign to change a particular law, then it may be decades before the question of establishing transnational links arises. Separate NGOs become well established in several countries before they decide to form an international NGO, as a loose federation, in order to exchange information and learn from each other's experience. Trade unions, women's organizations, charities for the elderly, and family-planning associations are examples.

2. Campaigning NGOs in one country may only have the goal of affecting their own government's policy, but decide for tactical reasons to obtain support from foreign governments and NGOs. Environmental NGOs in developing countries have found support from transnational networks to be crucial.

3. Sometimes campaigning NGOs decide from the start that they would be more effective as a transnational organization and they form sections simultaneously in several countries. Amnesty International and Friends of the Earth started in Britain and the United States respectively, but immediately appealed for support elsewhere.

4. NGOs can be based in just one country, while defining their goals in transnational terms. For many years Oxfam in Britain and CARE in the USA raised funds to spend on disaster relief and development overseas, before they too joined international federations and then later gained sections in other countries.

5. When regional or global intergovernmental organizations become the focus for policy-making, then NGOs seek to influence the proceedings. They use access to the international secretariat and the decision-making organs, as an

indirect route to influence the policy of individual governments.

NGOs are so diverse in their goals and their tactics that the above list only indicates the main processes by which they move from local to global politics.

When NGOs cooperate transnationally, they may use one of four different types of structures. In the past, a formal joint organization, known as an INGO (an international NGO) was usually established, with a permanent headquarters, a secretariat and a regular programme of meetings. With the advent of the Internet it is now just as likely that a looser network will be formed, often with a single NGO providing the technical support for e-mail communications and a joint web site. The most famous networks, such as Jubilee 2000, the Coalition for an International Criminal Court, and the International Campaign to Ban Landmines, have united around a single issue, brought together hundreds of NGOs from all around the world, and achieved major policy changes against the opposition of leading governments. These are known as advocacy networks. At the meetings of intergovernmental organizations, NGOs may combine in a caucus. This is a temporary network formed solely for the purpose of lobbying on the agenda items at the particular meeting. Finally, there are governance networks, formed by NGOs to maintain and enhance the participation rights of NGOs in intergovernmental meetings. They differ from advocacy networks and caucuses in not having common political goals, other than their common interest in being allowed access to the policy-making process.

Key points

- Most transnational actors can expect to gain recognition as NGOs by the UN, provided they are not individual companies, criminals, or violent groups, and they do not exist solely to oppose an individual government.

- The ECOSOC statute provides an authoritative statement that NGOs have a legitimate place in intergovernmental diplomacy.

- The creation of a global economy leads to the globalization of unions, commercial bodies, the professions, and scientists in international NGOs, which participate in the relevant international regimes.

- Governments can no longer control the flow of information across the borders of their country.

- Improved communications make it more likely that NGOs will operate transnationally and make it very simple and cheap for them to do so.

- NGOs from each country may combine in four ways, as international NGOs, as advocacy networks, as caucuses, and as governance networks.

International organizations as structures of global politics

International organizations provide the focus for global politics. The new physical infrastructure of global communications makes it easier for them to operate. In addition, when the sessions of the organizations take place, they become distinct structures for political communication. Face-to-face meetings produce different outcomes from telephone or written communications. Multilateral discussion produces different outcomes from interactions in networks of bilateral communications.

International organizations as systems

It was argued earlier that it inconsistent to see 'states' as coherent entities, while asserting anarchy exists at the global level. We can be consistent by accepting the existence of systems at all levels of world politics. In the modern world, human groups are never so coherent that they are independent, closed systems (perhaps excepting monastic orders). Equally, once distinct organizational processes are established, they are never so open that the boundaries become insignificant. Thus international organizations of all types transcend country boundaries and have a major impact on the governmental actors and transnational actors composing them.

For a system to exist, there must be a sufficient density of interactions, involving each of its elements, at a sufficient intensity to result both in the emergence of properties for the system as a whole and in some consistent effect on the behaviour of the elements. Generally, international organizations will have founding documents defining their goals, rules of procedure constraining the modes of behaviour, secretariats committed to the status and identity of the organization (or at least committed to their own careers), past decisions that provide norms for future policy, and interaction processes that socialize new participants. All these features at the systemic level will be part of the explanation of the behaviour of the members and thus the political outcomes will not be determined solely by the initial goals of the members. The statement that international organizations form systems is a statement that they are politically significant and that global politics cannot be reduced to 'inter-state' relations.

The intergovernmental versus non-governmental distinction

Normally a sharp distinction is made between intergovernmental organizations (IGOs) and international non-governmental organizations (INGOs). This conveys the impression that inter-state diplomacy and transnational relations are separate from each other. In practice governments do not rigidly maintain the separation. There is an overlapping pattern of relations in another category of international organizations, hybrid INGOs, in which governments work with NGOs. Among the most important hybrids are the International Red Cross, the World Conservation Union (IUCN), the International Council of Scientific Unions, the International Air Transport Association, and other economic bodies combining companies and governments.

In order to be regarded as a hybrid the organization must admit as full members *both* NGOs, parties, or companies *and* governments or governmental agencies. Both types of members must have full rights of participation in policymaking, including the right to vote on the final decisions. Voting may

---

Box 19.6	Key concepts

International organization: any institution with formal procedures and formal membership from three or more countries. The minimum number of countries is set at three rather than two, because multilateral relationships have significantly greater complexity than bilateral relationships.

Intergovernmental organization (IGO): an international organization in which full legal membership is officially solely open to states and the decisionmaking authority lies with representatives from governments.

International non-governmental organization (INGO): an international organization in which membership is open to transnational actors. There are many different types, with membership from 'national' NGOs, local NGOs, companies, political parties, or individual people. A few have other INGOs as members and some have mixed membership structures.

Hybrid INGO: a third type of international organization, in which governments and NGOs form joint organizations in which they are each allowed to be members. Logically they should be hybrid international organizations, but in diplomatic practice they are identified among the international NGOs and so hybrid INGOs is perhaps a more appropriate term.

International regime: a concept developed by Neo-realists to analyse the paradox—for them—that international cooperation occurs in some issue-areas, despite the struggle for power between states. They assume regimes are created and maintained by a dominant state and/or participation in a regime is the result of a rational cost–benefit calculation by each state. In contrast, Pluralists would also stress the independent impact of institutions, the importance of leadership, the involvement of transnational NGOs and companies, and processes of cognitive change, such as growing concern about human rights or the environment.

be with all members counted together, as in the International Conference of the Red Cross, or with separate majorities required in two categories of membership, as in the World Conservation Union. In hybrid INGOs there is usually also a joint obliga-

tion to fund the activities of the organization. When the principle of formal equality of NGOs and governments is acknowledged by both sides in such a manner, the assumption that governments can dominate must be totally abandoned.

Key points

- International organizations are structures for political communication. They are systems that constrain the behaviour of their members.

- Governments form intergovernmental organizations and transnational actors form international non-governmental organizations. In addition governments

and transnational actors accord each other equal status by jointly creating hybrid international NGOs.

- International organizations are more than the collective will of their members. They have a distinct impact upon other global actors.

Issues and policy systems in global politics

One way state-centric writers accommodate transnational activity is by distinguishing the high politics of peace and security, taking place in military alliances and UN diplomacy, from the low politics of other policy questions, debated in specialist UN bodies, other IGOs, and INGOs. Then, by asserting it is more important to analyse peace and war, actors in low politics are defined out of the analysis. In practice it is not so simple. Scientists, the Red Cross, religious groups, and other NGOs are involved in arms control negotiations; economic events may be treated as crises; social policy can concern matters of life and death; and heads of government do at times make the environment a top priority. It is useful to analyse global politics in terms of a variety of dimensions describing each policy domain and the actors within it, but the different dimensions do not correlate. A single high/low classification does not work.

The move from a state-centric to a Pluralist model, in which governments and transnational actors interact with each other bilaterally and multilaterally, depends on rejecting a static unidimensional concept of power. Actors enter a political process possessing resources and seeking particular goals: however, contrary to the Realist view, capabilities

do not determine influence. Explaining outcomes requires examining whether the resources of actors are relevant to the goals being pursued, describing the degree of divergence between the goals of the different actors, and analysing how they are changed by the interaction processes.

Governments are usually characterized as having legal authority and control over military capabilities and economic resources. They may also have high status, possess specialist information, have access to communications, and be able to articulate widely shared values in support of their goals, but all these latter four capabilities can also be attributes of transnational actors and international organizations. In the process of political debate something else is crucial. It is the ability to communicate in a manner that commands the attention and respect of other actors. While this is enhanced by possession of status and resources, in a particular time and place—through the news media, in a speech before a public audience, during negotiations, or when lobbying in private—the ability to communicate is a personal attribute of the speaker. Some presidents and prime ministers fail to command respect, while some NGO activists are inspiring and cannot be ignored. If power is seen solely in military terms, governments

Box 19.7   Key concepts

An **issue** consists of a set of political questions that are seen as being related, because they all invoke the same value conflicts, e.g. the issue of human rights concerns questions that invoke freedom versus order.

A **policy domain** consists of a set of political questions that have to be decided together because they are linked by the political processes in an international organization, e.g. financial policy is resolved in the IMF. A policy domain may cover several issues: financial policy includes development, environment, and gender issues.

Power: in the most general sense, the ability of a political actor to achieve its goals. In the Realist approach, it is assumed that possession of capabilities will result in influence, so the single word, power, is often used ambiguously to cover both. In the Pluralist approach, it is assumed that political interactions can modify the

translation of capabilities into influence and therefore it is important to distinguish between the two.

Capabilities: the resources that are under an actor's direct control.

Interaction processes: the flows of people, materials, energy, money, and information (including political ideas and proposals for policy), between the elements of a system. War is primarily determined by flows of people as soldiers and materials as weapons; economics by the exchange of money for all the other four types of flows; and politics by the flow of information. Thus, for a Pluralist, unless and until an issue involves armed conflict, structures of communication are the fundamental political structures.

Influence: the ability of one actor to change the values or the behaviour of another actor.

are expected to be dominant. If power is seen solely in economic terms, TNCs are expected to be dominant. However, if power includes possession of status, information, and communication skills, then it is possible for NGOs and international organizations to mobilize support for their values and to exercise influence over governments. Most real-world situations will see a mix of different capabilities being brought to bear upon the policy debate.

The types of authority, status, resources, informa-

tion, and skills that are relevant to political success are issue-specific. (They vary from one issue to another.) Thus the governments, the TNCs, the NGOs, the intergovernmental organizations, and the international NGOs that have the ability to exercise influence will vary according to the issues invoked by a policy problem. **Table 19.1** illustrates the point that there is not a single international system of nearly 200 'states', but a variety of **policy domains**, each involving their own distinct actors.

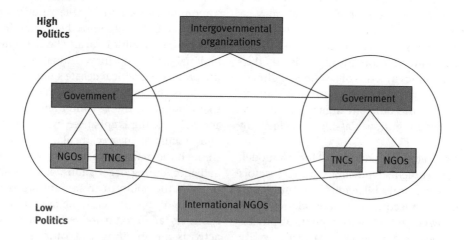

Fig. 19.3   The orthodox view of international relations

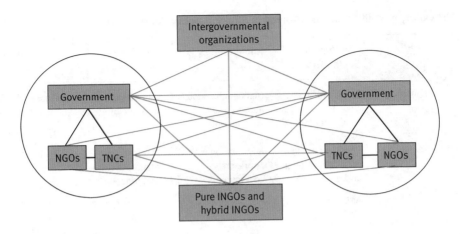

Fig. 19.4 The full range of international connections

Governments have a special role, linking the different domains, because membership of the UN obliges governments to form policy and vote on most issues. In practice, they are less central and cohesive than it appears in the UN, because different departments of government handle the different policy questions. The transnational actors and international organizations generally are more specialist and involved in a limited range of policy questions. Amnesty International rarely has significance in environmental politics and Greenpeace rarely is concerned with human rights, but each is central to their own domain. Being a specialist actor is a weakness in relation to situations where issue linkages become important, but usually it is a great strength for NGOs and international secretariats. Being a specialist generates high status, achieves command over information, and enhances communication skills. These capabilities enable a challenge to be made to the governments that control military and economic resources.

Within both domestic and global politics, civil society is the source of change. Companies usually initiate economic change and NGOs are usually the source of new ideas for political action. At any one point in time, economics and politics may seem to be relatively stable and under governmental control. Under the exceptional circumstances of war or under exceptional leadership, governments can generate change. However, NGOs generally provide the dynamics of politics. The European empires were dismembered by nationalist movements, with support from lawyers, journalists, unions, and the churches. Democracy and human rights have been extended by women's groups, ethnic minorities, and dissident groups. The environment has moved up the agenda in response to grassroots anger at the loss of natural beauty, protests against threats to health, and warnings from scientists about ecosystems being at risk of collapse. The right to have access to family planning supplies, sexual information, and reproductive health services has been established as a global norm. In some countries, notably the USA, this initially required women to go to jail to challenge repressive laws, but since 1953 the International Planned Parenthood Federation has grown to become the world's second largest NGO, even operating in virtually all Catholic and Islamic countries. The start of the cold war was not simply the formation of military alliances: it was a political struggle of communism as a transnational movement against the transnational appeal of democracy, the Catholic Church, and nationalism. The arms race and the process of **détente** included conflict between arms manufacturers and peace movements, with scientists being crucial to both sides. The end of the cold war was driven by economic failure within communist countries and the political failure in response to demands from unions, human rights dissidents, the churches, and environmentalists. The response to refugee crises produced by natural and human-made disasters has been dominated by the

Table 19.1 The variety of political actors involved in different policy domains

	Apartheid in South Africa	Human rights	Population planning	Environment
Main governments involved	South Africa, UK, USA versus African governments	Democratic versus authoritarian governments	All types of governments	Those who feel threatened by problems versus those who do not
Transnational companies	Wide range, but especially mining and oil	Any working with oppressive governments	Medical, pharmaceutical, and food	Mainly industrial, energy, and transport
Guerrillas	ANC, PAC, and SWAPO	Any taking hostages	Any in control of territory	Generally not concerned
Grass-roots NGOs	Anti-Apartheid Movement	Human rights groups and the oppressed	Religious, women's, and health groups	Friends of the Earth, WWF, Greenpeace, etc.
UN inter-governmental policy forum	Committee Against Apartheid and Security Council	Human Rights Commission	Commission on Population and Development	Commission on Sustainable Development
UN Secretariat	Centre Against Apartheid	Centre for Human Rights	UNICEF, UN Pop. Fund	UNDP, UNEP
Other IGOs	Organization of African Unity	Council of Europe, OAS, and OAU	WHO, World Bank	World Bank
International NGOs	Many involved, with a secondary concern	Amnesty International and others	International Planned Parenthood Federation	Environment Liaison Centre International and other networks
Hybrid INGOs	Those concerned with trade	None	None	World Conservation Union (IUCN)

Key points

- The high politics/low politics distinction is used to marginalize transnational actors. It is invalid because politics does not reduce to these two categories.

- A simple concept of power will not explain outcomes. Military and economic resources are not the only capabilities: communication facilities, information, authority, and status are also important political assets. In addition, an ability to use the interaction processes to mobilize support will contribute to influence over policy.

- Different policy domains contain different actors, depending upon the salience of the issues being debated.

- TNCs gain influence through the control of economic resources. NGOs gain influence through possessing information, gaining high status, and communicating effectively. TNCs and NGOs have been the main source of economic and political change in global politics.

media, the UN, and NGOs. The shift from seeing development as increasing a country's GNP to meeting ordinary people's basic needs and using resources in a sustainable manner was driven by development NGOs and the environmental movement. The international relations of the twentieth century have all occurred within complex, Pluralist political systems.

For further information and case studies on this subject, please visit the companion web site at **www.oup.com/uk/booksites/politics**.

CWS

QUESTIONS

1   Outline three meanings of the concept of a 'state' and explain the implications of each for the study of transnational actors.

2   What are the different types of transnational actors? Give examples of each type.

3   What is a nation? How does the concept differ from that of a state

4   How do transnational companies affect the sovereignty of governments?

5   List all the NGOs that you, and your family, have joined. Assess from their newsletters how many are global organizations, how many are national, or local with global connections, and how many have no transnational relations.

6   What measures could you use to compare the size of countries, TNCs, NGOs, and international organizations? Are countries always larger than transnational actors?

7   How could a local women's group have a significant effect upon global politics?

8   What types of NGOs are, and what types are not, eligible to obtain consultative status with the Economic and Social Council of the United Nations?

9   Explain the expansion in the number of NGOs engaging in transnational activities.

10   What is a hybrid international NGO?

11   How is it possible for NGOs to exercise influence in global politics? (Note: this question can be answered both in theoretical terms and in practical empirical terms.)

12   Explain the difference between analysing international relations as a single international system and as the global politics of many different policy domains

GUIDE TO FURTHER READING

Case study materials

Keohane, R. O., and Nye, J. S. (eds) (1972), *Transnational Relations and World Politics* (Cambridge, Mass.: Harvard University Press): the first major academic study of transnational relations, limited by the explicit decision to downplay non-economic actors.

Weiss, T. G., and Gordenker, L. (eds) (1996), *NGOs, the UN and Global Governance* (Boulder, Col.: Lynne Rienner): six studies of NGO activity and three chapters addressing cross-cutting themes, set within a Pluralist approach.

Willetts, P. (ed.) (1982), *Pressure Groups in the Global System: The Transnational Relations of Issue-Oriented Non-Governmental Organizations* (London: Pinter): in reaction against the omission of non-economic groups by Keohane and Nye, examines how pressure groups move from single-country to global activity.

Willetts, P. (ed.) (1996), *'The Conscience of the World'. The Influence of Non-Governmental Organizations in the UN System* (London: Hurst and Co.): defines what is an NGO, gives the history of the League and the UN consultative arrangements, and offers seven case studies of the influence of NGOs in the UN system.

Risse-Kappen, T. (ed.) (1995), *Bringing Transnational Relations Back In* (Cambridge: Cambridge University Press): provides a set of six case studies around the theme that transnational influence depends upon the structures of governance for an issue-area both at the domestic level and in international institutions

Keck, M. E., and Sikkink, K. (1998), *Activists Beyond Borders: Advocacy Networks in International Politics* (Ithaca, NY: Cornell University Press): a major contribution to the literature on the nature of modern transnational advocacy networks, with case studies on Latin America, the environment, and violence against women.

Theoretical debate

Rosenau, J. N. (1980), *The Study of Global Interdependence: Essays on the Transnationalisation of World Affairs* (London: Pinter): a fruitful source of theoretical ideas for a Pluralist approach.

Viotti, P. R., and Kauppi, M. V. (1998), *International Relations Theory. Realism, Pluralism Globalism* (New York: Macmillan, 3rd edn): gives excellent focus on the fundamentals of the theoretical debate.

Willetts, P. (1990), 'Transactions, Networks and Systems', in A. J. R. Groom and P. Taylor, *Frameworks for International Co-operation* (London: Pinter), ch.17: more detailed coverage of the development of International Relations theory on transnational and intergovernmental relations.

See also the editors' chapters in the case study books.

UN materials

Kaul, I., *et al.* (1993), *Human Development Report 1993* (New York: Oxford University Press): an official UN annual report, which in this edition concentrates on the contribution made by NGOs to development.

UNCTAD, Division on Transnational Corporations and Investment (1991–), *World Investment Report* (New York: UN): an official UN annual report, which assesses the scale of TNC participation in global production, investment, and trade.

See also documents on the web sites cited below.

WEB LINKS

www.un.org The United Nations home page, with separate links for the main organs and the major conferences. The site provides access to official documents and reports, but not any political analysis.

www.un.org/partners/index.html An index page, with links for the United Nations relations with civil society and with business.

www.oneworld.org A gateway to most of the active international NGOs. It can be used both to learn about particular organizations and to explore controversy about global issues.

www.staff.city.ac.uk/p.willetts/NGOS/NGO-HOME.HTM An index page, with links to primary sources on consultative status for NGOs at the UN and to NGO networks.

NOTES

1. Data on transnational corporations are given in annual reports from the United Nations: the figures quoted come from *World Investment Report 2003* (Geneva: UN, 2003): 222–4. The numbers of transnational and international organizations of different types are given in the statistical tables of the various editions of the Union of International Associations (UIA) yearbook: the figures quoted come from *Yearbook of International Organizations 2003–2004*, Vol. 1B (Munich: K. G. Saur, for the Union of International Associations, 40th edn, 2003): 2738. In each case, the current author has rounded the figures. The total number of global actors has increased significantly compared to the data given in the first edition of this book: TNCs are up by 66 per cent and there are three and a half times as many affiliates, while INGOs are up by 40 per cent.

2. The *Financial Times* lists the 500 largest TNCs in a special supplement each year. The figures quoted are from the edition published on 28 May 2003, which gives 53 companies as having sales of more than $40 bn. in 2002. Data for each country are given in the *World Development Indicators, 2002* (Washington, DC: World Bank, 2002). The total number of small states is more than 142, but this is the figure for UN members with a GNP of less than $40 bn.

3. *World Investment Report 2003*, Annex tables A.I.1–3 and A.I.15.

4. ECOSOC Resolution 288(X)B Arrangements for Consultation with Non-Governmental Organizations was passed in February 1950. It was amended and replaced by Resolution 1296(XLIV) in May 1968 and again by Resolution 1996/31 in July 1996.

Part Four

INTERNATIONAL ISSUES

In this part of the book we want to give you a wide-ranging overview of the main issues in contemporary world politics. The previous three parts have been designed to give you a comprehensive foundation for the study of contemporary international issues. As with the other sections, this one also has two aims: **first**, we want to give you an understanding of some of the more important pressing problems which appear every day in the media headlines and which, directly and indirectly, affect the lives of each of us. These issues are the stuff of globalization, and they take a number of different forms. Some, like the environment and nuclear proliferation, pose dangers of global catastrophe. Others, like nationalism, cultural differences, and humanitarian intervention, together with regionalism and integration, raise important questions and dilemmas about the twin processes of fragmentation and unification which characterize the world in which we live. Yet other issues such as terrorism, global trade and finance, gender, human rights, poverty, development, and hunger are fundamentally intertwined with globalization, while the development of the Internet represents a transformation of the ways in which people communicate and access information. Our **second** aim, of course, is that by providing overviews of these issues we are posing questions about the nature of globalization. Is it new? Is it beneficial? Is it unavoidable? Does it serve specific interests? Does it make it more or less easy to deal with the problems dealt with in these chapters? The picture that emerges from these chapters is that the process of globalization is a highly complex one, with major disagreements existing about its significance and its impact. Some contributors see opportunities for greater cooperation because of globalization while others see dangers of increased levels of conflict as the end of the century beckons. What do you think?

CHAPTER 20

Environmental issues

OWEN GREENE

READER'S GUIDE

Environmental issues emerged in the late twentieth century as a major focus of international concern and activity. Understanding the causes and impacts of global environmental change is an urgent task. So too is improving knowledge of how to develop effective responses. Approaches and concepts developed within International Relations can contribute substantially to such understanding. At the same time, international environmental issues pose important challenges for International Relations theory. This chapter introduces these issues, and discusses some key characteristics of the causes and risks of global environmental change and responses to it. It outlines the historical development of international environmental politics and agreements, and then examines issues and phases in the development of environmental regimes (particularly the ozone regime), and the Earth Summit agreements and their outcomes.

Introduction: international environmental issues

By the early twenty-first century, environmental issues had been high on the international agenda for a whole generation of political leaders, government officials, scientists, industrialists, and concerned citizens. Since the late 1960s, awareness of the risks and implications, of a wide range of international environmental problems has increased greatly, and justifiably so.

Since that time, it has become clear that most of the world's seas and oceans are over-fished. Soil is being degraded and eroded on a large scale throughout the world. Natural habitats are being destroyed: for example the area of tropical rainforest has reduced by over 50 per cent since 1950, and the process continues largely unabated. As a result, tens of thousands of species of plants and animals are probably becoming extinct each year. The dumping of waste products into the sea, air, and land means that pollution problems are ubiquitous. Huge quantities of waste, including hazardous chemicals, heavy metals, and radioactive materials, have been dumped at sea, either directly or carried by rivers. Together with sewage and oil spills, these have profoundly damaged sea environments, with lakes and semi-enclosed seas proving particularly vulnerable. Billions of people suffer daily air pollution. Acid rain, stratospheric ozone depletion, and climate change are major regional or global problems arising from atmospheric pollution.

Environmental problems are not new. Human societies have long had a major impact on their environment. Their tendency to exploit it as if it were an inexhaustible resource has repeatedly led to disaster, sometimes leading to the loss of entire human communities. Over much of human history, however, the environmental impacts of over-exploitation or pollution have typically been quite local. Communities could often escape the consequences of such activities by moving on to relatively unspoilt areas. Even if they could not, the local impoverishment did not necessarily affect the continued well-being of neighbouring societies. Widespread industrialization and rapid population growth changed this situation. Severe environmental damage and unsustainable exploitation occurred over whole regions of the world. By the late twentieth century, the impacts had become truly global.

This chapter examines the politics of **global environmental issues**. However, there are several senses in which the environment can be said to have become a global issue. **First**, some environmental problems are inherently global. CFCs (chlorofluorocarbons) released into the atmosphere contribute to the global problem of stratospheric ozone depletion irrespective of where they are emitted, just as carbon dioxide emissions contribute to global climate change. The effects are global, and the problems can only be tackled through **cooperation** on a global scale.

Second, some problems relate to the exploitation of **global commons**: resources shared by all members of the international **community**, such as the oceans, deep-sea bed, atmosphere, and outer space. Many argue that the world's genetic resources are a global resource, which should be preserved in the common interest.

Third, many environmental problems are intrinsically **transnational**, in that by their nature they cross **state** boundaries, even if they are not entirely global. For example, emissions of sulphur dioxide by one state will be carried by winds and deposited as acid rain on downwind countries. Wastes dumped into an enclosed or semi-enclosed sea affect all littoral states. Such transnational or regional problems exist in many parts of the world, and pose similar technical and political challenges to those of truly global problems. Moreover, states or **non-state actors** from outside the region may contribute to the problems or to efforts to tackle them.

Fourth, and following on from this, many processes of **over-exploitation** or environmental degradation are relatively local or national in scale, and yet they are experienced in such a large number of localities around the world that they can be considered to be global problems. Examples include unsustainable agricultural practices, soil degradation and erosion, deforestation, river pollution, and the many environmental problems associated with urbanization and industrial practices.

Finally, the processes leading to over-exploitation and environmental degradation are intimately linked to broader political and socio-economic processes, which themselves are part of a global political economy. Thus it is widely recognized that the causes of most environmental problems are closely related to the generation and distribution of wealth, knowledge, and power, and to patterns of energy consumption, industrialization, population growth, affluence, and poverty. In this respect, the processes of globalization and interdependence in the economic and other spheres of life, as discussed in Chapter 1, increasingly give all environmental issues a global dimension.

Thus, the phrase 'global environmental issues' encompasses a wide range of types of problems and issues, posing different challenges to those who wish to develop effective responses. Although they share some common characteristics, each issue is specific and needs to be analysed in its own right.

Key points

- International environmental issues emerged as a major focus for international politics and concern in the last three decades of the twentieth century.

- Although environmental problems are not new in themselves, industrialization and rapid population growth have greatly increased the scale and intensity of the over-exploitation of natural resources and environmental degradation, generating a wide range of urgent international and global problems.

- Environmental issues have become international and global in several senses. Many environmental problems are intrinsically transnational or global, or relate to global commons. Other local or national problems are experienced widely across the Earth. Finally, the processes generating most environmental problems are closely related to broader political or socio-economic processes, which are themselves part of an increasingly global system.

- Global environmental issues exist in many different forms, and though they share some common characteristics, each needs specific examination in its own right.

Environmental issues on the international agenda: a historical outline

The early years

Environmental issues first emerged as a focus for international politics in the nineteenth century in the context of international agreements to manage resources. For example, the River Commissions for the Rhine and the Danube, which are now deeply involved with environmental policy, began life as arrangements to facilitate economic use of the rivers as waterways. The International Maritime Organization (IMO) was formed in 1948, more or less as a 'shipowners' club' to facilitate international shipping and navigation and promote safety. But in 1954 the IMO was given responsibility for implementing a landmark treaty on marine pollution: the Convention for the Prevention of Pollution of the Sea by Oil.

The first international treaty on flora, signed in Berne in 1889, was primarily concerned with preventing the spread of a disease (Phylloxera) which threatened to destroy European vineyards. This was followed by a series of global and regional agreements on flora in the 1920s and 1950s, which were all similarly concerned with maintaining healthy stocks of cultivated plants or preventing disease. Likewise, the first agreement on fauna was the 1902 Convention for the Protection of Birds useful to Agriculture. In 1911 the USA, Canada, and Russia agreed a Convention for the Protection of Fur Seals, which were being unsustainably culled. In 1945, the UN Food and Agriculture Organization (FAO) was set up, with the conservation of natural resources included in its mandate. The 1946 International

Whaling Convention essentially established a club of whaling nations to manage the 'harvesting' of whales.

Even at that time, however, there was emerging concern to protect wildlife for its own sake as well as an economic resource. Conventions were signed to protect birds, in large part due to public pressures mobilized by groups such as the Royal Society for the Protection of Birds. The first international efforts to establish wildlife parks and reserves began as early as 1900 (among the colonial powers in Africa), and were further advanced through a series of Conventions from the 1930s onwards.

It was in the 1960s, however, that international concern about pollution and the preservation of the natural environment began to develop rapidly, particularly in developed countries. Rachel Carson's book *Silent Spring* not only stimulated intense concern about the widespread use of DDT and other pesticides, but also helped to launch the modern environmental movement (Carson 1962). Wide awareness of the health risks posed by radioactive fall-out contributed to the pressures to conclude the ban on nuclear warhead tests in the atmosphere, agreed in 1963. Concern about sea pollution grew, stimulated by disasters such as the spill from the *Torrey Canyon* oil tanker in 1967, and the IMO became increasingly engaged with preventing oil pollution at sea. The problem of transboundary air pollution, and 'acid rain', attracted increasing attention, particularly in Scandinavia and Canada where damage to vulnerable forest and lake ecosystems was becoming manifest. In the mid-1960s, informal discussions began on the development of a new Law of the Sea to govern access to, and use of, the international seas and the seabed: the old regime was collapsing as unilateral claims were being made on transit rights and for economic control of waters up to 200 miles from coasts.

The Stockholm Conference

The 1972 UN Conference on the Human Environment was organized in response to this dramatic increase in international environmental concern in the 1960s. The aim was to establish an international framework to promote a more coordinated approach to pollution and other environmental problems. The conference, which was held in Stockholm, marked a turning point in the development of international environmental politics. Some of the principles that were agreed, and the institutions and programmes that were established, had an enduring effect (see Box 20.1). Just as significantly, the debates at the conference established themes and practices that would remain central to international environmental politics for the next thirty years and beyond.

The importance of international environmental issues as a focus for international concern became institutionalized, along with the principle that states have a responsibility to cooperate with efforts to manage the global commons and reduce transboundary pollution. Developing countries insisted that they had less historical responsibility for global pollution and resource depletion than industrialized countries, and that actions to protect the environment had to be linked to efforts to promote their economic and social development—arguments that developed states accepted in principle. That is, the general relationship between **environment and development** in the context of North–South relations was for the first time formally elaborated at an intergovernmental meeting. At the same time, **environmental non-governmental organizations** (NGOs) from many countries gathered to monitor the entire proceedings of the Conference, to exert political pressure on the participants, and to network, thus establishing a practice that has continued ever since.

From Stockholm to Rio

In the 1970s and 1980s, dozens of international environmental agreements and programmes were established. For example, a series of conventions was set up to protect the environment of the Mediterranean, North Sea, Baltic Sea, and other regional seas, with UNEP playing an important leadership role. The 1972 London Dumping Convention established a framework for restricting the dumping of toxic wastes (including nuclear wastes) at sea. In 1973, an international convention was agreed to prevent intentional oil pollution from ships (the

MARPOL Convention) which was further strengthened in 1978, after further public outcries about continuing oil spills. In 1979, European and North American countries set up the Long Range Transboundary Air Pollution (LRTAP) agreement to limit emissions of sulphur dioxide and other pollutants causing air pollution and acid rain. In 1985 the Vienna Convention for the Protection of the Ozone Layer was signed, followed two years later by the Montreal Protocol which imposed substantial limits on the use of CFCs and other ozone-depleting substances.

Box 20.1　The Stockholm Conference and its legacy

The UN Conference on the Human Environment, held in Stockholm in 1972, was the UN's first major conference on international environmental issues. The Stockholm Conference attracted wide publicity, and many of the participants and observers no doubt learned a lot from the discussions of a wide range of specific environmental issues. The meeting agreed upon: a Declaration containing 26 principles concerning the environment and development; an Action Plan with 109 recommendations spanning six broad areas (human settlements, natural resource management, pollution, educational and social aspects of the environment, development and the environment, and international organizations); and a Resolution on various institutional and financial arrangements.

In the following years dozens of international environmental agreements were achieved. However, apart from galvanizing public concern and educating governments, the most enduring specific contributions of the Stockholm Conference are widely believed to be the following.

First, some of the agreed principles significantly strengthened the framework for future environmental cooperation They did not immediately command universal acceptance, not least because Soviet bloc countries boycotted the Stockholm Conference for broader foreign policy reasons. But over time they gained substantial international stature, and provided a basis for much subsequent environmental diplomacy. Principle 21 had particular significance, for example. It acknowledged states' sovereignty over their natural resources but stipulated that states have 'the responsibility to ensure that activities within their jurisdiction or control do not cause damage to the environment of other states or of areas beyond the limits of national jurisdiction'. Other principles established that: the international community should determine limits on the use and abuse of 'global commons'; resources identified as the **'Common Heritage of Mankind'** (such as the deep-sea bed) should be collectively managed, preserved, or used to common benefit; measures to prevent pollution and protect the natural environment should be balanced against the economic and social goals; and international agreements should take into account the different circumstances and responsibilities of developed and developing states.

Second, the Stockholm Conference led to the establishment of global and regional environmental monitoring networks, which have improved monitoring of environmental problems, such as marine pollution and ozone depletion, and have indirectly stimulated action to tackle them.

Third, the Conference led to the creation of the **UN Environment Programme (UNEP),** which was given the task of coordinating the environment-related activities of other UN agencies and promoting the integration of environmental considerations into their work. In practice, UNEP subsequently played a key role in: raising political awareness of environmental problems; helping with the formation of scientific consensus on problems and responses to them; facilitating negotiations (particularly for the protection of regional seas and the ozone layer); and improving countries' environmental management capacities. Further, UNEP provided institutional frameworks through which broader agenda-setting activities could develop. For example, since the 1980s UNEP provided an important forum for raising awareness of the linkages between environmental degradation and women's lives, developing agendas to promote gender awareness in environmental projects and specific engagement in environment and development institutions through the 1990s. Overall, the broader institutionalization of international environmental politics after the Stockholm Conference meant that the process acquired momentum to continue through periods when public and political concerns about the environment waned.

Finally, the Conference stimulated broader political and institutional changes. For example, many governments subsequently created Ministries for the Environment and national agencies for environmental monitoring or regulation. The development of international networks of environmental NGOs was stimulated. Moreover environmental NGOs, which at that time were primarily based in Europe or North America, began to engage more systematically with development issues and developing-country groups.

Largely as a result of sustained pressure by environmental NGOs, the Ramsar Convention to preserve wetland habitats of waterfowl was established in 1971, followed by the Convention on International Trade in Endangered Species (CITES) a year later. These were followed by a series of agreements to conserve habitats and animals including seals and polar bears. Furthermore, well-established resource-management regimes, such as the Antarctica Treaty and the International Whaling Convention were transformed into environmental protection agreements. Moratoriums on whaling and on the exploitation of Antarctic resources were established—marking a considerable departure from the original aims and priorities of these regimes.

It increasingly became the norm that non-governmental groups should have wide access to intergovernmental meetings on the environment, to an extent that would have shocked earlier generations of diplomats and is still unknown in some other spheres of international activity. Moreover, in many areas environmental NGOs came to command sufficient expertise and resources that they became substantial forces in international politics in their own right. Delegations from organizations such as Greenpeace, World Wildlife Fund, or Friends of the Earth at international meetings were frequently larger and more expert than those of all but the largest states, and through their access to the media and their expertise were able to shape international agendas. Industrial associations representing interested groups in the business community likewise became directly involved in seeking to shape international environmental regimes, rather than simply working through their governments.

However, the development agendas included in the Action Plan and Declaration of Principles agreed at Stockholm were never seriously followed up. Most of the international agreements listed above focused on environmental protection or pollution, without seriously integrating development concerns. Moreover, UNEP lacked the institutional weight seriously to coordinate other UN agencies, which typically vigorously protect their 'turf', and thus largely failed to achieve integration of environmental and development agendas in the UN system. This caused increasing international concern, particularly amongst developing countries.

The UN established a World Commission on Environment and Development, chaired by the then Prime Minister of Norway, Gro Harlem Brundtland, to propose ways forward. The 1987 **Brundtland Report** argued for priority to be given to achieving 'sustainable development', and received wide international support (World Commission on Environment and Development, 1987). Though the Report discussed a variety of issues and institutional reforms, the exact meaning of the concept of 'sustainable development' remained contested or unclear. Nevertheless, it was important because it developed an agenda which could attract strong support from a variety of important constituencies. As a result, the UN General Assembly decided in December 1989 to convene an **'Earth Summit'** as a twenty-year follow-up to the Stockholm Meeting, so that the international community could carry the sustainable development agenda forward. A **UN Conference on Environment and Development (UNCED)** was fixed to take place in Rio de Janeiro in June 1992.

Key points

- Environmental issues first emerged on the international agenda in the late nineteenth century.

- Environmental awareness and concern developed strongly after the 1960s, particularly in relation to pollution problems.

- The 1972 Stockholm Conference established a number of principles, institutions, and programmes which helped to provide a framework promoting the further development of international responses to transnational environmental problems.

- In the 1970s and 1980s, international environmental politics developed and matured. Green movements, environmental and industrial NGOs, and international organizations established themselves as key actors in international environmental politics alongside states.

- The Brundtland Commission promoted the concept of 'sustainable development', and preparations began for a 1992 UN Conference on Environment and Development.

Box 20.2 Sustainable development

The concept of 'sustainable development' was crystallized and popularized in the 1987 report of the UN World Commission on Environment and Development (the Brundtland Commission), which drew upon long established lines of thought that had developed substantially over the previous 20 years.

The Brundtland Commission's shorthand characterization of 'sustainable development' is development that meets the needs of the present without compromising the ability of future generations to meet their own needs. The prominence given to 'needs' reflects a concern to eradicate poverty and meet human basic needs, broadly understood.

The concept of sustainable development focused attention on finding strategies to promote economic and social development in ways that avoided environmental degradation, over-exploitation, or pollution, and sidelined less productive debates about whether to prioritize development or the environment. A variety of important constituencies could support this concept. The emphasis on 'development' could be widely endorsed, and was particularly welcomed by developing-country representatives, development agencies, and groups primarily concerned about poverty and social deprivation. The link with 'sustainability' satisfied a variety of environmental constituencies. It addressed those who were concerned that present patterns of economic and population growth would have to change because humankind was reaching the limits of the Earth's finite natural resources and 'carrying capacity', first popularized by the Club of Rome in the early 1970s (Meadows *et al.* 1972, 1992). It could also be welcomed by those who doubted this, and were more concerned about problems such as pollution, climate change, and threats to habitats and biodiversity.

Issues and challenges in international environmental politics

Some challenges for International Relations

As International Relations scholars came to study international environmental politics, they not surprisingly brought their established theoretical perspectives and prejudices with them. Such is the variety and complexity of the environmental issue-area that advocates of each such perspective can find plenty of evidence that seems to support their case, be it Realist, neo-realist, Liberal, Liberal Institutionalist, Marxist, Social Constructivist or feminist. Moreover, each perspective provides important insights into aspects of global environmental change or international environmental politics.

However, it is perhaps more interesting and important to note at the outset that international environmental issues pose particular challenges for some of the dominant approaches in International Relations. Theories and simplifying assumptions developed through other areas of study, such as security studies (Ch.13) or international political economy (Ch.14), should not be assumed to apply equally well to this area without careful examination of the evidence. In practice, they often require significant revision to take proper account of the particular characteristics of environmental issues.

One example relates to the significance and role of states. The dominant tradition within International Relations is state-centric, centred around concepts of state sovereignty and the belief that states are the primary actors in international affairs and that international politics is largely driven by states pursuing their interests (see Ch.7). However, transnational environmental problems pose real problems for established notions about the nature and limits of state sovereignty. Moreover, international environmental problems are rarely caused by deliberate acts of national policy, but are rather unintended side-effects of broader socio-economic processes. A wide range and large number of non-state actors—including companies, local authorities, financial institutions, social groups, and individuals—are typically at least as important as states as actors in these processes.

It is true, however, that states retain a relatively privileged position in the international politics of responding to global environmental problems. Whereas states and their central governments do not generally directly control the economic, social, and environmental activities of concern, they do have sovereign authority to legislate within their territories and thus must play a central role in developing and implementing any environmental regulations. Thus, while the rise of environmental problems has brought state power and sovereignty into question, the responses to these problems may often extend and strengthen aspects of state authority and involvement in society. Moreover, to the extent that international agreements are important for cooperative responses to environmental problems, interstate diplomacy must come to the fore and states will be the legal parties to any treaties.

But, as already illustrated, even in relation to the politics of responding to international environmental problems, non-state actors typically also play a primary role. **Supranational organizations** such as the EU play a key international role alongside states, as well as being able to regulate activities within their member states. The EU is itself a party to several international environmental treaties. **International organizations**, international financial institutions, **transnational organizations** (such as industrial associations or environmental **nongovernmental organizations** (NGOs)), **social movements**, womens groups, consumer groups, and scientists can all play a key role. Even in relation to international environmental negotiations and agreements, there are numerous examples of non-state actors playing central roles. Moreover, as states become enmeshed in international institutions or **regimes** established to tackle environmental problems, the policy process often acquires an important transnational or international dimension which in practice can substantially limit national autonomy.

Finally, implementing international environmental commitments typically has to involve a mixture of international institutions, states, and transnational and domestic organizations. Limiting atmospheric or sea pollution, for example, can rarely be directly carried out by government decision, like dismantling a missile or withdrawing a tank division

in arms control. It involves a complex process of changing a variety of often well-established industrial or social activities, involving a wide range of non-governmental groups, local authorities, and individuals.

Just as studies of international environmental politics oblige us to take full account of a range of non-state actors, and to review the significance and role of states, they also raise questions about the relationship between the 'international' and 'domestic' spheres of political activity. Several strands of International Relations theory have been developed on the basis of there being a radical distinction between these two spheres. However, global environmental issues involve a range of connections between local, national, and international processes that raise questions about such distinctions. This is true not only for patterns of causation and impacts of environmental problems in an interdependent world, but also for responses to such problems. Transnational organizations and networks—for example, environmental NGOs, multinational companies, financial institutions, scientists—typically play a relatively important role, and these by definition cut across international/domestic boundaries. International organizations are sometimes directly involved in local projects with only nominal involvement of the national authorities. The relationship between international organizations and institutions, states, and non-state actors within countries is normally complex in this context, and particularly when it comes to implementing international programmes for environmental protection.

A third issue for International Relations raised particularly by studies of international environmental issues is the relationship between knowledge, power, and interests. Scientific or expert knowledge often plays an especially important role in environmental politics. Careful scientific monitoring and modelling of the environment is usually needed to identify and assess problems and to frame debates about possible responses. 'Knowledge' helps to set agendas, affects patterns of **influence** and power, and shapes assessments by key actors of their priorities and interests. Typically, there is considerable scientific uncertainty—about the problems, impacts, and effective responses. Nevertheless, communities of scientists and experts can exert substantial influence. International environmental issues therefore provide an important area for exploring the ways in which power relations, patterns of interests, knowledge and learning processes, and values interact in determining outcomes. Attempts to explain the outcomes of international policy debates on environmental issues in terms of just one or two of these factors have normally failed.

The 'tragedy of the commons': an instructive parable

In 1968 Garrett Hardin proposed a particularly influential model to explain why communities may over-exploit shared environmental resources even where they know that they are doing so and are aware that it is against their long-term interests (Hardin 1968). This is known as the '**tragedy of the commons**'.

The notion of the 'tragedy of the commons' can be explained using a hypothetical example—or 'parable'—of the use of common fish resources (see Box 20.3). In brief, the notion shows how it is possible that 'rational' individual actions can lead to 'irrational' collective practices resulting in catastrophic over-exploitation of common resources. Where access to a common resource is open and unregulated, each user continues to have an individual interest in exploiting it to the maximum. Each user gains the full extra benefit of further resource extraction, while the cost of over-exploitation is shared by all of the communities that use the resource.

The 'tragedy of the commons' is that this depletion of 'open access' common resources can continue remorselessly to its destructive conclusion, even if each user involved is well intentioned, well informed, and exercising only its traditional and legal rights. Unilateral acts of public-spirited restraint are insufficient to tackle the problem. If the rest of the user community continues in its old ways, the public-spirited suffer along with the selfish without even having benefited from the 'good times' in the meantime.

Many environmental problems of industrial society appear to have a similar **structure**. The owners of

---

Box 20.3 | **The 'tragedy of the commons': a parable**

Consider a sea or large lake on which many local fishing communities depend as a source of food and income. Each fisher has an immediate interest in making as large a catch of fish as s/he can sell or eat, in order to improve his or her standard of living. For centuries, this arrangement has worked satisfactorily. Human populations were sufficiently low, and fishing technologies were sufficiently primitive, that there was no over-fishing. Gradually, however, living conditions improved and human populations grew, increasing the number of people fishing and also the demand for fish. At the same time, fishing technologies improved. In recent years, the sea or lake has been fished at unsustainable levels, and the total fish stock is falling.

In spite of this, each individual fisher continues to have an interest in maintaining or improving their catch. Each fisher gains the full extra benefit of catching additional fish, but bears only a small part of the extra cost of fishing a depleted fish stock because this cost is shared throughout the whole community. Even concerned and environmentally aware fishers may be sorely tempted to continue to make large catches: they know that even if they desist, others are likely to continue to maximize their own catches while they can. The 'tragedy of the commons', in this parable, is that this process continues until the fish stock is destroyed along with the fishing communities that depended on it.

---

a factory have an interest in continuing to produce goods in the cheapest way, even if that involves dispersing untreated pollutants into the rivers or atmosphere. They gain most of the benefits of cheap production, while the pollution costs are uncertain and in any case shared by the whole 'downstream' community and other species of life. That is, the costs of pollution are **externalized**, since the polluter does not have to include them in its production costs. In this way some governments have been relatively tolerant of sulphur emissions from power stations in their **territory**, since the resulting acid rain was dispersed over a number of downwind states. Moreover, the damage caused by acid rain to buildings and forests typically does not appear in power-generation budgets, whereas the costs of cleaning the emissions would do so.

Preventing the over-exploitation of the commons

The notion of the 'tragedy of the commons' demonstrates the vulnerability of open access resources to over-exploitation. In principle, a range of types of responses to such over-exploitation are available. One traditional response is to **'exploit and move on'**. This has been the approach taken by 'slash and burn' agricultural communities in the tropical forests, cattle herdsmen in regions of Africa, and many international timber companies. Increasingly, however, this is no longer an option. The environment cannot recover (or is given insufficient time and space in which to do so), and there are fewer places to move on to.

Another type of response is **'privatization'**. Hardin himself drew the conclusion that the solution to the 'tragedy of the commons' was a change in property rights, arguing that the problem of the commons is that they are 'owned' by everyone and that no one in particular had the authority or interest in managing them sustainably. Thus, in relation to the over-grazing of common land, for example, if ownership of the common grazing land were divided amongst the herd-keepers, each of these would have a direct interest in maintaining the value of his or her own land by grazing it at sustainable levels. Each would bear the full costs of any unsustainable practices, and each would have the ability to control how his or her land was managed.

In principle, the 'privatization' approach could play a significant role in improving resource management of the global commons. For example, the new UN Convention on the Law of the Sea, agreed in 1982, transferred effective ownership of much of the world's ocean resources to coastal states, with a broad obligation on these states to manage sustainably their Exclusive Economic Zones (EEZ) which stretched 200 miles from their coasts. However, in general, in order for this approach to be effective the new 'owners' would need to have a clear interest in the long-term conservation and management of the resources under their control, and have the capacity and knowledge necessary for effectively carrying out their management role. In practice, such conditions would often not be met. For example, without regu-lation, it is not clear that owners of 'privatized' forest could be relied on to manage their forests sustainably rather than sell the timber and invest the proceeds in other businesses. Moreover, the approach would be difficult to apply to tackle resources or problems which by their nature do not respect artificial 'property' boundaries, such as atmospheric or sea pollution or migratory fish.

The third type of approach to promoting environmental conservation and sustainable management of the commons is to establish systems of **governance** to prevent unsustainable or damaging practices. This approach tackles the problem by regulating access to shared resources rather than by changing patterns of ownership.

This third approach is in principle applicable to the widest range of problems. But it is clear that establishing any system of **norms, rules**, regulations, or taxes to tackle environmental problems is bound to be controversial, particularly when traditional rules of access have to be made more restrictive. Experience with attempts to prevent over-fishing, for example, has shown that some fishers can be expected to deny that there is an over-fishing problem. Others might dispute the maximum sustainable yield. Moreover, the ways in which fishing quotas or the burdens of implementing taxes or regulations are distributed amongst the community are also sure to be controversial. The benefits or costs of any environmental policy or regulation are bound to be distributed unevenly, leading to disputes about which regulations or policies to adopt and also to possible compliance problems in the future.

Such disputes and challenges are characteristic of all attempts to tackle environmental problems or to manage common resources. Nevertheless, the prospects for overcoming them and establishing effective management could be expected to be greatly improved if there is a strong hierarchical authority capable of taking decisions and enforcing them on dissenting groups. Thus most would agree that state regulation and control is a potentially effective approach to managing local or national resources within a well-developed state.

However, there is no **world government** with the power or authority to impose rules on the use of global commons. Authority for legislation and enforcement is dispersed amongst some 190 sovereign states, none of which can legally be obliged to obey an international law to which they do not subscribe. In this context, Hardin and many others have been deeply sceptical about the prospects for developing effective systems for **collective governance** of the global commons.

This focuses attention on the extent to which effective collective management systems can be developed and maintained. Such systems involve the development of collective institutions—in the form of sets of agreed principles, norms, rules, common understandings, organizations, consultation processes, and suchlike—governing or shaping uses of the shared environmental resources. Ostrom and others examined the conditions for the successful formation of such institutions amongst local or regional communities in the absence of a central authority (Ostrom 1990). Perhaps unsurprisingly, they found them to be similar in character to the conditions conducive to the establishment of international regimes, particularly those identified by Liberal Institutionalists, as discussed in Chapters 9 and 16.

In practice, much of the international politics of responding to global environmental problems has been focused around the development, implementation, and effectiveness of international environmental regimes. In this context, an **international environmental regime** is an international agreement or social institution with (more or less) agreed-upon principles, norms, rules, decisionmaking procedures and programmes that govern the activities and shape the expectations of actors in a specific environmental issue-area.

Understandings of how international environmental regimes develop and operate, and what determines their effectiveness, remain contested. As discussed in Chapter 16, for example, Realists and Liberal Institutionalists generally agree on the importance of the development of international rule-based behaviour, but differ between and among themselves on how to understand it. Realists tend to regard international regimes, including environmental regimes, as agreements that reflect particular patterns of power and interests of states, which are quite vulnerable to changes in such patterns. However, they accept that regimes may prove robust where participating states have strong interest in

coordination, and where the regime enables them to operate on the so-called Pareto frontier of optimal coordination. Liberal Institutionalists tend to see wider scope for developing robust environmental regimes, and emphasize their potential role in establishing collective environmental governance to tackle problems like the 'tragedy of the commons', involving collaboration among states that fear 'free-riding' or defection by competitors. Since the early 1990s, many analysts from the liberal tradition have emphasized the importance of seeing environmental regimes as international social institutions, through which rules-based behaviour is induced not only through rational calculations of interest but also through the absorption of norms and values and through processes of social learning. In this way, environmental and other regimes may shape and transform governments' perceptions of state interests.

It is important to note that the above working definition of an environmental regime deliberately does not prejudge any of the above debates. It provides scope for environmental regimes to be an important focus not only for Realist or Liberal Institutionalist investigations, but also for others including reflectivists and Social Constructivists (see Ch.12). Environmental regimes, from this perspective, can provide an important framework for the interactions between a wide variety of international and domestic actors, and between power, interests, knowledge, and values.

An environmental regime provides a focus for the formulation and implementation of policies to tackle a particular international environmental problem, including the organization of relevant resource transfers and capacity-building activities. For many, however, regimes provide too restrictive and 'reformist' a framework for examining responses to global environmental change. Insufficient attention may be devoted to the activities and struggles of local groups around the world that do not explicitly engage with the regime politics or focus on particular environmental 'issue-areas'. Similarly, environmental regimes have naturally tended to develop in issue-areas where influential international actors perceive international cooperation to be most useful or essential. Nevertheless, as international environmental regimes and institutions have developed, and become interlinked, their forums and programmes have provided a focus for international efforts to promote awareness of such local issues, and also of broader concerns such as the importance of gender awareness in environmental programmes and the specific roles that women might play.

Finally, regimes are typically developed to shape and restrict the activities of relevant actors in order to tackle specific environmental problems, not to challenge or transform the socio-economic or political structures and processes that generate the global patterns of development, resource distribution, and environmental degradation. Thus an emphasis on regimes can be criticized by those who focus on 'world-system' approaches or those for whom anything other than clearly transformatory agendas are inadequate. However, the scope of such agendas soon extends far beyond specifically environmental political issues.

Key points

- Each of the main approaches within International Relations theory provides important insights into international environmental politics. At the same time, environmental issues pose major challenges, particularly relating to: the role and significance of states and the notion of sovereignty; the relationship between international and domestic spheres of political activity; and the relationship between knowledge, values, power, and interests in determining outcomes in international processes.

- The notion of the 'tragedy of the commons' provides an instructive model of how common resources can become over-exploited.

- The collective management of global commons in principle is more widely applicable than approaches focusing on 'privatization', though the development of international collective management regimes poses particular challenges.

- Much international environmental politics can be said to focus around the development and implementation of international environmental regimes.

The development and implementation of environmental regimes

By the year 2000, there were over 130 multilateral environmental agreements (and hundreds of bilateral ones). As indicated in Chapter 16, some of these must be regarded as 'dead letters'. Others are symbolic or weak, and have probably had little or no independent effect on the behaviour of relevant actors, or on the problem which they address. Nevertheless, case studies have shown that numerous environmental regimes have really been effective, in that they have changed behaviour in line with their aims and have at least helped to tackle the problems for which they were established (Haas *et al.* 1993; Levy *et al.* 1995). The Montreal Protocol for the Protection of the Ozone Layer is a prime example. Such effective regimes are dynamic: they tend to develop and change over time, according to chan-

ging needs and opportunities and as the international context develops.

In this section we first outline the characteristic phases in the development of environmental regimes, and then illustrate some key issues through a short case study of the regimes to protect the ozone layer. The processes of regime development can, in principle, be divided into several phases: agenda formation; negotiation and decision-making; implementation; and further development. In practice, these phases often overlap and interact—particularly as a dynamic regime becomes established.

The **agenda-formation** stage includes the processes by which the problem becomes recognized, emerges on to the political stage, is framed for consideration and debate by the relevant policy communities, and rises high enough on the international political agenda to initiate negotiations and decisionmaking processes. For environmental issues, it can often be difficult even to secure recognition that there is a problem. Without careful scientific monitoring and assessment, problems such as pollution, depletion of fish stocks, decline in biodiversity, and climate change, may emerge slowly and not become clear until it is too late to prevent major impacts or even disaster. This is a major reason why science and 'knowledge-production' processes are particularly important in environmental politics, as discussed above.

Such scientific findings are used in attempts to place the issue on the political agenda and to frame the debates about possible responses. However this process is by no means straightforward. The science enters a political arena with competing interest groups, and is in any case often uncertain. NGOs have typically been particularly important in agenda setting, often in implicit coalitions with concerned scientific bodies, international secretariats, and sympathetic governments.

Vivid or dramatic events or discoveries have played an important role in mobilizing public concern and capturing political attention. Measures against oil pollution at sea were stimulated by oil tanker disasters, even though routine spillage had been posing at least as wide an environmental threat. Similarly, public concern in the UK about North Sea pollution was only mobilized sufficiently to persuade the government to support more stringent international action when it was linked to an epidemic among the (photogenic) seal population. In the 1970s, UNEP felt obliged to present the problem of desertification in terms of (scientifically dubious) images of desert sand-dunes advancing on farming areas in order stimulate international action.

The stage of **negotiating and agreeing commitments** takes a political process on an issue from the point where it becomes a priority item on the agenda of relevant policymaking or negotiating fora to the point where international decisions are made about which policies and rules will be adopted to address the issue. It is at this stage that choices are made about commitments, policies, and measures.

In principle, there are normally a number of possible ways to respond to a given environmental problem. The ways in which the main policy response options are actually framed, considered, and assessed are a key part of environmental politics, and constitute another important dimension to the relationship between policy, science, and 'knowledge'. Some approaches may be assessed to be more effective in tackling the problem than others. In this context, transnational 'knowledge-based' communities of experts with shared understanding of the problem and preferred policy responses (i.e. **epistemic communities**') have proved particularly influential.

Moreover, policies also differ in the ways they distribute the costs and benefits among different social groups and actors, and this also has a profound effect on the policymaking process and on final decisions. The problems of achieving agreement typically multiply as the number of participants and the variety of their interests increase.

Equity issues are generally central to the negotiation process. To be negotiable and have legitimacy, commitments generally need to be perceived to be reasonably fair and equitable. Sometimes it is possible to achieve agreement on a single principle to guide 'fair' distributions of burdens, such as the 'polluter pays' principle. In practice, however, many notions of equity are typically in play, including: equal quotas; equal percentage changes from the status quo; equality of burden in implementing commitments; burdens distributed according to historic responsibility for the problem, or according to capacity to pay; 'first come, first served'; historic ("grandfathered") rights; and many others. Application of different principles would have very different implications for the distribution of costs and benefits from the agreement. Particularly in global negotiations, agreement on basic equity principles often cannot be achieved. In such cases, parties have to find ways to define commitments so that they at least appear "arguably" equitable from a number of basic standpoints.

Successfully negotiating an effective environmental agreement typically requires **leadership**. When powerful states or groups of states, such as the United States or the EU, adopt a leading role, the prospects for achieving an agreement improve greatly. For example, US leadership in achieving a whaling moratorium in the IWC was critical. In any set of negotiations it is normally possible to identify 'leaders' that want an agreement and work hard to get one through a combination of active diplomacy promoting the production and dissemination of relevant knowledge, or (informal or formal) sanctions or 'side payments'. In this way 'laggards'—states that are reluctant to achieve agreement or to agree to effective commitments—may be persuaded to sign. Further, coordination and persuasion can be achieved of the (often large number) of states that are willing in principle to join an agreement provided it is not too costly, but are not going to work hard to achieve one.

Naturally leader states aim to shape the commitments in line with their interests. But they usually have to compromise to get an agreement. Moreover, in any given issue-area, there are likely to be 'veto states', without whose agreement and participation an effective regime cannot be established.

The **implementation** phase includes all of the activities involved in implementing the decisions and policies adopted in response to the problem. This can include: the incorporation of international commitments into domestic law; the development and operationalization of agreed programmes; and all other measures aimed at appropriately changing government, social, and economic practices in line with agreed rules and norms.

This stage is typically no less complex than the other two. On the contrary, experience shows that it is one thing to agree to international obligations, and quite another to bring them into operation and to achieve the desired effects on the behaviour of relevant actors. Those charged with implementing the decisions may lack necessary commitment or resources, and will typically interpret the decisions in their own ways. In practice, some countries tend to take legal obligations very seriously, whereas others tend to regard them as symbols of general intentions and a stage in an ongoing negotiation process, not to be interpreted too literally. Actors whose interests are substantially affected by the changes in policy can be expected to continue to try to influence the policy and the ways it is implemented. Compliance may leave much to be desired. In any case, the actual effects of decisions and rules can be very different from the expected ones.

Whether or not international agreements are implemented can depend greatly on the nature of the commitments themselves. Governments may not try hard to implement if they believe themselves to have been coerced into an unfair agreement, which is a reason why it is important that agreements should be regarded as legitimate and reasonably fair or in each participant's overall interest. This highlights the importance of equity and legitimacy for the implementation and effectiveness of regimes as well as for their negotiation.

The will to implement may be weak if parties suspect that others may not be complying, and attempting to 'free-ride'. Thus whether or not the implementation and compliance of commitments can be monitored or verified may be an important factor. Similarly, international systems to review countries' progress in implementation can help, by increasing awareness of obligations and by identifying and facilitating timely responses to any emerging problems. Further, mechanisms to provide international aid can both increase countries' capacity to implement their commitments and increase their interest in doing so.

Finally, regimes usually need to **further develop** once they have been established in order to maintain or improve their effectiveness. Institutions and commitments may be strengthened and revised to adapt to changing circumstances, such as improved understandings of the problems and policy responses, or new political or economic challenges or opportunities. As outlined above and below, 'framework' conventions are explicitly designed to facilitate further development. More broadly, at least since the 1980s, such capacity to adapt has been widely regarded as a critical characteristic of effective agreements.

The development and implementation of the ozone regime

The Montreal Protocol, signed in 1987 (see Box 20.4), stands at the centre of the regime to prevent the depletion of the ozone layer. It is widely regarded as one of the success stories in international environmental regimes. Before it was signed, global consumption and production of the main

Box 20.4 Ozone depletion and the Montreal Protocol

Ozone is a molecule consisting of three oxygen atoms. It is relatively unstable and quite rare in the atmosphere. Most of it is found in the 'stratosphere' between 10 and 50 kilometres above the Earth's surface—the 'ozone layer'. There it absorbs nearly all of the high-energy ultraviolet radiation (UV-B) from the sun, protecting plants and animals from its damaging effects. The ozone layer is highly vulnerable to destruction by chlorine, fluorine, and bromine, which are highly reactive chemicals. However, until recently, it was relatively safe from these chemicals. Precisely because they were so reactive, their atmospheric lifetimes were too short for emissions from the Earth's surface to have time to drift up as high as the ozone layer.

Unfortunately, when humankind manufactured CFCs and halons, they created highly stable compounds containing chlorine, fluorine, or bromine. Indeed, they were so stable that they did not react in the lower atmosphere, allowing a proportion of them to drift gradually up to the ozone layer. There they were broken apart by the incoming ultraviolet radiation, releasing the chlorine and other chemicals to act as catalysts in destroying the ozone. Each atom of chlorine, for example, can destroy an average of about 100,000 ozone molecules before it is removed from the stratosphere.

For complex reasons, the losses of ozone are worst in the spring. By 1995, stratospheric ozone levels over Europe and North America, for example, were about 10 per cent lower than in the 1970s, and in places 20–50 per cent lower. Over the Antarctic, a particularly deep 'ozone hole' appeared annually, virtually wiping out all ozone in thick bands of the ozone layer. This led to substantial increases in the intensity of UV-B radiation at the Earth's surface. UV-B depresses immune systems, causes cataracts and skin cancers, damages the development of crops, and reduces the productivity of phytoplankton in the sea—undermining the marine food chain.

As awareness of the risks of ozone depletion grew in the 1970s, the USA, Canada, Sweden, and Norway unilaterally banned non-essential uses of CFCs. However it was not until 1985 that an international agreement was achieved: the Vienna Convention. This was a framework convention, which did not oblige parties to reduce their consumption of CFCs or other ODS. In 1987, the Montreal Protocol was agreed by 24 mainly industrialized states and the European Community. Parties to this protocol were obliged to cut their consumption of five types of CFCs by 50 per cent by 1999 and to freeze consumption of three halons.

Between 1987 and 2000, the Montreal Protocol was progressively strengthened: most importantly in London (1990), Copenhagen (1992), Vienna (1995), and Montreal (1997). The 1990 London Amendment committed developed countries to phase out an extended range of ODS (including the halons, methyl chloroform, carbon tetrachloride, and a longer list of 15 CFCs) by 2000. Developing countries were committed to phase out by 2010, with assistance from a new Multilateral Fund (MLF), created for the purpose. In 1992, the phase out dates for developed states were brought forward to 1995, and new controls were agreed to phase out HCFCs by 2030—which had been introduced as a less destructive substitute for CFCs—and to freeze use of methyl bromide. In 1995, developing countries also accepted some controls on HCFCs and methyl bromide. In 1997, more ozone-depleting chemicals were added to the list of restricted substances, and more stringent limits on methyl bromide and HCFCs were agreed. By 1999, 95 ozone-depleting chemicals were controlled under the Protocol, and worldwide CFC consumption had reduced from 1.1 million tonnes in 1986 to less than 150,000 tonnes per year. Moreover, the Montreal Protocol had become truly global, with over 160 parties.

ozone-depleting substances (ODS) was increasing rapidly. By the mid-1990s, this trend had been halted and reversed, and most developed countries had virtually phased out consumption of CFCs and halons (the most important ODS). Natural time-lags mean that the depletion of the ozone layer will nevertheless continue to get worse until after the first decade of the twenty-first century, but thereafter it is expected gradually to recover—returning to its pre-1970 levels by about 2060.

The agenda-formation phase of the regime began

in the early 1970s. In 1974, Rowland and Molina—two US-based scientists—published an analysis arguing that CFCs emitted into the atmosphere could lead to the destruction of stratospheric ozone (Molina and Rowland 1974). Coming at a time of intense debates in the United States about the risks that emissions from high-flying supersonic aircraft might pose to the upper atmosphere, this hypothesis immediately attracted public attention. CFCs were invented in 1928, as a coolant for refrigeration, but since the 1960s production had increased rapidly as further uses were found in: air-conditioners; expanded foams for cushions and insulation; solvents to clean electronics; sterilants; and aerosol propellants. Halons—related chemicals including bromine—were also increasingly used as fire extinguishers and suppressants.

Environmental movements and the US Environmental Protection Agency (EPA) argued that at least non-essential uses of CFCs, as in aerosols, should be banned as a precautionary measure. DuPont and the other major chemical companies producing CFCs strongly disputed this, arguing that strong scientific evidence that the problem was real and serious should be required before any restrictions were introduced. The so-called 'spray can war' raged in the USA through the mid-1970s. After a US National Academy of Science report in 1976 judged that the risks were sufficiently large that precautionary measures would be justified, the balance of influence shifted towards the environmentalists and the EPA, and domestic legislation restricting CFC uses followed in 1978. These unilateral US actions had the effect of temporarily decreasing global CFC production, since the USA accounted for some 50 per cent of world consumption in the mid-1970s.

Internationally, the North American and Scandinavian countries became leaders in supporting UNEP's efforts to establish international restrictions on ozone-depleting chemicals. However, initially the countries of the EU and Japan—the other major producers and consumers of CFCs at the time—were 'laggards': sceptical about the threat and supportive of their major chemical companies.

Thus began the international process of negotiating and decisionmaking. In the first half of the 1980s, progress was extremely slow. During the first Reagan administration, the USA joined the sceptics and showed little enthusiasm for pressuring the EU and Japan on ozone issues. Under the charismatic leadership of Mostapha Tolba, UNEP played a key brokering role. In March 1985 the Vienna Convention for the Protection of the Ozone Layer was signed. However, this was a framework convention which obliged its signatories to do little more than to establish the principle that international action should be taken as necessary, carry out further research, exchange information, and periodically meet to review the adequacy of commitments.

Within two months, however, the discovery of a deep 'ozone hole' over the Antarctic was announced by scientists from the British Antarctic Survey. The political impact of this discovery provided a key illustration of the galvanizing effect of vivid or dramatic events in regime politics. The image of being exposed to UV radiation from space was already one that resonated with the general public. However, a surprise 'ozone hole' had much greater political impact than possible average depletion of 1–2 per cent per year, particularly when reinforced by NASA satellite images. Moreover, experiments in 1987 definitively showed the link between ozone depletion and the presence of chlorine: changes in chlorine and ozone concentrations were measured while an aircraft was flown across the edge of the ozone hole.

After this, DuPont, ICI, and other major CFC producers recognized that tough international restrictions on CFCs or other ODS had become virtually inevitable. Instead of continuing to oppose them, they focused on influencing any international agreement. In particular, they realized that stringent international controls on CFCs would create a market for substitutes, which they were in a better position to produce than their less sophisticated or wealthy competitors. By this time, green parties and environmental movements were becoming powerful in most West European countries. In this context, governments that had previously vetoed stringent international controls had every interest in reversing their position. For example, the UK Prime Minister Mrs Thatcher removed her objections and declared her government to be a world leader in efforts to ban CFCs. The 1987 Montreal Protocol committed parties to cut their CFC consumption by 50 per cent by 1999, and within two years a consensus was emerging among developed Western countries in favour of adopting a complete ban.

However, before a phase-out of CFCs and other ODS could be agreed, it was important to extend membership of the regime beyond developed Western states to include the Soviet bloc countries (as they were then) and developing countries. By the late 1980s production and consumption of CFCs in these countries were increasing rapidly, although still in much smaller quantities than in OECD states, and it was clear that countries like Russia, India, and

China would have to join the regime if it was to be successful in the long term. The Soviet Union and its allies were persuaded to join (with some transitional concessions) at the end of the 1980s. However, developing countries refused to accept any commitments to phase out CFCs and halons unless industrialized countries paid the 'incremental' costs they incurred in implementation. After much haggling, this was agreed in 1990. A Multilateral Fund (MLF) was established for this purpose, and developing countries agreed to phase out consumption of CFCs and halons by 2010.

From that stage, the processes of implementing and further developing the Montreal Protocol proceeded in tandem. Experience with implementing the Protocol's commitments, though complex, turned out to be easier and cheaper than many had feared. The chemical producers had a strong commercial incentive to develop substitutes quickly and also to monitor compliance amongst competitors. The Technology and Economic Assessement Panel (TEAP), established to advise on the availability and effectiveness of substitutes or alternatives for controlled substances, proved very effective in identifying opportunities and persuading users to accept them. Meanwhile the international Scientific Assessment Panel and the Environmental Impacts Panel produced authoritative reports on the need for ever more stringent commitments. UNEP continued to play a key role in brokering stringent agreements, supported by sympathetic states and environmental NGOs. In 1992, 1995, and 1997, the range of ODS controlled by the Montreal Protocol was widened, and phase-out dates for CFCs and halons were brought forward to 1995 and 1994 respectively for industrialized countries.

Implementation of these phase-outs proceeded on time and reasonably effectively in Western developed states, though there were continuing problems with black-market trading of illicit CFCs in the mid-1990s. The process turned out to be much more difficult in the 'countries with economies in transition' (the former Soviet bloc countries). The profound social and economic transitions in these countries meant that several of them neglected their Montreal Protocol commitments. The ozone regime's systems for reporting and reviewing implementation picked this up in 1995, and coordinated international responses aimed at bringing the 'culprits' (primarily Russia, Ukraine, Belarus, and Bulgaria) into compliance as quickly as possible. This was done through a mixture of 'carrots and sticks', including conditional offers of international aid. Thus a crisis that could have substantially weakened the regime was averted, and the institutions of the regime played a key role in achieving this. As far as developing countries are concerned, the operation of the MLF was a continuing source of friction between them and donor countries. Nevertheless, after initial problems, many projects to phase out controlled substances in developing countries were under way by the mid-1990s, and in many cases these countries were on track to phase out significantly before their legal deadline. By 1999, over $900 million had been disbursed by the MLF. Moreover, procedures for reviewing implementation of MLF-funded projects were developed in the mid-1990s to verify that such phase-outs actually took place. However, the ozone regime continues to adapt and develop, with major reviews every two to three years, and will probably have to do so for decades to come.

Key points

- The development of international environmental regimes can roughly be divided into four phases: agenda formation; negotiation and decision-making; implementation; and further development.

- The regime developed to limit and reverse ozone layer depletion illustrates each of these phases, and is justifiably regarded as an important and effective environmental regime.

The Rio Conference and its outcomes

As mentioned above, in 1989 the UN General Assembly decided to convene an 'Earth Summit' in Rio in 1992 in order to promote and develop sustainable development.

Preparing for Rio

The agenda for the Rio Conference quickly developed. By the end of the 1980s, there was great international concern that anthropogenic emissions of 'greenhouse gases', such as carbon dioxide, methane, nitrous oxides, and CFCs, could be affecting the Earth's overall energy balance and causing rapid global warming and climate change. In 1988, an international panel of scientists (the Intergovernmental Panel on Climate Change (IPCC)) was set up under the auspices of UNEP and the World Meteorological Organization (WMO) to examine the risk of such climate change. On the basis of the IPCC's 1990 report (Houghton *et al.* 1990), representatives of 137 countries at the Second World Climate Conference in Geneva in November 1990 agreed that an international convention was urgently needed to address the problem. Negotiations began three months later, with a view to completing a Framework Convention on Climate Change (FCCC) in time for signing at the Rio Conference.

Similarly, there was also wide concern about the loss of natural habitats and the consequent rapid extinctions of many species of life. Between 1988 and 1990 UNEP had convened a group of experts to examine the issue, and negotiations for a Convention on Biological Diversity started in June 1991, working to the same timetable.

In addition, there was wide support in many industrialized countries for an international forestry convention to limit deforestation, particularly of tropical rainforests. However, this proposal was strongly opposed by some developing countries possessing such forests, such as Malaysia and Brazil, on the grounds that it was their sovereign right to use their forests as they chose—just as industrialized countries had done centuries before. In an effort to win African governments' support in this debate, Western governments agreed to support negotiations to establish a Convention to Combat Desertification. This was a priority issue for African countries, many of which suffered from land degradation in arid areas, and also one on which UNEP had campaigned since the mid-1970s.

In addition to these specific conventions, attention focused on preparing agreements to define and promote the goal of sustainable development. Negotiations centred on preparing two main documents for agreement at the Rio Conference. The first of these was a statement of agreed principles, which later emerged as the Rio Declaration. The second document was to be a detailed programme of action for sustainable development, which became known as Agenda 21.

The Rio Conference

The 1992 Rio Conference turned out to be one of the biggest summit meetings ever held. Some 150 states were represented, and at one stage 135 heads of state were present. About 45,000 people attended, including government delegations, over 10,000 media people, and representatives of 1,500 NGOs, including environment, development, and business organizations, a women's caucus, and indigenous peoples groups. NGOs had their own parallel conference in Rio, but were also entitled to attend the intergovernmental meetings. The meeting attracted great public attention, and received enormous media coverage.

The Rio Declaration, Agenda 21, and the Declaration of Forest Principles were all agreed, and the conventions on climate change and biodiversity were respectively signed by 154 and 150 governments. The Convention on Desertification was not ready in time, and was not agreed until June 1994. Nevertheless, it is customarily included among the Earth Summit agreements (see Box 20.5).

Box 20.5 **The UNCED agreements**

The Rio Declaration proclaims 27 general principles to guide action on environment and development. They include principles relating to: national responsibilities and international cooperation on environmental protection; the needs for development and eradication of poverty; and the roles and rights of citizens, women, and indigenous peoples. For example, Principle 7 affirms the 'common but differentiated responsibilities' of developed and developing states in environmental protection. Principle 10 states that environmental issues are best handled with the participation of all citizens, at the relevant level, and thus public education, participation, and access to information and redress should all be promoted. Principle 15 affirms that a precautionary approach should be adopted: 'lack of full scientific certainty shall not be used as a reason for postponing cost-effective measures to prevent environmental degradation'.

Agenda 21 is a 400-page document with 40 chapters aiming to provide a programme of action for sustainable development. The chapters cover a wide range of topics, such as: promoting sustainable urban development; combating deforestation; biotechnology management; managing fragile mountain ecosystems; and hazardous waste management. Several chapters are on strengthening the role of 'major groups', including local authorities, trade unions, business and industry, scientists, women, indigenous peoples, youth, and farmers. The last eight chapters address implementation issues, including financial mechanisms and institutional arrangements. The Global Environment Facility is to provide 'agreed incremental costs' to help developing countries implement aspects of the Agenda 21 programme. The Commission for Sustainable Development is established as part of the UN system, to promote and review progress on implementation and to help to coordinate activities of UN Agencies in this context.

The Framework Convention on Climate Change (FCCC) was signed by 153 states, and subsequently came into force within 18 months, on 21 March 1994. It is a **'framework convention'**, establishing principles, aims, institutions, and procedures which should subsequently be developed. The declared objective of the FCCC, as stated in Article 2, is to 'achieve stabilisation of greenhouse gas concentrations in the atmosphere at a level that would prevent dangerous anthropogenic interference with the climate system. Such a level should be achieved within a time frame sufficient to allow ecosystems to adapt naturally to climate change, to

ensure that food production is not threatened and to enable economic development to proceed in a sustainable manner'. Recognizing that developed states should take the lead, these states should as a first step 'individually or jointly return to their 1990 levels' of greenhouse gas emissions. However, this was not a legally binding obligation. The most important obligations in the FCCC are that parties must provide regular reports on: their national greenhouse gas emissions; their emissions projections; and their policies and measures to limit such emissions. These are then carefully reviewed and assessed internationally. This review process aims not only to stimulate negotiation of further commitments as required, but also to promote the development and implementation of national targets.

The Convention on Biological Diversity was signed by 155 states, and came into force on 29 December 1993. It is a framework convention, which aims to preserve the biological diversity of the Earth, through protection of species, ecosystems, and habitats, and to establish terms for the use of genetic resources and bio-technologies. Parties must develop plans to protect biodiversity, and to submit reports which will be internationally reviewed. The principles clarifying states' sovereign rights to genetic resources on their territory were highly contentious and thus vague and highly qualified: such rights were affirmed, provided that the fruits of such resources are shared in a fair and equitable way on terms to be mutually agreed.

The Forest Principles were the residue of the failed attempts to negotiate a forestry convention. It proclaims principles for forest protection and management while emphasizing that states have a sovereign right to exploit forests on their territory.

The Convention to Combat Desertification was not open for signature until June 1994, but it is nevertheless considered to be an UNCED agreement. It aims to promote coordinated international actions to address problems of 'land degradation in arid, semi-arid, and dry sub-humid areas resulting from various factors, including climatic variations and human activities'. It provides a code of good practices for the management of marginal lands, for governments of affected regions, and for donors. It aims to provide a framework for cooperation between local land-users, NGOs, governments, international organizations funding agencies, and donor countries, but includes no binding obligations.

The implementation and development of the Rio conventions

The 1992 Rio Conference was widely regarded as an overall success. However, its real impact could only be judged according to how the Earth Summit agreements and conventions were subsequently developed and implemented.

It is worth noting that the conventions on climate change and biodiversity were '**framework conventions**'. That is, they established basic aims, principles, norms, institutions, and procedures for coordinated international actions, including procedures for regularly reviewing commitments and for strengthening or revising them and developing other rules and institutions of the regime as deemed appropriate by the parties. However, the initial obligations on parties in the conventions were weak. Moreover, in order to achieve agreement in time for either of these conventions to be signed at Rio, it had proved necessary for many contentious or complex issues to be sidestepped or fudged. Thus many key rules, institutions, and procedures remained to be worked out before the convention could even begin to operate. Indeed, in the case of the Biodiversity Convention, even the aims and priorities of the agreement remained unclear. Thus, the Intergovernmental Negotiating Committees (INC) that were responsible for negotiating each agreement were immediately reconvened to sort out these issues before the conventions came into force.

Before they come into force, international treaties need to be **ratified** by a minimum number of parties (with this number being defined in the treaty). In the case of the Climate Convention, for example, ratification by 50 states was needed. The ratification process involves the relevant national legislature of each signatory state (such as the US Senate or the UK Parliament) confirming that the state will be legally bound by the treaty. It normally takes several years for enough countries to ratify a treaty for it to come into force (the UN Law of the Sea, signed in 1982, did not come into force until 1994). However, the three Earth Summit conventions came into force remarkably quickly: all within two years of being signed.

In many respects, the early progress in implementing commitments in the Climate Convention was striking. Developed country parties mostly prepared relatively detailed national reports on their national greenhouse gas emissions, their projected future emissions, and their policies and measures to reduce them. These reports were internationally reviewed in detail, in a way that established promising precedents for the future. However, the lack of legally binding commitments to limit emissions caused wide concern. The first Conference of the Parties (CoP) of the Climate Convention, meeting in Berlin in March 1995, decided immediately to begin negotiations to establish more stringent commitments on industrial countries to limit their emissions of greenhouse gases. The aim was to establish a new protocol, including legally binding limits on greenhouse gas emissions of industrialized states, at the December 1997 CoP due to take place in Kyoto, Japan. By 1995 almost all OECD countries and the EU had unilaterally pledged themselves to aim at least to stabilize their greenhouse gas emissions at 1990 levels by the year 2000, and some including Germany and the Netherlands had promised reductions by that time. However, it soon became clear that most developed countries were not on track to achieve such stabilization pledges.

In this context, negotiations for a **Kyoto Protocol** including more stringent commitments for industrial states were bound to be difficult, and so it proved. An Alliance of Small Island States (AOSIS), threatened as they were with inundation as a result of sea-level rise, advocated a 20 per cent reduction in industrial country emissions by 2005. However, oil-exporting OPEC countries—their nominal allies in the G77 group of developing countries—campaigned strongly against any substantial commitments for developed countries, fearing that emission-reduction measures would reduce demand for oil, and thus threaten their incomes. Similarly, the EU and some other West European states broadly supported emission-reduction targets of 5–10 per cent by 2010, but several other developed countries, including the USA, Japan, Australia, and Canada, were reluctant to support any obligations requiring emission reductions. Former communist countries in Eastern Europe and the former Soviet Union were typically suspicious of any obligations that could impede their economic recovery, and several did not think it fair that they should be classed as developed countries when relatively wealthy states such as South Korea, and Malaysia were classed as developing countries and thus under no immediate pressure to limit their emissions.

These debates highlight how complex equity issues rapidly become in global negotiations. The differences in circumstances of states within the groups of developed and developing states are in many ways as great as the differences between these groups. Even within Western developed countries, Southern European governments argued that their countries are comparatively poor and should not have to stabilize their emissions yet; Japan and others argued that they should not have to accept the same percentage cuts in emissions as the USA, for example, because they have already implemented energy efficiency measures. Moreover, elites within developing countries live 'First World' lifestyles, and in countries like Brazil, India, and China their numbers far exceed the populations of medium or small developed countries. Surely, some say, these elites

should not be entirely exempt from pressure to adopt more 'climate-friendly' lifestyles. However, negotiators were aware that any attempt in the name of equity to negotiate separate targets for each country, taking into account its individual circumstances, is a recipe for failure. Special pleading and complexity would bog the negotiations down.

In the event, the Kyoto Protocol was succesfully agreed in December 1997, and involved more stringent limits on most developed countries emissions than many had expected in the circumstances, as outlined in Box 20.6. This was a major achievement, but many challenges remain. Many technical issues needed to be resolved on which the effectiveness of the Protocol depends; these were the subject of further negotiations between 1998 and 2001, and beyond. Moreover, there is the political challenge of achieving ratification of the Kyoto Protocol so that it comes legally into force. Particularly in the United States, political opposition to the Kyoto Protocol (and to the emission-reduction measures it implies)

Box 20.6   The 1997 Kyoto Protocol to the Framework Convention on Climate Change

At the core of the 1997 Kyoto Protocol are legally binding commitments by industrialized states to limit their greenhouse gas emissions. The EU, USA, and Japan respectively committed themselves to reduce their annual greenhouse gas emissions by 2008–12 to 8, 7, and 6 per cent less than 1990 levels. Prospective EU members such as Poland adopted EU targets, while Russia, Ukraine, and New Zealand agreed to stabilize their emissions at 1990 levels and Australia, Iceland, and Norway managed to negotiate limited increases in their permitted emissions. These commitments refer to net emissions, so that greenhouse gas emissions may be offset by absorption of such gases in sinks such as afforestation projects. Overall, these commitments would imply a 5 per cent reduction in greenhouse gas emissions in industrialized countries.

To achieve this agreement, a number of so-called flexibility mechanisms were established in the Protocol: Joint Implementation (allowing industrialized states to share the credit for emission reductions achieved in specific joint projects); Emissions Trading (allowing industrialized states to exchange part of their national emission allowances); and the Clean Development Mechanism (allowing industrialized states to obtain emission credits for financing approved climate-friendly projects in developing countries). Thus, for

example, the USA is allowed to achieve its commitments not only by reducing net emissions from domestic sources, but also by buying spare emissions quotas from other industrialized parties such as Russia, and by getting credit for emission reductions achieved in approved Joint Implementation or Clean Development Mechanism projects which it supports in other countries. EU member states also had their own flexibility mechanism. They are permitted to distribute emissions targets among themselves, provided that their overall emissions reduced by 8 per cent. Within the EU Austria, Denmark, Germany, Luxembourg, and the UK agreed to achieve reductions of more than 8 per cent, enabling Southern European countries, France, and Ireland to be allocated much less stringent targets.

The agreement achieved in Kyoto in 1997 left many key issues open, requiring further negotiation. These included the design of each of the above flexiblity mechanisms, the rules for offsetting emissions with absorption by sinks, methodologies for calculating and reporting national emissions, and systems for assessing implementation and compliance and for responding to compliance problems. These were the focus for detailed negotiations between 1998 and 2000, with the aim of achieving agreements at the Amsterdam CoP in November 2000.

became highly mobilized in the late 1990s, and in 2001 President Bush finally withdrew the US signature from the Protocol, significantly undermining the prospects of its success. Also in 2001 it was clear that most industrialized countries needed to take much more active emission-reduction measures if they were to achieve their Kyoto Protocol commitments. This is a prerequisite to meeting the longer-term challenge of negotiating and establishing the further commitments, including commitments of developing countries to limit their increases in the greenhouse gas emissions as they industrialize, that are required to reduce substantially the risk of catastrophic climate change.

The challenges of making the Biodiversity Convention effective have proved to be at least as fundamental. Although in formal terms it also got off to a reasonably prompt start, fundamental disputes about its aims and priorities continued. Little progress was made on what many in the developed countries regarded as the primary objective: to protect natural habitats and thus the diversity of species of wildlife that depend upon them. Many developing countries had a wider agenda, including securing international financial and technology assistance and gaining a share of the economic benefits of biodiversity and bio-technology by securing intellectual property rights over any genetic resources from their territory and any products made from them. These were demands that most developed countries were reluctant to concede.

Some progress was achieved in implementing those parts of the Convention concerned with the development and reporting of national data on biodiversity and of national plans to protect and promote biodiversity in the future. However, after 1995, negotiating efforts soon focused on the elaboration of a protocol on 'biosafety', and particularly on regulating the movement of genetically engineered organisms across borders. After almost five years of difficult negotiations, the parties agreed on the **Cartegena Protocol on Biosafety** on 29 January 2000. It established a requirement for 'advanced informed agreement' before genetically modified organisms (GMOs) may be transferred. In view of the increasingly highly charged debates surrounding the use and trade in GMOs, particularly intended for use in agriculture, this protocol was a significant

achievement. However, it will clearly do little to prevent loss of species or natural habitats. The effectiveness of the Biodiversity Convention in promoting these goals therefore remained in doubt at the turn of the century.

Similarly, although the Convention to Combat Desertification came into force by 1996, it was primarily designed to encourage donor countries to provide aid and assistance to developing countries in dry regions that are facing problems of land degradation. Donor countries are thereby intimately linked with broader development programmes, and this is how most of them have preferred to approach the issue during a period when development aid budgets were generally declining. In practice, only slow progress was made in establishing specific MLF mechanisms, and it proved difficult to attract additional donor interest.

Agenda 21: promoting sustainable development

The 1992 Rio Conference established several institutions to promote the overall implementation and further development of Agenda 21. The most significant of these were the Commission for Sustainable Development (CSD) and the Global Environment Facility (GEF), working in association with UNEP, UNDP, and other UN bodies. Clearly it was not expected that these institutions could directly implement Agenda 21, or force others to do so. Rather the hope was that they could help to stimulate or shape broader international or domestic processes in a useful way.

The CSD consists of representatives of 53 states, elected for three-year terms in a way that ensures equitable geographical representation. It began its work in 1993, and has met annually since then to review progress on different aspects of Agenda 21, with numerous preparatory meetings. Ministerial participation in these meetings has been substantial, giving the process more political weight than some had feared. Moreover, NGOs can participate in the proceedings, making each CSD meeting a sort of mini-Earth Summit. Coalitions between environmental NGOs and sympathetic states have made the CSD a forum in which environmental agendas can be set and pursued.

Broadly, the CSD process has aimed to promote sustainable development in three ways. Its role in promoting coordinated approaches towards sustainable development by international agencies has had some real but modest successes. However, its second role of reviewing national reports on aspects of sustainable development may be of wider significance. The significance of the CSD process in simply stimulating governments to review their practices and prepare policies for inclusion in their national reports should not be underestimated. Moreover, the CSD has provided a forum where governments can be called to account, for the contents of their policies or for the gap between these and reality. The presence of NGOs has helped to make this process more substantial.

The third role of the CSD process has been to follow-up on unfinished business of UNCED and to promote the formation of new regimes where opportunities arise. For example, after discussions on deforestation at the CSD, an intergovernmental panel was established to review the issues. In 1996, this led to an agreement to begin international negotiations on a forestry convention: providing a second chance after the failure in the lead-up to UNCED.

Another aspect of follow-up to UNCED has been a series of follow-up summit meetings on particular issues such as population and development (Cairo, 1994), social development (Copenhagen, 1995), the role and rights of women (Beijing, 1995), and urban development (Istanbul, 1996). The significance of such summits is controversial, but they have helped to promote political awareness and concern, and to develop international networks of concerned experts, NGOs, citizens groups, and local authorities, which it is hoped can then become more effective in their local activities. Five years on, there were a number of follow-up conferences (labelled, for example, as 'Copenhagen + 5') to review and stimulate further progress in implementing and developing sustainable development in the relevant policy spheres.

Global Environment Facility (GEF) funds only amount to a few billion dollars ($3 billion was allocated for 1994–7), which is a tiny amount compared to the massive international flows of funds that take place through normal economic transactions, and also compared to the funds needed to implement sustainable development. However, numerous relatively small GEF grants to developing countries and to former communist states have contributed significantly to the preparation of national plans to promote sustainability. Moreover, in such countries, modest funds can contribute significantly to 'institutional capacity building' where local expertise or resources are lacking. GEF funds for large-scale projects have been much slower to flow, and are a continual source of friction between recipients and donor countries.

Overall, therefore, the UNCED institutions to promote implementation of Agenda 21 have had some limited significance. But it is clear that they have had only a marginal impact on the broader economic and social processes that drive patterns of development.

At the end of the twentieth century, debates increasingly focused on the challenges of developing international mechanisms to shape broader patterns of trade and investment in line with environmental goals. Some believe that the norms and rules of the World Trade Organization (WTO), with their focus on removing constraints on international trade and investment, are inimical to efforts to promote environmental protection, sustainable development, and other social goals. Transnational NGO campaigns to challenge the dominance of WTO norms and rules proved resonant in 2000, for example, when they succeeded in disrupting the Seattle meeting of the WTO. In contrast, others believe that **trade and environment** regimes can be complementary and even mutually reinforcing (for example, by promoting international investment in modern, and more environmentally friendly, technologies). Principles have arguably been established whereby global environmental regimes, such as the ozone layer protection regime, may restrict trade in direct pursuit of its goals without falling foul of WTO rules. For example, the Montreal Protocol specifically includes provisions for restricting trade to non-parties or non-compliant parties, as well as restricting trade in goods containing ozone-depleting substances. However, the situation is much less clear when restrictions on trade for environmental purposes are imposed as part of national or regional measures that do not command

Box 20.7   Key concepts for international environmental issues

Agenda formation: the processes by which an issue or problem becomes recognized, emerges on to the political stage, is framed for consideration and debate by the relevant policy communities, and rises high enough on the political agenda to initiate negotiations or decisionmaking processes.

Collective governance: non-hierarchical (in the sense of the absence of a central coercive power) systems of management or governance.

Environmental regime: an international regime addressing an environmental issue.

Epistemic communities: knowledge-based transnational communities of experts with shared understandings of an issue or problem or preferred policy responses.

Framework convention: an international convention establishing principles, norms, goals, organizations, and procedures for consultation, decisionmaking, and review, with provision for flexible subsequent revision or development of rules or commitments.

Global commons: resources open for use by the international community, and not under the jurisdiction of any state, such as: oceans, atmosphere, deep-sea bed, Antarctica.

International institutions: sets of internationally agreed principles, norms, rules, common understandings, organizations, and consultation and decisionmaking procedures that govern or shape activities in a particular area.

Implementation: carrying out adopted decisions or policies.

Over-exploitation: the unsustainable exploitation of a resource.

Sustainable development: economic and social development that meets the needs of the present without compromising the ability of future generations to meet their own needs; programmes which maintain an appropriate balance between economic development, social development, and environmental protection. In practice, this is a contested concept, in that groups with differing political, economic, social, and environmental perspectives disagree about its exact meaning.

Tragedy of the commons: the over-exploitation of open-access resources by users 'rationally' pursuing their individual interests.

Transnational: cutting across national boundaries; linking the international and domestic sphere. Thus, for example, transnational processes are non-state processes that cut across national boundaries.

wide support at the global level. In this context, tensions between environmental and trading regimes are likely to be a continuing source of friction. For example, in the mid-1990s international free trade rules were used to overturn measures by the USA to restrict imports of tuna in response to fishing methods that damage dolphin populations. In general, however, there is increasing international interest in designing the rules and mechanisms of international environmental regimes so that they work with the grain of globalized economic processes and market mechanisms, and seek to shape international patterns of trade and investment in line with environmental goals. The flexibility mechanisms agreed in the Kyoto Protocol to the Framework Convention on Climate Change, discussed above, are just one illustration of this trend.

Key points

- Three new conventions were agreed at the Rio Conference, aimed at limiting climate change, preserving biodiversity, and combating desertification. Each of these came rapidly into force, but the process of making these conventions effective has proved a long-term task.

- The negotiations to develop further the Climate Change Convention demonstrated the immense challenges involved in achieving a sufficient response to prevent substantial anthropogenic climate change, and also the complexity of equity issues in negotiations. The Kyoto Protocol agreed in 1997 established substantial legally binding commitments, but many challenges remain.

- There are still major disputes about the main aims and objectives of the Biodiversity Convention and means to achieve them.

- The institutions established to promote the implementation of Agenda 21 have stimulated the production of national plans for sustainable development and provided a forum where plans can be reviewed and where networks of NGOs, government representatives, and international secretariats can develop and influence agendas. However, their influence on overall patterns of development has been small.

- The relationship between environment and trade regimes has emerged as a key issue.

Conclusion

Environmental issues emerged in the late twentieth century as a major focus of international concern and activity. They relate to globalization themes in several ways. Many environmental problems are intrinsically international or global, stimulating international political activities in response. Others, though local, are experienced across the world. Virtually all environmental issues are intimately linked to the dynamics of globalized political economic processes.

Awareness and concern about environmental issues grew substantially since the late 1960s. Since the 1970s, a wide range of agreements, institutions, and regimes for international environmental governance have developed. Much international political activity related to the environment has focused on the development and implementation of these regimes, involving a wide range of actors and processes. Since the late 1980s and particularly since the UNCED summit in 1992, many international political processes have engaged with the linked issues of development and environment, and the contested notion of sustainable development. By the end of the 1990s, the relationship between the WTO regimes to promote and govern a globalized market economy and international environmental regimes was high on the political agenda, influencing the design of the rules of environmental regimes as well as providing a focus for political mobilization and dispute.

Although established perspectives within International Relations theory provide important

insights into the character and outcomes of such activities, international environmental issues nevertheless pose significant new challenges for students of International Relations. They raise questions about the significance and role of states in environmental politics, about the relationship between power and knowledge, and about the distinction between the 'international' and 'domestic' spheres of activity. Historical experience shows that, alongside many failures, some effective institutions for collective management—or regimes—have been developed to help to prevent the degradation of 'global commons' or to tackle other international environmental problems. Moreover, these systems for international governance are no longer isolated regimes dealing with narrow problems. At least since the 1990s they have formed a complex of interlinked institutions shaping the activities and expectations of all relevant actors across a wide range of activities. The primary challenge for the 1990s and beyond is to shape patterns of development to promote sustainability, including preserving biodiversity and preventing damaging climate change. The 1992 UNCED agreements continue to provide a framework for international efforts to promote and coordinate efforts to achieve this. But the challenges are immense.

For further information and case studies on this subject, please visit the companion web site at www.oup.com/uk/booksites/politics.

QUESTIONS

1   In what ways has 'the environment' become a global issue in the late twentieth century?

2   What was the significance of the 1972 Stockholm Conference for international environmental politics?

3   What is meant by 'sustainable development', and why has this 'contested' concept become important in international environmental politics?

4   How does the study of international environmental issues pose particular challenges for International Relations theory?

5   What is the relevance of the notion of the 'tragedy of the commons' to global environmental problems, and what approaches are available for preventing the over-exploitation of global commons such as the open seas, the deep-sea bed, the atmosphere, and Antarctica?

6   'The nature of international society makes the prospects poor for developing collective institutions that can effectively tackle international environmental problems.' Discuss.

7   How effective has either the Montreal Protocol for the Protection of the Ozone Layer or the Climate Change Convention been?

8   What factors can contribute to (i) the formation and (ii) the implementation of international environmental regimes? Illustrate these factors with reference to the ozone layer and climate change regimes.

9   What are the key characteristics of a 'framework' convention? Illustrate these with reference to some existing framework conventions.

10 How important was the 1992 UN Conference on Environment and Development (UNCED, or the 'Earth Summit') for environmental protection and the promotion of 'sustainable development'?

11 How have 'North–South' issues shaped international environmental politics?

12 Discuss the relationship between environment regimes and the rules of the World Trade Organization, and the challenges and opportunities that globalized trade and investment processes pose for those who want to promote sustainable development.

13 Assess the significance of non-governmental organizations in international environmental politics. How is their role affected by international environmental institutions and regimes?

GUIDE TO FURTHER READING

There are now many good books on international environmental issues and on the environment in international relations. For example, the following books provide good introductions, including historical reviews up to at least the mid-1990s: R. Blakemore and A. Reddish (eds) (1996), *Global Environmental Issues*, 2nd edn (London: Hodder & Stoughton); J. Vogler and M. Imber (eds) (1996), *The Environment in International Relations* (London: Routledge); A. Blowers and P. Glasbergen (eds) (1996), *Environmental Policy in an International Context, Vols 1–4* (London: Arnold; and New York: John Wiley and Son); J. Vogler (2000), *The Global Commons: Environmental and Technological Governance*, 2nd edn (Chichester, John Wiley and Son); L. C. Hempel (1996), *Environmental Governance: The Global Challenge* (Washington, DC: Island Press); L. Elliott (1998), *The Global Politics of the Environment* (London: Macmillan); and S. Buck (1998), *The Global Commons: An Introduction* (Washington, DC: Island Press).

There are a number of journals and yearbooks of particular value in this context. For example, *Environment* (Washington, DC: Heldref Publications) is a monthly journal that provides detailed but accessible discussions of contemporary global environmental issues (broadly understood, as outlined in this chapter). Useful annual yearbooks include: the WorldWatch Institute's *State of the World* (London: Earthscan); the Fridtjof Nansen Institute' *Green Globe Yearbook* (Oxford: Oxford University Press); and VERTIC's *Verification: Arms Control and the Environment* (London: VERTIC). There are a number of more scholarly journals of direct relevance, such as *Environmental Politics* (London: Frank Cass) and the *Journal of Environment and Development* (London: Sage).

E. Ostrom (1990), *Governing the Commons: The Evolution of Institutions for Collective Action* (Cambridge: Cambridge University Press) is an important text analysing collective governance of open-access commons. On the development and effectiveness of international environmental institutions, O. Young (ed.) (1997), *Global Governance: Drawing Insights from the Environmental Experience* (London: Cornell University Press); P. M. Haas, R. O. Keohane, and M. Levy (eds) (1993), *Institutions for the Earth: Sources of Effective International Environmental Action* (London: MIT Press), and D. Victor, K. Raustiala, and G. Skolnikof (eds) (1998), *The Effectiveness of International Environmental Agreements* (Cambridge, Mass.: MIT Press), provide good thematic and empirical examinations. Much of the best and most influential work on international environmental issues has focused on particular issues or regimes. For example, R. E. Benedick (1991), *Ozone Diplomacy: New Directions in Safeguarding the Planet* (London: Harvard University Press) provides a readable 'insider's' story of the international negotiations to establish the Montreal Protocol; and I. Rowlands (1995), *The Politics of Global Atmospheric Change* (Manchester: Manchester University Press) and E. Parson and O. Greene (1995), 'The Complex Chemistry of Ozone Agreements', *Environment*, 37(2): 16–20, 35–43, examine the subsequent development of the ozone regime. Similarly, there are many good books on the development of climate change politics and the development of the climate change regime, including: T. O'Riordan and J. Jager (eds) (1996), *Politics of Climate Change: A European Perspective* (London: Routledge) and M. Grubb *et al.* (1999), *The Kyoto Protocol: a Guide and Assessment* (London: Earthscan). For an examination of the Convention on Biological Diversity, see K. Raustiala and D. Victor (1996), 'Biodiversity since Rio: the Future of the Convention on Biological Diversity', *Environment* (May): 16–20, 37–45.

The UNCED agreements, including Agenda 21, are clearly outlined and examined by M. Grubb *et al.* (1993), *The Earth Summit Agreements: A Guide and Assessment* (London: Earthscan). On sustainable development, the Brundtland Report, or World Commission on Environment and Development (1987), *Our Common Future* (Oxford: Oxford University Press), and the Agenda 21 document itself (*Agenda 21: The United Nations Programme of Action from Rio* (New York: United Nations, 1992)) remain essential texts, but chapters in the WorldWatch Institute's annual *State of the World Report* are just one of many texts providing more recent detailed examinations. On the politics of environmental activism, see e.g. D. Pepper (1996), *Modern Environmentalism: An Introduction* (London: Routledge), J. Dryzek (1997), *The Politics of the Earth: Environmental Discourses* (Oxford: Oxford University Press), P. Wapner (1997), *Environmental Activism and World Civic Politics* (New York: SUNY Press), and R. Lipshutz and J. Mayer (1996), *Global Civil Society and Global Environmental Governance: Politics of Nature from Place to Planet* (New York: SUNY Press). M. Redclift and T. Benton (eds) (1994), *Social Theory and the Global Environment* (London: Routledge) provides an excellent collection of articles on different social science perspectives on global environmental change issues.

WEB LINKS

There are many relevant web sites. The International Institute for Sustainable Development maintains a site (at www.iisd.ca) that includes much detailed information, including Climate News and Earth Negotiations Bulletin (detailing progress in international negotiations relating to the environment or sustainable development). Similarly, Global Change (www.globalchange.org) maintains a web site with many useful links. Virtually every international institute, substantial NGO, and international secretariat associated with an environmental agreement now maintains a home page, e.g. UN Environment Programme (www.unep.org), European Environment Agency (www.eea.eu.int), UN Framework Convention on Climate Change Secretariat (www.unfccc.de), The Biodiversity Convention (www.biodiv.org), Global Environmental Facility (www.gefweb.org), and World Wildlife Fund (www.panda.org).

CHAPTER 21

Terrorism and globalization

JAMES D. KIRAS

READER'S GUIDE

The technologies and processes linked with globalization have enabled terrorism to grow from a regional phenomenon into a global one. Precisely how globalization has influenced terrorism, however, is difficult to determine. The difficulty lies in the complex nature and local variations of terrorism as a form of irregular warfare, almost as much as it does with different interpretations of what comprises globalization. The current manifestation of terrorist violence has been explained in cultural, economic, and religious terms linked to globalization. Comprehensive explanations of terrorism using such prisms, however, are open to interpretation and debate. What is incontrovertible is that the technologies associated with globalization have enabled terrorist groups to conduct operations that are deadlier, more distributed, and more difficult to combat than those of their predecessors. Technological advantage, however, cuts both ways. The same systems and processes that terrorists can exploit can be harnessed to defeat terrorism by those governments with the will and resources to combat it.

Introduction

The relationship between terrorism and globalization is difficult to describe. Both are complicated, interdisciplinary phenomena that defy simple characterization. That relationship can be examined in cultural, economic, and religious terms. Technology has enabled many of the processes of globalization and terrorists can exploit its benefits. In particular, technologies have improved terrorists' abilities to conduct extremely lethal attacks and grow and sustain a global network of associates and sympathizers. But technologies have a limited ability to change the character of the terrorist message or the nature of the struggle. Terrorism is a weapon of the weak conducted by a minority of individuals who promote an extremist ideology. In order to effect change, terrorist groups must either make their message more appealing, to generate widespread support for their cause, and/or weaken their adversaries to the point of exhaustion or collapse. The global community, in response, must utilize the resources at their disposal collaboratively to diminish support for terrorism and demonstrate the illegitimacy of terrorist messages and causes.

Definitions

Terrorism and globalization share at least one thing in common—both are complex phenomena open to subjective interpretation. Definitions of terrorism vary widely but all start from a common point of departure. Terrorism is characterized, first and foremost, by the use of violence. Such violence includes hostage-taking, hijacking, bombing, and other indiscriminate attacks, usually targeting civilians. However, the purpose towards which violence is used, and the motivation behind it, is where most of the disagreements related to terrorism begin. Traditionally, terrorism has been separated from criminal acts on the basis of its political legitimacy. According to those sympathetic to terrorist causes, the violence undertaken is the only way to draw attention to the plight and grievances of a specific group, as opposed to an individual. With little recourse to change other than through violence, some view terrorism as an acceptable method of righting an injustice while others see it as an egregious act. Historically, such causes have included ideological, ethnic, and religious exclusion or persecution.

One of the difficulties in defining terrorism is that groups often espouse multiple grievances. For example, the Chechens are seeking independence from the Russian Federation but a number of them are also motivated by religious imperatives. Those targeted by terrorists are less inclined to see any justification, much less legitimacy, behind attacks that kill and maim civilians. As a result, the term 'terrorist' has a pejorative value ascribed to it that further complicates understanding of the subject.

Reaching consensus on what constitutes terrorism

Box 21.1 | Types of terrorist groups

Audrey Kurth Cronin has outlined different types of terrorist groups and their historical importance in the following way:

'There are four types of terrorist organizations currently operating around the world, categorized mainly by their source of motivation: left-wing terrorists, right-wing terrorists, ethnonationalist/separatist terrorists, and religious or "sacred" terrorists. All four types have enjoyed periods of relative prominence in the modern era, with left-wing terrorism intertwined with the Communist movement, right-wing terrorism drawing its inspiration from fascism, and the bulk of ethnonationalist/separatist terrorism accompanying the wave of decolonization especially in the immediate post-World War II years. Currently, "sacred" terrorism is becoming more significant. Although groups in all categories continue to exist today, left-wing and right-wing terrorist groups were more numerous in earlier decades. Of course, these categories are not perfect, as many groups have a mix of motivating ideologies—some ethnonationalist groups, for example, have religious characteristics or agendas—but usually one ideology or motivation dominates.'

(Kurth Cronin 2002/03: 39)

is difficult and one of the foremost reasons for disagreement relates to different interpretations of the legitimacy of terrorist means and methods. Some view forms of political violence such as terrorism as legitimate only if they meet the criteria associated with the 'just war' tradition established by Saint Thomas Aquinas. These criteria, which apply to all applications of force, have been expanded to include a just cause, proportional use of violence, and the use of force as a last resort.

Realists suggest that the political violence used by terrorist groups is illegitimate on the basis that **states** alone have a '**monopoly on the legitimate use of physical force**'.

Yet even as regards the use of violence by states,

there is disagreement on what constitutes legitimate application of armed force. For example, Libya sponsored terrorist groups as a method of responding to the United States, France, and the United Kingdom. Those states, in turn, condemned Libyan sponsorship as against international **norms**, and they responded with sanctions, international court cases, and occasional uses of force. Much of the disagreement relating to the legitimacy of coalition actions against Iraq in 2003, led by the United States, relates to interpretations over whether or not the conditions for 'just war' were met prior to commencement of military operations. Some suggest that the conditions were not met, and that actions by the coalition should be considered as an '**act of terrorism**' conducted by states. Leaders in the United States and the United Kingdom dismiss the charge on the basis that a greater evil was averted against a regime that had demonstrated its willingness to break international norms against neighbouring states, as well as religious and ethnic minorities domestically.

Critical theorists, in particular, reject such arguments by Western state leaders as subjective rhetoric. By classifying any political violence, including acts of terrorism, as illegitimate in international forums they control, Western states preserve the monopoly on the legitimacy of violence in the **international system**. Using relativist arguments, critical theorists suggest that Western states cannot claim moral superiority, and its associated legitimacy, on the basis of their willingness to contravene international norms as its suits them. If anything, the historical track record of Western states as colonial and/or imperial **powers** only legitimizes the acts of the disenfranchised who have no other option to combat their continued oppression and **poverty**

As with other forms of irregular warfare, including insurgencies and revolution, terrorism has as its goal political change for the purpose of obtaining power in order to right the perceived wrong. Terrorism, however, is the weakest form of irregular warfare with which to alter the political landscape that lacks the broader support of the population that characterizes insurgencies and revolutions. Terrorist groups lack broader support for their objectives because their goals for change often are absolute and based on radical ideas that do not have widespread appeal. In order to **influence** change, terrorists must provoke

---

Box 21.2 Legitimacy

Martha Crenshaw provides an analytic, albeit subjective approach to determine the legitimacy of terrorist acts of violence:

'The value of the normative approach (to terrorism) is that it confronts squarely a critical problem in the analysis of terrorism, and indeed any form of political violence: the issue of legitimacy. Terrorists of the left deny the legitimacy of the state and claim that the use of violence against it is morally justified. Terrorists of the right deny the legitimacy of the opposition and hold that the violence in the service of order is sanctioned by the values of the status quo . . . the need for scholarly objectivity and abstraction does not excuse use from the obligation to judge the morality of the use of force, whether by the state or against.'

She adds that morality can be judged in two ways:

'morality of the ends and the morality of the means. First, are the goals of the terrorists democratic or non-democratic? That is, is their aim to create or perpetuate a regime of privilege and inequality, to deny liberty to other people, or to further the ends of justice, freedom, and equality . . . Terrorism must not, as the terrorists can foresee, result in *worse* injustice than the condition the terrorists oppose . . . The morality of the means of terrorism is also open to judgment. The targets of terrorism are morally significant; witness the difference between material objects and human casualties.'

(Crenshaw 1983: 2–4)

drastic responses that act as a catalyst for change or weaken their opponent's moral resolve. The multiple bombings in Madrid in 2004, for example, influenced the outcome of elections in Spain in a dramatic fashion. Many terrorist leaders hope that their actions will lead to disproportionate reactions by a state that in turn disaffects public or international opinion and increases support for their cause. International reaction to Israel's invasion of Lebanon in 1982, prompted by attacks by the **Palestinian Liberation Organization** and **Abu Nidal**, is an example. Terrorism, however, is a prolonged undertaking in which states and the terrorist groups struggle for legitimacy that can lead to dilemmas associated with the amount and nature of the force applied. Attacks by terrorists that are so horrific run the risk of distancing sympathy and support for their cause. Some groups, such as **Hezballah** in Lebanon, have opted to wear down the resolve and force the withdrawal of their adversary, in this case Israel, as occurred in May 2000. Given the factors discussed above, the working definition of terrorism for this chapter is 'the use of violence by sub-state groups to inspire fear, by attacking civilians and/or symbolic targets, for purposes such as drawing widespread attention to a grievance, provoking a severe response, or wearing down their opponent's moral resolve, to effect political change'.

As with definitions of terrorism, there is general agreement on at least one aspect of globalization. Technologies allow the transfer of goods, services, and information almost anywhere quickly and efficiently. In the case of information, the transfer can be secure and is nearly simultaneous. There is little doubt that the technologies associated with globalization have been leveraged by terrorists. The extent of social, cultural, and political change brought on by globalization, including increasing interconnectedness and homogeneity in the international system, remain the subject of much disagreement and debate, as other chapters in this volume have outlined. These disagreements influence discussions of how globalization has affected terrorism since the latter became a transnational phenomenon in the 1960s. In order to understand the changes perceived in terrorism globally, it is useful to review the evolution of terrorism from a transnational to a global phenomenon.

Key points

- Agreement on what constitutes terrorism continues to be difficult given the range of potential acts involving violence.

- Terrorism, or acts of violence by sub-state groups, has been separated from criminal acts on the basis of the purpose for which violence is applied, namely political change.

- Terrorist groups succeed when their motivations or grievances are perceived to be legitimate by a wider audience. Disproportionate or heavy-handed responses by states to acts of terrorism serve to legitimize terrorist groups.

- The definition of globalization, as with terrorism, is open to subjective interpretation but the technologies associated with globalization have improved terrorist capabilities.

Terrorism: from transnational to global phenomenon (1968–2001)

Although incidents of terrorism existed prior to 1968, three factors led to the birth of transnational terrorism: the expansion of air travel; the wider availability of televised news coverage; and broad common political and ideological interests. These changes allowed terrorism to grow from a local and regional phenomenon into an international threat.

Air travel gave terrorists unprecedented mobility. Prior to the implementation of passport controls, terrorists could travel relatively freely between countries and regions. For example, terrorists of the **Japanese Red Army** could train in one country and conduct operations half a world away, as they did in the Lod Airport suicide attack in Israel in 1972. Air travel was also appealing to terrorists for another reason. Airport security measures were almost non-existent when terrorists began hijacking airlines. These 'sky-jackings', as they were eventually labelled, suited terrorist purposes well. Hijacked aircraft offered a degree of protection and security for the terrorists involved, and states initially acquiesced to terrorist demands, which encouraged further incidents. The high success rate of hijacking as a technique spurred other terrorist groups, as well as criminals and political refugees, to follow suit. As a result, incidents of hijacking skyrocketed from five in 1966 to 94 in 1969. Shared political ideologies stimulated cooperation and limited exchanges between groups as diverse as the **Irish Republican Army** (IRA) and the Basque separatist **Euzkadi Ta Askatasuna** (ETA). Besides sharing techniques and technical experience, groups demanded the release of imprisoned 'fellow revolutionaries' in different countries, giving the impression of a coordinated terrorist network.

CWS

Televised news coverage also played a role in expanding the audience who could witness the **'theatre of terrorism'** in their own homes. Individuals who had never heard of 'the plight of the Palestinians' became notionally aware of the issue after incidents such as the triple-hijacking and blowing up of airliners by the **Popular Front for the Liberation of Palestine** (PFLP) in September 1970, or live coverage of the hostage-taking conducted by **Black September** during the 1972 Munich Olympics. Although media coverage was termed **'the oxygen that sustains terrorism'**, terrorist groups discovered that reporters and audiences lost interest in repeat performances of the same incidents. In order to sustain viewer interest and compete for coverage, terrorist groups undertook increasingly spectacular attacks, such as the seizure of the Organization of Petroleum Exporting Countries (OPEC) delegates by 'Carlos the Jackal' in Austria in December 1975. Terrorism experts speculated that terrorist leaders understood that a horrific, mass casualty attack would alienate support for the group and delegitimize their cause. This helps explain, in part, why few terrorist groups attempted to acquire or use weapons of mass destruction, including nuclear, chemical, and biological weapons, to conduct the most shocking attack imaginable.

The Iranian 'Islamic Revolution' of 1979 was a watershed event in transnational terrorism. Although Israeli interests remained primary targets for attack, due in large part to continued sympathy for the Palestinian cause, the emphasis of a number of transnational groups shifted to attacks on symbols of the United States. In the **'decade of terrorism'** between 1980 and 1990, major attacks against US interests and citizens by groups such as the **Islamic Jihad Organization** included the bombings of the embassy (April 1983) and Marine Corps barracks (October 1983) in Lebanon. Although the majority of attacks consisted of car bombings, assassinations, or kidnappings by groups such as the German **Red Army Faction** and the Italian **Red Brigades**, three disturbing trends emerged: attacks were less frequent but more deadly and indiscriminate; some terrorist groups, such as the IRA, were becoming more technologically proficient; and terrorists appeared more willing to sacrifice their own lives in order to kill others.

With the end of the cold war and the collapse of the Soviet Union, many transnational leftist groups found that their sources of sponsorship and support had disappeared. In addition, the law-enforcement and paramilitary measures of states became increasingly effective, especially in Western Europe. For other organizations, transnational attacks were counterproductive. The **Palestine Liberation Organization** abandoned transnational attacks and focused instead on a conventional uprising, punctuated by terrorist attacks, within Israel to provoke a response. Other groups including ETA and the IRA sought to negotiate a political compromise although they still conducted occasional domestic attacks as a bargaining ploy. Although leftist transnational terrorism was decreasing in scale and intensity, another type of terrorism with global connections and reach was evolving: **Al Qaeda**, or 'The Base'.

> **Key points**
>
> - Many of the technologies and processes associated with globalization have enabled terrorism to have an impact internationally since 1968.
> - The majority of transnational terrorist attacks from 1979 onwards targeted American citizens and symbols.
> - The collapse of the Soviet Union denied leftist groups their major source of direct or indirect sponsorship, allowing the rise of religious terrorist groups.

Terrorism: the impact of globalization

Al Qaeda is a terrorist group, a sub-state financial provider, and an ideological rallying point for groups striving towards a broad, common goal. Indeed, some analysts portray the organization as the 'nexus' of global terrorism, with connections to almost all other terrorist groups.

The message of Al Qaeda's founder, Osama bin Laden, combines a number of disparate elements.

These elements include: the restoration of the former greatness of Islam through selective historical interpretation; the defence of oppressed Muslims and the defeat of the theological enemies of Islam; the requirement for absolute religious piety and devotion; global economic conspiracy theory that links to international poverty and suffering; and a rejection of secular materialism. His message has

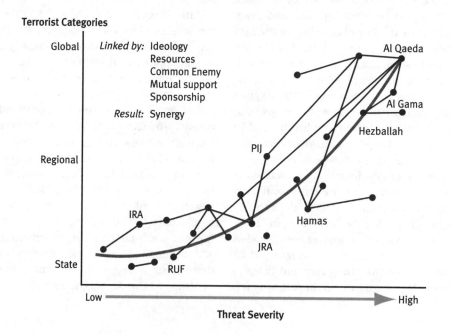

Fig. 21.1 The global terrorism nexus

Source: National War College Student Task Force on Combating Terrorism (2002: 12).

proven appealing to individuals and groups in areas as diverse as Egypt (**Egyptian Islamic Jihad**), Indonesia (**Jemaah Islamiyah**), and Uzbekistan (**Islamic Movement of Uzbekistan**). Bin Laden's message has enough different elements, woven into an overarching theory that links local suffering and poverty to a vast international Zionist and Christian network, that it taps into suspicions and anger in underdeveloped sections of the world where conspiracy theories form part of the indigenous culture. Efforts to describe the growth of terrorism into a global phenomenon (and its popularity), including its linkages to globalization, have focused on three areas: culture, economics, and religion.

Cultural explanations

'Culture' is one way to explain how armed struggle is used to preserve traditions and values against a wave of Western products and influence as the underdeveloped world perceives it (see Ch.24). Once sought after as an entry method to economic prosperity, Western secular, materialist cultural values are increasingly rejected by those seeking to regain or preserve their own unique cultural identity. The social changes associated with globalization and the spread of free market capitalism can seem to overwhelm the ethnic identity or religious values of smaller groups who believe that they are the losers in the new international system. In an attempt to preserve their threatened identity and values, groups actively distinguish themselves from 'others' who have different norms. At the local level, this may translate into conflicts divided along religious or ethnic lines in a struggle to safeguard their uniqueness.

On a global level, however, the number of civilizations is limited. They include Western, Confucian, Japanese, Islamic, Hindu, Slavic-Orthodox, and Latin American (Huntington 1993: 25). Geography and relative cultural stability limit the potential friction between some of the civilizations. Where individuals within a culture perceive their civilization to be weakened, insecure, or stagnant, and interaction is high between weak and strong civilizations, conflict may be inevitable. Huntington suggests that a major '**fault-line**' exists between the liberal

Western civilization and an Islamic one 'humiliated and resentful of the West's military presence in the Persian Gulf, the West's overwhelming military dominance, and . . . [unable] to shape their own destiny' (ibid.: 32).

Critics of Huntington suggest that he ascribes a degree of homogeneity within the Islamic world that simply does not exist. Theologically and socially, the Islamic 'civilization' contains a number of deep fault-lines that impede the cooperation required to challenge the West. Although attractive to some, Osama bin Laden's ideology is uncompromising towards non-believers, including fellow Muslims. Non-believers, who fall into the categories of infidels (those of different religion) and apostates (those who do not share his interpretation of the Koran), are all equal in Bin Laden's eyes. As a result, although Al Qaeda dismisses the collateral death of scores of Arabs and Muslims on 11 September and after the bombing of an apartment block in Saudi Arabia in November 2003 as 'mistakes', such actions increasingly call into question the morality of the means, and therefore the legitimacy of the organization as the champion of Muslim values among the wider and moderate Islamic community.

Economic explanations

Not everyone agrees that the defence of culture or identity is the primary motivation for globalized terrorist violence. Others see economic aspects as the fundamental motivating factor in the use of violence to effect political change. Although globalization provides access to a world market for goods and services, and has stimulated the growth of the economies of Asia, the processes and technologies favour the West and have created a new form of '**economic imperialism**'. In this system, the United States and the post-industrial states of Western Europe that are the global economic '**core**', through their domination of international economic institutions such as the World Bank, set exchange rates and determine fiscal policies that are by and large unfavourable to the underdeveloped countries that comprise the '**periphery**' or '**gap**'.

Wealth is also linked to personal security and violence. With little possible opportunity to obtain wealth in an increasingly competitive globalized system, especially in states where considerable social inequalities exist, many individuals will leave to pursue opportunities elsewhere. The result will be emigration and/or the rapid growth of burgeoning urban centres that act as regional hubs for the flow of global resources. Movement, however, is no guarantee that individual aspirations will be realized. In that case, individuals may turn to violence for criminal reasons (i.e., personal gain) or political reasons (i.e., to change the existing political system, through insurgency or terrorism). Paradoxically, rising standards of living and greater access to educational opportunities associated with globalization may lead to increased expectations that if unrealized could lead to the adoption of extreme political views and action against 'the system' that has thwarted more conventional ambitions. As justification for the necessity and use of political violence, to right the economic wrongs, the works of authors such as Franz Fanon take on new significance to explain the globalization of terrorism (Onwudiwe 2001: 52–6). For example, Fanon suggested the end of colonialism is not the end of the struggle between the West and the oppressed. It would be replaced by another form of struggle until the economic and power imbalances between the two were equalled (Fanon 1990: 74). Terrorist violence, therefore, is motivated by the inequalities of the global economy. The two attacks against the World Trade Center, in 1993 and 2001, were not reactions against the United States per se, but rather against the icon of global capitalism instead.

The explanation that recent terrorist violence is a reaction to economic globalization contains a number of contradictions related to the wealth of some of the members of terrorist groups and regional patterns of terrorist recruiting. Many former leaders and members of transnational terrorist groups, including the German Red Army Faction and the Italian Red Brigades, came from affluent families. A number of leaders within Al Qaeda, or groups affiliated with the organization, attended graduate schools around the globe in fields as diverse as engineering and theology and were neither poor nor downtrodden. The link between terrorism and poverty also varies considerably between regions. Although terrorist groups have conducted operations in Africa, including

bombings and attacks in Kenya and Tanzania in 1998 and 2002, foreign *jihadists* were responsible. In other words, despite conditions that favour the outbreak of terrorist violence in Africa against economic imperialism and global capitalism, the continent has been the location of operations but not necessarily a breeding ground for terrorism.

Religion and 'new' terrorism

In the decade prior to 11 September, a number of scholars and experts perceived that fundamental changes taking place in the character of terrorism. The use of violence for political purposes, to change state ideology or the representation of ethnic minority groups, had failed in its purpose and a new trend was emerging. **'Post-modern terrorism'**, also known as 'New' terrorism, was conducted for different reasons altogether. Motivated by promises of rewards in the afterlife, some terrorists are driven by religious reasons to kill as many of the non-believers and unfaithful as possible (Laqueur 1996: 32–3). Although suicide tactics had been observed in Lebanon as early as 1983, with the bombings of the US embassy and Marine Corps barracks, **'militant Islam'** had previously been viewed as a state-sponsored, regional phenomenon conducted by sub-state actors (Wright 1986: 19–21).

New terrorism, which some authors use to explain the underlying rationale of the global *jihad*, is seen as a reaction to the perceived oppression of Muslims worldwide and the spiritual bankruptcy of the West. As globalization spreads and societies become increasingly interconnected, Muslims have a choice: reject their beliefs to integrate with the system, or preserve their spiritual purity and fight against it. Those who believe in the global *jihad* view the rulers of 'Islamic' countries such as Egypt and Pakistan as apostates who have compromised their values in the pursuit and maintenance of secular, state-based power. Rather than submit to the system or seek to change it from within, the only response to oppression for those who espouse a radical view of Islam is *jihad*. Although *jihad* is accepted within most Islamic sects as the internal spiritual struggle for purity of the soul or to legitimize the shedding of blood in self-defence of a community under attack, other

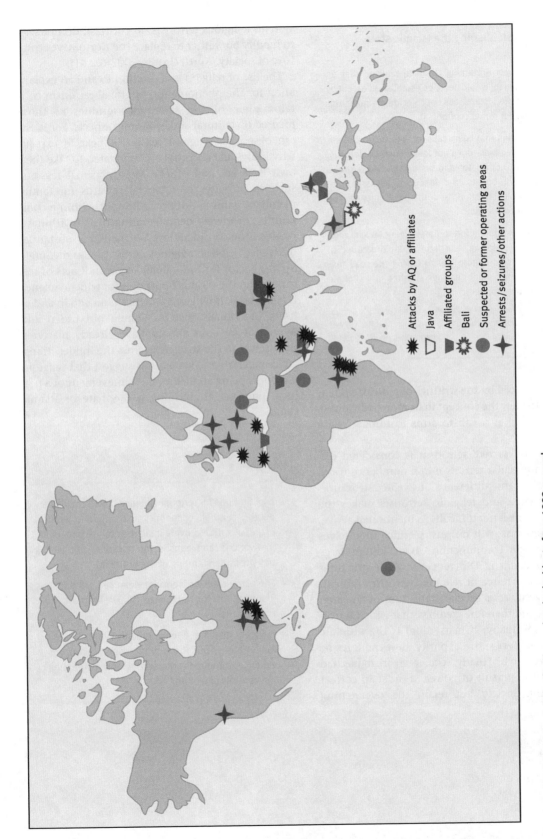

Fig. 21.2 Al Qaeda's global activities and major incidents from 1993 onward

Attacks by AQ or affiliates

Java

Affiliated groups

Bali

Suspected or former operating areas

Arrests/seizures/other actions

Box 21.3   Establishing the Islamic state

'These young men [returning to Allah] realized that an Islamic Government would never be established except by the bomb and rifle. Islam does not coincide or make truce with unbelief, but rather confronts it.

'The confrontation that Islam calls for with these godless and apostate regimes, does not know Socratic debates, Platonic ideals, nor Aristotelian diplomacy. But it knows the dialogue of bullets, the ideals of assassination, bombing, and destruction, and the diplomacy of the cannon and machine-gun . . .

'I present this humble effort to these young Muslim men who are pure, believing, and fighting for the cause of Allah. It is my contribution toward paving the road that leads to majestic Allah and establishes a caliphate according to the prophecy.'

(Declaration of Jihad Against the Country's Tyrants: Military Series (n.d.), Government Exhibit 1677-T; UK translation, pp.BM-8–BM-9)

groups influenced by the writings of radicals such as Sayyid Qutb view the concept in its more radicalized, historical usage as a call to arms to impose Islam globally.

Religious or 'sacred' terrorism is considered dissimilar from secular terrorism in a number of ways. In particular, the difference in value structures between secular and religious terrorists makes the responses to the latter difficult. As mentioned above, religious terrorists will not just sacrifice themselves but have little compunction about killing large numbers of civilians. Differences in value structures make the deterrence of religious terrorism difficult if not impossible, as secular states cannot threaten materially, and therefore credibly, that which terrorists value spiritually. If martyrdom is the ultimate purpose to achieve spiritual purity, how can force be used to threaten it? Finally, secular terrorism has had as its goal the pursuit of power in order to correct flaws within society but retain the overarching

system. Religious terrorists, in contrast, do not seek to modify but rather to replace the normative structure of society (Kurth Cronin 2002/03: 41).

The use of religion as a reaction to and an explanation for the phenomenon of global terrorism contains some of the same incongruities as those focused on cultural and economic aspects. For Western observers, religious reasons appear to explain why individual terrorists are motivated to take their own lives and kill others. More personal reasons, such as promises of financial rewards for family members, gaining esteem or honour within a community, or merely demonstrating their worthiness, receive little consideration. Yet there is a substantial difference between religious motivation as the single driving factor for individuals to commit acts of terrorism and the ultimate purposes for which violence is being used. If religious violence is an end in and of itself, individuals such as Osama bin Laden and Ayman al-Zawahiri should have already martyred themselves in the struggle against the infidel. Translated materials and statements suggest that religious fervour is being applied to the achievement of a political purpose: establishing a caliphate or Islamic state.

Key points

- Explanations for terrorist violence based exclusively on the cultural, economic, and religious aspects of globalization provide insights into the underlying motivations and causes for terrorism but lack a holistic understanding of the problem.

- The current wave of terrorist violence uses religious justifications to legitimize the killing of non-combatants.

- Religion may be a powerful motivating element for terrorists, but the ultimate purpose for which violence is applied is the seizing and remoulding of the controls of a state.

Globalization, technology, and terrorism

There is little debate that terrorism has become much more pervasive worldwide due to the processes and technologies of globalization. The technological advances associated with globalization have improved the capabilities of terrorist groups to plan and conduct operations with far more devastation and coordination than their predecessors could have imagined. In particular, technologies have improved the capability of groups and cells in the following areas: proselytizing, coordination, security, mobility, and lethality.

Proselytizing

Terrorist movements and insurgencies have traditionally sought sympathy and support within national boundaries or in neighbouring countries as a means to sustain their efforts. The sustainment of terrorist causes has traditionally been more difficult to achieve as terrorist messages, goals, and grievances have tended to be more extreme and less appealing than those of insurgents. For example, land reform and government corruption have motivated individuals to attempt to change the political system by supporting or joining insurgencies, whereas the radical political ideology espoused by groups such as the **Japanese Red Army** and the **Weather Underground** had little appeal in largely prosperous and stable democratic societies. A traditional advantage that states had over sub-state groups was their ability to control information flows and utilize superior resources to delegitimize the terrorist cause and win '**the battle of hearts and minds**'.

The continued expansion of the number of Internet service providers, especially in states with relaxed or ambivalent content policies or legal authorities, as well as more capable and cheaper computers, software, peripherals, and wireless technologies, has '**empowered**' individuals and groups with the ability to post tracts on or send messages throughout the World Wide Web. Once limited to mimeographed manifestos, some terrorists and their

supporters are now capable of building web sites to post any information they choose. For example, a web site sympathetic to the **Tupac Amaru Revolutionary Movement** posted the group's communiqués and videos, which were accessed by international news agencies during the seizure of the Japanese embassy in Lima in 1997. Webmasters, who can be either groups or individuals, selectively control the content posted on their web sites. The web site of the **Liberation Tigers of Tamil Eelam** posts items that cast the group as a responsible, internationally 'accepted' organization (meeting delegates from the World Bank) committed to conflict resolution. As well as handling content control, and depending on the resources available and the intended audience, webmasters can tailor messages electronically in ways more appealing to specific segments of the population. For example, a posted Internet video entitled 'Dirty Kuffar' (non-believer) by 'Sheikh Terra' presents *jihadist* exhortations to a reggae beat. Messages, files, and polemics can be dispatched to almost anywhere on the globe with a connection to the Internet, or via text messaging, almost instantaneously.

For the purposes of spreading messages to the widest possible audience for those without Internet or text messaging capabilities, and where speed of communication is not a requirement or a possibility for security reasons, terrorists need not rely exclusively on virtual methods. With a computer with modest capabilities, readily available software packages, and equipment such as printers and CD/DVD burners, members of terrorist groups and their sympathizers can create propaganda leaflets, distance learning materials, and multimedia presentations at very low cost in large quantities. Difficult to intercept and trace, the files for such materials can be e-mailed to other cells or groups to be modified to suit their specific message or mission with little chance of interception or prevention. More importantly, whereas offset printing machines and photocopiers are difficult to move, a laptop computer and printer can be packed in a suitcase, increasing the mobility of the terrorist cell generating the material and making them more difficult to locate. Terrorist groups in Chechnya and the Middle East have also made increasing use of video cameras to record the preparations for and results of attacks, including successful roadside bombings and bringing down of helicopters. Video footage is useful in inspiring potential recruits, as well as improving future attacks, and can be distributed to recruiters within the organization. The competition between global news outlets ensures that the images of successful and/or dramatic attacks reach the widest audience possible.

Coordination

During the era of transnational terrorism, groups planned and conducted individual attacks or mounted multiple attacks from a single staging base. The technologies associated with globalization have enabled terrorist cells and groups to mount coordinated attacks in different countries. Indeed, a hallmark of Al Qaeda and its affiliated groups is the conduct of multiple attacks in different locations concurrently. The simultaneous bombings of the US embassies in neighbouring countries in Africa in 1998 is one example. Another was the synchronized detonation of 10 of 13 bombs on packed commuter trains in Madrid in March 2004.

The technologies associated with globalization have allowed terrorist cell members and groups to operate independently at substantial distances from one another with a large degree of coordination. The Global System for Mobile Communications (GSM) standard, for example, ensures that any compliant phone will work anywhere in the world where a GSM network has been established. E-mail and cell phone contact among group members allows geographically separated to conduct their attacks in separate locations or converge on a specific target area. For example, the 11 September 2001 hijackers utilized cheap and readily available pre-paid phone cards to communicate between cell leaders and senior leadership and, according to at least one press account, coordinated final attack authorization prior to the jets taking off from different locations. In the Madrid bombings mentioned above, cell phones were put to a more operational use as detonators.

The more successful terrorist groups have demonstrated an ability to retain a level of coordination in the face of tactical setbacks through technological and organizational adaptation. The Liberation Tigers of Tamil Eelam, for example, fielded 'stealth' suicide boats designed to thwart Sri Lankan Navy radar systems. Surviving IRA bomb manufacturers were known for the technical complexity and ability to respond rapidly to British electronic countermeasures. A disturbing quality possessed by Al Qaeda is its ability to draw upon different levels of the organization to continue attacks even as the senior leaders regroup from setbacks suffered since December 2001. For example, they have provided funding and enabled other loosely affiliated groups such as Jemaah Islamiyah in Indonesia, or sleeper cells have undertaken independent operations, to spread terrorist violence to another region. In addition, individuals considered expendable to Al Qaeda, such as Richard Reid (the 'Shoe Bomber'), are used to test out new methods designed to defeat security measures at little or no risk to the organization. The actions of affiliated groups, sleeper cells, and individuals sustain general fear by maintaining the perception of the depth, power, and reach of terrorist groups as global threats even as the senior leadership recovers from setbacks.

Security

Without adequate security terrorist cells can be detected, monitored, penetrated, and/or neutralized. Translations of captured Al Qaeda manuals, for example, make it clear that the senior leaders of the organization place a high value on security, including surveillance and counter-surveillance techniques. The technological enablers of globalization assist terrorist cells and leaders in preserving security in a number of ways, including distributing elements (see preceding section), moving around (see section below), and utilizing clandestine and/or encrypted communications.

The security of terrorist organizations has traditionally been assured by allowing only limited communication and information exchanges between cells, to ensure that if one cell is compromised its members only know each other's identities and not those of other cells. In this way, the damage done to the organization is minimized. The use of specific codes and ciphers, known only to a few individuals, has been one way of preserving the security of an organization. Although code and ciphers inevitably have been broken, and information is obtained during interrogations, such activities take time. During that time, terrorist groups adjust their location and operating methods in an attempt to stay ahead of security and counter-terrorist forces. Computer advances, such as faster processing speeds, improved global connectivity, as well as **developments** in software technologies, enable clandestine communications between those with the capabilities to retrieve and decrypt them.

Terrorist groups have been able to leverage technological developments designed to shield a user's identity from unauthorized commercial or private exploitation (Gunartna 2002: 35). Concerns about infringements on civil liberties and privacy during the early years of the Internet led to the private development of encryption programs such as Pretty Good Privacy (PGP). Available online as shareware, to be downloaded by anyone, PGP provides levels of encryption that are extremely costly and time consuming to break. In addition, access to hardware such as cell phones, personal data assistants, and computers can be restricted via the use of passwords. The use of Internet protocol address generators, anonymity protection programs, and rerouted communications, as well as private chat rooms where password-protected or encrypted files can be shared, also provide a degree of security. According to some press accounts, terrorists have also made ingenious use of common, remote-access e-mail accounts to leave messages for cell members without actually sending out anything that could be intercepted.

Mobility

As noted previously, the reduced size and increased power of personal electronics gives terrorists both unprecedented capabilities to proselytize and coordinate the activities of dispersed cells, but also to improve mobility as well. Mobility has always been a crucial consideration for terrorists and insurgents alike, given the superior resources that states have been able to bring to bear against them. In open societies that have well-developed infrastructures, terrorists have been able to move rapidly within and between borders, complicating the efforts of law enforcement and security services to track them. The globalization of commerce has influenced terrorist mobility as well. The volume of air travel and goods that pass through ports has increased exponentially over the past two decades. Between states, measures have been taken to ease the flow of goods, services, and ideas in a less restrictive fashion to improve efficiency and lower costs. Market demands for efficiencies of supply, manufacture, delivery, and cost have complicated efforts of states to prevent members of terrorist groups from exploiting gaps in security measures designed to deter or prevent illicit activities. Additional mobility also allows terrorist groups to train one another and share tactics, techniques, and methods, as the arrest of three members of the IRA suspected of training counterparts in the Fuerzas Armadas Revolucionarias de Columbia (FARC) in Bogota in August 2001 appears to demonstrate.

The use of air travel by terrorists, as a means of mobility and attack, has been described in a number of books and newspaper accounts. Mohammed Atta, the suspected leader of the 11 September attacks, travelled extensively between Egypt, Germany, and the United States while studying and working. In this respect, the latest generation of terrorists resembles their transnational predecessors in exploiting travel methods for attacks. Terrorists' use of forms of transportation need not necessarily be overt in nature, as the volume of goods transported in support of a globalized economy is staggering and difficult to scrutinize effectively. For example, customs officials are hard-pressed to inspect every vehicle or container passing across a border or through a port. In the port of Los Angeles, the equivalent of 12,000 twenty-foot containers are processed daily. In at least one case in Italy in 2001, a suspected Al Qaeda terrorist was discovered inside a shipping container, modified for comfort, which was bound for the United States.

Lethality

Although the net effect that elements of globalization have had on terrorism is troubling, the one element that concerns counter-terrorism experts and practitioners the most is future catastrophic attacks using weapons of mass destruction. During the transnational era, terrorists could obtain advanced weapons to conduct attacks, including guided missiles, rudimentary radiological weapons (more commonly known as '**dirty bombs**'), and biological or chemical weapons, but they largely did not. Only a few groups tried to acquire them and fewer still, including the Weather Underground, threatened their use. The precise reasons why terrorists did not acquire and use radiological, biological, or chemical weapons during this era are unclear. Experts speculated, however, that terrorist leaders understood that the more lethal their attacks were, the greater the likelihood that a state or the international community would focus their entire efforts on hunting them down and eradicating them.

More recently, senior leaders and operatives of terrorist groups have not only expressed a desire to acquire such weapons—but demonstrated the will to use them as well. For example, the Japanese cult Aum Shinryko manufactured and used nerve gas in the Tokyo subway system in 1995. The Al Qaeda manual entitled 'Military Studies in the Jihad Against the Tyrants', discovered during a raid on a suspected cell in Manchester, England in May 2000, outlines the basic steps for manufacturing and using biological and chemical toxins. Documents recovered in Afghanistan survey plans by Al Qaeda to produce specific types of biological and chemical weapons in quantity. In addition, other evidence appears to show the live testing of a chemical agent to determine its lethality. Statements by Osama bin Laden have underscored that all available means, including weapons of mass destruction, should be used in attacks to kill as many infidels and apostates as possible and cripple the US economy, which is both the icon for and the main engine of globalization. In an ironic twist related to the interconnection between terrorism and the influence of globalized media, a motivating element behind the fascination of senior Al Qaeda leaders with mass casualty attacks such as 'Operation Bojinka' is allegedly the spectacular scenes of destruction contained in a number of Hollywood blockbuster films.

Although the senior leaders of Al Qaeda would prefer to conduct another dramatic attack to restore

---

Box 21.4   Operation Bojinka

During the 1998 trial of Ramzi Yousef, for his role in the 1993 World Trade Center bombing, the details of a planned set of attacks codenamed 'Operation Bojinka' were revealed which demonstrate Al Qaeda's ambitious goals. Bojinka was conceived as a two-part operation. During the first phase, the terrorist cell operating in the Philippines would assassinate Pope John Paul II during a scheduled visit in January 1995. With international attention diverted by the death of the pontiff, Al Qaeda operatives would carry out the second phase the following week. Five or more terrorists would plant bombs on between 11 and 14 aircraft, designed to detonate almost simultaneously while the flights were transiting across the Pacific Ocean. Modest estimates, should the attacks have succeeded, place the number of casualties close to the figure for those who perished in the World Trade Center on 11 September 2001.

(Derived from 'Operation Bojinka' (n.d.), *Wikipedia, the free Encyclopedia*, online at: http://en.wikipedia.org/wiki/Operation_Bojinka)

Box 21.5   Key concepts

Terrorism: the use of illegitimate violence by sub-state groups to inspire fear, by attacking civilians and/or symbolic targets. This is done for purposes such as drawing widespread attention to a grievance, provoking a severe response, or wearing down their opponent's moral resolve, to effect political change. Determining when the use of violence is legitimate, which is based on the contextual morality of the act as opposed to its effects, is the source for disagreement over what constitutes acts of terrorism.

Combating terrorism: this is comprised of anti-terrorism efforts (measures to protect against or mitigate future terrorist attacks) and counter-terrorism efforts (proactive actions designed to retaliate against or forestall terrorist actions).

---

some of their credibility lost since the collapse of the Taliban in Afghanistan, such attacks take time to plan, organize, and conduct even without inevitable delays. Globalization has facilitated access to weapons and resources required to conduct smaller, but still lethal attacks. In particular, affiliated groups have obtained and used or tried to obtain from black and grey market sources advanced weapons such as **manportable air defence systems** (MANPADS, or portable surface-to-air missiles) to bring down civilian airliners. Terrorist groups from Chechnya to Sri Lanka have shared their expertise in the manufacturing of lethal bombs triggered by increasingly sophisticated, but commercially available, communications and remote control devices. **Improved explosive devices** (IEDs), especially those packed into large vehicles, are likely to remain the preferred terrorist method of attack, given the ease of manufacture and use, as well as the difficulties associated with countering them.

Key points

- Elements of globalization that permit the rapid exchange of ideas and goods can also be leveraged and exploited by terrorist groups.

- The technologies associated with globalization allow terrorists to operate in a highly distributed global 'network' that shares information and allows small cells to conduct highly coordinated, lethal attacks.

- Globalization may allow some terrorist groups to acquire, manufacture, and use weapons of mass destruction in order to conduct catastrophic attacks.

Combating terrorism

The leaders of states plagued by transnational terrorism responded individually and collectively to combat it. Individual states undertook a range of activities that varied in scope, breadth, and quality, including the passage of anti-terrorism laws, preventive measures such as security precautions at airports, and the creation of military and paramilitary counter-terrorism forces such as the West German Grenzschutzgruppe-9 (GSG-9). Successful hostage rescues in Entebbe (1976), Mogadishu (1977), and Prince's Gate, London (1980) demonstrated that national counter-terrorism forces could operate effectively both domestically and abroad. A rules-based approach to tackling the problem, founded on the principles of international law and collective action, proved to be less successful. Although attempts to define and proscribe transnational terrorism in the United Nations bogged down in debate in the General Assembly over semantics, other cooperative initiatives were successfully implemented. These included the conventions adopted through the International Civil Aviation Organization (ICAO) to improve information-sharing, and legal cooperation including the Hague Convention for the Suppression of Unlawful Seizure of Aircraft (1970). Another collective response to improve information sharing and collaborate action was the creation of the Public Safety and Terrorism Sub-Directorate within Interpol in 1985. Additional legislative measures were undertaken against terrorism during this period, such as the Convention against the Taking of Hostages (1979), but most initiatives and responses throughout this decade were largely unilateral or regional and ad hoc in nature.

State leaders disagree on how best to deal with the current form of global terrorist violence on the basis of expediency, legitimacy, and legality. Much of the controversy relates to the nature of the threat and approach that should be taken to deal with it. Some national leaders view Al Qaeda as the nexus of a global consortium of terrorist groups, which have repeatedly demonstrated a desire to inflict as many casualties as possible upon civilian targets. With no possible latitude for negotiation or compromise with terrorist groups who seek to replace the existing international system with a much more restrictive one, these leaders suggest that all states have an interest in engaging in a '**war on terrorism**', led by the United States, to deal with the threat. The stakes in this war consist of the preservation of basic freedoms and a way of life. Some freedoms may have to be constrained, but not abrogated, as the war will last for a decade or longer. In addition, the war should be viewed in terms of a prolonged global counter-insurgency campaign, where all instruments of national power must be integrated and harnessed to separate the most extreme terrorist elements from their sources of support, capture or destroy them, mitigate the underlying causes that motivate individuals to become terrorists, and protect civilian populations. Given the global, distributed, and elusive nature of the threat, which can strike at any time, the best approach for dealing with global terrorism before other catastrophic attacks occur is to leverage military forces in a '**coalition of the willing**'. Coalition military forces, working with national forces, are structured and have the capabilities to lead efforts that will deny terrorist groups sanctuaries in ungoverned or ungovernable sections of the globe, while law enforcement officials locate and deny access to international sources of funding and support. By dealing with threats to the common rights and welfare of nations overseas now, as well as bolstering domestic capabilities to identify, track, and respond to internal terrorist threats, those in favour of a war on terror seek to prevent more devastating attacks from occurring on national soil.

Other national leaders are uneasy with the concept of 'war' against terrorism. They view actions led by the military as likely to lead to terrorist reprisals in an unending cycle of violence. In their eyes, terrorism is a crime that is best dealt with through law-enforcement methods. By dealing with terrorism as a police problem, states uphold the rule of law, maintain the high moral ground, preserve democratic principles, and prevent the establishment of martial law. Military force should only be used in extreme circumstances and even then its use may have negative consequences. Terrorism is best dealt with inside state borders and through cooperative international law-enforcement efforts to arrest subjects and provide them with due process. The law-enforcement approach to terrorism must balance taking enough measures against terrorist groups without crossing

over into the realm of ' "political justice," where the rules and rights enshrined in the principle of due process are either willfully misinterpreted or completely disregarded' (Chalk 1996: 98). To do little against domestic or global terrorism, in the name of upholding the rule of law, risks offering terrorist groups a sanctuary and the security of rights and laws to which they are not entitled, as terrorists are seeking to subvert the systems which protect them.

Although disagreements still exist over the best approach to pursue terrorists actively, the two biggest problems are locating terrorists and isolating them from their means of support and sustenance. Locating and identifying terrorists is a tedious and time-consuming process that requires acquiring, assessing, and analysing information collected from a range of technical and human sources. Information technologies associated with globalization, which many states possess, are useful in assisting this process. Such technologies allow terrorist patterns to be identified prior to attacks and assist in evaluating evidence collected after attacks, with systems capable of performing calculations measured in the trillions per second (floating point operations, or flops). Terrorist financial and organizational information can be compared using forms of link analysis to construct a more comprehensive picture of how the terrorist elements interact. In addition, huge volumes of information can be reduced and exchanged electronically between departments, agencies, and other governments or made available on secure servers whose capacities are measured in terabytes. Discovering terrorist cells, however, has as much to do with pursuing non-technical leads and mistakes. Although technology speeds the process, rebuilding key intelligence deficiencies, pursuing individuals globally, and adequately mapping the network of organizations and individuals still takes time.

In order to deal with global terrorism, the international community must address one of its most problematic aspects: the appeal of messages that inspire terrorists to commit horrific acts of violence. Collective law-enforcement and military actions are successful in removing temporarily or permanently current members of terrorist organizations. Although such actions may dissuade some individuals from taking up terrorist causes, they do little to halt the promotion of extremist interpretations of religion or political theory that occurs under the guise of 'education'. In the case of Islam, for example, radical mullahs and imams twist the tenets of the religion into a doctrine of action and hatred, where spiritual achievement occurs through destruction rather than personal enlightenment. In other words, suicide attacks offer the promise of immediate spiritual accomplishment and relieve the individual of the burden of a lifetime of piety and positive contributions to the community. Precisely how the processes and technologies of globalization can assist in delegitimizing the pedagogy that incites terrorists will remain one of the most vexing challenges for the international community for years, if not decades, to come.

> **Key points**
>
> - States, individually and collectively, have political, military, legal, economic, and technological advantages in the struggle against terrorist groups.
> - Differences between states over the nature and scope of the current terrorist threat, and the most appropriate responses to combat it, reflect subjective characterizations based on national biases and experiences.

Conclusion

Terrorism remains a complex phenomenon in which violence is used to obtain power and redress political, social, and/or economic grievances that have grown more widespread, or acute, to many through the process of globalization. Globalization has improved the technical capabilities of terrorists and given them global reach, but has not altered the fundamental fact that terrorism is the weakest form of irregular warfare, representing the extreme views of a limited minority of the global population. In other words, globalization has changed the scope of terrorism but not its nature. Although globalization has improved the technical capabilities of sub-state groups and individuals, it has not conveyed one-sided or absolute benefits to terrorists. The same technologies and processes giving terrorism its global reach also enable more effective means of states to combat them. The only hope for success that terrorists have in the long run is the widespread uprising of the disaffected and oppressed, or the collapse of their adversary after a crippling attack. Terrorist and counter-terrorist campaigns are characterized by prolonged struggle to maintain advantages in legitimacy domestically and internationally. The challenge for the global community will be in utilizing its advantages to win the war of ideas that motivates and sustains those responsible for the current wave of terrorist violence.

For further information and case studies on this subject, please visit the companion web site at www.oup.com/uk/booksites/politics.

> **QUESTIONS**
>
> 1 Why is linking terrorism with globalization so difficult to do theoretically?
>
> 2 When did terrorism become a truly global phenomenon and what enabled it to do so?
>
> 3 In what ways are the technologies and processes associated with globalization more beneficial to states or terrorists?

4   Given that terrorism has been both a transnational and a global phenomenon, why has it not been more successful in effecting change?

5   Of all of the factors that motivate terrorists, is any one more important than others and if so, why?

6   What has changed in terrorism over the past half century and have any factors remained the same? If so, what are they and why have they remained constant?

7   What is the role that technology plays in terrorism and will it change how terrorists operate in the future? If so, how?

8   What are the dilemmas that terrorist groups face with respect to weapons of mass destruction?

9   What is the primary challenge that individual states and the international community as whole face in confronting terrorism?

10 How can globalization be useful in diminishing the underlying causes of terrorism?

GUIDE TO FURTHER READING

Burton, P. (ed.) (2003), *Jane's World Insurgency and Terrorism* (Surrey: Jane's Information Group). An annual reference work containing summaries of insurgent and terrorist group issues, important events, and evolving trends.

Davis, P., and Jenkins, B. M. (2002), *Deterrence and Influence in Counter-terrorism: A Component in the War on Al Qaeda* (Santa Monica, Cal.: RAND). The authors offer a holistic strategy to combat Al Qaeda that accounts for deterring and influencing terrorist groups but recognizes the difficulties in doing so against a networked, adaptive adversary.

Drake, C. J. M. (1998), *Terrorists' Target Selection* (New York: St Martin's). The author captures similarities in the selection rationale, targeting process, and priorities of different terrorist groups.

Greenberg, M. (2002), *Terrorist Financing* (New York: Council on Foreign Relations). This report, available online from the Council on Foreign Relations web site (**www.cfr.org**), assesses Al Qaeda's financial network, US responses since 9/11 to dismantle it, and recommendations on how to improve national and international cooperation against this aspect of terrorism.

Hoffman, B. (1998), *Inside Terrorism* (New York: Columbia University Press). A lucid survey of the problems, trends, and developments in terrorism and a useful starting point for those interested in understanding the complex phenomenon of terrorism.

Juergensmeyer, M. (2000), *Terror in the Mind of God: The Global Rise of Religious Violence* (Berkeley, Cal.: University of California Press). An excellent study that highlights the commonalities among disparate and theologically diverse group leaders who use religion to justify the use of violence against civilians.

National War College Student Task Force on Combating Terrorism (2002), *Combating Terrorism in a Globalized World* (Washington, DC: National War College). A student project undertaken after 9/11, this document subsequently became the basis for the *U.S. National Strategy for Combating Terrorism*.

Pillar, P. (2001), *Terrorism and U.S. Foreign Policy* (Washington: Brookings Institution Press). An interesting overview of the actions that the United States should take against international terrorism based on the author's practical experience in counter-terrorism.

Schmid, A. P., Jongman, A. J., *et al.* (1988), *Political Terrorism: A New Guide to Actors, Authors, Concepts, Data Bases, Theories, and Literature* (New Brunswick, NJ: Transaction Books). A helpful, if at times elusive, reference work for further research that highlights the methodological problems associated with the study of terrorism.

Stern, J. (1999), *The Ultimate Terrorists* (Cambridge, Mass.: Harvard University Press). Provides much information on weapons of mass destruction and the ease with which terrorists can acquire them.

WEB LINKS

Terrorism Research Centre: **www.terrorism.com/index.shtml**.

This useful site has an excellent links section, including links to relevant reports and terrorism news.

This is Baader-Meinhof: **www.baader-meinhof.com/index.htm**.

This site contains information related to transnational terrorism, and in particular, the German Baader-Meinhof group. It has a section for students and researchers as well as links to or the complete text of seminal works such as Carlos Marighella's 'Minimanual of the Urban Guerrilla'. **www.baader-meinhof.com/students/resources/print/ manual.html**.

US State Department—Patterns of Global Terrorism Annual Report: **www.state.gov/s/ct/rls/pgtrpt/**.

Archived from 1995 upwards, these reports contains valuable information and trends analysis on American perceptions of terrorism and the threat it poses.

Terrorism Files: **www.terrorismfiles.org**.

A useful collection of news items, terrorist group overviews, individuals, and incidents.

Special Operations Web site: **www.specialoperations.com**.

Exhaustive collection devoted to all aspects of special operations, including national counter-terrorism units and historical operations.

RAND Corporation: **www.rand.org/publications/electronic/gse.html**.

Well known for the quality of its reports and established interest in terrorism, this link points to a number of reports on issues related to terrorism and other global security issues.

The 'Terrorism as a Global Issue' Web portal: **www.un.org/partners/civil_society/m-terror.htm**.

This Web portal, hosted by the United Nations, provides links to historical documents, summaries of events, and other web sites on international issues and actions related to terrorism.

CHAPTER 22

Nuclear proliferation

DARRYL HOWLETT

READER'S GUIDE

This chapter identifies those factors that have made nuclear proliferation a global phenomenon since 1945. Over this period, the nature of nuclear weapons has transformed military and political relationships, while the global diffusion of nuclear and ballistic missile technology has meant that more actors are in a position both to acquire a nuclear capability and potentially to deliver it over longer distances. This chapter also reveals the complexities associated with the globalization of the nuclear proliferation issue and some of the theoretical aspects related to it. There are difficulties in determining both the motivations, which lead to the acquisition of nuclear weapons, and the capabilities that might be constructed once acquisition has occurred. This complexity has been made more acute as a result of novel proliferation concerns, such as: ensuring the safety and security of nuclear and radiological materials around the world, including in what was formerly the Soviet Union; the arrival of nuclear-weapons capable states in South Asia and possibly elsewhere; the emergence of transnational nuclear supply networks operating outside established arrangements; and the prospect that non-state actors will acquire a nuclear capability and use it. To add a further dimension, there are those who argue that the spread of nuclear weapons to additional states is no bad thing as this may induce stability in conflict-prone regional situations. This contrasts with the alternative view, which argues that further nuclear proliferation is likely to increase instability and the potential for conflict between states.

As a result of these developments, efforts have focused primarily on measures designed: to raise the costs of nuclear acquisition; to develop standards of nuclear and missile behaviour; and to create the conditions that allow for reductions in nuclear stock-piles to occur in a safe and secure manner. What has also emerged in recent times is a debate about the conceptual and practical aspects of these measures and whether the international treaty approach, or what traditionally has been termed the nuclear non-proliferation regime, is sufficient to contain contemporary and future proliferation dynamics. Consequently, some consider that what is now required is a fresh appraisal of measures and responses so they meet the requirements of global nuclear governance in the twenty-first century.

Introduction

The issue of nuclear proliferation represents one of the more marked illustrations of the globalization of world politics. The advent of nuclear weapons and their unprecedented capacity for wreaking destruction across territorial boundaries has transformed the globe. Although only five states (China, France, Russia (formerly, the Soviet Union), the United Kingdom, and the United States) are acknowledged by the Treaty on the Non-Proliferation of Nuclear Weapons (NPT) as possessing nuclear weapons, others have the capability to construct nuclear devices and deliver them, if necessary, by increasingly sophisticated means. This latter aspect was emphasized in May 1998 when India and Pakistan, two states previously associated with having a 'threshold' or near-nuclear weapons position, demonstrated their respective capabilities by conducting a series of nuclear tests followed by ballistic missile launches. These events also highlighted another aspect concerning the globalization of the nuclear proliferation issue: the potential emergence of a regionally differentiated world. While some regions have moved from a situation where nuclear weapons once had a high profile in strategic thinking to one where these weapons have assumed much lower significance, other regions may be moving in the opposite direction. In Latin America, South-East Asia, Africa, and Central Asia, the trend has been towards developing the region as a **Nuclear-Weapon-Free Zone** (NWFZ). In other regions, such as South Asia and possibly North-East Asia and elsewhere, the contrasting trend appears to be towards a higher profile for nuclear capabilities. What is less clear is the impact that possible **nuclearization** (meaning the acquisition of nuclear weapons) in some regions will have on those that have been moving towards **denuclearization** (meaning a process of removing such capabilities).

Concern about the proliferation of nuclear capabilities has undoubtedly increased in significance on the global agenda since the end of the East–West cold war, yet many of the factors that have made it such an important issue have been under way for several decades. Knowledge of the enormous destructive effects of nuclear weapons against human populations, for example, dates back to the bombings of the Japanese cities Hiroshima and Nagasaki at the end of the Second World War. Similarly, the fire that destroyed the civil nuclear power plant at Chernobyl in the former Soviet Union in 1986 revealed the devastating effects of nuclear radiation and its potential for long-term damage across frontiers when carried on the prevailing winds.

Equally significant, in 1945 only the United States possessed the capacity to manufacture a nuclear weapon. Today, several states have acquired an infrastructure to construct at least crude nuclear devices, either as a direct result of a dedicated nuclear weapons programme or as a consequence of the acquisition of particular civil nuclear technologies. Additionally, the diffusion of ballistic missile technology has meant that the capacity to deliver nuclear weapons by this means has become more commonplace.

Developments stemming from the dissolution of the former Soviet Union in the early 1990s have also raised novel problems. This is the only case where a previously acknowledged **nuclear-weapon state** (NWS) has been subjected to political and territorial disintegration. At the time, there was little understanding of what the precise nuclear consequences from such a tumultuous state implosion would be and only in hindsight can we judge its full significance. That it was a period of unprecedented nuclear transformation, which ultimately called for long-term cooperation between previously hostile states, is not in doubt. Potentially less obvious is the observation that this period of transition was facilitated by the foresight of policymakers from both sides of the former cold war divide and by the framework of arms control and disarmament agreements in place at the time. Consequently, one judgement, which could be made, is that the maintenance of nuclear stability during this period would have been more difficult had it not been for policies such as the **Co-operative Threat Reduction Programme** and agreements like the multilateral NPT and bilateral **Strategic Arms Reduction Treaties** (START), signed initially between the USA and the former Soviet Union (and later between the USA and Russia).

Another development that has gained in momentum is the attention devoted both to theorizing why some states acquire nuclear weapons while others do not, and to the role of norms and taboos in this context. Aspects of these debates also featured in earlier texts written during the period of the East–West cold war. For example, when Hedley Bull published the first edition of *The Control of the Arms Race* in 1961, the issue of why states might seek a nuclear weapons capability and the consequences of such an action was already exercising the minds of policy-makers and strategic analysts. Nuclear proliferation at this time was often considered in the context of the 'Nth power problem', or as Bull expressed it (1961: 147):

the problem of preventing the expansion of the nuclear club, or of making adjustments to it, is a single one faced by international society as a whole (The Problem), and that it is one raised by any addition to the club's membership (Nth power).

Bull also noted the tension within this debate over how each state views their own possession of nuclear weapons and those of other possessors (that is, whether or not they are viewed as a threat); and the type of state possessing these weapons (1961: 147). Another aspect of Bull's 1961 analysis is his reference to a US study that identified 26 states, which to varying degrees depending on their economic and scientific resources could develop a nuclear weapons capability within a relatively short time-span (1961: 150). It is noteworthy that the number of states in possession of nuclear weapons has not reached the estimate suggested in the US study—although today it is probable that the number of states which could develop such a capability has increased since 1961.

One debate that has sparked diverging responses, at least since the early 1980s, has been a thesis asserting that the gradual spread of nuclear weapons to additional states is to be welcomed rather than feared. This thesis is based on the proposition that just as nuclear deterrence maintained stability between East and West during the cold war, so can it induce similar stabilizing effects on other conflict situations. The assumptions underpinning this thesis have been challenged by those who hold that

more will be worse not better and that measures to stem nuclear proliferation represent the best way forward (Sagan and Waltz 1995—see Boxes 22.1 and 22.2).

The responses to nuclear proliferation have embraced a wide range of unilateral, bilateral, regional, and global measures that collectively have

---

Box 22.1   The main arguments of the Waltz thesis

1. Nuclear weapons have spread rather than proliferated because these weapons have proliferated only vertically as the Nuclear Weapon States have increased their arsenals.

2. Nuclear weapons have spread horizontally to other states only slowly. However, this slowness of pace is fortunate as rapid changes in international conditions can be unsettling.

3. The gradual spread of nuclear weapons is better than either no spread or rapid spread.

4. New nuclear states will feel the constraints that nuclear weapons impose and this will induce a sense of responsibility on the part of their possessors and a strong element of caution on their use.

5. The likelihood of war decreases as deterrent and defensive capabilities increase; nuclear weapons, responsibly used, make wars hard to start.

(Sagan and Waltz 1995)

Box 22.2   Sagan's 'proliferation pessimism' argument

1. Professional military organizations, because of common biases, inflexible routines, and parochial interests, display organizational behaviours that are likely to lead to deterrence failures and deliberate or accidental war.

2. Because future nuclear-armed states are likely to have military-run or weak civilian governments, they will lack the positive constraining mechanisms of civilian control while military biases may serve to encourage nuclear weapons use, especially during crisis.

(Sagan and Waltz 1995)

traditionally been termed the nuclear non-proliferation regime. Advocates of this regime argue it is the evolution of these measures (which include arms control and disarmament treaties like the NPT, export controls, international monitoring procedures, nuclear supplier and trading agreements, and other standard setting arrangements) that has constrained nuclear acquisition since the 1960s. Conversely, there have been several criticisms of this regime and even some long-term supporters acknowledge it is in 'need of intensive care' if it is to meet the requirements of the coming decades (Ogilvie-White and Simpson 2003).

Among the criticisms of the nuclear non-proliferation regime are that it: is a product of a bygone **'first nuclear age'** (1945–90) and is not well suited to the demands of the complex and potentially more dangerous **'second nuclear age'** (1990–); is unable to alleviate the security dilemma that many states confront and, hence, does not adequately address the security motivation which leads states to acquire nuclear weapons; and is a discriminatory arrangement because the NPT only requires that the five NWS pursue nuclear disarmament in good faith (under its Article VI) while all other parties (designated as **Non-Nuclear-Weapon States** (NNWS)) must forgo the acquisition of nuclear weapons on signing the Treaty. Hence, there has always been a tension between whether the NPT is primarily a non-proliferation agreement designed to prevent additional nuclear weapon states emerging or a disarmament arrangement to achieve the eventual elimination of nuclear weapons. This aspect became a major factor at the NPT Review and Extension Conference in 1995 when the Treaty was extended indefinitely

after an initial 25 years in operation. It was also in evidence five years later when, at the 2000 NPT Conference, the five NWS acknowledged by the Treaty issued a joint statement reiterating their commitment to pursue the goal of the eventual elimination of their nuclear weapons. In the context of this discussion, emphasis was also placed on the need for all NPT parties to improve transparency in their nuclear transactions and operations, and for new measures to enhance verification and compliance.

It was noted earlier that a debate has emerged over future responses, particularly relating to the worth of the nuclear non-proliferation regime as an instrument of global nuclear policy. What is noticeable about this current debate is that it is being addressed in a manner that potentially has not been seen since the 1960s and 1970s, and against an international backdrop that differs radically from the earlier period. At the heart of this debate are key issues relating to the future global security environment, including: what are likely to be the main proliferation challenges of the coming decades; and whether the traditional treaty-based approach (centred around the nuclear non-proliferation regime) needs to be supplemented with additional arrangements or supplanted altogether with a new more fluid response involving a mix of instruments and measures depending on the particular circumstances and the actors involved (Saunders 2001; Ayson 2001; Bohlen 2003; Bracken 2003 and 2004; Feinstein and Slaughter 2004; Allison 2004). The outcome of this debate will consequently set the tone and content of what some envisage as the basis for global nuclear governance in the twenty-first century.

The nature of nuclear weapons and their effects

The technical basis of nuclear weapons

Unless a nuclear weapon or the key nuclear materials required for their manufacture can be obtained 'off the shelf' as a result of purchase or theft, a concern

that has become more pronounced in recent years, the usual route for any state or non-state actor seeking to acquire nuclear weapons would be via the development of the necessary technological infrastructure. The latter would include a range of

nuclear, conventional, computational, and electronic technologies and individuals with key scientific and technical skills.

Nuclear reactors and nuclear weapons differ in
their management of the nuclear chain reaction, and
in the nature of the energy produced. Whereas in a
reactor energy output is achieved through a sustained and regulated process, in a nuclear weapon
the objective is to attain a large explosive yield by
creating a critical mass of nuclear material as a result
of an uncontrolled and rapid chain reaction (Gardner 1994: 6–7). Nuclear weapons consequently
derive their explosive energy from techniques
designed either to split the atoms rapidly in order to
create a chain reaction (so-called fission weapons), or
by using fission weapons as a primary initiator to
compress and heat hydrogen atoms so that they
combine or fuse (so-called thermonuclear or fusion
weapons). In contrast, energy production in a
nuclear reactor involves a means for regulating the
chain reaction, a moderator that surrounds the fissile
core for maintaining the chain reaction, and a means
for removing the heat produced from the reactor
core by the chain reaction, which can also provide
the steam to drive turbines and generate electricity.

Nuclear weapons effects

The effects of nuclear weapons are considerable.
Because of this, the United Nations Commission for
Conventional Armaments in 1948 introduced a new
category of **'weapons of mass destruction'**
(WMD) to distinguish nuclear weapons from conventional forms. As the Commission outlined the
category, WMD included 'atomic explosive
weapons, radioactive material weapons, lethal chemical and biological weapons, and any weapons
developed in the future which have characteristics
comparable in destructive effect to those of the
atomic bomb or other weapons mentioned above'.
In recent years, an alternative term has appeared,
namely **CBRN** (referring to Chemical, Biological,
Radiological, and Nuclear capabilities). Some analysts have also argued that the term WMD should be
unravelled because each of the weapons types has
different effects, with nuclear weapons being the
true WMD (Panofsky 1998).

Box 22.3 | **The technology of nuclear weapons**

Separate processes are required to obtain the two fissile
materials needed to construct a nuclear weapon. Uranium
is found in nature and comprises 99.3% uranium 238
(U-238) and 0.7% uranium 235 (U-235). The U-235 has
the same chemical properties as the U-238 but has a
different atomic weight. It is the latter isotopic form that
is used in a nuclear weapon. To produce the weapon, the
amount of U-235 in a quantity of natural uranium is
increased to weapons grade by a process called enrichment so that eventually it becomes 90%+ of the sample.
Once a sufficient quantity of weapons grade U-235
has been accumulated to achieve a critical mass, defined
by the International Atomic Energy Agency (IAEA) as 25
kilograms—although the amount could be smaller—then
there is enough fissile material to construct one nuclear
weapon.

Plutonium does not occur naturally. Rather, it is one
of the end products of the irradiation of natural or
only very slightly enriched (2–3%) uranium in a nuclear
reactor. Plutonium 239 (Pu-239) is thus the result of a
controlled nuclear reaction process. Because the two are
chemically different, it is possible to separate plutonium
and uranium through a process known as reprocessing.
The figure of 6 to 8 kilograms is usually the quantity
quoted for one weapon although again some designs may
use less than that.

A nuclear weapon produces its energy in three
distinct forms: **blast; heat or thermal radiation;**
and **nuclear radiation**. Experience of nuclear
testing has also indicated another feature of a
nuclear weapons explosion, the phenomenon
known as electro-magnetic pulse (EMP). This can
cause acute disruption to electronic equipment
(Grace 1994: 1).

Extensive damage to human populations may
result from a nuclear weapons detonation. Awareness of these effects stems from the two weapons
dropped on Hiroshima and Nagasaki at the end of
the Second World War; this remains the only time
nuclear weapons have been used. What is also
known is that the weapons that destroyed these
Japanese cities were relatively small in comparison to
the destructive forces generated by later testing of
thermonuclear weapons. The largest weapon of this
kind known to have been tested was estimated to be

a 50-megaton device (i.e. 50 million tonnes of TNT) produced by the Soviet Union in 1961 during the height of the cold war. It is also understood that the Soviet Union stockpiled a 100-megaton weapon, although this device was never tested. One noticeable trend in recent years, however, has been a movement away from nuclear weapons with large explosive potential towards designs with much lower yields.

The long-term and widespread effects of nuclear radiation were also confirmed when, at 1.23 a.m. on 26 April 1986, the No. 4 power unit at the Chernobyl nuclear complex in the former Soviet Union went out of control. The devastation caused by a massive fire within an operating nuclear power plant shook the world, and while a more serious nuclear accident was prevented by the bravery of those who dealt with the immediate aftermath, the long-term consequences were still profound. Nuclear radiation was carried on the prevailing winds across several borders, resulting in large numbers of animals having to be destroyed and humans well outside the initial disaster area suffering varying degrees of radiation-induced illnesses.

Key points

- Nuclear weapon production requires a broad-based technological infrastructure and individuals with key scientific and technical skills.

- Nuclear reactors and nuclear weapons differ in their management of the chain reaction, and in the nature of the energy produced.

- In 1948, the United Nations introduced the category known as Weapons of Mass Destruction (WMD), which included atomic explosive weapons and radioactive material weapons.

- More recently, a new category has appeared known as CBRN (chemical, biological, radiological, and nuclear capabilities).

- Nuclear weapons produce energy in three forms—blast, heat and nuclear radiation—and the phenomenon known as electro-magnetic pulse (EMP).

- Nuclear weapons were used at the end of the Second World War and have not been used in conflict since that time.

- The testing of thermonuclear weapons indicated the greater explosive capacity of this type of weapon, although the trend in recent years have been towards weapon designs with much lower yields.

The global diffusion of nuclear and ballistic missile technology

The diffusion of nuclear technology

Since 1945, nuclear technology for civil and military uses has disseminated on a global scale. In the immediate post-Second World War years only the United States possessed the technological capability to manufacture a nuclear weapon. By 1964, four other states had crossed the nuclear weapons threshold, an event traditionally understood as the testing of a nuclear explosive device (Soviet Union (1949), the United Kingdom (1952), France (1960), and China (1964)).

Complications with regard to the definition of a NWS contained in the NPT (referring to a state that has exploded a nuclear weapon or other explosive nuclear device before 1 January 1967), were raised by the detonation of nuclear devices by India and Pakistan in May 1998. Neither state was party to the NPT at the time (and both have remained outside the Treaty subsequently), so they were not in breach of any international legal obligation. Yet, India and Pakistan's move from a presumed 'threshold' position to demonstrating an overt nuclear-weapons capability not only questioned the NPT's definition of a NWS, but also raised the issue of whether other states that had signed the Treaty might follow the nuclear path trodden by these two states.

In addition to this development there are concerns about the future evolution of nuclear supply arrangements and the role of transnational non-state networks in this context. At the inter-state level, there has been a structural change in the civil nuclear trading market since 1945. For several years after the Second World War, the United States remained the pre-eminent nuclear supplier. By the 1970s, this position was challenged, first by European nuclear suppliers such as France and Germany, and then by Japan (Walker and Lönnroth 1983). Today, there are several nuclear suppliers, including transnational non-state supply networks that operate outside established export control and supplier guidelines. This situation has generated the prospect that the acquisition of at least rudimentary nuclear capabilities has become easier and raised additional dilemmas for policymakers who have to respond to it.

The increasing sophistication of nuclear delivery

During the 1950s, nuclear weapons required large bomber aircraft designed specifically to carry these weapons to their target. Thereafter, as the technology developed for manufacturing ballistic missiles and for nuclear ordnance that was compact enough to be carried by these missiles, so the possibility increased that more states would seek to deliver nuclear weapons by this means.

Ballistic missiles consequently represent the most sophisticated method of nuclear delivery and were once restricted to a few technologically advanced states. But just as the diffusion of nuclear technology is a global phenomenon, so has the capability to deploy a ballistic missile become more commonplace. Should these missiles be linked to the delivery of nuclear ordnance, then more states will have the capacity to hit targets over longer distances and, by implication, also to widen their potential for political and strategic engagement. It is this aspect, probably more than any other, that increased the profile of the nuclear issue at the end of the 1990s and brought to the fore once more the debate over the merits of deploying defences against ballistic missiles.

The debate entered a new phase when the US Congress passed the National Missile Defense (NMD) Act in 1999. This Act proposed that the United States should develop the technical means to counter a possible small-scale ballistic missile attack on the US mainland. The timetable for the initial deployment, of what subsequently became known as the **Ballistic Missile Defence** (BMD) system, was set at 2005.

Following the announcement of the proposal for missile defences there was a range of reactions both within the United States and from states elsewhere. The overall programme cost and the technical feasibility became central elements of the US domestic debate: for unlike the Strategic Defence Initiative proposal of 1983, which intended to use a range of technologies including nuclear explosions to intercept incoming missiles, the new system has been developed primarily using kinetic energy. This means the intention is to hit an incoming missile with another defensive missile during its flight path. Such a system inevitably requires considerable early warning and computational capabilities, and a missile that is fast and manoeuvrable enough to hit a target potentially travelling at 7 kilometres per second.

International reaction to US missile defence proposals met with concerns in Russia and China about the impact on stability if the ABM Treaty was eroded, while in **Europe** similar reservations were expressed. The United States eventually announced its withdrawal from the ABM Treaty on 13 December 2001, negotiated a new agreement with Russia known as the **Strategic Offensive Reductions Treaty** (SORT), and continued with the plans for a BMD system. However, the issue of missile defences and their implications for global and regional security is likely to remain a topic on the international agenda.

Key points

- The nature of nuclear weapons and the dissemination of the capabilities to manufacture them around the world since 1945 makes the issue of nuclear proliferation a good illustration of the globalization of world politics.

- The end of the cold war and the dissolution of the former Soviet Union have generated new problems concerning nuclear proliferation.

- Greater attention has recently been paid to the theoretical aspects of nuclear proliferation and anti-proliferation.

- A debate has emerged over the merits of the further proliferation/spread of nuclear weapons.

- Because of new proliferation challenges generated by what some analysts call the 'second nuclear age', a debate has begun over whether the nuclear non-proliferation regime should be supplemented or supplanted by a new more flexible approach to the problems of global nuclear governance.

- A major element of the nuclear proliferation process is the acquisition of the key technologies to produce fissile materials to construct either a fission (nuclear) or fusion (thermonuclear) weapon.

- The effects of nuclear weapons are considerable and are manifest in the form of blast, heat, and nuclear radiation.

- Since 1945, the spread of nuclear technology for civil and military purposes has meant that states beyond the five which possess nuclear weapons now have the capacity to produce nuclear devices at relatively short notice, if they have not already done so.

- Over the same period the structure of the civil nuclear trading market has also changed, leading to proliferation concerns because there are more nuclear suppliers around, including transnational supply networks operating outside the established export control guidelines.

- There has also been a diffusion of ballistic missile and space-launch technology since 1945.

- A debate over the merits of deploying defensive systems to counter ballistic missiles has emerged and the ABM Treaty agreed in 1972 between the United States and the former Soviet Union is no longer in force.

Theorizing nuclear proliferation and non-proliferation

Conceptual issues

Considerable attention has been paid to the theoretical aspects of nuclear proliferation. One question that has provoked concerted interest is what constitutes nuclear proliferation: does it refer to a single decision to acquire a nuclear weapon or is it part of a process that may stretch over several years and consequently no one identifiable decision can be located? Research on what has been referred to as 'the proliferation puzzle' has thus embraced an increasingly complex array of variables and conceptual issues (Davis and Frankel 1993; Meyer 1984; Lavoy 1995; Ogilvie-White 1996). Similarly, while

much literature endorses the propositions derived from political realism, which asserts that in an anarchic international environment states will seek nuclear weapons to enhance their security, insights from other theoretical positions have become more commonplace in recent years. This has led to questions concerning what the appropriate 'level of analysis' should be in studying nuclear proliferation. Should the focus be on the individual, the organization, the cultural group, the state, the international system, or some combination of these? Similarly, in the context of fostering nuclear non-proliferation dialogues, some analysts have indicated the importance played by culture and identity factors (Krause and Williams 1997).

The argument has also been advanced that norms, taboos, and epistemic communities have played an important role in the nuclear context (Adler 1992; Price and Tannenwald 1996). One viewpoint sees international norms as increasingly significant both as constraints on nuclear behaviour and in setting appropriate standards among a range of actors. In this context, a proposition often voiced is that a non-proliferation norm has evolved which has assisted in limiting the numbers of nuclear weapon states in existence, certainly from the numbers expected by studies in the early 1960s.

Another issue with enduring resonance concerns the question of what can explain the lengthy period of nuclear 'non-use' since 1945. It is noteworthy that this debate started very early in the nuclear calendar as authors like Bernard Brodie, writing not long after the Second World War, argued that nuclear weapons were useful only in their non-use (Gray 1996; Brodie 1946). Over the years, the main explanation of non-use has centred on the notion of nuclear deterrence: states have been deterred from using nuclear weapons because of the concerns of retaliation in kind by adversaries.

In looking to alternative accounts of non-use, some have focused more on the nature of the weapon and the impact this has on normative judgements. Nina Tannenwald, for example, has challenged those arguments that rely on rational cost–benefit analysis relating to power, capabilities, and interests by exploring other non-material aspects, such as the constraining influence of what is termed the 'nuclear taboo' (1999). In identifying such a taboo, Barry Buzan and Eric Herring define it as 'a strategic cultural prohibition against the use of nuclear weapons . . . an assumption that nuclear weapons should not be used rather than a conscious cost–benefit calculation' (1998: 165).

The role that 'epistemic communities' and other transnational and non-governmental organizations play in the debate over nuclear proliferation and arms control generally has also provoked interest. Some writers have consequently drawn attention to the importance of groups of individuals, often from different disciplines and countries (the 'epistemic community'), who operate as conduits for ideas and proposals on nuclear policy issues, particularly if the intergovernmental fora are in stalemate.

Nuclear motivations

Traditional analysis of the motivations for nuclear proliferation has tended to focus at the state and inter-state levels. For much of the post-Second World War period the pattern of nuclear weapon acquisition established by the five acknowledged NWS was considered to be the one most likely to be followed by any future proliferating state. Analysis of the motivational aspect consequently focused on the strategic, political, and prestige rationales that led these states to seek nuclear weapons. The **strategic motivation** focused on the role that nuclear weapons played in the context of the Second World War and its immediate aftermath when initially they were seen as war-fighting or war-winning weapons. Later, attention shifted to the role that nuclear weapons played in deterrence, leading to the assumption that one of the principal motivations for acquisition was the deterrence of other nuclear weapons-capable states. Similarly, the **political and prestige benefits** that nuclear weapons conferred on those states with the wherewithal to manufacture them were also deemed significant. Nuclear weapons were seen as the most modern form of weaponry and their custodians, by dint of their technological prowess, were automatically afforded a seat at the 'top table of international affairs'.

Inherent in traditional analysis of nuclear proliferation was also a form of technological determinism, that once a state had acquired the necessary infrastructure it would automatically develop nuclear weapons. Supporting this assumption was the view that these states would also tread the same acquisition path as the five NWS. Thus, it could be predicted that any new nuclear state would pursue a dedicated military nuclear programme, conduct an overt nuclear test, produce a stockpile of weapons, and finally acquire an effective means for delivering the weapons to their target. While this explanation of the acquisition process and the motivations for embarking on a nuclear weapon programme is still relevant, over time, the understanding of the dynamics of nuclear proliferation have become more complex.

It is now more difficult to explain nuclear proliferation by focusing on a single variable. Increasingly analysts have argued that it is necessary to consider a range of factors that may influence nuclear weapons acquisition. These may include: traditional technological factors, the availability of nuclear technology, and a cadre of trained nuclear scientists who encourage acquisition; domestic politics, imperatives within a political party, or the domestic political situation may propel a state towards nuclear weapons; diplomatic bargaining, that acquisition of a nuclear capability can be used to influence or bargain politically or economically with both perceived allies and enemies; and non-intervention, that a nuclear capability can deter or prevent intervention by other states.

Other features of the 'proliferation puzzle' that need to be understood are the instances of nuclear restraint—why some states abandon the nuclear weapons option, and nuclear reversal—why some states relinquish their nuclear capabilities (Reiss 1995). One observation that can be made is that since 1945 developments have questioned the technological determinist argument. A number of factors have been identified to account for this. There may have been a change in strategic circumstances, such as the forging or the renegotiation of an alliance with a NWS. Similarly, technical difficulties encountered in the construction of the nuclear weapon, or the emergence of a perception that the acquisition of nuclear weapons would increase vulnerabilities, could create the necessary conditions for abandoning the nuclear option.

Further complexity is added when attention is focused at the **sub-state or** transnational actor level as the motivations of non-state actors may be different from those associated with states. In much traditional thinking, only states were considered to have the wherewithal to acquire nuclear capabilities. Nuclear commerce was conducted on a state-to-state basis, and it was states that entered into international arms control and disarmament treaties. Today, states are no longer the sole focus of attention as non-state actors have also featured.

Studies conducted during the 1970s and 1980s on **nuclear** terrorism indicated that there were risks associated with particular groups acquiring a nuclear device or threatening to attack civil or military nuclear installations. One study conducted by the International Task Force on Prevention of Nuclear Terrorism concluded that it was possible for a dedicated terrorist group to build a crude nuclear device provided it had sufficient quantities of chemical high-explosives and weapons-usable fissile materials. More significantly perhaps, in terms of thinking about the risks involved, it was felt that such a group would be more interested in causing panic and social disruption by making a credible nuclear threat rather than actually detonating a nuclear device and causing mass killing and destruction (Leventhal and Alexander 1987). More recent occurrences have served to alter this latter judgement.

Events in the mid-1990s, such as the first bombing of the World Trade Center in New York in 1993 and the attack against the US Government building in Oklahoma in April 1995, revealed the extent of damage and loss of life that could be caused. While both these instances involved traditional methods of inflicting damage, the use of nerve agents (chemical weapons) in an underground train network in central Tokyo in March 1995 to cause both death and widespread panic has been viewed as representing a quantum change in methods. These concerns have intensified since the tragic events of 11 September 2001, when the Twin Towers of the World Trade Center this time were completely destroyed by a coordinated attack using civilian aircraft loaded with aviation fuel as the method of destruction. The attack not only produced mass casualties but also changed the assumption about terrorist use of CBRN capabilities (Wilkinson 2003).

In addition to these factors, attention has focused on **nuclear smuggling** and the possibility that ethnic groups involved in civil conflict might seek a nuclear option to further their political or military objectives. As indicated earlier, nuclear smuggling has been given heightened attention since the discovery that materials and technology suitable for making nuclear weapons are being trafficked by transnational networks. Similarly, the fear that ethnic groups involved in civil conflict might resort to nuclear threats has become a feature of the post-cold war security debate. The concern in this context is that the situations in which such threats might occur would be highly unpredictable. It would be very difficult to determine whether the leaders of these groups would act responsibly or predictably in situations where the political and military conditions were unstable. Moreover, the possession of a single or small number of nuclear or radiological devices might encourage usage or pre-emptive strategies because of fear of discovery.

Nuclear capabilities and intentions

Closely paralleling the problems of analysing the motivational aspect are those associated with determining whether a state or terrorist group actually possesses a nuclear or radiological capability: that is, whether a form of nuclear proliferation has actually occurred. The case of South Africa, for example, indicates the difficulties in this area. On 24 March 1993, the then President F. W. de Klerk announced that South Africa had produced six nuclear devices prior to 1989 but had dismantled them before signing the NPT. While this announcement confirmed what many previously speculated—that South Africa possessed a nuclear capability during the 1980s—it also suggested a state did not need to test a nuclear device to be in possession of a nuclear stockpile. Additionally, there are currently around the world other advanced industrialized states with large operating nuclear power programmes, which could be used to produce quantities of fissile materials for military purposes if a political decision was taken to do so. The main barrier to nuclear weapon acquisition in such cases may therefore be political not technological.

One of the most significant developments in recent years has stemmed from the break-up of the former Soviet Union in 1991. Prior to its demise, the Soviet Union had deployed a vast nuclear weapon complex throughout its entire territory This complex embraced a large nuclear weapons arsenal, which included several tactical and strategic systems and a sophisticated technical infrastructure estimated to be around 100,000 personnel. Dealing with this infrastructure subsequently raised questions concerning: How to ensure secure employment for all the personnel involved in the weapons manufacturing process? Are the physical protection measures around the nuclear installations adequate? What should be done with any surplus nuclear materials? And are the export controls operating in the new republics adequate

---

Box 22.4 | **Compliance and non-compliance**

Compliance with international treaty obligations has been a perennial issue in the nuclear proliferation context. It has raised complex questions related to both the nature of any violation of agreements and the type of response to it. Violations, for example, may be only minor and relate to misinterpretation of procedures: conversely, they may be major and linked to breaches of specific treaty obligations. The type of response could therefore vary depending on how the violation is judged and, as a consequence, may involve a spectrum that could involve a procedural warning issued through an international organization like the IAEA or more stringent measures such as special inspection arrangements, sanctions, and the use of force. Where consideration of these aspects has been most pronounced since the early 1990s has been in the context of the DPRK and Iraq, although other cases have also come to the fore. The issue of compliance is therefore likely to receive continuing attention in the years ahead as it is not just responses to states that will be the subject of attention but responses to non-state actors as well.

---

now that the Soviet Union's overarching system has disappeared?

In response to this situation, efforts have focused on improving the prospects of those formerly working in the nuclear weapons complex, strengthening export control procedures in Russia and the new republics, and introducing tighter security arrangements around storage sites where nuclear weapons or materials are located.

In addition to developments that unfolded over Iraq after 1991, another party to the NPT that has been the subject of attention concerning capabilities and intentions is the Democratic People's Republic of Korea (DPRK). Both Iraq and the DPRK have revealed the difficulties in obtaining consensus in international fora on how to respond to compliance issues and the problems associated with verifying non-compliance in situations where special inspection or nuclear development arrangements are agreed.

In the case of Iraq, a special inspection arrangement known as UNSCOM (United Nations Special Committee) was established following the 1991 Gulf War to oversee the dismantlement of the WMD programme in Iraq that had come to light as a result of the conflict. By the late 1990s, problems were encountered over access to particular sites and UNSCOM inspectors were withdrawn. Disagreements also surfaced among the five Permanent Members of the United Nations Security Council concerning how to implement the UN resolutions that had been passed in connection with Iraq since 1991. These had not been resolved at the time of the intervention in Iraq that occurred in 2003.

The case of the DPRK since the early 1990s similarly highlights the difficulties associated with compliance. Following the attention that focused on the nuclear situation in the DPRK between 1991 and 1993, a special nuclear development arrangement was instituted in that country in 1994. Known as the 'Agreed Framework', this arrangement provided the DPRK with Light-Water Reactor technology and additional fuel supplies in exchange for that country's agreement that it would not produce nuclear weapons. However, since 1994 this arrangement has experienced several problems, which have resulted in continuing uncertainty surrounding the DPRK's nuclear intentions. This situation was exacerbated in August 1998 when the DPRK tested a ballistic missile whose trajectory took it over the territory of Japan and indicates the impact that emerging ballistic missiles and nuclear capabilities can have on threat perceptions. Tensions have subsequently heightened in the North-East Asia region with the DPRK stating in January 2003 that it has finally withdrawn from the NPT and will continue its nuclear programme. At the same time, efforts have been under way to find an appropriate response, including: high-level talks between the two Koreas; the initiation of security discussions involving the United States, China, Russia, and other regional states; and broader multilateral initiatives generated in the forums of the International Atomic Energy Association (IAEA) and the United Nations.

Another instance where the issue of nuclear intentions has generated uncertainty is Iran, also an NPT party. In the 1970s, German companies began constructing a nuclear power complex at Bushehr on the Persian Gulf coast. This complex was subsequently bombed during the Iran–Iraq war in the 1980s before it could be completed. Iran has subsequently attempted either to have the damage to the Bushehr nuclear complex repaired or to obtain alternative nuclear reactors. Additionally, the country became the subject of attention from the IAEA over delays in signing an additional protocol to Iran's safeguards agreement that requires increased transparency on the part of a NNWS in respect of its nuclear programme. Although Iran did sign the protocol to give the IAEA greater inspection rights on its territory in December 2003, the situation generated speculation because the IAEA discovered facilities that had not been declared to it and which once more highlighted the complexities in this area.

Key points

- Over time, the characterization of motivations for acquiring nuclear weapons has become more complex.

- There are also difficulties associated with determining whether nuclear proliferation has actually occurred due to technical ambiguities and the observation that a nuclear capability can be constructed without the need for a nuclear test.

- A number of states have the potential to manufacture nuclear weapons if they wanted, and a few actually embarked on military nuclear programmes before abandoning them.

- The role of non-state actors and transnational nuclear supply networks have added a further dimension to the nuclear proliferation issue.

- There is an ongoing task of ensuring the safety and security of nuclear materials around the world and efforts have been made to improve the prospects of personnel who formerly worked in the Soviet Union's nuclear weapon complex.

- The complexity surrounding compliance and non-compliance with international obligations has been a key feature of debate since the early 1990s.

The evolution of global nuclear control and anti-proliferation measures

Early efforts to control nuclear weapons, 1945–1970

Global efforts to constrain nuclear weapons acquisition began soon after the conclusion to the Second World War. In January 1946, the United Nations General Assembly passed a resolution establishing the UN Atomic Energy Commission (UNAEC). The remit of the UNAEC was to make proposals for the elimination of nuclear weapons and the use of nuclear energy for peaceful purposes under **international control**. Due to disagreements between the United States and the Soviet Union, these proposals were never implemented.

The issue of international atomic energy control was revisited following President Eisenhower's '**Atoms for Peace**' speech on 8 December 1953. It was stressed that Eisenhower's proposal was not a disarmament plan, but an initiative to open the benefits of atomic energy to the world community. Negotiations to implement 'Atoms for Peace' culminated in the establishment of the IAEA on 29 July 1957, although it was not until the mid-1960s that this organization was able to implement a comprehensive monitoring system (or **safeguards**) to ensure that materials in the nuclear energy programmes were not diverted for military use.

In the late 1950s, negotiations also began on a Comprehensive Test Ban Treaty (CTBT). These occurred in the context of a Soviet Union–United Kingdom–United States moratorium on nuclear testing (from 1958 to 1961), and against a backdrop of calls for the three NWS to engage in nuclear disarmament. The negotiations did not result in an agreement, largely because the three states were unable to overcome differences concerning **verification**: namely, the provisions for a system of inspections and controls that could provide adequate assurance of detection of violation, especially for underground testing. However, in 1963, the Soviet Union, the United Kingdom, the and United States did agree the Partial Test Ban Treaty (PTBT). This prohibited nuclear testing in the atmosphere, in outer space, and underwater. It meant, in effect, that future testing by states party to the PTBT had to be conducted underground.

Since the late 1950s, attention has also focused on measures to prevent the nuclearization of specific environments and geographical areas (Goldblat 2002). The first NWFZ applied to a populated geographic region is the Treaty for the Prohibition of Nuclear Weapons in Latin America (the Tlatelolco Treaty), which was opened for signature in 1967. Additionally, between 1958 and 1968 there was a greater focus on the issues posed by more states acquiring possessing weapons. In 1961, the UN General Assembly adopted what became known as the '**Irish Resolution**', which called for measures to limit the possibilities for additional states to acquire nuclear weapons and for all states to refrain from transfer or acquisition of such weapons. A breakthrough in the negotiation of a non-proliferation treaty came as a result of Resolution 2028 adopted by the UN General Assembly in 1965. Finally, on 11 March 1968 the Soviet Union and the United States tabled a joint draft treaty. Following some further amendments, this draft was passed by the UN General Assembly on 12 June 1968, opened for signature on 1 July 1968, and the NPT formerly entered into force on 5 March 1970 (Shaker 1980).

Anti-proliferation efforts since 1970

Since 1970, anti-proliferation measures have continued to evolve. In March 1971, the IAEA negotiated its so-called INFCIRC/153 safeguards document, which provides a model for all safeguards negotiated with parties to the NPT. Additional arrangements have been established for the conduct of international nuclear trade. In 1971, the Zangger Committee adopted guidelines or a 'trigger list' pursuant to the NPT allowing for IAEA safeguards to be applied on nuclear transfers, especially those involving the equipment or material for the processing, use, or production of special fissionable materials. But following the global expansion of nuclear power programmes, the increasing trade with non-NPT parties, and what India referred to as a 'peaceful' nuclear explosion it conducted in 1974, some nuclear suppliers decided that further export guidelines were necessary. The Nuclear Suppliers Group (NSG), formed in 1975 to respond to the new developments, agreed that additional conditions should be attached to sensitive nuclear exports, such as nuclear reprocessing and uranium enrichment plants.

At the First United Nations Special Session on Disarmament (UNSSOD-1) in 1978, China, France, the Soviet Union, the United Kingdom, and the United States all issued unilateral statements on so-called negative security assurances on the use or threat of use of nuclear weapons against NNWS. These assurances embraced specific qualifications related to each state's nuclear doctrine and security arrangements, but only China's was unconditional. China stated that it would not be the first to use nuclear weapons and undertook not to threaten to use nuclear weapons against any NNWS.

In 1987, seven missile technology exporters established identical export guidelines to cover the sale of nuclear-capable ballistic or cruise missiles. Known as the **Missile Technology Control Regime** (MTCR), this supply arrangement seeks 'to limit the risks of nuclear proliferation by controlling transfers of technology which could make a contribution to nuclear weapons delivery systems other than manned aircraft' (Karp 1995). Over the years, membership of the MTCR has expanded to include many of the major missile producers and the guidelines have been modified to embrace missile systems capable of carrying chemical and biological payloads. Yet, concerns have still been expressed about the long-term viability of the MTCR. Many consider that while this arrangement has fulfilled its initial purpose in slowing down missile proliferation, new measures are necessary. Missile defences are one means for dealing with the problem, but other suggestions include global or regional ballistic test notification centres and multilateral arms limitation measures for missiles with certain ranges. Also, in 2002 a new initiative, known as '**The Hague Code of Conduct**', was launched (Smith 2002). As the name implies, the Code seeks to develop standards of appropriate behaviour in the transfer of missiles and missile parts.

In 1995 a conference was held that extended the

Box 22.5	**The 1995 NPT Review and Extension Conference**

On 11 May 1995 the NPT Review and Extension Conference decided to extend the Nuclear Proliferation Treaty indefinitely without a vote. This extension decision was adopted in conjunction with two other documents and a resolution which established a set of principles and objectives for nuclear non-proliferation and disarmament; outlined new procedures for strengthening the Treaty review process; and called for the establishment of a Middle East zone free of nuclear weapons and other weapons of mass destruction within the context of the Middle East peace process. However, the parties were unable to agree a consolidated text on the review of the Treaty and, as in 1980 and 1990, the Conference concluded on 12 May without a final declaration. Even then, the outcome of the 1995 NPT Conference was still largely hailed as a success. This was because, as a result of decisions taken, the Treaty became permanent, new measures were established to strengthen future NPT review conferences, and a plan of action for non-proliferation and disarmament was outlined. In particular, the Conference agreed to continue holding review conferences every five years and for the preparatory process in advance of these conferences to be strengthened.

NPT indefinitely. At that time, expectations were high that the documents adopted by consensus at the conference would provide the foundation for strengthening the Treaty. Events afterwards indicated this assessment was premature, as differences surfaced between the parties over how the documents agreed at the 1995 conference should be interpreted. Similarly, in 1995, expectations were high that a CTBT would soon be agreed and implemented, but again this proved premature. Although a CTBT was opened for signature in 1996, it has not entered into force. This will only occur once a group of 44 states (including the five NWS and states such as India, Pakistan, and the DPRK), have signed and ratified the Treaty. This has meant that the success or otherwise of the CTBT is dependent on developments in several key states. Significantly, also, not everyone agrees that this Treaty is a worthwhile measure. Proponents claim that the restriction on nuclear testing will limit both **vertical proliferation** (meaning increases in the number of nuclear weapons by those states already in possession of such weapons) and **horizontal proliferation** (meaning an increase in the number of actors who possess nuclear weapons). Critics, in contrast, argue that any such testing prohibition is unverifiable and will therefore be unable to constrain proliferation.

Problems have similarly been encountered over what is called the Fissile Material Cut-Off Treaty (FMCT). Here the principal issue has been whether the FMCT should prevent future production of **fissile materials** only or deal with this aspect in conjunction with an agreement to remove existing stockpiles. One feature of this debate that inevitably will demand innovative thinking is how, as safely and cost effectively as possible, any excess fissile material can be disposed of, given the large quantities involved.

The document tabled at the 1995 NPT Conference by the Arab states party to the NPT, known as the Resolution on the Middle East, calls on all states in the region to accede to the NPT. The debate over this Resolution has highlighted the problems associated with the attempt to ensure universal adherence to the Treaty. For although signatories to the NPT have increased to the point where 189 states are now party (with Cuba being the latest signatory), three states have remained non-signatories: Israel, India, and Pakistan. The key question is, therefore, how, if at all, these states can be brought into the Treaty.

It is against this background that the events in South Asia have significance. The nuclear tests by India and Pakistan have provoked an array of commentary, on the consequences both for anti-proliferation efforts and for future stability in the region. The South Asian tests, combined with the difficulties encountered over certain aspects suggested the globalization of the nuclear proliferation issue was entering a new phase. Whereas the early-to-mid-1990s had witnessed a period of relative optimism that anti-proliferation efforts were being strengthened and that nuclear weapons were becoming marginalized, the latter part of the decade gave way to an alternative observation of the future. In particular, a view emerged that a 'second nuclear age' was already upon us in which a key feature is the potentially greater risks associated with this age than those experienced during the 'first nuclear age' between 1945 and 1990.

Yet, several aspects of this debate assumed a new guise as a range of complex questions emerged. Would the 'second nuclear age' be characterized by a rapid proliferation or slow spread of new overt nuclear weapon capabilities? Would there be a greater propensity to resort to actual nuclear use? What sort of relationship existed between nuclear weapons, on the one hand, and chemical and biological weapons, on the other, and could the former deter the latter? Would new precision-guided conventional and computer-generated capabilities, the so-called Revolution in Military Affairs (RMA), alter perceptions about the future role of nuclear weapons? And, would the nuclear non-proliferation regime prove robust enough if universality is not achieved and the impetus for nuclear disarmament appears to be faltering (Gray 1999; Baylis and O'Neill 2000)?

In response to this emerging situation new measures and responses were called for. One strategy that began during this period is **counter-proliferation**, which emphasizes the use of measures such as ballistic missile defences and a more proactive stance in prevention of nuclear proliferation. Another concept known as '**anti-proliferation**' also emerged and this was deemed to incorporate 'the traditional nonproliferation agenda as well as new elements responding to the political and military implications of the proliferation process itself' (Roberts 1993: 140).

Thus, by the turn of the millennium, the context of nuclear proliferation was undergoing profound change. Developments thereafter would add a greater sense of urgency to find a way forward that would be responsive to the complexities of the globalization of the nuclear proliferation issue in the twenty-first century. This has generated new measures, such as the **Proliferation Security Initiative (PSI)** established originally by 11 states in June 2003 and designed as a means for the interdiction of trafficking in WMD, delivery systems, and related materials. There have also been calls for tighter restrictions on sensitive technologies and materials, and a reappraisal of the prospects for creating new multilateral nuclear fuel centres (an idea that has been around for several decades). Regional safeguards organizations like the one established in the European Union (known as

EURATOM) have similarly been the subject of attention as possible models for facilitating greater regional oversight of nuclear energy developments.

Key points

- Nuclear control and anti-proliferation measures have been evolving since the end of the Second World War.

- The IAEA has established a global safeguards system.

- Attempts to implement a CTBT and negotiate a fissile material cut-off have stalled following a period of renewed impetus after 1995.

- A number of NWFZs have been negotiated.

- The NPT now has 189 parties, although three key states remain non-signatories.

- Since 1987, the MTCR has been operating as an export control agreement among suppliers to constrain the proliferation of missile technology and a new measure, The Hague Code of Conduct was introduced in 2002.

- In 1995, the NPT was extended indefinitely and review conferences have been held every five years since 1970.

- Since 1995, the NPT has encountered several challenges related to new incidences of nuclear testing, attempts to achieve universality of the Treaty, disposal of fissile material, compliance, and verification.

- It has been suggested that a 'second nuclear age' has emerged and this raises new risks for nuclear proliferation in the future.

- New measures have been implemented in response to the continuing globalization of the nuclear proliferation issue.

Conclusion

Since 1945, both the nature and the context of nuclear proliferation have altered markedly. At the end of the Second World War only the United States was in a position to build a nuclear weapon. Since then, knowledge of how to make nuclear weapons has diffused more widely. This has been coupled, throughout this period, by profound changes to global politics and epitomized by the momentous dislocation that occurred in the former Soviet Union following the end of the cold war.

As a result of these developments, nuclear proliferation has become a major issue on the global agenda. Yet, understanding the dimensions and complexity of this issue will represent a major challenge in the years ahead. However, since the 1990s greater theoretical attention has been paid to nuclear proliferation and insights from several areas have sought to add pieces to the 'puzzle'. Similarly, while aspects of traditional analyses of nuclear proliferation continue to have resonance, determining nuclear motivations, capabilities, and intentions is not straightforward. This is therefore an issue that is likely to receive increasing attention in the years ahead.

Some analysts have also argued that the spread of nuclear weapons cannot be prevented, so the most appropriate way forward is to try to manage the diffusion of nuclear capabilities to additional states so that stabilizing deterrent relationships can evolve. One feature of this latter strategy is that it assumes the process can be managed in all situations without breakdown and that the deterrent relationship will ultimately produce stability. The alternative view of nuclear spread suggests this assumption is questionable.

At the heart of the current debate are thus issues related to the future global security environment.

Box 22.6   Chronology

1945	The United States detonates the world's first nuclear weapon.
1946/7	The United States and the Soviet Union submit plans for the international control of atomic energy to the newly formed United Nations Atomic Energy Commission (UNAEC).
1949	The Soviet Union tests its first nuclear weapon.
1952	The United Kingdom tests its first nuclear weapon.
1953	President Eisenhower of the United States introduces his 'Atoms for Peace' proposal to the United Nations General Assembly.
1957	The International Atomic Energy Agency (IAEA) was inaugurated.
1958	The European Atomic Energy Community (EURATOM) begins its operation within the European Community.
1960	France becomes the fourth state to test a nuclear weapon.
1961	The United Nations General Assembly adopts the 'Irish Resolution' calling for measures to limit the spread of nuclear weapons to additional states.
1963	The Partial Test Ban Treaty (PTBT) entered into force.
1964	China becomes the fifth state to test a nuclear weapon.
1967	The Treaty for the Prohibition of Nuclear Weapons in Latin America (the Tlatelolco Treaty) was opened for signature.
1968	The Treaty on the Non-Proliferation of Nuclear Weapons (the NPT) was opened for signature.
1969	The Tlatelolco Treaty entered into force.
1970	The NPT entered into force.
1971	The IAEA concludes the INFCIRC (Information Circular)/153 Safeguards Agreement and the Zangger Committee also adopted a set of nuclear export guidelines pursuant to the NPT.
1972	The Anti-Ballistic Missile (ABM) Treaty is signed between the United States and the Soviet Union.
1974	India detonates a nuclear explosive device declared to be for peaceful purposes and the Nuclear Suppliers Group (NSG) is formed.
1975	The First Review Conference of the NPT is held in Geneva, and by the end of the year 97 states had become party to the Treaty.
1978	The First United Nations Special Session on Disarmament (UNSSOD-1) provides the forum for the five Nuclear Weapon States to issue unilateral statements on negative security assurances.
1980	Second NPT Review Conference is held in Geneva.
1983	The United States announces its Strategic Defence Initiative (SDI).
1985	Third NPT Review Conference is held in Geneva.
1987	The Missile Technology Control Regime (MTCR) is established.
1990	Fourth NPT Review Conference is held in Geneva.
1991	A United Nations Special Committee (UNSCOM) is established to oversee the dismantling of Iraq's undeclared nuclear weapons programme. The United States announces its Safety, Security, Dismantlement (SSD) Programme following the dissolution of the Soviet Union.
1993	South Africa announces that it had produced six nuclear devices up until 1989 and then dismantled them prior to signing the NPT. The Democratic People's Republic of Korea announced its intention to withdraw from the NPT following allegations concerning its nuclear programme.
1995	The Review and Extension Conference of the NPT is held in New York and the then 179 parties to the Treaty decide to extend the NPT indefinitely and also establish a new Treaty Review Process and a set of principles and objectives for non-proliferation and disarmament.
1996	The Comprehensive Test Ban Treaty (CTBT) is opened for signature.
1997	The first Preparatory Committee (PrepCom) for the new NPT Treaty Review process convenes in Geneva.
1998	India and Pakistan conduct a series of nuclear and missile tests.
1999	The United States announces its National Missile Defense (NMD) Act.
2000	The Sixth NPT Review Conference is held in New York for the now 188 parties to the Treaty. The five NWS reiterate the undertaking 'to accomplish the total elimination of their nuclear arsenals'.
2002	Cuba becomes the 189th party to the NPT and The Hague Code of Conduct for missile technology transfers is initiated.
2003	The issue of non-compliance and responses to it become the focus of attention as the DPRK announces its 'withdrawal' from the NPT and intervention occurs in Iraq.
2004	A transnational non-state nuclear supply network is discovered and Libya agrees unconditionally to dismantle its WMD infrastructure in compliance with international agreements.

Among the questions being asked in this context are: what are likely to be the main proliferation challenges of the coming decades; and, in order to address these, does the traditional treaty-based approach (centred around the nuclear non-proliferation regime), need to be supplemented with additional arrangements or supplanted altogether with a new more flexible response involving a mix of measures depending on the particular circumstances and the actors involved? One answer to the latter question could be to combine aspects of the two by developing a more comprehensive approach for long-term global nuclear governance though still situating it on the original treaty-based foundations. The NPT is now an old treaty with many limitations, but it also provides an international legal framework that allows for collective actions to address pressing global security issues. Such an approach might thus encompass: attempts to resolve disputes and build confidence at the bilateral and regional levels; the strengthening of international norms; innovation in areas such as compliance, verification, safeguards, intelligence, and fissile and radiological material production, security and disposal; the involvement of non-parties to the NPT; ongoing efforts aimed at nuclear disarmament; and continuing commitment by all parties to the treaty's objectives.

For further information and case studies on this subject, please visit the companion web site at **www.oup.com/uk/booksites/politics**.

QUESTIONS

1 What properties make nuclear weapons different from conventional forms?

2 What are the implications of the global diffusion of nuclear and long-range delivery vehicle technology?

3 What role have norms, taboos, and epistemic communities played in the context of nuclear proliferation?

4 How have the motivations for acquiring nuclear weapons changed since 1945?

5 In what ways has it become more difficult to determine whether nuclear proliferation has actually occurred?

6 Does the non-state actor represent a new nuclear proliferation challenge?

7 What nuclear proliferation concerns have stemmed from the dissolution of the Soviet Union?

8 What are the main arguments for and against the proliferation/spread of nuclear weapons?

9 Were the early efforts to control nuclear weapons doomed to failure?

10 What initiatives are needed to ensure global nuclear governance for the twenty-first century?

GUIDE TO FURTHER READING

Theoretical aspects

Buzan, Barry, and Herring, Eric (1998), *The Arms Dynamic in World Politics* (London: Lynne Rienner).

Sagan, Scott D., and Waltz, Kenneth N. (1995), *The Spread of Nuclear Weapons. A Debate* (New York and London: W. W. Norton).

On nuclear use and non-use

Herring, Eric (ed.) (2000), *Preventing the Use of Weapons of Mass Destruction* (special issue), *Journal of Strategic Studies*, 23: 1 (March).

WMD and terrorism

Hoffman, Bruce (1997), 'Terrorism; and WMD: Some Preliminary Hypotheses', *The Nonproliferation Review*, 4:3 (Spring/Summer): 45–53.

Ballistic missile proliferation and control issues

Bowen, Wyn (2000), *The Politics of Ballistic Missile Nonproliferation* (London: Macmillan).

Historical context and background

Brodie, Bernard (ed.) (1946), *The Absolute Weapon: Atomic Power and World Order* (New York: Harcourt Brace).

Bull, Hedley (1961), *The Control of the Arms Race. Disarmament and Arms Control in the Missile Age* (London: International Institute for Strategic Studies, 1st edn).

Non-proliferation/anti-proliferation measures

Simpson, John, and Howlett, Darryl (eds) (1995), *The Future of the Non-Proliferation Treaty* (New York: St Martin's Press).

Nuclear weapons technology

Grace, Charles S. (1994), *Nuclear Weapons: Principles, Effects and Survivability* (London: Brassey's).

Nuclear technology and trade

Potter, William C. (ed.) (1990), *International Nuclear Trade and Nonproliferation: The Challenge of the Emerging Suppliers* (Lexington, Mass.: Lexington Books).

Walker, William, and Lönnroth, Mans (1983), *Nuclear Power Struggles: Industrial Competition and Proliferation Control* (London: Allen & Unwin).

Alternative nuclear futures

Baylis, John and O'Neill, Robert (eds) (2000), *Alternative Nuclear Futures* (Oxford: Oxford University Press).

WEB LINKS

www.mcis.soton.ac.uk/ Mountbatten Centre for International Studies.

http://cns.miis.edu/research/nuclear.htm Center for Nonproliferation Studies, Monterey Institute of International Studies.

http://armscontrol.org/subject/nup/ Arms Control Association.

http://acronym.org.uk/npt/index.htm Nuclear documents and analysis.

www.ceip.org/files/nonprolif/weapons/weapons.asp?ID=3&weapons=nuclear Carnegie on nuclear weapons.

http://nci.org/index.htm Nuclear news and data links.

CHAPTER 23

Nationalism

FRED HALLIDAY

READER'S GUIDE

Nationalism, as a system of belief, an ideology, and as a political movement has been one of the formative processes in the creation of the contemporary world. It remains central to the conflictual processes of globalization. As an ideology it provides a set of ideas about the organization of humanity into communities, about the appropriate political form for organizing these, and about how relations between states representing nations should be conducted. Nationalism has occasioned many disputes in social science in general, and in international relations in particular: some of these concern the explanation of why nationalism became such a worldwide phenomenon, others concern the difficulties of reconciling nationalist claims with the requirements of international order. Once regarded as a thing of the past, nationalism has been both resistant to, and in some ways promoted by, processes of globalization—migration, free trade, cultural transnationalism, political violence. It has also been a major source of conflict in the post-cold war era. The ultimate paradox of nationalism is that while, as an ideology, it stresses the distinct character of states and peoples, it is itself a result of a global process whereby all countries are incorporated into a single political and normative system, and it is this global incorporation which, in turn, provokes particularist and often angry responses.

Introduction: nationalism and globalization

The chance observer of an average week in modern times, taking as an example one in April 2004, would soon notice a curious contradiction. While leaders and opinion makers were busy discussing the spread of world integration, a process subsumed under the word 'globalization', politicians in many specific countries were moving in the opposite direction, emphasizing in policy and symbol their adherence to national concerns: the Japanese premier visiting the Yakasuni shrine, which reveres Japan's Second World War heroes; the US Presidential candidate Kerry making clear he favoured limitations on free trade to protect US jobs; the French President Chirac emphasizing 'French' republican values on the Islamic veil, even as the head of his party, the UMP, declared that Turkey should not be admitted to Europe. Meanwhile, in Slovakia, two nationalist militants were competing for the Presidency; in neighbouring Slovenia, voters decided by an overwhelming majority to deny the franchise to members of ethnic minorities; in Serbia President Kostunica opposed collaboration with the attempts of the International Tribunal for Former Yugoslavia in the Hague to bring Serbian suspects to trial; in Palestine Israeli settlers and Palestinian opponents seemed to be digging in for a long period of violence and hatred; in Iraq, thousands took up arms to fight an American force seen as 'invaders', and more. There were plenty of other countries where such events could be observed. Yet, amidst all this, world trade seemed set to rise by 4 or 5 per cent and across the world, in what was a practical denial of one of the classic standard claims of nationalism, that it could protect its people by constructing a 'national' economy, millions of people continued to prepare to leave their, supposedly beloved, homelands to seek employment and a new life elsewhere. Faced with the tensions invoked in the relation between globalization and nationalism, neither the ongoing course of world events, nor the sophistication and rules of IR theory, could offer easy, or certain, answers.

Nationalism, as both ideology and social movement, has been one of the formative processes of the modern world. Yet until relatively recently, the topic of nationalism was not covered in most introductions to international relations. Nationalism was seen as a thing of the past, a cause of wars in Europe up to 1945, a relic of colonialism in the Third World an irrational if necessary feature of international relations. It had been left behind as a result of the establishment of international peace between the Great Powers and the independence of former colonial countries. It was generally assumed that states would resort less and less to nationalism in dealings with each other and would, instead, use the new institutions of international order, be they the UN or the European Union, to promote greater cooperation. Globalization, seen as a form of closer integration of states and societies, was expected to further this process: differences mattered less between states, populations became more open to cooperation and trade, and even identities and loyalties, hitherto based on the nation-state, were being affected. Indeed nothing could be seen as more contrary to the spirit of globalization than nationalism.

This approach is now no longer tenable, and there are many who would argue a contrary case. Nationalism, in both the developed and developing worlds, has been very much in evidence, be this in the demands of peoples for secession or greater autonomy within states, or in protests about migration and free trade. In relations between established states nationalism is invoked as a basis for disputes about economic advantage. In some earlier periods, the emphasis in domestic and international politics was on convergence, on universalization, even the creation of a single world community. There is now much more stress on the importance of what distinguishes people—on tradition, identity, authenticity, the politics of difference. In the post-communist world, the fall of authoritarian states has led to secession and ethnic conflict.

The implications of this for globalization are many. In the first place, it is evident, in retrospect, that nationalism never died, it just pretended to go to sleep. In the post-imperial powers of Europe, and the USA, let alone Japan during the 1950s and 1960s, a sense of national interest, national pride, and

Box 23.1	Globalization and nationalism: contradictory processes

Factors opposing nationalism	Factors promoting nationalism
• international law	• loss of control to foreign investors
• maintenance of international peace and security	• hostility to immigration
• shared prosperity	• fears of unemployment
• economic integration	• resentment at supranational institutions
• migration	• dislike of alien cultures
• travel and tourism	• fears of terrorism and subversion
• employment abroad	• hostility to global media
• global threats	• attractions of secession
• worldwide communications	
• end of belief in economic sovereignty	

national mission was very much present; it was just not called 'nationalism'. Moreover it is clear that globalization sets in train different, often contradictory, processes. By creating a world market and flows of goods, technology, and people between states it also provokes responses, and resistance, by those who feel their interests are threatened. This is as true in developed countries, for example in hostility to migration or free trade, as in Third World countries which feel they are being overwhelmed by the developed world. Nationalism can therefore, in the first instance, be seen as a *reaction against* globalization. But in another sense nationalism is also a *product of* globalization. On the one hand, the upsurge in nationalism of the 1980s and 1990s reflects the failure of other forms of state building, above all in the former multiethnic countries of the communist world. After the collapse of Soviet communism in 1991 four states disintegrated along national lines—the USSR, Czechoslovakia, Yugoslavia, and Ethiopia. Twenty-two new states came into existence. A central reason for this process was the impact on the hitherto insulated communist world of social and economic pressures from the West. In a world of globalization, peoples began to demand not integration into larger states but **secession**, independence, and access to the world market on their own terms. On the other hand, the collapse of communism also led to another form of nationalist drive, that for **national unification**—evident in

Germany, Yemen, China, Korea. The link between globalization and nationalism in the one case is **fragmentation**, through secession, while in the second case it was through unification, through fusion.

The argument on nationalism and globalization can, however, be taken back much further, to the very formation of the modern international system itself. Nationalism, as a doctrine, calls for the establishment of separate states. It invokes the distinct culture and history of peoples. It is, therefore, about how unique peoples are. But the doctrine itself has spread across the world over the past two centuries as a part of an international process: as a result of global changes, old forms of solidarity and loyalty have been broken down and a new idea has been promoted and diffused. This diffusion has itself been promoted by the transformation of the international system: the increasing integration of the world market, the establishment of European colonial empires, the rise of movements of resistance to these empires, the world wars, and the spread of democracy. The paradox is, therefore, that nationalism, the doctrine that proclaims the separateness of peoples, has spread because of, and in reaction against, the international and globalizing trends of the past two hundred years.

This link between nationalism and the modern international system is, however, more than historical. It is also **normative**, that means concerned with values, with ideas of how people **should** live, and to whom they **owe obedience**. Nationalism has, through this spreading across the world, become the main justifying or legitimizing doctrine of the international system itself. Prior to the modern period, states were justified by reference to their rulers, their dynasties, and their religion. The spread of nationalism has removed this justification and produced instead a system in which states are justified on the grounds that **they represent their peoples**. From this we get the modern term '**nation-state**', which implies that all states can, and do, represent a people. We also get the principle of **national** self-determination, according to which every nation has the right to decide on its own fate, to be independent, or, if not, to choose freely to be part of a larger state. This has meant that all the principles of international order, law, legitimacy, derived originally from other bases, are now justified by reference to this principle. Nationalism has become the ethical and moral, basis of international relations, so much so that the body grouping the states of the world is called the United Nations.

Key points

- Nationalism was only fully recognized as relevant by International Relations in the past two decades.
- Nationalism is both opposed to globalization and a product of it.
- The spread of nationalism is a result of the transformation of the international system over the past two centuries.
- Nationalism is now the moral basis of states and of the international system.

Nationalism as ideology

Nationalism, like many other terms in social science, such as 'democracy', 'revolution', 'liberalism', or 'socialism', is a broad one, and is used to describe two quite distinct things: a **political doctrine** or **ideology**, i.e. a set of political principles that movements and individuals espouse, and a **social and political movement**, a tendency that has, over the whole globe and for the past two centuries, affected all societies and transformed their politics. It is important, in this as in the other cases, to keep discussion of the two separate.

As an ideology nationalism has, like the other concepts mentioned above, many variants and permits of no easy one-line definition. This is all the more so because, unlike most other political doctrines, nationalism has no clear founding theorist, no classical text which others can refer to, or argue about. It is what philosophers sometimes call a 'cluster-concept', i.e. an idea with several elements usually attached. One of the major analysts of nationalism, Anthony Smith, has provided a clear set of seven themes which comprise the core doctrine, what we can term here 'the cluster', of nationalist ideology. Another writer, Ernest Gellner, has provided a notably succinct definition: 'Nationalism is primarily a political principle, which holds that the political and the national should be congruent' (Gellner 1983: 1). This can be said to mean that nationalism is above all a moral principle, which claims that nations do exist, that they should coincide with, i.e. cover the same people as, political communities and that they should be self-ruling. Nationalism as an ideology is, therefore, above all a moral or normative principle, a belief about how the world is and should be.

One of the claims of nationalism is that individual 'nations' and indeed the very sentiment of nationalism have existed throughout time or for at least hundreds of years. The invocation of history is very central to the whole nationalist view of the world: ideas of the 'ancient', the 'primordial', the 'traditional', the 'age-old' are commonly invoked. But the doctrine itself is of more recent origin, and is a result of changes in the international system during the latter part of the eighteenth and the first part of the nineteenth centuries. The word '**nation**', or

Box 23.2 The core themes of nationalist ideology

1. Humanity is naturally divided into nations.

2. Each nation has its peculiar character.

3. The source of all political power is the nation, the whole collectivity.

4. For freedom and self-realization, men must identify with a nation.

5. Nations can only be fulfilled in their own states.

6. Loyalty to the nation-state overrides other loyalties.

7. The primary condition of global freedom and harmony is the strengthening of the nation-state.

(Smith 1983: 21)

equivalent words in other traditions, has existed for many centuries, variously describing what today would be called tribes, peoples, groups of subjects of a monarch, communities. Some idea of community, with its own history and identity, and often its own language or religion, has existed in all cultures. However, the contemporary usage of the word 'nation' and its associated doctrine 'nationalism' dates from the eighteenth century. It can be seen as having been created in three separate, but interlinked, phases.

The **first phase** is associated with the thinking of the **Enlightenment** and in particular with the principle of the self-determination of communities, i.e. the idea that a group of people have a certain set of shared interests and should be allowed to express their wishes on how these interests should best be promoted. Derived from the ancient Greek idea of the *polis*, or **political community**, this idea was most influentially expressed in the thinking of Jean-Jacques Rousseau. Rousseau laid the basis for modern ideas of democracy and the legitimacy of majority rule. Later democratic thinkers, notably John Stuart Mill, added to this with their stress on representative government as being the most desirable form of political system: once the idea of representative government is accepted, as a means of realizing in a collective form the principle of individual self-determination, then it is a short step to the idea of the self-determination of nations (see Ch.8).

The **second phase** in the evolution of the idea of nationalism came with the French Revolution of 1789: the opponents of the monarch called themselves *la nation*, i.e. 'the nation', meaning by this the community of all French people irrespective of previous title or status. Here the concept 'nation' expressed above all the idea of a shared, common, equal **citizenship**, the unity of the people. The slogan of the French Revolution, 'Liberty, Equality, Fraternity', embodied this idea: perhaps the most common cry of the revolution was 'Vive la Nation', 'Long Live the Nation'. The concept of 'nation' was, therefore tied to the principle of **equality** of all those living within states, to an early concept of democracy. This evolution in France was paralleled in the Americas, North and South: in the revolt against British rule in the North (1776–83), and in the later uprising against Spanish rule in the South (1820–8). Here the basis for revolt was political—i.e. rejection of rule from the imperial centres in Europe by a group of people, a settler elite, drawn from similar ethnic and linguistic backgrounds to those they were rejecting, but opposed to the denial of their political rights and of the self-determination of the community they represented.

This democratic and political conception of 'nation' was then joined by its **third**, and final, component, the German romantic idea of the *Volk* or people, a community based not so much on political identity but on history, tradition, and culture. In essence, the idea of the *Volk*, promoted by such thinkers as Herder and Fichte, argued that humanity was divided up into separate peoples whose distinctiveness and identity could be discovered through investigation. Just as scientists were mapping the plants, minerals, and animals of the world, and as linguists were mapping the different languages of the world, so it would be possible to identify the different peoples of the world, each with its own character.

Out of the combination of these three trends there emerged, by the early nineteenth century, the political doctrine we recognize today as nationalism. One of those who most vigorously expressed it was the Italian Giuseppe Mazzini. For Mazzini nations were a given, with their national **territory**, and should have independence. The Italian case involved the unification of hitherto fragmented entities. But Mazzini

 CWS

<table>
<tr><td>

Box 23.3   Mazzini on nationhood

'the divine design will infallibly be fulfilled. Natural division, the innate spontaneous tendencies of the peoples will replace the arbitrary divisions sanctioned by bad governments. The map of Europe will be remade. The Countries of the People will rise, defined by the voice of the free, upon the ruins of the Countries of Kings and privileged castes. Between these Countries there will be harmony and brotherhood. And then the work of Humanity for the general amelioration, for the discovery and application of the real law of life, carried on in association and distributed according to local capacities, will be accomplished by peaceful and progressive development; then each of you, strong in the affections and in the aid of many millions of men speaking the same language, endowed with the same tendencies, and educated by the same historic tradition, may hope by your personal effort to benefit the whole of Humanity.'

(J. Mazzini, *The Duties of Man* (London, 1907),
as quoted in Luard 1992: 198–9)

</td></tr>
</table>

also espoused two other elements of what has come to be our modern concept of nationalism. One was the *moral* conception of the nation, according to which each individual not only belongs to a nation, but also owes the nation unquestioning obedience (see Box 23.2, point 6).

In this way earlier concepts of loyalty, patriotism, identification with the community became part of the modern state system. The other idea which Mazzini promoted was the idea of a **'family of nations'**: if the world was divided up into nations, then they could, through identification and self-determination, be encouraged to acquire independence. The result would, he expected, be peace between nations, on this new basis. For the French writer Ernest Renan nationalism was 'a daily plebiscite', a process by which a community, created by history, could constantly reaffirm, by its continued existence, its self-determination and its wishes.

Key points

- Nationalism as ideology is a normative idea; nations exist objectively and should have the right to self-determination.

- The modern idea of nationalism is a combination of (1) Enlightenment and liberal concepts of the self-ruling community; (2) the French revolutionary idea of the community of equal citizens; (3) German conceptions of a people formed by history, tradition, and culture.

- Nationalism propounds both an idea of history and tradition, and a claim of obligation.

Nationalism as a movement

From its origins in the late eighteenth century nationalism, evolving into the ideology we recognize today, has spread across the whole world. In the early nineteenth century, Europe saw the emergence of nationalism in Greece, Germany, Italy, and Ireland, and later in the multiethnic empires of Central and Eastern Europe—the Austro-Hungarian, Prussian, Russian, and Ottoman empires. Under pressure from within and without these empires gradually ceded to demands for independence until, in the cataclysm of the First World War, all four empires foundered and a map of newly independent states was created. In Western Europe a fifth multinational entity was forced to concede independence to one of its rebellious regions, when the British granted independence to Ireland in 1921. It can, indeed, be argued, and in various theoretical idioms, that it was nationalism itself which brought the First World War about. In a transnational 'non-governmental', or Marxist, view it can be claimed that it was the popular revolts *preceding* 1914 (in Russia 1905, Persia 1906, Portugal and Mexico 1910, China 1911) that unsettled world order. Realists and Weberian international sociologists would point to the role of militarized inter-state competition fuelled by nationalism.

The First World War was, in any event, the occasion on which the principle of **national self-determination**, hitherto confined to Europe and the white elites of the Americas, was now proclaimed as a universal principle, in radical revolutionary form by the Bolshevik Revolution in Russia (1917) and in liberal form by President Woodrow Wilson of the USA (1918). Prior to the First World War many nationalists had argued that their rights could be realized short of secession—through the creation of federal or regional rights within states, or by forms of cultural autonomy: in some countries—Czechoslovakia, Belgium, Switzerland—this remained so. But after the First World War self-determination came, increasingly, to be associated with full independence. It seemed that the era of national self-determination and of the emergence of the 'family of nations' envisioned by Mazzini was at hand. But this was not to be, for three reasons.

In the **first** place, the European colonial powers refused to allow the subject peoples of Asia and Africa to attain independence: it was only after the Second World War, which weakened the victors as well as destroying the vanquished, that Britain, France, Holland, and Belgium became disposed to granting independence to their Third World colonies, a process that lasted through the 1950s and 1960s. In the **second** place, nationalism, where it did achieve fulfilment, led not to peace between states but to conflict, dictatorship, and in the end world war: if there was a 'family of nations' it was a very quarrelsome and unhappy family indeed. One reason for this was the fact that peoples, in the sense of communities with one language or religion, were often mixed up with each other, or had competing historical claims: there was no simple fit between national and territorial claims. Disputes over territory and communities led in the Balkans and elsewhere to inter-ethnic quarrels that no amount of mediation or redrawing of frontiers could resolve. The independence of Ireland, conceded by Britain but excluding six of the thirty-two counties of the island, led to similar rancour. More explosively still, the nationalism that came to dominate in two European countries, Germany and Italy, was one based on an idea of power aggrandizement, military expansion and, in the case of Germany, forceful revision of frontiers and

the genocidal liquidation of Jews. All of this served to underline the dangers, as much as the benefits, of nationalism.

There was, however, a **third** reason for the failure of the 1918 hopes being realized—one that became more evident after the Second World War. This was that, even in states that were independent and where the issue of national identity and self-determination had supposedly been recognized, new tensions began to develop: there is no finality in the definition and formation of nations, nor, as the postmodernists like to put it, 'closure'. This was at first evident in the developed world, in Western Europe and in the USA, where from the 1960s onwards new demands for national self-determination, or the recognition of ethnic diversity and rights within states, began to emerge: among the Basques in Spain, among the Catholic population in Northern Ireland, in Scotland, in Belgium, in Corsica. In the USA, meanwhile, a massive upsurge of protest, associated first with the issue of civil rights for blacks, and then with growing ethnic awareness amongst a wide range of non-white ethnic communities, began to develop. In Canada the French-speaking population of Quebec began to demand greater autonomy and, in many cases, independence. This revival of national and ethnic politics in Western Europe and North America was, for all its international implications, contained: in no case did states fragment.

The same was not so for the even more explosive **development** of nationalism in the communist countries of the East. Nationalism, i.e. hostility to Soviet rule and a desire to re-establish links with the pre-communist past, and linked to demands for economic improvement and for democracy, played an important part in the growing opposition to communism in Eastern Europe. It also, however, challenged the USSR itself: the Soviet Union had been created after the First World War as a new multi-ethnic state. Once coercive control was relaxed, in 1991, the constituent states broke away to form 15 independent states: in many cases this independence was carried out under the aegis of the local communist elites, who feared, as much as anything, the democratic trends emerging in Russia itself. The end result was, nonetheless, the greatest tide of secession and fragmentation of states—in the USSR and elsewhere—ever seen in the history of the modern international system. As we shall see later, even now the issue of nationalism's impact on the international system is far from resolved.

Key points

- Nationalism was evident first in Western Europe and in the Americas.

- After the First World War, the collapse of the multi-ethnic empires in Eastern Europe, after the Second World War the end of the European empires in Asia and Africa.

- Decades of conflict followed the proclamation of self-determination by President Wilson in 1918.

Nationalism and international relations

The consequences of the emergence and spread of this doctrine for international relations are many, both at the level of the impact of nationalism on the international system and at the level of the problems—analytic and ethical—which nationalism poses for the study, and practice, of international relations.

In terms of **consequences**, four major ones can be identified. In the **first** place, nationalism has provided a new set of values, a new system of legitimation, for the system of states. Beyond justifications in terms of traditional understandings of sovereignty and its corollary, non-interference, represented in the **Westphalian system**, the states system can now claim to represent the interests of separate, individually legitimate, peoples. Hence the importance of the concept 'nation-state' and the implication, which many contest, that states do indeed represent nations. (The very term 'international' embodies this ambiguity: it was invented in 1780 by Jeremy Bentham, the English utilitarian political theorist, to denote the form of law existing between different Roman tribes. It has since come to mean 'inter-state', with the added implication that this is equivalent to 'inter-nation'.) Self-determination has come to be a universally accepted principle, and the supposed basis of the current international order. Both the Covenant of the League of Nations and the Charter of the United Nations rest on this assumption, and from it is derived the whole system of international law. State

> **Box 23.4** **The UN Charter, Article 1(2)**
>
> '2. To develop friendly relations among nations based on respect for the principle of equal rights and self-determination of peoples, and to take other appropriate measures to strengthen universal peace.'

may or may not in practice represent their peoples but in the international system of today, in **diplomacy** and law, they are deemed to do so.

Second, nationalism has served as an important, essential, component of state building and for the formation of a **common identity and consciousness** within societies. Pre-existing forms of loyalty certainly existed. Throughout history people have asserted that it is an individual's duty to die for his or her community. But the modern state, faced with the movement of large numbers of people into the cities, and with the need to mobilize resources against external competitors and threats, has been particularly keen to promote a sense of national identity and purpose. The means of doing so include education, conscription into national armies, the promoting of national histories, the making of patriotic films. All contribute to giving a people a sense of common identity and of promoting acceptance of the state. In this way nationalism serves to consolidate support for elites and the established **order** Writers on nationalism often argue that this promotion of nationalism is especially strong in former colonial countries where the very boundaries and identity of the state may be of a recent, externally imposed, character. Promotion of official nationalism undoubtedly has been part of this Third World, state-directed, nation building. But it is by no means exclusive to the Third World: in developed countries—be it France, the USA, or Britain—the state has also sought to promote a sense of national identity and purpose, through education and the other means available to it. It has become part of the very formation of the link between state and society throughout the world, the indispensable domestic accompaniment of the consolidation of state power internationally. No state can survive and compete in the international arena without the promotion of a sense of national identity and purpose domestically. This top-down sense of identity is often reinforced by factors operating in society—the press, popular attitudes, educational and cultural trends.

Third, nationalism has provided a powerful impetus to the **drawing** and **redrawing** of the international map, i.e. to defining the territories of states and the frontiers between them. In theory this means that the map of the world reflects a pre-existing reality—the distribution of peoples across the globe. The map of states we see on an atlas today is supposed to be of pre-existing peoples, a reality like that of a geological survey or of the physical features of a part of the earth: but this is far from being the case. In practice it reflects where history has, often by accident, led the lines to be drawn—in Europe where armies grew tired of fighting, elsewhere in the world where colonial administrators and soldiers chose to draw them. Even such a settled frontier as that between the USA and Canada, or between Spain and Portugal, reflects haphazard history. However, the norm that the map of states should correspond to that of peoples has continued to push against these inherited frontiers. As already noted in the context of the collapse of communism, this challenge to the map has taken the form of both **fission** and **fusion**. Thus some nationalism has involved movements that aim to break-up existing

states, through secession or fragmentation of various forms. Other cases have involved the drive to unite parts previously divided: Italian and German unification in the nineteenth century, Irish, Arab, Korean, Somali, and many other nationalisms in the twentieth.

A **fourth** consequence of nationalism for the international system has been that it has been a source of **conflict**, and often of **war**. In the inter-war period disputes over territorial division soured the belief that, once accepted, the principle of self-determination would produce peace between peoples. In the more recent past, frontier disputes and disputes where peoples are mixed together in multiethnic society have occasioned many conflicts: in the Arab–Israeli context, in former Yugoslavia, Kashmir, Sri Lanka to name but some. Even more catastrophically, nationalism has become a factor, both cause and pretext, in inter-state wars, most dramatically of all in the drive of Germany to dominate Europe, and of Japan to dominate East Asia, through a combination of annexation and subjugation, in the Second World War. From the Nazi and Japanese imperial experiences we have derived the sense of nationalism as a destructive force. This hostility to nationalism is all the greater because, as in the German and Japanese cases, ferocious nationalism abroad is often combined with dictatorial and racist policies at home: nationalism is used by dictatorial **regimes** to crush dissent at home, even as it is deployed to mobilize support for aggression abroad.

Key points

- Nationalism for the past two centuries has been the moral, normative, basis for the system of states.

- Nationalism both legitimates states and has been promoted by states as part of nation building.

- Nationalism has been the justification for secession and territorial claims.

- Nationalism closely relates to the incidence of war.

Four debates

The topic of nationalism is one that, at least as much as that of any other powerful ideological force, has provoked widespread controversy, in public political debate but also in the social sciences. The fact that, for many decades, only historians discussed it indicates that it presents difficulties: the lack of clear ideological definition, the apparent irrationality, the very denial of universal rational categories which it implies have all contributed to this. An important part of the difficulty has, however, been the controversy it has provoked within social science in general. Much of the debate about nationalism has taken place not in International Relations but in another social science, Sociology. But the sociological debates, and others in political theory, have important implications for International Relations and have affected or underlain much of the discussion about the subject. Here we shall look at four of these debates.

Justice versus order

The international system has rested on two principles—the sovereignty of states and the maintenance of peace between them. It has often been assumed that national self-determination and the expression of legitimate nationalist demands are compatible with these general principles. Often they are, and when disputes occur then there are mechanisms—arbitration, plebiscites, negotiated compromises—for securing peaceful and binding agreement. But one does not have to look far in the history of the international system over the past two centuries to see that there often is a conflict, and one that has led to conflict and injustice. In the first place, the principles of **balance of power** politics often conflict with those of self-determination: the maintenance of peace between Great Powers may involve carving out **spheres of influence** or agreeing to each having colonies. In the 1790s, for example, Russia and Prussia partitioned Poland, before that an independent kingdom, between them as part of the maintenance of the balance of power. In the late nineteenth and early twentieth centuries European states agreed to the creation of **colonies** and **spheres of influence** in Asia and Africa. During the cold war, and after, the Western world permitted Russia to exercise domination over peoples within Eastern Europe and within the USSR or Russia itself in order not to compromise broader considerations of stability and **security**. (To take two obvious examples: the Hungarian uprising of 1956, the Chechen rising of 1994 onwards. In both cases there was no Western official reaction to obvious denials of the right of peoples to self-determination.) In other parts of the world undoubtedly legitimate claims to independence have been ignored for reasons of regional security: from 1961, when war there began, the African states refused, until 1991, when it was a *fait accompli*, to recognize the right of Eritrea to independence from Ethiopia: equally no state in the world is prepared to grant the right of the over 20 million Kurds resident in Iran, Turkey, and Iraq to a separate state. When the communist system collapsed the international community was prepared to welcome the newly seceded states and recognize their independence: but this was done reluctantly, and the general consensus was that the process had to end as quickly as possible. No wonder that at a meeting at the Royal Institute of International Affairs in London, in June 1993, the then British Foreign Secretary Douglas Hurd declared: 'I hope we do not see the creation of any more nation-states.' The international community therefore accepted those peoples that seceded immediately afterwards, up to 1993, but for those in former Yugoslavia who tried to do so later in the decade—Kosovo, Montenegro, Macedonia—there was no such welcome.

Box 23.5	A limit on self-determination

'I hope we do not see the creation of any more nation-states.'

(Douglas Hurd, British Foreign Secretary, Royal Institute of International Affairs, London, June 1993)

Uncertainty on this issue underlay the confusion of Western policymaking on former Yugoslavia in the early 1990s: it was not clear how much support should be given for self-determination nor where this support should stop. But this case also raised another, related, problem. If one community was entitled to secede, then the issue of secession for minorities within that community's territory also arose: this concerned the Serbs of Bosnia and Croatia, but it is also posed in Northern Ireland, for Russians living in Ukraine, for Arabs in Israel, as it was, earlier, for Germans living outside Hitler's Reich. No one can argue that every community in the world with a legitimate claim to its own identity should have its own state. There are, for example, up to ten thousand languages yet no one envisages ten thousand states. Even peoples of the same language can have separate states—as speakers of Arabic, Spanish, English, French, German, Malay, Persian do. The question is where to draw the line: for this, some **balance of justice and order** has to be found. The right to self-determination, conceived of as the right and need of peoples of one community to have an independent, single, state has always had to be set against other principles of international relations.

History versus modernity

Nationalism rests upon a claim of historical continuity—this people has existed for centuries, going back to some founding moment, real or imagined, or to the mists of time. The attainment of national independence and of statehood is the culmination of this history. Hence the use of words like 'reawakening' and 'rebirth', the interest in archaeology and ancestors. Claims derived from history are also used to settle arguments within a community about what is, or is not, 'authentic' and, with great consequences for international relations, what the historic, natural, sometimes 'God-given' extent of the national territory is. When people want to deny the legitimacy of another nation's claims it is common to claim that they are 'not really' a nation, or have not existed for long, or if they have then they existed somewhere else, or were, and may still be, agents of foreign powers. History in such a context is everything.

This approach to nationalism is the one common to all nationalist movements. It has been termed the **perennialist** approach. By contrast many social scientists adopted the view that nations are (a) arbitrary and (b) recent creations. This is generally held to be the **modernist** approach. In this view today's map of nations could have been very different from what it is, and reflects arbitrary and recent processes—the drawing of colonial boundaries, accidents of war, the triumph of particular political groups claiming to represent peoples they then set about creating. Nationalism is not the working out of some historical destiny: it is a response to the breakdown of old forms of community, based on religion, dynastic rule, and rural life, and a way of giving the inhabitants of modern cities a sense of meaning and purpose. It creates a new sense of belonging—hence the term **imagined community**, coined by Benedict Anderson, to convey the idea of a group of people one knows one is part of, but all of whose members one can never meet. The past—tradition, history, language, folklore—is not what determines the present but is, rather, used to provide material, is used as a reserve, by political and intellectual leaders. Where the past is lacking, traditions are invented. There is not necessarily anything wrong with this, and, beyond its many benefits, nationalism may be unavoidable: but this **contingency** needs to be recognized. In the words of one modernist, 'it is the magic of nationalism to turn chance into destiny' (Anderson 1991: 19).

In between these two positions there are other less extreme approaches. Some theorists argue that while nations and nationalism in the contemporary political sense are recent creations, they rest upon earlier cultural, linguistic, and political roots that mean they are more than just contingent creations. Thus, without accepting the perennialist case, it is possible to write a history of, say, the English, Russian, Chinese, Egyptian, or Italian peoples. This is the position of the well-known writer Anthony Smith, who focuses on symbolism (A. Smith 1991). Smith has, in particular, argued for the use of the concept *ethnie*, based on a French term for an ethnic group, to denote the communities which, in a pre-nationalist age, still form the basis for modern nations. Some writers have taken this approach to distinguish between different kinds of nations, those with a longer history derived from an ethnic basis—obvious candidates would be the Chinese or the Germans—and those which are more recent creations, a product of the European colonial system—the USA, Australia, and many countries in Latin America and Africa would be candidates. Here a distinction can be made between **ethnic** and **political** nationalisms, or 'historic' and 'newly created' forms, i.e. between cases where the state and its associated nationalism came to represent an already existing community, and ones where it was the state itself that created the nationalism and forged a sense of solidarity amongst the people. There may be some truth in such a distinction, but it may also understate the degree to which all states have promoted and to a considerable degree created modern nationalism: such states as the British, the French, the German, the Japanese have devoted considerable energy to instilling a particular sense of identity, history, language into their peoples and to tidying up what had hitherto been a much less packaged sense of national tradition.

Positive and negative

In discussions of the role of nationalism in international relations it has been common to counterpoise what are the positive, desirable functions of nationalism from those that are deemed to be negative and undesirable. On the positive side four arguments at least can be made. **First**, nationalism does provide a **principle of legitimacy** that underpins the modern state system. It suggests that states can, and should, represent their peoples and hence that they derive legitimacy from them: the Rousseau–Mill theme of representative government finds its international fulfilment in this way. **Second**, nationalism is a **realization of democratic principles**: nationalism is the means by which the Enlightenment principles of representative government should be realized in the international arena. **Third**, nationalism serves a very important **psychological function**: it provides a sense of belonging, of where one is coming from, of a past and a future, and of what the appropriate forms of cultural expression should be. Everyone has such needs and without them there would be chaos and despair: it is nationalism which answers those needs in modern conditions. **Fourth**, nationalism has been and remains one of the great sources of **human creativity and diversity**—the explosion of nationalism has had enormous consequences for art, literature, music, language, sport, and much else besides, not least gastronomy. It has enriched not only the individual peoples it has affected but the whole of humanity: the world would be a greyer, more boring, place without it. The explosion of multiculturalism, of cultural expression by ethnic groups living in larger communities, is the latest example of this.

There are also several powerful arguments on the negative side. The **first** is that nationalism is a cause of conflict, and war. By making unreconcilable claims to territory, and by raising the emotional temperature of national and international politics, nationalism has become the curse of the modern age, responsible for world wars, ethnic massacres, genocide, and unending low-level crises across the world. Nationalism may present itself as a reasonable, legitimate ideology but it very soon lapses into other forms of political thinking—**xenophobia**,

---

Box 23.6   National symbols

(1) General

- Language
- Food and drink
- Clothing
- Commemorative holidays
- Military heroes
- Flags, colours, and anthems
- Terms of abuse for non-nationals

(2) 'Invented' traditions in the British Isles

- Christmas
- Morris dancing
- The kilt
- The shamrock
- The leek
- The ploughman's lunch

hatred of foreigners, **chauvinism**, an aggressive approach to foreigners and foreign countries, **militarism**, the use of force to resolve problems, and imperialism, the desire to create empires that subject other peoples. **Second**, nationalism, even when it avoids military confrontation, may serve as an **obstacle to cooperation** on international issues— be this trade, migration, the environment, or any other issue in contemporary international politics. The world needs greater international cooperation and recognition not of separate, competing, national concerns but of common, global, interests: if this was always so it is all the more so in an era of potential nuclear proliferation or ecological challenge. **Third**, nationalism by promoting the **break-up of states** destroys viable political and economic units. Nothing is served by the fragmentation of larger states: problems of political equity and resource allocation arise in any society but can be solved in other ways than by secession. **Fourth**, nationalism is undesirable on domestic grounds: it creates a climate within states of **intolerance and dictatorship**. This may take the form of a particular ruler using nationalism and arguments of security to justify their own holding of power. It may also involve the use of nationalism by one majority group, to oppress, expel, or in extreme cases exterminate those not considered part of that majority. Such a climate makes international pressure on human rights grounds all the easier to resist: states violating the rights of their peoples resort to standard defences— that all criticism is a form of interference in the nation's life, that critics are enemies of the nation, that the values of the critics are those of another nation. On the cultural level, nationalism provokes a small-mindedness, a mean, inward-looking, approach that is inimical to cultural exchange and which denies the rich interaction that has always characterized culture, religion, and language in the modern world. As long as there has been nationalism there has been criticism of it, by those who see and experience it as a tool of domination *within* societies.

Objects of primary loyalty

The moral claim underlying nationalism is one that raises issues central to political theory, but it is one that is also raised by the whole process of globalization. This is the claim that the individual, by dint of birth or subsequently acquired citizenship, owes loyalty first and foremost to the nation, and, in most circumstances, the nation as represented by the state. This is the basis upon which order within states and the legitimacy of the international states system has existed for the past two centuries or so.

The arguments for this claim are, as also noted, strong ones, but they are an answer to a question that allows, not least in an era of globalization, of other answers. In effect, an individual has *three* possible objects on to which to attach his or her primary loyalty: the nation-state, some community that is larger than or goes beyond the state (religion, the working class, humanity as a whole, Europe), or a grouping that is smaller than, contained within, the state (the family, tribe, local community, business enterprise). The choice of which of these one owes primary loyalty to is not a new one: prior to the rise of nationalism the choice was usually for some combination of the religious and the local or family unit. Many modern political or social movements— communism, Catholicism, radical Islam, feminism Freemasonry, the Mafia—call on their supporters to have loyalty to something beyond the state. In some cases the decision to declare loyalty to one minority or oppressed nation means one rejects loyalty to a broader state-centred nation: this would be the case for a person of Scottish or Welsh nationalist orientation in Britain, or for someone belonging to any of the many ethnic groups in the USA. Many individuals have chosen to adhere primarily to one of the sub-groups. The writer E. M. Forster once said he would prefer to betray his country than betray a friend. Feminist writers have criticized the way in which the nation, defined and controlled by men, and used for the advantage of men, has served to oppress women. Virginia Woolf declared: 'As a woman I have no country.'

Such choices, as between the three possible categories of objects of loyalty, need not be absolute: most individuals owe some form of loyalty to all three and seek, usually without too much problem, to combine them. But the tension is always there, and in an era of globalization, when both broader international loyalties are invoked, and the weakening of the state in some areas of life allows of more

Box 23.7   Critics of nationalism

Communist

'The working men have no country. We cannot take from them what they have not got ... National differences, and antagonisms between peoples, are daily more and more vanishing, owing to the development of the bourgeoisie, to freedom of commerce, to the world market, to uniformity in the mode of production and in the conditions of life corresponding thereto.'

(Karl Marx and Friedrich Engels, *Manifesto of the Communist Party* in Karl Marx, *The Revolutions of 1848* (London: Penguin Books in association with *New Left Review*, 1973), 84–5)

Feminist

'Therefore you insist upon fighting to gratify a sex instinct which I cannot share; to procure benefits which I have not shared and probably will not share; but not to gratify my instincts, or to protect either myself or my country. "For", the outsider will say, "in fact, as a woman I have no country. As a woman I want no country. As a woman my country is the whole world." '

(Woolf 1992: 313)

local, small-scale centres of legitimacy, the question is more present than is always the case: such processes as European integration, the growth of worldwide 'youth' and consumerist cultures, or employment in multinational enterprises may create complex shifts in loyalty. As with the other issues in debate concerning nationalism, however, there is no easy or quick answer to this question.

Key points

- Nationalism both underpins and challenges the security of states.

- Nationalism can be thought of as the fulfilment of a long historical development of peoples, or as a recent, modern, response to social change.

- There are strong arguments as to the benefits of nationalism to the international system, and also as to the harm it causes relations between states.

- Nationalism is one among several answers to the question of loyalty and identity.

Conclusion: the effects of globalization: towards a post-nationalist age?

Nationalism is part of, not an alternative to, the increasing integration of the globe. Since the emergence of nationalism in the early nineteenth century, there have been those who have predicted, and wished, that it would decline, and be swept away in the tide of international processes that go beyond states and separate nations. Nineteenth-century Liberals and communists believed the creation of the world market would sweep away differences between states. After the First World War it was hoped that international law, the spread of democracy, and the very triumph of self-determination could eliminate national conflict. Since the 1970s, first in the literature on interdependence and then in that on globalization, it has been argued that we are moving towards a more unified and cosmopolitan world, where national differences, and the nation-state, will be less influential and less necessary. Hence, as part

of debates on globalization, and the emergence of a 'global civil society'.

Nationalism remains an enduring part of international relations, yet for all the persistence of nationalism and of problems associated with it, it can, in certain respects, be argued that there is nonetheless a changed situation as far as nationalism is concerned. We are not simply seeing a recurrence of the pattern of national conflict that has marked the world for the past two centuries. In the **first** place, and despite all the 'new' nationalisms that have arisen and will do so, the classical justification for nationalism and for demands for independence, namely rule by an alien, colonial power, has almost entirely gone. The collapse of the USSR and the other multiethnic communist states has ended that chapter of human history. So when claims for independence are made it will in the future be much harder for

The European Union

date of joining

- 1957
- 1973
- 1981
- 1986
- 1990
- 1995
- 2004
- negotiating membership

★ headquarters

€ denotes country within the Euro zone

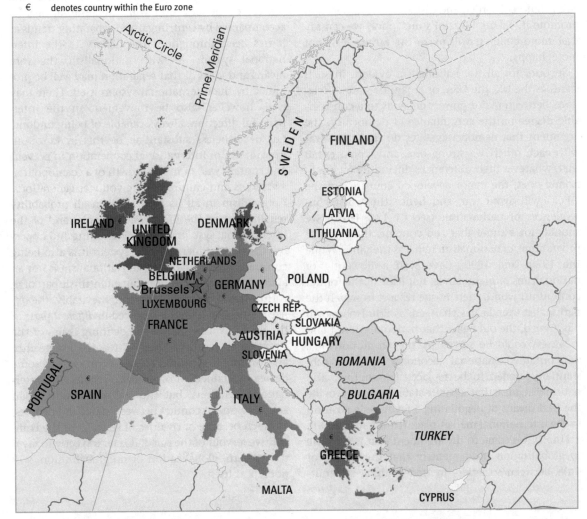

Fig. 23.1 Map of The European Union including the Euro zone

aspirant nationalisms to demand international recognition. There is the further constraint that following the end of European colonial rule and the fragmentation of the communist world the international system has, with close on two hundred sovereign states, decided that that is basically enough: this is not based on considerations of justice, but rather on a tired, but widespread, belief that the world now has enough states and that adding large numbers of other ones will create disorder, overload, and indecision. The argument of Mazzini and Woodrow Wilson has now been turned on its head: the general belief is that the creation of more states will promote disorder, and disharmony, rather than promote it. Taking Mazzini's metaphor, we can say that more children will make the family less, not more, happy.

Second, for all the nationalism evident in such states as the UK, the USA, or Japan, the fate of relations between major powers depends to a considerable degree on the continuance of democracy: the argument that democratic states do not go to war with each other is a strong one, and would entail that, whatever their differences, including over economic ones, the major developed countries of the OECD will avoid war, and hence the worst consequences of nationalism (see Ch.13). **Third**, we should not assume that the content, the political programme, of nationalism remains the same. While the 1980s and 1990s have seen a flowering of nationalisms of many kinds, not least in the former communist world, there is one respect in which the nationalist agenda has changed: as Eric Hobsbawm has argued, the old belief that national interest and greatness could be served by the promotion of a self-contained, 'national', economy has been substantially eroded to be replaced by another, also nationalist, idea, that separate statehood can provide the best means of negotiating a favourable position in the international market-place (Hobsbawm 1990).

Finally we come to the argument that is intrinsic to globalization itself, namely that the spread of links between societies—in trade, migration, tour-ism, communications—will erode national identities just as the growth of instruments and institutions of international and global governance, together with the globalization of markets, will erode the power of states. It is not necessary to adopt the most extreme variants of the globalization thesis, or to envisage or welcome the disappearance of the nation-state, to see that there could be some truth in this cosmopolitan argument (see Ch.32). The counter-arguments have already been made: that integration produces a fragmenting counter-reaction, that much of what passes for globalization is the imposition of one country's values and interests on others. The process of globalization will, therefore, always be accompanied by centrifugal and separating trends as it has been throughout the history of the international system. As with nationalism, the very means and ideas of that separation may well be promoted by the international system itself. There may well, however, also be movement in the international direction, always capable of being undone, but nevertheless substantial: be this in European integration, or international cooperation to prevent and contain war, or in the growth of a cosmopolitan awareness and culture among younger generations. Nationalism in all its forms will in all probability remain part of the life of each people, and of the international system, yet as it is resisting and opposing the development of that system it is also being constrained and shaped by it. Nationalism is not an alternative to globalization, but an intrinsic part of it.

How this issue is resolved and, inevitably, the *different* ways in which it is resolved in *different* parts of the world, will be one of the defining issues of the twenty-first century. The eighteenth, nineteenth, and twentieth centuries all began on, and to some degree sustained, universalist visions of international relations, but the reality was more than anything one of conflict between states and peoples, as much because of rivalries of states as of the competitive fervour of the ruled. It is far too early to say if this pattern, globalization or no globalization, will not repeat itself.

Key points

- Nationalism remains an important part of relations between states and also of the domestic politics of many countries.

- Expectations of a disappearance of nationalism, made over the past century and a half, were mistaken.

- Nationalism is a response to the new international context: in part benefiting from resentment at globalization, in part adjusting those parts of its programme that are no longer so relevant.

For further information and case studies on this subject, please visit the companion web site at www.oup.com/uk/booksites/politics.

QUESTIONS

1 Why should students of international relations pay attention to nationalism?

2 What accounts for the spread of nationalism across the globe in the past two centuries?

3 Can nationalism be defined?

4 What have been the consequences for the international states system of the rise of nationalism?

5 Is nationalism a 'good thing'?

6 What has been the function of nationalism in the development of the modern state

7 'Nations have always existed.' Discuss.

8 To what extent can the main theories of international relations provide an explanation for nationalism?

9 How has the international system dealt with demands for secession?

10 Can the world do without nationalism?

11 What is the relation of nationalism to the study of international political economy?

12 What are the implications for nationalism of globalization?

GUIDE TO FURTHER READING

Smith A. (1995), *Nations and Nationalism in a Global Era* (Cambridge: Polity Press) assesses the relation of nationalism to globalization.

Mayall J. (1990), *Nationalism and International Society* (Cambridge: Cambridge University Press), Hinsley F. H. (1973), *Nationalism and the International System* (London: Hodder & Stoughton), Deutsch K. (1996), *Nationalism and Social Communication* (Cambridge, Mass.: MIT Press), and Heraclides A. (1990), *The Self-Determination of Minorities in International Politics* (London: Cass) provide accounts of the impact of nationalism on international relations.

Ozkirimli U. (ed.) (2003), *Nationalism and its Futures* (London: Palgrave) assesses the relationship of nationalism to human rights.

Anderson B. (1991), *Imagined Communities: Reflections on the Origin and Spread of Nationalism* (London: Verso), Gellner E. (1983), *Nations and Nationalism* (Oxford: Blackwell), and Hobsbawm E. (1990), *Nations and Nationalism Since 1780: Programme, Myth, Reality* (Cambridge: Cambridge University Press) give modernist accounts of nationalism as ideology and political movement, while Smith A. (1991), *National Identity* (London: Penguin) and (2004) *Chosen Peoples: Sacred Sources of National Identity* (Oxford: Oxford University Press) offer an alternative, more historical, account.

CHAPTER 24

Culture in world affairs

SIMON MURDEN

READER'S GUIDE

The human experience is one of cultures. Culture and cultural differences have been at the heart of human behaviour throughout history. Indeed, as the twentieth century drew to a close, the significance of cultural explanations appeared to be reaffirmed amid the reorganization of world politics that followed the end of the cold war and the release of distinctive new wave of globalization. The new wave of globalization brought different cultures into closer contact and represented a challenge to traditional patterns of culture and social order. For all peoples, late-twentieth-century globalization meant finding some way of **meshing** their cultural values with the imperatives of the global economic system and its ideological software, Western Liberalism. The pressures for change were great and so were the frictions produced. When people of one culture perceive those of another not just as alien but also as threatening, conflict is likely. Peoples clashed at a local level, but there was also a broader tension between global and local forces. The culture of the West was the dominant force in globalization, and while Western culture seemed to be making the human experience more alike, it was also prompting cultural counter-reactions. New cultural suspicions created new frontiers of international security.

Introduction: culture in human affairs

Wherever human beings form communities, a culture comes into existence. Cultures may be constructed on a number of levels: in village or city locations, or across family, clan, ethnic, national, religious, and other **networks**. All communities produce a linguistic, literary, and artistic genre, as well as beliefs and practices that characterize social life and indicate how society should be run. Culture transcends ideology, and is about the substance of **identity** for individuals in a society. An **awareness of a common language, ethnicity, history, religion, and landscape represent the building blocks of culture**. Few cultures are completely insular or unchanging but, to be recognizable, totems of identity must enjoy some consensus and persistence within the **community**. Societies also define internal and external boundaries by inducing individuals and communities to believe in the value of their culture and the importance of its distinctiveness. Cultures almost always embody ideas and practices that support patterns of domination or **hegemony** within and between societies.

Cultures refer to a variety of totems and boundaries, but religious affiliation has historically been amongst the most powerful of **influences**. Religions transmit values about the existence of god/gods, and how such knowledge must shape human life. The model established by religious doctrines gives most worshippers and worshipping societies a moral core, a community spirit, and a guide to social stability. While some religions—Judaism, Hinduism, and Sikhism—define a limited community and have little appeal to outsiders, other religions—Christianity and **Islam**—offer universal values to the community of mankind. When claims are made in societies about 'cultural authenticity', they are most often made about religious totems, and by those priests, mullahs, and gurus that claim to be qualified to transmit them.

The rational and scientific foundations of Western modernity have challenged all religious faiths since the eighteenth century. The Western **Enlightenment** gradually allowed individuals to challenge God and His worldly government with questions and doubt.

However, religion has retained a grip on the mind of humanity to this day. The Islamic revival from the 1970s was one of the great phenomena of the twentieth century. In India, the secular foundations of the political system have been challenged by the rise of the Hindu revivalist, Bharatiya Janata Party (BJP). In China, the relaxation of communist totalitarianism allowed an explosion of local superstitions, most notably the Falun Gong movement, a cult inspired by a Chinese guru based in the United States. Across South-East Asia, Islamic, Christian, and Buddhist revivalism was evident, as was increasing intercommunal conflict. In Russia and Eastern **Europe** Orthodox and other Christian sects retook a public space in former communist societies.

Culture is clearly important to human beings then, but using it as an analytical tool can be problematic. Culture is such a multifaceted concept that it may only be possible to apply it in rather vague and intuitive ways. Deciding what culture is and isolating its influence is the key problem. Cultures can never really be described in their entirety, partly because they are too complex and dynamic. In practice, seeing through the cultural maze requires the identification of cultural totems: the images, meanings, **norms**, values, stories, and practices that seem particularly significant in determining what political or social life looks like. Thinking about culture in international relations is worthwhile. It is difficult to look at the world and not see the significance of culture. Culture can help us understand why humans act in the way they do, and what similarities and differences exist among them. The world is divided into distinct communities, and a taxonomy of belonging and exclusion is the vital job that cultural analysis can do.

Culture writ large: the civilization

The broadest construction of cultural identity is the civilization. In the eighteenth and nineteenth centuries, the European notion of civilization was linked to social and intellectual accomplishment. The superiority of European civilization, with its Greek and Roman heritage and its modernity expressed in the nation-state and science, was implicit in the term. Defining those outside civilization—**the Other**—made the idea more meaningful, and shaped the way in which areas and peoples of the world were regarded. Within Europe 'civilized' rules were applicable, outside they were not. As Europeans built their world empires, they imposed their culture by force. Only by the mid-twentieth century did European beliefs about their cultural superiority begin to change, although the idea that the West represented a model of progress continued. Civilization was redefined as a descriptive term to categorize the broadest groups of people that were able to identify with a sufficiently coherent set of aesthetic, philosophic, historic, and social traditions.

Civilizations represent coherent traditions, but are dynamic over time and place. For instance, medieval Christendom drew on ancient and eastern civilizations for many of its philosophical and technological advances; subsequently, Christendom was remoulded into a European civilization based around the nation-state and, finally, was expanded and adapted in North America and eventually redesignated as Western civilization. The process embodied both physical and conceptual reformulation, with theocratic, monarchical, and nationalist values superseded by the liberal ideal of human rights, democracy, and free markets. What is import-

ant to understand about the rise of the liberal ideal as the definitive marker of Western civilization was that, even for its principal promoters in Britain and the United States, it emerged from a long process of meshing and disentangling with quite contradictory ideas and practices. In the nineteenth and twentieth centuries, Britons and Americans meshed their Liberalism with a concept of civilization that claimed cultural and racial superiority over non-Europeans. Liberalism ran alongside the contradictions of imperial conquest, racial enslavement, and colonial rule. In the second half of the twentieth century—with the signing of the Atlantic Charter in 1941 being an important moment of future intentions—the most outrageous contradictions in Anglo-American Liberalism were ironed out, and the liberal ideal became synonymous with what it was to be Western.

Today, a number of civilizations clearly exist, notably the Western, Islamic, Indian, and Chinese. Other peoples are not so easily pigeonholed, either because they are not united around sufficiently distinct or powerful cultural totems, or because they are torn between different civilizations; in this respect, the location of peoples in South America, Africa, and Russia is problematic. However, no civilization is completely distinct from the influence of others and, in particular, all have been affected by the influence of the West.

The significance of cultures today

During the cold war, cultural differences ostensibly took a back seat to the global geopolitical struggle between the United States and the Soviet Union. Differences were defined in ideological and economic terms, and superimposed upon world politics regardless of cultural characteristics. Both superpowers offered their model to the world for imitation, and alignment to one of the two great blocs defined the 'Other'.

The end of the cold war saw a radical reshaping of world politics, with the triumph of the West reinforced by a revolution in the technology of communications. A new age of globalized capitalism was in the making. Cultural analysis was central in a number of seminal texts that appeared to explain what was happening in the post-cold war world, especially Francis Fukuyama's End of History (1992), Samuel Huntington's Clash of Civilizations (1996), and Benjamin Barber's *Jihad vs McWorld* (1996). Above all, culture offered a way of understanding the similarities and differences of the new age, where a globalized culture met a multicultural world, and where existing communities and cultures were in closer contact with each other.

The power of global capitalism and its consumer culture looked immense. The United States, and its European and Japanese allies, dominated an emerging pattern of global hegemony. John Agnew and Stewart Corbridge perceived that a new 'deterritorialized' geopolitical order—**the hegemony of 'transnational Liberalism'**—was emerging, and commented that 'a new ideology of the market (and of market access) [was] being embedded in and reproduced by a powerful constituency of liberal states, international institutions, and what might be called the "circuits of capital" themselves' (Agnew and Corbridge 1995: 166). Much of the world was brought into the world market economy and indoctrinated with its values. In most of the developing world, state-centred socialism was abandoned, and engagement with the West sought. Francis Fukuyama certainly thought that the great debates about how societies should be run were basically over. What Fukuyama termed the **'liberal idea'**—the combination of liberal democracy and the

market—had drawn a finishing line in the history of political and social development (Fukuyama 1992: 45). The liberal idea was the best that anybody was going to get.

The degree of cultural penetration embodied in the new hegemony was profound. A wave of democratization passed through much of the world. Just as significant was the influence of what Benjamin Barber called McWorld: the inescapable experience of consumer icons, such as Coca-Cola, McDonald's, Disney, Nike, and Sony, and the ubiquitous landscape of shopping malls, cinemas, sports stadiums, and branded restaurants. Beside the phenomenon of cultural 'crowding out', liberal reformism also drove the transformation of non-Western societies by drawing women and young people into a world of

---

Box 24.3	Francis Fukuyama on Islam after the cold war

For Francis Fukuyama, the end of the cold war had left the 'liberal idea'—liberal democracy and market capitalism—as mankind's universal project. To Fukuyama, it seemed that there was 'no ideology with pretensions to universality that [was] in a position to challenge liberal-democracy, and no universal principle of legitimacy other than the sovereignty of the people'. Fukuyama could only see localized resistance to the liberal idea, notably in the form of Islam. Fukuyama perceived that:

'The appeal of Islam [was] potentially universal, reaching out to all men as men ... And Islam has indeed defeated liberal democracy in many parts of the Islamic world, posing a grave threat to liberal practices even in countries where it has not achieved political power directly ... Despite the power demonstrated by Islam in its current revival, however, it remains the case that this religion has virtually no appeal outside those areas that were culturally Islamic to begin with. The days of Islam's cultural conquests, it would seem, are over. It can win back lapsed adherents, but has no resonance for the young people of Berlin, Tokyo, or Moscow. And while nearly a billion are culturally Islamic—one-fifth of the world's population—they cannot challenge liberal-democracy on its own territory on the level of ideas. Indeed, the Islamic world would seem more vulnerable to liberal ideas in the long run than the reverse.'

(Fukuyama 1992: 45–6)

wage-earning work and consumption. Traditional socio-economic hegemonies were liable to be blown apart as men and women were encouraged to count value in terms of money, consumption, and entertainment rather than duty, community, and piety. 'Economic man' was disinclined to care about any socio-cultural being. The cultural impact of the new wave of globalization was felt worldwide, including in the West itself, although the discontinuities were much greater for non-Westerners.

The multiculturalism of globalization

Globalized culture itself was multicultural, and while it was dominated by the West, it drew on many influences. The liberal idea embraced a certain degree of multiculturalism. The never-ending quest of global and local capitalists to entertain and sell did much to further cultural synthesis, most obviously in the realms of dress, art, film, television, and food. One only has to think of the output of Disney to see how the stories and images of local cultures are absorbed into a globalized mainstream. Elsewhere, Western images and aspirations are mediated to the Middle East and Asian continent through India's Bollywood film industry. Chinese, Indian, and French culinary culture coexists with McDonald's and Kentucky Fried Chicken almost everywhere on earth.

Globalization created common references, but the world was not about to become identical. Local ethnic and religious cultures survive alongside globalized culture and, as people and ideas increasingly flow around the world, exist in closer proximity to other cultures. The arenas for cultural mixing were the world's great cities—London, Paris, Berlin, Moscow, New York, Los Angeles, Sydney, and others—and living in such places required embracing toler-

ance and multiculturalism, or it meant an urban nightmare of inter-communal suspicion and conflict. Today, Muslims, Christians, Jews, Hindus, Sikhs, Buddhists, and pagans from all races and sects do live side by side in varying degrees of conflict and cooperation. The consequences of cultural proximity are complex. Multicultural settings create multiple identities, and so challenge the totems of existing cultures as well as the interests of some of those within them. Above all, multiculturalism tends to undermine patriarchal culture. The uplifting of women in the West was the most significant social phenomenon of the twentieth century, and one that multiculturalism and globalization promises to extend everywhere.

> **Key points**
>
> - Culture defines the identity of individuals in a society. A culture is composed of the customs, norms, and genres that inform social life. Religion remains a key influence.
>
> - Civilization is the broadest form of cultural identity, and represents a level of identity that may spread across nations and states.
>
> - Cultural groups often define themselves by representing different cultures as alien, or as the 'Other'.
>
> - The West has been the dominant civilization in the modern age, and all other civilizations have had to absorb its influence, whether this was welcome or not.
>
> - The end of the cold war heightened the significance of cultural identity. The hegemony of the West and of its liberal capitalism challenged the culture and social order of most societies. Globalization also fostered multicultural landscapes across the world.

The counter-revolutionaries of the global age

As globalized modernity challenged all societies, the forces of reaction gathered in the non-Western world. The West was widely stereotyped for its arro-

gance, irresponsible individualism, and permissive sexual practices, and its liberal capitalism denounced as exploitative and morally bankrupt. In the absence of a global-level theory of resistance, the opposition to globalization was largely parochial and led cultural conservatives, a fact reflected in the religious core of much of it. Across the world, societies clung to the familiar by remembering religion and associated values, for not everyone wishes the freedom to question, to doubt, and to be troubled. As ever, religion helped humans deal with uncertainty and fear, clarifying the purpose of human life and regulating the behaviour of individuals, families, and groups in worldly society. If religious doctrines were not taken on wholesale, then they were often translated into backward-looking moral prescriptions about such things as the role of women, the education of youth, the nature of personal responsibility, the punishment of deviancy, and the definition of the outsider. Wherever religious values made ground, it was clear that they could not be kept out of politics.

Popular culture was at the forefront of the cultural counter-revolution. In Saudi Arabia and Iran, the Islamic regimes sought to exclude news, films, music videos, and the world's rising tide of pornography by banning satellite television and restricting access to the Internet. It was a battle that was difficult to win. The place of women in society, and especially the issue of veiling (the *hijab*), was the key totem for Islamists who sought to bolster the institutions of traditional culture and social control. In Asia, a debate about the importance of 'Asian values' also got under way, with the state and business elite turning the 'liberal idea' on its head, and arguing that individualism and Pluralism actually negated economic success. 'Asian values' in Malaysia and Singapore meant illiberal legislation to control the aspirations and behaviour of youth. Even in the United States, the voice of pious Christians against the secular state, popular culture, liberal politics, abortion, and the teaching of evolution remained a force to be reckoned with.

Religious revivalism sometimes took the form of extreme literalism, often termed **fundamentalism**. The roots of fundamentalism varied. The charisma of messianic preachers has historically found an audience. More significantly, fundamentalism was a reaction to modernity, and to the insensitivity of the secular capitalist state and the market. Many fundamentalist groups were born in opposition to the perceived evils of modernity's secularism, Pluralism, social atomization, and moral emptiness. Claiming the legitimacy of God, fundamentalists could formulate interpretations of their faith that allowed for political and social violence, and sometimes even looked forward to some apocalyptic final vision.

Fundamentalists often sought to purify society in the most extreme ways. Just as the Marxist-inspired revolutionaries of the 1950s and 1960s disappeared, a new breed of religious militants became a principal cause of sub-state terrorism in the world. Islamic fundamentalism led the way into violence. In Algeria and Egypt, Islamists sought to prove themselves to God by committing the most terrible acts of brutality. In India, fundamentalist Muslim and Sikh secessionists fought pitched battles with the Indian Army, while Hindu extremists responded with force. Extremism could also be found in Christianity. In the United States, the Waco siege and the Oklahoma bombing were the most spectacular manifestations of violent paranoia against minorities, foreigners, and the federal government. Even eastern religion produced the Aum Shindri Kyo sect in the 1990s, a group that sought to commit mass murder on the Tokyo underground with the use of nerve gas. Where fundamentalists did find a credible voice the prospects for meshing global and local cultures successfully was much reduced.

Box 24.4   Fundamentalism

'Fundamentalism is more than a political protest against the West or the prevailing establishment. It also reflects deep-seated fear of modern institutions and has paranoid visions of demonic enemies everywhere. It is alarming that so many people in so many different parts are so pessimistic about the world that they can only find hope in fantasies of apocalyptic catastrophe. Fundamentalism shows a growing sense of grievance, resentment, displacement, disorientation, and anomie that any humane, enlightened government must attempt to address.'

(Armstrong 1997: 17)

A clash of civilizations?

The significance of culture following the cold war was reflected in a debate led by Harvard professor, Samuel Huntington. In an article entitled 'The Clash of Civilizations' (1993) and in a subsequent book (1996), Huntington offered a new paradigm of world politics in which the principal patterns of conflict and cooperation were shaped by culture and, ultimately, by civilization. Huntington suggested that the civilizations that would determine the future of international politics were the 'Western, Confucian, Japanese, Islamic, Hindu, Slavic-Orthodox, Latin American, and possibly African' (Huntington 1993: 25).

For Huntington, the clash of civilizations was a historic development. The history of the inter-national system had essentially been about the struggles between monarchs, nations, and ideologies within Western civilization. The end of the cold war inaugurated a new era, where non-Westerners were no longer the helpless recipients of Western power, but now counted among the movers of history. The rise of civilizational politics intersected four long-run processes at play in the international system:

1. The relative decline of the West.

2. The rise of the Asian economy and its associated 'cultural affirmation', with China poised to become the greatest power in human history.

3. A population explosion in the Muslim world, and the associated resurgence of Islam.

4. The impact of globalization, including the extraordinary expansion of transnational flows of commerce, information, and people.

The coincidence of these factors was forging a new international order

Underpinning the new politics were cultural revivals on a grand scale. The world was becoming a smaller place, and this was raising human consciousness about cultural differences. Global economic changes had also weakened local loyalties. With Western-originated ideas widely seen to have failed, communities sought to re-create some rooted past. Socialism and nationalism gave way to 'Islamization, Hinduization, and Russianization'. The 'liberal idea' may have been presented as a new universal by the West, but its individualism, secularism, Pluralism, democracy, and human rights had only superficial resonance in Islamic, Sinic, Hindu, Buddhist, and Orthodox cultures. In reality, the differences between civilizations ran deep: they were about man and God, man and woman, the individual and the state, and notions of rights, authority, obligation, and justice. Culture was about the basic perceptions of life that had been constructed over centuries.

For Huntington, culture worked at the level of motivation. States remained key actors, but civilizational politics became real when states and peoples identified with each other's cultural concerns or rallied around the 'core state' of a civilization. The Orthodox, Hindu, Sinic, and Japanese civilizations were clearly centred in powerful unitary states. The West had a closely linked core that included the United States, Britain, France, and Germany. Islam was without a clear core state, and for this reason experienced much more intra-civilizational conflict as a number of contenders—Turkey, Iran, Iraq, Egypt, Saudi Arabia—competed for influence. The fact that Islam was divided did not refute the idea that a pan-Islamic consciousness existed.

CWS

Cultural conflict could be found at a 'micro' and a 'macro' level. At the 'micro-level', groups from different civilizations were prone to conflict across local 'fault-lines', and by means of a 'kin-country syndrome' were liable to bring in their wider brethren. Huntington observed that Islam had particularly 'bloody borders', a situation that would continue until Muslim population growth slowed in the second or third decade of the twenty-first century. At the 'macro-level', a more general competition was evident, with the principal division between the 'West' and, to varying degrees, the 'Rest'. According to Huntington, the West's dominance was most contested by the two most dynamic non-Western civilizations, the Sinic and Islamic. Resistance to the West was most evident over issues such as arms control and the promotion of Western political values, which were regarded as a form of neo-imperialism.

Huntington's thesis was highly contentious, with critics pointing to conceptual and empirical problems (Murden 1999). The treatment of culture was brief, and the conclusions very pessimistic.

Huntington failed to tell the stories of interaction and synthesis that have always gone on between civilizations. Some thought Huntington was needlessly constructing new enemies for the West, once it had lost the Soviet Union as its Other, and that the *Clash of Civilizations* could become a self-fulfilling prophecy. Much of the criticism was based on caricature, but some reflected the enduring difficulty of using culture to analyse. Unpacking the myriad of factors that cause conflicts with such an all-encompassing tool as the notion of civilization is problematic. Where Huntington could really be criticized, though, was in his downplaying of the power of global economics and its culture. Huntington failed to recognize the extent to which traditional cultures are penetrated by global society and markets, and how the belligerency of even the keenest of civilizational warriors is usually tempered by the imperatives of the international system.

Notwithstanding the problems, Huntington initiated an important discussion about human motivations following the cold war, and about the emerging patterns of international conflict and cooperation. The civilization may be not a particularly coherent unit, but that did not mean that underlying cultural preferences do not exert specific and general influences. The *Clash of Civilizations* may not have told the whole story of what was happening in the post-cold war world, but it told part of it.

> **Key points**
>
> - The new wave of globalization has met local resistance in some places from those seeking to preserve their cultures from unbridled change. Religious revivalism has been a global phenomenon since the 1970s.
>
> - Religious fundamentalism has become the most important cause of domestic and international terrorism in many parts of the world.
>
> - As the cold war came to an end, a discourse was led by Samuel Huntington that suggested that a 'clash of civilizations' was about to become the principal cause of international conflict.

The counter-revolution at the civilizational level: the case of Islam

In much of the post-cold war debate about culture, it was Islam that came into the frame. Islam seemed to represent a particular source of conflict. Islamic peoples were locked in violent conflicts against adjoining civilizations and secular states across the Balkans, West and East Africa, the Middle East, the Caucasus, Central Asia, India, Indonesia, and the Philippines, with their efforts to promulgate Islamic law a particularly explosive issue. An Islamic militancy that emphasized the corrupt character of Western modernity had also been a clear factor in world politics since the Iranian revolution of 1978–9.

Islamic culture in the modern age

The Islamic world represents an example par excellence of the experience of almost all non-Western societies in the modern age. Islamic peoples have had to deal with the geopolitical and cultural hegemony of the West since the eighteenth century. The collapse of the Ottoman Empire at the end of the First World War heralded a new era in which the secular, nationalist, and authoritarian state became the dominant form of political organization. Modernizers in the Muslim world argued that Islam was the cause of backwardness and decline, and that modernization required the imitation of Western forms of culture and organization. In Mustafa Kemal's Turkey, the Ottoman Caliphate was abolished in 1924, and Western forms of law, script, and dress enforced. Women were forcibly unveiled. A similar model was adopted in Iran and the Arab world, although the attack on Islam was never quite so thoroughly pursued. Islam was divided by Turkish, Iranian, and Arab nationalism.

Secular nationalism was to be a failure in the Middle East. In some places, notably Syria and Iraq, the state was hijacked by minority groups. Arab nationalism also foundered on its demonstrable inability to take on Israel, with the Six Day War of June 1967 being a shattering blow. Jerusalem was lost. The June War was a turning point, and although the idea of an Arab nation retained an appeal, a new force was stirring: that force was revivalist Islam. Economic failure deepened the crisis. Rapid population growth and rural–urban migration meant that urban life was characterized by poor housing, strained services, and widespread underemployment. The young urban poor had little hope of a better life. In the 1950s and 1960s, secular elites had at least appealed to the masses with socialism and nationalism, but after the *infitah* (opening) model was initiated in Anwar Sadat's Egypt, the interests, values, and lifestyles of the elites turned towards the West. The elites essentially abandoned the masses, leaving Islam as the voice of opposition not only to the ruling regimes, but also to the cultural invasion that came with *infitah*. A deeper malaise within Islamic societies also drove the revival. According to Sohail Hashemi,

the Islamic revival [was] a complex mix of elements both unique to the Muslim world and shared with other post-colonial societies. The Islamic challenge is trivialized if explained as merely resentment of the power and wealth of the West. It derives its vitality and its appeal from a much more elemental factor: the widespread conviction that Islamic history has gone horribly astray, and that Muslim realities for centuries have been widely divergent from Islamic ethics. The fact today that Muslim countries are characterized by some of the most notoriously authoritarian regimes provides a powerful internal dynamic to the use of Islam as a revolutionary force. The fact that Muslim countries range in economic prosperity from the fabulously wealthy to the hopelessly impoverished provides a second powerful internal dynamic to the upsurge of religiously based calls for social justice (Hashemi 1996: 17).

The Islamic revival that began in the Middle East would eventually spread across the entire Muslim world. The conservative Islamic monarchies of the Gulf promoted missionary (*da'wa*) activities, but the Islamic revival was really a mass movement born in the crisis of modernization. Many young Muslims, especially those in the urban poor and lower middle class, turned to Islam as a culture that gave the forgotten and the hopeless self-worth.

Key points

- The impact of the West has been the principal issue facing Islamic civilization since the eighteenth century. Muslim modernizers sought to imitate the West, but the secular state went on to fail in much of the Middle East.

- A crisis of modernization exists in many Muslim societies. Poor economic performance has left large numbers of the urban population poor and frustrated.

- Islam remains a powerful influence in the Muslim world. When secular states faltered, Islam was there to fill the vacuum of leadership.

Islamic fundamentalism

The Islamic revival had many manifestations, but it was a new militant politics that had the most dramatic effects. Sayyid Qutb in Egypt (d. 1966), Abu al-Ala al-Mawdudi in Pakistan (d. 1979), and Ruhollah Khomeini in Iran (d. 1989) led a militant Islamic discourse that struck a chord across the Muslim world. Most militants advocated a return to the basic texts of Islam—thus, the term **Islamic fundamentalists**—and the implementation of an Islamic state through Islamic law (the *sharia*). The militants spoke of striving for the faith in the language of *jihad* (Holy struggle) and martyrdom.

Militant Islam also stood in opposition to Western modernity. Liberalism and Islam do represent two different ontologies for understanding, appreciating, and behaving in the world. Liberalism is a vision of economic liberation, individual choice, and the removal of social restraints. Islam is a vision of submission to God, the believer community, and social order. Islamic societies tend to frown on the idea of individual consciousness and choice. In the post-Enlightenment West, the idea of a better future has been a central one. In militant Islam, Muslims look forward to a better past. The perfect Islamic polity was established in the first years of Islam, and its eternal **principles** recorded in the Koran and other early scripts. The Koran and *sharia* represented the perfect constitution, in which sovereignty resided in

God, not in human beings. Many Islamists recognized the validity of consultation (*shura*), but the idea of popular democracy was alien. Islamic injunctions—notably, a criminal law that still conducts public executions and amputations, and the archaic regulation of women and non-Muslims—were totems of an authentic Islamic community and could not be reformed.

The Muslim Brotherhood (*Ikhwan al-Muslimin*)—an organization originally founded in Egypt by Hasan al-Banna in 1928, and spread to Syria, Palestine, Jordan, and North Africa—organized the Islamic revival. Muslim Brotherhoods were both political organizations and benevolent social foundations. Much of the time, Muslim Brotherhoods focused on supporting Muslims in their communities, but on occasions members turned to politics and even to violence. In Egypt, the Muslim Brotherhood led a violent protest against the secular socialist state led by Gamal Abdul Nasser. Sayyid Qutb, executed by Nasser's regime in 1966, became the icon of Sunni Muslim radicalism. Qutb argued that Islam was subject to a modern state of *jahiliyya*, a term referring to the condition of ignorance that existed before the Prophet Muhammad's time. Refusing to accept the legitimacy of the state or nation, Qutb denounced Nasser as an infidel; it was an individual Muslim's duty to wage a *jihad* against such corruption.

Shia Muslims were moving in a separate but similar direction to militant Sunnis in the 1960s and 1970s. The driving force of Shia revivalism was Grand Ayatollah Ruhollah Khomeini. Khomeini proposed a state dominated by religious scholars in which both **political and religious primacy** was vested in a supreme religious figure or council; the new system was termed the *velayet-e faqih* (the guardianship of the jurisconsult). The most senior Islamic expert would have the last word in ruling the state; it was a position that Khomeini was to fill himself. The Iranian Revolution that followed in 1978–9 would be about entrenching the *velayet-e faqih* in power, a process that was to take a number of years, and require the elimination of the Shia clergy's partners in the rebellion against the Shah's regime.

The Iranian Revolution itself provided great impetus to the Islamic revival. While Iran's revolution was of limited theological significance to Sunni radicals, it was an example to emulate. A populist Islamic movement had overthrown a powerful secular state; what had seemed impossible had been done, and the language of *jihad* and martyrdom vindicated. In fact, Islamic revolution was not about to sweep across the Arab world, but during the 1970s and 1980s a crescendo of Islamic protest shook the Middle East. Most Islamic violence was directed at Muslim societies themselves. While most Islamic revivalists broadly agreed over ends—an Islamic state and *sharia* law—they differed over means. The most militant wanted a revolution, but most were reluctant to engage in an all-out war. Mainstream Islamists sought to conduct a dialogue over gradually extending their values. For Muslim governments, keeping the mainstream away from the extremists was the central dynamic of politics. In Jordan, the Muslim Brotherhood was brought into a democratization process quite successfully. In Egypt, the state struggled to keep the Muslim Brotherhood and violent secret societies apart, but eventually ground the Islamists down. In Algeria, the army took decisions that brought mainstream and militants together in agreement over means, and produced a savage civil war. For the time being, the Islamic militants had met their match in the Middle Eastern state.

11 September 2001 and its aftermath

By the early 1990s, the Islamic revival appeared to have peaked. Grand dreams of seizing the state were superseded by a new cadre of puritanical preachers committed to reviving Islam from the grassroots. The threat to the Middle Eastern state receded, but the result was a chronic social violence as these grassroots Islamists sought to take back the streets. Just as the Islamic revival seemed to have been blocked, the new wave of globalization that followed the end of the cold war as well as the Gulf War of 1991 gave it new life. Following Iraq's defeat in 1991, the United States created a security regime across the Middle East, which included the garrisoning of Western forces in Saudi Arabia. The presence of infidel troops in the land of the two Holy cities of Mecca and Medina was so outrageous to some Islamic opinion that it galvanized a new phenomenon: a cadre of wealthy, well-educated Islamists in Saudi Arabia that had the ideas, money, and contacts to forge a new global alliance of militants, dedicated to fighting the West and its version of modernity. A new wave of international terrorism followed. Under the steward-ship of Osama bin Laden, a key alliance between some Saudi and Egyptian militants was formed, and from a base in the Islamic milieu of Afghanistan-Pakistan-Kashmir they organized a global network to give ideological, training, and financial support to Islamic militants everywhere. Drawing on the religious references to *jihad* and martyrdom, the organization fostered the cult of the suicide bomber—an innovation in Sunni Islam—not simply as an act of nihilism, but as the ultimate act of wor-ship of God and resistance to what they considered to be evil. Attacks on US interests in Saudi Arabia and East Africa in the late 1990s were but a prelude to the colossal event that took place at the World Trade Center in New York and the Pentagon in Washing-ton on 11 September 2001 (see Ch.21).

The attacks of 11 September were a profound moment, and not only led to so-called 'war on terror-ism', but also brought a new clarity in the discourse about civilization. The US Administration of George W. Bush steered its definition of civilization back toward an association with a standard of good: of course, this was the standard of universal Liberalism which was regarded as good for all peoples in all places. The conceptual guru was Fukuyama, not Huntington. The subsequent meshing of universal Liberalism with a revival of American Realism pro-duced the inclination for crusading; a new liberal imperialism was being forged. The world was divided into the civilized and the uncivilized, with Bush insisting that 'you were either for us or against us'. Bush declared that an 'axis of evil'—including Iraq, Iran, and North Korea—was the leader of the uncivil-ized, but Pakistan and Saudi Arabia also had ques-tions to answer. In the months after 9/11, though, Western leaders were keen to emphasize that the West had no fundamental quarrel with Islam itself, but only with the uncivilized rejects of modernity, or, as Fukuyama termed them, Islamo-fascists. Indeed, when the Italian Prime Minister, Silvio Ber-lusconi, broke ranks to articulate the Huntington-style argument that Western and Islamic standards of civilization were very different, adding that Mus-lims lagged behind, he was widely condemned in

both the Western and Muslim worlds, although for different reasons. Whether the 'war on terrorism' would have lasting consequences for the structure of international relations and the discourse about civil-izations remained to be seen. Anglo-American cru-sading might be interrupted by elections, and Afghans and Iraqis also seemed to be having some trouble in meshing their cultural inclinations with the interests of the United States and the culture of Liberalism.

In the meantime, one of the consequences of 9/11 and its aftermath was that all kinds of borders were going back up. In the West, there was a wave of unease, and the growing angst about immigrants and asylum seekers was a manifestation of this, as were fears about a Muslim fifth column within Western societies. New laws made the West a less liberal place. For those who believed—in the style of Fukuyama—that the struggle between liberal democracy and Islamo-fascism eventually would be resolved in favour of the far superior Western system, this rolling back of liberal values was a temporary expedient.

CWS

However, other Western thinkers believed that the security problem of globalization was more pro-found. Benjamin Barber believed that the problem lay in global capitalism's assault on local societies which created the climate of alienation, despair, and chaos. For Barber, McWorld and *jihad* existed in a 'parasitic dialectic', and what was needed was new civic approach to manage interdependency better: one that did not simply spread the worst features of globalization—organized crime, consumerism, and immorality—but gave local peoples more time and space to adapt (Barber 2002a: 262). Democracy might help find some way between the banal mon-ism of McWorld and the rage of the *jihadists*, but real democracy was also one of the victims of globalized capitalism. Reflecting some of the themes developed by Huntington, the British thinker, Roger Scruton, took an even more pessimistic view. For Scruton, Western civilization had developed in a way that embodied the seeds of its own self-destruction. Cosmopolitan Liberalism was devoid of values and community, while the weakening of territorial juris-diction was disempowering the democracy that mitigated the tensions inherent in capitalist society. Scruton urged that the nation-state be bolstered and some of the free-flowing exchanges of globalization controlled in order to preserve the territorialized existence of the Western societies as well as to stop so many other people from becoming lost, disillusioned, and vengeful (Scruton 2002: 159–60).

The future of Islam in the global age

The events of 9/11 and its aftermath set back the march of globalization and the process of meshing global and local. Yet, while it was easy to emphasize the compatibility problems and conflicts between the Western and Islamic worlds, Muslim countries could not escape the realities of practical politics and economics. Even Islamists have had to be pragmatic whether in opposition or power.

The case of Iran is illuminating. The Revolution of 1978–9 promoted a missionary Islam that sought to take on all the forces of corruption on earth, especially the United States. The Islamic Republic neglected the realities of power, but the costs were

---

Box 24.5   The crescendo of revivalist Islam from the late 1970s

- The Iranian Revolution (1978–9) talked of the United States as the 'Great Satan'. In November 1979, Iranian students took the US embassy in Tehran and held its staff hostage. The revolution spilled over into the Middle East, prompting the Iran–Iraq war.

- The seizure of the Grand Mosque in Mecca on the first day of *Hijra* 1400 by the charismatic Islamic primitivist, Juhayman al-Utaiba. In the bitter fighting that followed in Nov.–Dec. 1979, hundreds were killed.

- The assassination of President Anwar Sadat at a public parade on 6 October 1981 by the Islamic militants in the Egyptian Army.

- The rise of Shia militancy in Lebanon after the Israeli invasion of 1982. Amal and Hizbollah waged a *jihad* against Israel and the West, notably with the bombing of the US Marine Corps barracks in Beirut in 1983, the hijacking of a TWA airliner in 1985, and the kidnapping of Westerners in Beirut.

- The conflict over Salman Rushdie's book, *The Satanic Verses*. When the book that Muslims believed to be blasphemous led to anti-US riots in Pakistan in February 1989, Iran's Ayatollah Khomeini issued a *fatwa* condemning Rushdie to death.

- The Algerian Civil War. When the Front Islamique du Salut (FIS) was denied office by the Algerian Army after winning the general election in Dec. 1991–Jan. 1992, a civil war broke out in which tens of thousands were killed.

- The long-running campaign of Islamic terrorism in Egypt, directed not only at the Mubarak regime but also at foreign tourists.

- After the outbreak of the *intifadah* in 1987, the growth of HAMAS and Islamic Jihad re-energized the violence of the Palestinian struggle against Israel.

- After the *jihad* against Soviet and Soviet-backed forces in Afghanistan, militant Islamists descended into a civil war with conservative forces. Subsequently, Islamic 'students' formed an army, the Taliban, and seized most of the country to enforce a rigorous version of *sharia* law.

- In Bosnia, a travelling band of Islamic radicals assembled to fight for the mainly Muslim Bosnian government in its war against the Serbs. At the end of the 1990s, Albanian Muslim secessionism in Kosovo was suppressed by the Serbian state, prompting Western military intervention in 1999.

- After the Russian Republic of Chechnya seceded, Islamic fighters engaged in a bitter struggle with the Russian state. After achieving a brief period of independence in the mid-1990s, Russian troops returned in 1999–2000 to violently restore Moscow's rule.

- The long-running dispute between India and Pakistan over Kashmir was given impetus in the 1990s by Islamic militants. In 1999, an invasion of Indian Kashmir by Islamic militants threatened to escalate into a war between India and Pakistan.

- The Saudi dissident, Osama bin Laden, presided over the creation of a global network of militants that took up *jihad* against the United States. A low-level war between the USA and the bin Laden militants escalated into the dominant issue of international security following the 9/11 attacks on the USA. The USA responded by overthrowing the Taliban in Afghanistan and moving on to occupy Iraq. The so-called 'war on terrorism' went on and seemed liable to take new directions.

- From Nigeria to the Philippines, the effort of Muslims to assert Islamic principles and laws led to inter-communal fighting with Christians and secular states.

unsustainable and by the mid-1980s, the revolution had produced its 'pragmatists'. Fences were mended, and while the Islamic Republic continued to speak up for Muslim rights everywhere, it was less prone to act on them. The death of Ayatollah Khomeini in 1989 led to further reorganization. The presidencies of Hashemi Rafsanjani and Mohammad Khatami speeded attempts to reform politics, the economy, and society. The reformers realized that an Islamic insularity was not tenable in the global age. The young, women, and the middle class wanted more freedom, although there was a powerful conservative establishment determined to stop them having it. The process of Islamic-liberal meshing was bound not to be straightforward, with the reformists suffering ups and downs in their sparring with the conservative incumbents of the theocratic institutions of the state. The fairness of parliamentary elections in February 2004, for instance, was undermined by the banning of hundreds of reformist candidates by the unelected Council of Guardians. The struggle to define the future of Iranian society would be prolonged, but the fundamentalism of 1978–9 was disappearing and the Islamic Republic held out the potential of becoming an important model of Islamic democratization.

The inescapable dilemma for Islamists was that they could not promote their values without political and economic pragmatism, yet engaging with the world opened the door to a feared cultural synthesis. Finding the 'right path' was at the heart of contemporary Islamic discourse. By the 1990s, a breeze of Islamic reformism in the Arab world also appeared to be growing, with the Islamic idea of *shura* acting as a touchstone for political and social reform. In the 1990s, Morocco, Jordan, and most of the Gulf States referred to *shura* when they introduced limited forms of representative assembly. Even among the ranks of some Islamic fundamentalists, there was recognition that many ordinary Muslims wanted a voice. Using the principles of *shura* and *maslaha* (the public interest) some Islamic thinkers began to work up the arguments for representative government and human rights not only as permissible features of Muslim society, but as part of Islamic duty. The struggle for the body and soul of Arab societies would also be prolonged, and may have no clear outcome. The forces of globalization may demand a degree of conformity from all those engaged with it, but that does not mean that all traditional cultures will be tamed in the same way.

Key points

- Islam revivalists have embraced a cultural conflict with the West. In the 1980s, the Iranian Revolution led militant Islamists against the West. In the 1990s, the Sunni Islamists of the Al Qaeda network took up the torch of conservative rejectionism.

- Islamic movements are suspicious of the global, but the pressures to be pragmatic are strong. The Iranian Revolution is a good example of how political and economic realities can force compromise on Islamists.

- Islam does not have a single voice. Muslims will meet the forces of globalization in different ways. Muslim societies will continue to change in the twenty-first century.

Conclusion

The new wave of globalization that emerged in the late twentieth century brought an unknown level of inter-cultural interaction. Existing societies absorbed new global influences and a great deal of cultural synthesis was under way everywhere. A growing awareness of traditional cultural identities was a global response, although whether this translated itself into a fundamental reorganization of world politics in the way suggested by Samuel Huntington is still to be proven. What is clear, though, is that the new globalization stressed societies and produced belligerent forms of cultural revivalism. A revival of religions was one of the most important manifestations of cultural and social insecurity: religion appeared to offer fixed cultural totems, even if it did not. While most societies adapted to the momentous changes brought by globalization, violent resistance accompanied cultural revivalism. Religious fundamentalism was the most significant form of resistance, and although it was unlikely that these fundamentalists could stop the new global hegemony, the aggregate level of **anarchy** that they created and the West's response to it, especially after 9/11, did begin to slow the progress of liberal globalization. Localized cultural rearguard actions would continue to be fought well into the twenty-first century, but the imaginings of cultural authenticity were not only those of the parochial backwater, but an impossible dream in the age of globalization. We are all global now.

For further information and case studies on this subject, please visit the companion web site at www.oup.com/uk/booksites/politics.

QUESTIONS

1   What is culture?

2   How useful is the concept of culture when thinking about international relations?

3   How does religion influence cultural identity, and why has religion remained such powerful influence in the world?

4   Why did Samuel Huntington argue that differences between civilizations would become the principal cause of international conflict after the end of the cold war?

5   How have Middle Eastern peoples responded to the dominance of the West in the twentieth century?

6   Can the doctrines of the Islamic revival forge an alternative model of modernity?

7   How have the 11 September 2001 attacks on the United States changed the debate about culture?

8   How have the 11 September 2001 attacks on the United States changed the debate about globalization?

9   Will any changes be lasting or just short-lived?

10   How serious is the threat that Islam poses to the West, and vice versa?

GUIDE TO FURTHER READING

Agnew, John, and Corbridge, Stuart (1995), *Mastering Space: Hegemony, Territory, and International Political Economy* (London: Routledge). A study on hegemony and cultural discourse since the nineteenth century, which argues that globalization has created a 'deterritorialized' global hegemony.

Axford, Barrie (1995), *The Global System: Economics, Politics and Culture* (Cambridge: Polity Press). A study of Western modernity, and how it has been extended across the world.

Barber, Benjamin (1996), *Jihad vs McWorld* (New York: Ballantine Books). An eloquent account of global culture and capitalism, and ways that it challenges local social systems and identities.

Booth, Ken, and Dunne, Tim (eds) (2002), *Worlds in Collision: Terror and the Future of Global Order* (Basingstoke: Palgrave Macmillan). An edited volume reflecting on many aspects of 9/11, including chapters by Fukuyama, Der Derian, Chomsky, Cox, Barber, Halliday, and Waltz.

Fukuyama, Francis (1992), *The End of History and the Last Man* (London: Penguin Books). The book that explained the power of the liberal idea, and proclaimed that the history of political development was now at an end.

Huntington, Samuel (1996), *The Clash of Civilizations and the Remaking of the World Order* (New York: Touchstone). The follow-up to his *Foreign Affairs* article (1993) that argued that civilizational references were becoming the driving force of international affairs.

Scruton, Roger (2002), *The West and the Rest: Globalization and the Terrorist Threat* (London: Continuum). An opinion piece that reflects some of the anxieties about globalization within the West following 9/11. It argues that civilizations are different and that all have been damaged by liberal globalization, including the West.

WEB LINKS

www.incore.ulst.ac.uk The initiative on Conflict Resolution and Ethnicity (INCORE) is a joint project of the United Nations University and the University of Ulster. The web site contains research resources on ethnic conflicts around the world.

www.ceifo.su.se The Centre for Research in International Migration and Ethnic Relations at the University of Stockholm has a web site detailing its research on migration, nationalism, and ethnic relations.

www.lamp.ac.uk/cis/pathways The Department of Theology, Religious and Islamic Studies at the University of Wales in Lampeter has an extensive list of Internet links related to the study of Islam.

www.irna.com The Islamic Republic News Agency posts news, features, and photographs on contemporary life and politics in Iran.

CHAPTER 25

Humanitarian intervention in world politics

NICHOLAS J. WHEELER • ALEX J. BELLAMY

READER'S GUIDE

Non-intervention is the norm in international society, but should military intervention be legitimated in contravention of the sovereignty principle when governments massively violate the human rights of their citizens, or if states have collapsed into civil war and disorder? This is the guiding question addressed in this chapter. The society of states has outlawed war except for purposes of self-defence and collective enforcement action authorized by the UN Security Council (UNSC). The challenge posed by humanitarian intervention is whether it also should be exempted from the general ban on the use of force. This chapter examines the arguments for and against forcible humanitarian intervention, focusing on the tensions between considerations of power, order, and justice in world politics. This theoretical analysis is explored in relation to cold war and post-cold war cases of forcible humanitarian intervention and the humanitarian aspects of the 'war on terror'. The final section of the chapter examines the claim that the traditional definition of humanitarian intervention should be broadened to include non-military forms of humanitarian intervention practised by states and non-state actors.

Introduction

Humanitarian intervention poses the hardest test for an international society built on principles of sovereignty, non-intervention, and the non-use of force. The society of states has committed itself in the post-holocaust world to a 'human rights culture'[1] which outlaws genocide and mass killing, but these humanitarian principles can and do conflict with those of sovereignty and non-intervention. Sovereign states are expected to act as guardians of their citizens' security, but what happens if states behave as gangsters towards their own people, treating sovereignty as a licence to kill? Should tyrannical[2] states be recognized as legitimate members of international society, and accorded the protection afforded by the non-intervention principle? Or, should such states forfeit their sovereign rights, and be exposed to legitimate intervention by international society? Related to this, what responsibilities do other states have to enforce global human rights norms against governments that massively violate them? Armed humanitarian intervention was not a legitimate practice during the cold war But there was a significant shift of attitudes on this question during the 1990s, especially within liberal-democratic states, which led the way in pressing new humanitarian claims within international society. UN Secretary General Kofi Annan registered the extent of this change in a speech to the General Assembly in September 1999. He declared that there was a 'developing international norm' to forcibly protect civilians who were at risk from genocide and large-scale killing. The character of this new liberal interventionism, its moral limitations, and its likely future evolution in a post-9/11 world are central questions that are taken up later in the chapter.

We will show how the early optimism associated with the international intervention to rescue the Kurds in northern Iraq, in the immediate aftermath of the 1991 Gulf War, gave way to a mood of pessimism and moral cynicism. This was the product of the UN's failures in Bosnia and Somalia, and the appalling moral catastrophe of Rwanda where Western state leaders and publics stood by while a genocide took place. The experience of military intervention in Bosnia and Somalia led to a questioning of the efficacy of the means that had been employed to promote humanitarian ends. Some argued that what had been needed in these cases was a greater willingness to employ military force in defence of fundamental human rights. But others contended that while governments and citizens have moral duties to rescue suffering humanity, these should be discharged by non-violent means since the use of force is always inimical to moral ends. If there is debate over whether the use of force can promote humanitarian values and long-term reconstruction in murderous and/or failed states, then there is also the question as to whether states can be trusted with the responsibility to act as armed agents of common humanity. The abdication of moral responsibility on the part of the society of states in the face of the genocide in Rwanda—most crucially in the capitals of Western states—suggests that we should be cautious about investing too much faith in state leaders as guardians of human rights in world politics, and suspicious about their motivation when they do invoke human rights to legitimize military action. This was the lesson that many drew from NATO's use of force against the Federal Republic of Yugoslavia (hereafter Yugoslavia) in March 1999. But for others NATO's action represented a new-found commitment on the part of Western states to use force in defence of human rights. Nevertheless, even among those who supported the use of force against the Milosevic regime, there was considerable disquiet that the means chosen to save the Kosovars—a bombing campaign against targets in Kosovo and Yugoslavia—contradicted the humanitarian rationale behind 'Operation Allied Force'. Scepticism that force can ever be a servant of humanitarian values leads some analysts to argue for a post-statist reconceptualization of humanitarian intervention, which they label non-forcible humanitarian intervention (Ramsbotham and Woodhouse 1996).

This chapter is divided into seven sections. The first part of the chapter sets out the traditional definition of humanitarian intervention. The second part identifies five key objections to the practice of forcible humanitarianism advanced by Realism (see Ch.7) and Pluralist international society theory (hereafter Pluralism). The third section examines the counter-arguments advanced by **Solidarist international society theory** (hereafter Solidarism). Next, we look at the legitimacy of humanitarian intervention in state practice during the cold war, focusing on two case studies of intervention which led to the ending of genocidal practices: Tanzania's intervention against Idi Amin's Uganda and Vietnam's removal of the Pol Pot regime in Cambodia. The fifth part of the chapter focuses on international interventions in northern Iraq, Somalia, Rwanda, and Kosovo. The analysis here is subdivided into three key areas: the role of public opinion and the media in pressurizing state leaders to intervene; the legality and legitimacy of these interventions; and an evaluation of their success in promoting humanitarian outcomes. The sixth section investigates the impact of 9/11 and the 'war on terror' on humanitarian intervention. The final section of the chapter explores alternative conceptions of humanitarian intervention and considers the implications of globalization for practices of humanitarianism in world politics.

What is humanitarian intervention?

In his now classic definition in *Nonintervention and International Order*, R. J. Vincent defined intervention as set out in Box 25.1. Vincent was not writing specifically of humanitarian intervention but his definition sums up the traditional view. Traditionally, intervention has been defined in terms of a coercive breach of the walls of the castle of sovereignty. Such a breach violates the cardinal norm of sovereignty, and its logical corollary the rule of non-intervention, which is enshrined in customary international law and codified in Article 2(7) of the UN Charter. This prohibits the UN from intervening in matters that are 'essentially within the domestic jurisdiction of any state'. Vincent's description of intervention does not offer a definitive judgement on its legality, and this is a very controversial issue in relation to humanitarian intervention. The majority of international lawyers, labelled restrictionists, argue that the prohibition of the use of force in Article 2(4) of the UN Charter renders forcible humanitarian intervention illegal. The only legitimate exception to this general ban is the right of self-defence in Article 51 of the Charter. We will explore the reasoning behind this prohibition in the next section, but this position is contested by the counter-restrictionists who argue that there is a legal right of unilateral and collective humanitarian intervention in the society of states (this position is discussed in the fourth section of the chapter).

Box 25.1	R. J. Vincent's definition of intervention

'Activity undertaken by a state, a group within a state a group of states or an international organization which interferes coercively in the domestic affairs of another state. It is a discrete event having a beginning and an end, and it is aimed at the authority structure of the target state. It is not necessarily lawful or unlawful, but it does break a conventional pattern of international relations.'

(Vincent 1974: 13)

Key points

- Traditionally, intervention has been defined as a forcible breach of sovereignty that interferes in a state's internal affairs.

- The legality of **forcible humanitarian intervention** is a matter of dispute between **restrictionists** and **counter-restrictionists**.

Objections to legitimizing humanitarian intervention

Five key objections to legitimizing a practice of for-cible humanitarian intervention have been advanced, at various times, by scholars, inter-national lawyers, and policymakers. These objec-tions are not mutually exclusive and they can be found in the writings of both Realists and Liberals. For example, Liberals recognize that principles of humanitarianism are often applied selectively, but in contrast to Realists, they believe that state practice can be changed. This Liberal aspiration is embodied in Solidarism but the latter's commitment to legitim-izing a practice of humanitarian intervention in international society is challenged by both Realism and Pluralism.

States do not intervene for primarily humanitarian reasons

Bhikhu Parekh argues that humanitarian interven-tion should be 'an act wholly or primarily guided by the sentiment of humanity, compassion or fellow-feeling, and is in that sense disinterested' (Parekh 1997: 54). Realism tells us that states only pursue their national interest (see Ch.7) and thus humani-tarian intervention is ruled out since states are motivated solely by what they judge to be their national interest.

States are not allowed to risk the lives of their armed forces on humanitarian crusades

Realists not only argue that states do not intervene for humanitarian reasons; they are also asserting that states should not behave in this way. State leaders—those men and women who think and act in the name of states—do not have the moral right to shed blood on behalf of suffering humanity. Parekh expresses well the core postulates of the statist para-digm:[3] 'Citizens are the exclusive responsibility of their state, and their state is entirely their own busi-ness' (Parekh 1997: 56). Thus, if a civil authority has broken down or is behaving in an appalling way towards its citizens, this is the responsibility of that state's citizens and its political leaders. Outsiders have no moral duty to intervene even if they would be able to improve the situation and stop the killing.

The problem of abuse

A key Realist argument against humanitarian inter-vention is that it should not be legitimated as an exception to the general ban on the use of force in Article 2(4) because this will lead to abuse, a problem identified by Thomas Franck and Nigel Rodley. They contend that Article 2(4) is already vulnerable to states abusing it in the name of self-defence without creating a new legal right of humanitarian interven-tion that would be equally open to abuse. In the absence of an impartial mechanism for deciding when humanitarian intervention was permissible, states might espouse humanitarian motives as a pre-text to cover the pursuit of national self-interest (Franck and Rodley 1973: 275–305). The problem of abuse leads some to argue that humanitarian inter-vention will always be a weapon that the strong use against the weak.

Selectivity of response

The argument here is that states always apply prin-ciples of humanitarian intervention selectively, resulting in an inconsistency in policy. Because states will be governed by what they judge to be their national interest, they intervene only when they deem this to be at stake. The problem of selectivity arises when an agreed moral principle is at stake in more than one situation, but national interest dic-tates a divergence of responses. A good recent example of the selectivity of response is the claim by critics of NATO that its intervention in Kosovo could not have been driven by humanitarian motives because the Alliance had done nothing to address the equally terrible plight of the Turkish Kurds, the Chechens, or the East Timorese. Selectivity of response is the problem of failing to treat like cases alike.

Disagreement on what moral principles should govern a right of humanitarian intervention

Pluralism[4] identifies an additional objection to humanitarian intervention, namely, the problem of how to reach a consensus on what moral principles should underpin it. Hedley Bull defined the Pluralist conception of international society as one in which states are capable of agreement only for certain minimum purposes, the most crucial being recognition of each state's sovereignty and respect for the rule of non-intervention. The subject of humanitarian intervention is a difficult one for theorists of international society since it is the archetypal case where it might be expected that the society of states would agree to privilege individual justice over the non-intervention principle. Pluralism is sensitive to human rights concerns, but argues that humanitarian intervention should not be permitted in the face of disagreement about what constitutes extreme human rights violations in international society. The concern is that in the absence of a consensus on what principles should govern a right of individual or collective humanitarian intervention, the most powerful states would be free to impose their own

culturally determined moral values on weaker members of international society. This moral defence of the non-intervention rule is based on what philosophers call rule-consequentialism. International order, and hence the general well-being of all individuals, is better served by upholding a rule of non-intervention than by allowing humanitarian intervention in the absence of a consensus on the threshold of human suffering that should trigger intervention.

Key points

- States will not intervene for primarily humanitarian reasons.

- States should not place their armed forces in harm's way for primarily humanitarian reasons as this violates the compact between state and citizen.

- A new legal right of humanitarian intervention would be vulnerable to abuse as states employed humanitarian claims to cloak the pursuit of traditional national interests.

- States will apply principles of humanitarian intervention selectively.

- In the absence of a consensus on what principles should govern a right of individual or collective humanitarian intervention, such a right would undermine international order.

- Humanitarian intervention will always be based on the cultural preferences of the powerful.

The Solidarist case for humanitarian intervention

In contrast to Pluralism, Solidarism argues that states have both a legal right and a moral duty to intervene in situations of genocide and mass killing that offend against minimum standards of humanity. This section is divided into two parts. The counter-restrictionist case for a legal right of humanitarian intervention is explored in the first part, and in the second part we investigate the Solidarist claim that whatever the legality of humanitarian intervention,

there is a moral duty of forcible intervention in situations of extreme humanitarian emergency. It was pointed out earlier that there is a dispute among international lawyers concerning the legality of humanitarian intervention. Anthony Clark Arend and Robert J. Beck argue that the counter-restrictionist case for a legal right of individual and collective humanitarian intervention rests on two key claims: first, the UN Charter commits states to protecting fundamental human rights, and second, there is a right of humanitarian intervention in customary international law (Arend and Beck 1993: 132–7).

Protection of human rights

Counter-restrictionists challenge the view of restrictionists that the UN's primary purpose is to maintain international peace and security. They contend that the promotion of human rights should rank alongside the maintenance of international peace and security in the hierarchy of Charter principles. Here, they point to the preamble to the UN Charter and Articles 1(3), 55, and 56 of the Charter. Some counter-restrictionists are prepared to go even further, asserting that if the UN fails to take remedial action in cases of genocide and mass killing—as was so often the case during the cold war—individual states gain the legal right to intervene with force to reduce human suffering. Michael Reisman and Mryes McDougal assert that the human rights provisions of the Charter provide a secure legal basis for unilateral forcible intervention. They claim that were this not the case it 'would be suicidally destructive of the explicit purposes for which the United Nations was established' (quoted in Arend and Beck 1993: 133). As with the right to self-defence, humanitarian intervention is argued to be a legitimate exception to the general ban on the unilateral recourse to force in the UN Charter.

A customary right of humanitarian intervention

An alternative grounding for a legal right of unilateral humanitarian intervention is found in the contention that such a right exists in customary international law. Arend and Beck define this in the following terms: 'If, over a period of time, states begin to act in a certain way and come to regard that behaviour as being required by law, a norm of customary international law has developed' (Arend and Beck 1993: 6). Not only must states actually engage in the practice that is claimed to have the status of

customary law, they must do so because they believe that this practice is permitted by the law. This is described in the language of international law as opinio juris. Counter-restrictionists contend that states were permitted to engage in humanitarian intervention under pre-Charter customary international law. However, this is a very controversial claim and it is rejected by restrictionists like Franck and Rodley who argue that there is little or no support in pre-1945 state practice for a right of humanitarian intervention (Franck and Rodley 1973: 275–305). The legitimacy of humanitarian intervention in cold war state practice is the subject of the next section, but no discussion of the Solidarist case would be complete without an examination of the claim that humanitarian intervention is sometimes morally required.

Is humanitarian intervention morally required?

Some lawyers argue that whatever the legality of humanitarian intervention, it might be morally required in those cases where the use of force is the only means of ending the slaughter. Thus, Franck and Rodley write that humanitarian intervention 'belongs in the realm not of law but of moral choice, which nations, like individuals, must sometimes make' (Franck and Rodley 1973: 304). Their position is that this moral imperative cannot be legally recognized because of the dangers that such a legal right would be abused. The claim that humanitarian intervention is morally required is a much stronger one than the proposition that there is a legal right to engage in this practice because while the existence of a right enables action it does not determine it.

Even if an individual state, or group of states, feel sufficiently troubled by gross violations of human rights in another state to intervene, how should the society of states decide whether this action is legitimate? Put crudely, how many people have to die—or be in imminent peril—before the use of force is justified? Solidarism has not provided a satisfactory response to this question, but a pioneering attempt can be found in R. J. Vincent's discussion of this question as set out in Box 25.2.

Box 25.2 **R. J. Vincent's exceptions to the non-intervention principle**

'The international community has produced a number of conventions setting standards on human rights that go well beyond the proclamation of basic rights. The hard question is whether these standards legitimize action, either by international society as a whole or by states as its agents. Or, to put it another way, does a threat to life on the New York subway or in the Sahara desert trigger an international obligation to respond? Is intervention legitimate in these circumstances?

The answer is plainly no in these circumstances. Humanitarian intervention is, as Walzer puts it, reserved for extraordinary oppression, not the day-to-day variety. If the threat to life on the New York subway became the systematic killing of all commuters from New Jersey, or the threat to life in the Sahara desert reached famine proportions, in which local governments were implicated by failing to meet their responsibilities, *then* there might fall to the international community a duty of humanitarian intervention.'

(Vincent 1986: 126–7)

Writing with Peter Wilson in a posthumous work, Vincent expressed his reservations with a 'morality of states' which requires that 'we have to act as if other states are legitimate, not because they are legitimate [in their upholding of plural conceptions of the good] but because to do otherwise would lead to chaos ... states ought to satisfy certain basic requirements of decency before they qualify for the protection which the principle of non-intervention provides'.

(Vincent and Wilson 1993: 124–5)

Box 25.3 **Summary of key concepts in the theory of humanitarian intervention**

Abuse	States cloak power political interests in the guise of humanitarianism.
Common humanity	We all have human rights by virtue of our common humanity, and these rights generate correlative moral duties for individuals and states.
Failed states	States that have collapsed into civil war and disorder, and where the government of the state has ceased to exist inside the territorial borders of the state. Citizens find themselves in a quasi-state of nature.
Counter-restrictionists	International lawyers who argue that there is a legal right of humanitarian intervention in both UN Charter law and customary international law.
Forcible humanitarian intervention	Military intervention which breaches the principle of state sovereignty where the primary purpose is to alleviate the human suffering of some or all within a state's borders.
Murderous states	States where the sovereign government is massively abusing the human rights of its citizens, engaging in acts of mass killing and/or genocide.
Non-forcible/non-violent intervention	Pacific intervention which can be either consensual (Red Cross) or non-consensual (Médecins Sans Frontières) and which is practised by states, international organizations, and INGOs (international non-governmental organizations). It can be short term (delivery of humanitarian aid) or long term (conflict resolution and reconstruction of political life within failed states).
Pluralist international society theory	States are conscious of sharing common interests and common values, but these are limited to norms of sovereignty and non-intervention.
Restrictionists	International lawyers who argue that humanitarian intervention violates Article 2(4) of the UN Charter and is illegal under both UN Charter law and customary international law.

(continues)

Summary of key concepts in the theory of humanitarian intervention—continued

Rule-consequentialism	International order and hence general well-being is better served by a general prohibition against humanitarian intervention than by sanctioning humanitarian intervention in the absence of agreement on what principles should govern a right of unilateral humanitarian intervention.
Selectivity	An agreed moral principle is at stake in more than one situation, but national interest dictates a divergence of response.
Solidarist international society theory	International society is agreed or capable of agreeing on universal standards of justice and morality which would legitimize practices of humanitarian intervention.
Statism	The moral claim that states only have duties to their own citizens, and that they should not risk their soldiers' lives on humanitarian crusades.
Chapter VII	Article 39 of Chapter VII of the UN Charter authorizes the UN Security Council to 'decide what measures shall be taken in accordance with Articles 41 and 42, to maintain international peace and security'. Article 42 empowers the Security Council to 'take such action by air, sea, or land forces as may be necessary to maintain or restore international peace and security'.

Key points

- Solidarism is committed to developing consensual moral principles that would legitimate a practice of humanitarian intervention in international society.

- Counter-restrictionists argue for a legal right of forcible humanitarian intervention based on an interpretation of the human rights provisions in the UN Charter and the existence of customary international law.

- A legal right of humanitarian intervention enables intervention but it does not determine it. To ensure intervention in cases where it is desperately needed states would have to recognize a duty or obligation to act.

State practice during the cold war

This section assesses the extent to which humanitarian intervention was a legitimate practice of states during the cold war. Here, we will briefly focus upon two cases in the post-1945 period where interventionary action by a neighbouring state led to the ending of state-sponsored mass murder: Vietnam's intervention in Cambodia in December 1978 and Tanzania's intervention in Uganda a few weeks later. Three key issues will be explored in relation to these cases: the place of humanitarian motives in the decision to intervene; the justifications offered by

Tanzania and Vietnam for their actions; and the divergent responses of the society of states to these two cases.

The motives and justifications of Vietnam and Tanzania

Gross human rights violations characterized Idi Amin's Ugandan Government from start to finish. Amnesty International estimated that up to 300,000 people had been killed during the eight years in which he had been in power. The record is even more appalling in the case of the Khmer Rouge which seized power in Cambodia in April 1975, and immediately embarked upon policies which involved some of the most appalling human rights abuses in the brutally long twentieth century. While accurate figures are difficult to obtain, there is broad agreement that of a population of about seven million, some two to three million people lost their lives during the three and a half years in which the Khmer Rouge were in power. Despite this level of human rights abuses, there was no collective intervention to remove these murderous regimes, and it was left to Tanzania and Vietnam to take the law into their own hands. But in neither case did the intervening state claim that its motives were humanitarian. Instead, both Tanzania and Vietnam argued that they were acting in self-defence—the legitimate right of all states under Article 51 of the UN Charter. They claimed with some legitimacy that they were the victims of armed aggression since both Cambodia, and especially Uganda, had undertaken cross-border incursions in the months prior to the invasions. At no point did the governments of Tanzania or Vietnam argue that they had a legal right to use force to remove a tyrannical government from power.

What explains the reluctance on the part of Tanzania and Vietnam to claim a right of humanitarian intervention? Three explanations have been advanced. First, it is argued that neither of them acted for primarily humanitarian reasons confirming the Realist view that states do not risk their soldiers' lives unless vital interests are at stake. Gary Klintworth's study of these cases led him to conclude that, 'while saving human beings from being killed was an inevitable consequence of intervention by Vietnam and . . . Tanzania . . . it was always secondary to the overriding priority imposed by concern for vital security interests' (Klintworth 1989: 59). A further reason for the reluctance of the intervening states to claim a right of humanitarian intervention has been suggested by Adam Roberts. He writes, 'there was probably also a thought that to sanctify a doctrine of humanitarian intervention would be to store up trouble for themselves or their friends' (Roberts 1993: 434). The argument here is that states with dubious human rights records are fearful of

setting precedents for a doctrine of humanitarian intervention because this might be employed against them at some future date. However, there is no evidence to substantiate the claim in relation to Vietnam, and in the case of Tanzania, President Julius Nyerere was a rare and outspoken exponent of humanitarian values. A final explanation is offered by Hedley Bull, who suggests that the society of states was highly sensitive to the consequences of actions that eroded the non-intervention principle in international society. Writing in the mid-1980s, Bull stated:

There is no present tendency for states to claim, or for the international community to recognize, any such right [of humanitarian intervention] . . . The reluctance evident in the international community even to experiment with the conception of a right of humanitarian intervention reflects not only an unwillingness to jeopardise the rules of sovereignty and non-intervention by conceding such a right to individual states, but also the lack of any agreed doctrine as to what human rights are (Bull 1984a: 193).

The response of international society

Bull's judgement noted above reflected the fact that the actions of neither Vietnam nor Tanzania were legitimated by wider international society as humanitarian exceptions to the rules of sovereignty, non-intervention, and non-use of force. However, the international response that greeted the two interventions was radically different: Vietnam's use of force was almost universally condemned whereas Tanzania's intervention that breached the same rules as Vietnam's was treated much more leniently. What, then, explains this divergence of response? The international response was to a large degree conditioned by the political and strategic imperatives of the cold war. The case where armed intervention was arguably most justifiable on humanitarian grounds—Vietnam's intervention to overthrow the Pol Pot regime in Cambodia—received the greater censure. Rather than legitimize the overthrow of the Pol Pot regime on humanitarian grounds, both the US-led Western bloc and China castigated and sanctioned Vietnam for acting as an agent of Soviet imperialism. At the regional level, the Association of South-East Asian Nations (ASEAN) was deeply suspicious of Vietnam's intentions, fearing that Hanoi's adventurism in Cambodia heralded a wider bid for regional hegemony.

In stark contrast, Tanzania's overthrow of Idi Amin received no such public denunciation, with the new Ugandan Government rapidly receiving widespread recognition and financial aid from a number of foreign governments. Cold war geopolitics were not as strong a motivating influence in this case as they were with Cambodia, and Amin had almost totally alienated the Soviet Union, his superpower patron and only ally outside of Africa. The wider African response to Tanzania's violation of the non-intervention rule, a bedrock principle of the Organization of African Unity (OAU), was a muted one. With the exception of Nigeria, and the outgoing chair of the OAU Sudan, which roundly condemned Tanzania, the rest of the OAU reacted in a way which amounted to what Caroline Thomas calls 'almost tacit approval' (Thomas 1985: 122–3). This reflected the following considerations: the belief among most African leaders that Tanzania had been the victim of a prior act of Ugandan aggression in late 1978 when Amin had seized the Kegara Salient; the perception

that Tanzania as one of the poorest African countries was not a predatory state; and finally Amin's excesses at home and abroad had become an embarrassment to other African governments.

> ### Key points
>
> - Humanitarian considerations do not seem to have been decisive in the decisions of Vietnam and Tanzania to intervene.
>
> - Vietnam and Tanzania justified their interventions in terms of the traditional norms of the society of states.
>
> - The reluctance of the society of states to legitimize humanitarian intervention reflected fears about setting precedents which could erode the non-intervention principle.
>
> - In the polarized world of the late 1970s, reactions to the Tanzanian and Vietnamese interventions were conditioned by cold war geopolitics.

Post-cold war humanitarian interventions

This section discusses the international interventions in northern Iraq, Somalia, Rwanda, and Kosovo. It is divided into three parts: first, the place of humanitarian impulses in state decisions to intervene; second, the legality and legitimacy of the interventions; and finally, the humanitarian success of these military interventions.

The role of humanitarian sentiments in state decisions to intervene

In the cases of northern Iraq and Somalia, the principal force behind intervention was not state leaders taking the lead in persuading reluctant publics to respond to a humanitarian emergency. Rather, it was the media and domestic public opinion that pressurized policymakers into taking humanitarian actions.

In the face of a massive refugee crisis caused by Saddam Hussein's oppression of the Kurds, US, British, and French military forces intervened in April 1991 to create protected 'safe havens' for the Kurdish people. James Mayall argues that action was only taken to protect the Kurds 'because the attention devoted by the Western media to the plight of the Kurds along the Turkish border threatened the political dividends that Western governments had secured from their conduct of the war itself' (Mayall 1991: 426).

Similarly, the US military intervention in Somalia in December 1992 was a response to sentiments of compassion on the part of US citizens. However, this sense of solidarity disappeared once Americans saw the blood of their fellow countrymen being spilled on the streets of Mogadishu. The fact that the USA pulled the plug on its Somali intervention after the loss of 18 US Rangers in a fire-fight in October 1993 indicates how capricious public opinion is. Television pictures of starving and dying Somalis had persuaded the outgoing Bush Administration to launch a humanitarian rescue mission, but once the US public saw the consequences of this in terms of dead Americans being dragged through the streets of Mogadishu, the Clinton Administration was forced to announce a timetable for the removal of all US forces from Somalia. What this case demonstrates is that the 'CNN factor' is a double-edged sword: it can pressurize governments into humanitarian intervention, yet with equal rapidity, pictures of casualties arriving home can lead to public disillusionment and calls for an end to the intervention.

In the cases of intervention in northern Iraq and Somalia, policymakers primarily acted to appease the humanitarian sentiments of domestic publics. But while sensitivity to public opinion was probably the key factor, it would be churlish to deny that moral concerns played some part in leading Western governments to embark on these interventions. What these cases suggest is that even if there are no vital national interests at stake, liberal states might launch humanitarian rescue missions if sufficient public pressure is mobilized. Certainly, there is no evidence in either of these cases to support the Realist claim that states cloak power political motives in the guise of humanitarianism. Nevertheless, humanitarian interventions that are motivated by the primary concern of responding to pressures from domestic constituencies fail Bhikhu Parekh's definiton of humanitarian intervention as actions 'primarily guided by the sentiment of humanity, compassion or fellow-feeling' (Parekh 1997: 54).

But if the motives driving the interventions in Somalia and northern Iraq fail Parekh's stringent criteria for a genuine humanitarian intervention, how much more so does the French intervention in Rwanda in July 1994 which was a clear-cut case of abuse. The French Government emphasized the strictly humanitarian character of the operation, but this interpretation lacks credibility given the evidence that they seem to have been covertly pursuing national self-interest behind the figleaf of humanitarianism. France had propped up the one-party Hutu state for twenty years, even providing troops when the Rwandan Patriotic Front (RPF), operating

out of neighbouring Uganda, threatened to overrun the country in 1990 and 1993. The French President, François Mitterrand, was reportedly anxious to restore waning French credibility in Africa, and was fearful that an RPF victory in French-speaking Rwanda would result in the country coming under the influence of Anglophones.

According to Bruce Jones, the Rwandan case should lead us to broaden the traditional definition of humanitarian intervention, with its focus on the primacy of humanitarian motives, to encompass humanitarian outcomes. Figure 25.1 sets out Jones's matrix for judging the humanitarian character of interventions. For illustrative purposes, we have filled in three of the boxes with cases drawn from this chapter. Jones does not develop his understanding of humanitarian motives but it is helpful to think of the horizontal line of the matrix as a continuum with pure humanitarian motives at one end and the complete absence of humanitarian motives at the other. Humanitarian interventions launched to appease domestic publics are not examples where the humanitarian motive is primary, but they should be located nearer this end of the continuum than cases where state leaders espouse humanitarian motives to cloak the pursuit of national self-interest. The vertical line of the matrix indicates the success or failure of interventions in humanitarian terms, but this raises the question as to what counts as a successful humanitarian intervention. This is discussed later in the chapter.

The moral question raised by French intervention in Rwanda provides the answer to why international society failed to intervene as soon as the genocide began in early April 1994. French intervention saved some lives but it came far too late to halt the genocide. The failure of international society to prevent and end the genocide demonstrates the limits of states as guardians of human rights. It is some two decades since the 'killing fields' in Cambodia—the chilling description of Pol Pot's mass killing—but the response to Rwanda indicates that state leaders remain gripped by the mind-set of statism. The expression of international solidarity in the face of genocide was limited to moral outrage and the provision of humanitarian aid to its victims.

If the French intervention in Rwanda can be criticized for being too little, too late, NATO's

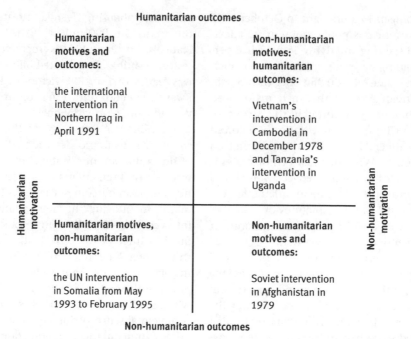

Humanitarian outcomes

Humanitarian motives and outcomes:

the international intervention in Northern Iraq in April 1991

Non-humanitarian motives: humanitarian outcomes:

Vietnam's intervention in Cambodia in December 1978 and Tanzania's intervention in Uganda

Humanitarian motives, non-humanitarian outcomes:

the UN intervention in Somalia from May 1993 to February 1995

Non-humanitarian motives and outcomes:

Soviet intervention in Afghanistan in 1979

Humanitarian motivation

Non-humanitarian motivation

Non-humanitarian outcomes

Fig. 25.1 Matrix of humanitarian intervention—motivation and outcomes

Source: Adapted from a matrix in B.D. Jones (1995: 239).

intervention in Kosovo in 1999 has been criticized for being too much, too soon. Three arguments were adduced to support NATO's claim that the resort to force was justifiable: first, it was argued that Serbian actions in forcibly expelling the Kosovars was creating a supreme humanitarian emergency which breached a whole range of international legal commitments accepted by Yugoslavia. Second, NATO governments pointed to the ad-hoc war crimes tribunal set up to deal with crimes committed in the wars in Croatia and Bosnia, and argued that the Serbs were again committing crimes against humanity, possibly including genocide. Third, it was contended that the Milosevic regime's use of force against the Kosovar Albanians challenged global norms of common humanity, and that NATO had a moral obligation to act to stop such criminal actions as otherwise it would be complicit in Serb atrocities.

Closer analysis of the justifications articulated by Western leaders suggests that while humanitarianism may have provided the primary impulse for action, it was by no means the exclusive impulse. While insisting that humanitarian need was the primary motive, the then British Foreign Secretary Robin Cook argued that NATO credibility was also a key determinant, particularly as the previous 12 months of **diplomacy** with Milosevic had been underpinned by the supposed credible threat of force. The USA was particularly concerned with the regional implications of continuing violence in Kosovo. Viewing the Dayton Agreement, which brought peace to Bosnia in 1995, as an American diplomatic triumph, the Clinton Administration's main interest in the region was Dayton's preservation. Thus, Clinton emphasized that the Kosovo tragedy was unfolding 'in the heart of **Europe**' and 'NATO's backyard' when he justified his policy to his electorate. Western states were also concerned that the massive flow of refugees in the southern Balkans could threaten the stability of the already weak states of Macedonia and Albania, and generate a massive inflow of asylum seekers in the West.

How legal and legitimate were the interventions?

In contrast with state practice during the cold war, the interventions in northern Iraq, Somalia, Rwanda, and Kosovo were all legitimated in humanitarian terms by the intervening states. As we show below, justifying the use of force on humanitarian grounds was contested by some states, which defended a traditional interpretation of the sovereignty principle. However, this position became less and less tenable as the 1990s progressed, and by the end of the decade most states were prepared to accept that the enforcement provisions in Chapter VII of the UN Charter could reasonably be stretched to legitimate armed intervention in cases of genocide and mass killing. Chapter VII enables the Security Council to authorize military enforcement action only in cases where it finds a threat to 'international peace and security', and this attempt to justify humanitarian intervention was first controversially employed by Western states in the case of northern Iraq.

Resolution 688 adopted on 5 April 1991 identified the refugee crisis caused by Saddam Hussein's repression as constituting a threat to 'international peace and security'. However, the resolution was not passed under Chapter VII and there was no explicit authorization of military enforcement action to defend the Kurds in northern Iraq. The reason for this was that Resolution 688 was highly controversial in the eyes of the Soviet Union, China, and a number of other non-Western states on the Council. These states were fearful that authorizing the use of force to protect human rights would set a precedent for humanitarian intervention that might be employed against them and/or undermine the non-intervention norm in the society of states. The refusal of the Security Council to provide a military enforcement mandate for international intervention in northern Iraq forced the Western powers to justify their military intervention as authorized by Resolution 688. This attempt at securing legitimacy was not expressly endorsed by other states, but it was either tacitly accepted or acquiesced in because no one wanted to challenge the legality of an intervention that was saving lives.

In stark contrast to its position on northern Iraq, the Security Council approved unanimously the US military intervention in Somalia to create a secure environment for the delivery of humanitarian aid. Resolution 794 passed under Chapter VII in December 1992 represented a sharp break in existing practice, for as Christopher Greenwood notes, 'it was the plight of the Somali people which was given as the reason for invoking Chapter VII of the Charter and authorizing intervention' (Greenwood 1993: 37). The reason why the Security Council legitimated US military intervention in Somalia, in contrast to the position it had taken over intervention in northern Iraq, was because it did not conform to the classical model of intervention against a government's will. The Somali state had effectively collapsed and humanitarian intervention was legitimated because it was perceived as not undermining the principles of sovereignty and non-intervention (Roberts 1993: 429–49). Nevertheless, non-Western states were sufficiently sensitive to the dangers of being seen to sanction exceptions to the non-intervention principle that they ensured that the drafting of Resolution 794 undermined its import as a case of humanitarian intervention. For example, immediately prior to noting the relationship between human suffering and threats to international peace and security, the resolution recognizes the 'unique character of the present situation in Somalia and mindful of its deteriorating, complex and extraordinary nature, requiring an immediate and exceptional response'. The use of terms such as 'unique', 'extraordinary', and 'exceptional' have to be seen as an attempt to differentiate the humanitarian crisis in Somalia from other cases of **failed states** hence reducing the chance of setting a precedent for future humanitarian interventions. They seem to have been inserted specifically to appease the fears of states such as China which may otherwise have blocked a Chapter VII enforcement action.

More than any other case analysed here, NATO's intervention in Kosovo raised the question of how international society should treat intervention where a state, or in this case a group of states, use force to alleviate human suffering without the explicit authorization of the Security Council. Although the UN did not expressly sanction NATO's use of force, the Security Council also chose not to condemn it. Immediately after NATO launched its first attacks against Yugoslavia, Russia tabled a draft Security Council resolution condemning NATO's use of force and demanding an immediate halt to the bombing. While the NATO members on the Council voted against the resolution, what was surprising was that only Russia, China, and Namibia supported it, leading to a resounding defeat of the resolution. The Security Council's response to NATO's breach of the UN Charter's rules governing the use of force indicated that while it was not prepared to legitimate unilateral humanitarian intervention, it was not necessarily going to condemn it. Instead, the law would be interpreted flexibly depending upon the persuasiveness of the case marshalled to justify such an infraction of the rules.

What emerges from post-cold war state practice is how Western states have taken the lead in advancing a new norm of armed humanitarian intervention in international society. Although many states, notably Russia, China, and India, have been uneasy with this development, there was by the end of the 1990s growing acceptance of the idea that UN military intervention was justifiable in cases of genocide and mass killing. The best illustration of this is the fact that no member of the Security Council tried to oppose intervention in Rwanda on the grounds that this violated its sovereignty. Instead, the barrier to intervention was the lack of political will on the part of states to incur the costs and risks of armed intervention to save Rwandans. It is extremely unlikely that Russia or China would veto Security Council action in a clear-cut case of genocide or wholesale slaughter, unless they had vital interests at stake that dictated another course of action.

The Solidarist idea that the exercise of sovereignty should be conditional on states satisfying basic standards of common humanity was given its most eloquent expression in the 2001 report *The Responsibility to Protect* which was produced by the International Commission on Intervention and State Sovereignty (ICISS). The Commission argued that states have the primary responsibility to protect the security of their citizens. When they are unable or unwilling to do so, or when they deliberately terrorize their citizens, then 'the principle of non-intervention yields to the international responsibility to protect' (ICISS 2001: xi). The report broadens this responsibility to encompass not only the responsibility to react to humanitarian crises, but also the responsibility to prevent such crises and the 'responsibility to rebuild' failed and murderous states. This reframing of the debate, away from the question of whether states have a right of intervention towards the question of where responsibility rests for protecting endangered peoples, has the potential to generate a new political consensus supporting what the ICISS report calls 'intervention for human protection purposes' (ICISS 2001: xiii).

A crucial motivating factor behind the setting up of ICISS was the aspiration to avoid another Kosovo-type situation where Security Council action had been paralysed by the threat of a veto, and individual states had intervened to protect human rights. There is no consensus in international society on the legality of unilateral (non-UN authorized) humanitarian intervention and the report's recommendations in this regard have failed to move the debate significantly forward. The ICISS insisted that potential interveners should secure the backing of the Security Council before acting, considering that the challenge was to make this body work better as a protector of human rights. To this end, the Commission proposed that there should be an agreement among the five permanent members of the Council not to exercise the veto to prevent the passage of a resolution aimed at averting or stopping 'a significant humanitarian crisis ... where [their] vital national interests were not claimed to be involved' (ICISS 2001: 51). Given that the key disagreement in the Council over Kosovo was whether the humanitarian crisis met the threshold that should trigger UN military intervention, the Commission's proposal to restrict the veto fails to address the fundamental problem that divided the Council in this case, and which is likely to bedevil it in future situations.

In arguing that the Security Council had a central responsibility for the protection of humanitarian values, the ICISS recognized that if it failed to discharge this obligation in particularly appalling situations, then others might act to enforce basic human rights norms in international society. An important contribution of the report is the setting out of specific criteria that should be used to judge the legitimacy of such interventions (see Box 25.4)).

| Box 25.4 | The responsibility to protect: principles for military intervention |

'(1) The Just Cause Threshold

Military intervention for human protection purposes is an exceptional and extraordinary measure. To be warranted, there must be serious and irreparable harm occurring to human beings, or imminently likely to occur, of the following kind:

A. **large scale loss of life**, actual or apprehended, with genocidal intent or not, which is the product either of deliberate state action, or state neglect or inability to act, or a failed state situation; or

B. **large scale "ethnic cleansing"**, actual or apprehended, whether carried out by killing, forced expulsion, acts of terror or rape.

(2) The Precautionary Principles

A. **Right intention:** The primary purpose of the intervention, whatever other motives intervening states may have, must be to halt or avert human suffering. Right intention is better assured with multilateral operations, clearly supported by regional opinion and the victims concerned.

B. **Last resort:** Military intervention can only be justified when every non-military option for the prevention or peaceful resolution of the crisis has been explored, with reasonable grounds for believing lesser measures would not have succeeded.

C. **Proportional means:** The scale, duration and intensity of the planned military intervention should be the minimum necessary to secure the defined human protection objective.

D. **Reasonable prospects:** There must be a reasonable chance of success in halting or averting the suffering which has justified the intervention, with the consequences of action not likely to be worse than the consequences of inaction.

(3) Right Authority

A. There is no better or more appropriate body than the United Nations Security Council to authorize military intervention for human protection purposes. The task is not to find alternatives to the Security Council as a source of authority, but to make the Security Council work better than it has.

B. Security Council authorization should in all cases be sought prior to any military intervention action being carried out. Those calling for an intervention should formally request such authorization, or have the Council raise the matter on its own initiative, or have the Secretary-General raise it under Article 99 of the UN Charter.

C. The Security Council should deal promptly with any request for authority to intervene where there are allegations of large scale loss of human life or ethnic cleansing. It should in this context seek adequate verification of facts or conditions on the ground that might support a military intervention.

D. The Permanent Five members of the Security Council should agree not to apply their veto power, in matters where their vital state interests are not involved, to obstruct the passage of resolutions authorizing military intervention for human protection purposes for which there is otherwise majority support.

E. If the Security Council rejects a proposal or fails to deal with it in a reasonable time, alternative options are:

I. consideration of the matter by the General Assembly in Emergency Special Session under the "Uniting for Peace" procedure; and

II. action within area of jurisdiction by regional or sub-regional organizations under Chapter VIII of the Charter, subject to their seeking subsequent authorization from the Security Council.

F. The Security Council should take into account in all its deliberations that, if it fails to discharge its responsibility to protect in conscience-shocking situations crying out for action, concerned states may not rule out other means to meet the gravity and urgency of that situation—and that the stature and credibility of the United Nations may suffer thereby.

(continues)

The responsibility to protect: principles for military intervention—continued

(4) Operational Principles

A. Clear objectives; clear and unambiguous mandate at all times; and resources to match.

B. Common military approach among involved partners; unity of command; clear and unequivocal communications and chain of command.

C. Acceptance of limitations, incrementalism and gradualism in the application of force, the objective being protection of a population, not defeat of a state.

D. Rules of engagement which fit the operational concept; are precise; reflect the principle of proportionality; and involve total adherence to international humanitarian law.

E. Acceptance that force protection cannot become the principal objective.

F. Maximum possible coordination with humanitarian organizations.'

(International Commission on Intervention and State Sovereignty 2001: xii–xiii)

In the event that the Council failed to act in cases like Rwanda and Kosovo, the report argued that the criteria established the benchmarks against which to judge the legitimacy of armed intervention taken outside the UN framework. A key criterion in assessing whether an intervention is justified, according to the report, is whether there is a reasonable prospect of success. And central to this in the Commission's thinking was the idea that interveners should take on a long-term responsibility for human rights protection in the target state. It is to the success of the interventions in Iraq, Somalia, and Kosovo that we turn next.

Were the interventions successful?

Does the record of post-cold war forcible interventions lend support to the proposition that the use of force can promote humanitarian values? Humanitarian outcomes can be usefully divided into short- and long-term ones. The former would refer to the immediate alleviation of human suffering through the termination of mass killing and/or the delivery of humanitarian aid to civilians trapped in war zones. Long-term humanitarian outcomes focus on how far intervention addresses the underlying causes of human suffering by facilitating conflict resolution and the reconstruction of viable polities.

This approach to defining a positive humanitarian outcome is favoured by Parekh and Michael Walzer. The former argues that the delivery of aid in complex humanitarian emergencies is not humanitarian intervention, which he defines as a political act 'intended to help create ... a structure of civil authority acceptable to the people involved' (Parekh 1997: 55–6). His contention is that humanitarian intervention differs from other forms of intervention in aiming to ensure that new structures of government are evolved in consultation with local political actors, rather than being imposed from outside. This is also the argument of Walzer who challenges the traditional counter-restrictionist assumption that humanitarian interveners should conduct a quick military intervention and then withdraw having removed the source of the human rights abuses. This might have been realistic in the cold war period when forcible intervention could end the human rights abuses of genocidal regimes. However, Walzer argues that this type of intervention is not appropriate to post-cold war humanitarian crises where the sources of human suffering are often deeply rooted in the political, economic, and social structures of societies. He contends that if intervention does not address the underlying roots of these conflicts, the exit of the intervening force will simply lead to the resumption of violent conflict. He argues that the use of force in complex humanitarian emergencies should be employed as part of a long-term project of conflict resolution and political, economic, and social reconstruction (Walzer 1995*b*: 35–6).

Given this conceptualization of short-term and long-term humanitarian outcomes, how should we evaluate the international interventions in northern Iraq, Somalia, and Kosovo? 'Operation Safe Haven' enjoyed initial success in dealing with the refugee problem in northern Iraq and clearly saved lives. However, as the media spotlight began to shift elsewhere and public interest waned, so did the commitment of Western governments to protect the Kurds. While Western air forces policed a 'no-fly zone' over northern Iraq that extended some protection to the Kurds, the intervening states quickly handed over the running of the safe havens to what they knew was an ill-equipped and badly supported UN relief operation. This faced enormous problems given Iraq's enduring hostility towards its Kurdish minority. Despite its success in alleviating the immediate suffering of the Kurds, the intervention failed to put in place effective guarantees for their protection.

Some commentators identify the initial US intervention in Somalia in the period between December 1992 and March 1993 as evidence of a successful humanitarian intervention. In terms of short-term success, the USA claimed that it saved thousands of Somalis from starvation. There is disagreement over how far 'Operation Restore Hope' really saved lives (Weiss 1999: 82–7), but what is not disputed is that the mission eventually ended in disaster. This can be traced to the attempt by UNOSOM II (this UN force took over from the Americans in May 1993 but its main military power was provided by a US Quick Reaction Force of 1,200 men under US control) to go beyond the initial US mission of famine relief to the disarmament of the warring factions, and the provision of law and order in Somali society. Suffering always has political causes, and the rationale behind the expanded UN mandate of UNOSOM II was to establish a law-governed polity that would prevent a return to civil war and famine. However, this attempt to convert a short-term humanitarian outcome (famine relief) into the longer-term one of conflict resolution and political reconstruction proved a failure. The problem was that once the UN Security Council sanctioned the arrest of one of the

warlords, General Aidid, after his forces had killed 24 UN peacekeepers on 5 June 1993, UNOSOM II acted like an imperial power, relying on high-tech American weaponry to police the streets of southern Mogadishu. Indeed, the shift from famine relief to war-making was graphically illustrated by the television footage of US helicopter gunships firing missiles into the crowded urban areas of southern Mogadishu. The haunting question raised by Somalia is whether intervention that tries to combine both the short-term and long-term goals of rescuing victims from starvation and lawlessness, and restoring legitimate authority, is *always* doomed to end in a humiliating exit.

The jury remains out in Kosovo on whether the international community can succeed in rebuilding a new multiethnic state. The NATO-led force that went into Kosovo immediately after the air campaign (KFOR) did succeed in returning virtually all the refugees to their homes remarkably quickly. However, most of the Serbian population fled Kosovo out of fear of reprisals from the majority Albanian community, and those that are left live in a constant climate of fear and insecurity in ghettos protected by KFOR troops. The grim truth is that some of the Kosovar Albanians who suffered at the hands of the Serbs through the 1990s have inflicted their own brand of ethnic apartheid on those Serbs who continue to live in Kosovo. Set against this, the majority people of Kosovo, as a result of NATO's action, enjoy new freedoms, and projects such as the EU's Stability Pact offer the possibility of both future prosperity and security.

The conclusion that emerges from this brief overview is that forcible intervention in humanitarian crises is most likely to be a short-term palliative that does little to address the underlying political causes of the violence and suffering. The problem is that the initial determination to employ force in defence of humanitarian goals has not been backed up by a long-term political, military, economic, and social commitment to provide long-term human rights protection. States that intervene militarily as agents of common humanity need to have a clear formulation of short-term and long-term objectives, which balances immediate responses to the humanitarian crisis with a sustained commitment to long-term reconstruction.

Key points

- Solidarism is committed to developing consensual moral principles that would legitimate a practice of humanitarian intervention in international society.

- Counter-restrictionists argue for a legal right of forcible humanitarian intervention based on an interpretation of the human rights provisions in the UN Charter and the existence of customary international law.

- A legal right of humanitarian intervention enables intervention but it does not determine it. To ensure intervention in cases where it is desperately needed states would have to recognize a duty or obligation to act.

Humanitarian intervention after 11 September 2001

What effect did the terrorist attacks on 11 September have on humanitarian intervention? Has the 'war on terror' made it less likely that powerful states will use their militaries to save strangers? Is there a danger that the USA will return to its cold war policy of prioritizing strategic advantage over human rights? There are two important perspectives on these questions.

The first is a pessimistic position. It holds that since the 'war on terror' began, the USA has placed its own strategic interests ahead of concern for human rights, both overseas and at home. Michael Ignatieff, for example, argues that the United States is prepared to align itself with repressive governments that support its anti-terror strategy (Ignatieff 2002). According to this view, where it might have been difficult to marshal Western commitment to humanitarian intervention in the 1990s, it has become virtually impossible after 9/11. In 2002, the West was unwilling to make anything other than token gestures in response to the unfolding humanitarian catastrophes in Sierra Leone, the Democratic Republic of Congo (DRC), and Ivory Coast.

The second perspective is more optimistic. It springs from the core premise that Western states will only militarily intervene in humanitarian emergencies if they believe vital security interests are at stake. And since, as Afghanistan shows, there is often a critical linkage between failed states and **terrorism** it is contended that the war on terrorism could pro-

vide the necessary strategic interests to motivate intervention that is defensible on grounds of both human rights and **national security** (Wheeler 2004; Chesterman 2004). What do the two principal conflicts of the era since 9/11 tell us about the future direction of humanitarian intervention?

Although the US-led intervention in Afghanistan was a war of self-defence, the US President nevertheless felt the need to make a humanitarian argument to support his case. He told Afghans that, 'the oppressed people of Afghanistan will know the generosity of America and its allies. As we strike military targets, we'll also drop food, medicine and supplies to the starving and suffering men and women and children of Afghanistan' (Bush 2001). The USA took steps to minimize non-combatant suffering in Afghanistan but at least two operational choices undermined the humanitarian credentials of the war. The first was the decision to rely heavily on intelligence provided by different Afghan factions for the identification and targeting of Taliban and Al Qaeda forces. This reflected the US determination to reduce the risks to its armed forces. But this decision left the USA open to manipulation by Afghans eager to settle scores with their rivals, resulting in a number of attacks where innocent civilians were killed. The second failure was Washington's refusal to contribute ground troops to the UN-mandated International Security Assistance Force (ISAF). The latter has only been able to provide security in Kabul and the surrounding areas, and the continuing insecurity across the rest of the country is severely hampering the ongoing international effort to rebuild Afghanistan.

The Iraq war was primarily justified as one necessitated by the danger posed by Saddam Hussein's weapons of mass destruction (WMD). However, as the offending weapons became more elusive both before, and especially after, the war, those justifying the use of force increasingly resorted to humanitarian rationales. During the war itself, Bush told the media that 'we're working to free the Iraqi people . . . slowly, but surely, the grip of terror around the throats of the Iraqi people is being loosened' (Bush 2004). And as criticism of the war mounted in the following months, both Bush and the British Prime Minister, Tony Blair, frequently retorted that regardless of WMD, the war was justifiable because 'Iraq is a better place' without Saddam. Leaving aside the WMD question, was the invasion of Iraq justifiable in humanitarian terms? In opening Human Rights Watch's 2004 report, Executive Director Kenneth Roth argued in an important essay that Iraq failed as a humanitarian intervention on two important counts: first, the level of human rights abuses perpetrated by the regime, though appalling and unacceptable, did not meet the threshold of mass killing—actual or anticipated—that alone justifies

the death and destruction that accompanies military action. Second, to qualify as humanitarian, an intervention must be motivated primarily by humanitarian purposes, and Roth contended that this factor was not the prime reason why Bush and Blair had launched the war (Roth 2004).

The fact that the USA and the UK felt it necessary to employ humanitarian arguments highlights the extent to which this justification has become a legitimating basis for military intervention in the post-cold war era. This is in marked contrast to the cold war period when interventions that produced a humanitarian good—such as Tanzania's overthrow of the Idi Amin regime in Uganda—had to be justified as self-defence, whatever the humanitarian considerations motivating the action. But the reluctance of Western governments to wage war, without dressing it up in humanitarian terms, does not presage a new-found commitment to protecting civilians in danger. In both Afghanistan and Iraq, this was a low priority compared to securing the strategic and political goals of the intervening states. This dismal conclusion raises the deeper question of whether militarized and statist approaches to intervention can ever promote human rights on a global scale. The final part of the chapter takes up this issue by exploring the possibilities for a non-violent politics of humanitarianism.

Globalization and non-forcible humanitarian intervention

As we have seen, the traditional approach to humanitarian intervention focuses on states and forcible intervention. Intervention is characterized by coercion, by a breach of sovereignty, and is non-consensual. By contrast, non-forcible humanitarian intervention emphasizes the pacific activities of states, international organizations, and non-governmental organizations in delivering humanitarian aid and facilitating third party conflict resolution and reconstruction. Non-forcible humanitarian intervention can be consensual or non-consensual. An example of the latter is the activities of Médecins Sans Frontières which frequently operates without the consent of host governments, but which works through non-violent methods to bring humanitarian relief. Consensual acts include the diplomacy of third party mediation and the practices of the International Committee of the Red Cross which normally only operates with the consent of sovereign governments. The weakness, then, of restricting humanitarian intervention to coercive/forcible acts is that such a definition provides no framework for accommodating the non-military humanitarian activities of states and non-state actors.

The activities of humanitarian agencies in complex humanitarian emergencies reflect the growth of a global society in which humanitarian organiza-

Box 25.5	The mission of Médecins Sans Frontières

'Médecins Sans Frontières (MSF) is the leading non-governmental organization for emergency medical aid. We provide independent medical relief to victims of war, disasters, and epidemics in 80 countries around the world. We strive to provide assistance to those who need it most, regardless of ethnic origin, religion, or political affiliation.

To get access to care for the most vulnerable, MSF must remain scrupulously independent of governments, as well as religious and economic powers. We rely on private individuals for the majority of our funding. In the field, we conduct our own assessments, manage projects directly and monitor the impact of our aid. We campaign locally and internationally for greater respect for humanitarian law and the right of civilians to impartial humanitarian assistance. We also campaign for fairer access to medicines and healthcare for the world's poorest people.'

(Médecins Sans Frontières 2000)

tions operate transnationally. Globalization has generated many of the ills of contemporary life but it has also created that growing sense of 'cosmopolitan moral awareness' (Bull 1984b: 12) that is beginning to make a reality of Kant's vision of a right's violation in one place being felt everywhere. Television presents images of humanity in peril across the world, and it is simply no longer possible for state leaders and publics to isolate themselves and say that they do not know what is happening in places like Rwanda, Chechnya, and Sierra Leone. Rather, governments are required to justify their moral choices when confronted by states and local actors committing crimes against humanity. The challenge for those individuals and organizations committed to the defence of minimum standards of humanity is to ensure that governments are held accountable for their moral choices when confronted by acts of genocide and mass killing.

The global human rights culture seeks to protect human rights and humanitarian values everywhere. This culture is a product of the post-holocaust world and it is embedded in the ideas and practices of international civil servants, media, local non-governmental organizations (NGOs), and a global network of humanitarian international non-governmental organizations (INGOs) that are sustained and supported by that transnational global citizenry committed to human rights and humanitarianism (Minear and Weiss 1995; B. D. Jones 1995). This community is anti-statist but not necessarily anti-state; governments often fail to act as local agents of common humanity, but a key challenge for those who want to deepen global moral solidarities is to harness state power to the purposes of global humanitarianism.

The global human rights culture is a unique and progressive feature of the globalization of world politics at the start of the new millennium. Its existence reflects the growing recognition that the causes of human rights abuses and humanitarian crises are global ones that require global solutions. Non-forcible humanitarian intervention is usually defined in terms of the activities of non-state actors and third party mediators in complex humanitarian emergencies, but it also needs to encompass global interventionary strategies designed to address the underlying causes of human suffering in world politics.

The question of how and why human suffering gets constructed in the way it does is beyond the scope of this chapter. However, consider the following question posed by Parekh: Why, he asks, 'should suffering and death only become a matter of humanitarian intervention when they are caused by the breakdown of the state or by an outrageous abuse of its power?' (Parekh 1997: 55). The answer to this question is that what counts as human suffering is a product of the ideological biases of global political and economic elites. It suits dominant elites to construct humanitarian intervention in terms of crisis management rather than developing the global political and economic policies to address the underlying structural causes of poverty and malnutrition. There is nothing natural or inevitable about the facts of global poverty; it is a product of the handiwork of individuals and social classes whose interactions have constructed global capitalism. These structure are deeply rooted and produce a global alienated underclass, and their transformation must be the objective of an emancipatory global politics of non-forcible humanitarian intervention.

Key points

- Non-forcible humanitarian intervention is characterized by the pacific activities of states, international organizations, NGOs, and INGOs in the global humanitarian community.

- INGOs and NGOs have succeeded in broadening the humanitarian agenda to include issues of development, the environment, and women' rights.

- Dominant Western political and economic elites encourage a crisis management approach to complex humanitarian emergencies that does nothing to tackle the underlying causes of these emergencies.

- Humanitarian crises like Somalia and Rwanda are the tip of the iceberg of human suffering. The slow death of millions through poverty and malnutrition are just as pressing cases for humanitarian intervention.

Conclusion

Humanitarian intervention remains a contested issue. Realism and Pluralism seek to interpret the cases we have discussed in this chapter as confirming their different theoretical positions. Realism purports to describe and explain the 'realities' of statecraft but the problem with this claim to objectivity is that it is the Realist mind-set that has constructed the very practices that Realist theory seeks to explain. Realism identifies some important objections to the practice of humanitarian intervention, but this chapter has argued that Pluralism is essential to any understanding of why the society of states has proven so reluctant to legitimate humanitarian intervention. Pluralism produces the dominant practices of the society of states, which continue to privilege the principles of sovereignty and non-intervention over respect for human rights. But crucially, there is nothing natural or inevitable about this hierarchy between order and justice. Indeed, changing values and norms could lead to the growth of new Solidarist sentiments that produce a more just world order

This chapter is sympathetic to Solidarism but the latter is a muted voice in contemporary global politics. Solidarism relies on states acting as trustees of common humanity, but what emerges from a study of state practice in the 1990s is that it is not states but global civil society that is the principal agent promoting humanitarian values in global politics.

Globalization is bringing nearer Kant's vision of moral interconnectedness, but as the Rwandan genocide so brutally demonstrates, this growth in 'cosmopolitan moral awareness' has not yet been translated into the Solidarist project of forcible humanitarian intervention. Western publics living in the relatively secure sphere of global politics are increasingly sensitized to the human suffering of others, but this media-nurtured sense of compassion is very selective in its response to human suffering. The media spotlight ensured that governments directed their humanitarian energies to the crises in northern Iraq, Somalia, and Bosnia, but during the same period millions perished in the brutal civil wars in Angola, Liberia, and the Democratic Republic of the Congo.

A growing consciousness of common humanity permeates the emerging global civil society, but how can this society best promote humanitarianism? Is forcible humanitarian intervention sometimes the only way to respond to massive human rights abuses? Or is the use of violence to stop even greater violence a strategy that can only result in a spiral of bloodletting to the detriment of humanitarian goals? Each case has to be judged on its merits but as the example of Somalia, and perhaps Kosovo, demonstrate, interventions that begin with humanitarian credentials can all too easily degenerate into 'a range of policies and activities which go beyond, or even conflict with, the label "humanitarian" ' (Roberts 1993: 448). A further fundamental problem with armed intervention concerns the so-called 'body-bag' factor. Is domestic public opinion, especially in Western states, prepared to see their military personnel die in the cause of humanitarian intervention? The USA withdrew from Somalia after the killing of 18 US Rangers, and its refusal to put American forces in harm's way to save Rwandans, demonstrates that the world's most powerful liberal state is not prepared to pay the human costs to save others. Indeed, a striking feature of all post-cold war humanitarian interventions is that no Western Government has risked its military personnel in situations where it believed there was a high risk of casualties.

The security concerns following the attacks of 11 September 2001, which motivated the US-led interventions in Afghanistan and Iraq, have increased the likelihood that Western states will risk their own soldiers if it can be shown that specific failed states are a breeding ground for international terrorism. How far this leads to greater protection for civilians in these states depends upon whether intervening forces are successful in tailoring military means to the effective promotion of humanitarian values. If intervention is primarily driven by the logic of the war on terror, the worry is that it will only occur in those humanitarian crises which directly impact on this. The other lesson from both Afghanistan and Iraq is that if intervention does take place, the effective protection of human rights requires a long-term military, political, and economic commitment by the international community.

This chapter has examined the case for non-forcible humanitarian intervention, which, it has been argued, is a progressive manifestation of the globalization of world politics. The actors in this drama are frequently not states and the means employed are always non-violent. This type of intervention spans a continuum ranging from humanitarian crisis management to crisis prevention, and connects the subject of humanitarian intervention to broader issues of conflict resolution and the role of third-party mediation. The unresolved question here concerns the issue of how far forcible intervention might have an important role to play in stimulating and supporting processes of conflict resolution in complex humanitarian emergencies. Beyond this, the non-forcible approach to humanitarian intervention opens up the normative question of what counts as human suffering at the end of the twentieth century. The 'loud emergencies' of genocide, ethnic cleansing, and famine receive media attention, and command the limited resources of the international donor community. This conception of humanitarianism is not rooted in objective facts; instead, it is the product of globally dominant beliefs and values which privilege the 'loud emergencies' and exclude the 'silent emergency' of slow death through poverty and malnutrition. The question for the future is why the eradication of global poverty is not as urgent a subject for humanitarian intervention as the deaths of those killed by men in uniform with machine guns. If humanitarianism is what we have made of it, we do not have to make it like this in our global future.

For further information and case studies on this subject, please visit the companion web site at www.oup.com/uk/booksites/politics.

4   Should considerations of international order always be privileged over concerns of individual justice in the society of states?

5   Why has the society of states failed to arrive at a collective consensus on what principles should underpin a right of humanitarian intervention?

6   Does the illegitimacy of humanitarian intervention in cold war state practice support the theoretical arguments of Realism or Pluralism?

7   Does a study of post-cold war state practice support the contention that there is a new developing norm of humanitarian intervention?

8   How far is military force an effective instrument for the promotion of humanitarian values?

9   What are the strengths and weaknesses of a strategy of non-forcible humanitarian intervention?

10   Has the 'war on terror' made it less likely that powerful states will use their armed forces to 'save strangers'?

11   Does the reliance on humanitarian rationales to justify the interventions in Afghanistan and Iraq discredit the claims for a new norm of humanitarian intervention in international society?

12   Are prevalent conceptions of humanitarianism infused with the ideological biases and cultural preferences of the dominant Western states?

GUIDE TO FURTHER READING

Wheeler, N. J. (2000), *Saving Strangers: Humanitarian Intervention in International Society* (Oxford: Oxford University Press). Offers a new way of evaluating humanitarian interventions and considers a wide range of interventions in the cold war and post-cold war eras.

Chesterman, S. (2001), *Just War or Just Peace: Humanitarian Intervention in International Law* (Oxford: Oxford University Press). An excellent analysis of the legality of humanitarian intervention which strongly supports a 'restrictionist' view.

Holzgrefe, J. F., and Keohane, R. (eds) (2002), *Humanitarian Intervention: Ethical, Legal and Political Dilemmas* (Cambridge: Cambridge University Press). A superb edited collection that explores the practice of humanitarian intervention from the perspectives of moral philosophy, international law, and political practice.

Welsh, Jennifer (ed.) (2004), *Humanitarian Intervention in International Relations Theory* (Oxford: Oxford University Press). Another first-rate edited volume which brings together International Relations theorists and practitioners who have been involved in interventions during the past decade.

Ramsbotham, O., and Woodhouse, T. (1996), *Humanitarian Intervention in Contemporary Conflict* (Cambridge: Polity Press). Presents a powerful case for broadening humanitarian intervention to include non-forcible approaches. Also contains very good case study material on Bosnia and Somalia.

WEB LINKS

www.un.org The official web site of the United Nations. Includes links to all the UN's major institutions and agencies concerned with humanitarian invention, including the Security Council and UNHCR.

www.nato.int/kosovo NATO web site containing information on Operation Allied Force and the subsequent KFOR operation.

www.fco.gov.uk Home page of the British Foreign Office, containing speeches and briefing papers on the concept and practice of humanitarian intervention.

www.hrw.org Home page of Human Rights Watch. Provides detailed human rights reports for around 100 states and up-to-date reports on the human rights implications of current interventions.

www.amnesty.org.uk Provides details of Amnesty International's work and includes press briefings and links to detailed human rights reports.

www/isn.ethz.ch Vast archive on all aspects of security and intervention, including many links to institutes working in the field.

www.osce.org Home page of the Organization for Security and Co-operation in Europe (OSCE), which has been at the forefront of several interventions in Europe and Central Asia.

www.usip.org United States Institute for Peace. Research institute carrying out a lot of work in this area.

www.crisisweb.org Home page of the International Crisis Group, a liberal advocacy group working throughout Africa and south-east Europe.

NOTES

1. The term is Eduardo Rabossi's and was discussed by Richard Rorty in his 1993 Amnesty International lecture, 'Sentimentality and Human Rights' (Rorty 1993).

2. The term is Stanley Hoffmann's (Hoffman 1995–6: 31).

3. We are following Tim Dunne and Brian Schmidt in this volume in conceptualizing statism as one of the common elements which make up the core of Realism in world politics. They identify self-help and survival as the other two. For the purposes of this chapter, we define **statism** as the belief that states only have duties to their own citizens, and that they should not risk their soldiers' lives on humanitarian crusades.

4. The term Pluralism here should not be confused with the idea of Pluralism found in the literature on interdependence and transnationalism (see Ch.8). Bull first used this term to refer to the debate within the international society tradition in his chapter 'The Grotian conception of international society' (Bull 1996).

CHAPTER 26

European integration and regional cooperation

THOMAS CHRISTIANSEN

READER'S GUIDE

This chapter discusses the dynamics of regional integration, with a special focus on the European Union. Charting the integration process from the beginnings in the post-war period, it distinguishes between supranational and intergovernmental features of the European Union. The rationale of European integration is viewed in the context of globalization and differing interpretations of the nature of the European response to it. A further section looks beyond Europe to the efforts of regional cooperation in Asia, Africa, and the Americas and contrasts these developments with the more firmly institutionalized process of integration in Europe. The EU emerges as a post-sovereign polity that, despite its imperfections, has firmly established a new form of governance at an intermediate level between the global and the state.

Introduction

Since the Second World War, global politics have witnessed the emergence of a new political phenomenon: the cooperation and integration of states on 'regional'—meaning continental—scale. The prime example among these regional groupings is the European Union (EU), but all over the globe states seek to institutionalize cooperation in different ways. The EU is a particular case in this respect not so much because it came first, but because it has gone furthest in terms of the powers transferred from its member states to the central institutions. Regional alliances of states elsewhere are still essentially about *cooperation* among states rather than, as in Europe their *integration* and the resultant creation of a new polity. While observing the global phenomenon of regional cooperation it is important, therefore, to emphasize the similarities as well as the differences between individual cases. Either way this process throws up interesting and to some extent fundamental questions about the nature of inter-state politics in the twenty-first century. To what extent are states willing to submit themselves to systems of collective rule? What are the dynamics that explain the emergence and evolution of regional blocs? And what relationship do processes of regional integration and cooperation have with the wider phenomenon of globalization? This chapter addresses these and related questions, first looking at the evolution of the European Union, the workings of its main institutions, and its relationship with the member states as well as with the wider world. Separate sections will then look at the relationship between the processes of integration and globalization and the emergence of regional cooperation in other parts of the globe.

Box 26.1	**Key concepts**

Regionalism: development of institutionalized cooperation among states and other actors on the basis of regional contiguity as a feature of global politics.

Integration: creation of a new polity bringing together a number of different constituent parts (member states).

Intergovernmentalism: concept in integration theory that indicates that states remain in control of the process and that common institutions merely facilitate decisionmaking among state representatives.

Supranationalism: concept in integration theory that implies the creation of common institutions having independent decisionmaking authority and thus the ability to impose certain decisions and rules on member states.

Cooperation: Regular and sustained interaction among states on one or more policy issues, possibly leading to and making use of common institutions set up to facilitate deepening of such exchanges.

Spillover: concept developed in neo-functionalist integration theory, indicating that there is integration 'spillover' from one policy area to the next, due to the functional logic and/or the transfer of political loyalties among the policymakers involved.

Bargaining: mode of interaction in intergovernmental meetings when the search for compromise is based on the representation of interests rather than the search for solutions to a particular problem.

Negotiation: mode of interaction across longer periods of time, allowing for problem-solving and learning among participants.

European integration: from international treaty to constitutional polity

In the course of a process of regional integration, the EU has gradually become an important factor in the domestic affairs of states as well as in the relations between them. It was founded through a series of

Box 26.2	Current and prospective member states of the European Union

Member states of the EU (year of accession)	Candidate countries negotiating or seeking to negotiate entry to the EU	Countries participating in the Stability Pact for South-Eastern Europe[a]	Non-member states with strong bilateral or multilateral links with the EU[b]
• Austria (1995)	• Bulgaria	• Bosnia and Hercegovina	• Iceland
• Cyprus (2004)	• Croatia	• Serbia and Montenegro	• Norway
• Czech Republic (2004)	• Romania	• Macedonia	• Switzerland
• Belgium (1953)	• Turkey[c]	• Albania	
• Denmark (1973)			
• Estonia (2004)			
• Finland (1995)			
• France (1953)			
• Germany (1953)			
• Greece (1981)			
• Hungary (2004)			
• Ireland (1973)			
• Italy (1952)			
• Latvia (2004)			
• Lithuania (2004)			
• Luxembourg (1953)			
• Malta (2004)			
• Netherlands (1953)			
• Poland (2004)			
• Portugal (1986)			
• Slovakia (2004)			
• Slovenia (2004)			
• Spain (1986)			
• Sweden (1995)			
• United Kingdom (1973)			

[a] The Stability Pact, launched in June 1999 in the wake of the Kosovo conflict, contains not only the promise of financial and economic assistance from the EU for the region, but also the prospect of eventual EU membership for the participating countries.
[b] Norway and Iceland are, together with the EU member states, participants in the European Economic Area (EEA) which provides for special access to the EU's Single European Market. After a negative referendum on the issue, Switzerland decided not to participate in the EEA, but instead maintains strong bilateral links with the EU.
[c] Turkey's application for EU membership was accepted in 1999, but—in contrast to Bulgaria and Romania—accession negotiations have not yet begun as the EU is monitoring internal reforms in Turkey. A date for the start of negotiations may be set at the end of 2004.

international treaties among the 'original Six' member states, but has since expanded to include most of the European continent (see Box 26.2). There were numerous influences leading to the creation of this nucleus of supranational governance: the condition of physical, economic, and social devastation in post-war Europe, the ambitions for a federal Europe developed during the war, often within the ideology of resistance movements, the division of Europe in the course of the cold war, the desire among Western powers, especially the USA, to strengthen Western Europe politically and economically. The most visible driving force at the time, and for most of the EU's history, has been the reconciliation between France and Germany, of which European integration has been both a consequence and a guarantee.

Initially responsible for the regulation of specific sectors of the economy (coal, steel, agriculture), over time the European institutions have been entrusted with responsibility over an ever-increasing range of tasks. At the end of the twentieth century, these included monetary policy, the protection of human rights, and coordination in foreign policy and military security, thus encroaching on what many regard as the core of state sovereignty

In line with its growing role in economic and social regulation in Western Europe has come a greater weight in international affairs for the EU. The EU's power to negotiate external trade agreements went hand in hand with the establishment of a customs union in the 1960s. But in the 1970s came the first attempts to cooperate in foreign policy matters for the member states—an ambition that was upgraded to a 'Common Foreign and Security Policy' of the Union in the 1992 Maastricht Treaty. The same treaty also contained plans for a single European currency—the euro—that was launched at the beginning of 1999.

Since the end of the cold war the perspectives for European integration have changed fundamentally. With the Iron Curtain gone, an originally *Western* European project has received a pan-European dimension. Central and East European states, as well as Malta and Cyprus, joined the EU in 2004, and the resulting challenges of a 'wider European Union' has raised fundamental questions about the nature and direction of the integration process. The 'Eastern

Enlargement' has generally been seen as a qualitative leap for the EU, promising—or threatening as the view may be—to transform it. Concerns that the enlarged Union, if not reformed substantially, would find it difficult to take decisions and maintain a reliable legal framework led to several attempts to reform the treaties. The most wide-ranging proposals, and the most significant step-change in the language of integration, came with the Treaty for a Constitution of the European Union which was signed by EU Heads of State in 2004. This Constitutional Treaty, if ratified within each state (in many cases involving referenda), would be a recognition of how far the EU has developed from its modest beginnings as a small international organization While not a constitution as commonly understood, it would symbolize the degree to which member states and the peoples of Europe have accepted that they are part of a constitutional polity with shared rules and norms. But it is precisely this symbolic power of a 'European constitution' that may also make adoption and ratification difficult, and the original idea to ensure such key reforms *before* the enlargement to 25 member states has clearly not

---

Box 26.3   Aspects of gradualism in the process of European integration

- **Gradual expansion of competences:** the sectoral responsibilities of common institutions are gradually expanded to include ever-wider areas of socio-economic and political life.

- **Gradual expansion of membership:** rather than depending on a wider membership, the underlying dynamic has been for a smaller number of countries to forge ahead and be joined subsequently by new member states.

- **Gradual expansion of majority vote:** over time, an increasing number of decisions can be taken by 'qualified majority vote', i.e. national governments have agreed to give up their veto in more and more areas of policymaking.

- **Gradual expansion of parliamentary powers:** in line with national governments losing their veto, the European Parliament has acquired greater powers to scrutinize institutions and pass legislation.

been achieved. Thus, the EU finds itself, as often in its history, having to strike a balance between the lengthy search for compromise and the continuing pursuit of great ambitions for the future. The estab-

lished path of a succession of a gradual development rather than big leaps is therefore likely to continue (see Box 26.3).

Key points

- The Second World War and its aftermath provided much impetus for a change in the nature of relations between the European states.

- Sectoral integration, driven by a smaller core of six countries, led to the creation of the European Communities.

- Powers and competences of the European institutions were gradually expanded in a move from economic to political integration.

- In line with enlargement to a membership of 25 or more countries in the first decade of the twenty-first century, the EU has embarked on an ambitious process of constitutionalization.

Conceptualizing European integration

Emphasizing the gradual nature of the integration process allows us to distinguish between two different processes at work in the course of integration: the first of these is the reform of the treaties which first established the European Union ('Paris Treaty', 'Rome Treaties') or subsequently reformed it ('Single European Act', 'Maastricht Treaty', 'Amsterdam Treaty', 'Nice Treaty', 'Constitutional Treaty') (see Box 26.4). These are the result of **Inter-governmental Conferences** (IGC), where representatives of national governments negotiate the legal framework within which the EU institutions operate. These treaty changes require ratification in each of the member states in order to come into force and—because of the significance of achieving agreement among all member states on what have usually been substantial reforms—can be considered as the 'grand bargains' in the evolution of the EU (Moravcsik 1993).

Within the framework of these treaties, which are referred to as the Union's 'primary legislation', a number of institutions operate that have more specific tasks and possess a degree of autonomy from the member states (see Box 26.5). They are responsible for running the day-to-day affairs of the Union, developing public policies, deciding on the annual

budget, and passing 'secondary' legislation such as EU directives and regulations (Wincott 1995).

It is important to recognize that the dynamics of decisionmaking differ significantly between the arenas of treaty reform and policymaking. Supranational institutions may have considerable autonomy in running the day-to-day affairs of the Union, but decisions about treaty change or substantial institutional reforms are dominated by national governments. In this respect, the existence of the **national** veto often leads to difficult and lengthy negotiations. The message here is that, in seeking to understand the integration process, we need to take account of the role played by both member states and supranational institutions. And **member states** are not just represented by national governments, as a host of state, non-state, and transnational actors participate in processes of domestic preference formation or in direct representation of interest in Brussels (Greenwood 1998). The relative openness of the European policy process means that political groups or economic interests will try and influence EU decisionmaking if they feel that their position is not sufficiently represented by national governments. That is one reason why the EU is increasingly seen as a system of multilevel

Box 26.4	Important agreements in the history of the European Union

Year	Treaty	Main subjects
1952	Paris Treaty	Regulation of coal and steel production in the member states, creation of supranational institutions.
1957	Rome Treaties	Plans for a common market and a customs union, agreement on the removal of all industrial tariffs on internal trade.
1985	Single European Act	Removal of all non-tariff barriers to the mobility of persons, goods, services, and capital (the '1992 programme'); foreign policy cooperation included in the treaty provisions.
1992	Maastricht Treaty	Economic and monetary union (the euro), political union (incl. change of name from; European Community to European Union), justice and home affairs included in the pillar structure of the EU treaties established.
1997	Amsterdam Treaty	Various institutional reforms, High Representative for CFSP, provisions for enhanced cooperation.
2000	Nice Treaty	Reform of Commission and Council (voting weights), expansion of majority voting; European Charter of Fundamental Rights.
2004	Constitutional Treaty	Simplification of the treaties, incorporation of the Fundamental Rights Charter, creation of the post of President of the Council and EU Foreign Minister.

governance, involving a plurality of actors on different territorial levels: supranational, national, and subnational (Marks *et al.* 1996*a*).

One therefore needs to be clear about the issue one is talking about: whether, for example, it is possible to claim that the EU is 'imposing' a decision or a policy on a member state, or whether, on the other hand, a member state may be able to 'block' a decision, crucially depends on the decisionmaking mechanism that is applicable in any given situation. The EU possesses a very complex institutional machinery, and general answers to such questions are not very meaningful.

This complexity, together with continuous change over time, has spawned a lively debate among integration theorists. Among the contributions to this debate are a variety of approaches (Rosamond 2000; Wiener and Diez 2004), some of which are applications of more general theories of International Relations: the literature on both Realism and interdependence has contributed to theorizing of integration (see Ch.9). Other scholars have regarded the European Union as *sui generis*—in a category of its own—and therefore in need of the development of dedicated theories of integration. The most prominent among these has been neo-functionalism, which sought to explain the evolution of integration in terms of spillover from one sector to another as resources and loyalties of elites where being transferred to the European level (Haas 1958; Schmitter 2004). More recently, as aspects of EU politics have come to resemble the domestic politics of states, scholars have turned to approaches drawn from Comparative Politics (Hix 1994).

However, while there have been these and other theoretical debates, it has been the exchange between 'supranational' and 'intergovernmental' approaches which has had the greatest impact on the study of European integration. **Supranational approaches** regard the emergence of supranational institutions in Europe as a distinct feature and turn these into the main object of analysis. Here, the politics *above* the level of states are regarded as the most significant, and consequently the political actors, institutions at the European level, receive most attention (see Box 26.6). **Intergovernmentalist approaches**, on the other hand, continue to regard states as the most important aspect of the

| Box 26.5 | Institutions of the European Union |

EU institutions	Responsibilities	Location
European Commission	Initiating, administering, and overseeing the implementation of EU policies and legislation	Brussels and Luxembourg
European Parliament (EP)	Directly elected representatives of EU citizens, scrutinizing the operation of the other institutions, and, in certain areas, sharing with the Council the power to determine EU legislation	Strasbourg (plenary sessions); Brussels (MEP offices, committee meetings and some plenary sessions); Luxembourg (administration)
Council of Ministers	Representing the views of national governments and determining, in many areas jointly with the EP, the ultimate shape of EU legislation	Brussels (some meetings in Luxembourg)
European Council	Regular summits of Heads of State and Government, setting the EU's broad agenda and a forum of last resort to find agreement on divisive issues (NB: different from the Council of Europe)	City in the member state holding the presidency
European Court of Justice	The EU's highest court, ruling in disputes on matters of EU law between member states and EU institutions, as well as providing preliminary rulings on request from national courts in cases involving private persons	Luxembourg
European Central Bank	Central bank responsible for setting the interest rates and controlling the money supply of the single European currency, the euro	Frankfurt am Main
Committee of the Regions	Advisory committee of 317 members representing the interests of local and regional authorities in the EU	Brussels
Economic and Social	Advisory committee of 317 members representing the interests of labour, employers, and consumer organizations in the EU	Brussels
Court of Auditors	The EU's audit office, responsible for auditing the revenues and the expenditure under the EU budget	Luxembourg

integration process and consequently concentrate on the study of politics *between* and *within* states (see Box 26.7). But whatever one's theoretical preferences, most scholars would agree that no analysis of the EU is complete without studying both the oper-

ation and evolution of the central institutions and the input from political actors in the member states.

More recently, debate in EU studies has also centred on a wider fault-line in the social sciences:

Box 26.6 | **Key arguments of supranational approaches to European integration**

- Integration as a gradual process.

- Supranational institutions are political actors in their own right.

- Emergence of a new polity above the level of the state.

- Integration process is to some extent driven by institutional dynamics.

- Supranational laws provide constraints for member states.

Box 26.7 | **Key arguments of intergovernmentalist approaches to European integration**

- Integration as a series of 'bargains' among states.

- Supranational institutions assist and facilitate negotiations among states.

- EU as the framework for the execution of inter-state politics by different means.

- Bargains reflect national interests of the member states.

- Supranational laws reflect the interests of powerful states.

---

the difference between **rationalist and Constructivist approaches**. Constructivists have challenged the implicit rationalism of much of the mainstream of integration research until the 1990s. Their critique focused on the tendency of rationalist studies to privilege decisionmaking over agenda-setting, and outcomes over process. The Social Constructivist research agenda instead concentrates on the framing of issues *before* decisions about them are made, and therefore emphasizes the role of ideas, discourses, and social interaction in shaping interests (Christiansen, Jørgensen, and Wiener 2001). One prominent example of Constructivist analysis of European integration is the 'puzzle' of the EU eastward enlargement: in terms of rational calculation of interests it is hard to explain why 15 relatively wealthy West European states would invite 10 new

members to join their 'club', to share power and receive substantial financial transfers. However, as Constructivists have sought to show, the discourse of a 'promise' by the EU to the countries of Central and Eastern Europe became a structural constraint that made it difficult, if not impossible, to propose anything other than full EU membership to these countries (Risse 2004; Fierke and Wiener 2001). Rationalists in turn have criticized the apparent inability or unwillingness of Constructivists to provide specific hypotheses and to submit these to empirical tests (Moravcsik 2001). At the same time, an explicitly rationalist research programme, often making use of quantitative methods, has developed and established itself, not least through the journal *European Union Politics*. One area in which quantitative methods have been used extensively is that of roll-call analysis in the European Parliament and voting models in the Council of Ministers.

These developments in integration theory demonstrate that the EU continues to provide interesting and enduring conceptual challenges, and that an ever-greater number of scholars is willing to take them up. The result is a rich menu of theoretical approaches and conceptual tools which are on offer to those who seek to engage systematically with the study of European integration.

Key points

- The development of integration theory originated as a branch of International Relations.

- Key debates in integration theory are between supranationalists, emphasizing the role of central institutions, and intergovernmentalists, arguing for the continued relevance of states, their resources, and processes of domestic preference formation.

- Contending approaches emphasize different aspects of the integration process. Important distinctions in their focus are: institutional dynamics/state preferences; policymaking/treaty reform; long-term/short-term developments; ideas/interests; and process/events and outcomes.

- Greater theoretical Pluralism, moving beyond the established debate, has developed from the late 1990s onwards.

The global context to European integration

The early phase of European integration developed in the context of the cold war. Encouragement from the United States, the need to strengthen economic defences against a perceived Soviet threat, and the desire among some European countries to give some weight to European views in the emerging bipolar world all contributed to the speed of developments in that early phase of integration. In the same vein, external developments have been regarded as partially responsible for the **Eurosclerosis** of the 1970s and early 1980s: as successive oil crises led to economic recession in Europe, there was retrenchment within national boundaries. Keeping the integration project moving in the face of minimal or even negative economic growth became difficult, and thus the external environment has had a negative impact on the process.

The more recent phase of integration has occurred against the backdrop of globalization. Three dynamics of globalization, in particular, have been mirrored by developments in the EU. **First**, in terms of economic governance, European integration has fed on, and contributed to, the global trend towards neo-liberal economic policy, with its emphasis on liberal trade, low inflation, **deregulation**, and tight fiscal budgets. To the extent to which this has shifted power from states to markets, the trend of 'marketization' is clearly visible in the EU. **Second**, the trend towards greater social and cultural exchange across national borders has also intensified in the European Union. Common policies and institutions in Europe are specifically designed to enhance possibilities of **greater mobility** across national borders, adding to secular trends on the global scale. As a matter of course, political parties, local and regional authorities, social movements, interest groups, and non-governmental organizations (NGOs) are now active, alongside national governments and supranational institutions, on a European scale. One example of how European integration has contributed to this trend is in the area of higher education where both teaching (through the successful Socrates student exchange programme) and research (through funding in the form of a series of large-scale 'framework' programmes) has received a European dimension. Here we have existing transnational trends that the EU has fed into rather than causing them. **Third**, despite the creation of an integrated market and the growth of trans-border economic, social, and cultural exchange, the development of a transnational civil society has been limited by factors such as, for example, the diversity of languages. At the mass level, national and regional identities continue to take precedence over any emerging European identity. This lack of identification—the absence of European *demos*—and the institutional limitations of the European Union hamper the democratization of supranational governance.

In the academic literature, attention has been drawn to the dual nature of the relationship between integration and globalization—with the EU acting both as a shelter from, and as an accelerator of, global processes (Wallace 2000). In the wider political and public debate, however, one or the other side of these aspects is being emphasized. In this respect, two very different interpretations of this interaction are on offer: European integration is regarded either as an expression of turbo-charged globalization or as a protective shield against the negative 'fall-out' from globalization. The following sections reproduce some of the arguments of this political debate, emphasizing that in their political interpretations observers often come to contrasting conclusions in their assessment of the integration process.

Integration as turbo-charged globalization?

In this perspective, the EU is little more than the local variant of the kind of the global trends mentioned above. If anything, globalization is being accelerated by the policies of the European Union. **Multinational corporations** benefit from the improved access to markets, and there is a general trend towards greater concentration of economic power in certain regions and large firms. States are abdicating their traditional welfare responsibilities in order to satisfy the demands of efficiency and price stability imposed by the single market and single currency. Supranational institutions have little to put in place instead, and the trend is towards an unevenly regulated market-place. The development of a supranational legal order is based on the needs of economic integration, not the result of an explicit programme of political integration.

In the EU, there may be efforts to establish transnational social policies, citizenship rights, and environmental protection, but such attempts have been haphazard and have remained secondary to the overarching aim of market liberalization. The latter, on the other hand, has been more effective and more far-reaching than elsewhere. Within the EU, capital mobility and market access are hardly different from those within the nation-state, and as a result there are ever greater competitive pressures for firms as well as for public authorities.

In the face of the dynamic effects of economic integration, the political process at the European level remains imperfect. Supranational institutions have not been given effective tools to regulate economic exchange, as national governments and political parties maintain increasingly symbolic debates about the protection of 'national sovereignty'. Even to the extent to which these institutions can act, they are far removed from the citizens they are supposed to serve. Given the limitations alluded to earlier, the democratic process at the European level is hardly effective: EU decisionmaking lacks transparency, is complex and difficult to communicate, and as a result there is hardly any transnational debate on the priorities of European governance. The political process may function well at the national level—though even that is frequently questioned—but the setting of domestic preferences is hollowed out as individual countries have lost the capacity to act unilaterally.

Those who want to see political responses to these trends are faced with a dilemma: a more efficient EU with greater decisionmaking capacity and better able to respond to the challenges of globalization, is likely to be more centralized and even less responsive to the preferences of citizens and elected governments. Yet the 're-nationalization' of economic policymaking at the national level, where voters could directly register their influence, risks reducing the effectiveness of political authority over internationalized markets even further. Nevertheless, the voters in countries such as Norway and Switzerland, who have opted to remain outside the EU, believe that the loss of autonomy implied by European integration is greater than the political control over the process gained by membership. The same logic applies to the choice of the UK, Denmark, and Sweden to remain outside the single currency when this was launched in 1999: as with many other policies of the EU, the euro is regarded as a reduction of national options in economic and fiscal policy and as being, not so much a European solution to the problems caused by globalization, as a further, even more damaging variety of these pressures (see Box 26.8).

Integration as protection against globalization?

Yet the advocates of the single currency, and of European integration generally, advertise it as precisely the opposite. In their view, integration provides nation-states and electorates in Europe with a mechanism to confront the challenges of globalization. There may be a dynamic process of economic integration, but the EU provides an institutional response to regulate this. Ultimately, the transnational market is regulated and political control is exercised, through the collaboration of supranational institutions and national governments (see Ch.10). Individual citizens may have less influence on this process than they have on the traditional political process, but—as in the case of the move democratic theory made from the city-state to the nation-state—direct participation and representation must give way to the enhanced effectiveness of a greater polity (Dahl 1994).

Though uneven, there is the growth of such a supranational polity. Its development may have been led by the market, but eventually an effective legal order, a system of political rights and duties, and a political community have been established. Both states and firms are now subject to rules and regulations that go much further than anything that is available at the global scale. Indeed, global

Box 26.8   Case study: economic and monetary union and the euro

A long-standing and fundamental aim of the EU has been the removal of all barriers to the movement of goods, services, and capital between its member states. But the more tariff and non-tariff barriers were being dismantled in the 1960s, 1970s, and 1980s, the more the significance of fluctuating exchange rates in affecting intra-EU trade became evident. Flexible exchange rates produce uncertainty about the future cost of foreign supplies, the price of exported goods, and the return on foreign direct investment (FDI), and this in turn acts as a major disincentive to trade and FDI—and therefore as a hidden barrier to trade in the EU.

In response to these problems, some European countries had begun in the 1970s to search for greater exchange rate stability. The European Monetary System—the EMS—was an agreement among participating central banks to ensure that their currencies would only fluctuate within certain bands. During the 1980s the EMS went some way to ameliorate the situation, but as the single market liberalized the movement of capital, it became increasingly difficult to maintain exchange rate stability based solely on agreements among central banks.

A first plan for a monetary union had already been launched in 1970, but had fallen victim to the economic turmoil that followed the wars in Vietnam and the Middle East. By the end of the 1980s, the EU was ready to try again. A committee chaired by Commission President Jacques Delors was set up in 1988 and delivered a report in the following year. This 'Delors Report', which envisaged the achievement of Economic and Monetary Union (EMU) in three stages, was accepted by the great majority of governments as the basis for an Intergovernmental Conference (IGC) which was launched in Rome in 1990.

The IGC resulted in the Maastricht Treaty and demonstrated that governments were willing to move ahead towards EMU and a single currency. Only the UK, later joined by Denmark and Sweden, opted out of this project and sought to maintain their own monetary policies, but agreed that the other member states could go ahead with the project, and utilize the EU institutions to do so. Despite some delays due to the problems of treaty ratification—in turn caused by substantial opposition to the project in some member states—and subsequent turbulence in the currency markets, the treaty was implemented, the exchange rates between participating currencies fixed, and the euro became a reality on 1 January 1999. Initially the euro was only a virtual currency used for bank transfers and electronic payments, but euro notes and coins began to circulate and to replace national currencies from January 2002.

The agreement at Maastricht is remarkable because monetary union is much more than a question of economic efficiency. The single currency does indeed provide greater certainty and transparency over prices within the single market, but it also incurs substantial 'political cost': by transferring monetary policy to a single European Central Bank (ECB), governments and national central banks not only accept the loss of important instruments of economic management, but in fact agree to run their economic and fiscal policies in a manner compliant with the 'stability criteria' set by the EU. This means that there are tight controls to ensure that state debt and public deficits are within the limits set by the EU—if states exceed these limits, they face reprimands and even fines from the European institutions.

The constraints imposed on states by the move to EMU have made the single currency highly controversial. One of these concerned the degree of independence of the ECB. The Maastricht Treaty, essentially exporting the German model of monetary policymaking, stipulated that the ECB must be sufficiently independent to pursue the aim of price stability without interference from governments. But both the independence of the ECB and the dominance of the price stability criterion in its decisionmaking have been contested, as some member states, in particular France, have sought an enhanced role for national governments in the setting of priorities. The weakness of the euro after its launch—having lost by mid-2000 as much as a third of its value against the dollar—was a further bone of contention, as governments and institutions appeared divided on how to respond: while some seemed to welcome the boost the weak euro gave to exports, others feared that it would result in a rise in inflation.

In the long term, what is bound to weigh heavier in the public debate is the political dimension of monetary union. For many critics and supporters alike the euro is not just a functional tool which may assist trade and investment. EMU, though often presented in purely economic terms, is also seen as a mechanism which either creates a political union, or necessitates the creation of one. There is an expectation that a single currency threatens the continuation of national economic, tax, and social policies. Many therefore regard the euro as a substantial loss of national sovereignty—a debate that is bound to continue for some time.

EMU exemplifies the underlying rationale of the wider integration project: the use of economic means towards political ends. Countries opting out of the euro have refused to pay this 'political price' in return for the expected

(continues)

Case study: economic and monetary union and the euro—continued

economic gains. There is an expectation that, as the economic and political cost of remaining outside the 'eurozone' grows, they may reconsider their position. But even among, and within, the countries committed to EMU, debates about the ultimate implications of creating a single currency have continued.

The single currency had been launched in the context of a favourable economic climate—more difficult economic conditions in the future are likely to provide more serious tests of the strength of the currency, the reliability of the decisionmaking procedures of EMU, and of its legitimacy in the public eye. In terms of its aims and methods, but also in terms of the difficult issues it raises, the euro is closely tied to the wider integration project. Monetary union therefore remains an opportunity as well as a challenge for the future development of the European Union.

---

environmental and social regulation receives much impetus from the political consensus among the EU member states.

European integration has also helped to provide a **counterweight** to the economic interests of the USA, the remaining superpower. It is difficult to see how individual states in Europe would respond to the demands for unregulated market access from US firms and the US Administration. The EU, on the other hand, has regularly resisted such demands, often couched in complaints about protectionism, whether in response to preferential market access for developing countries, concerns over health or environmental safety, or simply because of the economic interests of the member states. In multilateral negotiations, the EU has permitted member states substantially to increase their voice and thus extend their influence in the international trade regime. A 'success story' in this respect has been the EU's ability, in 2004, to get the USA to drop its increased steel tariffs, making use of the World Trade Organization's (WTO) dispute-settlement process.

Supranational institutions, though distant from the individual citizen, have spawned an impressive network of transnational interests. Commission and Parliament provide the focus for political as well as economic interest representation, and a culture of political debate (and occasional conflict) is emerging in the wider public. Depending on the degree of integration in specific sectors, this reaches further in some areas than in others: farmers have consistently presented their case in Brussels, but other professions, less affected by EU decisions, may not have as high a profile as farmers. Even without a shift in loyalties or identity, there are the beginnings of a political community—not on a general, Europe-wide scale, but in certain areas and around certain issues. The agreement, in June 2004, to adopt a Constitutional Treaty is both a sign of this process and a further stepping-stone towards greater 'political' union. Then again, the widespread scepticism as to whether the electorates in those member states where referenda will be held will ratify this document, indicates that at the wider level of the mass public a political community is still doubtful.

Key points

- The process of integration has interacted with, and received much impetus from, developments at the global level.

- The relationship between processes of globalization and integration is contested: some see integration as a regional expression of globalization, accelerating the transnational nature of markets and thus further disenfranchising states and societies.

- However, the EU can also be regarded as a mechanism through which states and societies regain a degree of control over markets and are able to address transborder issues such as environmental protection, health, migration, or international crime more effectively.

The global phenomenon of regional cooperation

The interaction between processes of globalization and efforts to integrate regional economies is not limited to Europe alone. In fact, there was a substantial increase in the regionally based institutionalized cooperation among states during the 1990s—to the extent that observers have termed this feature the **new regionalism** (Hettne, Inotai, and Sunkel 1999). This section will briefly scan developments in North America, Latin America, Asia, and Africa before comparing these to the experience of regional integration in Europe.

The critical point to be made at the outset of this discussion of the 'new regionalism' is the **dynamic relationship** between developments in different parts of the world. As countries in one continent agree to integrate their economies, creating free trade zones, customs unions, or more, the effects are felt elsewhere. Frequently, there has been a response 'in kind', i.e. the attempt to match the efforts of economic integration elsewhere. An important driving force for these processes has been the end of the cold war: the removal of superpower conflict with its repercussions in many parts of the world provided new opportunities for regions to cooperate in matters of trade and security (see Ch.6). Further impetus came from the EU, both purposefully— the EU has a history of establishing and institutionalizing links with other regional groupings (Edwards and Regelsberger 1990)—and unintentionally through the competitive pressures exerted by the Single European Market. In North America and in South-East Asia—regions which had been strongly competing with Western Europe in the preceding decade—there were concerns that the facilitation of easier market access within the European Community would lead to trade diversion and therefore be achieved at the expense of exports from overseas (Mattli 1999). This concern about the emergence of a **Fortress Europe** provided much of the impetus behind the dynamic development of the **North American Free Trade Agreement** (NAFTA), the **Association of South-East Asian States** (ASEAN), and **Asia Pacific Economic Co-operation** (APEC), respectively. Regional groupings

have also come to the fore in Latin America with the creation of **MERCOSUR** while in Africa there has been renewed dynamism with the transformation of the Organization of African Unity (OAU) into the **African Union**.

CWS

The case of regionalism which is most frequently compared to the European Union is NAFTA which brings together the economies of Canada, Mexico, and the United States. NAFTA was based on an initial free trade agreement between the USA and Canada which led, in 1992, to the conclusion of the wider, North American agreement including Mexico. It aims at abolishing barriers to the trade in goods and services between the three countries. To support this aim, the agreement provides for the progressive elimination of customs tariffs in many—though not all—areas of trade, and for a dispute-settlement mechanism to deal with cases where disagreements between the partners arise. There is a small secretariat consisting of national offices in the three capitals, but essentially the administration of the agreement relies on national ministers—meeting in the Free Trade Commission—or on their appointed representatives in more specialized working groups and committees. NAFTA, being concerned with trade matters, does not provide for collective action in other areas. There are provisions for dispute settlement, but they imply the setting of arbitration panels when individual cases are raised rather than a permanent court. An agreement on labour cooperation was signed by the three countries in 1993 in order to provide a 'social dimension' to NAFTA, but it explicitly affirms each party's right to set its own labour standards and essentially provides for cooperation and consultation between national authorities, the exchange of information, and the conduct of policy reviews rather than the setting of common standards for the region as a whole.

It is an important departure in global politics because it is the most far-reaching example of a regional cooperation project spanning the North–South divide. The diversity in the economic **structures** and levels of development between the participating countries makes the creation of a single free trade area among them a great challenge—one that was put to the test, in particular, when Mexico suffered a deep financial crisis in 1997 and had to rely on support from its larger neighbour. But NAFTA weathered the storm well—indeed it assisted the search for collaborative solutions to the crisis. NAFTA has led further proposals to conclude trade agreements also with the countries of South America (in particular the Free Trade Area of the Americas Treaty signed in Quebec City in 2001). The EU also engaged with the United States in a series of transatlantic agreements, most recently through the Transatlantic Economic Partnership which was agreed in 1998.

The desire to liberalize trade, engage in regular economic cooperation, and thus create a greater degree of stability has also fed into efforts in the Pacific area, where a total of 34 countries have come together to form APEC. Again under leadership from the USA, this highly diverse group of countries seeks to coordinate economic policies, reduce tariffs and duties, and enhance its negotiating position in global trade negotiations and within the WTO. There are annual summit meetings, but the more regular work is done in meetings of ministers and officials, coordinated by a secretariat based in Singapore. There is much emphasis on the role of **non-state actors**, especially business leaders, to contribute to APEC's goals of **enhancing trade**, **investment**, and a sense of **community** in the region. APEC's progress towards free trade has been severely limited, though, not only because of the great disparity among the economies of the region, but also because of the disturbances of the Asian financial crisis of the late 1990s (see Ch.10). At the same time, the inclusiveness of APEC as a regional forum has been useful in order to discuss political and security issues among its members.

In terms of effective regional cooperation in South-East Asia, ASEAN, an older organization with a more limited membership, has probably been more significant. It dates back to an agreement among Indonesia, Malaysia, Thailand, Singapore, and the Philippines in the 1960s, but after successive enlargements in the 1980s and 1990s it now comprises also Brunei, Vietnam, Laos, Burma/Myanmar, and Cambodia. This membership bringing together neo-liberal and authoritarian **tiger economies** on the one hand, and socialist **transition** economies, on the other, is still highly diverse. What weighs more than similarities in size, common economic ties, and shared environmental and social problems is the external environment. ASEAN is a useful caucus for its members to agree negotiating positions *vis-à-vis* the larger economies of China, Japan, and South Korea and—occasionally together with these three—the United States and the EU. Beyond trade, ASEAN serves as a useful forum to discuss security issues and, in the context of global debates about workers' and wider human rights issues, as the institutional support for arguments about 'Asian values'. But human rights, above all, have strained relations among members, given the continuing problems in Burma in this regard, and the resultant controversies surrounding its accession (see Ch.31).

In **Latin America**, again spurred by the developments in Europe and North America, there has also been renewed dynamism in regional efforts to integrate economies more closely. Projects dating back to the early 1960s to create a Latin American Free Trade Association in the South and a Central American Common Market in the centre of the hemisphere floundered in the 1970s as they went against the grain of economic trends and political relations among their members. But plans for a **Common Market of the South**—known as MERCOSUR, its Spanish acronym—took off in the mid-1990s.

The aim of the contracting states of Argentina, Brazil, Paraguay, and Uruguay is to progressively abolish tariff barriers, establish a common external tariff, and thus enhance trade and investment between their economies. As with its counterpart in the North, the institutional framework is very thin, relying only on intergovernmental mechanisms for decisionmaking. There are ambitious aims to move integration further via the coordination of member states' economic policies, but at the end of the 1990s—some five years after the original deadline—the customs union remained imperfect. Nevertheless, even these more modest advances have borne fruit, given that there have been substantial increases in the trade among MERCOSUR countries.

At the same time, the Rio Group has brought all the countries of South and Central America together in a looser framework. With an inclusive membership it has provided a forum for the exchange of views on a broad range of issues. These have included the search for peace and stability in the region, the fight against the drugs trade and against organized crime as well as more general economic cooperation. And just as the USA has sought to establish permanent cooperation with Latin America via the FTAA, the EU has institutionalized its relationships with Latin America through regular summits and ministerial meetings with both the MERCOSUR and the Rio Group countries.

In **Africa**, there had been a long history of cooperation in the context of the Organization of African Unity (OAU). It was an organization that reflected the common problems and ambitions of the African states during the process of decolonization. It did suffer, however, from the great heterogeneity of its membership and did not become an effective institution. In global trade negotiations

African states represented their common interests through other alliances such as the Group of 77, and intra-African economic cooperation has been organized on a smaller, geographical scale (e.g. the Economic Community of West African States or the South African Development Community). The OAU, left as an arena for essentially declaratory politics, exhibited unity with respect to some issues, for example the struggle against Apartheid in South Africa, but was generally a weak institution with little authority either over its own membership or *vis-à-vis* the rest of the world. It is difficult to see how the OAU's the transformation in 2000 into the **African Union** (AU) will change that—it appears to add further to the ambitions and expectations without the political will among member states to accept the constraints on their autonomy that would go with it. In setting up central institutions—e.g. the AU Commission and an African Court of Justice—the AU

Box 26.9	Differences between regional integration in Europe and regional cooperation in other continents

Parameters	Regional cooperation	European integration
Institutional characteristics	Reliance on purely intergovernmental forms of decisionmaking	Presence of autonomous supranational institutions that initiate and enforce common policies
Forms of decisionmaking	Consensual decisionmaking (i.e. states have veto over decisions)	Extensive use of qualified majority voting (i.e. states have no veto over decisions)
Degree of legal integration	Arbitration and dispute settlement of individual cases	Permanent court system developing a supranational legal order
Extent of political integration	Concentration on economic cooperation among states	Development of a political union with a system of economic, social, and political rights for citizens
Range of issues covered	Emphasis on trade, investment, and related economic issues	Expansion of competences into much wider areas (single currency environments, culture, etc.)
Presence of democratic procedures	Minimal, if any, involvement of parliaments	Establishment of a democratic process, based on a directly elected parliament
Foreign policy cooperation	Coordination of external relations limited to participation in multilateral trade negotiations	Development of a common foreign, security, and defence policy

appears to intend a step-change, but it remains to be seen what authority these organs will have in relation to the member states.

The organizations mentioned here are only the more prominent among the plethora of regional cooperation ventures across the world. In the context of a globalizing world, the end of the cold war, and frequent economic and political instability there is greater need, and greater incentives, for countries to cooperate on a regional basis. As trade and other economic issues have become more salient in global politics, states increasingly seek to ally themselves with like-minded and similarly structured partners, and these are often neighbouring countries with which there are already established trade patterns. Above all, a **domino effect** is at work: when countries in one region club together in order to pursue common economic interests, then other regions are bound to follow suit. This dynamic results from the need not only to counter the anticipated negative impact on the trade with other regions, but above all to maintain a strong voice in multilateral and global trade negotiations. Thus the negotiations in the Doha Round and the ongoing discussions within the WTO have strongly encouraged the instances of regionalism discussed here (Fawcett and Hurrell 1995).

As a result, the 1990s witnessed the growth of 'new regionalism'—regional organizations in all parts of the world forming an integral part of the process of globalization. As we have seen, there are several similarities between these efforts at regional cooperation, which warrants its recognition as a global phenomenon. On the other hand, there are important distinctions between the established integration process in Europe and the more recent developments elsewhere (see Box 26.9). In any case, it is apparent that the rise of regional cooperation in the context of globalization is not a paradox—indeed the two processes are closely related to one another (see Ch.33).

> ## Key points
>
> - Multilateral negotiations and global economic competition have provided powerful incentives for cooperation among states on a regional basis.
> - Efforts to establish free trade areas and customs unions in Asia and in North and South America received a boost during the 1990s.
> - On the whole, these forms of regionalism differ from European integration in only focusing on economic matters and relying on a very limited degree of institutionalization.

Conclusion

This chapter has illustrated the dynamics and dilemmas underlying the process of regional integration. In Europe, supranational institutions were created to oversee integration in a number of specific economic sectors. Gradually, their powers were extended, and ever-wider areas of economic and social regulation became the responsibility of the European Union. With growing membership and expanding competences, member states progressively gave up their veto over decisionmaking in order to ensure efficient governance. The EU now takes decisions on a wide range of issues of direct relevance to the wider public, but citizens are only indirectly, and imperfectly, empowered to influence

these. As a result, the legitimacy of the EU's institutional structure and of individual policies is fragile, and often under attack in the member states.

In other parts of the world, in particular in North America, South America, and Asia, there have also been intensifying efforts to cooperate on a regional basis. Here there has been more emphasis on encouraging free trade through progressive tariff reductions without the establishment of an extensive central bureaucracy. Economically, this method of regional cooperation has shown itself to be effective, though politically such ventures remain close to established forms of inter-state relations.

The EU, in contrast, has made considerable

advances towards the creation of a novel system of governance. This has been particularly effective in the economic realm, with a single market and a single currency creating a more competitive environment for business in Europe. Externally, economic integration has led to a common trade policy that has made the EU a key player in international trade negotiations. Political integration has somewhat lagged behind, and efforts at creating a common foreign and security policy have tended to promise more than they were able to deliver (see Ch.13).

Much of what happens in the course of European integration is specific to its time and place, but at the same time we have seen that the EU receives the same dynamic effects from globalization as regional cooperation elsewhere. But the **end of sovereignty**, heralded by globalization, is more pronounced in the EU, where supranational institutions and national governments share political authority, and where market forces play an important role in the setting of standards and regulations. Yet while unilateral action has become all but unthinkable, **states are not at all withering away**. States continue to be an elementary part of the system, with much scope for affecting decisions and regulating their own affairs. Crucially, it is, on the whole, *within* states that electorates seek redress, citizens exercise their rights, and communities share their identity—in this respect the EU constitutes an addition to, not a replacement of, the nation-state.

Regional integration, more so than globalization, raises questions about transnational democracy, and the development of the European Parliament and the growth of transnational interest representation in Brussels demonstrate both the possibilities, and the limitations, of democracy beyond the nation-state (see Ch.32). Most importantly, in the shadow of the often difficult institutional development of the EU, social and economic mobility has increased substantially, transforming the nature of the regional economy and the way it is regulated. But this transformation has affected different countries, and different segments of society, unevenly. As a growing number of decisions affecting societies are taken on the European level, the tension between common rules and national diversity is bound to grow, something that will be further exacerbated following the accession of 25 new member states from Central and Eastern Europe in 2004.

Regional integration will continue to face such tensions and dilemmas. This has already led to greater flexibility, with some agreements applying only to some countries, or individual countries opting out of common policies. As the EU grows, such flexibility will become more important in order to allow the entire organization to function, but it will also make the institutional structure even more complex.

For further information and case studies on this subject, please visit the companion web site at www.oup.com/uk/booksites/politics.

CWS

QUESTIONS

1   What have been the driving forces behind the process of European integration?

2   What are the main differences between supranationalist and intergovernmentalist approaches to the study of the EU?

3   What role do the supranational institutions play in the European policy process?

4   In which ways can member states influence decisionmaking in the EU?

5   How effective has the EU been in the handling of its external affairs?

6   Has European integration improved or hindered the capacity of member states to respond to the challenges of globalization?

7   What are the main differences and similarities between the European integration and regional cooperation in other parts of the world?

8   What are the dynamics behind the 'new regionalism'?

9   What are the main challenges the EU has to face in the coming years?

10   What impact do processes of regional integration and cooperation hold for the future of the Westphalian state?

GUIDE TO FURTHER READING

Armstrong, K., and Bulmer, S. (1997), *The Governance of the Single European Market* (Manchester: Manchester University Press). Provides a thorough, theoretically grounded analysis of the way in which the Single Market is governed.

Börzel, T., and Cichowski, R. A. (2003), *The State of the European Union; Law Politics and Society* (Oxford: Oxford University Press). The most recent in a regular series of books on key themes in EU studies, published under the auspices of the American EU Studies Association.

Christiansen, T., Jørgensen, K. E., and Wiener, A. (2001), *The Social Construction of Europe* (London: Sage). Provides a discussion of different aspects of European integration applying insights from Social Constructivism, and also includes debates with critics of this approach.

Fawcett, L., and Hurrell, A. (1995), *Regionalism in World Politics* (Oxford: Oxford University Press). Covers various forms of regional cooperation in different parts of the globe, looking at both the conceptual and empirical issues arising from the revival of regionalism.

Hix, S. (1999), *The Political System of the European Union* (Basingstoke: Macmillan). This advanced textbook approaches the subject from a comparative politics angle, looking in detail at the executive, legislative, and judicial politics as well as at developments in various policy areas.

Laffan., B., O'Donnell, R., and Smith, M. (1999), *Europe's Experimental Union* (London: Routledge). This co-authored volume puts the study of European integration into the context of world politics and the international political economy.

Marks, G. *et al.* (1996b), *Governance in the European Union* (London: Sage). Brings together contributions to the theoretical debate from some of the leading scholars in the field.

Moravcsik, A. (1998), *The Choice for Europe: Social Purpose and State Power from Messina to Maastricht* (Ithaca, NY: Cornell University Press). This important text approaches the study of European integration from an intergovernmental angle. It provides an in-depth analysis of the key decisions in the history of the EU.

Scharpf, F. W. (1999), *Governing in Europe* (Oxford: Oxford University Press). A study of the EU with approaches informed by rational choice and political economy. The author concentrates in particular on the tension between efficient decisionmaking and democratic legitimation in the EU.

Wallace, H., and Wallace, W. (eds) (2000), *Policy-making in the European Union* (Oxford: Oxford University Press). This is a wide-ranging textbook that covers all major policies and also examines ways of studying the institutional setting and the dynamics of governance in the EU.

Weiler, J. H. H. (1999), *The Constitution of Europe* (Cambridge: Cambridge University Press). This collection of essays from a leading legal scholar of European integration provides important insights and original ideas regarding the interaction of law and politics in the EU.

Wiener, A., and Diez, T. (2004), *European Integration Theory* (Oxford: Oxford University Press). A comprehensive and topical reader bringing together the most important contributions to the theoretical debates in the study of European integration.

WEB LINKS

www.europa.eu.int This is the official web site of the European Union, leading to separate sites of the EU institutions, and also has links to the various policies. There is also a useful 'ABC' section providing basic information on the EU.

www.eurotext.ulst.ac.uk Access to this web site, providing full text copies of key documents as well as brief academic introductions to the main institutions and policies of the EU, is free for students at UK universities.

www.eiop.or.at/euroint This web site is an invaluable research resource, providing an extensive and well-organized collection of links to private and public web sites with further information, debate, or publications about European integration.

www.euractiv.com This private news service provides up-to-date information on a range of policy and institutional developments in the EU. Focused on current affairs but also containing substantive background analysis, it is a very useful resource whereby to gain a quick entry into the state of play in a certain area of EU politics.

CHAPTER 27

Global trade and finance

JAN AART SCHOLTE

READER'S GUIDE

This chapter explores various economic aspects of contemporary globalization. It begins by distinguishing three general conceptions of economic globalization and highlights the third, geographical notion of increasing transborder production, markets, and investment. This global dimension of contemporary world commerce is then described in more detail under headings of global trade and global finance. A fourth section of the chapter counters exaggerated claims about economic globalization by emphasizing some qualifications about its nature and extent. Finally, globalization of commerce is linked to several major problems of injustice and insecurity in contemporary world politics.

Introduction

The globalization of world politics involves, among other things, a globalization of economics. As Ngaire Woods has emphasized elsewhere (Ch.14), politics and economics are inseparable within social relations. Politics (the acquisition, distribution, and exercise of power) is integral to economics (the production, exchange, and consumption of resources). At the same time, and equally, economics is integral to politics, helping to determine where power lies and how it is exercised. Economics does not explain everything, but no account of world politics (and hence no analysis of globalization as a key issue of contemporary world history) is adequate if it does not explore the economic dimension.

Countless discussions of globalization have highlighted its economic aspects. For example, Milton Friedman, the Nobel Prize-winning economist, remarks that it has become possible 'to produce a product anywhere, using resources from anywhere, by a company located anywhere, to be sold anywhere' (cited in Naisbitt 1994: 19). Management consultants have ceaselessly extolled the virtues of global markets (e.g. Ohmae 1990). A senior researcher with American Express has described global financial integration of recent decades as marking 'the end of geography' (O'Brien 1992). Global governance bodies like the Bank for International Settlements (BIS), the Group of Eight (G8),

the International Monetary Fund (IMF), the Organization of Economic Co-operation and Development (OECD), the United Nations Conference on Trade and Development (UNCTAD), the World Bank Group (WBG), and the World Trade Organization (WTO) have all put economic globalization high on their agendas. (On these and other institutions of global economic governance, see Box 27.1.) Usually these official circles have endorsed and encouraged the trend, as have most states. Meanwhile many social movements have focused their critiques of globalization on economic aspects of the process. Their analyses have depicted contemporary globalization of trade and finance as a major cause of higher unemployment, a general decline in working standards, increased inequality, greater poverty for some, recurrent financial crises, and large-scale environmental degradation.

In their different ways, all of these assessments agree that economic globalization is a key development of contemporary history. True, the trend is often exaggerated. However, it is just as wrong to argue, as some sceptics have done, that claims about a new globalizing economy rest on nothing but hype and myth. Instead—as in the case of most historical developments—economic globalization involves an intricate interplay of changes and continuities.

A globalizing economy

One key reason for disagreements over the extent and significance of economic globalization relates to the contrasting definitions that different analysts have applied to notions of globality. What, more precisely, is 'global' about the global economy? The following paragraphs distinguish three contrasting ways that the globalization of trade and finance has been broadly conceived, namely, in terms of: (a) the crossing of borders; (b) the opening of borders; and (c) the transcendence of borders. Although the three

conceptions overlap to some extent, they involve important differences of emphasis. Most arguments concerning economic globalization have pitted sceptics who adopt the first perspective against enthusiasts who apply the second notion. However, the third conception of globality offers a more distinctive and revealing approach. Later sections of the present chapter therefore develop that alternative notion in relation to trade and finance.

Box 27.1   Major public global governance agencies for trade and finance

BIS Bank for International Settlements. Established in 1930 with headquarters in Basle. Membership (2004) of 55 shareholding central banks, although many other public financial institutions also use BIS facilities. Promotes cooperation among central banks and provides various services for global financial operations. For example, the Basle Committee on Banking Supervision, formed through the BIS in 1974, has spearheaded efforts at multilateral regulation of global banking. See further www.bis.org.

G8 Group of Eight. Established in 1975 as the G5 (France, Germany, Japan, the UK, and the USA); subsequently expanded as the G7 to include Canada and Italy and since 1998 as the G8 to include the Russian Federation. The G8 conducts semi-formal collaboration on world economic problems. Government leaders meet in annual G8 Summits, while finance ministers and/or their leading officials periodically hold other consultations. See further www.g8online.org.

GATT General Agreement on Tariffs and Trade. Established in 1947 with offices in Geneva. Membership had reached 122 states when it was absorbed into the WTO in 1995. The GATT coordinated eight 'rounds' of multilateral negotiations to reduce state restrictions on cross-border merchandise trade.

IMF International Monetary Fund. Established in 1945 with headquarters in Washington, DC. Membership (2004) of 184 states. The IMF monitors short-term cross-border payments and foreign exchange positions. When a country develops chronic imbalances in its external accounts, the IMF supports corrective policy reforms, often called 'structural adjustment programmes'. Since 1978 the IMF has undertaken comprehensive surveillance both of the economic performance of individual member states and of the world-economy as a whole. The IMF also provides extensive technical assistance. In recent years the Fund has pursued various initiatives to promote efficiency and stability in global financial markets. See further www.imf.org.

IOSCO International Organization of Securities Commissions. Established in 1983 with headquarters in Montreal; secretariat now in Madrid. Membership (2004) of 181 official securities regulators and (non-voting) trade associ-

ations and other agencies. IOSCO aims to promote high standards of regulation in stock and bond markets, to establish effective surveillance of transborder securities transactions, and to foster collaboration between securities markets in the detection and punishment of offences. See further www.iosco.org/.

OECD Organization of Economic Co-operation and Development. Founded in 1962 with headquarters in Paris. Membership (2004) of 30 states with advanced industrial economies and further relationships with 70 other states. Provides a forum for multilateral intergovernmental consultations on a wide range of economic and social issues. OECD measures have especially addressed environmental questions, taxation, and transborder corporations. At regular intervals the OECD Secretariat produces an assessment of the macroeconomic performance of each member, including suggestions for policy changes. See further www.oecd.org.

UNCTAD United Nations Conference on Trade and Development. Established in 1964 with offices in Geneva. Membership (2004) of 192 states. UNCTAD monitors the effects of world trade and investment on economic development, especially in the South. It provided a key forum in the 1970s for discussions of a New International Economic Order. See further www.unctad.org.

WBG World Bank Group. A collection of five agencies, the first established in 1945, with head offices in Washington, DC. The WBG promotes development in medium- and low-income countries with project loans, structural adjustment programmes, and various advisory services. See further www.worldbank.org.

WTO World Trade Organization. Established in 1995 with headquarters in Geneva. Membership (2004) of 146 states. The WTO is a permanent instititution to replace the provisional GATT. It has a wider agenda, covering services, intellectual property, and investment issues as well as merchandise trade. The WTO also has greater powers of enforcement through its dispute-settlement mechanism. The organization's Trade Policy Review Body conducts surveillance of members' commercial measures. See further www.wto.org.

Cross-border transactions

Scepticism about the significance of contemporary economic globalization has often arisen when analysts have conceived of the process in terms of increased cross-border movements between countries of people, goods, money, investments, messages, and ideas. From this perspective, globalization is seen as equivalent to internationalization. No significant distinction is drawn between global companies and international companies, between global trade and international trade, between global money and international money, between global finance and international finance.

When conceived in this way, economic globalization is nothing particularly new. Long-distance commerce has existed for centuries and in some cases even millennia. Ancient Babylon and the Roman Empire knew forms of long-distance lending and trade, for example. Shipments between Arabia and China via South and South-East Asia occurred with fair regularity more than a thousand years ago. Certain coins circulated widely around maritime South-East Asia in a prototypical 'international monetary regime' of the tenth century. Long-distance monies of the pre-modern Mediterranean world included the Byzantine *solidus* from the fifth century onwards and the Muslim *dinar* from the eighth to the thirteenth centuries. Banks based in Italian city-states maintained (temporary) offices along long-distance trade routes as early as the twelfth century. The Hanseatic League in the fourteenth century and companies based in Amsterdam, Copenhagen, London, and Paris in the seventeenth century operated overseas trading posts. The first brokerage houses with cross-border operations appeared in the eighteenth century with Amsterdam-based Hope & Co. and London-based Barings.

Indeed, on certain (though far from all) measures, cross-border economic activity reached similar levels in the late nineteenth century as it did a hundred years later. Relative to world population of the time, the magnitude of permanent migration was in fact considerably greater than today. When measured in relation to world output, cross-border investment in production facilities stood at roughly the same level on the eve of the First World War as it did in the early 1990s. International markets in loans and securities also flourished during the heyday of the gold–sterling standard between 1870 and 1914. Under this regime the British pound, fixed to a certain value in gold, served as a transworld currency and thereby greatly facilitated cross-border payments. Again citing proportional (rather than aggregate) statistics, several researchers (for example, Zevin 1992) have argued that these years witnessed larger capital flows between countries than in the late twentieth century. Meanwhile the volume of international trade grew at some 3.4 per cent per annum in the period 1870–1913, until its value was equivalent to 33 per cent of world output (Barraclough 1984: 256; Hirst and Thompson 1999: 21). By this particular calculation, cross-border trade was greater at the beginning than at the end of the twentieth century.

For the sceptics, then, the contemporary globalizing economy is nothing new. In their eyes recent decades have merely experienced a phase of increased cross-border trade and finance, much as occurred a hundred years before. Moreover, they note, just as growth of international interdependence in the late nineteenth century was substantially reversed with a forty-year wave of protectionism after 1914, so economic globalization of the present day may prove to be temporary. Governments can block cross-border flows if they wish, say the sceptics, and 'national interest' may well dictate that states once more tighten restrictions on international trade, travel, foreign exchange, and capital movements. Contemporary economic globalization gives little evidence, say these doubters, of an impending demise of the state, a weakening of national loyalties, and an end of war. Thus, for example, sceptics regularly point out that most so-called 'global' companies: (a) still conduct the majority of their business in their country of origin; (b) retain a strong national character and allegiances; and (c) remain heavily dependent on states for the success of their enterprises.

Open-border transactions

In contrast to the sceptics, enthusiasts for contemporary globalization of trade and finance generally define these developments as part of the long-term evolution towards a global society. In this second conception, globalization entails not an extension of internationalization, but the progressive removal of official restrictions on transfers of resources between countries. In the resultant world of **open borders**, global companies replace international companies, global trade replaces international trade, global money replaces international money, global finance replaces international finance. From this perspective, globalization is a function of liberalization, that is, the degree to which articles, communications, financial instruments, fixed assets, and people can circulate throughout the world-economy free from state-imposed controls. Whereas sceptics generally back up their arguments of historical repetition with proportional data, globalists usually substantiate their claims of historical change with aggregate statistics, many of which do indeed appear quite staggering. (See Table 27.1.)

Globalists regard the forty-year interlude of protectionism (*c.*1910–50) as a temporary detour from a longer historical trend towards the construction of a single integrated world-economy. In their eyes the tightening of border controls in the first half of the twentieth century was a major cause of economic depressions, authoritarian regimes, and international conflicts such as the world wars. In contrast, the emergent open world-economy will (so runs the globalist promise) yield prosperity, liberty, democracy, and peace for all humanity. From this perspective—which is often termed neo-liberalism—contemporary economic globalization continues the project of modernity launched several centuries ago.

Recent history has indeed witnessed considerable opening of borders in the world economy. For one thing, a succession of inter-state accords through the General Agreement on Tariffs and Trade (GATT) has since 1948 brought major reductions in customs duties, quotas, and other measures that previously inhibited cross-border movements of merchandise. Average tariffs on manufactures in countries of the North fell from over 40 per cent in the 1930s to less than 4 per cent by 1999. Following the Uruguay Round of multilateral trade negotiations (1986–94), the GATT was subsumed within the World Trade Organization. This successor agency has greater competences both to enforce existing trade agreements and to pursue new avenues of liberalization, for example, in respect of shipping, telecommunications, and investment flows. Meanwhile, as indicated in Chapter 26, regional frameworks in most areas of the world have (to varying degrees) removed official restrictions on trade between participating countries. Encouraged by such liberalization, cross-border trade expanded between 1950 and 1994 at an annual rate of just over 6 per cent: thus almost twice as fast as in the late nineteenth century. Total international trade multiplied fourteen-fold in real terms over this period, while expansion in respect of manufactures was even greater, with a twenty-six-fold increase (WTO 1995).

Table 27.1 Some indicators of contemporary economic globalization ($US billion)

Measure (worldwide figures)	Earlier level	Recent level
Foreign direct investment	$66 (1960)	$7,100 (2002)
Exports	$629 (1960)	$7,300 (2003)
Official foreign exchange reserves	$100 (1970)	$1,579 (1997)
Daily turnover on foreign exchange markets	$100 (1979)	$1,210 (2001)
Bank deposits by non-residents	$20 (1964)	$7,876 (1995)
Cross-border loan announcements	$9 (1972)	$1,465 (2000)
Cross-border bond issues	$1 (1960)	$1,157 (1999)
Euroequity issues	Initiated 1984	$50 (1995)
Cross-border share dealing	$10 (1980)	$120 (1994)
Daily turnover of financial derivatives contracts	Small before 1980	$1,162 (1995)

Sources: BIS, IMF, OECD, UNCTAD.

Borders have also opened considerably to money flows since 1950. A **gold–dollar standard** became fully operational through the International Monetary Fund in 1959. Under this regime major currencies—and especially the United States dollar—could circulate worldwide (though not in communist-ruled countries) and be converted to local monies at an official **fixed exchange rate**. The gold–dollar standard thereby broadly recreated the situation that prevailed under the gold–sterling standard in the late nineteenth century. Contrary to many expectations, the US government's termination of dollar–gold convertibility on demand in 1971 did not trigger new restrictions on cross-border payments. Instead, a regime of **floating exchange rates** developed: de facto from 1973 and formalized through the IMF in 1976. Moreover, from the mid-1970s onwards most states reduced or eliminated restrictions on the import and export of national currencies. In these circumstances the average volume of daily transactions on the world's wholesale foreign exchange markets burgeoned from $15 billion in 1973 to $1,500 billion in 1998, before slipping to the still enormous sum of $1,200 billion in 2001.

Alongside the liberalization of trade and money movements between countries, recent decades have also witnessed the widespread opening of borders to investment flows. These movements involve both direct investments (that is, fixed assets like research facilities and factories) and portfolio investments (that is, liquid assets like loans, bonds, and shares).

Apart from a wave of expropriations in the South during the 1970s (many of them subsequently reversed), states have generally welcomed **foreign direct investment (FDI)** into their jurisdictions in contemporary history. Indeed, many governments have actively lured externally based business by lowering corporate tax rates, reducing restrictions on the repatriation of profits, relaxing labour and environmental standards, and so on. Since 1960 there has been a proliferation of what are variously called 'international', 'multinational', 'transnational', or 'global' corporations (hence the frequently encountered abbreviations **MNC** and **TNC**). The number of such companies grew from 3,500 in 1960 to 65,000 in 2001. The aggregate stock of FDI worldwide increased in tandem from $68 billion in 1960 to $7,100 billion in 2002, as compared with only $14 billion in 1914 (UNCTAD 1996: ix, 4; UNCTAD 1999). In this world of more open borders, various globalists have described MNCs as 'footloose' and 'stateless'.

Substantial liberalization has also occurred since the 1970s in respect of cross-border portfolio investments. For example, many a state now permits non-residents to hold bank accounts within its jurisdiction. Other deregulation has removed legal restrictions on ownership and trading of stocks and bonds by non-resident investors. Further legislation has reduced controls on participation in a country's financial markets by externally based banks, brokers, and fund managers. As a result of such deregulation (for example, the City of London's so-called 'Big Bang' in 1986) financial institutions from all over the world have converged on **global cities** like Hong Kong, New York, Paris, and Tokyo. Levels of cross-border banking and securities business have risen markedly since the 1960s in tandem with such liberalization, as several statistics in Table 27.1 indicate. Corresponding indicators for the 1870–1914 period come nowhere close to these aggregate figures.

In sum, legal obstructions to economic transactions between countries have greatly diminished worldwide in contemporary history. At the same time, cross-border flows of merchandise, services, money, and investments have reached unprecedented levels, at least in aggregate terms. To this extent enthusiasts for globalization as liberalization can argue, against the sceptics, that borders have opened more than ever.

That said, significant official restrictions on cross-border economic activity persist. They include countless trade restrictions and continuing **capital controls** in many countries. While states have on the whole welcomed FDI, there is as yet no multilateral regime to liberalize investment flows comparable to the GATT/WTO in respect of trade or the IMF in respect of money. (Negotiations for a **Multilateral Agreement on Investment** were abandoned at the end of 1998, although hundreds of liberalizing bilateral investment treaties have been concluded.) In addition, while many governments have loosened visa and travel restrictions in recent times, **immigration controls** are on the whole as tight as ever. Indeed, many have recently been reinforced. To this extent sceptics have grounds to affirm that international borders remain very much in place and can be opened or closed as states choose to do.

Transborder transactions

As mentioned earlier, most debates concerning economic globalization have unfolded between, on the one hand, sceptics who regard the current situation as a limited and reversible expansion of cross-border transactions and, on the other hand, globalists who see an inexorable trend towards an open world economy. However, these two most common positions do not exhaust the possible interpretations. Indeed, neither of these conventional perspectives requires a distinct concept of 'globalization'. Both views resurrect arguments that were elaborated using other vocabulary long before the word 'globalization' entered widespread circulation in the 1980s.

In a third conception, globalization refers to **processes whereby social relations acquire relatively distanceless and borderless qualities**, so that human lives are increasingly played out in the world as a single place. In this usage, 'globalization' refers to a transformation of geography that occurs when a host of social conditions become less tied to territorial spaces.

On these lines a globalizing economy is one in which patterns of production, exchange, and consumption become increasingly delinked from a geography of territorial distances and territorial borders. 'Global' economic activity extends across widely dispersed terrestrial locations at the same time and moves between locations scattered across the world in effectively no time. While the patterns of 'international' economic interdependence are strongly influenced by territorial distances and national-state divisions, patterns of 'global' trade and finance often have little correspondence to distance and state boundaries. With air travel, satellite links, telecommunications, transworld organizations, global consciousness (that is, a mind-set that conceives of the world as a single place) and more, much contemporary economic activity transcends

borders. In this third sense globalization involves the growth of a **transborder** (as opposed to cross-border or open-border) economy.

This rise of **supraterritoriality** is reflected *inter alia* in increased transactions between countries. However, the geographical character of these **transworld** (as opposed to long-distance) movements is different from the territorial framework that has traditionally defined international interdependence. This qualitative shift means that contemporary statistics on international trade, money, and investment can only be crudely compared with figures relating to earlier times. Hence the issue is not so much the amount of trade between countries, but the way that much of this commerce forms part of transborder production processes and global marketing **networks**. The problem is not only the quantity of money that moves between countries, but also the instantaneity with which most funds are transferred. The question is not simply the number of international securities deals so much as the emergence of stock and bond issues that involve participants from multiple countries at the same time. In short, if one accepts this third conception of globalization, then both the sceptics and the enthusiasts are largely missing the crucial point of historical change. The next sections elaborate further.

Key points

- The 'globalization' of economic activity can be understood in several different ways.

- Sceptical interpretations emphasize that current levels of cross-border trade, money movements, and investment flows are neither new nor as great as some claim.

- Globalist interpretations argue that large-scale relaxations of border controls have taken international economic activity to unprecedented levels.

- Geographical conceptions of globalization highlight the proliferation of economic transactions in which territorial distance and borders present limited if any constraint.

Global trade

The distinctiveness of transborder, supraterritorial economic relations should become clearer with illustrations. Examples relating to global trade are given in the present section. Others concerning global finance follow in the next section. In each case it is seen that, although the phenomena in question made some earlier appearances, their significance relates mainly to contemporary history.

Transborder production

Transborder production arises when a single process is spread across widely dispersed locations both within and between countries. Global coordination links research centres, design units, procurement offices, materials processing installations, fabrication plants, finishing points, assembly lines, quality control operations, advertising and marketing bureaux, data-processing offices, after-sales service, and so on. Describing a global production operation, the head of Levi Strauss has noted that:

our company buys denim in North Carolina, ships it to France where it is sewn into jeans, launders these jeans in Belgium, and markets them in Germany using TV commercials developed in England (R. D. Haas 1993: 103)

Transborder production can be contrasted with territorially centred production. In the latter instance, all stages of a given production process—from initial research to after-sales service—occur within the same local or national unit. In global production, however, the stages are dispersed across different and often widely scattered countries. Each of the various links in the transborder chain specializes in one or several functions, thereby creating economies of scale and/or exploiting cost differentials between locations. Through **global sourcing**, the company draws materials, components, machinery, finance, and services from anywhere in the world. Distance and borders figure only secondarily, if at all, in determining the sites. Indeed, a firm may relocate certain stages of production several times in short succession in search of profit maximization. In one striking example of **country-hopping**, athletic suppliers Nike during a five-year period opened or closed 55 factories in North America and East Asia in response to changes in relative costs of production (Abegglen 1994: 26).

What others have called **global factories** were unknown before the 1940s. They did not gain major prominence until the 1960s and have mainly spread since the 1970s. Supraterritorial production has developed mainly in the manufacture of textiles, garments, motor vehicles, leather goods, sports articles, toys, optical products, consumer electronics, semiconductors, aeroplanes, and construction equipment.

With the growth of global production, a large proportion of purportedly 'international' transfers of goods and services has entailed intra-firm trade within transborder companies. When the intermediate inputs and finished goods pass from one country to another they are officially counted as 'international' commerce; yet they primarily involve movements within a global company rather than between national economies. Conventional statistics do not measure intra-firm transfers, but estimates of the share of such exchanges in total cross-border trade have ranged from 25 to over 40 per cent.

Much (though far from all) transborder production has taken advantage of what are variously called special economic zones (SEZs), export processing zones (EPZs), or free production zones (FPZs). Within these enclaves the ruling national or provincial government exempts assembly plants and other facilities for transborder production from the usual import and export duties. The authorities may also grant other tax reductions, subsidies, and waivers of certain labour and environmental regulations. The first such zone was established in 1954 in Ireland, but most were created after 1970, mainly in Asia, the Caribbean, and the so-called *maquiladora* areas along the Mexican frontier with the USA. Nearly 850 EPZs were in place worldwide at the turn of the century (UNDP 1999: 86). Among other things, these manufacturing centres have been distinguished by their frequent heavy reliance on female labour.

Transborder products

Much of the output of both transborder and country-based production has acquired a **supraterritorial market** in the contemporary globalizing economy. Hence a considerable proportion of 'international' trade now involves the distribution and sale of **global goods**, often under a transworld brand name. Consumers dispersed across many corners of the planet purchase the same articles at the same time. The country location of a potential customer for, say, a Xerox photocopier, a Britney Spears CD, or Kellogg's corn flakes is of limited importance. Design, packaging, and advertising determine the market far more than territorial distance and borders.

Like other aspects of globalization, supraterritorial markets have a longer history than many contemporary observers appreciate. For example, Campbell Soup and Heinz began to become household names at widely dispersed locations across the world in the mid-1880s, following the introduction of automatic canning. From the outset Henry Ford regarded his first automobile, the Model T, as a world car. Coca-Cola was bottled in 27 countries and sold in 78 by 1929 (Pendergrast 1993: 174). On the whole, however, the numbers of goods, customers, and countries involved in these earlier global markets were relatively small.

In contrast, global goods pervade the contemporary world economy. They encompass a host of packaged foods, bottled beverages, tobacco products, designer clothes, household articles, music recordings, audio-visual productions, printed publications, interactive communications, office and hospital equipment, armaments, transport vehicles, and travel services. In all of these sectors and more, global products inject a touch of the familiar almost wherever on earth a person might visit. The countless examples include Nescafé (sold in 200 varieties worldwide), Heineken beer (drunk in 170 countries), Kiwi shoe polish (applied in 130 countries), Nokia mobile phones (used in 120 countries), Thomas Cook tourist bureaux (available in 140 countries), American International Group insurance policies (offered in 130 countries), television programmes by Globo of Brazil (distributed in 128 countries), and

the *Financial Times* newspaper (read in 160 countries). Covering smokers in 170 lands, 'Marlboro Country' is a distinctly supraterritorial place.

Today many shops are mainly stocked with transborder articles. Moreover, since the 1970s a number of **retail chains** have gone global. Examples include Italy-based Benetton, Japan-based 7-Eleven, Sweden-based IKEA, UK-based Body Shop, and US-based Toys 'R' Us (Treadgold 1993). Owing largely to

---

Box 27.2   Case study: Moscow in global markets

The current reach and power of global markets became acutely—and indeed somewhat painfully—apparent to me on a visit to Moscow at the turn of the year 1994–5. Less than a decade after the launch of perestroika, the city was flooded with global cigarettes, to the point that it had become nearly impossible to find a Russian brand. Dove Bars and Perrier were available for anyone who could pay, but it took me five days to find a sack of potatoes. Everywhere the eye turned, Nike was competing with Reebok, Pizza Hut with Burger King, Pepsi with Coke, Martini with Asti Spumanti, Wrigley's with Hershey, Pioneer with JVC, Philips with Bosch, Gold Star with TDK, Tide with Ajax, Wella with Flex, Cosmopolitan with Burda (each in Russian-language editions), Barbie with Cindy, Konica with Kodak, Casio with Rolex, Whiskas with Pedigree Chum. Moscow travel agents were beginning to flog fun-in-the-sun package holidays and time-share vacation homes, while US Global Health offered private medical insurance for the monied few. VDNH, once the communist Exhibition to the Achievements of the People's Economy, had been turned into a consumer playground. Its pavilions were now crammed with make-shift stalls selling global products, especially consumer electronics, many of them bought duty-free in the Persian Gulf region. In the north-west corner of the park, the large Cosmos hangar had been converted into a showroom for shiny Fords and Mercedes. Lenin's statue stared blandly as hordes of buyers scuttled past now-silent fountains with televisions, portable stereos, cordless telephones, and car alarms, while public loudspeakers pumped out strains of Brian Adams: 'Baby it's hard to believe, we're in heaven'. Comrades had become customers. (The situation on subsequent return visits to Moscow has remained broadly the same, although it should be noted that the impact of global markets on Russia is much less pronounced outside the major cities.)

the various 'megabrands' and transborder stores, shopping centres of the twenty-first century are in good part global emporia. (See Box 27.2.)

Other supraterritorial markets have developed since the 1990s through **electronic commerce**. Today's global consumer can—equipped with a credit card and telephone, television, or Internet links—shop the world from home. Mail-order outlets and telesales units have undergone exponential growth, while e-commerce on the World Wide Web has expanded greatly from its 1996 level of $2.6 billion (Bacchetta *et al.* 1998: 23; UNDP 1999: 60).

Through transborder production and transworld products, global trade has become an integral part of everyday life for a notable proportion of the world's firms and consumers. Indeed, these developments could help to explain why the recessions of contemporary history have not, in spite of frequently expressed fears of 'trade wars', provoked a wave of protectionism. In previous prolonged periods of commercial instability and economic hardship (for example, during the 1870s–1890s and 1920s–1930s) most states responded by imposing major pro-

tectionist restrictions on cross-border trade. Reactions to contemporary recession have been more complicated (cf. Milner 1988). While many territorial interests have pressed for protectionism, global commercial interests have generally resisted it. Thus many transborder companies actively promoted the Uruguay Round and have on the whole vigorously supported the new World Trade Organization.

Key points

- Transborder production and associated intra-firm trade have developed in a number of industries since the middle of the twentieth century.

- Many states have created special economic zones in order to attract so-called 'global factories'.

- Much contemporary commerce involves transborder marketing of global brand-name products.

- The growth of a substantial global dimension to world trade may have discouraged protectionism.

Global finance

Finance has attracted some of the greatest attention in contemporary debates on globalization, especially following a string of crises in Latin America (1994–5), Asia (1997–8), Russia (1998), Brazil (1999), and Argentina (2001–2). The rise of supraterritoriality has affected both the forms that money takes and the ways that it is deployed in banking, securities, derivatives, and (although not detailed below) insurance markets. (See Box 27.3 regarding terminology.) As international, cross-border activities, such dealings have quite a long history. However, as commerce that unfolds through telephone and computer networks that make the world a single place, global finance has experienced its greatest growth since the 1980s.

Transworld money

The development of global production and the growth of global markets have each encouraged—and been facilitated by—the spread of global monies. It was noted earlier that the fixed and later floating exchange regimes operated through the IMF have allowed a number of 'national' currencies to enter transworld use. As familiar 'bureau de change' signs indicate, today retail outlets in scores of countries deal in multiple currencies on demand.

No national denomination has been more global in this context than the US dollar. About as many dollars circulate outside as inside the USA. Indeed, in certain financial crises this global money has displaced the locally issued currency in the everyday life of a national economy. Such 'dollarization' has occurred in parts of Latin America and Eastern Europe. Since the 1970s the German Mark (now superseded by the euro), Japanese yen, Swiss franc, and other major currencies have also acquired a substantial global character. Hence huge stocks of notionally 'national' money are now used in countless transactions that never touch the 'home' soil.

Foreign exchange dealing has become a thoroughly supraterritorial business. This round-the-clock, round-the-world market has no central meeting place. Many of the deals have nothing directly to do with the countries where the currencies involved are initially issued or eventually spent. The trading itself also taken place without distance. Transactions are generally concluded over the telephone and confirmed by telex or e-mail between buyers and sellers across whatever distance. Meanwhile shifts in exchange rates are flashed instantaneously and simultaneously on video monitors across the main dealing rooms worldwide.

Transborder money also takes other forms besides certain national currencies. Gold has already circulated across the planet for several centuries, although it moves cumbersomely through territorial space rather than instantly through telecommunication lines. A newer and more fully supraterritorial denomination is the Special Drawing Right, issue through the IMF since 1969. SDRs reside only in computer memories and not in wallets for everyday transactions.

Meanwhile other supraterritorial money has entered daily use in plastic form. For example, many bank cards can extract local currency from automated teller machines (**ATMs**) worldwide. In

---

| **Box 27.3** | **A glossary of global finance terms** |

Bond: a contractual obligation of a corporation, association, or governance agency to make payments of interest and repayments of principal on borrowed funds at certain fixed times.

Derivative: a financial contract that 'derives' its value from an underlying asset, exchange rate, interest level, or market index.

Equity: also called stock or share; a number of equal portions in the nominal capital of a company; the shareholder thereby owns part of the enterprise.

Eurobond: a bond denominated in a currency that is alien to a substantial proportion of the underwriters through whom it is distributed and investors to whom it is sold; the borrower, the syndicate of managers, the investors, and the securities exchange on which the bond is listed are spread over a number of countries.

Eurocurrency: national money in the hands of persons and institutions domiciled outside the currency's territorial 'home': hence 'eurodollar', 'eurozloty', etc.

Euroequity: a share issue that is offered simultaneously in different stock-markets, usually across several time zones; also called global equity.

Merchant bank: also called an investment bank or securities house; a bank specializing in securities business, as opposed to a commercial bank engaged primarily in deposit and lending business. (That said, many major investment banks have in recent years become arms of global commercial banks: for example, Deutsche Morgan Grenfell and UBS Warburg.)

Offshore finance centre: a site for financial business offering inducements such as tax reductions, regulation waivers, subsidies and rebates, secrecy guarantees, and so on; most are located in island and other mini-states, though offshore provisions also cover arrangements like International Banking Facilities in New York (since 1981), the Tokyo-based Japan Offshore Market (since 1986) and the Bangkok International Banking Facility (since 1993).

Petrodollars: earnings from oil exports deposited outside the USA; they provided the largest single spur to growth in the euromarkets in the 1970s.

Security: a contract with a claim to future payments in which (in contrast to bank credits) there is a direct and formally identified relationship between the investor and the borrower; also unlike bank loans, securities are traded in markets.

Special Drawing Right: the supraterritorial denomination issued since 1969 through the International Monetary Fund and used as its unit of account. As of April 2004, 21.4 billion SDRs were in circulation at a value of 1 SDR = US$1.47. A further allocation to double the amount of SDRs is pending.

Syndicated eurocredit: a loan provided in the euromarkets by an ad hoc association of a number of commercial banks.

addition, several types of **smart cards** (e.g. Mondex and the Clip card of Europay International) can simultaneously hold several currencies as digital cash on a microchip. Certain **credit cards** like Visa and MasterCard are accepted at several million venues the world over to make purchases in whatever local denomination.

In sum, then, contemporary globalization has—through the spread of transborder currencies, distinctly supraterritorial denominations, digital purses, and global credit and debit cards—significantly altered the shape of money. No longer is money restricted to the national-state-territorial form that prevailed from the nineteenth to the middle of the twentieth century.

Transworld banking

Globalization has touched banking mainly in terms of: (a) the growth of transborder deposits; (b) the advent of transborder bank lending; (c) the expansion of transborder branch networks; and (d) the emergence of instantaneous transworld interbank fund transfers.

So-called eurocurrency deposits are bank assets denominated in a national money different from the official currency in the country where the funds are held. For instance, euroyen are 'Japanese' yen deposited in, say, Canada. Eurocurrency accounts first appeared in the 1950s, but mainly expanded after 1970, especially with the flood of so-called petrodollars that followed major rises of oil prices in 1973–4 and 1979–80. Eurocurrencies are supraterritorial: they do not attach neatly to any country's money supply; nor are they systematically regulated by the national central bank that issued them.

Globalization has also entered the lending side of banking. Credit creation from eurocurrency deposits first occurred in 1957, when 'American' dollars were borrowed through the 'British' office of a 'Soviet' bank. However, euroloans mainly proliferated after 1973 following the petrodollar deluge. Today it is common for a loan to be issued in one country, denominated in the currency of a second country (or perhaps a basket of currencies of several countries), for a borrower in a third country, by a bank or syndicate of banks in fourth and more countries.

Global banking takes place not only at age-old sites of world finance like London, New York, Tokyo, and Zurich, but also through multiple offshore finance centres. Much like EPZs in respect of manufacturing, offshore financial arrangements offer investors low levels of taxation and regulation. Although a few offshore finance centres including Luxembourg and Jersey predate the Second World War, most have emerged since 1960 and are now found in over forty countries. Most of the world's major banks now have branch networks across the principal 'onshore' (i.e. normally taxed and regulated) and offshore locations. For example, less than thirty years after passing relevant legislation in 1967, the Cayman Islands hosted over 500 offshore banks, with total deposits of $442 billion, none of them in the local currency (Roberts 1994; BIS 1996: 7).

The supraterritorial character of much contemporary banking also lies in the instantaneity of **interbank fund transfers**. Electronic messages have largely replaced territorial transfers by cheque or draft—and cost far less. The largest conduit for such movements is the Society for Worldwide Interbank Financial Telecommunications. Launched in 1977, SWIFT interconnected around 7,500 financial institutions in 199 countries by 2003, carrying an average of nearly nine million payments per day.

Transworld securities

Globalization has altered not only banking, but also the shape of securities markets. First, some of the bonds and stocks themselves have become relatively detached from territorial space. Second, many investor portfolios have acquired a transborder character. Third, electronic interlinkage of trading sites has created conditions of anywhere/anytime securities dealing.

In regard to the first point, contemporary globalization has seen the emergence of several major securities instruments with a transborder character. These bonds and equities involve issuers, currencies, brokers, and/or exchanges across multiple countries at the same time. For example, a so-called eurobond is denominated in a currency that is alien to a substantial proportion of the parties involved: the borrower who issues it; the underwriters who distribute it; the investors who hold it; and/or the exchange(s) that list it. This transborder financial instrument is thereby different from a **foreign bond**, which is handled in one country for an external borrower. Cross-border bonds of the latter type have existed for several hundred years, but eurobonds first appeared in 1963. In that year the state highways authority in Italy issued bonds denominated in US dollars through managers in Belgium, Britain, Germany, and the Netherlands, with subsequent quotation on the London Stock Exchange. By the late 1980s eurobonds constituted the second largest bond market in the world, behind that for US domestic issues (Honeygold 1989: 19).

On a similar pattern, a euroequity issue involves transborder syndicate of brokers selling a new share release for simultaneous listing on stock exchanges in several countries. This supraterritorial process contrasts with an international offer, where a company based in one country issues **equity** in a second country. Like foreign bonds, international share quotations have existed almost as long as stockmarkets themselves. However, the first transborder equity issue occurred in 1984, when 15 per cent of a privatization of British Telecommunications was offered on exchanges in Japan, North America, and Switzerland concurrently with the majority share release in the UK. Transworld placements of new shares have occurred less frequently than eurobond issues. However, it has become quite common for major transborder firms to list their equity on different stock exchanges across several time zones. For example, equity in Alcatel Alsthom is quoted on twelve exchanges, stock in Nestlé on eleven, and shares in Imperial Chemical Industries on nine.

Not only various securities instruments, but also many **investor portfolios** have acquired a transborder character in the context of contemporary financial globalization. Thus, for example, an investor in one country may leave assets with a fund manager in a second country who in turn places those sums on markets in a collection of third countries. In other words, even when individual securities have a territorial character, they can be combined in a supraterritorial investment package. Indeed, a number of pension funds, insurance companies, and unit trusts have created explicitly designated 'global funds' whose component securities are drawn from multiple corners of the world. Many transborder institutional investors have furthermore registered offshore for tax and other cost advantages. For example, the Africa Emerging Markets Fund has its investments in Africa, its listing in Ireland, and its management base in the USA. As of 1995 Luxembourg hosted some $350 billion in offshore investment funds, largely outside the regulatory reach of the managers' home governments.

Finally, securities markets have gone global through the growing supraterritorial character of many exchanges since the 1970s. The open-outcry trading floors of old have largely given way to electronic transactions by telephone and computer networks. These telecommunications provide the infrastructure for distanceless deals (so-called **remote trading**), in which the brokers can in principle be located anywhere on earth. Most major investment banks (Daiwa Securities, Dresdner Kleinwort Benson, Merrill Lynch, etc.) now coordinate offices across several time zones in round-the-clock, round-the-world trading of bonds and shares. The first computerized order-routing system became operational in 1976, connecting brokers across the USA instantly to the trading floor of the New York Stock Exchange. Similar developments have since 1996 begun to link brokers anywhere in the European Union directly to its main exchanges. For its part the wholly computer-based National Association of Securities Dealers Automated Quotation system (Nasdaq) has since its launch in 1971 had no central meeting place at all, but instead links 11,000 traders in 790 firms across more than 1,000 locations. This transborder cyberspatial network has become the world's second largest stock-market, listing around 3,500 companies, with total capitalization of $2 trillion and annual trading of $7.3 trillion as of 2002. The Europe-wide Easdaq system launched a similar screen-based market in 1996, although its proportions have thus far remained modest. Meanwhile, beginning with the Toronto and American Stock Exchanges in 1985, a number of securities markets have established electronic links to enable transborder dealing between them. This extensive growth of supraterritoriality in the securities markets helps to explain why, for example, the Wall Street crash of October 1987 triggered transworld reverberations within hours.

Much like global banking, transborder securities trading is mainly conducted through computerized clearing systems. The equivalents of SWIFT are the Euroclear network, established in 1968, and Cedel (now renamed Clearstream), launched in 1971. Between them these two global electronic bookkeeping operations handled a turnover of nearly $60 trillion in 1999.

Transworld derivatives

A fourth area of finance suffused with globalization is the derivatives industry. A derivative product is a contract, the value of which depends on (hence is 'derived' from) the price of some underlying asset (for example, a raw material or an equity) or a particular reference rate (e.g. an interest level or stock-market index). Derivatives connected to 'tangible' assets like raw minerals and land date from the middle of the nineteenth century, while derivatives based on financial indicators have proliferated since their introduction in 1972.

Derivatives contracts take two principal forms. The first type, called **futures** or **forwards**, oblige a buyer and seller to complete a transaction at a pre-determined time in the future at a price agreed upon today. The second main type, called **options**, give parties a right (without obligation) to buy or sell at a specified price for a stipulated period of time up to the contract's expiry date. Other kinds of derivatives include 'swaps', 'warrants', and further—seemingly ever more obscure—financial instruments (Banks 1994).

Additional technical details and the various rationales relating to derivatives need not detain us here. It suffices for present purposes to emphasize the magnitude of this financial industry. Public derivatives exchanges have proliferated worldwide since 1982 along with even larger over-the-counter (OTC) markets. By 1995 the volume of trading on world derivatives markets totalled some $1.2 trillion per day. The notional value of outstanding OTC financial derivatives contracts alone reached $88 trillion at the end of 1999 (Sharpe 1996; BIS 1996: 27; BIS 2000: 26).

Like banking and securities, much derivatives business has become relatively distanceless and bor-

derless. For example, a number of the contracts relate to supraterritorial indicators: e.g. the world price of copper; the interest rate on euroswiss franc deposits; and so on. In addition, much derivatives trading is undertaken through global securities houses and transworld telecommunications links. A number of derivatives instruments are traded simultaneously on several exchanges in a round-the-world, round-the-clock market. For example, contracts related to three-month eurodollar interest rates have been traded concurrently on the London International Financial Futures and Options Exchange (LIFFE), the New York Futures Exchange (NYFE), the Sydney Futures Exchange (SFE), and the Singapore International Monetary Exchange (SIMEX). Starting with a connection between SIMEX and the Chicago Mercantile Exchange in 1984, electronic links have enabled distanceless, transborder trading between various market sites.

Owing to these tight global interconnections, major losses in the derivatives markets can have immediate worldwide repercussions. For example, deficits of $1.3 billion accumulated by the Singapore-based futures trader Nick Leeson triggered a transborder collapse of the venerable Barings investment bank in 1995. A succession of similarly huge losses in other quarters has caused some to worry that global derivatives trading could undermine the world financial system as a whole.

Key points

- Globalization has changed forms of money with the spread of transborder currencies, distinctly supraterritorial denominations, digital cash, and global credit cards.

- Globalization has reshaped banking with the growth of supraterritorial deposits, loans, branch networks, and fund transfers.

- Securities markets have gained a global dimension through the development of transborder bonds and stocks, transworld portfolios, and electronic round-the-world trading.

- Globalization has likewise affected the instruments and modes of trading on derivatives markets.

Continuity and change in economic globalization

Having now reviewed the development of a supraterritorial dimension in the contemporary world-economy (summarized chronologically in Box 27.4), and emphasized its significance, we must also recognize continuities alongside these changes. As noted earlier in the present chapter, many assessments of globalization are suffused with hype and exaggeration. However, one can appreciate the importance of globalization without slipping into such 'globalism'. Four main points are highlighted in this respect below: (*a*) the unevenness with which the globalization of trade and finance has spread; (*b*) the continuing importance of **territoriality** in the con-

temporary globalizing economy; (*c*) the continuing key place of the state amidst these changes; and (*d*) the continuing significance of national attachments, and cultural diversity more generally, in the present era of economic globalization.

Irregular incidence

Globalization has not been experienced everywhere and by everyone to the same extent. In general, transborder trade and finance have developed furthest: (a) in East Asia, North America, and Western

---

Box 27.4	Some key events in global trade and finance

1880s	Development of first global products.		1974	Formation of Basle Committee on Banking Supervision following the collapse of two banks heavily involved in foreign exchange dealing.
1929	Institution of the first offshore finance arrangements (in Luxembourg).			
1944	Bretton Woods Conference drafts constitutions of the IMF and the World Bank.		1974	US Government relaxes foreign exchange controls (other states follow in later years).
1954	Establishment of the first export processing zone (in Ireland).		1976	IMF meeting in Jamaica formalizes the regime of floating exchange rates.
1954	Launch of the 'Marlboro cowboy' as a global commercial icon.		1977	Inauguration of the SWIFT system of electronic interbank fund transfers worldwide.
1955	First McDonald's restaurant opened (operating in 119 countries 50 years later).		1982	Mexico's threatened default on global loans triggers Third World debt crisis.
1957	Issuance of the first eurocurrency loan.		1983	Formation of the International Organization of Securities Commissions.
1959	Gold–dollar standard enters into full operation.			
1963	Issuance of the first eurobond.		1984	First transborder equity issue (by British Telecommunications).
1965	Start of the *maquiladora* programme in Mexico.			
1968	Launch of Euroclear computerized transworld settlement of securities deals.		1985	First transborder electronic link between stock exchanges.
1969	Introduction of the Special Drawing Right.		1987	Stock-market crash on Wall Street reverberates worldwide within hours.
1971	Establishment of the first wholly electronic stock exchange (Nasdaq).		1994	Conclusion of the Uruguay Round of the GATT.
1972	Launch of markets in financial derivatives, starting with currency futures.		1995	Inauguration of the World Trade Organization.
			1995	Leeson Affair highlights the volatility of global derivatives markets.
1973	Quadrupling of oil prices floods euromarkets with petrodollars.		1997–2002	Crises in Asia, Russia, Brazil, and Argentina raise concerns about underregulated global finance.

Europe; (b) in urban areas relative to rural districts worldwide; and (c) in wealthier and professional circles. On the other hand, few people and places are today completely untouched by economic globalization.

Supraterritorial trade and finance have transpired disproportionately in the so-called **North**, and then most especially in its **cities**. For example, in the 1990s over half of world manufacturing output and a third of merchandise exports were centred in just three countries: the USA, Japan, and Germany (Kidron and Segal 1995: 86–9). Usually only the labour-intensive assembly stage of a transborder production process has been located in the South. The sale of most global products has also been heavily concentrated in the North. For instance, although McDonald's fast food is dished up in 119 countries, the vast majority of these meals are consumed in a handful of those lands. In contrast to currencies issued in the North, the national denominations of countries in Africa have had scarcely any mutual convertibility. At the time of writing, three-quarters and more of foreign direct investment, credit card transactions, stock-market capitalization, derivatives trade, and transborder loans flowed within the North. In the light of such inequalities, a number of promoters as well as critics of globalization have worried that the trend is substantially bypassing the South.

This exclusion is far from complete, however. For instance, certain products originating in the South have figured significantly in global markets (for example, wines from Chile and package holidays in the Caribbean). Electronic banking has even reached parts of rural China. A number of offshore finance centres and large sums of transborder bank debt are found in the South. Global portfolios have figured strongly in the development of new securities markets in major cities of Africa, Asia, Eastern Europe, and Latin America since the mid-1980s. SIMEX and the Saõ Paulo-based Bolsa de Mercadorias & Futuros (BM&F) have played a part in the burgeoning derivatives markets of recent decades.

Indeed, involvement in global trade and finance is often as much a function of **class** as the North–South divide. The vast majority of the world's population—including many in the North—have lacked the means to purchase most global products. Michael Porter of the Harvard Business School puts this point more euphemistically by noting that markets 'today seem based less on country differences and more on buyer differences that transcend country boundaries' (1986: 44). Likewise, placing investments in global financial markets depends on wealth, the distribution of which does not always follow a North–South pattern. For example, petro-dollars have been mostly owned by elites in the oil-exporting countries of Africa, Latin America, and the Middle East. Country comparisons have indicated that the populations of Brazil and Botswana have the world's largest income inequalities.

Space limitations do not permit full elaboration of the point here, but transborder markets and investments can be shown to have contributed significantly to **growing wealth gaps** within countries as well as between North and South (Scholte 2000: ch.10). For example, the global mobility of capital, in particular to low-wage production sites and offshore finance centres, has encouraged many states to reduce upper-tax brackets and to downgrade some social welfare provisions. Such steps have contributed to growing inequality across much of the contemporary world. Increasingly, poverty has become connected as much to supraterritorial class, gender and race structures as to country of domicile (see further Chs 29 and 30).

The persistence of territory

On the other hand, the transcendence of territorial space in the contemporary world economy must not be overestimated. True, evidence presented in earlier sections of this chapter suggests that distance and borders have often lost the determining influence on economic geography that they once had. However, this is not to say that territoriality has lost all significance in the contemporary organization of production, exchange, and consumption. Robert Reich exaggerated when, shortly before joining the Clinton Administration, he declared that economic globalization yielded a situation of 'no *national* products or technologies, no national corporations, no national industries' (1991: 3, his emphasis).

On the contrary, after several decades of accelerated globalization a great deal of commercial activity still has only a secondary if any supraterritorial dimension. For example, although transborder manufacturing through global factories has affected a significant proportion of certain industries, it has involved but a small percentage of overall world production. Most processes have remained contained within one country, and only a tiny percentage of the world's workforce has so far been employed in EPZs. Even many global products (Boeing jets, Ceylon teas) are prepared within a single country although their distribution extends worldwide. While transborder products have generally been more prevalent than supraterritorial production, far from all sales items have acquired global circulation.

Many types of money, too, have remained restricted to a national or local domain. Likewise, the great bulk of retail banking has stayed territorial, as clients deal with their local branch offices. In spite of substantial growth since the 1980s, transborder share dealing remains a small fraction of total equity trading. Moreover, a large majority of turnover on most stock exchanges continues to involve shares of firms headquartered in the same country. The London Stock Exchange provides the only major case where externally based equity accounted for over half of business in the 1990s. Similarly, despite exponential expansion of the eurobond market, in 1995 the total value of outstanding transborder bonds ($2.8 trillion) was still dwarfed by the aggregate value of outstanding domestic issues ($23.9 trillion) (BIS 1996: 20).

Nor has most global commercial activity been wholly divorced from territorial geography. For example, local circumstances have strongly influenced corporate decisions regarding the location of transborder production facilities. In the foreign exchange markets dealers have mainly been clustered in half a dozen cities, even if their transactions are largely cyberspatial and can have immediate consequences anywhere in the world. It remains rare for a transborder company to issue a large proportion of its stock outside its country of origin. In the light of such qualifications Richard O'Brien has readily conceded the hyperbole in his depiction of global finance as 'the end of geography' (1992: 2).

Hence the importance of globalization is that it has ended the monopoly of territoriality in defining the spatial character of the world economy. This is not to say that the trend has eliminated territoriality altogether. The global dimension of contemporary world commerce has grown alongside, and in complex relations with, its territorial aspects. Globalization has been reconfiguring geography rather than obliterating **territory**

The survival of the state

Similarly, globalization has repositioned the (territorial) state rather than signalled its demise. The expansion of transborder trade and finance has made claims of **Westphalian sovereign statehood** obsolete, but the significance of states themselves remains. Through both unilateral decisions and multilaterally coordinated policies, states have done much to facilitate economic globalization and influence its course.

As already mentioned, states have encouraged the globalization of commerce *inter alia* through various policies of liberalization and the creation of special economic zones and offshore finance centres. At the same time, some governments have also slowed globalization within their jurisdiction by retaining certain restrictions on transborder activity. However, most states—including those still nominally 'communist'—have sooner or later responded to strong pressures to liberalize. In any case, governments have often lacked effective means fully to enforce their territorially bound controls on globally mobile capital. Only in respect of immigration restrictions have states largely sustained their borders against economic globalization, and even then substantial traffic in unregistered migrants has developed.

Yet states are by no means powerless in the face of economic globalization. Even the common claim that global finance lies beyond the state requires qualification. After all, governments and central banks continue to exert major influence on money supplies and interest rates, even if they no longer monopolize money creation and lack direct control over the euromarkets. Likewise, particularly through cooperative action, states can significantly shift exchange rates, even if they have lost the capacity to fix the conversion ratios and are sometimes overridden by currency dealers. Governments have also pursued collective regulation of transborder banking to some effect via the Basle Committee on Banking Supervision, set up through the BIS in 1974. The survival of offshore finance centres, too, depends to a considerable extent on the goodwill of governments, both the host regime and external authorities. Recent years have seen increased intergovernmental consultations, particularly through the OECD, to obtain tighter official oversight of offshore finance. Similarly, national regulators of securities markets have collaborated since 1984 through the International Organization of Securities Commissions (IOSCO). State oversight of derivatives trading may also intensify as those transactions become better understood.

In short, there is little sign that global commerce and the state are inherently antithetical. On the contrary, the two have shown considerable mutual dependence. States have provided much of the regulatory framework for global trade and finance, albeit that they have shared these competences with other regulatory agencies.

The continuance of cultural diversity

Much evidence also confounds the common presumption that economic globalization is effecting cultural homogenization and a rise of cosmopolitan orientations over national identities. The growth of transborder production, the proliferation of global products, the multiplication of supraterritorial monies, and the expansion of transworld financial flows have shown little sign of heralding an end of cultural difference in the world economy.

True, global trade and finance are moved by much more than national loyalties. Consumers have repeatedly ignored exhortations to 'buy British' and the like in favour of global products. Shareholders and managers have rarely put national sentiments ahead of the profit margin. For example, the global media magnate Rupert Murdoch happily traded Australian for US citizenship when it suited his commercial purposes. Foreign exchange dealers readily desert their national currency in order to reap financial gain.

However, in other respects national identities and solidarities have survived—and sometimes positively thrived—in the contemporary globalizing economy. Most transborder companies have retained a readily recognized national affiliation, even if the situation is in practice not always so clear-cut. Most firms involved in global trade and finance have kept a mononational board of directors, and the operations of many of these enterprises continue to reflect a national style of business practice connected with the country of origin. Different national conventions have persisted in global finance as well. For instance, since equities have traditionally held a smaller place in German finance, globalization in that country has mainly involved banks and the bond markets.

Cultural diversity has also persisted in transborder marketing. Local peculiarities have often affected the way that a global product is sold and used in different places. Advertising has often been adjusted to local tastes to be more effective. New technologies like computer-aided design have moreover allowed companies to tailor some global products to local proclivities. In this vein Michael Porter has argued that 'national differences in character and culture, far from being threatened by global competition, prove integral to success in it' (1990: 30).

In sum, then, like globalization in general, its economic dimension has not had universal scope. Nor has the rise of global trade and finance marked the end of territorial space, the demise of the state, or full-scale cultural homogenization. However, recognition of these qualifications does not entail a rejection of notions of globalization altogether, on the lines of the sceptics noted earlier. After discounting for exaggeration and non sequiturs, the growth of globality remains a highly significant development in the contemporary world economy. The challenge for analysis is to tease out the interplay in economic globalization between territoriality and supraterritoriality, between territorial states and other governance arrangements, and between territorial identities and transborder affiliations.

Key points

- Global trade and finance have spread unevenly between different regions and different circles of people.

- Transborder commerce has to date often widened material inequalities within and between countries.

- Territorial geography continues to be important in the contemporary globalizing economy.

- Although lacking Westphalian sovereign powers, states exercise significant influence in global trade and finance.

- While economic globalization has weakened cultural diversity and national attachments in some respects, it has promoted them in others.

Conclusion

The present chapter has shown that, among other things, the globalization of world politics is a deeply economic affair. The growth of global trade and finance has deeply shaped—and been shaped by— the general developments described in Chapter 1. Economic globalization has affected different places and people to different extents, and it has far from eliminated older core structures of world politics: territory, state, and nation. However, these developments have already shifted many contours of geography, governance, and community; and economic globalization seems likely to unfold further still in the future.

The preceding pages have only touched on the wide-ranging and deeply significant questions of global trade and finance. In particular, this discussion has but hinted at the substantial problems of human security, social justice, and democracy that contemporary economic globalization has raised. Chapter 29 by Caroline Thomas addresses a number of these matters at greater length. For its part the present chapter will, I hope, have established the far-reaching importance of economic globalization when it is understood as the growth of a supraterritorial dimension in world commerce.

For further information and case studies on this subject, please visit the companion web site at www.oup.com/uk/booksites/politics.

QUESTIONS

1 Distinguish different conceptions of economic globalization.

2 To what extent is economic globalization new to contemporary history?

3 How does transborder production differ from territorial production?

4 How has globalization been manifested in changed forms of money?

5 What makes financial dealings in the euromarkets 'supraterritorial'?

6 What is an offshore financial centre?

7 To what extent has contemporary economic globalization marked 'the end of geography'?

8 How has globalization of trade and finance affected state capacities for economic regulation?

9 Discuss the impact of global products on cultural diversity.

10 To what extent can it be said that global capital carries no national flag?

11 Assess the relationship between globalization and income inequality.

12 In what ways might global commerce be reshaped to promote greater distributive justice?

GUIDE TO FURTHER READING

Barnet, R. J., and Cavanagh, J. (1994), *Global Dreams: Imperial Corporations and the New World Order* (New York: Simon & Schuster). A highly readable critical examination of transborder companies and global consumerism.

Held, D. *et al.* (1999), *Global Transformations: Politics, Economics and Culture* (Cambridge: Polity Press). Excellent on indicators and repercussions of economic globalization.

Hirst, P., and Thompson, G. (1999), *Globalization in Question: The International Economy and the Possibilities of Governance*, 2nd edn (Cambridge: Polity Press). A critique of 'globalist' presumptions that economic globalization is new, irreversible, and wholly beyond state control.

O'Brien, R., and Williams, M. (2004), *Global Political Economy: Evolution and Dynamics* (Basingstoke: Palgrave Macmillan). A thorough overview of the history and current challenges of global production and exchange.

Ohmae, K. (1990), *The Borderless World: Power and Strategy in the Interlinked Economy* (London: Fontana). A management consultant's celebration of global business.

Peterson, V. S., and Runyan, A. S. (1999), *Global Gender Issues*, 2nd edn (Boulder, Col.: Westview Press). A critical examination of the impacts of globalization on, *inter alia*, women's employment and the feminization of poverty

Porter, M. E. (ed.) (1986), *Competition in Global Industries* (Boston: Harvard Business School Press). A general discussion of global trade supplemented with numerous case studies from the Harvard Business School.

Porter, T. (2005), *Globalization and Finance* (Cambridge: Polity Press). A thorough analysis of global finance and its governance.

Scholte, J. A. (2005), *Globalization: A Critical Introduction*, 2nd edn (Basingstoke: Palgrave Macmillan). Elaborates the arguments presented in this chapter, including the implications of economic globalization for human security, social justice, and democracy.

Stubbs, R., and Underhill, G. R. D. (eds) (2000), *Political Economy and the Changing Global Order*, 2nd edn (Basingstoke: Palgrave). A textbook in International Political Economy with much concerning global trade and finance.

UNDP (1990–), *Human Development Report* (New York: Oxford University Press). This annual publication of the United Nations Development Programme includes much on the welfare consequences of economic globalization. See especially the 1999 edition.

WEB LINKS

www.iccwbo.org International Chamber of Commerce. Grouping thousands of member companies and associations from over 130 countries, the ICC is a strong business-sector proponent of market-led economic globalization.

www.nasdaq.com Nasdaq Stock Market. Covers the history, organization, and current trading activities of the world's largest completely screen-based stock exchange.

www.new-academy.ac.uk New Academy of Business. An education and research project, inspired by Body Shop founder Anita Roddick, to promote socially and environmentally responsible global companies.

www.oneworld.net OneWorld. An online gateway on global development issues that links over 2,000 civil society and media organizations in 89 countries.

CHAPTER 28

Causes and consequences of the communications and Internet revolution

JONATHAN D. ARONSON

READER'S GUIDE

During the 1990s the Internet and the World Wide Web exploded on to the scene. Communications always were critical in the conduct of international relations, but the onset of globalized networks makes the practice of foreign affairs even more complicated today. After providing a brief historical backdrop and an overview of global communications as of 2004, the chapter focuses on the key drivers that shape the global communication and information network and their security, political, economic, social, and cultural consequences. The chapter concludes with a review of the kinds of new global political issues raised by the globalization of communications and the demands for governance in this arena.

The author thanks Peter Cowhey and Steve Weber for comments and Lars Kavli for research assistance.

Introduction and historical background

The microprocessor and cheap memory revolutionized the communication industry in the 1980s. The Web was born in the 1990s. By 2000 the price of international telephone calls was a fraction of what it had been 15 years earlier, torrents of data pulsed through global digital networks, and the ways people communicated were transformed. Communications and information technology are now at the core of a new world information economy. As globalization proceeds we need to understand why global networking grew as it did, and the consequences of these developments for the workings of contemporary international relations.

A significant driver of globalization is the advent of faster, cheaper communications that are critical to growth, innovation, higher productivity, and job creation. The rise of affordable global communications also had two major consequences that fundamentally altered the practice of international relations, making it more difficult for policymakers to keep control. First, global communications upset the power balance among states, firms, and non-governmental organizations. The empowerment of new players on key issues and the restructuring of power relationships among existing actors forced change. Just as the cold war ended and bipolar competition gave way to new, more complex policy challenges, the rise of global communications augmented the loss of control of governments over traditional foreign and economic policy issues. Second, the instant saturation of broadcast and Internet channels with the latest news from anywhere on the planet pushed decisionmakers to act more quickly in response to breaking crises. Policymakers often did not have the luxury of time in which to deliberate about their decisions.

Until the early 1980s almost all national communications were provided by government-owned or government-controlled monopolies that were slow to innovate. Internationally there was limited voice traffic, occasional satellite broadcasts, and no commercial e-mail. There was no competition in the provision of international calls, so international calls were extremely expensive for callers, profitable for the phone companies, but not that numerous. The scheme for managing international voice

---

Box 28.1 The 1997 WTO agreement on basic telecommunications services

The WTO negotiations on basic telecommunications resulted in an agreement in which signatories adopted rules to encourage market access, adopt non-discriminatory regulations, and liberalize foreign investment restrictions by taking some, but not necessarily all, of the following steps:

1. to separate the regulatory body from the operators and to ensure that they treat all participants in the same manner;

2. to regulate closely suppliers of telecommunications services which exercise considerable market power;

3. to take measures to ensure that major suppliers do not engage in anti-competitive practices;

4. to ensure interconnection with a major supplier for competitors at any technically feasible point in the network

5. to enforce rules designed to ensure universal services in ways that are transparent, non-discriminatory, and competitively neutral;

6. to use procedures for the allocation and use of scarce resources such as radio frequencies that are timely, objective, transparent, and non-discriminatory.

Fifty-nine countries agreed to adopt transparent, pro-competitive regulatory principles, representing 99 per cent of the WTO telecommunications market. Forty-four countries agreed to permit significant inward foreign investment. Fifty countries guaranteed market access for all domestic and international satellite services and facilities.

The results of the WTO negotiations exceeded expectations. Twenty-three of the 25 European and Eastern European countries made full offers in all four categories. Eleven of the 20 offers from the Americas were strong across the board. Australia, Japan, New Zealand, and Singapore were far ahead of the other 12 Asian countries in fully liberalizing their markets. None of the eight African and Middle Eastern countries made full opening offers.

communications remained almost unchanged for more than a century, from the first telegraphic submarine cable until the mid-1970s. At its core was the International Telecommunication Union (ITU) that set technical standards, allocated spectrum, provided technical assistance to poorer **nations**, and later gave out orbital slots. In essence, the ITU was a cartel controlled by the national telephone monopolies.

At the start of the 1980s the British introduced limited competition and began privatizing British Telecom and Cable & Wireless. In the United States AT&T was broken up on 1 January 1984, but also was permitted, for the first time, to provide value-added and enhanced information services. Many countries followed Britain and the United States to embrace greater telecom competition, privatization, and **liberalization**. Convergence became the watchword as boundaries separating local and long-distance, voice and data, cable and telephone, and wireline and wireless services eroded. Service providers were permitted to provide content and broadcasters, studios, and other content providers could provide voice and data services.

On the international level, a series of trade negotiations pushed trade liberalization in new communications and information services and promoted competition by multiple competitors on a playing field that was made more level. Box 28.1 summarizes the results of the WTO agreement on basic telecommunications services that moved this process forward. In addition, the US Federal Communications Commission acted unilaterally to force a sharp reduction in international calling rates.

Key points

- Communications and IT firms are at the core of a new world information economy.

- The rise of cheap global communications added new players to the decisionmaking mix and often forced decisions to be taken more rapidly.

- National monopolies provided telephone services in almost all countries for decades. They used the International Telecommunication Union to prevent competition in the provision of international communications services.

- The introduction of domestic and international communications competition liberalized national and international communications, and unleashed significant technological innovation.

Globalization, the Internet, and the World Wide Web revolution

The global telecom and information landscape is in flux. Consider telephone, cellular, and Internet penetration. Table 28.1 shows the number of main telephone lines, cellular subscribers, and Internet users per 1,000 inhabitants in 1990 and 2001. In 2001 Scandinavia, the Benelux countries, Switzerland, and North America led on installed telephone lines. Most major European countries had closed the gap with North America on wireline telephone. **Europe** and Japan enjoyed substantially larger cellular penetration in 2001 than either the United States or Canada, which lagged far behind. By contrast, Internet penetration was higher in the United States than in every country except Korea, Sweden, and Iceland, but the gap is closing.

An examination of the flows of telecommunications traffic written within Europe and Asia demonstrates that geography still matters. The United States is the linchpin of interregional voice and data flows. Combined traffic flows between Europe and Asia/and the Pacific were about a third of what passed between North America and the three main regions. Note that international bandwidth is available for data transmission hubs through North America. The USA–Europe traffic is almost four times greater than the available bandwidth for USA–Asia traffic and almost 90 times as great as the link connecting Europe and Asia. Within Europe, Germany and the United Kingdom are the main hubs of international traffic flows with France in a strong third

Table 28.1 Connectivity in relation to the UN's Human Development Index ranking (per 1,000 people)

HDI ranking		Telephone mainlines		Cellular subscribers		Internet users	
		1990	2001	1990	2001	1990	2001
1	Norway	502	732	46	815	7.1	463.8
2	Iceland	510	664	39	865	5	599.3
3	Sweden	681	739	54	790	5.8	516.3
4	Australia	456	541	11	574	5.9	371.4
5	Netherlands	464	621	5	767	3.3	490.5
6	Belgium	393	498	4	747	(.)	310.4
7	United States	547	667	21	451	8	501.5
8	Canada	565	676	22	362	3.7	466.6
9	Japan	441	586	7	588	0.2	384.2
10	Switzerland	574	732	18	728	5.8	307
12	Ireland	281	485	7	774	0.6	233.1
13	United Kingdom	441	587	19	770	0.9	329.6
14	Finland	534	548	52	804	4	430.3
17	France	495	573	5	605	0.5	263.8
18	Germany	441	634	4	682	1.4	373.6
19	Spain	316	434	1	734	0.1	182.7
21	Italy	388	471	5	883	0.2	268.9
30	South Korea	306	486	2	621	0.2	521
55	Mexico	55	137	1	217	0.1	36.2
63	Russian Fed.	140	243	0	53	—	29.3
65	Brazil	65	128	—	167	—	46.6
104	China	6	137	—	110	—	25.7
	High Income	461	592	13	608	3.2	396.9
	Middle Income	41	152	—	128	—	36.8
	Low Income	10	30	—	10	—	6.4
	WORLD	98	169	2	153	—	79.6

Source: UN Human Development Report 2003.

position. The most recent data from Telegeography indicate that Europe generated 44.1 per cent of all outgoing international telecommunications flows in 2002, up from 41.4 per cent in 1996. Within Asia the five main hubs are Hong Kong, Australia, Japan, China, and Singapore. Taiwan and South Korea trail, but also are substantial hubs. North America originated 31.3 per cent of international traffic in 2002, down from 32.3 per cent in 1996.

One way to interpret these statistics is that competition and innovation have promoted three major trends that are transforming global communications, reshaping the world information economy, and reshaping world politics and international relations.

Trend 1. The Rise of Data: First, although telephone penetration and international voice traffic proceeds incrementally, the growth of data transmission is far outdistancing the growth of domestic and international voice traffic. The changes in the size of market segments reflect these trends. In 1994 the world telecommunication services market of

$517 billion was about 16 per cent data and 10 per cent mobile. In 2001 the world telecommunications services market was $968 billion even though competition had caused prices to plunge in many of the world's largest markets. Data revenues were about 18.5 per cent even though data were, by volume, now equal in size to voice traffic. Mobile had grown to about 33 per cent of world telecommunications revenues. International traffic had slipped from more than 8 per cent of the total revenue to less than 8 per cent (ITU 2001). The success of the Internet and the Web and the rapid growth of e-commerce all help to explain this trend. However, there is another way to look at this trend. The rise of global digital networks made much less meaningful the distinction between voice and data. Streaming bits can now be reassembled in much richer, more textured forms as voice, data, images, films, or music. From this perspective the real change is that people, governments, firms, and computers are using communication networks to interact much more than in the past.

Trend 2. The rise of the Internet and the Web: The Internet changes how a network is organized, the services it can provide, and its cost **structure**. Internet architectures are cheaper and more powerful than traditional phone networks. Voice is being supplemented by more complex communication flows that require more bits to be transmitted thanks to the Internet, the Web, and the continuing sharp declines in computing costs. In addition phones are becoming interchangeable with computers, as witnessed by the latest cell phones (which have powerful microprocessors). Further, just as banks sometimes give away mobile phone handsets to new customers, cable companies soon will bundle domestic and long-distance telephone services in their service packages. As a result, every network of any competitive economy will need to support data applications reliably. Modern economies require modern networks that efficiently carry vast amounts of information. This means that the cost of sending large amounts of data needs to be minimal. This, in turn, means that the price of traditional phone services—domestic, long-distance, and international—will rapidly begin to approach zero. Indeed, voice services that use Internet connections and allow free calls, including international ones, are already proliferating.

Trend 3. The rise of wireless networking: The third significant trend is the emergence of **wireless networks** that now connect more users than do wired networks. Satellite and microwave systems began the movement away from wireline to the first major fixed wireless system of the modern era. Satellite services were originally provided almost exclusively through monopoly systems, mainly through the Intelsat system. Terrestrial mobile wireless systems followed. New fixed, wireless (**WiFi**) systems that can deliver large bandwidth for short distances are now proliferating. In addition, videophones now provide many of the international stories on CNN and the BBC. All of these are substitutes for conventional phone services that use transmission cables and make possible alternative choices. The new systems provide affordable voice and data links for many poor countries with little or no connectivity to international submarine cables. Wireless voice traffic and data transfer could shortly compete strongly with wireline voice and data transfer for dominance worldwide.

The significance of wireless for society, regulation, and international relations is huge. The early leaders are Korea, Japan, and Finland, but the rest of Europe is now moving quickly, with North America trailing. Wireless has opened the way to a vast increase in the connectivity of the developing countries' populations. It is cheaper and faster to deploy than wired networks. However, communications regulators in developing countries have so far treated it as if it were a luxury premium service for the better-off and business. As a result, they allowed mobile operators to charge higher prices for service but also encouraged competition in these services earlier than for wired networks. The pace of globalization was accelerated by competition which pushed down prices for long-distance and international calls and unleashed innovation, stimulating tremendous investment in and growth of global communications. National firms partnered and merged, often across national borders, to achieve the scale and scope necessary to operate **global networks**. In essence the emergence of affordable, integrated global networks provided the backbone of the World Wide Web and was a huge catalyst that juggled the priorities and agenda of international relations.

Key points

- The United States is the linchpin of interregional telecommunications and data traffic, but European countries generate a third more international traffic flows than North America.

- Growth rates are higher in Europe, Latin America, the Pacific, and Africa than in North America or Asia.

- International data traffic has grown faster than international voice traffic and is now the larger of the two. The distinction between voice and data is losing its meaning. The rise of the Internet, the Web, and e-commerce complements this trend.

- Wireless Internet voice traffic and international videophones will increase in popularity.

Drivers that shape globalization

Figure 28.1 presents a dynamic model of telecommunications and IT globalization. This section focuses on the drivers that shape globalization. Later the consequences of globalization will be considered. Start with the assumption that firms work to make money and dominate markets. To do so they use expertise from different disciplines to try to guide globalization in ways that help them and

undermine their competitors. Their strategies may involve influencing the policy and regulations that shape how **global networks** operate, the hardware that comprises the network, the content that flows through the network, or the software that mediates between the hardware and content. Firms employ different strategic tools to win at each level. The interdisciplinary nature of these tools is one reason

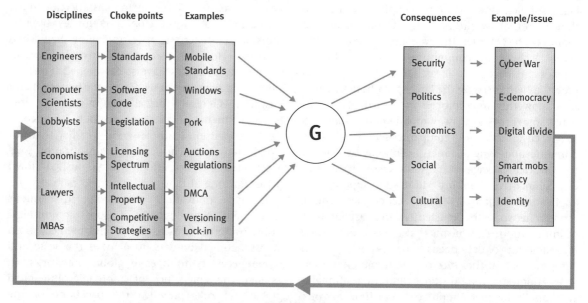

Governance efforts using various regulations, laws, and institutions

Fig. 28.1 A dynamic model of telecommunications/IT globalization

that the role of communications in determining the structure of global networks is not well understood. Six separate strategies that depend on different professional expertise are noted in Fig. 28.1 to illustrate how firms try to advantage themselves.

First, engineers create the technical **standards** for equipment and the mechanisms for physically linking them. This can be accomplished cooperatively or conflict may arise. Whoever controls standards that triumph in the market-place holds a significant competitive advantage. But the 'best' standard is not always the winning standard. Famously, the once ubiquitous VHS standard for videorecording vanquished Sony's Beta standard, even though at the time Beta was the superior technical standard. Nonetheless, a strong alliance of companies that did not want Sony to dominate the market successfully supported the VHS standard that ultimately was embraced everywhere. At present there is significant competition between Europe, the United States, and China over which wireless standards will triumph.

Second, computer programmers write the *software* that instructs the hardware how to operate and allow content to flow through networks. Those that design and own the software determine how networks operate. The obvious example is Windows. The battle for control of communications was initially waged between AT&T (which controlled the communication network) and IBM (which dominated the terminals attached to the network). They battled over where the intelligence should be located in the network. To try to leverage their strengths, AT&T favoured a smart network with dumb terminals; IBM advocated smart terminals and a dumb network. But they were debating the wrong issue, so both firms lost. Microsoft, by designing the operating system now run by most personal computers, won the battle that traditional powers did not understand was being fought until it was too late. However, there is a backlash against Microsoft. Hackers delight in exposing the weaknesses in Windows' security and many programmers (and IBM) champion Linux, as an alternative to Windows.

Third, firms hire lobbyists to try to create advantage for them by persuading politicians and regulators to adopt laws and public policies that benefit them. Firms may try to obtain trade protection, subsidies, or tax breaks for national firms versus foreign

ones from their own governments, for their industries over other industries, and even for one firm or process over another. At a minimum, lobbyists for established interests work hard to block laws and regulations that might undermine their favoured position. Lobbyists and the firms they represent try to elect politicians who favour their positions and lobby for changes in policy that enhance their clients' interests.

Fourth, economists worry about money and its distribution. If governments implement successful economic strategies that play to the strengths of some firms or sectors more than others, then those firms or sectors are more likely to prosper. Economists associated with firms and with government regulatory agencies continually joust with one another trying to devise policies that will skew benefits to their clients or citizens. Their focus is on the generation of revenue and **influence** and its distribution among the governments, firms, and consumers. Firms working within markets or under government guidance **rules** set prices. Government economists advise legislators and policymakers about taxation issues. In the telecommunications arena government economists have been critical in developing schemes for spectrum allocation and licensing that are meant to generate revenue for the government, spur growth and innovation, and ensure customers receive the best possible service at a fair price. One reason that privatization of government-owned telecommunications monopolists proved popular was that the sale of their **equity** generated large sums of cash for government coffers. More recently, economists urged governments to auction off scarce spectrum instead of distributing it free to existing operators or in lotteries.

Fifth, intellectual property lawyers have allowed firms to make the ownership of content into a key issue of control. Intellectual property in the network environment is critical because information is expensive to create, but additional, perfect copies are cheap to produce. Owners of content have gained a boost in the past decade because of unanticipated advances achieved in the protection of international **intellectual property rights** during the NAFTA and Uruguay Round of trade negotiations. The United States also unilaterally extended the intellectual property rights of US firms through such measures as the Digital Millennium Copyright Act of 1998. However, the owners of information are concerned that the technology now exists to enable the simpler and cheaper manufacture of perfect copies of software, films, and music than ever before. Critics worry that the balance between innovators and users has tilted too far in favour of the owners of intellectual property and that consumers, the poor, and those in developing countries are being disadvantaged. Specifically, the extension and strengthening of intellectual property laws in the telecommunications/IT arena give a new weapon to firms that own intellectual property, but some believe that the laws are now so one-sided that some firms are using them to stifle competition. Firms trying to claim ownership of key technologies on the Internet could hold progress and innovation hostage.

Sixth, business executives, many with MBA qualifications, seek competitive strategies to lock in customers, manage their corporate alliances, and legally undermine opponents (Shapiro and Varian). Executives are paid to design marketing and pricing strategies that will attract a broad range of customers who are willing to pay different prices for different versions of the same product. Similarly, it may be possible to sell different versions of a product with quite different features in different countries and cultures. To the extent possible firms try to lock in their more profitable customers either by making it expensive for them to switch vendors in mid-process or by providing huge incentives to good customers to stick with the same vendor.

> **Key points**
>
> - Different professional expertise is used by firms to create advantage. Computer programmers and engineers can design software and standards to create competitive advantages for firms within networks.
> - Lobbyists work to shape laws and public policy to advantage their clients.
> - Economists try to devise systems to increase the revenue and profits of their clients, firms, or governments.
> - Lawyers use intellectual property laws to maximize the power of firms over content.
> - Business executives are paid to find ways to create advantages and profits for their firms relative to their competitors.

The impact of the information revolution on international relations and institutions

The impact of the deregulatory push in America and Britain during the 1980s also tilted the balance of influence from government towards firms and markets. The rebalancing of power among actors in international affairs was accelerated by the information revolution. The Web and the information revolution already have had tremendous security, political, economic, social, and cultural consequences. This section briefly notes the altered roles of countries, companies, non-governmental organizations (NGOs), international institutions, and individuals and then examines the consequences for international relations already evident.

The information revolution altered the role of government policymakers in four main ways. First, policymakers now have access to much more information, perhaps too much information. As the run-up to 9/11 makes clear, paralysis through information overload is a real danger. Second, global networks mean that decisionmaking can be centralized or decentralized. Governments generally have centralized decisionmaking, reducing the importance of ambassadors and embassies and tempting political leaders to micro-manage military situations and economic negotiations in distant locations because they can, not because they should. Third, global networks erode the monopoly of information in the hands of governments, democratizing access to breaking information. Firms, journalists, and NGOs often have better information than governments. Fourth, global networks provide transparency to everybody, making it difficult for countries unilaterally to take national policy decisions when the problems are global.

Globalization and global networks also allow business firms to think and act in terms of global production and a global market-place, heightening their international influence. The global movement of money and information allows firms to achieve global production strategies, including the use of strategies such as outsourcing, and simultaneously makes it more difficult for national governments to regulate them effectively. In the absence of effective international regulation, these firms are gaining in influence.

Global networks empowered and vastly increased the numbers of NGOs and even individuals on the international stage. NGOs now create, track, and disseminate information and organize people and groups sympathetic to their goals to pursue specific policy outcomes in areas such as human rights advocacy, environmental protection, and women's rights. The most striking example of the positive influence of NGOs was their major role in the negotiations to ban landmines and their success in raising human rights concerns. NGO efforts to ban land mines are summarized in Box 28.2. A more visible impact of NGOs came when environmental NGOs and labour unions joined to disrupt the attempt by governments to launch a WTO Trade Round in Seattle in November 1999. The round was finally launched in Doha, Qatar, a city not noted for public demonstrations and dissent.

Ironically, international institutions like the WTO and the IMF are both more important and less effective international actors because of the rise of global networks. They are more important because in the absence of effective national policies to deal with globalization, these institutions are the logical venues through which to organize cooperative international policies. They are less effective because critics of such institutions, who complain that they are neither democratic nor even-handed, have stymied their initiatives at major junctures.

Box 28.2 | **The campaign to ban landmines**

In 1997 the Nobel Peace Prize was awarded to the International Campaign to Ban Landmines (**www.icbl.org/**), a consortium of about 1,000 NGOs that helped mobilize public opinion and motivated governments. The cause was championed by Princess Diana, the International Committee of the Red Cross, and a handful of NGOs such as the Vietnam Veterans of America, which first advocated the ban. The Web allowed NGOs and individuals to organize support for the ban and assist sympathetic political leaders such as UN Secretary General Kofi Annan, Canadian Foreign Minister Lloyd Axworthy, and US Senator Patrick Leahy to move the process forward.

The Mine Ban Treaty of December 1997 bans the use, production, stockpiling, and transfer of antipersonnel landmines. The treaty became international law on 1 March 1999. As of 10 September 2004 the treaty had been ratified by 143 countries. Another nine countries had signed but had not completed their ratification process, bringing the total number of countries supporting the treaty to 152. At that date, 42 countries had not joined the treaty. Major states that have so far not signed or ratified the treaty include the United States, Russia, China, India, Pakistan, the two Koreas, Egypt, Iran, Iraq, Israel, Cuba, Saudi Arabia, Finland, and Vietnam.

These kinds of shifts influenced world politics and the theory of international relations. Global communications enabled and empowered new nongovernmental institutions and accelerated and broadened transnational contacts between states and non-state actors in other countries. Non-state actors, firms, and smaller, interest-driven NGOs proliferated because their internal communications made them more cohesive and transnational. In addition, global networks and new communication technologies produced a democratization of intelligence-like information that narrowed the information gap between states and others. For example, although official intelligence efforts to find weapons of mass destruction in Iraq have so far failed, in late 2002 photos taken by a commercial satellite documented Iran's active nuclear programme and forced this issue on to the Bush Administration's agenda.

International relations theories have adapted to incorporate globalization and global networks into

CWS

their approaches. Globalization did not banish high-level state-to-state relations, but did add several layers of complexity. The variants of theory that begin with 'neo' and/or end with 'ism' continue to proliferate, but in essence the impact of global networks is to undermine government control and to make it possible for those at the top and those at the bottom of society to interact in new ways. Supranational and subnational players matter in different ways, at different times, on different issues. Leaders isolate themselves from grassroots opinion at their own risk. The democratization of information in real time levels the field in terms of who knows what, when, and where. Every crisis is aired on CNN and BBC as it happens, often forcing decisionmakers to act quickly instead of deliberating over their responses. The same breaking news and, importantly, a flood of vivid images of the breaking news is available from all but the most remote points and is instantly available in countries around the world. Today the trendiest place in Timbuktu, Mali is the MCT (Multipurpose Community Telecentre) opened in May 1998. In Tibet tourists and residents can check their e-mail at the Barkhor Caf, not too far from the Lhasa Holiday Inn. The percentage of the world's population linked to the global communications network in one or more ways is growing rapidly. Those on the outside truly suffer from a digital divide, but this gap may be closing more rapidly than most people appreciate because nodes are proliferating, costs are declining, and governments more and more understand that building a telecommunications/IT infrastructure needs to be a development priority.

Key points

- The information revolution increased the influence of the market and of giant firms relative to governments.

- Global networks allowed NGOs to increase in number and influence. NGOs sometimes promote positive changes, but may hamper initiatives that governments and firms launch through international institutions.

- Global networks and new communication technologies empowered non-state actors and democratized access to information. The information gap between states and others narrowed.

- Decisionmakers must act more quickly because every crisis is aired on CNN and BBC as it happens. A flood of information, often with vivid images, is narrowing the global news gaps. Democracy slows down decisions, so governments are having a more difficult time keeping up with changing situations.

Security, political, economic, social, and cultural consequences

The consequences of global networks and communications cut across borders and issues. The results are both positive and disruptive, raising new opportunities and challenges for global stability. This section surveys both the positive and negative consequences of globalization and global networks for international security, politics, economics, and social/cultural identity. The final section of this chapter examines the challenges for governance raised by these developments.

Security consequences: intelligence gathering, activism, and cyberwar

The information revolution altered the nature of intelligence operations, political opposition, and the waging of war. However, access to more information does not automatically translate into better policy decisions or greater national security. Components of this sea change include: intelligence gathering and its impact on foreign policy; the rise of 'activism, hacktivism, and cyberterrorism' (Arquilla and Ronfeldt 2001) and the use of networked information to

CWS

initiate terrorist actions or to use in military conflict. Table 28.2, for example, indicates the benefits and drawbacks faced by netwar terrorists trying to use IT to further their aims.

First, global communication networks help governments collect and analyse vast quantities of information to inform their decisions. But greater intelligence collection often does not always translate into better policy or prevention of terrorism. The information-collection capabilities of modern intelligence services were already evident in the 1980s after a Soviet fighter downed Korean Airlines 007. Within hours, President Reagan released the taped conversations between the Soviet pilot who shot down the plane and his ground base. Two decades later, despite extensive efforts and technological advances in intelligence gathering, efforts failed to prevent the terrorist attacks on 11 September 2001 on the World Trade Center and the Pentagon or the Madrid train bombings two and a half years to the day later. Similarly, despite confident claims by American and British leaders that Iraq was poised to unleash weapons of mass destruction (WMD), a year after the invasion of Iraq in 2003, no WMDs have been found. Even when important information exists, locating it and recognizing its importance in time to prevent disasters can be challenging.

Thus, deciding what intelligence matters becomes imperative in the conduct of electronic espionage, especially because cyberterrorists have access to almost the same information on the Web. Information overload may also leave less room for intuition, trust, and secret understandings that were traditional instruments of the process. In short, more information may be a blessing when bureaucrats and political leaders can manage, analyse, and synthesize the data. It can be a curse when abundant information overloads or dehumanizes the decisionmaking process to the detriment of creativity and flexibility. Similarly, global networks allow governments to centralize decisionmaking, increasing the influence of a narrow range of top leaders. This may not translate into sound, efficient policy choices. Indeed, many large firms have decided to decentralize their decisionmaking processes and to give more authority to those closer to the customers.

Second, governments and others now routinely try to use 'soft power' to influence the views of others through television, radio, and print media and via the Web. Those who generate the information view it as 'public diplomacy'. Those on the receiving end are more likely to see such broadcasts as propaganda. The United States, in the aftermath of 9/11, began to focus more on public diplomacy initiatives. In March 2002 the United States launched Radio Sawa, an Arabic-language radio station to provide an

Table 28.2 Benefits and drawbacks of IT use for netwar terrorists (facilitating and mitigating factors)

IT use	Facilitating	Mitigating
Organizational	Enables dispersed activities with reasonable security Helps maintain a loose and flexible network Lessens need for state sponsorship	Susceptibility to wire and wireless tapping Digitally stored information can be easily retrievable unless well protected Cannot itself energize a network; common ideology and direct contact still essential
Offensive	Generally lower entry costs Eradication of national boundaries Physically safer Spillover benefits for recruitment/fundraising	Current bombing techniques already effective Significant technical hurdles for disruptive and destructive information operations Unique computer security risks impose recurring costs of 'technological treadmill'

Source: Reprinted with permission from Michele Zanini and Sean J. A. Edwards, 'The Networking of Terror In the Information Age', in John Arquilla and David Ronfeldt (eds), *Networks and Netwars* (Santa Monica, Cal.: RAND, 2001): 48.

American perspective mixed with music to attract those who otherwise might not listen. In February 2004 Al Hurra, a US-funded Arabic language television news station, went on the air throughout the Middle East. Famously, in the mid-1990s the Zapatistas in Chiapas, Mexico, knowing they could never win a military struggle, launched a social netwar spearheaded by 'Subcommander Marcos' to make their case against the Mexican Government to the world. By making their plight transparent to the world, they created a media playing field on which they could compete and sometimes triumph.

Those dissatisfied with the current order found in global networks a tool that allowed diverse individuals to organize to make their voice heard. Activists and NGOs of all political persuasions have seized on the Web as a mechanism to maximize their influence and lobbying clout. Advocacy networks in support of human rights issues, the environment, to oppose violence against women, and to seek the end of landmine use have been especially noteworthy (Keck and Sikking). Similarly, in the 'Battle at Seattle' anti-globalization activists used new global communications technologies to organize against the WTO and the forces of globalization that they opposed. A more virulent form of activism occurs when hackers, for fun, fame, or politics, break into networks and try to cripple or sabotage them or infect them with viruses, worms, and other forms of attack.

Third, global data communication networks and new information technologies are changing modern warfare. Knowledge is the key to destruction as well as to production. The potential power of information weapons was demonstrated in the 1990 and 2003 invasions of Iraq. The military was bolstered by AWACS (an Airborne Warning and Control System) which scanned the sky for enemy aircraft and missiles and sent targeting data to allied forces from modified Boeing 707s. In parallel, J-STARS (the Joint Surveillance and Target Attack System) helped detect, disrupt, and destroy Iraqi ground forces during Desert Storm with speed and precision. Similarly, the battle for Kosovo was fought from the air. Smart bombs were delivered by smart planes directed by smart computers. In this virtual war the attacking forces suffered no fatalities during the fighting.

In addition, the Pentagon apparently has considered launching direct cyberattacks on its foes to bring down their computer and communications systems, but there is reluctance to go as far as this because there remains uncertainty regarding cyberwarfare's place amid the rules of armed conflict. Weaker states and terrorist organizations cannot compete with the military firepower of the United States and Britain, but they have tried to mount cyberattacks on vulnerable US computer systems and networks. For example, in 2001 at the nadir of US-Chinese relations, Chinese hackers launched waves of cyber attacks on US Government computer systems in an effort to penetrate and sabotage them.

Political consequences: from e-democracy to e-terrorism

The political consequences of globalization and global networks also are both positive and negative. E-government that engages citizens more directly in the political process is technologically feasible. At the same time, the process, politics, and political implications that result from the new technologies could foment civil unrest and confusion.

On the positive side, new communications and information technologies are beginning to enable advances in e-government, e-democracy, and e-participation (United Nations Economic and Social Council 2003). Governments and candidates now routinely use the Web to provide citizens and supporters with information. Increasingly politicians and parties use the Web to solicit contributions. More rarely, governments and candidates use the Web to elicit views from their people and to seek input to assist them in their decisionmaking. A few isolated localities have also experimented with e-voting in elections. The lasting legacy of Governor Howard Dean, the unsuccessful US Democratic Party presidential candidate in 2004, may be that his use of the Internet to motivate and involve supporters and raise funds for his campaign was a precursor of what it is to come.

At the same time, governments are losing their hegemony over the political process. New communications and information technologies empower NGOs, firms, revolutionaries, terrorists, fundamentalist religious leaders, extremists of all stripes, criminal syndicates, and political subversives as well as well-meaning social movements, reformers, and activists. This raises concerns that decentralized, fragmented, anarchic chaos is on the horizon that may overwhelm the positive benefits of communications and information technology. Alternatively, governments may emulate China and crack down and reassert their control over the Internet and their citizens.

Economic consequences: growth, digital divide, and criminal organizations

The strongest case for globalization and global networks is that they promote economic growth through increased trade and investment. Companies and countries that are early adopters of communications and information technologies may enjoy an information edge as they compete and grow. Globalization and global communications do not, however, guarantee that growth will be distributed equitably within or between countries. Furthermore, global flows of funds and information may undermine national policies and facilitate crime and corruption. It is unclear, for example, whether national monetary authorities can control money supply or exchange rates in a globalized economy, especially when large sums of money are being illegally laundered. In short, national governments are challenged as they try effectively to manage global firms and markets.

The teledensity gap between upper and middle income and the poorest countries results in a 'digital divide' relative to the industrial world that is especially poignant. The Benton Foundation estimates that 'there are an estimated 429 million people online globally, but even this staggering number is small when considered in context. For example, of those 429 million, fully 41% are in North America. Also, 429 million represents only 6% of the world's entire population.' Such statistics suggest that large segments of the world's population have no way of participating in the information economy. Without Internet access, economically marginalized populations will experience even greater development gaps than they already face.

The World Bank's InfoDev project concisely summarizes the dilemma: the Internet revolution is both an opportunity and a threat for developing countries. The Internet presents the opportunity to leapfrog communications into a new level beyond voice communications and incorporates entirely new applications and services. It presents the opportunity to enhance social and economic conditions through this higher level of communications, thus presenting the potential for convergence in the social and economic status of nations around the world. At the other extreme, however, is the threat that the Internet revolution results in an increased gap in the communications infrastructure and that this gap could inevitably hinder the pace of social and economic development *vis-à-vis* the developed world, thus resulting in a world where the global economic order diverges further. Box 28.3 describes this dilemma in greater detail.

Some developing countries have successfully narrowed the gap. China now has more mobile phone users than any country in the world and South Korea is the world's leader in advanced telecommunications services. Until recently most analysts worried that the digital divide would devastate poor countries' prospects. More recently this concern has been called into question. A debate rages over whether the digital divide is widening or narrowing. In the parallel case of the Internet, in the United States, according to the Center for Communication Policy at the University of California at Los Angeles, the digital divide seems to be closing. Latinos and African-Americans are the fastest-growing Internet users. The gender gap is also narrowing so that only a slightly larger percentage of men than women are online. By 2014 80 to 85 per cent of Americans are predicted to be connected to the Internet, approaching the predicted percentage penetration among the leading Internet adopters—Sweden, Finland, and South Korea. By that time Britain, Germany, and Japan should be approaching 75 per cent penetration.

But for populations and countries with only sparse connectivity to the world, Manuel Castells argues, 'uneven development is the most dramatic expression of the digital divide'. Moreover, the digital divide within and between countries should not be 'measured by the number of connections to the Internet, but by the consequences of both connection and lack of connection'. The 'social unevenness of the development process is linked to the networking logic and global reach of the new economy. ... Education, information, science, and technology become the critical sources of value creation in the Internet-based economy' (Castells 2001: 265–9). To be competitive within a networked

world-economy countries and firms and individuals within them must have access to global flows of capital and information. It is but a short logical jump from this starting point to contend that if legitimate, legal capital flows and especially information flows are restricted, alternatives will be found. If large parts of the population in poorer countries are shut out of

---

Box 28.3 | **The digital divide challenge: examining the gap between haves and have-nots**

Without basic connectivity countries cannot participate in a communications revolution and the gap between the haves and have-nots in the short and medium term could widen. The digital divide for mobile, Internet, and broadband access accounts varies substantially across countries. **Leaders** have the highest penetration levels in all areas of communications and are entering the multimedia phase of the Internet revolution. **Latecomers** have low penetration levels, moderate literacy rates, low income levels, and economic and social conditions that discourage ready availability of financial capital. They could be left behind in the absence of serious external intervention. **Adopters** are in between and many will unleash the Internet revolution in the near future.

Mobile

Mobile service is fast becoming the preferred medium for basic voice communications. In the medium term, mobile markets offer the greatest hope for narrowing the connectivity gap. The gap between Leaders and Adopters should shrink as markets in the Leader countries mature and growth in the Adopter countries stays strong. Competition should promote lower prices and entry costs; the spread of prepaid and calling party pay services should increase mass market penetration, reduce prices, improving quality and greater geographic coverage should boost mobile phones over fixed lines. Although mobile prices usually are higher, the level of service innovation, customer service, and price reductions competition has led to greater dynamism in mobile markets than in the fixed-line sector.

Internet

The Internet gap between developed and developing countries is less likely to narrow in the medium term. Even with the falling prices for personal computers, the cost is a significant barrier to individuals in developing countries. Low literacy and low levels of connectivity limit the growth of Internet connections. Weak postal systems, poor financial systems, and lower utility because there are few local

language sites also may limit Internet growth. Although the high cost of service probably will encourage multiple user accounts and a greater reliance on community access centres, such as Internet cafés, the Internet audience should grow. Further, the Internet is a low-cost alternative to international voice communications and should attract business from price-sensitive firms and individuals in developing countries.

Broadband access

There is considerable danger that the gap in broadband access could widen because of its high price and because the initial target market in most developing countries may be too small to spur the private sector and investments. Carriers, with limited financial resources, first focus on basic connectivity. So, few carriers in the developing world have concrete plans for the deployment of broadband access technology. Poor prospects for broadband access in developing nations also raise the risk of divergence that could sabotage the chance of Latecomers to benefit from the 'Internet Economy'.

Recommendations

Adopter and Latecomer countries need to emphasize three priorities: (1) **Connectivity**—at least 5 per cent connectivity probably is needed to leapfrog to Internet connectivity. (2) **Competition** is needed to spur investment, decrease prices, and boost subscriber growth and new technology development. The challenge is successfully to initiate and regulate competition. (3) Widespread **literacy and IT technology knowledge** are needed to participate in the Internet revolution. In short, to narrow the digital divide Adopters need to build the foundations necessary to launch affordable and ubiquitous broadband access. Latecomers must first concentrate on providing broad, basic connectivity and worry about deploying broadband infrastructure later.

Source: Greatly condensed from the Executive Summary of World Bank/InfoDev 2001.

the new economy, global criminal activities will arise to create illicit transnational networks instead. Inevitably, such activities will undermine the legitimacy and stability of governments and the civic culture and can, in extreme instances, result in the destruction of the rule of law, the collapse of state authority, and sometimes to violence and civil war.

Similarly, illegal activities could undermine the trust in and functioning of the world-economy. Organized crime has a long history. The Sicilian mafia, the Cali cartel, Chinese triads, Japanese Yakuza, Russian criminal networks, and their predecessors have operated for centuries. But globalization and global networks have prompted criminal networks to form transnational strategic partnerships to ply their illegal, often violent trade. Since the 1980s sophisticated transnational criminal organizations using global communications and transportation technologies have expanded their grasp and become more efficient. The United Nations Conference on Transnational Crime noted in 1994 that criminal organizations were active in crimes involving the transnational movement of drugs, weapons and weapon-grade materials, people and body parts, and money. **Drug smuggling** is the dominant global criminal activity from Colombia to Thailand. Ironically, the greatest threat facing the drug trade may be drug legalization, not government success at shutting down the supply side. **Weapons trafficking** is a multi-billion dollar business that can easily spill over to supply arms and munitions to revolutionaries, terrorists, and criminals. Smuggling of **nuclear weapons-grade material** for possible use by 'rogue' states or terrorists is a real risk. Concern for the safekeeping of Russian nuclear material has long worried specialists; in 2004 the head of Pakistan's nuclear programme confessed that he had sold materials abroad illegally. The smuggling of **illegal immigrants** eager for a better life has increased as opportunities diverged in richer and poorer countries. The **trafficking in women** for menial work and prostitution, of **children**, and of **body parts** also has increased. **Money laundering** through global networks is the glue that holds all of the other transnational criminal activities together.

Social and cultural consequences: smart mobs and transnational identities

The rise of new information and communications technologies creates a second digital divide separating those who are comfortable using new technologies from those who are not. Those who are connected to the technology also are increasingly connected to virtual communities with which they regularly share information and ideas, even if they have never met in physical space. These smart mobs gather and disperse, intellectually and physically, with remarkable speed (Rheingold 2003). In short, one consequence of global networks is that they enable actors to relate to and interact with institutions and one another in new ways. Another consequence, related to the transparency created in an interconnected world, is that individuals lose significant amounts of their privacy. It now is routine to 'google' those you meet. A slightly deeper examination will reveal credit reports, parking tickets, and employment and criminal records. Ironically, those plotting terrorism may choose not to use new communications sources precisely because that could expose their activities in advance.

On the cultural side, communications networks redefine questions of identity, of determining 'Who is us?' Again technology pulls identity in conflicting directions. On the one hand, the Internet allows people to get in touch or stay in touch with their roots and maintain their family, ethnic, religious, and cultural ties. Unlike travellers and immigrants in previous generations, those who move across the globe today do not cut ties with family, friends, and their workplace because phone and e-mail connections are usually cheap and available. At the same time, cultures blend into one another and become more global today because of shared attachments to news, movies, video games, fashion, design, and even cuisine. Thus, hyphenated identities are slowly giving way to multiple identities shared among global citizens.

In summary, globalization has tremendous consequences in different arenas. But globalization is a dynamic process. As new consequences emerge, companies, countries, and individuals adjust. These adjustments provide feedback and impact on factors driving globalization, so the process continues to

unfold. But globalization is a journey, not a destination.

Key points

- The information revolution altered intelligence gathering and its impact on foreign policy; allowed activists and cyberterrorists to gain more influence; and networked information has transformed military conflict.

- New communications and information technologies are beginning to enable advances in e-government, e-democracy, and e-participation. But they also empower NGOs, firms, revolutionaries, terrorists, fundamentalist religious leaders, extremists of all stripes, criminal syndicates, and political subversives as well as well-meaning social movements, reformers,

and activists. These forces threaten stability, raising concerns that decentralized, fragmented anarchy could occur.

- Global networks promote economic growth but may lead to uneven development. Faced with a growing digital divide, legal and illegal activities could undermine the trust in and functioning of the world-economy.

- Virtual communities build on new network connections and change the identity of those participating.

Governance in a time of information revolution

As globalization proceeds, governance issues grow more complicated. At each stage governments and private firms react to new developments and consequences which in turn alter the dynamics of globalization. At the same time, social movements, terrorists, revolutionaries, and criminal organizations which are focused on their own goals and interests try to manipulate globalization and global networks to their own advantage. As complexity and numbers increase, the chance that networks will fall apart, leading to system breakdown, economic collapse, and violence also grows. Unless a flexible system of governance emerges, problems are likely to intensify and could spiral out of control.

There are four main options. First, governments can try to muddle through, reacting as new circumstances and issues arise. The problem is that national regulations are less and less effective when dealing with global issues and transnational movements. Second, governments can deregulate, step aside, and put their faith in the magic of markets. However, as they pursue power and profit large firms frequently distort markets. Over time firms may behave better and increasingly practise 'self-regulation' because

their behaviour can and probably will be exposed globally, but the record of self-regulation is spotty at best. Further, malicious hackers, criminal organizations, terrorists, and other rogue actors can be counted on to 'cheat' whenever it is in their interest. Third, governments may try to work through international institutions like the ITU, the WTO, or the IMF. Here too there is a problem. Activists and NGOs fear that international institutions are undemocratic and serve as puppets for rich firms and governments. Thus, although governments have transformed the international telecommunications regime since 1984, the effort to create an equitable **international regime** to govern the world information economy has proceeded in fits and starts. Fourth, there are now a few instances in which individuals and grassroots users take responsibility for managing and maintaining international **cooperation**. Prominent examples include **open source software** efforts such as Linux or Apache that are maintained by programmers around the world and the California-based, but internationally organized NGO, the Internet Corporation for Assigned Names and Numbers (ICANN), which administers the Internet's domain name system. Linux has enjoyed significant successes, but the ICANN experience to date has been uneven.

With technology changing so rapidly, rules negotiated in prolonged trade negotiations are always going to be out of date before they come into force. Rules and regulations can only remain relevant if they are flexible enough to evolve along with the system. But that is so complicated that critics worry that if the wrong rules are negotiated or misguided policies are introduced, problems will inevitably arise. The challenge for policymakers is to be sensitive to inputs from firms and NGOs, to figure out which rules are needed (and which are not) and how they should be structured, implemented, and enforced in ways that benefit individuals and the society as a whole.

Nobody has solved the challenge of constructing and implementing a sustainable regime for managing global networks, global firms, and global economies. The task grows ever more complex because there are more and more relevant players—developing countries, global firms, labour unions, and NGOs. Moreover, as the Web powers the **transition** towards globalization, every country, large firm, and NGO is actively engaged in the process because they realize that the agreements that are struck will determine whether they are winners or losers in the emerging world information economy. Their future is at stake.

There is considerable debate about the impact of globalization on risk and uncertainty, growth and inequality, democracy and freedom, family and social relationships, and international affairs. But globalization is a dynamic process that governments and other actors continuously influence. The information revolution caught policymakers unprepared but, as it continues to unfold, the choices that governments (and other actors) make about policy do matter. So far governments and international institutions have advanced no coherent plan about how or even whether they should guide the information revolution or about how to create an international regime for cyberspace. Here, we consider four key challenges facing policymakers with regard to cyberspace, that links all countries and an increasing percentage the world's population.

The legal and policy areas most directly affected by the communication and Web revolution can be grouped into five main areas that impact (1) individuals, (2) the content that flows over global networks, (3) the global communication infrastructure, (4) the global regulatory environment, and (5) international relations. Each of these areas requires attention because of the global nature of cyberspace, all of them may require global cooperation and **coordination**. The relative influence of governments, firms, NGOs, and international government organizations (IGOs), social movements, criminal and terrorist organizations, and individuals will all shape globalization and the information revolution as it continues to unfold. Yet the balance of influence among these actors varies from issue to issue.

Policies affecting individuals: privacy and secrecy

Privacy rights and data security concerns are heightened in cyberspace (including data security and encryption issues, sometimes referred to as the 'Balkans of the cyber age'). Data communications and especially electronic commerce transactions take place in a new form of 'space' in which much greater surveillance by governments, employers, or individuals is possible. How should the rights and privacy of individuals be protected and balanced in light of the pressing data security needs of governments and firms in an age of rising terrorism? Similarly, in many countries officials try to control content that is viewed as containing pornography, excessive violence, bigotry, and hatred, or that is relevant to national security concerns. This becomes especially sensitive and may lead to international dissension because different countries focus on different issues—Europe is more worried about Nazi memorabilia than America; China blocks Internet sites related to Tibet.

Policies affecting content: intellectual property

In a global digital age content that flows across global networks has great value. Intellectual property rules that protect the owners of content through copyright, patents, trade marks, and trade secrets are more important now that perfect digital copies are cheap to make. The potential for software or film piracy in China or music piracy by students is immense. Firms and innovators argue that investment and *research and development* will dry up if innovators are not fairly compensated for their inventions. By contrast, if intellectual property fees are so high that users, in developing countries, cannot afford to pay to license new technologies they face immense barriers to their development. Should, for example, Africans with HIV-AIDs, who cannot afford to pay for expensive drug treatments, be condemned to early death?

One of the most visible successes of the Uruguay Round trade negotiations was the TRIPs (Trade-Related Intellectual Property) agreement of 1994 that strengthened international intellectual property protection and established new enforcement mechanisms and dispute-settlement procedures. Critics in industrial and developing countries worry, however, that the TRIPs agreement and the similar arrangements agreed to by the United States, Canada, and Mexico negotiated under the NAFTA accord tilted the balance between the rights of innovators and of users too far towards the creators of intellectual property. Finding appropriate ways to balance and harmonize the rights of users and innovators across borders may prove a significant and ongoing challenge.

For example any successful governance scheme for international intellectual property will need to balance the interests involved in three interdependent power relationships. First, can the balance between the interests of transnational firms and users be kept roughly equal? The legal and treaty advantage has shifted in favour of owners of intellectual property, but given the significant technology and information technology advances in areas such as file sharing and open source, is it possible for countries and firms to enforce international intellectual property laws and agreements? Second, now that progress in NAFTA and TRIPs has succeeded in creating stricter international intellectual property protection for industrial countries' interests, can the needs of developing countries be safeguarded in the trading system? Third, what is the relationship between international intellectual property rights, innov-

ation, and creativity? Specifically, should large companies that are subsidized by military, government, and academic infusions of money and talent be allowed to reap all the rents from 'their' intellectual property? Also, if users are innovators, not separate from them, are we in danger of establishing an international intellectual property regime that discourages innovation?

Policies affecting the network: standard setting

The global communications network is the largest single human creation. It is a logistical marvel that allows anyone anywhere to dial a few numbers on their phone or type a few strokes at a keyboard and be connected in moments to any other phone or computer in the world. With the advent of mobile, wireless communications this is true even when the communications devices are in motion, even across borders. Globalization depends on the smooth functioning of this global network. The computers, telephones, and personal digital assistants (PDAs) connected to the network must be compatible with each other or nothing happens. Therefore technical standards, set mainly by engineers, make global networking possible. Predictably firms which control key standards get rich and powerful. Losers lag or vanish altogether. Therefore countries and companies engage in ongoing standards wars. The outcome of these intense, but almost invisible battles delineates the shape of networks, competition, and advantage in an era of globalization. Not surprisingly, governments and users want to encourage competition and discourage bottlenecks to promote efficient global networks. As a result, the regulation and setting of technical standards to ensure network interconnectivity and interoperability is critical.

Policies affecting global competition: competition (anti-trust) policy

Liberalization and the decline of micro-management is not the same as deregulation and free markets. To cope with global networks policymakers need to know when to act, and when not to act. They will need to understand how to act, and how not to act. They will need to balance domestic politics and national interests against international realities enhanced by globalization. They will need to develop mechanisms flexible and robust enough to withstand attacks by rebels and terrorists intent on abusing or undermining the network and the existing order.

Specifically, there is growing attention being paid to cross-national and international governance and rule making as the idea that markets and corporate self-governance will suffice recedes. The pressures of determining jurisdiction and the limits of sovereignty are growing. Although the pendulum of influence may have swung towards markets and firms, government policymakers and regulators will not go away. If they are savvy, they adapt to new circumstances and develop new tools. Competition is on the rise nationally and internationally, but, predictably, established incumbents continue to try to take advantage of their dominant position whenever they have the opportunity. One consequence is

that regulators nationally and internationally are concluding that **competition policy** (or **anti-trust policy** as it is called in the United States) is trade policy. These *new-style regulators* are intent on promoting competition by curbing potential global monopolists. They want to be proactive without being micro-managers. But regulators and policymakers on different continents may not agree and harmonized policies are unlikely to emerge soon. For example, the EU blocked the merger between General Electric and Honeywell which had already been approved by the US Justice Department and continued to prosecute Microsoft after it had settled in the United States.

Global networks operated by global firms are under increasing scrutiny. In Europe, the Competition Directorate of the European Commission has intervened to stop transborder mergers within Europe and has expressed strong concerns that caused mergers within the United States to be restructured or even abandoned (General Electric and Honeywell). Even after the US Government

---

Box 28.4 Key concepts

Competition (anti-trust) policy: policies that prohibit anti-competitive action and transactions by firms, especially monopolists, including state-owned enterprises.

Deregulation: the removal of all regulation so that market forces, not government policy, control economic developments.

Digital divide: the gap in technology access/ownership between those who have access to advanced communications and information services and those who are either too poor to afford such access or live in rural or remote areas with no access. Most often, the gap is that between the Internet 'haves' and 'have nots'.

E-government: the use of technology to engage people in the political process.

Global network: digital networks that span the globe allowing instant voice and data communication worldwide—the global information highway.

Intellectual property rights: rules that protect the owners of content through copyright, patents, trade marks and trade secrets.

Netwar (or cyberwar): the use of digital networks and communications to attack enemies as an act of war or terrorism.

Non-governmental organization (NGO): an organization with policy goals. NGOs, often grassroots ones, are neither governmental nor corporate in their make-up. Examples include Amnesty International and the International Campaign to Ban Landmines.

Open source software: software that is built on the idea that software should be freely distributed and that potential users should not be excluded.

Standards war: conflict between countries or firms over which standards to adopt.

WiFi: Wireless Fidelity, fixed, wireless systems that can deliver large bandwidth for short distances.

Wireless network: communication data and voice traffic networked through microwave and satellite connections.

settled with Microsoft, Europe continued to prosecute it in relation to its practices. More generally, as telecommunications and IT firms are transformed into global networking giants, regulators are trying to promote the efficient and affordable flow of information across national borders by ensuring that multiple carriers are positioned to compete to provide comparable services. Where they succeed in promoting competition, less regulation is needed.

The effect on international relations

In 1989 the fall of the Berlin Wall precipitated the collapse of the Soviet Union, the end of the cold war, and if not the end of history, at least a major shake-up in international relations. That same year the launching of commercial Internet operations went unnoticed, but it too led in time to the World Web and to fundamental changes in international affairs. The latest information revolution that is hurtling forward on the wings of global communication networks also raises new opportunities and challenges that will rewrite the way that the existing order works. The ultimate impact on international affairs will be far ranging. But, just as was the case with the introduction of the printing press authorities do not want to accept that the world as they knew it is gone. If governments, firms, and NGOs fail to use instant, affordable access to vast troves of information and knowledge to promote equality and cooperation and instead concentrate on maximizing their wealth,

power, and narrow self-interest, prospects for peace and sustainability will be bleak. But if leaders and individuals, men and women, of all ages and from all nations and backgrounds, are allowed to share in the possibilities of global networks, then perhaps we will begin to move in a better direction.

Key points

- The nature of cyberspace impacts individuals, the content that flows over global networks, the communication infrastructure, and the global regulatory environment.

- A balance is needed between protecting the rights of individuals and the data security needs of governments and firms.

- A balance is needed between the rights of users of information and those of the creators of information. Therefore, valuing intellectual property on global networks is important.

- Whoever controls the winning standards wins. Therefore, 'standards wars' are fierce.

- Competition (anti-trust) policy is becoming trade policy for the world information economy.

- The advent of global networks will transform international relations as much as the end of the cold war did. Whether the results will be positive or negative is unclear.

Conclusion

Global communications networks are a driving force propelling globalization and challenging policy-makers to adapt to new international challenges. But it is not enough to say that global networks and the Web 'will change everything'. It also is necessary to find out which changes are short-term fads driven by speedier delivery of more information and which constitute fundamental long-term shifts in the way people, organizations, and governments deal with one another. In the future international relations

will involve more actors interacting about more issues on a transparent, but complex field of play. To succeed leaders will need to use the abundance of information at their disposal to help them decide what matters and how to achieve their goals. But the democratization of information means that others will have much the same information that they possess. In that sense, all the forces that traditionally shaped international relations remain the same, but global networks have accelerated the intensity and speed of the interactions. The challenge will be to find ways for national governments, working alone or together, to guide globalization through its next phase.

For further information and case studies on this subject, please visit the companion web site at www.oup.com/uk/booksites/politics.

QUESTIONS

1 Why did economists and policymakers traditionally decide that the monopoly provision of telecommunications services made more sense than competition in the provision of telecommunications services?

2 Why did policymakers start to promote competition and reduce regulation in the provision of communication and information services during the 1980s and 1990s?

3 How are the Internet and the World Wide Web connected to globalization?

4 How do firms use choke points to enhance their global competitive position?

5 How would easy, affordable wireless Internet connections change your life?

6 Is it possible for any country to develop and progress without being fully integrated into global networks? Why or why not?

7 To what extent should policymakers be concerned with the 'digital divide', 'transparency', and 'universal service'? Which should be the first priority and why?

8 After the GATT/WTO entered into the trade in telecommunications services arena how do you expect that the ITU reacted to the trespassing on its turf? On balance did this improve the ITU?

9 If globalization is irreversible and national policies are increasingly ineffective, what should be done? Muddle through? Deregulate and get out of the way? Depend on international agreements and institutions? Or do something else?

10 How does the way you communicate today differ from the way you connected to the world three years ago? What changes in the way you communicate do you expect during the next few years?

GUIDE TO FURTHER READING

Arquilla, J., and Ronfeldt, D. (eds) (2001), *Networks and Netwars* (Santa Monica, Cal.: RAND). An examination of violent and social netwars, past, present, and future.

Berners-Lee, T., with Fischetti, M. (1999), *Weaving the Web: The Original Design and Ultimate Destiny of the World Wide Web by Its Inventor* (New York: Harper San Francisco). A first-hand account of the creation and evolution of the World Wide Web.

Cairncross, F. (1997), *The Death of Distance: How the Communications Revolution Will Change Our Lives* (Boston: Harvard Business School Press). Senior editor at *The Economist* explores how the communications revolution and the Internet will change everything.

Castells, M. (2001), *The Internet Galaxy* (New York: Oxford University Press). A short set of reflections on the Internet, business, and society.

—— (2000, 2004), *The Rise of Network Society*, 3 vols, 2nd edn (Oxford: Blackwell). Brilliant, dense, multilayered account of the economic and social dynamics of the information age. Castells sweeps across time and continents in an effort to formulate a systematic theory of the information society.

International Telecommunication Union (2002), *Internet for a Mobile Generation* (Geneva: ITU). The international telecommunications union provides analysis and statistics.

—— (various), *World Telecommunication Development Report* (Geneva: ITU). The best available source of comparative data on communications. New reports are issued every year or so and also contain essays on specific issues, in 2003 it focused on measuring access to the information society.

Kalathil, S., and Boas, T. C. (2003), *Open Networks Closed Regimes* (Washington, DC: Carnegie Endowment for International Peace). The impact of the Internet on authoritarian rule in China, Cuba, Singapore, Vietnam, Burma, Saudi Arabia, and Egypt.

Keck, M., and Sikkink, K. (1998), *Activists Beyond Borders* (Ithaca, NY: Cornell University Press). The rise of advocacy networks as significant players in international politics.

Kogut, B. (ed.) (2003), *The Global Internet Economy* (Cambridge, Mass.: MIT Press). A business school professor has brought together chapters on the Internet in the United States Sweden, France, Germany, South Korea, and Japan. There are also cross-cutting chapters on issues of regulation and governance.

Lessig, L. (1999), *Code and Other Laws of Cyberspace* (New York: Basic Books). A Stanford Law School professor provides a lucid analysis of the relationship between law, cyberspace, and social organization. How the code is written determines who wins and loses.

—— (2004), *Free Culture* (New York: Penguin). How the media use technology and the law to lock down culture and control creativity. Available free online at: www.msnbc.msn.com/id/4585579/#040329.

Levy, B., and Spiller, P. T. (eds) (1996), *Regulations, Institutions, and Commitment: Comparative Studies of Telecommunications* (New York: Cambridge University Press). Economists assess the impact of core political and social institutions on regulatory structures and performance in the telecommunications industry in Jamaica, the United Kingdom, Chile, Argentina, and the Philippines.

Price, M. (2002), *Media and Sovereignty: The Global Information Revolution and Its Challenge to State Power* (Cambridge, Mass.: MIT Press). A law school professor assesses how the media impacts states and their sovereignty.

Rheingold, H. (2003), *Smart Mobs: The Next Social Revolution* (Cambridge, Mass.: Perseus). A keen observer of the social implications of technology considers how new forms of communication will change our lives and our identities.

UNESCO (1998), *World Culture Report: Culture, Creativity and Markets* (Paris: UNESCO). Excellent report on the impact of communications on culture and society. It includes extensive comparative statistical tables on cultural indicators.

United Nations Economic and Social Council (2003), *World Public Sector Report 2002: E-Government at the Crossroads* (New York: UN). Prospects for e-democracy and e-government.

Weber, S. (2004), *The Success of Open Source* (Cambridge, Mass.: Harvard University Press).

World Bank/InfoDev (2001), *Global Information Infrastructure*. Report prepared by Pyramid Research—EIU (Washington, DC: World Bank). Comprehensive report on the digital divide.

WEB LINKS

www.apectelwg.org Asia-Pacific Economic Cooperation Telecommunications & Information Working Group (APECTEL). Projects and reports on telecommunications and information infrastructure in the APEC region.

www.fcc.gov Federal Communications Commission (USA). This is the first stop for those wanting to understand US domestic and international communications policy.

www.intug.net International Telecommunications Users Group. Position papers, speeches, and surveys on issues related to global telecommunications policy and emergent problems.

www.itu.int/indicators International Telecommunications Union (USA). The best source on international communication statistics.

www.oecd.org/sti/telecom OECD, Directorate of Science, Technology, and Industry—Information and Communications Policy section. Data on the communication sectors of OECD countries including OECD Communications Outlook, OECD Information Technology Outlook.

www.ofcom.org.uk/ Office of Communication (OFCOM) (UK). The site of the new regulator of British communications industries.

www.sciencedirect.com/science/journal/03085961 *Telecommunications Policy* journal.

www.telecommunications.com Latest telecommunications news from the World News Network.

www.telegeography.com Database and reports about the global geography of the Internet, voice traffic, and networks.

www.totaltele.com A comprehensive site on international communications developments that includes *Communications Week International*, a journal focusing on telecommunications reform, management, and regulation.

www.worldbank.org/ict and info.worldbank.org/ict World Bank, Global Information & Communication Technologies Department. Publications, reports, and links to related web sites including Telecoms Virtual Library.

CHAPTER 29

Poverty, development, and hunger

CAROLINE THOMAS

READER'S GUIDE

This chapter explores and illustrates the contested nature of a number of important concepts in International Relations. It examines the orthodox mainstream understanding of poverty, development, and hunger, and contrasts this with a critical alternative approach. Consideration is given to how successful the development orthodoxy has been in incorporating and thereby neutralizing the concerns of the critical alternative. The chapter then closes with an assessment of the likelihood of a globalization with a human face in the twenty-first century.

Introduction

Since 1945 we have witnessed over fifty years of unprecedented official development policies and impressive global economic growth. Yet global polarization is increasing, with the economic gap between rich and poor states and people growing (see Table 29.1). Box 29.1 shows that as a discipline International Relations has been slow to engage with these issues

Poverty, hunger, and disease remain widespread, and women and girls continue to comprise the majority of the world's poorest people. Moreover, this general situation is not confined to that part of the world that we have traditionally termed the 'South' or the 'Third World'. Particularly since the 1980s and 1990s, the worldwide promotion of neo-liberal economic policies (the so-called Washington consensus) by global governance institutions has been accompanied by increasing inequalities within and between states. During this period the Second World countries of the former Eastern bloc have been incorporated into the Third World grouping of states, and millions of people previously cushioned by the state have been thrown into poverty with the transition to market economies. In the developed world, rising social inequalities characterized the social landscape of the 1980s and 1990s. Within the Third World countries, the adverse impact of globalization has been felt acutely, as countries have been forced to adopt free market policies as a condition of debt rescheduling and in the hope of attracting new investment to spur development. Gendered outcomes of these neo-liberal economic policies have been noted, though the global picture is very mixed,

Table 29.1 Changing income ratios

Year	Income ratio of 20% global population in richest countries to 20% in poorest
1960	30 : 1
1990	60 : 1
1997	74 : 1

Source: Adapted from UNDP 1999: 3.

Box 29.1   International Relations theory and the marginalization of priority issues for the Third World

- Traditionally, the discipline focused on issues relating to inter-state conflict, and regarded security and development as separate areas.

- Mainstream Realist and Liberal scholars neglected the challenges presented to human well-being by the existence of global underdevelopment.

- Dependency theorists were interested in persistent and deepening inequality and relations between North and South, but they received little attention in the discipline.

- During the 1990s, debate flourished, and several sub-fields developed or emerged which touched on matters of poverty, development, and hunger, albeit tangentially (e.g. global environmental politics, gender, international political economy).

- More significant in the 1990s in raising within the discipline the concerns of the majority of humanity and states, were the contributions from post-colonial theorists, Marxist theorists (Hardt and Negri), scholars adopting a human security approach (Nef, Thomas), and the few concerned directly with development (Saurin, Weber).

- At the beginning of the twenty-first century, the discipline is better placed to engage with the inter-related issues of poverty, development, and hunger.

- And therefore to influence the diplomatic world, where interest in these issues is increasing, spurred on by fears of terrorist threats and recognition of the uneven impact of globalization.

(Thomas and Wilkin 2004)

---

with other factors such as class, race, and ethnicity contributing to local outcomes (Buvinic 1997: 39).

The enormity of the current challenges was recognized in the UN in 2000 with the acceptance of the

Box 29.2	Mapping mainstream and alternative approaches to poverty, development, and hunger		
	Poverty	**Development**	**Hunger**
Mainstream approach	Unfulfilled material needs	Linear path—traditional to modern	Not enough food to go around everyone
Critical alternative approach	Unfulfilled material and non-material needs	Diverse paths, locally driven	There is enough food, the problem is distribution and entitlement

Millennium Development Goals (www.undp.org). These set time-limited, quantifiable targets across eight areas, ranging from poverty to health, gender education, environment, and development. The first goal was the eradication of extreme poverty and hunger, with the target of halving the proportion of people living on less than a dollar a day by 2015.

The attempts of the majority of governments, intergovernmental organizations, and non-governmental organizations (NGOs) since 1945 to address global hunger and poverty can be categorized into two very broad types, depending on the explanations they provide for the existence of these problems and the respective solutions that they prescribe. These can be identified as the dominant mainstream or **orthodox approach**, which provides and values a particular body of developmental knowledge, and a **critical alternative approach**, which incorporates other more marginalized understandings of the development challenge and process. Most of this chapter will be devoted to an examination of the differences between these two approaches in relationship to the three related topics of poverty, development, and hunger, with particular emphasis being placed upon the topic of development. The chapter concludes with an assessment of whether the desperate conditions in which so many of the world's citizens find themselves today are likely to improve. Again, two contrasting approaches are outlined.

Poverty

Different conceptions of poverty underpin the mainstream and alternative views of development. There is basic agreement on the material aspect of poverty, such as lack of food, clean water, and sanitation, but disagreement on the importance of non-material aspects. Also, key differences emerge in regard to how material needs should be met, and hence about the goal of development.

Most governments, international organizations citizens in the West, and many elsewhere adhere to the orthodox conception of poverty. This refers to a situation where people do not have the money to buy adequate food or satisfy other basic needs, and are often classified as un- or underemployed. This mainstream understanding of poverty based on money has arisen as a result of the globalization of Western culture and the attendant expansion of the market. Thus a community which provides for itself outside of monetized cash transactions and wage labour, such as a hunter-gatherer pygmy group, is regarded as poor.

Since 1945, this meaning of poverty has been almost universalized. Poverty is seen as an economic condition dependent on cash transactions in the market-place for its eradication. These transactions in turn are dependent on development defined as economic growth. An economic yardstick is used to measure and to judge all societies.

Poverty has widely been regarded as characterizing the Third World, and it has a gendered face. An approach has developed whereby it is seen as incumbent upon the developed countries to 'help' the Third World eradicate 'poverty', and increasingly to address female poverty. James Wolfensohn, Managing Director of the World Bank, declared in February 2000 that 'The World Bank is committed to making gender equality central to its fight against poverty' (cited in World Bank 2000). The solution advocated to overcome global poverty is the further integration of the global economy (Thomas 2000) and of women into this process (Pearson 2000; Weber 2002). Increasingly however, as globalization has intensifed, poverty defined in such economic terms has come to characterize significant sectors of population in advanced developed countries such as the USA (see Bello 1994).

Critical, alternative views of poverty exist in other cultures where the emphasis is not simply on money, but on spiritual values, community ties, and availability of common resources. In traditional subsistence methods, a common strategy for survival is provision for oneself and one's family via community-regulated access to common water, land, and fodder. The autonomy characteristic of such methods may be highly valued by those who have traditionally practised them. Indeed some such methods have been sustained over thousands of years. For many people in the developing world the ability to provide for oneself and one's family may be preferable to dependence on an unpredictable market and/or an unreliable government.

Critical views on poverty have emanated from within Western society also. For example, it has been asserted that our emphasis on monetary values has led to the creation of 'a system of production that ravishes nature and a society that mutilates man' (Schumacher 1973).

Some global institutions have been important in promoting a conception of poverty that extends beyond material indicators. The work of the UNDP since the early 1990s is significant here for distinguishing between income poverty (a material condition) and human poverty (encompassing human dignity, agency, opportunity, and choices). The issue of poverty and the challenge of poverty alleviation moved up the global political agenda at

the close of the twentieth century, as evidenced in the UN's first Millennium Development Goals cited earlier. While World Bank figures for the 1990s showed a global improvement in reducing the number of people living on less than a dollar a day (its orthodox measurement of extreme poverty), the picture was uneven: in sub-Saharan Africa the situation deteriorated, and elsewhere, such as the Russian Federation, the Commonwealth of Independent States, Latin America and the Caribbean, and some Middle Eastern states, the picture remains bleak. Most of the global improvement resulted from trends in China and India, and even there, deep pockets of poverty remain.

Key points

- The monetary-based conception of poverty has been almost universalized among governments and international organizations since 1945.

- Poverty is interpreted as a condition suffered by people—the majority of whom are female—who do not earn enough money to satisfy their basic material requirements in the market-place.

- Developed countries have regarded poverty as being something external to them and a defining feature of the Third World. This view has provided justification for the former to help 'develop' the latter by promoting their further integration into the global market.

- However, such poverty is increasingly endured by significant sectors of the population in the North, as well as the Third World, hence rendering traditional categories less useful.

- A critical alternative view of poverty places more emphasis on lack of access to community-regulated common resources, community ties, and spiritual values.

- Poverty moved up the global political agenda at the start of the twenty-first century.

Having considered the orthodox and critical alternative views of poverty, we will now turn to an examination of the important topic of development. This examination will be conducted in three main parts.

The first part will start by examining the orthodox view of development and will then proceed to an assessment of its effect on post-war development in the Third World. The second part will examine the critical alternative view of development and its application to subjects such as empowerment and democracy. In the third part consideration will be given to the ways in which the orthodox approach to development has responded to some of the criticisms made of it by the critical alternative approach.

Development

When we consider the topic of **development** it is important to realize that all conceptions of development necessarily reflect a particular set of social and political values. Indeed, it is true to say that 'Development can be conceived only within an ideological framework' (Roberts 1984: 7).

Since the Second World War the dominant understanding, favoured by the majority of governments and multilateral agencies, has seen development as synonymous with economic growth within the context of a free market international economy. Economic growth is identified as necessary for combating poverty, defined as the inability of people to meet their basic material needs through cash transactions. This is seen in the influential reports of the World Bank, where countries are categorized according to whether they are low-income, lower middle-income, upper middle-income, or high-income countries. Those countries that have the lower national incomes per head of population are regarded as being less developed than those with higher incomes, and they are perceived as being in need of increased integration into the global marketplace.

An alternative view of development has, however, emerged from the occasional government, UN agency, grassroots movements, NGOs, and some academics. Their concerns have centred broadly on entitlement and distribution. Poverty is identified as the inability to provide for the material needs of oneself and one's family by subsistence or cash transactions, and by the absence of an environment conducive to human well-being broadly conceived in spiritual and community terms. These voices of opposition are growing significantly louder, as ideas polarize following the apparent universal triumph of economic **liberalism**. The language of opposition is changing to incorporate matters of democracy such as political empowerment, participation, meaningful **self-determination** for the majority, protection of the commons, and an emphasis on pro-poor growth. The differences between the orthodox and the alternative views of development are summarized in Box 29.3. In the following two sections we will examine how the orthodox view of development has been applied at a global level and assess what measure of success it has achieved.

Economic liberalism and the post-1945 international economic order

During the Second World War there was a strong belief amongst the allied **Powers** that the protectionist trade policies of the 1930s had contributed significantly to the outbreak of the war. Plans were drawn up by the USA and the UK for the creation of a stable post-war **international order** with the United Nations (UN), its affiliates the **International Monetary Fund** (IMF) and the World Bank, plus the **General Agreement on Tariffs and Trade** (GATT), providing the institutional bases. The latter three provided the foundations of a liberal international economic **order** based on the pursuit of free trade, but allowing an appropriate role for state intervention in the market in support of **national security** and national and global stability (Rapley 1996). This has been called **embedded liberalism**. The **decisionmaking procedures** of these international economic institutions favoured a small group of developed Western states. Their relationship with the UN, which in the General Assembly has more democratic procedures, has not always been an easy one.

In the early post-war years, reconstruction of

Box 29.3	Development: a contested concept

The orthodox view

Poverty: a situation suffered by people who do not have the *money to buy food* and satisfy other basic *material needs*.

Purpose: transformation of traditional subsistence economies defined as 'backward' into industrial, commodified economies defined as 'modern'. Production of surplus. Individuals sell their labour for money, rather than producing to meet their family's needs.

Core ideas and assumptions: the possibility of unlimited economic growth in a free-market system. Economies would reach a 'take-off' point and thereafter wealth would trickle down to those at the bottom. Superiority of the 'Western' model and knowledge. Belief that the process would ultimately benefit everyone. Domination, exploitation of nature.

Measurement: economic growth; Gross Domestic Product (GDP) per capita: industrialization, including of agriculture.

Process: top-down; reliance on 'expert knowledge', usually Western and definitely external; large capital investments in large projects; advanced technology; expansion of the private sphere.

The alternative view

Poverty: a situation suffered by people who are not able to meet their *material and non-material needs* through their own effort.

Purpose: creation of human well-being through sustainable societies in social, cultural, political, and economic terms.

Core ideas and assumptions: sufficiency. The inherent value of nature, cultural diversity, and the community-controlled commons (water, land, air, forest). Human activity in balance with nature. Self-reliance. Democratic inclusion, participation, for example, voice for marginalized groups, e.g. women, indigenous groups. Local control.

Measurement: fulfilment of basic material and non-material human needs of everyone; condition of the natural environment. Political empowerment of marginalized.

Process: bottom-up; participatory; reliance on appropriate (often local) knowledge and technology; small investments in small-scale projects; protection of the commons.

previously developed states took priority over assisting developing states. This reconstruction process really took off in the context of the **cold war**, with the transfer of huge sums of money from the United States to **Europe** in the form of bilateral aid from the Marshall Plan of 1947. In the 1950s and 1960s as decolonization progressed, the focus of the World Bank and the UN system generally shifted to the perceived needs of developing countries. The USA was heavily involved as the most important funder of the World Bank and the UN, and also in a bilateral capacity.

There was a widespread belief in the developed Western countries, amongst the managers of the major multilateral institutions, and throughout the UN system, that Third World states were economically backward and needed to be 'developed'. This process would require intervention in their economies. This attitude was widely shared by Western-educated elites in those countries. In the context of independence movements the development imperative came to be shared by many citizens in the Third

World. The underlying assumption was that the Western lifestyle and mode of economic organization were superior and should be universally aspired to.

The cold war provided a context in which there was a competition between the West and the Eastern bloc to win allies in the 'Third World'. The USA believed that the path of liberal economic growth would result in development, and that development would result in hostility to socialist ideals. The USSR, by contrast, attempted to sell its economic system as the most rapid means for the newly independent states to achieve industrialization and development. The process of industrialization underpinned conceptions of development in both East and West, but whereas in the capitalist sphere the market was to be the engine of growth, in the socialist sphere central planning by the state was the preferred method. The majority of Third World states were born into and accepted a place within the Western, capitalist orbit, while a few either by choice or lack of options ended up in the socialist camp. Yet in the early post-war and post-colonial decades, all states, whether in the West, East, or Third World, favoured an important role for the state in development. Many Third World countries pursued a strategy of import substitution industrialization, in order to try to break out of their dependent position in the world-economy as peripheral producers of primary commodities for the core developed countries.

With the ending of the cold war and the collapse of the Eastern bloc after 1989, neo-liberal economic and political philosophy came to dominate development thinking across the globe. The championing of unadulterated liberal economic values played an important role in accelerating the globalization process. This represented an important ideological shift. The 'embedded liberalism' of the early post-war decades gave way to the unadulterated neoclassical economic policies which favoured a minimalist state and an enhanced role for the market: the so-called 'Washington consensus'. The belief was that global welfare would be maximized by the liberalization of trade, finance, and investment, and by the restructuring of national economies to provide an enabling environment for capital. Such policies would also ensure the repayment of debt. The former Eastern bloc countries were now seen to be in transition from centrally planned to market economies, and throughout the Third World the state was rolled back and the market given the role of major engine of growth and associated development. This approach was presented as common sense, with the attendant idea that 'There is No Alternative' or TINA (Thomas 2000).

By the end of the 1990s the G7 (later the G8) and associated international financial institutions were championing a slightly modified version of the neo-liberal economic orthodoxy, labelled the 'post Washington consensus', which stressed pro-poor growth and poverty reduction based on continued domestic policy reform and growth through trade liberalization. Henceforth, locally owned national poverty reduction strategy papers would be the focus for funding (Cammack 2002). These papers quickly became the litmus test for funding from an increasingly integrated line-up of global financial institutions and donors.

The achievements of the post-1945 international economic order

There have been major gains for developing countries since 1945 as measured by the orthodox criteria of economic growth, GDP per capita and industrialization. The rates of total and per capita growth for developing countries in the periods 1960–70, 1970–80, and 1980–7 are shown in Fig. 29.1. With respect to economic growth, from 1950 to the end of the 1980s, the economies of developing countries grew on average at 4.9 per cent per year, compared with a growth of 3.5 per cent for developed economies (Adams 1993: 8). In countries with over 90 per cent of the population of the developing world, the annual average growth rate of the GDP per capita remained positive over the period 1960–87. However, a striking feature of the per capita economic growth of developing countries revealed in Table 29.2 is its marked **regional diversity**, with some countries (largely in Asia and the Americas) achieving substantial growth rates, and others (largely in Africa) not doing so well.

CWS

In the 1990s, the picture was far less positive. The UNDP reports that: 'no fewer than 100 countries—all developing or in transition—have experienced serious economic decline over the past three decades. As a result, per capita income in these 100 countries is lower than it was 10, 20, even 30 years ago' (UNDP 1998: 37). Moreover the 1990s saw 21 countries experience decade-long declines in social and economic indicators, compared with only four in the 1980s (UNDP 2003). Financial crises spread across the globe and indicated marked reversals in Mexico, the East Asian states, Brazil, and Russia. The African continent looked increasingly excluded from any economic benefits of globalization, and 33 countries there ended the 1990s more heavily indebted than they had been two decades earlier (Easterly 2002). By the end of the century, not a single former Second or Third World country had joined the ranks of the First World in a solid sense. Significant growth occurred in a handful of countries such as China, India, and Mexico—the 'new globalizers'—but the benefits were not well distributed within those countries. Despite significant improvements in global social indicators such as adult literacy, access

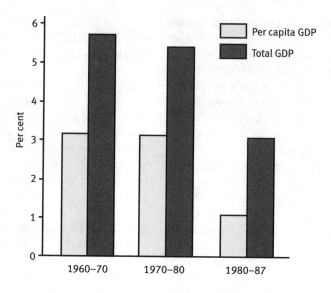

Fig. 29.1 Per capita and total GDP growth rates in the South between 1960 and 1987

Source: South Commission 1990: 33 (based on UNCTAD data).

Table 29.2 Annual average rates of growth of per capita GDP of individual developing countries, 1960–1989

	<0%	0–2%	2–4%	>4%	Totals
No. of countries with growth rates falling within designated ranges	26	43	26	11	106
Breakdown of countries by major geographical region					
Americas	4	13	11	0	28
Africa	19	20	6	3	48
Asia	3	10	9	8	30
Share of total population* accounted for by countries in each growth range (%)	7.0	56.4	30.7	5.0	100

Source: Adams (1993: 12; based on UNCTAD data for 1989).
* Total population of those countries covered in the table.

to safe water, and infant mortality rates, global deprivation continues. This is illustrated vividly in Fig. 29.2.

Having looked briefly at the broad achievements of the post-war international economic order, we will now proceed to an assessment of these achievements from, first of all, the perspective of the mainstream orthodox view of development, and then the critical alternative view of development.

The orthodox assessment of the post-war international economic order

Prior to the late 1970s, the rate of industrial growth was higher in the developing world as a whole than in the developed capitalist countries taken as a group. Many developing countries exhibited an impressive economic performance, and average per capita incomes in many developing states were

Income poverty
(Living on less than $1 a day)

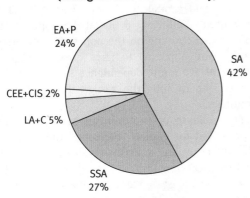

Child mortality
(Under 5s deaths)

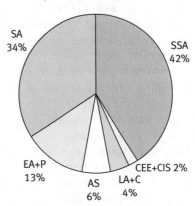

Access to water
(People without access to improved water)

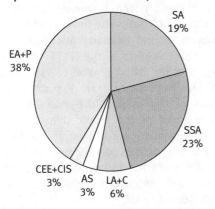

Gender equality
(Primary age girls not enrolled in school)

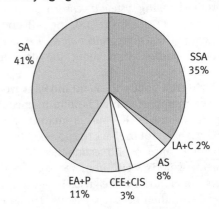

Access to sanitation

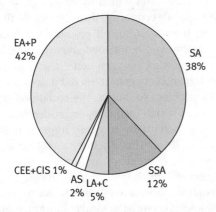

Key:

EA+P	⬤	East Asia & the Pacific
CEE+CIS	◯	Central & Eastern Europe & the Commonwealth of Independent States
SA	⬤	South Asia
LA+C	◯	Latin American & the Caribbean
SSA	⬤	Sub-Saharan Africa
AS	◯	Arab States

Fig. 29.2 Global deprivation

Source: Adapted from UNDP 2003: 53–9.

rising. Following the first oil price shock of 1973, developing countries undertook large-scale borrowing of recycled petrodollars from Western commercial banks in an attempt to sustain their rates of economic growth. However, during the 1980s there was a serious regression in much of the developing world as a result of the rich countries' strategy for dealing with the second oil price hike in 1979, which resulted in massive rises in interest rates and steep falls in commodity prices in the early 1980s.

These changes precipitated the debt crisis. Once the debt crisis had come to a head in 1982, following Mexico's threat to default, the Group of Seven (G7) leading developed Western countries decided to deal with the debt problem on a country-by-country basis, with the goal of avoiding the collapse of the international banking system by ensuring continued repayment of debt. In this regard, the IMF and the World Bank pursued a vigorous policy of **structural adjustment lending** throughout the developing world.

In applying this policy, the Fund and Bank worked together in an unprecedented fashion to encourage developing countries to pursue market-oriented strategies based on rolling back the power of the state and opening Third World economies to foreign investment. Exports were promoted so that these countries would earn the foreign exchange necessary to keep up with their debt repayments. The strategy worked, in that debt repayments have largely been met, the exposure of Western banks has been very significantly reduced, and the associated threat to the international financial system has receded. (It has since been replaced by other threats, such as the instability created by rapid capital liberalization in the 1990s.) However, the anticipated influx of foreign investment into developing countries did not occur.

Despite the negative effects of the debt crisis upon many countries within the South, others among them enjoyed significant and sustained economic growth over the 1980s. China's economy grew at 9.4 per cent per annum, while India and South-East Asia averaged 5.5 per cent per annum. China and India benefited in this respect from their large size, the fact that they had negligible foreign debts at the beginning of the decade, and that they were self-sufficient in food and capital goods. The East Asian Tigers, purportedly following a liberal development path (but in fact thriving on the policy of **state-assisted capitalism**) appeared to have broken out of the chains of economic dependence on the West and looked set to join the ranks of the developed countries.

The collapse of communism in the late 1980s represented for Francis Fukuyama 'the triumph of the West ... an unabashed victory of economic and political liberalism ... [and] the total exhaustion of viable systematic alternatives to Western [neo-] liberalism' (Fukuyama 1989: 3). The Western countries continued to advocate free market policies throughout the rest of the world. This strategy was pursued not just through the IMF and the World Bank, but very importantly, through the Uruguay Round of trade discussions carried out under the auspices of the GATT which resulted in the creation of the World Trade Organization (WTO). Importantly this expanded the private realm of the market into areas previously considered part of the public domain or subject to national regulation: for example, **intellectual property rights**, such as patents on seeds. It also created a **rules**-based institution to promote and oversee further integration of the global economy through trade liberalization.

The orthodox liberal assessment of the 1990s suggests that states which integrated most deeply into the global economy through trade liberalization grew the fastest, and it praises these 'new globalizers'. However, it acknowledges that neo-liberal economic policy has resulted in greater inequalities within and between states. But it does not regard this as a problem so long as the social and political discontent which inequality engenders is not so extensive as potentially to derail implementation of the project itself. This discontent will be alleviated by the development of national poverty reduction strategies, which it is claimed put countries and their peoples in the driving seat of development policy, thus empowering the local community and ensuring a better distribution of benefits.

A critical alternative assessment of the post-war international economic order

Critics of the development orthodoxy do not believe that, on their own, statistical measurements of economic growth and per capita GDP give us an adequate picture of what is happening in developing countries, or indeed to human beings wherever they are located across the world. For example, Glyn Roberts points out that 'GNP growth statistics might mean a good deal to an economist or to a maharajah, but they do not tell us a thing about the quality of life in a Third World fishing village' (Roberts 1984: 6). Those who advocate an alternative approach therefore place more emphasis on the pattern of distribution of gains within global society and within individual states. They believe that the economic liberalism which underpins the process of globalization has resulted, and continues to result, in increasing economic differentiation between and within countries, and that this is problematic.

As indicated above, there has been an explosive widening of the gap between the rich and the poor since 1945 compared with previous history, and more particularly in the 1990s (Adams 1993: vii; Thomas 2000). This trend has been evident over the very period when key global actors have been committed to promoting development worldwide, and indeed when there were fairly continuous world economic growth rates and positive rates of GDP growth per capita, at least until 1990 (Brown and Kane 1995).

The increasing gap between rich and poor was regarded as inevitable by dependency theorists such as André Gunder Frank (Frank 1967). Writing in the 1960s and 1970s, they stressed how the periphery, or Third World, was actively underdeveloped by activities which promoted the growth in wealth of the core Western countries, and of elites in the periphery. The periphery produced cheap primary products which were exported to the core. There, they were processed or converted into manufactured goods, then re-exported to the periphery with value added. Raul Prebisch (1963; 1964) of UNCTAD had argued that inevitably the periphery suffered from declining terms of trade, by which he meant that the selling price of primary commodities relative to the buying price of manufactured goods tends to decline over the long term, and as a result conditions generally worsen in the periphery.

Informed by such concerns in the 1970s the developing countries campaigned unsuccessfully for a **New International Economic Order**. In fact they were calling for reforms of the existing order, and were especially concerned about declining terms of trade. They wanted the prevailing order to be made more user friendly for the producers of primary commodities through such mechanisms as index-linking the prices of primary products to the prices of manufactured goods. They were also concerned to defend their right to exercise sovereignty over their natural resources and to form producer cartels. The success of OPEC had resulted in the illusion of commodity power, an illusion that was short-lived.

By the end of the 1970s it was clear that the orthodox conception of 'trickle-down' (the idea that overall economic growth as measured by increases in the GDP would automatically bring benefits for the poorer classes) had not worked. Despite impressive rates of growth in GDP per capita enjoyed by developing countries, this success was not reflected in their societies at large, and while a minority became substantially wealthier, the mass of the population saw no significant change. The South Commission concluded of this period that:

Inequalities tended to widen as the economy grew and became more industrialized ... Increasingly, the rich and powerful in the countries of the South were able to enjoy the life-style and consumption patterns of developed countries of the North. But large segments of the population experienced no significant improvement in their standard of living, while being able to see the growing affluence of the few. (South Commission 1990: 38)

There was consequently a dawning recognition in some quarters that growth reduces poverty only if accompanied by specific economic and social policies directed to that end (ibid.: 36).

The 1980s have been described as the 'lost decade' for the majority of Southern states, with sub-Saharan Africa suffering the most. In the first half of the 1980s, over half of developing countries experienced a declining per capita GDP, while over the whole decade, developing countries as a group faced a 10 per cent decline in per capita GDP. As well as the stringent structural adjustment policies, they were faced with rising floating interest rates which increased their debt burden; commodity price fluctuations; declining terms of trade; uncertain markets for their goods as developed countries pursued protectionist policies while advocating free market policies for the rest of the world; and insufficient financial and technological transfers from the developed world. Not surprisingly therefore the international economic structure was perceived by developing states as being inherently unfair and disadvantageous to their interests. Moreover, increasingly it came to be seen by some groups as unfair in terms of gendered outcomes disadvantageous to women (UN 1999).

In 1987, UNICEF published a report entitled *Adjustment with A Human Face* (Cornia *et al.* 1987). This study highlighted the social cost of structural adjustment policies (SAPs) and argued for a redesign of structural adjustment to take these costs into account. Some authors took a more critical stance, arguing that adjustment amounted to economic genocide and was beyond reform (Chossudovsky 1997; Bello 1994). For the majority of debtor states and their populations the pursuit of SAPs in the context of an unsupportive external economic environment has resulted in increased debt, social hardship, political tension, and environmental degradation. As a group, debtor states entered the 1990s 61 per cent more indebted than in 1982, while sub-Saharan Africa's debt increased by 113 per cent over the same period (George 1992: xvi). Those paying the price are not the people who borrowed the money in the first place, nor the wealthy elites, but the poor. More specifically, poor women have been identified as losers in this process (Elson 1991; Tsikata 1995).

In 1990 the UNDP developed the Human Development Index (HDI) to measure the development achievements of individual countries. Giving equal weight to life expectancy, adult literacy, and average local purchasing power, HDI results in a very differ-

ent assessment of countries' achievements than does the traditional measurement of development based on per capita GDP (Thomas *et al.* 1994: 22). For example, China, Sri Lanka, Poland, and Cuba fare much better under HDI assessments than they do under more orthodox assessments, while Saudi Arabia and Kuwait fare much worse. The HDI have been refined over the 1990s, and data for the HDI have been disaggregated in certain countries along racial, gender, regional, and ethnic groups. The Human Poverty Index (HPI) reflects the distribution of progress on HDI measurements, while the Gender Empowerment Index (GEI) has been developed to monitor the relative position of women. However, the picture is very complex. As the UNDP Human Development Report 1996 shows, to disaggregate in India by gender is insufficient, for there may be disparities in female capabilities among regions, between ethnic groups, or between urban and rural areas (UNDP 1996: 34). The promotion of the HDI reveals the contrasting approaches to development of some of the UN agencies on the one hand, and the IMF and World Bank on the other. It also reveals the complex and diverse nature of local situations on the ground.

At the beginning of the twenty-first century, critics of the development orthodoxy turned their attention to the national poverty reduction strategies (PRSs) which had become the focus for all concessional lending. They challenged claims of local ownership and empowerment of Third World states and people, and suggested the opposite: that these PRSs actually enabled the IMF, the World Bank, and donors to assume more extensive powers over developing countries, as these lenders are able to validate an entire national development strategy, including its social and political aspects. They also criticized the policy content of these strategies, arguing that while a new focus on issues such as health and education was important, the more fundamental issue of discussion of possible links between Washington-consensus policies and poverty creation was ignored.

Key points

- In 1945 the USA had carte blanche to set up a liberal international economic order, the institutional pillars of which were the IMF, the World Bank, and the GATT Yet governments were responsive to the demands of national security, and embedded liberalism was the order of the day.

- The cold war stimulated competition between the West and the East to win allies in the developing world. Most of the latter were born into the Western international economy and saw their development within the context of that system, i.e. based on growth within a free market, but also they stressed the role of the state in promoting development.

- Progress was achieved up to the 1980s according to the orthodox development criteria of GDP per capita, economic growth, and industrialization. Yet despite apparent success in conventional terms, there has been an explosive widening of the gap between the richest and poorest 20 per cent of the world's population, and the developing countries as a group entered the 1990s more indebted than the 1980s. Most of the countries of the former Eastern bloc or Second World, now known as the economies in transition from central planning to free market, have suffered a rapid economic decline in the 1990s and effectively joined the Third World.

- Trickle-down has been discredited, and it has been recognized that economic growth only reduces poverty if accompanied by specific economic and social policies.

- In recognition of the failure of economic growth-based indices of development, the UNDP Human Development Index was designed in 1990 to measure development in terms of longevity, education, and average purchasing power.

- National poverty reduction strategies, a response to perceived shortcomings in the development orthodoxy, are criticized on issues of national ownership and policy content.

- Dependency theorists see the current predicament of the Third World as predictable, arguing that export-oriented, free-market development promoted in the Third World has increased the wealth of the West and of Southern elites.

A critical alternative view of development

Since the early 1970s there have been numerous efforts to stimulate debate about development and to highlight its contested nature. Critical alternative ideas have been put forward that we can synthesize into an alternative approach. These have originated with various NGOs, grassroots development organizations, individuals, UN organizations, and private foundations. Disparate social movements not directly related to the development agenda have contributed to the flourishing of the alternative viewpoints: for example, the women's movement, the peace movement, and movements for democracy and green movements (Thomas 2000). Noteworthy was the publication in 1975 by the Dag Hammarskjöld Foundation of *What Now? Another Development?* This alternative conception of development (see Ekins 1992: 99) argued that the **process of development** should be:

1. need-oriented (material and non-material);
2. endogenous (coming from within a society);
3. self-reliant (in terms of human, natural, and cultural resources);
4. ecologically sound; and
5. based on structural transformations (of economy, society, gender, power relations).

Since then various NGOs, such as the World Development Movement, have campaigned for a form of development that takes aspects of this alternative approach on board. Grassroots movements have often grown up around specific issues, such as dams (Narmada in India) or access to common resources (the rubber tappers of the Brazilian Amazon; the Chipko movement, which began as a women's movement to secure trees in the Himalayas). Such campaigns received a great impetus in the 1980s with the growth of the green movement worldwide. The two-year preparatory process before the UN Conference on Environment and Development (UNCED) in Rio, in June 1992, gave indigenous groups, women, children, and other previously voiceless groups a chance to express their views. This momentum has continued, and it has become the norm to hold alternative NGO fora, parallel to all major UN conferences. Also the World Social Forum meets annually, apart from any UN event.

Democracy, empowerment, and development

Democracy is at the heart of the alternative conception of development. The worldwide democratic transition over the the 1980s and 1990s was characterized more by the establishment of the formal institutions of Western democracy, such as regular multiparty elections, than by substantive changes in the power structure of societies and the associated entitlements of their members to resources (Gills *et al.* 1993). Thus the government may have changed from military to civilian, but its membership is often drawn from the same elite and shares similar values. The quality of life for the majority will have changed very little.

Grassroots movements are playing an important role in challenging entrenched structures of power in formal democratic societies. In the face of increasing globalization, with the further erosion of local community control over daily life and the further extension of the power of the market and transnational corporations, people are standing up for their rights as they define them. They are making a case for local control and local empowerment as the heart of development. They are protecting what they identify as the immediate source of their survival—water, forest, and land. They are rejecting the dominant agenda of private and public (government-controlled) spheres and setting an alternative one. Examples include the Chipkos in India, the Rubber Tappers in the Amazon, the Chiapas uprising in Mexico, and Indian peasant protests against foreign-owned seed factories. The protests at the WTO meeting in Seattle, in November 1999, and at the IMF/World Bank Washington spring meeting in April 2000, were indicative of an increasingly widespread discontent with the process of globalization and with the distribution of its benefits. Such protests

symbolize the struggle for substantive democracy which communities across the world are working for. In this context development is about facilitating a community's participation and lead role in deciding what sort of development is appropriate for it; it is not about assuming the desirability of the Western model and its associated values. This alternative conception of development therefore values diversity above universality, and is based on a different conception of rights.

The Alternative Declaration produced by the NGO Forum at the Copenhagen Summit enshrined principles of community participation and empowerment. It laid stress on equity, participation, self-reliance, and sustainability. The role of women and youth was singled out. With women comprising over half the global population, and with half of the world population under 15 years old by 2000, these groups are very important. The Alternative Declaration represents an alternative vision of past, present, and future that rejects the importance of the private sphere. It rejects the economic Liberalism accepted by governments of North and South, seeing it as a path to aggravation rather than alleviation of the global social crisis. Moreover it identified trade liberalization and privatization as causes of the growing concentration of wealth globally. It called for immediate cancellation of all debt, improved terms of trade, transparency and accountability of the IMF and World Bank, and the regulation of multinationals. An alternative view of democracy was central to its conception of development. Similar ideas emanated from the parallel NGO fora, which accompanied all the UN global conferences in the 1990s. NGO statements have also been accompanied by follow-up. For example, the Women's Eyes on the World Bank Campaign was launched at Beijing to keep up the pressure on the World Bank to mainstream gender concerns in its work.

For some commentators, national poverty reduction strategies offer the opportunity—albeit as yet unrealized—for greater community participation in development policymaking in the South. If all parties operate in the spirit which was intended, the PRS process could enhance representation and voice for states and peoples in the South, and it offers the best hope available for expanding national ownership of economic policy.

Key points

- The last two decades of the twentieth century saw increasing debate about what constitutes development, with NGOs and grassroots activists playing significant role.

- An alternative view of development emerged, based on the transformation of existing power structures which uphold the status quo. Such structures vary in scope from the global to the local, and these are often interlinked; for example, the global economy severely disadvantages the poorest 20 per cent of the global population, while at a local level access to common resources affects the ability of people to provide for themselves.

- Grassroots organizations challenge entrenched power structures as people defend their rights, and as they define them, seeking local control and empowerment. Development in this alternative view can be seen as facilitating a community's progress on its own terms. The Alternative Declarations of NGOs at global conferences have stressed community participation, empowerment, equity self-reliance, and sustainability.

Now that we have looked at the critical alternative view of development, we will look at the way in which the orthodox view has attempted to respond to the criticisms of the alternative view.

The orthodoxy incorporates criticisms

In the mainstream debate the focus has shifted from growth to sustainable development. The concept was championed in the late 1980s by the influential Brundtland Commission (officially entitled the World Commission on Environment and Development—see WCED 1987), and supported in the 1990s by a series of UN global conferences. Central to the concept of sustainable development is the idea that the pursuit of development by the present generation should not be at the expense of future generations. In other words, it stressed inter-generational equity as well as intra-generational equity. The importance of maintaining the environmental resource base was highlighted, and with this comes the idea that there are natural limits to growth. The Brundtland Report made clear, however, that further growth was essential; but it needed to be made environment-friendly. The Report did not address the belief, widespread among a sector of the NGO community, that the emphasis on growth had caused the environmental crisis in the first place. The World Bank accepted the concerns of the Report to some degree. When faced with an NGO spotlight on the adverse environmental implications of its projects, the Bank moved to introduce more rigorous environmental assessments of its funding activities. Similarly concerning gender, when faced with critical NGO voices, the World Bank eventually in 1994 came up with its Operational Policy 4.20 on gender. The latter aimed to 'reduce gender disparities and enhance women particularly in the economic development of their countries by integrating gender considerations in its country assistance programmes' (www.worldbank.org).

With the United Nations Conference on the Environment and Development (UNCED— sometimes referred to as the Rio Summit) in June 1992, the idea that the environment and development were inextricably interlinked was taken further. However, what came out of the official inter-state process was legitimation of market-based development policies to further sustainable development, with self-regulation for transnational corporations. Official output from Rio, such as Agenda 21, however, recognized the huge importance of the sub-state level for addressing sustainability issues, and supported the involvement of marginalized groups. But while the groups had a role in the preparatory process, they have not been given an official role in the follow-up to UNCED. At the alternative summit, where the largest selection of non-governmental views ever expressed was aired, the viability of this strategy was challenged. For example, the possibility of structural adjustment policies being made environment-friendly was seriously questioned.

The process of incorporation has continued ever since. This is seen most recently in the language of poverty reduction being incorporated into World Bank and IMF policies: growth with equity, and pro-poor growth are the buzzwords, yet underlying macroeconomic policy remains unchanged. An examination of the contribution of the development orthodoxy to increasing global inequality is not on the agenda. The gendered outcomes of macro-economic policies are largely ignored. Despite promises of new funding at the UN Monterrey Conference on Financing for Development in 2002, new transfers of finance from developed to developing countries are slow in coming, and debt write-off for the poorest still has along way to go. The North/South agenda has changed little in the years since the Rio Summit, when sustainable development hit the headlines.

An appraisal of the responses of the orthodox approach to its critics

The Fourth World Conference on Women at Beijing gave the appearance of the global mainstreaming of gender concerns. Yet the orthodox view of development remains largely unaltered, and the Washington consensus of the 1980s and 1990s remains largely intact. During 2000, a series of official '+ 5' mini-conferences were held, such as Rio + 5, Copenhagen + 5, and Beijing + 5, to assess progress in specific areas since the major UN conferences five years earlier. The assessments suggested that the international community had fallen short in its efforts to operationalize conference action plans and to mainstream these concerns in global politics. For example, a critical reading of Beijing suggests that the conference represented a continuation of the attempts of the 1970s and 1980s to integrate women into prevailing development practice (so-called 'WID'), in other words to increase their economic opportunities within the existing economic system. This stands in contrast to an attempt fundamentally to alter the social and economic power of women relative to men, which would require a transformation in prevailing development practice via the promotion of a gender and development ('GAD') approach. The World Bank's own assessment of its mainstreaming of gender, undertaken by the Social Development Task Force in 1996, concluded that gender concerns are not incorporated systematically into projects and are regarded by many as 'add-ons'. An even more critical evaluation of the World Bank

was published by the Women's Eyes on the World Bank and the Fifty Years is Enough Campaigns in 1997, which wanted the Bank to 'challenge women's subordination as the root cause of gender inequity' (Women's Eyes on the World Bank 1997: 1).

Voices of criticism are growing in number and range. Even among supporters of the mainstream approach, voices of disquiet are heard as increasingly the maldistribution of the benefits of economic Liberalism are seen to have been a threat to local, national, regional, and even global order. Moreover, the social protest which accompanies economic globalization is regarded by some as a potential obstacle to the neo-liberal project. Thus supporters of globalization are keen to temper its most unpopular effects by modification of neo-liberal policies. Small but nevertheless important changes are taking place. For example, the World Bank has guidelines on the treatment of indigenous peoples, on resettlement, and on the environmental impact of its projects. It has guidelines on gender, and on disclosure of information. It is implementing social safety nets when pursuing structural adjustment policies. It is promoting microcredit as a way to empower women. With the IMF, it developed a Heavily Indebted Poor Country Initiative to reduce the debt burden of the poorest states. The IMF has launched a Poverty Reduction with Growth Facility, which aims to reduce debt and free up more resources for education and healthcare. What is important, however, is whether these guidelines and concerns really inform policy, and whether these new policies and facilities result in practical outcomes that impact on the fundamental causes of poverty.

The Bank has admitted that such changes have been incorporated largely due to the efforts of NGOs which have monitored its work closely and undertaken vigorous international campaigns to change the way the Bank funds projects, and to change its general operational processes. These campaigns continue, with the Bretton Woods Campaign, the Fifty Years is Enough Campaign, and Jubilee 2000 being particularly significant in calling for open, transparent, and accountable decisionmaking by global economic institutions, for local involvement in project planning and implementation, and for debt write-off. In addition to the NGO pressure for change, pressure is building within the

Key points

- The development orthodoxy remains essentially unchanged. However, the mainstream debate has shifted from growth to sustainable development—the view that current development should not be at the expense of future generations or the natural environment.

- The orthodox view asserts that sustainable development is to be achieved by further growth within a global free-market economy. This is the most effective way to maximize global wealth creation. Supporters believe that this will free up resources to care for the environment and to ensure social progress.

- This approach has been approved by the UNCED and the Copenhagen Summit, both of which legitimated further global integration via the free market. However,

- in the run-up to Copenhagen, many developing countries advocated embedded Liberalism rather than pure free-market economics, as necessary to help meet the basic needs of their people and ensure political stability.

- Critical alternative views of development have been effectively neutralized by the formal incorporation of their language and concerns into the orthodox view. Nevertheless, the process of incorporation has resulted in some small positive changes in the implementation of the orthodox view, for example by the World Bank.

- Nevertheless, despite semantic changes, fundamental questions remain about the sustainability of the dominant model of development.

institutional champions of the neo-liberal development orthodoxy.

There is a tremendously long way to go in terms of gaining credence for the core values of the alternative model of development in the corridors of power nationally, and internationally. Nevertheless, the alternative view, marginal though it is, has had some noteworthy successes in modifying orthodox development. These may not be insignificant for those whose destinies have up till now been largely determined by the attempted universal application of a selective set of local, essentially Western values.

We have now concluded our examination of the topic of development from the orthodox and alternative approaches and will turn our attention to the topic of hunger.

Hunger

In addressing the topic of global hunger, it is necessary to face the paradox that while 'the production of food to meet the needs of a burgeoning population has been one of the outstanding global achievements of the post-war period' (ICPF 1994: 104, 106), there are nevertheless around 827.5 million people in over 50 countries who are malnourished (UNDP 2003: 54), and at least 40,000 die every day from hunger-related causes. While famines may be exceptional phenomena, hunger is ongoing. Why is this so?

Broadly speaking there are two schools of thought with regard to hunger: the orthodox, nature-focused approach which identifies the problem largely as one of overpopulation, and the entitlement, society-focused approach, which sees the problem more in terms of distribution. Let us consider each of these two approaches in turn.

The orthodox, nature-focused explanation of hunger

The orthodox explanation of hunger, first mapped out in its essentials by Thomas Robert Malthus in his *Essay on the Principle of Population* in 1798, focuses on the relationship between human population growth and the food supply. It asserts that population growth naturally outstrips the growth in food production, so that a decrease in the per capita availability of food is inevitable, until eventually a point is reached at which starvation, or some other disaster, drastically reduces the human population to a level which can be sustained by the available food supply. This approach therefore places great stress on human overpopulation as being the cause of the problem, and seeks for ways to reduce the fertility of the human race, or rather, that part of the human race which seems to breed faster than the rest—the poor of the 'Third World'. Recent supporters of this approach, such as Paul Ehrlich and Denis and Donella Meadows (1972), argue that there are nat-ural limits to population growth—principally that of the carrying capacity of the land—and that when these limits are exceeded disaster is inevitable.

The available data on the growth of the global human population indicate that it has quintupled since the early 1800s, and is expected to grow from six billion in 1999 to ten billion in 2050. Over 50 per cent of this increase is expected to occur in seven countries: Bangladesh, Brazil, China, India, Indonesia, Nigeria, and Pakistan. Figure 29.3 provides data on world population growth from 1800, with projections through to 2050, and shows that the rate of world population growth is set to increase over the coming decades. Figure 29.4 focuses on the most populous countries—almost all of which are located in the Third World—and only 11 of them account for over half of the world's population. It is figures such as these that have convinced many adherents of the orthodox approach to hunger that it is essential that Third World countries adhere to strict family-planning policies which one way or another limit their population growth rates. Indeed, in the case of the World Bank, most women-related efforts

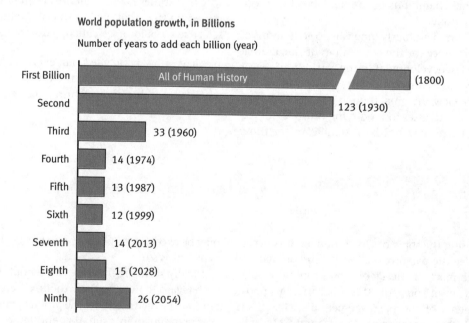

World population growth, in Billions

Number of years to add each billion (year)

- First Billion — All of Human History — (1800)
- Second — 123 (1930)
- Third — 33 (1960)
- Fourth — 14 (1974)
- Fifth — 13 (1987)
- Sixth — 12 (1999)
- Seventh — 14 (2013)
- Eighth — 15 (2028)
- Ninth — 26 (2054)

Fig. 29.3 World population growth from 1800 with projections to 2050

Sources: First and second billion: Population Reference Bureau. Third through ninth billion: United Nations, *World Population Prospects: The 1998 Revision* (medium scenario). Accessed online at www.prb.org on 6 Feb. 2004.

Most populous countries, 2003

Rank	Country	Population (millions)
1	China	1,289
2	India	1,069
3	United States	292
4	Indonesia	220
5	Brazil	176
6	Pakistan	149
7	Bangladesh	147
8	Russia	146
9	Nigeria	134
10	Japan	128

Most populous countries, 2050

Rank	Country	Population (millions)
1	India	1,628
2	China	1,394
3	United States	422
4	Pakistan	349
5	Indonesia	316
6	Nigeria	307
7	Bangladesh	255
8	Brazil	221
9	Congo, Dem. Rep. of	181
10	Ethiopia	173

Fig. 29.4 Most populous countries, 2003, with projections to 2050

Source: Accessed online at www.prb.org on 6 Feb. 2004.

until very recently were in the area of family planning.

The entitlement, society-focused explanation of hunger

Critics of the orthodox approach to hunger and its associated implications argue that it is too simplistic in its analysis and ignores the vital factor of food distribution. They point out that it fails to account for the paradox we observed at the beginning of this discussion on hunger: that despite the enormous increase in food production per capita that has occurred over the post-war period (largely due to the development of high-yielding seeds and industrial agricultural techniques), little impact has been made on the huge numbers of people in the world who experience chronic hunger. For example, the UN Food and Agriculture Organization estimates that although there is enough grain alone to provide everyone in the world with 3,600 calories a day (i.e. 1,200 more than

the UN's recommended minimum daily intake), there are still over 800 million hungry people.

Furthermore critics note that the Third World, where the majority of starving people are found, produces much of the world's food, while those who consume most of it are located in the Western world. This latter point is supported by evidence such as that shown in Table 29.3, which demonstrates that the Third World countries of China and India, despite their enormous agricultural outputs, consume far less grain and livestock products per capita than do the two Western countries of Italy and the United States. Such evidence leads opponents of the orthodox approach to argue that we need to look much more closely at the social, political, and economic factors that determine how food is distributed and why access to food is achieved by some and denied to others.

A convincing alternative to the orthodox explanation of hunger was set forward in Amartya Sen's pioneering book, *Poverty and Famines: An Essay on Entitlement and Deprivation*, which was first

Table 29.3 Annual per capita grain use and consumption of livestock products in selected countries, 1990

Country	Consumption (in kilograms)						
	Grain	Beef	Pork	Poultry	Lamb	Milk	Eggs
USA	800	42	28	44	1	271	16
Italy	400	16	20	19	1	182	12
China	300	1	21	3	1	4	7
India	200	—	0.4	0.4	0.2	31	13

Source: Brown and Kane (1995: 64).

published in 1981. From the results of his empirical research work on the causes of famines, Sen concluded that hunger is due to people not having enough to eat, rather than there not being enough to eat. He discovered that famines have frequently occurred when there has been no significant reduction in the level of per capita food availability and, furthermore, that some famines have occurred during years of peak food availability. For example, the Bangladesh famine of 1974 occurred in a year of peak food availability, yet because floods wiped out the normal employment opportunities of rural labourers, the latter were left with no money to purchase the food which was readily available, and many of them starved.

Therefore, what determines whether a person starves or eats is not so much the amount of food available to them, but whether or not they can establish an entitlement to that food. For example, if there is plenty of food available in the shops, but a family does not have the money to purchase that food, and does not have the means of growing their own food, then they are likely to starve. The key issue is not therefore per capita food availability, but the distribution of food as determined by the ability of people to establish entitlements to food. With the globalization of the market, and the associated curtailing of subsistence agriculture, the predominant method of establishing an entitlement to food has become that of the exercise of purchasing power, and consequently it is those without purchasing power who will go hungry amidst a world of plenty (Sen 1981; 1983).

Sen's focus on entitlement enables him to identify two groups who are particularly at risk of losing their access to food: landless rural labourers—such as in South Asia and Latin America—and pastoralists—such as in sub-Saharan Africa. The landless rural labourers are especially at risk because no arrangements are in place to protect their access to food. In the traditional peasant economy there is some security of land ownership, and therefore rural labourers have the possibility of growing their own food. However, this possibility is lost in the early stages of the transition to capitalist agriculture, when the labourers are obliged to sell their land and join the wage-based economy. Unlike in the developed countries of the West, no social security arrangements are in place to ensure that their access to food is maintained. In this context it is important to note that the IMF/World Bank austerity policies of the 1980s ensured that any little welfare arrangements that were previously enjoyed by vulnerable groups in developing countries were largely removed, and therefore these policies directly contributed to a higher risk of hunger in the Third World.

Building upon the work of Sen, the researcher Susan George in *The Hunger Machine* (Bennett and George 1987: 1–10) details how different groups of people experience unequal levels of access to food. She identifies six factors which are important in determining who goes hungry: the North–South divide between developed and developing countries; national policies on how wealth is shared; the rural–urban bias; social class; gender; and age. In addition, one could add to the list two other very important, and often neglected, factors determining hunger— that of race and disability. Consequently a person is more likely to experience hunger if they are disabled rather than able-bodied, black rather than white, a child rather than an adult, poor rather than wealthy, a rural dweller rather than a town dweller, and an inhabitant of a developing country rather than a developed country.

Globalization and hunger

It is possible to explain the contemporary occurrence of hunger by reference to the process of globalization. Globalization means that events occurring in one part of the globe can affect, and be affected by, events occurring in other, distant parts of the globe. Often as individuals we remain unaware of our role in this process and its ramifications. When we drink a cup of tea or smoke a cigarette in the developed countries, we tend not to reflect on the changes experienced at the site of production of these cash crops in the developing world. However, it is possible to look at the effect of the establishment of a global, as opposed to a local, national, or regional system of food production. This has been done by David Goodman and Michael Redclift in their book, *Refashioning Nature: Food, Ecology and Culture* (1991), and the closing part of this discussion on hunger is largely based on their findings.

Since 1945 a global food regime has been established, and as we enter the twenty-first century we are witnessing an increasingly global organization of food provision and of access to food, with transnational corporations playing the major role. This has been based on the incorporation of local systems of food production into a global system of food production. In other words, local subsistence producers who traditionally have produced to meet the needs of their family and community may now be involved in cash-crop production for a distant market. Alternatively they may have left the land and become involved in the process of industrialization. The most important actor in the development and expansion of this global food regime has been the USA, which, at the end of the Second World War, was producing large food surpluses. These surpluses became cheap food exports and initially were welcomed by the war-ravaged countries of Europe. They were also welcomed by many developing countries, for the model of development prevalent then depended on the creation of a pool of cheap wage labour to serve the industrialization process. Hence in order to encourage people off the land and away from subsistence production, the incentive to produce for oneself and one's family had to be removed. Cheap imported food provided this incentive, while the resulting low prices paid for domestic subsistence crops made them unattractive to grow; indeed, for those who continued to produce for the local market, such as in Sudan, the consequence has been the production of food at a loss (Bennett and George 1987: 78). Not surprisingly therefore the production of subsistence crops in the developing world for local consumption has drastically declined in the post-war period.

The post-war, US-dominated, global food regime has therefore had a number of unforeseen consequences. First, the domestic production of food staples in developing countries was disrupted. Second, consumer preferences in the importing countries changed in line with the cheap imports, and export markets for American-produced food were created. Effectively, a dependence on food aid was created (Goodman and Redclift 1991: 123). Third, there has been a stress on cash-crop production. The result has been the drive towards export-oriented, large-scale, intensively mechanized agriculture in the South. Technical progress resulted in the 'Green Revolution', with massively increased yields being produced from high-yield seeds and industrialized agricultural practices. This has in some respects been an important achievement. However the cost has been millions of peasants thrown off the land because their labour was no longer required, greater concentration of land in a smaller number of hands, and environmental damage from pesticides, fertilizers, and inappropriate irrigation techniques.

Since the early 1980s, the reform of national economies via SAPs has given a further boost to the undermining of the national organization of agriculture, and a further fillip to the activities of agribusiness. Also the aggressive pursuit of unilateralist trade policies by the USA, such as the invocation of free trade to legitimize prising open the Korean agricultural market, has added to this. Global trade liberalization since the early 1980s, and especially the Uruguay Round's Agreement on Agriculture (the original text of which was drafted by the multinational Cargill's Vice President Dan

| Box 29.4 | Case study: destruction of local agriculture, booming food imports, and rising malnutrition in Haiti |

With its per capita income of $556, Haiti is the poorest country in the Western hemisphere. Two-thirds of people live in rural areas; 80 per cent are poor. Nearly half the population consumes less than 75 per cent of the recommended intake of food energy. Rice is a major staple of the diet, and mainly produced by small farmers. Twenty per cent of people depend on rice cultivation for their livelihoods, and the sector has a major economic spin-off, with thousands of agricultural labourers, traders, and millers earning their living from it.

In recent years Haiti has undergone rapid trade liberalization, and is now one of the most open economies in the world. Liberalization of the rice market started in the 1980s, but the final stroke came in 1994/5 when, under pressure from the international community (notably the IMF and the USA), the tariff on rice was cut from 35 per cent to 3 per cent.

Rice producers reported that prices fell by 50 per cent during 1986–7, after the first wave of liberalization. In 1995, local production fell by 27 per cent. Rice imports increased by 30 times between 1985 and 1999 as a result of the market slump. Food aid in rice surged from zero in 1994 to 16,000 tonnes in 1999. Most rice imports are of subsidized US rice.

These trends have severely undermined the livelihoods of more than 50,000 rice-farming families and led to a rural exodus. While cheap imports initially benefited poor consumers, in recent years these benefits have vanished . . . the FAO says that overall malnutrition has increased since the start of the trade liberalization, affecting 48 per cent of the population in 1979–81, and 62 per cent in 1996–98. Almost half of Haiti's food needs are now met by imports.

(Oxfam 2003: 10)

Amstutz—Oxfam 2003: 23), are further eroding local food security and throwing peasant producers and their families off the land, and this has fuelled resentment in the South about the global rules governing agriculture. For example, in India disputes over intellectual property rights in regard to high-yielding crop seeds have resulted in violent protest by peasant farmers at foreign-owned seed factories. In the North, NGOs have campaigned against the double standards operated by their governments in expecting Southern countries to liberalize their food markets while Northern economies continue to be protected and while Northern agriculture is heavily subsidized.

 CWS

Key points

- In recent decades global food production has burgeoned, but paradoxically hunger and malnourishment remain widespread.

- The orthodox explanation for the continued existence of hunger is that population growth outstrips food production.

- An alternative explanation for the continuation of hunger focuses on lack of access or entitlement to available food. Access and entitlement are affected by factors such as the North–South global divide; particular national policies; rural–urban divides; class; gender; and race.

- Globalization can simultaneously contribute to increased food production and increased hunger.

We have now concluded our discussion of the three topics of poverty, development, and hunger, and in the last part of this chapter we will assess the likelihood of globalization with a more human face.

Conclusion: looking to the future—globalization with a human face?

It is clear when we consider the competing conceptions of poverty, development, and hunger explored above that there is no consensus on definitions, causes, or solutions.

We are faced with an awesome development challenge. Early indications suggest that the UN Millennium Development Goal (MDG) targets will not be met. Most gains are being made in very few countries like China and India, and even within those states there remain deep pockets of poverty. Beyond, the picture is less encouraging. If sub-Saharan Africa continues on its current course, it will take another 150 years to reach the MDG target of halving poverty, and the hunger situation continues to worsen there (UNDP 2003).

The orthodox model of development is being held up for closer scrutiny, as we become more aware of the risks as well as the opportunities which globalization and the Washington consensus bring in their wake. The key question is: can globalization develop a human face?

Opinions differ. For Michel Camdessus, speaking as Head of the IMF, it is clear that a new reformist paradigm of development is already emerging which entails the 'progressive humanization of basic economic concepts' (Camdessus 2000). However, more critical voices see in the reforms under way a complete failure to tackle fundamental issues of redistribution, which require valuing an economic system only if it works for people and the planet.

The current development orthodoxy is following the reformist pathway. History will reveal whether this pathway bears the seeds of its own destruction by delivering too little, too late to too few people. As students of International Relations it is imperative that we bring these issues in from the margins of our discipline and pursue them as central to our study.

For further information and case studies on this subject, please visit the companion web site at www.oup.com/uk/booksites/politics.

QUESTIONS

1 What does poverty mean?

2 Explain the orthodox approach to development and outline the criteria by which it measures development.

3 Assess the critical alternative model of development.

4 How effectively has the orthodox model of development neutralized the critical, alternative view?

5 Compare and contrast the orthodox and alternative explanations of hunger.

6 What are the pros and cons of the global food regime established since the Second World War?

7 Account for the increasing gap between rich and poor states and people after fifty years of official development policies.

8 Critically explore the gendered nature of poverty.

9 Is the recent World Bank focus on poverty reduction evidence of a change of direction by the Bank?

10 Which development pathway—the reformist or the alternative—do you regard as the more likely to contribute to global peace in the twenty-first century?

11 Are national poverty reduction strategies contributing to national ownership of development policies in the Third World

12 Why has the discipline of International Relations been slow to engage with issues of poverty and development?

GUIDE TO FURTHER READING

General

Adams, N. B. (1993), *Worlds Apart: The North–South Divide and the International System* (London: Zed) presents a broad economic and political history of the North–South divide, and focuses on the role of the international economic system. This book provides an effective introduction to the politics of North–South economic relations over the past half century.

Rapley, J. (1996), *Understanding Development* (Boulder, Col.: Lynne Rienner) analyses the theory and practice of development in the Third World since the Second World War in a straightforward, succinct manner. It provides the reader with a firm grasp of changing development policies at the international level and their take-up over time in different states.

Thomas, C. (2000), *Global Governance, Development and Human Security* (London: Pluto) examines the global development policies pursued by global governance institutions, especially the IMF and the World Bank, in the 1980s and 1990s. It assesses the impact of these policies on human security, and analyses different paths towards the achievement of human security for the twenty-first century.

Development

Rahnema, M., with Bawtree, V. (eds) (1997), *The Post Development Reader* (Dhaka: University Press, and London: Zed) challenges the reader to think critically about the nature of development and assumptions about meanings. This is an extremely stimulating interdisciplinary reader.

Hunger

Dreze, J., Sen, A., Hussain, A. (eds) (1995), *The Political Economy of Hunger* (Oxford: Clarendon Press) is an excellent collection on the political economy of hunger.

Sen, A. (1981), *Poverty and Famines* (Oxford: Clarendon Press) provides a ground-breaking analysis of the causes of hunger which incorporates detailed studies of a number of famines and convincingly challenges the orthodox view of the causes of hunger.

WEB LINKS

www.oneworld.net The fastest growing online civil society analysis of broad development issues and global problems.

www.twnside.org Provides an extremely interesting view from the developing world. This site, arranged by the Third World Network, Malaysia, provides an excellent range of papers and information on international political economy, development, environment, and human rights issues.

www.eurodad.org Provides policy studies from a network of 48 development NGOs in 15 European countries focusing on development and finance, especially debt issues. Its aim is poverty eradication and the empowerment of the poor.

CHAPTER 30

Gender issues

JAN JINDY PETTMAN

READER'S GUIDE

This chapter asks why feminist scholarship and gender issues have come so late to the study of international politics, and suggests how asking feminist questions might make a difference. It then identifies different kinds of feminism, and traces the shifting debates about gender relations and sexual difference. The rest of the chapter explores a gender analysis of several aspects of globalization: deregulation and structural adjustment politics, the changing international division of labour, and the 'export' of women workers; rising identity politics, and the uses these politics make of women, and issues of gender and militarism; and the ways women's transnational alliances and international conferences have globalized gender issues.

Introduction

International Relations has long been taught and theorized as if women were invisible: as if either there were no women in world politics, which was only men's business; or as if women and men were active in and affected by world politics in the same ways, in which case there would be no need to 'gen-der' the analysis. Now feminist scholarship is visible, if still marginal, and women's and gender issues are the focus of transnational politics. Both feminist understandings and women's organizing provide us with perspectives that contribute a more inclusive view of globalization.

Gendering international politics

This section explores the late coming of feminism to International Relations and issues of women and gender in global politics. It makes the case for 'gendering' IR.

Feminist international politics

Feminist scholarship is often strongly resisted by academic gatekeepers, for it reveals the partial and gendered nature of intellectual work which is built on (elite?) men's experiences. But feminism has come even later to International Relations, one of the most masculinist of the social sciences. Suggested explanations include that the discipline is male dominated, and so more likely to reflect men's interests and fears; and that the way the discipline constructs its subject matter makes most people, including almost all women, disappear. Its focus on the 'high politics' of diplomacy, war, and statecraft called up a world of statesmen and soldiers, who were assumed to be male. Even when international political economy became a concern, this often took the form of analysis of relations between states and markets, or of structures of domination and exploitation. In either case, gender relations were rarely considered a necessary part of the analysis.

The intellectual field, or territory, further disguised women and gender relations through its distinction between the domestic or the inside of states, and the international or the in-between of states. In the process differences within states, including gender differences, were relegated away from its interest, and left to other disciplines like Political Science and Sociology. At the same time, world politics was often characterized in terms of conflict, competition, security (defined as military security), and power (demonstrated through the threat or use of force), drawing on a particular notion of human nature that was gendered, and also perhaps class and culture specific.

But many women have written on and thought about war and peace. The discipline of International Relations was established in 1919 in the wake of the First World War, in the hope that there should never again be such a war. However, it ignored the critiques of women organizing for peace, including those who had held the Hague peace conference in 1915, in the midst of that war, and who opposed the punishing conditions imposed on Germany at its conclusion on the grounds that it would spread poverty, disease, and enmity through Europe, and generate further conflict (which it did). This is why feminists are concerned to ask whose experiences are being taken seriously. Whose understandings of politics, including international politics, become the material for theorizing about, and acting in, 'the world'?

Where are women in global politics?

Feminist questions unsettle assumptions which reflect only (some) men's experiences. In an early feminist intervention in the discipline, Cynthia

Enloe asked the question: **'Where are the women?'** (1989). She found that women often were there, even where we might not expect them: keeping a military base going, for example, or as the majority of workers in export-processing zones (see Ch.12).

Asking the question 'Where are the women?' can suggest different kinds of answers. For some, it leads to 'the famous few'—Indira Gandhi and Margaret Thatcher, for example. These particular women were strong leaders who showed no hesitation to use force in international conflicts. This led some to say that the only difference between men and women is that women are so rarely in power; if they are, they behave like men. Others argue that in national and world politics, only those who play the main game well will succeed. It may show more about contemporary politics as **masculinist**, than about whether women and men are 'different'. So, too, men who appear compassionate or seek to negotiate away from conflict may be accused of being wimps, 'women', or girls.

Others use the question 'Where are the women?' to identify places where women are not, because they are women. Until very recently, and still in many states, women were prohibited from combat roles, which in turn made it impossible for them to rise to commanding levels in their state's armed forces. But not just any man is seen as a soldier. The fierce debates over whether gay men should be allowed to serve are similar to those used against women soldiers: that they may break down under fire, or threaten group cohesion. Here military service is associated with men, and with certain kinds of **masculinity**.

Asking 'Where are the women?' reveals women in places where, otherwise, we might not look for them. Feminists take women seriously as knowledge-makers about the world. This means seeking to learn from their experiences of politics and global processes. Women are often under-represented in formal politics, as heads of state or parliamentary representatives or executive bureaucrats for example, though in Rwanda and the Scandinavian states, they are now close to equal (see Table 30.1). Women are more likely to organize in other politics, in social movements, and in non-governmental organizations (NGOs) for example. Through these politics,

Table 30.1 Women in national parliaments, January 2004: Selected countries in descending order of percentage of women in lower or single house

Rank	Country	% Women
1	Rwanda	48.8
2	Sweden	45.3
3	Denmark	38.0
4	Finland	37.5
5	Netherlands	36.7
6	Norway	36.4
7	Cuba	36.0
8	Belgium	35.3
14	Mozambique	30.0
18	Vietnam	27.3
37	China	20.2
47	United Kingdom	17.9
57	United States	14.3
78	Russian Federation	9.8
96	Japan	7.1
108	Armenia	4.6
121	Papua New Guinea	0.9

World average: both houses 15.2%, lower houses 15.2%
Source: Reproduced with permission from the IPU PARLINE database www.ipu.org/wmn-e/world.htm, accessed 30 Jan. 2004.

women were actors in global politics long before they were noticed in the study of International Relations.

Discovering gender

Asking 'Where are the women?' usually reveals women in different roles, for example, different relations to the military, or the market, compared with men. When we find women, we find gender relations. So war stories from very different states tell of brave soldier men, the protectors, and the women they protect, who wait, and weep, and have more sons for the killing (Elshtain 1987). These stories construct men as the agents of the state or **nation** and women as passive, regardless of what actual men and women are doing. These constructions in turn place pressure on peaceful or unwilling men to fight, to protect 'womenandchildren'. They disguise some women's active support of or participation in wars, including as warriors. And they force conditions of dependence on women, who are expected to be grateful for this protection, even when they do not wish it.

The gendered war script is not an exception. The citizen is often presumed to be male, with public responsibilities, while women are relegated to the family, the domestic world. In foundation stories in political theory, women were also relegated away from the world of reason to one of emotions and passions, making them unreliable citizens, and even dangerous to men. The **public/private** split coincides with other splits, like reason/emotion, mind/body, and male/female. These are gendered divisions: they associate certain kinds of character or behaviour with a particular gender. The 'male' side of the dichotomy is usually given more value, and privileged, while the female side is devalued. In the process, 'gender' becomes both relational and a power relationship.

Feminism makes several very important strategic claims here. The first is that women's experiences are **systematically** different from men's, even from men of their own family or group. Another is that all social relations are gendered; so we experience

our class, or race, for example, in gendered forms. We do not experience our gender alone, or in isolation from other social identities, including for example whether we are citizens, where we live, or our age. And gender is constitutive of other social relations. This reveals as partial those representations of social relations including global politics that appear gender neutral, but on closer examination turn out to universalize (elite) men's experiences and knowledge.

> ## Key points
>
> - Gender analysis and feminism came late to International Relations.
>
> - Women's experiences of and ideas about world politics were rarely admitted to the discipline.
>
> - Asking the question 'Where are the women?' makes women visible in world politics.
>
> - Making women visible also reveals gender relations as power relations.
>
> - Feminism claims that women's experiences are systematically different from men's and that all social relations are gendered.

Feminisms

Feminism is often identified as Western. There is a very complicated politics here about who names feminism, and whether other women's struggles for equal rights can be called feminist, even if they themselves do not use that name. But it is not true that either feminism or women's rights movements were only or largely of Western origin. In a number of Asian and Middle Eastern colonies, 'the woman question' arose in the late nineteenth and early twentieth centuries, alongside or in connection with early anti-colonial nationalism. These early feminists were familiar with suffrage struggles in other places, and some travelled to participate in international conferences.

The politics of feminism

Second-wave feminism came to prominence in a number of Western states in the 1970s, alongside or in uneasy relations with other social movements for more inclusive citizenship and social rights. Feminism had a rather different relation to socialist states, whose treatment of women as workers and their support for women working outside the home allowed state leaders to declare that they had solved the woman question. That has made post-cold war feminist organizing in these states very difficult, both because of the association of women's rights language with state socialism, and because the rush to marketization and deregulation of their economies swept away many of the gains that had led socialist state women to see Western feminists as 'coming from behind'. This helps explain the declining numbers of women in parliamentary politics in East European states. Generalizing to 'Third World' states is even more difficult, given the variety of pre-colonial, colonial, and post-colonial experiences to include.

We might describe feminism as a **political project** to understand and, therefore, to change women's inequality, exploitation, or oppression. But any generalizations about feminist politics globally are made even more difficult by the **differences** within feminism, within and between states. First-wave feminism was concerned with suffrage, with women's legal and civil rights, including their rights to education. Many of these early feminists were active in other politics—as socialists, or anti-colonial nationalists, or pacifists for example. So too second-wave feminists had very different politics, that affected their understanding of sexual difference, for example their views on the possibility of alliances with progressive men. In the 1970s and 1980s, these differences were often summed up under labels of liberal, radical, and socialist feminist. While many feminists are not easily put under one label, and the lines of difference and alliance shift over time and place, the differences between them are important for thinking about gender, and about strategies necessary to overcome gender inequality or oppression.

Very broadly, **liberal feminists** are equality feminists, seeking an end to women's exclusion from or under-representation in office, power, and employment. They seek women's equal rights in the military, including in combat, for they see women's 'protection' as a way of keeping them from power, and their dependence on men as compromising their claims to full citizenship, which is usually understood to include fighting for one's country.

Other feminists are critical of liberal feminists as seeking equality in masculinist **institutions** on men' terms. In different ways, they seek to change the institutions themselves to be women friendly. They disagree, however, on what lies at the heart of the problem. So **radical feminists** see women's sub-ordination as universal, though taking different forms at different times. Some argue women are a sex-class, systematically and everywhere subject to men's sex-right, or their claims for access to their bodies, children, and labour. Violence against women is seen as key to keeping women resourceless and 'in their place'. They also draw attention to sexuality as politics.

Cultural feminists include those who see women as different from men, more nurturing and peaceable for example. They do not reject 'women's values', as liberal feminists do, but they argue that these values are just what world politics, and ecology, now need. Some cultural feminists are accused of essentialism, of representing these values as naturally women's, and so reinforcing the gendered stereotypes that underpin women's oppression. Others see women's values more as learned skills, as women are almost always those responsible for the care of children, health, and **community**. They argue that men, too, can learn to nurture.

Socialist feminists put together class and gender, finding that a class analysis alone leaves out much that women experience. It cannot explain why women are those responsible for reproductive and family labour, why women are so over-represented among the poor, or why gender inequities, often reinforced by violence against women, continue even where women are integrated into the workforce.

These classic lines of difference in feminism are less clear these days, and are now supplemented by naming other feminisms. So in the 1980s **black** and **'Third World' feminists** accused white feminists of ignoring race, culture, and colonial relations as also affecting women. These locate white women in ambiguous ways, as oppressed in relation to gender and perhaps class, but privileged by their membership of the dominant race and/or culture, and by citizenship rights in rich countries. However, geographic location or social identity cannot predict person's politics. Some Third World feminists are liberal feminists, seeking admission to their state or profession on equal terms with men, while others are socialist or left feminists who are concerned to build alliances across class lines between elite and poorer women, for example. Some white feminists also pursue anti-racist theories and politics.

Developments within feminism in recent years have shifted both theory and practical politics, for example, **post-modern feminists** have added to growing recognition of differences between women (see Ch.12). These shifts have unsettled the category 'woman', raising issues about who speaks for 'women'. Whose experiences as women are not reflected in feminist knowledge-making and politicking? There is an ongoing tension in much feminism between equality and difference claims; between trying to build-up the category 'woman' for political purposes; while trying to tear it down in the face of its use against women. This is made even more difficult in these times of growing right-wing and fundamentalist movements, which seek to discredit feminism and attack women's rights.

Sex and gender

Different feminisms, then, have different views on gender relations, and how to change them so they do not routinely count against women. The conversations and sometimes conflicts between these feminisms have taken us further in understanding gender relations and sexual difference. Jane Flax (1987) asks 'how do we think, or do not think or avoid thinking about gender?' Just because gender is not made visible in many accounts of the world or our lives does not mean that it is absent. What then does a gender analysis contribute to our understanding of international and increasingly globalized politics?

Gender is often used as a code word for women. This does draw our attention to the ways in which dominant groups can normalize or naturalize their own identities—they name others while remaining themselves unnamed. But of course men have gender too, just as white people are also 'raced', and dominant culture members have culture.

An important early second-wave feminist intervention made a distinction between sex and gender. Sex was seen as biology: we are born male or female. Gender was seen as a social construction: what it means to be male or female in any particular place or time. This distinction was politically very important, for women have been badly done by biology, in its explanations of their inequality or

extra burdens as natural, an inevitable extension of their child-bearing difference. It built on the fact that while women's work appeared to be universal, just what that work involved, and how sexual difference was understood, varied from society to society, group to group, and over time (see Box 30.1). More recently, Men's Studies have explored the social construction of masculinities.

The distinction between sex and gender made room for a feminist project—for if gender is a social construction, it can be changed. It has also enabled us to explore different meanings of gender. Gender is a **personal identity**—how do I experience being a woman? a **social identity**—what do others expect of me, as a woman? and a **power relation**—why are women as a social category almost always under-represented in relations of power? Gender is political—it is contested, by men and women

---

Box 30.1	Women at work

Key statistics

- Of the 192 countries in the world, only 12 have a female head of state.

- Seventy per cent of the world's 1.3 billion poor—those who are living on the equivalent of less than US$1 per day—are women.

- Women spend twice as much time as men (or more time) on unpaid work.

- Worldwide, women on average earn two-thirds of what men earn.

- Women make up the majority of the world's part-time workers—between 60 per cent and 90 per cent. In the European Union, 83 per cent of part-time workers are women.

- In countries such as Australia, Canada, Thailand, and the United States, over 30 per cent of all businesses are now owned or operated by women, with Thailand topping the list at almost 40 per cent.

- In some countries of sub-Saharan Africa, most of the female labour force is in the informal economy; for example, 97 per cent in Benin, 95 per cent in Chad, 85 per cent in Guinea, and 83 per cent in Kenya.

- In Europe, women are the heads of household in nine out of ten single-parent families.

(International Labour Organization n.d.)

who regularly subvert, challenge, or bolster gender difference, at home or in other places, by feminists who seek women's liberation, and by anti-feminists, who seek to take back what women have won through struggle. Gender may be the basis for a **mobilized political identity**—of which 'feminist' is one. So too is the Australian anti-feminist women's group called Women Who Want to be Women.

Lately, some feminists have developed more fluid representations of gender. 'Doing gender', or gender as performance, suggests that we select and negotiate our ways through social possibilities and expectations. Gender as process reminds us that gender never just is, but rather that much work goes into its reproduction. Some feminists fault gender constructionists who continue to use the sex–gender distinction, for reinforcing yet another dichotomy, nature and nurture—and for treating the body as a neutral 'thing' on which gender difference is written. They find it more productive to think about sexual difference, and stress embodiment—that our first place of location is our body. By drawing attention to bodies, they say, attention is inevitably drawn to sexual difference.

Women's politics and contests around gender, though still anchored often in local and particular sexual politics, are now increasingly globalized.

These politics are a response to the gendered impact of **globalization**, and also take advantage of the opportunities for communication and organization transnationally that globalization offers. The rest of this chapter will pursue the changing international sexual division of labour, crises of the state in the face of globalization and restructuring, and rising identity conflicts. It will conclude by looking at women's politics, which are also being globalized.

> ### Key points
>
> - Feminism is not restricted to Western states.
>
> - Contemporary feminisms are diverse in their understandings of the difference gender makes, and how to stop this difference from counting against women.
>
> - Since the early 1980s, the issue of differences between women has become visible in feminist politics.
>
> - Women's rights are not being progressively achieved. Today there is a global-wide backlash against women's rights.

Gender in the global political economy

Until recently, women and gender relations rarely appeared in studies of the international political economy (IPE). An exception was development studies (though these often remained separate from IPE). From 1970, feminist critiques and women's NGOs made visible the ways in which development planners overlooked women, including their roles as workers, owners, and entrepreneurs, as well as in subsistence and family production. They pointed out both that women were differently affected by development, often losing access to land and resources, and expected to take on additional work; and that the outcomes of development policies were affected by already existing gender relations, including local notions of what was women's work.

Women in development

The international Decade for Women (1976–85) generated a huge amount of material on women's lives, and the discriminations they faced. It also documented the gendered effects of development, and provided a base for the themes of peace, justice, development—which came out of the third women's conference in Nairobi in 1985. In the process, it supported a new field, known as **Women in Development** (WID).

There are very different approaches to WID, including between liberal feminists who seek to integrate women more equally into development, and other feminists who see development, currently defined, as damaging to women. They seek the empowerment of women, including through participation in development decisions that affect their own lives and choices.

Not all women are poor, in the 'Third World' or elsewhere. But no state treats its women as well as its men (see Box 30.2). Some years ago, it was said that women did one-third of the paid work, two-thirds of the productive work, for one-tenth of the income and less than one-hundredth of the property. Now it is likely that the figures are even more against women.

The Human Development Index (HDI) is based on three measures: life expectancy at birth, educational attainment, and standard of living. The Gender Development Index (GDI) measures these too, but adjusts for the disparity between women and men in each case. The Gender Empowerment Index (GEM) measures relative empowerment between men and women in political and economic spheres, and in terms of political representation (see Table 30.2).

A series of **global crises**, in terms of trade dependence, debt, and restructuring, have hit women especially hard. The conditions imposed on states in return for loans include structural adjustment policies, deregulating finance, liberalizing trade, favouring export industries, and reducing social services and public support, including food subsidies.

These policies are not restricted to poorer 'Third World' states. They are evident in former and some existing communist states, where marketization has similar effects, including removing state provision of many services that supported working women. They are reshaping Western states, too, as their governments give up on much economic regulation and cut back on social security and public enterprise.

These dramatic changes are part of the globalization of production and of 'the market'. Within states, they represent a dramatic shift from public to private expenditure, and from state to family, especially women's, responsibilities. We live in times of high unemployment, polarizing wealth within and between states, reducing state provision, and growing impoverishment. These are gendered in their effects. **First**, cut-backs in state services like health, education, and social security especially affect women's employment opportunities. **Second**, women are everywhere overwhelmingly responsible for family and household maintenance, and must compensate through their own time and labour when (often inadequate) state support is reduced or removed. **Third**, the cost of globalization is not evenly spread: the 'feminization of poverty' refers to the growing proportion, as well as numbers, of women and their children living in poverty. This is in part a reflection of the worldwide trend, so that now between a third and a half of all families do not have a male breadwinner. The gendered effects of restructuring, then, amount to a massive crisis in reproduction. This has led UNICEF to identify an

---

Box 30.2 Women's world statistics

- Women possess roughly 1 per cent of the land in the world.

- Today only six countries can boast the following: close to complete sexual equality in the area of secondary education, 30 per cent representation of women in elected government positions, roughly 50 per cent of non-agricultural jobs occupied by women.

- In nearly 100 years, only 24 women have been elected as head of state.

- Around 80 per cent of the 27 million refugees around the planet are women.

- Two-thirds of the 300 million children who have no access to education are girls.

- Out of almost a billion people who are unable to read and write, two-thirds of them are women.

- Over 200,000 women die every year as a result of back street abortions.

- Women produce 80 per cent of the food in the poorest areas of the world; in some places, this figure is as high as 95 per cent.

- Officially, 110 million girls worldwide between the ages of 5 and 14 work, and this does not include domestic tasks.

(World March of Women 2000)

Table 30.2 Global gender disparity: GEM, GDI, and HDI rankings, 2003

Country	GEM rank	GDI rank	HDI rank
Iceland	1	2	2
Norway	2	1	1
Sweden	3	3	3
Denmark	4	9	11
Finland	5	10	14
Netherlands	6	7	5
Austria	7	14	16
Germany	8	15	18
Canada	9	6	8
United States	10	5	7
United Arab Emirates	65	49	48
Turkey	66	81	96
Sri Lanka	67	80	99
Egypt	68	99	120
Bangladesh	69	112	139
Yemen	70	127	148

Note: GEM ranks are for 70 countries.
Source: UNDP 2003.

invisible adjustment, which is women's responsibility, largely unaided by those who allocate resources and wealth elsewhere.

The changing international division of labour

Fourth, the changing international division of labour is gendered. Transnational corporations go on the global prowl for cheap labour, which often means women's labour (Enloe 1992). Especially since the 1980s, increasingly competitive trading and labour deregulation in many states has accompanied the rise of a largely female marginalized workforce, with a core of skilled and professional workers who are mainly male.

Women are concentrated in poorly paid work, including part-time and outwork. This partly reflects many women's juggling between their domestic and their paid work. But it also reflects the construction of women workers as cheap labour—or, more

accurately, as 'labour made cheap'. In many different cultures and states, women's labour is seen to be temporary, filling in before marriage, or supplementing husbands' income. At the same time, they are seen as 'naturally' good with their hands, patient and docile, and so particularly fitted to do work which men would not tolerate. Assumptions about women's work mean that it is often classified as unskilled, even where, like sewing, it is seen as skilled if men do it. In these ways, particular constructions of femininity enter into the organization of work, and shape its status and rewards. So women are now the vast majority of workers on the global assembly line, in factories and in export-processing zones, where their gender and often their youth help keep wages down.

CWS

The export of women

Women or girls come from rural areas into the towns or cities, into export-processing zones or to military base servicing areas, or cross state borders in search of work. They may be their family's only income earner. This in turn unsettles gender relations, and gives those women experiences which range from liberating to exploitative or downright dangerous.

Where once the labour migrant was presumed to be male (and often was), now about half of all those outside their country of birth are women. In some particular migrant labour flows, women are in the overwhelming majority. Many are domestic workers and child carers. They are part of a **global flow** of women from poorer states to wealthier ones, from Indonesia, Sri Lanka and the Philippines to Japan, Hong Kong, and oil-rich Middle East states, and from Central and South American states into the United States. This labour migration was largely unnoticed until the Gulf War revealed some 400,000 Asian women workers in Kuwait and a further 100,000 in Iraq. There are between 1.0 and 1.7 million women in the domestic worker trade from South and South-East Asia alone. This trade reinforces the assumption that it is women who are responsible for domestic labour, even where that labour is paid for and releases other women to go into paid work.

Exporting women is big business. Recruitment agencies, banks, and airlines profit from it. So do the exporting states, in the form of remittances, for example, an estimated $3 billion per year to the Philippines. This trade contributes to those states' search for hard currency in the face of growing debt pressures, and relieves unemployment at home. It is therefore unlikely that the home state will act strongly in support of their citizens' rights when women are subject to abuse in other states; though another factor is their own poor record in labour and women's rights.

This trade in women reflects power and wealth relations globally. Poorer South-East Asian states export domestic workers, while richer ones import these women. In the process, some states become associated with servant status. In a further complication, the gendered representations of national difference reinforce earlier colonial and racist images of South-East Asian women as exotic and sexually available. In this way, the export of domestic workers is not so different from the international purchase of 'mail-order brides', and the international sex tourist industry (see Box 30.3). Women's organizations work transnationally to publicize the dangers in all these forms of trafficking in women, and to support the women caught up in these traffics.

Other forms of labour migration are not so obviously sexualized, though they may also involve exploitative working conditions and insecure rights in relation to both work and residence or citizenship. Many migrants move to and take up work in older industrial cities in Western states, and do work in clothing, textiles, electronics, and information services, for example, that is not so different from that which women do in some 'Third World' states. In conditions of urban decay, high unemployment, and cut-backs in public expenditure and services, migrants can easily become scapegoats for other people's troubles. In this way, globalization and migration become targets in politics against 'outsiders'. **Racism** marks the boundaries of national

---

> ### Box 30.3   The global sex trade
>
> **Mail-order brides**
>
> - An estimated 150,000 women are advertised each year through marriage bureaux and catalogues as being available for international marriage. There are 250 mail-order bride companies in the USA alone.
>
> - Main sending countries: China, Indonesia, Malaysia, Philippines, Russia, South Korea, Thailand, Ukraine, Vietnam.
>
> - Main receiving countries: Germany, Japan, Taiwan, Thailand, and USA.
>
> **Trafficking of women and children**
>
> Minimum estimates of women and children trafficked out of regions, 2001–2:
>
> - South-East Asia: 225,000
> - South Asia: 150,000
> - New Independent States: 100,000
> - Latin America/Caribbean: 100,000
> - Eastern Europe: 75,000
> - Africa: 50,000
>
> (Seager 2003, online at www.MyriadEditions.com)

belonging, and immigration and citizenship become major political issues. In these circumstances, those who are seen as different often organize in defence of their own rights, and may use their perceived difference as a basis for organizing. Instead of reducing differences between people, these aspects of globalization appear to heighten difference and intolerance.

Key points

- Feminist critiques, women's NGOs, and the Decade for Women helped generate 'Women in Development' (WID).

- WID includes very different approaches to gender and development.

- Recent crises associated with intensifying globaliza-

tion and restructuring impact on women in particular, generating a crisis in reproduction.

- The 'export of women' is big business, and also contributes significantly through remittances to poorer states' economies.

- Migrants and foreign workers are often scapegoated for rising unemployment and social distress.

Gender, nationalism, and militarism

While we do now live in 'the world as a whole' for some purposes, we also live in a world where difference and particular political identities are as important as ever—perhaps more so. This can be seen in the 1990s resurgence of nationalisms and ethnonationalisms, the parallel rise of fundamentalist religious politics globally, and the 'war on terror'. Women's roles and gender relations are a key element in these identity politics, and gender figures in global militarization too.

Gendered nationalism

Since the end of the cold war, there has been an upsurge in identity conflicts. **Nationalism** has unsettled the presumed coincidence of nation and state (see Ch.23). While in the past nationalism was more associated with progressive politics, for example in anti-colonial nationalism, nowadays it is often cast in exclusivist terms against 'the other'. In the process, women get caught up in nationalist politics in different ways, and identity politics come to impact on gender relations.

The language of nationalism is **familial language**—home, blood, kin. The state is often imagined as male, and the nation as female. The nation is often represented as a woman under threat of violation or domination, so that her citizen-sons must fight for her honour. The 'rape of Kuwait' told a typical story—of a feminized victim, with male villain and male hero fighting for her possession. These stories associate boundary transgression with sexual danger, and also associate proving manhood with nationalism and war. In these ways, regardless of what actual men and women are doing, men become the agents of nationalism and women passive or national possessions.

Where the nation is feminized, men are the responsible protectors. But women have obligations to the nation, too. Here we can trace a move from **nation-as-woman** to women as **mothers-of-the-nation**. This symbolic use of women and their confinement within roles as mothers can mean the policing of their bodies and behaviour, especially in wartime or in times of heightened identity conflicts.

Women, nationalism, and militarism

Women are seen as the physical **reproducers** of the nation: they are 'nationalist wombs' (Enloe 2000). This makes it important that women have the right children, with the right men. They are also seen as social reproducers and cultural transmitters, bringing up their children as Palestinian for example, even—or especially—if they do not have a state of their own. Women are also seen as **signifiers of difference**, marking the boundaries of belonging. For this reason, much importance is attached to women's clothing and movements, especially their relations with those outside the nation. Beyond the symbolic uses made of them, women are also agents in or against nationalist politics in their own right.

It is easier for women to mobilize in support of nationalist causes, if this cause is in power in their state or region. Some women do organize in movements that are dangerous for others, including other women. So there are many women supporters and some leaders of the Indian right-wing Hindu movement, and some of these women participated in violence against Muslim women and children. Many Serbian women supported the Serbian nationalist project, which involved systematic violence against women as part of 'ethnic cleansing'.

However, in some states women from dominant nationalist groups or states have organized in support for other women. Israeli **Women in Black** demonstrated in support of Palestinian women, and Belgrade feminists also demonstrated as Women in Black against Serbian nationalist aggression. These women have been subjected to much threat and sometimes violence, for their loyalty is supposed to be to their community, and not to women, or people more generally. At the same time, the idea of Women in Black has been taken up in many states experiencing nationalist violence, in expressions of solidarity with women across nationalist lines (see Box 30.4).

The high **symbolic** value attached to women in community conflicts makes them susceptible to attack from their own men, if they are seen as disloyal or rebellious. It also makes them especially vulnerable to attack from men on the other side, as a way of getting at their men. So mass rape in war and identity conflicts are not only war spoils. They are

---

Box 30.4 Women at the peace table

In conflict and war women bear great responsibility for the physical, educational, and economic well-being of their families, for caring for the wounded, for maintaining the national economy. They have also been increasingly targeted as weapons of war as they are raped, forced into marriage, abducted, and attacked. However women are not invited to the tense and delicate negotiations for peace. Indeed the culture of militarism so present during conflict tends to reinforce gender-based discrimination. In spite of resistance to their participation women are developing strategies for their voices to be heard at the peace table. They form community groups and non-government organizations that campaign and lobby the peace process and international forums. Their strategies have been creative—in the Philippines women initiated peace zones to protect their children from recruitment by the militias and the army.

Women often take the lead in developing grassroots movements to bring about peace because the men are away fighting. In Northern Ireland issues such as child care, education, health, and micro-enterprise brought women together—Catholic and Protestant—to cooperate in resolving shared problems. It was from here that women came to launch a powerful campaign to bring about peace and be included in the peace process. The numerous grassroots women's organizations came together to politicize and form the Northern Ireland Women's Coalition.

Sustaining peace requires commitment from people at the grass roots, it is they who must build lasting reconciliation and peace. The involvement of women in peace negotiations leads to ensuring a peace agreement that builds lasting peace at all levels.

(United Nations Development Fund for Women, 2000, *Women at the Peace Table*)

---

also a war strategy aimed at humiliating the enemy men by showing they are unable to protect their women. The recent visibility of **war rape**, especially in the former Yugoslavia, and of women forcibly recruited in to Japanese military brothels in the Second World War, is partly due to feminist work within states, to name rape and other violence against women as crimes against women, not against the honour of men. It is also a sign of globalizing gender issues, especially in the form of women's rights' claims.

Women's peace-building in many war zones and

Box 30.5 Gender, peace, and conflict

Excerpts from United Nations Security Council Resolution 1325 (2000)

'1. *Urges* Member States to ensure increased representation of women at all decision-making levels in national, regional and international institutions and mechanisms for the prevention, management, and resolution of conflict; ...

5. *Expresses* its willingness to incorporate a gender perspective into peacekeeping operations, and *urges* the Secretary-General to ensure that, where appropriate, field operations include a gender component; ...

8. *Calls on* all actors involved, when negotiating and implementing peace agreements, to adopt a gender perspective, including, inter alia:

   (a) The special needs of women and girls during repatriation and resettlement and for rehabilitation, reintegration and post-conflict reconstruction;

   (b) Measures that support local women's peace initiatives and indigenous processes for conflict resolution, and that involve women in all of the implementation mechanisms of the peace agreements;

   (c) Measures that ensure the protection of and respect for human rights of women and girls, particularly as they relate to the constitution, the electoral system, the police and the judiciary; ...

10. *Calls on* all parties to armed conflict to take special measures to protect women and girls from gender-based violence, particularly rape and other forms of sexual abuse, and all other forms of violence in situations of armed conflict; ...

13. *Encourages* all those involved in the planning for disarmament, demobilization and reintegration to consider the different needs of female and male ex-combatants and to take into account the needs of their dependants; ...

16. *Invites* the Secretary-General to carry out a study on the impact of armed conflict on women and girls, the role of women in peace-building and the gender dimensions of peace processes and conflict resolution, and *further invites* him to submit a report to the Security Council on the results of this study and to make this available to all Member States of the United Nations;

17. *Requests* the Secretary-General, where appropriate, to include in his reporting to the Security Council progress on gender mainstreaming throughout peacekeeping missions and all other aspects relating to women and girls.'

(Available online at www.peacewomen.org/un/UN1325)

---

feminist scholarship critiquing militarized responses to conflicts came together in the UN Security Council Resolution 1325 in 2000. This resolution calls for gender mainstreaming in peace and conflict too, including the involvement of women at all stages of peace negotiation and reconstruction (see Box 30.5). However, 9/11 and the 'war on terror' further militarized and masculinized global politics in the new millennium (Pettman 2004). At first women were rarely visible, outside their usual role in the war story, as victims and those in need of protection, and markers of difference between Islam and the West. Feminists organized globally to reject the proferred understandings of security as military security, and the hard masculinity that dominated both sides of the war on terror. Once again, their campaigns frequently declared 'Not in Our Name', as well as highlighting the ongoing effects of heightened surveillance and gendered insecurity within and between states.

Key points

- Nationalism is usually called up in gendered language.

- Women get caught up in nationalist politics in their construction as mothers of the nation and as markers of difference.

- Women also participate in or oppose nationalist politics.

- Women's symbolic significance in nationalism makes them vulnerable to violence, including war rape.

- 9/11 and the war on terror had the effect of further militarizing, and masculinizing, international politics.

Globalizing gender issues

Women organizing in the face of global processes and documenting the impact on women become players in new global politics.

Naming **gender-specific violence** against women has been part of women's transnational politics. Violence against women in their homes is the most common crime in the world. It knows no boundaries, in terms of class, culture, or nationality. Other kinds of violence against women vary by region or take culture-specific forms. There has been an increase in dowry-burnings in India; in many states there are still 'honour' crimes which see husbands, fathers, and brothers exempt from punishment after killing women whose behaviour the family opposes; female genital mutilation maims and often kills girl children and women in some North African states.

Transnational women's movements

In some states, women are subjected to bodily violence through forced contraception or abortion, as in the China one-child policy. Many poor, racialized, and minority women in Western states face discrimination and lack of care in terms of health and social choices. Women and girls are now the majority of HIV/AIDs victims, both directly in terms of infection and death (see Fig. 30.1), and indirectly as those most responsible for the healthcare and support of HIV-affected households. There is now an **international women's health movement**, which struggles with different state policies and practices, and different views within women's NGOs and outside them, over how to secure women's sexuality and reproductive rights. 'Third World' women point out that these must go beyond individual rights, to ensure enabling conditions to access choice, including maternal and child health more generally. The 1994 international conference on population and development in Cairo was crucial in mobilizing women and building regional and global linkages. But even rhetorical gains are at risk in these backlash days. And there is no easy unity or single political position on these issues among women either.

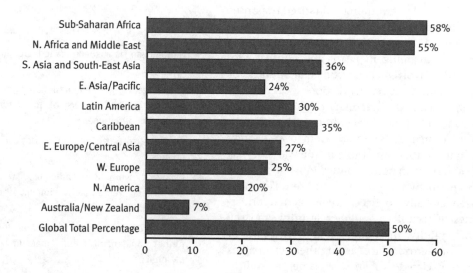

Fig. 30.1 Women's infection rate as a percentage of total HIV/AIDS cases

Source: Reproduced with permission from Centre for Reproductive Rights, New York, UNAIDS & WHO, AIDS epidemic update (2002) www.crlp.org/.

International women's conferences

International conferences and preparations for them have been especially important in globalizing women's issues, networks, and alliances. The first two women's conferences in 1975 and 1980 (see Box 30.6) witnessed conflicting priorities between First World and Third World women. By the Nairobi conference in 1985 there were alliances across these divides, and more evident splits among women from the same state or region, especially between state-sponsored women's organizations and more radical dissident or exiled women. But Nairobi did place women's issues on the international agenda, and generated webs of connection between women's NGOs across state borders.

Women's activism has impacted on other kinds of international conferences. At the 1992 Earth Summit for example women named gender as shaping relations with the **environment**, including women's primary responsibilities for fuel and water in much of the world. They also identified militarism as the cause of much environmental degradation. The 1993 Human Rights conference was even more significant in highlighting **women's rights** claims internationally. In the lead-up to the conference, a series of preparatory committees and regional women's NGO meetings made their concerns visible. The Bangkok (Asia-Pacific) regional forum identified **five priority issues** to take to Vienna. These were violence against women, the international traffic in women, rising fundamentalisms (which usually target women's rights), military rape as a crime, and women's reproductive rights.

Women's global political campaigns helped win the adoption of the UN General Assembly Declaration against Violence against Women in 1993. This represents a significant advance in global gender issues. It recognizes violence as gender based, supported by structural conditions which include women's subordination, and calls on states to punish perpetrators of violence whether in public or private places. It rejects religion or culture as excuses to abuse or discriminate against women. There are still huge problems with implementation, but this declaration does politicize violence against women, and give states formal responsibility for the security of women.

Over 30,000 women attended the NGO forum at Huairoou, which ran parallel to the official fourth international women's conference in Beijing in 1995. In many states and in regional meetings, there was a process of consultation which culminated in the Platform for Action, which identified 12 crucial areas and strategies for pursuing them, which continue to guide UN and government targets (see Fig. 30.2). The conference recognized the disproportionate costs to women of restructuring. Of the themes of equality, development, and peace, the first took priority, though the NGO forum especially recognized the interconnections here.

The 1994 Cairo conference was the first to see a concerted, global reaction against women's rights claims, led by the Vatican and conservative Islamist states. At the Beijing conference much effort went into defending earlier gains. Recent changes in global politics are even more hostile to women, and feminist agendas. The combined effect of intensifying globalization, exclusivist and anti-women identity politics, and resurgent global militarism has led some transnational feminists to advise against holding another women's international conference in these circumstances.

Box 30.6	**Globalizing gender issues through the UN system**
1946	The Commission on the Status of Women
1975	International Women's Year
1975	Mexico Women's Conference
1976–85	UN Decade for Women
1979	UN Convention on the Elimination of All Forms of Discrimination Against Women
1980	Copenhagen Women's Conference
1985	Nairobi Women's Conference
1993	Vienna Human Rights Conference
1993	UN General Assembly Declaration on the Elimination of Violence Against Women
1994	Cairo International Conference on Population and Development
1995	Beijing Women's Conference
2000	Beijing + 5, New York
2002	Durban World Conference Against Racism

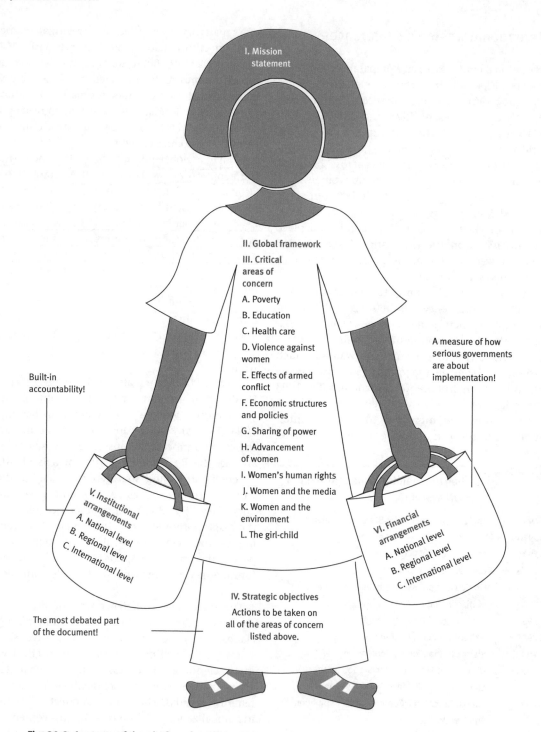

Fig. 30.2 Anatomy of the platform for action

Source: Tribune, no. 54, August 1995.

Box 30.7 Key concepts related to gendering global issues

Sex: biological difference, born male or female; the sex act; sexual difference.

Gender: what it means to be male or female in a particular place or time; the social construction of sexual difference.

Gender relations: power relations: the relational construction of masculinity and femininity, in which the masculine is usually privileged; and which are contested, and changing.

Sexuality: including normalized heterosexuality, and other, often stigmatized sexualities: homosexuality, minority masculinities, shifting or multiple sexualities.

Feminism: a political project to understand so as to change women's inequality, exploitation, or oppression. For some, aiming to move beyond gender, so that it no longer matters; for others, to validate women's interests, experiences, and choices; for others, to work for more equal and inclusive social relations overall.

Gendered Division of Labour (GDL): the notion of 'women's work', which everywhere includes women's primary responsibility for childcare and housework, and which designates many public and paid forms of work as 'women's' or 'men's', too.

Feminization of labour: recognizing the increasing global demand for women as 'cheap labour', on the global assembly line and in the provision of paid as well as unpaid reproductive labour and care.

Global care economy: recognizing the growing global demand for women's domestic and sexual services, which often see poorer, minority, or 'Third World' women providing domestic or sexual labour in other households and countries.

Transnational feminism: a sustained cross-border response to globalization, especially in its negative impacts on women, taking advantage of new opportunities for women's organizing through UN and other international conferences and global communications technology.

Gendering globalization: applying a 'gender lens' to globalization, to reveal that women are differently positioned in relation to globalization processes and differently impacted upon by them; and that women become global players in response to these gendered effects.

Key points

- There are now different transnational women's movements, for example, for women's health and reproductive rights.

- International conferences, especially women's conferences, have been very important in building transnational women's networks, and in putting women' issues on the global agenda.

- The Beijing conference is seen by some as an example of global feminism in action, while for others it illustrated the difficulties facing women's rights struggles globally.

- Contemporary global politics are strongly anti-feminist, and threaten the gains of the last two decades.

Conclusion

Gender is a relevant, and indeed necessary, category for analysis in global politics. Globalization affects women somewhat differently from men, though how it does so also depends on women's other identities and interests. In times of intensifying globalization which affects everyone, the state is no longer either willing or able to act in support of a global response. As well, the politics of identity and global militarism threaten hard-won gains, and make global politics even less amenable to feminist action.

At the same time, this 'triad' of contemporary global politics—liberal **capitalism**, exclusivist identities, and militarism—generate more women's activism. Growing numbers of women and women's NGOs are organizing transnationally, including in solidarity with other progressive movements and organizations. Utilizing congenial aspects of global-ization, especially new communications technology, they are ensuring that gender issues are increasingly globalized.

For further information and case studies on this subject, please visit the companion web site at www.oup.com/uk/booksites/politics.

QUESTIONS

1   Why did feminism come so late to International Relations?

2   What difference does it make to ask the question 'Where are the women?' about global politics?

3   What difference does it make being female, or male, in your experience?

4   What do you understand by gender?

5   What is feminism? What might different kinds of feminism contribute to our study of globalization?

6   What effects has globalization had on women, and on gender relations?

7   Why is there an increasing feminization of migrant labour, and of the global assembly line?

8   Are notions like the export of women, the global trade in women, or international traffic in women useful for tracking some global flows?

9   Discuss women's contradictory relations with nationalism.

10   What would a feminist position on 11 September 2001 and the war on terror look like?

11   Do you believe that holding another international women's conference would help or undermine women's rights struggles in the global arena?

12   Can we talk about global feminism, or transnational sisterhood?

GUIDE TO FURTHER READING

Enloe, C. (2001), *Bananas, Bases and Beaches: Making Feminist Sense of International Politics*, 2nd edn (London, Pinter). This book asks 'Where are the women?' and reveals them in many different roles in international politics, in militaries, in export production, in prostitution and the sex trade, and in diplomacy.

Marchand, M., and Runyan, A. S. (eds) (2000), *Gender and Global Restructuring* (London: Routledge). This collection applies a gender lens to global restructuring, in states economies, and households, and documents resistance to globalization.

Moser, C., and Clarke, F. (eds) (2001), *Victims, Perpetrators or Actors? Gender, Armed Conflict and Political Violence* (London: Zed Books). This collection explores the range of women's roles and responses to different kinds of violence, including the experiences of women in different war zones.

Peterson, V. S., and Runyan, A. S. (1999), *Global Gender Issues*, 2nd edn (Boulder, Col.: Westview Press). This text analyses gender in global politics, the gendered divisions of power, violence, and labour; and the politics of resistance, including women's politics.

Pettman, J. J. (1996), *Worlding Women: A Feminist International Politics* (London: Routledge). This book explores aspects of global politics only briefly touched on in this chapter. It is organized in three sections: the gendered politics of identities, of war and peace, and of the international political economy.

Pettman, J. J. (2004), 'Feminist International Relations After September 11, 2001', *Brown Journal of World Affairs*, 10:2: 85–96. This article reviews feminist contributions to IR, and develops a feminist position on 11 September 2001 and the war on terror.

Sen, G., and Grown, C. (1987), *Development, Crises and Alternative Visions: Third World Women's Perspectives* (New York: Monthly Review Press). This is a brief but broad-ranging review of the gendered impact of debt, dependence, and exploitation in Third World countries, and women's responses to these challenges.

Steans, J. (1998), *Gender and International Relations* (Cambridge, Polity Press). An accessible exploration of feminist critique in IR, and gender analysis of nationalism, war, security international political economy, and development.

Tickner, A. (2001), *Gendering World Politics* (New York: Columbia University Press). A careful feminist critique and revisioning of mainstream IR approaches to security, international political economy, and ecology.

WEB LINKS

www.dawn.org.fj The Southern feminist network Development Alternatives for a New Era is research and advocacy group which pursues gender and economic justice, democracy, and anti-militarism.

www.unifem.undp.org The United Nations Development Fund for Women (UNIFEM) works to ensure the participation of women in development planning and practice.

www.cwgl.rutgers.edu The Center for Women's Global Leadership engages in networking and advocacy in policymaking and campaigns against violence against women, and for women's human rights, sexual and reproductive rights, and social and economic justice and well-being.

www.un.org/womenwatch Women Watch: an Internet gateway for the advancement and empowerment of women.

CHAPTER 31

Human rights

CHRIS BROWN

READER'S GUIDE

Over the last fifty years the growth of an international human rights regime based on the idea that human rights should be internationally protected has been striking, and seems a prime example of globalization. However, the record of compliance with human rights law is patchy, and states seem unwilling to give international action in support of human rights a high priority. Moreover there are serious conceptual problems involved in widening the notion of 'rights' to incorporate economic and collective rights. The Western origin of the doctrine of rights has also come to be seen as problematic in the post-colonial era, as the proponents of 'Asian values' have stressed. However, recent developments such as, in different ways, the International Criminal Court and the war on terror have reaffirmed the centrality of human rights for twenty-first-century international politics.

Introduction

On the face of it, human rights are an ideal focus for a consideration of processes of globalization Whereas it was once the case that rights were almost always associated with domestic legal and political systems, in the last half century a complex network of international law and practice (the 'international human rights regime') has grown up around the idea that individuals possess rights simply by virtue of being human, of sharing in a common humanity The purpose of this chapter is to explain how this came about, but also, and in particular, to examine the many problems associated with the idea of universal human rights. This introduction will set the scene; the next section will examine some basic issues raised by rights language; the liberal position on human rights will then be examined, followed by discussion of the politics of international human rights protection as this has developed since 1945.

Many cultures and civilizations have developed ideas about the intrinsic worth and dignity of

human beings, but the notion that humans are 'rights bearers' is specifically European. Medieval in origin, this notion was embodied in the positive law of a few countries in the early modern era; and by the late eighteenth century the slow process of broadening the idea of the 'rights of man' by recognizing the rights of women, and, via campaigns against the slave trade, those of non-Europeans, began. These preliminary moves set the scene for the globalization processes of the post-1945 era. Here we have seen a number of global and regional treaties and declarations concerning human rights, and the emergence of non-governmental organizations (NGOs) such as Amnesty International dedicated to their enforcement. Moreover, governments such as that of the United States, and intergovernmental bodies such as the International Monetary Fund and the Commonwealth have increasingly (and controversially) seen it as part of their remit to promote human rights.

All of this amounts to an impressive body of international law and diplomatic practice, which has led to a further broadening and deepening of the idea of rights, often conceptualized in terms of three generations. Early statements concentrated on *First Generation* rights such as freedom of speech and assembly and 'the right to take part in the government of his [*sic*] country, directly or through freely chosen representatives' (**Universal Declaration, Article 21**). But the same declaration also recognized *Second Generation* rights to the 'economic, social and cultural rights indispensable for his dignity and the free development of his personality' (Article 22) and these economic and social rights feature very largely in later UN documents, especially, of course, the **International Covenant on Economic, Social, and Cultural Rights**. Both first and second generation rights are, in essence, possessed by individuals. *Third Generation* rights build on this a collective dimension and concern the rights of 'peoples'; for example, under the **Banjul Charter** (see Box 31.1) peoples have the right to 'freely dispose of their wealth and natural resources' (**Article 21(1)**), while the individual has a duty 'to serve his natural

---

Box 31.1 | **The international protection of human rights**

The **Universal Declaration of Human Rights** adopted by the United Nations General Assembly in 1948

The **International Covenant on Civil and Political Rights** and the **International Covenant on Economic, Social, and Cultural Rights** of 1966

The **European Convention for the Protection of Human Rights and Fundamental Freedoms** of 1950

The **American Convention on Human Rights** of 1969

The **African Charter on Human and Peoples' Rights** of 1981, usually referred to as the **Banjul Charter**

The **Convention on the Prevention and Punishment of the Crime of Genocide** of 1948

The **International Convention on the Elimination of All Forms of Racial Discrimination** of 1965

The **International Convention on the Elimination of Discrimination Against Women** of 1979

The **Vienna Declaration** and **Action Programme** of 1993

community by placing his physical and intellectual abilities at its service' and to 'preserve and strengthen positive African cultural values in his relations with other members of the society' (Article 29(2) and (7)).

This international human rights regime provides a mixed and varied menu of items for discussion. There are legal issues concerning the ratification of these treaties, the interpretation of particular clauses, and so on. These legal issues lead into polit-ico-legal questions such as the vexed issue of 'compliance'. This in turn raises foreign policy issues such as whether it is either practicable or prudent to make compliance with human rights law a touchstone of one's foreign relations. Clearly, there are straight-forward political and moral issues here concerning the trade-off between particular values—is it worth risking a trading contract in order to make a point about a violation of human rights? The political problems posed by US trade policy towards the People's Republic of China over the last decade illus-trate the difficulties here. Again, should foreign aid to poor countries be made dependent on the estab-lishment of effective human rights? Realists who privilege the **national interest**, and communitarian political philosophies which assert the right of communities to determine their own forms of rule, inevitably clash with the cosmopolitan universalism of the international human rights regime.

Finally, there are philosophical questions that cannot be avoided even by an account of human rights that tries to keep both feet firmly planted on the ground. For example, are first, second, and third generation rights compatible with each other? Indeed, are second or third generation 'rights', rights at all?

Each of these dimensions of human rights is worthy of discussion although the early items on this menu have been discussed so often that it is dif-ficult to think that anything new is likely to be said about them; nowadays the latter, political and philo-sophical, issues are increasingly coming to the fore. This is because of a general change of atmosphere after the end of the **cold war**. Until comparatively recently, few objected to the notion that human rights are universal; the *content* of human rights Dec-larations and Conventions was regarded by practical people as being rather less problematic than the issue

| Box 31.2 | **Key concepts: cosmopolitanism and communitarianism** |

One rough-and-ready classification of normative theories of international relations is in terms of cosmopolitan and communitarian thought on the ultimate source of meaning and value in human life—for the cosmo-politan, such value resides with the individual (or perhaps with God), while the communitarian looks to the community, whether ethnic, national, or per-haps even 'virtual'. This classification maps on to the Realist–Liberal dichotomy discussed elsewhere in this volume, but imperfectly; in any event virtually no serious political philosopher can be placed un-ambiguously within either camp. Still, the implica-tions for human rights are clear—cosmopolitans are disposed to favour very extensive accounts of universal human rights, while communitarians will look to, at best, a basic minimum of universal standards with emphasis on the community setting its own standards for most purposes.

of *compliance*. The key human rights problem was seen as one of forcing states to adhere to reasonably uncontroversial standards of behaviour.

Since the cold war, this problem has not gone away but some progress has been made: the estab-lishment of international tribunals after the Rwanda and Bosnia conflicts, the Pinochet case in London, and the International Criminal Court established in 2002 suggest that there is a spreading consensus that at least extreme human rights violations are a matter for the international community. As against this, the association of human rights with '**democracy pro-motion**' and the 'war on terror' since 9/11 may dam-age this consensus. In any event this marginal but significant progress has been accompanied by the emergence of another set of issues putting in ques-tion the **universality** of human rights. Clearly one of the (third generation) rights of a *'people'* must be to be different from other people and could such differ-ence be achieved other than at the expense of uni-versal standards? In any event, does not the alleged universality of human rights hide the actual privil-eging of an essentially Western notion of politics, as is suggested by, among others, advocates of 'Asian values'? Moreover, the 'masculinist' assumptions of human rights language have already been noted, and feminists have been critical of articles in the various Declarations and Covenants which assume traditional **gender** roles. These new issue challenge, indeed reverse, the normal assumption of a process of globalization. The development of rights thinking from local and national to global and universal is usually seen as the great, albeit incomplete, achievement of the human rights movement—but a return to a more limited conception of basic rights may be the only way the regime can, in fact, survive.

Key points

- The international human rights regime is an established feature of contemporary world society, and a good example of the processes of globalization.

- Modern thinking distinguishes between three generations of rights: first, broadly political; second, economic and social; third, the rights of peoples.

- One major set of contemporary problems concerns compliance, enforcement, and the politics of human rights.

- More recently, the universal status of human rights has come to be challenged by critics who stress the Western, masculine, intolerant nature of this universalism.

On rights in general

As we can no longer take the idea of rights for granted, we must now ask some fundamental questions: What kinds of rights might there be? Do rights necessarily imply **duties**? The standard legal answer to the first two questions is to distinguish different kinds of 'rights' some of which involve 'duties'; these same categories can be used in a wider political and moral context. On what **foundations** do rights rest? The answer in legal terms must be that they rest within a legal system, but what kind of legal system? Here we must return and re-examine the starting point of this chapter—the theory and practice of medieval European politics.

The theory of rights in the Middle Ages rested on the idea of **natural law**. Natural law theorists differed on many issues, but the central proposition is clear. Universal moral standards exist upon which the rights that individuals have are founded and there is a general duty to adhere to these standards. The most important feature of this position is that it is not limited in application to any particular legal system, community, state, race, creed, or civilization. Here is to be found the origin of much of the rhetoric of universal human rights.

Box 31.3   Key concepts: kinds of rights

A standard analysis here, deriving from the American jurist Wesley Hofeld (Jones 1994 for a modern version) distinguishes four kinds of rights. Claim-rights are the most basic rights—the only true rights, Hofeld believed; the classic example of a claim-right is a right generated by a contract and accompanied by correlative duties. Liberty-rights occur when I have the right to do something in the sense that I have no obligation *not* to do it—for example, to dress as I please. Here there is no correlative duty, except perhaps the duty to let me do as I choose. Sometimes a right involves the exercise of a power. For example, to have the *right* to vote means to be *empowered* to vote, to be enfranchised. Finally, a right sometimes means an immunity, the essence of which is that others are disbarred from making claims under certain circumstances, for example, to be legally insane, or under age, is to be *immune* from criminal prosecution.

Natural law provided the basis for a theory of rights in the Middle Ages; however, in the rougher

Key concepts: natural law

The origin of natural law thinking can be traced to the classical Greeks and early Christians, but in its modern form it is based on medieval Catholic theology. The central idea is that human beings have an essential nature which dictates that certain kinds of human goods are always and everywhere desired; because of this there are common moral standards that govern all human relations and these common standards can be discerned by the application of reason to human affairs. For a modern defender of the traditional Catholic doctrine, see Finnis 1980.

world of medieval political practice, rights had rather different connotations. Here a right was a concession one extracted from a nominal superior, probably by force. The **Magna Carta** (1215) is a case in point. The barons of England obliged King John to grant to them and their heirs in perpetuity a series of liberties which are, for the most part, very specific and related to particular grievances. The Great Charter as a whole was based on the important principle that the subjects of the king owe him duty only if he meets their claims. This is clearly a political bargain or contract.

There is no necessary incompatibility between the rights established by political bargaining between monarch and subjects and the rights entailed by natural law, but it should not be forgotten that these two sources of the notion of rights are actually based not simply on different, but on opposed principles Whereas rights based on **natural law** are derived from reason and the notion of human flourishing and are universal in time and space, 'charter rights' simply describe in legal terms the result of a political bargain or contract and, by definition, are limited to the parties to the bargain, and thus restricted in time and space.

Key points

- We need to establish the *status* of rights—what a right is, what kind of rights people have, whether rights imply duties, and why.

- The distinction between rights as claims, liberties, powers, and immunities helps to clarify these questions.

- The origin of thinking about rights can be traced to two features of medieval political and intellectual life, the doctrine of natural law and the political practice of extracting charters of liberties.

- Natural law generates universal rights and duties, while a charter confers local and particular liberties. The actual rights and liberties conveyed by charters may be compatible with natural law, but this compatibility cannot be relied upon and a potential conflict exists between these two sources of the idea of rights.

The modern Liberal synthesis on human rights

The complex language of medieval thinking on rights carried over into the modern period. Political philosophers such as **Hugo Grotius, Thomas Hobbes**, and **John Locke** continued to use notions of natural law, albeit in radically different ways from their predecessors. Political activists such as the Parliamentarians in the English Civil War drew on the rights and privileges they believed to have been granted to their forebears to sustain their notion of themselves as *'free-born Englishmen'*. Gradually, a synthesis emerged which can be termed the **Liberal position on rights**. This position is made up of two basic components:

1. Human beings possess rights to life, liberty, the secure possession of property, the exercise of freedom of speech, and so on which are inalienable—cannot be traded away—and unconditional—the only acceptable reason for constraining any one individual is to protect the rights of another.

2. The primary function of government is to protect

these rights, political institutions are to be judged on their performance of this function, and political obligation rests on their success in this—in short, political life is based on a kind of implicit or explicit contract between people and government.

From a philosophical and conceptual point of view this position is easy to denigrate as a mish-mash of half-digested medieval ideas. As **G. W. F. Hegel** and many subsequent communitarian thinkers have pointed out, it assumes that individual rights, indeed individuals, predate society—and yet it is difficult to see how one could exist as an individual without being part of a society. For **Jeremy Bentham** the function of government was to promote the general good (which he called utility) and the idea that individuals might have the right to undermine this seemed to him madness, especially since no one could tell him where these rights came from; the whole idea was 'nonsense upon stilts'. **Karl Marx**, on the other hand, and many subsequent radicals, pointed to the way in which the liberal position stresses property rights to the advantage of the rich and powerful.

All these points raise compelling questions, but they underestimate the powerful *rhetorical* appeal of the liberal position. Perhaps fortunately, most people are not political philosophers, and are less likely to be worried about the conceptual inadequacies associated with the liberal position on human rights than they are to be attracted by the obvious benefits of living in a political system based on or influenced by it. The plain fact is that the relatively few liberal democratic polities that have attempted to order their life along these lines have been the freest, safest, most congenial and civilized societies known to history—which, of course, is not to deny that these societies have also seen great and continuing injustices, injustices perhaps psychologically more difficult to bear because they exist in broadly just regimes.

One of the uncertain features of the liberal position is the extent to which the rights it generates are considered to be universal. For example, the French Revolutionary **Declaration of the Rights of Man and of the Citizen** clearly by its very title is intended to be of universal scope, but even here the universalism of Article 1, 'Men are born and remain free and equal in respect of rights', is soon followed by Article 3, 'The nation is essentially the source of all sovereignty', and when Revolutionary and Napoleonic France moved to bring the Rights of Man to the rest of Europe the end result looked to most contemporaries remarkably like a French Empire. The liberal position, while universal in principle, is particularistic in application and state boundaries are more or less taken for granted.

The humanitarianism and international standard setting of the nineteenth and twentieth centuries brought these issues to the fore. The Congress of Vienna of 1815 saw the Great Powers accept an obligation to end the slave trade, which was finally abolished by the **Brussels Convention** of 1890, while slavery itself was formally outlawed by the **Slavery Convention** of 1926. The **Hague Conventions** of 1907 and the **Geneva Conventions** of 1926 were designed to introduce humanitarian considerations into the conduct of war. The International Labour Office formed in 1901, and its successor the International Labour Organization, attempted to set standards in the workplace via measures such as the **Convention Concerning Forced or Compulsory Labour** of 1930.

However, although these and other subsequent measures taken together do provide a quite elaborate framework for some kind of 'global governance', they exist within a context in which notions of sovereignty and non-intervention are taken for granted and only to be overridden with great reluctance; for example, abolishing the slave trade, which involves international transactions, was much easier than abolishing slavery, which concerns what states do to their own people—indeed, pockets of slavery survive to this day in parts of West Africa and the Middle East.

All the while sovereignty remains a norm of the system, humanitarian impulses can only take the form of exhortation and standard-setting. In nineteenth-century England, Manchester School radical Liberals such as John Bright and Richard Cobden were bitterly critical of traditional diplomacy, but supported the norm of non-intervention on the grounds that their opponents used moral arguments in support of interventions which were really engaged in for reasons of power politics and general

Key concepts: sovereignty and the standards of civilization

When nineteenth-century Europeans travelled to China, Japan, and other non-European countries in pursuit of trade, they were reluctant to put themselves (and their property) under the jurisdiction of local legal systems, which often violated what Europeans regarded as basic principles of justice, for example, by allowing the aristocracy and military elite to dispense summary justice. However, a basic principle of international society is the sovereignty of states, which required respect towards and non-interference with the institutions of the states which were its members. Where they had the power to do so, Europeans solved this problem by requiring that the countries concerned respected European legal conventions (the 'standards of civilization') before they were allowed full membership of international society. In the meantime, special courts would be established by and for Europeans and those who dealt with them. These restrictions were bitterly resented as implying inferior status, and removing the regime of 'capitulations'—as it was called—was a key nationalist demand everywhere in which they were set in place.

rent conventional wisdom on human rights is based on quite similar ideas.

The willingness of Liberals to extend their thinking on human rights in a more interventionist direction was characteristic of the second half of the twentieth century. The horrors of the 1914–18 war stimulated attempts to create a peace system based on a form of international government, and although the **League of Nations** of 1919 had no explicit human rights provision, the underlying assumption was that its members would be states governed by the rule of law and respecting individual rights. The **Charter of the United Nations** of 1945 in the wake of the Second World War does have some explicit reference to human rights—a tribute to the impact on the general climate of thought of the horrors of that war, and, in particular of the murder of millions of Jews, Gypsies, and Slavs in the extermination camps of National Socialist Germany. In this context the need to assert a universal position was deeply felt, and the scene was set for the burst of international human rights legislation of the postwar era.

mischief-making. This is, of course, a familiar line of argument most likely in the twenty-first century to be directed at the American heirs of Britain's position in the world.

Cobden was a consistent anti-interventionist and anti-imperialist—other Liberals were more selective; Gladstone's 1870s campaign to throw the Ottoman Empire out of Europe bag and baggage was based on the more common view that different standards applied as between 'civilized' eand 'uncivilized' peoples. In Gladstone's view the Ottoman Empire—although, since 1856, a full member of international society—could not claim the rights of a sovereign state because its institutions did not come up to the requisite standards. Indeed this latter position was briefly established in international law in the notion of **standards of civilization**. In the late twentieth century, this notion disturbs and unsettles, yet cur-

Key points

- From out of medieval theory and practice a synthesis emerged, the liberal position on human rights, which combines universal and particularist thinking—universal rights established by a contract between rulers and ruled.

- This position is conceptually suspect, but politically and rhetorically powerful.

- Nineteenth-century Liberalism supported international humanitarian reform but within the limits of the norms of sovereignty and non-intervention.

- For some Liberals these latter norms did not apply when the standards of civilization were in question. Twentieth-century thinking on human rights has been less restrictive, largely because of the horrors of the world wars and the Holocaust.

1948 and the modern agenda

The post-1945 humanitarian impulse identified above led to the burst of lawmaking and standard-setting described in the introduction to this chapter. Although the 1966 covenants now have the status of international law, and although the **European Convention** of 1950 has the most effective enforcement machinery, nonetheless, for all its declamatory status and lack of teeth, the **Universal Declaration of Human Rights** by the UN General Assembly in 1948 is, symbolically, central. This was the first time in history that the international community had attempted to define a comprehensive code for the internal government of its members. During the late 1940s the United Nations was dominated by the West, and the contents of the declaration represented this fact, with its emphasis on political freedom. The voting was 48 for and none against. Eight states abstained, for interestingly different reasons.

South Africa abstained. The white-dominated regime in South Africa denied political rights to the majority of its people and clearly could not accept that 'all are born free and equal in dignity and rights' (Article 1). The South African Government objected to the Declaration on the grounds that it violated the protection of the domestic jurisdiction of states guaranteed by Article 2(7) of the **United Nations Charter**. This is a clear and uncomplicated case of a first generation rights issue.

The Soviet Union and five Soviet bloc countries abstained. Although Stalin's Russia was clearly a tyranny, the Soviet Government did not officially object to the political freedoms set forth in the Declaration. Instead the Soviet objection was to the absence of sufficient attention to social and economic rights by comparison to the detailed elaboration of 'bourgeois' freedoms and property rights. The Soviets saw the Declaration as a cold war document, designed to stigmatize socialist regimes—a not wholly inaccurate description of the motives of its promulgators. Here we see the first expression of second generation rights issues, which would later be taken up by more worthy proponents.

Saudi Arabia abstained. Saudi Arabia was one of the few non-Western members of the United Nations in 1948 and just about the only one whose system of government was not, in principle, based on some Western model. Saudi Arabia objected to the Declaration on religious grounds, specifically objecting to Article 18 which specifies the freedom to change and practise the religion of one's choice. These provisions did not simply contravene specific Saudi laws which, for example, forbade (and still forbid) the practice of the Christian religion in Saudi Arabia, they contravened the tenets of Islam which does not recognize a right of apostasy. Here, to complete the picture, we have an assertion of third generation rights and a denial of the universalism of the Declaration.

Thus, the opening moment of the **universal human rights regime** sees the emergence of the themes which will make up the politics of human rights over the subsequent fifty years.

Key points

- The politics of the Universal Declaration of 1948 allow us to identify the three major human rights issues of the post-1945 era.

- First, there is the contest between the old norm of sovereignty and the new norm of universal domestic standards.

- Second, there is the contest between political and liberal and social and economic formulations of human rights.

- Finally, there is the assertion of the rights of peoples to be different.

The politics of human rights promotion

'No one shall be subjected to torture or to cruel, inhuman or degrading treatment or punishment' (UN Declaration Article 5, Covenant on Civil and Political Rights Article 7, etc). This is an *immunity* that is now so well established as to be part of **customary international law**. What in practice does this mean for someone faced with the prospect of such treatment?

If an individual is fortunate enough to live in a country governed by the rule of law, its domestic courts may well uphold his or her immunity, and the international side of things will come into play only on the margins. Thus, a European dissatisfied with his or her treatment at home may be able to continue a legal dispute over a particular practice beyond his or her national courts to the **European Commission on Human Rights** and the **European Court of Human Rights**. In non-European countries governed by the rule of law no such direct remedy is available, but, in any event, the international, universal side of human rights, at best, merely reinforces rights which are established elsewhere, in the domestic political order.

The more interesting case emerges if potential victims do not live in such a law-governed society, if, that is, 'their' government and courts are the problem and not a possible solution. What assistance have they the right to expect from the international community in such circumstances? What consequences will flow from their government's failure to live up to its obligations? The problem is that even in cases where violations are quite blatant it may be difficult to see what other states are able to actually do, even supposing they are willing to act, which, since states rarely if ever act simply in terms of human rights considerations cannot be taken for granted.

Thus, during the cold war, the West regularly issued verbal condemnations of human rights violations by the Soviet Union and its associates, but rarely acted on these condemnations—the power of the Soviet Union made direct intervention imprudent, while even relatively minor sanctions would only be adopted if the general state of East–West relations suggested this would be appropriate. Conversely, violations by countries associated with the West were routinely overlooked or, in some cases, even justified. With the ending of the cold war it seemed possible that a more even-handed approach to human rights violations might emerge, and, indeed, more active policies have been pursued in some cases but expectations of major changes in attitude have not been met. In 1997, for example, the incoming Labour Government in Britain declared its determination to place human rights at the heart of its foreign policy. Perhaps predictably, the actual policy of the new government has frequently been seen to be as determined by political and commercial considerations as in the past, and the 'ethical dimension' promised has not delivered much in the way of a new emphasis on human rights (Smith and Light 2001).

All told it seems unlikely that individuals ill-treated by non-constitutional regimes will find any real support from the international community unless their persecutors are weak, of no strategic significance, and commercially unimportant—and even then it is unlikely that effective action will be taken unless one further factor is present, namely the force of public opinion. This is the one positive factor that may goad states into action—the post-war growth of humanitarian **NGOs** has produced a context in which sometimes the force of public opinion can make itself felt, not necessarily in the oppressing regime, but in the policy-formation processes of the potential providers of succour.

The situation with respect to *second generation* rights is more complicated. Consider, for example, 'the right of everyone to an adequate standard of living for himself and his family, including adequate food, clothing and housing, and to the continuous improvement of living conditions' (Covenant on Economic, Social, and Cultural Rights, Article 11.1), or the 'right of everyone to be free from hunger' (Article 11.2).

The Covenant makes the realization of these rights an obligation on its signatories, but this is a different kind of obligation to the obligation to refrain from,

---

| Box 31.6 | **Case study: the ending of apartheid in South Africa** |

White-dominated South Africa was commercially important to many Western businesses, and of some strategic
importance in the cold war; initial attempts to boycott
South African goods and stem the flow of investment to
the country were unsuccessful. However, the impact of
public opinion—reinforced in the United States by the
power of the Black Congressional lobby, and African-
American pressure groups—gradually made it commercially unwise to be associated with South Africa, while
pressure in the United Nations and elsewhere produced
a reasonably effective arms embargo. This international
pressure certainly contributed to the decision of the
South African regime to end apartheid and enter into
negotiation with the African National Congress. However,
this comparatively rare success story for the international
human rights community may be a product of some of
the peculiarities of the South African system. Although
blatantly unjust, the old South Africa claimed to be preserving Western 'civilization', and did indeed have a freer
judiciary and press than might have been expected. This
made it more vulnerable to Western pressure than is the
case with those repressive regimes that do not make this
claim, or possess those institutions.

---

for example, 'cruel or degrading' punishments. In
the latter case, as with other basically political
rights, the remedy is clearly in the hands of
national governments. The way to end torture is for
states to stop torturing. The right not to be tortured
is associated with a duty not to torture. The right to
be free from hunger, on the other hand, is not simply a matter of a duty on the part of one's own and
other states not to pursue policies that lead to starvation—it also involves a positive duty to 'ensure
an equitable distribution of world food supplies in
relation to need' (Covenant on Economic, Social,
and Cultural Rights, Article 11.2(b)). This is
problematic.

First, it is by no means clear that, even assuming
goodwill, these social and economic goals could
always be met, and to think in terms of having a
right to something that could not be achieved is to

misuse language. In such circumstances a right simply means 'a generally desirable state of affairs'—and
this weakening of the concept may have the effect of
undermining more precise claims to rights which
can be achieved (such as the right not to be tortured).
Second, some states may seek to use economic and
social rights more directly to undermine political
rights. Thus, dictatorial regimes in poor countries
quite frequently justify the curtailment of political
rights in the alleged name of promoting economic
growth, or economic equality. In fact, there is no
reason to accept the general validity of this argument—Amartya Sen's work, for example, makes it
clear that development and freedom go together
(Sen 1999)—but it will still be made, and not always
in bad faith. Finally, if it is accepted that all states
have a positive duty to promote economic well-
being and freedom from hunger everywhere, then
the consequences go beyond the requirement of the
rich to share with the poor, revolutionary though
such a requirement would be. They also make virtually all national social and economic policies a matter for international regulation. Clearly rich states
would have a duty to make economic and social policy with a view to its consequences on the poor, but
so would poor states. The poor's right to assistance
creates a duty on the rich to assist, but this in turn
creates a right of the rich to insist that the poor have
a duty not to worsen their plight—for example, by
failing to restrict population growth or by
inappropriate economic policies. Aid programmes
promoted by the Commonwealth and World Bank,
and the structural adjustment programmes of the
IMF regularly include conditions of this kind. They
are, however, widely resented because they contradict another widely supported economic and social
right, that 'All peoples have the right of self-
determination. By virtue of that right they freely
determine their political status and freely pursue
their economic, social and cultural development'
(Covenant on Economic, Social, and Cultural Rights,
Article 1.1). Even when applied in a well-meaning
and consistent way external pressures to change policy are rarely popular, even with those they are
intended to benefit.

Key points

- The politics of rights varies according to whether constitutional or non-constitutional regimes are involved.

- In any event, the international community rarely acts on human rights cases unless public opinion is engaged.

- Economic and social rights are conceptually different from political rights, and present a more basic challenge to existing norms of sovereignty and non-intervention.

Universalism challenged

The very idea of human rights implies limits to the range of variation in domestic political regimes that is acceptable internationally. Post-1945 human rights law, if taken seriously and at face value, would create a situation where all states would be obliged to conform to a quite rigid template which dictated most aspects of their political, social, and economic structures and policies.

Conventional defenders of human rights argue that this would be a Good Thing—the universal spread of best practice in human rights matters is in the interest of all people. Others disagree. Does post-1945 law actually constitute best practice? The feminist critique of universal human rights is particularly apposite here. The universal documents all, in varying degrees, privilege a patriarchal view of the family as the basic unit of society. Even such documents as the Convention on Elimination of Discrimination against Women (CEDAW) of 1979 do no more than extend to women the standard liberal package of rights, and modern feminists debate whether this constitutes a genuine advance (Peters and Wolper 1995).

More fundamentally, is the very idea of best practice sound? We have already met one objection to the idea in the Saudi abstention of 1948. The argument is simple: universalism is destructive not just of undesirable differences between societies but of desirable and desired differences. The human rights movement stresses the common humanity of the peoples of the world, but for many, the things that distinguish us from one another are as important as the things that unify us. The **Declaration of Prin-**

Box 31.7   The feminist critique of human rights

Until recently it has been conventional for human rights treaties to be cast in language that assumes that the rights-bearer is a man and the head of a household. Many feminists argue that this reflects more than an old-fashioned linguistic convention. The classic political and civil rights (freedom of speech, association, from arbitrary arrest, and so on) assume that the rights-bearer will be living, or would wish to live, a life of active citizenship—but, until very recently, such a life was denied to nearly all women in nearly all cultures. Instead of this public life, women were limited to the private sphere and subjected to the arbitrary and capricious power of the male head of the household. It is only very recently in the Western liberal democracies that women have been able to vote, to stand for office, or to own property in their own name, and such issues as the criminalization of rape in marriage and effective measures to prevent domestic violence against women are still controversial. The situation is, if anything, rather worse in non-Western polities, which is why although the feminist critique of the privileging of the interests of men is structurally quite similar to the 'Asian' critique of the privileging of the interests of Western conceptions of what it is to be human, the politics of the two positions are very different. It may be that a genuinely gender-neutral account of human rights is possible, but some radical feminists argue that a different kind of thinking altogether is required (see Catherine Mackinnon in Shute and Hurley 1993).

---

ciples of **Indigenous Rights** adopted in Panama in 1984 by a non-governmental group, the **World**

Council of Indigenous Peoples, lays out positions which are designed to preserve the traditions, customs, institutions, and practices of indigenous peoples (many of which, it need hardly be said, contradict contemporary liberal norms).

A more basic challenge to universalism emerged in the 1990s. In the immediate post-cold war world, and especially after the election of US President Bill Clinton in 1992, there was some talk of adopting active policies of 'democracy promotion', and a number of East Asian governments and intellectuals asserted in response the notion that there were specifically 'Asian values' that required defending from this development. The argument was not simply that Western governments, intergovernmental bodies, NGOs, and journalists are engaging in a new form of imperialism by using universal human rights to attack various state practices in South-East Asia (and elsewhere) but also that these rights boil down to no more than a set of particular social choices which need not to be considered binding by those whose values (and hence social choices) are differently formed, for example, by Islam or Confucianism rather than by a secularized Christianity. The wording of the **Vienna Declaration on Human Rights** of 1993 which refers to the need to bear in mind 'the significance of national and regional particularities and various historical, cultural and religious backgrounds' when considering human rights partially reflects this viewpoint—and has been criticized for this by some human rights activists.

Returning to the history of rights, it is here that the distinction between rights grounded in natural law and rights grounded in a contract becomes crucial. As was noted above, it is only if rights are grounded in some account of human flourishing and reason that they are genuinely universal in scope. But is this position, as its adherents insist, free of cultural bias, a set of ideas that all rational beings must accept? It seems not, at least in so far as many apparently rational Muslims, Hindus, Buddhists, Atheists, Utilitarians, and so on clearly do not accept its doctrines! It seems that either the standards derived from natural law, or some such doctrine, are cast in such general terms that virtually any continuing social system will exemplify them—in which case the cutting edge of the doctrine is lost; or, if cast more specifically, the standards described are not in fact universally desired—in which case the claim that they are based on general features of human nature or the human condition is suspect.

Of course, we are under no obligation to accept all critiques of universalism at face value. Human rights may have first emerged in the West, but this does not

---

Box 31.8   Key concepts: 'Asian values'

That Western states, intergovernmental bodies, and NGOs have sometimes taken it upon themselves to promote human rights has always been resented as hypocritical in the non-Western world, where the imperialist record of the West over the last four centuries has not been forgotten. In the 1990s, this resentment led a number of the leaders of the quasi-authoritarian newly industrializing nations of South-East Asia to assert the existence of 'Asian values' that could be counterposed to the (allegedly) Western values associated with the international human rights regime—in this they seemed to confirm the forthcoming 'clash of civilizations' forecast by Huntington (1996). Such thinking was partially reflected in the **Bangkok Declaration** of 1993, made by Asian ministers in the run-up to the **Vienna Conference** of that year (for text see Tang 1994). Western notions of human rights were seen as excessively individualistic, as opposed to the stress on the family of Asian societies, and insufficiently supportive of (if not downright hostile to) religion. Some, especially Prime Minister Mahathir Mohamad of Malaysia, regarded the West as morally decadent because of the growth of gay rights and the relative success of the women's movement in combating gender discrimination. Critics accused Mahathir and others of justifying their own authoritarian rule, although it should be noted that 'Asian values' can only perform this task if the argument strikes a chord with ordinary people. More to the point, it may be doubted whether the conservative positions expressed by proponents of Asian values are in any genuine sense 'Asian'; many Western conservatives and fundamentalists share their critique of the West, while progressive Asian human rights activists are critical. Notions such as 'the West' or 'Asia' are unacceptably 'essentialist'—all cultures and civilizations contain different and often conflicting tendencies; the world of Islam, or of 'Confucian capitalism', is no more monolithic than is Christianity or Western secularism.

in itself make rights thinking 'Western'. It may be that an apparently principled rejection of universalism is, in fact, no more than a rationalization of tyranny. How do we know that the inhabitants of Saudi Arabia or Malaysia actually prefer not to live in a democratic system with Western liberal rights, as their governments assert? There is an obvious dilemma here: if we insist that we will only accept democratically validated regimes we will be imposing an alien test of legitimacy on these societies—yet what other form of validation is not open to the charge that it simply reflects the interests and values of the privileged?

In any event, does not the body of legal acts for the protection of universal human rights outlined in earlier sections of this chapter override local considerations? Again, defenders of difference will argue that international law is itself a Western, universalist notion and that to pose the issue in these terms is to beg the question; in any event, they rightly note, the Western record of adherence to universal norms is not such as to justify any claim to moral superiority, pointing to the many crimes of the age of imperialism as well as to contemporary issues such as the treatment of asylum seekers and refugees.

The general point is that there is no neutral language with which to discuss human rights; whatever way the question is posed reflects a particular viewpoint, and this is no accident, it is built into the nature of the discourse. Is there any way in which the notion of universal rights can be saved from its critics? Two modern approaches seem fruitful. Even if we find it difficult to specify human rights, it may still be possible to talk of human wrongs—similarly, some have argued it is easier to specify what is *unjust* than what is *just*. To use Michael Walzer's terminology (1994*a*) there may be no thick moral code that is universally acceptable, to which all local codes conform, but there may be a thin code which at least can be used to delegitimize some actions. Thus, for example, the **Genocide Convention** of 1948 seems a plausible example of a piece of international legislation that outlaws an obvious wrong, and, similarly,

while some local variations in the rights associated with gender may be unavoidable, it is still possible to say that practices such as **female genital mutilation** are simply wrong, which means, in both cases, that any code which did not condemn such suffering would be unworthy of respect.

This may not take us as far as some would wish—essential to this approach is the notion that there are going to be some practices which many would condemn but which will have to be tolerated—but it may be the most appropriate response to contemporary Pluralism. An alternative approach is more supportive of universal ideas but on a non-foundationalist basis. This involves recognizing that human rights are based on a particular culture—Richard Rorty (1993) actually calls this the 'human rights culture'—and defending them in these terms rather than by reference to some universal cross-cultural code. This approach would involve abandoning the idea that it is possible to demonstrate that human rights exist; instead, it involves proselytizing on behalf of the sort of culture in which rights exist. The basic point is that human life is safer, pleasanter, and more dignified when rights are acknowledged than when they are not.

Key points

- The human rights template severely limits the degree of acceptable variation in social practices.

- This universalism can be challenged on feminist grounds as privileging patriarchy.

- More generally, the liberal position on rights privileges a particular account of human dignity.

- Cultural critics of universal rights such as proponents of 'Asian values' can be seen as self-serving, but no neutral criteria for assessing this criticism can exist.

- But a set of basic rights may be defensible, likewise the idea of a human rights culture.

Conclusion

Along with 'democracy promotion' the last decade has seen the elaboration of the notion of humanitarian intervention and the emergence of international legal doctrines which support 'universal jurisdiction' in respect of severe human rights violations and the establishment of an **International Criminal Court (ICC)** in 2002. Each of these developments suggests that human rights will be taken more seriously in the future, although each also actually assumes a degree of global consensus which, as suggested above, may not actually exist. It is striking, for example, that three of the five 'veto powers' in the UN have not signed up to the **ICC** (China, Russia, and the USA), and even more striking that no major Asian power has joined, or intends to join. Still, setting aside these innovations, the most significant recent development in the area of human rights has been the fallout from the terrorist attacks on New York City and Washington on 11 September 2001.

This awful event has had consequences in two different directions. On the one hand, the political exigencies of the 'war on terror' that followed 9/11 have meant that many of the worst habits of the cold war have come back in fashion. First, the human rights failings of allies in this war are now routinely overlooked by the West in general and the USA in particular; Russia, China, and Pakistan have benefited greatly from this dispensation. Second, most of the Western countries that are the prime targets of terrorism have introduced restrictions on the civil rights of their citizens in the name of 'homeland security'—such restrictions may be necessary, but they are certainly regrettable. On the other hand, it may be that the need to address the root causes of terrorism will actually focus attention more clearly on the human rights abuses that have characterized so many of the Arab countries whose citizens carried out the attacks on 11 September 2001. It is certainly the intention of the influential 'neo-conservative' movement that US power should be used in the Middle East to promote democratic forms of government and the observance of human rights. Cosmopolitan Liberals challenge the neo-conservative lack of interest in social and economic rights, and conventional Realists criticize the alleged *naïveté* they show in assuming that liberal democracy will be easy to transplant to the Middle East; more seriously, it is possible that greater democracy in the region might make things worse in some areas of human rights, especially those connected to gender—still, the possibility that, in the long run, 9/11 will revitalize the international human rights regime should not be completely discounted.

In any event, whatever politicians and philosophers of right and left may say or do, it is on the strength of popular support for universal human rights that the idea will flourish or die in the twenty-first century. If the idea of human rights captures the imagination of the peoples of the world, then the shortcomings of Western leaders, and the opposition of authoritarian rulers elsewhere, will be of little long-run significance. If, on the other hand, people insist on defining themselves in terms which deny the existence of universal rights, whether those terms are religious, ethnic, or national, then the work of human rights activists will be equally fruitless. There is no predetermined outcome to this contest.

For further information and case studies on this subject, please visit the companion web site at www.oup.com/uk/booksites/politics.

QUESTIONS

1   Can first, second, and third generation rights be distinguished?

2   Does a right always involve a correlative duty?

3   Are there such things as natural rights?

4   Can the promotion of human rights be a foreign policy goal of states? Are there moral as well as practical objections to such a policy?

5   In what sense can one speak of a right to an adequate standard of living?

6   Should peoples as well as individuals have rights? If so, do the rights in question include the right to override individual rights?

7   Are advocates of human rights necessarily cultural imperialists?

8   Is there a distinctively feminist approach to human rights?

9   How important is public opinion in mobilizing support for victims of human rights violations?

10 Is a democratic form of government a necessary precondition for the existence of human rights?

11 Are there specifically 'Asian values' which provide the basis for a critique of universal human rights?

12 What have been the consequences for the international human rights regime of the terrorist attacks of 11 September 2001?

GUIDE TO FURTHER READING

Brownlie, I. (ed.) (2002), *Basic Instruments on Human Rights*, 5th edn (Oxford: Clarendon Press) contains the texts of all the most important treaties and declarations.

Steiner, H. J., and Alston, P. (2000), *International Human Rights in Context: Law, Politics, Morals: Texts and Materials*, 2nd edn (Oxford: Clarendon Press) contains abbreviated texts and a great deal of useful commentary in its over 1,500 pages! It is the single most useful book for the study of international human rights.

Jones, P. (1994), *Rights* (Basingstoke: Macmillan) is a good source for a discussion of the philosophical problems posed by the idea of rights.

Finnis, J. (1980), *Natural Law and Natural Rights* (Oxford: Clarendon Press) is more difficult, but the best introduction to modern natural law thinking.

For on international human rights

Dunne, T., and Wheeler, N. J. (eds) (1999), *Human Rights in Global Politics* (Cambridge: Cambridge University Press) is the best introductory collection.

Vincent, R. J. (1986), *Human Rights and International Relations* (Cambridge: Cambridge University Press), which links human rights protection to the theory of international society is an older but still useful study.

Donnelly, J. (1993), *International Human Rights* (Boulder, Col.: Westview) is a good summary of the standard liberal position.

Smith, K. E., and Light, M. (eds) (2001), *Ethics and Foreign Policy* (Cambridge: Cambridge University Press) sets out some of the problems involved in making human rights central to foreign policy.

Shue, H. (1983), *Basic Rights* (Princeton, Princeton University Press) is a very influential defence of second generation rights as genuine rights.

Pogge, T. (2002), *World Poverty and Human Rights* (Cambridge: Polity Press) is a more recent view.

For third generation rights and so-called 'Asian values'

Crawford, J. (ed.) (1958), *The Rights of Peoples* (Oxford: Clarendon Press).

Tang, J. H. (ed.) (1994), *Human Rights and International Relations in the Asia-Pacific Region* (London: Pinter Press).

Bauer, J., and Bell, D. A. (eds) (1999), *The East Asian Challenge for Human Rights* (Cambridge: Cambridge University Press).

Bell, D. A. (2000), *East meets West: Human Rights and Democracy in East Asia* (Princeton, NJ: Princeton University Press) presents the argument brilliantly in dialogue form.

For the argument that development requires the curtailment of human rights

Sen, A. (1999), *Development as Freedom* (Oxford: Oxford University Press).

For a wider, very controversial, but since 9/11 very topical, context for these arguments

Huntington, S. (1996), *The Clash of Civilizations and the Remaking of World Order* (New York: Simon & Schuster).

Walzer, M. (1994*a*), *Thick and Thin: Moral Argument at Home and Abroad* (Notre Dame, Ind.: University of Notre Dame Press) makes the case for a 'thin' moral code that can operate cross-culturally.

Shute, S., and Hurley, S. (eds) (1993), *On Human Rights* (New York: Basic Books) is an excellent collection of papers on the philosophy of human rights, including essays by John Rawls, Richard Rorty, and Catherine Mackinnon. The latter offers one feminist view.

Peters, J. S., and Wolper, A. (eds) (1995), *Women's Rights, Human Rights: International Feminist Perspectives* (New York: Routledge) is a good collection of other feminist views.

Cox, M., Ikenberry, J., and Inoguchi, T. (eds) (2000), *American Democracy Promotion: Impulses, Strategies and Impacts* (New York: Oxford University Press) is a good survey of democracy promotion before 9/11.

Ignatief, M. (2003), *Human Rights as Politics and Idolatry* (Princeton, NJ: Princeton University Press) is a provocative look at the theory and practice of human rights in the world since 9/11.

Schultz, W. (2003), *Tainted Legacy: September 11, 2001 and the Ruin of Human Rights* (New York: Nation Books) offers a more depressed account focusing on civil rights in the USA by the director of the American branch of Amnesty International.

The most useful journals in the field are: *Human Rights Quarterly: a Comparative and International Journal of the Social Sciences, Philosophy and Law* (Baltimore: Johns Hopkins University Press) and the *International Journal of Human Rights* (London: Frank Cass).

WEB LINKS

Some of the best web sites on human rights are associated with American law schools: the Project Diana Online Human Rights Archive at Yale Law School (named after a Yale librarian) is particularly good: www.yale.edu/lawweb/avalon/diana; as is the University of Minnesota Human Rights Library at: www.umn.edu/humanrts and the University of Denver's Institute of International Human Rights at www.du.edu/humanrights. UN sites such as: www.un.org/rights and, for the UN Commissioner for Human Rights: www.unhchr.ch are also valuable resources. Amnesty International is served at www.amnesty.org.

Part Five

GLOBALIZATION IN THE FUTURE

In this final part of the book we want to offer you some reflections on the impact of globalization for world politics in the new millennium. We thought long and hard about whether we, as editors, should write a conclusion to the second edition of this book given that some readers of the first edition wrote to us to suggest that there should be a concluding section to the book. But we eventually decided that it was impossible to do this given all the very different perspectives on globalization found in the preceding chapters. This is an approach we have continued in this third edition. Our intention all along has been to show you that there are very distinct ways of looking at globalization, and writing a conclusion would have meant taking sides on which of these we preferred: we think that this is something that you, the reader, should do! Therefore we asked two scholars to contribute chapters in this part, and, although neither of them is intended as a conclusion, together they outline the main questions concerning the nature of world politics in the current world. Andrew Linklater's chapter examines the forms of political community that are emerging under globalization, while Ian Clark's chapter looks at the question of what kind of order exists in the post-cold war period. We have two main aims for this part of the book: **first,** we want to end the book by returning to world politics, rather than international politics, by asking about the relationship between political community and globalization; **second,** we want to summarize the main arguments about the nature of world politics since the cold war, to bring the historical story up to date, so to speak. Each of these chapters problematizes the traditional international politics notion of hermetically sealed states acting within a states-system. Above all, we want to leave you with a series of deep questions about the effect of globalization both on the state and on world politics. Is the form of political community found in the globalized world different from that found before? Is the state still the unit for political community or does globalization make cosmopolitan politics more possible? Is there order in the post-cold war world? Is there much difference between the form of order found in the contemporary period and that found in the cold war? Does globalization help or hinder the creation of a more just, or a more equal, world order? We hope that these two chapters will raise a series of questions that will allow you to come to judgements about the overall impact of globalization on politics in the world.

CHAPTER 32

Globalization and the transformation of political community

ANDREW LINKLATER

READER'S GUIDE

Realist approaches to international relations focus on relations between independent political communities. They ask how far political communities—nation-states that wish to retain their sovereignty—can control force and maintain order through the balance of power. In the main, Realists assume the human race will remain divided into separate states. They are right to emphasize the state's power; however, several important challenges to traditional conceptions of political community have developed in recent times. Globalization has led many to ask whether the nation-state should be the dominant form of political community in an era of global problems which include environmental devastation. Many ethnic movements have called for the transformation of political community to overcome their 'second-class citizenship'. This chapter explains how the nation-state became the dominant form of political community in the modern world. It then analyses conceptions of new forms of community and citizenship which have emerged in the context of globalization and ethnic fragmentation.

Introduction: what is a political community?

Many different types of **community** exist in the modern world. They include local communities such as neighbourhood groups, political associations such as sovereign states, transnational movements such as scientific associations or international non-governmental organizations and 'virtual communities' made possible by instant forms of global communication. Each of these communities has its particular kind of human solidarity and distinctive pattern of political cooperation

Politics exist in all such communities because members do not have identical views about the goals of society and about how they should be realized. In modern states, for example, there are differences of opinion about how far governments should redistribute wealth and how far markets should allocate resources. Like states, religious communities have their politics but they may not be political communities according to the definition used in this chapter. The desire to worship with others is central to religious community but it is the desire for **self-rule**—the desire to be free from the dominion of others—which turns a religious association, or any collectivity, into a political community (see Ch.23).

In all forms of community, special loyalties and attachments exist between members who prefer cooperation with each other rather than with 'outsiders'. References to a common past which often includes the shared experience of suffering in war are frequently used to bind a community together. A British example is the memory of the struggle against fascism during the Second World War; other illustrations include memories of national liberation struggles in the former colonies of Africa and Asia. The place of war in histories of the national past is a reminder that individuals may be asked to die for their political community. Some religious communities have expected the same of their members in the form of martyrdom. However, the duty to be prepared to die for the larger group has been central to virtually all independent political communities.

Most people belong to several communities simultaneously—to national and religious groups, for example, as well as to the nation-state. Some political and religious communities have tried to persuade their members to forsake these other loyalties. Totalitarian states such as Stalin's Russia demanded this from their citizens but they failed because their populations valued their membership of communities which were not coterminous with the state. Many Soviet citizens attached more importance to their church or ethnic group than to the state. Liberal-democratic forms of political community recognize that citizens value many different loyalties at any given time whether directed towards local communities, political parties, or international non-governmental associations such as Greenpeace and Amnesty International. Most of these states also believe they have moral duties to peoples elsewhere. Most believe that they should obey international law and promote respect for human rights in other parts of the world.

Even so, war has had a massive impact on the evolution of modern political communities, and states have wanted to ensure that they can count on their citizens' loyalty when national survival is threatened (see Ch.13). States have tried to ensure that national loyalties are the central political attachments in the lives of their citizens, but not the only ones they have. The importance of this demand on citizens has declined in those political communities which have been spared the ordeal of war in recent decades. The period since the end of the Second World War is the longest period of peace between the Great Powers since the Treaty of Westphalia in 1648. This is also the era in which globalization, the condition in which social relations are increasingly non-territorial, has become as important as Great Power conflict in shaping world politics. An intriguing question is what the declining role of Great Power rivalry or war, and the growing importance of globalization, mean for the future of political community. A crucial question is whether political communities will become more cosmopolitan because of globalization (see also Ch.24).

Key points

- The members of a political community are committed to governing themselves.

- Totalitarian states attempted to make the political community absolute but liberal-democratic states recognize that their citizens value their membership of many communities including the nation-state.

- Because they expected to be involved in major wars,

states have tried to persuade their citizens to place obligations to the state ahead of duties to other communities, whether local or global.

- Globalization and the declining significance of military competition between the Great Powers have raised the question of whether political communities will become more cosmopolitan in future.

Box 32.1 Some political theorists on political community

'The primary good that we distribute to one another is membership in some human community.' (Michael Walzer)

'Clearly then, as all associations aim at some good, that association which is most sovereign among them all and embraces all others will aim highest, i.e. at the most sovereign of all goods. This is the association which we call the state, the association which is "political".' (Aristotle)

'What makes a man a citizen [is] the mutual obligation between subject and sovereign.' (Jean Bodin)

'Individuals are so constituted that they could accomplish but little by themselves and could scarcely get on without the assistance of civil society and its laws. But as soon as a sufficient number have united under a government, they are able to provide for most of their needs, and they find the help of other political societies not so necessary to them as the State is itself to individuals.' (Emmerich de Vattel)

'It is through the small fatherland, which is the family, that we attach ourselves to the great fatherland; it is the good father, the good husband, the good son, who makes the good citizen.' (Jean-Jacques Rousseau)

'Do we want peoples to be virtuous? If so, let us begin by making them love their homeland. But how will they come to love it, if their homeland means nothing more to them than it does to foreigners, and if it grants to them only what it cannot refuse to anyone?' (Jean-Jacques Rousseau)

'should we have been so slow to see that . . . each one of us

being in the civil state as regards our fellow citizens, but in the state of nature as regards the rest of the world, we have taken all kinds of precautions against private wars only to kindle national wars a thousand times more terrible? And that in joining a particular group of men, we have really declared ourselves to be enemies of the whole race?' (Jean-Jacques Rousseau)

'War has the higher significance of [preserving] the ethical health of peoples.' (George Wilhelm Friedrich Hegel)

'both routine and extraordinary decisions taken by representatives of nations and nation-states profoundly affect citizens of other nation-states—who in all probability have had no opportunity to signal consent or lack of it—but . . . the international order is structured by agencies and forces over which citizens have minimum, if any, control, and in regard to which they have little basis to signal their [disagreement].' (David Held)

'I am a citizen of the world.' (Diogenes)

'I am not a citizen of the world . . . I am not even aware that there is a world such that one could be a citizen of it. No one has ever offered me citizenship, or described the naturalisation process, or enlisted me in the world's institutional structures, or given me an account of its decision procedures . . . or provided me with a list of the benefits and obligations of citizenship, or shown me the world's calendar and the common celebrations and commemorations of its citizens.' (Michael Walzer)

Nationalism and political community

The nation-state has been the dominant form of political community since the French Revolution but very different kinds of political community existed in other times. The first city-states of Mesopotamia and Ancient Greece, the early empires of Assyria, Persia, and Rome, and the more recent Ottoman and Chinese empires were all political communities but they were very different from nation-states. Ancient Greek city-states, for example, cherished their independence but they had highly exclusionary conceptions of community compared with modern democracies. In Greece, the right to participate in politics was restricted to adult males; women, resident aliens, and slaves were denied citizenship and were not full members of the community. Indeed, most forms of political community in human history have been hostile to the idea of popular rule. Empires, for example, have usually been ruled by military elites and not by the people at large; governing elites certainly did not believe that states should represent nations or that each nation should have its own state. These are modern ideas which have dominated political life for just over two centuries.

If we look at European states in the seventeenth century we will see that they were not nation-states but territorial states governed by absolutist monarchs engaged in a struggle for economic and political power. It is important to explain how territorial states differed from earlier states, how they were replaced by nation-states, and how further changes in the nature of political community have arisen in the recent phase of globalization.

Territorial states

As Max Weber argued, all states aim to monopolize control of the instruments of violence. But they differ in what they can do with their coercive power. Pre-modern states had a limited ability to direct the lives of their subjects whereas modern territorial states have the capacity to regulate (if not control) most aspects of society, including the economy and relations within the family. Regarding this differ-

ence, Michael Mann (1986: 7–10) argues that modern states have built up very high levels of 'intensive power': power that can be projected deep into society. In addition, pre-modern states had poorly defined frontiers and a limited ability to control frontier populations whereas the modern state has clearly demarcated borders and the ability to project its will across its territory. Commenting on this second difference, Mann (ibid.) argues that modern territorial states acquired a high level of 'extensive power': power that can be projected across whole territories. The vast colonial empires which encompassed the Americas, Asia-Pacific, and Africa were evidence of the modern state's capacity to acquire 'global reach'. This is crucial for understanding the history of globalization. When the Spanish and Portuguese colonized Central and South America in the sixteenth century, and when Europe embarked on second wave of imperial expansion in the nineteenth century, it was the state that drove globalization (Held *et al.* 1999).

From territorial states to nation-states

The territorial states which established these empires gradually turned into nation-states. As Norbert Elias (2000) argued, the modern state's monopoly control of the instruments of violence led to the pacification of society; in this context, closer emotional ties between citizens then developed. There are at least two reasons for this second development: the rise of capitalism and endemic warfare. Benedict Anderson (1991) has argued that 'print capitalism' made national consciousness possible. Books, pamphlets, and, in more recent times, national newspapers, radio, and television disseminated national symbols, shared narratives about the past, and a common destiny. Print capitalism meant that strangers who would never actually meet could identify emotionally with what Anderson calls the 'imagined community' of the nation. Ernest Gellner (1983) argued that industrialization was a principal reason for the emergence of national languages and cultures. The sheer number of commercial exchanges which are a feature of modern industrial societies could not take place unless strangers could communicate in the same language. The crucial point is that the world is not naturally divided into nations. States played a central role in creating national cultures not least by building education systems that promoted common values and loyalties.

Modern territorial states emerged in the context of war and they were largely instruments for waging war. It has been said that in Europe in the sixteenth century the successful states were small enough to be governed from a central administrative point and large enough to resist external threats (Mattingly 1955; see also Tilly 1992). War was also an important reason for the transition from territorial states to national states. Warring states promoted national solidarity to ensure that citizens would prove loyal in times of war. The turning point in modern history was the **French Revolution**, which created the idea of the 'nation in arms' along with national conscription. From the time of the French Revolution, nationalism has been the ideology with the greatest influence on the evolution of political communities.

It is important to remember then that warfare and industrialization created modern peoples with a strong sense of national consciousness. By claiming to represent the nation, states increased their ability to mobilize their populations for war and for the task of building new overseas empires. At the end of the nineteenth century, European nation-states expanded their worldwide empires by drawing non-European peoples into global economic and political relations. The nation-state has played a central role in unifying the human race.

Nationalism was a European invention which was subsequently exported to the rest of the world. **Third World nationalist movements** used European ideas to replace alien government with self-rule. Their success meant that the number of sovereign states more than tripled in the three decades following the Second World War, but many of these new political units failed to become nation-states. Frequently, ethnic rivalries meant that a sense of identification with the state did not develop. In many regions, such as the Indian subcontinent, divided peoples dismembered the former colonial territories in the hope of building their own nation-states. The

---

Box 32.2 | **Key concepts**

Community: a human association in which members share common symbols and wish to cooperate to realize common objectives.

Political community: a community that wishes to govern itself and to be free from alien rule.

Territorial state: a state that has power over the population which resides on its territory but which does not seek to represent the nation or the people as a whole.

Nation-state: a political community in which the state claims legitimacy on the grounds that it represents the nation.

Capitalism: a system of production in which human labour and its products are commodities that are bought and sold in the market-place.

Endemic warfare: the condition in which warfare is recurrent feature of the relations between states not least because they regard it as inevitable.

Loyalty: an emotional disposition in which people give institutions (or each other) some degree of unconditional support.

Citizenship: the status of having the right to participate in and to be represented in politics.

Group rights: rights which are said to belong to groups such as minority nations or indigenous peoples rather than to individuals.

Quasi-state: a state which has 'negative sovereignty' because other states respect its sovereign independence but lacks 'positive sovereignty' because it does not have the resources or the will to satisfy the needs of its people.

Failed state: a state that has collapsed and cannot provide for its citizens without substantial external support.

Cosmopolitan democracy: a condition in which international organizations, transnational corporations, global markets, and so forth are accountable to the peoples of the world.

Neo-medievalism: a condition in which political power is dispersed between local, national, and supranational institutions, none of which commands supreme loyalty.

separation of India and Pakistan, and of East Pakistan (Bangladesh) from West Pakistan, are two examples. However, because of decolonization, the modern state which is not indigenous to non-

European societies became the principal form of political community across the world. The globalization of the sovereign state is one of the central features of globalization.

Key points

- Most forms of political community in human history have not represented the nation or the people.

- The idea that the state should represent the nation is a European development which has dominated politics for just over two hundred years.

- War and capitalism are two reasons why the nation-state became the dominant form of political community.

- The extraordinary power of modern states—the growth of their 'intensive' and 'extensive' power—made global empires possible.

- States have been the principal architects of globalization over the last four centuries.

- The global spread of the sovereign state and nationalism are key examples of globalization.

Community and citizenship

We have seen that modern political communities accumulated extraordinary powers, and that the rise of vast overseas empires illustrated the point. It may seem odd that these political communities have also been the site for experiments in liberal-democratic forms of governance but there is no paradox here. Nation-states created national peoples which they mobilized for war. But the peoples which were formed in this way began to resist the state's increasing power over their lives. They organized politically to win **citizenship** rights from the state. Demands for citizenship were first heard within the major European states but they are now a powerful theme in political communities in all parts of the world. These demands along with the spread of the language of universal human rights reveal that a global political culture has appeared in recent decades (see Ch.31).

Citizenship and rights

We have to remember that territorial states in early modern Europe were governed by absolute monarchs who saw the state as their property. In the eighteenth and nineteenth centuries, the rising

commercial and industrial classes challenged monarchical power and sought **political rights** commensurate with their economic role. The middle classes sought to destroy royal privileges and promote constitutional government. They demanded the right to the **rule of law** and **representation** in politics. They succeeded in winning democratic rights but they refused to grant the same rights to subordinate groups such as the working classes. The struggle to extend the suffrage to all adult men and women was a dominant theme in all modern industrial societies during the latter part of the nineteenth century and the first part of the twentieth century. Demands for welfare rights quickly followed.

The fundamental point here is that labour movements and political parties on the Left argued that inequalities of power and wealth had increased under capitalism, the result being that the poor did not enjoy full membership of the political community. The contention was that legal and political rights do not mean very much unless individuals have the power to exercise them. (The claim that everyone is free to dine in the Ritz but not everyone can actually dine there captures the crucial point.) Pressures mounted to deepen the meaning of citizenship by adding **social or welfare rights** to the legal and political rights which had been won earlier. In the first part of the twentieth century, many Western states introduced national health services, welfare provision for the poor, and more open educational systems as a result of social struggles to create more inclusive communities.

The most influential account of the evolution of citizenship, at least in the British context, can be found in the writings of **T. H. Marshall** although later in this chapter we shall see that the struggle to deepen the meaning of citizenship has unfolded in ways that Marshall could not have anticipated. The key point to stress for now is that writers such as Marshall believed that political communities would enjoy greater legitimacy if they became more inclusive, and if their citizens enjoyed the full range of legal, political, and social rights. Certainly, many governments in the industrialized West supported this package of citizenship to defuse dangerous social tensions. Although it may seem extraordinary now, many writers in the 1950s and 1960s believed that

'the end of ideology' had arrived in societies such as the United States. What they meant was that Western liberal democracies had solved—or would shortly solve—the social conflicts which had threatened domestic stability.

In the 1950s and 1960s, many believed that new states in the Third World—Europe's former colonies in other words—would follow the Western pattern of development. Modernization theorists, as they were called, spoke about the impending 'modernization' or 'development' of traditional, non-Western societies. They thought that new states would undergo the nation-building process which had started in the West. They would undergo democratization and imitate the West in following the course of capitalist development.

Modernization theory and the end of ideology thesis were seriously flawed doctrines. Civil rights movements, the student revolt, opposition to the Vietnam War, **feminism**, and environmental movements revealed that the end of ideology thesis was mistaken. Ethnic and religious conflict in many new states, the rise of military government as opposed to democratization, and economic stagnation rather than capitalist development, demonstrated that modernization theorists had misunderstood the forms of political community that were emerging in the Third World. What was striking about modernization theory, though, was its belief that all societies were heading in the same direction and following the Western path of economic and political development. A similar claim has resurfaced since the end of the bipolar world, namely that liberal-democratic capitalist forms of political organization are spreading to most parts of the globe, just as nationalism and the idea of the modern state spread across the world in an earlier epoch (Fukuyama 1989). This is a contentious thesis which has been famously rejected by the notion of a coming '**clash of civilizations**' (Huntington 1993).

Box 32.3	**T. H. Marshall's analysis of citizenship in Britain**

T. H. Marshall (1973) identified three stages in the development of citizenship rights in Britain. In the eighteenth century the struggle for citizenship revolved around the quest for legal rights, specifically around the demand for the rule of law. In the nineteenth century, the emphasis shifted to political rights—to the right not only to be governed by law but to be represented in legislatures which make the law. In the twentieth century, the emphasis shifted again to social or welfare rights. The critical point here was that massive inequalities of wealth meant that the poor were not full members of the community. Significant transfers of wealth and more equal educational opportunities were essential if the poor were to be equal members of the political community.

The changing nature of political community

One of the paradoxes of the modern world is that the globalization of economic and political life has increased in recent years with the result that the global influence of Western capitalist democracies has never been greater, and yet the national fragmentation of political communities has not declined. These two processes, **globalization** and **fragmentation**, are two major influences on political communities at the present time.

As we saw earlier, the fragmentation of societies has been pronounced in many regions of the Third World. The division of India and Pakistan in 1947, the civil war in Nigeria in the late 1960s, and the creation of the separate state of Bangladesh in 1970 were part of a larger trend that included civil war in Ethiopia and the establishment in 1993 of the new state of Eritrea. New approaches to precarious Third World states appeared in the early 1990s. The concept of the quasi-state has been used to describe states which are regarded as sovereign but cannot satisfy the basic needs of their peoples (Jackson 1990). The notion of the failed state has been used to describe states which are unable to govern their societies without significant international support (Helman and Ratner 1992/93).

Many thinkers have asked whether liberal democratic societies have moral responsibilities to the peoples of failed states which include the right of humanitarian intervention to prevent violations of human rights (see Ch.25). But in an extraordinary and largely unforeseen development, the failed state is no longer a problem which is limited to the Third World. The disintegration of the former Yugoslavia was a striking example of a failed state in what was widely regarded as one of the most liberal and affluent socialist societies in Eastern Europe.

In this example, violent nationalism destroyed a multicultural political community which seemed to have succeeded in preserving harmony between different national groups. The more general point that needs to be made is illustrated by developments in political communities such as Canada, Belgium, Italy, and the United Kingdom. It is that collective demands for respect for national or ethnic differences exist in virtually all nation-states. These political demands are part of a worldwide movement in which minority nations and indigenous peoples seek respect for their languages and cultures. Nationalist reactions to the influx of Western values are widespread in India and throughout the Muslim world, but they are rarely a challenge to globalization per se (see Ch.24). Many give expression to a globalizing political culture which places pressure on national governments to respect national and cultural differences within their boundaries and within the world at large. Al Qaeda is an unusually violent example of this trend notwithstanding the fact that it relies on globalization (the global banking system, modern communications, and air travel) to promote its religious and political ends. There is no more dramatic example of the rejection of Western forms of political community in many parts of the Islamic world.

The politics of cultural difference

Another way of expressing the points made in the last section is to suggest that traditional ideas about citizenship are being reconsidered across the world in the current phase of globalization. To understand what is changing we need to return to the relationship between war and the evolution of modern political communities. When states sought to create national cultures in modern Europe the usual trend was that the language and customs of a dominant culture were imposed on subordinate groups. Success in war went to states which succeeded in creating an overarching idea of the nation with its sense of a shared history and common symbols evident in national flags, commemorations, and so forth. But as British politics reveal, the sense of Scottish, Welsh, or Irish identity survived alongside efforts to create more encompassing national identity.

The desire to preserve local cultures and to achieve some degree of political autonomy if not outright independence can be found in all modern nation-states but its success was limited when political communities faced the permanent threat of major war. The 'long peace' between the Great Powers has given national movements new opportunities to assert their rights. Core industrial states no longer need to mobilize their citizens for war and they are less able to wield national symbols effectively because of the combined power of globalization and fragmentation. Of course, the 'war against terror' and the 2003 invasion of Iraq have shown that states can mobilize national populations by highlighting threats to personal and national security, but public opposition to the Iraq war in the Western democracies indicates that for many loyalty to the state is conditional on its compliance with international law and respect for the United Nations system. The increasingly conditional nature of loyalties is one of the most important characteristics of political communities in the modern age (Waller and Linklater

2003). However, the ethnic revolt has long indicated that many minority nations and indigenous peoples give qualified loyalty to the nation-state.

Group rights

Claims for group rights have produced global changes in attitudes to citizenship (Young 1990). Earlier struggles for legal, political, and social rights usually assumed there were no significant cultural differences between citizens. Feminists have been prominent in arguing that the advancement of citizenship was gender blind since no account was taken of the special needs of women (see Ch.30). Exponents of new conceptions of citizenship have maintained that the differences between citizens— differences of culture and also gender—must be reflected in public policy. Minority nations throughout the world and indigenous peoples in societies such as Australia, Canada, and New Zealand have spearheaded the claim that group rights should be respected by the wider polity, for example by assisting self-government. These are not simply important developments within nation-states; the political representatives of these movements belong to transnational alliances which work—through their involvement in international organizations— to create a global political culture which is positive about group rights.

The mass movement of peoples is one consequence of globalization that feeds into this process. Here too an important argument is that traditional conceptions of citizenship should be adapted to fit the multicultural nature of modern societies. Moreover, no discussion of changing attitudes towards political community and national citizenship would be complete without noting how feminist movements have challenged gendered conceptions of the nation shaped by the male experience of war. Various forms of religious fundamentalism—Christian, Hindu, Islamic, etc.—demonstrate that powerful nationalist, racist, and patriarchal reactions against these challenges to traditional notions of political community exist in most societies. Discontent with traditional forms of community and efforts to preserve or revitalize them are global trends affecting all peoples.

Box 32.4 | **Kymlicka on Liberalism and group rights**

Kymlicka (1989) maintains that in a liberal-democratic society the individual has the right to free movement, to own private property, and to vote in elections. Traditional liberal thought does not recognize group rights, especially if these are in conflict with the fundamental rights of individuals. Kymlicka argues that indigenous cultures in societies such as Canada will not survive unless individual rights are curtailed. Indigenous cultures need to have a degree of self-government and for that to work limits have to be placed on the rights of members of the dominant culture. If members of the dominant culture have the right to purchase property in territories managed by individual peoples and the right to vote in their municipal elections then the indigenous culture will simply be overwhelmed. Respect for the rights of indigenous peoples entails the curtailment of certain individual rights which lie at the heart of the liberal-democratic polity.

Cosmopolitan democracy and transnational citizenship

One of the most intriguing dimensions of political communities is how they deal with differences of class, gender, sexual identity, religion, race, and ethnicity; and one of the most interesting aspects of globalization is that subordinate groups across the world often reject claims that these differences justify the unequal distribution of rights and resources (see Ch.1). Resistance to doctrines which claim that one race or nation has the right to dominate another, or that men are naturally entitled to more rights than women, is pronounced in most parts of the world.

Rethinking relations between citizens and aliens

No less important is how political communities understand differences between citizens and aliens. This leads to the question of whether globalization is changing one of the fundamental assumptions of modern political communities, namely that citizens have special duties to each other which necessitate much weaker responsibilities to the rest of the human race. As already noted, the continuing strength of nationalist emotions in most regions of the world is not in question. Powerful nationalist and religious responses to globalization are triggered by the intrusion of what are seen as alien values.

But globalization has unleashed other tendencies which question the idea that political communities are primarily responsible for promoting the interests of their citizens. The more affluent populations are often disturbed by images of human suffering caused by state terror, civil conflict, natural disaster, and famine. Public support for humanitarian intervention in Somalia and Kosovo developed in the wake of images of suffering disseminated by the global media. How far emotional identification between peoples can extend in a world of nation-states is a central question for the student of political community. Various global problems which states cannot hope to solve on their own—atmospheric pollution and global warming for example—have encouraged the development of non-governmental organizations which are concerned with the fate of the earth. Many think that global civil society reveals the dawn of a new era of human cooperation, although sceptics are quick to point to the continuing appeal of nationalism, the tenacity of the state, and the weakness of cosmopolitan loyalties (see Ch.23). Certainly, interventions in Somalia and Kosovo—and inaction in the case of the genocide in Rwanda—reveal that national populations hold back from risking the lives of co-nationals for the sake of 'distant strangers' (see Ch.25).

CWS

Cosmopolitan democracy

Cosmopolitan approaches to political community have enjoyed a renaissance in recent years. The idea of world citizenship is a concept used by international non-governmental organizations to promote a stronger sense of responsibility for the global environment and for the human species. Proponents of cosmopolitan democracy have argued that national democracies have little control over global markets and a limited ability to influence decisions taken by transnational corporations which influence currency values, employment prospects, and so forth (see Held 1995). They maintain that democracy may not survive in any meaningful form if it remains tied to the nation-state. They argue for democratizing international organizations such as the World Trade

Box 32.5	Contrasting views about the scope of human sympathy

'Whether we can conceive of a way to think of morality that extends some form of sympathy further than our own group remains perhaps the fundamental moral question for contemporary life.' (Jean Tronto)

'We should all agree that each of us is bound to show kindness to his parents and spouse and children, and to other kinsmen in a less degree: and to those who have rendered services to him, and any others whom he may have admitted into his intimacy and called friends: and to neighbours and to fellow-countryman more than others: and perhaps we may say to those of our own race more than to black or yellow men, and generally to human beings in proportion to their affinity to ourselves.' (Henry Sidgwick)

'If he was to lose his little finger to-morrow, he would not sleep tonight; but provided he never saw them, he will snore with the most profound security over the ruin of a hundred millions of his brethren, and the destruction of that immense multitude seems plainly an object less interesting to him, than this paltry misfortune of his own.' (Adam Smith)

'[O]ur sense of solidarity is strongest when those with whom solidarity is expressed are thought of as "one of us", where

"us" means something smaller and more local than the human race.' (Richard Rorty)

'The fact that a person is physically near to us . . . may make it more likely that we shall assist him, but this does not show that we ought to help him rather than another who happens to be further away.' (Peter Singer)

'Those closer to us will *tend* to be more vulnerable to our actions and choices than those distant from us, and thus we are not obliged to weigh everyone's interests exactly equally. Yet in so far as those distant from us *are* particularly vulnerable to our actions and choices, we have special obligations to care for them.' (Grace Clement)

'We are nowadays more strongly than ever aware that an enormously large part of humanity live their entire lives on the verge of starvation, that in fact there are always and in many places people dying of hunger . . . Many members of richer communities feel it to be almost a duty to do something about the misery of other human groups. To avoid misunderstanding on the issue, let it be said that relatively little is done.' (Norbert Elias)

Do the 'oceans make a community of nations impossible?' (Immanuel Kant)

Organization and for ensuring that transnational corporations are held accountable for decisions that may harm vulnerable persons. One response to globalization argues then for new forms of **cosmopolitan political community** in which the members of different societies come together as **cosmopolitan citizens** to influence decisions that affect the whole world. Critics argue that the vision of cosmopolitan democracy is utopian. They maintain that democracy is unlikely to flourish at the global level because there is no counterpart to the nation which can engage the moral and political emotions. Democracy requires a level of trust and a commitment to the public good which only exist—at least at this stage in human history—between those who share a common nationality (Miller 1999).

Neo-medievalist approaches

Neo-medievalism is a second and related vision of new form of political community which has

attracted attention in recent years. Neo-medievalism refers to an ideal political order in which individuals are governed by several overlapping authorities—which is how political community was organized in Europe in the Middle Ages prior to the rise of modern states. The forces of globalization and fragmentation have renewed interest in a neo-medieval model of world order (Linklater 1998; Falk 2000). According to this vision, states should transfer some powers to international institutions which will deal with global problems while other powers should be transferred to the domestic regions where the sense of cultural difference remains strong. National governments would retain many powers according to this conception of world order and citizens would remain loyal to the state which would, however, be only one tier of government; loyalty to the state would exist alongside emotional attachments to sub-state and transnational authorities. None of those political authorities or loyalties would reign supreme.

Box 32.6   Visions of new forms of community and citizenship

'The bourgeoisie has through its exploitation of the world-market given a cosmopolitan character to production and consumption in every country . . . All old-fashioned national industries have been destroyed or are daily being destroyed . . . In place of the old wants, satisfied by the productions of the country, we find new wants, requiring for their satisfaction the products of different lands and climes. In place of the old local and national seclusion and self-sufficiency, we have intercourse in every direction, universal interdependence of nations . . . The bourgeoisie, by the rapid improvement of all instruments of production, by the immensely facilitated means of communication, draws all, even the most barbarian nations, into civilisation. It compels all nations, on pain of extinction, to adopt the bourgeois mode of production . . . i.e. to become bourgeois themselves. In one word, it creates a world after its own image.' (Karl Marx)

'We have a system of national citizenship in a social context which requires a new theory of internationalism and universalistic citizenship.' (Bryan Turner)

'Every person holding the nationality of a Member State shall be a citizen of the Union.' (The Maastricht Treaty)

It is 'time to go higher in our search for citizenship, but also lower and wider. Higher to the world, lower to the locality . . . The citizen has been too puffed and too compressed.' (Andrew Wright)

'We may envisage a situation in which, say, a Scottish authority in Edinburgh, a British authority in London, and a European authority in Brussels were all actors in world politics and all enjoyed representations in world political organisations, together with rights and duties of various kinds in world law, but in which none of them claimed sovereignty or supremacy over the others, and a person living in Glasgow had no exclusive or overriding loyalty to any one of them. Such an outcome would take us truly "beyond the sovereign state" and is by no means implausible.' (Hedley Bull)

'The preference of Western powers, especially the United States, for air strikes, despite the physical and psychological damage caused even with highly accurate munitions, arises from [the] privileging of nationals or Westerners. This type of national or statist thinking has not yet come to terms with the concept of a common human community . . . Whereas the soldier, as the traditional bearer of arms, had to be prepared to die for his country, the international soldier/policeman [would risk] his or her life for humanity.' (Mary Kaldor)

'Even if we still have a long way to go before fully achieving it, the cosmopolitan condition is no longer merely a mirage. State citizenship and world citizenship form a continuum whose contours, at least, are already becoming visible.' (Jurgen Habermas)

'Europeans have stepped out of the Hobbesian world of anarchy into the Kantian world of perpetual peace.' (Robert Kagan)

The best prospects for neo-medievalism lie in those parts of Europe (such as the societies that belong to the European Union) where the erosion of national sovereignty is taking place (see Ch.26). Whether this normative vision will ever appeal in other regions is a moot point. It has been regarded as a striking illustration of how far Europe has moved beyond power politics, of how far Europe is divorced from the currently more powerful Hobbesian conception of world politics which is evident in the war against terror initiated by the Bush Administration after the terrorist attacks of 11 September 2001 (Kagan 2003). It is no small achievement, however, that the neo-medieval vision has commanded significant support in a region which was frequently embroiled in major wars.

Key points

- Globalization and fragmentation are two phenomena challenging traditional conceptions of political community and national citizenship.

- Ethnic fragmentation is one reason for the failed state in Europe as well as in the Third World, but demands for the recognition of cultural differences exist in all political communities.

- Globalization theorists have argued for cosmopolitan democracy on the grounds that national democracies are less able to influence global forces which affect them.

- The 'war against terror' has sharpened the division between a 'Hobbesian' conception of national security politics and the 'Kantian' belief in the possibility of perpetual peace.

The dangers of new forms of political community?

In recent years, globalization and fragmentation have weakened or destroyed centralized nation-states as different as Indonesia, Ethiopia, Italy, the USSR, and Canada. Perhaps new forms of political community which are more respectful of cultural differences and more cosmopolitan than their predecessors will emerge in future. However, the disintegration of the former Yugoslavia reveals it is unwise to generalize about such matters. Violent nationalism can be the main beneficiary of the collapse or the erosion of the nation-state.

As far as relations between the Great Powers are concerned, the apex of violent nationalism was reached in the first half of the twentieth century (see Ch.3). In 1914 European governments led their populations into the most destructive war in human history. Two decades later, a more devastating international conflict took place following the rise of totalitarianism in Europe. The desire not to return to major war was the main reason for the development of the European Community after the Second World War (see Ch.26). War no longer seems likely to engulf the continent, and it is improbable that it will be waged between the core industrial powers in the foreseeable future. This may be a revolution in world politics although the Realist approach to international relations insists there is no warranty that peace between the Great Powers will survive indefinitely. It is impossible to say that the kind of nationalism which characterized international politics in the first half of the twentieth century has run its course. Certainly the 'war against terror' has made security politics more central than they were in the 1990s. The level of public support which Bush and Blair commanded during the war against Iraq demonstrated that the state matters more than the United Nations when fears for personal and national security are high (although against this must be noted public concerns about needless civilian suffering in war). Since 9/11 we have witnessed the revival of an old theme which is that the state remains the only political association which will take effective measures to protect the security of its citizens. From this perspective, support for new forms of community ignores the most basic fact of political life.

Beyond Realism and neo-realism

There have been several recent attempts to explain how globalization and fragmentation are transforming political communities, and there have been several efforts to develop visions of alternative forms of community and citizenship (Brown 1992; Linklater 1998). These are important developments in a discipline that has been powerfully influenced by Realism and neo-realism. The latter perspective has focused on continuities rather than change in world politics—war, the balance of power, the rise and fall of Great Powers, and so forth. In consequence, the respects in which political communities are changing—or should change—have been left to the exponents of other approaches. Three broad approaches merit consideration because they have been especially interested in whether globalization and fragmentation will lead to new forms of political community. They are **cosmopolitanism**, **communitarianism**, and post-modernism (see Ch.12).

Cosmopolitanism

Globalization may seem to create new opportunities for promoting the cosmopolitan idea that all human beings are equal. Cosmopolitans argue that efforts to solve global problems (such as environmental destruction) should promote the welfare of the species as a whole. Writers on the international law of war argue that the international community should defend the victims of war crimes wherever they may live. From this vantage point, the establishment of an International Criminal Court is to be welcomed as an important step in promoting what Mary Kaldor (1999: 124ff.) has called 'cosmopolitan law enforcement'. Many cosmopolitans applauded the UK House of Lords' ruling that leaders who are guilty of human rights violations cannot claim immunity from prosecution by appealing to the principle of sovereign immunity. (This decision was a response to the legal claim that General Pinochet should be extradited to Spain to be tried for human rights violations in Chile.) Following NATO's military action against Serbia in 1999, some cosmopolitans referred to the birth of a new era of humanitarian war (Beck 1998). Opponents of NATO's action, and they included many with equally good claims to be cosmopolitan, stressed the dangers associated with military action to defend human rights (see Ch.25). One of their concerns is that Great Powers will use cosmopolitanism to breach national sovereignty when it is in their interests to do so. It is worth noting that Realists have long warned that universalist ideologies can all too easily be distorted to legitimize a crusading foreign policy which pitches 'good' against 'evil'.

Post-modernism

This takes us to post-modernism, and specifically to Foucault's claim that all forms of knowledge, including those that are designed to promote progress, are potentially dangerous. His point was that all forms of knowledge can lay the foundations for new forms of power and domination (see Ch.12). This is a telling criticism of Marxism which set out to liberate the human race but became an instrument of totalitarian domination (see Ch.10). Richard Ashley and R. B. J. Walker (1990) have argued that all political perspectives that claim to have uncovered universal truths contain this danger. Their point is that distinctions between those who possess the truth and those who live in ignorance are intrinsic to such worldviews, and therein lies the danger of domination. So in the case of cosmopolitanism, the distinction between those who think globally and those who remain wedded to particular communities may lead to new forms of power and exclusion. This argument resonates with claims that the universal human rights culture and doctrines of humanitarian intervention may simply extend Western power over the rest of the world. Similar themes are present in recent discussions about the dangers inherent in efforts to create a new international community in Europe. Jacques Derrida (1992) has argued that a

Europe which weakens the nation-state and reduces its monopoly powers is desirable. But movement in this direction is not risk free since it is possible that efforts to promote close cooperation within Europe will engender pernicious distinctions between, for example, Europe and the Islamic world. The danger is that Europe might close in on itself by extending restrictions on migrants and refugees.

Communitarianism

The claim that cosmopolitans underestimate the role that separate communities play in the lives of human beings is a central theme in communitarianism. Its proponents maintain that individuals acquire their most fundamental rights and responsibilities as members of particular communities, not as members of the human race (Walzer 1995a). Communitarians do not deny that societies have obligations to one another but rather insist that it is right that most human beings are usually moved by attachments to their community rather than by arguments about what is good for humanity. On this view, it is erroneous to suppose that globalization will so weaken particular communities that human beings will replace national ties with cosmopolitan loyalties. To act on the assumption that this is likely would be to endanger the most viable political communities in the modern world.

Walzer's position on the idea of world citizenship is a good example of the communitarian critique of cosmopolitanism (Walzer 1994a). He argues that citizenship refers to a web of political rights and duties which only exist when there is a strong sense of identification with the nation-state. In his view, it is highly unlikely that any meaningful sense of citizenship (which includes the right to participate in politics and a willingness to make personal sacrifices for the good of society as a whole) will develop outside the nation-state. For example, the citizens of member states of the European Union are European citizens according to the Maastricht Treaty, but this is a pale imitation of the forms of citizenship which exist within nation-states. In short, citizenship is a national achievement; cosmopolitan citizenship is illusory.

This is a powerful argument but one that it is criticized by many post-modern thinkers and feminist writers. They have argued that communitarians often fail to recognize that the dominant conceptions of community in any place do not represent all sections of the population. Members of minority nations and indigenous peoples belong to this category, and feminists have argued that large numbers of women have also suffered exclusion at the hands of 'their' community (see Ch.30). The main lesson to draw is that all communities include some human beings but exclude others. This is why post-modern writers have been keen to emphasize how the dominant language of any community can be used to marginalize or oppress subordinate groups (Ashley and Walker 1990). They argue that this danger will remain whether peoples remain loyal to sovereign states or try to build new forms of political community.

Key points

- The apex of nationalism in relations between the Great Powers occurred in the first half of the twentieth century.

- Nationalism remains a powerful force in the modern world but globalization and fragmentation have led to discussions about the possibility of new forms of political community.

- Cosmopolitan approaches which envisage an international system in which all individuals are respected as equal have flourished in the contemporary phase of globalization.

- Communitarians argue that most people value their membership of a particular political community; they are unlikely to shift their loyalty from the nation-state to the human race.

- Post-modern writers argue that all forms of political community contain the danger of generating the domination or exclusion of significant sections of society.

Conclusion

The study of international politics has been largely concerned with understanding the relations between separate political communities, and particularly the relations between Great Powers. Realists and neo-realists argue that all states are forced to compete for security and survival in the context of anarchy. They contend that separate states look to their own interests first and foremost. They maintain that the sense of community which exists between the citizens of particular states is unlikely to develop within the world at large. They also argue that close cooperation is generally more highly developed within separate states. Realists and neo-realists do not expect this condition to change while international anarchy survives.

There is no reason to think that sovereign states are about to be replaced by some new form of political association but, equally, there can be little doubt that globalization and fragmentation pose novel challenges for political communities across the world. The most recent phase in the development of globalization invites a discussion of how far the forms of cooperation which exist within viable nation-states can develop globally.

Optimists may stress the existence of a global civil society which shows that transnational cooperation involving the members of different political communities is flourishing. Pessimists may argue that the US response to 9/11 has demonstrated the centrality of geopolitics; fear of the globalization of 'weapons of mass destruction' has checked what some hope for, namely the transformation of political communities and world politics.

Pessimists may also argue that increasing inequalities between the global rich and the global poor is the main consequence of globalization (see Ch.29).

The question then is whether privileged groups in world society will conclude that they have a fundamental moral duty to rescue the poorest human beings from terrible poverty. The shift from the territorial state to the modern state involved the extension of emotional identification between citizens, including the belief that the more fortunate members of the political community had obligations to assist the poor within their midst. The global mass media have made more people aware of human suffering in other societies but this particular facet of globalization has not had much influence on the course of world politics. Whether human sympathy will develop beyond the nation-state—and whether more cosmopolitan political communities will emerge as a result—are crucial questions for students of globalization.

For further information and case studies on this subject, please visit the companion web site at www.oup.com/uk/booksitespolitics.

QUESTIONS

1 What is community, and what makes a community a political community?

2 Why has the modern state been the dominant form of political community?

3 What is the relationship between nationalism, citizenship, and political community?

4 What is the relationship between war and political community?

5 To what extent are globalization and fragmentation transforming political communities?

6 Can one be a citizen of the world?

7 What are the arguments for and against cosmopolitan democracy

8 What are the main differences between the cosmopolitan, communitarian, and post-modern approaches to political community?

9 Has the 'war against terror' strengthened the link between the citizen and the state?

10 How far can human sympathy extend beyond the nation-state?

GUIDE TO FURTHER READING

General

Linklater, A. (1998), *The Transformation of Political Community: Ethical Foundations of the Post-Westphalian Era* (Cambridge: Polity Press). Provides a more detailed analysis of many of the themes considered in this chapter.

Waller, M., and Linklater, A. (eds) (2003), *Political Loyalty and the Nation-State* (London: Routledge). A recent collection of papers on whether the European nation-state continues to command the loyalty of its citizens.

Communitarianism and cosmopolitanism

Nussbaum, M. (2002), *In Defence of Country* (Boston: Beacon Press). An excellent collection of essays on patriotism and cosmopolitanism

The modern state

Elias, N. (2000), *The Civilizing Process: Sociogenetic and Psychogenetic Investigations* (Oxford: Basil Blackwell). A landmark analysis of the rise of the modern state.

Mann, M. (1986; 1993), *Sources of Social Power, Vol. 1: A History of Power from the Beginning to AD 1760* and *Vol. 2: The Rise of Classes and Nation-States, 1760–1914* (Cambridge: Cambridge University Press). This two-volume work contains a wealth of information about city-states and ancient empires as well as the modern state.

Tilly, C. (1992), *Coercion, Capital and European States: AD 990–1992* (Oxford: Blackwell). An outstanding account of how the modern state eclipsed other forms of political organization.

Nationalism and group rights

Anderson, B. (1983; revised 1991), *Imagined Communities: Reflections on the Origin and Spread of Nationalism* (London: Verso). A key reference point in discussions about the rise of modern nationalism.

Gellner, E. (1983), *Nations and Nationalism* (Oxford: Basil Blackwell). A classic study of the relationship between industrialization and nationalism.

Kymlicka, W. (1989), *Liberalism, Community and Culture* (Oxford: Oxford University Press). A pathbreaking study of the significance of the struggle for 'indigenous' rights for liberal-democratic communities.

National and world citizenship

Dower, N., and Williams, J. (eds) (2002), *Global Citizenship* (Edinburgh: Edinburgh University Press). A comprehensive collection of essays on world citizenship.

Hutchings, K., and Danreuther, R. (eds) (1999), *Cosmopolitan Citizenship* (London: Macmillan). A useful set of debates about the strengths and weaknesses of the idea of cosmopolitan citizenship.

Marshall, T. H. (1973), *Class, Citizenship and Social Development* (Westport, Conn.: Greenwood Press). A central study of the development of legal, political, and social rights.

Emotional responses to suffering in other societies

Cohen, S. (2001), *States of Denial: Knowing about Atrocities and Suffering* (Cambridge: Polity Press). An excellent sociological study of attitudes to human suffering.

Sontag, S. (2003), *Regarding the Pain of Others* (London: Hamish Hamilton). An excellent recent work on photographic images of suffering in other societies.

Alternatives to the nation-state

Held, D. (1995), *Democracy and the Global Order: From the Modern State to Global Governance* (Cambridge: Polity Press). An influential defence of cosmopolitan democracy.

Tilly, C. (1992), 'The Futures of European States', *Social Research*, 59: 705–17. An inspiring short essay on possible developments in Europe.

CHAPTER 33

Globalization and the post-cold war order

IAN CLARK

READER'S GUIDE

This chapter explores the nature of the order that is developing in the period since the end of the cold war. It asks whether that order is distinctive. It asks also whether globalization is the defining feature that sets it apart from earlier patterns of order. After distinguishing between various types of order—international, world, and global—the chapter sketches out the main ingredients of the contemporary order. These extend well beyond the traditional domain of international military security. The argument then addresses the forces that helped to bring the cold war to an end, and investigates the trend towards globalization as one of these. It explores also the ways in which globalization now causes problems and tensions in the present order, especially with regard to its legitimacy. The chapter ends by suggesting that globalization is a condition that reflects changes in states, not just between them, and that what is distinctive about the present order is the continuation of a system of international order, the constituent units of which are increasingly globalized states.

Introduction

This chapter is concerned with two key questions. The first is whether there is now a distinctive pattern of order in the post-cold war world and, if so, what are its principal elements. The second is whether this order should be defined in terms of globalization.

Is there now a pattern of international politics sufficiently distinctive to mark it off from that in existence prior to the end of the cold war? Implicit in this is the need to devise a description of the present period that tells us something substantive about how it functions. This goes beyond the indeterminate chronological label 'post-cold war', since that informs us merely that it followed on where the cold war left off. To understand our present period, we need to know more than that it was the phase that came after the cold war.

The second question directs attention to whether contemporary order can be captured by the imagery of globalization. There is, of course, intense debate as to the precise meaning, novelty, and extent of globalization. But that some kind of transformation is under way is scarcely in doubt, even if commentators are unable to agree on its significance, or on whether the changes are to be welcomed or not. If some

degree of globalization is indeed occurring, is this simply one feature among many others of the post-cold war order? Or is it so central to the nature of the present order that we can define the order in terms of it? Is the contemporary order above all a globalized order, and what might this mean in practice?

Serious study of the overall character of the post-cold war order remains in its infancy. We are still too immersed in living it to have any real sense of perspective; because we do not know how it culminates (c.f. what we call 'the inter-war period'), it is not an 'enclosed' period with a determinate ending, and we consequently find difficulty in assigning specific characteristics to it. While there have been studies aplenty of individual aspects of this present order (ethnicity, identity, peacekeeping, humanitarian intervention, globalization, regionalism, economic transition, democratization, integration, financial instability, terrorism and the war against it, weapons of mass destruction, regime change, etc.), we still lack the makings of any grand evaluation of its essential nature.

In analysing the contemporary order, we need to be mindful of how much greater are the demands

---

Box 33.1   Elements of discontinuity and continuity between cold war and post-cold war orders

Cold war		Post-cold war
	Discontinuity	
Soviet power in Eastern Europe		*Dissolution of Soviet Union*
Bipolar competition		*Unipolar peacemaking*
Rival ideologies		*Supremacy of liberal capitalism*
Global security integration		*Greater regional autonomy*
Military security as high politics		*National identity as high politics*
	Continuity	
	Some security structures, e.g. NATO	
	Economic globalization	
	Human rights	
	Reaction against secular state	
	Multiple identities	
	Environmental agendas	
	Poverty in South	

upon, and the expectations about, the **international order** today than previously. In earlier periods, the interest in the international order was largely 'negative', and lay in ensuring that no threats emerged from it. Given present high levels of integration and **interdependence**, the interest is now 'positive' as well, and about the international order as a much greater source and provider than hitherto of a range of social goods. The international order can deliver information, economic resources, human rights, intervention, access to global **social movements** and international non-governmental organizations, and permits the sharing of an abundance of cultural artefacts. Many of these 'goods' are regarded as unwelcome intrusions, but at the same time they are also desired by governments, and/or peoples, around the world.

> **Key points**
>
> - It is difficult to make out the characteristics of the contemporary order.
>
> - Because we live in the midst of it, it is hard to get any sense of historical perspective.
>
> - Our understanding of, say, the inter-war period (1919–39) is coloured by how it ended, but we do not yet know how our present period will 'end'.
>
> - We can see that international and transnational connections are a very important element of contemporary order because of currently high levels of interdependence.

A typology of order

At the present moment, thinking about order is being pulled in a number of different directions. At the one end of the spectrum, it continues to be largely state-centred and to be concerned with traditional models of order, such as the **structure** of the **balance of power**, the polarity of the **international system**, and the current forms of **collective security** At the other end is a widening agenda of order that encompasses the relationship between economic and political dimensions, **new thinking** about human security, debates about the consequences of globalization, the role of human rights, the impact of environmentalism, and strategies for human emancipation. Clearly, in these various analyses, a number of differing, and potentially competing, conceptions of order are at work.

This was nicely illustrated in the early 1990s when then US President George Bush spoke about his vision of a New World Order. In an address to Congress on 11 September 1990, Bush outlined

A new era—freer from the threat of terror, stronger in pursuit of justice and more secure in quest for peace, an era in which nations of the world . . . can prosper—a world where rule of law supplants the rule of the jungle, a world in which nations recognize the shared responsibility for freedom and justice, a world where the strong respect the rights of the weak.

Individually, these goals might all be highly desirable, but the troublesome question is whether they fit together into a consistent whole and, if some elements are in tension, what priority is to be assigned amongst them. Underlying the separate elements of this vision, we can distinguish competing frameworks of order. Some derive from traditional state-centric models and emphasize stability and peace amongst states. Others take the individual human being as the unit of account and construct order in terms of rights, justice, and prosperity.

This draws our attention to a number of semantic distinctions important to any assessment of the contemporary order. Are we to judge the degree and effectiveness of order solely as an aspect of the **inter-state system**, and thus speak of international order Or are we to widen the discussion and consider order in terms of its impact on individual human lives and aspirations and thus talk of a **world order**? Such a distinction is widely noted in the literature. However, what are we to make of the introduction of the concept of globalization into the analysis? Does globalized order signify the same as world order or something different? An attempt will be made to answer that question in the final section of this chapter.

Box 33.2   Key concepts

Collectivization of security: the tendency for security to be organized on a multilateral basis, but without the institutional formality of a fully fledged collective security system.

Concert: the directorial role played by a number of Great Powers, based on norms of mutual consent.

Global governance: the loose framework of global regulation, both institutional and normative, that constrains conduct. It has many elements: international organizations and law; transnational organizations and frameworks; elements of global civil society; and shared normative principles.

Globalized state: the notion of a particular kind of state that helps sustain globalization, as well as responding to its pressures. The distinctive feature of this concept is that the state is not 'in retreat' but simply behaving differently.

Hegemony: a system regulated by a dominant leader.

International order: the normative and the institutional pattern in the relationship between states. The elements of this might be thought to include such things as sovereignty the forms of diplomacy, international law, the role of the Great Powers, and the codes circumscribing the use of force.

Internationalization: this term is used to denote high levels of international interaction and interdependence, most commonly with regard to the world-economy. In this context it refers to the volume of international trade and investment and to the organization of production. The term is often used to distinguish this condition from globalization as the latter implies that there are no longer distinct national economies in a position to interact.

Liberal rights: the agenda of human rights that is driven largely from a Western perspective and derived from classical liberal positions.

Minimum order: a view of international order that is concerned with peace and stability, rather than with the attainment of other values, such as justice.

Multipolarity: a distribution of power among a number (at least three) of major powers or 'poles'.

Multilateralism: the tendency for functional aspects of international relations (such as security, trade, or environmental management) to be organized around large numbers of states, or universally, rather than by unilateral state action.

Order: this may denote any regular or discernible pattern of relationships that are stable over time, or may additionally refer to a condition that allows certain goals to be achieved.

Primordialism: the belief that certain human or social characteristics, such as ethnicity, are deeply embedded in historical conditions.

State system: the regular patterns of interaction between states, but without implying any shared values between them. This is distinguished from the view of a 'society' of states.

Triads: the three economic groupings (North America, Europe, and East Asia).

Unipolarity: a distribution of power internationally in which there is clearly only one dominant power or 'pole'. Some analysts argue that the international system became unipolar in the 1990s since there was no longer any rival to American power.

World order: this is a wider category of order than the 'international'. It takes as its units of order, not states, but individual human beings, and assesses the degree of order on the basis of the delivery of certain kinds of goods (be it security, human rights, basic needs, or justice) for humanity as a whole.

Theoretically, the result is that the search for the definitive elements of the contemporary order proceeds within quite separate frameworks. The first direction from which these issues have been approached is the broadly Realist one. This concentrates upon the structure of the post-cold war system, especially upon the number of Great Power actors and the distribution of capabilities amongst them. It defines order largely in terms of the operative secur-

ity structure within the system. It spawned a debate in the early 1990s about the polarity of the post-cold war system, about the prospects for a renewed concert, and about the worrisome prospect that return to multipolarity could herald the erosion of the stability generated by the cold war's bipolarity.

The second line is broadly Liberal in derivation and focuses upon regimes and institutions towards one end of its spectrum, and a variety of norms and values towards the other. Its central claim is that patterns of integration and interdependence had become so deeply embedded in the cold war period, albeit for strategic and geopolitical reasons, that they now have a self-sustaining momentum that precludes any return to war and autarchy. Since complex systems of global governance have been spawned in the interim, these regimes will survive the collapse of the 'Realist' conditions that gave rise to them in the first place.

A third line is the one that adjudges order in terms of its achievement of human emancipation. The evidence from either of the two former approaches is thereby deemed inadequate to the task. The mere fact of stability amongst the major powers, or the institutionalization of relations amongst the dominant groups of states, tells us little of importance about the quality of life for most inhabitants of the globe. If it is true, as writers like Ken Booth (1999) argue, that governments are the main source of the abuse of human rights, we need to do more than study the international human rights agreements that these very governments enter into, but look also at what is happening to people on the ground.

The fourth line of exploration is via the literature on globalization. This is not the place to rehearse the complex arguments about the nature of globalization in general (see Ch.1). This chapter asks simply whether globalization may be thought to constitute a form of order or not. Must we speak of globalization as an ongoing process without an end state, or can we reasonably speak of a globalized order as a

distinctive political form? The latter view is clearly set forth, for instance, in the suggestion that the contemporary Western state conglomerate, collectively, constitutes an 'emergent *global state*' (Shaw 1997: 503–4; 2000). Globalization, to this extent and with whatever qualifications, represents an incipient political order.

Key points

- When we speak of order, we need to specify order for whom—states, peoples, groups, or individuals.

- International order focuses on stable and peaceful relations between states, often related to the balance of power. It is primarily about military security.

- World order is concerned with other values, such as justice, development, rights, and emancipation.

- A pattern of order may advance some values at the expense of others. There is often a tension, for example, between state-centred concepts of order, and those that promote individual values. For instance, policies based on the balance of power might lead to assistance being given to regimes with bad human rights records.

- A key question about globalization is whether it supersedes all ideas of international order, or whether it can be incorporated into more traditional ideas.

Box 33.3	**Typologies of order**

	Units	Characteristics
Globalized	Global system	End of national polities, societies, and economies
International	States	Concern with agenda of sovereignty and stability
World	Humanity	Concern with agenda of rights, needs, and justice
Globalized international	Globalized states	Agenda of managing relations between states penetrated by global system but still distinguishable within it

The elements of contemporary order

The 'social-state' system

Initially, there is the basic nature of the contemporary state system itself. The state system is 'social', first, in the sense that states over the past century have performed a range of social functions that distinguish them from states in earlier phases of the state system. The great revival in the political credibility of states, from its nadir in the Second World War, is attributable to the largely successful undertaking of this task. While states are not all equal in the ability to deliver these functions, most would now list responsibility for development and economic management, health, welfare, and social planning as desirable roles for the state, even where effectiveness of delivery is variable.

It is 'social' also in the second sense that there are pressures for emulation within the system and this tends to reinforce common patterns of behaviour, and similar forms of state institutional structure. Historically, states have emulated each other in developing the social and economic infrastructures for generating military power. Now this task has broadened as states seek to adopt 'best practice' in terms of economic competitiveness and efficiency. They also face the social pressure to conform to certain standards of civil rights, and this has permitted a measure of dilution and delegation of the state's exclusive jurisdiction over its own domestic affairs. In consequence, some of the key rules of the state system (sovereignty, non-intervention) are undergoing considerable adaptation, and this gives the contemporary state system many of its complex and ambivalent qualities.

Identity and the nation-state

A second feature is the multiplicity of issues about identity that have become prevalent since the 1990s. Some of these revolve around contemporary forms of nationalism, and are subject to contested assessments as to whether they represent a 'new' national-

ism, or a reversion to a pre-existing primordialism. The state is both challenged and reinforced by a welter of additional crises of identity—tendencies towards apparently new forms of political community driven by ethnic separatism, regional identities, new transnational projects, new social movements, and the return to culture/religion. Clearly, the key question here is the extent to which these are wholly new tendencies or represent some kind of historical atavism. The politics of identity at the beginning of the new millennium itself impacts on the social nature of the state as it raises explicit questions about the nature of citizenship—who is to count as a citizen, and what is the nature of the contract between state and citizen (see Ch.32).

It must not, however, be imagined that all such issues of identity have emerged only in the aftermath of the cold war. For example, it could be said that there has been a widespread reaction in much of the developing world against what has been seen as the imposition of a modernizing, Westernizing, and secular form of state. The revolution in Iran in 1979 is a case in point, and cautions us not to assume that 'identity politics' were invented only after the end of the cold war.

Polarity and the collectivization of security

A key area of concern remains the primary attributes of the contemporary security order. This addresses the debates about the present distribution of power, and whether that distribution should be assessed as unipolarity, or as being bipolar, multipolar, or some kind of hybrid of them all. This debate has shifted considerably since the early 1990s. At that point, expectations of some kind of resumption of multipolarity were widespread, and a US-centred unipolarity thought likely to last for a 'moment', at most. Since then US predominance has become much more clearly established, so that analysts now routinely refer to American **hegemony** (see Ch.6), or some kind of American empire. This trend is a result of US economic successes during the 1990s, coupled with the ongoing difficulties of its other competitors. Japan's economy has stagnated. Russia was embroiled in domestic political and economic transformation. The European Union, although it has both widened and deepened, continues to have difficulty in acting decisively on its own in international crises. China's power remains a long-term prospect. In consequence, a key determinant of the present security order relates to the role of the United States, and its willingness to become involved in general order-maintenance. This element has been highly variable, with the prominent US role in Kosovo in 1999 and in Iraq in 2003 standing in marked contrast to its unwillingness to become engaged in Rwanda in 1994. Without doubt, there was a marked shift in US policy in the early 2000s under the administration of President George W. Bush. This was crystallized by the terrorist attacks of 11 September 2001: these did not change the facts of US power on the ground so much as they intensified the political will of US policymakers to deploy that power in a direct fashion. This was demonstrated in the open-ended **'war on terror'** that was declared shortly after 9/11

CWS

More generally, there are several contemporary trends towards **'collectivization'** of security (as distinct from collective security, properly speaking). These cover the various forms of **multilateralism** in security, the role of coalitions, the rise and partial demise of peacekeeping and **peace enforcement**, and the trend to (as well as limits of) humanitarian interventionism. There are analysts, such as Mary Kaldor (1999), who argue that fundamental restructuring in the nature of organized violence is taking place. Such conceptions are important as they link the discussion of violence to the other elements of order, and treat it as a dynamic problem—rather than holding a static view that 'war is war is war'. Violence then becomes symptomatic of changes in other social spheres, and not simply a structural constant produced by the 'anarchic' state system.

The organization of production and exchange

Another prominent dimension is the political economy of the present order. Central to the theme of order is our assessment of the degree of stability within the international trading and financial systems. The former remains beset by disputes between the world's three great trading groups or **'triads'**, and their trading relationship with the developing world; the latter shows periodic signs of undergoing meltdown, most recently during the financial turmoil that afflicted the East Asian economies in the late 1990s. This economic order is partially managed by those elements of governance institutionalized in bodies such as the IMF, the World Bank, and the WTO. The economic order penetrates more deeply than these obvious instances of it would seem to indicate. Such bodies do not determine just the rules for international trade and borrowing, nor shape exchange rates alone. The full effects of this **'internationalization'** of production can be appreciated only by taking into account its impact on those many other things that determine the quality of human lives: production of military equipment, the condition of the environment, social welfare, human (and specifically child) rights in the area of labour, and **gender** inequalities within the economy and in processes of development.

Multilateral management and governance

A remarkable aspect of the order is the highly dense and complex **network** of contemporary forms of international governance (regimes, **international organizations**, and international non-governmental organizations (INGOs)). These cover most aspects of life, including developments in legal (human rights, war crimes, the International Criminal Court), environmental, and economic regimes, as well as in the core peacekeeping activities of universal organizations like the UN. To what extent can we sensibly refer to globalization as giving rise, in turn, to a system of global governance? What is its potential for further development? Are current **international regimes** dependent on the underlying power

Box 33.4	Elements of order	
Structural elements		**Purposive elements**
Polarity		Social-state
Multilateralism		Identity
Regionalism		Economic order
Two worlds		Liberal rights

structure of Western dominance and reflective of Western preferences, and how sustainable are they given the value and cultural diversity of the present world? These issues link the discussion directly to the next element of order, since much of this regime base is emerging at a regional level.

Regionalism

The development of contemporary regionalism is another key to understanding the emerging order (see Ch.26). This takes various forms, including economic (trading regions), security (such as NATO), and cultural activities. The intensification of regionalism is occasionally viewed as a refutation of trends towards globalization, but is more plausibly regarded as one aspect of globalization, rather than as evidence against it. The fact that a number of regions feel the need to develop regional institutions is itself a manifestation of globalization, in the same way that the universal spread of the nation-state, as the principal political form, was earlier a product of globalization. Nonetheless, there are interesting questions about the significance of regionalism for the post-cold war order, such as the seemingly greater degree of security autonomy 'enjoyed' by regions since the end of the cold war, and the role of regions in constituting new forms of identity. There is perhaps a paradox to be noted that, with the loss of cold war constraints, regions now have greater autonomy—while, at the same time, levels of inter-penetration and globalization indicate diminished possibilities for regional insulation.

CWS

The liberal rights order

Arguably, the liberal rights order is the feature with the most striking continuities to the cold war period, and in contrast to the pre-1945 world. Human rights programmes had become a conspicuous feature of post-1945 international politics, largely in reaction to the catastrophic experiences of the period before 1945 (see Ch.31). This theme was a paramount aspect of the cold war period itself and was again highlighted with the collapse of the Soviet bloc, since that event was portrayed as a major step forward in extending the liberal order. In this respect, the focus on liberal rights is another element of continuity between the two periods, rather than a concern that has materialized only since the demise of the cold war. Indeed, it is often argued that it was the growth of concern with rights in the former Eastern Europe that had a corrosive effect on the maintenance of authoritarian political systems within the region. However, as commonly noted, the post-cold war order is paradoxically under pressure precisely because of its seemingly greater promotion of types of universalism, and it is this which could be evoking forms of religious and cultural resistance to it.

This relates directly to wider questions about the future of democratization. How this develops is of momentous import for the future stability of the international order and touches on a series of inter-related issues: about the status of democracy as a universal norm; the current variable experience with democratization; the pressures upon democracy arising from globalization (and hence the appeals for cosmopolitan forms of democracy); and the future of democracy as a source of inter-state peace and stability (see Ch.32).

North–South and the two world orders

Any examination of the contemporary order must give a high profile to the apparent gulf within it, separating the experience of the industrialized North from the increasingly marginalized South. Some see the tensions to which this gives rise as undermining the prospects for longer-term stability (see Ch.29). Are North–South relations more stable now than in the previous eras, or do they remain precariously rooted in inequalities of power, massive gaps in quality of life, and incompatibilities of cultural values? It is also a very moot point, and a key area of disagreement, whether globalization is aggravating these inequalities, or, as its supporters believe, whether it remains the best available means of rectifying them in the longer term. Otherwise expressed, are the problems of the South due to the processes of globalization, or due to the South's relative exclusion from the current trends in globalization? In any case, does this divide threaten the durability of the post-cold war order or must we simply recognize it as a key component of that order, and for that reason understand it as an element of structural continuity with its predecessors?

As against this image of two monolithic blocs of North and South, other analysts insist that such a conception is now out of date. The impacts of globalization cut across states and not just between them, yielding complex patterns of stratification that defy easy classification into North and South. There are enormous variations and inequalities within states, and regions, and not just between them. For this reason, it may be too artificial to speak of two such orders, as there is much more diversity than such crude dichotomies tend to imply.

> **Key points**
>
> - Order is shaped by the changed nature of states and of the tasks they perform.
> - There are complex questions about whether the end of the cold war has released a new agenda of nationalism and national identity or whether these issues have been present all along.
> - Security is increasingly being dealt with on a multilateral basis even when this does not conform to classical 'collective security' models.
> - The global economy is primarily shaped by relations between the three key groupings (America, Western Europe, and East Asia), and is managed by a panoply of Western-dominated institutions.
> - There are dense patterns of international institutions in all functional areas.
> - There are strong trends towards regionalism, but they take different forms in various regions.
> - Matters to do with human rights have a much higher profile than in earlier historical periods.

Globalization and the end of the cold war

There is a tendency to regard the high degree of globalization as being a consequence of the end of the cold war. This is especially so with regard to the geographical extent of globalization. Areas of the world that were formerly excluded from the full force of global capitalism, global communications, and global cultural intrusions are now much more integrated into these networks than at any previous time. In that sense, the main effect of the end of the cold war has been precisely to break down the barriers that previously held globalization at bay, at least in so far as the 'Second' or 'socialist' world had been concerned.

Not surprisingly, many commentators see the post-cold war period as being characterized by the intensification of the processes of globalization, particularly with regard to financial integration. The global financial order is now virtually universal in its reach, as is the influence of its principal institutions such as the World Bank and the IMF.

On this reasoning, it is the ending of the cold war that has allowed the further spread of globalization to occur, and we can therefore regard the scope of globalization as a point of difference between the cold war, and post-cold war worlds. Unfortunately, there is a danger in such an analysis. The problem is that to regard globalization as simply the consequence of the end of the cold war is to neglect the extent to which globalization also served as a cause of its end. This being so, globalization marks a point

Interpretations of globalization and the end of the cold war

'The end of the cold war division into competing world orders marks a crucial substantive and symbolic transition to single-world economic, cultural and political orders.' (Shaw 1999: 194)

'America has ceased to be a superpower, because it has met its match: globalization—a globalization which, moreover, it helps to promote despite not managing to master totally its meaning.' (Laidi 1998: 170)

'Globalization is the most significant development and theme in contemporary life and social theory to emerge since the collapse of Marxist systems.' (Albrow 1996: 89)

'Globalization and globalism were thus the product of specific historical conditions in the last three decades of the twentieth century.' (Cox 1996a: 34)

'Globalists continue to maintain that there are big, *fin-de-siècle* transformations under way in the world at large, which can be laid at the door of something called globalization. This new era—popularized as "a world without borders" and symbolized by the dismantling of the Berlin Wall—ostensibly came into its own where the cold war left off.' (Weiss 1999: 59)

of continuity, rather than discontinuity, between the two periods.

In a wider sense, the danger with such a procedure is that it neglects other dimensions of continuity, such as in the construction of a liberal capitalist order (Ikenberry 2000). What is the historical evidence for this type of argument? Its principal element is the view that globalization grew out of the core of Western capitalist states that formed during the cold war. This became such a powerful force that it finally weakened the other cold war protagonist, namely the Soviet Union, but also made the point of the cold war increasingly irrelevant. As regards the Soviet Union, what damaged and eroded the effectiveness of the USSR as a military power was precisely the fact that it was not integrated into the financial and technological sinews of global capitalism. As regards the logic of the cold war as a whole, the existence of a hostile Soviet bloc was a crucial element in the initial integration of the Western system. But by the 1980s, this system was effectively

self-sustaining, and no longer required any external enemy to provide its dynamic for growth. In this sense, the Soviet Union had become redundant as far as the needs of the dominant Western system were concerned.

If globalization both was an element of the pre-existing cold war system, but also stands out sharply as an element of the contemporary order, it needs to be seen as a point of continuity between the two periods. The logic of this, in turn, requires us to concede that the present order is not *sui generis*, as it contains within it elements that were present also during the cold war. This suggests that the contemporary order should not be understood as wholly separate from that which preceded it. But if globalization is the element that binds both together, can it be the key to understanding the present order? Is it the defining quality of today's world?

The claim that globalization defines the essential quality of the present order has been denied for a number of reasons. Most generally of all, if globalization is seen as a long-term historical trend—with various waves—then to interpret the present order in terms of globalization does not say enough about what is specific to it alone.

Beyond this, globalization has been described as the dystopic absence of order: negative qualities appear in abundance but without any seeming coherence. The clearest example is provided in Falk's description of globalization as 'a constellation of market, technological, ideological and civilizational developments that have nothing in common' (1997: 125). The general claim is that 'no one seems now to be in control' (Bauman 1998: 58). Even at the most basic level, globalization seems not to constitute a 'minimum' order of the kind that has traditionally underpinned international society (Bull 1977). It has no common institutions fulfilling minimally agreed societal functions.

All of these arguments suggest that globalization is inadequate as the conceptual basis for understanding the contemporary order because of what globalization *does*. It is too varied in its effects, and so lacking in purpose and goals, that we cannot visualize an order constructed on that basis. Indeed, the main theme of these writings on globalization is to draw attention to just how disorderly is the process of globalization. But a different form of argument can be made also on the basis of what globalization is, not just what it does. We need to be more precise about its nature, and not look only at its effects. This will be set out in the final section, after we have reviewed some of the political problems that appear to be attached to globalization today. These derive exactly from that sense of purposelessness and lack of control.

Key points

- Globalization is often portrayed as an effect of the end of the cold war because this led to its further geographical spread.

- At the same time, globalization has to be understood as one of the factors that caused the end of the cold war. It was the Soviet Union's marginalization from processes of globalization that revealed, and intensified, its weaknesses.

- Accordingly, globalization is an element of continuity between the cold war and post-cold war orders, and the latter should not be regarded as wholly new.

- A variety of authors are sceptical about the claim that globalization is the hallmark of contemporary order.

- One of the reasons is that, as a long-term historical trend, globalization is not specific to the late twentieth, nor the early twenty-first, century.

- Globalization embodies a range of often competing values.

- Globalization is too much outside our control to form an order. We are its objects rather than its subjects.

Globalization and legitimacy

On the face of it, globalization potentially creates several problems for the political stability of the current order. Not least is this so with regard to its legitimacy. There is a widely shared view that the emergence of a diffuse protest movement against globalization is symptomatic of a new wave of resistance to it. The central problem is understood to be one of the limited bounds of democratic practice in present world conditions. At a time when so much emphasis is placed on the virtues of democracy, many question its viability if organized on a purely national basis, but within a context of globalization. There are two facets to this issue: representation and accountability. It is all very well for citizens to be represented in national electoral institutions, but what voice does this give them in controlling those very economic, social, and cultural forces that cut across national borders, if their own governments do not have the capacity to deal with these? Conversely, this creates an issue of accountability. There may be little point in holding national and local politicians accountable through elections, if these politicians remain relatively powerless to exercise influence over global corporations, global technology, global environmental changes, or the global financial system. These concerns are specifically related to just how democratic are bodies such as the World Bank and the IMF, as well as international organizations such as the United Nations. On a more regional level, there has been recurrent anxiety about the so-called legitimacy deficits that afflict the structures of the European Union (see Ch.26).

In the face of these concerns, there has been much debate about the role to be played by an emerging global civil society. This embraces a variety of cross-national social movements, including anti-globalization activists, as well as a multitude of INGOs, such as Greenpeace and Amnesty International. Their proponents see these movements as

> ### Box 33.6   The debate about globalization and legitimacy
>
> 'The process of globalization has had a mixed impact on the legitimacy of international organizations. The demand for international co-ordination and common action has obviously increased. But at the same time, the effectiveness of IOs has diminished.' (Junne 2001: 218–19)
>
> 'Global structures violate commitments to the politics of consent: there is a global democratic deficit that must be reduced if world-wide arrangements are to be legitimate.' (Linklater 1999: 477)
>
> 'The democratic project is to globalize democracy as we have globalized the economy.' (Barber 2002: 255)
>
> 'Some theorists have pointed to the activity of social movements working beyond state borders as a method of increasing democratic practice. They see a contradiction between the fact that the structures of power . . . are firmly rooted in the global context, but participation, representation and legitimacy are fixed at the state level.' (O'Brien, Goetz, Scholte, and Williams 2000: 21–2)
>
> 'However much individual INGOs and global social movements may have contributed to the extension of democratic politics across the world, they do not currently possess the requisite degree of legitimacy and accountability to be considered as democratic representatives in a globalized political community.' (Colas 2002: 163)
>
> 'Rather than reform, these critics insist that what is required is an alternative system of global governance, privileging people over profits, and the local over the global.' (Held and McGrew 2002: 64)

the only feasible way of directly influencing global policies on such matters as development, the environment, human rights, and international security, and hence as the best way of democratizing global governance. Others, however, remain sceptical. There is nothing inherently democratic about global civil society as such, as there is no legitimate basis of representation or accountability to many of these movements. Indeed, from the perspective of many governments in the South, global civil society is resented as an extension of the power of the North, for the reason that such movements have a much more solid basis in the developed world, and are more likely to speak for its interests. This is illustrated, for example, in the tension between the economic development objectives of many governments in the South, and the preferred policies of many environmental movements in the North.

Key points

- There is evidence of resistance to globalization.

- Some of this is generated by the feeling that traditional democracy does not offer effective representation in the global order.

- National elections may not make politicians accountable if they cannot control wider global forces.

- There is a heated debate about whether global civil society can help democratize international institutions, or whether they themselves are largely undemocratic.

- Some governments in the South remain suspicious of social movements that may be better organized in developed countries.

An international order of globalized states?

Finally, the chapter returns to the matter of the extent to which globalization can be regarded as the defining element in contemporary order. Globalization could be taken to represent the mainstay of today's order only if it superseded all traditional elements of the international order itself. But if globalization is an addition to, but not a substitute for, the existing international order, then it is scarcely surprising that it is not adequate to the task of providing us with the single key to the post-cold war order.

The point can be taken further. If it can be convincingly held that globalization is not some process over and above the activities of states, but is instead an element within state transformation, it is not unreasonable to develop on this basis a conception of the globalized state. Globalization does not make the state disappear, but is a way of thinking about its present form. By extension of the same logic, globalization does not make redundant any notion of international order but instead requires us to think about a *globalized international order*. In short, what is required is a notion of international order that is based on a membership of globalized states. Only when this has been set in place will we be able to assess the role of globalization in the order that currently prevails.

Much of the confusion enters the debate about globalization by the tendency to see it as exclusively something pertaining to the environment in which states find themselves: globalization is a force wholly external to the individual states. On this view, globalization is presented as a claim about the degree of interconnectedness between states, such that the significance of borders, and the reality of separate national actors, is called seriously into question. There is no denying that this is part of what globalization signifies. But what such a one-sided interpretation leaves out of account is the extent to which globalization refers also to a 'domestic' process of change within states. Regarded in this alternative way, globalization can be understood as an expression of the profound transformations in the nature of the state, and in state–society relations, that have developed in recent decades. These lead us to think in terms, not of the demise or retreat of the state, but about its changing functionality: states still exist but do different things, do some things less well than they used to, but also have taken on new responsibilities in exchange.

The extension of this argument is that, even in an age of globalization, there remain both states and a state system. While, as noted above, the idea of international order is more limited than that of world or global order, the suggestion that globalization refers (at least in part) to a condition within states invites us to develop a theory about the nature of international order appropriate for globalized states. We need to face the seeming paradox that there can indeed be an international order of globalized states. To be sure, this does not address all issues of order, but it still engages with a number of significant aspects of it. For example, one key respect in which states have become globalized is with regard to the provision of human rights, since they are by no means the sole providers of such rights. To the extent that this is the case, the recent attempts by the international community to articulate a modified practice of non-intervention, thereby to allow for some modest degree of intervention on behalf of human rights, can be understood as the quest for a set of ground rules—an international order—appropriate to the nature of the 'new' globalized states that form its membership. In a word, the principles of international order are not currently developing simply as rules between anonymous 'billiard balls', but are a natural outgrowth of the kinds of creatures that states are in process of becoming. The mistake then is to imagine that globalization signifies the end of all projects for international order, when what in fact is under way is the reconfiguration of the principles of international order to reflect the new realities of globalized states.

Fig. 33.1 **Structural view of globalization as state form**

Key points

- Globalization is often thought of as an extreme form of interdependence. This sees it largely as a change in the external environment in which states find themselves.

- The implication of such analyses is that states are now much weaker as actors. Consequently, they are in retreat or becoming obsolete.

- If this were the case, ideas of international order would be much less relevant to our concept of order.

- But if globalization is considered as a transformation in the nature of states themselves, it suggests states are still central to the discussion of order: they are different but not obsolete. This leads to the idea of a globalized state as a state form.

- In this case, there is no contradiction between the norms and rules of a state system, operating alongside globalized states.

- This international order will nonetheless have different norms and rules in recognition of the new nature of states and their transformed functions. Rules of sovereignty and non-intervention are undergoing change as symptoms of this adaptation.

Conclusion

In short, we now face a hybrid situation in which states share a host of responsibilities with both intergovernmental organizations and a multiplicity of non-governmental and **transnational actors**. Formerly, the function of the international order was largely to cushion and protect the states so that they might go about their business as the principal providers of social goods to their citizens. This situation is now vastly more complex. Much of that provision (economic goods, monitoring of human rights, access to information, security, and so on) originates beyond the individual state itself, and indeed in non-state components that fall outside the jurisdiction of the international order narrowly conceived.

This does not, however, mean that the international order has become redundant. It means simply that it needs to be redesigned to take account of the new division of labour between states, **global networks,** and the rudimentary forms of global governance. As long as states persist as important sources of political agency, they will construct a state system with its own rules and norms. It is this that we regard as the essential basis of the international order. Currently, the identity of states is undergoing considerable change, to the extent that we can describe them as globalized states. But these globalized states still coexist within an international order, albeit one that now differs from its recent historical forms. This order is currently seeking to develop a set of principles to reflect that transformation. The quest for a post-cold war order is the expression of this uneasy search.

For further information and case studies on this subject, please visit the companion web site at www.oup.com/uk/booksites/politics.

QUESTIONS

1   Is the post-cold war order still an international order?

2   How important an element in the contemporary order is the condition of globalization?

3   How would you distinguish between an international and a world order, and which is the more important framework for assessing the contemporary situation?

4   In which respects are the 'identities' of states undergoing change?

5   How would you define the polarity of the contemporary international system

6   Is global governance a significant element of today's order

7   Is regionalism a contradiction of globalization?

8   Is the prominence of democracy and liberal rights convincing evidence of the impact of globalization? If so, why is globalization so problematic for democracy?

9   Can globalization be considered the basis of the present order if its impact is so variable on different regions, states, and individuals?

10 Is the idea of an international order of globalized states contradictory?

GUIDE TO FURTHER READING

International order

Bull, H. (1977), *The Anarchical Society: A Study of Order in World Politics* (London: Macmillan), especially Part 1, provides the standard introduction to this issue from an international society perspective.

Cox, R. (1996a), 'Social Forces, States, and World Orders: Beyond International Relations Theory', in R. Cox with T. J. Sinclair, *Approaches to World Order* (Cambridge: Cambridge University Press) is an alternative to the 'English School' approach and steps outside the state-centric framework.

Vincent, R. J. (1990), 'Order in International Politics', in J. D. B. Miller and R. J. Vincent (eds), *Order and Violence* (Oxford: Oxford University Press) gives a useful commentary on Bull's position.

New world orders and the post-cold war world

Clark, I. (2001), *The Post-Cold War Order: The Spoils of Peace* (Oxford: Oxford University Press) presents a guide to the debates about the post-cold war period, viewing the order as the equivalent of a historical peace settlement.

Ikenberry, G. J. (2000), *After Victory: Institutions, Strategic Restraint, and the Rebuilding of Order after Major Wars* (Princeton: Princeton University Press) also sets post-cold war developments in historical context and argues for the emergence of an increasingly 'constitutional' international order after 1945.

Williams, A. (1998), *Failed Imagination? New World Orders of the Twentieth Century* (Manchester: Manchester University Press) discusses the historical precedents for new orders during the twentieth century.

Globalization in the present order

Clark, I. (1999), *Globalization and International Relations Theory* (Oxford: Oxford University Press) develops a theoretical account of globalization in terms of state transformation.

—— (1997), *Globalization and Fragmentation: International Relations in the Twentieth Century* (Oxford: Oxford University Press) places the contemporary debates about globalization in historical perspective.

Held, D., and McGrew, A. (eds) (2003), *The Global Transformations Reader: An Introduction to the Globalization Debate*, 2nd edn (Cambridge: Polity Press) is a detailed selection of readings about contemporary globalization and its implications.

Scholte, J. A. (2004), *Globalization: A Critical Introduction*, 2nd edn (Basingstoke: Palgrave).

WEB LINKS

www.un.org/rights This UN site gives information about international human rights and their protection.

There are many examples of 'global civil society' networks actively involved in issues of globalization, human rights, and development:

www.oneworld.net This network promotes 'a more just global society'.

www.globalexchange.org This is an international human rights organization.

www.ifg.org The International Forum on Globalization is an activists network concerned with economic globalization.

REFERENCES

Abbott, K., Keohane, R. O., Moravcsik, A., Slaughter, A.-M., and Snidal, D. (2000), 'The Concept of Legalization', *International Organization*, 54(3): 401–20.

Abegglen, J. C. (1994), *Sea Change: Pacific Asia as the New World Industrial Center* (New York: Free Press).

Abu-Lughod, J. L. (1989), *Before European Hegemony: The World System AD 1250–1350* (Oxford: Oxford University Press).

Adams, N. B. (1993), *Worlds Apart: The North–South Divide and the International System* (London: Zed).

Adler, E. (1996), 'The Emergence of Cooperation: National Epistemic Communities and the International Evolution of the Idea of Nuclear Arms Control', *International Organization*, 50(1): 101–45.

——(1997), 'Seizing the Middle Ground: Constructivism in World Politics', *European Journal of International Relations*, 3(3): 291–318.

——(2000), 'Seizing the Middle Ground: Constructivism in World Politics', *European Journal of International Affairs*, 3 (Sept. 1997): 319–63.

——and Haas, P. (1992), 'Conclusion: Epistemic Communities, World Order, and the Creation of a Reflective Research Program', *International Organization*, 46(1): 367–90.

——and Barnett, M. (eds) (1998), *Security Communities* (Cambridge: Cambridge University Press).

Agnew, J., and Corbridge, S. (1995), *Mastering Space: Hegemony, Territory, and International Political-Economy* (London: Routledge).

Ahmed, A. S. (1992), *Post-Modernism and Islam: Predicament and Promise* (London: Routledge).

Albrow, M. (1990), 'Introduction', in M. Albrow and Elizabeth King (eds), *Globalization, Knowledge and Society* (London: Sage).

——(1996), *The Global Age* (Cambridge: Polity Press).

Allison, G. (2000), 'The Impact of Globalization on National and International Security', in J. S. Nye and J. D. Donahue (eds), *Governance in a Globalizing World* (Washington, DC: Brookings Institution): 72–85.

——(2004), 'How to Stop Nuclear Terror', *Foreign Affairs*, 83(1) (Jan./Feb.): 64–74.

——Carter, A. B., Miller, S. E., and Zelikow, P. (eds) (1993), *Cooperative Denuclearisation*, CSIA Studies in International Security, 2 (Cambridge, Mass.: Harvard University Press).

Alperovitz, G. (1965), *Atomic Diplomacy: Hiroshima and Potsdam: The Use of the Atomic Bomb and the American Confrontation with Soviet Power* (New York: Simon & Schuster).

Amin, S. (1997), *Capitalism in the Age of Globalization* (London: Zed Press).

Anderson, B. (1983; revised 1991), *Imagined Communities: Reflections on the Origin and Spread of Nationalism* (London: Verso).

Anderson, P. (1974a), *Passages from Antiquity to Feudalism* (London: New Left Books).

——(1974b), *Lineages of the Absolutist State* (London: New Left Books).

Angelo, S. (1969), *Machiavelli: A Dissection* (New York: Harcourt Brace).

Archibugi, D., and Held, D. (eds) (1995), *Cosmopolitan Democracy: An Agenda for a New World Order* (Cambridge: Polity Press).

Arend, A. C., and Beck, R. J. (1993), *International Law and the Use of Force* (London: Routledge).

Armstrong, D. (1982), *The Rise of the International Organisation: A Short History* (London: Macmillan).

Armstrong, K. (1997), 'Fundamentalism', *Demos*, 11: 15–17.

Arrighi, G. (1994), *The Long Twentieth Century: Money, Power and the Origins of Our Times* (London: Verso).

Ashley, R. K. (1981), 'Political Realism and Human Interests', *International Studies Quarterly*, 25(2): 204–36.

——(1984), 'The Poverty of Neo-realism', *International Organisation*, 38(2): 225–86.

——(1987), 'The Geopolitics of Geopolitical Space: Toward a Critical Social Theory of International Politics', *Alternatives*, 12(4): 403–34.

——(1988), 'Untying the Sovereign State: A Double Reading of the Anarchy Problematique', *Millennium*, 17(2): 227–62.

——and Walker, R. B. J. (1990), 'Reading Dissidence/Writing the Discipline: Crisis and the Question of Sovereignty in International Studies', *International Studies Quarterly*, 34: 367–416.

Austin, J. (1996), *Lectures in Jurisprudence*, Vol. 1 (Bristol: Thoemmes Press).

Axford, B. (1995), *The Global System: Economics, Politics, and Culture* (Cambridge: Polity Press).

Ayson, R. (2001), 'Management, Abolition, and Nullification: Nuclear Nonproliferation Strategies in the 21st Century', *The Nonproliferation Review*, 8(3) (Fall/Winter): 67–81.

Bacchetta, M. *et al.* (1998), *Electronic Commerce and the Role of the WTO* (Geneva: World Trade Organization).

Bailey, K. C. (1991), *Doomsday Weapons in the Hands of Many* (Champaign, Ill.: Illinois Press).

Bailey, T. A. (1974), *A Diplomatic History of the American People* (Englewood Cliffs, NJ: Prentice-Hall).

Baldwin, D. (ed.) (1993), *Neo-realism and Neo-liberalism: The Contemporary Debate* (New York: Columbia University Press).

Banks, E. (1994), *Complex Derivatives: Understanding and Managing the Risks of Exotic Options, Complex Swaps, Warrants and Other Synthetic Derivatives* (Chicago: Probus).

Baran, P. (1957), *The Political Economy of Growth* (New York: Monthly Review Press).

Barber, B. (1996), *Jihad vs McWorld* (New York: Ballantine Books).

——(2002), *Fear's Empire: War, Terrorism, and Democracy* (New York: W. W. Norton).

——(2002*a*), 'Democracy and Terror in the Era of Jihad vs. McWorld', in K. Booth and T. Dunne (eds), *Worlds in Collision: Terror and the Future of Global Order* (Basingstoke: Palgrave Macmillan): 245–62.

Barber, P. (1979), *Diplomacy: The World of the Honest Spy* (London: The British Library).

Barkawi, T. (2004), 'On the Pedagogy of Small Wars', *International Affairs*, 80(1): 19–38.

——and Laffey, M. (2002), 'Retrieving the Imperial: *Empire* and International Relations', *Millennium: Journal of International Studies*, 31(1): 109–27.

Barker, D., and Mander, J. (1999), *Invisible Government: The World Trade Organization: Global Government for the Millennium?* (San Francisco, Cal.: International Forum on Globalization).

Barnett, M. (1998), *Dialogues in Arab Politics: Negotiations in Regional Order* (New York: Columbia University Press).

Barraclough, G. (ed.) (1984), *The Times Atlas of World History* (London: Times Books).

Barry, B. (1989), *Theories of Justice* (Hemel Hempstead: Harvester Wheatsheaf).

Barston, R. P. (1988), *Modern Diplomacy* (London: Longmans).

Bartelson, J. (1995), *A Genealogy of Sovereignty* (Cambridge: Cambridge University Press).

Bauman, Z. (1998), *Globalization: The Human Consequences* (Cambridge: Polity Press).

Baylis, J., and O'Neill, R. (eds) (2000), *Alternative Nuclear Futures* (Oxford: Oxford University Press).

Beck, U. (1998), 'The Cosmopolitan Manifesto', *New Statesman*, 20 March.

Beitz, C. (1979), *Political Theory and International Relations* (Princeton, NJ: Princeton University Press).

——(1994), 'Cosmopolitan Liberalism and the States System', in C. Brown (ed.), *Political Restructuring in Europe: Ethical Perspectives* (London: Routledge).

Bello, W. (1994), *Dark Victory: The United States, Structural Adjustment and Global Poverty* (London: Pluto Press).

Bennett, A. L. (1991), *International Organisations: Principles and Issues*, 5th edn (Englewood Cliffs, NJ: Prentice-Hall).

Bennett, J., and George, S. (1987), *The Hunger Machine* (Cambridge: Polity Press).

Berners-Lee, T., with Fischetti, M. (1999), *Weaving the Web: The Original Design and Ultimate Destiny of the World Wide Web by Its Inventor* (New York: Harper San Francisco).

Berridge, G. R. (1995), *Diplomacy: Theory and Practice* (Hemel Hempstead: Harvester Wheatsheaf).

——and James, A. (2001), *A Dictionary of Diplomacy* (Basingstoke: Palgrave).

Bethell, L. (1970), *The Abolition of the Brazilian Slave Trade: Britain, Brazil and the Slave Trade Question 1807–1869* (Cambridge: Cambridge University Press).

Bhabha, H. K. (1994), *The Location of Culture* (London: Routledge).

——(ed.) (1990), *Nation and Narration* (London: Routledge).

Bhagwati, J. (1998), 'The Capital Myth: The Difference between Trade in Widgets and Trade in Dollars', *Foreign Affairs*, 73(3).

Bialer, S. (1986), *The Soviet Paradox: External Expansion, Internal Decline* (New York: Knopf).

Bill, J., and Springborg, R. (1990), *Politics in the Middle East* (London: Scott, Foresman/Little Brown Higher Education).

BIS (1996), *International Banking and Financial Market Developments* (Basle: Bank for International Settlements).

——(2000), *Quarterly Review: International Banking and Financial Market Developments* (Basle: Bank for International Settlements).

Black, M. (1992), *A Cause for our Times: Oxfam, the First 50 Years* (Oxford: Oxford University Press).

Bodin, J. (1967), *Six Books of the Commonwealth* (Oxford: Basil Blackwell).

Bohlen, A. (2003), 'The Rise and Fall of Arms Control', *Survival* (Autumn): 7–34.

Boli, J. and Thomas, G. (1999), *Constructing World Culture* (Palo Alto, Cal.: Stanford University Press).

Bonanate, L. (1995), 'Peace or Democracy', in D. Archibugi and D. Held (eds), *Cosmopolitan Democracy* (Cambridge: Polity Press): 42–67.

Bond, B. (1998), *War and Society in Europe: 1870–1970* (Stroud, Gloucestershire: Sutton Publishing).

Booth, J., and Walker, T. (1993), *Understanding Central America* (Boulder, Col.: Westview Press).

Booth, K. (1991), 'Security Emancipation', *Review of International Studies*, 17(4): 313–26.

——(1995*a*), 'Dare not to Know: International Relations Theory versus the Future', in K. Booth and S. Smith (eds), *International Relations Theory Today* (Cambridge: Polity Press): 103–26.

——(1995*b*), 'Human Wrongs and International Relations', *International Affairs*, 71(1): 103–26.

——(1999), 'Three Tyrannies', in T. Dunne and N. J. Wheeler (eds), *Human Rights in Global Politics* (Cambridge: Cambridge University Press).

——(ed.) (2004), *Critical Security Studies in World Politics* (Boulder, Col.: Lynne Rienner).

——and Dunne, T. (1999), 'Learning beyond Frontiers', in T. Dunne and N. J. Wheeler (eds), *Human Rights in Global Politics* (Cambridge: Cambridge University Press): 303–28.

————(eds) (2002), *Worlds in Collision: Terror and the Future of Global Order* (London: Palgrave Macmillan).

——and Smith, S. (eds) (1995), *International Relations Theory Today* (Cambridge: Polity Press).

Boutros-Ghali, B. (1992), *An Agenda for Peace* (New York: United Nations).

Bowker, M. (1997), *Russian Foreign Policy and the End of the Cold War* (Aldershot: Dartmouth).

——and Cameron, R. (eds) (2000), *Russia after the Cold War* (London: Longman).

Boyer, R., and Drache, D. (eds) (1996), *States against Markets: The Limits of Globalization* (New York: Routledge).

Bracken, P. (2003), 'The Structure of the Second Nuclear Age', *Orbis*, 47(3) (Summer): 399–413.

——(2004), 'Thinking (Again) About Arms Control', *Orbis*, 48(1) (Winter): 149–59.

Braudel, F. (1975), *The Mediterranean and the Mediterranean World in the Age of Philip II*, 2 vols (London: Fontana).

Braun, L. (1987), *Selected Writings on Feminism and Socialism* (Bloomington: Indiana University Press).

Brecher, M., and Wilkenfeld, J. (1991), 'International Crises and Global Instability: The Myth of the "Long Peace" ', in C. Kegley (ed.), *The Long Post-war Peace: Contending Explanations and Projections* (New York: HarperCollins).

Brenner, R. (1977), 'The Origins of Capitalist Development: A Critique of Neo-Smithian Marxism', *New Left Review*, 104.

Bretherton, C., and Ponton, G. (eds) (1996), *Global Politics: An Introduction* (Oxford: Blackwell).

Brewer, A. (1990), *Marxist Theories of Imperialism: A Critical Survey*, 2nd edn (London: Routledge).

Brittan, A. (1989), *Masculinity and Power* (Oxford: Basil Blackwell).

Brock, G. W. (1994), *Telecommunications Policy for the Information Age: From Monopoly to Competition* (Cambridge, Mass.: Harvard University Press).

Brodie, B. (ed.) (1946), *The Absolute Weapon: Atomic Power and World Order* (New York: Harcourt Brace).

Brown, C. (1992), *International Relations Theory: New Normative Approaches* (Hemel Hempstead: Harvester Wheatsheaf).

——(1999), 'History Ends, Worlds Collide', in M. Cox, K. Booth, and T. Dunne (eds), *The Interregnum: Controversies in World Politics 1989–1999* (Cambridge: Cambridge University Press): 41–57.

——(2000), 'John Rawls, The Law of the *Peoples*, and International Political Theory', *Ethics and International Affairs*, 14: 125–32.

Brown, L. R., and Kane, H. (1995), *Full House: Reassessing the Earth's Population Carrying Capacity* (London: Earthscan).

——*et al.* (1990), *State of the World 1990* (London: Unwin).

Brown, S., *et al.* (1977), *Regimes for the Ocean, Outer Space and the Weather* (Washington, DC: Brookings Institution).

Brownlie, I. (1979), *Principles of Public International Law* (Oxford: Clarendon).

——(ed.) (1971), *Basic Documents on African Affairs* (Oxford: Clarendon).

Bruce, D. (1995), 'Intervention without Borders: Humanitarian Intervention in Rwanda, 1990–4', *Millennium*, 24(2).

Brundtland, G. H., *et al.* (1987), (The Brundtland Report), *Our Common Future: Report of the World Commission on Environment and Development* (Oxford: Oxford University Press).

Bukharin, O. (1994/5), 'Nuclear Safeguards and Security in the Former Soviet Union', *Survival*, 36(4).

Bull, H. (1961), *The Control of the Arms Race: Disarmament and Arms Control in the Missile Age* (London: International Institute for Strategic Studies).

——(1966), 'The Grotian conception of international society', in H. Butterfield and M. Wright (eds), *Diplomatic Investigations* (London: Allen & Unwin).

——(1977), *The Anarchical Society. A Study of Order in World Politics* (London: Macmillan).

——(ed.) (1984*a*), *Intervention in World Politics* (Oxford: Clarendon Press).

——(1984*b*), *Justice in International Relations* (Ontario: Hagey Lectures, University of Waterloo).

——and Watson, A. (1984), *The Expansion of International Society* (Oxford: Clarendon Press).

Burchill, S., Linklater, A., *et al.* (1996), *Theories of International Relations* (Basingstoke: Macmillan).

Burckhardt, J. (1958), *The Civilization of the Renaissance in Italy*, Vol. 1 (New York: Harper).

Burnham, P. (1991), 'Neo-Gramscian Hegemony and International Order', *Capital & Class*, 45: 73–93.

——(1994), 'Open Marxism and Vulgar International Political Economy', *Review of International Political Economy*, 1(2).

——(1999), 'The Politics of Economic Management', *New Political Economy*, 4(1): 37–54.

Burrows, W., and Windrem, R. (1994), *Critical Mass: The Dangerous Race for Superpowers in a Fragmented World* (New York: Simon & Schuster).

Burtless, G., *et al.* (1998), *Globalphobia: Confronting Fears About Open Trade* (Washington, DC: Brookings Institution).

Burton, J. (1972), *World Society* (Cambridge: Cambridge University Press).

——(1990), 'International Relations or World Society', in J. A. Vasquez (ed.), *Classics of International Relations* (Englewood Cliffs, NJ: Prentice Hall).

Bush, G. W. (2001), 'Bush announces military strikes in Afghanistan', 9 October, available online at www.usinfo.state.gov, accessed 27 July 2004.

——(2003), 'Remarks by President George W. Bush', Press Conference, Camp David, 27 March, available online at www.acronym.org.uk/docs/0303/doc29.htm (downloaded 19 April 2004).

Butler, J. (1990), *Gender Trouble: Feminism and the Subversion of Identity* (London: Routledge).

Butterfield, H. (1951), *History and Human Relations* (London: Collins).

Buvinic, M. (1997), 'Women in Poverty: A New Global Underclass', *Foreign Policy* (Fall): 38–53.

Buzan, B. (1983), *People, States and Fear* (London: Harvester Wheatsheaf).

——and Herring, E. (1998), *The Arms Dynamic in World Politics* (London: Lynne Rienner).

——and Little, R. (2000), *International Systems in World History* (Oxford: Oxford University Press).

Byers, M. (1999), *Custom, Power, and the Power of Rules: International Relations and Customary International Law* (Cambridge: Cambridge University Press).

Cable, V. (1994), *The World's New Fissures: The Politics of Identity* (London: Demos).

Cairncross, F. (1997), *The Death of Distance: How the Communications Revolution Will Change Our Lives* (Boston: Harvard Business School Press).

Callaghy, T. M. (1995), 'Africa and the World Political Economy: Still Caught between a Rock and a Hard Place', in J. W. Harbeson and D. Rothchild (eds), *Africa in World Politics: Post-Cold War Challenges* (Oxford: Westview Press).

Calvert, P. (1994), *The International Politics of Latin America* (Manchester: Manchester University Press).

Camdessus, M. (2000), 'Address to the Tenth UNCTAD', Bangkok, February, *World Bank Development News* (Washington, DC: World Bank).

Camilleri, J. A., and Falk, J. (1992), *The End of Sovereignty* (Aldershot: Edward Elgar).

Cammack, P. (2002), 'The mother of all governments: the World Bank's matrix for global governance', in R. Wilkinson and S. Hughes (eds), *Global Governance: Critical Perspectives* (London: Routledge).

Campbell, D. (1992), *Writing Security: United States Foreign Policy and the Politics of Identity* (Manchester: Manchester University Press).

——(1993), *Politics Without Principle: Sovereignty, Ethics and the Narratives of the Gulf War* (Boulder, Col.: Lynne Rienner).

——(1998), *National Deconstruction: Violence, Identity, and Justice in Bosnia* (Minneapolis: University of Minnesota Press).

Caporaso, L., and Levine, D. (1992), *Theories of Political Economy* (New York: Cambridge University Press).

Cardoso, F. H., and Faletto, E. (1979), *Dependency and Development in Latin America* (Berkeley: University of California Press).

Carpenter, C. (2003), ' "Women and Children First": Gender, Norms and Humanitarian Evacuation in the Balkans 1991–1995', *International Organization*, 57(4) (Fall): 66–94.

Carr, E. H. (1939; 2nd edn. 1946), *The Twenty Years' Crisis 1919–1939: An Introduction to the Study of International Relations* (London: Macmillan).

——(1961), *What is History?* (Harmondsworth: Penguin).

Carson, R. (1962), *Silent Spring* (Harmondsworth: Penguin).

Carver, T. (1996), *Gender Is Not a Synonym for Women* (Boulder, Col.: Lynne Rienner).

Castells, M. (1996), *The Rise of Network Society*, 3 vols (Oxford: Blackwell).

——(2000), *The Rise of the Network Society* (Oxford: Blackwell).

——(2001), *The Internet Galaxy* (New York: Oxford University Press).

Castles, S. (2000), 'The Racisms of Globalization', in *Ethnicity and Globalization: From Migrant Worker to Transnational Citizen* (London: Sage).

Cavanagh, J., Wysham, D., and Arruda, M. (eds) (1994), *Beyond Bretton Woods, Alternatives to the Global Economic Order* (London: Pluto Press).

Center for Reproductive Rights, UNAIDS, and WHO (2002), *AIDS epidemic update* (New York: Center for Reproductive Rights). Available online at www.crlp.org/.

Cerny, P. (1993), 'Plurilateralism: Structural Differentiation and Functional Conflict in the Post-Cold War World Order', *Millennium*, 22(1).

Chalk, P. (1996), *West European Terrorism and Counter-Terrorism: The Evolving Dynamic* (New York: St Martin's Press).

Chase-Dunn, C. (1989), *Global Formation: Structures of the World-Economy* (Oxford: Blackwell).

——(1994), 'Technology and the Logic of World-Systems', in R. Palan and B. K. Gills (eds), *Transcending the State–Global Divide: A Neostructuralist Agenda in International Relations* (Boulder, Col.: Lynne Rienner): 84–105.

——(1998), *Global Formation: Structures of the World-Economy*, updated edition (London: Rowman & Littlefield).

Chesterman, S. (2004), 'Humanitarian intervention and Afghanistan', in J. Welsh (ed.), *Humanitarian Intervention in*

International Relations Theory (Oxford: Oxford University Press).

Chirot, D. (1982), Review of Wallerstein's 'The Modern World-System Vol. 2', *Journal of Social History*, 15(3).

Chomsky, N. (1994), *World Orders, Old and New* (London: Pluto Press).

——(1999), *The New Military Humanism: Lessons from Kosovo* (Monroe, Maine: Common Courage Press).

Chossudovsky, M. (1997), *The Globalization of Poverty* (London: Zed Press).

Christiansen, T., Jørgensen, K. E., and Wiener, A. (eds) (2001), *The Social Construction of Europe* (London: Sage).

Clark, I. (1989), *The Hierarchy of States: Reform and Resistance in the International Order* (Cambridge: Cambridge University Press).

——(1997), *Globalization and Fragmentation: International Relations in the Twentieth Century* (Oxford: Oxford University Press).

——(1999), *Globalization and International Relations Theory* (Oxford: Oxford University Press).

Claude Jr., I. (1955), *National Minorities: An International Problem* (Cambridge, Mass.: Harvard University Press).

——(1971), *Swords into Plowshares: The Progress and Problems of International Organization*, 4th edn (New York: Random House).

——(1984), *Swords into Plowshares* (New York: Random House).

Cochran, M. (1999), *Normative Theory in International Relations: A Pragmatic Approach* (Cambridge: Cambridge University Press).

Cohen, A. (1998), *Israel and the Bomb* (New York: Columbia University Press).

Cohen, R. (1995), 'Diplomacy 2000 BC–2000 AD', paper presented to the 20th Annual Conference of the British International Studies Association, Southampton, December.

Cohn, J. (1999), 'What Did Political Science Forget About Politics?', *The New Republic*, 25 Oct., 25–31.

Colas, A. (2002), *International Civil Society: Social Movements in World Politics* (Cambridge: Polity Press).

Computer Science and Telecommunications Board, National Research Council (2000), *The Digital Dilemma: Intellectual Property in the Information Age* (Washington, DC: National Academy Press).

Connell, R. W. (1995), *Masculinities* (London: Routledge).

Cooper, A. F., and English, J. with Thakur, R. (2002), *Enhancing Global Governance: Towards a New Diplomacy* (Tokyo: United Nations University Press).

——and Hocking, B. (2000), 'Governments, Non-governmental Organizations and the Re-calibration of Diplomacy', *Global Society*, 14(3): 361–76.

Cooper, R. (1968), *The Economics of Interdependence* (New York: McGraw Hill).

Copeland, D. C. (2000), *The Origins of Major War* (London: Cornell University Press).

Cornia, G. A., *et al.* (1987), *Adjustment with a Human Face* (Oxford: UNICEF/Clarendon Press).

Cowhey, P., 'The International Telecommunications Regime: The Political Roots of Regimes for High Technology', *International Organization*, 44(2): 169–99.

Cox, M. (1994), 'Rethinking the End of the Cold War', *Review of International Studies*, 20(20): 187–200.

——(1995), *US Foreign Policy after the Cold War: Superpower Without a Mission?* (London: The Royal Institute of International Affairs).

——(1998), 'Rebels Without A Cause? Radical Theorists and the World System after the Cold War', *New Political Economy*, 3(3): 445–60.

——Booth, K., and Dunne, T. (eds) (1999), *The Interregnum: Controversies in World Politics, 1989–1999* (Cambridge: Cambridge University Press).

——Ikenberry, G. J., and Inoguchi, T. (eds) (2000), *American Democracy Promotions: Impulses, Strategies, and Impacts* (Oxford: Oxford University Press).

Cox, R. (1981), 'Social Forces, States and World Orders: Beyond International Relations Theory', *Millennium Journal of International Studies*, 10(2): 126–55.

——(1986), 'Social Forces, States and World Orders: Beyond International Relations Theory', in R. Keohane (ed.), *Neo-realism and its Critics* (New York: Columbia University Press): 204–54.

——(1992), 'Towards a Post-Hegemonic Conceptualization of World Order: Reflections on the Relevancy of Ibn Khaldun', in J. Rosenau and E.-O. Czempiel (eds), *Governance without Government: Order and Change in World Politics* (Cambridge: Cambridge University Press).

——(1994), 'Multilateralism and the Democratization of World Order', Paper for International Symposium on Sources of Innovation in Multilateralism, 26–28 May, Lausanne.

——(1996a), 'Social Forces, States, and World Orders: Beyond International Relations Theory', in R. Cox with T. J. Sinclair, *Approaches to World Order* (Cambridge: Cambridge University Press).

——(1996b), 'A Perspective on Globalization', in J. H. Mittelman (ed.), *Globalization: Critical Reflections* (Boulder, Col.: Lynne Rienner).

——with Sinclair, T. (1996), *Approaches to World Order* (Cambridge: Cambridge University Press).

Cram, L. (1994), 'The European Commission as a Multi-Organization: Social Policy and IT Policy in the EU', *Journal of European Public Policy*, 1(2): 194–217.

Crawford, J. (ed.) (1988), *The Rights of Peoples* (Oxford: Clarendon Press).

Crawford, N. (2002), *Argument and Change in World Politics: Ethics, Decolonization and Humanitarian Intervention* (Cambridge: Cambridge University Press).

Crenshaw, M. (ed.) (1983), *Terrorism, Legitimacy, and Power* (Middletown, Conn.: Wesleyan University Press).

Crockatt, R. (1995), *The Fifty Years War: The United States and the Soviet Union in World Politics, 1941–1991* (London: Routledge).

Cronin, B. (2003), *Institutions for the Common Good: International Protection Regimes in International Society* (Cambridge: Cambridge University Press).

Cumings, B. (1999), 'Still the American Century', *Review of International Studies*, 25 (Dec.): 271–99.

Cusimano, M. K. (ed.) (2000), *Beyond Sovereignty* (New York: St Martins Press).

Dag Hammarskjöld Foundation (1975), *What Now? Another Development?* (Uppsala: DHF).

Dahl, R. (1994), 'A Democratic Dilemma: System Effectiveness versus Citizen Participation', *Political Science Quarterly*, 109(1): 23–32.

Damrosch, L. F. (ed.) (1993), *Enforcing Restraint: Collective Intervention in Internal Conflicts* (New York: Council on Foreign Relations).

Daniel, D., and Hayes, B. (eds) (1995), *Beyond Traditional Peacekeeping* (New York: St Martin's Press).

Davis, Z. S., and Frankel, B. (eds) (1993), *The Proliferation Puzzle: Why Nuclear Weapons Spread and What Results* (London: Frank Cass).

Dawisha, K. (1990), *Eastern Europe, Gorbachev and Reform: The Great Challenge* (Cambridge: Cambridge University Press).

De Soto, H. (2001), *The Mystery of Capital. Why Capitalism Triumphs in the West and Fails Elsewhere* (New York: Black Swan).

Dean, M. (1994), *Critical and Effective Histories: Foucault's Methods and Historical Sociology* (London: Routledge).

Declaration of Jihad Against the Country's Tyrants: Military Series (n.d.), US Government Exhibit 1677-T; UK translation, pp. BM-8-BM-9.

Dehousse, R. (1995), 'Institutional Reform in the European Community: Are there Alternatives to the Majoritarian Avenue?', *West European Politics*, 18(3).

——(ed.) (1997), *Europe: The Impossible Status Quo* (London: Macmillan).

——*et al.* (1992), *Europe after 1992: New Regulatory Strategies (EUI Working Paper LAW No. 92/31)* (Florence: European University Institute).

Denemark, R. A., Freidman, J., Gills, B. K., and Modelski, G. (eds) (2000), *World System History* (London: Routledge).

Der Derian, J. (1987), *On Diplomacy: a Genealogy of Western Estrangement* (Oxford: Blackwell).

——(1992), *Antidiplomacy: Spies, Terror, Speed, and War* (Oxford: Blackwell).

——(2001), *Virtuous War: Mapping the Military-Industrial-Media-Entertainment Network* (Boulder, Col.: Westview).

Derrida, J. (1976), *Of Grammatology* (Baltimore: Johns Hopkins University Press).

——(1992), *The Other Heading: Reflections on Today's Europe* (Bloomington: Indiana University Press, 1992).

Desch, M. (2003), 'The Humanity of American Realism', *Review of International Studies*, 29(3) (July): 415–26.

Destexhe, A. (1995), *Rwanda and Genocide in the Twentieth Century* (London: Pluto Press).

Deutsch, K. W. (1968), *The Analysis of International Relations* (Englewood Cliffs, NJ: Prentice Hall).

——(1996), *Nationalism and Social Communication* (Cambridge, Mass.: MIT Press).

——*et al.* (1957), *Political community and the North Atlantic area; international organization in the light of historical experience* (Princeton, NJ: Princeton University Press).

Devetak, R. (1996a), 'Critical Theory', in S. Burchill, A. Linklater, *et al.*, *Theories of International Relations* (Basingstoke: Macmillan): 145–78.

——(1996b), 'Post-modernism', in S. Burchill, A. Linklater, *et al.*, *Theories of International Relations* (Basingstoke: Macmillan): 179–209.

——and Higgott, R. (1999), 'Justice Unbound—Globalisation, States and the Transformation of the Social Bond', *International Affairs*, 75(3): 515–30.

Dibb, P. (1988), *The Soviet Union: The Incomplete Superpower* (London: International Institute for Strategic Studies/ Macmillan).

Dicken, P. (1992), *Global Shift: The Internationalisation of Economic Activity* (London: Paul Chapman).

Donelan, M. (1990), *Elements of International Political Theory* (Oxford: Clarendon Press).

Donnelly, J. (1993), *International Human Rights* (Boulder, Col.: Westview).

Doty, R. L. (1993), 'The Bounds of "Race" in International Relations', *Millennium*, 22(3): 443–61.

——(1996), *Imperial Encounters: The Politics of Representation in North-South Relations* (Minneapolis: University of Minnesota Press).

Doyle, M. W. (1982), 'Kant, Liberal Legacies and Foreign Affairs', *Philosophy and Public Affairs*, 12: 205–35 and 323–53.

——(1983a), 'Kant, Liberal Legacies, and Foreign Affairs, part 1', *Philosophy and Public Affairs*, 12(3).

——(1983b), 'Kant, Liberal Legacies, and Foreign Affairs, part 2', *Philosophy and Public Affairs*, 12(4).

——(1995a), 'On the Democratic Peace', *International Security*, 19(4): 164–84.

——(1995b), 'Liberalism and World Politics Revisited', in Charles W. Kegley (ed.), *Controversies in International*

Relations Theory: Realism and the Neoliberal Challenge (New York: St Martin's Press), 83–105.

——(1997), *Ways of War and Peace: Realism, Liberalism, and Socialism* (New York: W. W. Norton).

——(1999), 'A Liberal View: Preserving and Expanding the Liberal Pacific Union', in T. V. Paul and John A. Hall, *International Order and the Future of World Politics* (Oxford: Oxford University Press): 41–66.

Drake, M. (2003), *Problematics of Military Power: Government, Discipline and the Subject of Violence* (London: Frank Cass).

Dreze, J., Sen, A., and Hussain, A. (eds) (1995), *The Political Economy of Hunger* (Oxford: Clarendon Press).

Drower, G. (1992), *Britain's Dependent Territories* (Aldershot: Dartmouth).

Drucker, P. (1993), *Managing in Turbulent Times* (Oxford: Butterworth & Heinemann).

DuBois, W. E. B (1993), *The Souls of Black Folk* (New York: Knopf).

Duffield, M. (2001), *Global Governance and the New Wars* (London: Zed Books).

Dugard, J. (1987), *Recognition and the United Nations* (Cambridge: Grotius Publications Ltd).

Dunn, L. A. (1991), *Containing Nuclear Proliferation, Adelphi Papers, 263* (London: Brassey's for IISS).

Dunne, T. (1995), 'The Social Construction of International Society', *European Journal of International Relations* 1(3).

——(1998), *Inventing International Society* (London: Macmillan).

——(2003), 'Society and Hierarchy in International Relations', *International Relations*, 17(3): 303–20.

——Hill, C., and Hanson, M. (2000), 'New Interventionism', in W. T. Tow and M. Hanson (eds), *International Relations in the New Century: An Australian Perspective* (Melbourne: Oxford University Press): 93–116.

Durch, W. J. (ed.) (1993), *The Evolution of UN Peacekeeping* (New York: St Martin's Press).

Easterly, W. (2002), 'How Did Heavily Indebted Poor Countries Become Heavily Indebted? Reviewing Two Decades of Debt Relief', *World Development*, 30(10): 1677–96.

Ecologist (1993), 'Whose Common Future? Reclaiming the Commons' (London: Earthscan).

Economides, S., and Taylor, P. (1996), 'Former Yugoslavia', in J. Mayall (ed.), *The New Interventionism, 1991–1994* (Cambridge: Cambridge University Press).

Eden, L. (1991), 'Bringing the Firm back in: Multinationals and IPE', *Millennium: Journal of International Studies*, 20(1): 197–224.

Edkins, J. (1999), *Poststructuralism and International Relations: Bringing the Political Back in* (Boulder, Col.: Lynne Rienner).

——(2000), *Whose Hunger?: Concepts of Famine, Practices of Aid* (Minneapolis: University of Minnesota Press).

——(2003), *Trauma and the Memory of Politics* (Cambridge: Cambridge University Press).

——Persram, N., and Pin-Fat, V. (1999), *Sovereignty and Subjectivity* (Boulder, Col.: Lynne Rienner).

Edwards, G., and Regelsberger, E. (1990), *Europe's Global Links* (London: Pinter).

Edwards, P. (1996), *The Closed World: Computers and the Politics of Discourse in Cold War America* (Cambridge, Mass.: MIT Press).

Eichengreen, B. (1998), 'Dental Hygiene and Nuclear War: How International Relations Looks at Economics', *International Organization*, 52(4): 993–1012.

Ekins, P. (1992), *A New World Order: Grassroots Movements for Global Change* (London: Routledge).

Elias, N. (2000), *The Civilizing Process: Sociogenetic and Psychogenetic Investigations* (Oxford: Basil Blackwell).

Elshtain, J. B. (1987), *Women and War* (New York: Basic Books).

——and Tobias, S. (eds) (1990), *Women, Militarism, and War: Essays in History, Politics, and Social Theory* (Totowa, NJ: Rowman & Littlefield).

Elson, D. (1991), 'Structural Adjustment: Its Effects on Women', in T. Wallace with C. March (eds), *Changing Peceptions* (Oxford: Oxfam).

Enloe, C. (1989), *Bananas, Beaches and Bases: Making Feminist Sense of International Politics* (London: Pandora Books).

——(1992), 'Silicon Tricks and the Two Dollar Woman', *New Internationalist*, July.

——(1993), *The Morning After: Sexual Politics at the End of the Cold War* (Berkeley: University of California Press).

——(2000), *Maneuvers: The International Politics of Militarizing Women's Lives* (Berkeley: University of California Press).

Erksine, T. (2003), *Can Institutions Have Responsibilities? Collective Moral Agency and International Relations* (London: Palgrave).

Ertekun, N. M. (1984), *The Cyprus Dispute and the Birth of the Turkish Republic of Northern Cyprus* (Nicosia: Rustem and Brother).

Esposito, J. (1991), *The Straight Path* (Oxford: Oxford University Press).

——(ed.) (1983), *Voices of Resurgent Islam* (Oxford: Oxford University Press).

——and Piscatori, J. (1991), 'Democratization and Islam', *Middle East Journal*, Washington, 45(3).

European Journal of International Relations, 1(3): 267–331.

Evans, G., and Grant, B. (1995), *Australia's Foreign Relations: In the World of the 1990s* (Melbourne: Melbourne University Press).

Falk, R. (1975), *A Study of Future Worlds* (New York: Free Press).

——(1993), 'Global Apartheid: The Structure of the World-Economy', *Third World Resurgence*, 37 (Nov.).

——(1995a), 'Liberalism at the Global Level: The Last of the Independent Commissions', *Millennium Special Issue: The Globalization of Liberalism?*, 24(3): 563–76.

——(1995b), *On Humane Governance: Toward a New Global Politics* (Cambridge: Polity Press).

——(1997), 'State of Siege: Will Globalization Win Out?', *International Affairs*, 73(1).

——(2000), 'A "New Medievalism" ', in G. Fry and J. O'Hagan (eds), *Contending Images of World Politics* (Basingstoke: Macmillan).

——and Mendlovitz, S. (eds) (1973), *Regional Politics and World Order* (San Francisco: W. H. Freeman).

Fanon, F. (1967a), *Black Skin, White Masks* (New York: Grove Press).

——(1967b; reissued 1990), *The Wretched of the Earth* (Harmondsworth: Penguin).

Fausto-Sterling, A. (1992), *Myths of Gender: Biological Theories about Women and Men* (New York: Basic Books).

——(2000), *Sexing the Body: Gender Politics and the Construction of Sexuality* (New York: Basic Books)

Fawcett, L., and Hurrell, A. (1995), *Regionalism in World Politics* (Oxford: Oxford University Press).

Fearon, J., and Wendt, A. (2002), 'Rationalism vs. Constructivism', in W. Carlneas, B. Simmons, and T. Risse (eds), *Handbook of International Relations* (London: Sage).

Feinstein, L., and Slaughter, A.-M. (2004), 'A Duty to Prevent', *Foreign Affairs*, 83(1) (Jan./Feb.): 136–50.

Feldstein, M. (1998), 'Refocusing the IMF', *Foreign Affairs*, 77: 24.

Fierke, K., and Wiener, A. (2001), 'Constructing Institutional Interests: EU and NATO Enlargement', in T. Christiansen, K. E. Jørgensen, and A. Wiener (eds), *The Social Construction of Europe* (London: Sage): 121–39.

Fine, B. (1998), 'The Triumph of Economics: "Rationality Can Be Dangerous To Your Reasoning" ', in J. G. Carrier and D. Miller (eds), *Virtualism: A New Political Economy* (New York: Berg).

Finnemore, M. (1996a), 'Norms, Culture, and World Politics: Insights from Sociology's Institutionalism', *International Organization*, 50(2): 325–47.

——(1996b), *National Interests in International Society* (Ithaca, NY: Cornell University Press).

——(2000), 'Are Legal Norms Distinctive?', *International Law and Politics*, 32.

——and Sikkink, K. (1998), 'International Norm Dynamics and Political Change', *International Organization*, 52 (Oct.): 887–918.

————(2001), 'Taking Stock; The Constructivist Research Program in International Relations and Comparative Politics', *Annual Review of Political Science*, 4: 391–416.

Finney, M. (1997), *The Origins of the Second World War* (London: Arnold).

Finnis, J. (1980), *Natural Law and Natural Rights* (Oxford: Clarendon Press).

Fischer, B. (1997), *The Reagan Reversal: Foreign Policy and the End of the Cold War* (Columbia, Mo.: University of Missouri Press).

Fischer, D. A. V. (1992), *Stopping the Spread of Nuclear Weapons: the Past and the Prospects* (New York and London: Routledge).

Fischer, F. (1961), *Griff Nach der Weltmacht* (Dusseldorf: Drosle Verlag).

Fishlow, A. (1994), 'Latin America and the United States in a Changing World-Economy', in A. F. Lowenthal and G. F. Treverton (eds), *Latin America in a New World* (Boulder, Col.: Westview).

Flax, J. (1987), 'Postmodernism and Gender Relations in Feminist Theory', *Signs*.

Foot, R., and Walter, A. (1999), 'Whatever Happened to the Pacific Century?', *Review of International Studies*, 25 (Dec.): 245–69.

Forde, S. (1992), 'Classical Realism', in T. Nardin and D. Mapel (eds), *Traditions of International Ethics* (Cambridge: Cambridge University Press): 372–93.

Forsythe, D. P. (1988), 'The United Nations and Human Rights', in L. S. Finkelstein (ed.), *Politics in the United Nations System* (Durham, NC, and London: Duke University Press).

Foucault, M. (1977), *Discipline and Punish: The Birth of the Prison* (New York: Vintage Books).

——(1978), *The History of Sexuality* (Harmondsworth: Penguin).

——(1984), *The Foucault Reader* (New York: Pantheon Books).

——(1994), *Power* (New York: New Press).

Fox-Keller. E. (1985), *Reflections on Gender and Science* (New Haven, Conn.: Yale University Press).

Franck, T., and Rodley, N. (1973), 'After Bangladesh: The Law of Humanitarian Intervention by Force', *American Journal of International Law*, 67: 275–305.

Frank, A. G. (1967), *Capitalism and Underdevelopment in Latin America* (New York: Monthly Review Press).

——(1979), *Dependent Accumulation and Underdevelopment* (New York: Monthly Review Press).

——(1998), *ReORIENT: Global Economy in the Asian Age* (Berkeley: University of California Press).

——and Gills, B. (eds) (1996), *The World System: Five Hundred Years or Five Thousand?* (London: Routledge).

Frankel, B. (ed.) (1991), *Opaque Nuclear Proliferation* (London: Frank Cass).

Friedman, J. (ed.) (2003), *Globalization, The State and Violence* (Oxford: AltaMira Press).

Friedman, T. (1999), *The Lexus and the Olive Tree* (New York: HarperCollins).

Friori, G. (1990), *Antonio Gramsci: Life of a Revolutionary*, trans. Tom Nairn (London: Verso).

Frost, M. (1996), *Ethics in International Relations: A Constitutive Theory* (Cambridge: Cambridge University Press).

Fukuyama, F. (1989), 'The End of History', *The National Interest*, 16.

——(1992), *The End of History and the Last Man* (London: Hamish Hamilton).

Gaddis, J. (1986), 'The Long Peace: Elements of Stability in the Post-war International System', *International Security* 10(4): 99–142.

——(1992), *The United States and the End of the Cold War: Implications, Reconsiderations, Provocations* (New York: Oxford University Press).

Galtung, J. (1971), 'A Structural Theory of Imperialism', *Journal of Peace Research*, 8(1).

Gamble, A. (1999), 'Marxism after Communism: Beyond Realism and Historicism', *Review of International Studies*, Special Issue (Dec.): 127–44.

Gamble, C. (1994), *Timewalkers: The Prehistory of Global Colonization* (Cambridge, Mass.: Harvard University Press).

Gardner, G. T. (1994), *Nuclear Nonproliferation. A Primer* (London and Boulder, Col.: Lynne Rienner).

Garthoff, R. (1994), *The Great Transition: American-Soviet Relations and the End of the Cold War* (Washington, DC: Brookings Institution).

Garton Ash, T. (2002), 'The Perils of Too Much Power', *New York Times*, 9 April.

Gates Jr., H. L. (ed.) (1987), *Classic Slave Narratives* (New York: Mentor).

Gati, C. (1990), *The Bloc that Failed: Soviet-East European Relations in Transition* (Bloomington: Indiana University Press).

Gellner, E. (1983), *Nations and Nationalism* (Oxford: Blackwell).

George, J. (1994), *Discourses of Global Politics: A Critical (Re)Introduction to International Relations* (Boulder, Col.: Lynne Rienner).

George, S. (1992), *The Debt Boomerang* (Boulder, Col.: Westview).

Germain, R. (ed.) (1999), *Globalization and its Critics* (Basingstoke: Macmillan).

——and Kenny, M. (1998), 'Engaging Gramsci: International Relations Theory and the New Gramscians', *Review of International Studies*, 24(1): 3–21.

Giddens, A. (1990), *The Consequences of Modernity: Self and Society in the Late Modern Age* (Cambridge: Polity Press, and Stanford, Cal.: Stanford University Press).

Gierke, O. (1987), *Political Theories of the Middle Ages*, trans. F. W. Maitland (Cambridge: Cambridge University Press).

Gill, S. (1995), 'Globalization, Market Civilisation and Disciplinary Neo-liberalism', *Millennium: Journal of International Studies*, 24(3): 399–423.

——(ed.) (1993), *Gramsci, Historical Materialism and International Relations* (Cambridge: Cambridge University Press).

——and Law, D. (1988), *The Global Political Economy: Perspectives, Problems and Policies* (Hemel Hempstead: Harvester Wheatsheaf).

Gills, B. K., *et al.* (eds) (1993), *Low Intensity Democracy: Political Power in the New World Order* (London: Pluto Press).

Gilmore, R. W. (1998/9), 'Globalisation and US Prison Growth: From Military Keynesianism to post-Keynesian Militarism', *Race and Class*, 40(2–3): 171–88.

Gilpin, R. (1981), *War and Change in World Politics* (New York: Cambridge University Press).

——(1986), 'The Richness of the Tradition of Political Realism', in R. Keohane (ed.), *Neo-realism and its Critics* (New York: Columbia University Press): 301–21.

——(1987), *The Political Economy of International Relations* (Princeton, NJ: Princeton University Press).

——(2001), *Global Political Economy* (Princeton, NJ: Princeton University Press).

——(2002), *The Challenge of Global Capitalism* (Princeton, NJ: Princeton University Press).

Gioseffi, D. (ed.) (2003), *Women on War: an International Anthology of Women's Writings from Antiquity to the Present*, 2nd edn (New York: Feminist Press at the City University of New York).

Glaser, C. (1994/5), 'Realists as Optimists: Cooperation as Self-Help', *International Security*, 19(3): 50–90.

Goldman, M. (1992), *What Went Wrong With Perestroika* (New York: W. W. Norton).

Goldstein, J., Kahler, M., Keohane, R. O., and Slaughter, A. (2000), 'Legalization in World Politics', *International Organization*, 54(3).

Goldstein, J. S. (1994), *International Relations* (New York: HarperCollins).

Goodman, D., and Redclift, M. (1991), *Refashioning Nature: Food, Ecology and Culture* (London: Routledge).

Gorbachev, M. (1988), *Perestroika: New Thinking for Our Country and the World* (London: Fontana).

Gottlieb, R. S. (ed.) (1989), *An Anthology of Western Marxism: from Lukacs and Gramsci to Socialist-Feminism* (Oxford: Oxford University Press).

Gowa, J. (1983), *Closing the Cold Window: Domestic Politics and the End of Bretton Woods* (Ithaca, NY: Cornell University Press).

Grace, C. S. (1994), *Nuclear Weapons. Principles, Effects and Survivability* (London: Brassey's).

Gramsci, A. (1971), *Selections from the Prison Notebooks*, ed. and trans. Q. Hoare and G. Nowell Smith (London: Lawrence & Wishart).

Gray, C. S. (1996), 'The Second Nuclear Age: Insecurity, Proliferation, and the Control of Arms', in W. Murrey (ed.), *The Brassey's Mershon American Defense Annual, 1995–1996: The United States and the Emerging Strategic Environment* (Washington, DC: Brassey's): 135–54.

——(1999), *The Second Nuclear Age* (Boulder, Col. and London: Lynne Rienner).

——(2002), Realism Vindicated? World Politics as usual after September 11', in K. Booth and T. Dunne (eds), *Worlds in Collision: Terror and the Future of Global Order* (London: Palgrave Macmillan).

Gray, J. (1995), *Enlightenment's Wake: Politics and Culture at the Close of the Modern Age* (London: Routledge).

Green, D. (1995), *Silent Revolution: The Rise of Market Economic in Latin America* (London: Latin America Bureau).

Greenwood, C. (1993), 'Is there a Right of Humanitarian Intervention?', *The World Today*, 49.

Greenwood, J. (1998), *Representing Interests in the European Union* (Basingstoke: Macmillan).

Grieco, J. (1988a), 'Anarchy and the Limits of Cooperation: A Realist Critique of the Newest Liberal Institution', *International Organization*, 42 (Aug.): 485–507.

——(1988b), 'Realist Theory and the Problem of International Cooperation', *Journal of Politics*, 50 (Summer): 600–24.

——(1993a), 'Anarchy and the Limits of Cooperation: A Realist Critique of the Newest Liberal Institutionalism', in D. Baldwin (ed.), *Neo-realism and Neo-liberalism: The Contemporary Debate* (New York: Columbia University Press).

——(1993b), 'Understanding the Problem of International Cooperation', in D. Baldwin (ed.), *Neo-realism and Neo-liberalism: The Contemporary Debate* (New York: Columbia University Press).

——(1997), 'Realist International Theory and the Study of World Politics', in M. Doyle and G. J. Ikenberry (eds), *New Thinking in International Relations Theory* (Boulder, Col.: Westview): 163–201.

Groom, A. J. R., and Taylor, P. (1990), *Frameworks for International Cooperation* (London: Pinter).

Grotius, H. (1925), *The Law of War and Peace: De Jure Belli ac Pacis Libri Trea* (New York: Bobbs-Merrill). First published 1625.

Grovogui, S. N. (1996), *Sovereigns and Quasi Sovereigns, and Africans: Race and Self-Determination in International Law* (Minneapolis: University of Minnesota Press).

Grubb, M., Koch, M., Munson, A., Sullivan, F., and Thompson, K. (1993), *The Earth Summit Agreements: A Guide and Assessment* (London: Royal Institute for International Affairs).

Gunaratna, R. (2002), *Inside Al Qaeda: Global Network of Terror* (New York: Columbia University Press).

Haas, E. (1958), *The Uniting of Europe* (Stanford, Cal.: Stanford University Press).

——(1968), 'Technology, Pluralism, and the New Europe', in J. S. Nye (ed.), *International Regionalism* (Boston: Little, Brown).

Haas, P. M., Keohane, R. O., and Levy, M. (eds) (1993), *Institutions for the Earth: Sources of Effective International Environmental Action* (London: MIT Press).

Haas, R. D. (1993), 'The Corporation without Boundaries', in M. Ray and A. Rinzler (eds), *The New Paradigm in Business: Emerging Strategies for Leadership and Organizational Change* (New York: Tarcher/Perigee).

Hall, C. (1992), *White, Male, and Middle Class: Explorations in Feminism and History* (Cambridge: Polity Press).

——(2002), *Civilising Subjects: Metropole and Colony in the English Imagination 1830–1867* (Cambridge: Polity Press).

Hall, J. A. (1985), *Powers and Liberties: the Causes and Consequences of the Rise of the West* (Oxford: Blackwell).

——(1994), *Coercion and Consent: Studies on the Modern State* (Cambridge: Polity Press).

Halliday, F. (1983), *The Making of the Second Cold War* (London: Verso; 2nd edn 1986).

——(1994), *Rethinking International Relations* (London: Macmillan)

——(1999), 'The Potentials of Enlightenment', *Review of International Studies*, 25 (Dec.): 105–25.

Ham, P. van (1993), *Managing Non-Proliferation Regimes in the 1990s* (London: Royal Institute of International Affairs/ Pinter Publishers).

Hamilton, K., and Langhorne, R. (1995), *The Practice of Diplomacy* (London: Routledge).

Haraway, D. (1989), *Primate Visions: Gender, Race, and Nature in the World of Modern Science* (New York: Routledge).

——(1991), *Symians, Cyborgs and Women: The Re-Invention of Nature* (New York: Routledge).

Hardin, G. (1968), 'The Tragedy of the Commons', *Science*, 162: 1243–8.

Harding, S. (1986), *The Science Question in Feminism* (Milton Keynes: Open University Press).

——and Narayan, U. (eds) (1998), *Border Crossings: Multicultural and Postcolonial Feminist Challenges to Philosophy 1* and *2* (Bloomington: Indiana University Press).

Hardt, M., and Negri, A. (2000), *Empire* (Cambridge, Mass.: Harvard University Press).

Hart, H. L. A. (1994), *The Concept of Law*, 2nd edn (Oxford: Oxford University Press).

Hartsock, N. (1998), *The Feminist Standpoint Revisited and Other Essays* (Boulder, Col.: Westview).

Harvey, D. (1987), 'The World Systems Theory Trap', *Studies in Comparative International Development*, 22(1).

——(1989), *The Condition of Postmodernity: An Enquiry into the Conditions of Cultural Change* (Oxford: Blackwell).

Harvey, F., and Brecher, M., (eds) (2002), *Critical Perspectives in International Studies* (Ann Arbor: University of Michigan Press).

Hasenclever, A. (2000), 'Integrating theories of regimes', *Review of International Studies*, 26: 3–33.

——Mayer, P., and Rittberger, V. (1997), *Theories of International Regimes* (Cambridge: Cambridge University Press).

Hashemi, S. (1996), 'International Society and its Islamic Malcontents', *The Fletcher Forum of World Affairs*, 20(2).

Hay, C. (2000), 'Contemporary capitalism, globalization, regionalization and the persistence of national variation', *Review of International Studies*, 26(4): 509–32.

Heilbroner, R., and Milberg, W. S. (1995), *The Crisis of Vision in Modern Economic Thought* (Cambridge: Cambridge University Press).

Held, D. (1993), 'Democracy: From City-states to a Cosmopolitan Order?', in D. Held (ed.), *Prospects for Democracy: North, South, East, West* (Cambridge: Polity Press): 13–52.

——(1995), *Democracy and the Global Order: From the Modern State to Cosmopolitan Governance* (Cambridge: Polity Press).

——(2002), 'Cosmopolitanism: Ideas, Realities, Deficits', in D. Held and A. McGrew (eds), *Governing Globalization* (Cambridge: Polity Press): 305–24.

——and McGrew, A. (2002), *Globalization/Anti-Globalization* (Cambridge: Polity Press).

————Goldblatt, D., and Perraton, J. (1999), *Global Transformations: Politics, Economics and Culture* (Cambridge: Polity Press).

Helleiner, E. (1995), 'Explaining the Globalization of Financial Markets: Bringing the State back in', *The Review of International Political Economy*, 2(2): 315–41.

Helman, G. B., and Ratner, S. R. (1992/3), 'Saving Failed States', *Foreign Policy*, 89: 3–20.

Hempel, L. C. (1996), *Environmental Governance: The Global Challenge* (Washington, DC: Island Press).

Henkin, L. (1968), *How Nations Behave: Law and Foreign Policy* (London: Pall Mall Press).

——(1995), *International Law: Politics and Values* (Dordrecht: Martinus Nijhoff).

Hennessy, R., and Ingraham, C. (eds) (1997), *Materialist Feminism: a Reader in Class, Difference, and Women's Lives* (London: Routledge).

Heraclides, A. (1990), *The Self-Determination of Minorities in International Politics* (London: Cass).

Hersh, S. M. (1983), *The Price of Power: Kissinger in the Nixon White House* (New York: Summit Books).

Hertz, J. H. (1962), *International Politics in the Atomic Age* (New York: Columbia University Press).

Herz, J. (1950), 'Idealist Internationalism and the Security Dilemma', *World Politics*, 2(2).

——(1981), 'Political Realism Revisited', *International Studies Quarterly*, 25: 182–97.

Hettne, B., Inotai, A., and Sunkel, O. (eds) (1999), *Globalization and the New Regionalism* (Basingstoke: Macmillan).

Higate, P. (ed.) (2003), *Military Masculinities: Identity and the State* (London: Praeger).

Higgins, R. (1994), *Problems and Process: International Law and How We Use It* (Oxford: Oxford University Press).

Higgott, R. A. (1998), 'The Asian Economic Crisis: A Case Study in the Politics of Resentment', *New Political Economy*, 3(3): 333–56.

——(1999), 'Economics, Politics and (International) Political Economy: The Need for a Balanced Diet in an Era of Globalisation', *New Political Economy*, 4(1): 23–36.

——(2001), 'Taming Economics, Emboldening International Relations: The Theory and Practice of IPE 10 Years after the Cold War', in S. Lawson (ed.), *After the Wall: International Relations after the Cold War* (Cambridge: Polity Press).

Hill, C. (1993), 'The Capability–Expectations Gap, or Conceptualizing Europe's International Role', *Journal of Common Market Studies*, (31)1: 305–28.

——(1996), 'World Opinion and the Empire of Circumstance', *International Affairs*, 72(1).

——(2003), *The Changing Politics of Foreign Policy* (Basingstoke: Palgrave).

Hinsley, F. H. (1967), *Power and the Pursuit of Peace* (Cambridge: Cambridge University Press).

——(1973), *Nationalism and the International System* (London: Hodder & Stoughton).

Hirschmann, A. O. (1945), *National Power and the Structure of Foreign Trade* (Berkeley: University of California Press).

——(1977), *The Passions and the Interests* (Princeton, NJ: Princeton University Press).

——(1986), 'Against Parsimony: Three Easy Ways of Complicating Some Categories of Economic Discourse', in A. O. Hirschmann (ed.), *Rival Views of Market Society and Other Recent Essays* (New York: Viking Books).

Hirst, J. (1996), 'In Defence of Appeasement: Indonesia and Australian Foreign Policy', *Quadrant*, 40(4).

Hirst, P. (2001), *War and Power in the 21st Century: the State, Military Conflict, and the International System* (Cambridge: Polity Press).

——and Thompson, G. (1996; 2nd edn. 1999), *Globalization in Question: The International Economy and the Possibilities of Governance* (Cambridge: Polity Press).

————(2003), 'Globalization—a necessary myth?', in D. Held and A. McGrew (eds), *The Global Transformations Reader*, 2nd edn (Cambridge: Polity Press): 98–106.

Hix, S. (1994), 'Approaches to the Study of the EC: The Challenge to Comparative Politics', *West European Politics*, 17(1): 1–30.

Hobbes, T. (1991), *Leviathan*, ed. R. Tuck (Cambridge: Cambridge University Press).

Hobden, S. (1998), *International Relations and Historical Sociology: Breaking Down Boundaries* (London: Routledge).

——and Hobson, J. M. (2002), *Historical Sociology of International Relations* (Cambridge: Cambridge University Press).

Hobsbawm, E. (1990), *Nations and Nationalism Since 1780: Programme, Myth, Reality* (Cambridge: Cambridge University Press).

——(1994), *Age of Extremes: The Short Twentieth Century, 1914– 1991* (London: Michael Joseph).

——(1995), 'Pax Americana: Bosnia is its First Success', *Independent*, 22 Nov.

Hobson, J. M. (2000), *The State and International Relations* (Cambridge: Cambridge University Press).

Hocking, B. (2004), 'Diplomacy', in W. Carlsnaes, H. Sjursen, and B. White (eds), *Contemporary European Foreign Policy* (London: Sage): 91–109.

——(ed.) (1999), *Foreign Ministries: Change and Adaptation* (Basingstoke: Macmillan).

——and Smith, M. (1990), *World Politics: An Introduction to International Relations* (London: Harvester Wheatsheaf).

Hoffman, J. (2003), 'Reconstructing Diplomacy', *British Journal of Politics and International Relations*, 5(4): 525–42.

Hoffman, M. (1987), 'Critical Theory and the Inter-Paradigm Debate', *Millennium*, 16(2): 231–49.

——(1993), 'Agency, Identity and Intervention', in I. Forbes and M. Hoffman (eds), *Political Theory, International Relations and the Ethics of Intervention* (Houndmills, Basingstoke: St Martin's Press).

Hoffmann, S. (1987), *Janus and Minerva: Essays on the Theory and Practice of International Politics* (Boulder, Col.: Westview).

——(1995–6), 'The Politics and Ethics of Military Intervention', *Survival*, 37(4): 29–51.

Hogan, M. (ed.) (1992), *The End of the Cold War: Its Meaning and Implications* (Cambridge: Cambridge University Press).

Holden, P., and Rupel, R. J. (eds) (2003), *Imperial Desire: Dissident Sexualities and Colonial Literature* (London: University of Minnesota Press).

Hollis, M., and Smith, S. (1990), *Explaining and Understanding International Relations* (Oxford: Clarendon Press).

Holsti, K. J. (1996), *War, the State, and the State of War* (Cambridge: Cambridge University Press).

Holt, P. M., Lambton, A., and Lewis, B. (1970), *The Cambridge History of Islam*, vols 1 and 2 (Cambridge: Cambridge University Press).

Homer-Dixon, T. F. (1994), 'Environmental Scarcities and Violent Conflict: Evidence from Cases', *International Security* 19(1): 5–40.

Honeygold, D. (1989), *International Financial Markets* (Cambridge: Woodhead-Faulkner).

Hoogvelt, A. (2001), *Globalization and the Post-Colonial World* (Basingstoke: Palgrave).

Hopkins, A. G. (ed.) (2002), *Globalization in World History* (London: W. W. Norton).

Horsman, M., and Marshall, A. (1994), *After the Nation-State: Citizens, Tribalism and the New World Disorder* (New York: HarperCollins).

Hough, J. (1988), *Opening up the Soviet Economy* (Washington, DC: Brookings Institution).

Houghton, J., Jenkins, G., and Ephraums, J. (eds) (1990), *Climate Change: The Ipcc Assessment* (Cambridge: Cambridge University Press).

Howlett, D., and Simpson, J. (1993), 'Nuclearisation and Denuclearisation in South Africa', *Survival*, 35(3).

——Leigh-Phippard, H., and Simpson, J. (1996), 'After the 1995 NPT Renewal Conference: Can the Treaty Survive the Outcome?', in J. B. Poole and R. Guthrie (eds), *Verification Report 1996. Arms Control, Peacekeeping and the Environment* (Boulder, Col., San Francisco, and Oxford: Westview).

Hunger Project (1985), *Ending Hunger: An Idea whose Time has Come* (New York: Praeger).

Hunter, S. (ed.) (1988), *The Politics of Islamic Revivalism: Diversity and Unity* (Bloomington: Indiana University Press).

Huntington, S. (1993), 'The Clash of Civilizations', *Foreign Affairs*, 72(3): 22–169.

——(1996), *The Clash of Civilizations and the Remaking of the World Order* (New York: Simon & Schuster).

Hurrell, A. (1994), 'Regionalism in the Americas', in A. Lowenthal and G. Treverton (eds), *Latin America in a New World Order* (Boulder, Col.: Westview).

——(1995), 'Explaining the Resurgence of Regionalism in World Politics', *Review of International Studies*, 21(4).

——and Kingsbury, B. (eds) (1992), *The International Politics of the Environment: Actors, Interests and Institutions* (Oxford: Clarendon Press).

——and Woods, N. (1995), 'Globalization and Inequality', *Millennium*, 24(3): 447–70.

Hutchings, K. (1999), *International Political Theory: Rethinking Ethics in a Global Era* (London: Sage).

Hutton, W. (1995), *The State We're In* (London: Jonathan Cape).

ICPF (1994), *Uncommon Opportunities: An Agenda for Peace and Equitable Development* (London: Zed).

Ignatieff, M. (1995), 'The Show that Europe Missed', *Independent*, 22 Nov.

——(2000), *Virtual War: Kosovo and Beyond* (New York: Henry Holt).

——(2002), 'Is the human rights era ending?', *New York Times*, 5 Feb.

Ikenberry, G. J. (1999), 'Liberal Hegemony and the Future of American Post-war Order', in T. V. Paul and J. A. Hall (eds), *International Order and the Future of World Politics* (Cambridge: Cambridge University Press): 123–45.

——(2000), *After Victory: Institutions, Strategic Restraint, and the Rebuilding of Order after Major Wars* (Princeton, NJ: Princeton University Press).

Independent Commission on International Development Issues (Chairman: Willy Brandt) (1980), *North–South: a programme for survival: report of the Independent Commission on International Development Issues* (London: Pan).

International Affairs (2000), *Europe: Where does it begin and where does it end?* Special Issue, 76(3): 437–574.

International Commission on Intervention and State Sovereignty (2001), *The Responsibility to Protect* (Ottawa: ICISS).

International Labour Organization (n.d.), *Fact sheet*, available online at **www.ilo.org/communication**.

International Parliamentary Union, *IPU PARLINE database*, available online at **www.ipu.org/wmn-e/world.htm**, accessed 30 Jan. 2004.

International Studies Perspectives (2004), 'ISP Policy Forum: Public Advocates for Private Interests? The Rise of Commercial Diplomacy', *International Studies Perspectives*, 5(1): 50–70.

International Telecommunication Union (2001), ITU-D, 'Key Global Telecom Indicators for the World Telecommunication Service Sector', available online at **www.itu.int/ITU-D/ict/statistics/at_glance/KeyTelecom-99.html**, accessed 26 July 2004.

Iriye, A. (1987), *The Origins of the Second World War in Asia and the Pacific* (London: Longmans).

Jackson, B. (1990), *Poverty and the Planet* (London: Penguin).

Jackson, R. H. (1990), *Quasi-States: Sovereignty, International Relations and the Third World* (Cambridge: Cambridge University Press).

Jacobson, H. K. (1984), *Networks of Interdependence: International Organizations and the Global Political System*, 2nd edn (New York: Knopf).

James, A. (1986), *Sovereign Statehood: The Basis of International Society* (London: Allen & Unwin).

——(1990), *Peacekeeping in International Politics* (Basingstoke: Macmillan).

——(1993), 'System or Society?', *Review of International Studies*, 19(3).

Jensen, E., and Fisher, T. (eds) (1990), *The United Kingdom—The United Nations* (London: Macmillan).

Jervis, R. (1983a), *The Illogic of American Nuclear Strategy* (Ithaca, NY: Cornell University Press).

——(1983b), 'Security Regimes', in S. D. Krasner (ed.) (1983), *International Regimes* (Ithaca, NY: Cornell University Press).

——(1999), 'Realism, Neo-liberalism, and Cooperation: Understanding the Debate', *International Security*, 24 (Summer): 42–63.

John, I. M. W., and Garnett, J. (1972), 'International Politics at Aberystwyth 1919–1969', in B. Porter, *The Aberystwyth Papers: International Politics 1919–1969* (London: Oxford University Press): 86–102.

Jones, B. D. (1995), ' "Intervention Without Borders": Humanitarian Intervention in Rwanda, 1990–94', *Millennium: Journal of International Studies*, 24.

Jones, P. (1994), *Rights* (Basingstoke: Macmillan).

Jones, R. W. (1995), ' "Message in a Bottle"—Theory and Praxis in Critical Security Studies', *Contemporary Security Policy*, 16(3).

——(1999), *Security, Strategy and Critical Theory* (Boulder, Col.: Lynne Rienner).

——(ed.) (2000), *Critical Theory and World Politics* (Boulder, Col.: Lynne Rienner).

Jørgensen, K. E. (1998), 'Sleeping Beauty is Awake!', *Studia Diplomatica*, 51(1–2).

Joseph, A., and Sharma, K. (eds) (2003), *Terror, Counter Terror: Women Speak Out* (London and New York: Zed Books).

Junne, G. C. A. (2001), 'International Organizations in a Period of Globalization: New (Problems of) Legitimacy', in J.-M. Coicaud and V. Heiskanen (eds), *The Legitimacy of International Organizations* (Tokyo: United Nations University Press).

Kagan, R. (2003), *Paradise and Power: America and Europe in the New World Order* (London: Atlantic Books).

Kaldor, M. (1995), 'Who Killed the Cold War?', *The Bulletin of The Atomic Scientists*, July/Aug.: 57–60.

——(1999), *New and Old Wars: Organized Violence in a Global Era* (Cambridge: Polity Press).

Kant, I. (1970), 'Perpetual Peace', in M. Forsyth, H. M. A. Keens-Soper, and P. Savigear (eds), *The Theory of International Relations: Selected Texts from Gentili to Treitschke* (London: Allen & Unwin).

——(1991), *Political Writings*, ed. Hans Reiss (Cambridge: Cambridge University Press).

Kanter, R. M. (1995), *World Class: Thriving Locally in the Global Economy* (New York: Simon & Schuster).

Kaplan, R. D. (1994), 'The Coming Anarchy', *Atlantic Monthly*.

——(2000), *The Coming Anarchy: Shattering the Dreams of the Post-Cold War* (New York: Random House).

Karp, A. (1995), *Ballistic Missile Proliferation: The Politics and Technics* (Oxford: Oxford University Press for SIPRI).

Katzenstein, P. (ed.) (1996), *The Culture of National Security:*

Norms and Identity in World Politics (New York: Columbia University Press).

——Keohane, R. O., and Krasner, S. (1998), 'International Organization and the Study of World Politics', *International Organization*, 52(4): 463–85, 645–85.

Keck, M., and Sikkink, K. (1998), *Activists beyond Borders: Transnational Advocacy Networks in International Politics* (Ithaca, NY: Cornell University Press).

Keene, E. (2002), *Beyond the Anarchical Society: Grotius, Colonialism and Order in World Politics* (Cambridge: Cambridge University Press).

Kegley, C. (ed.) (1995), *Controversies in International Relations Theory: Realism and the Neoliberal Challenge* (New York: St Martin's Press).

——and Wittkopf, E. (1999), *World Politics: Trend and Transformation*, 7th edn (New York: St Martin's Press).

Kelsen, H. (1952), *Principles of International Law* (New York: Rinehart).

Kendall, G., and Wickham, G. (1999), *Using Foucault's Methods* (London: Sage).

Kennan, G. F. (1992), 'The GOP Won the Cold War—Ridiculous', *New York Times*, 28 Oct.

——(1996), 'Diplomacy in the Modern World', in R. J. Beck, A. Clark Arend, and R. D. Vanger Lugt (eds), *International Rules: Approaches from International Law and International Relations* (Oxford: Oxford University Press): 99–106.

Kennedy, P. (1988), *The Rise and Fall of Great Powers: Economic Change and Military Conflict from 1500–2000* (Harmondsworth: Penguin).

Keohane, R. (1984), *After Hegemony: Cooperation and Discord in the World Political Economy* (Princeton, NJ: Princeton University Press).

——(1988), 'International Institutions: Two Approaches', *International Studies Quarterly*, 32(4): 379–96.

——(ed.) (1989a), *International Institutions and State Power: Essays in International Relations Theory* (Boulder, Col.: Westview).

——(1989b), 'Theory of World Politics: Structural Realism and Beyond', in R. Keohane (ed.), *International Institutions and State Power: Essays in International Relations Theory* (Boulder, Col.: Westview).

——(2002), 'The Public Delegitimation of Terrorism and Coalitional Politics', in K. Booth and T. Dunne (eds), *Worlds in Collision: Terror and the Future of Global Order* (London: Palgrave Macmillan): 141–51.

——and Martin, L. (1995), 'The Promise of Institutionalist Theory', *International Security*, 20(1): 39–51.

——and Nye, J. (1977), *Power and Interdependence: World Politics in Transition* (Boston: Little, Brown).

————(2003), 'Globalization: What's New? What's Not? (And so what?)', in D. Held and A. McGrew (eds), *The Global Transformations Reader* (Cambridge: Polity Press): 75–84.

————(eds) (1972), *Transnational Relations and World Politics* (Cambridge, Mass.: Harvard University Press).

————and Hoffmann, S. (eds) (1993), *After the Cold War: International Institutions and State Strategies in Europe 1989–1991* (London: Harvard University Press).

Keylor, W. (1992), *The Twentieth Century World: An International History* (New York: Oxford University Press).

Keynes, J. M. (1919), *The Economic Consequences of the Peace* (London: Macmillan).

Khoman, T. (1992), 'ASEAN: Conception and Evolution', in K. S. Sandhu (ed.), *The ASEAN Reader* (Singapore: Institute of South East Asian Studies).

Khor, M. (1995), 'Remarks to the International Forum on Globalization', New York, November.

Kidron, M., and Segal, R. (1995), *The State of the World Atlas* (London: Penguin).

Kinsella, H. (2003), 'For a Careful Reading: The Conservativism of Gender Constructivism', *International Studies Review*, 5: 294–7.

Kirkpatrick, J. (1979), 'Dictatorships and Double Standards', *Commentary*, 68.

Kissinger, H. A. (1977), *American Foreign Policy*, 3rd edn (New York: W. W. Norton).

Klein, N. (2000), *No Logo* (London: Flamingo).

Klintworth, G. (1989), *Vietnam's Intervention in Cambodia in International Law* (Canberra: AGPS Press).

Knox, P., and Agnew, J. (1994), *The Geography of the World-Economy* (London: Edward Arnold).

Kofman, E., and Youngs, G. (eds) (2003), *Globalization: Theory and Practice*, 2nd edn (London: Continuum).

Kohli, A. (1985), 'The Politics of Land Reform', in A. Gauhar (ed.), *Third World Affairs* (London: Third World Foundation).

Kolawoski, L. (1978), *The Main Currents of Marxism*. Vol. 1 *The Founders*. Vol. 2 *The Golden Age*. Vol. 3 *The Breakdown* (Oxford: Oxford University Press).

Koskenniemi, M. (1989), *From Apology to Utopia: The Structure of International Legal Argument* (Helsinki: Finnish Lawyers Publishing Co.).

Kotschwar, B. R. (1995), 'South–South Economic Cooperation: Regional Trade Agreements among Developing Countries', *Cooperation South* (New York: UN Development Programme).

Krasner, S. D. (1985), *Structural Conflict: The Third World Against Global Liberalism* (Berkeley: University of California Press).

——(1991), 'Global Communications and National Power: Life on the Pareto Frontier', *World Politics*, 43: 336–66.

——(1993), 'Sovereignty, Regimes and Human Rights', in V. Rittberger (ed.), *Regime Theory and International Relations* (Oxford: Clarendon Press).

——(1999), *Sovereignty: Organized Hypocrisy* (Princeton, NJ: Princeton University Press).

——(ed.) (1983), *International Regimes* (Ithaca, NY: Cornell University Press).

Kratochwil, F. (1989), *Rules, Norms, and Decisions* (Cambridge: Cambridge University Press).

——(1993), 'The Embarrassment of Changes: Neo-Realism as the Science of *Realpolitik* without Politics', *Review of International Studies*, 19(1): 63–80.

Krause, K. (ed.) (1999), *Culture and Security. Multilateral Arms Control and Security Building* (London: Frank Cass).

——and Williams, M. C. (eds) (1997), *Critical Security Studies: Concepts and Cases* (London: UCL Press).

Krauthammer, C. (1990–1), 'The Unipolar Moment', *Foreign Affairs*, 70: 23–33.

——(1992), 'In Bosnia, Partition Might Do', *International Herald Tribune*, 9 Sept.

Krugman, P. (1999), *The Return of Depression Economics* (London: Allen Lane, Penguin Press).

Kupchan, Charles A. (2002), *The End of the American Era: US Foreign Policy and the Geopolitics of the Twenty-first Century* (New York: Knopf).

——and Kupchan, Clifford A. (1991), 'Concerts, Collective Security and the Future of Europe', *International Security*, 16(1).

————(1993), 'The Promise of Collective Security', *International Security*, 20(1).

————(1995), 'The Promise of Collective Security', *International Security*, 20(10) (Summer).

Kurth Cronin, A. K. (2002), 'Behind the Curve: Globalization and International Terrorism', *International Security*, 27(3): 30–58.

Kymlicka, W. (1989), *Liberalism, Community, and Culture* (Oxford: Oxford University Press).

Laidi, Z. (1998), *A World Without Meaning: The Crisis of Meaning in International Politics* (London: Routledge).

Lang Jr., A. F. (2002), *Agency and Ethics: the Politics of Military Intervention* (New York: State University of New York Press).

Lapid, Y. (1989), 'The Third Debate: On the Prospects of International Theory in a Post-Positivist Era', *International Studies Quarterly*, 33(3): 225–35.

Laqueur, W. (1996), 'Post-modern Terrorism', *Foreign Affairs*, 75(5): 24–37.

Latham, R. (1997), *The Liberal Moment: Modernity, Security, and the Making of Post-war International Order* (New York: Columbia University Press).

Lavoy, P. (1995), 'The Strategic Consequences of Nuclear Proliferation. A Review Essay', *Security Studies*, 4(4): 695–753.

Lawler, L. (1995), 'The Core Assumptions and Presumptions of "Cooperative Security" ', in S. Lawson (ed.), *The New Agenda for Global Security: Cooperating for Peace and Beyond* (St Leonards: Allen & Unwin).

Lebow, R., and Stein, J. (1994), 'Reagan and the Russians', *Atlantic Monthly*, 273(2) Feb.: 35–7.

Lenin, V. I. ([1917] 1966), *Imperialism, the Highest Stage of Capitalism: A Popular Outline*, 13th edn (Moscow: Progress Publishers).

Lessig, L. (1999), *Code and Other Laws of Cyberspace* (New York: Basic Books).

Leventhal, P., and Alexander, Y. (eds) (1987), *Preventing Nuclear Terrorism* (Lexington, Mass., and Toronto: Lexington Books).

Levy, B., and Spiller, P. T. (eds) (1996), *Regulations, Institutions, and Commitment: Comparative Studies of Telecommunications* (New York: Cambridge University Press).

Levy, M. A., Young, O. R., and Zurn, M. (1995), 'The Study of International Regimes', *European Journal of International Relations*, 1(3): 267–330.

Linklater, A. (1990a), *Men and Citizens in the Theory of International Relations*, 2nd edn; 1st edn 1982 (London: Macmillan).

——(1990b), *Beyond Realism and Marxism: Critical Theory and International Relations* (London: Macmillan).

——(1996), 'The Achievements of Critical Theory', in S. Smith, K. Booth, and M. Zalewski (eds), *International Theory: Positivism and Beyond* (Cambridge: Cambridge University Press): 279–98.

——(1998), *The Transformation of Political Community: Ethical Foundations of the Post-Westphalian Era* (Cambridge: Polity).

——(1999), 'The Evolving Spheres of International Justice', *International Affairs*, 75(3).

Little, R. (1996), 'The Growing Relevance of Pluralism?', in S. Smith, K. Booth, and M. Zalewski (eds), *International Theory: Positivism and Beyond* (Cambridge: Cambridge University Press): 66–86.

Long, D. (1996), 'The Harvard School of International Theory: A Case for Closure', *Millennium*, 24(3): 489–506.

Longino, H. E. (1990), *Science as Social Knowledge: Values and Objectivity in Scientific Inquiry* (Princeton, NJ: Princeton University Press).

Luard, E. (ed.) (1992), *Basic Texts in International Relations* (London: Macmillan).

Luttwak, E. (1998), *Turbo Capitalism: Winners and Losers in the Global Economy* (London: Weidenfield & Nicolson).

Lynch, C. (1998), 'Social Movements and the Problem of Globalization', *Alternatives*, 23(2): 149–73.

Lyons, G. M., and Mastanduno, M. (eds) (1995), *Beyond Westphalia—State Sovereignty and International Intervention* (Baltimore and London: Johns Hopkins University Press).

Lyotard, J.-F. (1984), *The Post-modern Condition: A Report on Knowledge* (Manchester: Manchester University Press).

McDougal, M., and Reisman, M. (1983), 'International Law in Policy-Oriented Perspective', in R. MacDonald and D. Johnston (eds), *The Structure and Process of International Law* (The Hague: Martinus Nijhoff).

McGrew, A. (2002), 'From Global Governance to Good Governance: Theories and Prospects of Democratizing the Global Polity', in M. Ougaard and R. Higgott (eds), *Towards a Global Polity?* (London: Routledge).

——Lewis, P., *et al.* (1992), *Global Politics* (Cambridge: Polity Press).

Machiavelli, N. (1965), *The Art of War*, ed. N. Wood (New York: Da Capo Press).

——(1988), *The Prince*, ed. Q. Skinner (Cambridge: Cambridge University Press).

Mackinnon, C. (1993), 'Crimes of War, Crimes of Peace', in S. Shute and S. Hurley (eds), *On Human Rights* (New York: Basic Books).

McLuhan, M. (1964), *Understanding Media* (London: Routledge).

McMichael, P. (1996), 'Globalization: Myths and Realities', *Rural Sociology*, 61(1): 257–77.

McNamara, R. S. (1999), 'Reflecting on War in the Twenty-first Century: The Context for Nuclear Abolition', in J. Baylis and R. O'Neill (eds), *Alternative Nuclear Futures: The Role of Nuclear Weapons in the Post-Cold War World* (Oxford: Oxford University Press): 167–82).

McNeill, W. H. (1982), *The Pursuit of Power: Armed Force, Technology and Society* (Oxford: Blackwell).

Malone, D. (ed.) (2004), *The UN Security Council: From the Cold War to the 21st Century* (Boulder, Col.: Lynne Rienner).

Mann, M. (1986), *The Sources of Social Power*, Vol. 1. *A History of Power from the Beginning to AD 1760* (Cambridge: Cambridge University Press).

——(1992), *States, War and Capitalism: Studies in Political Sociology* (Oxford: Blackwell).

——(1993), *The Sources of Social Power*, Vol. 2. *The Rise of Classes and Nation States, 1760–1914* (Cambridge: Cambridge University Press).

——(2003), *Incoherent Empire* (London: Verso).

Mansbach, R., Ferguson, Y., and Lampert, D. (1976), *The Web of World Politics* (Englewood Cliffs, NJ: Prentice-Hall).

Marks, G., *et al.* (1996*a*), 'European Integration from the 1980s: State-Centric v. Multilevel Governance', *Journal of Common Market Studies*, 34(3): 341–79.

Marshall, J. (ed.) (1996), *The New Interventionism 1991–1994* (Cambridge: Cambridge University Press).

Marshall, T. H. (1973), *Class, Citizenship and Social Development* (Westport, Conn.: Greenwood Press).

Martel, G. (1986) (ed.), *The Origins of the Second World War Reconsidered* (London: Allen & Unwin).

Marx, K. (1992), *Capital: Student Edition*, ed. C. J. Arthur (London: Lawrence & Wishart). First published 1867.

——and Engels, F. (1967), *The Communist Manifesto*, with an Introduction by A. J. P. Taylor (Harmondsworth: Penguin): 83–4.

Mastanduno, M. (2000), 'Models, Markets and Power: Political Economy and the Asia-Pacific, 1989–1999', *Review of International Studies*, 26(4): 493–508.

Mathews, J. T. (1997), 'Power Shift', *Foreign Affairs*, Jan./Feb.

Mattingly, G. (1955), *Renaissance Diplomacy* (Harmondsworth: Penguin).

Mattli, W. (1999), *The Logic of Regional Integration: Europe and Beyond* (Cambridge: Cambridge University Press).

——and Slaughter, A. (1995), 'Law and Politics in the European Union: A Reply to Garrett', *International Organization*, 49(1): 183–90.

————(1998), 'Revisiting the European Court of Justice', *International Organization*, 52(1): 177–210.

Mayall, J. (1990), *Nationalism and International Society* (Cambridge: Cambridge University Press).

——(1991), 'Non-Intervention, Self-Determination and the "New World Order" ', *International Affairs*, 67.

——(1996), *Interventionism, 1991–1994* (Cambridge: Cambridge University Press).

Mazarr, M. (1995), 'Virtual Nuclear Arsenals', *Survival*, 37(3).

Mazower, M. (1999), *Dark Continent: Europe's Twentieth Century* (Harmondsworth: Penguin).

Meadows, D. H., Meadows, D. L., and Randers, J. (1972), *The Limits to Growth* (London: Earth Island).

————(1992), *Beyond the Limits: Global Collapse or a Sustainable Future* (London: Earthscan).

Mearsheimer, J. (1990), 'Back to the Future: Instability After the Cold War', *International Security*, 15(1): 5–56.

——(1994/5), 'The False Promise of International Institutions', *International Security* 19(3): 5–49.

——(2001), *The Tragedy of Great Power Politics* (New York: W. W. Norton).

——and Walt, S. (2003), 'An Unnecessary War', *Foreign Policy* (Jan.–Feb.): 51–9.

Médecins Sans Frontières (2000), *Notes from the Field: The Work of Médecins Sans Frontières* (London: Médecins Sans Frontières).

Meinecke, F. (1957), *Machiavellism: The Doctrine of 'Raison d'Etat' and Its Place in Modern History*, trans. D. Scott (London: Routledge).

Mendlovitz, S. (1975), *On the Creation of a Just World Order* (New York: Free Press).

Merrill, D., and Paterson, T. (eds) (2000), *Major Problems in American Foreign Relations*, Vol. 2, 6th edn (Boston, Mass.: Houghton Mifflin).

Metcalf, T. (1997), *Ideologies of the Raj* (Cambridge: Cambridge University Press).

Meyer, M., and Prugl, E. (eds) (1999), *Gender Politics and Global Governance* (New York: Rowan & Littlefield).

Meyer, S. M. (1984), *The Dynamics of Nuclear Proliferation* (Chicago: University of Chicago Press).

Michalet, C.-A. (1982), 'From International Trade to World-Economy: A New Paradigm', in H. Makler *et al.*, *The New International Economy* (London: Sage): 37–58.

Miller, D., (1999), 'Bounded Citizenship', in K. Hutchings and R. Danreuther (eds), *Cosmopolitan Citizenship* (London: Macmillan).

Miller, J. (1993), 'The Challenge of Radical Islam', *Foreign Affairs*, 72.

Miller, P. (1998), *Transformations of Patriarchy in the West, 1500–1900* (Bloomington: Indiana University Press).

Milner, H. V. (1988), *Resisting Protectionism: Global Industries and the Politics of International Trade* (Princeton, NJ: Princeton University Press).

Minear, L., and Weiss, T. G. (1995), *Mercy Under Fire: War and the Global Humanitarian Community* (Boulder, Col.: Westview).

Mitchell, R. (1995), *Bridled Ambition—Why Countries Constrain their Nuclear Capabilities* (Washington, DC: Woodrow Wilson Center).

Mitrany, D. (1943), *A Working Peace System* (London: RIIA).

Modelski, G. (1972), *Principles of World Politics* (New York: Free Press).

——(1988), *Sea Power in Global Politics* 1494–1943 (Seattle: University of Washington Press).

Moellendorf, D. (2002), *Cosmopolitan Justice* (Cambridge, Mass.: Westview).

Mohanty, C., *et al.* (eds) (1991), *Third World Women and the Politics of Feminism* (Bloomington: Indiana University Press).

Molina, M. J., and Rowland, F. S. (1974), 'Stratospheric Sink for Chlorofluoromethanes: Chlorine Atom Catalysed Destruction of Ozone', *Nature*, 249: 810–14.

Moore-Gilbert, B. (1997), *Postcolonial Theory: Contexts, Practices, Politics* (London: Verso).

Moravcsik, A., (1993), 'Preferences and Power in the European Community: A Liberal Intergovernmentalist Approach', *Journal of Common Market Studies*, 31(4): 473–523.

——(1997), 'Taking Preferences Seriously: A Liberal Theory of International Relations', *International Organization*, 51(4): 513–54.

——(2001), ' Constructivism and European Integration: A Critique', in T. Christiansen, K. E. Jørgensen, and A. Wiener (eds), *The Social Construction of Europe* (London: Sage): 176–88.

Morgenthau, H. J. (1940), 'Positivism, Functionalism, and International Law', *American Journal of International Law*, 34(2): 260–84.

——([1948] 1955, 1962, 1978), *Politics Among Nations: The Struggle for Power and Peace*, 2nd edn (New York: Knopf).

——(1985), *Politics Among Nations*, 6th edn (New York: McGraw Hill).

Morse, E. (1976), *Modernization and the Transformation of International Relations* (New York: Free Press).

Morton, A. (1999), 'On Gramsci', *Politics*, 19(1): 1–8.

Moulton, H., and Pasvolsky, L. (1932), *War Debts and World Prosperity* (Washington, DC: Brookings Institution).

Munting, R. (1982), *The Economic Development of the USSR* (London: Macmillan).

Murden, S. (1999), 'Review Article: Huntington and His Critics', *Political Geography*, 18: 1017–22.

Murphy, C. N. (1994), *International Organization and Industrial Change* (Cambridge: Polity Press).

Naím, M. (2002), 'Post-terror surprises', *Foreign Policy*, Sept.–Oct.

Naisbitt, J. (1994), *Global Paradox: The Bigger the World-Economy, the More Powerful its Smallest Players* (London: Brealey).

Nardin, T. (1983), *Law, Morality and the Relations of States* (Princeton, NJ: Princeton University Press).

Naya, S., and Imada, P. (1992), 'Implementing AFTA, 1992–2007', in K. S. Sandhu (ed.), *The ASEAN Reader* (Singapore: Institute of South East Asian Studies).

Nef, J. (1999), *Human Security and Mutual Vulnerability*, 2nd edn (Ottawa: IDRC).

Newman, E., and Richmond, O. P. (eds) (2001), *The United Nations and Human Security* (London: Palgrave).

Nicolson, H. (1954), *The Evolution of Diplomatic Method* (London: Constable).

Nye, J. (2004), *Soft Power: The Means to Success in World Politics* (New York: Public Affairs Ltd).

——(ed.) (1968), *International Regionalism: Readings* (Boston, Mass.: Little, Brown).

Oberdorfer, D. (1992), *The Turn: From the Cold War to a New Era* (New York: Touchstone Books).

O'Brien, P. (1984), 'Europe in the World-Economy', in H. Bull and A. Watson (eds), *The Expansion of International Society* (Oxford: Clarendon Press).

O'Brien, R. (1992), *Global Financial Integration: The End of Geography* (London: Pinter).

——Goetz, A. M., Scholte, J. A., and Williams, M. (2000), *Contesting Global Governance: Multilateral Economic Institutions and Global Social Movements* (Cambridge: Cambridge University Press).

Ogilvie-White, T. (1996), 'Is There A Theory of Nuclear Proliferation?', *The Nonproliferation Review*, 4(1): 43–60.

——and Simpson, J. (2003), 'The NPT and Its PrepCom Session: A Regime in Need of Intensive Care', *The Nonproliferation Review*, 10(1) (Spring): 40–58.

Ohmae, K. (1990), *The Borderless World: Power and Strategy in the Interlinked Economy* (London: Fontana).

Ohmae, K. (1995), *The End of the Nation State: The Rise of Regional Economies* (New York: Free Press).

Olson, M. (1965), *The Logic of Collective Action* (Cambridge: Harvard University Press).

Onuf, N. (1989), *A World of our Making: Rules and Rule in Social Theory and International Relations* (Columbia, SC: University of South Carolina Press).

Onwudiwe, I. D. (2001), *The Globalization of Terror* (Burlington, VT: Ashgate).

'Operation Bojinka' (n.d.), *Wikipedia, the free Encyclopedia*, available online at http://en.wikipedia.org/wiki/Operation_Bojinka, accessed 13 July 2004.

O'Rourke, K. H., and Williamson, J. J. (1999), *Globalization and History: The Evolution of the Nineteenth-Century Atlantic Economy* (Cambridge, Mass.: MIT Press).

Ostrom, E. (1990), *Governing the Commons: Evolution of Institutions for Collective Action* (Cambridge: Cambridge University Press).

Ougaard, M. (2004), *Political Globalization—State, Power and Social Forces* (London: Palgrave).

Owen, R. (1992), *State, Power and Politics in the Making of the Modern Middle East* (London: Routledge).

Oxfam (2003), 'Boxing Match in Agricultural Trade', Briefing Paper No. 32, available online at **www.oxfam.org**.

Oye, K. A. (ed.) (1986), *Cooperation Under Anarchy* (Princeton, NJ: Princeton University Press).

Panagariya, A. (1994), 'East Asia; A New Trading Bloc?', *Finance and Development*, March.

Panofsky, W. K. H. (1998), 'Dismantling The Concept of "Weapons of Mass Destruction" ', *Arms Control Today*, 28(3) (April): 3–8.

Parekh, B. (1997), 'Rethinking Humanitarian Intervention', *International Political Science Review*, 18(1): 49–70.

——(1997a), 'When religion meets politics', *Demos*, 11: 5–7.

Parsons, Sir A. (1995), *From Cold War to Hot Peace: UN Interventions 1947–1995* (Harmondsworth: Penguin).

Pauly, L., and Reich, S. (1997), 'National Structures and Multinational Corporate Behavior: Enduring Differences in the Age of Globalization', *International Organisation*, 51(1): 1–30.

Pearson, R. (2000), 'Rethinking Gender Matters in Development', in T. Allen and A. Thomas (eds), *Poverty and Development into the Twenty-first Century* (Oxford: Oxford University Press): 383–402.

Pendergrast, M. (1993), *For God, Country and Coca-Cola: The Unauthorized History of the Great American Soft Drink and the Company that Makes It* (London: Weidenfeld & Nicolson).

Persaud, R. B. (2002), 'Situating Race in International Relations: The Dialectics of Civilizational Security in American Immigration', in G. Chowdhry and S. Nair (eds), *Power, Post-colonialism and International Relations: Reading Race, Gender and Class* (London: Routledge).

Peters, J. S., and Wolper, A. (eds) (1995), *Women's Rights, Human Rights: International Feminist Perspectives* (New York: Routledge).

Peterson, V. S. (1990), 'Whose Rights? A Critique of the "Givens" in Human Rights Discourse', *Alternatives*, 15.

——(1992), 'Security and Sovereign States: What is at Stake in Taking Feminism Seriously?', in V. S. Peterson (ed.), *Gendered States: Feminist (Re)Visions of International Relations Theory* (London: Lynne Rienner)

——(1994), 'Gendered Nationalism', *Peace Review*, 6.

——(2003), *A Critical Rewriting of Global Political Economy: Reproductive, Productive and Virtual Economies* (London and New York: Routledge).

Petrella, R. (1996), 'Globalization and Internationalization: The Dynamics of the Emerging World Order', in R. Boyer and D. Drache (eds), *States against Markets: The Limits of Globalization* (New York: Routledge).

Pettman, J. J. (1996), *Worlding Women: A Feminist International Politics* (St Leonards: Allen & Unwin).

——(2004), 'Feminist International Relations After September 11, 2001', *Brown Journal of World Affairs*, 10(2): 85–96.

Phillip, D. (1998), *The Fiction of Imperialism: Reading Between International Relations and Postcolonialism* (Washington, DC: Cassell)

Phillips, A. (2000), 'The Political Economy of Russia: Transition or Condition?', in M. Bowker and C. Ross (eds), *Russia after the Cold War* (Harlow: Pearson Education): 121–34.

Pipes, R. (1992), Letter to the Editor, *New York Times*, 6 Nov.

Piscatori, J. (1992), 'Islam and World Politics', in J. Baylis and N. J. Rengger (eds), *Dilemmas of World Politics; International Issues in a Changing World* (Oxford: Oxford University Press).

Ponting, C. (1998), *Progress and Barbarism: The World in the Twentieth Century* (London: Chatto & Windus).

Pope Atkins, G. (1995), *Latin America in the International Political System* (Oxford: Westview).

Porter, G., and Brown, J. W. (1991), *Global Environmental Politics* (Boulder, Col.: Westview).

Porter, M. E. (1990), *The Competitive Advantage of Nations* (London: Macmillan).

——(ed.) (1986), *Competition in Global Industries* (Boston, Mass.: Harvard Business School Press).

Potter, W. (1995), 'Before the Deluge? Assessing the Threat of Nuclear Leakage From the Post-Soviet States', *Arms Control Today*, Oct.

Prebisch, R. (1963), *Towards a Dynamic Development Policy in Latin America* (New York: United Nations).

——(1964), *Towards a New Trade Policy for Development* (New York: United Nations).

Price, R. (1998), 'Reversing the Gun Sights: Transnational Civil Society Targets Land Mines', *International Organization*, 52(3).

——(2004), 'Emerging Customary Norms and Anti-Personnel Landmines', in C. Reus-Smit (ed.), *The Politics of International Law* (Cambridge: Cambridge University Press): 106–30.

——and Reus-Smit, C. (1998), 'Dangerous Liaisons? Critical International Relations Theory and Constructivism', *European Journal of International Relations*, 4(2): 259–94.

——and Tannenwald, N. (1996), 'Norms and Deterrence: The Nuclear and Chemical Weapons Taboos', in P. J. Katzenstein (ed.), *The Culture of National Security: Norms and Identity in World Politics* (New York: Columbia University Press): 114–52.

Pugh, M. (2001), 'Peacekeeping and Humanitarian Intervention', in B. White, R. Little, and M. Smith (eds), *Issues in World Politics*, 2nd edn (London: Palgrave).

Purvis, N. (1991), 'Critical Legal Studies in Public International Law', *Harvard International Law Journal*, 32(1): 81–127.

Raffety, F. W. (1928), *The Works of the Right Honourable Edmund Burke*, Vol. 6 (Oxford: Oxford University Press).

Ramsbotham, O., and Woodhouse, T. (1996), *Humanitarian Intervention in Contemporary Conflict* (Cambridge: Polity Press).

Rapley, J. (1996), *Understanding Development* (Boulder, Col.: Lynne Rienner).

Rawls, J. (1971), *A Theory of Justice* (Oxford: Oxford University Press).

Reich, R. B. (1991), *The Work of Nations: Preparing Ourselves for 21st-Century Capitalism* (New York: Simon & Schuster).

Reinecke, W. (1988), *Global Public Policy: Governing without Government* (Washington, DC: Brookings Institution).

Reiser, O. L., and Davies, B. (1944), *Planetary Democracy: An Introduction to Scientific Humanism and Applied Semantics* (New York: Creative Age Press).

Reiss, H. (ed.) (1989), *Kant's Political Writings* (Cambridge: Cambridge University Press).

Reiss, M. (1995), *Bridled Ambition—Why Countries Constrain Their Nuclear Capabilities* (Washington, DC: Woodrow Wilson Center Press; distributed by the Johns Hopkins University Press, Baltimore).

——and Lutwak, R. (eds) (1994), *Nuclear Proliferation After the Cold War* (Washington, DC: Woodrow Wilson Center Press).

Rengger, N. (1992), 'Culture, Society and Order in World Politics', in J. Baylis and N. J. Rengger (eds), *Dilemmas of World Politics: International Issues in a Changing World* (Oxford: Oxford University Press).

——(2000), *International Relations, Political Theory and the Problem of Order: Beyond International Relations Theory?* (London: Routledge).

Reus-Smit, C. (1999), *The Moral Purpose of the State* (Princeton, NJ: Princeton University Press).

——(2001), 'The Strange Death of Liberal International Theory', *European Journal of International Law*, 12(3): 573–93.

——(2003), 'Politics and International Legal Obligation', *European Journal of International Relations*, 9(4): 591–625.

——(ed.) (2004), *The Politics of International Law* (Cambridge: Cambridge University Press).

Review of International Studies (2000), Special Section on 'The Asian-Pacific Crisis', 26(3): 359–428.

Rheingold, H. (2003), *Smart Mobs: The Next Social Revolution* (Cambridge, Mass.: Perseus).

Rhodes, E. (2003), 'The Imperial Logic of Bush's Liberal Agenda', *Survival* 45: 131–54.

Richardson, J. L. (1994), *Crisis Diplomacy: The Great Powers since the Mid-Nineteenth Century* (Cambridge: Cambridge University Press).

——(1997), 'Contending Liberalisms: Past and Present', *European Journal of International Relations*, 3(1): 5–33.

Risse, T. (2004), 'Social Constructivism and European Integration', in A. Wiener and T. Diez (eds), *European Integration Theory* (Oxford: Oxford University Press): 159–76.

Rittberger, V. (ed.) (1993), *Regime Theory and International Relations* (Oxford: Clarendon Press).

Roberts, A. (1993), 'Humanitarian War: Military Intervention and Human Rights', *International Affairs*, 69.

——(1996), 'The United Nations: Variants of Collective Security', in N. Woods, *Explaining International Relations Since 1945* (Oxford: Oxford University Press): 309–36.

——and Kingsbury, B. (1993), 'Introduction: The UN's Roles in International Society since 1945', in A. Roberts and B. Kingsbury (eds), *United Nations, Divided World* (Oxford: Clarendon Press).

Roberts, G. (1984), *Questioning Development* (London: Returned Volunteer Action).

Roberts, S. (1994), 'Fictitious Capital, Fictitious Spaces: The Geography of Offshore Financial Flows', in S. Corbridge *et al.* (eds), *Money, Power and Space* (Oxford: Blackwell).

Robertson, E. M. (ed.) (1971), *The Origins of the Second World War: Historical Interpretations* (London: Macmillan).

Robertson, R. (1992), *Globalization: Social Theory and Global Culture* (London: Sage).

——(2003), *Three Waves of Globalization: A History of Developing Global Consciousness* (London: Zed Books).

Rodley, N. S. (ed.) (1992), *To Loose the Bonds of Wickedness: International Intervention in Defence of Human Rights* (London: Brasseys).

Rodney, W. (1972), *How Europe Underdeveloped Africa* (London: Bogle–L'Ouverture).

Rodrik, D. (1998), *Has Globalization Gone Too Far?* (Washington, DC: Institute for International Economics).

——(1999), *The New Global Economy and Developing Countries: Making Openness Work* (Washington, DC: Overseas Development Council): 148.

Rorty, R. (1993), 'Sentimentality and Human Rights', in S. Shute and S. Hurley (eds), *On Human Rights* (New York: Basic Books).

Rosamond, B. (2000), *Theories of European Integration* (Basingstoke: Macmillan).

Rosenau, J. N. (1990), *Turbulence in World Politics* (Princeton, NJ: Princeton University Press).

——(1997), 'The Dynamics of Globalization: Toward an Operational Formula', *Security Dialogue*, 27(3): 247–62.

——and Czempiel, E.-O. (1992), *Governance without Government: Order and Change in World Politics* (Cambridge: Cambridge University Press).

Rosenberg, J. (1994), *The Empire of Civil Society: A Critique of the Realist Theory of International Relations* (London: Verso).

——(2000), *The Follies of Globalisation Theory: Polemical Essays* (London: Verso).

Rostow, W. (1960), *The Stages of Economic Growth: A Non-Communist Manifesto* (London: Cambridge University Press).

Rotblat, J. (ed.) (1998), *Nuclear Weapons. The Road to Zero* (Boulder, Col.: Westview).

Roth, K. (2004), 'War in Iraq: Not a Humanitarian Intervention', *Human Rights Watch World Report*. Available online at www.hrw.org/wr2k4/3.htm.

Rousseau, J.-J. (1987), *The Basic Political Writings*, trans. Donald A. Cress (Cambridge: Hackett).

——(1991), 'The State of War', in S. Hoffmann and D. P. Fidler (eds), *Rousseau on International Relations* (Oxford: Clarendon Press).

Roxburgh, A. (1991), *The Second Russian Revolution* (London: BBC Publications).

Ruggie, J. G. (1982), 'International Regimes, Transactions and Change: Embedded Liberalism in the Post-War Economic Order', *International Organisation*, 36(2).

——(1983), 'Continuity and Transformation in the World Polity: Toward a Neo-realist Synthesis', *World Politics*, 35(2) (Jan.): 261–85.

——(1993), 'Multilateralism: The Anatomy of an Institution', in J. G. Ruggie (ed.), *Multilateralism Matters* (New York: Columbia University Press): 3–50.

——(1995), 'At Home Abroad, Abroad at Home: International Liberalisation and Domestic Stability in the New World-Economy', *Millennium: Journal of International Studies*, 24(3): 507–26.

——(1998), *Constructing the World Polity: Essays on International Institutionalization* (London: Routledge).

Rupert, M. (1995), *Producing Hegemony: The Politics of Mass Production and American Global Power* (Cambridge: Cambridge University Press).

Rusi, A. (1997), *Dangerous Peace: New Rivalry in World Politics* (Boulder, Col.: Westview).

Russett, B. (1993), *Grasping the Democratic Peace: Principles for a Post-Cold War World* (Princeton, NJ: Princeton University Press).

——(1995), 'The Democratic Peace', *International Security* 19(4): 164–84.

Sagan, S. D. (1993), *The Limits of Safety: Organisations, Accidents and Nuclear Weapons* (Princeton, NJ: Princeton University Press).

——(1996/7), 'Three Theories in Search of a Bomb', *International Security*, 21(3): 54–86.

——and Waltz, K. N. (1995), *The Spread of Nuclear Weapons: A Debate* (New York and London: W. W. Norton).

Said, E. (1993), *Culture and Imperialism* (New York: Vintage Books).

——(1995), *Orientalism: Western Conceptions of the Orient* (London: Penguin).

Sakwa, R. (1990), *Gorbachev and his Reforms 1985–1990* (London: Routledge).

Sandhu, K. S. (ed.) (1992), *The ASEAN Reader* (Singapore: Institute of South East Asian Studies).

Sargent, L. (ed.) (1981), *Women and Revolution: a Discussion of the Unhappy Marriage of Marxism and Feminism* (Boston, Mass.: South End).

Saurin, J. (1996), 'Globalisation, Poverty and the Promises of Modernity', *Millennium: Journal of International Studies*, 25(3): 657–80.

Scharpf, F. W. (1996), 'Positive and Negative Integration in the Political Economy of European Welfare States', in G. Marks, *et al.*, *Governance in the European Union* (London: Sage).

Scheinman, L. (1987), *The International Atomic Energy Agency and World Nuclear Order* (Washington, DC: Johns Hopkins University Press).

Schelling, T. C. (1960), *The Strategy of Conflict* (Oxford: Oxford University Press).

——and Halperin, M. H. (1961), *Strategy and Arms Control* (New York: The Twentieth Century Fund).

Schlesinger, P. R. (1994), 'Europe's Contradictory Communicative Space', *Daedalus*, 123(2).

Schmidt, B. C. (1998), *The Political Discourse of Anarchy: A Disciplinary History of International Relations* (Albany, NY: State University of New York Press).

Schmitter, P. (1992), 'Representation and the Future Euro-Polity', *Staatswissenschaften und Staatspraxis*, 2(3).

——(2004), 'Neo-Neofunctionalism', in A. Wiener and T. Diez (eds), *European Integration Theory* (Oxford: Oxford University Press): 45–74.

Scholte, J. A. (1993), *International Relations of Social Change* (Buckingham: Open University Press).

——(1996), 'Globalisation and Collective Identities', in J. Krause and N. Renwick (eds), *Identities in International Relations* (London: Macmillan).

——(1997a), *Globalisation: A Critical Introduction* (London: Macmillan).

——(1997b), 'Global Capitalism and the State', *International Affairs*, 73(3): 427–52.

——(2000), *Globalization: A Critical Introduction* (Basingstoke: Macmillan).

Schumacher, E. F. (1973), *Small is Beautiful: Economics as if People Mattered* (New York: Harper & Row).

Schweller, R. L. (1996), 'Neo-realism's Status-Quo Bias: What Security Dilemma?', *Security Studies*, 5: 90–121.

Scruton, R. (2002), *The West and the Rest: Globalization and the Terrorist Threat* (London: Continuum).

Seager, J. (2003), *The Penguin Atlas of Women in the World* (New York: Penguin). Available online at www.MyriadEditions.com.

Seaman, J. (1996), 'The International System of Humanitarian Relief in the "New World Order" ', in J. Harriss (ed.), *The Politics of Humanitarian Intervention* (London: Pinter): 17–32.

Seidler, V. (1989), *Rediscovering Masculinity: Reason, Language and Sexuality* (London: Routledge).

Sen, A. (1981), *Poverty and Famines* (Oxford: Clarendon Press).

——(1983), 'The Food Problem: Theory and Policy', in A. Gauhar (ed.), *South–South Strategy* (London: Zed).

——(1997), 'Rational Fools: A Critique of the Behavioural Foundations of Economic Theory', *Philosophy and Public Affairs*, 6(4): 713–44.

——(1999), *Development as Freedom* (Oxford: Oxford University Press).

Shaker, M. I. (1980), *The Nuclear Non-Proliferation Treaty*, Vols 1–2 (London: Oceana).

Shannon, T. R. (1989 and 1996), *An Introduction to the World-System Perspective* (Boulder, Col.: Westview).

Sharpe, A. (1996), 'Exotic Derivatives "Less Favoured" ', *Financial Times*, 12 Feb.: 8.

Shaw, M. (1994), *Global Society and International Relations* (Cambridge: Polity Press).

——(1997), 'The State of Globalization: Towards a Theory of State Transformation', *Review of International Political Economy*, 4(3).

——(1999), 'The Global Revolution and the Twenty-first Century: From International Relations to Global Politics', in S. Chan and J. Wiener (eds), *Twentieth Century International History* (London: I. B. Tauris).

——(2000), *Theory of the Global State: Globality as an Unfinished Revolution* (Cambridge: Cambridge University Press).

——(2003), *War and Genocide: Organized Killing in Modern Society* (Cambridge: Polity Press).

——(ed.) (1984), *War, State, and Society* (New York: St Martin's Press).

Shue, H. (1980), *Basic Rights* (Princeton, NJ: Princeton University Press).

Shute, S., and Hurley, S. (eds) (1993), *On Human Rights* (New York: Basic Books).

Simon, J. (1998), 'Refugees in a Carceral Age: The Rebirth of Immigration Prisons in the United States', *Public Culture*, 10(3): 577–607.

Simpson, J., and Howlett, D. (eds) (1995), *The Future of the Non-Proliferation Treaty* (New York: St Martin's Press).

Sinclair, T. J. (1994), 'Passing Judgement: Credit Rating Processes as Regulatory Mechanisms of Governance in the Emerging World Order', *Review of International Political Economy*, 1 (Spring).

Singer, H., and Roy, S. (1993), *Economic Progress and Prospects in the Third World* (Aldershot: Edward Elgar).

Singer, M., and Wildavsky, A. (1993), *The Real World Order: Zones of Peace/Zones of Turmoil* (New Jersey: Chatham House Publishers).

Singer, P. (1985), *Marx* (Oxford: Oxford University Press).

Sivan, E. (1989), 'Sunni Radicalism in the Middle East and the Iranian Revolution', *International Journal of Middle Eastern Studies*, 21(1).

Skinner, Q. (1988), 'Meaning and Understanding in the History of Ideas', in J. Tully (ed.), *Meaning and Context: Quentin Skinner and his Critics* (Cambridge: Polity Press): 29–67.

Skocpol, T. (1977), 'Wallerstein's World Capitalist System: A Theoretical and Historical Critique', *American Journal of Sociology*, 82(5).

——(1979), *States and Social Revolutions: a Comparative Analysis of France, Russia, and China* (Cambridge: Cambridge University Press).

——(1992), *Protecting Soldiers and Mothers* (Cambridge, Mass.: Harvard University Press).

——(ed.) (1984), *Vision and Method in Historical Sociology* (Cambridge: Cambridge University Press).

Slaughter, A. (1995), 'International Law in a World of Liberal States', *European Journal of International Law*, 6.

——(2000), 'A Liberal Theory of International Law' (unpublished manuscript).

——(2004), *A New World Order* (Princeton, NJ: Princeton University Press).

Smith, A. (1983), *Theories of Nationalism*, 2nd edn (London: Duckworth).

—— (1991), *National Identity* (London: Penguin).

Smith, D. (1991), *The Rise of Historical Sociology* (Cambridge: Polity Press).

Smith, K. E., and Light, M. (eds) (2001), *Ethics and Foreign Policy* (Cambridge: Cambridge University Press).

Smith, M. (1986), *Realist Thought from Weber to Kissinger* (Baton Rouge: Louisiana State University Press).

Smith, M. (2002), 'On Thin Ice: First Steps for the Ballistic Missile Code of Conduct', *Arms Control Today*, 32(6) (July): 9–13.

Smith, S. (2000), 'Wendt's World', *Review of International Studies*, 26(1): 151–63.

—— Booth, K., and Zalewski, M. (eds) (1996), *International Theory: Positivism and Beyond* (Cambridge: Cambridge University Press).

Snidal, D. (2000), 'The Concept of Legalization', *International Organization*, 54: 401–20.

Snitow, A. (1989), 'Pages from a Gender Diary: Basic Divisions in Feminism', *Dissent*, 36: 205–24.

Snyder, J. (1991), *Myths of Empire: Domestic Politics and International Ambition* (Ithaca, NY: Cornell University Press).

Soros, G. (1998), *The Crisis of Global Capitalism* (London: Little, Brown).

South Commission (1990), *The Challenge to the South* (Oxford: Oxford University Press).

Spector, L., McDonough, M., with Medeiros, E. (1995), *Tracking Nuclear Proliferation: A Guide to Maps and Charts*, (Washington, DC: Carnegie Endowment for International Peace).

Spero, J. (1981), *The Politics of International Economic Relations* (New York: St Martin's Press).

Spivak, G. C. (1987), *In Other Worlds: Essays in Cultural Politics* (London: Routledge).

—— (1988), 'Can the Subaltern Speak?', in C. Nelson and L. Grossberg (eds), *Marxism and the Interpretation of Culture* (Basingstoke: Macmillan).

—— (1998), 'Cultural Talks on the Hot Peace: Revisiting the "Global Village" ', in P. Cheah and B. Robbins (eds), *Cosmopolitics: Thinking and Feeling Beyond the Nation* (Minneapolis: University of Minnesota Press).

Staar, H. (1999), *Anarchy, Order, and Integration: How to Manage Interdependence* (Ann Arbor, Mich.: University of Michigan Press).

State, Department of, International Intervention Programmes (2002), available at www.usinfo.state.gov/regional/eur/terrorism/bush1007.htm (accessed 16 March 2002).

Steans, J. (1998), *Gender and International Relations: An Introduction* (Cambridge: Polity Press).

Stein, A. (1982), 'Coordination and Collaboration in an Anarchic World', *International Organization*, 36(2): 299–324.

—— (1983), 'Coordination and Collaboration in an Anarchic World', in S. D. Krasner (ed.), *International Regimes* (Ithaca, NY: Cornell University Press): 115–40.

Stiglitz, J. (1998), 'Towards a New Paradigm for Development: Strategies, Policies and Processes', The Prebisch Lecture (Geneva, UNCTAD, 19 Oct.). Available online at www.worldbank.org/html/etme/jssp101998.htm.

Stopford, J., and Strange, S. (1991), *Rival States, Rival Firms: Competition for World Market Shares* (Cambridge: Cambridge University Press).

Strange, S. (1970), 'International Relations and International Economics: A Case of Mutual Neglect', *International Affairs*, 46(2): 304–15.

—— (1988), *States and Markets* (London: Pinter).

—— (1994a), 'Wake up, Krasner! The world HAS changed', *Review of International Political Economy*, 1(2).

—— (1994b), *States and Markets*, 2nd edn. (London: Pinter).

Stubbs, R. (2002), Review of 'The Many Faces of Asian Security' (ed. Sheldon W. Simon), *Contemporary South-east Asia*, 24: 1.

Suganami, H. (1989), *The Domestic Analogy and World Order Proposals* (Cambridge: Cambridge University Press).

Tang, J. H. (ed.) (1994), *Human Rights and International Relations in the Asia-Pacific Region* (London: Pinter).

Tannenwald, N. (1999), 'The Nuclear Taboo: The United States and the Normative Basis of Nuclear Non-Use', *International Organization*, 53(3): 433–68.

Taylor, A. J. P. (1961), *The Origins of the Second World War* (Harmondsworth: Penguin).

—— (1983), *A Personal History* (London: Hamish Hamilton).

Taylor, P. (1995), *International Organization in the Modern World* (London: Pinter).

—— (1996a), *The European Union since the 1990s* (Oxford: Oxford University Press).

—— (1996b), 'Options for the Reform of the International System for Humanitarian Assistance', in J. Harriss (ed.), *The Politics of Humanitarian Intervention* (London: Pinter).

—— (2003), *The United Nations in the Age of Globalization* (London: Continuum).

—— and Groom, A. J. R. (1992), *The United Nations and the Gulf War, 1990–91*, RIIS Discussion Paper No. 38.

—— —— (eds) (1989), *Global Issues in the United Nations Framework* (Basingstoke: Macmillan).

Terriff, T., Croft, S., James, L., and Morgan, P. (1999), *Security Studies Today* (Cambridge: Polity Press).

Thomas, A., *et al.* (1994), *Third World Atlas*, 2nd edn (Milton Keynes: Open University Press).

Thomas, C. (1985), *New States, Sovereignty and Intervention* (Aldershot: Gower).

—— (1993), 'The Pragmatic Case Against Intervention', in I. Forbes and M. Hoffmann (eds), *Political Theory*,

International Relations and the Ethics of Intervention (Basingstoke: St Martin's Press).

——(1999), 'Where is the Third World Now?', *Review of International Studies*, Dec., special millennium edn.

——(2000), *Global Governance, Development and Human Security* (London: Pluto).

——and Wilkin, P. (2004), 'Still waiting after all these years: the Third World on the periphery of International Relations', *British Journal of Politics and International Relations*, 6: 223–40.

Thomas, Sir J., and Tickell, Sir C. (1993), *The Expanding Role of the United Nations and its Implications* (London: HMSO).

Thompson, E. (1990), 'The Ends of Cold War', *New Left Review*, 182 (July/Aug.): 139–46.

Thucydides ([1954] 1972), *The Peloponnesian War*, trans. R. Warner (London: Penguin).

Tickner, J. A. (1988), 'Hans Morgenthau's Principles of Political Realism: A Feminist Reformulation', *Millennium*, 17(3): 429–40.

——(1992), *Gender in International Relations: Feminist Perspectives on Achieving Global Security* (New York: Columbia University Press).

Tilly, C. (1981), *As Sociology Meets History* (New York: Academic Press).

——(1990), *Coercion, Capital, and European States, AD 990–1990* (Oxford: Blackwell).

——(1992), *Coercion, Capital and European States, AD 900–1992* (Cambridge, Mass.: Blackwell).

Tocqueville, A. (1933), *De Tocqueville's Ancien Regime*, trans. M. W. Patterson (Oxford: Blackwell).

Treadgold, A. (1993), 'Cross-Border Retailing in Europe: Present Status and Future Prospects', in H. Cox *et al.* (eds), *The Growth of Global Business* (London: Routledge).

Tsikata, D. (1995), 'Effects of Structural Adjustment on Women and the Poor', *Third World Resurgence*, 61(2): 56–9.

Tucker, R. W. (1977), *The Inequality of Nations* (New York: Basic Books).

UN (1999), *1999 World Survey on the Role of Women in Development: Globalization, Gender and Work* (New York: UN).

UN Centre on Transnational Corporations (1988), *Transnational Corporations in World Development. Trends and Prospects* (New York: United Nations).

UN Conference on Environment and Development (1992), *Nations of the Earth* (New York: United Nations).

UN Conference on Trade and Development, Division on Transnational Corporations and Investment (1995), *World Investment Report 1995* (New York: United Nations).

UNCTAD (1996), *Transnational Corporations and World Development* (London: International Thomson Business Press).

——(1999), *World Investment Report 1999: Foreign Direct Investment and the Challenge of Development* (Geneva: United Nations Conference on Trade and Development).

UNDP (1994–), *United Nations Human Development Report* (New York: Oxford University Press).

——(2003), *United Nations Human Development Report* (New York: UNDP).

UNESCO (1998), *World Culture Report: Culture, Creativity and Markets* (Paris: UNESCO).

UNFPA/Myers, N. (1991), *Population, Resources and the Environment* (New York: UNFPA).

United Nations Development Fund for Women (2000), *Women at the Peace Table* (New York: UN).

United Nations Economic and Social Council (2003), *World Public Sector Report 2002: E-Government at the Crossroads* (New York: UN).

United Nations Human Development Commission (2003), *United Nations Human Development Report*. Available online at http://hdr.undp.org/reports/global/2003/.

Urquhart, Sir B. (1991), *A Life in Peace and War* (New York: Harper & Row).

Urwin, D. (1995), *The Community of Europe: A History of European Integration Since 1945 (The Post-war World)* (London: Addison-Wesley Longman).

Van der Wee, H. (1987), *Prosperity and Upheaval: The World-Economy 1945–1980* (Harmondsworth: Penguin).

Vasquez, J. A. (1983), *The Power of Power Politics: A Critique* (London: Pinter).

——(1993), *The War Puzzle* (Cambridge: Cambridge University Press).

——(1998), *The Power of Power Politics: From Classical Realism to Neotraditionalism* (Cambridge: Cambridge University Press).

Vincent, R. J. (1974), *Nonintervention and International Order* (Princeton, NJ: Princeton University Press).

——(1981), 'The Hobbesian Tradition in Twentieth Century International Thought', *Millennium*, 10(2).

——(1982), 'Realpolitik', in J. Mayall (ed.), *The Community of States* (London: George Allen & Unwin).

——(1986), *Human Rights and International Relations* (Cambridge: Cambridge University Press).

——and Wilson, P. (1993), 'Beyond Non-intervention', in I. Forbes and M. Hoffmann (eds), *Political Theory, International Relations and the Ethics of Intervention* (London: Macmillan): 122–32.

Viner, J. (1948), 'Power versus Plenty as Objectives of Foreign Policy in the Seventeenth and Eighteenth Centuries', *World Politics*, 1(1): 1–29.

Viotti, P. R., and Kauppi, M. V. (1993), *International Relations Theory: Realism, Pluralism, Globalism* (New York: Macmillan).

Viotti, P. R., and Kauppi, M. V. (eds) (1999), *International Relations Theory: Realism, Pluralism, Globalism and Beyond* (Boston: Allyn and Bacon).

Virilio, P. (1989), *War and Cinema: the Logistics of Perception* (London: Verso).

——(1998), *The Virilio Reader* (ed. James Der Derian) (Oxford: Blackwell).

——(2002), *Desert Screen: War at the Speed of Light* (London: Continuum).

Vitalis, R. (2000), 'The Graceful and Generous Liberal Gesture: Making Racism Invisible in American International Relations', *Millennium*, 29(2): 331–56.

Vogel, L. (1995), *Woman Questions: Essays for a Materialist Feminism* (London: Routledge).

Von Martens, G. F. (1795), *Summary of the Law of Nations Founded on the Treaties and Customs of Modern Nations* (Philadelphia: Thomas Bradford).

Wade, R. (1996), 'Globalization and its Limits: Reports of the Death of the National Economy are Greatly Exaggerated', in S. Berger and R. Dore (eds), *National Diversity and Global Capitalism* (Ithaca, NY: Cornell University Press).

Waever, O. (1996), 'The Rise and Fall of the Inter-Paradigm Debate', in S. Smith, K. Booth, and M. Zalewski (eds), *International Theory: Positivism and Beyond* (Cambridge: Cambridge University Press): 149–85.

——Buzan, B., Kelstrup, M., and Lemaitre, P. (1993), *Identity, Migration and the New Security Agenda in Europe* (London: Pinter).

Walker, R. B. J. (1993), *Inside/Outside: International Relations as Political Theory* (Cambridge: Cambridge University Press).

Walker, W., and Lönnroth, M. (1983), *Nuclear Power Struggles: Industrial Competition and Proliferation Control* (London: Allen & Unwin).

Wallace, H. (2000), 'The Policy Process', in H. Wallace and W. Wallace (eds), *Policy-making in the European Union* (Oxford: Oxford University Press).

Wallace, W. (ed.) (1990), *The Dynamics of European Integration* (London: Pinter).

Waller, M., and Linklater, A. (eds) (2003), *Political Loyalty and the Nation-State* (London: Routledge).

Wallerstein, I. (1974), *The Modern World-System*. Vol. 1 *Capitalist Agriculture and the Origins of the European World-Economy in the Sixteenth Century* (San Diego: Academic Press).

——(1979), *The Capitalist World-Economy* (Cambridge: Cambridge University Press).

——(1980), *The Modern World-System*. Vol. 2 *Mercantilism and the Consolidation of the European World-Economy, 1600–1750* (San Diego: Academic Press).

——(1984), *The Politics of the World-Economy: The States, the Movements, and the Civilisations* (Cambridge: Cambridge University Press).

——(1989), *The Modern World-System*. Vol. 3 *The Second Era of Great Expansion of the Capitalist World-Economy* (San Diego: Academic Press).

——(1991a), *Unthinking Social Science: The Limits of Nineteenth-Century Paradigms* (Cambridge: Polity Press).

——(1991b), *Geopolitics and Geoculture: Essays on the Changing World-System* (Cambridge: Cambridge University Press).

——(1994), 'The Agonies of Liberalism—What Hope Progress?', *New Left Review*, 204.

——(1995), *After Liberalism* (New York: New Press).

——(1996), 'The Inter-State Structure of the Modern World-System', in S. Smith, K. Booth, and M. Zalewski (eds), *International Theory: Positivism and Beyond* (Cambridge: Cambridge University Press).

——(1998), *Utopistics: Or Historical Choices of the Twenty-First Century* (New York: New Press).

——(1999), *The End of the World as We Know it: Social Science for the Twenty-First Century* (Minneapolis: University of Minnesota Press).

——(2003), *The Decline of American Power: The US in a Chaotic World* (New York: New Press).

Walt, S. (1998), 'International Relations: One World, Many Theories', *Foreign Policy*, 110: 29–46.

——(2002), 'The Enduring Relevance of the Realist Tradition', in I. Katznelson and H. V. Milner (eds), *Political Science: The State of the Discipline* (New York: W. W. Norton).

Waltz, K. (1954), *Man, the State and War* (New York: Columbia University Press).

——(1959), *Man, the State and War* (New York: Columbia University Press).

——(1979), *Theory of International Politics* (Reading, Mass.: Addison-Wesley).

——(1981), *The Spread of Nuclear Weapons: More May Be Better*, Adelphi Paper 171 (London: International Institute for Strategic Studies).

——(1989), 'The Origins of War in Neorealist Theory', in R. I. Rotberg and T. K. Rabb (eds), *The Origin and Prevention of Major Wars* (Cambridge: Cambridge University Press): 39–52.

——(2000), 'Globalization and American Power', *The National Interest*, 59 (Spring): 46–56.

——(2002), 'The Continuity of International Politics', in K. Booth and T. Dunne (eds), *Worlds in Collision: Terror and the Future of Global Order* (London: Palgrave Macmillan).

Walzer, M. (1977), *Just and Unjust Wars: A Moral Argument with Historical Illustration* (Harmondsworth: Penguin, and New York: Basic Books).

——(1994a), *Thick and Thin: Moral Argument at Home and Abroad* (Notre Dame, Ind.: University of Notre Dame Press).

——(1994b), 'Spheres of Affection', *Boston Review*, 19(5): 29.

——(1995a), *The Spheres of Justice: A Defence of Pluralism and Equality* (Oxford: Blackwell).

——(1995*b*), 'The Politics of Rescue', *Dissent* (Winter).

Warren, B. (1980), *Imperialism: Pioneer of Capitalism* (London: New Left Books).

Washbrook, D. (1990), 'South Asia, The World System and World Capitalism', *Journal of Asian Studies*, 49(3).

Waters, M. (1995), *Globalization* (London: Routledge).

Watson, A. (1982), *Diplomacy: The Dialogue Between States* (London: Methuen)

Watson, A. (1992), *The Evolution of International Society* (London: Routledge).

Weber, C. (1995), *Simulating Sovereignty: Intervention, the State and Symbolic Exchange* (Cambridge: Cambridge University Press).

Weber, H. (2001), *The Politics of Microcredit: Global Governance and Poverty Reduction* (London: Pluto).

——(2002), 'Global Governance and Poverty Reduction', in S. Hughes and R. Wilkinson (eds), *Global Governance: Critical Perspectives* (London: Palgrave): ch. 8.

——(2004), 'Reconstituting the "Third World"? Poverty Reduction and Territoriality in the Global Politics of Development', *Third World Quarterly*, 25(1): 187–206.

Weber, M. (1949), *The Methodology of the Social Sciences*, E. Shils and H. Finch (eds) (New York: Free Press).

Webster (1961), *Webster's Third New International Dictionary of the English Language Unabridged* (Springfield, Mass.: Merriam).

Wedgwood, C. V. (1992), *The Thirty Years War* (London: Pimlico).

Weiler, J. (1991*a*), 'Problems of Legitimacy in Post-1992 Europe', *Aussenwirtschaft*, 46(3–4).

——(1991*b*), 'The Transformation of Europe', *Yale Law Journal*, 100(8): 2403–83.

Weiss, L. (1998), *The Myth of the Powerless State* (Ithaca, NY: Cornell University Press).

——(1999), 'Globalization and Governance', *Review of International Studies*, 25 (Special Issue).

Weiss, T. G., *et al.* (1994), *The United Nations and Changing World Politics* (Boulder, Col.: Westview).

Wendt, A. (1987), 'The Agent-Structure Problem in International Relations', *International Organization*, 41(3): 335–70.

——(1992), 'Anarchy is What States Make of It: The Social Construction of Power Politics', *International Organisation*, 46(2): 391–425.

——(1994), 'Collective Identity Formation and the International State', *American Political Science Review*, 88(2): 384–96.

——(1995), 'Constructing International Politics', *International Security* 20(1).

——(1998), 'Constitution and Causation in International Relations', *Review of International Studies*, 24: 101–18.

——(1999), *Social Theory of International Politics* (Cambridge: Cambridge University Press).

Weston, B. H., Falk, R., and D'Amato, A. (1990), *Basic Documents in International Law*, 2nd edn (St. Paul, Minn.: West Publishing).

Wheeler, N. J. (1996), 'Guardian Angel or Global Gangster? A Review of the Ethical Claims of the Society of States', *Political Studies*, 44(2).

——(2000), *Saving Strangers: Humanitarian Intervention in International Society* (Oxford: Oxford University Press).

——(2004*a*), 'Humanitarian Intervention after September 11', in A. Lang (ed.), *Just Intervention* (Georgetown: Georgetown University Press).

——(2004*b*), 'The Kosovo Bombing Campaign', in C. Reus-Smit (ed.), *The Politics of International Law* (Cambridge: Cambridge University Press): 189–216.

——and Booth, K. (1992), 'The Security Dilemma', in J. Baylis and N. J. Rengger (eds), *Dilemmas of World Politics: International Issues in a Changing World* (Oxford: Oxford University Press).

Wheen, F. (1999), *Karl Marx* (London: Fourth Estate).

White, B. (2001), *Understanding European Foreign Policy* (Basingstoke: Palgrave).

White, S. (1990), *Gorbachev in Power* (Cambridge: Cambridge University Press).

Whitworth, S. (1994), *Feminism and International Relations: Towards a Political Economy of Gender in Inter-state and Non-Governmental Institutions* (Basingstoke: Macmillan).

Wiener, A., and Diez, T. (eds) (2004), *European Integration Theory* (Oxford: Oxford University Press).

Wight, M. (1977), *Systems of States* (Leicester: Leicester University Press).

——(1986), *Power Politics*, 2nd edn (Harmondsworth: Penguin).

Wilkinson, P. (2003), 'Implications of the attacks of 9/11 for the future of terrorism', in M. Buckley and R. Fawn (eds), *Global Responses to Terrorism* (London: Routledge).

——(ed.) (1996), '*The Conscience of the World': The Influence of Non-Governmental Organizations in the UN System* (London: Hurst and Co.).

Williams, D. (1987), *The Specialised Agencies and the United Nations: the System in Crisis* (London: Hurst and Co.).

Williams, M. (1994), *International Economic Institutions and the Third World* (London: Harvester Wheatsheaf).

Williams, P., and Black, S. (1994), 'Transnational Threats: Drug Trafficking and Weapons Proliferation', *Contemporary Security Policy*, 15(1).

Williamson, J. (1990), 'What Washington Means by Policy Reform', in J. Williamson (ed.), *Latin American Adjustment, How Much Has Happened?* (Washington, DC: Institute for International Economics).

Wilson, P. (1998), 'The Myth of the "First Great Debate" ', *Review of International Studies*, 24 (Special Issue).

Wincott, D. (1995), 'Institutional Interaction and European Integration: Towards an Everyday Critique of Liberal Intergovernmentalism', *Journal of Common Market Studies*, 33(4): 597–610.

Winham, G. (1977), 'Negotiation as a Management Process', *World Politics*, 30(1) (Oct.), reprinted in F. S. Sondermann, D. S. McClellan, and W. C. Olsen, *The Theory and Practice of International Relations* (Englewood Cliffs, NJ: Prentice-Hall).

Wippman, D. (2004), 'The International Criminal Court', in C. Reus-Smit (ed.), *The Politics of International Law* (Cambridge: Cambridge University Press): 151–88.

Wolfensohn, J. (1995), 'President Wolfensohn's speech at the 1995 Beijing conference', available online at www.worldbank.org/gender/how/policy.htm.

Wolin, S. (1960), *Politics and Vision* (Boston: Little, Brown).

Women's Eyes on the World Bank—US Chapter and 50 Years Campaign (1997), *Gender Equity and the World Bank Group: A Post-Beijing Assessment* (Washington, DC).

Wood, E. M. (2003), *Empire of Capital* (London: Verso).

Woodward, B. (2004), *Plan of Attack* (New York: Simon & Schuster).

Woolcock, S. (2000), 'European Trade Policy', H. Wallace and W. Wallace (eds), *Policy-making in the European Union* (Oxford: Oxford University Press): 373–400.

Woolf, Virginia (1992), *A Room of One's Own. Three Guineas* (Oxford: Oxford University Press). First published 1929.

World Bank (2000), *Addressing Gender Equity: World Bank Action Since Beijing* (Washington, DC: World Bank), also available online on the World Bank web site.

World Bank/InfoDev (2001), *Global Information Infrastructure* report prepared by Pyramid Research–EIU (Washington, DC: World Bank).

World Commission on Environment and Development (1987), *Our Common Future* (the Brundtland Report) (Oxford: Oxford University Press).

World March of Women (2000), report available online at www.marchemondiale.org/en/cahier/sexisme.html.

World Trade Organization (WTO) (1995), *International Trade: Trends and Statistics* (Geneva: WTO).

Worsley, P. (1980), 'One World or Three? A Critique of the World-System Theory of Immanuel Wallerstein', *Socialist Register* (London: Merlin Press).

Wright, R. (1986), *Sacred Rage: The Wrath of Militant Islam* (New York: Simon & Schuster).

Wyatt-Walter, A. (1996), 'Adam Smith and the Liberal Tradition in International Relations', *Review of International Studies*, 22(1): 142–72.

Young, I. M. (1990), *Justice and the Politics of Difference* (Princeton, NJ: Princeton University Press).

Young, O. (1997), *Global Governance* (Cambridge, Mass.: MIT Press).

Zacher, M. W., with Sutton, B. A. (1996), *Governing Global Networks: International Regimes for Transportation and Communications* (Cambridge: Cambridge University Press).

Zakaria, F. (1998), *From Wealth to Power: The Unusual Origins of America's World Role* (Princeton, NJ: Princeton University Press).

Zalewski, M. (1993a), 'Feminist Standpoint Theory Meets International Relations Theory: A Feminist Version of David and Goliath', *Fletcher Forum of World Affairs*, 17(2).

——(1993b), 'Feminist Theory and International Relations', in M. Bowker and R. Brown (eds), *From Cold War to Collapse: Theory and World Politics in the 1980s* (Cambridge: Cambridge University Press).

——and Parpart, J. (eds) (1988), *The 'Man' Question in International Relations* (Boulder, Col.: Westview).

Zanini, M., and Edwards, S. J. A. (2001), 'The Networking of Terror in the Information Age', in J. Arquilla and D. Ronfeldt (eds), *Networks and Netwars* (Santa Monica, Cal.: RAND).

Zartman, I. W. (1995), *Collapsed States* (Boulder and London: Lynne Rienner).

Zevin, R. (1992), 'Are World Financial Markets More Open? If So, Why and With What Effects?', in T. Banuri and J. B. Schor (eds), *Financial Openness and National Autonomy: Opportunities and Constraints* (Oxford: Clarendon Press).

GLOSSARY

Agent-structure problem: the problem is how to think about the relationship between agents and structures. One view is that agents are born with already formed identities and interests and then treat other actors and the broad structure that their interactions produce as a constraint on their interests. But this suggests that actors are pre-social to the extent that there is little interest in their identities or possibility that they might change their interests through their interactions with others. Another view is to treat the structure not as a constraint but rather as constituting the actors themselves. Yet this might treat agents as cultural dupes because they are nothing more than artefacts of that structure. The proposed solution to the agent-structure problem is to try and find a way to understand how agents and structures constitute each other.

Anarchic system: the 'ordering principle' of international politics according to Realism, and that which defines its structure.

Anarchy: a system operating in the absence of any central government. Does not imply chaos, but in Realist theory the absence of political authority.

Anomie: a system operating in the absence of norms or rules.

Apartheid: system of racial segregation introduced in South Africa in 1948, designed to ensure white minority domination.

Appeasement: a policy of making concessions to a revanchist (or otherwise territorially acquisitive) state in the hope that settlement of more modest claims will assuage that state's expansionist appetites. Appeasement remains most (in)famously associated with British Prime Minister Neville Chamberlain's acquiescence to Hitler's incursions into Austria and then Czechoslovakia, culminating in the Munich Agreement of September 1938. Since then, appeasement has generally been seen as synonymous with a craven collapse before the demands of dictators—encouraging, not disarming, their aggressive designs.

Asymmetrical globalization: describes the way in which contemporary globalization is unequally experienced across the world and among different social groups in such a way that it produces a distinctive geography of inclusion in, and exclusion from, the global system.

Autarky: the pursuit of national economic self-sufficiency—a policy pursued by several states in the wake of the Depression, as they sought to disentangle their economies from reliance on unstable global commodity markets and foreign loans.

Axis of evil: phrase deliberately used by George W. Bush in January 2001 to characterize Iran, North Korea, and Iraq.

Balance of power: in Realist theory, refers to an equilibrium between states; historical Realists regard it as the product of diplomacy (contrived balance) whereas structural Realists regard the system as having a tendency towards a natural equilibrium (fortuitous balance). It is a doctrine and an arrangement whereby the power of one state (or group of states) is checked by the countervailing power of other states.

Bank for International Settlements: established in 1930 with headquarters in Basle. Membership (2004) of 55 shareholding central banks, although many other public financial institutions also use BIS facilities. Promotes cooperation among central banks and provides various services for global financial operations. For example, the Basle Committee on Banking Supervision, formed through the BIS in 1974, has spearheaded efforts at multilateral regulation of global banking. See further www.bis.org.

Battle of the sexes: a scenario in game theory illustrating the need for a coordination strategy.

Bipolarity: term employed by scholars of International Relations to describe the post-war order before the USSR fell apart in 1991, leaving the United States as the sole superpower.

Bond: a contractual obligation of a corporation, association, or governance agency to make payments of interest and repayments of principal on borrowed funds at certain fixed times.

Brezhnev doctrine: declaration by Soviet premier Leonid Brezhnev in November 1968 that members of the Warsaw Pact would enjoy only 'limited sovereignty' in their political development. It was associated with the idea of 'limited sovereignty' for Soviet bloc nations, which was used to justify the crushing of the reform movement in Czechoslovakia in 1968.

Capabilities: the resources that are under an actor's direct control such as population and size of territory, resources, economic strength, military capability, and competence (Waltz 1979: 131).

Capitalism: a system of production in which human labour and its products are commodities that are bought and sold in the market-place. In Marxist analysis, the capitalist mode of production involved a specific set of social relations that were particular to a specific historical period. For Marx there were three main characteristics of capitalism: (1) Everything involved in production (e.g. raw materials, machines, labour involved in the creation of commodities, and the commodities themselves) is given an exchange value, and all can be exchanged, one for the other. In essence, under capitalism everything has its price, including people's working time. (2) Everything that is needed to undertake production (i.e. the factories, and the raw materials) is owned by one class—the capitalists. (3) Workers are 'free', but in order to survive must sell their labour to the capitalist class in order to survive, and because the capitalist class own the *means of production*, and control the *relations of production*, they also control the profit that results from the labour of workers.

Citizenship: the status of having the right to participate in and to be represented in politics.

Civil society: (1) the totality of all individuals and groups in a society who are not acting as participants in any government institutions, or (2) all individuals and groups who are neither participants in government nor acting in the interests of commercial companies. The two meanings are incompatible and contested. There is a third meaning: the network of social institutions and practices (economic relationships, family and kinship groups, religious, and other social affiliations) which underlie strictly political institutions. For democratic theorists the voluntary character of these associations is taken to be essential to the workings of democratic politics.

Claim-rights: the most basic rights—the only true rights, the American jurist Wesley Hofeld believed (see Jones 1994 for a modern version); the classic example of a claim-right is a right generated by a contract and accompanied by correlative duties.

Clash of civilizations: controversial idea first used by Samuel Huntington in 1993 to describe the main cultural fault-line of international conflict in a world without communism; the notion has become more popular still since 9/11.

Coexistence: the doctrine of live and let live between political communities, or states.

Cold war: extended worldwide conflict between communism and capitalism that is normally taken to have begun in 1947 and concluded in 1989 with the collapse of Soviet power in Europe.

Collaboration: a form of cooperation requiring parties not to defect from a mutually desirable strategy for an individually preferable strategy.

Collective security: refers to an arrangement where 'each state in the system accepts that the security of one is the concern of all, and agrees to join in a collective response to aggression' (Roberts and Kingsbury 1993: 30). It is also the foundational principle of the League of Nations: namely, that member states would take a threat or attack on one member as an assault on them all (and on international norms more generally). The League would accordingly respond in unison to such violations of international law. Appreciating that such concerted action would ensue, putative violators—the League's framers hoped—would be duly deterred from launching aggressive strikes in the first place. As the 1920s and 1930s showed, however, theory and practice diverged wildly, with League members failing to take concerted action against Japanese imperialism in Asia, and German and Italian expansionism in Europe and Africa.

Collectivization of security: the tendency for security to be organized on a multilateral basis, but without the institutional formality of a fully fledged collective security system.

Combating terrorism: Combating terrorism is comprised of anti-terrorism efforts (measures to protect against or mitigate future terrorist attacks) and counter-terrorism efforts (proactive actions designed to retaliate against or forestall terrorist actions).

Common European home: Soviet premier Mikhail Gorbachev's concept (associated with his New Thinking in foreign policy) of the essential unity of Europe and of the need to overcome the 'artificiality and temporariness of the bloc-to-bloc confrontation and the archaic nature of the "iron curtain"'.

Common humanity: we all have human rights by virtue of our common humanity, and these rights generate correlative moral duties for individuals and states.

Common security: to accept 'as the organizing principle for efforts to reduce the risk of war, limit arms, and move towards disarmament, means, in principle, that co-operation will replace confrontation in resolving conflicts of interest. This is not to say that differences among nations should be expected to disappear . . . The task is only to ensure that these conflicts do not come to be expressed in acts of war, or in preparations for war. It means that nations must come to understand that the maintenance of world peace must be given a higher priority than the assertion of their own ideological or political positions.' (Palme Report 1992).

Communitarianism: the ultimate source of meaning and value in human life resides in the community, whether ethnic, national, or perhaps even 'virtual'. In terms of human rights, communitarians will look to, at best, a basic minimum of universal standards with emphasis on the community setting its own standards for most purposes.

Community: a human association in which members share common symbols and wish to cooperate to realize common objectives.

Community-based organization (CBO): any group of people organized in a local village, small town, or local district of a city. Logically, a CBO is a local NGO. However, in political debate, CBOs are sometimes contrasted with NGOs and seen as being more radical.

Compellence: the use or threat of force to make an actor do something they would not otherwise do.

Competition (anti-trust) policy: policy that prohibits anti-competitive action and transactions by firms, especially monopolists, including state-owned enterprises.

Concert: the directorial role played by a number of Great Powers, based on norms of mutual consent.

Constructivism: an approach to international politics that concerns itself with the centrality of ideas and human consciousness and stresses a holistic and Idealist view of structures. As Constructivists have examined world politics they have been broadly interested in how the structure constructs the actors' identities and interests, how their interactions are organized and constrained by that structure, and how their very interaction serves to either reproduce or transform that structure.

Containment: American political strategy for resisting perceived Soviet expansion, first publicly espoused by an American diplomat, George Kennan, in 1947. Containment became a powerful factor in American policy towards the Soviet Union for the next forty years, and a self-image of Western policymakers.

Cooperation: is required in any situation where parties must act together in order to achieve a mutually acceptable outcome.

Coordination: a form of cooperation requiring parties to pursue a common strategy in order to avoid the mutually undesirable outcome arising from the pursuit of divergent strategies.

Cosmopolitan democracy: a condition in which international organizations, transnational corporations, global markets, and so forth are accountable to the peoples of the world. Associated with David Held, Daniele Archibugi, Mary Kaldor, and others, a cosmopolitan model of democracy requires the following: the creation of regional parliaments and the extension of the authority of such regional bodies (like the European Union) which are already in existence; human rights conventions must be entrenched in national parliaments and monitored by a new International Court of Human Rights; the UN must be replaced with a genuinely democratic and accountable global parliament.

Cosmopolitanism: the ultimate source of meaning and value in human life resides with the individual (or perhaps with God). Cosmopolitans are disposed to favour very extensive accounts of universal human rights.

Counter-restrictionists: international lawyers who argue that there is a legal right of humanitarian intervention in both UN Charter law and customary international law.

Crisis diplomacy: refers to the delicate communications and negotiations involved in a crisis. A crisis may be defined as a short, intensive period in which the possibility of (nuclear) war is perceived to increase dramatically.

Customary international law: this comprises a wide range of rules that are binding upon all states, regardless of their explicit consent. Two things are considered necessary before a rule can be considered customary law: evidence of general state practice (that is, states habitually acting in a manner consistent with the rule); and evidence that states accepted such practice as law (*opinio juris*).

Decisionmaking procedures: there identify specific prescriptions for behaviour, the system of voting, for example, which will regularly change as a regime is consolidated and extended. The rules and procedures governing the GATT, for example, underwent substantial modification during its history. Indeed, the purpose of the successive conferences was to change the rules and decisionmaking procedures (Krasner 1985: 4–5).

Defensive Realism: a structural theory of Realism that views states as security maximizers.

Democracy promotion: the strategy adopted by leading Western states and institutions—particularly the USA—to use instruments of foreign and economic policy to spread liberal values. Advocates make an explicit linkage between the mutually reinforcing effects of democratization and open markets.

Democratic peace: a central plank of liberal internationalist thought, the democratic peace thesis makes two claims: first, liberal polities exhibit restraint in their relations with other liberal polities (the so-called separate peace) but are imprudent in relations with authoritarian states. The validity of the democratic peace thesis has been fiercely debated in the IR literature.

Deregulation: the removal of all regulation so that market forces, not government policy, control economic developments.

Derivative: a financial contract that 'derives' its value from an underlying asset, exchange rate, interest level, or market index.

Détente: relaxation of tension between East and West; Soviet–American détente lasted from the late 1960s to the late 1970s, and was characterized by negotiations and nuclear arms control agreements.

Deterrence: the threat or use of force to prevent an actor from doing something they would otherwise do.

Deterritorialization: a process in which the organization of social activities is increasingly less constrained by geographical proximity and national territorial boundaries. Accelerated by the technological revolution and refers to the diminuition of influence of territorial places, distances, and boundaries over the way people collectively identify themselves or seek political recognition. This permits an expansion of global civil society but equally an expansion of global criminal or terrorist networks.

Development, core ideas, and assumptions: in the orthodox view, the possibility of unlimited economic growth in a free-market system. Economies would reach a 'take-off' point and thereafter wealth would trickle down to those at the bottom. Superiority of the 'Western' model and knowledge. Belief that the process would ultimately benefit everyone. Domination, exploitation of nature. In the alternative view, sufficiency. The inherent value of nature, cultural diversity, and the community-controlled commons (water, land, air, forest). Human activity in balance with nature. Self-reliance. Democratic inclusion, participation, for example, voice for marginalized groups, e.g. women, indigenous groups. Local control.

Development, measurement of: in the orthodox view, economic growth; Gross Domestic Product (GDP) per capita: industrialization, including of agriculture. In the alternative view, fulfilment of basic material and non-material human needs of everyone; condition of the natural environment. Political empowerment of marginalized.

Development, process of: in the orthodox view, top-down; reliance on 'expert knowledge', usually Western and definitely external; large capital investments in large projects; advanced technology; expansion of the private sphere. In the alternative view, bottom-up; participatory; reliance on appropriate (often local) knowledge and technology; small investments in small-scale projects; protection of the commons.

Development, purpose of: in the orthodox view, transformation of traditional subsistence economies defined as 'backward' into industrial, commodified economies defined as 'modern'. Production of surplus. Individuals sell their labour for money, rather than producing to meet their family's needs. In the alternative view, the creation of human well-being through sustainable societies in social, cultural, political, and economic terms.

Developmental diplomacy: refers to 'the process whereby third world countries attempt to negotiate improvements in their position in the international political economy. These negotiations largely take the form of bargaining with Western industrialised countries' (Williams 1994: 46).

Digital divide: the gap in technology access/ownership between those who have access to advanced communications and information services and those who are either too poor to afford such access or live in rural or remote areas with no access. Most often, the gap between the Internet 'haves' and 'have nots'.

Diplomacy: in foreign policy it refers to the use of diplomacy as a policy instrument possibly in association with other instruments such as economic or military force to enable an international actor to achieve its policy objectives. Diplomacy in world politics refers to a communications process between international actors that seeks through negotiation to resolve conflict short of war. This process has been refined, institutionalized, and professionalized over many centuries.

Disaggregated state: the tendency for states to become increasingly fragmented actors in global politics as every part of the government machine becomes entangled with its foreign counterparts and others in dealing with global issues through proliferating transgovernmental and global policy networks.

Dual moral standards: in Realist theory, the idea that there are two principles or standards of right and wrong: one for the individual citizen and a different one for the state.

E-government: the use of technology to engage people in the political process.

Empire: a distinct type of political entity, which may or may not be a state, possessing both a home territory and foreign territories. It is a disputed concept that some have tried to apply to the United States to describe its international reach, huge capabilities, and vital global role of underwriting world order.

End of history: famous phrase employed by Francis Fukuyama in 1989; this argued that one phase of history shaped by the antagonism between collectivism and individualism had (two hundred years after the French Revolution) come to an end, leaving Liberalism triumphant.

Endemic warfare: the condition in which warfare is a recurrent feature of the relations between states not least because they regard it as inevitable.

Enlightenment: associated with rationalist thinkers of the eighteenth century. Key ideas (which some would argue remain mottoes for our age) include: secularism, progress, reason, science, knowledge, and freedom. The motto of the Enlightenment is: '*Sapere aude*! Have courage to use your *own* understanding' (Kant 1991: 54).

Equity: also called stock or share; a number of equal portions in the nominal capital of a company; the shareholder thereby owns part of the enterprise.

Ethic of responsibility: for historicalRealists, an ethic of responsibility is the limits of ethics in international politics; it involves the weighing up of consequences and the realization that positive outcomes may result from amoral actions.

Eurobond: a bond denominated in a currency that is alien to a substantial proportion of the underwriters through whom it is distributed and investors to whom it is sold; the borrower, the syndicate of managers, the investors, and the securities exchange on which the bond is listed are spread over a number of countries.

Eurocurrency: national money in the hands of persons and institutions domiciled outside the currency's territorial 'home': hence 'eurodollar', 'eurozloty', etc.

Euroequity: a share issue that is offered simultaneously in different stock-markets, usually across several time zones; also called global equity.

Europe: a geographical expression that during the course of the cold war came to be identified with Western Europe, but since 1989 has once again come to be associated with the whole of the European continent.

Evil empire: Reagan's term, used in a speech of 1983, to describe the Soviet Union.

Exponential growth: a situation where the rate of growth is not constant or linear but increases over time.

Extraterritoriality: occurs when one government attempts to exercise its legal authority in the territory of another state. It mainly arises when the US federal government deliberately tries to use domestic law to control the global activities of TNCs.

Failed state: this is a state that has collapsed and cannot provide for its citizens without substantial external support and where the government of the state has ceased to exist inside the territorial borders of the state.

Feminization of labour: recognizing the increasing global demand for women as 'cheap labour', on the global assembly line, and in the provision of paid as well as unpaid reproductive labour and care.

Feminism: a political project to understand so as to change women's inequality, liberation, or oppression. For some, aiming to move beyond gender, so that it no longer matters; for others, to validate women's interests, experiences, and choices; for others, to work for more equal and inclusive social relations overall.

Forcible humanitarian intervention: military intervention which breaches the principle of state sovereignty where the primary purpose is to alleviate the human suffering of some or all within a state's borders.

G8 (Group of Eight): established in 1975 as the G5 (France, Germany, Japan, the UK, and the USA); subsequently expanded as the G7 to include Canada and Italy and since 1998 the G8 to include the Russian Federation. The G8 conducts semi-formal collaboration on world economic problems. Government leaders meet in annual G8 Summits, while finance ministers and/or their leading officials periodically hold other consultations. See further **www.g8online.org**.

Game theory: a branch of mathematics which explores strategic interaction.

Gender relations: power relations: the relational construction of masculinity and femininity, in which the masculine is usually privileged; and which are contested, and changing.

Gender: what it means to be male or female in a particular place or time; the social construction of sexual difference.

Gendered division of labour (GDL): the notion of 'women's work', which everywhere includes women's primary responsibility for childcare and housework, and which designates many public and paid forms of work as 'women's' or 'men's', too.

Gendering globalization: applying a 'gender lens' to globalization, to reveal that women are differently positioned in relation to globalization processes and differently impacted upon by them; and that women become global players in response to these gendered effects.

General Agreement on Tariffs and Trade (GATT): established in 1947 with offices in Geneva. Membership had reached 122 states when it was absorbed into the World Trade Organization (WTO) in 1995. The GATT coordinated eight 'rounds' of multilateral negotiations to reduce state restrictions on cross-border merchandise trade.

Glasnost: policy of greater openness pursued by Soviet premier Mikhail Gorbachev from 1985, involving greater toleration of internal dissent and criticism.

Global care economy: recognizing the growing global demand for women's domestic and sexual services, which often see poorer, minority, or 'Third World' women providing domestic or sexual labour in other households and countries.

Global covenant: the rules, values, and norms which govern the global society of states.

Global governance: the evolving system of (formal and informal) political coordination—across multiple levels from the local to the global—among public authorities (states and intergovernmental organizations) and private agencies (NGOs and corporate actors) seeking to realize common purposes or resolve collective problems through the making and implementing of global or transnational norms, rules, programmes, and policies. The loose framework of global regulation, both institutional and normative, that constrains conduct. It has many elements: international organizations and law; transnational organizations and frameworks; elements of global civil society; and shared normative principles.

Global network: digital networks that span the globe allowing instant voice and data communication worldwide—the global information highway.

Global policy networks: complexes which bring together the representatives of governments, international organizations, NGOs, and the corporate sector for the formulation and implementation of global public policy.

Global politics: the politics of global social relations in which the pursuit of power, interests, order, and justice transcends regions and continents.

Global polity: the collective structures and processes by which 'interests are articulated and aggregated, decisions are made, values allocated and policies conducted through international or transnational political processes' (Ougaard 2004: 5).

Globalism: the condition of globalization at any point in time usually gauged by its thickness or thinness.

Globalization: a historical process involving a fundamental shift or transformation in the spatial scale of human social organization that links distant communities and expands the reach of power relations across regions and continents. It is also something of a catch-all phrase often used to describe a single world-economy after the collapse of communism, though sometimes employed to define the growing integration of the international capitalist system in the post-war period.

Globalized state: the notion of a particular kind of state that helps sustain globalization, as well as responding to its pressures. The distinctive feature of this concept is that the state is not 'in retreat' but simply behaving differently.

Great Depression: a byword for the global economic collapse that ensued following the US Wall Street stock-market crash in October 1929. Economic shockwaves soon rippled around a world already densely interconnected by webs of trade and foreign direct investment with the result that the events of October 1929 were felt in countries as distant as Brazil and Japan.

Group rights: rights that are said to belong to groups such as minority nations or indigenous peoples rather than to individuals.

Harmony of interests: common among nineteenth-century Liberals was the idea of a natural order between peoples which had been corrupted by undemocratic state leaders and outdated policies such as the balance of power. If these distortions could be swept away, they believed, we would find that there were no *real* conflicts between peoples.

Hegemonic stability theory: a Realist-based explanation for cooperation that argues that a dominant state is required to ensure a liberal, free-trade, international political economy.

Hegemony: a system regulated by a dominant leader, or political (and/or economic) domination of a region, usually by a superpower. In Realist theory, the influence a Great Power is able to establish on other states in the system; extent of influence ranges from leadership to dominance. It is also power and control exercised by a leading state over other states.

Holism: the view that structures cannot be decomposed to the individual units and their interactions because structures are more than the sum of their parts and are irreducibly social. The effects of structures, moreover, go beyond merely constraining the actors but also construct them. Constructivism holds that the international structure shapes the identities and interests of the actors.

Hybrid international non-governmental organization (INGO): a third type of international organization, in which governments and NGOs form joint organizations in which they are each allowed to be members. Logically they should be hybrid international organizations, but in diplomatic practice they are identified among the international NGOs and so hybrid INGOs is perhaps a more appropriate term.

Idealism: holds that ideas have important causal effect on events in international politics, and that ideas can change. Referred to by Realists as utopianism since it underestimates the logic of power politics and the constraints this imposes upon political action. Idealism as a substantive theory of international relations is generally associated with the claim that it is possible to create a world of peace. But Idealism as a social theory refers to the claim that the most fundamental feature of society is social consciousness. Ideas shape how we see ourselves and our interests, the knowledge that we use to categorize and understand the world, the beliefs we have of others, and the possible and impossible solutions to challenges and threats. The emphasis on ideas does not mean a neglect of material forces such as technology and geography. Instead it is to suggest that the meanings and consequences of these material forces are not given by nature but rather driven by human interpretations and understandings. Idealists seek to apply liberal thinking in domestic politics to international relations, in other words, institutionalize the rule of law. This reasoning is known as the domestic analogy. According to Idealists in the early twentieth century, there were two principal requirements for a new world order. First: state leaders, intellectuals, and public opinion had to believe that progress was possible. Second: an international organization had to be created to facilitate peaceful change, disarmament, arbitration, and (where necessary) enforcement. The League of Nations was founded in 1920 but its collective security system failed to prevent the descent into world war in the 1930s.

Identity: the understanding of the self in relationship to an 'other'. Identities are social and thus are always formed in relationship to others. Constructivists generally hold that identities shape interests; we cannot know what we want unless we know who we are. But because identities are social and are produced through interactions, identities can change.

Immunity rights: the essence of there is that others are disbarred from making claims under certain circumstances, for example, to be legally insane, or under age, is to be *immune* from criminal prosecution.

Imperialism: the practice of foreign conquest and rule in the context of global relations of hierarchy and subordination. It can lead to the establishment of an empire.

Individualism: the view that structures can be reduced to the aggregation of individuals and their interactions. International relations theories that ascribe to individualism begin with some assumption of the nature of the units and their interests, usually states and the pursuit of power or wealth, and then examine how the broad structure, usually the distribution of power, constrains how states can act and generates certain patterns in international politics. Individualism stands in contrast to holism.

Influence: the ability of one actor to change the values or the behaviour of another actor.

Institutionalization: the degree to which networks or patterns of social interaction are formally constituted as organizations with specific purposes.

Institutions: persistent and having connected sets of rules and practices that prescribe roles, constrain activity, and shape the expectations of actors. Institutions may include organizations, bureaucratic agencies, treaties and agreements, and informal practices that states accept as binding. The balance of power in the international system is an example of an institution. (Adapted from Haas, Keohane, and Levy 1993: 4–5.)

Integration: a process of ever closer union between states, in a regional or international context. The process often begins with cooperation to solve technical problems, referred to by Mitrany (1943) as ramification.

Intellectual property rights: rules that protect the owners of content through copyright, patents, trade marks and trade secrets.

Interaction processes: the flows of people, materials, energy, money, and information (including political ideas and proposals for policy) between the elements of a system. War is primarily determined by flows of people as soldiers and materials as weapons; economics by the exchange of money for all the other four types of flows; and politics by the flow of information. Thus, for a Pluralist, unless and until an issue involves armed conflict, structures of communication are the fundamental political structures.

Interdependence: a condition where states (or peoples) are affected by decisions taken by others; for example, a decision to raise interest rates in the USA automatically exerts upward pressure on interest rates in other states. Interdependence can be symmetric, i.e. both sets of actors are affected equally, or it can be asymmetric, where the impact varies between actors. A condition where the actions of one state impact upon other states (can be strategic interdependence or economic). Realists equate interdependence with vulnerability.

Intergovernmental organization (IGO): an international organization in which full legal membership is officially solely open to states and the decisionmaking authority lies with representatives from governments.

International law: the formal rules of conduct that states acknowledge or contract between themselves.

International Monetary Fund: Established in 1945 with headquarters in Washington, DC. Membership (2004) of 184 states. The IMF monitors short-term cross-border payments and foreign exchange positions. When a country develops chronic imbalances in its external accounts, the IMF supports corrective policy reforms, often called 'structural adjustment programmes'. Since 1978 the IMF has undertaken comprehensive surveillance both of the economic performance of individual member states and of the world-economy as a whole. The IMF also provides extensive technical assistance. In recent years the Fund has pursued various initiatives to promote efficiency and stability in global financial markets. See further **www.imf.org**.

International non-governmental organization (INGOs): an international organization in which membership is open to transnational actors. There are many different types, with membership from 'national' NGOs, local NGOs, companies, political parties, or individual people. A few have other INGOs as members and some have mixed membership structures.

International order: the normative and the institutional pattern in the relationship between states. The elements of this might be thought to include such things as sovereignty, the forms of diplomacy, international law, the role of the Great Powers, and the codes circumscribing the use of force. It is a shared value and condition of stability and predictability in the relations of states.

International Organization of Securities Commissions: Established in 1983 with headquarters in Montreal; secretariat now in Madrid. Membership (2004) of 181 official securities regulators and (non-voting) trade associations and other agencies. IOSCO aims to promote high standards of regulation in stock- and bond markets, to establish effective surveillance of transborder securities transactions, and to foster collaboration between securities markets in the detection and punishment of offences.

International organization: any institution with formal procedures and formal membership from three or more countries. The minimum number of countries is set at three rather than two, because multilateral relationships have significantly greater complexity than bilateral relationships.

International regime: a concept developed by neo-realists to analyse the paradox—for them—that international cooperation occurs in some issue-areas, despite the struggle for power between states. They assume regimes are created and maintained by a dominant state and/or participation in a regime is the result of a rational cost–benefit calculation by each state. In contrast, Pluralists would also stress the independent impact of institutions, the importance of leadership, the involvement of transnational NGOs and companies, and processes of cognitive change, such as growing concern about human rights or the environment.

International system: a set of interrelated parts connected to form a whole. In Realist theory, systems have defining principles such as hierarchy (in domestic politics) and anarchy (in international politics).

Internationalization: growing interactions between national states. This term is used to denote high levels of international interaction and interdependence, most commonly with regard to the world-economy. In this context it refers to the volume of international trade and investment and to the organization of production. The term is often used to distinguish this condition from globalization as the latter implies that there are no longer distinct national economies in a position to interact. It also describes the increase in transactions among states reflected in flows of trade, investment, and capital (cf. the argument that these flows have not increased as much as is claimed: UNDP 1997). The processes of internationalization have been facilitated and are shaped by inter-state agreements on trade, investment, and capital, as well as by domestic policies permitting the private sector to transact abroad.

Intra-firm trade: international trade from one branch of a TNC to an affiliate of the same company in a different country.

Islam: a religious faith developed by the Prophet Muhammaed which in the contemporary period functions as a form of political identity for millions and the inspiration of what some at least now regard as the most important ideological opposition to Western modern values.

Issue, an: consists of a set of political questions that are seen as being related, because they all invoke the same value conflicts, e.g. the issue of human rights concerns questions that invoke freedom versus order.

Jus ad bellum: The laws of war governing when it is legally permitted to use force or wage war. Chapter 7 of the United Nations Charter, for example, restricts the legitimate use of force to two areas: international peace-enforcement actions authorized by the Security Council, and individual or collective self-defence in response to an armed attack.

Jus cogens: the term used to describe peremptory norms of international law. These are norms that are considered so fundamental that states are not permitted to contract out of them. Commonly cited examples of peremptory norms are the norm against aggression and the norm governing the inviolability of diplomatic agents.

Jus in bello: The laws of war governing the conduct of war once launched. These laws cover, among other things, the proportionate use of force, the targeting of civilians, the treatment of political prisoners. The principal legal instruments in this area are the Geneva Conventions of 1949, and the Additional Protocols to the Conventions of 1977.

Liberal rights: the agenda of human rights that is driven largely from a Western perspective and derived from classical Liberal positions.

Liberalism: according to Doyle (1997: 207), Liberalism includes the following four claims. First, all citizens are juridically equal and have equal rights to education, access to a free press, and religious toleration. Second, the legislative assembly of the state possesses only the authority invested in it by the people, whose basic rights it is not permitted to abuse. Third, a key dimension of the liberty of the individual is the right to own property including productive forces. Fourth, Liberalism contends that the most effective system of economic exchange is one that is largely market driven and not one that is subordinate to bureaucratic regulation and control either domestically or internationally.

Liberalization: describes government policies which reduce the role of the state in the economy such as through the dismantling of trade tariffs and barriers, the deregulation and opening of the financial sector to foreign investors, and the privatization of state enterprises.

Liberty-rights occur when an individual has the right to do something in the sense that he or she has no obligation *not to* do it—for example, to dress as he or she pleases. Here there is no correlative duty, except perhaps the duty to let the individual do as he or she chooses. Sometimes a right involves the exercise of a power. For example, to have the *right* to vote means to be *empowered* to vote, to be enfranchised.

Loyalty: an emotional disposition in which people give institutions (or each other) some degree of unconditional support.

Market failure: results from the inability of the market to produce goods which require collaborative strategies.

Market Stalinism: ironic coupling of two words sometimes used by critics to describe the system in China which combines an authoritarian political order with a highly dynamic capitalism.

Materialism: the view that the most fundamental feature of society is the organization of material forces. Material forces include natural resources, geography, military power, and technology. To understand how the world works, therefore, requires taking these fundamentals into account. For international relations scholars, this leads to forms of technological determinism or the distribution of military power for understanding the state's foreign policy and patterns of international politics.

Means (or forces) of production: in Marxist theory, these are the elements that combine in the production process. They include labour as well as the tools and technology available during any given historical period.

Merchant bank: also called an investment bank or securities house; a bank specializing in securities business, as opposed to a commercial bank engaged primarily in deposit and lending business. (That said, many major investment banks have in recent years become arms of global commercial banks: for example, Deutsche Morgan Grenfell and UBS Warburg.)

Microeconomics: the branch of economics studying the behaviour of the firm in a market setting.

Minimum order: a view of international order that is concerned with peace and stability, rather than with the attainment of other values, such as justice.

Multilateralism: the tendency for functional aspects of international relations (such as security, trade, or environmental management) to be organized around large numbers of states, or universally, rather than by unilateral state action.

Multipolarity: a distribution of power among a number (at least three) of major powers or 'poles'.

Murderous states: those where the sovereign government is massively abusing the human rights of its citizens, engaging in acts of mass killing and/or genocide.

Mutually Assured Destruction (MAD): condition in which both superpowers possessed the capacity to destroy their adversary even after being attacked first with nuclear weapons.

Nation: a group of people who recognize each other as sharing a common identity, with a focus on a homeland.

National interest: invoked by Realists and state leaders to signify that which is most important to the state—survival being at the top of the list.

National security: a fundamental value in the foreign policy of states.

Nation-state: a political community in which the state claims legitimacy on the grounds that it represents the nation. The nation-state would exist if nearly all the members of a single nation were organized in a single state, without any other national communities being present. Although the term is widely used, no such entities exist.

Natural law: the origin of natural law thinking can be traced to the classical Greeks and early Christians, but in its modern form it is based on medieval Catholic theology. The central idea is that human beings have an essential nature which dictates that certain kinds of human goods are always and everywhere desired; because of this there are common moral standards that govern all human relations and these common standards can be discerned by the application of reason to human affairs.

Neoclassical Realism: a version of Realism that combines both structural factors such as the distribution of power and unit-level factors such as the interests of states (status quo or revisionist).

Neo-medievalism: a condition in which political power is dispersed between local, national, and supranational institutions none of which commands supreme loyalty.

Neo-realism: modification of the Realist approach, by recognizing economic resources—in addition to military capabilities—are a basis for exercising influence. Also, the concept of a single international system is abandoned in favour of analysing issue-specific systems, each characterized by their own power structure. Thus Saudi Arabia may be the most powerful state in the politics of oil, while Brazil is the most powerful in the politics of rainforests.

Netwar (or cyberwar): The use of digital networks and communications to attack enemies as an act of war or terrorism.

Network: any structure of communication for individuals

and/or organizations to exchange information, share experiences, or discuss political goals and tactics. There is no clear boundary between a network and an NGO. A network is less likely than an NGO to become permanent, to have formal membership, to have identifiable leaders or to engage in collective action.

New thinking: the general label given by former Soviet premier Mikhail Gorbachev to his reforms in domestic and foreign policy.

Non-discrimination: a doctrine of equal treatment between states.

Non-forcible/non-violent intervention: pacific intervention which can be either consensual (Red Cross) or non-consensual (Médecins Sans Frontières) and which is practised by states, international organizations, and INGOs (international non-governmental organizations). It can be short term (delivery of humanitarian aid) or long term (conflict resolution and reconstruction of political life within failed states).

Non-governmental organization (NGO): an organization, usually a grassroots one, with policy goals, but neither governmental nor corporate in make-up. Examples include Amnesty International and the International Campaign to Ban Landmines. An NGO is any group of people relating to each other regularly in some formal manner and engaging in collective action, provided that the activities are non-commercial and non-violent, and are not on behalf of a government. People are often baffled by the dry, bland term, 'non-governmental organization'. Nevertheless, some of the international NGOs, such as Amnesty International, Greenpeace, or the Red Cross are better known than some smaller countries.

Non-state actor: a term widely used to mean any actor that is not a government. Often it is not clear whether the term is being used to cover bodies such as the United Nations. Ambiguity is best avoided by referring separately to two categories, transnational actors and international organizations.

Normative structure: international relations theory traditionally defines structure in material terms, such as the distribution of power, and then treats structure as a constraint on actors. By identifying a normative structure, Constructivists are noting how structures also are defined by collectively held ideas such as knowledge, rules, beliefs, and norms that not only constrain actors, but also construct categories of meaning, constitute their identities and interests, and define standards of appropriate conduct. Critical here is the concept of a norm, a standard of appropriate behaviour for actors with a given identity. Actors adhere to norms not only because of benefits and costs for doing so but also because they are related to a sense of self.

Normative theory: systematic analyses of the ethical, moral, and political principles which either govern or ought to govern the organization or conduct of global politics. The belief that theories should be concerned with what ought to be, rather than merely diagnosing what is. Norm creation refers to the setting of standards in international relations which governments (and other actors) ought to meet.

Norms: specify general standards of behaviour, and identify the rights and obligations of states. So, in the case of the GATT, the basic norm is that tariffs and non-tariff barriers should be reduced and eventually eliminated. Together, norms and principles define the essential character of a regime and these cannot be changed without transforming the nature of the regime.

North Atlantic Treaty Organization (NATO): organization established by treaty in April 1949 comprising 12 (later 16) countries from Western Europe and North America. The most important aspect of the NATO alliance was the American commitment to the defence of Western Europe.

Nuclear diplomacy: refers to the interactions between nuclear-armed states where one or more of them threatens to use nuclear weapons either to dissuade an opponent from undertaking an action or to persuade them to call a halt to some action that has begun. The former is also known as deterrence and the latter as compellence.

Offensive Realism: a structural theory of Realism that views states as security maximizers.

Offshore finance centre: a site for financial business offering inducements such as tax reductions, regulation waivers, subsidies and rebates, secrecy guarantees, and so on; most are located in island and other mini-states, though offshore provisions also cover arrangements like International Banking Facilities in New York (since 1981), the Tokyo-based Japan Offshore Market (since 1986), and the Bangkok International Banking Facility (since 1993).

Open door policy: pursuit of an 'open door' was the aspiration of US foreign policy in China since 1900. What this meant was that China would agree to cede equal access and commercial opportunities to all foreign powers that sought to participate in the lucrative 'China trade', rather than surrendering exclusive access to single foreign states in its many treaty ports. The 'open door' has also, however, been taken as a signifier more broadly for the US approach to the pursuit of asymmetric advantage in trading relations, often involving a bulldozing down of barriers to 'free trade' erected by those less economically powerful than itself.

Open source software: software that is built on the idea that software should be freely distributed and that potential users should not be excluded.

Opinio juris: the conviction on the part of states that a certain form of action is required or permitted by international law.

Order: this may denote any regular or discernible pattern of relationships that are stable over time, or may additionally refer to a condition that allows certain goals to be achieved.

Organization of Economic Co-operation and Development: founded in 1962 with headquarters in Paris. Membership (2004) of 30 states with advanced industrial economies and other relationships with 70 states. Provides a forum for multilateral intergovernmental consultations on a wide range of economic and social issues. OECD measures have especially addressed environmental questions, taxation, and transborder corporations. At regular intervals the OECD Secretariat produces an assessment of the macroeconomic performance of each member, including suggestions for policy changes. See further **www.oecd.org**.

Ostpolitik: the West German government's 'Eastern Policy' of the mid- to late 1960s, designed to develop relations between West Germany and members of the Warsaw Pact.

Pacta sunt servanda: the principle, central to the international legal order, that states must observe in good faith treaties to which they are parties.

Pax Americana: Latin phrase (literally American peace, adapted from Pax Romana) implying a global peace dictated by American power.

Peace enforcement: designed to bring hostile parties to agreement, which may occur without the consent of the parties.

Peace Treaty of Versailles, 1919: the Treaty of Versailles formally ended the First World War (1914–18). The Treaty established the League of Nations, specified the rights and obligations of the victorious and defeated powers (including the notorious regime of reparations on Germany), and created the 'Mandatories' system under which 'advanced nations' were given legal tutelage over colonial peoples.

Peacekeeping: the deployment of a UN presence in the field with the consent of all parties (this refers to classical peacekeeping).

Peacemaking: designed to bring hostile parties to agreement, essentially through peaceful means. However, when all peaceful means have failed peace enforcement authorized under Chapter VII of the Charter may be necessary.

Perestroika: policy of restructuring, pursued by former Soviet premier, Mikhail Gorbachev in tandem with *glasnost*, and intended to modernize the Soviet political and economic system.

Petrodollars: earnings from oil exports deposited outside the USA; they provided the largest single spur to growth in the euromarkets in the 1970s.

Pluralism: an umbrella term, borrowed from American political science, used to signify international relations theorists who rejected the Realist view of the primacy of the state, the priority of national security, and the assumption that states are unitary actors. It is the theoretical approach that considers all organized groups as being potential political actors and analyses the processes by which actors mobilize support to achieve policy goals. Pluralists can accept that transnational actors and international organizations may influence governments. Equated by some writers with Liberalism, but Pluralists reject any such link, denying that theory necessarily has a normative component, and holding that Liberals are still highly state-centric.

Pluralist international society theory: states are conscious of sharing common interests and common values, but these are limited to norms of sovereignty and non-intervention.

Policy domain: consists of a set of political questions that have to be decided together because they are linked by the political processes in an international organization, e.g. financial policy is resolved in the IMF. A policy domain may cover several issues: financial policy includes development, the environment, and gender issues.

Political community: a community that wishes to govern itself and to be free from alien rule.

Post-conflict peacebuilding: to develop the social, political, and economic infrastructure to prevent further violence and to consolidate peace.

Poverty: in the orthodox view, a situation suffered by people who do not have the *money to buy food* and satisfy other basic *material needs*. In the alternative view, a situation suffered by people who are not able to meet their *material and non-material needs* through their own effort.

Power: in the most general sense, the ability of a political actor to achieve its goals. In the Realist approach, it is assumed that possession of capabilities will result in influence, so the single word, power, is often used ambiguously to cover both. In the Pluralist approach, it is assumed that political interactions can modify the translation of capabilities into influence and therefore it is important to distinguish between the two. Power is defined by most Realists in terms of the important resources such as size of armed forces, gross national product, and population that a state possesses. There is the implicit belief that material resources translate into influence.

Preventive diplomacy: involving confidence-building measures, fact finding, and preventive deployment of UN authorized forces.

Primordialism: the belief that certain human or social characteristics, such as ethnicity, are deeply embedded in historical conditions.

Principles: in regime theory, they are represented by coherent bodies of theoretical statements about how the world works. The GATT operated on the basis of liberal principles which assert that global welfare will be maximized by free trade.

Prisoners' dilemma: a scenario in game theory illustrating the need for a collaboration strategy.

Public bads: the negative consequences which can arise when actors fail to collaborate.

Public goods: goods which can only be produced by a collective decision, and which cannot, therefore, be produced in the market-place.

Quasi-state: a state which has 'negative sovereignty' because other states respect its sovereign independence but lacks 'positive sovereignty' because it does not have the resources or the will to satisfy the needs of its people.

Rapprochement: re-establishment of more friendly relations between the People's Republic of China and the United States in the early 1970s.

Rational choice: an approach that emphasizes how actors attempt to maximize their interests, how they attempt to select the most efficient means to achieve those interests, and attempts to explain collective outcomes by virtue of the attempt by actors to maximize their preferences under a set of constraints. Deriving largely from economic theorizing, the rational choice to politics and international politics has been immensely influential and applied to a range of issues.

Rationality: reflected in the ability of individuals to place their preferences in rank order and choose the best available preference.

Reason of state: the practical application of the doctrine of Realism and virtually synonymous with it.

Reasonable sufficiency: Former Soviet premier, Mikhail Gorbachev's term (associated with his New Thinking in foreign policy) for a defence policy which relied on the minimum necessary level of weaponry consistent with national security, and designed to overcome the spiralling dynamics of the nuclear arms race.

Reciprocity: reflects a 'tit for tat' strategy, only cooperating if others do likewise.

Regimes: these are sets of implicit or explicit principles, norms, rules, and decisionmaking procedures around which actors' expectations converge in a given area of international relations. They are are social institutions that are based on agreed rules, norms, principles, and decisionmaking procedures. These govern the interactions of various state and non-state actors in issue-areas such as the environment or human rights. The global market in coffee, for example, is governed by a variety of treaties, trade agreements, scientific and research protocols, market protocols, and the interests of producers, consumers, and distributors. States organize these interests and consider the practices, rules, and procedures to create a governing arrangement or regime that controls the production of coffee, monitors its distribution, and ultimately determines the price for consumers. (Adapted from Young 1997: 6.)

Regionalization: growing interdependence between geographically contiguous states, as in the European Union.

Regulatory arbitrage: in the world of banking, the process of moving funds or business activity from one country to another, in order to increase profits by escaping the constraints imposed by government regulations. By analogy the term can be applied to any transfer of economic activity by any company in response to government policy.

Relations of production: in Marxist theory, relations of production link and organize the means of production in the production process. They involve both the technical and institutional relationships necessary to allow the production process to proceed, as well as the broader structures that govern the control of the means of production, and control of the end product(s) of that process. Private property and wage labour are two of the key features of the relations of production in capitalist society.

Relative gains: one of the factors that Realists argue constrain the willingness of states to cooperate. States are less concerned about whether everyone benefits (absolute gains) and more concerned about whether someone may benefit more than someone else.

Reparations: dues owed (as money or *matériel*) by vanquished nations to their victorious former enemies at a war's end. In 1919, the issue of reparations owed by Germany caused the peacemakers considerable difficulty, with much debate over the precise amount that Germany could be expected to repay, and with what consequences for that country's economic reconstruction. Whether or not Germany should be squeezed dry—and the economic sense that made (or did not make) for Europe's wider recovery—was coupled with the contentious issue of 'war guilt'. Germans thus smarted not only at the punitively high scale of the reparations bill with which they were confronted but also at its coupling to a clause insisting on Germany's singular responsibility for the war.

Restrictionists: international lawyers who argue that humanitarian intervention violates Article 2(4) of the UN Charter and is illegal under both UN Charter law and customary international law.

Right of self-defence: a state's right to wage war in its own defence.

Rules: operate at a lower level of generality to principles and norms, and they are often designed to reconcile conflicts which may exist between the principles and norms. Third World states, for example, wanted rules which differentiated between developed and underdeveloped countries.

Security community: 'A group of people which has become "integrated". By integration we mean the attainment, within a territory, of a "sense of community" and of institutions and practices strong enough and widespread enough to assure . . . dependable expectations of "peaceful change" among its population. By a "sense of community" we mean a belief . . . that common social problems must and can be resolved by processes of "peaceful change"' (Karl Deutsch *et al.* 1957).

Security complex: involves 'a group of states whose primary security concerns link together sufficiently closely that their national securities cannot realistically be considered apart from one another' (Barry Buzan 1983).

Security regimes: these occur 'when a group of states cooperate to manage their disputes and avoid war by seeking to mute the security dilemma both by their own actions and by their assumptions about the behaviour of others' (Robert Jervis 1983*b*).

Security: in finance, a contract with a claim to future payments in which (in contrast to bank credits) there is a direct and formally identified relationship between the investor and the borrower; also unlike bank loans, securities are traded in markets.

Self-determination: a principle ardently, but selectively, espoused by US President Woodrow Wilson in the peacemaking that followed the First World War: namely that each 'people' should enjoy self-government over its own sovereign nation-state. Wilson pressed for application of this principle to East/Central Europe, but did not believe that other nationalities (in colonized Asia, Africa, the Pacific and Caribbean) were fit for self-rule.

Self-determination: the right of a political community or state to become a sovereign state.

Self-help: in Realist theory, in an anarchical environment, states cannot assume other states will come to their defence even if they are allies. *Each state must take care of itself.*

Separate paths to socialism: former Soviet premier Nikita Khrushchev's acknowledgement of the existence of diversity in the Soviet bloc and of the validity (within strict limits) of separate routes to the common socialist goal.

11 September 2001: often referred to in popular parlance as '9/11', the day when four aircraft were hijacked by Islamic terrorists in the United States—two of which destroyed the World Trade Center in New York, one which partially destroyed the Pentagon, and a fourth which crash-landed in a field in Pennsylvania.

Sex: biological difference, born male or female; the sex act; sexual difference.

Sexuality: including normalized heterosexuality, and other, often stigmatized sexualities: homosexuality, minority masculinities, shifting or multiple sexualities.

Shadow of the future: a metaphor indicating that decision-makers are conscious of the future when making decisions.

Sinatra doctrine: statement by the Soviet foreign ministry in October 1989 that countries of Eastern Europe were 'doing it their way' (a reference to Frank Sinatra's song 'I did it my way') and which marked the end of the Brezhnev doctrine and Soviet hegemony in Eastern Europe.

Social movement: people with a diffuse sense of collective identity, solidarity, and common purpose that usually leads to collective political behaviour. The concept covers all the different NGOs and networks, plus all their members and all the other individuals who share the common value(s). Thus, the women's movement and the environmental movement are much more than the specific NGOs that provide leadership and focus the desire for social change.

Socialism in one country: Stalin's term used to justify the Soviet Union's departure from the orthodox Marxist view that socialism in the Soviet Union could succeed only in conjunction with socialist revolutions in advanced industrial nations.

Society of states: an association of sovereign states based on their common interests, values, and norms.

Sovereignty: the condition of a state being free from any higher legal authority. It is related to, but distinct from, the condition of a government being free from any external political constraints. It is the rightful entitlement to exclusive, unqualified, and supreme rule within a delimited territory. The state has supreme authority domestically and independence internationally.

Special Drawing Right (SDR): the supraterritorial denomination issued since 1969 through the International Monetary Fund (IMF) and used as its unit of account. As of April 2004, 21.4 billion SDRs were in circulation at a value of 1 SDR = US$1.47. A further allocation to double the amount of SDRs is pending.

Standards war: conflict between countries or firms over which standards to adopt.

State autonomy: in a more interdependent world, simply to achieve domestic objectives national governments are forced to engage in extensive multilateral collaboration and cooperation. But in becoming more embedded in frameworks of global and regional governance states confront a real dilemma: in return for more effective public policy and meeting their citizens' demands, whether in relation to the drugs trade or employment, their capacity for self-governance—that is state autonomy—is compromised.

State of war: the conditions (often described by classical Realists) where there is no actual conflict, but a permanent cold war that could become a 'hot' war at any time.

State sovereignty: in any post Westphalian order the sovereign power and authority of national government—the entitlement of states to rule within their own territorial space—is being transformed but not necessarily eroded. Sovereignty today is increasingly understood as the shared exercise of public power and authority between national, regional, and global authorities.

State system: the regular patterns of interaction between states, but without implying any shared values between them. This is distinguished from the view of a 'society' of states.

State: a legal territorial entity composed of a stable population and a government; it possesses a monopoly over the legitimate use of force; its sovereignty is recognized by other states in the international system. This one word is used to refer to three distinct concepts: 1. In international law, a state is an entity that is recognized to exist when a government is in control of a community of people within a defined territory. It is comparable to the idea in domestic law of a company being a legal person. 2. In the study of international politics, each state is a country. It is a community of people who interact in the same political system and who have some common values. 3. In philosophy and sociology, the state consists of the apparatus of government, in its broadest sense, covering the executive, the legislature, the administration, the judiciary, the armed forces, and the police.

Statism: in Realist theory, the ideology that supports the organization of humankind into particular communities; the values and beliefs of that community are protected and sustained by the state.

Strategic interaction: occurs when an outcome is the product of decisions arrived at independently.

Structure: in the philosophy of the social sciences a structure is something that exists independently of the actor (e.g. social class) but is an important determinant in the nature of the action (e.g. revolution). For contemporary structural Realists, the number of Great Powers in the international system constitutes the structure.

Summit diplomacy: refers to a direct meeting between heads of government (of the superpowers in particular) to resolve major problems. The 'summit' became a regular mode of contact during the cold war.

Superpower: term used to describe the United States and the Soviet Union after 1945, denoting their global political involvements and military capabilities, including in particular their nuclear arsenals.

Survival: the first priority for state leaders, emphasized by historical Realists such as Machiavelli, Meinecke, and Weber.

Suzerain state: a state which dominates and subordinates neighbouring states, without taking them over.

Syndicated eurocredit: a loan provided in the euromarkets by an ad hoc association of a number of commercial banks.

Technological revolution: refers to the way modern communications (the Internet, satellite communications, high-tech computers) made possible by technological advances have made distance and location less important factors not just for government (including at local and regional levels) but equally in the calculations of other actors such as firms' investment decisions or in the activities of social movements.

Territorial state: a state that has power over the population which resides on its territory but which does not seek to represent the nation or the people as a whole.

Territoriality: borders and territory still remain important, not least for administrative purposes. Under conditions of globalization, however, a new geography of political organization and political power is emerging which transcends territories and borders.

Territory: a portion of the earth's surface appropriated by a political community, or state.

Terrorism: the use of illegitimate violence by sub-state groups to inspire fear, by attacking civilians and/or symbolic targets. This is done for purposes such as drawing widespread attention to a grievance, provoking a severe response, or wearing down their opponent's moral resolve, to affect political change. Determining when the use of violence is legitimate, which is based on contextual morality of the act as opposed to its effects, is the source for disagreement over what constitutes acts of terrorism.

Theocracy: a state based on religion.

Third World: a notion that was first used in the late 1950s to define both the underdeveloped world and the political and economic project that would help overcome underdevelopment: employed less in the post-cold war era.

Time-space compression: the technologically induced erosion of distance and time giving the appearance of a world that is in communication terms shrinking.

Total war: a term given to the twentieth century's two world wars to denote not only their global scale but also the combatants' pursuit of their opponents' 'unconditional surrender'

(a phrase particularly associated with the Western allies in the Second World War). Total war also signifies the mobilization of whole populations—including women into factory work, auxiliary civil defence units, and as paramilitaries and paramedics—as part of the total call-up of all able-bodied citizens in pursuit of victory.

Transfer price: the price set by a TNC for intra-firm trade of goods or services. For accounting purposes, a price must be set for exports, but it need not be related to any market price.

Transgovernmental networks: formal and informal mechanisms which link government officials in one agency with their foreign counterparts for purposes of policy coordination, harmonization, dialogue, and enforcement.

Transition: usually taken to mean the lengthy period between the end of communist planning in the Soviet bloc and the final emergence of a fully functioning democratic capitalist system.

Transnational actor: any civil society actor from one country that has relations with any actor from another country or with an international organization.

Transnational civil society: a political arena in which citizens and private interests collaborate across borders to advance their mutual goals or to bring governments and the formal institutions of global governance to account for their activities.

Transnational company (TNC): a company that has affiliates in a foreign country. The affiliates may be branches of the parent company, separately incorporated subsidiaries, or associates, with large minority shareholdings.

Transnational feminism: a sustained cross-border response to globalization, especially in its negative impacts on women, taking advantage of new opportunities for women's organizing through UN and other international conferences and global communications technology.

Treaties of Utrecht 1713: the Treaties of Utrecht, which brought an end to the Wars of Spanish Succession, consolidated the move to territorial sovereignty in Europe. The Treaties of Westphalia 1648 did little to define the territorial scope of sovereign rights, the geographical domain over which such rights could extend. By establishing that fixed territorial boundaries, rather than the reach of family ties, should define the reach of sovereign authority, the Treaties of Utrecht were crucial in establishing the present link between sovereign authority and territorial boundaries.

Treaties of Westphalia 1648: the Treaties of Osnabruck and Munster, which together form the 'Peace of Westphalia', ended the Thirty Years War and were crucial in delimiting the political rights and authority of European monarchs. Among other things, the Treaties granted monarchs rights to maintain standing armies, build fortifications, and levy taxes.

Treaty of Paris 1814: the Treaty of Paris ended the Napoleonic Wars and paved the way for the Congress of Vienna (1814–15). The Congress of Vienna, in turn, defined the nature of the post-Napoleonic War settlement, and ultimately led to the

Concert of Europe. The Concert has often been credited with successfully limiting Great Power warfare for a good part of the nineteenth century, but it is also noteworthy as an institution for upholding monarchical authority and combatting liberal and nationalist movements in Europe.

Triads: the three economic groupings (North America, Europe, and East Asia).

Triangulation: occurs when trade between two countries is routed indirectly via a third country. For example, in the early 1980s, neither the Argentine Government nor the British Government permitted trade between the two countries, but companies simply sent their exports via Brazil or Western Europe.

Truman doctrine: statement made by US President Harry Truman in March 1947 that it 'must be the policy of the United States to support free people who are resisting attempted subjugation by armed minorities or by outside pressures'. Intended to persuade Congress to support limited aid to Turkey and Greece, the doctrine came to underpin the policy of containment and American economic and political support for its allies.

Unipolarity: theoretical notion that takes as its working assumption the fact that the United States has now become and is likely to remain the only major power in the world. It is a distribution of power internationally in which there is clearly only one dominant power or 'pole'. Some analysts argue that the international system became unipolar in the 1990s since there was no longer any rival to American power.

United Nations Charter (1945): the Charter of the United Nations is the legal regime that created the United Nations as the world's only 'supranational' organization. The Charter defines the structure of the United Nations, the powers of its constitutive agencies, and the rights and obligations of sovereign states party to the Charter. Among other things, the Charter is the key legal document limiting the use of force to instances of self-defence and collective peace enforcement endorsed by the United Nations Security Council.

United Nations Conference on Trade and Development: established in 1964 with offices in Geneva. Membership (2004) of 192 states. UNCTAD monitors the effects of world trade and investment on economic development, especially in the South. It provided a key forum in the 1970s for discussions of a New International Economic Order. See further www.unctad.org.

US decline: an argument that gained currency in the United States in the 1970s, subsequently made popular by the historian Paul Kennedy who in 1987 suggested that because of domestic economic problems and imperial overextension, America was entering a period of global retreat.

War on terror: announced after the attacks of 11 September 2001 to suggest an extensive and global struggle to combat and finally defeat international terrorism.

WiFi: Wireless Fidelity, fixed, wireless systems that can deliver large bandwidth for short distances.

Wind of change: reference by British Prime Minister Harold Macmillan in a speech in South Africa in 1960 to the political changes taking place across Africa heralding the end of European imperialism.

Wireless network: communication data and voice traffic networked through microwave and satellite connections.

World Bank Group: a collection of five agencies, the first established in 1945, with head offices in Washington, DC. The WBG promotes development in medium- and low-income countries with project loans, structural adjustment programmes, and various advisory services. See further www.worldbank.org.

World government: associated in particular with those Idealists who believe that peace can never be achieved in a world divided into separate sovereign states. Just as governments abolished the state of nature in civil society, the establishment of a world government must end the state of war in international society.

World order: this is a wider category of order than the 'international'. It takes as its units of order, not states, but individual human beings, and assesses the degree of order on the basis of the delivery of certain kinds of goods (be it security, human rights, basic needs, or justice) for humanity as a whole.

World society: the society produced by globalization.

World Trade Organization (WTO): established in 1995 with headquarters in Geneva. Membership (2004) of 146 states. The WTO is a permanent instititution to replace the provisional GATT. It has a wider agenda, covering services, intellectual property, and investment issues as well as merchandise trade. The WTO also has greater powers of enforcement through its dispute-settlement mechanism. The organization's Trade Policy Review Body conducts surveillance of members' commercial measures.

INDEX

C